International Maritime Security Law

International Maritime Security Law

By

James Kraska and Raul Pedrozo

MARTINUS
NIJHOFF
PUBLISHERS

LEIDEN • BOSTON
2013

Library of Congress Cataloging-in-Publication Data

Kraska, James.
 International maritime security law / by James Kraska and Raul Pedrozo.
   pages cm
 Includes index.
 ISBN 978-90-04-23356-0 (hardback : alk. paper)—ISBN 978-90-04-23357-7 (e-book) 1. Freedom of the seas. 2. Law of the sea. 3. Security, International. 4. Maritime terrorism—Prevention—Law and legislation. 5. Merchant marine—Security measures. I. Pedrozo, Raul A. II. Title.

 KZA1348.K73 2013
 341.4'5—dc23

2012049101

This publication has been typeset in the multilingual "Brill" typeface. With over 5,100 characters covering Latin, IPA, Greek, and Cyrillic, this typeface is especially suitable for use in the humanities. For more information, please see www.brill.com/brill-typeface.

ISBN 978-90-04-23356-0 (hardback)
ISBN 978-90-04-23357-7 (e-book)

Copyright 2013 by Koninklijke Brill NV, Leiden, The Netherlands.
Koninklijke Brill NV incorporates the imprints Brill, Global Oriental, Hotei Publishing, IDC Publishers and Martinus Nijhoff Publishers.

All rights reserved. No part of this publication may be reproduced, translated, stored in a retrieval system, or transmitted in any form or by any means, electronic, mechanical, photocopying, recording or otherwise, without prior written permission from the publisher.

Authorization to photocopy items for internal or personal use is granted by Koninklijke Brill NV provided that the appropriate fees are paid directly to The Copyright Clearance Center, 222 Rosewood Drive, Suite 910, Danvers, MA 01923, USA.
Fees are subject to change.

This book is printed on acid-free paper.

PRINTED BY DRUKKERIJ WILCO B.V. - AMERSFOORT, THE NETHERLANDS

CONTENTS

List of Tables xxiii

List of Annexes and Appendices xxv

Chapter One   Introduction to Maritime Security Law 1
  1.1   Introduction 1
  1.2   What is "Maritime Security Law"? 5
       1.2.1   The Protean Nature of Maritime Security Law 7
       1.2.2   The Influence of Law on Sea Power 11
       1.2.3   Influence of Law on Maritime Security 12
  1.3   Building a Public Order of the Oceans 15
       1.3.1   From Westphalia to Montego Bay 16
       1.3.2   Building a Global Maritime Partnership 19
  1.4   Conclusion 23

Chapter Two   American Maritime Security Policy and Strategy 25
  2.1   Introduction 25
  2.2   U.S. Maritime Security Policy 27
  2.3   National Strategy for Maritime Security 30
  2.4   National Strategy for Global Supply Chain Security 33
  2.5   U.S. Maritime Strategy for Homeland Security 35
  2.6   Cooperative Strategy for 21st Century Sea Power 36
       2.6.1   Naval Operations Concept 38
       2.6.2   Expeditionary Sea Power 40
       2.6.3   Pivot to Asia and the Air-Sea Battle Concept 42

Chapter Three   European Maritime Strategy and Policy 47
  3.1   North Atlantic Treaty Organization 47
       3.1.1   NATO Alliance Maritime Strategy 49
              3.1.1.1   Collective Defense 50

		3.1.1.2	Crisis Management	50
		3.1.1.3	Cooperative Security	51
		3.1.1.4	Maritime Security Operations	52
			a. Nato Maritime Organization	53
			b. Operation Active Endeavor	54
			c. Ocean Shield: Counter-piracy	55
		3.1.1.5	Promotion of International Law	57
	3.2	European Union		58
		3.2.1	Blue Book—Integrated Maritime Policy	62
		3.2.1.1	Maritime Surveillance	62
		3.2.1.2	Naval Capabilities	64
		3.2.1.3	Anti-piracy Operations	64
		3.2.1.4	A Security Strategy for the Global Maritime Domain	66
	3.3	Chiefs of European Navies Maritime Operational Concept		66
	3.4	U.K. Future Maritime Operational Concept		70

Chapter Four   Peacetime Zones and Control Measures 75

4.1	Temporary Suspension of Innocent Passage			75
4.2	Offshore Installation Safety Zones			76
	4.2.1	IMO Safety Zones		78
	4.2.2	U.S. Safety Zones		82
	4.2.3	U.K. Safety Zones		84
4.3	World-Wide Navigational Warning Service			85
	4.3.1	U.S. Navigational Warnings		88
		4.3.1.1	HYDROPAC: Strait of Hormuz—Iranian Naval Exercises	88
		4.3.1.2	HYDROLANT: Mediterranean Sea—Hazardous Operations	89
		4.3.1.3	Special Warning: Cuba	90
		4.3.1.4	Special Warning: Papua New Guinea—Political Unrest	90
		4.3.1.5	Special Warning: Morocco—Aggressive Maritime Enforcement	91
		4.3.1.6	Special Warning: Persian Gulf—UN Security Council Enforcement Action	91
		4.3.1.7	Special Warning: Sri Lanka—Combating Terrorist Threats	92
		4.3.1.8	Special Warning: Yemen—Threats to U.S. Citizens	93
		4.3.1.9	Special Warning: Iran—Danger to Shipping	93
		4.3.1.10	Special Warning: Sierra Leone—Dangerous Port	94
		4.3.1.11	Special Warning: United States—Worldwide Defensive Measures	94

		4.3.1.12	Special Warning: Persian Gulf—Military Operations	95
		4.3.1.13	Special Warning: East Africa—Terrorist Threat	96
		4.3.1.14	Special Warning: Yemen—Terrorist Threat	96
		4.3.1.15	Special Warning: Somalia—Piracy	97
	4.3.2	U.S. Maritime Administration Advisories		97
		4.3.2.1	Reporting Terrorist Incidents	98
		4.3.2.2	Regional Terrorist and Piracy Threat	98
		4.3.2.3	Vessels Transiting High Risk Waters (HRW)—Maritime Piracy	99
		4.3.2.4	Japan Tsunami Radiological Threat and Debris Field	102
4.4	Aeronautical Information Services			103
	4.4.1	ICAO Aeronautical Information Service		103
	4.4.2	U.S. Notice to Airmen (NOTAM)		105

Chapter Five	Marine Environmental Protection and Control Measures	113
5.1	The Marine Environment	113
	5.1.1 Evolution of Marine Environmental Law	113
	5.1.2 Framework Agreements to Protect the Marine Environment	116
5.2	Particularly Sensitive Sea Areas	117
	5.2.1 Western Europe PSSA and the 2005 Guidelines	121
	5.2.2 Malpelo Island PSSA (Colombia)—Regulation without Protection	126
	5.2.3 Baltic Sea Area PSSA—Regulation without Concurrence	130
	5.2.4 Papahānaumokuākea PSSA (United States)—Regulation without Need	131
	5.2.5 Mid-Pacific Ocean National Monuments (United States)	135
5.3	Ships' Routeing, Vessel Traffic Services, and Ships' Reporting	137
5.4	Mandatory Ship Reporting (United States)	141
5.5	Marine Mammals	146
	5.5.1 Natural Resources Defense Council v. Winter (Sonar Litigation)	147
	5.5.2 Navy Mitigation Measures during Sonar Operations	151

Chapter Six	U.S. Safety and Security Zones and Airspace Control Measures	155
6.1	Introduction to U.S. Zones	155
6.2	Jurisdiction over the Navigable Waters of the United States	156
	6.2.1 Ports and Waterways Safety Act	156
	6.2.2 Presidential Proclamation No. 5928	157
6.3	Safety Zones	160

CONTENTS

- 6.4 Security Zones ... 162
  - 6.4.1 Regulated Navigation Areas and Restricted Waterfront Areas ... 165
    - 6.4.1.1 Naval Vessel Protection Zones ... 165
    - 6.4.1.2 Restricted Areas and Danger Zones ... 168
      - a. Pacific Ocean, Hawaii; danger zones ... 169
      - b. Pacific Ocean, Island of Oahu, Hawaii; danger zone ... 169
      - c. Pacific Ocean at Barber's Point, Island of Oahu, Hawaii; danger zone ... 170
      - d. Pacific Ocean at Keahi Point, Island of Oahu, Hawaii; danger zone ... 170
      - e. Kaneohe Bay, Island of Oahu, Hawaii—Ulupau Crater Weapons Training Range; danger zone ... 170
      - f. Pacific Ocean at Barking Sands, Island of Kauai, Hawaii; missile range facility ... 171
      - g. Pacific Ocean, at Barbers Point, Island of Oahu, Hawaii; restricted area ... 172
      - h. Pacific Ocean, at Makapuu Point, Waimanalo, Island of Oahu, Hawaii, Makai Undersea Test Range ... 172
    - 6.4.1.3 Naval Defensive Sea Areas and Naval Airspace Reservations ... 173
    - 6.4.1.4 Trust Territory of the Pacific Islands ... 175
  - 6.4.2 Airspace Control Measures ... 178
    - 6.4.2.1 Air Defense Identification Zone ... 178
    - 6.4.2.2 Special Use Airspace ... 181
      - a. Prohibited Areas ... 181
      - b. Restricted Areas ... 181
      - c. Warning Areas ... 182
      - d. Military Operation Areas ... 182
      - e. Alert Areas ... 183
      - f. Controlled Firing Areas ... 183
      - g. National Security Areas ... 183

Chapter Seven   Sea Power, Grand Strategy, and Freedom of the Seas ... 185
- 7.1 Seapower and Grand Strategy ... 185
  - 7.1.1 Littoral Regions ... 186
  - 7.1.2 Global System ... 187
  - 7.1.3 Freedom of the Seas in the Early Modern Period ... 189
  - 7.1.4 Freedom of the Seas in the World Wars and the Cold War ... 191
  - 7.1.5 Freedom of the Seas, the Law of the Sea, and U.S. Policy ... 196
- 7.2 U.S. Freedom of Navigation Program ... 201

Chapter Eight		Freedom of Navigation in the Law of the Sea	215
8.1	Baselines		216
8.2	Internal Waters		217
8.3	Territorial Sea		218
8.4	Straits Used for International Navigation		219
	8.4.1	Corfu Channel Case	219
	8.4.2	The Straits Regime in UNCLOS	222
	8.4.3	Types of Straits Used for International Navigation	224
		8.4.3.1 Geographic Straits	224
		8.4.3.2 Long-standing Conventions	225
		8.4.3.3 Route of Similar Convenience	226
		8.4.3.4 Island Forming a Strait (Route of Similar Convenience)	227
		8.4.3.5 Archipelagic Straits	227
		8.4.3.6 Dead-end Straits	228
	8.4.4	Transit Passage in the Approaches to the Strait	229
	8.4.5	Archipelagic Sea Lanes Passage	230
		8.4.5.1 Indonesia	231
8.5	Contiguous Zone		232
8.6	Exclusive Economic Zone		233
	8.6.1	Coastal State Competence in the EEZ	234
8.7	Continental Shelf		241
8.8	High Seas		242
Chapter Nine		Excessive Maritime Claims: Territorial Seas, Straits, and Archipelagos	243
9.1	Introduction		243
9.2	Illegal Straight Baselines		246
	9.2.1	Libya's "Line of Death" in the Gulf of Sirte	247
9.3	Excessive Claims over the Territorial Sea and Contiguous Zone		252
	9.3.1	Black Sea Bumping Incident	255
	9.3.2	Jackson Hole Agreement	258
9.4	Excessive Claims over Straits Used for International Navigation		259
	9.4.1	Strait of Hainan	261
	9.4.2	Head Harbor Passage	261
	9.4.3	Northwest Passage	262
	9.4.4	Torres Strait	264
	9.4.5	Strait of Hormuz	269
9.5	Excessive Claims over Archipelagic Sea Lanes		270
	9.5.1	Indonesia's 1960s Archipelagic Claims	271
	9.5.2	The Philippines	273
	9.5.3	Maldives	275

CONTENTS

Chapter Ten   Security Claims in the Exclusive Economic Zone 277
10.1   Security Claims in the Exclusive Economic Zone 277
10.2   China's Oceans Law and the EEZ 279
10.3   North Korea's Military Zone 283
10.4   Military Activities in the EEZ 284
    10.4.1   Marine Data Collection 285
    10.4.2   International Airspace of the EEZ 289
        10.4.2.1   Peruvian Attack on a U.S. C-130 State Aircraft (1992) 289
        10.4.2.2   Chinese Collision with a U.S. EP-3 State Aircraft (2001) 290
            10.4.2.2.1   Law of the Sea 291
            10.4.2.2.2   Aviation Law 292
        10.4.2.3   State Aircraft Sovereign Immunity 293
        10.4.2.4   Schooner Exchange 294
        10.4.2.5   Military Interception of Civil Aircraft in International Airspace 296
            10.4.2.5.1   U.S. Practice 299
    10.4.3   "Peaceful Purposes" 304
    10.4.4   Offshore Environmental Regulation as Maritime Strategy 309

Chapter Eleven   Flashpoint: South China Sea 313
11.1   The Political Seascape and Regional Stability 313
    11.1.1   Chinese Maritime Claims 315
        11.1.1.1   The U-Shaped Line (The "Cow Tongue") 316
        11.1.1.2   Sansha City 318
        11.1.1.3   Regional Reaction to China's Claims 319
    11.1.2   Vietnam's Maritime Claims 321
    11.1.3   The Philippines' Maritime Claims 325
    11.1.4   ASEAN and the Declaration on the Conduct of Parties 330
11.2   American Security Relationships and the South China Sea 334
    11.2.1   U.S.-Philippine Cooperation 340
    11.2.2   U.S.-Australian Cooperation 348
    11.2.3   U.S.-New Zealand Cooperation 351
    11.2.4   Trans-Pacific Partnership 353

Chapter Twelve   Securing the Marine Transportation System 355
12.1   Threats to International Ship and Port Facility Security 355
    12.1.1   Piracy and Armed Robbery at Sea 358
    12.1.2   Maritime Terrorism 358
    12.1.3   Cargo Tampering, Sabotage, or Theft 359
    12.1.4   Smuggling of Contraband 359
    12.1.5   Illegal Migrants, Stowaways, Refugees, and Asylum Seekers 359

		12.1.6	Environmental Extremists	359
		12.1.7	Weather and Natural Disasters	360
		12.1.8	Accidents	360
		12.1.9	Organized Labor Activities and Labor Violence	360
	12.2	The Law of the Sea and the IMO		362
	12.3	Exclusive Flag State Jurisdiction		365
		12.3.1	SOLAS	368
		12.3.2	Load Lines	372
		12.3.3	MARPOL	373
		12.3.4	STCW	373
		12.3.5	TONNAGE 69	374
		12.3.6	IMO Member State Audit Scheme	375
		12.3.7	ILO Instruments	376
	12.4	The ISPS Code		378
		12.4.1	Special Measures	385
		12.4.2	Security Levels	387
		12.4.3	Declaration of Security	389
		12.4.4	Security Plans for Port Facilities and Ships	392
		12.4.5	Interagency Government Coordination	393
		12.4.6	Regional Organizations	395
		12.4.7	Recognized Security Organizations	395
		12.4.8	Government Oversight and Enforcement	397
	12.5	Maritime Domain Awareness		399
		12.5.1	U.S. Maritime Domain Awareness Policy	400
		12.5.2	Automatic Identification System	404
		12.5.3	Long-Range Identification and Tracking	408
Chapter Thirteen		Port and Port Facility Security		411
	13.1	Ports in the Global Transportation System		411
	13.2	Port State Control		416
		13.2.1	IMO Protocols	418
		13.2.2	Port State Regional MoUs	423
			13.2.2.1 Paris MoU	424
			13.2.2.2 Acuerdo de Viña del Mar	424
			13.2.2.3 Tokyo MoU	425
			13.2.2.4 Caribbean MoU	425
			13.2.2.5 Mediterranean MoU	425
			13.2.2.6 Indian Ocean MoU	426
			13.2.2.7 Abuja MoU	427
			13.2.2.8 Black Sea MoU	427
			13.2.2.9 Riyadh MoU	427
			13.2.2.10 PERSGA	428
		13.2.3	U.S. Port State Control	429

13.3	Port Facility Security			434
	13.3.1	Designated Authority		436
	13.3.2	Declaration of Security		436
	13.3.3	Port Facility Security Officer		438
	13.3.4	Port Facility Security Plan		439
	13.3.5	Port Facility Security Level		442
		13.3.5.1 Port Access		443
		13.3.5.2 Restricted Areas within the Port Facility		444
		13.3.5.3 Cargo Handling		445
		13.3.5.4 Delivery of Ships' Stores		446
			13.3.5.4.1 Security Level 1	446
			13.3.5.4.2 Security Level 2	447
			13.3.5.4.3 Security Level 3	447
		13.3.5.5 Monitoring the Port Facility		448
	13.3.6	Port Facility Security Assessment		449
13.4	Port State Control Certifications and Documents			451
13.5	Questionnaire for Designated Authorities			452
13.6	Security Checklist for Port Facility Operators			455
	13.6.1	Guidance for Port Facility Operators		456
		13.6.1.1 Performance of Port Facility Security Duties		456
			Part A	456
			Part B	457
		13.6.1.2 Controlling Access to the Port Facility		458
			Part A	458
			Part B	458
		13.6.1.3 Monitoring of the Port Facility, Anchoring and Berthing Area		459
			Part A	459
			Part B	459
		13.6.1.4 Monitoring of Restricted Areas		460
			Part A	460
			Part B Establishment of Restricted Areas	460
			Part C Security Measures	461
		13.6.1.5 Supervising the Handling of Cargo		462
			Part A	462
			Part B	462
		13.6.1.6 Supervising the Handling of Ship's Stores		463
			Part A	463
			Part B Ship's Stores Security Measures	463
		13.6.1.7 Communications Security		464
			Part A	464
			Part B Effectiveness and Protection of Communications	464

		13.6.1.8	Training, Drills, and Exercises	464
			Part A	464
			Part B Training, Drills, and Exercises	465
		13.6.1.9	Miscellaneous	465
			Part B	465

Chapter Fourteen   Ship and Ship Operator Security 467

14.1 Shipping Company Responsibilities 467

  14.1.1 Applicability of IMO Maritime Security Measures 467
  14.1.2 Alternative Security Agreements 468
  14.1.3 Equivalent Security Agreements 470

14.2 Checklist for Shipping Companies 471

  14.2.1 Checklist 471
    14.2.1.1 Continuous Synopsis Record 471
    14.2.1.2 Ship Security Alert System 471
    14.2.1.3 Master's Discretion for Ship Safety and Security .. 472
    14.2.1.4 Obligations of the Company 472
      Part A Obligations of the Company 472
      Part B Obligations of the Company 473
    14.2.1.5 Control and Compliance Measures 473
    14.2.1.6 Verification and Certification for Ships 474
      Part A Verification and Certification for Ships   474
    14.2.1.7 Ship Security Assessment 474
      Part A Ship Security Assessment 474
      Part B Company Security Officer
              Requirements to Conduct an
              Assessment 475
      Part C Content of the Ship Security
              Assessment 476
    14.2.1.8 Ship Security Plan 477
      Part A Ship Security Plan 478
      Part B Content of the Ship Security Plan 479
    14.2.1.9 Records 479
      Part A Records 479
    14.2.1.10 Company Security Officer 480
      Part A Company Security Officer 480
    14.2.1.11 Training, Drills, and Exercises on Ship Security ... 481
      Part A Training, Drills, and Exercises 481
      Part B Training, Drills, and Exercises 481
    14.2.1.12 Information and Cooperation (Best Practice) 482

14.3 Ship Security 482

  14.3.1 Ship Security Levels 482
  14.3.2 Declarations of Security 483

	14.3.3	Model Declaration of Security for a Ship-to-Ship Interface	484
	14.3.4	Ship Security Personnel	486
		14.3.4.1 Company Security Officers	486
		14.3.4.2 Ship Security Officers	487
	14.3.5	Ship Security Alert Systems	488
	14.3.6	Ship Security Assessments	489
	14.3.7	Ship Security Plans	490
	14.3.8	Responding to Requests to Board the Ship in Port or at Sea	494
	14.3.9	Vessel Pre-arrival Information	496
		14.3.9.1 Ship and Contact Details	496
		14.3.9.2 Port and Port Facility Information	497
		14.3.9.3 Information Required by SOLAS Regulation XI-2/9.2.1	497
		14.3.9.4 Other Security-related Information	498
		14.3.9.5 Agent of the Ship at the Intended Port of Arrival	498
		14.3.9.6 Identification of the Person Providing the Information	499
	14.3.10	The International Ship Security Certificate	499
	14.3.11	Checklist for Flag State Administrations	500
14.4	Checklist for Ship Security Personnel		503
	14.4.1	Basic Information for Ship Security Personnel	503
		14.4.1.1 Company and Ship Overview	503
		14.4.1.2 Total Manning of the Ship and Crew with Security Duties on Board	504
		14.4.1.3 Ship Security Information in the Last 12 Months	504
		14.4.1.4 Security Agreements and Arrangements	504
	14.4.2	Checklist	504
		14.4.2.1 Ensuring the Performance of All Ship Security Duties	504
		Part A Ensuring the Performance of All Ship Security Duties	504
		Part B Organization and Performance of Ship Security Duties	505
		14.4.2.2 Controlling Access to the Ship	506
		Part A Access to the Ship	506
		Part B Access to the Ship	506
		14.4.2.3 Controlling the Embarkation of Persons and Their Effects	508

		Part A	Embarkation of Persons and Their Effects	508
		Part B.1	Embarkation of Persons and Their Effects	508
		Part B.2	Handling Unaccompanied Baggage	508
	14.4.2.4	Monitoring of Restricted Areas		509
		Part A	Restricted Areas on the Ship	509
		Part B	Restricted Areas on the Ship	509
	14.4.2.5	Monitoring of Deck Areas and Areas Surrounding the Ship		510
		Part A	Access to the Ship	510
		Part B.1	Access to the Ship	510
		Part B.2	Monitoring the Security of the Ship	510
	14.4.2.6	Supervising the Handling of Cargo and Ship's Stores		511
		Part A	Handling of Cargo	511
		Part B.1	Handling of Cargo	511
		Part B.2	Delivery of Ship's Stores	512
	14.4.2.7	Ensuring Security Communication is Readily Available		512
		Part A	Ensuring Security Communication	512
	14.4.2.8	Training, Drills, and Exercises		513
		Part A	Training, Drills, and Exercises	513
		Part B	Training, Drills, and Exercises	513
	14.4.2.9	Miscellaneous		513
		Part A	Miscellaneous	513
		Part B	Miscellaneous	515
14.5	Yachts and Other Non-SOLAS Vessels			515

Chapter Fifteen	Global Authorities to Counter Drug Trafficking	519
15.1	International Law and the Trade in Illegal Drugs	519
15.2	The Multilateral Treaty Framework	522
	15.2.1 United Nations Convention on the Law of the Sea	522
	15.2.2 1961 Single Convention on Narcotic Drugs, As Amended	524
	15.2.3 1971 Convention on Psychotropic Substances	529
	15.2.4 1988 Vienna Drug Convention	531
	15.2.4.1 Illicit Traffic by Sea	538
15.3	International Maritime Organization	541
	15.3.1 IMO Guidelines	541
	15.3.2 Maritime Trafficking	543
15.4	UN Basic Principles on the Use of Force	549
	15.4.1 Basic Principles on the Use of Force and Firearms	549
	15.4.2 Use of Force in the Case of the M/V Saiga	552

Chapter Sixteen		Regional Authorities to Counter Drug Trafficking	555
16.1		Regional Cooperation in Countering Maritime Drug Trafficking	555
16.2		Caribbean Regional Maritime Agreement	555
	16.2.1	U.S. Declaration of the Agreement	563
16.3		Caribbean Basin Security Initiative	566
	16.3.1	CBSI Joint Statement	568
16.4		Organization of American States Model Operating Procedure	569
16.5		The Paris Pact Initiative	573
16.6		Republic of the Philippines National Coast Watch System	578
	16.6.1	Executive Order 57	579
16.7		Mérida Initiative	582
16.8		The Central America Regional Security Initiative	585
Chapter Seventeen		U.S. Maritime Counterdrug Law	587
17.1		Maritime Drug Law Enforcement Act	587
	17.1.1	Jurisdiction under MDLEA	587
	17.1.2	Offenses under MDLEA	588
	17.1.3	Intent to Commit an Offense under MDLEA	589
17.2		Drug Trafficking Vessel Interdiction Act	590
	17.2.1	Self-propelled Semi-submersible (SPSS) Watercraft	591
	17.2.2	Criminal and Civil Penalties for Operation of SPSS	592
	17.2.3	Legal Challenges to DTVIA	594
	17.2.4	SPSS Model Law of the Organization of American States	597
17.3		Foreign Narcotics Kingpin Designation Act	598
	17.3.1	Executive Order 12978	599
	17.3.2	Purpose of the Kingpin Act	599
17.4		U.S. Coast Guard Authorities	602
	17.4.1	Plenary U.S. Maritime Law Enforcement Authority	603
	17.4.2	Use of Force	604
	17.4.3	Airborne Use of Force	605
	17.4.4	Maritime Enforcement of U.S. Immigration Law	607
17.5		Department of Defense Legal Authorities	607
	17.5.1	Lead Agency for Detection and Monitoring	608
	17.5.2	Military Support for Civilian Law Enforcement	608
		17.5.2.1 Department of Defense Directive 5525.5	613
		17.5.2.2 Chairman of the Joint Chiefs of Staff Instruction 3710.01B	617
		17.5.2.3 Geographic Combatant Commander Counterdrug Authority	620
		17.5.2.4 Maritime Counterdrug Rules of Engagement	621
	17.5.3	Joint Publication 3-07.4, Counterdrug Operations	622
		17.5.3.1 Coast Guard Law Enforcement Detachments	622

		17.5.3.2	Department of Defense Joint Interagency Task Forces	623

Chapter Eighteen U.S. International Maritime Counterdrug Policy 627
- 18.1 The U.S. Policy and Operational Framework 627
  - 18.1.1 U.S. National Drug Threat Assessment 628
  - 18.1.2 U.S. National Drug Control Strategy 632
  - 18.1.3 Strategy to Combat Transnational Organized Crime 634
  - 18.1.4 Department of Defense U.S. Southern Command 636
- 18.2 U.S. Bilateral Maritime Counterdrug Instruments 639
  - 18.2.1 Agreement to Suppress Illicit Traffic by Sea (U.S.-Colombia) 641
  - 18.2.2 Air Bridge Denial Agreement (U.S.-Colombia) 643
- 18.3 Conclusion 650
- 18.4 U.S. International Maritime Law Enforcement Instruments 650
  - 18.4.1 Bilateral Maritime Counterdrug Agreements 650
  - 18.4.2 Memorandums of Understanding and Operational Procedures 654
  - 18.4.3 Forward Operating Location/Cooperative Security Location Agreements 655
  - 18.4.4 Multilateral Counterdrug Agreements 656

Chapter Nineteen Migrant Smuggling at Sea 657
- 19.1 Transnational Threat of Irregular Migration 657
- 19.2 Law of the Sea Convention 659
- 19.3 Transnational Organized Crime Convention 660
  - 19.3.1 Executive Order 13581 661
- 19.4 Migrant Smuggling Protocol 662
- 19.5 IMO Initiatives 666
  - 19.5.1 Assembly Resolution A.773(18) 667
  - 19.5.2 Assembly Resolution A.867(20) 668
  - 19.5.3 Maritime Safety Committee Circular 896 668
  - 19.5.4 Guidelines on the Treatment of Persons Rescued at Sea 673
- 19.6 Duty to Assist 675
- 19.7 Salvage Conventions 675
- 19.8 International Convention for the Safety of Life at Sea 676
- 19.9 International Convention on Maritime Search and Rescue 679
- 19.10 Refugee Convention 680
- 19.11 The U.S. Experience in Law and Practice 682
  - 19.11.1 *USS Morton* (DD 948) 683
  - 19.11.2 *USS Dubuque* (LPD 8) 684
  - 19.11.3 U.S. Counter-Migrant Smuggling Initiatives 686
- 19.12 Conclusion 689

CONTENTS

Chapter Twenty Maritime Piracy and Armed Robbery at Sea 691
20.1 The Historical Roots of the Law of Piracy 692
    20.1.1 Mediterranean Sea and the Rise of the Nation State 693
    20.1.2 Renaissance Scholars Shape the Law 693
    20.1.3 Anglo-American Law of Piracy 695
20.2 Contemporary Law of Maritime Piracy 697
    20.2.1 UN Convention on the Law of the Sea 698
    20.2.2 UN Security Council 701
        20.2.2.1 Somalia 701
        20.2.2.2 African Union Mission to Somalia 707
        20.2.2.3 Gulf of Guinea 712
    20.2.3 International Maritime Organization 713
    20.2.4 Djibouti Code of Conduct 718
20.3 Counter-piracy Operations 723
    20.3.1 Combined Maritime Force—Task Force 151 724
    20.3.2 North Atlantic Treaty Organization—Operation Ocean Shield 725
    20.3.3 European Union Naval Force Somalia—Operation Atalanta 727
    20.3.4 Japan Maritime Self-Defense Force 733
    20.3.5 Flag State Administrations and Best Management Practices 736

Chapter Twenty-One Maritime Terrorism and Weapons of Mass Destruction at Sea 739
21.1 Prevalence of Maritime Terrorism 739
    21.1.1 Palestine Liberation Front and the *Achille Lauro* 740
    21.1.2 Sri Lanka and the Tamil Tigers 741
    21.1.3 Al Qaeda and the *USS Cole* 743
21.2 Non-Proliferation Treaty 745
    21.2.1 North Korea 746
    21.2.2 Iran 747
    21.2.3 Is the NPT Viable? 750
21.3 Coastal State and Flag State Jurisdiction 752
    21.3.1 Coastal State Authorities 752
    21.3.2 Exclusive Flag State Jurisdiction 754
    21.3.3 Stateless Vessels 756
    21.3.4 Consent of the Master 757
21.4 Cases on the Use of Force in Shipboarding 758
    21.4.1 *The Caroline* 758
    21.4.2 *I'm Alone* 760
    21.4.3 *Red Crusader* 762
    21.4.4 M/V *Saiga* 763

21.5	UN Security Council		766
	21.5.1	Resolution 1540	767
	21.5.2	North Korea	768
	21.5.3	Iran	774
	21.5.4	Ineffectiveness of the Security Council	783
21.6	Proliferation Security Initiative		785
	21.6.1	Statement of Interdiction Principles	786
	21.6.2	Bilateral Shipboarding Agreements	787
21.7	Can the NPT Survive?		795

Chapter Twenty-Two   Commentary for the Convention on the Suppression of Unlawful Acts against the Safety of Maritime Navigation 801

22.1	Convention for the Suppression of Unlawful Acts (SUA)		801
	22.1.1	1988 Convention	804
		Article 1	805
		Article 2	806
		Article 3	806
		Article 4	809
		Article 5	810
		Article 6	810
		Article 7	813
		Article 8	814
		Article 9	814
		Article 10	814
		Article 11	815
		Article 12	816
		Article 13	816
		Article 14	817
		Article 15	817
		Article 16	817
		Article 17	818
		Article 18	818
		Article 19	818
		Article 20	818
		Article 21	819
		Article 22	819
	22.1.2	2005 Convention	820
		Article 1	822
		Article 2	823
		Article 2*bis*	824
		Article 3	826
		Article 3*bis*	826

	Article 3*ter*	828
	Article 3*quater*	829
	Article 4	830
	Article 5 and Article 5*bis*	831
	Article 6	832
	Article 7	832
	Article 8	833
	Article 8*bis*	833
	Article 9	842
	Article 10	843
	Article 11	843
	Article 11*bis*	844
	Article 11*ter*	844
	Article 12	845
	Article 12*bis*	845
	Article 13	846
	Article 14	847
	Article 15	847
	Article 16	847
	Article 16*bis*	848
	Article 17	848
	Article 18	849
	Article 19	849
	Article 20	849
	Article 21	850
	Article 22	850
	Article 23	851
	Article 24	852
22.1.3	2005 Protocol (Safety of Fixed Platforms)	853
	Article 1	853
	Article 2	854
	Article 2*bis*	854
	Article 2*ter*	854
	Article 3	855
	Article 4	855
	Article 4*bis*	856
	Article 8	856
	Article 9	856
	Article 10	857
	Article 11	857
	Article 12	857
	Article 13	858

Chapter Twenty-Three		Irregular Naval Warfare and Blockade	859
23.1	Irregular Naval Warfare		859
	23.1.1	Law of the Sea during Armed Conflict	864
	23.1.2	Combatants at Sea	867
23.2	Quarantine		869
	23.2.1	Cuban Missile Crisis	870
	23.2.2	Legality of Quarantine	877
23.3	*Cordon Sanitaire*		880
23.4	Neutrality and Maritime Blockade		882
	23.4.1	Blockade in History	882
	23.4.2	Law of Blockade	885
		23.4.2.1 Object of Blockade	886
		23.4.2.2 Geographic Scope	886
		23.4.2.3 Absolute and Conditional Contraband	887
		23.4.2.4 Belligerent Right of Visit and Search	888
		23.4.2.5 Attempted Breach	889
	23.4.3	Law of Neutrality	891
23.5	Blockade in Non-International Armed Conflict		892
	23.5.1	U.S. Civil War	892
	23.5.2	Spanish Civil War	895
	23.5.3	Israel's Blockade of Gaza	895
Appendix 1: Agreement on the Gaza Strip and Jericho Area			900
Chapter Twenty-Four		Security Council Maritime Enforcement	903
24.1	Rhodesia Sanctions and the Beira Patrol (1965)		904
24.2	The Maritime Blockade of Iraq (1990–91)		907
24.3	Former Republic of Yugoslavia Armaments Embargo (1991–96)		912
24.4	Haiti Sanctions (1994)		915
24.5	Libya Embargo (2011)		918
Index			923

LIST OF TABLES

Table 3.1.	NATO SNMG1 and SNMG2 Anti-piracy Rotations	56
Table 4.1.	Notice to Airmen D (NOTAM D) Key Word Indicators	106
Table 8.1.	Examples of Lawful Military Activities in the EEZ	236
Table 10.1.	Signals Initiated by Intercepting Aircraft and Responses by Intercepted Aircraft (United States)	301
Table 12.1.	Maritime Conventions and Protocols Revised by the Maritime Labor Convention, Feb. 23, 2006	378
Table 12.2.	Declaration of Security Matrix for Port Facilities	390
Table 13.1.	Applicability of Treaties in Port State Control	428
Table 13.2.	The ISPS Code and U.S. Port State Control, 2004–2010	432
Table 13.3.	Compliance Targeting Matrix for U.S. Ports	433
Table 13.4.	Flag States Targeted by Port State Control	434
Table 14.1.	Vessel Pre-Arrival Template for Last Ten Ports of Call	497
Table 15.1.	Chemical Processing in Manufacture of Illegal Drugs	548
Table 18.1.	Mexican-based Transnational Criminal Organizations	629
Table 20.1.	Djibouti Code of Conduct Information Sharing Network	722
Table 20.2.	Japanese Counter-piracy Legal Authorities	735
Table 21.1.	U.S. Bilateral PSI Shipboarding Agreements	794
Table 22.1.	United Nations Terrorism Conventions	852
Table 22.2.	Original Contracting States for the 2005 SUA Protocol	853
Table 22.3.	Original Contracting States for the Fixed Platforms Protocol of 2005	858

LIST OF ANNEXES AND APPENDICES

Annex 1	National Security Decision Directive 20 (1982)	204
Annex 2	National Security Decision Directive 265 (1987)	206
Annex 3	National Security Directive 49 (1990)	209
Annex 4	Presidential Decision Directive 32 (1995)	213
Annex 5	U.S. Freedom of Navigation Challenges 1995–2003	214
Appendix 1	Agreement on the Gaza Strip and Jericho Area	900

ONE

INTRODUCTION TO MARITIME SECURITY LAW

1.1 Introduction

There is no uniform or universally accepted definition of "maritime security," but we regard it as a stable order of the oceans subject to the rule of law at sea. Threats to international maritime security include maritime piracy and ship hijacking, use of the sea by terrorists, smugglers of illicit cargo, human traffickers, international criminal and extremist organizations, low-intensity or irregular maritime militia, and sometimes even conventional naval forces employing asymmetric tactics or operating in tandem with other governmental or nongovernmental organizations. Threats to the maritime domain also include intentional and unlawful damage to the marine environment, intentional or illegal dumping and vessel discharge of pollutants, illegal, unreported and unregulated fishing, as well as more attenuated threats, such as the spread of infectious disease, and accidental marine environmental degradation. In this volume, these "softer" or non-violent threats are dealt with only as they relate to the more violent threats mentioned above.[1]

The lines between law enforcement and military operations first blurred in 1989 when, the U.S. military was flush with the capability purchased during a decade of defense buildup right at the point that the threat of the Soviet Union evaporated. The United States began to employ surplus Department of Defense warships, aircraft, and other military capabilities in a "war" on illegal drugs. The emergence of Al Qaeda in the 1990s and the spectacular strikes against the United States by agents of that organization on September 11, 2001, thrust into the public consciousness and political and legal dialogue the question of how we should think about contemporary terrorism within the old models of war

---

[1] UN Doc. A/63/63, Oceans and Law of the Sea, Report of the Secretary-General, Mar. 10, 2008, para. 40.

and peace. More than a decade later debates over whether counter-terrorism is best described as a law enforcement endeavor or the conduct of armed conflict still bedevils virtually all efforts to suppress it. Meanwhile, barriers to international travel and trade have fallen, leading to a rapid expansion of the vast global maritime network. Just as the cultural, political, and economic phenomena that generated globalization have contributed to instability on land, they have also affected stability and the rule of law at sea.

The superpower competition from 1945–1989 contained internecine conflicts on land, while American and Soviet fleets imposed order at sea. Western European navies provided a powerful supplement to the U.S. Navy. Today, the Russian fleet and European navies have atrophied; the U.S. Navy is half the size it was during the 1980s. At the same time, while the bipolar balance of terror is thankfully an historic relic, lower order maritime threats have multiplied and give rise to a new breed of maritime security operations.

Maritime security operations lie at the uncomfortable nexus between maritime law enforcement and naval warfare. Just like efforts to ensure security on land and in the air, maritime security requires an ability to combat threats without undermining, harming, or excessively restricting legitimate activities at sea.[2] The rules, regimes, and norms that apply to maritime security activities are the subject of this volume—maritime security law. Maritime security law is a hybrid sub-discipline of international law, combining principally elements of the international law of the sea, international criminal law, international human rights law, and the law of naval warfare, which is a subset of international humanitarian law. Maritime security law also involves aspects of national and international administrative regulation of immigration, trade and customs.

Hybrid laws guide responses to hybrid threats. Maritime security law has much in common with its greatest land-based forerunners, law enforcement and international humanitarian law (also called the law of armed conflict), and poses the same dilemmas that are present in national security law, such as detention and the use of force. Much like the questions concerning the use of force and the geography of war in the law of armed conflict, maritime security law opens new questions of the exercise of law enforcement jurisdiction or application of naval power in different areas of the oceans.

Contemporary threats effortlessly involve international criminal organizations, non-state armed groups and insurgencies, and terrorism simultaneously with conventional theater war. The 2006 Summer War between Israel and Hezbollah, for example, was both conventional and asymmetric, and the conflict affected both land and sea, with peacetime and wartime rules applying at the same time,

---

[2] UN Doc. A/63/174, Report on the work of the United Nations Open-ended Informal Consultative Process on Oceans and Law of the Sea at its ninth meeting, July 25, 2008, para. 38.

often in the same location. Likewise, Iran's thirty-year campaign of destabilizing the Persian Gulf and the Levant has been led by the Iranian Revolutionary Guard Corps employing a mixture of criminal conduct, such as counterfeiting U.S. dollars, with terrorist methods, and the application of military force involving advanced weapons, such as missiles. Likewise, sub-national armed groups are destabilizing the Niger Delta and the Gulf of Guinea, the Western Indian Ocean, and the maritime drug trafficking corridor from the Andean Ridge to the Caribbean—generating political and economic effects that are well beyond the scope of ordinary crime but under the threshold of classic warfare.

Ensuring maritime security involves law enforcement, conventional military forces, and irregular, clandestine and special operations forces. The naval, coast guard, marine police, coastal and maritime forces are joined by ground and air elements of the joint armed forces, other departments and agencies, including oceanographic and fisheries services, the intelligence community, and international partners.

The fluidity and complexity of the nature of maritime threats and the interdisciplinary responses to them requires an understanding of policies, regulations, national civil and criminal laws of participating states, and public international law. This volume brings many of the most important legal and policy authorities into a single book, which we hope will be useful to maritime security policy planners, company and ship operators and flag registries, maritime law enforcement, the naval defense and marine security sector, the intelligence community, and international law and international relations scholars and academics. Although this is a volume on law, our aim is to provide the political-military context within which it applies by integrating into the text additional material and judgments about international maritime security. An interdisciplinary approach involving international law and international relations offers greater coherence than would be the case with a volume focused solely on "black letter" law, and should be particularly useful for the many persons less familiar with life at sea. This approach is informed not just by legal theory and doctrinal law, but also by decades of practice and experience in providing legal and policy counsel to senior joint and naval task force commanders operating throughout the world, in Pentagon and interagency decision-making, and in numerous international negotiations.

The formation and exercise of the rule of law in the oceans is important for the grand strategy of the major maritime powers, and especially the United States. Mahan suggested that maritime forces, which freely transit the seas, are an especially flexible instrument of national power, able to assert influence "where the national armies cannot go."[3] Over the last five hundred years, all of the world's

---

[3] Philip A. Crowl, *Alfred Thayer Mahan: The Naval Historian*, in Makers of Modern Strategy: From Machiavelli to the Nuclear Age 444–477, at 462 (Peter Paret ed.).

leading states achieved their position of leadership through reliance on preeminent sea power and naval capabilities. When tested empirically, the theory holds true for Portugal, the Netherlands, Great Britain and the United States.[4] There is a close relationship between a strong navy and the maintenance of global power, and the United States is uniquely positioned to capitalize on it.

By adopting the role of an offshore balancer, the United States can remain diplomatically engaged everywhere while supporting the weaker side or most stabilizing partner in any regional conflict. The international law of the sea provides political-legal infrastructure that supports the ability of air and naval forces to maneuver freely throughout the world. By exercising "command of the commons," the United States and its alliance partners leverage the entire world as maneuver space and are prepared to insert locally superior military forces into any single locality.[5] Playing the role of "offshore balancer" reduces the chances that the United States is dragged into a costly and bloody land war like Vietnam, Iraq, and Afghanistan.[6] Instead, the United States and other maritime powers can leverage capacity-building programs that boost regional self-reliance and promote regional stability.[7]

Our objective in writing this book is not just to provide a description or even analysis of the law, although we hope we do that. Our primary goal is to provide description and analysis that reflects experience in the application of the law in the real world—marrying the theory and the practice of maritime security law. In this regard, we are disciples of the legal realist movement. One of the first champions of legal realism, Dean Roscoe Pound, exhorted, "Let us not become legal monks. Let us not allow our legal texts to acquire sanctity and go the way of all sacred writings."[8] Consequently, although we provide the essential features of maritime security law, we also are unafraid to identify some glaring shortcomings in the legal architecture, and to point out a lack of convergence in law and state practice, particularly in the areas of freedom of navigation and maritime counter-proliferation.

As international law attorneys, we also believe in and borrow heavily from the liberal internationalist school of international relations; our careers have been spent in the advancement of a liberal world order. At the same time we are mindful of the explanatory power of classic political realism and its variant, structural realism. China's activities in the South China Sea, for example, may be viewed through a structural realist paradigm as an attempt to establish hegemony in

---

[4] *See generally*, GEORGE MODELSKI & WILLIAM R. THOMPSON, SEAPOWER IN GLOBAL POLITICS 1493–1993 (1988).
[5] Barry R. Posen, *Command of the Commons: The Military Foundations of U.S. Hegemony*, 28 INT'L SECURITY, Summer 2003, at 5–46.
[6] John J. Mearsheimer, *Know the Limits of US Power*, NEWSWEEK, Dec. 8, 2008, at 41.
[7] EU Strategy Against the Proliferation of Weapons of Mass Destruction (Aug. 2004).
[8] Roscoe Pound, *Law in Books and Law in Action*, 44 AM. L. REV. 12, 36 (1910).

East Asia. Yet the promise and attraction of liberal internationalism to fashion a more stable international order persists, and we are unwilling to give up on it. Finally, our research reflects the value of constructivist approaches to international law—the importance of the concepts and language to shape what Myres S. McDougal and William T. Burke so aptly called the "public order of the oceans."[9] The research and convictions reflected in this volume leverage these three methods of international relations theory in the pursuit of developing more effective maritime security law.

1.2 WHAT IS "MARITIME SECURITY LAW"?

Just as states seek to maximize national security and yet often disagree on what means should be employed to do so, the pursuit of maritime security is both ubiquitous and ambiguous. During the Cold War, the terms "naval power," or "naval diplomacy," or the more nuanced, "seapower," were common parlance. In the contemporary era, however, naval forces are just one element—albeit an essential or even dominant one—for ensuring security in the maritime domain. Any definition of maritime security, however, must at least include all four elements of national power that constitute "DIME"—diplomacy, intelligence or information, military, and economic means. Beyond the marine or oceans aspects of "DIME," maritime security may involve environmental or cultural interests. Furthermore, there is difficulty in separating maritime safety from maritime security, and the two sets of activities, which developed independently, have become intertwined. The division between oceans law and oceans policy or maritime law and maritime policy is similarly blurred.

In many respects the fusion of maritime security and maritime safety is unavoidable. The legal regimes that regulate each activity are less distinct today than in the past and now share common and mutually reinforcing objectives. "[A] secure maritime space is certainly a safer one; and a maritime regime that prioritizes safety is less vulnerable to . . . threats to security."[10] The world economy depends on a free and secure maritime transportation system. The "just in time" global trading regime, for example, appears able to absorb only about a week of disruption before dire economic consequences ensue.[11] Strengthening safety or security in the maritime domain generates cascading benefits, spinning off

---

[9] MYRES S. MCDOUGAL & WILLIAM T. BURKE, THE PUBLIC ORDER OF THE OCEANS 562 (1962).
[10] UN Doc. A/63/63, Oceans and Law of the Sea, Report of the Secretary-General, Mar. 10, 2008, para. 36.
[11] BERNICE LEE & FELIX PRESTON, WITH GEMMA GREEN, PREPARING FOR HIGH-IMPACT, LOW-PROBABILITY EVENTS: LESSONS FROM EYJAFJALLAJÖKULL viii and 12 (Chatham House Jan. 2012).

positive and reinforcing externalities for advancing McDougal & Burke's vision of a public order of the oceans.

Maritime security law includes legal authorities to counter traditional and conventional threats, as well as irregular or asymmetric dangers, against the territorial integrity or political independence of flag, port, coastal, and land-locked states. The breadth of issues that may constitute maritime security law can easily overwhelm any effort to capture them in a single, comprehensible volume. Consequently, the contents of this book are a product of certain subjective decisions concerning the amount of description and analysis afforded each topic, the scope of interdisciplinary material, and perhaps the most challenging decision—which subjects to exclude. In particular, our work concentrates on international law to a greater extent than domestic law, although we make special reference to some authorities of state practice and laws of the United States because of its dispositive presence in global maritime security operations.

The U.S. sea services of the Navy, Marine Corps and Coast Guard describe the maintenance of maritime security as "essential to mitigating threats short of war, including piracy, terrorism, weapons proliferation, drug trafficking, and other illicit activities."[12] Furthermore, "Countering these irregular and transnational threats protects our homeland, enhances global stability, and secures freedom of navigation for the benefit of all nations."[13] The tri-service *Naval Operations Concept 2010* that implements the U.S. maritime strategy proposes a definition for maritime security that reads, "Those operations conducted to protect sovereignty and resources, ensure free and open commerce, and to counter maritime-related terrorism, transnational crime, piracy, environmental destruction, and illegal seaborne immigration."[14] Thus, as amorphous as the term maritime security is, it is distinct from traditional naval power.

Maritime security operations are also called maritime constabulary operations, and they address maritime transnational crime, terrorism, maritime piracy, illicit trafficking, and maritime proliferation of chemical, biological, nuclear, radiological weapons and high explosives that constitute some of the most vexing threats to maritime security.[15] These threats cannot adequately be addressed merely by law enforcement, but also do not normally call for the full measure of naval fleet action. Similarly, in some regions, such as the South China Sea or the Eastern Mediterranean, there is not a definable separation between civil activities and naval operations. There is a real risk in such circumstances that civil activities involving fishing or exploring for oil and gas deposits may erupt in violence.

---

[12] Dep't of the U.S. Navy, A Cooperative Strategy for 21st Century Sea Power 14 (Oct. 2007).
[13] Id.
[14] Dep't of the U.S. Navy, Naval Operations Concept 2010 at 98 (2010).
[15] UN Doc. A/63/63, Oceans and Law of the Sea, Report of the Secretary-General, Mar. 10, 2008, para. 39.

Maritime law enforcement is a subset of maritime security law, giving rise to questions of both substantive law and issues of national criminal jurisdiction and procedure. Rules for maritime law enforcement generally flow from the nationality of the flag state of the ship on which the crime occurred (*lex locus delicti*), the geographic location of the ship at sea and the relationship of the offense to a coastal state, the nationality of the perpetrators or conspirators, and the nationalities of the victims. How states interpret and apply national and international rules, however, leads to contending notions of compliance and law enforcement.

Even when nations agree upon the substance of customary international law or treaty law, they may disagree on how those rules are implemented by individual states. In some sense, the lack of uniformity is a function of differences among states over international law more generally, since nations vary in their acceptance of different sources of international law, and in their national or constitutional criteria for implementing international rules. National laws concerning self-execution of treaties and recognition of customary international law and legislative embodiment mean that even when nations agree in principle, they may diverge in practice.

1.2.1 *The Protean Nature of Maritime Security Law*

Armed attack or armed aggression in the maritime domain may involve conventional sea mines, missiles, and traditional military aviation, surface combats, and submarine platforms. During a period that extended from the first Hague conference in 1899, through two world wars, and continuing until the end of the Cold War, the predominant influence of law on sea power were naval arms control regimes. Arms control sought to limit the risk or effects of naval warfare. Naval arms control refined the laws of naval warfare and prescribed conduct at sea by erecting "firewalls" that separated opposing fleets or by creating limitations on the means of naval warfare, such as the use of sea mines, or restrictions on the methods of naval warfare, such as the proscription against unrestricted submarine warfare. These rules were designed to maintain the peace or prevent the expansion of war at sea by controlling the types and numbers of warships, the types of permissible weapons, and how those weapons may be employed.

During the period between the two world wars, the Washington Treaty of 1922 fixed battleship ratios for all of the major maritime powers.[16] While the agreement actually did slow the construction of capital warships, it also had the

---

[16] Treaty Between the United States of America, The British Empire, France, Italy, and Japan, Limiting Naval Armament (Five Power Treaty or Washington Treaty), Feb. 6, 1922, 43 STAT. 1655, 2 BEVANS 35. The treaty limited United States, British and Japanese battleship strength in a 5:5:3 ration. For an analysis, *see* THE WASHINGTON NAVAL CONFERENCE 1921–22: NAVAL RIVALRY, EAST ASIAN STABILITY AND THE ROAD TO PEARL HARBOR (Erik Goldstein & John Maurer eds. 1994).

perverse effect of creating conditions and incentives to redirect naval ambitions into other systems, such as submarines, that were not explicitly controlled. The last major fleet engagement ended with the Battle of Leyte Gulf in October 23–26, 1944. The final naval battle of the war, the Battle of Okinawa in the spring of 1945, was the largest amphibious assault of the Pacific theater.

The Western alliance and the Soviet Union engaged in an uneasy face-off, brushing close to naval warfare in the Caribbean during the U.S. quarantine of Cuba in 1962, and in the Mediterranean Sea during the Yom Kippur War of 1973. The superpowers, however, never met in battle at sea, despite decades of tense political drama.

A set of nuclear arms control agreements underscored that the primary function of international law was to prevent superpower war, and nuclear war in particular. In that setting, international law, in the form of nuclear and conventional arms control regimes, was an important part of the broader equation of containment. The 1971 Seabed Treaty, for example, slowed the spread of nuclear weapons by banning their emplacement on the floor of the ocean beyond 12 nautical miles from the coastline.[17] Law served a controlling function—complementing the INCSEA agreements to avoid unintended confrontation by American and Soviet naval forces. The 1972 USSR-United States Incidents at Sea Agreement (INCSEA)[18] and the follow-on agreements between the Soviet Union and the United Kingdom (1986), West Germany and France (1988), Canada and Italy (1989), Spain and the Netherlands (1990), and between West Germany and the Republic of Poland (1990), were aimed at reducing provocative or risky behavior by maintaining physical separation of rival naval forces.[19]

---

[17] Treaty on the Prohibition of the Emplacement of Nuclear Weapons and Other Weapons of Mass Destruction on the Seabed and the Ocean Floor and in the Subsoil Thereof, Washington, London and Moscow, Feb. 11, 1971, entered into force May 18, 1972, 23 UST 701, TIAS 7337, 955 UNTS 115.

[18] Agreement between the Government of the United States and the Government of the Union of Soviet Socialist Republics on the Prevention of Incidents on or over the High Seas, Moscow May 25, 1972, entered into force May 25, 1972, 23 UST 1168, TIAS 7379, 852 UNTS 151, amended by the Protocol of May 22, 1973, 24 UST 1063, TIAS 7624, 925 UNTS 174 [Hereinafter INCSEA].

[19] *See*, USSR-UK: Agreement between the Government of the United Kingdom of Great Britain and Northern Ireland and the Government of the Union of Soviet Socialist Republics concerning the Prevention of Incidents at Sea beyond the Territorial Sea, London July 15, 1986, entered into force July 15, 1986, 1505 UNTS 89, UKTS No. 5 (1987), 37 ICLQ 420 (1988), UN LAW OF THE SEA BULL. NO. 10, Nov. 1987, at 97.

USSR-France: Agreement Between the Government of the Federal Republic of Germany and the Government of the Union of Soviet Socialist Republics Concerning the Prevention of Incidents at Sea Beyond the Territorial Sea, Moscow Oct. 25, 1988, entered into force Nov. 25, 1988, 1546 UNTS 203; Agreement Between the Government of the Union of Soviet Socialist Republics and the Government of the French Republic Concerning the Prevention of Incidents at Sea Outside Territorial Waters, Paris July 4,

This volume avoids a complete discussion of legacy maritime security agreements designed to control high-end sea power, only bringing them into sharper focus when they pertain to conflict and war prevention at the lower end of the spectrum of conflict. Operation Praying Mantis, for example, was as much a counter-terrorism operation as it was a naval battle. The U.S. response to Iranian attacks on merchant oil tanker shipping traffic in the Persian Gulf in 1987–88 remains the greatest U.S. naval battle since World War II. The rules governing irregular maritime conflict and the law of naval warfare had currency alongside the peacetime law of the sea—hybrid law for a hybrid conflict. The Tanker War represents the most likely type of naval warfare at sea today—asymmetric, unconventional, and low in intensity, involving a combination of traditional naval forces and non-state or irregular forces, yet capable of producing strategic effects in regional politics and global markets.

Since the Iran-Iraq War of the 1980s, however, international law in the maritime domain has reoriented, moving away from the law of naval warfare and toward producing legal frameworks and informal networks to achieve stability and security at sea. The new maritime security law facilitates collaboration among states rather than reinforcing their separation through arms control, limits on the use of force, or the promulgation of confidence-building measures. Contemporary maritime security law spreads safety and security through networks or coalitions that are linking states together in a common enterprise to secure the global maritime system. Laws and international institutions have become catalysts for

---

1989, entered into force July 4, 1989, UN Law of the Sea Bull. No. 16, at 23, 1548 UNTS 223, amended by the Protocol signed at Kaliningrad Dec. 17, 1997, entered into force Dec. 17, 1997, 2090 UNTS 219;

USSR-Italy: Agreement Between the Government of the Union of Soviet Socialist Republics and the Government of the Italian Republic Concerning the Prevention of Incidents at Sea Outside Territorial Waters, Rome Nov. 30, 1989, entered into force Dec. 31, 1989, 1590 UNTS 22.

USSR-Canada: Agreement Between the Government of the Union of Soviet Socialist Republics and the Government of Canada Concerning the Prevention of Incidents at Sea Beyond the Territorial Sea, Moscow Nov. 20, 1989, entered into force Nov. 20, 1989, UN Law of the Sea Bull. No. 18, at 25, 1568 UNTS 11;

Germany-Poland: Agreement Between the Government of the Federal Republic of Germany and the Government of the Republic of Poland Concerning the Prevention of Incidents at Sea Beyond the Territorial Sea, Bonn Nov. 27, 1990, entered into force Dec. 27, 1990, 1910 UNTS 39;

USSR-Spain: Agreement Between the Government of Spain and the Government of the Union of Soviet Socialist Republics Concerning the Prevention of Incidents at Sea Beyond the Territorial Sea, Madrid Oct. 26, 1990, entered into force Oct. 10, 1991, 1656 UNTS 429;

USSR-Netherlands: Agreement Between the Government of the Union of Soviet Socialist Republics and the Government of the Netherlands Concerning the Prevention of Incidents at Sea Beyond the Territorial Sea, Moscow June 19, 1990, entered into force Oct. 1, 1991, 1604 UNTS 3;

fostering collaboration among states. Distributed maritime forces from a coalition of nations are spreading the rule of law at sea—building a public order of the oceans that is broad, robust, and inclusive. Much as changes in international politics opened the door to a new paradigm in maritime security law, the law itself influences the strategic, operational, and political seascape in decisive ways.

Maritime security law is experiencing a renaissance. Over the past two decades, the international laws pertaining to maritime security evolved from a set of rules designed to avoid naval warfare by keeping maritime powers apart, toward a new global framework designed to facilitate maritime security cooperation by bringing countries together to reach common goals.[20] The effects of this change are far-reaching—for the first time, law is a force multiplier for pursuing shared responsibilities in the oceans. In a departure from the past hundred years of state practice, the contemporary focus of international maritime security law now is constructive and prospective, broadening international partnerships for enhancing port security, as well as coastal and inshore safety, extending maritime domain awareness, and countering threats at sea.

Traditional institutions are still important for constructing a more secure maritime order. The United Nations Security Council and the International Maritime Organization (IMO), a specialized agency of the United Nations, are more active than ever in promoting security in the maritime commons. The prospect of greater maritime threats has made legacy organizations and institutions adapt, with the IMO taking the lead. In 2002, member States of the IMO adopted major revisions to the 1974 Convention on the Safety of Life at Sea (SOLAS) and in 2005 the international body completely revised the 1988 Convention for the Suppression of Unlawful Acts against the Safety of Maritime Navigation (SUA). Three years later, at the urging of the Secretary-General of the IMO, the Security Council became involved in efforts to repress maritime piracy.

Informal networks and frameworks have emerged to fill in gaps not covered by formal agreements. Ten years after it was founded, the 2003 Proliferation Security Initiative to disrupt the spread of weapons of mass destruction has more than 100 participating nations. The 2008 Shared Awareness and Deconfliction (SHADE) initiative has met in Bahrain to coordinate operational counter-piracy operations for 27 nations. The 2009 Contact Group on Piracy off the Coast of Somali counts 50 states and international organizations as active associates. Industry is also doing more, recognizing that international shipping has an affirmative responsibility to protect seafarers and ships through adoption of Best Management Practices that include passive vessel security measures, or even by hiring privately contracted armed security.

---

[20] James Kraska, *Grasping 'The Influence of Law on Sea Power'*, 62 NAVAL WAR COLL. REV., Summer 2009, at 113, 113–114.

1.2.2 *The Influence of Law on Sea Power*

In 1975 the eminent scholar D. P. O'Connell published his influential study, *The Influence of Law on Sea Power*, which reflects an approach to sea power and international law tied to the bipolar strategic order of that time.[21] O'Connell portrayed the role of international law in naval operations and planning largely as a function of the law of naval warfare. His seminal volume epitomized the relationship between sea power and international law over the previous century. In many respects O'Connell's approach, with its focus on Hague and Geneva law, is antiquated, but his attention to irregular maritime incidents was a prescient glimpse into the "return of history" after the Cold War.[22] His review of the legality of unrestricted submarine warfare has only marginal value today, whereas other sections of the book, including the investigation of how naval forces view the law of self-defense in light of hostile acts or demonstrations of hostile intent at sea, retain considerable currency. Within a decade of its publication, however, the demise of the USSR and the absence of a peer competitor to the US Navy meant that for the most part O'Connell's scholarship has gathered dust.

Since O'Connell's volume appeared, both international law and naval warfare have evolved to fit changes in the distribution of maritime power in the world system. Today there is no contemporary guide that explains the relationship between international law and maritime security in the era that began with September 11 in the same way that O'Connell did for international law and naval power in the Cold War. The dramatic political changes in the world system as it shifted from a bipolar order during the 1950s to 1980s to a unipolar model during the 1990s, and now toward a multi-polar globe are axiomatic. We hope this volume helps to fill the legal space created by these tectonic shifts in sea power.

International law has experienced dramatic growth and change since the 1970s by becoming both more diffuse and exerting more influence on the world system. Over the past twenty years, the seismic changes in the world system have meant that international law has evolved relatively quickly to accommodate and then to influence the shape of the world system. In contrast, because it takes decades to design and construct warships and modern aircraft, and since those platforms remain in service for additional decades, naval force structure and doctrine have progressed comparatively slowly. While measures of naval power have been a lagging indicator of change in power in the international system, both the international law of the sea and maritime security law are at the vanguard, driving those changes.

---

[21] D. P. O'Connell, The Influence of Law on Sea Power (1975).
[22] Robert W. Kagan, The Return of History and the End of Dreams 3–4 (2009) (The world is becoming a multipolar system based on ethnic, religious, and civilizational struggle for power in which America is dominant but lacks power to dominate).

Since 1989 international law has served a more complicated, if not more ambitious purpose: to hold the fractured Westphalian international system together by favoring integration over autonomy and stability over change. International law also serves to tie together the public order of the oceans. In 1994, the United Nations Convention on the Law of the Sea (UNCLOS) entered into force, and states began to actively pursue the full range of oceans policies under the umbrella of the treaty.[23] These efforts include molding interpretations of UNCLOS to promote inconsistent and competing state interests in maritime security. Ivan Shearer, for example, suggested in 1998 that the primary value of international law to sea power was in the creation of a normative framework for law enforcement at sea.[24] For Shearer, international law is a mechanism for the coastal state to enforce its laws in waters superjacent to the coastline, including criminal laws in the territorial sea, customs infringement and public health laws in the contiguous zone, and resource conservation regulations in the exclusive economic zone. Extending seaward from the beach, the coastal state could assert jurisdiction over certain offenses involving marine pollution or protection of the natural environment. Traditionalists, however, still adhere to the meme of freedom of the seas that runs through a line of oceans law jurisprudence dating from the discovery of the New World to Hugo Grotius to McDougal and Burke, and that is championed more recently by John Norton Moore, Bernard H. Oxman, and others.[25]

1.2.3 *Influence of Law on Maritime Security*

The US' *Cooperative Strategy for 21st Century Sea Power* reflects a shift in the theory of sea power away from the concept of command of the sea, the linchpin of geostrategist Alfred Thayer Mahan conception of maritime power,[26] toward British

---

[23] United Nations Convention on the Law of the Sea, Montego Bay Dec. 10, 1982, entered into force Nov. 10, 1994, UN Doc. A/CONF.62/122, 21 I.L.M. 1621–1354 (1982), 1833 UNTS 397 [Hereinafter UNCLOS].

[24] Ivan A. Shearer, *Development of International Law with Respect to the Law Enforcement Role of Navies and Coast Guards in Peacetime*, 71 NAVAL WAR COLL. INT'L LEG. STUD. 429 (1998).

[25] *See*, Lawrence S. Eagleberger & John Norton Moore, *Opportunity on the Oceans*, WASH. POST, July 30, 2007, Bernard H. Oxman, *The Territorial Temptation: Siren Song at Sea*, 100 AM. J. INT'L L. 830 (2006), JAMES KRASKA, MARITIME POWER AND THE LAW OF THE SEA: EXPEDITIONARY OPERATIONS IN WORLD POLITICS (2011), and James Kraska, *Law of the Sea Convention—Global Strategic Mobility through the Rule of Law*, 39 GEO. WASH. INT'L L. REV. 543 (2007), *cf.* STEVEN GROVES, ACCESSION TO THE U.N. CONVENTION ON THE LAW OF THE SEA IS UNNECESSARY TO SECURE U.S. NAVIGATIONAL RIGHTS AND FREEDOMS, THE HERITAGE FOUNDATION BACKGROUNDER NO. 2599 (Aug. 24, 2011).

[26] ALFRED THAYER MAHAN, THE INFLUENCE OF SEA POWER UPON HISTORY 1660–1783 14–24 (1890) (Little Brown, 12th ed. 1918) (Sea control an essential feature of power politics).

historian Sir Julian S. Corbett's notion of constabulary sea control.[27] Mahan envisioned naval forces taking command of the sea through large-scale engagements such as the Battle of Jutland. For Corbett, it is not enough just to control the seas. Force structure should include not only major combatants, but also widely distributed engagement forces capable of exercising constabulary authority.[28] In today's world, international maritime law is the medium for developing a collaborative approach to expanding constabulary authority. As a result, international maritime law has gravitated from the periphery to the center of maritime strategy. The relationship between international law and maritime security should be understood, and even redefined, in light of these changes.

The aggression against the United States on September 11 and the specter of corresponding terrorist assaults from the sea caused a sudden and far-reaching reappraisal of the role of law in maritime security. Although the attacks in 2001 came from the air, the maritime community feared that a mass casualty terrorist assault against a ship or port would be equally catastrophic. An oil tanker could ram into the Golden Gate Bridge; a Liquefied Natural Gas tanker could be detonated in Boston Harbor, creating nuclear bomb-like effects, a cruise ship could be seized by masked gunmen, holding thousands hostage. These prospects led to negotiation of new agreements under the framework of international law of the sea that have awakened a renaissance in maritime security collaboration.

The law is contributing substantively to maritime security by creating new norms, regimes, and expectations, and procedurally by building trust and collaborative decision-making. The emerging global maritime security regime is inclusive, multilateral and consensual, in sharp distinction to the disparate and competing national perspectives on international law concerning counter-terrorism. The vehement disagreement among nations over issues of detention, interrogation, drone strikes, and targeting of terrorists does not exist in the maritime domain. Furthermore, the important role of law in facilitating maritime security cooperation is at odds with conventional wisdom that suggests the oceans are subject to a legal vacuum—a sort of wild and ungoverned space.[29]

Working alongside states, international and intergovernmental organizations play a key role in the process of developing authoritative and controlling decisions for maritime security law.[30] The United Nations Security Council can adopt

---

[27] JULIAN STAFFORD CORBETT, SOME PRINCIPLES OF MARITIME STRATEGY 190–204 (Longmans, Green & Co. 1918).
[28] Id., at 104–07.
[29] WILLIAM LANGEWIESCHE, THE OUTLAW SEA: A WORLD OF FREEDOM, CHAOS, AND CRIME 3–4 (2005).
[30] In the New Haven School of policy-oriented jurisprudence, law is a process of decision that is both authoritative and controlling against the "guiding light of a preferred world public order of human dignity." W. Michael Reisman, Siegfried Wiessner, & Andrew R. Willard, *The New Haven School: A Brief Introduction*, 32 YALE. J. INT'L L. 575, 576 (2007).

binding resolutions that determine a threat to international peace and security. The UN Secretariat includes the Division of Ocean Affairs and Law of the Sea (DOALOS); the UN General Assembly, which convened the Third United Nations Conference on the Law of the Sea from 1973–1982, is an all-inclusive forum for considering different approaches to oceans governance. The International Maritime Organization (IMO) plays the leading role in building out the international law of the sea, developing conventions, codes, and guidelines to make shipping safer and more secure. The International Atomic Energy Agency (IAEA), the International Criminal Police Organization (INTERPOL), and the UN Environment Program (UNEP), to name just a few organizations, also contribute to the development of global oceans law and policy.

The New Haven School of jurisprudence stresses that virtually anyone may mediate their voice through groups large and small to participate in the process of authoritative decision.[31] Private commercial and industry organizations participate in meetings of the IMO and other international organizations to shape the law of the sea. The International Maritime Bureau (IMB), part of the International Chamber of Commerce and funded by the shipping industry, has been instrumental in reducing the risk of maritime piracy. Shipping industry groups, including the Baltic and International Maritime Council (BIMCO) and the International Chamber of Shipping (ICS) wield great influence. Individuals working with environmental nongovernmental organizations also enjoy influence on the shape of international marine environmental protection.

Despite differences among nations in normative goals and legal institutions, varying interpretations of international law, and competing interests, there is accord on the legal frameworks necessary for ensuring maritime security. Since the United States was the principle sponsor of the international system developed in the wake of World War II, the evolution of sea power as an outgrowth of international maritime law plays to a rather unique American strength. The trend converts traditional competition arising from naval power—a "struggle for power," to a contest over interpretation and application of legal norms and regimes of the global maritime partnership—a "struggle for law."

The United States has become the world's leader in advancing these positive relationships, which include nonbinding political arrangements such as the Proliferation Security Initiative, the Department of Energy's Megaports program to detect radiation sources secreted in cargoes inbound to the United States from foreign ports, and the Department of Homeland Security's Container Security Initiative, which uses forward deployed Coast Guardsmen overseas to screen every container entering the country. The United States also serves as a principal advocate of binding legal instruments, including Security Council Resolution 1540,

---

[31] Id., at 576–77.

the 2002 overhaul of the 1974 Safety of Life at Sea Convention (SOLAS)[32] and comprehensive revisions to the 1988 Convention for the Suppression of Unlawful Acts against the Safety of Maritime Navigation (SUA).[33] If the United States is to continue to have influence over the course of maritime security law it will have to address a major piece of unfinished business—U.S. accession to UNCLOS. UNCLOS is the foremost international instrument for realizing collaborative approaches to maritime security.[34]

1.3 Building a Public Order of the Oceans

The oceans are primarily a spatial extension resource, and their foremost use is as a means of transit and communication, which is why freedom of navigation is the bedrock maritime interest.[35] Moreover, the interconnected nature of the oceans and the important position of the doctrine of precedent in international law mean that international maritime law in one area affects the progression of the law everywhere. Unlike a stock resource such as fish, the value of a spatial resource does not diminish as more users enjoy and exploit it.

"All politics is local," is the most memorable utterance from Thomas P. "Tip" O'Neil, the iconic speaker of the House of Representatives from 1977–87. The New Deal politician learned the hard lesson when he lost his first election—a run for the Cambridge City Council during the Great Depression. While on land, all politics is local; at sea, all politics necessarily is global, since the oceans constitute the greatest global common. Oceans law and policy issues occupy a classic functional arena of governance, and maritime security and freedom of the seas ensure that the community resource of the ocean is safe and open to all users, cross-cutting every other use of the sea.

With increasing reliance on just-in-time delivery of goods, countries are closely bound together by maritime shipping. More than two billion passengers and 35 percent of the international trade (in terms of value) transits international

---

[32] International Convention for the Safety of Life at Sea, London Nov. 1, 1974, entered into force May 25, 1980, 32 UST 47, TIAS 9700, 1184 UNTS 277.

[33] *See*, Ch. 16. Convention for the Suppression of Unlawful Acts Against the Safety of Maritime Navigation, Rome March 10, 1988, entered into force Mar. 1, 1992, 27 I.L.M. 672 (1988), UN Law of the Sea Bull. No. 11, July 1988, at 14, 1678 UNTS 221 [SUA 1988] and Convention for the Suppression of Unlawful Acts Against the Safety of Maritime Navigation, done at London, Oct. 14, 2005, entered into force July 28, 2010, IMO Doc. SUA.3/Circ.11, May 4, 2010 (SUA 2005).

[34] United Nations Convention on the Law of the Sea, *opened for signature* Dec. 10, 1982, UN Doc. A/CONF.62/122 (1982), 1833 U.N.T.S. 3, 397, 21 I.L.M. 1261 (1982) [hereinafter UNCLOS] (*entered into force* Nov. 16, 1994), Article 17.

[35] McDougal & Burke, The Public Order of the Oceans, at 564.

airspace annually.[36] By volume, however, more than 90 percent of global trade (in terms of weight) is conducted over the sea lanes.[37] Globalization would be impossible without the 50,000 ships that travel the Earth on international voyages. The vessels are flagged in 150 states and are operated by over one million seafarers representing virtually every nationality. Since the end of World War II, one billion people have been lifted out of poverty as a result of this grand orchestration of trade.[38]

Ensuring maritime security requires littoral and coastal states, landlocked states, flag states, and port states to work in concert with international organizations and the maritime industry. Each state has an interest in the development and maintenance of maritime security, stability and the maintenance of good order at sea. Nearly every maritime security scenario involves multiple states—all with an interest in the collaborative process of authoritative decision. The key to order is creating and enforcing a stability of expectations based upon a commonly understood rule set.

Determining jurisdiction in maritime security cases is particularly vexing. A vessel hijacked by pirates or engaged in smuggling most likely is registered in one nation, such as Greece,[39] owned by a corporation located in South Korea, and operated by a crew comprised of nationals from the Philippines and Pakistan. Furthermore, the vessel is likely to be transporting either containerized cargo or bulk commodities owned by companies in one or more additional states. Port officials or naval forces from several nations may be involved in tracking and intercepting the pirated ship. The cosmopolitan rules governing negotiations among these disparate players emerged from hundreds of years of oceans law.

1.3.1 *From Westphalia to Montego Bay*

The development of modern oceans law may be traced to the seventeenth century, when Bourbon and Hapsburg rivalry engulfed central Europe in the Thirty Years War. The war was brought to a close with the Peace of Westphalia in 1648.[40]

---

[36] GENERAL NORTON A. SCHWARTZ & ADMIRAL JONATHAN W. GREENERT, AIR-SEA BATTLE: PROMOTING STABILITY IN AN ERA OF UNCERTAINTY (Feb. 20, 2012).
[37] DEP'T OF THE U.S. NAVY, A COOPERATIVE STRATEGY FOR 21ST CENTURY SEA POWER 5 (Oct. 2007).
[38] SCHWARTZ & GREENERT, AIR-SEA BATTLE.
[39] The term "flag state" is understood to be the administration or the government of the state whose flag the ship is entitled to fly. MARITIME INTERNATIONAL SECRETARIAT SERVICES LIMITED, SHIPPING INDUSTRY GUIDELINES ON FLAG STATE PERFORMANCE 5 (2d ed. 2006).
[40] The Peace of Westphalia was constructed from a series of treaties ending the Thirty Years War, and signed between May and October 1648 in Osnabrück and Münster, Germany. Leo Gross, *The Peace of Westphalia, 1648–1948*, 42 AM. J. INT'L L. 20, 24 (Jan. 1948) and Rainer Grote, *Westphalian System*, MAX PLANCK ENCYCLOPEDIA OF PUBLIC

The Treaty of Westphalia was an epochal document, recognizing sovereignty over land areas under individual autonomous rulers and ushering in the modern nation state. Whereas the complex treaty recognized that states exercise complete authority and are responsible for maintaining security inside their borders, it was manifest that no nation could exercise sovereignty over the oceans.

Decades earlier, in 1618, Dutch jurist Hugo de Groot (Grotius) cogently set forth the natural law doctrine of freedom of the seas that preserved access to the oceans for all nations and thereby fueled an explosion in international trade. "For do not the oceans," Grotius wrote, "navigable in every direction with which God has encompassed all the earth, and the regular and occasional winds which blow now from one quarter and now from another, offer sufficient proof that Nature has given to all peoples a right of access to all other peoples?"[41]

In crafting Westphalia, Europe accomplished "what may fairly be described as an international constitution...."[42] For four hundred years international law regarding land territory was stable, governed by the canon of state sovereignty evident in the treaties of Westphalia.

> These treaties contain the clauses by which Sweden and France not only make peace with the Emperor on certain terms, but pledge themselves to their allies, the subordinate German Princes, that they will ensure that the privileges and immunities conferred on the Princes and free cities of Germany in the treaty shall be upheld and maintained. This is constantly referred to in later treaties as the guarantee for the execution of the terms of the treaty and, as Sir Ernest Satow has pointed out, it continued to be regarded as valid almost down to the outbreak of the French Revolution. Here, again, the fact of the guarantee was of the highest importance in ensuring that the treaties should be observed and that they should continue to hold their place as part of the general European System.[43]

While the Peace of Westphalia was Europe's first constitution, UNCLOS, declared Singapore Ambassador Tommy T. B. Koh at the Third UN Conference on the Law of the Sea in Montego Bay, Jamaica, represents the world's "constitution" for the oceans. The Convention has contributed directly to international peace and security by replacing abundant conflicting maritime claims with universally agreed limits and associated regulations for the territorial sea, archipelagic waters, the contiguous zone, the exclusive economic zone and the continental shelf. In recognizing the importance of these functional zones, the international community

---

INTERNATIONAL LAW (Rüdiger Wolfrum ed., 2009), *cf.* Andreas Osiander, *Sovereignty, International Relations, and the Westphalian Myth*, 55 INT'L ORG. 251–87 (2001).

[41] HUGO GROTIUS, THE FREEDOM OF THE SEAS OR THE RIGHT WHICH BELONGS TO THE DUTCH TO TAKE PART IN THE EAST INDIAN TRADE 8 (1608) (Trans. Ralph Van Deman Magoffin, ed. James Brown Scott, Oxford 1916).

[42] DAVID JAYNE HILL, II A HISTORY OF DIPLOMACY IN THE INTERNATIONAL DEVELOPMENT OF EUROPE 602 (1906) (Cornell University Library 2009).

[43] Gross, *The Peace of Westphalia*, at 24, *citing* C. VAN VOLLENHOVEN, THE LAW OF PEACE 85 (1936).

acknowledged what Grotius had so eloquently argued: freedom of the seas and international security and stability are intertwined.

D. P. O'Connell wrote that UNCLOS picks us out of the "intellectual morass," where competing opinions and views serve as a substitute for law, and the occasions for controversy and dispute became numerous and frequent.[44] The interest of the world community in freedom of navigation and overflight is preserved by delicate compromise. Finally, the treaty provides a stable and widely accepted legal order of the oceans that effectively balances the rights of flag, port and coastal states, providing a sound basis for states to cooperate in enhancing maritime security.

The process of negotiating UNCLOS flowed from three distinct elements—interaction among the maritime states and ocean users, the rights of access of the international community to ocean space and the rights of coastal states to claim jurisdiction over ocean space, and the decisions made by others in response to these rival claims.[45] It took nine years to reach agreement on these issues, and the process was contentious. "It was like playing no-limit poker and three-dimension chess at the same time," said chief U.S. delegate to the conference Elliot Richardson, in an interview with *Time Magazine* in 1980. The unfolding process of reaching authoritative decision on questions of competing oceans interests plays out in the context of UNCLOS, against a backdrop of maritime operations and diplomatic theater.

The Convention sets forth rules for the status of ships and their nationality, the rights of port states to secure internal waters and the offshore rights and duties of coastal states. As a peacetime agreement, UNCLOS reduces military risk by protecting key navigational rights and freedoms. The exercise of these global freedoms includes the right of transit through international straits by ballistic missile submarines—the most survivable component of the nuclear force—and the right, regardless of cargo or means of propulsion, to exercise innocent passage in the territorial sea, and the exercise of high seas freedoms in the exclusive economic zone.

Besides the key parts of the treaty pertaining to navigational rights and freedoms, UNCLOS recognizes that, with limited exceptions, the flag state exercises exclusive jurisdiction over ships listed on its registry. Vessels may sail under only one flag and a ship that is not registered in any nation is deemed "stateless," enjoying no flag state rights.[46] Article 94 of UNCLOS sets forth the rule that states have a duty to exercise effective control and jurisdiction over their vessels and everything on them. The rule reflects state practice through the ages—flag states exercise the exclusive right of jurisdiction over vessels flying their flag regard-

---

[44] D. P. O'Connell, The Influence of Law on Sea Power 13 (1975).
[45] McDougal & Burke, The Public Order of the Oceans vii.
[46] *United States v. Cortes*, 588 F.2d 106 (5th Cir. 1979).

less of the location of the vessel.[47] Years of ineffective flag state control by some registries, however, has led to the expansion of port state control regimes that assert greater authority over foreign-flagged ships in port in matters relating to the criminal or civil laws of the port state.

UNCLOS also contains provisions relating specifically to the tactical conduct of maritime security. Article 99 pertains to trafficking in human slaves, articles 100–107 address maritime piracy. International maritime drug trafficking became more prevalent during the decade of negotiations, and UNCLOS provides for the control of the illicit traffic in narcotic drugs in article 108. Article 110 incorporates the customary right of approach by warships of commercial vessels in order to determine their nationality. Normally the exercise of the right of approach by a warship does not impose a requirement on the part of the queried vessel to respond to the queries and a refusal to do so does not automatically trigger a right of visit on the hailing ship.[48] This peacetime right should not be confused with the belligerent right of visit and search of neutral vessels in order to search for contraband or determine the enemy character of the ship or its cargo under the law of neutrality, an offshoot of the law of armed conflict.[49] Finally, Article 111 recognizes that coastal states may initiate hot pursuit in internal waters, archipelagic waters, or the territorial sea in order to interdict ships fleeing those areas onto the high seas when the coastal state has "good reason to believe that the ship has violated the laws and regulations of that State."

1.3.2   *Building a Global Maritime Partnership*

The concept of a "Thousand Ship Navy" was introduced in 2004 and represents a figurative rather than a literal fleet comprised of a thousand vessels. Navy chiefs from over thirty nations endorsed the concept as a way for the sea services to coordinate to meet common maritime challenges. For example, the maritime relief effort in response to the tsunami off the coast of Sumatra in December 2004 was spontaneous and effective, involving coordination among international naval and coast guard forces, the civil shipping industry, and non-governmental organizations. Likewise, the U.S. Pacific Command's *Operation Tomadachi*, in response to the 2011 Tōhoku earthquake and tsunami involved 24 U.S. Navy ships and 24,000 personnel. The response rejuvenated U.S.-Japan relations and underscored the fact that no single nation can accomplish the complex mission of maritime security, even along its immediate littoral.[50]

---

[47] *Case of the SS. Lotus* (Fr. V. Turk.) Permanent Court of International Justice (Ser. A) No. 10 at p. 25 (1927).
[48] *The Mariana-Flora*, 24 U.S. (11 Wheat.) 1, 44 (1826).
[49] SAN REMO MANUAL ON THE LAW APPLICABLE TO ARMED CONFLICT AT SEA 31–32, paras. 118–121 (Louise Doswald-Beck ed., 1995).
[50] Eric Johnston, *After the Disaster, Better Ties?*, JAPAN TIMES, Apr. 5, 2011, at 2.

Over the course of a decade, the original concept of a "Thousand Ship Navy" has broadened into a combined, interagency Global Maritime Partnership (GMP) that includes not just naval forces, but civilian law enforcement and regulatory agencies and the shipping industry. The partnership approach leverages treaty relationships, formal institutions, informal coalitions, and government and non-governmental organizations. As an activity-based approach to cooperation, GMP is a new method for building greater consensus on policy to address maritime challenges. GMP is not a formal organization or agreement led by any country, however, and it does not have a structure requiring formal membership.

The North Pacific and North Atlantic Coast Guard Forums are two examples of how regimes are fostering closer relationships. The North Pacific Coast Guard Forum (NPCGF) is focused on increasing the ability of regional coast guard services to conduct combined operations and exchange information to accomplish maritime homeland security missions such as counterdrug operations, fisheries enforcement, and interdiction of illegal migrants. The first Forum was held in Tokyo in 2000 and participants include Canada, China, Japan, Korea, Russia, and the United States. Since its inception, the NPCGF has followed an alternating semi-annual cycle of technical meetings and principal summits. The NPCGF has been helpful in integrating maritime security operations throughout the North Pacific.

Building on the achievements of the NPCGF, the North Atlantic Coast Guard Forum (NACGF) was initiated in 2007 to promote multilateral maritime cooperation among states situated on the Atlantic Ocean. Coast guards and service equivalents from 18 countries participate in the NACGF.[51] No single country dominates either forum, and each is structured around shared interests. All of the participants are self-reliant and directly contribute assets and other resources in support of the shared objectives. Moreover, because the mission areas are non-confrontational the parties are willing to share experiences and best practices, increasing the potential for surge cooperation in the event of a crisis.

The Cooperative Mechanism to enhance safety and environmental protection in the Straits of Malacca and Singapore is one of the most prominent IMO-sponsored efforts to improve regional response. The initiative began in 2005 at a meeting in Jakarta as a process aimed at increasing regional cooperation and building local capacity among the littoral states to patrol the straits used for international navigation.[52] Follow-up meetings were held in Kuala Lumpur in 2006, and a third

---

[51] Belgium, Canada, Denmark (the 2008 host nation), Estonia, Finland, France, Germany, Iceland, Ireland, Latvia, Lithuania, the Netherlands, Norway, Poland, Russia, Sweden, the United States and the United Kingdom. Spain and Portugal participated in the 2008 in the North Atlantic Coast Guard Forum.

[52] J. Ashley Roach, *Enhancing Security in the Straits of Malacca and Singapore*, 59 J. INT'L AFF. 97, 102–03, 107–08, Fall/Winter 2005 (Columbia University SIPA).

meeting was held in Singapore in 2007.[53] Indonesia, Singapore and Malaysia, and 25 trading nations that are the greatest users of the straits, participated in the meetings. On September 6, 2007, at the meeting in Singapore, participant states signed the Cooperative Mechanism.[54] The Cooperative Mechanism is composed of a Cooperation Forum, a Project Coordination Committee, and an "Aids to Navigation" Fund, and is supported by the IMO.[55] The agreement marks the only time nations have come together under Article 43 of UNCLOS to cooperatively manage a strait used for international navigation.[56]

Asian counter-piracy cooperation has been even more successful. In 2004 and with the leadership of Japan, sixteen Asian nations signed the Regional Agreement on Combating Piracy and Armed Robbery against Ships in Asia (ReCAAP). ReCAAP is the first multilateral treaty dedicated solely to combating piracy. The treaty entered into force in 2006 and established a modern Information Sharing Center (ISC) in Singapore to serve as an operational coordination and information fusion point for member states.

The IMO also has been instrumental in helping the twenty-five nations of the Maritime Organization of West and Central Africa (MOWCA) more effectively cooperate to improve safety, security and environmental protection.[57] The organization is the only sub-regional body on the continent of Africa dedicated to maritime security. Since its inception in 1975, MOWCA has served as a forum for limited objectives in the maritime domain, helping states coordinate port management, for example, but it was hampered by lack of capacity, political

---

[53] IMO Doc. C/ES.24/7 (Secretary-General) Report on the Meeting on the Straits of Malacca and Singapore: Enhancing Safety, Security and Environmental Protection held in Singapore, from September 4 to 6, 2007 (Singapore Meeting). The Singapore Statement is set out in Annex 2 to document C/ES.24/7.

[54] IMO Doc. SGP/2.1/1, The Cooperative Mechanism Between the Littoral States and User States on the Safety of Navigation and Environmental Protection in the Straits of Malacca and Singapore, Singapore Meeting on the Straits of Malacca and Singapore: Enhancing Safety, Security and Environmental Protection, September 4 to 6, 2007, Aug. 16, 2007 (Indonesia, Malaysia, and Singapore) and UN Doc. A/62/518, Letter of Oct. 22, 2007 from the Permanent Representative of Indonesia, Malaysia, and Singapore, to the United Nations, Nov. 2, 2007.

[55] IMO Doc. C 100/7/Add.1, Protection of Vital Shipping Lanes: Follow-up to the 2007 Singapore Meeting and the Cooperative Mechanism, May 22, 2008.

[56] Robert C. Beckman, *Towards Implementation of UNCLOS Article 43 for the Straits of Malacca and Singapore—Rapporteur's Report on the 1999 IPS/IMO Conference on the Straits of Malacca and Singapore*, 2 SING. Y. B. INT'L L. 253, 255–61 and 274–75 (1999).

[57] MOWCA consists of the coastal states of Angola, Benin, Cameroon, Cape Verde, Republic of the Congo, Democratic Republic of the Congo, Cote d'Ivoire, Gabon, The Gambia, Ghana, Guinea, Guinea-Bissau, Equatorial Guinea, Liberia, Mauritania, Nigeria, Sao Tome & Principe, Senegal, Sierra Leone, and Togo, and the land-locked states of Burkina Faso, Central African Republic, Mali, Niger and Chad.

instability and protectionist policies. In the last few years, however, MOWCA has flourished.

The 2006 MOWCA meeting in Dakar led to release of a functional memorandum of understanding on the establishment of a Sub-regional Coastguard Network for the West and Central African region in July 2008.[58] The comprehensive agreement establishes an institutional framework for closer cooperation on suppression of piracy and armed robbery at sea, countering maritime terrorism, illegal, unregulated and unreported (IUU) fishing, interdiction of drug trafficking, prevention of oil platform and pipeline theft, anti-smuggling and pipeline security, and maritime accident response. The sub-region is divided into four coast guard zones comprised of five states each. Each zone has a coast guard center, with two principal coordinating centers in Luanda, Angola and Accra, Ghana. The agreement also provides guidelines for enhancing coastal surveillance, maintaining a maritime presence in the exclusive economic zone, and enforcement of international treaties.

Efforts to broaden maritime security partnerships can be supported through transfer of boats, equipment, and training by nations with greater resources, as well as through legal and policy capacity building. The U.S. Coast Guard's Model Maritime Service Code (MMSC), for example, was developed in 1994 to assist nations in improving their legislative infrastructure and maritime regulations to create a maritime service.[59] The Code is modular, meaning that nations may select and adapt the entire document, or extract sections to address particular issues such as border security, search and rescue, or counterterrorism, which could supplement existing laws. The Code was updated in 2008 in order to reflect recent developments in international law.[60] At the 2008 meeting of the IMO, a large group of states proposed that the Organization lead development of comparable model legislation of a maritime security code.[61] The IMO's model code would assist states that are party to SOLAS to comply with the requirements contained in the ISPS Code by proposed responsibilities for national authorities, a recommended leadership structure for ship and port facilities, a framework for

---

[58] IMO Briefing No. 39, West and Central African states to Cooperate in Sub-regional Coastguard Network, Aug. 12, 2008, http://www.imo.org/blast/mainframe.asp?topic_id=1709&doc_id=9939.

[59] U.S. Coast Guard, Model Maritime Service Code (2008), http://www.uscg.mil/international/affairs/Publications/MMSCode/english/contents.htm.

[60] Tamara Wallen, *The Model Maritime Service Code: Advancing and Updating the Coast Guard's International Outreach*, U.S. Coast Guard Proceedings, Summer 2009, at 32, 34.

[61] IMO Doc. MSC/84/4/4, Development of Model Legislation on Maritime Security, Mar. 5, 2008, *submitted by* Austria, Belgium, Bulgaria, Cyprus, Czech Republic, Denmark, Estonia, Finland, France, Germany, Greece, Hungary, Iceland, Ireland, Italy, Latvia, Lithuania, Luxembourg, the Netherlands, Malta, Norway, Poland, Portugal, Romania, Slovakia, Slovenia, Spain, Sweden, United Kingdom and the European Commission.

interagency cooperation, criteria for port facility and ship security assessments, and development of metrics for measuring compliance.

1.4 CONCLUSION

Maritime security law promotes the best of the realist and idealist strands of grand strategy. Partnerships are woven together by law, and construction of a worldwide coalition is an effective strategy for integrating disparate conceptions of security. While continuing to develop maritime security law, states should focus especially on compliance—folding existing commitments into national law and action. Adding new layers of international law without integrating commensurate authorities into national law whitewashes maritime security challenges and forms a dangerous illusion of security and community. Adjusting national laws and policies to new international commitments takes time. Nations are still implementing the post-9-11 amendments to the SOLAS Convention and the 2005 SUA Convention, for example. These amendments and complementary instruments constitute the greatest package of multilateral maritime security commitments since the interwar period of the 1930s. Although the United States led development of the new regimes, it is less clear whether the country will continue to enjoy that sort of influence in the future.

There is a widespread perception that the American brand has suffered from the war in Iraq and the Great Recession that began in 2008. At the same time, however, the diplomatic influence of the states of the European Union has diminished in the wake of a slowly unfolding economic calamity.[62] The EU's decline at the UN, for example, is apparent in three key forums: the General Assembly, the Human Rights Council, and the Security Council. After a review of voting patterns at the UN, one study concluded:

> Yet the EU is losing political credibility. It confronts a changed international context, with China and Russia emerging as alternative poles of attraction, and blocs of states from the Middle East, Africa and elsewhere setting themselves in opposition to the values that Europe espouses. And the West is in disarray: the EU's rifts with the US on many human rights issues at the UN in the Bush era have weakened both.[63]

Meanwhile, the diplomatic influence of states not entirely plugged into the international system of maritime security law—China, Iran, and Russia, for example—has expanded. These developments mean even greater investments will be needed to realize stronger maritime security laws, regimes, and institutions necessary to realize McDougal & Burke's vision of a minimum public order of the oceans.

---

[62] RICHARD GOWAN & FRANZISKA BRANTNER, A GLOBAL FORCE FOR HUMAN RIGHTS? AN AUDIT OF EUROPEAN POWER AT THE UN 3 (EUROPEAN COUNCIL ON FOREIGN RELATIONS, Sept. 2008).
[63] Id.

TWO

AMERICAN MARITIME SECURITY POLICY AND STRATEGY

2.1 INTRODUCTION

With the twilight of U.S. involvement in the wars in Iraq and Afghanistan, the United States has embarked on a strategic pivot to the Asia-Pacific region.[1] The shift is accompanied by reorientation from land-based missions—ground operations—toward an enhanced sea-based and offshore defense posture. Even before the announcement, however, there was change afoot in U.S. naval force structure in every theater.

In Europe, the U.S. Navy is forward deploying four Aegis guided missile destroyers to Rota, Spain. With massive over-the-horizon radars and anti-ballistic missile systems, these powerful warships provide ballistic missile defense to American allies in Europe. In the Americas, interdiction of maritime drug trafficking continues to be a major focus of U.S. Southern Command, located in Miami. Meanwhile, since 2007, the Arctic Ocean has become a new and important area of interest for U.S. Northern Command and U.S. European Command. The United States and Canada are expanding hemispheric cooperation beyond the North American Air Defense Command, to include Arctic maritime security.

In Asia, the newest U.S. surface combatant, the configurable Littoral Combat Ship (LCS), will be deployed to Singapore, complementing the massive power of the U.S. Seventh Fleet in Yokosuka, Japan and its associated amphibious flotilla in Sasebo and the 31st Marine Expeditionary Unit in Okinawa. The expeditionary Marine Corps is set to rotate 2,500 marines through Darwin, Australia, providing a quick reaction force on the southern edge of Southeast Asia. These

---

[1] PRESIDENT BARACK OBAMA, THE WHITE HOUSE, FOREWORD: SUSTAINING U.S. GLOBAL LEADERSHIP: PRIORITIES FOR 21ST CENTURY DEFENSE, Jan. 3, 2012 [Hereinafter SUSTAINING U.S. GLOBAL LEADERSHIP].

developments come after a decade of repositioning forces to Guam, turning the island into a forward bastion of joint maritime and air power. Guam hosts three fast attack submarines and maintains facilities to handle strategic stealth bomber aircraft and unmanned aerial vehicles.

Homeland security has acquired a maritime dimension for the first time since the Japanese invasion scare on the West Coast during the darker days of World War II. The terrorist attacks of September 11 exposed the vulnerabilities of the marine transportation system to non-state threats. The global network of container ships and oil tankers, port facilities and roadsteads are vulnerable to new forms of destruction. Multi-ethnic seafarers co-mingle with huge volumes of cargo throughout a global shipping industry dominated by weakly regulated open registries.

A major focus of the U.S. maritime security effort is strengthening international norms and legal regimes. Both political parties in Washington believe that investments in global and regional rules bring stability to the maritime domain. The United States promotes maritime agreements and is especially supportive of the work at the International Maritime Organization (IMO). Over the past decade, however, the nation also has come to value informal cooperative relationships. Joining 11 key nations,[2] for example, President George W. Bush announced the Proliferation Security Initiative (PSI) on May 31, 2003. PSI was created to address what the G8 calls the "preeminent threat"[3]—the spread of weapons of mass destruction (WMD)—through a "sticky" web of domestic and international laws and relationships designed to ensnare WMD hidden in the stream of commerce. PSI now has more than 100 participating states and is credited with a handful of significant, but unheralded, silent successes.

The Department of Energy launched the Megaports initiative to detect radioactive sources in international shipping inbound to the United States from foreign ports of departure, while the Department of Homeland Security's Container Security Initiative (CSI) forged close cooperation with exporting states to screen and inspect cargo overseas that is destined for U.S. ports.

Beginning in 2002, the United States worked with other nations at the IMO to develop a major overhaul of the 1988 Convention for the Suppression of Unlawful Acts against the Safety of Maritime Navigation (SUA) to deter the use of ships by terrorists or to transfer WMD. The result was the 2005 Protocol—now called the 2005 SUA Convention—that introduced a comprehensive shipboarding frame-

---

[2] ARMS CONTROL ASS'N, FACT SHEET: THE PROLIFERATION SECURITY INITIATIVE (PSI) AT A GLANCE, June 2004. The original PSI countries are Australia, France, Germany, Italy, Japan, the Netherlands, Poland, Portugal, Spain, the United Kingdom and the United States.

[3] *G-8 Call Proliferation 'Pre-eminent Threat' to International Security: Officials Note 'Significant Progress' On Pu Disposition*, NUCLEAR WEAPONS & MATERIALS MONITOR, June 9, 2003, at 10–11.

work and criminalized the transfer of dual use items, such as fertilizer, being misused as a weapon.

The United States also proposed amendments to the 1974 Safety of Life at Sea Convention (SOLAS), which were reflected in the 2002 International Shipping and Port Facility Security (ISPS) Code.[4] The ISPS Code requires governments and the shipping industry to cooperate in global cargo chain security. Finally, the United States advocated binding legal instruments proscribing the marine transport of WMD, including UN Security Council resolution 1540 of April 28, 2004. Adopted under Chapter VII of the Charter, the resolution mandates nations refrain from providing any form of support to terrorist groups that seek to develop, possess, or transport nuclear, chemical or biological weapons or their means of delivery.

2.2 U.S. MARITIME SECURITY POLICY

The attacks of September 11 were a catalyst for development of a new approach to maritime security. Immediately after the attacks, virtually the entire apparatus of the defense, security, and intelligence community inside the Washington Beltway obsessively focused on the war against Al Qaeda and the impending war with Iraq. By 2003 and early-2004, however, at least some of the U.S. government's attention began to be diverted back toward maritime security. At the time, the ground war was still in the hands of the Army and Marines—it was only in 2004 that the Navy would begin to pledge and provide thousands of officers and enlisted sailors to fill "individual augmentation" slots in Central Asia to supplement the war on the ground. The Navy Staff was gutted as large numbers of junior and mid-level officers were deployed to support the war effort in Iraq or Afghanistan.

Within this austere environment for maritime policy making, the Pentagon and the Coast Guard began the process of developing a national maritime security policy, working in conjunction with the Department of State, the National Security Council and the Homeland Security Council. The result of the effort was the production of National Security Presidential Directive (NSPD)-41, *Maritime Security Policy*.[5] President Bush signed the policy on December 21, 2004.

NSPD-41 was the highest U.S. outline of American interests in maritime security. The policy established guidelines to enhance U.S. national security and

---

[4] 68 FR 60449–60472, General Provisions of Maritime Security, Oct. 22, 2003, 68 FR 60545–60559, Outer Continental Shelf Facility Security, Oct. 22, 2003, 68 FR 60483–60515, Vessels; Security Measures, Oct. 22, 2003, 68 FR 60472–60483, Area Maritime Security, Oct. 22, 2003, 68 FR 60559–60570, Automatic Identification System; Vessel Carriage Requirements, Oct. 22, 2003.

[5] The policy also was designated as Homeland Security Presidential Directive -13 (HSPD-13).

homeland security interests in the oceans, which were broadly defined to include littoral seas and inland waterways. The original maritime security policy covered the entire "maritime domain," which was defined as all areas and things "of, on, under, relating to, adjacent to, or bordering on a sea, ocean, or other navigable waterway, including all maritime-related activities, infrastructure, people, cargo, and vessels and other conveyances."[6] The policy was developed to provide strategic focus for the Federal interagency community to ensure that the United States implemented a "whole of government" approach to security at sea. Under the policy, the National Security Council could arbitrate differences among departments and agencies of the U.S. government, and any disputes would be resolved by the Assistant to the President for National Security Affairs. Furthermore, Federal, state, local, and private sector efforts were grafted on to the national policy in the hope of forming a single, coherent approach.

The U.S. maritime security policy asserted that the nation will "take all necessary and appropriate actions" consistent with domestic and international law to conduct the following activities: counter-terrorism, critical marine infrastructure protection (including ports, harbors, and industrial and population centers situated along the maritime domain), consequence management, and maritime domain awareness (to enhance indications and warnings).[7]

While NSPD-41 set forth national maritime security policy, it also established a process for implementing the directive. The White House created an interdepartmental committee at the National Security Council initially called the Maritime Security Policy Coordinating Committee (MSPCC). The Obama administration renamed the group the Maritime Security Interagency Policy Committee (MSIPC), and the group meets about twice per month to conduct deliberate planning and policy development. The group also gathers on an ad hoc basis to develop U.S. responses to time-sensitive security issues arising in the maritime domain, addressing events such as maritime drug trafficking or migrant interdiction incidents that have national or international implications and therefore require authoritative U.S. government decisions. About fifteen departments and agencies are represented in the MSIPC, which is co-chaired by a senior officer of the U.S. Navy representing the Department of Defense, and a member of the U.S. Coast Guard of equivalent rank—representing the Department of Homeland Security. MSIPC meetings are held in the Executive Office of the President and may meet in the Eisenhower Executive Office Building next to the West Wing of the White House or at the White House Situation Room, as warranted.

The MSIPC is a functional policy coordinating committee that implements and refines NSPD-41, executing American strategy relating to maritime security. In

---

[6] George W. Bush, *Maritime Security Policy*, National Security Presidential Directive/NSPD-41, Dec. 21, 2004.
[7] Id.

addition to officials from the Office of the Under Secretary of Defense for Policy, bureaus within the U.S. Department of State, and U.S. Coast Guard headquarters, the MSIPC includes senior representatives from the Office of the Vice President, the Office of the Director of Central Intelligence, and the Office of the Director of Strategic Plans and Policy of the Joint Chiefs of Staff. The committee develops new policies and initiatives for consideration by the deputies and principals of the major departments and agencies that serve as members of the National Security Council and the Homeland Security Council, to include the Secretary and Deputy Secretary of Defense, Secretary of Homeland Security, the Department of State, and Chairman and Vice Chairman of the Joint Chiefs of Staff, among others.

NSPD-41 called for creation of a coordinated and integrated government-wide effort to enhance maritime security, jointly led by the Secretaries of Defense and Homeland Security. The first order of business under the policy was to draft a national strategy for maritime security (NSMS), which was due 180 days from the December 21, 2004, inception of NSPD-41. The MSPCC led the effort to draft and circulate the national maritime strategy, which was released by President George W. Bush in September 2005.[8] The National Security Council and Homeland Security Council coordinated the draft strategy with the Department of Defense, Department of State, the U.S. Maritime Administration, and other departments and agencies. The Joint Chiefs of Staff received input from the worldwide combatant commands and the military services, particularly the Navy and Marine Corps. After more than one year of collaboration, the National Security Council submitted the *National Strategy for Maritime Security* to the president for approval.

On August 14, 2012, President Barack Obama rescinded NSPD-41 in a completely new policy, Presidential Policy Directive (PPD)-8, *Maritime Security*. PPD-8 reaffirms and extends the provisions of NSPD-41 and expresses support for the 2005 *National Strategy for Maritime Security*. PPD-8 describes the maritime domain, "covering more than 70 percent of the earth's surface," as "a valuable resource for many nations." Echoing the multilateral approach of the Global Maritime Partnership, PPD-8 states that protection of the maritime domain is a responsibility that should be shared among nations.

> The deliberate misuse of the maritime domain to commit harmful, hostile, or unlawful acts, including those against the marine transportation system, remains an enduring threat to the safety and security of the American people, to wider U.S. national security interests, and to the interests of our international allies and private sector partners.

---

[8] *New U.S. Maritime Security Strategy Includes Legal and Institutional Initiatives*, 100 AM. J. INT'L L. 222–24 (Jan. 2006).

> Priority attention by the nations of the world in partnership with the private sector is essential to maritime security, including preserving freedom of navigation, protecting the maritime transportation system, serving as good stewards of the maritime environment, and safeguarding this natural resource for other lawful public and private activities.[9]

The policy also identifies specific actions to be taken to counter maritime threats, including "galvanizing action through enhanced international cooperation and public-private partnerships, promotion of peaceful resolution of competing maritime claims in accordance with international law, enhancing maritime domain awareness, encouraging adoption of security measures by industry, deployment of layered security by the commercial sector, and the use risk based methods to identify and screen threats to the system in order to facilitate the free flow of commerce.[10] Finally, the policy pledges to "continue to support and observe the principles of established customary international law reflected in the Law of the Sea Convention and consistent with longstanding policy, continue to seek advice and consent of the United States Senate to accede to the Law of the Sea Convention to advance U.S. economic and national security interests."[11]

2.3 National Strategy for Maritime Security

The 2005 *National Strategy for Maritime Security* (NSMS) was released in September 2005 and, even after the release of PPD-8, remains the capstone U.S. document for maritime security under the *National Security Strategy*.[12] The NSMS sets forth the relationship between the worldwide maritime domain and broader themes of U.S. national security.[13]

The principal U.S. interest in the oceans relates to the use of the surface of the water, the water column, and the airspace above the water as a domain of movement. The United States has a deep interest in unfettered access to the Atlantic Ocean, Pacific Ocean, Caribbean Sea, and Beaufort Sea. The country also has responsibilities in distant oceans, such as the Indian Ocean and the Arctic Ocean. The maritime domain is a flow resource, rather than a stock resource. A stock

---

[9] Presidential Policy Directive (PPD)-8, Maritime Security, Aug. 14, 2012.
[10] Id.
[11] Id. The proponents of the United Nations Convention on the Law of the Sea (UNCLOS) traditionally have used the term "Law of the Sea Convention" in the United States, under the belief that the "United Nations" portion of the name of the treaty presents unfavorable political optics. Our view is that the treaty should be considered on its own terms and under its official name, just as the United Nations Charter is appreciated and referred to by its official title.
[12] *New U.S. Maritime Security Strategy Includes Legal and Institutional Initiatives*, 100 Am. J. Int'l L. 222–24 (Jan. 2006).
[13] The White House, National Strategy for Maritime Security 2005, Sept. 2005, at 2.

resource, such as a timber forest or a fishing ground, diminishes as the number of users begin to use the resource. A flow resource, on the other hand, is one in which one user does not appreciably reduce the value or potential of the resource for follow on users. Mankind's foremost use of the oceans facilitates "a unique freedom of movement and flow of goods while allowing people, cargo, and conveyances to transit with anonymity not generally available by movement over land or by air."[14]

The nature of the oceans as a flow resource has influenced the United States to view security in the maritime domain as a global issue. The United States seeks to "facilitate global commerce and protect freedom of the seas for legitimate military and commercial navigation and other legitimate activities...."[15] Free seas are liberalizing, generating positive externalities within the international system. While enriching nations and bringing them together through economic and trade relationships and cultural and political contacts, the oceans also contribute to international cultural, communications, and social integration that form the cosmopolitan interconnectedness of globalization.

In the strongest language of any national-level document in the United States or overseas on the issue of freedom of the seas, the NSMS states, "[t]hree broad principles provide overarching guidance to this Strategy. First, preserving the freedom of the seas is a top national priority.[16] The free, continuing, unthreatened intercourse of nations is an essential global freedom and helps ensure the smooth operation of the world's economy."[17] Maintaining a stable regime that ensures global maritime maneuverability and mobility is a cornerstone of the nation's global security posture.[18] "Maritime security is required to ensure freedom of the seas, facilitate freedom of navigation and commerce, advance prosperity and freedom, and protect the resources of the ocean."[19]

At the same time, however, the oceans are susceptible to misuse by organizations, individuals, and nations hostile to the United States. Consequently, the United States also seeks to ensure that the maritime stream of commerce is secure. The NSMS promotes standardized ship and port security practices in accordance with rules set by the World Customs Organization and the IMO. The strategy also recognizes a symbiotic relationship between maintaining maritime security and coastal state prerogatives in environmental protection, homeland security, and offshore sovereign rights and jurisdiction, suggesting that both maritime security and freedom of the seas are dependent on one another. The United States champions both the rights of distant water states in freedom of navigation, as well as

---

[14] Id.
[15] Id.
[16] Id.
[17] Id.
[18] Id.
[19] Id.

legitimate coastal state rights in littoral management and offshore security. Distant water states are those nations that operate ships, aircraft, and submarines in ocean areas located far from their own shore.

Consequently, U.S. policy is to maintain the full range of naval and maritime forces to prevent the seas from being misused by "terrorists, criminals, and hostile states" to inflict harm on the United States, its people, economy, property, territory, allies and friends.[20] By protecting the maritime sinews of the global system, the United States believes it is delivering a public good to the international community, while at the same time advancing its own national interest. Protection of the global system is, for the United States, tantamount to homeland security in depth, and this broad mandate has wide and deep support among presidential administrations from both major political parties.[21]

Perhaps ironically, just as the country moves to reduce and consolidate its far-flung military obligations throughout the world, the sea services of the Navy, Coast Guard, and Marine Corps will become even busier. Since ports, ships and seafarers naturally mix in a cosmopolitan and globalized milieu, building a coherent maritime security system requires close collaboration. The crowning piece of the American maritime security policy is the emphasis on building maritime relationships. The 2005 vision for a "Thousand Ship Navy"[22] or "global maritime partnership," stressed that maritime security could be achieved only by close collaboration with the naval forces and marine police of other countries. The concept of cooperation later was incorporated into the tri-service policy (and title) of the sea services' 2007 *Cooperative Strategy for 21st Century Seapower*.[23]

Ultimately, burden sharing is the endgame for bringing other nations' forces into a greater role in maritime security. The United States hopes that by helping other nations increase their capacity to police the oceans they will do so more often, freeing up the United States to do less, or at least relieve U.S. forces to accomplish other higher order duties, such as deterring great power naval conflict. The U.S. approach to "leading from behind" in Operation Odyssey Dawn, the UN Security Council operation in Libya, reflects this new approach.

---

[20] Id.

[21] As more than a decade of war in Afghanistan ends, however, the ability of the United States to continue to maintain a defense posture designed to defend the entire global system is called into question. Neo-isolationists, such as former Republican presidential hopeful Ron Paul, Boston University political scientist Andrew Bacevich, Chalmers Johnson, and Noam Chomsky, as well as offshore balancers, including John Mearsheimer and Barry Posen, advocate a much more selective use of American military power.

[22] Vice Admiral John G. Morgan Jr., & Rear Admiral Charles. W. Martoglio, *The 1,000 Ship Navy: Global Maritime Network*, U.S. NAVAL INSTITUTE PROCEEDINGS, Nov. 20005, at 14–17. *See also*, John Morgan Jr., *A Navy of Navies*, RUSI DEFENCE SYSTEMS, Summer 2006, at 66.

[23] DEP'T OF THE NAVY, COOPERATIVE STRATEGY FOR 21ST CENTURY SEA POWER 2007 [Hereinafter CS21].

Caught between doing nothing in Rwanda, and what many view as an over commitment in Iraq, the new model leverages the capabilities of friends and allies to bring stability to situations of crisis.[24] Even with capable NATO allies involved in Libya, however, the entire mission depended on decisive U.S. intervention in the opening stage to suppress the country's sophisticated air defense system.[25] Whether the maritime security partnerships formed to increase the capability of other states will entice them to play a greater role in maintaining the security of the global maritime system is not guaranteed. For example, the Royal Navy of the United Kingdom has begun training Libyan naval forces after the downfall of that country's dictator, but it remains to be seen whether the efforts will help to depoliticize and professionalize the force.

2.4 NATIONAL STRATEGY FOR GLOBAL SUPPLY CHAIN SECURITY

Maritime transport is a cornerstone of globalization. Combined with telecommunications (most of which travel on intercontinental submarine cables lying on the seabed), trade liberalization, and international standardization, the worldwide maritime transportation network is essential for a healthy and progressive global economy.[26] Jan Hoffman at the United Nations Conference on Trade and Development suggested that the maritime business is the most globalized of all industries.[27] Rules for securing the system are necessarily multinational.

The United States consciously initiated the policy of globalization under President William J. Clinton during the 1990s to reduce and eliminate trade barriers. For the United States, international trade is not just about the economy—Americans believe that liberal international economic relationships reinforce peace and stability. World trade is believed to promote and solidify democracy and it is an important component of the belief in a "democratic peace."[28] Thus, the United States is compelled to protect the U.S. maritime shipping system, while

---

[24] David W. Sanger, *Letting Others Lead in Libya*, N.Y. TIMES, Apr. 23, 2011.
[25] The operation was enabled by strike against Libyan air-defense systems with 110 U.S. and British Tomahawk cruise missiles and strikes by three B-2 Spirit stealth bombers delivering 45 Joint Direct Attack Munitions (JDAMs). Dep't of Defense Media Press briefing by Vice Admiral Bill Gortney, Director of the Joint Staff, Mar. 19, 2011.
[26] Jan Hoffman, *Shipping Out of the Economic Crisis*, XVI BROWN J. GLOBAL AFF., Spring/Summer 2010, 121, 121.
[27] Id.
[28] BRUCE RUSSETT, GRASPING THE DEMOCRATIC PEACE: PRINCIPLES FOR A POST-COLD WAR WORLD 3–23 (1993), John M. Owen, *How Liberalism Produces Democratic Peace*, 19 INT'L SECURITY, Autumn, 1994, at 87 (liberal ideas essential for democratic peace), and Michael Mousseau, *Market Prosperity, Democratic Consolidation, and Democratic Peace*, 44 J. CONFLICT RESOLUTION, 472, 502–03 (Aug. 2000) (market cooperation promotes shared liberal ideology among states).

at the same time avoiding security measures so stringent that they hamper the free flow of commerce.

On January 23, 2012, President Barack Obama released the U.S. government's policy designed to harden the global supply chain "...in order to protect the welfare and interests of the American people and secure our Nation's economic prosperity."[29] Consistent with the NSMS, the *National Strategy for Global Supply Chain Security* focuses on protection of the worldwide marine transportation system. The document was crafted in order to counter the threats to the worldwide network of maritime and related transportation nodes and shipping pathways by which raw materials are delivered to manufacturers and finished goods are moved from points of production to consumers. The task of protecting the global shipping network is daunting because it requires an ability to separate legitimate cargo from unlawful weapons or dangerous persons intent on damaging the system or wreaking havoc in society.

Seaborne trade includes imports and exports by ship, but it also encompasses stationary or moving cargo throughout the inter-modal freight transportation system, including ports and roadsteads, oil and gas pipelines under the water or at points of landfall, and submarine cables, essential for Internet communications and banking and finance transactions. Physical cargo is moved seamlessly from land to air to sea. Commercial air, land, and sea nodes of transportation are interlinked, and the entire system is vulnerable to disruption at its weakest link.[30] Protection of the system is a prerogative of national defense and not just economic security because military cargo often travels by commercial conveyances and through commercial transport modes, such as on chartered or leased commercial ships and aircraft.

Against this backdrop the locus of effort also includes preparation to recover from attacks on the system.[31] The United States endorses the goal of making the movement of goods more efficient and secure. The flow of legitimate commerce has to be expedited, while at the same time the supply chain must be secure from exploitation or disruption. This goal is achieved by enhanced confidence in the integrity of goods as they move through the supply chain. Sealing, screening, monitoring, and targeted inspection of shipping containers increases confidence. The second goal of the Strategy focuses on consequence management. In a vast and complex system, resiliency and recovery is just as important as deterrence and prevention. The United States wants to be able to quickly withstand and rebound from attacks against the system. Containing the effects of attack helps to stabilize economic expectations following an incident. The *Strategy for Global*

---

[29] THE WHITE HOUSE, NATIONAL STRATEGY FOR GLOBAL SUPPLY CHAIN SECURITY, JAN. 23, 2012.
[30] Id., at note 3, at p. 4.
[31] Id., at 2–3.

Supply Chain Security presents a roadmap for accomplishing these goals through integration of efforts across Federal, state, local, tribal and territorial governments, the private sector and the international community.[32]

Risks to the supply chain are identified, assessed and prioritized, and implementation of layered defense secures the system. Toward this end, the Federal government regularly updates its threat and risk assessments. Broad engagement with the private sector and international stakeholders is designed to further deepen systemic security. The Strategy is an evolving or dynamic template that informs and guides promulgation of more specific regulations.

The United States also works to identify infrastructure projects that can be used by other components of the system as models of best practice. Advanced technology and research, development, testing, and evaluation (RDT&E) help to improve cargo chain security in the air, on the ground, and at sea. The United States also incorporates global supply chain resiliency into the Federal infrastructure investment plan, with construction of new ports, highways, and railway nodes. Finally, the U.S. approach values customized solutions to speed the flow of legitimate commerce. One such measure, the use of "trusted trader" programs, standardizes procedures in lower-risk parts of the cargo chain.[33]

2.5 U.S. Maritime Strategy for Homeland Security

After September 11 the United States supplemented the NSMS with a national homeland security strategy. Since the *National Security Strategy* already set forth U.S. goals and objectives in homeland security, the additional document does not provide much more by way of maritime security policy. The only mention concerning maritime security in the 2002 *Homeland Security Strategy* pertains to the need to enhance maritime domain awareness in order to better track vessels along the 95,000 miles of American coastline.[34]

Driving home the importance of securing maritime approaches to the United States is valuable, but risks a myopic view of U.S. national security and foreign policy interests in the oceans. Most of the military is focused on operating overseas and maintaining a forward presence in the oceans and continents distant from the shores of the United States. The *Homeland Security Strategy*, however, like the *National Military Strategy*, focuses on the need to maintain "strategic access" in the waterway approaches to the country to ensure maritime homeland security, without a corresponding and complementary mention of the even greater importance of global strategic access for overseas power projection.

---

[32] Id., at 4.
[33] Id., at 5.
[34] White House Office of Homeland Security, Homeland Security Strategy of the United States 2002, at 68.

The *U.S. Maritime Strategy for Homeland Security* is subordinate to and expounds on the *Homeland Security Strategy*. The *Maritime Strategy* adds granularity to the maritime aspects of homeland security, and the document is respectful of the importance of freedom of navigation.[35] The commandant of the Coast Guard signed the strategy, which was released just one year after the attacks of 9–11. The strategy acknowledges that the maritime domain is divided into areas of shared use and that the United States should accommodate the "long-standing international respect for freedom of navigation" even as it establishes a protective maritime belt around the country.[36] Although the Coast Guard was the primary institutional author of the *Maritime Strategy for Homeland Security*, the sea service also produced a complementary vision in the *U.S. Coast Guard Strategy for Maritime Safety, Security and Stewardship*. The strategy should have contained a stronger statement on the importance of freedom of navigation to the United States, although it does indicate that as maritime piracy has increased since the 1980s, maritime crime threatens U.S. interests in freedom of the seas.[37]

2.6 Cooperative Strategy for 21st Century Sea Power

With the collapse of international peacekeeping efforts in Somalia in 1992, the United States sought to understand the lessons of Mogadishu. The U.S. Navy white paper ... *From the Sea* distilled the importance of U.S. naval power to solving crises ashore. The doctrine was revised in 1994 and re-released as *Forward ... From the Sea* to emphasize the force multiplier effect of forward deployed naval forces, which increase in-theater combat power by a factor of three to five times over similar forces stationed in the continental United States. Naval forces already in theater are able to meet challenges more quickly, rather than depleting overseas patrol time through long transits to and from major naval ports in the United States.

At the 2005 International Sea power Symposium, then Chief of Naval Operations Admiral Michael Mullen observed that all of the world's regions shared a common set of challenges—maritime piracy, illegal maritime trafficking, and terrorism at sea. The seas are not simply a collection of regional bodies of water or an assortment of separate theaters of maritime operation. The seas oceans transect and connect the globe—there is one gigantic world ocean. The idea that the United States is best served by a maritime strategy that encompasses virtually all of the nations of the world culminated in release of the *Cooperative Strategy for 21st Century Seapower* (CS21) in 2007.

---

[35] Admiral Thomas H. Collins, U.S. Coast Guard Maritime Strategy for Homeland Security 2002, Dec. 23, 2002, at 1.
[36] Id.
[37] Admiral Thad W. Allen, U.S. Coast Guard Strategy for Safety, Security and Stewardship 2007, Jan. 19, 2007, at 22.

The *Cooperative Strategy* is built on the lessons learned in the fight against terrorism by recognizing that no nation is individually powerful enough to maintain peace and stability in the international system. Cooperation requires countries to share a common vision for a liberal world order, and that they enjoy some level of mutual trust and embrace shared responsibility. The new strategy was applauded by many nations because it reflected a more benign U.S. leadership coupled with a multilateral approach to maintenance of good order at sea.

The cornerstone of CS21 is the idea that deeper coordination with more partners at sea will yield concrete benefits for maritime security:

> Sea power in this century cannot be harnessed by a single nation, acting alone. If we are to build a fleet for the future capable of keeping pace with globalization, we must leverage the capacity of our partners with common interests. The positive potential of sea power and freedom of the seas can only be achieved through a collective and cooperative approach focused on international rule of law and freedom of the maritime commons.[38]

"The old *Maritime Strategy* [of the Cold War] focused on sea control," Admiral Mullen suggested, while the new one recognizes that the "economic tide of all nations rises—not when the seas are controlled by one—but rather when they are made safe and free for all."[39] The 2008 *National Defense Strategy*, however, was more ambitious, if not more magnanimous, stating: "For more than sixty years, the United States has secured the global commons for the benefit of all." Today, the challenge for the United States is to reconcile American sea power with a penchant to champion Wilsonian notions of salvation. The United States is trying to convert hegemonic inclinations into a cooperative approach that incorporates—or even accommodates—the interests of other nations, and yet still maintains a peaceful order of the sea based upon the rule of law.[40]

Though an important expression of the U.S. commitment to multilateralism, CS21 did not scratch every itch. Some complained that it was not a strategy at all, but rather a means to achieve singularly U.S. goals through co-opting friends and allies into an American project. The vision reassured other nations that the United States would not go it alone, but it also appeared to obscure U.S. interests in an amorphous cloud of "feel good" multilateralism that did not always reflect realities of power. CS21 attracted criticism because it set forth *how* the United States would promote maritime security—through cooperation with other states—without specifying exactly *what* was to be accomplished. As the economic crisis hit the United States in the fall of 2008, still others began to wonder whether U.S. maritime power was sufficient to orchestrate global maritime

---

[38] Statement of Admiral Michael G. Mullen, Chief of Naval Operations, before the Senate Armed Services Committee, Mar. 29, 2007.
[39] Remarks by Admiral Mike G. Mullen, Chief of Naval Operations, at the Argentine Naval Staff Headquarters, Apr. 7, 2005.
[40] SECRETARY OF DEFENSE ROBERT GATES, NATIONAL DEFENSE STRATEGY 2008, at 16.

security, even if other countries were successfully enlisted into the project. As an apparent recognition of the relative stagnation of U.S. naval power, the strategy also failed to capture the unparalleled lethality of American sea power. While the U.S. Navy banked on numerous capacity-building partnerships with the weakest navies, it still honed an incredibly capable multi-mission combat force able to fight and win throughout the spectrum of conflict.

Finally, as though to avoid a self-fulfilling prophecy, CS21 purposefully chose not to call out the potential threat posed by the breathtaking expansion in Chinese naval power over the previous fifteen years. Would ignoring the rise of the People's Liberation Army Navy generate goodwill and prevent a maritime Cold War? Would this approach be seen in Asia as weakness, or appear out of touch with changes in the international system? These questions stalked CS21 in 2011–12 as the Chief of Naval Operations considered a review of the strategy. After five years, CS21 is seen as having been a success for its time, but it has become stale, being outpaced by events in Asia.

CS21 is on the way out. Just as China's enormous investments in naval, air, and missile forces began to pay off with the introduction of sophisticated new classes of weapons, CS21 was reexamined. A less radical approach that merely refreshed CS21, much as the 1992 white paper *From the Sea*, was updated by the 1994 strategy, *Forward...From the Sea*, was considered and rejected. The most likely outcome is that the document will be completely rewritten to look more like the nascent *Air-Sea Battle Concept*, described in section 2.6.3, below.

2.6.1 *Naval Operations Concept*

In the hierarchy of national and cabinet department-level strategy documents, the Navy and Marine Corps developed service-specific strategies. The *Naval Operation Concept* (NOC) was first introduced by the Navy and Marine Corps in 2006, and then revised in 2010, adding the Coast Guard. The current NOC serves as the "commander's intent" for the Navy, Coast Guard and Marine Corps, implementing CS21.[41] The Chief of Naval Operations and the Commandant of the Marine Corps created the NOC to provide essential principles for modern naval operations. The *Concept* sets forth the extensive maritime missions of the country, and includes tactical, operational, and strategic applications of sea power. The Navy conducts missions across the range of sea-air-land operations, maintaining a forward presence with scalable, adaptable, and globally distributed, mission-tailored sea power.[42] The missions arise throughout the continuum of peace and war.

First, at the strategic level, the Navy is on the front line of nuclear deterrence, and it operates the most survivable component of the nuclear triad comprised of

---

[41] GENERAL JAMES T. CONWAY, ADMIRAL GARY ROUGHEAD, & ADMIRAL THAD W. ALLEN, NAVAL OPERATIONS CONCEPT: IMPLEMENTING THE MARITIME STRATEGY (2010) [Hereinafter NOC 2010].

[42] CAPTAIN WAYNE P. HUGHES, FLEET TACTICS AND COASTAL COMBAT 35 (2d. ed. 2000).

ballistic missile nuclear submarines (SSBNs), land-based bombers, and intercontinental ballistic missiles.[43] The sophisticated Aegis warship platforms possess phased array radar and surface-to-air missiles that are ideal for anti-air warfare, theater air control, and the variants of the Standard Missile-3 are a proven capability for ballistic missile defense.[44]

The service can reach strategic targets in distant lands with advanced conventional capabilities. Cruise missiles launched from four ballistic missile submarines that have been converted to a conventional role, and aircraft from ten deployable aircraft carriers can strike targets at sea and land. These manned forces ensure a conventional global strike, and technology already exists to add unmanned strike platforms in the fleet.[45] Direct tactical attack with missiles, naval gunfire, and forced entry special mission forces generates decisive effects ashore. Sea control,[46] forward presence,[47] protection of the sea lines of communication (SLOCs)[48] and naval control and protection of shipping (NCAPS)[49] are classic sea power missions that are part of the contemporary arsenal.

As people congregate along the shore—both on land and at sea—the boundary between sea and shore activities has blurred. Expeditionary and amphibious operations in littoral areas have risen in importance because littoral regions are now a center of gravity, rather than just a point of egress into a country.[50] The Navy is able to employ a variety of special operations forces (SOF) and Marine air-ground task forces (MAGTFs) for these missions, which include counterinsurgency and counterterrorism.[51] Likewise, joint Coast Guard and Navy assets conduct maritime constabulary patrols and maritime security operations, including counter-drug operations,[52] anti-piracy missions,[53] and counter-proliferation

---

[43] John Norton Moore, *The Regime of Straits and the Third United Nations Conference on the Law of the Sea*, 74 AM. J. INT'L L. 77, 88 (1980).
[44] NOC 2010, at 10, 21, 54, 56, and 74.
[45] Michael R. Gordon, *Pentagon Seeks Non-nuclear Tips for Subs Missiles*, N.Y. TIMES, May 29, 2006 at A1. For a chronology of global strike events prepared by the Federation of American Scientists, *see generally*, HANS M. KRISTENSEN, GLOBAL STRIKE: A CHRONOLOGY OF THE PENTAGON'S NEW STRIKE PLAN, Mar. 15, 2006.
[46] NOC 2010, at Ch. 7.
[47] Id., at Ch. 4.
[48] Id., at 31.
[49] LIEUTENANT MICHAEL C. GRUBB, PROTECTION OF SHIPPING: A FORGOTTEN MISSION WITH MANY NEW CHALLENGES Oct. 10, 2006 (Naval War College).
[50] NOC 2010, at 16–17, 22 and Andrew Scutro, *Navy and Marine Corps Plan Together for Future*, NAVY TIMES, Sept. 18, 2006, at 18.
[51] NOC 2010, at 28. *See also*, David Longshore, *American Naval Power and the Prevention of Terror* 1 HOMELAND SECURITY AFF., Summer 2005, at 5–7 (new Navy strategy, tactics, and technology conducive to deterring terrorism against the homeland).
[52] NOC 2010, at 37. *See also*, James Kraska, *Counterdrug Operations in U.S. Pacific Command*, JOINT FORCE QUARTERLY, Winter, 1997–98, at 81.
[53] NOC 2010, at 39.

activities.[54] Several tactical doctrinal concepts support maritime security operations, such as maritime interception operations (MIO) and the application of visit, board, search and seizure (VBSS).[55] The tactics, techniques, and procedures to execute these operations are not publicly available.

Finally, the Navy has new capabilities to conduct missions that are not considered classic maritime endeavors, but that are becoming more important as the boundary between land and sea are erased. Naval forces have resident cyber warfare and information operations capacity that are fused to joint and interagency efforts. The maritime services also perform ad hoc missions that include humanitarian assistance and disaster relief,[56] overseas civil-military affairs,[57] security cooperation and capacity building, and naval peacekeeping and peace enforcement.[58]

Each of these missions is dependent on the Pentagon's ability to exercise mobility and maneuverability throughout the global commons. In the past, freedom of navigation and overflight were taken for granted by U.S. forces, which operated throughout the oceans with impunity. More recently, however, many coastal states, especially in Europe, Asia and the Middle East, have acquired advanced warships, weapons, and aircraft capable of effectively implementing anti-access and area denial (A2/AD) strategies. The A2/AD capabilities are designed to prevent foreign flagged ships and aircraft from operating freely in offshore littoral areas and semi-enclosed seas. The United States can bring a preponderance of power to bear throughout the coastal zone and up to hundreds of miles inland by operating from the sea. The A2/AD strategies are being designed to blunt America's unique and powerful expeditionary capabilities.

2.6.2 *Expeditionary Sea Power*

Until World War I,[59] virtually the entire history of U.S. sea power sprang from operations in the littoral or coastal and near shore areas of the world's oceans.[60] The Marine Corps has been the principal armed service to campaign at the inter-

---

[54] Id., at 9–10, 18, 64.
[55] Id., at Ch. 5.
[56] Id., at Ch. 6.
[57] Id., at 18, 29–30.
[58] Id., at 64.
[59] The global circumnavigation of the Great White Fleet by two squadrons of battleships from 1907–09 was a rare exception to the rule that nearly all Navy operations were conducted near shore. The Great White Fleet was comprised of 16 battleships, and in combination with U.S. activities in the Philippines and Hawaii, established the United States as a major Pacific power. David Starr Jordan, *The Pageant of the Ships*, XIX THE PACIFIC MONTHLY 491, 493 (May 1908),
[60] This section draws heavily from the interdisciplinary study, JAMES KRASKA, MARITIME POWER AND LAW OF THE SEA: EXPEDITIONARY OPERATIONS IN WORLD POLITICS 179–220 (2010).

face of the sea and land. The United States continues to place a premium on the operational reach and agility of what once were called amphibious forces, but today are more commonly referred to as expeditionary forces.[61] In March 2009 in an effort to reaffirm the importance of these forces, the Marine Corps released the white paper, *Amphibious Operations in the 21st Century*. The framework bridges the divide between sea power and events on the land.[62]

As the United States began to consider reductions in defense spending after the war in Iraq, it became obvious that the four military services would compete for a smaller share of the Federal budget. In order to dispel the idea that equal cuts in defense spending should be made to each service, General James F. Amos, Commandant of the Marine Corps, outlined the special role and importance of the service in expeditionary operations in a September 2011 letter to the Secretary of Defense. Amos stated that naval and marine forces have special qualities that make them uniquely suited in an era of uncertain threats and constabulary operations. Power projected from the sea is "not reliant on host nation support or permission."[63] With ample loiter time measured in terms of months, not hours, expeditionary forces are positioned to buy time and decision space for national leaders to deescalate a crisis.

The 82nd Congress directed that the Marine Corps continues to serve as the nation's force in readiness and determined that it is "the most ready when the nation is least ready."[64] The Marines provide the United States with viable options for forcible entry worldwide that no other armed force can even consider. After the terrorist attacks of September 11, for example, the Marines' Task Force 58 seized Forward Operating Base (FOB) Rhino located 450 miles inland.[65] The Afghan base was the first major footprint of American forces into the country and was captured only ten weeks after the attacks on the Pentagon and the World Trade Center. FOB Rhino was used to rush 1,000 troops into Afghanistan, and then used as a staging area to strike and take the large airfields at Kandahar and Bagram. Supplies were flown in to support a larger ground presence until road convoys could be established.

The example of FOB Rhino illustrates why the United States is so keen to preserve freedom of navigation and overflight and other internationally lawful uses

---

[61] ROBERT O. WORK, THE US NAVY: CHARTING A COURSE FOR TOMORROW'S FLEET 30–32 (2008) and GEOFFREY TILL, NAVAL TRANSFORMATION, GROUND FORCES, AND THE EXPEDITIONARY IMPULSE: THE SEA-BASING DEBATE 18 (Dec. 2006).

[62] G. J. FLYNN, LIEUTENANT GENERAL, U.S. MARINE CORPS, AMPHIBIOUS OPERATIONS IN THE 21ST CENTURY, Mar. 18, 2009 (Commanding General, Marine Corps Combat Development Command, Washington, D.C.).

[63] General James F. Amos, Headquarters United States Marine Corps, Department of the Navy, Memorandum for Secretary of Defense, Role of the United States Marine Corps, Sept. 12, 2011.

[64] Id.

[65] Id.

of the sea in the littoral zone. Launching expeditions nearer the coastline extends the range of penetration of the force, enabling missions like the one that stood up FOB Rhino. In order to repel these operations potential adversaries try to erect A2/AD barriers that diminish the special capability.[66] In an effort to preserve the U.S. advantages in operating in the littoral zone, the United States has begun to think more carefully about how to suppress and defeat coastal states' A2/AD strategies.

2.6.3 Pivot to Asia and the Air-Sea Battle Concept

What is conspicuous about American grand strategy is its consistency; regardless of which of the two major political parties holds the presidency, U.S. strategy has been remarkably constant since 1941. Both Republican and Democratic presidents have been inspired by the liberal ideas of President Woodrow Wilson to promote a just and sustainable world order where the rights and responsibilities of nations and peoples are upheld, especially the fundamental rights of every human being.[67] Despite the routine political bickering between the two major political parties or election-year posturing for votes, Americans are united in the need to remain engaged globally to contribute in a meaningful—and sometimes decisive way—to a more peaceful and stable world order. This messianic zeal is part of the American character, perhaps to a fault. For example, the decade long military detour into Iraq and Afghanistan had bipartisan support in the White House and Congress. Supplemental budget appropriations funded both wars, approved overwhelmingly by Democrats and Republicans in Congress, and by presidents from both parties—just as the Vietnam War was supported by both Democratic and Republican presidents and members of Congress. Neither political party has challenged the lawfulness of the operations in Iraq and Afghanistan under the War Powers Act.

Members from both political parties also recognize that since 2001, while America was focused on counterinsurgency war in Central Asia, the Chinese military has reaped the rewards of inexorable rise from the position of the world's second largest economy. In terms of purchasing power parity, China's economy overtaking the United States' appears almost imminent. Economic power fuels military power. Beijing's massive investment in military power has created dangerous uncertainty in Asia, raising the prospect that the United States is slowly being edged to the sideline in the region. Thus, President Obama's January 3, 2012, announcement of a U.S. strategic pivot toward Asia has strong bipartisan support.[68] Even while the United States maintains global commitments, increasingly, it will define its global maritime posture with a keen focus on the Pacific

---

[66] Kraska, Maritime Power and Law of the Sea at, 179–220.
[67] Sustaining U.S. Global Leadership.
[68] Id.

Ocean and Indian Ocean, much as the Central Front and Fulda Gap became the epicenter of U.S. strategic focus during the Cold War.

The Asia-Pacific is a littoral region, comprised of island nations such as Japan, archipelagic states, including the Philippines and Indonesia, and large coastal states, Vietnam and China. The central geographic feature of the area is the interface of the sea and the shore, interspersed by land and semi-enclosed seas, including the East China Sea, the Sea of Japan, the Yellow Sea, and the South China Sea (which, in the Philippines, is known as the West Philippine Sea). Geopolitically, Asia is a maritime theater.

The United States has seven bilateral defense agreements throughout the world: five of them are in Asia—Thailand, Australia, South Korea, the Philippines, and Japan. (The other two—the Rio Treaty and NATO—are multilateral agreements). Among the defense relationships in Asia, the U.S.-Japan alliance is the cornerstone for stability in the region. The U.S. Seventh Fleet, forward deployed to Yokosuka, the expeditionary strike group in Sasebo, and the associated Marine Expeditionary Force in Okinawa entail a huge commitment of American power and prestige to defend Japan and protect American interests in the region. This physical forward presence is essential to deterrence in the region and cannot be achieved remotely through a "virtual presence," such as by reliance on U.S. airpower based in Guam or farther away. Virtual presence means actual absence. There is no substitute for forward deployment.

The U.S. naval presence in Japan includes the *USS George Washington* in Yokosuka, one of only ten deployable U.S. aircraft carriers, and the *USS Essex*, a Wasp-class amphibious assault ship, homeported in Sasebo. Because these forward deployed naval forces already are located in Asia, they are on a short tether, able to respond quickly to regional crises without the need for a long transit time from Pearl Harbor, San Diego, or Seattle. But as the legacy conflicts in Central Asia are put in the rearview mirror, the country is once again prioritizing maritime challenges even as the U.S. Navy struggles to maintain a fleet commensurate with worldwide commitments.[69] In order to provide greater forward presence with a smaller force at risk of further erosion, change is afoot in every naval theater.

The U.S. Navy is forward deploying four Aegis guided missile destroyers to Rota, Spain.[70] With over-the-horizon radars and anti-ballistic missile systems, the powerful warships will provide ballistic missile defense to American allies in Europe, as well as participate in NATO exercises and maritime security missions. Similarly, on June 4, 2011, speaking at the Shangri-La Dialogue, Secretary of Defense Robert Gates announced that the United States would forward deploy

---

[69] Craig Whitlock, *Obama's Asia Strategy Gives Navy Key Role, Fewer Ships*, WASH. POST, Feb. 15, 2012 (Navy hopes to increase force from 285 to 313 vessels by 2020).

[70] DEP'T OF DEFENSE, *SECDEF Announces Stationing of Aegis Ships at Rota, Spain*, Statement made by Secretary of Defense Leon E. Panetta on stationing Aegis ships at Rota, Spain, Story Number: NNS111005-12, Oct. 5, 2011.

four new U.S. surface combatants, the configurable Littoral Combat Ship (LCS), to Singapore.[71] The move is significant because these are the first U.S. warships to be forward deployed to the tiny city-state. The modular ships can conduct a variety of missions, such as anti-submarine warfare, maritime security operations, and partnership and capacity building exercises, throughout the strategic crossroads of the Indian Ocean and South China Sea.

The Marine Corps will begin rotating 2,500 soldiers through Darwin, Australia, providing a quick reaction force at the southern edge of Southeast Asia.[72] Washington is also in talks with Manila to enlarge the U.S. military presence in the Philippines, which since 2002 has included 600 special operations forces in Mindanao to help suppress armed Islamist extremists from the Abu Sayyaf group.[73] These developments come after a decade in which the United States has turned Guam into a forward bastion of joint maritime and air power. The Navy-Air Force Joint Region Marianas facility is home to three fast attack submarines, *USS Okinawa* (SSN 723), *USS Chicago*, (SSN 721) and *USS Buffalo* (SSN 715), three Coast Guard cutters, Navy SEALs, and rotational B-2 stealth bomber aircraft supported at Anderson Air Force Base by the 36th Wing, as well as RQ-4 Global Hawk unmanned aerial vehicles.

It is unmistakable that the flow of new forces into the Asia-Pacific is intended to telegraph a reassurance of U.S. commitment to the region and to deter a rising China from dominating East Asia. In recent years China has catalogued a growing list of incidents at sea with its neighbors, typically involving Chinese military or civilian government forces and authorities, such as the Chinese State Oceanic Administration, or purportedly private Chinese fishing or merchant vessels that nonetheless appear to operate in concert with the government. These occurrences, which once were uncommon, have startled countries in the region.

One of the most arresting incidents occurred in April 2001, when two Chinese F-8 fighter jet aircraft conducted an aggressive interception of a U.S. P-3C propeller-driven spy plane overflying international airspace 75 nautical miles off the coast of China. The aircraft overflew China's exclusive economic zone, an area subject to resource rights and jurisdiction of the coastal state, but devoid of any prohibition on the exercise of military activities and high seas freedoms. While attempting a razor-close approach to intimidate the larger and slower aircraft to force it off course, one of the Chinese fighter jets accidently collided with the P-3C. The Chinese interceptor jet and pilot were lost at sea and the badly damaged P-3C made an emergency landing on Hainan Island, China. The Navy crew and aircraft were detained by the Chinese government for nearly two weeks,

---

[71] Whitlock, *Obama's Asia Strategy Gives Navy Key Role, Fewer Ships*.
[72] David Nakamura, *U.S. Troops Heading to Australia, Irking China*, WASH. POST, Nov. 16, 2011.
[73] Craig Whitlock, *Philippines May Allow Greater U.S. Military Presence in Reaction to China's Rise*, WASH. POST, Jan. 25, 2011 (updated Mar. 25, 2011).

which created a diplomatic stand-off that placed the United States on notice that China would risk conflict in order to assert control over portions of the global commons.

The P-3C incident came after a string of similar incidents in the Yellow Sea, the South China Sea, and the East China Sea, in which Chinese warships and aircraft aggressively intercepted unarmed U.S. naval auxiliary ships conducting military activities beyond China's territorial waters. As the Chinese military budget grew tenfold during the 2000s, the Pentagon began to worry about its ability to maintain access to the littoral waters of East Asia. By 2011, China was nearing completion of a revolutionary anti-ship ballistic missile (ASBM), the Dong-Feng 21, which reportedly can hit a moving aircraft carrier at sea.

As concern began to grow that China sought to decouple the U.S. strategic link to Asia in order to politically dominate the region, the United States began to contemplate new approaches to defeat Chinese A2/AD.[74] By precipitously and perhaps prohibitively raising the costs of the U.S. naval presence in the Asia-Pacific, China is trying to curtail the ability of the United States to project power in the region. In addition to holding U.S. forces at risk, Beijing also employs a relentless campaign of media and legal "warfare," to delegitimize the American presence in the region.[75]

In response, the Pentagon began to look at the Air-Sea Battle concept to ensure that U.S. maritime forces continue to maintain freedom of movement in the airspace and ocean commons of Asia. The Air-Sea Battle concept is still being developed, but its basic contours are clear. Joint Navy and Air Force operating concepts are being designed to roll-up the A2/AD capabilities of China and other land-based adversaries through dynamic and innovative application of naval and air power. Air-Sea Battle encompasses operational concepts to enable the ships, submarines, and aircraft of the United States and its allies to continue to command the maritime commons, even in the highest threat environments. The Pentagon has established a joint Air-Sea Battle Office staffed with mostly Navy and Air Force officers, but it also includes representatives from the Army and Marine Corps.

---

[74] ANDREW KREPINEVICH, WHY AIR-SEA BATTLE? 7 (2010).
[75] KRASKA, MARITIME POWER AND LAW OF THE SEA at 18.

THREE

EUROPEAN MARITIME STRATEGY AND POLICY

3.1 NORTH ATLANTIC TREATY ORGANIZATION

As its name implies, the North Atlantic Treaty Organization (NATO) fundamentally is a maritime strategy.[1] The Alliance began as a way to ensure the United States and Canada maintained a maritime bridge to Western Europe—a connection placed at risk by Germany and the Soviet Union during two world wars and the Cold War.[2] During all three conflicts European navies practiced higher end naval warfare—principally anti-submarine warfare and major fleet action—to keep the lifeline open to North America.

Since the demise of the Soviet threat, NATO has broadened its horizon and now conducts war in Afghanistan, as well as out-of-area naval operations. At any given moment, NATO warships may be engaged in anti-piracy patrols in the Indian Ocean as part of Operation Ocean Shield, conducting counter-terrorism operations in the Mediterranean Sea pursuant to Operation Active Endeavor,

---

[1] Jason Alderwick & Bastian Giegerich, *Navigating Troubled Waters: NATO's Maritime Strategy*, SURVIVAL, Aug.–Sept. 2010, at 13–20 and Robert S. Jordan, *The Maritime Strategy and the Atlantic Alliance*, J. OF THE ROYAL UNITED SERVICES INSTITUTE FOR DEFENCE STUDIES, Sept. 1987, at 45–54.

[2] Our judgment is that the NATO Alliance is essentially a maritime endeavor to maintain collective security in the North Atlantic region by connecting North America with Western Europe. Consequently, maritime forces were the essential military foundation of the Alliance during the Cold War. Not all scholars agree. *See,* John J. Mearsheimer, *A Strategic Misstep: The Maritime Strategy and Deterrence in Europe*, INT'L SECURITY, Fall 1986, 3–57 (Reagan administration's *Maritime Strategy* did nothing to enhance deterrence in Europe and diverted resources away from more important ground and air forces), *cf.* Linton F. Brooks, *Naval Power and National Security: The Case for the Maritime Strategy*, INT'L SECURITY, Fall 1986, 58–88 and Colin S. Gray, MARITIME STRATEGY, GEOPOLITICS AND THE DEFENSE OF THE WEST 85 (1986).

completing Mediterranean naval exercises with NATO's Istanbul Cooperative Initiative, which includes Bahrain, Kuwait, Qatar and the United Arab Emirates, or working with a Partnership for Peace state, such as Sweden, in the context of the NATO Response Force.[3]

The war in Georgia during the summer of 2008 provided a vivid reminder that even the prospect of naval warfare in the European theater is not unthinkable. Early on in the conflict, warships from the Russian Black Sea Fleet deployed off the coast of Abkhazia and into the Georgian port of Poti in support of Russia's invasion of its neighbor. Several Georgian ships lying at anchor were destroyed, and Russian and Georgian patrol ships clashed at sea. Responding to the humanitarian needs of Georgia after the ceasefire, first a Coast Guard cutter and then NATO warships delivered humanitarian aid to the country. As the conflict wound down, four NATO warships were operated in the Black Sea, engaged in scheduled port visits with Romania and Bulgaria.

In 1984, NATO published the *Maritime Strategy*, but it was focused on how NATO might prevail in Cold War scenarios. Twenty years later, the strategy was long overdue for a re-write. Meeting in Norfolk, Virginia, in July 2008, NATO's senior civilian official in charge of operations and the top maritime commanders determined that they should develop the *Alliance Maritime Strategy* (AMS) and a supporting *Maritime Security Operations Concept* (MSO), analogous to the U.S.' 2007 *Cooperative Strategy for 21st Century Sea Power* and the 2006 *Naval Operations Concept*.[4] In the spring of 2009, the North Atlantic Council endorsed the idea to develop the *Alliance Maritime Strategy*. The Alliance's MSO Concept was completed on July 21, 2009, and it added further definition to the project to draft an AMS.[5] At an Alliance summit in Lisbon in November 2010, member states adopted a new Strategic Concept, recommitting them to the fundamental purpose of safeguarding freedom and security. This document provides overall policy direction for the AMS.[6]

---

[3] Diego A. Ruiz, *The End of the Naval Era?*, NATO REVIEW (2010).
[4] DEP'T OF THE NAVY, COOPERATIVE STRATEGY FOR 21ST CENTURY SEA POWER 2007 and General JAMES T. CONWAY, ADMIRAL GARY ROUGHEAD, & ADMIRAL THAD W. ALLEN, NAVAL OPERATIONS CONCEPT: IMPLEMENTING THE MARITIME STRATEGY (2010) (Although the 2010 version was signed by all three chiefs of the sea services, the original version, released in 2006, was signed by the Commandant of the Marine Corps and the Chief of Naval Operations only).
[5] NORTH ATLANTIC TREATY ORGANIZATION, NEW ALLIANCE MARITIME SECURITY OPERATIONS CONCEPT, July 21, 2009 (SH/J5/2009–207387.3000 TC-538/TT-4427/Ser: NC0027) [Hereinafter MSO].
[6] ACTIVE ENGAGEMENT, MODERN DEFENSE, NATO STRATEGIC CONCEPT FOR THE DEFENCE AND SECURITY OF THE MEMBERS OF THE NORTH ATLANTIC TREATY ORGANIZATIONS, adopted by the Heads of State and Government in Lisbon, Nov. 19, 2010, http://www.nato.int/cps/en/natolive/official_texts_68580.htm.

3.1.1 *NATO Alliance Maritime Strategy*

NATO nations possess greater collective naval power than any other alliance in history, offering speed, lethality, reach, interoperability and endurance. Speaking in Bahrain on March 7, 2010, former NATO Secretary General Anders Fogh Rasmussen acknowledged, "the [NATO] Alliance has a maritime capability that no other organization can match."[7] In a world without great power war, these capabilities are harnessed toward conducting maritime security operations—constabulary missions aimed at protecting the world maritime transportation system, rather than war fighting.

In 2011, NATO released the *Alliance Maritime Strategy* as a fairly substantial reappraisal of the contribution of maritime forces in supporting NATO's objectives.[8] Just as the new Alliance *Strategic Concept* took account of the evolving geopolitical security environment, the AMS and the associated MSO reflect emerging threats at the intersection of law enforcement and warfare. The AMS provides a long-term framework to fulfill NATO's roles and missions in the maritime domain over the next 20–30 years, as well as a guide for the development of new capabilities. In contrast, the MSO *Concept* provides immediate operational guidance on the use of allied naval forces in support of maritime security operations.

In decades past, NATO's maritime security posture was directed at bolstering collective self-defense against the Soviet bloc menace. The contemporary threats, however, are diffuse and complex, combining rash and unpredictable dangers from rogue states and non-state actors with the proliferation of advanced and emerging weapons. Within this dynamic marine environment NATO naval and maritime forces prepare for five overarching roles: deterrence and collective defense, crisis management, cooperative security, building partnership capacity, and maritime security operations. The first three tasks—collective defense, crisis management, and cooperative security—mirror the three core tasks of the Alliance that are the centerpiece of the 2010 *Strategic Concept*.

The AMS provides guidance to the NATO Defense Planning Process so that the ways and means of the Alliance are directed toward common ends. Rather than seeking to impose change on allied maritime capabilities, however, the *Strategy* provides a guidepost toward which those capabilities can aspire and evolve.

---

[7] Speech by NATO Secretary General Anders Fogh Rasmussen at the occasion of his visit to the Kingdom of Bahrain, Ritz Carlton Hotel, Manama, Bahrain, Mar. 7, 2010, http://www.nato.int/cps/en/natolive/opinions_62052.htm.

[8] North Atlantic Treaty Organization Alliance Maritime Strategy, Annex 1, C-M(2011)0023, Mar. 18, 2011 [Hereinafter AMS].

3.1.1.1 Collective Defense

At its most basic level the NATO Alliance is an exercise in collective defense, as the concept is reflected in customary international law and codified in Article 51 of the UN Charter. The maritime forces of NATO contribute to high-end collective defense and promote security and confidence in the North Atlantic region. The 2010 *NATO Strategic Concept* states:

> NATO members will always assist each other against attack, in accordance with Article 5 of the Washington Treaty. That commitment remains firm and binding. NATO will deter and defend against any threat of aggression, and against emerging security challenges where they threaten the fundamental security of individual Allies or the Alliance as a whole.[9]

Self-defense for NATO includes nuclear deterrence, which depends on extended deterrence under the U.S. nuclear umbrella, supplemented by associated nuclear deterrent forces operated by the United Kingdom and France. Capability and political will are the benchmarks of deterrence, and the Alliance has both a robust capability and credibility. The large NATO military exercise Brilliant Mariner in April 2010, for example, brought together 31 warships (including an aircraft carrier, numerous frigates, oil tankers and mine countermeasure vessels), four submarines and 28 aircraft from ten NATO nations and one partner country (Sweden), in order to demonstrate the ability to defeat a major maritime power.

NATO maritime forces are also engaged in countering the proliferation of weapons of mass destruction, and more recently, U.S. warships provide missile defense to deter ballistic missile attack or nuclear blackmail against member states. Thus, the nuclear and strategic deterrent posture of the Alliance will continue to include a range of conventional and nuclear naval strike forces, amphibious and expeditionary capabilities that can forcibly enter and then dominate the littoral space at sea and ashore, and classic sea power missions, such as sea control and protection of sea lines of communication.

3.1.1.2 Crisis Management

Maritime forces were a key component of NATOs historic evolution away from Massive Retaliation and toward a posture of graduated or Flexible Response. Flexible Response was a military doctrine implemented by President John F. Kennedy in 1961, in order to provide more options for dealing with Soviet aggression. Skeptical of President Dwight D. Eisenhower's emphasis on the doctrine of Massive Retaliation against any level of Soviet aggression, President Kennedy sought to expand the number of tools in the toolkit available to U.S. decision makers. Due

---

[9] STRATEGIC CONCEPT FOR THE DEFENCE AND SECURITY OF THE MEMBERS OF THE NORTH ATLANTIC TREATY ORGANIZATIONS, adopted by the Heads of State and Government in Lisbon, Nov. 2010, para. 4 [Hereinafter NATO STRATEGIC CONCEPT].

to their ability to operate without foreign bases or land-based forward operating locations and with a globally distributed force structure that can aggregate and disaggregate, naval forces were a key component of Flexible Response.

Naval forces are best suited for graduated reaction to a provocation because they are inherently scalable. The Alliance can conduct the full range of military responses, including demonstrations of force, deployment of mission tailored forces, sea control and sea denial, conventional and strategic deep strike, expeditionary and amphibious action, and an array of kinetic and decisive effects.

The 2010 *Strategic Concept* introduces crisis management as a core task for the Alliance:

> NATO has a unique and robust set of political and military capabilities to address the full spectrum of crises—before, during and after conflicts. NATO will actively employ an appropriate mix of those political and military tools to help manage developing crises that have the potential to affect Alliance security, before they escalate into conflicts; to stop ongoing conflicts where they affect Alliance security; and to help consolidate stability in post-conflict situations where that contributes to Euro-Atlantic security.[10]

The maritime contribution to Alliance crisis management includes rapid deployment of combined, joint forces that can operate effectively in austere environments lacking port facilities or modern communications, having degraded infrastructure, or fragile governments and unstable civil societies. Alliance crisis management includes conflict prevention, demonstration of resolve, crisis response operations, peace-enforcement, embargo operations, counter-terrorism, mine clearance, and consequence management, and the ability to perform any of these missions in non-permissive environments.

The AMS anticipates that naval forces will be engaged in arms embargoes and maritime interception or interdiction operations, maritime precision strike operations, employment of expeditionary and amphibious forces and special operations forces in the littoral zone, and humanitarian assistance and disaster relief. Naval forces, particularly aircraft and submarines, are also ideal platforms for conducting discreet surveillance and reconnaissance. Finally, NATO's at-sea presence is supplied through a well-developed logistical tail that provides depth and endurance to the forces afloat.

3.1.1.3 Cooperative Security

Alliance maritime activities make an important contribution to NATO's policy of outreach through partnerships, dialogue, and cooperation. The 2010 *Strategic Concept* explains the importance of collaborative approaches to international security:

---

[10] Id.

The Alliance is affected by, and can affect, political and security developments beyond its borders. The Alliance will engage actively to enhance international security, through partnership with relevant countries and other international organizations; by contributing actively to arms control, non-proliferation and disarmament; and by keeping the door to membership in the Alliance open to all European democracies that meet NATO's standards.

The Alliance's maritime partnerships include: diplomacy, port visits utilizing ships from the Standing NATO Maritime Groups, building partnership capacity, and, combined training and exercises.[11] Partnerships offer leverage with host nations that can prevent regional war through mediation, confidence building measures, and increased transparency. By building partnership capacity, NATO also enhances the exchange of information and the value of interoperability. The Alliance is made stronger by drawing on local and regional familiarity, and leveraging a wider set of assets and capabilities. Closer international relationships is particularly important during operations that require an enduring NATO presence and onshore access. At sea, a loitering presence reassures allies and deters potential aggressors ashore, helping to manage stable outcomes. For example, during the secession of East Timor from Indonesia, naval forces supported the United Nations International Force in East Timor (INTERFET).

By their very nature, naval forces regularly encounter merchant ships and foreign warships, and these interactions encourage the formation of closer ties among seafarers, shipping carriers, and foreign naval forces than exists between ground combat forces and land transportation industries. Through confidence-building activities, naval forces provide an easier way than territorial armies to reduce friction and alleviate suspicion by working with international partners. For example, in the November 2010 Lisbon summit, the member states agreed that Russia should become a strategic maritime partner—a decision that would have been less likely to occur if it had related to ground forces.[12]

NATO has adopted the *Comprehensive Approach Action Plan*, which was designed to leverage the full range of states and international organizations that play a constructive role in bringing order to the maritime environment. International and intergovernmental organizations, such as the United Nations, International Maritime Organization (IMO), and the European Union (EU), share NATO's goals of avoiding conflict and preventing war, building partner capacity, ensuring the freedom of the seas, and upholding international maritime law.

3.1.1.4 Maritime Security Operations

NATO forces are all-weather and full-spectrum instruments of sea power, designed to accomplish missions at both the higher and lower ends of the conflict spectrum.

---

[11] Id.
[12] Felix F. Seidler, *Slowing Alliance—NATO's New Maritime Strategy and the Need for Reform*, RUSI.org (Royal United Services Institute for Defence & Security Studies 2011).

While less capable navies are forever restricted to lower order tasks, NATO's higher-end force is flexible and adaptable, and thus capable of operating downward, effective at the lower end of the conflict spectrum, which includes maritime security operations (MSO). Less capable naval forces may be useful for MSO, but they are unable to operate in the high end of high-technology warfare.

The first major NATO MSO was the sustained maritime interception operation (MIO) to enforce the UN-mandated embargo on merchant shipping traffic in the Adriatic Sea during the Yugoslav civil war. Ships bound to or from the Federal Republic of Yugoslavia were interdicted at sea during the period June 1992 to October 1996. The Alliance screened 74,000 ships. Six thousand vessels were boarded and 1,500 ships were diverted to ports for inspections.

a. *NATO Maritime Organization*
There are two maritime components within NATO's integrated military command structure: Allied Maritime Command (MC) Northwood, United Kingdom, reports to Joint Forces Command Brunssum, in the Netherlands, while Maritime Command (MC) Naples, Italy, is under Joint Forces Command Naples. (A third NATO operational level command is located in Lisbon, Portugal). Two Standing NATO Maritime Groups (SNMGs) and the two Standing NATO Mine Countermeasures Maritime Groups (SNMCMGs) are comprised of integrated, multinational naval forces. Each group has between six to ten vessels that are provided by member states on a rotational basis for a period of four to six months. The forces of SNMGs and SNMCMGs participate in exercises, maritime diplomacy, and crisis intervention, and if need be, combat missions, providing the Alliance with credible sea power.

SNMG1 and SNMCMG1 are usually deployed in the Eastern Atlantic and report to MC Northwood, and SNMG2 and SNMCMG2 generally operate in the Mediterranean Sea, reporting to MC Naples. Additionally, NATO maintains five on-call High Readiness Maritime Headquarters for the Supreme Allied Commander Europe (SACEUR), which can control NATO naval task forces. Naval forces from Canada, Denmark, Germany, The Netherlands, Norway, Portugal, Spain and the United States routinely participate in SNMG1. The national headquarters of Italy, Spain, United Kingdom, and France, and the multinational, U.S.-led Striking Forces NATO headquarters based in Naples, can each support alliance maritime command and control.[13]

---

[13] Each headquarters provides the Maritime Component Command for the NATO Response Force on a rotational basis. SACEUR has available:
- Headquarters Commander Italian Maritime Forces.
- Headquarters Commander Spanish Maritime Forces
- Headquarters Commander United Kingdom Maritime Forces.
- Headquarters Commander French Maritime Forces.
- Headquarters Striking Forces NATO.

SNMG2 and SNMCMG2 come under the command of Allied Maritime Component Command (CC-Mar) Naples, which is one of the three Component Commands of Allied Joint Force Command Naples. Germany, Greece, Italy, The Netherlands, Spain, Turkey, the United Kingdom and the United States frequently provide ships for SNMG2. Normally SNMG2 and SNMCMG2 operate in the Mediterranean Sea, but they have deployed to the western Indian Ocean to fight against Somali piracy as part of Operation Ocean Shield. SNMG2 falls under the Operational Control of Component Command Maritime Headquarters Northwood and is under the overall responsibility of Joint Headquarters Lisbon.

The NATO naval and maritime forces are an important capability for the collective self-defense of the Alliance, which is embodied in Article 5 of the North Atlantic Treaty. The SNMGs and SNMCMGs constitute conventional sea power, whereas U.S., U.K., and more recently, French, nuclear naval forces provide a deterrent umbrella. The United Kingdom and France have a varied nuclear arsenal, including submarine-launched ballistic missiles. The U.K. 1999 *Strategic Concept* recounts, "The supreme guarantee of the security of the Allies is provided by the strategic nuclear forces of the Alliance, particularly those of the United States; the independent nuclear forces of the United Kingdom and France, which have a deterrent role of their own, contribute to the overall deterrence and security of the Allies."[14] The U.S. Navy is the workhorse of the Alliance and American ballistic missile submarines provide a powerful nuclear deterrent. Although the three NATO nuclear powers enhance alliance deterrence, the weapons remain under national control at all times.

NATO emphasizes forces that are ready on arrival. The NATO Response Force (NRF) provides the Alliance with an integrated force composed of land, air, sea, and special operations forces components. The NRF is designed to go into action anywhere in the world and operate successfully in a variety of threat environments. The forces are on a five-day tether and are self-sustaining for up to 30 days. The SNMGs and SNMCMGs provide the core maritime component of the NRF.

b. *Operation Active Endeavor*

Operation Active Endeavor (OAE) was launched on October 26, 2001, as a response to the terrorist attacks of September 11. Ironically, an alliance that was designed to secure the European continent from land attack from the East conducted its first operation under Article 5 of the North Atlantic Treaty as a maritime operation in collective self-defense of the United States in the West. OAE was conducted in the Mediterranean Sea to ensure the sea lanes were not being used by terrorists fleeing Afghanistan, particularly after the fall of the Taliban in 2001–02.

In March 2004, OAE was expanded to cover the entire Mediterranean Sea, rather than just the eastern end. As the geographic scope of OAE expanded, so

---

[14] NATO STRATEGIC CONCEPT, para. 62 (1999).

did its operational mission. During March 2003 to May 2004, for example, counterterrorist merchant ship escorts were conducted in the Strait of Gibraltar. In April 2003, OAE revised its rules of engagement to permit compliant boarding operations, which may be conducted with the consent of the merchant ship's master (under the expansive U.S. view that the master has plenary authority over the ship) or flag state. The warships also provided anti-terrorism support to Greece during the 2004 Olympic Games.

In October 2004, OAE was scaled back to be an intelligence-cued operation seeking specific targets based upon actionable information, rather than conducting routine patrols. OAE has provided a real world opportunity for NATO forces to develop information sharing and interoperability. Reaching beyond the NATO members, OAE operates with nations outside the Alliance, including Ukraine, Russia, and Albania (before accession) as well as Algeria, Georgia, Israel, and Morocco.

c. *Ocean Shield: Counter-piracy*

The Alliance's maritime security operations gained particular prominence in the suppression of Somali piracy. October 2008 was a high water mark in efforts to repress Somali piracy. That month, the UN Security Council adopted Resolution 1838 that called

> ... upon States whose naval vessels and military aircraft operate on the high seas and airspace off the coast of Somalia to use on the high seas and airspace off the coast of Somalia the necessary means, in conformity with international law, as reflected in the [Law of the Sea] Convention, for the repression of acts of piracy;[15]

In answering the call, the NATO Defense Ministers ordered deployment of three warships from SNMG2 to conduct counter-piracy operations off the coast of Somalia. The effort was code-named Operation Allied Provider, and it involved NATO ship escorts for African Union supply convoys for World Food Program (WFP) shipments into Somalia. Operation Allied Provider was halted in March 2009 when the EU assumed escort duty for WFP shipments.

Thereafter, however, NATO initiated Operation Allied Protector, which was stood up from April to August 2009, to conduct broader anti-piracy patrols. Warships from both SNMGs participated in the operation. Operation Ocean Shield (OOS) was launched on August 17, 2009, to maintain a long term NATO contribution to the fight against Somali piracy.[16] Ocean Shield has facilitated tactical cooperation between NATO and the EU counter-piracy deployments. The headquarters for both operations—Maritime Security Centre Horn of Africa (MSCHOA) and NATO Shipping Centre—are located in Northwood, United Kingdom. Surface warships from the two SNMGs have participated in OOS,

---

[15] UN Doc. S/RES/1838 (Oct. 7, 2008).
[16] In March 2012, Operation Ocean Shield was extended through December 2014.

Table 3.1. NATO SNMG1 and SNMG2 Anti-piracy Rotations[17]

June 2011 to Jan. 2012 SNMG2	
Rear Admiral Mattesi (Italian Navy)	ITS Andrea Doria (Flagship—Italy); USS Carney (USA); USS De Wert (USA); NRP D. Francisco De Almeida (Portugal)
Dec. 2010 to June 2011 SNMG2	
Commodore Michael Hijmans (Royal Netherlands Navy)	De Ruyter (Flagship—Netherlands); Eastern Snare (Denmark); TCG Gaziantep (Turkey); USS Laboon (United States)
Aug. 2010 to Dec. 2010 SNMG1	
Commodore Christian Rune (Denmark)	HDMS Esbern Snare (Flagship, Denmark); HMS Montrose and FTVR (United kingdom); USS Kauffman and Laboon (United States); ITS Bersagliere (Italy); Zeeleeuw (NL submarine)
Mar. 2010 to Aug. 2010 SNMG2	
12 March–30 June: Commodore Steve Chick (UK)	HMS Chatham (Flagship, Royal Navy); HS LIMNOS (Greek Navy)—under national control from 30 May; ITS SCIROCCO (Italian Navy)—under national control from 5 June TCG Gelibolu (Turkish Navy); USS Cole (US Navy)
1 July–6 August: Commodore Michiel Hijmans (Royal Netherlands Navy)	HNLMS De Zeven Provinciën (Flagship, the Netherlands); TCG Gelibolu (Turkey); USS Cole (United States)
Nov. 2009 to Mar. 2010 SNMG1	
Commodore Christian Rune (succeeded Rear Admiral Jose Pereira de Cunha (PO) from 25 January 2010).	NRP Álvares Cabral (outgoing flagship, Portugal); H DMS Absalon (incoming flagship, Denmark); HMS Fredericton (Canada); USS Boone (United States); HMS Chatham (United Kingdom)
Aug. 2009 to Nov. 2009 SNMG1	
Commodore Steve Chick (UK)	HS Navarinon (frigate F461, Greece); ITS Libeccio (Italian frigate); TCG Gediz (Turkish frigate); HMS Cornwall (United Kingdom frigate); USS Donald Cook (United States destroyer)

---

[17] The SNMG1 and SNMG2 are under the overall command of the commander, Allied Maritime Component Command Headquarters Northwood, in the United Kingdom, which is one of the three Component Commands of Allied Joint Force Command Brunssum.

joining a multinational coalition that utilizes maritime patrol aircraft, unmanned aerial vehicles, and even satellite imagery to disrupt piracy in the western Indian Ocean. The NATO Shipping Centre in Northwood and the Transport Planning Group under NATO's Senior Civil Emergency Planning Committee provide a connection between Ocean Shield and the international commercial shipping community.

Like all of the nations conducting anti-piracy operations off the coast of Somalia, the member states of NATO have had difficulty addressing the detention and criminal prosecution of suspected pirates in criminal court. Even after five years of counter-piracy experience, vexing legal and policy obstacles remain.[18] For example, certain NATO military forces, such as those from Spain or Germany, are constitutionally barred from law enforcement duties.

3.1.1.5 Promotion of International Law

NATO's activities are conducted in accordance with international law, including applicable treaties and customary international law and relevant UN Security Council resolutions. The 2010 *Strategic Concept* highlights the importance of "unique community values." These values inform both the purpose and the activities of the Alliance and include a commitment to "principles of individual liberty, democracy, human rights and the rule of law."[19] The Alliance is also "firmly committed" to the principles of the UN Charter and the North Atlantic Treaty (also known as the Washington Treaty), which affirm the primary standing of the UN Security Council for the maintenance of international peace and security.

In May 2010, General Stéphane Abrial, Supreme Allied Commander Transformation (SACT), chartered a study to identify the challenges and vulnerabilities that affect the use of the global commons by NATO. The effort reviewed the importance to the Alliance of the oceans, airspace, outer space, and cyberspace.[20] In each case, the existing legal architecture in the international law of the sea was found to provide sufficient authority for NATO operations. The maritime chapter of the study indicates the Alliance relies on the rules set forth in the United Nations Convention on the Law of the Sea (UNCLOS), which entered into force in 1994. Like the UN Charter, UNCLOS is an "umbrella" treaty in the sense that it is the basis for a number of follow-on treaties and laws. Furthermore, because UNCLOS

---

[18] Lord Jopling (United Kingdom), General Rapporteur, The Growing Threat of Piracy to Regional and Global Security, NATO Parliamentary Assembly 169 CDS 09 E rev.1, (2009).
[19] NATO Strategic Concept (2010).
[20] MAJ. GEN. MARK BARRETT, DICK BEDFORD, ELIZABETH SKINNER & EVA VERGLES, ASSURED ACCESS TO THE GLOBAL COMMONS 11–19 (Supreme Allied Command Transformation, North Atlantic Treaty Organization, Norfolk, Virginia, Apr. 3, 2011).

... balances the rights and duties of flag, port, and coastal states, the entire architecture of oceans law represents a "package deal," in which states are required to accept all of its provisions, enjoying rights and fulfilling concomitant responsibilities. This careful balance between the rights and duties of flag and coastal states represents a grand bargain that unfolded during the negotiation of the Convention.[21]

International law and the law of the sea do not receive special treatment in a separate section of the AMS, but rather the norms and rules are woven throughout the document as part of Alliance values in the rule of law. Because NATO is a maritime alliance, with the North Atlantic connecting North America and Western Europe, historically, it has promoted a particularly robust view of freedom of navigation and other internationally lawful uses of the sea.

3.2 European Union

Twenty-seven states belong to the European Union (EU), and all of them, as well as the European Community (EC), are party to UNCLOS.[22] Approximately 350 million passengers and about 3.5 billion tons of cargo per year pass through European seaports. European waterways include some of the most critical maritime chokepoints—the English Channel, the Danish Straits and the Strait of Gibraltar. The total sea area is nearly 4 million square kilometers. The littoral regions of Europe produce 40 percent of the continent's gross domestic product, and 22 European nations operate 1,200 seaports.[23] Rotterdam, Antwerp and Hamburg are among the largest ports in the world.

Like the United States, European nations are heavily dependent upon maritime trade. In 2010, 52 percent of the continent's trade was carried by sea, an increase from 45 percent a decade ago.[24] The European Commission reports that 90 percent of trade with nations outside of the EU and 43 percent of intra-EU trade travels by ship.[25] The member states include some of the largest flag state registries in the world, including Greece, which joined the EC in 1981, and Cyprus and Malta, which acceded to the treaty in 2004. Forty percent of the world's commercial fleet is owned by European shipowners.

---

[21] James Kraska, *Indistinct Legal Regimes, in* Securing Freedom in the Global Commons 51 (Scott Jasper ed., 2010).

[22] United Nations Convention on the Law of the Sea, Montego Bay Dec. 10, 1982, entered into force Nov. 10, 1994, UN Doc. A/CONF.62/122, 21 I.L.M. 1621–1354 (1982), 1833 U.N.T.S. 397 [Hereinafter UNCLOS].

[23] Analysis of Cyber Security Aspects in the Maritime Sector, para. 1.1 (European Network and Information Security Agency, Nov. 2011).

[24] Eurostat database: EXTRA EU 27 Trade Since 2000 By Mode of Transport (HS6) (DS_043328), as cited in Analysis of Cyber Security Aspects in the Maritime Sector, para. 1.1 (European Network and Information Security Agency, Nov. 2011).

[25] http://ec.europa.eu/maritimeaffairs/maritimeday/pdf/proceedings_en.pdf.

Since its inception in 1957, the expansion of a common shipping policy within the European Economic Community (EEC) Treaty (or Treaty of Rome) by the original members of Belgium, France, Germany, Italy, Luxembourg, and The Netherlands, has been remarkable.[26] The Treaty of Maastricht amended the European framework in 1992,[27] accelerating the integration of shipping policy, and which is reflected in Article 71(1)(c) of the EEC Treaty. By the mid-1990s, the EC Committee on Safe Seas had pledged to explore further coordination of safety at sea.[28] Article 80(2) of the EC Treaty provides that "The Council may, acting by a qualified majority, decide whether, to what extent and by what procedure appropriate provisions may be laid down for sea [and air transport]." Consequently, the EU has endeavored to develop and implement a common maritime transport policy that addresses maritime safety and environmental protection. Increasingly, this approach includes matters that edge into the realm of maritime security. EC maritime transport law now extends to Norway, Iceland, and Liechtenstein, none of which are members of the EC, but these states participate in the European Economic Area.

There are three key EU strategic documents: the 2003 *European Security Strategy* (ESS),[29] the 2008 *Report on the Implementation of the ESS*,[30] and the 2010 *Internal Security Strategy*.[31] These documents form the core of the EU's Common

---

[26] Treaty Establishing the European Economic Community, signed at Rome, Mar. 25, 1957, *entered into force*, Jan. 1, 1958, 298 U.N.T.S. 11 (*EEC Treaty*), amended by the Single European Act, signed at Luxembourg, Feb. 17, 1986 [1987] OFFICIAL J. OF THE EUROPEAN UNION L 169/1 (*Single European Act*), amended by the Treaty on European Union, signed at Maastricht, Feb. 7, 1992, [1992] OFFICIAL J. OF THE EUROPEAN UNION C191/1, 1757 U.N.T.S. 3, 31 I.L.M. 247 (*Maastricht Treaty*), amended by the Treaty on the European Union, signed at Maastricht on Feb. 7, 1992 [1992] OFFICIAL J. OF THE EUROPEAN UNION C191/1, 31 I.L.M. 247, Treaty of Amsterdam Amending the Treaty on European Union, the Treaties Establishing the European Communities and Certain Related Acts, signed at Amsterdam on Oct. 2, 1997, [1997] OFFICIAL J. OF THE EUROPEAN UNION C340/1 (*Treaty on European Union* or *Amsterdam Treaty*). The Treaty of Nice Amending the Treaty on European Union, the Treaties Establishing the European Communities and Certain Related Acts, Dec. 11, 2000, signed in Nice, Feb. 14, 2001 [2001] OFFICIAL J. OF THE EUROPEAN UNION C80/1 (*Treaty of Nice*).

[27] *Maastricht Treaty*, 1757 U.N.T.S. 3, 31 I.L.M. 247.

[28] Regulation 2099/2002 of the European Parliament and of the Council, Nov. 5, 2002, establishing a Committee on Safe Seas and the Prevention of Pollution from Ships (COSS) and amending the Regulations on maritime safety and the prevention of pollution from ships, 2002 Official J. of the European Communities L 324/1.

[29] COUNCIL OF THE EUROPEAN UNION, A SECURE EUROPE IN A BETTER WORLD: EUROPEAN SECURITY STRATEGY, Dec. 12, 2003.

[30] COUNCIL OF THE EUROPEAN UNION, REPORT ON THE IMPLEMENTATION OF THE EUROPEAN SECURITY STRATEGY—PROVIDING SECURITY IN A CHANGING WORLD, Dec. 12, 2008.

[31] COUNCIL OF THE EUROPEAN UNION, INTERNAL SECURITY STRATEGY FOR THE EUROPEAN UNION "TOWARDS A EUROPEAN SECURITY MODEL," Feb. 23, 2010.

Security and Defense Policy (CSDP). The ESS is the overarching document—it states, "Europe has never been so prosperous, so secure, nor so free," although the "world is full of new dangers and opportunities." Terrorism, proliferation of weapons of mass destruction, regional conflict, failed states, and organized crime, are listed as the greatest threats to the EU. None of these major EU strategy documents addresses maritime security in detail, although the ESS refers to piracy as "a new dimension to organized crime."[32] The 2008 *Report* recognizes that there is a maritime dimension to illegal maritime migration related to the EU's regional partnership with countries along the southern periphery of the Mediterranean Sea.

The common shipping policy emerged from concern over uniform standards for marine environmental protection, and began with pilotage requirements for transit in the North Sea and English Channel,[33] transference of registry within the Community,[34] safety and health requirements aboard ships,[35] minimum standards for the carriage of dangerous or polluting goods,[36] training for seafarers,[37] and port state control.[38] Thus, the initial focus was on European safety for purposes of marine environmental protection.

The EU places great emphasis on strengthening management of commercial shipping in port and in coastal waters as a way to enhance state security. In 2004, the European Parliament and Council of the EU adopted Regulation 725/2004 on enhancing ship and port facility security.[39] The EC Regulation clarifies Community obligations under the 1974 *International Convention for the Safety of Life at Sea* (SOLAS Convention) and the *International Ship and Port Facility Security Code* (ISPS Code). The focus of the Regulation is on intra-European and transcontinental marine shipping traffic operating on fixed and scheduled routes and associated ports. Member states had to apply the mandatory security measures of the ISPS Code to their international fleets and ports by July 1, 2005, and make a

---

[32] A SECURE EUROPE IN A BETTER WORLD, at p. 5.
[33] Directive 79/115/EEC, Dec. 21, 1978, OFFICIAL J. OF THE EUROPEAN COMMUNITIES 1979 L 33/32.
[34] Regulation 613/91/EEC, Mar. 4, 1991, OFFICIAL J. OF THE EUROPEAN COMMUNITIES 1991 L 68/1, as amended.
[35] Directive 92/29/EC, Mar. 31, 1992, OFFICIAL J. OF THE EUROPEAN COMMUNITIES 1992 L 113/19.
[36] Directive 93/75/EC, Sept. 13, 1993, OFFICIAL J. OF THE EUROPEAN COMMUNITIES 1993 L 247/19, as amended.
[37] Directive 2001/25/EC, Apr. 4, 2001, OFFICIAL J. OF THE EUROPEAN COMMUNITIES 2001 L 136/17, as amended.
[38] Directive 95/21/EC, June 19, 1995, OFFICIAL J. OF THE EUROPEAN COMMUNITIES 1995 L 157/1, as amended.
[39] Regulation (European Commission) No. 725/2004 of the European Parliament and of the Council, Mar. 31, 2004 on enhancing ship and port facility security, OFFICIAL J. OF THE EUROPEAN UNION L 129, 29.4.2004, at p. 6 and Directive 2005/65/EC of the European Parliament and the Council, Oct. 26, 2005, on enhancing port security, OFFICIAL J. OF THE EUROPEAN UNION L 310, 25.11.2005, at p. 28.

determination as to the application of the measures for ships operating domestic services by July 1, 2007.

Two of the major threats identified by the ESS, terrorism and proliferation of WMD, are not mentioned in EU maritime policy. Related issues, however, are addressed, and these include port state control,[40] maritime situational awareness, vessel traffic services, and traffic separation schemes. These programs amplify the traditional continental approach of maintaining a firm state hand to mitigate sea-related risk. Europeans have an inclusive view of maritime threats; they include vessel source pollution and safety of life at sea. Individual states of the EU have made great progress in harmonizing domestic law to international instruments, such as the ISPS Code, and bilateral engagements, such as the U.S. Container Security Initiative (CSI). The 2006 *Green Paper* on maritime policy promoted a holistic, integrated maritime policy within the EU, including the idea of creation of a European Coast Guard.[41]

The open societies of the EU member states pose a particularly difficult maritime security challenge. The states have a combined coastline of 100,000 kilometers, so protecting the EU from maritime threats is daunting. Furthermore, the *Maastricht Treaty* reflected the notion of "European citizenship," which afforded the rights of entry and exit without discrimination to all nationals of the member states and their families.[42] The 1999 *Treaty of Amsterdam*, amending the *Treaty on the European Union*, for example, imported the Schengen accords on visa-free entry within Europe into EU law. The Schengen rules erased most border controls for internal travel among 26 European countries.[43]

Border controls to enter or exit the Schengen Area were standardized and strengthened. As a result of the 1985 *Schengen Agreement*, signed in the town of Schengen, Luxembourg, the rules include four non-EU member states—Iceland, Liechtenstein, Norway, Switzerland—and *de facto* includes three European micro-states—Monaco, San Marino, and the Vatican. The rules cover 1.6 million square miles and include all of the EU member states except the United Kingdom and Ireland. But the EU has yet to realize the full potential for standardizing maritime security protocols under the *Schengen Agreement*.

---

[40] Council of the European Union Directive 95/21/EC of June 19, 1995 [1995] OFFICIAL J. OF THE EUROPEAN UNION L 157, July 7, 1995, at 1, as amended by Directive 2002/84/EC of the European Parliament and of the Council [2002] OFFICIAL J. OF THE EUROPEAN UNION L 324, 29.11.2002, at p. 53.

[41] COMMISSION OF THE EUROPEAN COMMUNITIES, TOWARDS A FUTURE MARITIME POLICY FOR THE UNION: A EUROPEAN VISION FOR THE OCEANS AND SEAS BRUSSELS, 7.6.2006 (COM (2006) 275) final Volume II—ANNEX (The Green Paper) (SEC (2006) 689), at 26–27.

[42] Consolidated EC Treaty, Article 12: "Within the scope of the application of this Treaty, and without prejudice to any special provisions contained therein, any discrimination on grounds of nationality shall be prohibited."

[43] Passport usage and regular border controls vary among Schengen countries.

3.2.1 Blue Book—Integrated Maritime Policy

The European Agency for the Management and Operational Cooperation at the External Borders (FRONTEX) is the lead EU body for harmonizing external border security through risk analysis, training, and operational cooperation among member states. In partnership with FRONTEX, member states established the European Patrols Network in 2007 in order to share operational information and coordinate patrols along the southern tier. With the October 2007 adoption of the *Blue Book*, an *Integrated Maritime Policy of the European Union*, a maritime dimension was added to these efforts.[44]

The *Blue Book* sets out oceans governance principles and links together regional and EU-wide initiatives from different sectors. The policy has limited application to maritime security, however, and focuses mostly on trade and fisheries. The *Blue Book* is a template for maritime and coastal economic development. The policy seeks to integrate the maritime affairs among national, regional, and EU institutions to maintain surveillance and better manage maritime space. Separate marine sectors of transport, environment, energy, employment, oceanographic research, and fisheries are combined into a single coherent policy.

A 2009 message from Commissioner of Fisheries and Maritime Affairs Joe Borg provides greater detail of EC development of the *Blue Book*.[45] By that year, the Commission and Council had launched or completed 56 of 65 actions contained in the *Blue Book*. Increased coordination at the intra-EU regional level promised even greater integration. Cooperation among states is driven by new instruments, which include the roadmap for planning a maritime area (2008), the *Baltic Sea Strategy* (2009), the June 2011 *Strategy for the Atlantic Area*, as well as support for better integrated coastal zone management.

3.2.1.1 Maritime Surveillance

The *Blue Book* includes text on maritime surveillance, naval force generation, and international coordination. The most effective contribution of the *Blue Book* to maritime security is the promotion of an interoperable maritime surveillance

---

[44] Communication from the European Commission to the European Parliament, the Council, the European Economic and Social Committee, and the Committee of the Regions on AN INTEGRATED MARITIME POLICY FOR THE EUROPEAN UNION (COM (2007) 575 final) adopted by the European Commission on Oct. 10, 2007 (Hereinafter BLUE BOOK), *reprinted in*, II TERROR ON THE HIGH SEAS: FROM PIRACY TO STRATEGIC CHALLENGE 473–75 (Yonah Alexander & Tyler B. Richardson eds., 2009). The BLUE BOOK consists of two Commission Communications on policy and two working documents—an Action Plan and an Impact Study.

[45] Anne Eckstein, *Maritime Policy: EU Executive Sets Out Priorities for Next Five Years*, EUROPOLITICS, Oct. 16, 2009.

system. National, regional, and EU systems are becoming integrated so that information is shared with authorities at each level.[46] The European Commission plans to make ocean surveillance among the member states interoperable by bringing together tracking systems used for safety and security with those used for marine environmental protection, IUU fisheries control, and maritime migration and marine law enforcement.[47] Coordinated maritime surveillance is a cost-effective way to enhance the EU's capacity to counter illegal maritime trafficking in people and illicit drugs. Maritime surveillance is also an element of the incomplete single European Border Surveillance System (EUROSUR). Over the longer term, maritime surveillance is expected to include data to inform maritime safety and security, protect of the marine environment, fisheries control, trade and economic interests, and marine law enforcement and maritime defense.

The European Defence Agency (EDA) was established by the EU in 2004 in order to promote a common vision of defense and security, assist member states with training and development of their armed forces, and aid in the collaboration of defense policy. The EDA is investigating the extent to which marine surveillance and maritime domain awareness (MDA) should be part of the Common Security and Defense Policy. On April 26, 2010, the EDA's "Wise Pen" team of five Vice-Admirals delivered its final report, *Maritime Surveillance in Support of the CSDP*.[48] The "Wise Pen" group does not favor a monolithic or hierarchical system of systems of European MDA,[49] but instead supports incremental advances in new technologies that eventually could create a "loosely coupled federated system."[50] The NATO Maritime Security and Safety Information System (MSSIS), for example, provides an Internet website that fuses data from numerous automatic identification system (AIS) receivers that pinpoint the location of international shipping.

Just as inertia has worked to slow full implementation of the Schengen Agreement, changing the culture of maritime information sharing from "need to know" to "need to share" is a long road. In November 2009, the Council of the EU tasked the Commission to develop a comprehensive approach to integrated maritime surveillance that includes civil and military tracking. The Commission presented a roadmap at the end of 2010, which was further detailed in 2011 to take into

---

[46] Proposed Measures include the achievement of an integrated network of vessel tracking, interoperable surveillance systems and improved cooperation among Member States' coast guards. BLUE BOOK, at 5–6.
[47] Id.
[48] The authors are Vice Admirals Fernando del Pozo, Anthony Dymock, Lutz Feldt, Patrick Hebrard, and Ferdinando Sanfelice di Monteforte.
[49] Vice Admiral Fernando del Pozo, et al., *Maritime Surveillance in Support of CSDP*, THE WISE PEN TEAM FINAL REPORT TO EDA STEERING BOARD, Apr. 26, 2010, para. 11, at 9 and para. 124, at 39.
[50] Id., at para. 119, p. 38.

account the full range of asymmetric maritime threats. As with all CSDP initiatives, however, policy makers still grapple with how to avoid duplicating NATO frameworks and obtain effective implementation.

3.2.1.2 Naval Capabilities

In 2004, the EU released *Headline Goal 2010*, which provides operational detail and depth to the political objectives in the ESS. The document asserts that the EU should be able "to respond with rapid and decisive action" across the "whole spectrum of crisis management" operations. The EU also seeks the ability to simultaneously conduct several distinct naval operations at different levels of engagement.

The *Headline Goal* identifies strategic lift, including strategic sealift, as a core capability for the EU's *Maritime Rapid Response Concept*. Under the *Rapid Response Concept*, the EU force structure should support a comprehensive maritime capability within a five to 30 day crisis window.

Member states of the EU already participate in several multinational naval initiatives, such as the European Maritime Force (EUROMARFOR) that can be stood up on a five-day notice through force contributions from France, Italy, Portugal, and Spain. EUROMARFOR warships deployed from October to November 2002 with NATO's Operation Active Endeavour, and since 2003, with the U.S.-led Operation Enduring Freedom.

3.2.1.3 Anti-piracy Operations

Since 2008, Somali pirates have attacked more than 1,000 ships in the Western Indian Ocean.[51] On November 10, 2008, the Council launched the EU Naval Force (NAVFOR) Operation Atalanta to deter Somali piracy attacks on humanitarian convoys from the World Food Program (WFP). Operation Atalanta is the first naval operation under the CSDP. The operational area was also expanded to cover the area out to the Seychelles archipelago. From the end of March 2010, two objectives were added to Atalanta's mission's mandate: controlling Somali ports where pirates are based and neutralizing roving pirate mother ships. By the spring of 2012, EUNAVFOR consisted of 1,600 personnel, nine warships, and five maritime surveillance aircraft.

On March 23, 2012, the EU Council extended the mandate of the counter-piracy operations until December 2014. The Council also expanded the area of operations to include the land territory and internal waters of Somalia, based upon the authority granted by UN Security Council Resolution 1851 of December 16, 2008. The authority was used to attack pirate boats and supplies on the beach.

---

[51] F. Brinley Bruton, *EU Forces Attack Somali Pirates on Land for First Time*, MSNBC.COM, May 15, 2012.

The attacks inside Somalia are meant to deprive pirates safe havens on the land that seem politically (but not legally) immune from attack, but the naval campaign has had limited success.

The EU effort is directed from the Maritime Security Centre Horn of Africa (MSCHOA) in Northwood, United Kingdom. The Centre serves as a link between the EU naval forces and international shipping in the western Indian Ocean. Operation Atalanta has been bedeviled by resource constraints and the legal policy relating to detention and criminal prosecution of captured pirate suspects. That is not to say, however, that the naval campaign has been unsuccessful, at least in ensuring the delivery of WFP shipments to Somalia and helping to reduce the success rate of Somali pirates. Like most other naval forces engaged in anti-piracy patrols, the EUNAVFOR effort has a dual purpose to exercise an ability to deploy a flotilla and conduct complex maritime security operations successfully.[52]

The greatest impact the EU has had on Somali piracy, however, is through its considerable political and economic clout ashore. The decision to create the EU military mission to contribute to training Somali Security Forces (EUTM Somalia) was taken in February 2010,[53] and the initiative was launched on the ground on March 31, 2010.[54] The training takes place in Uganda, with the headquarters in Kampala and actual instructions occurring in Bihanga, 350 kilometers southwest of Kampala. The headquarters also includes a rear element in Brussels and an office in Nairobi, Kenya. Uganda is also the principal contributor to the African Union's Mission in Somalia (AMISOM). A Ugandan general serves as force commander for AMISOM. EUTM Somalia coordinates training with AMISOM, the United States, and the United Nations. The training plan was amended in 2011 to focus on improving the command and control of the Somali National

---

[52] James Kraska & Brian Wilson, *Cooperative Strategy and Maritime Piracy*, 154 J. OF THE ROYAL UNITED SERVICES INSTITUTE FOR DEFENCE & SECURITY STUDIES, Apr. 2009, at 74–81 (counter-piracy deployments used to demonstrate ability to conduct out-of-area operations).

[53] On 15 February 2010, the Council adopted Decision 2010/96/CFSP on a European Union military mission to contribute to the training of Somali security forces. OFFICIAL J. OF THE EUROPEAN UNION L 44, 19.2.2010, at p. 16.

[54] European Council Decision, Common Security and Foreign Policy, 2010/96/CFSP on a European Union military mission to contribute to the training of Somali security forces, Mar. 31, 2010, OFFICIAL J. OF THE EUROPEAN UNION L 87, 7.4.2010, at p. 33. The Council Decision was amended by Corrigendum to Council Decision 2010/197 of Mar. 31, 2010 on the launch of a European Union Military Mission to Contribute to the Training of Somalia Security Forces (EUTM Somalia), OFFICIAL J. OF THE EUROPEAN UNION L 201 4.8.2011, at p. 19 and Corrigendum to Council Decision 2010/96 of Feb. 15, 2010 on the launch of a European Union Military Mission to Contribute to the Training of Somalia Security Forces (EUTM Somalia), OFFICIAL J. OF THE EUROPEAN UNION L 201 4.8.2011, at p. 19.

Security Forces (NSF), and now includes training local instructors in order to enable Somalis to transfer expertise to others inside the country.[55]

The EU training support promotes the peace and reconciliation process of the Transitional Federal Government and it aids the work of the African Union Mission in Somalia (AMISOM) to stabilize the country. The EU has poured money into additional programs to promote the rule of law, education, and rural development in Somalia. The EU is also training the Yemeni coast guard. The EU funded the construction of the anti-piracy operational coordination center in Sana'a, one of three in the region established under the Djibouti Code. The *Djibouti Code of Conduct concerning the Repression of Piracy and Armed Robbery against Ships in the Western Indian Ocean and the Gulf of Aden* is perhaps the most notable IMO effort to nurture regional capacity to repress Somali piracy.

3.2.1.4   A Security Strategy for the Global Maritime Domain

The EU continues to build out the frameworks necessary to implement the 2007 *Blue Book*. The Lisbon Treaty bridges the gap between areas of community competence and those under the primary authority of the member states. At the EU Foreign Ministers meeting on April 26, 2010, in Luxembourg, the principals invited the EU High Representative, the European Commission, and member states to begin "preparing options for the possible elaboration of a Security Strategy for the global maritime domain, including the possible establishment of a Task Force."

The Luxembourg decision was simply another early step to refine the EU approach to maritime security. The maritime security policy provides coherence to three disparate efforts—the civilian component, reflected in the IMP; the civil-military dimension, reflected by the CSDP focus on supporting civilian initiatives; and the military or naval dimension. From the military side, greater coordination with NATO could avoid duplication of effort and possibly tap into operational synergies. The NATO Secretary-General has offered to increase practical cooperation in the field of maritime security. For example, both NATO and the EU conduct patrols in the Mediterranean (under FRONTEX and Active Endeavour), but there is little coordination between the two efforts.

3.3   Chiefs of European Navies Maritime Operational Concept

The Chiefs of European Navies (CHENS) is an informal and independent forum with a membership that includes the chief of the navy of each European nation that is a member of either the EU or NATO. While CHENS does not have any

---

[55] European Council Decision, Common Security and Foreign Policy, 2011/483/CFSP, Jul. 28, 2011, Official J. of the European Union L 198 30.7.2011, at p. 37.

official authority in its own right, the high level membership suggests that recommendations from the group are given serious consideration.

The chiefs of navies consider the prosperity and security of their nations inextricable link to the sea. The littoral demography is particularly striking on the European Continent. There is an increase in urbanization and settlement in the coastal regions that brings greater competition for offshore areas, including:

> ... a substantial proliferation of artificial structures, energy farms, power generators and aquaculture. Coastal areas are also the destination for the majority of tourists in Europe, making the need to reconcile economic development, environmental sustainability and quality of life particularly acute in these regions. Gas and oil infrastructures and port facilities are also likely to increase in complexity and footprint. Sectors identified with most growth potential include: cruise shipping, ports, aquaculture, renewable energy—offshore wind energy, energy generation from ocean currents, waves and tidal movements—underwater marine telecommunications, marine biotechnology and ocean mining.[56]

With greater demands on littoral regions, the navy chiefs suggest that the ability of all peoples to freely use the offshore maritime commons is "dependent on respect for international law, treaties and conventions."[57]

On August 10, 2010, the commanders released a capstone document, the *Chiefs of European Navies Maritime Operational Concept* (MOC).[58] The MOC sets forth the maritime challenges facing Europe, including the array of threats to the significant and growing volume of trade by sea and the vast scale of damage that could be inflicted on Europe by a threat from the sea.[59] Other threats include "unregulated and unreported fishing, smuggling, arms trafficking—including proliferation of weapons of mass destruction, illegal immigration or human trafficking, narcotics trafficking, ... piracy and terrorism."[60] At the same time, the MOC embraces the opportunities that can be found in exploiting ocean resources and contemplates the possibility of new Arctic trade routes connecting Europe to Asia and North America.[61]

The Chiefs of European Navies are alarmed by the proliferation of weapons of mass destruction and the trade in chemical, biological, radiological and nuclear (CBRN) material that can be used in the production of missile warheads and dirty bombs. More than 15 nations are seeking a military nuclear capability, even

---

[56] CHIEFS OF EUROPEAN NAVIES MARITIME OPERATIONAL CONCEPT, at p. 3 [Hereinafter CHENS MOC].
[57] CHIEFS OF EUROPEAN NAVIES MARITIME OPERATIONAL CONCEPT, at p. 2. The CHENS MOC was written by CHENS Working Group for Strategic Dialogues, and was endorsed by the chiefs of the European navies in Copenhagen on August 13, 2010.
[58] Id. The MOC is available at http://www.chens.eu/products/CHENS_MOC_2010.pdf.
[59] Id., at 2.
[60] Id., at 5.
[61] Id., at 2.

68 CHAPTER THREE

though some of them are members of the Non Proliferation Treaty.[62] There is a certain "stickiness" connecting a fusion of conventional and irregular maritime threats with rogue states at the center. Extremist groups and individuals are joined to national armed forces. The result:

> Military nuclear technology is becoming more and more accessible making it harder to specify the nature of the threat, which in turn encourages proliferation. At the same time, the proliferation of cruise missile and ballistic missile programs is facilitated by the lack of international legal framework on missile technology development and exportation. The acquisition and development of long-range missile programs globally has increased the amount of these missiles that can be deployed rapidly. It could lead to a change in the strategic regional balance of some regions.
>
> The free use of the seas for transportation in general terms also gives vast opportunities for illegal, covert trafficking at sea of CBRN material for the production of missiles and dirty bombs, violating international non proliferation treaties.[63]

The CHENS view naval power and maritime security forces as ideally positioned to disrupt the dangerous relationships that foster trafficking. The navies are considered a "unique expression of state sovereign capacity at sea." European navies are structured to conduct four major maritime roles: maritime defense, maritime security operations, crisis response operations, and naval diplomacy. Maritime defense includes traditional deterrence and war fighting roles and power projection. Maritime security operations constitute constabulary missions, including counter-terrorism and disruption of weapons proliferation, drug smuggling, illegal migrant interdiction, and energy security.

Crisis response presents opportunities for expeditionary peacekeeping operations. Naval forces are uniquely tailored to provide a number of significant public goods in or by using the global maritime commons, including humanitarian assistance and disaster relief, and security capacity and confidence building. Finally, naval diplomacy permits graduated and scalable military commitments overseas, providing a forward maritime presence that reassures allies and friends and can signal resolve to potential adversaries. Each of these roles leverages the sovereign immune legal status in international law of warships and naval auxiliaries.[64]

Freedom of access to the oceans and freedom of navigation "on the high seas" are considered "strategic enablers."[65] Certainly this is true, as far as it goes, but the CHENS would have done better to recognize freedom of navigation and overflight over exclusive economic zones, considering that most of the countries of Europe do not have free access to the high seas without traversing the EEZ of one or more neighboring states. (This omission is most likely inadvertent, given that

---

[62] Id., at 6.
[63] Id., at 6.
[64] Id., at 4.
[65] Id., at 9.

Articles 58 and 87 of UNCLOS join the regime of high seas freedoms, for the most part, to the rules that pertain to the EEZ).

The CHENS also promote greater maritime situational awareness (MSA)—what the United States refers to as maritime domain awareness (MDA)—as another enabler of improved maritime security. Maritime security operations, in particular, are considered to be entirely dependent upon effective MSA; otherwise, trying to conduct security at sea is like looking for the proverbial needle in a haystack. Only by information and intelligence cueing can scarce maritime and air forces locate and address potential maritime threats. Finally, the CHENS believe that joint, combined, and interagency forces are required to address the complex nature of maritime threats and opportunities.

There is a high degree of similarity in the description of the maritime threat environment between the CHENS documents and the U.S. maritime strategy. Additionally, there is a great deal of overlap between CHENS and the *Cooperative Strategy for 21st Century Seapower*, including:

- Protection of trade—both the European and American approaches stress the importance of protection sea lines of communication; whereas the European approach is more regional, the American approach is global;
- Competition for resources—although both approaches consider the dynamic of competition for marine resources, the U.S. strategy is concerned with wider claims of excessive coastal state claims, which encroach on the rights of other coastal states and the international community;
- Social instability—the threat of coastal state instability is reflected in both documents, although CHENS documents do not explicitly mention the dangers posed by extremist ideologies;
- Proliferation of weapons of mass destruction—the growing risks of WMD proliferation are compelling for both Americans and Europeans, and it is a feature in documents generated on both sides of the Atlantic Ocean;
- Terrorism—the threats posed by maritime terrorism are addressed in each approach;
- Interagency coordination—whereas the CHENS focuses more deeply on interagency coordination, the United States has stresses the importance of international partnerships.[66]

In comparison to the U.S. perspective of maritime threats embodied in *A Cooperative Strategy for 21st Century Seapower*, the CHENS documents more often mention the protection of living resources of the oceans and the need to safeguard biodiversity—stretching the concept of maritime "security." The CHENS and U.S. documents raise concern over the proliferation of improvised explosive devices, and articulate a reliance on interagency cooperation.[67] The *Cooperative Strategy*, on the other hand, places a greater emphasis on the potential conflicts caused

---

[66] Comparison of the US New Maritime Strategy and the CHENS documents: A study conducted by the CHENS MSD working group, May 9, 2008, at p. 6.
[67] Id., at p. 5–7.

by wider claims of sovereignty exerted by coastal states, the risks associated with climate change, and the dangers presented by extremist ideologies and cyber threats to critical infrastructure, such as the banking system.

3.4 U.K. FUTURE MARITIME OPERATIONAL CONCEPT

The United Kingdom's 2007 *Future Maritime Operational Concept* (FOMC) sets forth the nation's military interests in maritime security in terms both sweeping and, looking backwards and forward, historic:

> The UK is a maritime nation whose prosperity, stability and security depend on the unique access provided by the sea and the maintenance of an international system of law and free trade. Out to 2025, an increasingly interdependent, yet competitive world will be characterized by intense, but uneven globalization, continuing tensions and rivalries between states, the accelerating exploitation of ocean resources and a variety of trans-national pressures. The UK will therefore need the means to continue to discharge its sovereign responsibilities and protect its political and economic interests in an era of increased maritime complexity and competition and as a result of more diverse dependencies on the sea.[68]

In the coming decades, the British expect the maritime domain to be characterized by two main themes: littoral complexity and increased oceanic competition. Even in non-combat situations, the urban coastal landscape poses significant challenges.[69] Littoral complexity is driven by the presence of large populations and human activity, coastal urbanization, and a proliferation of offshore installations, energy farms, pipelines and roadsteads, shore side power generation plants, aquaculture, and shipping traffic. Oceanic competition will mar cooperation on the high seas, the deep seabed, and in the Arctic and Antarctic regions. Increased access to the farthest reaches of the sea—a function of advanced marine technology and the effects of climate change in the Arctic Ocean—will produce more intensive resource exploitation of the seas. Fishing, seabed mining, and oil and gas drilling, and perhaps disputes over freedom of navigation, may produce conflict from the eastern Mediterranean to the Indian Ocean and the South China Sea. In short, the British view a "cluttered, busy seascape" as the "prime means for the transmission of risk" in a globalized world.[70]

The U.K. also views the risk of terrorism and the spread of WMD via the sea as a "permanent feature of the maritime scene."[71] Activist groups and other non-state actors will continue to challenge Britain's oceanic interests, and the pros-

---

[68] MINISTRY OF DEFENCE OF THE UNITED KINGDOM, THE FUTURE MARITIME OPERATIONAL CONCEPT (Nov. 13, 2007), para. 101 [Hereinafter FOMC].
[69] Id., at para. 129.
[70] Id., at para. 110.b. and para. 124.
[71] Id., para. 110.

pect for international naval conflict by 2015–2018 means that the Royal Navy should be "benchmarked at the war-fighting level."[72] Maritime forces will have to be prepared to operate in an increasingly crowded and dangerous physical and metaphorical oceanic space.

The most technologically worrisome threats in the maritime domain are increasing numbers of fast attack craft, which stress the ability of naval forces to react quickly under traditional rules of engagement, and the proliferation of cruise and ballistic missiles and missile technology. Major concerns also include:

- Improvised explosive devices that provide an asymmetric means of destroying large, friendly military or civilian ships in choke points or in port;
- Proliferation of submarines by states and minis-subs and unmanned underwater systems by non-state groups that afford a powerful and inexpensive means of covert surveillance and attack in the busy littoral waters;
- Mines, which are capable of stopping shipping. The examples of the mining of the Red Sea in 1984, the Gulf of Oman and Persian Gulf in 1987, and the approaches to Kuwait in 1991 demonstrate that just the suspicion or allegations that mines have been laid will cause significant disruption to international shipping;
- Electromagnetic pulse, directed energy, and chemical, biological, radiological, and nuclear attack threaten to confound and overwhelm advanced societies.[73]

These changes will be exacerbated if China's economy continues to rapidly expand, a resource-rich and "antagonist" Russia maintains its course away from the West, and middle powers, such as India, Brazil, South Africa, and Iran challenge the existing world order.[74] New and emerging threats from other nations may utilize directed energy weapons (DEW) (including energy 'bombs'), electromagnetic pulse, electronic warfare, quantum computing, cyber warfare, and proliferation of precision guided munitions. Without a check on these trends, the future of cooperation in the oceans could give way to naval conflict.

The Middle East remains an area of historic British influence. A Royal Navy Fleet Auxiliary support ship and four mine hunters are permanently based in Bahrain, for example. The ships are crewed by rotating personnel. The Royal Navy conducts counter-piracy operations off the coast of Somalia and warships and Merlin helicopters are engaged in disrupting terrorism, human trafficking, and drug smuggling in the region. The United Kingdom deployed thousands of soldiers and naval personnel to Iraq and Afghanistan. The magazine *IHS Fairplay* reported in 2009 that $952 billion of trade passed through the Gulf of Aden and the Suez Canal that year, including $840 billion in containerized cargo and $62 billion in oil, gas, and petro-chemicals.

After three decades as an energy exporter, in 2004, the United Kingdom began to be a net importer of energy. In 2010, 35 percent of the nation's gas imports

---

[72] Id.
[73] Id., Annex A, pp. A1–A4.
[74] Id., at para. 111.

arrived in liquefied natural gas tankers, and about 80 percent of that came from Qatar. Within less than a decade, the United Kingdom estimates that 70 percent of its natural gas will arrive by sea. The United Kingdom exports £15 billion worth of goods and services to the Gulf countries, and 160,000 British nationals live in the region.

The oceans are governed by a mix of "law, practice, custom and commerce," undergirded by the rules reflected in UNCLOS. Britain worries, however, that the legal regime "may not be sustainable in the face of competing claims to resources and unclaimed space, and in areas [of disagreement in which] international law remains unclear."[75] To maintain peace in this potentially chaotic maritime system, the United Kingdom is one of the few nations still capable of putting to sea a balanced fleet, with the ability to operate effectively throughout the spectrum of threats and conflicts with flexible and scalable, mission-tailored naval task forces. At the higher end, British sea power relies on powerful, agile, and versatile Carrier Strike (CS) and Littoral Manoeuver (LitM) Task Groups that have sustained reach. These powerful task forces are configured to dominate all dimensions of the maritime environment (air, surface and subsurface domains and the electromagnetic bandwidth) and project power ashore. Much like the United States, however, the United Kingdom expects to encounter "assertive, aspiring and adventurist powers" positioning to defeat expeditionary capabilities through large investments in "anti- access, surveillance, and sea denial systems and technologies."[76]

The United Kingdom expects to operate with other countries, including the NATO alliance, or under ad hoc UN or regional mandates, to secure its maritime goals. Interestingly, the UK *Maritime Concept* reflects an understanding that in order to preserve its influence with the United States and beyond, the country has to continue to play a "leading role" in NATO and the wider world.[77] At the same time, contingencies such as the Falklands dispute, may find Britain compelled to operate unilaterally. In order to prevail in U.K.-only contingencies, however, the country recognizes it needs an "irreducible minimum" of maritime power.[78]

Two types of forces will be needed—maritime force projection (MFP) and maritime security.[79] The MFP will be built around Carrier Strike (CS) and LitM Task Groups capable of conducting "high impact, low footprint Ship to Objective Maneuver (STOM) from Over the Horizon (OTH) through synchronized, simultaneous surface and/or air assault in support of both concentrated and distributed operations."[80] Sea-based forces obviate the need for large installations on

---

[75] Id., at para. 120.
[76] Id., at para. 113.
[77] Id., at para. 118.
[78] Id.
[79] Id., at para. 128.
[80] Id., at para. 141.

the ground. These forces suggest capability that includes forced entry of hostile shores, replicating U.S. sea power strategy, doctrine, and naval force structure.

The British conception of maritime security consists of three elements: maritime homeland security, maritime security operations to protect the global commons and the world system, and maritime protection to defend specific global choke points and maritime infrastructure. Maritime homeland security protects the UK mainland and Overseas Territories, such as the British Indian Ocean Territories and the atoll of Diego Garcia, and their associated territorial and jurisdictional waters and airspace. The homeland security aspects of maritime security include fisheries enforcement, protection of North Sea oil installations, and maritime surveillance along the approaches to the United Kingdom.[81]

Maritime Security Operations (MSO) addresses the "security of the international system."[82] MSO are marine constabulary operations, and are drawn from joint, interagency, and combined coalitions of like-minded states. Maritime protection is focused on the physical security of strategic maritime choke points and internationally recognized maritime infrastructure, such as the Suez Canal, Panama Canal, and the Strait of Hormuz.[83] These sea lines of communication are essential for what the British refer to as "maritime trade operations," or commercial shipping, including the uninterrupted flow of strategic materials, energy, and commercial goods that travel by sea.[84]

The *Fleet Operational Maritime Concept* is prescient, observing in 2007, when the 2008 Great Recession had not yet occurred nor the 2011 *Strategic Defense Review* had yet to gut the Royal Navy, that resources to ensure maritime security were in decline. Only an unexpected shock to the international system, the FOMC states, such as a "decisive discontinuity," is likely to reverse declining resources dedicated to maritime security.[85] The United Kingdom plans for its maritime forces to continue to support national security by "exploiting the sea as a strategic medium" to help to preserve international order at sea and promote the U.K.'s national values and interests in the world. This peculiarly global and systemic view of maritime security is a hallmark of the Anglo-Saxon-American perspective that a liberal order of the oceans is essential for shaping a free, stable, and secure liberal world order.[86]

---

[81] Id., Annex B-1.
[82] Maritime Security Operations—The Military Contribution, MWC 11/2/3/5, May 5, 2006.
[83] FOMC, at Annex B-2.
[84] Id., at B-2–B-3.
[85] Id., at para. 102.
[86] JAMES KRASKA, MARITIME POWER AND LAW OF THE SEA 11 and 51 (2011).

FOUR

PEACETIME ZONES AND CONTROL MEASURES

4.1 TEMPORARY SUSPENSION OF INNOCENT PASSAGE

Ships of all nations enjoy the right of innocent passage through the territorial sea of any coastal State. This rule of innocent passage is codified in Article 17 of the United Nations Convention on the Law of the Sea (UNCLOS).[1] Moreover, high seas freedoms of navigation and overflight apply seaward of the territorial sea.[2]

UNCLOS, however, also recognizes the counter-balancing right of the coastal State to employ maritime zones and other control measures in appropriate circumstances, such as to enhance safety of navigation and to preserve and protect the marine environment. Many of these measures are under the purview of the International Maritime Organization (IMO)—the specialized UN agency for maritime matters. Generally, restrictions or impediments to passage in territorial seas overlapped by straits used for international navigation must be adopted by the member states of the IMO. In other circumstances, however, restrictions on innocent passage in the territorial sea may be established unilaterally by the coastal State.

Nations routinely conduct naval weapons practice and exercises within their territorial seas. In order to ensure safety of navigation for commercial ships and aircraft that transit the exercise area, Article 25(3) of UNCLOS allows the coastal State to temporarily suspend innocent passage in specified areas of its territorial sea "if such suspension is essential for the protection of its security, including weapons exercises."

---

[1] United Nations Convention on the Law of the Sea, *opened for signature* Dec. 10, 1982, UN Doc. A/CONF.62/122 (1982), 1833 U.N.T.S. 3, 397, 21 I.L.M. 1261 (1982) (*entered into force* Nov. 16, 1994), Article 17 [Hereinafter UNCLOS].
[2] Id., Articles 58, 86 and 87.

For instance, the United States has elected to temporarily suspend innocent passage in very limited areas of the territorial sea. The Ulupau Crater Weapons Training Range off the island of Oahu, for example, is a designated danger zone in which innocent passage may be temporarily suspended to accommodate naval exercises.[3] One of over 60 U.S. armed forces training ranges at sea, the Ulupau Crater Range extends seaward to a distance of 3.8 nautical miles[4] and overlaps a 500-yard wide prohibited area.[5]

The U.S. Coast Guard is responsible for issuing a Notice to Mariner (NOTMAR) for the specific dates and times reserved for weapons firing. At the Ulupau Crater range, training may occur at any time of the week between 0600 and 2300. When the range is not in use "boaters...have complete access to the danger zone...."[6] But during periods when the range is live, ships are not allowed. In such case, all craft "shall expeditiously vacate the danger zone at best speed and by the most direct route whenever weapons firing is scheduled."[7]

4.2 Offshore Installation Safety Zones

Coastal States are also entitled to declare safety zones around artificial islands and installations in the 200-nautical mile Exclusive Economic Zone (EEZ) and on the Continental Shelf. As new land-based sources of hydrocarbons become increasingly scarce, coastal States turn to the sea to develop offshore oil and gas reserves located within the EEZ and on the Continental Shelf. Article 56 grants the coastal State jurisdiction over the establishment and use of artificial islands, installations and structures used to exploit these resources. In the exercise of its jurisdiction over resources, the coastal State has the "exclusive right to construct and to authorize and regulate the construction, operation and use" of:

(a) artificial islands;
(b) installations and structures for the purposes provided for in article 56 and other economic purposes;
(c) installations and structures which may interfere with the exercise of the rights of the coastal State in the zone.[8]

Included in this grant of jurisdiction is the authority to regulate matters related to customs, fiscal, health, safety and immigration issues that concern the coastal

---

[3] 33 C.F.R. § 334.1380.
[4] The area lies between radial lines bearing 357.1° true and 124.9° true, respectively, from a starting point on Mokapu Peninsula at latitude 21°27'11.84" N, longitude 157°43'53.83" W. Id.
[5] 33 C.F.R. Part 334 for a complete list of all U.S. training ranges.
[6] 33 C.F.R. § 334.1380.
[7] Id.
[8] Id., Articles 60 and 80.

State.[9] The remit in Article 56 raises an interesting point. The coastal State's jurisdiction over artificial islands and installations granted in Article 56 appears to apply only to those structures or features constructed "for the purposes provided for in Article 56 and other economic purposes." Presumably, installations used for other purposes are permitted, even without the consent of, and indeed even with the disapproval of, the coastal State. While there may be political arguments against such activities, the law appears to permit them.

A fair reading of Article 56 suggests that it does not limit artificial islands and installations constructed for non-economic purposes. Would a foreign state be entitled, for example, to place an installation for military purposes in the EEZ of a foreign coastal State? As autonomous and unmanned underwater technology becomes more sophisticated, there is a strong likelihood that states may surreptitiously emplace "smart" installations on the Continental Shelf or in the EEZ of coastal States. Those installations would appear to satisfy the rules in UNCLOS so long as they are not related to economic purposes and have due regard for the coastal State's resource rights in the EEZ and on the Continental Shelf. These technologies give rise to numerous military applications, such as positioning listening devices that keep track of coastal State submarines entering and exiting port, use of autonomous underwater installations that launch and recover submarine surveillance drones, and even installations that contain mines and torpedoes.

Article 60(4) of UNCLOS provides authority for coastal States to "establish reasonable safety zones around such artificial islands, installations and structures in which it may take appropriate measures to ensure the safety both of navigation and of the artificial islands, installations and structures." The size of the safety zone is determined by the coastal State, but cannot exceed 500 meters around them, "except as authorized by generally accepted international standards or as recommended by the competent international organization"[10] The IMO "is recognized as the only international body responsible for establishing and recommending measures on an international level concerning ships' routeing."[11] Routeing is promulgated by IMO in the *General Provision on Ships' Routeing* (GPSR), which can be supplemented by additional IMO Assembly resolutions.[12] The rules for navigation of ships in the vicinity of offshore installations and structures, for example, states that vessels should

>.1 [conduct] navigation with caution, giving due consideration to safe speed and safe passing distances taking into account the prevailing weather conditions and the presence of other vessels or dangers;

---

[9] Id.
[10] Id.
[11] IMO Doc. A.571(14), General Provisions on Ships' Routeing, Nov. 20, 1985.
[12] Id.

.2 where appropriate, take early and substantial avoiding action when approaching such installation or structure to facilitate the installation's or structure's awareness of the vessel's closest point of approach and provide information on any possible safety concerns, particularly where the offshore installation or structure may be used as an aid to navigation;
.3 use any routeing systems established in the area; and
.4 maintain a continuing listening watch on the navigating bridge on VHF channel 16 or other appropriate radio frequencies when navigating in the vicinity of offshore installations or structures, vessel traffic services and other vessels so that any uncertainty as to a vessel maintaining an adequate passing distance from the installations or structures can be alleviated.[13]

All ships navigating in the vicinity of manmade offshore features are required to respect lawfully designated safety zones and "comply with generally accepted international standards regarding navigation in the vicinity of artificial islands, installations, structures and safety zones."[14] Offshore structures and the safety zones around them may not, however, be "established where interference may be caused to [sic] the use of recognized sea lanes essential to international navigation."[15]

4.2.1 *IMO Safety Zones*

In recent years the member states of the IMO considered whether the 500-meter safety zone is sufficient to protect high-value offshore infrastructure. In 2007, Brazil proposed that the IMO approve an expansion of the maximum size of permissible safety zones around offshore energy installations. Brazil operates numerous Floating Production, Storage and Off-Loading (FPSO) Units in the South Atlantic, and sought larger zones "in order to meet the need for safety around each peculiar structure."[16] Accordingly, Brazil requested the IMO to extend the breadth of the safety zones to:

> [O]ne nautical mile around fixed oil rigs and offshore terminals [and two] nautical miles around [Floating Production, Storage and Off-Loading or FPSO Units] and [Dynamic Positioning or DP] oil rigs, in order to reduce the risk of a maritime casualty and resulting marine pollution in the area, due to damage of oil rigs.[17]

The proposal was designed to better protect Brazil's booming offshore oil industry, and to avoid vessel damage to an installation that could lead to a marine

---

[13] IMO Doc. A.671(16), Safety Zones and Safety of Navigation Around Offshore Installations and Structures, Oct. 19, 1989, para. 2.
[14] Id.
[15] Id.
[16] IMO Doc. NAV 53/3, Proposal for the establishment of an Area to be Avoided and modifications to the breadth of the Safety Zones around Oil Rigs located off the Brazilian Coast—Campos Basin Safety Zones, Feb. 26, 2007.
[17] Id.

environmental incident.[18] Brazil is trying to get a handle on managing an offshore energy sector that has burgeoned. Brazilian energy giant *Petrobras* estimates that the country's oil production and its proven oil reserves will nearly double by 2020, putting the country in the same league as major oil exporters as Qatar, Canada, and Nigeria.[19]

Although there was general support for the Brazilian proposal in the Sub-Committee on Safety of Navigation (NAV) at IMO, a number of delegations expressed concern that there were no established IMO procedures or guidelines in place to make determination for approving safety zones in excess of 500 meters.[20] The U.S. delegation emphasized that

> ...the [Navigation] Sub-Committee should develop uniform procedures, and guidelines by which safety zone proposals should be considered. Otherwise, the Sub-Committee would be considering proposals for safety zones greater than 500 meters on an *ad hoc* basis without guidelines, standards or objective measures by which to make a judgment. The development of uniform procedures would...ensure that safety of navigation was taken consistently into account. Proposals should be judged on an objective basis such that the size of any adopted safety zone was no larger than the minimum necessary to achieve safety of navigation.[21]

The U.S. statement reflects the general American preference to view with skepticism establishment of new limitations on freedom of navigation. If the rule permitted coastal States to unilaterally extend safety zones beyond 500 meters, it might tempt coastal States to try to use such zones inappropriately to impair freedom of navigation. By erecting a collection of offshore structures and linking zones together into a string of small outposts, a country effectively could construct a regulatory wall to prevent legitimate transit, all under the guise of enhancing navigational safety and environmental protection. Brazil ultimately agreed to maintain the breadth of the safety zones at 500 meters after a majority of delegations indicated that they "did not agree to the extension of the safety zones, taking into consideration that there were not any established procedures and guidelines in order to determine the proposed extension."[22]

During the following session of the IMO Maritime Safety Committee, the United States and Brazil submitted a joint proposal to add a new item to the work program "regarding the Development of Guidelines for Consideration of

---

[18] Juan Forero, *Brazil Girds for Massive Offshore Oil Extraction*, Wash. Post, Dec. 7, 2009.
[19] Id.
[20] IMO Doc. NAV 53/22, Report to the Maritime Safety Committee, Aug. 14, 2007, para. 3.14.
[21] Id., para. 3.16.
[22] Id., paras. 3.50 and 3.51.

Requests for Safety Zones Larger than 500 meters."[23] Based on this proposal, the Committee "agreed to include, in the work program...a high-priority item on 'Guidelines for consideration of requests for safety zones larger than 500 meters around artificial islands, installations and structures in the EEZ.' "[24]

At the next meeting of the NAV Sub-Committee, the matter was deferred to NAV 56 because no proposals had been submitted. Based on a recommendation by the United Kingdom, however, a correspondence group was established to work between sessions of the Sub-committee and report progress at NAV 56.[25] The group was specifically tasked to:

> .1 review [earlier] resolutions[26]...and develop relevant guidelines for recommending Safety Zones larger than 500 meters around artificial islands, installations and structures in the [EEZ] including multiple structure installations, taking into account the General Provisions on Ships' Routeing....;
>
> .2 address means for ensuring the safety of navigation and of the artificial island, installations, or structures from collisions or allisions of passing vessels, while at the same time assuring a reasonable relationship of the proposed safety zone to the nature and function of the artificial island, installation or structure, and while remaining fully consistent with the rights and duties of other States in the EEZ in accordance with international law as referenced in Article 58 of UNCLOS....[27]

At NAV 56, a working group was established to consider documents relating to safety zones and to prepare recommendations for consideration and approval by the Plenary. The group first considered the report of the correspondence group that had been established at NAV 55. That report offered two alternatives to resolve the issue:

> 16. The Sub-Committee is invited to consider and approve the draft amendments to the General Provisions on Ships' Routeing (Resolution A.572(14), as amended, relating to *Guidelines for consideration of requests for safety zones larger than*

---

[23] IMO Doc. MSC 84/22/4, Development of Guidelines for Consideration of Requests for Safety Zones Larger than 500 meters Around Artificial Islands, Installations and Structures in the Exclusive Economic Zone, Submitted by the United States and Brazil, Feb. 4, 2008.

[24] IMO Doc. MSC 84/24, Report of the Maritime Safety Committee on its Eighty-Fourth Session, May 23, 2008, para. 22.41. Two sessions were needed to complete the agenda item.

[25] IMO Doc. NAV 55/21, Report to the Maritime Safety Committee, Sept. 1, 2009, paras. 5.4 and 5.5.

[26] IMO Doc. A.671(16), Safety Zones and Safety of Navigation Around Offshore Installations and Structures, Oct. 19, 1989, IMO Doc. A.571(14), General Provisions on Ships' Routeing, Nov. 20, 1985, and IMO Doc. MSC 84/22/4, Development of Guidelines for Consideration of Requests for Safety Zones Larger than 500 meters Around Artificial Islands, Installations and Structures in the Exclusive Economic Zone, Submitted by the United States and Brazil, Feb. 4, 2008 (Brazil and United States).

[27] IMO Doc. NAV 55/21, Report to the Maritime Safety Committee, Sept. 1, 2009, para. 5.6.

500 meters around artificial islands, installations and structures in the EEZ (annex 1), and forward them to the Committee for adoption.

17. The Sub-Committee is also invited to consider as an alternative or supplement to the above a draft SN circular on *Safety zones and safety of navigation around offshore installations and structures* attached as annex 2.[28]

The United States, however, reversed its earlier position, indicating that there was "no demonstrated need at present for safety zones larger than 500 meters or the development of guidelines for such safety zones."[29] This change by the United States derived from disagreement by the Department of Defense, which had come to believe that the Coast Guard had gone too far on the issue and risked stumbling into endorsement of new rules that deplete navigational freedom.

Delegations from other States observed that safety zones "were not actually routeing measures, and, thus, might not be a proper subject to include in the *General Provisions on Ships' Routeing*."[30] Accordingly, a number of delegations, including the United States, did not support the recommendations of the Correspondence Group. Rather than developing guidelines in a new Annex to the *GPSR*, the United States proposed the adoption of an appropriate SN circular pertaining to safety zones and the safety of navigation around offshore installations and structures.[31]

Although a handful of delegations favored amending the *GPSR*, the majority of States "were of the opinion that safety zones were not routeing measures and should therefore not be addressed under *GPSR*."[32] A majority of the delegations also supported the U.S. proposal that "an SN [Safety of Navigation] circular would be the more appropriate way to address the issue."[33]

Ultimately, the Sub-Committee agreed to a draft SN circular titled *Guidelines for Safety Zones and Safety of Navigation Around Offshore Installations and Structures*.[34] The Sub-Committee also agreed with the U.S. position "that there was no demonstrated need, at present, to establish safety zones larger than

---

[28] IMO Doc. NAV 56/4, Guidelines for Consideration of Requests for Safety Zones Larger Than 500 Meters Around Artificial Islands, Installations and Structures in the EEZ, Report of the Correspondence Group, Submitted by the United Kingdom, Apr. 23, 2010.

[29] IMO Doc. NAV 56/4/1, Guidelines for Consideration of Requests for Safety Zones Larger Than 500 Meters Around Artificial Islands, Installations and Structures in the EEZ Submitted by the United States, June 4, 2010, para. 2.

[30] IMO Doc. NAV 56/20, Report to the Maritime Safety Committee, Aug. 31, 2010, para. 4.6.

[31] IMO Doc. NAV 56/4/1, Guidelines for Consideration of Requests for Safety Zones Larger Than 500 Meters Around Artificial Islands, Installations and Structures in the EEZ, Submitted by the United States, June 4, 2010, para. 7.

[32] IMO Doc. NAV 56/20, Report to the Maritime Safety Committee, Aug. 31, 2010, para. 4.9.

[33] Id.

[34] Id., para. 4.13.

500 meters around artificial islands, installations and structures in the exclusive economic zone or to develop guidelines to do so, and that the continuation of the work beyond 2010 for a Correspondence Group on Safety Zones was, at present, no longer necessary."[35]

In December 2010, at the 88th session of the Maritime Safety Committee, the member States approved *Guidelines for Safety Zones and Safety of Navigation Around Offshore Installations and Structures*.[36] The *Guidelines* were contained in *Safety of Navigation Circular 295*, which requested flag States to:

> .1 take all necessary steps to ensure that, unless specifically authorized, ships flying their flag observe any coastal State's conditions for entry into and/or navigation within duly established safety zones; and
>
> .2 draw the attention of seafarers to the need to navigate with extreme caution, including taking all necessary measures in regard to voyage planning required by SOLAS regulation V/34 and make timely radio contact with the offshore artificial islands, installations or structures, associated vessel traffic services and other vessels in the area, if an infringement of the safety zone cannot be avoided.[37]

While the IMO has struggled to maintain the size of safety zones in UNCLOS, individual States have promulgated national laws that adopt a precautionary approach around offshore structures. The Outer Continental Shelf Lands Act of the United States, for example, contains a system for safety zones around offshore installations.

4.2.2   U.S. Safety Zones

The Outer Continental Shelf Lands Act (OCSLA) provides for American jurisdiction over offshore structures, islands, and installations.[38] Pursuant to Title 43 of the U.S. Code:

> The Constitution and laws and civil and political jurisdiction of the United States are extended to the subsoil and seabed of the Outer Continental Shelf and to all artificial islands, and all installations and other devices permanently or temporarily attached to the seabed, which may be erected thereon for the purpose of exploring for, developing, or producing resources therefrom, or any such installation or other device (other than a ship or vessel) for the purpose of transporting such resources, to the same extent as if the outer Continental Shelf were an area of exclusive Federal jurisdiction located within a State: Provided, however, That mineral leases on the

---

[35] Id., para. 4.15.
[36] IMO Doc. MSC 88/26, Report of the Maritime Safety Committee on its Eighty-Eighth Session, Dec. 15, 2010, para. 11.8.
[37] IMO Doc. SN.1/Circ.295, Guidelines for Safety Zones and Safety of Navigation Around Offshore Installations and Structures, Dec. 7, 2010, para. 4.2.
[38] 43 U.S.C. § 1333 (2009). The history of U.S. continental shelf legislation dates to the 1950s. *See*, Aug. 7, 1953, ch. 345, § 4,67 Stat. 462; Pub. L. 93–627, § 19(f), Jan. 3, 1975, 88 Stat. 2146; Pub. L. 95–372, title II, § 203, Sept. 18, 1978, 92 Stat. 635; Pub. L. 98–426, § 27(d)(2), Sept. 28, 1984, 98 Stat. 1654.

outer Continental Shelf shall be maintained or issued only under the provisions of this subchapter.[39]

It is interesting to note that U.S. jurisdiction extends to offshore artificial islands and installations and "devices permanently or temporarily attached to the seabed," but only insofar as they are "for the purpose of exploring for, developing, or producing resources therefrom," or associated with "transporting such resources." Thus, in accordance with Article 56 of UNCLOS, the United States does not purport to exercise jurisdiction over non-resource-related installations or structures on its Continental Shelf.

The U.S. Coast Guard has authority to regulate offshore installations:

> ... promulgate and enforce such reasonable regulations with respect to lights and other warning devices, safety equipment ... on the artificial islands, installations, and other devices referred to in subsection (a) of this section or on the waters adjacent thereto....[40]

[and]

> mark for the protection of navigation any artificial island, installation, or other device referred to in subsection (a) of this section whenever the owner has failed suitably to mark such island, installation ... and the owner shall pay the cost of such marking.[41]

The Secretary of the U.S. Army has authority to prevent obstruction to navigation in U.S. navigable waters, and the remit is "extended to the artificial islands, installations, and other devices referred to in subsection (a) of this section."[42] Generally, Army responsibilities in the areas offshore are fulfilled by the Army Corps of Engineers.

In U.S. law, safety zones may be established around facilities located on the Outer Continental Shelf (OCS) that are constructed, maintained, or operated "to promote the safety of life and property on the facilities, their appurtenances and attending vessels, and on the adjacent waters within the safety zones."[43] Safety zone regulations "may extend to the prevention or control of specific activities and access by vessels or persons, and include measures to protect the living resources of the sea from harmful agents."[44]

Coast Guard District Commanders possess the authority to establish safety zones and issue and enforce safety zone regulations.[45] Consistent with UNCLOS Article 60, a U.S. safety zone "may extend to a maximum distance of 500 meters

---

[39] 43 U.S.C. § 1333(a)(1).
[40] Id., (d)(1).
[41] Id., (d)(2).
[42] Id., (e).
[43] 33 C.F.R. § 147.1 (2011).
[44] Id.
[45] 33 C.F.R. § 147.5 and § 147.10 (2011).

around the OCS facility measured from each point on its outer edge or from its construction site, but may not interfere with the use of recognized sea lanes essential to navigation."[46]

The United States has declared safety zones around 39 offshore installations, and each one is specified separately in the Code of Federal Regulations. The deepwater Boxer Platform, for example, has a fairly typical safety zone. The platform is a self-contained drilling and production platform installed by Shell Offshore, Inc. in the Gulf of Mexico during the late-1980s. Located about 140 miles south of Morgan City, Louisiana, the platform sits in 750 feet of water, and the installation is one of the early deepwater wells.[47] The zone around Boxer Platform extends "within 500 meters (1640.4 feet) from each point on the structure's outer edge, not to extend into the adjacent East-West Gulf of Mexico [Shipping] Fairway."[48] The regulation states, "[n]o vessel may enter or remain in this safety zone...." Exceptions, however, exist for "[a]n attending vessel; a vessel under 100 feet in length overall not engaged in towing; or, [a] vessel authorized by the Commander, Eighth Coast Guard District."[49]

4.2.3 U.K. Safety Zones

The United Kingdom also established offshore installation safety zones, which are issued under the Petroleum Act 1987.[50] For example, a rather typical 500-meter radius zone was established around Islay Pipeline End Manifold and Wellhead (Block 3.15, Islay Field). Vessels, including hovercraft, submersibles and installations in transit, are prohibited from entering or remaining in the zone, except with the consent of the Health and Safety Executive or in accordance with the Offshore Installations (Safety Zones) Regulations 1987.[51]

The section 2 of the 1987 Regulations provides exceptions to the prohibition on vessels entering or remaining in a safety zone:

> 2. The prohibition...on a vessel entering or remaining in a safety zone...shall not apply to a vessel entering or remaining in the safety zone—
> (a) in connection with the laying, inspection, testing, repair, alteration, renewal or removal of any submarine cable or pipeline in or near that safety zone;

---

[46] 33 C.F.R. § 147.15 (2011).
[47] The Boxer Platform is located at position 27°56'48" N, 90°59'48" W. *See*, 33 C.F.R. § 147.801 (2011).
[48] Id. Shipping fairways are established to provide for safe approaches through oil fields in the Gulf of Mexico and entrances to major ports along the Gulf Coast. *See*, 33 C.F.R. § 166.200 (2011).
[49] CGD 08-99-023, 65 FR § 16825, Mar. 30, 2000.
[50] Sections 21(7), 22(1), 22(2), 23(1) and 24(2A).
[51] The Offshore Installations (Safety Zones) (No. 4) Order 2011, http://www.legislation.gov.uk/uksi/2011/2492/made.

(b) to provide services for, to transport persons or goods to or from, or under the authority of a government department to inspect, any installation in that safety zone;
(c) if it is a vessel belonging to a general lighthouse authority performing duties relating to the safety of navigation;
(d) in connection with the saving or attempted saving of life or property;
(e) owing to stress of weather; or
(f) when in distress.[52]

4.3 World-Wide Navigational Warning Service

Navigational warnings provide timely information to ensure the safety of life at sea. The IMO defines a navigational warning as "a message containing urgent information relevant to safe navigation broadcast to ships in accordance with the provisions of the *International Convention for the Safety of Life at Sea, 1974....*"[53] The coordinated warnings are issued regularly and contain information about persons in distress or objects and events that pose an immediate hazard to navigation. The IMO and the International Hydrographic Organization (IHO) World-Wide Navigational Warning Service (WWNWS) have combined guidance on navigational warnings.[54]

There are four types of navigational warnings: Naval Area (NAVAREA) warnings, Sub-Area warnings, Coastal warnings and Local warnings. NAVAREA warnings include navigational warnings or in-force bulletins "promulgated as part of a numbered series by a NAVAREA coordinator."[55] There are about 30 NAVAREA coordinators. The coordinators for the Arctic region, for example, include the Norwegian Coastal Administration (NAVAREA XIX), the Federal State Unitary Hydrographic Department of the Russian Federation (NAVAREA XX and XXI), and the Canadian Coast Guard (NAVAREA XVII and XVIII).[56]

NAVAREA coordinators for other regions include the United Kingdom Hydrographic Office (NAVAREA I), the U.S. National Geospatial-Intelligence Agency (NAVAREA IV and XII), the *Diretoria de Hidrografia e Navegacão* in Brazil, the Swedish Maritime Administration, the *Service hydrographique et océanographique de la Marine* in France, the Navy Hydrographic Office in South Africa and India, the Australian Maritime Safety Authority, and the Japan Coast Guard. NAVAREA warnings may include "new navigational hazards and failures of important aids to navigation as well as information requiring alterations to planned navigation

---

[52] The Offshore Installations (Safety Zones) Regulations 1987.
[53] IMO Doc. MSC.1/Circ.1288, Amendments to Resolution A.706(17), World-Wide Navigational Warning Service, Dec. 9, 2008, para. 2.1.16.
[54] Id., para. 1.1.
[55] Id., para. 2.1.15.
[56] IMO Doc. COMSAR .1/Circ.51/Rev.3, List of NAVAREA Coordinators, Annex, Jan. 18, 2012.

routes."[57] Delimitation of NAVAREA responsibility does not prejudice marine boundary disputes between states.

A Sub-Area warning is defined as "a navigational warning promulgated as part of a numbered series by a Sub-Area coordinator."[58] Sub-Areas are subdivisions of NAVAREAs. Coastal warnings are broadcast in numbered series by the International NAVTEX service or the International SafetyNET service. The International NAVETX service is a coordinated broadcast and automatic reception on 518 kHz using narrow-band direct-printing telegraphy in the English language, and International SafetyNET service is a coordinated broadcast and automatic reception using the Inmarsat Enhanced Group Call system, and also utilizes the English language."[59]

Local warnings, which are not regulated by the WWNWS Guidance, include navigational warnings that cover "inshore waters, often within the limits of jurisdiction of a harbor or port authority."[60] Local warnings normally are broadcast by means other than NAVTEX or SafetyNET, and they may supplement coastal warnings, providing more detailed information on inshore waters.[61]

Provided information on the subject has not previously been disseminated via a Notice to Mariners (NOTMAR), the following warnings may be suitable for broadcast:

.1 casualties to lights, fog signals, buoys and other aids to navigation affecting main shipping lanes;
.2 dangerous wrecks in or near main shipping lanes;
.3 new aids to navigation or significant changes to existing ones;
.4 large unwieldy tows in congested waters;
.5 drifting hazards (including derelict ships, ice, mines, containers, etc.);
.6 areas of search and rescue or anti-pollution operations;
.7 newly discovered rocks, shoals, reefs and wrecks posing a danger to shipping;
.8 alteration or suspension of established routes;
.9 cable or pipe-laying activities, or the towing of large submerged objects;
.10 emplacement of marine scientific research instruments;
.11 offshore structures and installations;
.12 malfunctioning radio or satellite navigation services;
.13 naval exercises, missile firings, space missions, nuclear tests, ordnance dumping zones;
.14 acts of piracy and armed robbery against ships;
.15 tsunamis and other natural phenomena, such as abnormal changes to sea level;
.16 World Health Organization (WHO) health advisory information; and
.17 security related requirements.[62]

---

[57] IMO Doc. MSC.1/Circ.1288, Amendments to Resolution A.706(17), World-Wide Navigational Warning Service, Dec. 9, 2008, para. 4.2.1.1.
[58] Id., para. 2.1.20.
[59] Id., paras. 2.1.1 and 4.2.1.2.
[60] Id., para. 2.1.7.
[61] Id., para. 4.2.4.1.
[62] Id., at 4.2.1.3.

The same subjects may be broadcast as Sub-Area warnings, but doing so will normally alert only the Sub-Area.[63] Coastal warnings may be issued with regard to the same criteria identified in the list above.[64]

The following example from 1985 illustrates the use of a NAVAREA warning to announce a series of U.S. military exercises off the coast of Florida that could affect the safety of merchant or civil shipping. The precise latitude and longitude coordinates of the warning have been omitted:

PRIORITY
P 172202Z OCT 85
FM DMAHTC WASHINGTON DC//HNNM/
TO AIG FOUR FIVE ZERO ONE
AIG FOUR NINE ZERO NINE
UNCLAS

SUBJECT: NAVAREA IV 2911/85 (11). FLORIDA-EAST COAST. ORDNANCE.

1. MINING EXERCISES 221500Z TO 231700Z OCT IN AREA.
2. TORPEDO EXERCISES 231100Z TO 231700Z OCT IN AREA.
3. LIVE ORDNANCE DROPS 241500Z TO 261600Z OCT IN AREA.
4. GUNNERY EXERCISES 221900Z TO 222200Z AND 232000Z TO 232300Z OCT IN AREA.
5. FLARE SMOKE DROPS 210900Z TO 260300Z OCT IN AREA.
BT[65]

The message alerts mariners to military activities involving mines, torpedoes, live ordnance, gunnery exercises, and smoke exercises during the designated times and at specified locations, identified by latitude and longitude. The code "P 172202Z OCT 85" is a military date-time group stamp and refers to the time of the release of the message, as October 17, 1985, at 2202 "Zulu" time, or 10:02 PM. The warning was issued by "DMAHTC," or the Department of Defense, Defense Mapping Agency Hydrographic/Topographic Center, and it was sent to several "AIG" recipients, which denote address indicating groups, or a collection of staffs, units, or commands represented by plain language address designators, or shorthand message addresses.[66] Consistent with IMO guidance, the warning was issued five days before the actual events transpired.

---

[63] Id., para. 4.2.2.1.
[64] Id., para. 4.2.3.2.
[65] MARITIME OPERATIONAL ZONES (Richard Jaques et al. ed., Naval War College, 2006), Appendix C [Hereinafter MARITIME OPERATIONAL ZONES].
[66] An address indicating group (AIG) is a form of military address for a predetermined list of specific and frequently recurring combinations of addressees. The purpose of AIGs is to facilitate faster message handling and reduce long lists of recipients by bundling together the electronic plain language addresses (PLADs) of numerous commands or units.

4.3.1 U.S. Navigational Warnings

Navigational warnings promulgated by the United States in support of the Global Maritime Distress and Safety System (GMDSS) are issued and categorized by location, for example, NAVAREA IV, HYDROLANT [Atlantic Ocean] or HYDROPAC [Pacific Ocean].

Special Warnings and U.S. Maritime Administration (MARAD) Advisories contain information about potential hazards caused by the global political climate. Daily memorandums are issued each weekday and contain a summary of all Broadcast Warnings and Special Warnings promulgated during the past 24–72 hours. The Atlantic Edition contains HYDROLANT and NAVAREA IV Warnings. The Pacific Edition contains HYDROPAC and NAVAREA XII Warnings. Both editions include any Special Warnings issued during the same period.[67]

The following HYDROPAC warning advises mariners that Iranian naval exercises in the Persian Gulf may potentially disrupt shipping in the Strait of Hormuz between December 2011 and March 2012.

4.3.1.1 HYDROPAC: Strait of Hormuz—Iranian Naval Exercises

This HYDROPAC warns merchant ships that during Iranian naval exercises from December 2011 to March 2012 in the Strait of Hormuz, vessels are in danger. In the past, Iranian naval forces have conducted ship boarding and inspections of foreign-flagged merchant ships, and particularly ships flying the flag of a European nation, as part of its naval exercises in the Strait.

> HYDROPAC WARNINGS
> 3581/11(62). STRAIT OF HORMUZ
> 1. REPORTS FROM MARITIME FORCES AND COMMERICAL MARITIME INTERESTS INDICATE CONCERN WITH THE POTENTIAL FOR LOCALIZED DISRUPTION TO SHIPPING IN CONJUNCTION WITH FUTURE IRANIAN NAVAL EXERICISES. DURING PREVIOUS EXERCISES IRANIAN MARITIME FORCES CONDUCTED BOARDINGS AND INSPECTIONS OF MERCHANT SHIPS, INCLUDING THOSE FLAGGED TO EUROPEAN NATIONS. THE POSSIBILITY EXISTS THAT IRAN WILL ATTEMPT TO CONDUCT BOARDINGS AND INSPECTIONS DURING EXERCISES BETWEEN DEC 2011 AND MAR 2012. THE MOST LIKELY LOCATION FOR THIS ACTIVITY WOULD BE IN THE VICINITY OF THE STRAIT OF HORMUZ, PARTICULARLY IN AREAS CLOSER TO IRANIAN TERRITORIAL WATERS.
> 2. IF A US FLAG VESSEL IS HAILED FOR BOARDING BY THE IRANIAN NAVY IN INTERNATIONAL WATERS, THE SHIP'S MASTER SHOULD "PROTEST BUT COMPLY," IF CIRCUMSTANCES WARRANT. [Paragraph Two provides guidance to U.S.-flagged ships, indicating that boarding should be protested, but not resisted].
> 3. US FLAG VESSELS ARE ADVISED TO REPORT INCIDENTS TO THE COMUSNAVCENT BATTLEWATCH CAPTAIN (MARITIME OPERATIONS CENTER) [contact

---

[67] Dep't of Defense, National Geospatial-Intelligence Agency, U.S. Notice to Mariners No. 1, Jan. 7, 2012.

telephone numbers ommitted here]. [Paragraph Three informs U.S.-flagged commercial vessels to report incidents to the Battle Watch Captain at the Maritime Operations Center of Commander, Naval Forces, U.S. Central Command and the U.S. Marine Liaison Office, both located in Bahrain.][68]

4.3.1.2 HYDROLANT: Mediterranean Sea—Hazardous Operations

The United States also uses HYDROPAC and HYDROLANT messages to warn mariners that U.S. naval forces are on patrol in a heightened defensive posture as the result of political or military events, such as a heightened risk of terrorist attack. The following HYDROLANT message refers to U.S. naval operations during January 1983 in the eastern Mediterranean Sea, and it requests ships and submarines to maintain a standoff distance of five nautical miles from U.S. naval forces.

> P 271845Z DEC 83
> FM DMAHTC WASHINGTON DC//NVS//
> TO AIG FOUR FIVE ZERO ONE
> ...
> UNCLAS
>
> HYDROLANT 2420/83 (54, 56). MEDITERRANEAN SEA, HAZARDOUS OPERATIONS.
>
> 1. HAZARDOUS OPERATIONS WILL BE CONDUCTED BY U.S. NAVAL FORCES IN THE EASTERN MEDITERRANEAN 30 DEC 83 TO 31 JAN 84 IN AREA BOUND BY [latitude/longitude coordinates omitted].
> 2. ALL SURFACE AND SUBSURFACE CRAFT SHOULD ATTEMPT TO AVOID APPROACHING CLOSER THAN 5 NAUTICAL MILES TO U.S. NAVAL FORCES WITHIN THE BOUNDED AREA DUE TO POTENTIALLY HAZARDOUS OPERATIONS BEING CONDUCTED AND HEIGHTENED SECURITY AWARENESS RESULTING FROM TERRORIST THREATS. ON THEIR PART, U.S. NAVAL FORCES WILL ALSO ATTEMPT TO AVOID APPROACHING OTHER SURFACE AND SUBSURFACE CRAFT. IT IS REQUESTED THAT RADIO CONTACT WITH U.S. NAVAL FORCES BE MAINTAINED ON VHF CHANNEL 16, INTERNATIONAL SAFETY AND CALLING CHANNEL, WHEN WITHIN 5 NAUTICAL MILES OF U.S. NAVAL VESSELS.
> 3. THIS NOTICE IS PUBLISHED SOLELY TO ADVISE THAT HAZARDOUS OPERATIONS ARE BEING CONDUCTED ON AN UNSCHEDULED BASIS; IT DOES NOT AFFECT THE FREEDOM OF NAVIGATION OF ANY INDIVIDUAL OR STATE.[69]

The notice also makes clear that it constitutes an alert or request, rather than an order. Ships of all nations are entitled to continue to enjoy their right of freedom of navigation. In this regard, the notice merely requests that nations avoid U.S. warships and that they maintain contact on Channel 16 if approaching closer than five nautical miles. The warning does not indicate that U.S. naval forces will take automatic defensive action even if a ship disregards the warning. Still, the

---

[68] MARITIME OPERATIONAL ZONES, Appendix C.
[69] Id.

warning helps U.S. forces to sort and better monitor civilian vessels and craft. Not all merchant ships will comply with the request, and some may not even know about it. But most ships will comply, and their compliance reduces the number of suspicious vessels that the naval forces must contend with.

4.3.1.3 Special Warning: Cuba

Special Warnings are published in U.S. *Notice to Mariners No. 1* (NM 1/12) and contain information of general interest not covered by HYDROLANT and HYDROPAC messages. Transmitted by U.S. Navy and Coast Guard Stations authorized to broadcast HYDROLANT and HYDROPAC messages, Special Warnings identify unique risks that may affect maritime shipping. Maritime Administration advisories are also published in NM 1/12 on a weekly basis, and they may be accessed through the Internet web sites[70] of the National Geospatial-Intelligence Agency and the U.S. Maritime Administration.[71]

Special Warnings are utilized for a variety of situations, including warning mariners of actions taken by coastal states to enforce their national sovereignty, or even excessive maritime claims of national sovereignty, as is the case with Cuba, immediately below.

> Special Warning No. 29. Cuba[72]
>
> 1. Mariners are advised to use extreme caution in transiting the waters surrounding Cuba. Within distances extending in some cases upwards of 20 miles from the Cuban coast, vessels have been stopped and boarded by Cuban authorities. Cuba vigorously enforces a 12-mile territorial sea extending from straight baselines drawn from Cuban coastal points. The effect is that Cuba's claimed territorial sea extends in many cases beyond 12 miles from Cuba's physical coastline....

4.3.1.4 Special Warning: Papua New Guinea—Political Unrest

On May 22, 1990, Papua New Guinea issued a Notice to Mariners, which was recirculated by the United States as a Special Warning to alert U.S.-flagged vessels:

> Special Warning No. 77. Papua New Guinea—Bougainville Coast
>
> 1. Bougainville Island declared unilateral independence from Papua New Guinea on May 17, 1990. The government of Papua New Guinea does not recognize the declaration. Consequently, the political situation may be tense in the future.

---

[70] *See*, National Geospatial-Intelligence Agency http://msi.nga.mil/NGAPortal/MSI.portal and U.S Maritime Administration of the Department of Transportation http://marad.dot.gov.

[71] Dep't of Defense, National Geospatial-Intelligence Agency, U.S. Notice to Mariners No. 1, Jan. 7 2012.

[72] Id., para. 1-1.5 (Originally published on Mar. 1, 1962, updated Jan. 1, 1982, reviewed Nov. 9, 1994).

2. The following Notice to Mariners No. 36/90, issued by the government of Papua New Guinea, is quoted in its entirety:

Quote. Overseas vessels are advised to stand clear of the islands of Bougainville and Buka and to remain outside of territorial waters extending 12 nautical miles from the coast of Bougainville and immediately adjacent islands but excluding Solomon Islands territory, and excluding the groups of islands or atolls known as Feni, Green, Nuguria, Carteret (Kilinailau), Mortlock (Tauu) and Tasman (Nukumanu). Any vessel entering the waters adjacent to Bougainville or Buka will be subject to stop and search powers. This Notice to Mariners is effective immediately (May 22, 1990 EST) in respect to overseas shipping. Papua New Guinea coastal vessels will be restricted as of midnight local time on 20th May 1990. Restrictions will continue for an indefinite period. Charts affected are [nautical charts identified by number]. Dept. of Transport. Port Moresby. Papua New Guinea. *Unquote*

3. U.S. mariners are advised to exercise extreme caution in entering and transiting the waters of Bougainville.[73]

4.3.1.5 Special Warning: Morocco—Aggressive Maritime Enforcement

On August 31, 1990, the United States issued a Special Warning concerning aggressive maritime law enforcement tactics by Moroccan authorities at sea:

Special Warning No. 82. Morocco

1. U.S. mariners are advised to exercise caution within the territorial waters claimed by Morocco. Moroccan coastal protection warships, while engaged in anti-drug smuggling activities or enforcing territorial fishing rights, have been known to open fire on innocent vessels....[74]

4.3.1.6 Special Warning: Persian Gulf—UN Security Council Enforcement Action

On February 16, 2001, the United States issued the following Special Warning relating to coalition maritime interception operations (MIO) enforcement action against Iraq:

Special Warning No. 115. Persian Gulf

1. In the Persian Gulf, multi-national naval units continue to conduct a maritime operation to intercept the import and export of commodities and products to/from Iraq that are prohibited by UN Security Council Resolutions 661 and 687.
2. Vessels transiting the Persian Gulf and Gulf of Oman can expect to be queried and, if bound for or departing from Iraq or the Shatt-al-Arab waterway, also intercepted and boarded. Safe navigation may require vessels to be diverted to a port or anchorage prior to conducting an inspection.
3. Maritime interception operations in the Red Sea, Strait of Tiran and Strait of Hormuz have ceased. Cargo bound for Aqaba or transshipment from Aqaba may be

---

[73] Id. (Originally published by the U.S. Dep't of State, May 25, 1990).
[74] Id. (Originally published by the U.S. Dep't of State, Aug. 31, 1990).

inspected on shore according to an agreement worked out by the UN Sanctions Committee and Jordanian authorities.
4. Documentation requirements for the naval regime in the Persian Gulf and the shore-based regime in Aqaba are identical and can be found in the most recent HYDRPOACS covering the enforcement of UN sanctions against Iraq.
5. Stowage and other requirements for vessels transiting the Persian Gulf can also be found in the most recent HYDROPAC covering the UN sanctions against Iraq.
6. Ships, which after being intercepted, are determined to be in violation of UN Security Council Resolution 661, will not be allowed to proceed with their planned transit.
7. The intercepting ship may use all available communications, primarily VHF Channel 16, but including International Code of Signals, flag hoists, other radio equipment, signal lamps, loudspeakers, bow shots, and other appropriate means to communicate directions to a ship.
8. Failure of a ship to proceed as directed will result in the use of the minimum level of force necessary to ensure compliance.
9. Any ships, including waterborne craft and armed merchant ships, or aircraft, which threaten or interfere with multinational forces engaged in enforcing a maritime interception may be considered hostile....[75]

4.3.1.7 Special Warning: Sri Lanka—Combating Terrorist Threats

Sri Lanka fought a thirty-year war against the Liberation Tigers of Tamil Eelam (LTTE). The maritime forces of the LTTE waged an effective insurgency at sea. On December 1, 1997, the United States issued the following warning to alert U.S.-flagged ships in the vicinity of Sri Lanka:

Special Warning No. 107. Sri Lanka

1. Sri Lanka has announced that entrance by unauthorized vessels into the waters of Palk Strait and the eastern territorial waters of Sri Lanka is prohibited because of increased acts of terrorism against shipping and Sri Lankan Naval Vessels. Sri Lanka requires that vessels in the vicinity contact the Sri Lankan Command (Tel. ...) for authorization if they wish to enter these areas.
2. The government also has established a restrictive zone in coastal waters along the west coast from Kalpitiya to Colombo Port's southern backwaters. Written permission from the Sri Lankan Command is required for entry into these waters as well. Sri Lankan authorities have advised that they will fire on violators.
3. The U.S. Embassy in Colombo reports that between July and September 1997, at least three foreign flag merchant vessels were attacked by the Liberation Tigers of Tamil Eelam (LTTE). One vessel operating as a passenger ferry off Mannar on the northwest coast was set on fire and sunk. A second vessel departing north from the Jaffna Peninsula was hijacked, stripped of equipment, and its crew temporarily held by the terrorists. One crew member was killed during the hijacking. A third vessel was loading a mineral cargo off the northeast coast near Pulmoddai when it was attacked and at least five members of its crew killed.
4. Any anti-shipping activity should be reported to NGA NAVSAFETY, U.S. State Department, or the nearest U.S. Consulate. Refer to NGA Pub. 117, Chapter 4, for

---

[75] Id., at para. I-1.7 (Originally published by the U.S. Dep't of State, Feb. 16, 2001).

instructions on filing a Ship Hostile Action Report (SHAR) or Anti-Shipping Activity Message (ASAM)....[76]

4.3.1.8 Special Warning: Yemen—Threats to U.S. Citizens

On October 13, 2000, the United States issued the following Special Warning concerning Islamic extremists fighting the government and foreign nationals and interests inside Yemen:

Special Warning No. 113. Yemen

1. The level of risk for foreigners in Yemen remains high. On 12 October 2000, several U.S. citizens were killed and many more were injured in an incident involving a U.S. Navy ship in the port of Aden, Yemen in what may have been a terrorist attack. An explosion in the morning of 13 October 2000 caused minor damage to the British Embassy in Sana'a, Yemen and no casualties. While U.S. and Yemeni officials are still cooperating closely to determine the cause of the tragic explosion, the investigation has only started. Under these circumstances, U.S. mariners should avoid Yemeni ports for the present.
2. In light of this and other recent events, the U.S. Department of State warns U.S. citizens to defer travel to Yemen. U.S. citizens should exercise a very high level of caution and should only travel between cities by air or with an armed escort. They should register with the U.S. Embassy in Sana'a and remain in contact with the Embassy for updated security information at [telephone numbers].[77]

4.3.1.9 Special Warning: Iran—Danger to Shipping

Special Warnings may be temporary, or remain in effect for years. This Special Warning concerning Iran, originally issued on February 5, 2001, was still in effect on January 7, 2012:

Special Warning No. 114. Iran

1. Mariners are advised to exercise extreme caution when transiting the waters of the North Persian Gulf.
2. Iranian-flag speedboats and patrol craft operating in Iranian and international waters have boarded vessels and demanded payment before the vessels are allowed to proceed.
3. Mariners should exercise extreme caution and vigilance when operating in this area, and should obtain and evaluate current warning information broadcasted by the National Geospatial-Intelligence Agency (NGA) via HYDROPAC broadcasts.
4. Any anti-shipping activity should be reported to NGA NAVSAFETY Bethesda MD [telephone and e-mail contacts] via Ship Hostile Action Report (SHAR) procedures,[78] or directly to the U.S. State Department, or nearest U.S. Embassy or Consulate.

---

[76] Id., para. I-1.6 (Originally published by the U.S. Dep't of State, Dec. 1, 1997).
[77] Id., para. I-1.7 (Originally published by the U.S. Dep't of State, Oct. 13, 2000).
[78] *See*, Nat'l Geospatial Agency, Radio Navigation Aids, Pub. 117, Chapter 4 (2005).

5. The publication of this notice is solely for the purpose of advising U.S. mariners of information relevant to navigation safety, and in no way constitutes a legal recognition by the United States of the validity of any foreign rule, regulation, or proclamation so published.[79]

4.3.1.10   Special Warning: Sierra Leone—Dangerous Port

On March 16, 2001, the United States issued this Special Warning concerning a lack of adequate port security in Freetown, Sierra Leone:

Special Warning No. 119. Sierra Leone

1. Mariners are strongly advised not to use any ports in Sierra Leone except for the port of Freetown, which is currently considered to provide safe harborage. Mariners should note that the Department of State warns U.S. citizens against travel to Sierra Leone. Although the security situation in Freetown has improved somewhat, areas outside the capital are still very dangerous.
2. The Department of State has terminated the ordered departure status of U.S. Government personnel in non-emergency positions. However, the U.S. Embassy in Freetown currently operates with a reduced staff. Only emergency consular services to U.S. citizens are available, and the Embassy's ability to provide these services is limited. U.S. citizens in Sierra Leone should review their own personal security situations in determining whether to remain in the country.[80]

4.3.1.11   Special Warning: United States—Worldwide Defensive Measures

On November 16, 2001, the United States issued this worldwide Special Warning to U.S. mariners and ships, warning of heightened political instability and increased risk of terrorist attack, just two months after Islamic extremists destroyed the World Trade Center and flew a passenger aircraft into the Pentagon, killing nearly 3,000 people. The Special Warning reminds commercial vessels that U.S. naval forces operate on alert and are taking "defensive precautions" in force protection:

Special Warning No. 120. Worldwide.

1. Due to recent events in the Middle East and the American homeland, U.S. forces worldwide are operating at a heightened state of readiness and taking additional defensive precautions against terrorist and other potential threats. Consequently, all aircraft, surface vessels, and subsurface vessels approaching U.S. forces are requested to maintain radio contact with U.S. forces on Bridge-to-Bridge Channel 16, international air distress (121.5 MHz VHF) or MILAIR distress (243.0 MHz UHF).

---

[79] Dep't of Defense, National Geospatial-Intelligence Agency, U.S. Notice to Mariners No. 1, Jan. 7, 2012, para. I-1.7 (Originally published by the U.S. Dep't of State, Feb. 5, 2001).

[80] Id., para. I-1.8 (Originally published by the U.S. Dep't of State, Mar. 16, 2001).

2. U.S. forces will exercise appropriate measures in self-defense if warranted by the circumstances. Aircraft, surface vessels, and subsurface vessels approaching U.S. forces will, by making prior contact as described above, help make their intentions clear and avoid unnecessary initiation of such defensive measures.
3. U.S. forces, especially when operating in confined waters, shall remain mindful of navigational considerations of aircraft, surface vessels, and subsurface vessels in their immediate vicinity.
4. Nothing in the special warning is intended to impede or otherwise interfere with the freedom of navigation or overflight of any vessel or aircraft, or to limit or expand the inherent self-defense rights of U.S. forces. This special warning is published solely to advise of the heightened state of readiness of U.S. forces and to request that radio contact be maintained as described above.[81]

4.3.1.12 Special Warning: Persian Gulf—Military Operations

On March 20, 2003, the United States issued this Special Warning, which accounts for a large international naval coalition staging in the Persian Gulf. The coalition naval forces are in a higher state of readiness, and the Special Warning cautions civilian vessels and aircraft to avoid approaching the warships:

Special Warning No. 121. Persian Gulf

1. Coalition naval forces may conduct military operations in the Eastern Mediterranean Sea, Red Sea, Gulf of Aden, Arabian Sea, Gulf of Oman, and Arabian Gulf. The timely and accurate identification of all vessels and aircraft in these areas are critical to avoid the inadvertent use of force.
2. All vessels are advised that Coalition naval forces are prepared to exercise appropriate measures in self-defense to ensure their safety in the event they are approached by vessels or aircraft. Coalition forces are prepared to respond decisively to any hostile acts or indications of hostile intent. All maritime vessels or activities that are determined to be threats to Coalition naval forces will be subject to defensive measures, including boarding, seizure, disabling or destruction, without regard to registry or location. Consequently, surface vessels, subsurface vessels, and all aircraft approaching Coalition naval forces are advised to maintain radio contact on Bridge-to-Bridge Channel 16, international air distress (121.5 MHz VHF) or military air distress (243.0 MHz UHF).
3. Vessels operating in the Middle East, Eastern Mediterranean Sea, Red Sea, Gulf of Oman, Arabian Sea, and Arabian Gulf are subject to query, being stopped, boarded and searched by US/Coalition warships operating in support of operations against Iraq. Vessels found to be carrying contraband bound for Iraq or carrying and/or laying naval mines are subject to detention, seizure and destruction. This notice is effective immediately and will remain in effect until further notice.[82]

---

[81] Id., para. I-1.9 (Originally published by the U.S. Dep't of State, Nov. 16, 2001).
[82] Id., para. I-1.9 (Originally published by the U.S. Dep't of State, Mar. 20, 2003).

4.3.1.13 Special Warning: East Africa—Terrorist Threat

On March 11, 2005, the United States issued this Special Warning to relay information concerning planning for a terrorist attack against Western ships in East Africa. Although the Warning lacks specific detail, it provides a reminder to civilian ships to remain vigilant:

> Special Warning No. 122. East Africa
>
> As of early 2005, the United States Government has received unconfirmed information that terrorists may attempt to mount a maritime attack using speedboats against a Western ship possibly in East Africa. This information is unconfirmed and the United States is not aware of additional information on the planning, timing, or intended targets of the maritime attack.[83]

4.3.1.14 Special Warning: Yemen—Terrorist Threat

On November 16, 2010, the United States issued a Special Warning concerning Yemen-based Islamic extremists who were planning attacks in the region, and the continuing risk of Somali pirates attacking ships in the Gulf of Aden and the Red Sea:

> Special Warning No. 125. Worldwide
>
> 1. The Department of State warns U.S. citizens of the high security threat level in Yemen due to terrorist and recommends postponing non-essential to Yemen. The level of risk for foreigners in Yemen remains high. A recent body of information suggests that Yemen based extremists are planning an attack against port facilities, commercial or transiting warships. Although it is unclear exactly how the Yemen based extremists intend to conduct an attack, it may be similar in nature to the attack against the *USS Cole* in October 2000 or the M/V *Limburg* in October 2002, where a small to mid-size boat laden with explosives was detonated in the vicinity of the targeted ships. However, it cannot be ruled out that the extremists may be capable of other more sophisticated methods of targeting, such as the use of mortars or projectiles to target ships such as the missiles used to unsuccessfully strike a navy ship in Jordan in 2005. Although the time and location of such an attack is unknown, it is likely that ships in the Bab-al-Mandeb Strait, Southern Red Sea, and the Gulf of Aden along the coast of Yemen, as well as in associated ports or at offshore facilities are at the greatest risk of becoming targets of such an attack.
> 2. Travel by boat through the Red Sea or near the Socotra Islands in the Gulf of Aden also presents a continuing high risk of pirate attacks. In 2009, over 70 vessels were reportedly attacked. Since the beginning of 2010, four vessels reportedly have been seized in the area, one released in February. As of 15 March 2010, nine vessels and crew were being held for ransom, in addition to a British couple that was abducted from their yacht....[84]

---

[83] Id., para. I-1.9 (Originally published by the U.S. Dep't of State, Mar. 11, 2005).
[84] Id., paras. I.1.10–.11 (Originally published by the U.S. Dep't of State, Nov. 16, 2010).

4.3.1.15 Special Warning: Somalia—Piracy

On November 11, 2005, the United States issued a Special Warning concerning the risk of piracy off the coast of Somalia after the luxury cruise ship *Seabourn Spirit* was attacked by Somali pirates. When this Special Warning was issued, Somali pirates threatened the area of the Somali Basin immediately along the coast of East Africa. By 2010, pirates were attacking ships as far as the Lakshadweep Islands off the coast of India.

> Special Warning No. 123. Somalia
>
> 1. Due to continuing conditions of armed conflict and lawlessness in Somalia and waters off its coast, mariners are advised to avoid the Port of Muqdisho (Mogadishu) and to remain at least 200 nautical miles distant from the Somali coast. The U.S. Government does not have an Embassy in Somalia and cannot provide services to U.S. citizens.
> 2. Recent vessel hijackings off the east coast of Somalia demonstrate that pirates are able to conduct at sea hijackings from as far south as Kismaayo (Chisimayu) (00-22S)—though vessels are advised to transit no closer than 02-00S—to as far north as Eyl (08-00N), and out to a distance of 170 miles. The first known attempt to hijack a cruise vessel occurred in November 2005 [the attack on the luxury cruise ship *Seabourn Spirit*]. All merchant vessels transiting the coast of Somalia, no matter how far offshore, should increase antipiracy precautions and maintain a heightened state of vigilance. Pirates are reported to have used previously hijacked ships as bases for further attacks.
> 3. Another reported pirate tactic has been to issue a false distress call to lure a ship close inshore. Therefore, caution should be taken when responding to distress calls keeping in mind it may be a tactic to lure a vessel into a trap.
> 4. Victimized vessels have reported two to three (2–3) speedboats measuring six to nine meters...in length. Each vessel has a crew of three to six...armed men with AK-47s and shoulder launched rockets, which are opening fire on vessels in broad daylight in order to intimidate them into stopping.
> 5. To date, vessels that increase speed and take evasive maneuvers avoid boarding while those that slow down are boarded, taken to the Somali coastline, and released after successful ransom payment, often after protracted negotiations of as much as 11 weeks.[85]

4.3.2 *U.S. Maritime Administration Advisories*

The U.S. Maritime Administration is an agency within the Department of Transportation. Maritime Administration (MARAD) Advisories are designed to rapidly disseminate information on government policy, danger and safety issues pertaining to vessel operations, as well as other timely maritime matters.

---

[85] Id., para. I-1.10 (Originally published by the U.S. Dep't of State, Nov. 11, 2005).

4.3.2.1 Reporting Terrorist Incidents

MARAD Advisory No. 05-01 of July 22, 2005, provides U.S. reporting requirements for attacks ("hostile actions") directed against U.S. maritime shipping.

> MARAD ADVISORY NO. 05-01 (221817Z JUL 05)
>
> SUBJECT: THREAT INFORMATION AND MARITIME INDUSTRY REPORTING OF SUSPECTED/ACTUAL TERRORIST INCIDENTS
>
> TO: OPERATORS OF U.S. FLAG AND EFFECTIVE U.S. CONTROLLED VESSELS AND OTHER MARITIME INTERESTS
>
> . . .
>
> 1. The Coast Guard's National Response Center (NRC) should be notified of any suspected domestic terrorist incident, particularly those affecting transportation systems in addition to oil and hazardous substance releases....
> 2. Hostile actions directed at merchant shipping are a present and growing problem. These hostile actions include piracy, theft and terrorism. In order to establish a reliable database of incidents to define the area and degree of the problem, a database has been instituted by the National Geospatial-Intelligence Agency (NGA) as the Anti-Shipping Activity Messages (ASAM) file. This file can be accessed via the Internet at NGA's Maritime Safety Web site: [http://msi.nga.mil/NGAPortal/MSI.portal]. Another excellent threat assessment report produced weekly by the Office of Naval Intelligence (ONI) is the ONI Worldwide Threat to Shipping. This report is also available on the NGA Web site.
> 3. NGA has also established Ship Hostile Action Report (SHAR) procedures to rapidly disseminate information within the U.S. Government on hostile actions against U.S. merchant ships.[86]
> 4. It should be noted that neither the ASAM nor SHAR reports are a distress message. U.S. and effective U.S. controlled (EUSC) vessels under attack or threat of attack may request direct assistance from U.S. naval forces....
> 5. All U.S.-flag vessels required by MARAD regulation, agreement, or those who voluntarily file Amver[87] position reports, are reminded of the importance in filing voyage and update reports. Those ships operating in the north Arabian Sea, Gulf of Oman, Persian Gulf, Gulf of Aden, Red Sea and the Suez Canal are reminded to file Amver position update reports every 24 hours rather than every 48 hours.

4.3.2.2 Regional Terrorist and Piracy Threat

Similarly, MARAD Advisory No. 10–03 of March 9, 2010, warns vessels transiting the Strait of Bab el Mandeb, the Red Sea, and the Gulf of Aden near the coast of Yemen to be alert to the threat posed by Islamic terrorists and Somali pirates.

---

[86] Procedures for sending SHAR reports are detailed in NGA PUBLICATION 117, RADIO NAVIGATIONAL AIDS 4–15 (National Geospatial-Intelligence Agency, 2005).

[87] Note: AMVER is a worldwide voluntary vessel reporting system operated by the U.S. Coast Guard to promote safety of life and property at sea. AMVER's mission is to quickly provide search and rescue authorities, on demand accurate information on the positions and characteristics of vessels near a reported distress." *See*, UNITED STATES COAST GUARD, AMVER SHIP REPORTING SYSTEM MANUAL 2 (rev. ed., Jan. 2005).

MARAD ADVISORY NO. 10-03 (091953Z MAR 10)

SUBJECT: VESSELS TRANSITING THE BAB-AL-MANDEB STRAIT, RED SEA, AND THE GULF OF ADEN ALONG THE COAST OF YEMEN

1. This MARAD advisory provides guidance for vessels transiting the Bab-al-Mandeb Strait, Red Sea and the Gulf of Aden along the coast of Yemen.
2. Information suggests that Al-Qaeda remains interested in maritime attacks in the Bab-al-Mandeb Strait, Red Sea and the Gulf of Aden along the coast of Yemen. Although it is unclear how they would proceed, it may be similar in nature to the attack against the *USS Cole* in October 2000 or the M/V *Limburg* in October 2002, where a small to mid-size boat laden with explosives was detonated in the vicinity of the targeted ships. However, it cannot be ruled out that the extremists may be capable of other more sophisticated methods of targeting, such as the use of missile or projectiles to target ships such as the mortars used to target a navy ship in Jordan in 2005. Although the time and location of such an attack is unknown, it is likely that ships in the Bab-al-Mandeb Strait, Red Sea and the Gulf of Aden along the coast of Yemen are at the greatest risk of becoming targets of such an attack.
3. All vessels transiting the waters in the vicinity of Yemen are urged to operate at a heightened state of readiness and should maintain strict 24-hour visual and radar watches and regularly report their position/course/speed to the UK Maritime Trade Operations (UKMTO Dubai). Vessels are at greatest risk in areas of restricted maneuverability and while in port or at anchor.
4. Merchant vessels are requested to report any suspicious activity to the UKMTO... IMB Piracy Reporting Centre (PRC)... and Maritime Security Centre, Horn of Africa (MSCHOA)....[contact details provided for UKMTO, IMB PRC, and MSCHOA].

4.3.2.3 Vessels Transiting High Risk Waters (HRW)—Maritime Piracy

This MARAD advisory was issued on March 29, 2010, and provides guidance to vessels transiting the high-risk waters of the Gulf of Aden, Red Sea, the Indian Ocean and waters off the Horn of Africa (Somalia).

MARAD ADVISORY NO. 10-06 (291725Z MAR 10)

SUBJECT: GUIDANCE TO VESSELS TRANSITING HIGH RISK WATERS

...

6. The Maritime Security Centre, Horn of Africa (MSC-HOA), run by the European Union Naval Force (EUNAVFOR) is a coordination center tasked to safeguard merchant shipping operating in the region by preventing and deterring acts of piracy in the Gulf of Aden (GOA), off the Horn of Africa and in the Somali basin. Vessels should register for access to the MSCHOA website at [http://www.mschoa.org/. This site provides information and guidance for the shipping community transiting the high-risk waters.
7. Combined Maritime Forces (CMF), in cooperation with the European Union Naval Force (EUNAVFOR) Atalanta and the United Kingdom Maritime Trade Office (UKMTO), established the Internationally Recommended Transit Corridor (IRTC) through the GOA. This revised corridor was intended to de-conflict commercial transit traffic with Yemini fishermen, provide a measure of traffic separation and allow maritime forces to conduct deterrent operations in the GOA with a greater degree of flexibility. Detailed information on the IRTC can be found at http://www.mschoa.org/. CMF established the Maritime Security Patrol Area (MSPA) in

the region. The MSPA was established in support of the International Maritime Organization's (IMO) ongoing efforts to ensure the safety of ships and mariners at sea. The MSPA is a naval military term for use by warships when communicating with each other positioned to maximize deployment of available forces in areas of high risk. Coalition forces patrol the MSPA on a routine basis. Neither the IRTC nor MSPA are marked or defined by visual navigational means. The IRTC is not intended to be a dedicated traffic separation scheme.

8. In accordance with the MARSEC Directive and Port Security Advisory (PSA) 2-09, unless otherwise directed or advised by on-scene military forces, all U.S. flag ships navigating through the GOA shall plan voyages using the IRTC and follow the GOA Group Transit (GT) if speed ranges from 10 to 18 knots. Vessels that make less than 10 knots shall contact UKMTO for routing guidance. Information on IRTC and GOA GT can be found on the Maritime Security Centre-Horn of Africa (MSC-HOA) web site.

9. In addition to communications required by the Coast Guard MARSEC Directive, masters should remain in contact with UKMTO and the United States Maritime Liaison Office (MARLO) to the maximum extent possible. The EU has established a web-based resource for ships to receive the latest alerts and to register vessels prior to transiting high-risk areas in the region. In accordance with the MARSEC Directive, owners and operators of U.S. flag vessels that operate in the HOA/GOA shall register with the MSC-HOA, at www.mschoa.org. Additionally, they shall establish contact by e-mail or phone with UKMTO at ukmto@eim.ae.

10. In accordance with the U.S. Coast Guard MARSEC directive [104-6], U.S. flag vessels that operate in high-risk waters must consider supplementing vessel's crew with armed or unarmed security personnel. If transiting the HOA/GOA, all vessels shall supplement vessel's crew with armed or unarmed security personnel based on a piracy-specific vessel threat assessment conducted by the operator. Supplemental security personnel should meet the minimum training requirements and guidelines set forth in PSA (5-09) (Rev. 1).[88]

11. In accordance with the U.S. Coast guard MARSEC Directive and PSA 2-09,[89] as soon as the master thinks a threat is developing, [she should] contact UKMTO [by phone].... If attacked or boarded, masters should activate the Ship Security Alert System (SSAS). Broadcast attacks immediately on all available radio circuits, adjust speed and maneuver and activate all available defensive measures. Do not immediately surrender upon approach of suspected pirate boats. Attacks have been thwarted in many cases where defensive measures were used and the vessels became difficult targets. An attack has even been successfully thwarted when pirates were able to board a ship but were unable to gain access to the superstructure due to the careful preparations of the crew in securing all access points.

---

[88] U.S. Coast Guard Port Security Advisory 5-09 Mimimum Guidelines for Contracted Security Services in High Risk Waters, May 12, 2010 (requirements for contracted security, including vetting qualifications, and training).

[89] U.S. Coast Guard Port Security Advisory 2-09, Port Security Advisory related to the release of MARSEC Directive 104-6 (Series): Guidelines for U.S. vessels operating in High Risk Waters, Rev. 3, Jan. 2011.

12. Additional guidance regarding practices recommended for mariners operating in vicinity of high-risk areas has been published by IMO revised Maritime Safety Committee (MSC) circulars....
13. All vessels are advised to check in with UKMTO at least 96 hours prior to entering the IRTC through the GOA. Check in again upon entering the corridor and check out upon exiting the corridor. While in high-risk waters off the Horn of Africa it is recommended to report vessel positions to UKMTO a minimum of every six hours.
14. The following is the UKMTO report format:
    a. Ship name:
    b. IRCS:
    c. IMO #:
    d. Cargo:
    e. Last port:
    f. Noon position (GMT):
    g. Next port:
    h. Additional ports:
    i. Security team aboard (y/n):
    j. Reporting via AMVER?:
    k. Publication 117 aboard?:
    l. Present position:
15. Escort service may be requested for vessels by contacting MARLO Bahrain, phone: [number provided] or by e-mail: marlo.bahrain@me.navy.mil.
16. If attacked or boarded by pirates, communications must be limited to distress calling and response coordination per the vessel security plan. In accordance with the MARSEC Directive and PSA 2–09, information about the vessel's movement, capabilities or the incident itself should be considered sensitive security information and should not be released to family, friends or the media....

Finally, MARAD Advisories may be used to provide information on specific threats to vessels transiting high-risk waters. In this August 31, 2011 Advisory, international shipping and pleasure craft (yachts) are warned of the use of automatic weapons and rocket propelled grenades, and the annual rhythm of attack, which is set by the Indian Ocean monsoon.

MARAD ADVISORY NO. 11-05 (311400Z AUG 11)

SUBJECT: VESSELS TRANSITING THE HIGH-RISK WATERS (HRW) OF THE GULF OF ADEN (GOA), RED SEA, INDIAN OCEAN, ARABIAN SEA AND WATERS OFF THE HORN OF AFRICA (SOMALIA)

1. This MARAD Advisory provides information on the risk to vessels transiting the high risk waters (HRW) of the Gulf of Aden (GOA), Red Sea, Indian Ocean, Arabian Sea and waters off the Horn of Africa (Somalia).

...

5. Pirates are attacking vessels, including yachts and other non-commercial vessels—such as sailboats, in the Gulf of Aden, Arabian Sea, Indian Ocean, Southern Red Sea, and Mozambique Channel. Pirates are firing automatic weapons and rocket propelled grenades (RPGs) in an attempt to board and hijack vessels. If an attack is successful and the vessel is hijacked, pirates direct vessels to the Somali coast and thereafter demand ransom for the safe release of vessels and crew. Pirates

use hijacked fishing and merchant vessels to conduct piracy operations as mother vessels to sail far from the Somali coast to attack and hijack vessels in transit or at anchor. Smaller skiffs are launched from the pirate mother vessel to attack targeted vessels.

6. Recent attacks in the Southern Red Sea and to a ship at anchor in Oman should serve to warn all vessels operating in the HRW that the pirates have and will continue to adapt to ship protection measures. The transition between monsoon seasons between Oct thru Nov will be more favorable for pirate skiff attacks. Masters and operators should anticipate attacks that may vary from past tactics. In light of the extension of the threat to ports and territorial waters, masters and operators are advised to maintain all applicable defensive and protective measures that are legally permissible during the vessel's time in port or at anchor.
7. Transit by yachts and privately owned sailing vessels through HRW is extremely hazardous, and may result in capture by pirates. The Coast Guard advises against all operation of, or travel by, yacht and pleasure craft in HRW. Vessels that make this passage despite this warning should make contact in advance with the naval authorities. In addition, American citizens aboard should inform the nearest U.S. embassy or consulate of their plans to transit the area and/or update their information via the Smart Traveler Enrollment Program (STEP) on www.travel.state.gov.... If you are due to travel the area of high threat, please inform MSCHOA by emailing postmaster@mschoa.org, with the subject line "yacht vessel movement."

4.3.2.4 Japan Tsunami Radiological Threat and Debris Field

Advisories also are used to warn mariners of impending safety issues. Excerpts below are reproduced from MARAD Advisory No. 11-03 of June 8, 2011, and Advisory 11-06 of September 23, 2011, concerning the devastating earthquake and tsunami that struck Japan on March 11, 2011. The two advisories warn shipping of the potential radiological threat and debris field in the Pacific Ocean following the 9.0 Earthquake and tsunami:

MARAD ADVISORY NO. 11-03 (081036Z JUN 11)

SUBJECT: UPDATE TO VESSELS TRANSITING TO OR FROM JAPAN OR IN WATERS IN THE VICINITY OF HONSHU

1. This MARAD Advisory updates guidance to vessels transiting to or from ports in Japan or in waters in the vicinity of the northeast coast of the island of Honshu and cancels advisory 2011–02.

...

3. Mariners are advised to continue to monitor and comply with NAVTEX and NAVAREA XI warnings issued for Japanese waters.
4. Operators and mariners are also advised to review and follow the radiological information on ports and maritime transportation provided on the government of Japan's (GOJ) Ministry of Land, Infrastructure, Transport, and Tourism (MLIT) website: http://www.mlit.go.jp. Mariners should keep abreast of information being provided by the government of Japan relating to any further potential impacts.
5. Vessels that enter into the Japanese defined "Restricted Area" may be subject to additional screening by the USCG if the U.S. is their first port call after departing the restricted area.

MARAD ADVISORY NO. 11–06 (232239Z SEP 11)
SUBJECT: UPDATE TO VESSELS TRANSITING TO OR FROM JAPAN OR IN WATERS IN THE VICINITY OF HONSHU

1. This MARAD Advisory provides guidance to vessels transiting the North Pacific Ocean from Japan to the U.S. west coast.

...

3. The 9.0 magnitude earthquake that occurred March 11, 2011 off the east coast of Honshu Japan resulted in a debris field in the North Pacific Ocean.
4. Possible marine debris types include derelict vessels, fishing nets and floats, lumber, cargo containers, and household goods. Because different debris types move with currents or winds differently, the debris may be dispersed over a very broad area between Japan and the U.S. west coast. Some general information is available at website http://marinedebris.noaa.gov/info/japanfaqs.html.
5. U.S.-flag operators with ships transiting the subject area should advise such vessels to remain vigilant and to monitor all sources of available information affecting safe and secure navigation in this area.
6. Significant debris sightings can be reported to mdsightings@gmail.com. Please indicate if information can be displayed on public website....

4.4 Aeronautical Information Services

States also issue warning areas to alert civil aviation to potential hazards that can result from military operations and exercises. These warning areas are designed to help fulfill the duty owed by governments to exercise due regard for the safety of civil aviation. Matters affecting safety of civil aviation are governed by the *Convention on International Civil Aviation* (Chicago Convention).[90] The *Chicago Convention* established the International Civil Aviation Organization to promote cooperative regulation of commercial aviation.

4.4.1 *ICAO Aeronautical Information Service*

The objective of the ICAO Aeronautical Information Service is "to ensure the flow of information/data necessary for the safety, regularity and efficiency of international air navigation."[91] Information and data is particularly important with the "implementation of area navigation (RNAV),[92] performance-based navigation

---

[90] Int'l Civil Aviation Org., Convention on International Civil Aviation, Annex 15, International Standards and Recommended Practices, Aeronautical Information Services (13th ed. July 2010) [Hereinafter Aeronautical Information Services].
[91] Id., at 1-1.
[92] Area Navigation (RNAV) uses Instrument Flight Rules to permit aircraft to choose any desired course within the parameters of a station-referenced network of navigation signals from beacons, rather than navigating strictly from beacon to beacon. Area Navigation was developed in the 1960s and called Random Navigation, hence the acronym, RNAV. See, Aeronautical Information Services, at 2-2. RNAV was developed to

(PBN),[93] airborne computer-based navigation systems and data link systems."[94] Corrupted or erroneous data or information can reduce the safety of air navigation.[95] Consequently, the Aeronautical Information Service establishes uniform and consistent provisions for aeronautical information.

Under Chapter 5 of the Aeronautical Information Service, a notice to airmen (NOTAM)[96] shall be issued whenever one of the following events is of direct operational significance to civil aviation:

> ...establishment, closure, or significant change in:
> - closure of aerodromes or runways;
> - operation of aeronautical services;[97]
> - electronic and other aids to air navigation;
> - visual aids;
> - aerodrome lighting systems;
> - procedures for air navigation services;
> - maneuvering area;
> - availability of fuel, oil and oxygen;
> - search and rescue facilities and services;
> - hazard beacons;
> - hazards affecting air navigation (e.g. military exercises);
> - prohibited, restricted, or danger areas;
> - areas, routes, or indicators;
> - aerodrome rescue and fire-fighting;
> - hazardous conditions due to snow, slush, ice or water on the movement area;[98]
> - outbreaks of epidemics;
> - forecasts of solar cosmic radiation;
> - volcanic activity and horizontal and vertical extent of volcanic ash cloud;[99]
> - release into the atmosphere of radioactive materials or toxic chemicals;

---

permit greater lateral freedom and make more complete use of airspace. GPS, LORAN, Inertial Navigation Systems, and other systems provide RNAV capability.

[93] Performance-based Navigation (PBN) is a navigational framework that uses RNAV and Required Navigation Performance (RNP), which is onboard performance monitoring and alerting capabilities. The RNP increased the pilot's situational awareness. PBN is used as a framework for airspace design and implementation of obstacle clearance or closer routing without the need for air traffic control. *See*, FED. AVIATION ADMIN., FACT SHEET—NEXTGEN GOAL: PERFORMANCE-BASED NAVIGATION: RNAV AND RNP EVOLUTION THROUGH 2025, Apr. 24, 2009.

[94] AERONAUTICAL INFORMATION SERVICES, at 1-1.

[95] Id.

[96] NOTAMs are defined as notices "concerning the establishment, condition or change in any aeronautical facility, service, procedure or hazard..." affecting flight operations. Id., at 2-5.

[97] Id., at 5-1, 2. These capabilities include AGA, AIS, ATS, COM, MET, and SAR.

[98] Preferably, notification is made using SNOWTAM format in Appendix 2, AERONAUTICAL INFORMATION SERVICES, or in the NOTAM Code, INT'L CIVIL AVIATION ORG. DOC 8400, PROCEDURES FOR AIR NAVIGATION SERVICES (7th ed. July, 2007) and plain language.

[99] Preferably, notification is made using ASHTAM format in Appendix 3, AERONAUTICAL INFORMATION SERVICES, or in the NOTAM Code, INT'L CIVIL AVIATION ORG. DOC 8400, PROCEDURES FOR AIR NAVIGATION SERVICES (7th ed. July, 2007) and in plain language.

- humanitarian relief missions, such as those undertaken under the auspices of United Nations.[100]

Notice to Airmen are issued promptly when the "information to be distributed is of a temporary nature and of short duration or when operationally significant permanent changes, or temporary changes of long duration are made at short notice, except for extensive text and/or graphics."[101] Information of short duration containing extensive text and/or graphics is published as an AIP Supplement.[102]

4.4.2 U.S. Notice to Airmen (NOTAM)

Air navigation services and procedures in the United States are regulated by Federal Aviation Administration (FAA) orders,[103] the FAA Notice to Airmen (NOTAM) Domestic/International,[104] and the FAA Aeronautical Information Manual (AIM).[105] Guidance on the U.S. NOTAM System is provided in Section 1 of Chapter 5 of the AIM.

Tracking ICAO's AIS, U.S. NOTAMs include "[t]ime critical aeronautical information [that could affect a pilot's decision making], which is of either a temporary nature or not sufficiently known in advance to permit publication on aeronautical charts...."[106] Such information includes "airport or aerodrome primary runway closures, taxiways, ramps, obstructions, ... changes in the status of navigational aids, [and] radar service availability...."[107]

The FAA classifies NOTAMs into four categories: NOTAM (D) or distant, Flight Data Center (FDC) NOTAMs, Pointer NOTAMs, and Military NOTAMs. NOTAM (D)s are distributed automatically via the Service A telecommunications system "for all navigational facilities that are part of the National Airspace System (NAS), all public use airports, seaplane bases, and heliports listed in the Airport/Facility Directory (A/FD)."[108] NOTAM (D) information includes "taxiway closures, personnel and equipment near or crossing runways, and airport lighting aids that do not affect instrument approach criteria, such as VASI [visual approach slope

---

[100] AERONAUTICAL INFORMATION SERVICES, at 5-1, 2.
[101] Id.
[102] Id., at 4-4.
[103] U.S. Department of Transportation, Federal Aviation Administration Order 7930.2M (Change 1 Incorporated), Notices to Airmen (NOTAMS), Sept. 25, 2008.
[104] U.S. Department of Transportation, Federal Aviation Administration, Notices to Airmen Domestic/International, Jan. 12, 2012.
[105] U.S. DEP'T OF TRANSPORTATION, FEDERAL AVIATION ADMINISITRATION, AERONAUTICAL INFORMATION MANUAL (2010), Ch. 5, Air Traffic Procedures.
[106] Id., para. 5-1-3(a).
[107] Id.
[108] Id., para. 5-1-3(b)(1).

indicator]."[109] NOTAM (D)s will have one of the keywords contained in Table 4.1 as the first part of the text after the location identifier:

Table 4.1. Notice to Airmen D (NOTAM D) Key Word Indicators

Keyword	Definition
RWY	Runway
Example	ABC XX/XXX ABC RWY 3/21 CLSD
TWY	Taxiway
Example	ABC XX/XXX ABC TWY F LGTS OTS
RAMP	Ramp
Example	ABC XX/XXX ABC RAMP TERMINAL EAST SIDE CONSTRUCTION
APRON	Apron
Example	ABC XX/XXX ABC APRON SW TWY C NEAR HANGARS CLSD
AD	Aerodrome
Example	ABC XX/XXX ABC AD ABN OTS
OBST	Obstruction
Example	ABC XX/XXX ABC OBST TOWER 283 (246 AGL) 2.2 S LGTS OTS (ASR 1065881) TIL 1003282300
NAV	Navigation
Example	ABC XX/XXX ABC NAV VOR OTS
COM	Communications
Example	ABC XX/XXX ABC COM ATIS OTS
SVC	Services
Example	XX/XXX ABC SVC JET FUEL UNAVBL TIL 1003291600
AIRSPACE	Airspace
Example	ABC XX/XXX ABC AIRSPACE AIRSHOW ACFT 5000/BLW 5 NMR AIRPORT AVOIDANCE ADZD TIL 1003152200
U	Unverified Aeronautical Information[110]
	(for use only where authorized by Letter of Agreement)
O	Other Aeronautical Information[111]

---

[109] Id.

[110] Unverified Aeronautical Information can be movement area or other information received that meets NOTAM criteria and has not been confirmed by the Airport Manager (AMGR) or their designee. If Flight Service is unable to contact airport management, Flight Service shall forward (U) NOTAM information to the United States NOTAM System (USNS).

Subsequent to USNS distribution of a (U) NOTAM, Flight Service will inform airport management of the action taken as soon as practical. Any such NOTAM will be prefaced with "(U)" as the keyword and followed by the appropriate keyword contraction, following the location identifier.

[111] Other Aeronautical Information is that which is received from any authorized source that may be beneficial to aircraft operations and does not meet defined NOTAM criteria. Any such NOTAM will be prefaced with "(O)" as the keyword following the location identifier.

The following example of a NOTAM (D) indicates that Runways 6 and 24 are closed, except by 1-hour prior permission during the times indicated:

!BDL BDL RWY 6/24 CLSD EXC 1 HR PPR
203-627-3001 WEF 0909131300-0909132000

FDC NOTAMs are transmitted via Service A by the National Flight Data Center (NFDC) in Washington, D.C., when it becomes necessary to disseminate regulatory information, including "amendments to published IAPs and other current aeronautical charts..." and "to advertise temporary flight restrictions caused by such things as natural disasters or large scale public events that may generate a congestion of air traffic over a site."[112]

For example, FDC 1/2534 provides instructions for aircraft operating in the vicinity of the Tripoli Flight Information Region (FIR) during the "Arab Spring" uprising that toppled Muammar Qaddafi and NATO's enforcement of UN Security Council Resolution 1973:

> FDC 1/2534—PART 1 OF 2 SPECIAL ADVISORY FOR NORTH AFRICA... INSTRUCTIONS CONCERNING CERTAIN FLIGHTS WITHIN THE TRIPOLI FLIGHT INFORMATION REGION (HLLL)
>
> A. Applicability. this advisory applies to all U.S. air carriers and commercial operators and all persons exercising the privileges of an airman certificate issued by the faa except such persons operating U.S.-registered aircraft for a foreign air carrier, and all operators of aircraft registered in the united states except where the operator of such aircraft is a foreign air carrier.
> B. United nations security resolution 1973 has banned all flight operations within the tripoli (HLLL) FIR with the exception of those operations specifically authorized by the resolution. additionally, eurocontrol has suspended flight plans for all flight operations within the tripoli HLLL FIR.
> C. Caution for HLLL. no person described in paragraph a should conduct flight operations within HLLL.
>
> ...
>
> E. Emergency situations. In an emergency that requires immediate decision and action for the safety of the flight, the pilot in command of an aircraft may deviate from this special notice to the extent required by that emergency.
> F. Expiration. This special advisory will remain in effect until further notice. FAA air traffic system operations security (202–267–8276) is the point of contact.[113]

---

[112] U.S. Dep't of Transportation, Federal Aviation Administration, Aeronautical Information Manual (2010), Ch. 5, Air Traffic Procedures, para. 5-1-3(b)(2)(a).

[113] U.S. Dep't of Transportation, Federal Aviation Administration, Notices to Airmen Domestic/International, Jan. 12, 2012.

Pointer NOTAMs are issued by a flight service station to highlight or point out another NOTAM, such as an FDC or NOTAM (D) that can help users cross-reference important information that may not be found under an airport or NAVAID identifier.[114] The following is an example of a Pointer NOTAM providing information on a temporary flight restriction from a referenced Flight Data Center NOTAM:

!ACT ACT AIRSPACE SEE FDC 8/8989 ZFW 91.141 WEF 0904211200-0904251800
!BWI BWI NAV SEE DCA 04/006 EMI TIL 0904202359[115]

Finally, Special Use Airspace (SUA) NOTAMs are issued when special use airspace "will be active outside the published schedule times and when required by the published schedule."[116] An example of a SUA NOTAM is provided below, which illustrates military usage of airspace in the area of Killeen, Texas, for training purposes:

HOOD HIGH MILITARY OPERATIONS AREA
Effective Date: February 9, 2012.

The Hood High Military Operations Area (MOA) in the vicinity of Killeen, TX, supports fighter or bomber aircraft with more maneuvering airspace when training at Fort Hood in support of ground force activities providing close air support (CAS). This airspace will allow longer-look tactics and advanced targeting systems that use tactics developed and refined during operations over Kosovo and Afghanistan and overcomes significant limitations on "fast mover" jet aircraft due to the relatively small vertical dimensions of the Hood and Gray MOAs and the inability to transit in and out of restricted area R-6302 freely.

Although the Hood and Gray MOAs go up to 10,000 feet mean sea level (MSL), they do not provide the vertical distance from targets required by modern weapons systems and tactics. The Hood High MOA provides the vertical distance required today and allows combat air forces to practice effective integration/application of Basic Surface Attack, Surface Attack Tactics, Suppression/Destruction of Enemy Air Defense, Close Air Support, and Battlefield Air Interdiction training requirements.

The Hood High MOA will support 2 to 10 sorties per week, of any of the following type aircraft; F-16, AT-38, F/A-18, B-52, B-1, B-2, AC-130, A-10, F-22, F/A-35, AV-8, F-117, and F-15. Depending on the aircraft type, sorties may contain from one to four aircraft.[117]

---

[114] U.S. Dep't of Transportation, Federal Aviation Administration, Aeronautical Information Manual (2010), Chap. 5, Air Traffic Procedures, para. 5-1-3(b)(3).
[115] U.S. Dep't of Transportation, Federal Aviation Administration Order 7930.2M (Change 1 Incorporated), Notices to Airmen (NOTAMS), Sept. 25, 2008, para. 2-2-1(c).
[116] U.S. Dep't of Transportation, Federal Aviation Administration, Aeronautical Information Manual (2010), Chap. 5, Air Traffic Procedures, para. 5-1-3(b)(4).
[117] Hood High MOA, TX boundaries are set forth as follows:
Beginning at lat. 31_30'01"N., long. 98_03'01"W.;
to lat. 31_30'01"N., long. 97_36'41"W.;
to lat. 31_28'01"N., long. 97_34'31"W.;
to lat. 31_14'01"N., long. 97_33'01"W.;

* * *

Altitudes. 10,000 feet MSL to but not including FL 180, excluding Hood MOA and Gray MOA when active.
Times of use. By NOTAM, 48 hours in advance.
Controlling agency. FAA, Houston ARTCC.
Using agency. U.S. Army, Commanding General, III Corps and Fort Hood, TX.[118]

Military NOTAMs pertain to U.S. military navigational aids and airports that are part of the National Airspace System.[119] An example of a Military NOTAM for Robert Gray Army Air Field in Texas is provided below:

FORT HOOD/KILLEEN
Robert Gray AAF
FDC 1/8597 GRK FI/T IAP ROBERT GRAY AAF, FORT HOOD/KILLEEN, TX. RADAR-2, ORIG... THIS IS A MILITARY NOTAM PAR 15 DA 1215/HAT 200 ALL CATS. VISIBILITY RVR 2400 ALL CATS. PAR 33 DA 1187/HAT 213 ALL CATS. VISIBILITY 1/2 ALL CATS. FOR INOPERATIVE MALSR, INCREASE PAR 15 CAT E VISIBILITY TO RVR 4000 AND PAR 33 CAT E VISIBILITY TO 3/4 MILE. PAR 15: VGSI AND PAR GLIDEPATH NOT COINCIDENT....

The United States also uses NOTAMs to advise the international community that U.S. forces operating in a specific area are taking special defensive precautions in light of heightened tensions in the region or in response to a credible and ongoing terrorist threat.

The following NOTAM was issued on July 29, 1987, by the United States combatant commander for U.S. Central Command after the May 1987 attack on the *USS Stark* (FFG-31) by an Iraqi Mirage F-1 aircraft in the Persian Gulf. The NOTAM asks approaching ships and aircraft to remain clear of U.S. naval forces in order to avoid an inadvertent confrontation. More explicitly, the NOTAM warns that illumination of U.S. warships by fire control radar "will be viewed with suspicion" and may result in U.S. "defensive action." The term "will be viewed with suspicion" does not commit U.S. forces to any particular response. Under current Standing

---

to lat. 31_20'01"N., long. 97_41'01"W.;
to lat. 31_21'01"N., long. 97_41'01"W.;
to lat. 31_22'08"N., long. 97_41'56"W.;
to lat. 31_23'01"N., long. 97_43'01"W.;
to lat. 31_24'01"N., long. 97_48'01"W.;
to lat. 31_19'01"N., long. 97_51'01"W.;
to lat. 31_16'01"N., long. 97_54'01"W.;
to lat. 31_19'01"N., long. 97_55'01"W.;
to lat. 31_19'01"N., long. 98_03'01"W.;
to the point of beginning.

[118] U.S. DEP'T OF TRANSPORTATION, FEDERAL AVIATION ADMINISTRATION, NOTICES TO AIRMEN DOMESTIC/INTERNATIONAL, Jan. 12, 2012.

[119] U.S. DEP'T OF TRANSPORTATION, FEDERAL AVIATION ADMINISTRATION, AERONAUTICAL INFORMATION MANUAL (2010), Chap. 5, Air Traffic Procedures, para. 5-1-3(b)(5).

Rules of Engagement, illumination by fire control radar would be regarded as a demonstration of hostile intent, or even commission of a hostile act.

```
P 291950Z JUL 87
FM USCINCCENT MACDILL AFB FL//CCJ5//
TO AFCNF CARSWELL AFB TX//CC//
INFO JCS WASH DC//J3//
USCINCPAC HONOLULU HI
FAA WASHINGTON HQ WASHINGTON DC
UNCLAS
SUBJ: INTERNATIONAL NOTAMS
```

A. JCS/DJS 2123357 JUL 87. SUBJ: REVISED NOTAM/NOTMAR FOR PERSIAN GULF AREA (NOTAL)
1. USCINCCENT [Commander-in-Chief, U.S. Central Command] REQUESTS PUBLICATION OF THE FOLLOWING JCS [Joint Chiefs of Staff] APPROVED (REF A) NOTAM OVER THE INTERNATIONAL NOTAM SYSTEM. THIS NOTAM REPLACES THE NOTICE CURRENTLY IN EFFECT AS ORIGINALLY PUBLISHED IN JAN 84.
2. IT IS IMPERATIVE THAT NOTAM BE TRANSMITTED TO INTERNATIONAL NOTAM OFFICES IN THE MIDDLE EAST REGION WITHIN THE FOLLOWING COUNTRIES/FIRS.
   A. COUNTRIES:
      OMAN, UNITED ARAB EMIRATES, QATAR, BAHRAIN, SAUDI ARABIA, KUWAIT, IRAQ, IRAN, PAKISTAN.
   B. FIRS [Flight Information Regions]:
      KABUL—OAKX, TEHRAN—OIIX, BAHRAIN—OBBB, BAGHDAD—ORBB, AMMAN—OJAC, DAMASCUS—OSTT, JEDDAH—OFJN, MUSCAT—OOMM, KARACHI—OPKR.
3. NOTAM FOR THE PERSIAN GULF, STRAIT OF HORMUZ, GULF OF OMAN, AND NORTH ARABIAN SEA TO BE PUBLISHED WORLD WIDE IN THE ICAO ALERT SYSTEM:

Quote: a. in response to the recent attack on the *USS Stark*, and the continuing terrorist threat in the region, U.S. naval vessels operating within the persian gulf, strait of Hormuz, gulf of Oman and the Arabian sea, north of 20 degrees north, are taking additional defensive precautions. It is requested that aircraft (fixed wing and helicopters) approaching U.S. naval forces establish and maintain radio contact with U.S. naval forces on 121.5 Mhz Vhf or 243.0 Mhz Uhf. Unidentified aircraft, who's intentions are unclear, or who are approaching U.S. naval vessels, may be requested to identify themselves and state their intentions as soon as they are detected.

In order to avoid inadvertent confrontation, aircraft (fixed wing and helicopters) including military aircraft may be requested to remain well clear of U.S. vessels. Failure to respond to requests for identification and interntions, or to warnings, and operating in a threatening manner, could place the aircraft (fixed wing and helicopters) at risk by U.S. defensive measures. Illumination of a U.S. naval vessel with a weapons' fire control radar will be viewed with suspicion and could result in immediate U.S. defensive reaction.

B. This notice is published solely to advise that measures in self-defense are being exercised by U.S. naval forces in this region. The measures will be implemented in a manner that does not unduly interfere with the freedom of navigation and overflight. *Unquote.*[120]

---

[120] MARITIME OPERATIONAL ZONES Appendix C.

FIVE

MARINE ENVIRONMENTAL PROTECTION
AND CONTROL MEASURES

5.1 THE MARINE ENVIRONMENT

Environmental control measures are not designed for the maintenance of traditional maritime security, but indirectly they may promote security by enhancing shipping safety. Environmental control measures may be useful in channeling shipping traffic, reducing the number of contacts in the zone, and thereby indirectly facilitating maritime security for coastal state and port state authorities. At the same time, however, environmental regulations can impair maritime security and safety, mostly by impeding the transit of military and commercial ships. Thus, finding the right balance of measures to protect the marine environment, while preserving navigational freedom, is essential to the maintenance of the public order of the oceans.

5.1.1 *Evolution of Marine Environmental Law*

During the 1960s many people began to realize that ecology would touch all aspects of our lives and that the environment would affect and be influenced by every corner of society. In 1968 the UN General Assembly (UNGA) for the first time began to think about the environment within the context of social and political terms.[1] Writing before the conference, economist Barbara Ward and the microbiologist René Dubos captured the prognosis of the times, "The two worlds of man—the biosphere of his inheritance, the techno-sphere of his creation—are out of balance, indeed potentially in deep conflict.... This is the hinge of history

---

[1] UNGA Res. 2398 (XXII), *Problems of Human Environment*, Dec. 3, 1968.

at which we stand, the door to the future opening to a crises more sudden, more global, more inescapable and more bewildering than ever encountered by the human species...."[2]

In 1968, the UNGA adopted Resolution 2398, which proposed to convene a UN Conference on the Human Environment in 1972 for the purpose of creating a framework for "comprehensive consideration" of environmental problems. The Stockholm Conference convened from November 5–16, 1972, and was the first global intergovernmental conference dedicated solely to environmental issues. The final declaration found its influence and authority in tone and in its dedication to the idea of establishing basic rules of international environmental law.[3]

Non-governmental organizations (NGOs) burst onto the scene, fully engaged in negotiations at an international conference for the first time ever. The acceptance of NGOs as influential non-state actors in multilateral diplomacy permanently shaped how international law would be developed. The International Maritime Organization (IMO), for example, recognizes interventions by NGOs on a basis of equality with States during its deliberations, although only States have the right to vote.

Fundamental Principle 1 set forth in sweeping aspirational language the key to the Declaration, "Man has the fundamental right to freedom, equality and adequate conditions of life, in an environment of quality that permits a life of dignity and well-being, and bears solemn responsibility to protect and improve the environment for present and future generations."[4] Implicit in this definition was the concept of "sustainable development" or more simply, cost-benefit analysis conducted over time. The 1972 Stockholm Conference also turned attention toward the human impact on the global environment, including the marine environment.

Principle 7 of the Declaration called on all states to "take all possible steps to prevent pollution of the seas by substances that are liable to create hazards to human health, to harm living resources and marine life, to damage amenities or to interfere with other legitimate uses of the sea." Principle 7 became influential in the development of text for protection of the marine environment at the Third United Nations Conference on the Law of the Sea from 1973–1982.[5] The general obligation of States to protect the marine environment is reflected in Articles 192

---

[2] BARBARA WARD AND RENÉ DUBOS, ONLY ONE EARTH 12 (1972).
[3] Louis B. Sohn, *The Stockholm Declaration on the Human Environment*, 14 HARV. INT'L L. J. 423, 513–515 (Summer 1973).
[4] UN Doc A/CONF.48/14/Rev.1, Report of the United Nations Conference on the Human Environment, June 16, 1972, 11 I.L.M. 1416 (1972).
[5] IMO Doc. MEPC 30/10/3, Identification of Particularly Sensitive Areas, Including Development of Guidelines for Designating Special Areas Under Annexes I, II and IV: The Legal Concept of Particularly Sensitive Sea Areas (Submitted by Australia), Sept. 19, 1990.

and 194 of the *United Nations Convention on the Law of the Sea* (UNCLOS), and the language promotes terms borrowed from the *Stockholm Declaration*.[6]

Article 194 of UNCLOS requires States to "take ... all measures consistent with [the] Convention ... necessary to prevent, reduce and control pollution of the marine environment from any source...." This important article underscores that 80 percent of marine pollution is from land-based sources of marine pollution (LBSMP).[7] In general, UNCLOS has not been effective at curtailing LBSMP, partly because of weakness in the framework of the Convention, which focuses on the much smaller problem of vessel-source pollution. The greatest obstacle, however, has been the political preferences of coastal states to direct their efforts against foreign flagged ships offshore, rather than major sources of agricultural and industrial run-off pollution from their own shores.

Under UNCLOS, coastal states have appropriate legal architecture to deal effectively with vessel source pollution, so long as the political will to do so is present. Article 211(1) calls on States, acting through the "competent international organization," i.e., the IMO, or a general diplomatic conference, to "establish international rules and standards to prevent, reduce and control pollution of the marine environment from vessels and promote the adoption ... of routing systems designed to minimize the threat of accidents which might cause pollution of the marine environment, including the coastline, and pollution damage to the related interests of coastal States."

The coastal State may adopt within the territorial sea laws and regulations for the prevention, reduction and control of marine pollution from foreign vessels, including vessels exercising the right of innocent passage.[8] These laws and regulations may not, however, hamper innocent passage of foreign vessels.[9] Finally, coastal States may in respect of their EEZ "adopt laws and regulations for the prevention, reduction and control of pollution from vessels conforming to and giving effect to generally accepted international rules and standards established through the competent international organization or general diplomatic conference."[10]

---

[6] United Nations Convention on the Law of the Sea, Montego Bay Dec. 10, 1982, entered into force Nov. 10, 1994, UN Doc. A/CONF.62/122, 21 I.L.M. 1621–1354 (1982), 1833 U.N.T.S. 397 [Hereinafter UNCLOS].
[7] DAVID HASSAN, PROTECTING THE MARINE ENVIRONMENT FROM LAND-BASED SOURCES OF POLLUTION: TOWARDS EFFECTIVE INTERNATIONAL COOPERATION vii (2006).
[8] UNCLOS, Articles 21(1)(f) and 211(4).
[9] Id., Article 24.
[10] Id., Article 211(5).

5.1.2 *Framework Agreements to Protect the Marine Environment*

Today there exist a pantheon of international agreements designed, at least in part, to ensure the protection of the marine environment. These instruments include not only UNCLOS, but also the following instruments:

- 1972 *Convention for the Prevention of Marine Pollution by Dumping of Wastes and Other Matter (London Convention)*;
- 1969 *International Convention on Civil Liability for Oil Pollution Damage* and the 1976 *Protocol*;
- 1971 *International Convention on the Establishment of an International Fund for Compensation for Oil Pollution Damage*;
- 1969 *International Convention Relating to Intervention on the High Seas in Cases of Oil Pollution Casualties* and its 1973 *Protocol*;
- 1974 *Safety of Life at Sea* (SOLAS)[11] and its protocols and numerous amendments;
- 1977 *International Convention on Civil Liability for Oil Pollution Damage Resulting from the Exploration and Exploitation of Submarine Mineral Resources*;
- 1973/1978 *International Convention for the Prevention of Pollution from Ships* (MARPOL 73/78).

In addition to these treaties with global application, there exist regional treaties such as the 1974 *Convention on the Protection of the Marine Environment of the Baltic Sea Area (Helsinki Convention)*. Several of these agreements have had influence that extends outside their region. The *Helsinki Convention*, for example, influenced the creation of the UNEP Regional Seas Program, as well as the negotiations of UNCLOS.

In the event that international rules and standards are inadequate to meet the special circumstances of a specific area and a coastal State has reasonable grounds to believe that the particular, clearly defined area of its respective EEZ "is an area where the adoption of special mandatory measures for the prevention of pollution from vessels is required for recognized technical reasons in relation to its oceanographical [sic] and ecological conditions, as well as its character of its traffic," the coastal State may, after appropriate consultations through the IMO and other States concerned, communicate with the IMO to submit "scientific and technical evidence in support and information on necessary reception facilities."[12]

If the IMO determines that the prescribed conditions have been met, the coastal State "may, for that area, adopt laws and regulations for the prevention,

---

[11] International Convention for the Safety of Life at Sea, London Nov. 1, 1974, *entered into force* May 25, 1980, 32 UST 47, TIAS 9700, 1184 U.N.T.S. 277.
[12] UNCLOS, Article 211(6).

reduction and control of pollution from vessels implementing such international rules and standards or navigational practices as are made applicable, through the organization, for special areas."[13] Such laws and regulations may not, however, "require foreign vessels to observe design, construction, manning or equipment standards other than generally accepted international rules and standards."[14]

A number of international and regional instruments encourage States to protect areas with high ecological, cultural, historical, archaeological, socio-economic or scientific significance from damage or degradation from shipping activities. Consistent with these instruments, the international community has developed concepts that provide special status for these areas and allow for enhanced coastal State regulation of them to prevent, reduce and control pollution of the marine environment throughout large areas of the oceans, including parts of the EEZ and high seas.

These concepts include "special areas" under MARPOL 73/78, High Seas Marine Protected Areas (HSMPAs), the nascent control measures of Large Marine Ecosystems (LMEs), Locally Managed Marine Areas (LMMAs), Indigenous and Community Conserved Areas (ICCAs), and Particularly Sensitive Sea Areas (PSSAs).[15] In short, the definitions, regulatory measures, and other terms applied to each of these measures vary greatly among governments, scholars, and non-governmental organizations. No standard definition exists, nor even a standard understanding of terms used in their description. For example, people among States, and different constituencies within States, hold such divergent views on what constitutes the "precautionary approach" and the "precautionary principle" that any use of the terms, particularly in a comparative sense, is practically useless. The IMO has sought to bring about some standardization in the usage and application of these different control measures, which most often are referred to generically as marine protected areas (MPAs). The PSSA is a concept denoting a marine protected area, and it is a relatively new creation that arose from an especially circuitous pedigree.

5.2 Particularly Sensitive Sea Areas

A PSSA "is an area that needs special protection through action by IMO because of its significance for recognized ecological, socio-economic, or scientific attributes where such attributes may be vulnerable to damage by international shipping

---

[13] Id.
[14] Id.
[15] IMO Doc. A.982(24), Revised Guidelines for the Identification and Designation of Particularly Sensitive Sea Areas, Dec. 1, 2005. The revised guidelines supersede IMO Doc. A.927(22), Guidelines for the Identification of Designation of Particularly Sensitive Sea Areas, Nov. 29, 2001 (Annex 2).

activities."¹⁶ The current PSSA guidelines state that appropriate associated protective measures (APMs) designed to prevent, reduce or eliminate the threat or identified vulnerability of the area will be approved or adopted by the IMO at the same time the PSSA is designated. APMs include establishment of areas to be avoided (ATBAs), no-anchor areas, mandatory ship reporting (MSR) systems, and other rules that affect the operation of ships in exchange for reduced impact on the marine environment. This requirement is a departure from earlier IMO practice, in which a PSSA could be adopted without consideration of appropriate APMs—leading to establishment of several PSSAs without careful consideration beforehand of what protective measures, if any, should be applied within them.

Beginning in the early 1990s, the IMO demonstrated a growing willingness to place environmental considerations above traditional navigational rights and freedoms. The heightened concern over marine pollution, exacerbated by high-visibility oil spills like the *Exxon Valdez* (1989), *Sea Empress* (1996), *Erika* (1999), *Prestige* (2002), and much later, the *Deepwater Horizon* explosion (2010). These incidents placed a great deal of pressure on the IMO to adopt environmentally based routing measures, and by the early-2000s they began to encroach on freedom of navigation. The political pressure to be responsive to environmental constituencies, coupled with the IMO "spirit of cooperation" to be equally supportive of proposals from all states—has resulted in an unwillingness of some member States, including sometimes the United States, to adequately scrutinize other States' PSSA proposals. Furthermore, if a member State of the IMO challenges the proposals of other states, then they risk having their own proposals blocked at a later date. Thus, the incentive structure at IMO supports a proliferation of environmental regulations that may be disassociated with actual environmental risk or hazard. The result of this political dynamic is that protective measures have been adopted for some areas even though proponent States failed to adequately demonstrate that international shipping poses a serious threat of environmental damage, or that additional protective measures were necessary to protect the environment.

Unlike Special Areas created within the context of MARPOL, PSSAs are created outside of the architecture of a binding treaty regime. In enclosed or semi-enclosed sea areas designated as MARPOL Special Areas, States may restrict operational discharges, releases, or emissions of oil, garbage, or sulfur oxide (SOx) emissions, the latter being regulated by SOx Emissions Control Areas (SECAs) designated under Annex VI. Special Area designation involves a more rigorous process of adoption than PSSAs since the area must satisfy several criteria, including oceanographic conditions, ecological conditions and vessel traffic characteristics. Furthermore, protective measures or regulations may be applied in Special

---

[16] IMO Doc. A.982(24), Revised Guidelines for the Identification and Designation of Particularly Sensitive Sea Areas, Dec. 1, 2005, para. 1.2.

Areas only for the purpose of prevention of ocean pollution from the specific vectors identified in the annexes to MARPOL 73/78. The pollutants contained in those annexes include oil (Annex I), noxious liquid substances (Annex II), sewage (Annex IV) and garbage (Annex V).

A PSSA, on the other hand, need satisfy only one risk criterion for designation, such as heightened social or cultural importance or ecological sensitivity, so long as the area is also at risk from international shipping activities. Additionally, the evaluation of what it means for a proposed PSSA to be "at risk from international shipping" has become a fairly low bar. In more recent PSSAs, the test for whether an area is at risk from shipping has meant the rare presence of international shipping, rather than a specific attribute of either the shipping (e.g., oil tanker traffic) or the area (e.g., shifting shoals) that suggests heightened risk. If not developed through consensus and carefully and responsibly managed by coastal States, associated protective measures that arise from the PSSA process could lead to restrictions on the exercise of high seas freedoms in the Exclusive Economic Zone (EEZ), impair the right of transit passage through straits used for international navigation, and weaken the right of innocent passage in the territorial sea. Since the approval of the Great Barrier Reef PSSA (Australia) in 1990,[17] there has been an increase in the number of PSSAs, and especially those extending into the EEZ.

The list of PSSAs has risen to 14 and now includes the archipelago of Sabana-Camagüey (Cuba 1997),[18] Malpelo Island (Colombia 2002),[19] the Florida Keys (United States 2002),[20] the Wadden Sea (Netherlands, Denmark and Germany 2002),[21] Paraças Nature Reserve (Peru 2003),[22] Western European Waters (Belgium, France, Ireland, Portugal, Spain, United Kingdom 2004),[23] Canary Islands (Spain 2005),[24] the Baltic Sea (Denmark, Estonia, Finland, Germany, Latvia, Lithuania, Poland, Sweden 2005),[25] Galapagos Islands (Ecuador 2005),[26] the Torres Strait extension of the Great Barrier Reef (Australia and Papua New Guinea 2005),[27] the *Papahānaumokuākea* Marine National Monument (United States

---

[17] IMO Doc. MEPC.44(30).
[18] IMO Doc. MEPC.74(40).
[19] IMO Doc. MEPC.97(47).
[20] IMO Doc. MEPC.98(47).
[21] IMO Doc. MEPC.101(48).
[22] IMO Doc. MEPC.106(49).
[23] IMO Doc. MEPC.121(52).
[24] IMO Doc. MEPC.134(53).
[25] IMO Doc. MEPC.136(53).
[26] IMO Doc. MEPC.135(53).
[27] IMO Doc. MEPC.133(53).

2007),[28] and the Strait of Bonifacio (France and Italy 2011).[29] The Marine Environmental Protection Committee 53 was particularly busy, adopting four new PSSAs: Canary Islands, Baltic Sea Area, Galapagos Islands, and the Torres Strait. The Saba Bank in the Dutch Caribbean is the most recent PSSA, and it includes two associated protective measures: an area to be avoided and a mandatory no anchoring area.[30]

Although PSSA designation does not necessarily prohibit entry into the area by all shipping carriers, once a particular area is designated as a PSSA, expectations in government, private industry, and the NGO community are that shipping will remain outside of the area. Thus, whether a PSSA actually contains APMs that impede shipping as a matter of regulation, the practical effect is predictable; ships—both commercial vessels and warships—avoid the area. While the impact on navigation may tend to promote the environmental goals being pursued in the PSSA, it also diverts shipping and impairs freedom of navigation both for commercial vessels (by regulation) and warships (through policy, if not as a matter of law).

Unilateral national efforts to protect the marine environment also have expanded in recent years. Between 2003 and 2010, the total ocean area under protection worldwide increased by over 150 percent.[31] The total number of marine protected areas (MPAs) currently stands at nearly 5,900, comprising over 4.2 million square kilometers of the world's oceans.[32] Most of these measures are located within areas of national jurisdiction, but they have the potential to adversely affect navigational rights and freedoms enjoyed by the international community. For example, over 500 MPAs have been established in the Philippine archipelago alone.[33] Likewise, by 2009 the 76 MPAs in the Indonesian archipelago covered over 13 million square hectares (more than 32.5 million acres). Some of these areas, which have been ostensibly adopted to protect the marine biodiversity and sustain coastal resources, are located within and could potentially block access to internationally recognized archipelagic sea lanes, impeding archipelagic sea lanes passage.

Because PSSAs arise from *ad hoc* declarations at the IMO, which are approved by the Maritime Environmental Protection Committee and endorsed by the

---

[28] IMO Doc. MEPC.171(57).
[29] IMO Doc. 203(62). *See also*, IMO Doc. MEPC.1/Circ.778, List of Special Areas Under MARPOL and Particularly Sensitive Sea Areas, Jan. 26, 2012.
[30] The Saba Bank is to be designated by MEPC 64 in October 2012.
[31] INT'L UNION FOR THE CONSERVATION OF NATURE AND RESOURCES, GLOBAL OCEAN PROTECTION: PRESENT STATUS AND FUTURE POSSIBILITIES 7 (C. Toropova, et al., eds. 2010) (Hereinafter IUCN GLOBAL OCEAN PROTECTION).
[32] Id.
[33] TheFishSite, 500 Marine Protected Areas Established in the Philippines, http://www.thefishsite.com/fishnews/7343/500-marine-protected-areas-established-in-philippines.

Assembly, rather than from a binding treaty, they represent one of the least formal mechanisms for control of marine pollution and, if not properly adopted and implemented, a new device for diminishing freedom of the seas. The informal nature of their adoption and rapid growth of PSSAs has raised questions not only about their efficacy, but also of their impact on lawful uses of the seas other than freedom of navigation.

Developing nations are not alone in adopting environmental regulations that may adversely affect navigational rights and freedoms. Major maritime powers have similar measures in waters under their jurisdiction. Moreover, there are ongoing efforts to establish MPA networks across entire regions and seas.[34] As of 2010, there were 11 MPAs with an area greater than 100,000 square kilometers.[35] No single or particular reasonably sized MPA poses a threat to freedom of navigation, but the cumulative effect of their horizontal spread, particularly when they are unsupported by evidence that they are effective, has an insidious effect on freedom of navigation. The slow erosion of navigational rights and freedoms puts economic prosperity and military security at risk, and also carries a pernicious cost in terms of unwinding the liberal order of the oceans.

5.2.1 Western Europe PSSA and the 2005 Guidelines

The inception of the concept of the PSSA arose several years after Stockholm with the International Conference on Tanker Safety and Pollution Prevention, held in London in 1978. Resolution 9, "Protection of Particularly Sensitive Sea Areas," invited the IMO "to initiate making an inventory of sea areas around the world which are in special need of protection against marine pollution from ships and dumping, on account of the areas' particular sensitivity in respect of their renewable natural resources or in respect of their importance for scientific purposes." The second part of the proposal was for the IMO to assess the "extent of the need of protection, as well as the measures which might be considered appropriate, in order to achieve a reasonable degree of perfection, taking into account also other legitimate uses of the seas."

By 1990, there had been considerable development of both global and regional agreements to prevent or reduce the risk of pollution in the marine environment and the value in pursuing additional measures for areas determined to be particularly sensitive or at risk of international shipping. These efforts culminated in adoption of the first PSSA and promulgation of initial PSSA guidelines by IMO in 1991.[36]

---

[34] IUCN GLOBAL OCEAN PROTECTION, at 7, 73–82.
[35] Id.
[36] IMO Doc. A.720(17), Guidelines for the Designation of Special Areas and the Identification of Particularly Sensitive Sea Areas, Nov. 6, 1991.

The guidelines that emerged in 1991 focused on four issues: (1) ensuring the process for designation of PSSAs considers all interests (coastal State, flag State, and the shipping and vessel traffic communities); (2) develop considerations based on scientific, technical, economic and environmental information regarding the area (i.e. the criteria were not to be political in nature); (3) conduct of an assessment of the potential risk of environmental damage of the area from international shipping carrier activities (in contrast to the risk of damage from coastal State vessels which may be addressed through coastal State enforcement of its registered fleet); and, (4) introduction of regulatory or protective measures into the area that might minimize the risk from international shipping carriers. The guidelines were further clarified in 1999 and 2001, and were completely rewritten in 2005 by the National Oceanic and Atmospheric Administration with concurrence of the Law of the Sea Desk in the Office of the Judge Advocate General of the U.S. Navy.

The inception for the 2005 revised guidelines was the acrimonious process that led to of adoption of the Western Europe PSSA at IMO. During the debate over the Western Europe PSSA, "a number of delegations" at the IMO expressed concern over the enormous size of the area under consideration and the damaging precedent that was about to be set for freedom of navigation through encouragement of vast new PSSAs.[37] Additionally, a "large number of states" stressed that the significant restrictions on freedom of navigation, and in particular, the prohibition of single hull tankers through international straits, was contrary to international law.[38] States also suggested that there was no identified policy basis for the proposed protective measures, a common criticism of many PSSAs that would also be levied at the enormous *Papahānaumokuākea* PSSA in 2008.[39]

During the debate over the Western Europe PSSA, the delegation from the Russian Federation questioned whether there even existed a legal basis to designate as a PSSA a geographic sea region as big as the North Atlantic littoral of Western Europe. Russia noted that Article 8 of the *Convention on Biological Diversity* serves as a framework for establishing protected areas, and that the instrument does not recognize designation of wide sea regions. European states responded that the precedence for the Western Europe PSSA was set in 1990 with the establishment of the Great Barrier Reef PSSA.[40] The concern that application of navigational restrictions and other special measures over large areas, however, remained, with Russia even suggesting that their continued persistence could lead to the dismantling UNCLOS—unraveling the

---

[37] IMO Doc. MEPC 49/22, Report of the Marine Environmental Protection Committee on its Forty-ninth Session, Aug. 8, 2003, para. 8.14.1.
[38] Id., para. 8.14.2.
[39] Id., para. 8.14.4.
[40] Id., para. 8.14.1.

worldwide consensus on the carefully constructed "package deal."[41] Furthermore, it apparently did not occur to most delegations to join Russia to question whether enormous PSSAs remained a good idea, no matter what the worthy intentions were in adopting the Great Barrier Reef PSSA in 1990. Russia would revisit these same concerns during Marine Environmental Protection Committee (MEPC) 53, when the Committee approved four PSSAs, including the Baltic Sea Area PSSA, that Russia also initially protested with vigor but then accepted.

Consequently, tighter guidelines for designation of PSSAs were sorely needed. Much of the work on the revised guidelines was conducted between meetings of the IMO MEPC 52 and MEPC 53. Lindy Johnson of the National Oceanic and Atmospheric Administration in the U.S. Department of Commerce served as chair of the technical group that met to finish the work during MEPC 53. But MEPC 53 was also the meeting that recognized four new PSSAs, and the disagreements over the Baltic Sea PSSA and the Torres Strait PSSA exposed divisions among IMO delegations. Russia, in protesting the Baltic Sea PSSA, and the United States and Singapore, in rejecting Australia's initial bid for mandatory pilotage in the Torres Strait, guarded the principle of freedom of navigation.

The new guidelines were successful in making the process of designation of PSSAs somewhat more rigorous by ensuring that all associated protective measures (APMs), which serve as the actual regulatory "teeth" of a PSSA, have a clear basis in the law.[42] At least one APM must be included with the submission for a PSSA so that states understand the proposed limitation on vessel activities in the area at the time they consider its creation. The revised guidelines were adopted at IMO Assembly 24, and they are designed to:

   .1 provide guidance to IMO Member Governments in the formulation and submission of applications for designation of PSSAs;
   .2 ensure that in the process all interests—those of the coastal State, flag State, and the environmental and shipping communities—are thoroughly considered on the basis of relevant scientific, technical, economic, and environmental information regarding the area at risk of damage from international shipping activities and the associated protective measures to prevent, reduce, or eliminate that risk; and
   .3 provide for the assessment of [PSSA] applications by IMO.[43]

Potential environmental hazards to environmentally or ecologically sensitive areas associated with international shipping include: operational discharges; accidental or intentional pollution; and, physical damage to marine habitats or organisms.[44] IMO must take into consideration three factors in the PSSA

---

[41] Id., para. 8.24.3.
[42] IMO Doc. A.982(24), Revised Guidelines for the Identification and Designation of Particularly Sensitive Sea Areas, Dec. 1, 2005.
[43] Id., para. 1.4.
[44] Id., para. 2.1.

124   CHAPTER FIVE

designation process: "the particular attributes of the proposed area, the vulnerability of the area to damage by international shipping activities, and the availability of associated protective measures within the competence of IMO to prevent, reduce, or eliminate risks from these shipping activities."[45]

Before an area may be identified as a PSSA, it must meet at least one of the following criteria: "ecological criteria; social, cultural, and economic criteria; or scientific and educational criteria."[46] Ecological criteria include consideration of the uniqueness or rarity of the natural environment; critical nature of the habitat, biosphere dependency; representativeness; diversity; productivity; the presence of spawning or breeding grounds; naturalness or unspoiled nature of the area; integrity of the area as a separate ecology; and the fragility or bio-geographic importance of the area.[47]

Social, cultural and economic criteria include social or economic dependency upon the area; human dependency on the area; and the cultural heritage related to the area.[48] Finally, scientific and educational criteria include the value of the area to research, service of the area as a baseline for monitoring studies, and the importance of the area for education.[49] Of course, these criteria, while certainly an improvement over earlier checklists, are so vague as to invite any coastal State to easily articulate the need for PSSA designation for practically any area of the oceans.

In addition to meeting one of the above criteria, the area also must be at risk from international shipping activities. Factors to take into consideration in this regard include:

Vessel traffic characterisics

> 5.1.1. Operational factors—Types of maritime activities (e.g. small fishing boats, small pleasure craft, oil and gas rigs) in the proposed area that by their presence may reduce the safety of navigation.
> 5.1.2. Vessel types—Types of vessels passing through or adjacent to the area (e.g. high-speed vessels, large tankers, or bulk carriers with small under-keel clearances).
> 5.1.3. Traffic characteristics—Volume or concentration of traffic, vessel interaction, distance offshore or other dangers to navigation, are such as to involve greater risk of collision or grounding.
> 5.1.4. Harmful substances carried—Type and quantity of substances on board, whether cargo, fuel or stores, that would be harmful if released into the sea.

---

[45] Id., para. 1.5.
[46] Id., para. 4.4.
[47] Id., para. 4.4.1–4.4.11.
[48] Id., para. 4.4.12–4.4.14.
[49] Id., para. 4.4.15–4.4.17.

Natural factors

> 5.1.5. Hydrographical—Water depth, bottom and coastline topography, lack of proximate safe anchorages and other factors which call for increased navigational caution.
> 5.1.6. Meteorological—Prevailing weather, wind strength and direction, atmospheric visibility and other factors which increase the risk of collision and grounding and also the risk of damage to the sea area from discharges.
> 5.1.7. Oceanographic—Tidal streams, ocean currents, ice, and other factors which increase the risk of collision and grounding and also the risk of damage to the sea area from discharges.

Other factors that may be taken into consideration include any amount or measure of the following:

> .1 any evidence that international shipping activities are causing or may cause damage to the attributes of the proposed area, including the significance or risk of the potential damage, the degree of harm that may be expected to cause damage, and whether such damage is reasonably foreseeable, as well as whether damage is of a recurring or cumulative nature;
> [Note: this expansive definition reflects a classic precautionary approach because it uses as a factor *any* evidence that shipping *may* cause damage—a standard that applies to every cubic inch of the water column, providing a rather speculative walk of the plank to help establish the need for a PSSA—if everywhere is special, then nowhere is special]
> .2 any history of groundings, collisions, or spills in the area and any consequences of such incidents;
> [Note: this element allows for consideration of the consequences of groundings or collisions, even of coastal State ships, in considering creation of rules that are binding on foreign-flagged shipping]
> .3 any adverse impacts to the environment outside the proposed PSSA expected to be caused by changes to international shipping activities as a result of PSSA designation;
> .4 stresses from other environmental sources; and
> .5 any measures already in effect and their actual or anticipated beneficial impact.[50]

Associated protective measures that may be approved or adopted by the IMO to prevent, reduce or eliminate the threat or identified vulnerability of the PSSA include:

- designation ... as a Special Area under MARPOL Annexes I, II or V, or a SOx emission control area under MARPOL Annex VI, or application of special discharge restrictions to vessels operating in a PSSA;
- adoption of ships' routeing and reporting systems near or in the area under SOLAS and the *General Provisions on Ships' Routeing* (GPSR) and the *Guidelines and Criteria for Ship Reporting Systems*; and

---

[50] Id., para. 5.2.

- development and adoption of other measures aimed at protecting specific sea areas against environmental damage from ships, provided that they have an identified legal basis.[51]

There are several other options that are believed to offer supplementary protection of a PSSA, including listing it on the World Heritage List, declaring the area a Biosphere Reserve, or including it on a list of areas of international, regional, or national importance.[52] In assessing the APMs within each proposal, IMO must determine that they "are appropriate to prevent, reduce or eliminate the identified vulnerability of the area from international shipping," as well as confirm a "linkage between the recognized attributes, the identified vulnerability, the associated protective measure to prevent, reduce, or eliminate that vulnerability, and the overall size of the area, including whether the size is commensurate with that necessary to address the identified need."[53] Associated protective measures must be implemented in accordance with international law, including UNCLOS.[54]

5.2.2 *Malpelo Island PSSA (Colombia)—Regulation without Protection*

The Malpelo Island PSSA is a textbook example of how the IMO "spirit of cooperation" leads to unnecessary interference with navigational rights and freedoms without a concomitant increase in environmental protection. Even if the waters surrounding Malpelo Island possess the "morphological, geological and ecological characteristics" articulated by Colombia in its original proposal that make the island "a unique and special enclave," the proposed designation was initially justified on the need to curtail illegal fishing in and around the islands by domestic and foreign fishing boats—rather than addressing a "risk from international shipping," as required by IMO guidelines.[55] Adoption of the PSSA would not be the first time that coastal State vessel activities that imposed a risk on an area of the ocean triggered misguided regulations that controlled international shipping.

According to the original Colombian submission, the Government had passed various laws that designated the island and its surroundings as a "Wildlife and Plant Sanctuary."[56] Malpelo Island was identified as an "area designated for the preservation of species or populations of animals and plants to conserve the genetic resources of the country's fauna and flora, and lay down a series of tight restrictions on their use and management with a view to protecting them in

---

[51] Id., para. 6.1.
[52] Id., para. 6.2.
[53] Id., para. 8.2.1 and 8.2.3.
[54] Id., para. 92.
[55] IMO Doc. MEPC 43/6/7, Designation of Malpelo Island as a Particularly Sensitive Sea Area, Apr. 30, 1999, para. 2.1.
[56] Id., para. 2.4.

perpetuity, under the responsibility of the national environmental authorities."[57] These efforts, however, proved to be inadequate to prevent illegal fishing by Colombian and foreign fishing boats.[58]

Colombia therefore requested the MEPC to "study the identification of Malpelo Island as a particularly sensitive sea area...based on the ecological importance of Malpelo Island for the conservation of species unique to the region and to the world, and justified by the ecological, socio-economic, cultural and scientific criteria contained in the document to be distributed to each delegation at the forty-third session of the MEPC."[59] Following a discussion of the issue in the IMO plenary, the "Committee agreed to consider the matter further at MEPC 44, when it would have all the information required to make a decision on the matter."[60]

At the next session of the MEPC, Colombia submitted a revised proposal with the assistance of interested States, including members of the U.S. delegation, that expanded on the ecological importance of the area and the need to designate Malpelo Island as a PSSA based on a number of ecological, socioeconomic, cultural and scientific criteria.[61] But the proposal did not identify a risk to the island and its surrounding waters from international shipping carriers. Instead the submission still identified the threat of illegal fishing as the main problem in the area:

> 8. One of the main problems of this oceanic island, and of its surrounding waters in particular, is the permanent presence of fishing boats, both Colombian and foreign, which...engage in illegal fishing on the edge of the island platform.
> 9. These boats operate within the territorial waters of a number of countries without any authorization, or at least, in Colombian territorial waters, without any license to engage in fishing operations.... [F]ishing is strictly prohibited, but they ignore the fact that the area is protected and continue their operations...extracting many tons of fish without being subject to control of any kind....
> 10. In particular, they use mechanical trawling techniques, operating trawlers offshore or on the periphery of the island over banks and hollows of rocky substratum and layers of coral. The operational plan of these vessels includes the use of helicopters to locate shoals of small cetaceans and sharks, including a number of species of shark peculiar to the area.
> 11. Trawl fishing, which has been prohibited by Colombia since 1966 in any area less than one nautical mile off all coasts, islands and keys within Colombian territory...invariably includes seriously endangered species such as turtles, dolphins, sharks and manatees. It should also be noted that on many occasions

---

[57] Id., para. 2.5.
[58] Id., para. 2.6 and 2.7.
[59] Id., para. 3.1.
[60] IMO Doc. MEPC 43/21, Report of the Marine Environment Protection Committee on its Forty-Third Session, July 6, 1999, para. 6.33.
[61] IMO Doc. MEPC 44/7, Designation of Malpelo Island as a Particularly Sensitive Sea Area (Submitted by Colombia), Dec. 3, 1999.

> these illegal operations are carried out in the vicinity of areas where skin diving is practiced, without concern for the presence of divers, thus putting their lives in danger because trails of blood spreading over vast areas will attract the attention of sharks.

The attached multi-page annex to the Colombian proposal additionally provided that

> Colombia's difficulties arise from the fact that owing to the isolation of the island and its great distance from the mainland, supervision and control operations are difficult. Patrol vessels cannot be maintained at the site because it is physically impossible to establish anchorages or to build quays and harbors.
>
> The main purpose of a large number of fishing operations is to catch specimens of hammerhead shark, which are much prized by markets in the Indo-Pacific region, where high prices are paid for a kilogram of shark fins.... [Once] the sharks have been caught and their fins and tails cut off, they are thrown back into the sea still alive and bleeding, so that they can either be devoured by their fellows, thus attractil0ng more shark specimens, or simply left to die when they reach the bottom, defenseless and unable to move. Such scenes are entirely contrary to environmental ethics and morality.
>
> Reports are currently available from the Ministry of the Environment and the Colombian Navy on several dozen cases where foreign vessels have been caught in the act of conducting illegal fishing operations. When challenged by the Colombian authorities, these offenders disclaim all knowledge of Colombian laws and regulations protecting Malpelo Island as a wildlife and plant sanctuary.
>
> The Government of Colombia is seeking the adoption by [the IMO] of protective measures, which will make the international maritime community, and especially the fishing community, fully aware of the highly sensitive nature of the environmental resources of Malpelo Island, so that they will respect its status as a wildlife sanctuary and as the heritage of present and future generations.

While recognizing that the Colombian proposal met the ecological criteria for designating Malpelo Island as a PSSA, MEPC indicated that Colombia had failed, *inter alia*, to indicate the "extent of risk that [legitimate] international maritime activities" posed to the area or identify an associated protective measure to protect the area from such risks.[62] As a result, MEPC "requested Colombia to provide the additional information to a future session for further consideration."[63] It was already becoming clear that the tragic, indeed reprehensible destruction of marine animals and the marine environment around Malpelo Island was not due to legal shortcomings that could be fixed through new regulations imposed on international shipping, but rather stemmed from the inability of Colombian maritime forces to police existing rules in their territorial sea.

Colombia submitted the requested supplemental information at MEPC 46 and requested the Committee to "declare Malpelo Island a...PSSA on the basis of

---

[62] IMO Doc. MEPC 44/20, Report of the Marine Environment Protection Committee on its Forty-Fourth Session, Apr. 12, 2000, para. 7.20.
[63] Id., para. 7.21.

its ecological importance for the conservation of species which are unique both regionally and internationally, and also on the basis of the vulnerability of the area to damage caused by international maritime activities...."[64] The revised submission retained illegal fishing as a major cause of environmental degradation, but it also added that the presence of international cruise ships engaged in unregulated skin-diving and international vessel traffic, including "ships engaged in illegal drug trafficking activities," were also contributing to damage to the marine environment and ocean species.[65]

Colombia therefore requested that an "area to be avoided" (ATBA) be established as an associated protective measure around the island. The ATBA applies to all fishing vessels and all other ships in excess of 500 gross tons. The ATBA was drawn to connect the outer geographical points of the island.[66] Following general support for the Colombian proposal, MEPC agreed in principle to the revised submission and instructed the Navigation Sub-Committee (NAV) to review any navigational issues associated with the proposed ATBA and report back to the Marine Environmental Protection Committee.[67] NAV endorsed the ATBA in 2001 and conveyed its decision to MEPC.[68]

Five years after its original submission and after numerous revisions by IMO, and with the considerable assistance from other interested delegations to craft the proposal, the rewritten Colombian proposal was adopted in March 2002 at MEPC 47. In short, Colombia asked MEPC to designate a PSSA around the Malpelo Island because it lacked the capacity to enforce its domestic fishing laws or the ability to enforce existing regulations on international cruise ships operating in its territorial sea. Perhaps a better course of action would have been for the international community to assist Colombia in developing a more robust maritime patrol and law enforcement capability, rather than creating a new legal instrument of dubious value. Instead, new rules were imposed on international shipping that added nothing to the existing legal framework on the books to

---

[64] IMO Doc. MEPC 46/6/3, Additional information for the designation of Malpelo Island as a Particularly Sensitive Sea Area, Submitted by Colombia, Feb. 16, 2001, para. 3.

[65] Id., Annex, Additional Information for the Designation of Malpelo Island as Particularly Sensitive Sea Area, Part I.

[66] Id., para. 4 and Annex, Additional Information for the Designation of Malpelo Island as a Particularly Sensitive Sea Area, Part II. The coordinates are: A 81°43'18" North–04°04'48" West; B 81°28'07" North–04°04'48" West; C 81°28'07" North–03°52'09" West; and, D 81°43'18" North–03°52'09" West. Nautical reference charts INT 6105 Gulf of Cupica to Bay of Buenaventura and INT 6000 West Coast of Colombia.

[67] IMO Doc. MEPC 46/23, Report of the Marine Environment Protection Committee on its Forty-Sixth Session, May 16, 2001, para. 6.16 and 6.17.

[68] IMO Doc. NAV 47/13, Routeing measures other than Traffic Separation Schemes Associated Routeing Measures related to Particularly Sensitive Sea Areas around the Florida Keys and Malpelo Island, July 26, 2001, para. 3.59.

protect a marine environment at risk, and Colombia still lacks the capacity to patrol its waters or enforce either the legacy laws or the new IMO standards.

An ATBA to protect the newly designated PSSA was promulgated by IMO Circular SN/Circ.220 in May 2002.[69] It is naïve to suggest, however, that illegal fishing vessels, cruise ships engaged in unlicensed skin-diving or international drug trafficking vessels will observe the PSSA and its associated ATBA with any more regularity than they complied with existing Colombian national law. The ATBA generates external costs to legitimate maritime traffic, however, as vessels are directed to avoid the area entirely. Thus, cost is imposed on those acting lawfully, while those outside the law continue their repugnant mistreatment of the marine environment and desecration of marine wildlife with impunity. Greater enforcement capacity by Colombia, rather than yet another layer of redundant rules, would have been a more effective approach.

5.2.3 *Baltic Sea Area PSSA—Regulation without Concurrence*

The Baltic Sea is cold and shallow, and it has a low level of biodiversity. The area has unique fresh water and true brackish water species, however, and the shores of the Baltic Sea are a breeding ground for coastal birds and waterfowl. Many aquatic species are threatened, and the disappearance of one of these species could disrupt the entire system. Consequently, the marine ecosystem is particularly sensitive to manmade disturbances.

But the Baltic Sea hosts some of the densest maritime traffic lanes in the world. More than 2,000 ships transit the area in an average day. The area is a particularly important route for oil tankers, and 200 of these vessels are in the Baltic Sea daily.

The proposal for the Baltic Sea Area PSSA was submitted by Denmark, Estonia, Finland, Germany, Latvia, Lithuania, Poland, and Sweden. The Baltic Sea Area PSSA covers the Baltic Sea proper, the Gulf of Bothnia, the Gulf of Finland, and the entrance to the Baltic Sea, but excludes those marine areas within the sovereignty of the Russian Federation or subject to the sovereign rights and jurisdiction of the Russian Federation, i.e. the Russian EEZ.[70]

The Baltic Sea PSSA was approved by MEPC 53 and adopted by the 24th Assembly of the IMO. But the PSSA created a political storm at MEPC 53, when the Russian Federation initially objected to the designation of the area because it

---

[69] IMO Doc. MEPC 47/20, Report of the Marine Environment Protection Committee on its Forty-Seventh Session, Mar. 18, 2002, para. 8.10; IMO Doc. MEPC.97(47), Identification of the Sea Area Around Malpelo Island as a Particularly Sensitive Sea Area, Mar. 8, 2002, IMO Doc. MEPC 47/20, Routeing Measures other than Traffic Separation Schemes, Malpelo Island, Annex 4, Mar. 8, 2002, and IMO Doc. SN/Circ.220, Routeing Measures Other Than Traffic Separation Schemes, May 27, 2002.

[70] IMO Doc. MEPC 136(53), Designation of the Baltic Sea Area as a Particularly Sensitive Sea Area, July 22, 2005.

included all of the Baltic Sea, failing to exclude waters under Moscow's sovereign rights and jurisdiction. That is, the original proposal proposed to delegate the entire Baltic Sea as a PSSA, presumably including areas within Russia's EEZ. To complicate matters, the Russian Federation and other Baltic states were unable to agree on the precise coordinates of the outer boundary of Russian territorial waters or areas under Russian jurisdiction, such as EEZs. In response to Moscow's concerns, and the threat by the Russian delegate to the IMO that the Kremlin was sending a high-level diplomat to protest the proposal as constituting a political issue beyond the technical competence of IMO, text was redrafted and inserted into Annex I of the Resolution that explicitly excluded from the PSSA marine areas under the sovereignty or jurisdiction of the Russian Federation—a practical compromise that purchased Russia's grudging cooperation.

Furthermore, the Russian Federation received assurances that designation of the Baltic Sea Area PSSA did not prejudice its sovereignty or sovereign rights and jurisdiction in international law. This change accommodated Russia's resistance to the proposal. Once the deadlock between Russia and the other Baltic states was resolved, the Russian Federation did not object to the final resolution and abstained from the final vote.

The protective measures associated with the Baltic Sea PSSA are contained in IMO Resolution MEPC.136(53) and include a new and amended Traffic Separation Scheme (TSS) just south of Sweden between the areas of Götland Island and Bornholm Island (Denmark).[71] There also are several new ATBAs established in the southern Baltic Sea, with the largest one located in the vicinity of Hoburgs Bank (just south of Gotland Island). The ATBAs apply to all vessels of 500 gross tons or greater.

5.2.4 *Papahānaumokuākea PSSA (United States)—Regulation without Need*

The greatest instance of creating a large PSSA in a marine area not subject to any particular threat from international shipping is the *Papahānaumokuākea* Marine National Monument and subsequent recognition at IMO as a PSSA. Between 2006 and 2009, the United States established four Marine National Monuments in the Pacific Ocean. The monuments encompass 214,777,000 acres composed of pristine small islands, atolls, coral reefs, submerged islets, and deep blue waters.[72] The *Papahānaumokuākea* Marine National Monument was the first and largest of these monuments. The monument encompasses over 89 million acres (139,793

---

[71] IMO Doc. MEPC 136(53), Designation of the Baltic Sea Area as a Particularly Sensitive Sea Area, July 22, 2005.
[72] U.S. Fish and Wildlife Service, Marine National Monuments Internet Website, Mar. 30, 2011. The monuments include "214,777,000 acres composed of small islands, atolls, coral reefs, submerged lands, and deep blue waters." http://www.fws.gov/marinenationalmonuments/.

square miles or 362,073 square kilometers), and includes numerous coral islands, seamounts, banks and shoals within the Northwestern Hawaiian Islands. The island chain stretches 1,200 nm from Nihoa to Kure Atoll.

A presidential proclamation on June 15, 2006, established *Papahānaumokuākea* Monument under authority of the Antiquities Act.[73] The Antiquities Act authorizes the President of the United States to declare by public proclamation historic landmarks, historic and prehistoric structures, and other objects of historic or scientific interest that are situated upon lands owned or controlled by the U.S. Government to be national monuments.[74] The marine regulation may be legally unsupported under the Antiquities Act, since the law was never intended to apply to the natural environment. The Northwest Hawaiian Islands cannot be fairly said to constitute a "monument" or "object(s)" reasonably subject to regulation as an "Antiquity."

Still, the Monument was established by the decree of President George W. Bush. Entry into the monument is prohibited except as authorized by the Secretary of Commerce or Secretary of the Interior. Ships or persons passing through the monument must also provide notice prior to and upon departing the area. Vessels that have been issued a permit by either the Secretary of Commerce or Secretary of Interior to operate in the monument also must have a NOAA-approved vessel monitoring system on board. Furthermore, the following activities are prohibited within the designated area:

1. Oil, gas, or mineral exploration or development;
2. Use of poisons, electrical charges, or explosives to harvest a resource;
3. Introducing or otherwise releasing an introduced species from within or into the monument; and
4. Anchoring on or having a vessel anchored on any living or dead coral.[75]

The following activities are also prohbited, unless specifcally provided for in the Proclamation:

1. Removing, moving, taking, harvesting, possessing, injuring, disturbing, or damaging; . . . any living or nonliving monument resource;
2. Drilling into, dredging, or otherwise altering the submerged lands other than by anchoring a vessel; or constructing, placing, or abandoning any structure, material, or other matter on the submerged lands;
3. Anchoring a vessel;
4. Deserting a vessel aground, at anchor, or adrift;

---

[73] Pres. Proc. 8031, Establishment of the Northwestern Hawaiian Islands Marine National Monument, June 15, 2006, 71 FR 36443, June 26, 2006.
[74] 16 U.S.C. § 431, *et seq.*
[75] Northwest Hawaiian Islands Marine National Monument, 50 C.F.R. § 404.6, 71 FR 51134 (Aug. 29, 2006).

5. Discharging or depositing any material or other matter into Special Preservation Areas or the Midway Atoll Special Management Area except vessel engine cooling water, weather deck runoff, and vessel engine exhaust;
6. Discharging or depositing any material or other matter into the monument [...that...] injures any resources of the monument, except fish parts (i.e., chumming material or bait) used in and during authorized fishing operations, or discharges incidental to vessel use such as deck wash, approved marine sanitation device effluent, cooling water, and engine exhaust;
7. Touching coral, living or dead;
8. Possessing fishing gear except when stowed...;
9. Swimming, snorkeling, or closed or open circuit SCUBA diving within any Special Preservation Area or the Midway Atoll Special Management Area; and
10. Attracting any living monument resources.[76]

The Department of Defense sought to obtain exclusion from regulation for its activities in the area. During interagency meetings at the National Security Council and the Council on Environmental Quality within the Executive Office of the President, Pentagon officials from the Office of the Secretary of Defense, the Joint Chiefs of Staff, and the Office of the Navy Judge Advocate General argued that the sanctuary lies directly on the threat axis between North Asia and the Hawaiian Islands. Commander, U.S. Pacific Fleet set forth naval rationale for continued U.S. warship and submarine access to the area, and Commander, U.S. Pacific Command sought to continue to use the airspace above the PSSA for missile overflight.

Under the proposal, the U.S. Navy would have been compelled to obtain a permit from the Secretary of Interior or Secretary of Commerce to operate submarines in the area—highly classified missions that are not widely known even inside the armed forces. Not only would the requirement give another cabinet secretary regulatory authority over active missions of the armed forces, but ironically, foreign submarines would not (and under UNCLOS could not) be made subject to the rule—putting U.S. forces at an operational disadvantage by a burdensome new approval process.

The agencies and departments of the U.S. government had contending views on the appropriate scope of an exemption for military activities in the U.S. regulation. After extensive negotiations, however, a military exemption was crafted that reads: "all activities and exercises of the U.S. Armed Forces shall be carried out in a manner that avoids, to the extent practicable and consistent with operational requirements, adverse impacts on monument resources and qualities."[77] Moreover, "in the event of threatened or actual destruction of, loss of, or injury to a monument resource or quality resulting from an incident, including but not limited to spills and groundings," caused by the Department of Defense or the U.S. Coast Guard, the cognizant armed force is required to coordinate with the Secretaries of Commerce and Interior to take action to mitigate the

---

[76] Id., § 404.6.
[77] Id., § 404.9.

harm.[78] The Pentagon accepted the provisions, although the rules tend to impede training realism and operational flexibility within the monument.

The armed forces initially opposed a proposal to seek IMO designation of the Northwestern Hawaiian Islands Marine National Monument as a PSSA, which then would open the door for protective measures to be imposed on foreign flagged ships. General Peter Pace, Chairman of the Joint Chiefs of Staff, signed a letter of non-concurrence to reject the idea. The military objected because the area was deemed too large for designation as a PSSA—echoing Russia's concern over the Baltic Sea Area PSSA—and the proposal failed to demonstrate a threat of environmental damage from international shipping or other activities.

In the view of the military, the proposal was a regulation in search of a threat to the marine environment. The U.S. proposal, for example, stated that the extent of tourism and recreation in the area was "extremely low."[79] The incidence of international shipping was also quite minimal, suggesting that the potential for harm to the area did not warrant designation as a PSSA. The U.S. proposal stated:

> 4.4.1 Although due to its remoteness, the exact route of vessels through this area is unknown, it appears that most traffic passes to the north of the island chain, following the great circle routes to and from ports on the west coast of North America and East Asia. Other trans-Pacific ships travelling from ports in Hawaii transit at least 100 miles south of the [Northwestern Hawaiian Islands]. Occasionally, vessels transiting from the south pass within the boundaries of the proposed PSSA.
>
> 4.4.2 A preliminary analysis of vessel traffic patterns [...reveals that...] during a 21-month study period in 2004 and 2005, approximately 132 vessels reported from within the area of the proposed PSSA: 104 of these vessels were freighters, 8 were tankers, 4 were research vessels, 2 were passenger vessels, 2 were vessels used for educational purposes, 1 was a recreational vessel, 1 was a towing vessel with a 666 foot vessel in tow, and 10 were unidentified vessels. The 132 vessels were flagged in 23 different countries.[80]

The proposal sought mandatory ship reporting as part of the package of APMs, hoping to collect sufficient data of a greater number of ship movements through the area to justify regulations over time. But the associated protective measures proposed by NOAA to prevent harm to the monument area from international shipping could have been implemented through the IMO without designation of the entire Monument as a PSSA. The armed forces maintained that it was not in the security interests of the United States or its alliance structure with Japan, Australia, South Korea, Thailand, and the Philippines to promote designation of

---

[78] Id.
[79] IMO Doc. MEPC 56/8, Designation of the Papahānaumokuākea Marine National Monument as a Particularly Sensitive Sea Area, Apr. 5, 2007, para. 4.2.
[80] Id., at 4.4.1 and 4.4.2.

vast swaths of the Pacific Ocean as a PSSA, which could be seen to show a new tolerance for the erosion of navigational freedoms in the Asia-Pacific.

Nonetheless, the White House authorized the U.S. delegation at IMO to submit a proposal for designation of the monument as a PSSA. The U.S. delegation to MPEC 56 submitted a proposal, meeting at IMO in 2007.[81] In April 2008, MEPC 57 approved the request for designation of the Marine National Monument as a PSSA.[82] The associated protective measures adopted for the area include expansion of six existing ATBAs and establishment of a ship reporting system, which is recommendatory for transiting ships that are 300 gross tons or larger, and for fishing vessels and all ships in distress, and is mandatory as a condition of entry to a U.S. port or "U.S. place" for all ships 300 gross tons or larger, and for ships in distress.[83] Sovereign immune vessels, such as warships, however, are exempt from the reporting procedures.

Surprisingly, the *Papahānaumokuākea* PSSA was approved by IMO, even though there was minimal presence of international shipping through the area, let alone a demonstration of harm produced by vessel transits. There is scant evidence that foreign-flagged ships have been responsible for marine environmental harm in the area over the past three decades.[84] The last foreign-flagged vessel that is known to have created any remarkable environmental impact was the Greek-flagged *Anangel* that had to dump 2200 pounds of kaolin clay into the ocean to escape a reef, but that incident occurred thirty years ago.[85] Still, the criticism that the PSSA was a regulation in search of a risk did not sway either the Bush administration or the IMO.

Finally, on July 30, 2010, the monument was inscribed as a mixed (natural and cultural) World Heritage Site at the United Nations Educational, Scientific and Cultural Organization's (UNESCO) 34th World Heritage Convention in Brasilia, Brazil.

5.2.5 *Mid-Pacific Ocean National Monuments (United States)*

The United States has continued to expand its network of marine national monuments in the Pacific Ocean. On January 16, 2009, three marine national monuments were established: The Marianas Trench Marine National Monument, the

---

[81] Id., at 4.2.
[82] IMO Doc. MEPC 57/21Report of the Marine Environmental Protection Committee, Apr. 7, 2008, para. 7.1–7.4.
[83] IMO Doc. SN.1/Circ.264, Mandatory Ship Reporting Systems, Oct. 23, 2007, Annex 1.
[84] IMO Doc. 56/INF.2, Designation of the *Papahānaumokuākea* Marine National Monument as a Particularly Sensitive Sea Area, Apr. 5, 2007, Annex I.
[85] Id.

CHAPTER FIVE

Pacific Remote Islands Marine National Monument, and the Rose Atoll Marine National Monument.[86]

The Marianas Trench Marine National Monument encompasses nearly 61,100,000 acres (95,216 square miles) and includes the 1,100 mile long and 44 mile wide Mariana Trench. The Mariana Trench is the site of the deepest point on Earth. The Trench extends along an arc 2.3 miles in diameter, and consists of 21 undersea mud volcanoes and thermal vents. The area is home to unusual life forms that flourish in some of the harshest conditions of cold and pressure. The waters around the northernmost three islands of the Archipelago have the greatest diversity of seamount and hydrothermal vent life ever discovered.[87]

The Pacific Remote Islands Marine National Monument includes Howland Island, Baker Island, Jarvis Island, Johnston Atoll, Palmyra Atoll, Kingman Reef, Wake Atoll National Wildlife Refuges, and their surrounding waters. The Monument extends throughout 55,600,000 acres (86,888 square miles) of land and water, and it contains a widespread collection of coral reefs, seabirds, and shore bird protected areas. The Rose Atoll Marine National Monument is small by comparison, but covers 8,609,000 acres (13,451 square miles). NOAA has initiated the process to add the Monument's surrounding marine areas to the Fagatele Bay National Marine Sanctuary.

Commercial fishing is prohibited within all three of the monuments. Sustenance, recreational, and traditional indigenous fishing, however, is permitted, but it is managed as a sustainable activity in accordance with the Magnuson-Stevens Fishery Conservation and Management Act and an Executive Order.[88] Likewise, the Secretary of Interior may authorize scientific exploration and research within each of the monuments.

The Secretaries of Interior and Commerce approve management plans for the monuments. These plans, however, "shall impose no restrictions on innocent passage in the territorial sea or otherwise restrict navigation, overflight, and other internationally recognized lawful uses of the sea... in compliance with international law." The proclamations state that none of the navigation restrictions "shall apply to or be enforced against a person who is not a citizen, national, or resident alien of the United States (including foreign flag vessels) unless in accordance with international law."

---

[86] Pres. Proc. 8335, Establishment of the Marianas Trench Marine National Monument, Jan. 6, 2009, 74 FR 1557, Jan. 12, 2009; Pres. Proc. 8336, Establishment of the Pacific Remote Islands Marine National Monument, Jan. 6, 2009, 74 FR 1565, Jan. 12, 2009, and Pres. Proc. 8337, Establishment of the Rose Atoll Marine National Monument, Jan. 6, 2009, 74 FR 1577, Jan. 12, 2009.

[87] The Mariana Archipelago includes the islands of *Maug, Asuncion,* and *Farallon de Pajaros,* which is also known as *Uracas.*

[88] 16 U.S.C. § 1801, *et seq.* and Exec. Ord. 12962.

Exceptions similar to those found in the proclamation of the *Papahānaumokuākea* Marine National Monument concerning emergencies, national security, and law enforcement activities also apply to the Marianas Trench, the Pacific Remote Islands and the Rose Atoll Marine National Monuments. Nothing in any the proclamations tries to "limit agency actions to respond to emergencies posing an unacceptable threat to human health or safety or to the marine environment and admitting of no other feasible solution." Furthermore, none of the proclamations apply to activities of the Armed Forces, including those of the U.S. Coast Guard.[89]

Nonetheless, the Pentagon agreed that it will "ensure, by the adoption of appropriate measures not impairing operations or operational capabilities, that its vessels and aircraft act in a manner consistent, so far as is reasonable and practicable," with the proclamations. In the event of threatened or actual destruction of, loss of, or injury to a monument's living marine resource resulting from an incident caused by the Department of Defense or the U.S. Coast Guard, the responsible armed force is required to coordinate with the Secretary of the Interior or Commerce, as appropriate, for the purpose of taking actions to respond to and mitigate the harm. If possible, the Navy or Coast Guard is required to "restore or replace the Monument resource or quality." This charge is a broad and open-ended duty stapled to an equally large financial liability.

5.3 Ships' Routeing, Vessel Traffic Services, and Ships' Reporting

In addition to the establishment of PSSAs, a number of other IMO-adopted measures can be used by coastal States to enhance safety of navigation and to protect the marine environment. These measures, which include ship routeing systems, ATBAs, ship reporting systems, and vessel traffic services, can be used to channelize shipping traffic or regulate their movement through a prescribed area.

Traffic separation schemes (TSS) have been established in many of the major congested shipping areas in the world. Typically, the provisions include two-way routes, recommended tracks, deep-water routes, and precautionary areas. These measures help to improve safety of navigation in areas of converging or high-density traffic. The schemes are best for passage constrained by restricted sea room, obstructions to navigation, limited depths and challenging shoals and tides, or unfavorable meteorological conditions.[90]

Pursuant to Regulation 10 of Chapter V of the *Safety of Life at Sea Convention* (SOLAS), ships' routeing systems can be recommendatory or mandatory for all

---

[89] Pres. Proc. 8335, 74 FR 1557, 1561; Pres. Proc. 8336 74 FR 1565, 1569; and Pres. Proc. 8337, 74 FR 1577, 1579.

[90] IMO Doc. A.572(14), General Provisions on Ships' Routeing, as amended, Nov. 20, 1985.

ships or they may apply only to certain categories of ships or ships carrying certain cargoes. Routeing measures must be adopted in accordance with the guidelines and criteria developed by the IMO. However, ships' routeing systems and coastal State enforcement action shall be consistent with international law, including UNCLOS. Furthermore, neither SOLAS Regulation V/10 nor its associated guidelines "shall prejudice the rights and duties of Governments under international law or the legal regimes of straits used for international navigation and archipelagic sea lanes."[91]

A ships' routeing system may or may not have associated with it a vessel traffic service (VTS), adopted pursuant to SOLAS Regulation V/12. A VTS may be established when vessel characteristics or the degree of risk warrants close vessel tracking. There is no single architecture for VTS, and the term refers to any shore-side system that may "range from the provision of simple information messages to ships, such as position of other traffic or meteorological hazard warnings, to extensive management of traffic within a port or waterway."[92] Ships entering a VTS area normally report to the local authorities and may be tracked by the VTS control center. Ships within the area are required to maintain a specific frequency for navigational or other warnings so that they may be contacted directly by the VTS operator if there is an increased risk of an incident or, in areas where traffic flow is regulated, to receive advice or notice on when or how to proceed.

A VTS enhances safety of life at sea and efficiency of navigation, as well as protects the marine environment, adjacent shore areas, work sites and offshore installations from the potentially adverse effects of maritime traffic. Nothing in Regulation V/12 or its implementing guidelines, however, shall "prejudice the rights and duties of Governments under international law or the legal regimes of straits used for international navigation and archipelagic sea lanes."[93]

In 1994, SOLAS was amended to allow the establishment of mandatory ship reporting systems.[94] The updated SOLAS Regulation V/11 entered into force in 1996, and it provides that all ships, certain categories of ships, or ships carrying certain cargoes shall use reporting systems that have been adopted and implemented in accordance with IMO guidelines and criteria.[95] As is the case with

---

[91] SOLAS Regulation V/10.
[92] IMO Doc. MSC.65(68), Adoption of Amendments to the Convention for the Safety of Life at Sea, June 4, 1997, *reprinted in* IMO Doc. MSC 68/23/Add.1, Annex 2; IMO Doc. A.857(20), Guidelines on Vessel Traffic Services, Dec. 3, 1997.
[93] SOLAS Regulation V/12.
[94] IMO Doc. MSC.31(63), Adoption of Amendments to the Convention for the Safety of Life at Sea, 1974, May 23, 1994 and IMO Doc. MSC 63/23/Add.1, Annex 2, May 23, 1994.
[95] http://www.sailing.org/downloads/sailors/SOLASV.pdf.

mandatory ship routeing measures, all "ship reporting systems and actions taken to enforce compliance with those systems shall be consistent with international law, including...[UNCLOS]."[96] Furthermore, nothing in Regulation V/11 and its associated guidelines "shall prejudice the rights and duties of Governments under international law or the legal regimes of straits used for international navigation and archipelagic sea lanes." The use of ship reporting systems shall be free of charge to the ships concerned, a rule that prevents rent seeking by coastal states always searching for new sources of outside revenue.

In general, ships' routeing and reporting systems "can be established to improve safety of life at sea, safety and efficiency of navigation, and/or increase the protection of the marine environment."[97] In order to facilitate the assessment and approval of ship routeing and ship reporting systems by the Sub-Committee on Safety of Navigation and the Maritime Safety Committee, proposals should be prepared using IMO guidelines.[98] States should also consult Part A of the GPSR, which contains advice on how to craft proposals.

At a minimum, proposals should set out the "objectives of the routeing system, the demonstrated need for its establishment, and the reasons why the proposed system is preferred."[99] The "history of groundings, collisions, or damage to the marine environment" and "the proposed impact on navigation, including the expected impact on shipping," should be included in routeing system proposals.[100] Traffic considerations should be taken into account, including aids to navigation, traffic patterns, nautical charts for the area, and the presence of offshore structures. Environmental factors, such as prevailing weather conditions, tidal streams, currents, and sea ice concentrations, also should be set forth.[101] If the system is intended to protect the marine environment, the proposal should also "state whether the proposed routeing system can reasonably be expected to significantly prevent or reduce the risk of pollution...."[102]

The proponent must indicate whether they are seeking a recommendatory or mandatory routeing system. If a proposal is for a mandatory system, the submission must also include a justification for why a mandatory system is needed, whether such a system would adversely affect ports and harbors of neighboring states, and whether the mandatory routeing system is limited to what is

---

[96] IMO Doc. MSC.31(63), Adoption of Amendments to the Convention for the Safety of Life at Sea, 1974, May 23, 1994.
[97] Id., Annex, para. 1.2.
[98] IMO Doc. MSC/Circ.1060, Guidance Note on the Preparation of Proposals on Ships' Routeing Systems and Ship Reporting Systems for Submission to the Sub-Committee on Safety of Navigation, Jan. 6, 2003.
[99] Id., Annex, para. 3.1.
[100] Id.
[101] Id., para. 3.4 and 3.5.
[102] Id., para. 3.5.2.

essential in the interest of safety of navigation and protection of the marine environment.[103]

Other information that may be contained in a routeing system proposal includes:

.1 presence of fishing grounds; existing or foreseeable development of offshore exploration and exploitation of the seabed, offshore structures, and changes in the traffic pattern because of port or offshore terminal development;
.2 a summary of other measures taken;
.3 consultations that have taken place with mariners using the area, port authorities, or other groups with an interest in the area; and
.4 in the case of a mandatory system, the details of the measures to be taken to monitor compliance with the system and the actions intended if a ship fails to comply with its requirements.[104]

Proposals for ship reporting systems should include the following information:

.1 the objectives and demonstrated need;
.2 categories of ships required to participate;
.3 hydrographical and meteorological elements, and vessel traffic characteristics;
.4 geographic coverage;
.5 format and content of the reports required;
.6 information to be provided to participating ships;
.7 communication requirements for the system, including radio frequencies;
.8 regulations to be put into effect;
.9 shore-based facilities and personnel qualifications ashore;
.10 a summary of the measures used and reasons why they are inadequate;
.11 alternative communications protocols;
.12 plans for responding to an emergency;
.13 measures to enforce compliance; and
.14 effective date.[105]

Since mandatory ship reporting systems first were authorized in 1996, they have proliferated much like PSSAs. These systems have been adopted to enhance safety of navigation, as well as protect the marine environment. Although there was a demonstrated need for many of these systems to enhance safety of navigation, a number of other reporting systems, adopted for purposes of marine environmental protection, underwent only minimal scrutiny in the relevant IMO bodies. For example, a U.S. proposal to establish two mandatory ship reporting systems off the northeastern and southeastern United States was adopted by IMO. The ship reporting systems purportedly protect the endangered

---

[103] Id., para. 3.6.
[104] Id., para. 3.8.
[105] Id., para. 7.

northern right whale, although there is insufficient evidence that they have done so.[106]

5.4 Mandatory Ship Reporting (United States)

At NAV 44, the United States proposed the establishment of a mandatory ship reporting system off the eastern coast of the United States to protect the endangered northern right whale from the threat posed by international shipping.[107] The whales are especially vulnerable to ship strikes due to their distribution, behavior, and physical attributes. Because they have a largely coastal life, living along the continental shelf, right whales are brought into contact with human population centers and major shipping lanes.

The marine mammals are highly buoyant and spend long periods of time resting at or just below the water's surface. Right whales may be observed in active surface groups (i.e., four to twenty individuals engaged in frequent physical contact and courtship behavior), and they skim feed (i.e., gathering plankton by swimming slowly near the surface with their mouths open). During resting, feeding and surface active situations, whales may be unaware of approaching ships. Mothers nursing calves are frequently observed at the surface, and calves have limited ability to dive so they are especially vulnerable to ship strikes. Right whales are slow moving, with occasional speeds of up to only five or six knots. Moreover, the animals are difficult for mariners to see, especially in rough seas and at night, due to their low profile, dark color, broad back and lack of a dorsal fin.

The objective of the mandatory ship reporting system is to:

> ... provide mariners entering critical habitat areas with timely notice and other relevant information including recent sightings where available to reduce the potential for collisions between ships and right whales. This system will assist mariners to navigate safely through the area by informing them of a potential navigation hazard and other beneficial information and thus directly contribute to the survival and recovery of the right whale....[108]

---

[106] IMO Doc. MSC.85(70), Mandatory Ship Reporting Systems, Annex 1, Description of the Mandatory Ship Reporting Systems for Protection of Endangered North Atlantic Right Whales in Sea Areas off the Northeastern and Southeastern Coasts of the United States, Dec. 7, 1998, *reprinted in* IMO Doc. MSC 70/23/Add.2, Mandatory Ship Reporting Systems, Description of the Mandatory Ship Reporting Systems for Protection of Endangered North Atlantic Right Whales in Sea Areas off the Northeastern and Southeastern Coasts of the United States, Dec. 7, 1998, Annex 16, and IMO MSC 85/26/Add.1, Report of the Maritime Safety Committee on its Eighty-fifth Session, Establishment of a New Recommentatory Seasonal Area to be Avoided in the Great South Channel, off the East Coast of the United States, Annex 15, Jan. 6, 2009.

[107] IMO Doc. NAV 44/14, Report to the Maritime Safety Committee, Forty-fourth Session of the Navigation Sub-Committee, Sept. 4, 1998, para. 3.23.

[108] Id., para. 3.24.

Prior to NAV 44 in 1998, all mandatory ship reporting systems had been adopted to prevent marine pollution from ships, rather than to protect a particular marine species from ship collisions. The United States believed, however, that mandatory ship reporting for the specific purpose of protecting populations of single marine species from direct physical impacts of ships was warranted in cases of clear scientific evidence that:

.1.1 the population of a marine species is "immediately endangered with extinction;"
.1.2 major international shipping lanes pass through its critical habitat; and
.1.3 the greatest known threat to the survival and recovery of the population is posed by direct physical impacts from ship collisions.[109]

Although a majority of the IMO delegations thought that the U.S. proposal was justified, a substantial minority were not convinced that the proposed protective measures would be effective. The opposition preferred a recommendatory ship reporting system. Concern was also evident from a number of delegations that approval of the system would create an undesirable precedent, as it would lead to yet more mandatory ship reporting systems that impaired freedom of navigation.[110] In the end, despite these concerns, the Sub-Committee endorsed the U.S. view that a mandatory system was required in this case.[111]

The U.S. proposal received support from most of the delegations at MSC 70. In light of the scientific evidence proffered by the United States, the Maritime Safety Committee adopted the proposal in December 1998.[112] To alleviate any remaining concerns that the ship reporting system would lead to a proliferation of mandatory ship reporting systems elsewhere to protect single species, the U.S. delegation recommended a three-part test. MSC agreed that ship reporting systems for the specific purpose of protecting populations of single marine species from direct physical impacts of ships, such as collisions, may be warranted only in special circumstances. The test indicates single species rules are appropriate only if there is clear scientific evidence that:

.1 the population of a marine species is immediately endangered with extinction;
.2 major shipping routes pass through habitat critical for the population; and
.3 the greatest known threat to the survival and recovery of the population is posed by direct physical impacts of ships, such as collisions.[113]

---

[109] Id., para. 3.24 and Annex 8.
[110] Id., paras. 3.25 and 3.26.
[111] Id., para. 3.27.
[112] IMO Doc. MSC 70/23, Report of the Maritime Safety Committee on its Seventieth Session, Dec. 17, 1998, para. 11.41; IMO Doc. MSC.85(70), Report of the Maritime Safety Committee on its Seventieth Session, Dec. 17 1998, Annex 16, and IMO Doc. MSC 70/23/Add.2, Dec. 17, 1998, Annex 16.
[113] IMO Doc. MSC 70/23, Report of the Maritime Safety Committee on its Seventieth Session, Dec. 17, 1998, paras. 11.39 and 11.40.

The mandatory ship reporting system applicable off the northeastern and southeastern coasts of the United States took effect in July 1999.[114] The ship reporting system applies to all ships displacing 300 gross tonnage or greater, except sovereign immune vessels. The geographical coverage of the system includes:

> 2.1. Northeastern United States: Geographical boundaries of the proposed northeast area include the water of Cape Cod Bay, Massachusetts Bay, and the Great South Channel east and southeast of Massachusetts.[115]
> 2.2. Southeastern United States: Geographical boundaries of the proposed southeast area include coastal waters within about 25 nautical miles along a 90 nautical miles stretch of the Atlantic seaboard in Florida and Georgia.[116]

Ships entering the prescribed areas are instructed:

> 4.1. ...that they are entering an area of critical importance for the protection of the highly endangered right whale; that such whales are present; and that ship strikes pose a serious threat to whales and may cause damage to ships....
> 4.2. ...to monitor Coast Guard Broadcast Notice to Mariners, NAVTEX, NOAA Weather Radio, and, in the northeastern ship reporting system area only, the Cape Cod Canal Vessel Traffic Control and the Bay of Fundy Vessel Traffic Control [to obtain seasonal right whale advisories]....
> 4.3. ...to consult with NAVTEX, Inmarsat-C SafetyNET (satellite text broadcasts), the United States Coast Pilot, Notice to Mariners, and nautical charts for information on the boundaries of the right whale critical habitat and the national marine sanctuary, [and] applicable regulations, and precautionary measures that mariners may take to reduce the risk of hitting right whales....
> 4.4. ...to report any whale sightings, and dead, injured, or entangled marine mammals to the nearest local Coast Guard station....[117]

The two systems are implemented domestically through a U.S. Federal statute.[118] The Department of Defense was opposed to the compulsory nature of the concept

---

[114] 33 U.S.C. § 1230(d).
[115] IMO Doc. MSC.85(70), Report of the Maritime Safety Committee on its Seventieth Session, Dec. 17 1998, Annex 16, and IMO Doc. MSC 70/23/Add.2, Dec. 17, 1998, Annex 16, Appendix 1. Coordinates of the area are as follows: from a point on Cape Ann, Massachusetts at 42°39'.00 N, 70°37'.00 W; then northeast to 42°45'.00 N, 70°13'.00 W; then southeast to 42°10'.00 N, 68°31'.00 W; then south to 41°00'.00 N, 68°31'.00 W; then west to 41°00'.00 N, 69°17'.00 W; then northeast to 42°05'.00 N, 70°02'.00 W, then west to 42°04'.00 N, 70°10'.00 W; and then along the Massachusetts shoreline of Cape Cod Bay and Massachusetts Bay back to the point on Cape Anne at 42°39'.00 N, 70°37'.00 W. NOAA Chart No.13009.
[116] IMO Doc. MSC.85(70), Report of the Maritime Safety Committee on its Seventieth Session, Dec. 17 1998, Annex 16, and IMO Doc. MSC 70/23/Add.2, Dec. 17, 1998, Annex 16, Appendix 2. The area extends from the shoreline east to longitude 80°51'.60 W with the southern and northern boundary at latitudes 30°00'.00 N and 31°27'.00 N, respectively. NOAA Chart No.11009.
[117] IMO Doc. MSC.85(70), Report of the Maritime Safety Committee on its Seventieth Session, Dec. 17 1998, Annex 16.
[118] 33 U.S.C. § 1230(d).

during the U.S. interagency deliberations leading up to the decision to submit the proposal to the IMO. The armed forces were concerned about the adverse precedent the mandatory ship reporting system would have on worldwide freedom of navigation. President Clinton disagreed with his military advisers and rejected other less-intrusive options proposed by the Pentagon, such as a recommendatory system with all the same features proposed in the compulsory system. The Clinton administration insisted on pursuing a mandatory system, even though proponents had not presented evidence that a mandatory system would reduce ship strikes any more than a recommendatory system.

A 2007 report prepared for the Marine Mammal Commission by scientists at Woods Hole Oceanographic Institution supports the Pentagon's suspicion that the proposed system would not produce the desired effect. Commenting on the ship strike reduction strategy, the report determined that mandatory ship reporting systems "have not brought an end to ship strikes, nor is there any evidence that they have reduced the incidence of such events."[119] The report concludes, "[a]lthough the ship strike reduction strategy may have prevented some collisions, it has not been successful in addressing this threat to North Atlantic right whales."

The northern right whale population has remained fairly consistent for the past 40 years, numbering between 300–350 animals. Since 1999, compliance with the mandatory ship reporting systems has averaged only about 53 percent (64 percent in the northeast and 43 percent in the southeast).[120] Despite these lackluster compliance rates and the findings of the Woods Hole study, the United States continued to advocate the value of the systems.

In 2008, the United States proposed that the north-south leg of the existing traffic separation scheme (TSS) in the approach to Boston, Massachusetts, be amended to narrow the shipping lanes in order to, *inter alia*, "provide further protection to right whales from ship strikes because the lanes will be moved away from an area with a high seasonal density of right whales in April through July."[121] In conjunction with these amendments to the TSS, the United States also proposed the establishment of a recommendatory, seasonal area to be avoided (ATBA). The ATBA would apply to ships 300 gross tons and above, and from

---

[119] RANDALL REEVES, ET AL., REPORT OF THE NORTH ATLANTIC RIGHT WHALE PROGRAM REVIEW FOR THE MARINE MAMMAL COMMISSION 13–17 (2007) (Woods Hole, Massachusetts, Mar. 2006).

[120] IMO Doc. NAV 47/INF.2, Ship strikes of Endangered Northern Right Whales, Submitted by the United States, Apr. 23, 2001.

[121] IMO Doc. NAV 54/3, Amendment of the Traffic Separation Scheme In the Approach to Boston, Massachusetts, Submitted by the United States, Mar. 27, 2008, para. 3.

April 1 to July 31 in the Great South Channel, which was identified as "one of the most important feeding habitats for right whales within the species' range."[122]

Right whales engage in behavior in this area during the four-month period that makes them particularly susceptible to ship strikes.[123] One year earlier, Canada submitted a similar proposal to establish a seasonal ATBA, from June 1 to December 31, in Roseway Basin, south of Nova Scotia for ships of 300 gross tonnage and above.[124]

> In order to significantly reduce the risk of ship strikes of the highly endangered North Atlantic right whale, it is recommended that ships of 300 gross tonnage and upwards solely in transit during the period of 1 June through 31 December should avoid the area....[125]

The proposed area is "one of only two known, high-use, seasonal aggregation areas for North Atlantic right whales in Canadian waters and is an important feeding and socializing habitat" for the endangered species.[126] The purpose of establishing an ATBA is "to minimize ship traffic in this environmentally sensitive area where right whale densities are significant," and thereby reduce the risk of ship strikes.[127]

Most recently, NOAA proposed expanding the areas considered the right whale's critical habitat off the coast of Florida. Current critical habitats for the northern right whale have been established in the Great South Channel, Cape Cod Bay, Massachusetts, and the Southeastern United States.[128] If approved, the expansion of the southeastern critical habitat could have negative implications

---

[122] IMO Doc. NAV 54/3/1, Area to be Avoided in the Great South Channel, Submitted by the United States, Mar. 27, 2008, paras. 1–2. The coordinates are: (1) 41° 44'.14 N 069° 34'.83 W; (2) 42° 10'.00 N 068° 31'.00 W; (3) 41° 24'.89 N 068° 31'.00 W; and, (4) 40° 50'.47 N 068° 58'.67 W. Id. See also, IMO Doc. NAV 54/25, Report to the Maritime Safety Committee, Aug. 14, 2008, Annex 2.

[123] Id., para. 12.

[124] IMO Doc. NAV 53/3/13, Area to be Avoided in Roseway Basin, South of Nova Scotia (Submitted by Canada), Apr. 20, 2007, para. 1.

[125] Id. The area is bounded by: (1) 43° 16'.00 N 064° 55'.00 W; (2) 42° 47'.00 N 064° 59'.00 W; (3) 42° 39'.00 N 065° 31'.00 W; and, (4) 42° 52'.00 N 066° 05'.00 W. See also, IMO Doc. MSC 83/28/add.3, Annex 25, Report of the Maritime Safety Committee on its Eighty-Third Session, Nov. 2, 2007.

[126] Id.

[127] Id., paras. 2 and 8; IMO Doc. NAV 53/22, Report to the Maritime Safety Committee, Aug. 14, 2007, para. 3.27.

[128] The designated areas include:
(a) *Great South Channel.* The area bounded by 41° 40' N/69° 45' W; 41° 00' N/69° 05' W; 41° 38' N/68° 13' W; and 42° 10' N/68° 31' W.
(b) *Cape Cod Bay, Massachusetts.* The area bounded by 42° 04.8' N/70° 10' W; 42° 12' N/70° 15' W; 42° 12' N/70° 30' W; 41° 46.8' N/70° 30' W and on the south and east by the interior shoreline of Cape Cod, Massachusetts.

for the Navy's decision to build a 500–square mile undersea warfare training range (USWTR) off Jacksonville, Florida.[129]

The prospects for extinction of the right whale are disturbing, and many sense that only desperate measures can save the species. It is reasonable, however, to question whether the current approach helps maintain the marine mammal population at the lowest sacrifice of navigational freedoms. Expansion of the critical habitat for the right whale may not save any additional animals, but would be contrary to U.S. national security and global ocean interests.

5.5 Marine Mammals

Are U.S. naval operations, and particularly the use of sonar, hazardous to marine mammals?

The ability to test and train with sonar is critical to the Navy's operational readiness. Over 40 countries operate more than 400 submarines worldwide, many of which are quiet, modern diesel-electric boats, and some are super-quiet air independent propulsion (AIP) submarines with improved sensor performance, advanced weapons systems, and enhanced signature reduction. It has been more than ten years, for example, since China introduced the sophisticated *Song*-class diesel electric submarine.

Reportedly quieter than the U.S. fast attack *Los Angeles*-class boats, the *Song* is equipped with wake-homing torpedoes and anti-ship cruise missiles. In one incident on October 26, 2006, one of the ultra-quiet *Song* submarines surfaced inside the protective screen of the aircraft carrier *USS Kitty Hawk*, at a distance of about five miles. Admiral Gary Roughead, who served as commander of the U.S. Pacific Fleet, and who would later serve as Chief of Naval Operations, was visiting China at the time. He warned that the submarine risked igniting a "shootout."[130]

Advanced conventional submarines pose a significant threat to U.S. forces operating in littoral or near-shore environments. Active sonar is the best way to detect submarines lurking offshore. The U.S. Navy says it needs to be able to train in realistic conditions with a variety of ocean bottom topography in order to be prepared to face the threat posed by the new generation of diesel electric

---

(c) *Southeastern United States.* The coastal waters between 31° 15' N and 30° 15' N from the coast out 15 nautical miles; and the coastal waters between 30° 15' N and 28° 00' N from the coast out 5 nautical miles (Figure 8 to Part 226 C.F.R.).

50 C.F.R. § 226.203 [59 FR 28805, June 3, 1994. Re-designated and amended at 64 FR 14067, Mar. 23, 1999; 68 FR 17562, Apr. 10, 2003; 70 FR 1832, Jan. 11, 2005; 71 FR 38293, July 6, 2006; 73 FR 19011, Apr. 8, 2008].

[129] Jim Waymer, *Feds may extend right whale habitat off Brevard*, Florida Today, Dec. 28, 2009.

[130] *Admiral Says Sub Risked a Shootout*, Wash. Times, Nov. 15, 2006.

submarines.[131] Sonar is a key to anti-submarine warfare (ASW) training. Because ASW is a perishable skill, however, Navy technicians that operate sonar systems must practice regularly.

Navy ships routinely exercise with sonar in order to certify a task force before the group of ships may deploy overseas. But environmental organizations have maintained that sonar usage harms marine mammals. The Natural Resources Defense Council (NRDC) sought to halt the Navy's use of sonar during training. The Navy replied that there was little evidence to suggest that sonar affected marine mammals and, in any event, that the balance of interests for the United States augured in favor of national security rather than marine mammal conservation. In 2008, the U.S. Supreme Court decided a case that ended the controversy.[132]

5.5.1 *Natural Resources Defense Council v. Winter (Sonar Litigation)*

On March 22, 2007, NRDC sued the U.S. Navy in the District Court for the Central District of California seeking declaratory and injunctive relief on the grounds that the Navy's southern California training exercises that involve the use of sonar violate the National Environmental Policy Act of 1969 (NEPA), the Endangered Species Act of 1973 (ESA), and the Coastal Zone Management Act of 1972 (CZMA). In January 2008, the District Court granted plaintiffs' motion for a preliminary injunction and prohibited the Navy from using mid-frequency active (MFA) sonar during its training exercises because evidence suggested that sonar use harmed whales and other marine mammals.[133]

The Navy filed an emergency appeal to the Ninth Circuit Court of Appeals. The Court of Appeals agreed with the District Court that a preliminary injunction was appropriate. The appellate court also concluded that a blanket injunction prohibiting the Navy from using MFA sonar in the Southern California training area was overbroad, and remanded the case to the District Court "to narrow its injunction

---

[131] Dept' of the U.S. Navy, Navy's Need for Sonar and Marine Mammal Protection Efforts, Chief of Naval Operations Fact Sheet (2012).

[132] *Winter, Secretary of the Navy, et al. v. National Resources Defense Council, Inc., et al.*, 129 S. Ct. 365, 555 U.S. 7 (2008). *See also,* Stacey M. Valentine, *Case Summaries: Winter, Secretary of the Navy, et al. v. Natural Resources Defense Council, Inc., et al., 129 S.Ct. 365, No. 07-1239 (U.S. 2008)*, 1 Wash. & Lee J. Energy, Climate, & Env't 195 (2010).

[133] Active sonar involves emitting pulses of sound underwater and then receiving acoustic waves that echo off the target. Passive sonar, on the other hand, "'listens' for sound waves but does not introduce sound into the water. Passive sonar is not effective for tracking diesel-electric submarines because those vessels can operate almost silently. Passive sonar also has a more limited range than active sonar, and cannot identify the exact location of an enemy submarine." Id.

so as to provide mitigation conditions under which the Navy may conduct its [sonar] training exercises."[134]

On remand, the District Court entered a new preliminary injunction allowing the Navy to use MFA sonar, but only if it implemented a list of mitigation measures designed to reduce the effect of sonar on marine mammal populations. First, the Navy was required to observe a 12-mile "exclusion zone" from the coastline when operating with sonar. Second, warships must use lookouts to help avoid encounters with marine mammals. Third, the District Court restricted the use of "helicopter-dipping" sonar. Fourth, the use of MFA sonar in geographic choke points was restricted. Fifth, the Navy was required to shut down MFA sonar when a marine mammal was spotted within 2,200 yards of a warship. Finally, the Navy would power down MFA sonar by 6 dB during significant surface ducting conditions, in which sound travels farther than it otherwise would due to temperature differences in adjacent layers of water.[135] The Navy filed a notice of appeal, challenging only the last two restrictions. The mitigation measures were imposed on the Navy in addition to related measures the Navy previously had adopted pursuant to the Marine Mammal Protection Act.

Concurrently, the Navy sought relief from the Executive Branch. Accordingly, the President granted the Navy an exemption from the requirements of the Coastal Zone Management Act after determining that the naval exercises in question were "in the paramount interest of the United States."[136] The President concluded that compliance with the District Court's injunction would "undermine the Navy's ability to conduct realistic training exercises that are necessary to ensure the combat effectiveness of... [aircraft carrier] strike groups."[137]

The Navy then moved to vacate the District Court's injunction with respect to the 2,200-yard "shutdown" zone and the restrictions on training in surface ducting conditions. The District Court declined to do so, however, and the Court of Appeals affirmed the decision.[138] The Ninth Circuit agreed with the District Court's holding that the Navy's environmental assessment (EA), which resulted in a finding of no significant environmental impact from the use of Navy sonar, was "cursory, unsupported by cited evidence, or unconvincing."[139] The Court of Appeals further determined that, based on the Navy's own figures, the training exercises would cause 564 physical injuries to marine mammals, as well as 170,000 "disturbances of marine mammals' behavior."[140]

---

[134] 508 F. 3d 885, 887 (CA9 2007).
[135] 530 F. Supp. 2d 1110, 1118–1121 (C.D. Cal. 2008).
[136] 16 U. S. C. § 1456(c)(1)(B).
[137] 555 U.S. 7, 18 (2008).
[138] 527 F. Supp. 2d 1216 (C.D. Cal 2008).
[139] 518 F. 3d, at 658, 683 (9th Cir. 2008).
[140] Id., at 696.

The Ninth Circuit held that the balance of hardships and consideration of the public interest weighed in favor of the plaintiffs, emphasizing that the negative impact on the Navy's training exercises was "speculative," since the Navy had never before operated under the procedures required by the District Court.[141] In particular, the Court of Appeals determined the 2,200-yard shutdown zone imposed by the District Court was unlikely to affect the Navy's operations because the Navy often shuts down its mid-frequency active sonar systems during the course of training exercises. The power down requirement during significant surface ducting conditions was not unreasonable because such conditions are rare, and the Navy has previously certified strike groups that had not trained under such conditions.

The Navy appealed the case to the Supreme Court, arguing that the standard used by the District and Appellate Courts was too lax when deciding in favor of a preliminary injunction against Navy sonar usage. The Navy argued that the judiciary had improperly interfered with the Executive branch's authority to control the military. The Supreme Court granted *certiorari*, and upon hearing the case, reversed the lower courts' decisions and vacated the injunction.

In delivering the opinion of the Court, Chief Justice Roberts stated:

> 'To be prepared for war is one of the most effectual means of preserving peace.' [1 Messages and Papers of the Presidents 57 (J. Richardson comp. 1897)]. So said George Washington in his first Annual Address to Congress, 218 years ago. One of the most important ways the Navy prepares for war is through integrated training exercises at sea. These exercises include training in the use of modern sonar to detect and track enemy submarines, something the Navy has done for the past 40 years.
>
> ...the Court of Appeals upheld a preliminary injunction imposing restrictions on the Navy's sonar training, even though that court acknowledged that "the record contains no evidence that marine mammals have been harmed" by the Navy's exercises.... The Court of Appeals was wrong, and its decision is reversed.[142]

The Chief Justice elaborated:

> President Theodore Roosevelt explained that 'the only way in which a navy can ever be made efficient is by practice at sea, under all the conditions which would have to be met if war existed.' [President's Annual Message, 42 Cong. Rec. 67, 81 (1907)]. We do not discount the importance of plaintiffs' ecological, scientific, and recreational interests in marine mammals. Those interests, however, are plainly outweighed by the Navy's need to conduct realistic training exercises to ensure that it is able to neutralize the threat posed by enemy submarines.[143]

The U.S. Supreme Court recognized the Navy's need to conduct realistic training with active sonar as vital to American national security and held that the need for operational sonar training outweighed the claims of environmental groups

---

[141] Id., at 698–699.
[142] 555 U.S. 7, 12–13 (2008).
[143] Id., at 32.

opposed to sonar use. The landmark decision shapes U.S. law and may have persuasive effect overseas. For example, the *Winter* case was cited by the U.S. District Court for the District of Massachusetts in denying a lawsuit filed by Richard Strahan against the Navy.[144]

In the *Strahan* case, the plaintiff argued that by operating Navy vessels and conducting military training operations in U.S. coastal waters in a manner that kills and injures federally protected whale species, by adversely altering their federally-designated habitats, and by failing to consult with the National Marine Fisheries Service (NMFS) regarding the impact of its operations, the Navy was violating various provisions of the Endangered Species Act (ESA). Accordingly, Strahan asked the court to impose a number of restraints on all Navy ships operating along the Atlantic coastline within the region of responsibility assigned to the NMFS northeast regional office in Gloucester Massachusetts. Specifically, Strahan asked the Federal judge to:

(1) order all Navy ships to comply with the speed limit restrictions imposed by the NMFS on ships in the northeastern Atlantic when exiting or leaving ports;
(2) order the Navy to enter formal consultations with the NMFS over a Navy ship's 2004 killing of a pregnant northern right whale;
(3) order the Navy, in the absence of such consultation, to apply for an incidental "take" permit regarding the "takings" of "large whales" in the region;
(4) prohibit Navy ships from operating faster than 10 knots in the Stellwagens Bank National Marine Sanctuary between June 1 and November 1 each year;
(5) order all Navy ships to operate at least 1,000 yards from any sighted "large whale;"
(6) prohibit Navy ships from operating at speeds faster than 10 knots in any northern right whale critical habitat;
(7) order all Navy ships to post trained lookouts to spot "large whales" when navigating within 100 nautical miles of the coastline, to record the sighting of all "large whales," and to provide a copy of the record to Strahan "on a monthly basis for the duration of these proceedings."[145]

The court noted the case was analogous to the *Winter* case, "in which the Supreme Court held that 'any such injury [was] outweighed by the public interest and the Navy's interest in effective, realistic training of its sailors.'" In deciding in favor of the Navy, the court ruled that "the balance of equities and consideration of the overall public interest in this case tip strongly in favor of the Navy."[146] Strahan's motion for a preliminary injunction was therefore denied.

---

[144] *Strahan v. Roughead*, C.A. No. 08-cv-10919–MLW, 2010 WL 48278 (D.Mass. Nov. 22, 2010).
[145] Id.
[146] Id. citing, *Winter*, 129 S.Ct. at 378.

5.5.2 Navy Mitigation Measures during Sonar Operations

Despite the precedent of the *Winter* decision, environmental groups continue to challenge the Navy's use of sonar during training exercises. In January 2012, for example, a handful of environmental groups, including Earthjustice, the Natural Resources Defense Council, and ten Northern California Native American tribes, filed suit in U.S. Federal District Court in San Francisco to challenge NMFS' decision to approve a five-year Navy plan for expanded use of sonar during naval training exercises in the Pacific Northwest Training Range Complex located off the coast of the state of Washington.

The Navy has trained in the area for 60 years, but the suit claimed that underwater sound produced by Navy sonar harasses and kills whales and other marine mammals. The plaintiffs alleged that repeated use of sonar in breeding and feeding grounds, continuing over a number of years, can drive marine mammals from the area, making it harder for the species reproduce.[147]

In order to advance environmental stewardship, the Navy employs an extensive set of mitigation measures whenever it is using sonar. The mitigation measures are based on science and are designed to protect marine mammals without sacrificing operational capability. Moreover, there remains significant scientific uncertainty over the impact of sonar on marine mammals. For example, worldwide use of active sonar by the U.S. Navy has been correlated with the stranding of approximately 50 whales from 1996 to 2006. That number equates to less than one-quarter of one percent of the 3,500–plus marine mammal strandings that occur each year on U.S. shores alone.[148]

Some Navy ranges like the Hawaii Operating Area, meanwhile, are experiencing an increase in the estimated marine mammal population in the instrumented sonar range. Moreover, the Navy has operated mid-frequency active (MFA) sonar in offshore Southern California training areas for over 40 years without a single documented sonar-related injury to a marine mammal.[149]

The U.S. Navy is a world leader in marine mammal research, funding millions of dollars in research at universities, scientific institutions, and Federal laboratories. Between 2003 and 2008, for example, the Navy contributed over $100 million in marine mammal scientific research. The program of research focuses on the distribution and abundance of protected marine species and their habitats.[150] Scientists are trying to better understand the effects of sound on marine mammals, sea turtles, fish and birds.[151]

---

[147] Gene Johnson, *Groups Sue Over Navy Sonar Use off Northwest Coast*, SEATTLE TIMES, Jan. 26, 2012.
[148] DEP'T OF THE U.S. NAVY FACT SHEET, SONAR AND MARINE MAMMALS (2006).
[149] 555 U.S. 7 (2008).
[150] DEPT' OF THE U.S. NAVY, NAVY'S NEED FOR SONAR AND MARINE MAMMAL PROTECTION EFFORTS, CHIEF OF NAVAL OPERATIONS FACT SHEET (2012).
[151] Id.

The Navy's mitigation measures are publicly available and set forth in the *Final Undersea Warfare Training Range Overseas Environmental Impact Statement* (FOEIS). Chapter 6 of the EIS contains a detailed description of mitigation with respect to acoustic effects on marine animals.[152] Recognizing that use of sensors and weapons may adversely affect some marine mammals, the FOEIS outlines protective measures that have been developed by the Navy to minimize harmful acoustic effects. The measures include steps to mitigate the impact of vessel transits in the vicinity of mid-Atlantic ports during northern right whale migratory seasons and in the vicinity of NMFS-designated critical habitats off the southeastern United States.[153]

Navy sailors undergo extensive training to qualify as a lookout so that they can identify the presence of marine mammals. Lookout training includes apprenticeship with an experienced lookout, followed by completion of a Navy personal qualification program that certifies the individual sailor has acquired the skill to detect and report partially submerged objects, such as marine mammals."[154] Periodically, a two-day refresher course is provided to lookouts. Still, identifying a marine mammal just under the surface of the water from a distance is a daunting task.

Furthermore, lookouts also receive Marine Species Awareness Training (MSAT) to ensure they are integrated into the ship's environmental program. MSAT includes training on marine environmental laws governing the protection of marine species and the Navy's commitment to stewardship.[155] All Commanding Officers, Executive Officers, and officers standing watch on the bridge, maritime patrol aircraft aircrews, and Anti-submarine Warfare (ASW) helicopter crews will complete MSAT material prior to conducting a training activity employing mid-frequency active sonar.[156] Bridge personnel on ships and submarines, as well as sonar personnel on ships, submarines, and ASW aircraft, receive MSAT.[157]

Requirements for ship lookouts are particularly detailed, and include the following directives:

- On the bridge of surface ships, there should always be at least three personnel on watch whose duties include observing the water surface around the vessel.
- In addition to the three personnel on watch on the bridge, all surface ships participating in ASW exercises should have at least two additional personnel on watch as lookouts at all times during the exercises.

---

[152] DEP'T OF THE NAVY, FINAL UNDERSEA WARFARE TRAINING RANGE OVERSEAS ENVIRONMENTAL IMPACT STATEMENT 6.1 (June 26, 2009).
[153] Id., para. 6.2.
[154] Id., para. 6.1.1.
[155] Id.
[156] Id., para. 6.1.2.1.
[157] Id.

MARINE ENVIRONMENTAL PROTECTION AND CONTROL MEASURES   153

- Personnel on lookout and officers on watch on the bridge shall have at least one set of binoculars [per person].
- On surface vessels equipped with mid-frequency active sonar, pedestal-mounted "Big Eye" (20 × 110) binoculars shall be present.
- Personnel on lookout shall follow visual search procedures employing a scanning methodology in accordance with the *Lookout Training Handbook*.
- Surface lookouts should scan the water from the ship to the horizon and be responsible for all contacts in their sector. They should search the entire sector through the binoculars in approximately five-degree steps, pausing between steps for approximately five seconds to scan the field of view.
- After sunset and prior to sunrise, lookouts shall employ Night Lookout Techniques in accordance with the *Lookout Training Handbook*.
- At night, lookouts should not sweep the horizon with their eyes, as eyes do not perceive objects well when they are moving. Lookouts should scan the horizon in a series of short movements that would allow their eyes to come to periodic rests as they scan the sector.
- Personnel on lookout shall be responsible for informing the [Officer of the Deck] of all objects or anomalies sighted in the water (regardless of the distance from the vessel), since any object or disturbance (e.g., trash, periscope, surface disturbance, discoloration) in the water may indicate a threat to the vessel and its crew or the presence of a marine species.[158]

Sonar operating procedures to mitigate potential harm to marine mammals include:

- Helicopters shall survey the vicinity of a planned ASW exercise ten minutes prior to dipping of sonobuoys.
- Commanding officers should make use of marine species detection cues and information to limit interaction with marine species to the maximum extent possible, consistent with the safety of the ship.
- All personnel using all instrumentation capable of passive acoustic sonar operation (including aircraft, surface ships, or submarines) shall monitor for marine mammal vocalizations and report the detection of any marine mammal to the appropriate watch station for dissemination and appropriate action. The Navy can detect sounds within the human hearing range and passive acoustic detection systems are used during all ASW activities.
- Units shall use trained lookouts to survey for marine mammals and sea turtles prior to commencement and during the use of active sonar.
- During operations involving active sonar, personnel shall use all available sensors and optical systems (such as night vision goggles) to aid in the detection of marine mammals.
- Navy aircraft participating in exercises at sea shall conduct and maintain surveillance for marine species of concern.
- Sonobuoys deployed by aircraft shall be used only in the passive mode when marine mammals are detected within 183 meters (600 ft.) of the devices.
- Marine mammal detections by aircraft shall be immediately reported when it is reasonable to conclude that the course of the ship will likely close the distance between the ship and a detected marine mammal.

---

[158] Id., para. 6.1.2.2.

154   CHAPTER FIVE

- When marine mammals are detected by any means (aircraft, shipboard lookout, or acoustically) within 914 meters (3,000 ft.) of the sonar dome (the bow), the ship or submarine shall limit active transmission levels to at least 6 decibels (dB) below normal operating levels.
- Ships and submarines shall continue to limit maximum transmission levels by a 6 dB factor until the animal has been seen to leave the area, has not been detected for 30 minutes, or the vessel has transited more than 1,829 meters (6,000 ft.) beyond the location of the last detection.
- Should a marine mammal be detected within 457 meters (1,500 ft.) of the sonar dome, active sonar transmissions shall be limited to at least 10 dB below the equipment's normal operating level. Ships and submarines shall continue to limit maximum ping levels by a 10 dB factor until the animal has been seen to leave the area, has not been detected for 30 minutes, or the vessel has transited more than 1,829 m (6,000 ft.) beyond the location of the last detection.
- Should the marine mammal be detected within 183 m (600 ft.) of the sonar dome, active sonar transmissions shall cease. Sonar shall not resume until the animal has been seen to leave the area, has not been detected for 30 minutes, or the vessel has transited more than 1,829 meters (6,000 ft.) beyond the location of the last detection.
- Prior to start up or restart of active sonar, operators shall check that the shut down zone radius around the sound source is clear of marine mammals.
- Sonar levels: The Navy should operate sonar at the lowest practicable level, not to exceed 235 dB, except as required to meet tactical training objectives.
- Helicopters shall not dip their sonar within 183 meters (600 ft.) of a marine mammal and should cease pinging if a marine mammal closes within 183 meters (600 ft.) after pinging has begun.[159]

In summary, the U.S. Navy has taken extensive steps toward protecting marine life from the potential impact of sonar. The Navy exercises caution when operating in areas likely to contain marine mammals and implements a series of mitigation measures to minimize potential effect on marine mammals. While these protocols can never be perfect, they represent the most extensive measures undertaken by any civilian or naval force to ameliorate the potential effects of underwater sound on marine mammals.

---

[159] Id., para. 6.1.2.3.

SIX

U.S. SAFETY AND SECURITY ZONES AND AIRSPACE CONTROL MEASURES

6.1 INTRODUCTION TO U.S. ZONES

States employ a variety of maritime zones and other control measures in waters and airspace adjacent to their coasts or on the high seas to enhance safety of navigation and overflight, or to heighten the security and safety of their naval and air forces operating in the global commons. Because these zones and other measures are normally used to restrict or control access to a specified geographic area, the United States exercises care to ensure that they are implemented in a manner that is consistent with international law.

In peacetime, maritime zones and other control measures normally are used to improve the safety of air and surface navigation, control access to national airspace and internal waters, preserve and protect the marine environment, and augment physical security at port facilities, harbor works, and off-shore structures and installations. In times of heightened tensions, control measures can be employed to enhance force protection measures and the self-defense posture of ships in port or at sea. Maritime zones are used in time of war to exercise control over an area at sea, manage the battle space, seal off enemy ports and airfields, and to keep neutral vessels and aircraft out of harm's way or from interference with belligerent operations.

U.S. laws and regulations authorize various government agencies to employ a variety of zones and use other designated areas to regulate and control maritime surface and air traffic in internal waters, territorial sea, and national airspace. Maritime measures used by the United States include safety zones, security zones, regulated navigation areas, naval vessel protection zones, restricted waterfront areas, danger zones, restricted areas, naval defensive sea areas, naval airspace reservations, areas placed under the Secretary of the Navy for administrative purposes, and the Trust Territory of the Pacific Islands.

U.S. Coast Guard Maritime safety and security teams (MSST) can be used to enforce these zones and areas.[1] MSSTs are designed to enhance U.S. maritime security, and their missions include protecting "vessels, harbors, ports, facilities, and cargo in waters subject to the jurisdiction of the United States from destruction, loss or injury from crime, or sabotage due to terrorist activity...."[2] Each MSST may be used to:

(1) deter, protect against, and rapidly respond to threats of maritime terrorism;
(2) enforce moving or fixed safety or security zones established pursuant to law;
(3) conduct high speed intercepts;
(4) board, search, and seizure any vessel or facility;
(5) rapidly deploy to supplement the U.S. armed forces domestically or overseas;
(6) respond to criminal or terrorist acts within a port;
(7) assist with facility vulnerability assessments; and
(8) carry out any other missions of the Coast Guard.[3]

To the extent feasible, MSSTs will coordinate their activities with other Federal, state and local law enforcement and emergency response agencies.

6.2 Jurisdiction over the Navigable Waters of the United States

The Ports and Waterways Safety Act (PWSA) authorizes enactment and enforcement of zones and other control measures to regulate U.S. and foreign-flag shipping in U.S. navigable waters, as well as to control access to and security of U.S. ports, harbors and other coastal facilities.[4]

6.2.1 *Ports and Waterways Safety Act*

The Ports and Waterways Safety Act (PWSA) is a cornerstone authority, and it provides:

(a) that navigation and vessel safety, protection of the marine environment, and safety and security of United States ports and waterways are matters of major national importance;
(b) that increased vessel traffic in the Nation's ports and waterways creates substantial hazard to life, property, and the marine environment;
(c) that increased supervision of vessel and port operations is necessary in order to
   (1) reduce the possibility of vessel or cargo loss, or damage to life, property, or the marine environment;

---

[1] 46 U.S.C. § 70106 (2011).
[2] The teams operate in support of the Maritime Transportation Security Plan. Id., § 70103 (2011).
[3] Id., § 70106(b) (2011).
[4] The Ports and Waterways Safety Act or the Act of June 15, 1917, 33 U.S.C. §§ 1221–1236 (2012), *as amended by* the Magnuson Act (50 U.S.C. §§ 191–195) and § 104 of the Maritime Transportation Security Act of 2002 (Pub. L. 107–295).

(2) prevent damage to structures in, on, or immediately adjacent to the navigable waters of the United States or the resources within such waters;
(3) insure that vessels operating in the navigable waters of the United States shall comply with all applicable standards and requirements for vessel construction, equipment, manning, and operational procedures; and
(4) insure that the handling of dangerous articles and substances on the structures in, on, or immediately adjacent to the navigable waters of the United States is conducted in accordance with established standards and requirements; and
(d) that advance planning is critical in determining proper and adequate protective measures for the Nation's ports and waterways and the marine environment, with continuing consultation with other Federal agencies, state representatives, affected users, and the general public, in the development and implementation of such measures.[5]

6.2.2 *Presidential Proclamation No. 5928*

The "navigable waters of the United States" are defined as "all waters of the territorial sea of the United States as described in Presidential Proclamation No. 5928 of December 27, 1988."[6] Presidential Proclamation 5928 extended the U.S. territorial sea from 3 to 12 nautical miles:

Presidential Proclamation No. 5928, December 27, 1988

Territorial Sea of the United States of America

International law recognizes that coastal nations may exercise sovereignty and jurisdiction over their territorial seas.

The territorial sea of the United States is a maritime zone extending beyond the land territory and internal waters of the United States over which the United States exercises sovereignty and jurisdiction, a sovereignty and jurisdiction that extends to the airspace over the territorial sea, as well as to its bed and subsoil.

Extension of the territorial sea by the United States to the limits permitted by international law will advance the national security and other significant interests of the United States.

NOW, THEREFORE, I, RONALD REAGAN...do hereby proclaim the extension of the territorial sea of the United States of America, the Commonwealth of Puerto Rico, Guam, American Samoa, the United States Virgin Islands, the Commonwealth of the Northern Mariana Islands....

The territorial sea of the United States henceforth extends to 12 nautical miles from the baselines of the United States determined in accordance with international law.

In accordance with international law, as reflected in the applicable provisions of the 1982 United Nations Convention on the Law of the Sea, within the territorial sea of the United States, the ships of all countries enjoy the right of innocent passage

---

[5] 33 U.S.C. § 1221.
[6] Id., § 1222(5).

and the ships and aircraft of all countries enjoy the right of transit passage through international straits.[7]

Vessel traffic services, which consist of measures for controlling or supervising vessel traffic or for protecting navigation and preserving the marine environment, may be established in any port or place under U.S. jurisdiction or in U.S. navigable waters.[8] These services also may be established in any area covered by an international agreement, and may include reporting and operating requirements, surveillance and communications systems, routing systems and fairways.[9]

If the Secretary of Homeland Security determines that an area is hazardous or has reduced visibility, adverse weather, vessel congestion or other hazardous circumstances, then vessel traffic within U.S. jurisdiction may be controlled by specifying times of entry, movement, or departure, and establishing vessel traffic routing schemes, vessel size, speed, draft limitations and vessel operation conditions.[10]

Furthermore, as a condition of port entry, ships may be required to provide a pre-arrival message "in sufficient time to permit advance vessel traffic planning prior to port entry, which shall include any information which is not already a matter of record and which the Secretary [of Homeland Security] determines necessary for the control of the vessel and the safety of the port or the marine environment."[11]

Under certain circumstances, the Secretary of Homeland Security may order any vessel, in a port or place subject to U.S. jurisdiction or in U.S. navigable waters, to operate or anchor in a manner he directs if:

> (1) he has reasonable cause to believe such vessel does not comply with any regulation issued under [Title 33, Chapter 25, Ports and Waterways Safety Program] or any other applicable law or treaty;
> (2) he determines that such vessel does not satisfy the conditions for port entry set forth in section 1228 [relating to a history of accidents or vessel incidents, unlawful pollution, or unlicensed seafarers on board the ship] of the PWSA; or
> (3) by reason of weather, visibility, sea conditions, port congestion, other hazardous circumstances, or the condition of such vessel, he is satisfied that such directive is justified in the interest of safety.[12]

In order to provide safe access routes for the movement of vessel traffic proceeding to or from ports of places subject to U.S. jurisdiction, the Secretary of Homeland Security is also authorized to designate necessary fairways and traffic separation schemes (TSS) for vessels operating in the U.S. territorial sea and in

---

[7] PRESIDENT RONALD REAGAN, PRES. PROC. NO. 5928, TERRITORIAL SEA OF THE UNITED STATES, Dec. 27, 1988, 54 FR 777, Jan. 9, 1989.
[8] 33 U.S.C. § 1223(a)(1).
[9] Id., § 1230.
[10] Id., § 1223(a)(4).
[11] Id., § 1223(a)(5).
[12] Id., § 1223(b).

high seas approaches to ports.[13] Within these routes, the right of navigation takes precedence over all other uses. When designating access routes, the Secretary of Homeland Security is also required to issue regulations governing the use of such areas.[14] Finally, the Secretary shall notify the International Maritime Organization (IMO) of any designation and "take action to seek the cooperation of foreign States in making it mandatory for vessels under their control to use any fairway or traffic separation scheme designated ... in any area of the high seas...." to the same extent as required for U.S. vessels.[15] The Secretary has authority to conduct negotiations for agreements to establish vessel traffic services in the high seas.[16]

Consistent with international law, the PWSA does not apply automatically to foreign vessels conducting innocent passage through the territorial sea or transit passage through an international strait, and that are not destined for, or departing from, a U.S. port or place.[17]

The Secretary of Homeland Security is also authorized by the PWSA to "take any action necessary to prevent damage to, or the destruction of, any bridge or other structure on or in the navigable waters of the United States [as well as nearby land structures ashore] and to protect the navigable waters and waterfront infrastructure from harm."[18] The Secretary may take security measures to prevent or respond to an act of terrorism against any U.S. person or vessel, or an "individual, vessel, or public or commercial structure, that is subject to the jurisdiction of the United States, and located within or adjacent to the marine environment."[19]

The Secretary of Homeland Security may "... deny entry into the navigable waters of the United States, to any port or place under the jurisdiction of the United States or to any vessel not in compliance with the provisions of [Chapter 25 on the Ports and Waterways Safety Program]."[20] Consistent with a liberal understanding of the norm of distress entry, vessels may be exempt from the U.S. entry prohibitions if their owner or operator "proves, to the satisfaction of the Secretary, that such vessel is not unsafe or a threat to the marine environment, and if such entry is necessary for the safety of the vessel or persons aboard."[21]

The PWSA also includes enforcement authority.[22] Civil penalties for violation of the statute may not to exceed $25,000 for each violation, with each day a continuing violation constituting a separate basis for the fine.[23] Moreover, any

---

[13] Id., § 1223(c)(1).
[14] Id., § 1223(c)(5)(A) and (B).
[15] Id., § 1223(c)(5)(D).
[16] Id., § 1223(b).
[17] Id., § 1223(d).
[18] Id., § 1225(a).
[19] Id., § 1226(b).
[20] Id., § 1232(e).
[21] Id., § 1228(b).
[22] Id., §§ 1223(a)(2), 1227 and 1232.
[23] Id., § 1232(a).

vessel that "is used in violation of [Chapter 25 or its associated regulations] shall be liable *in rem* for any civil penalty assessed."[24] Criminal sanctions for violations may be as high as a class D felony [carrying a sentence of 5–10 years imprisonment]."[25] A person prosecuted under the PWSA who violates the Act using "a dangerous weapon, or engages in conduct that causes bodily injury or fear of imminent bodily injury to any officer authorized to enforce the provisions of [the] chapter…commits a class C felony [that carries a sentence of 10–25 years imprisonment]."[26]

The Secretary of Homeland Security has authority to issue regulations necessary to implement the Ports and Waterways Safety Act. The regulations are found in Part 165 of Title 33 Code of Federal Regulations (C.F.R.) and contain procedures for establishing limited or controlled access areas and regulated navigation areas.[27]

A safety zone, security zone, or regulated area may be established by any authorized Coast Guard official, such as the Captain of the Port (COTP). Any person may submit a request in writing to the COTP or the Coast Guard District Commander to request establishment of a safety zone, security zone, or regulated area.[28] The Coast Guard district commanders have plenary authority to issue regulations over the navigable waters of the United States. These one or two-star admirals are empowered to issue regulations to control vessel traffic in areas they determine contain hazardous conditions. The authority extends to:

(a) Specifying times of vessel entry, movement, or departure to, from, within, or through ports, harbors, or other waters;
(b) Establishing vessel size, speed, draft limitations, and operating conditions; and
(c) Restricting vessel operation, in a hazardous area or under hazardous conditions, to vessels which have particular operating characteristics or capabilities which are considered necessary for safe operation under the circumstances.[29]

6.3 Safety Zones

The United States defines a safety zone as "a water area, shore area, or water and shore area to which, for safety or environmental purposes, access is limited to authorized persons, vehicles, or vessels."[30] Safety zones are created under the authority of the PWSA and may be established in waters subject to U.S. jurisdic-

---

[24] Id., § 1232(c).
[25] Id., § 1232(b)(1).
[26] Id., § 1232(b)(2). *See also*, 33 C.F.R. Part 165. Specific areas and their boundaries are also listed in 33 C.F.R. Part 334.
[27] 33 U.S.C. § 1231(a) and 33 C.F.R. § 165.1.
[28] 33 C.F.R. § 165.5.
[29] Id., § 165.11.
[30] Id., § 165.20.

tion, including the territorial sea. The zones "may be stationary and described by fixed limits or...described as a zone around a vessel in motion."[31]

Safety zones also may be established around artificial installations and structures located on the continental shelf.[32] Consistent with UNCLOS, Article 60, safety zones established around continental shelf facilities may not exceed 500 meters distance beyond the facility and "may not interfere with the use of recognized sea lanes essential to navigation."[33]

The safety zones of Apra Harbor, Guam and Boxer Platform on the continental shelf, for example, are described below:

§ 165.1401   Apra Harbor, Guam—safety zones.

(a) The following is designated as Safety Zone A—The waters of the Pacific Ocean and Apra Outer Harbor encompassed within an arc of 725 yards radius centered at the center of Wharf H.

(b) The following is designated Safety Zone B—The waters of Apra Outer Harbor encompassed within an arc of 680 yards radius centered at the center of Naval Wharf Kilo....

(c) Special regulations. (1) Section 165.23 does not apply to Safety Zone A and/or Safety Zone B, except when Wharf H and/or Naval Wharf Kilo, or a vessel berthed at Wharf H and/or Naval Wharf Kilo, is displaying a red (BRAVO) flag by day or a red light by night.

(2) In accordance with the general regulations in 165.23 of this part, entry into these zones is prohibited unless authorized by the Captain of the Port, Guam.[34]

* * *

§ 147.801   Boxer Platform safety zone.

(a) Description. The Boxer Platform is located at position 27°56'48" N, 90°59'48" W. The area within 500 meters (1640.4 feet) from each point on the structure's outer edge, not to extend into the adjacent East—West Gulf of Mexico Fairway is a safety zone.

(b) Regulation. No vessel may enter or remain in this safety zone except:
1. An attending vessel;
2. A vessel under 100 feet in length overall not engaged in towing; or
3. A vessel authorized by the Commander, Eighth Coast Guard District.[35]

In general, unless otherwise provided by law or regulation, no person may enter a safety zone, bring or cause to be brought into a safety zone any vehicle, vessel or object, or remain in a safety zone or allow any vehicle, vessel or object to remain in a safety zone unless authorized by the COTP or the District Commander.[36]

---

[31] Id., §§ 165.9(b) and 165.20.
[32] Id., § 147.1.
[33] Id., § 147.15.
[34] COTP Guam Reg. 89–001, 55 FR 18725, May 4, 1990.
[35] Coast Guard District 08–99–023, Safety Zone: Outer Continental Shelf Platforms in the Gulf of Mexico. Final Rule, 65 FR 16825, Mar. 30, 2000.
[36] 33 C.F.R. § 165.23.

6.4 Security Zones

The PWSA also provides authority to create offshore security zones.[37] Security zones may be established in waters subject to the jurisdiction of the United States, including the territorial sea, which for purposes of the Act extends to three nautical miles from the shoreline. A security zone is defined as "an area of land, water, or land and water which is so designated by the [COTP] or District Commander for such time as is necessary to prevent damage or injury to any vessel or waterfront facility, to safeguard ports, harbors, territories, or waters of the United States, or to secure the observance of the rights and obligations of the United States."[38] The purpose of a security zone is "to safeguard from destruction, loss, or injury from sabotage or other subversive acts, accidents, or other causes of a similar nature... vessels, harbors, ports, and waterfront facilities... subject to the jurisdiction of the United States."[39]

Under the PWSA, as amended by the Magnuson Act, security zones regulating anchorage and movement of vessels may be established during a declared national emergency.

> Whenever the President by proclamation or Executive order declares a national emergency to exist by reason of actual or threatened war, insurrection, or invasion, or disturbance or threatened disturbance of the international relations of the United States, or whenever the Attorney General determines that an actual or anticipated mass migration of aliens en route to, or arriving off the coast of, the United States presents urgent circumstances requiring an immediate Federal response, the Secretary of Transportation may make, subject to the approval of the President, rules and regulations governing the anchorage and movement of any vessel, foreign or domestic, in the territorial waters of the United States...

> [The President is also] authorized to institute... regulations to govern the anchorage and movement of any foreign-flag vessels in the territorial waters of the United States, to inspect such vessels at any time, to place guards thereon, and... take for such purposes full possession and control of such vessels and remove therefrom the officers and crew thereof....[40]

For example, a security zone was established in 1996 by President William J. Clinton following the shoot-down by a Cuban fighter jet aircraft of two unarmed, U.S.-registered civilian aircraft flying in international airspace. The planes were looking for Cuban rafters in the Florida Straits when they were attacked by the

---

[37] Id., § 165.9(c) and Ports and Waterways Safety Act or the Act of June 15, 1917, *as amended by* the Magnuson Act (50 U.S.C. §§ 191–195) and § 104 of the Maritime Transportation Security Act of 2002 (Pub. L. 107–295).
[38] 33 C.F.R. § 165.30(a).
[39] Id., § 165.30(b).
[40] 50 U.S.C. § 191.

Cuban fighter jets. Four members of "Brothers to the Rescue," a Miami-based Cuban exile group, were killed in the attack.[41]

In response to the incident, President Clinton established a security zone to regulate the anchorage and movement of vessels in the U.S. territorial sea:

> ... NOW, THEREFORE, I, WILLIAM J. CLINTON, ... find and do hereby proclaim that a national emergency does exist by reason of a disturbance or threatened disturbance of international relations. In order to address this national emergency and to secure the observance of the rights and obligations of the United States, I hereby authorize and direct the Secretary of Transportation ... to regulate the anchorage and movement of vessels....
>
> ... which may be used, or [are] susceptible of being used, for voyage into Cuban territorial waters and that may create unsafe conditions and threaten a disturbance of international relations....
>
> ... to inspect any vessel, foreign or domestic, in the territorial waters of the United States, at any time; to place guards on any such vessel; and, with my consent expressly hereby granted, take full possession and control of any such vessel and remove the officers and crew....[42]

The scope of the national emergency declared by President Clinton in Proclamation 6867 was expanded by President Bush in February 2004 in order to deny monetary and material support to the Cuban Government."[43] President Bush made a determination that Cuba was a state sponsor of terrorism and that the government in Havana had "demonstrated a ready and reckless willingness to use excessive force, including deadly force, against U.S. citizens...."[44] Thus, entry of U.S. vessels into Cuban territorial waters was considered dangerous and "could threaten a disturbance of international relations."[45] Accordingly, the President placed Cuban territorial waters off limits to U.S.-flagged or registered vessels. The Presidential Proclamation stated:

> NOW, THEREFORE, I, GEORGE W. BUSH ... hereby authorize and direct the Secretary of Homeland Security to make ... regulate the anchorage and movement of vessels, and authorize and approve the Secretary's issuance of such rules....

---

[41] *Cuban Pilots Charged with Murder*, CNN JUSTICE, Aug. 22, 2003.
[42] PRESIDENT WILLIAM J. CLINTON, PRES. PROC. NO. 6867, DECLARATION OF NATIONAL EMERGENCY AND INVOCATION OF EMERGENCY AUTHORITY RELATING TO THE REGULATION OF THE ANCHORAGE AND MOVEMENT OF VESSELS, Mar. 1, 1996, 61 FR 8843, Mar. 5, 1996.
[43] PRESIDENT GEORGE W. BUSH, PRES. PROC. NO. 7757, EXPANDING THE SCOPE OF THE NATIONAL EMERGENCY AND INVOCATION OF EMERGENCY AUTHORITY RELATING TO THE REGULATION OF THE ANCHORAGE AND MOVEMENT OF VESSELS INTO CUBAN TERRITORIAL WATERS, Feb. 26, 2004, 69 FR 9515, Mar. 1, 2004.
[44] Id.
[45] Id.

> Section 1. The Secretary may make rules... governing the anchorage and movement of any vessel, foreign or domestic, in the territorial waters of the United States, which may be used, or is susceptible of being used, for voyage into Cuban territorial waters and that may create unsafe conditions, or result in unauthorized transactions....
>
> Section 2. The Secretary is authorized to inspect any vessel, foreign or domestic, in the territorial waters of the United States, at any time; to place guards on any such vessel; and, with my consent expressly hereby granted, take full possession and control of any such vessel and remove the officers and crew....[46]

As directed by the President, the Secretary of Homeland Security issued the following regulations governing the anchorage and movement of vessels into Cuban territorial waters:

> In furtherance of the purposes of Presidential Proclamation 7757, the Commandant of the United States Coast Guard, and subject to the direction of the Commandant, the Commanders of Coast Guard Areas or Districts... are directed and authorized to regulate the anchorage and movement of any vessel, foreign or domestic, in the territorial waters of the United States which may be used, or is susceptible of being used, for voyage into Cuban territorial waters and that may create unsafe conditions, or result in unauthorized transactions, and thereby threaten a disturbance of international relations..., including, but not limited to, inspection of any vessel, foreign or domestic, in the territorial waters of the United States, at any time; and placing guards on any such vessel; taking full possession and control of any such vessel and removing the officers and crew....[47]

The national emergency declared by Proclamation 6867 was also extended by President Barack Obama on February 23, 2012, after he determined that "[t]he Cuban government has not demonstrated that it will refrain from the use of excessive force against U.S. vessels or aircraft that may engage in memorial activities or peaceful protest north of Cuba."[48] Unauthorized entry of U.S.-registered vessels into Cuban territorial waters, however, is considered detrimental to U.S. foreign policy. Therefore, in accordance with section 202(d) of the National Emergencies Act,[49] President Obama continued the national emergency with respect to Cuba and the emergency authority relating to the regulation of the anchorage and movement of vessels set out in Proclamation 6867, and as amended previously by Presidential Proclamation 7757.[50]

---

[46] Id.
[47] DEP'T OF HOMELAND SECURITY, ORDER GOVERNING THE ANCHORAGE AND MOVEMENT OF VESSELS INTO CUBAN TERRITORIAL WATERS, 69 FR 41366, DHS 19–04, July 8, 2004.
[48] PRESIDENT BARACK OBAMA, CONTINUATION OF THE NATIONAL EMERGENCY WITH RESPECT TO CUBA AND THE EMERGENCY AUTHORITY RELATING TO THE REGULATION OF THE ANCHORAGE AND MOVEMENT OF VESSELS, Feb. 23, 2012, 77 FR 11379, Feb. 24, 2012.
[49] 50 U.S.C. § 1622(d) (2012).
[50] PRESIDENT BARACK OBAMA, CONTINUATION OF THE NATIONAL EMERGENCY WITH RESPECT TO CUBA AND THE EMERGENCY AUTHORITY RELATING TO THE REGULATION

No person or vessel may enter or remain in a security zone without the permission of the Captain of the Port, unless otherwise authorized by law. Persons and vessels within a security zone are under a legal obligation to comply with any direction or order of the COTP, who is authorized to take possession and control of any vessel found in a zone, as well as remove any person, vessel, article, or thing from a security zone.[51] Failure to obey PWSA security zone regulations can result in seizure and forfeiture of the offending vessel, as well as imposition of criminal fines of up to $10,000, and/or imprisonment for up to 10 years.[52] Civil penalties are also extensive, and may amount to up to $25,000 for each violation.[53]

6.4.1 Regulated Navigation Areas and Restricted Waterfront Areas

Regulated navigation areas are created under the authority of the Ports and Waterways Safety Act and may be established in waters subject to U.S. jurisdiction, including the territorial sea, out to a distance of three nautical miles.[54] A regulated navigation area is defined as "a water area within a defined boundary for which regulations for vessels navigating within the area have been established. . . ."[55] Vessels operating in a regulated navigation area may do so only in accordance with regulations issued by the Secretary of Homeland Security.[56] Acting on behalf of the Secretary, the Commandant of the Coast Guard can direct a COTP "to prevent access to waterfront facilities, and port and harbor areas, including vessels and harbor craft therein."[57]

6.4.1.1 Naval Vessel Protection Zones

Following the terrorist attacks on the World Trade Center and the Pentagon on September 11, 2001, the Navy became concerned that its warships operating in

---

OF THE ANCHORAGE AND MOVEMENT OF VESSELS, Feb. 23, 2012, 77 FR 11379, Feb. 24, 2012 and PRESIDENT BARACK OBAMA, CONTINUATION OF THE NATIONAL EMERGENCY RELATING TO CUBA AND OF THE EMERGENCY AUTHORITY RELATING TO THE REGULATION OF ANCHORAGE AND MOVEMENT OF VESSELS, 75 FR 8793, Feb. 23, 2010. The National Emergencies Act provides that "any national emergency declared by the President . . . , and not otherwise previously terminated, shall terminate on the anniversary of the declaration of that emergency if, within the ninety-day period prior to each anniversary date, the President does not publish in the Federal Register and transmit to the Congress a notice stating that such emergency is to continue in effect after such anniversary." National Emergencies Act, 50 U.S.C. § 1622(d) (2012).

[51] 33 U.S.C. § 165.33.
[52] 50 U.S.C. § 192(a) and (b).
[53] Id., § 192(c). Each day of a continuing violation constitutes a separate violation for purposes of computation of the penalty. Id.
[54] 33 C.F.R. § 165.9(b).
[55] Id., § 165.10.
[56] Id., § 165.13.
[57] Id., § 165.40.

U.S. waters were particularly vulnerable to a terrorist attack. One year earlier, the devastating attack on the *USS Cole* (DDG 67) in Aden, Yemen, by Al Qaeda terrorists was a stark wake-up call that perhaps the greatest danger to high value U.S. warships and submarines was a very low-technology threat. The Chief of Naval Operations and the Office of the Judge Advocate General of the Navy, working in conjunction with U.S. Coast Guard Headquarters, developed Naval Vessel Protection Zones (NVPZs) that authorize Coast Guard COTPs to control vessel traffic in the vicinity of U.S. warships. NVPZs have been established in both the Atlantic Area[58] and Pacific Area.[59]

NVPZs are a key counter-terrorism tool to protect high value, national assets and crews on submarines and warships. The NVPZ legislation states that the Secretary of Homeland Security "may control the anchorage and movement of any vessel in the navigable waters of the United States to ensure the safety or security of any United States naval vessel in those waters."[60]

The NVPZ is a 500-yard protective regulatory "bubble" surrounding large U.S. naval vessels, which are defined as ships or submarines greater than 100 feet in length.[61] The zone exists whether the naval vessel is "underway, anchored, moored, or within a floating dry dock, except when the ... naval vessel is moored or anchored within a restricted area or within a naval defensive sea area."[62] The term "U.S. naval vessel" includes "any vessel owned, operated, chartered, or leased by the U.S. Navy; any pre-commissioned vessel under construction for the U.S. Navy, once launched into the water; and any vessel under the operational control of the U.S. Navy or a Combatant Command."[63] Violations of NVPZ orders, such as refusal to make way for a warship, are at 33 U.S.C. § 1232.[64]

Traffic regulations in the zones supplement, but do not replace, other rules pertaining to the safety and security of U.S. naval vessels.[65] For example, the Collision Regulations (COLREGs) always apply within a NVPZ.[66]

Any Coast Guard commissioned, warrant or petty officer may enforce the rules and regulations pertaining to NVPZs.[67] In some cases, even U.S. naval officers may exercise authority under the statute. Where immediate action is required and Coast Guard representatives are not present or are not present in sufficient force to exercise effective control of a NVPZ, "the senior naval officer present in command may control the anchorage or movement of any vessel in the navigable

---

[58] Id., § 165.2025.
[59] Id., § 165.2030.
[60] 14 U.S.C. § 91.
[61] 33 C.F.R. § 165.2015.
[62] Id., § 165.2025(b) and § 165.2030(b).
[63] Id., § 165.2015.
[64] 14 U.S.C. § 91(c).
[65] Id., § 633. *See also,* 33 C.F.R. § 165.2010.
[66] 33 C.F.R. § 165.2025(c) and § 165.2030(c).
[67] Id., § 165.2020(a).

waters of the United States to ensure the safety and security of any United States naval vessel under the officer's command."[68] This grant of authority also includes assisting any Coast Guard enforcement personnel who are present.[69] Unless otherwise designated by competent authority, the "senior naval officer present in command" is "the senior line officer of the U.S. Navy on active duty, eligible for command at sea, who is present and in command of any part of the Department of Navy in the area."[70] The provision is interesting because it carves out a limited area in which an officer of the military forces may exercise control over civilians, or even civil authorities, inside the internal waters or territorial sea of the United States. Normally, American civil-military culture and the statutory prohibitions of the Posse Comitatus Act and 10 U.S.C. § 375 prohibit the military from exercising law enforcement functions inside the United States.[71]

All vessels within 500 yards of a U.S. naval vessel must operate at the minimum speed necessary to maintain a safe course, unless required to maintain speed by the COLREGS, and "shall proceed as directed by the Coast Guard, the senior naval officer present in command or the official patrol."[72] "Official patrols" include all "personnel designated and supervised by a senior naval officer present in command and tasked to monitor a naval vessel protection zone, permit entry into the zone, give legally enforceable orders to persons or vessels within the zone, and take other actions authorized by the U.S. Navy."[73]

In no case are other vessels allowed within 100 yards of a U.S. naval vessel, unless authorized by the Coast Guard, the senior officer present in command or the official patrol.[74] Vessels requesting to pass within 100 yards of a U.S. naval vessel must contact the Coast Guard, the senior naval officer present in command, or the official patrol on VHF-FM channel 16, in order to obtain permission.[75] Under appropriate circumstances, the Coast Guard, the senior naval officer present in command or the official patrol may:

---

[68] 14 U.S.C. § 91(b); 33 C.F.R. § 2020(b).
[69] 33 C.F.R. § 2020(b).
[70] Id., § 165.2015.
[71] 18 U.S.C. § 1385 (P.L. 112–123), Use of the Army and Air Force as a Posse Comitatus (May 31, 2012). The Act states:
   Whoever, except in cases and under circumstances expressly authorized by the Constitution or Act of Congress, willfully uses any part of the Army or the Air Force as a posse comitatus or otherwise to execute the laws shall be fined under this title or imprisoned not more than two years, or both.
The Air Force was added to the statute in 1956. The Navy and Marine Corps are not specifically included in the Act, but they are made subject to it by Department of Defense regulation, 32 C.F.R § 213.2.
[72] Id., § 165.2025(d) and § 165.2030(d).
[73] Id., § 165.2015.
[74] Id., § 165.2025(d) and § 165.2030(d).
[75] Id., § 165.2025(e) and § 165.2030(e).

... Permit vessels constrained by their navigational draft or restricted in their ability to maneuver to pass within 100 yards of a large U.S. naval vessel in order to ensure a safe passage in accordance with the Navigation Rules; and

... Permit commercial vessels anchored in a designated anchorage area to remain at anchor when within 100 yards of passing large U.S. naval vessels; and

... Permit vessels that must transit via a navigable channel or waterway to pass within 100 yards of a moored or anchored large U.S. naval vessel with minimal delay consistent with security.[76]

Although restrictive in nature, the effects of NVPZs on freedom of navigation for civil and commercial craft is minimal because the zones are limited in size, and the enforcement authorities may allow access to the zone. Furthermore, the NVPZs apply only in the "navigable waters of the United States," which include only internal waters and territorial seas. Since the zones follow or adhere to naval warships, they move with the ship and therefore are not permanent.

6.4.1.2 Restricted Areas and Danger Zones

The Secretary of the Army is authorized by 33 U.S.C. § 1 to administer and regulate use of U.S. "navigable waters" as may be necessary "for the protection of life and property ... covering all matters not specifically delegated by law to some other executive department." Under authority granted in 33 U.S.C. § 3, the Secretary may, in the interest of national defense and for the protection of life and property on U.S. navigable waters, prescribe

> such regulations as he may deem best for the use and navigation of any portion or area of the navigable waters of the United States or waters under the jurisdiction of the United States endangered or likely to be endangered by Artillery fire in target practice or otherwise, or by the proving operations of the Government ordnance proving grounds at Sandy Hook, New Jersey, or at any Government ordnance proving ground that may be established elsewhere on or near such waters, and of any portion or area of said waters occupied by submarine mines, mine fields, submarine cables, or other material and accessories pertaining to seacoast fortifications, or by any plant or facility engaged in the execution of any public project of river and harbor improvement....

Violators of regulations issued under 33 U.S.C. § 1 or 33 U.S.C. § 3 may be fined up to $500.00 or imprisoned up to six months.

Likewise, the Army Corps of Engineers has authority to establish restricted areas and danger zones.[77] A danger zone is "a defined water area (or areas) used for target practice, bombing, rocket firing or other especially hazardous operations, normally for the armed forces."[78] Such zones may be closed to the public

---

[76] Id., § 165.2025(f) and § 165.2030(f).
[77] Id., § 334.1.
[78] Id., § 334.2(a).

on a full-time or intermittent basis. A restricted area is "a defined water area for the purpose of prohibiting or limiting public access to the area."[79] These areas are used to "provide security for Government property and/or protection to the public from the risks of damage or injury arising from the Government's use of that area."[80]

Although entry into restricted areas and danger zones is normally controlled, regulations establishing such zones "shall provide for public access to the area to the maximum extent practicable."[81] Establishment of such areas may not "unreasonably interfere with or restrict the food fishing industry."[82] Use of restricted and danger areas shall be notified to the public (and other interested Federal, state and local officials) at least two weeks prior to the planned event by the agency requesting use of the water area through an appropriate notice to mariners (NOTMAR) requesting that vessels avoid the area.[83]

Over 175 restricted areas and danger areas have been established by the U.S. Government in U.S. navigable waters pursuant to 33 U.S.C. §§ 1 and 3. For example, a number of restricted areas and danger zones have been established around the Hawaiian Islands to ensure military training and exercises are carried out consistent with safety of navigation and overflight. In the following examples, the latitude and longitude coordinates of the zones are omitted.

a. *Pacific Ocean, Hawaii; danger zones*

    (a) Danger zones—
        (1) Aerial bombing and strafing target surrounding Kaula Rock, Hawaii. The waters within a circular area with a radius of three (3) miles having its center on Kaula Rock....
        (2) Submerged unexploded ordnance danger zone, Kahoolawe Island, Hawaii. The waters adjacent to Kahoolawe Island within the area encompassed by [the coordinates].
    (b) The regulations. No person, vessel or other craft shall enter or remain in any of the areas at any time except as authorized by the enforcing agency.
    (c) Enforcing agency. The regulations in this section shall be enforced by Commander, Naval Base, Pearl Harbor, Hawaii 96860–5020, and such agencies as he/she may designate.[84]

b. *Pacific Ocean, Island of Oahu, Hawaii; danger zone*

    (a) The danger zone. Beginning at point of origin at Kaena Point Light...thence along the arc of a circle centered at Kaena Point Light to...thence to point of origin.

---

[79] Id., § 334.2(b).
[80] Id.
[81] Id., § 334.3(a).
[82] Id., § 334.3(b).
[83] Id., § 334.3(c).
[84] Id., § 334.1340.

(b) The regulations.
  (1) The area will be closed to the public and all shipping on specific dates to be designated for actual firing and no person, vessel or other craft shall enter or remain in the area during the times designated for firing except as may be authorized by the enforcing agency. Notification to maritime interests of specific dates of firing will be disseminated through the U.S. Coast Guard media of the Local Notice to Mariners and the NOTAMs published by the Corps of Engineers. On dates not specified for firing, the area will be open to normal maritime traffic.
  (2) The regulations of this section shall be enforced by the Commanding General, U.S. Army, Hawaii/25th Infantry Division, APO 957, and such agencies as he may designate.[85]

c. *Pacific Ocean at Barber's Point, Island of Oahu, Hawaii; danger zone*

  (a) The danger zone. The waters within a rectangular area... thence along the shoreline at the high water mark along the southerly boundary of Naval Air Station, Barber's Point, to the point of beginning.
  (b) The regulations.
    (1) The area is closed to all surface craft, swimmers, divers and fishermen except to craft and personnel authorized by the enforcing agency.
    (2) The regulations in this section shall be enforced by the Commanding Officer, Naval Air Station, Barber's Point, Hawaii, 96862, and such agencies as he/she may designate.[86]

d. *Pacific Ocean at Keahi Point, Island of Oahu, Hawaii; danger zone*

  (a) The danger zone. The waters within an area beginning at a point in latitude 21°18'21.4" N., longitude 157°59'14.2" W.; thence to latitude 21°18'11" N., longitude 158°00'17.5" W.; thence to latitude 21°17'11.8" N., longitude 158°00'06.5" W.; and thence to latitude 21°17'22.5" N., longitude 157°59'03.1" W.
  (b) The regulations.
    (1) The area is closed to all surface craft, swimmers, divers, and fishermen except to craft and personnel authorized by the enforcing agency.
    (2) The regulations in this section shall be enforced by the Commanding Officer, Explosive Ordnance Disposal Training and Evaluation Unit One, Barbers Point, Hawaii 96862–5600.[87]

e. *Kaneohe Bay, Island of Oahu, Hawaii—Ulupau Crater Weapons Training Range; danger zone*

  (a) The danger zone. The area within a sector extending seaward a distance of 3.8 nautical miles between radial lines bearing 357.1° true and 124.9° true, respectively, from a starting point on Mokapu Peninsula... overlapping the existing 500-yard wide prohibited area. The danger zone is defined as a pie-shaped area bounded by the landward starting point on Mokapu Peninsula and the three

---

[85] Id., § 334.1350.
[86] Id., § 334.1360.
[87] Id., § 334.1370.

U.S. SAFETY AND SECURITY ZONES AND AIRSPACE CONTROL MEASURES 171

seaward points forming an arc with a 3.8 nautical-mile radius at its center (Point B) with a radial line bearing 56.9° true....

(b) The regulations.
  (1) Weapons firing at the Ulupau Crater Weapons Training Range may occur at any time between 6 a.m. and 11 p.m., Monday through Sunday. Specific dates and hours for weapons firing, along with information regarding onshore warning signals, will be promulgated by the U.S. Coast Guard's Local Notice to Mariners. Information on weapons firing schedules may also be obtained by calling the Marine Corps Base Hawaii Range Manager, AC/S G–3....
  (2) Whenever live firing is in progress during daylight hours, two large red triangular warning pennants will be flown at each of two highly visible and widely separated locations on the shore at Ulupau Crater.
  (3) Whenever any weapons firing is scheduled and in progress during periods of darkness, flashing red warning beacons will be displayed on the shore at Ulupau Crater.
  (4) Boaters will have complete access to the danger zone whenever there is no weapons firing scheduled, which will be indicated by the absence of any warning flags, pennants, or beacons displayed ashore.
  (5) The danger zone is not considered safe for boaters whenever weapons firing is in progress. Boaters shall expeditiously vacate the danger zone at best speed and by the most direct route whenever weapons firing is scheduled. Passage of vessels through the danger zone when weapons firing is in progress will be permitted, but boaters shall proceed directly through the area at best speed. Weapons firing will be suspended as long as there is a vessel in the danger zone. Whenever a boater disregards the publicized warning signals that hazardous weapons firing is scheduled, the boater will be personally requested to expeditiously vacate the danger zone by MCBH Kaneohe Bay military personnel utilizing by hailing the vessel on VHF channel 16 or contacting directly by U.S. Navy surface craft.
  (6) Observation posts will be manned whenever any weapons firing is scheduled and in progress. Visibility will be sufficient to maintain visual surveillance of the entire danger zone and for an additional distance of 5 miles in all directions whenever weapons firing is in progress.
(c) The enforcing agency. The regulations shall be enforced by the Commanding Officer, MCB Hawaii, Kaneohe Bay and such agencies as he/she may designate.[88]

f. *Pacific Ocean at Barking Sands, Island of Kauai, Hawaii; missile range facility*

  (a) The danger zone. The waters within an area [latitude and longitude coordinated omitted]; and thence southeasterly to point of beginning.
  (b) Markers.
    (1) Range markers at the control point at latitude 22°03'17.4" N., longitude 159°47'12.2" W., are separated 300 feet (one pole 95.5 feet northwest and the other pole 334.5 feet southeast of this point) along a line bearing 327°10' True.
    (2) Range markers at the control point at latitude 22°02'44.5" N., longitude 159°47'16.4" W., are separated 300 feet (one pole 75 feet west and the other pole 225 feet east of this point) along a line bearing 266°20' True.

---

[88] Id., § 334.1380.

(3) The range marker poles seaward from each control point are 25 feet in height above ground level. The other two poles are 45 feet above ground level.
(4) Each range marker consists of a 10-foot equilateral triangle with alternate red and white diagonal stripes.
(c) The regulations. Entry into the area by any person, boat, vessel or other craft is prohibited at all times. Special permission for transit through the area by the most direct route may be obtainable on an individual basis, by prior arrangement with the Commanding Officer, Pacific Missile Range Facility, Hawaiian Area, Barking Sands, Kauai, Hawaii.[89]

g. *Pacific Ocean, at Barbers Point, Island of Oahu, Hawaii; restricted area*

(a) The area. That portion of the Pacific Ocean lying offshore of Oahu between Ewa Beach and Barbers Point, basically outlined [by coordinates omitted].
(b) The regulations.
(1) Vessels shall not anchor within the area at any time.
(2) Dredging, dragging, seining, or other fishing operations which might foul underwater installations within the area are prohibited.
(3) Use of the restricted area for boating, fishing (except as prohibited in paragraph (b)(2) of this section) and other surface activities is authorized.
(4) The regulations in this section shall be enforced by the Officer in Charge, Fleet Area Control and Surveillance Facility, Pearl Harbor, Hawaii 96860–7625, and such agencies as he/she may designate.[90]

h. *Pacific Ocean, at Makapuu Point, Waimanalo, Island of Oahu, Hawaii, Makai Undersea Test Range*

...

(b) The regulations.
(1) During critical testing phases of surface and submerged units, the operating officials of the Makai Test Range will mark in a conspicuous manner the location of the equipment which might be subject to damage from navigation and fishing activities or might represent a hazard to persons or property in the vicinity. During the display of signals in the restricted area, all persons and surface craft will remain away from the area until such time as the signals are withdrawn. At all other times the area is open to unrestricted fishing, boating and general navigation.
(2) Operating officers and personnel of the Makai Test Range will be responsible for marking in a conspicuous manner the location of surface and underwater equipment which is subject to damage from navigation and fishing activities in the vicinity or represents a hazard to persons or property in the vicinity, and the location of the work area during critical testing phases. Surface communication by boat will be provided by the Makai Test Range during testing phases.[91]

---

[89] Id., § 334.1390.
[90] Id., § 334.1400.
[91] Id., § 334.1410.

6.4.1.3 Naval Defensive Sea Areas and Naval Airspace Reservations

The U.S. Government may also restrict free access to certain areas, such as military installations, due to their strategic importance. Restricted access to naval defensive sea areas, naval airspace reservations, administrative areas, and the Trust Territory of the Pacific Islands protects military installations and the personnel, property, and equipment assigned to or located therein."[92]

The entry or movement of persons, ships or aircraft in the areas is controlled.[93] Persons, ships and aircraft shall not enter designated defense areas without authorization. Every effort is made to avoid unnecessary interference with the free movement through the area, however.[94] Generally, cameras or photographs are prohibited within a naval defensive sea area.[95]

Entry into defense areas will only be authorized if the ship, aircraft, or person will not, under "existing or reasonably foreseeable future conditions," endanger or impose an undue burden upon, "the armed forces located within or contiguous to the area."[96] Entry can be denied for any of the following reasons:

(1) Prior noncompliance with entry control regulations;
(2) Willfully furnishing false, incomplete, or misleading;
(3) Advocacy of the overthrow or alteration of the Government of the United States by unconstitutional means;
(4) Commission of, or attempt or preparation to commit, an act of espionage, sabotage, sedition, or treason;
(5) Performing, or attempting to perform, duties, or otherwise acting so as to serve the interest of another government to the detriment of the United States;
(6) Deliberate unauthorized disclosure of classified defense information;
(7) Knowing membership with the specific intent of furthering the aims of ... acts of force or violence to prevent others from exercising their rights under the Constitution or laws of the United States or of any State, or which seeks to overthrow the Government of the United States or any State or subdivision thereof by unlawful means;
(8) Serious mental irresponsibility;
(9) Chronic alcoholism or addiction to the use of narcotic;
(10) Illegal presence in the United States;
(11) Being the subject of proceedings for deportation;
(12) Conviction of larceny of property of the United States.[97]

No person, except those aboard public vessels or aircraft of the U.S. armed forces, or those working on behalf of the armed forces or under military orders, shall

---

[92] 32 C.F.R. § 761.2(a).
[93] Id., § 761.2(b).
[94] Id.
[95] Id., § 761.20(1).
[96] Id., § 761.6(a)(1).
[97] Id., § 761.6(b).

enter a defense area without the permission of the Entry Control Commander.[98] The following officers of the armed forces are designated Entry Control Commanders with authority to approve or disapprove individual entry authorizations for persons, ships, or aircraft as indicated:

(a) Chief of Naval Operations. Authorization for all persons, ships, or aircraft to enter all defense areas.
(b) Commander in Chief, U.S. Atlantic Fleet. Authorization for all persons, ships, or aircraft to enter defense areas in the Atlantic.
(c) Commander in Chief, U.S. Pacific Fleet. Authorization for all persons, ships, or aircraft to enter defense areas in the Pacific.
(d) Commander U.S. Naval Forces Caribbean. Authorization for all persons, ships, and aircraft to enter the Guantanamo Bay Naval Defensive Sea Area and the Guantanamo Naval Airspace Reservation. (This authority is delegated to Commander U.S. Naval Base, Guantanamo Bay.)
. . .
(f) Commander Third Fleet. Authorization for U.S. citizens and U.S. registered private vessels to enter Midway Island, Kingman Reef, Kaneohe Bay Naval Defensive Sea Area, Pearl Harbor Defensive Sea Area and Filipino workers employed by U.S. contractors to enter Wake Island.
(g) Commander U.S. Naval Forces, Marianas. Authorization in conjunction with the High Commissioner, for non-U.S. citizens, ships, or aircraft documented under laws other than those of the United States or the Trust Territory to enter those portions of the Trust Territory where entry is not controlled by the Department of the Army or the Defense Nuclear Agency.
(h) Senior naval commander in defense area. Emergency authorization for persons, ships, or aircraft in cases of emergency or distress....
(i) U.S. Coast Guard. The U.S. Coast Guard regulates the movement of shipping within the Honolulu Harbor.... The Commandant, Fourteenth Naval District, as representative of the Secretary of the Navy, retains responsibility for security of the Honolulu Defensive Sea Area....[99]

Naval Defensive Sea Areas and Naval Airspace Reservations may be established by the President by Executive Order.[100] The following Naval Defensive Sea Areas and Naval Airspace Reservations are under the control of the Secretary of the Navy: Guantanamo Bay Naval Defensive Sea Area and Guantanamo Bay Naval Airspace Reservation;[101] Honolulu Defensive Sea Area;[102] Kaneohe Bay Naval Defensive Sea Area and Kaneohe Bay Naval Airspace Reservation;[103] Pearl

---

[98] Id., § 761.7(a) and § 761.10. Privately owned local craft that are pre-approved may enter the areas, foreign vessels traveling with diplomatic or special clearance and ships in distress, also may enter the areas, but subject to local clearances and control by senior officer present. 32 C.F.R. § 761.12 and § 761.14.
[99] Id., § 761.9. Commander Seventeenth Coast Guard District is also designated an Entry Control Commander by the Commandant, U.S. Coast Guard.
[100] 18 U.S.C. § 2152.
[101] Executive Order 8749, May 1, 1941 (6 FR 2252; 3 C.F.R. 1943 Cum. Supp., p. 931).
[102] Executive Order 8987, Dec. 20, 1941 (6 FR 6675; 3 C.F.R. 1943 Cum. Supp., p. 1048).
[103] Executive Order 8681, Feb. 14, 1941 (6 FR 1014; 3 C.F.R. 1943 Cum. Supp., p. 893).

Harbor Defensive Sea Area;[104] Johnston Island, Kingman Reef, Midway Island, Palmyra Island, and Wake Islands Naval Defensive Sea Areas and Naval Airspace Reservations;[105] Kiska Island Naval Defensive Sea Area and Kiska Island Naval Airspace Reservation;[106] Kodiak Naval Defensive Sea Area[107] and Unalaska Island Naval Defensive Sea Area and Unalaska Island Naval Air-space Reservation.[108]

The Secretary of the Interior is responsible for the civil administration of Wake Island, whereas the Secretary of the Navy is responsible for the civil administration of Midway Island.[109] On June 24, 1972, the Department of the Air Force assumed responsibility for the civil administration of Wake Island pursuant to an agreement between the Department of the Interior and the Department of the Air Force.[110]

6.4.1.4 Trust Territory of the Pacific Islands

The Trust Territory of the Pacific Islands is a strategic area administered by the United States under the provisions of a trusteeship agreement with the United Nations. Following the end of World War II, the United States submitted a proposal to the United Nations Security Council in accordance with Article 83 of the UN Charter to establish a trusteeship agreement for the Pacific Islands, formerly mandated to Japan under Article 22 of the Covenant of the League of Nations in December 1920, under which the United States would administer those islands.

On April 2, 1947, the UN Security Council unanimously approved the trusteeship agreement, and a Joint Resolution of Congress authorized the President to approve the agreement on July 18, 1947.[111] Article 3 of the Agreement grants the United States "full powers of administration, legislation, and jurisdiction over the

---

[104] Executive Order 8143, May 26, 1939 (4 FR 2179; 3 C.F.R. 1943 Cum. Supp., p. 504).
[105] Executive Order 8682, Feb. 14, 1941 (6 FR 1015; 3 C.F.R. 1943 Cum. Supp., p. 894) as amended by Executive Order 8729, Apr. 2, 1941 (6 FR 1791; 3 C.F.R. 1943 Cum. Supp., p. 919) and Executive Order 9881, Aug. 4, 1947 (12 FR 5325; 3 C.F.R. 1943–1948 Comp., p. 662).
[106] Executive Order 8680, Feb. 14, 1941 (6 FR 1014; 3 C.F.R. 1943 Cum. Supp., p. 892) as amended by Executive Order 8729, Apr. 2, 1941 (6 FR 1791; 3 C.F.R. 1943 Cum. Supp., p. 919).
[107] Executive Order 8717, Mar. 22, 1941 (6 FR 1621; 3 C.F.R. 1943 Cum. Supp., p. 915). Kodiak Naval Airspace Reservation: Executive Order 8597, Nov. 18, 1940 (5 FR 4559; 3 C.F.R. 1943 Cum. Supp., p. 837) as amended by Executive Order 9720 of May 8, 1946 (11 FR 5105; 3 C.F.R. 1943–1948 Comp., p. 527).
[108] Executive Order 8680, Feb. 14, 1941 (6 FR 1014; 3 C.F.R. 1943 Cum. Supp., p. 892) as amended by Executive Order 8729, Apr. 2, 1941 (6 FR 1791; 3 C.F.R. 1943 Cum. Supp., p. 919).
[109] Executive Order 11048, Administration of Wake Island and Midway Island, September 4, 1962, 27 FR 8851, 3 C.F.R., 1959–1963 Comp., 632.
[110] 32 C.F.R. § 935.11.
[111] Trusteeship Agreement for the Former Japanese Mandated Islands, 61 Stat. 3301, T.I.A.S. No. 1665, 8 U.N.T.S. 189 (Apr. 2, 1947).

territory...." Article 5 authorizes the United States to establish naval, military and air bases and to erect fortifications in the trust territory; position armed forces in the territory; and employ the local population for the defense and the maintenance of law and order within the trust territory.

The Trust Territory of the Pacific Islands initially included the Northern Mariana Islands, the Federated States of Micronesia (FSM), the Marshall Islands (RMI), and Palau. The Trusteeship Agreement terminated with respect to the Republic of the Marshall Islands on October 21, 1986, with respect to the Federated States of Micronesia and the Commonwealth of the Northern Mariana Islands on November 3, 1986, and with respect to the Republic of Palau on October 1, 1994.[112] The United States retains defense obligations and access rights with these independent nations pursuant to a Compact of Free Association.

The Compact of Free Association sets forth the relationship between the United States and the Pacific Islands.[113] Under Section 311 of each Compact, the United States exercises security and defense authority related to the islands, including the commitment to "defend the Federated States of Micronesia [and Republic of the Marshall Islands] and its people from attack or threats," the right to bar the armed forces of another country from using the islands, and the right to establish and maintain military areas and facilities on the islands.

Upon gaining its independence in 1994, Palau entered into a 50-year Compact of Free Association with the United States that is similar to the Compacts entered into between the United States and the FSM and RMI.[114]

The Compacts provide authority for the U.S. operation of nuclear capable and nuclear propelled vessels and aircraft without either confirming or denying the presence or absence of nuclear weapons on board those conveyances.[115]

The Secretary of the Interior is responsible for the administration of the civil government of the Trust Territory of the Pacific Islands.[116] Section 1 of Executive Order 11021 provides that the Secretary of the Interior has the "responsibility for the administration of civil government in all of the trust territory, and all executive, legislative, and judicial authority necessary for that administration...."[117] The Secretary of the Interior, however, has certain limitations on the exercise of administration over the islands.

> [T]he authority to specify parts or all of the trust territory as closed for security reasons and to determine the extent to which Articles 87 and 88 of the Charter of the

---

[112] 48 U.S.C. § 1682 Note.
[113] Pub. L. 99–239, Jan. 14, 1986, 99 Stat. 1770, amended by Pub. L. 108–188, Dec. 17, 2003, 117 Stat. 2720.
[114] Pub. L. 99–658, November 14, 1986, 100 Stat. 3673.
[115] Id., sec. 331.
[116] 32 C.F.R. § 761.3(c).
[117] Executive Order 11021, Administration of the Trust Territory of the Pacific Islands by the Secretary of the Interior, May 7, 1962, 27 FR 4409; 3 C.F.R. 1959–1963 Comp., at 600.

United Nations shall be applicable to such closed areas, in accordance with Article 13 of the trusteeship agreement, shall be exercised by the President.... [T]he Secretary of the Interior shall keep the Secretary of State currently informed of activities in the trust territory affecting the foreign policy of the United States and shall consult with the Secretary of State on questions of policy concerning the trust territory which relate to the foreign policy of the United States, and that all relations between the departments and agencies of the Government and appropriate organs of the United Nations with respect to the trust territory shall be conducted through the Secretary of State.

Pursuant to two agreements, effective July 1, 1951 and July 1, 1962, between the Department of the Navy and the Department of the Interior, the entry of individuals, ships and aircraft into the Trust Territory (except areas under the control of the Department of the Army (Kwajalein Atoll) and the Defense Nuclear Agency (Eniwetok Atoll), is controlled by the High Commissioner of the Trust Territory and the Department of the Navy.[118] The Department of the Army controls entry into islands in the Kwajalein Atoll under military jurisdiction.[119] Entry into Eniwetok Atoll and Johnston Atoll is controlled by the Defense Nuclear Agency.[120] Criminal and civil penalties for violating orders or regulations controlling access to the Trust Territory are provided in U.S. statutes.[121]

Restricted entry into all Naval Airspace Reservations, except the Guantanamo Bay Naval Airspace Reservation, has been suspended. Furthermore, restricted entry into several Naval Defensive Sea Areas and Administrative Areas also has been suspended, including Honolulu Defensive Sea Area; Kiska Island Naval Defensive Sea Area; Kodiak Island Naval Defensive Sea Area; Unalaska Island Naval Defensive Sea Area; Wake Island Naval Defensive Sea Area (except for entry of foreign flag ships and foreign nationals); and that part of Kaneohe Defensive Sea Area lying beyond a 500 yard buffer zone around the perimeter of the Kaneohe Marine Corps Air Station at Mokapu Peninsula and eastward to Kapoho

---

[118] 32 C.F.R. § 761.3(c).
[119] National Range Commander, U.S. Army Safeguard System Command.
[120] 32 C.F.R. § 761.4(a)–(c), Commander, Field Command and 32 C.F.R. § 761.3(f), Commander, Johnston Atoll.
[121] Sanctions for violations of orders governing persons or ships within the defensive sea areas is in 18 U.S.C. § 2152. Prohibited entry into military, naval or Coast Guard property may be punished pursuant to 18 U.S.C. § 1382. Penalties for violation of regulations imposed for the protection or security of military or naval aircraft, airports, air facilities, vessels, harbors, ports, piers, waterfront facilities, bases, forts, posts, laboratories, stations, vehicles, equipment, explosives, or other property or places subject to jurisdiction of the Department of Defense are set out in 50 U.S.C. § 797 and Department of Defense Directive 5200.8, Aug. 20, 1954. Individuals convicted of knowingly and willfully making a false or misleading statement or representation in any matter within the jurisdiction of any department or agency of the United States are punished under 18 U.S.C. § 1001.

Point, Oahu.[122] The suspension of restrictions on entry, however, does not obviate the authority of appropriate commanders to lift the suspension and reinstate controls on entry.[123]

6.4.2 *Airspace Control Measures*

As a matter of national security, the United States requires U.S. and foreign-registered aircraft flying into, out of, or through U.S. airspace to comply with air defense identification zones, special use airspace, prohibited areas, restricted areas, warning areas, military operations areas, alert areas, and controlled firing areas.

6.4.2.1 Air Defense Identification Zone

International law does not prohibit a nation from establishing an Air Defense Identification Zone (ADIZ) in international airspace adjacent to its national airspace. The term ADIZ is defined in Annex 15 of the Chicago Convention[124] as a special designated airspace of defined dimensions within which aircraft are required to comply with special identification and/or reporting procedures that supplement those related to civil air traffic services (ATS).

The United States defines an ADIZ as "an area of airspace over land or water in which the ready identification, location, and control of all aircraft (except for Department of Defense and law enforcement aircraft) is required in the interest of national security."[125] The legal basis for establishing these zones in times of peace is that states always enjoy the right to establish reasonable conditions of entry into their land territory. Thus, the legal theory for an ADIZ is analogous to imposition of conditions of port entry for ships entering into port or traversing internal waters. Accordingly, aircraft approaching national airspace may be required to provide identification even while in international airspace, but only as a condition of entry approval.[126]

The terrorist attacks on the World Trade Towers and the Pentagon in 2001 resulted in greater scrutiny of aircraft approaching the United States. Because aircraft inbound to the United States will at some point cross into a U.S. ADIZ, aircraft commanders should be aware of the possibility of being intercepted by U.S. military aircraft, particularly when entering U.S. airspace from abroad, and

---

[122] 32 C.F.R. § 761.4(d).
[123] Id., § 761.4(e).
[124] INT'L CIVIL AVIATION ORG., CONVENTION ON INTERNATIONAL CIVIL AVIATION, ANNEX 15, INTERNATIONAL STANDARDS AND RECOMMENDED PRACTICES, AERONAUTICAL INFORMATION SERVICES (13th ed. July 2010).
[125] 14 C.F.R. § 99.3.
[126] *See*, Peter A. Dutton, *Caelum Liberam: Air Defense Identification Zones Outside Sovereign Airspace*, 103 AM. J. INT'L L. 1, 9 (2009).

they should be prepared to comply with any instructions given by the intercepting aircraft. Non-compliance with instructions could result in the use of force. Further discussion on ICAO and U.S. intercept procedures is contained in Chapter 4 of this volume.

U.S. rules establishing ADIZs are contained in Chapter 5 of the *Federal Aviation Administration's Aeronautical Information Manual*.[127] The United States has established ADIZs to assist in early identification of aircraft in the vicinity of international U.S. airspace boundaries around the contiguous United States,[128] Alaska,[129] Hawaii,[130] and Guam.[131] The ADIZ regulations require aircraft bound for U.S. national airspace to file flight plans and provide periodic reports. Civil aircraft operating within a U.S. ADIZ "must have a functioning two-way radio, and the pilot must maintain a continuous listening watch on the appropriate aeronautical facility's frequency."[132] Persons are prohibited from operating an aircraft within an ADIZ unless they file a Defense Visual Flight Rules (DVFR) flight plan containing the time and point of ADIZ penetration, and the aircraft departs within five minutes of the estimated departure time contained in the flight plan.[133]

In cases where a pilot operating an aircraft under DVFR in a U.S. ADIZ cannot maintain two-way radio communications, "the pilot may proceed, in accordance with the original DVFR flight plan, or land as soon as practicable."[134] Persons are also prohibited from operating an aircraft into, within, or from a departure point within a U.S. ADIZ, "unless the person files, activates, and closes a flight plan with the appropriate aeronautical facility, or is otherwise authorized by air traffic control."[135] A pilot may not deviate from the filed Instrument Flight Rules (IFR) when operating in uncontrolled airspace or DVFR flight plan unless an appropriate aeronautical facility is notified before deviating.[136] Finally, the pilot of an aircraft operating in or penetrating an ADIZ under IFR to is required to make position reports.[137] Foreign civil aircraft may not enter the United States through an ADIZ unless the pilot makes the required reports or reports the position of

---

[127] 14 C.F.R. §§ 99.1–99.49.
[128] Doc. No. FAA–2001–10693, 66 FR 49822, Sept. 28, 2001. Redesignated at 69 FR 16756, Mar. 30, 2004.
[129] Doc. No. FAA–2001–10693, 66 FR 49822, Sept. 28, 2001. Redesignated at 69 FR 16756, Mar. 30, 2004.
[130] Doc. No. 25113, 53 FR 18217, May 20, 1988. Redesignated at 69 FR 16756, Mar. 30, 2004.
[131] Doc. No. 25113, 53 FR 18217, May 20, 1988. Redesignated at 69 FR 16756, Mar. 30, 2004.
[132] 14 C.F.R. § 99.9(a).
[133] Id., § 99.9(b).
[134] Id., § 99.9(c).
[135] Id., § 99.11(a).
[136] Id., § 99.17(b)–(c).
[137] Id., § 99.15(a) and § 91.183.

the aircraft when it is not less than one hour and not more than 2 hours average direct cruising distance from the United States."[138]

During an air defense emergency the United States may issue special security instructions pursuant to the Emergency Security Control of Air Traffic (ESCAT) Plan. Under ESCAT, military authorities "will direct the action to be taken in regard to landing, grounding, diversion, or dispersal of aircraft and the control of air navigation aids..." in the defense of the United States.[139] If ESCAT is implemented, "[Air Traffic Control] facilities will broadcast appropriate instructions received from the Air Traffic Control System Command Center (ATCSCC) over available ATC frequencies."[140] These transmissions may include directing all VFR flights to land at the nearest available airport. In such case, pilots on the ground may be required to file a flight plan and obtain an approval (through FAA) prior to conducting flight operations.[141] Deviations from the above rules are permitted during emergencies that require an immediate decision and action for the safety of flight.[142]

The United States does not recognize any claim by a state to apply its ADIZ procedures to foreign aircraft not intending to enter national airspace, nor does the United States apply its ADIZ procedures to foreign aircraft not intending to enter U.S. airspace. For example, in March and May 2008, U.S. F-15 fighter aircraft intercepted Russian Tu-95 Bear heavy bombers in the Alaska ADIZ. After a fifteen-year lapse, Russia restarted its bomber surveillance flights in the Arctic in 2007. In the representative cases that occurred in 2008, when it was determined that the Russian bombers were on a training flight and did not intend to enter U.S. national airspace, they were allowed to continue on their mission without harassment or interference from the U.S. aircraft.[143] Accordingly, U.S. military aircraft not intending to enter foreign national airspace normally will not identify themselves or otherwise comply with ADIZ procedures established by other nations. In some cases, such as in the operation of point-to-point flights, the United States specifically may agree to do so to facilitate air traffic control. Department of Defense guidance, however, states that U.S. "[m]ilitary aircraft transiting through a foreign ADIZ without intending to penetrate foreign sovereign airspace are not required to follow...[ADIZ] procedures."[144]

---

[138] Id., § 99.15(c).
[139] DEP'T OF TRANSPORTATION, FEDERAL AVIATION ADMINISTRATION, AERONAUTICAL INFORMATION MANUAL (2010), Chap. 5, Sec. 6, sec. 5-6-1(g) [Hereinafter FAA AERONAUTICAL INFORMATION MANUAL].
[140] Id.
[141] Id.
[142] 14 C.F.R § 99.5.
[143] Rowan Scarborough, *Russian Flights Smack of Cold War*, WASH. TIMES, June 26, 2008.
[144] DEP'T OF DEFENSE, DEPARTMENT OF DEFENSE INSTRUCTION, 4540.01, USE OF INTERNATIONAL AIRSPACE BY U.S. MILITARY AIRCRAFT AND FOR MISSILE/PROJECTILE FIRINGS, Mar. 28, 2007, para. 6.4.

6.4.2.2 Special Use Airspace

Special use airspace is defined as "airspace wherein activities must be confined because of their nature, or wherein limitations are imposed upon aircraft operations that are not a part of those activities, or both."[145] Prohibited areas, restricted areas, warning areas, military operations areas (MOA), alert areas, controlled firing areas (CFA), and national security areas are all included as special use airspace. The vertical limits of special use airspace are measured by designated altitude floors and ceilings expressed as flight levels or as feet above mean sea level, while the horizontal limits are measured by boundaries described by geographic coordinates or other appropriate references that clearly define their perimeter.[146]

Prohibited and restricted areas are established pursuant to 14 C.F.R. Part 73, while warning areas, MOAs, alert areas, and CFAs are non-regulatory special use airspace. Descriptions of the various special use airspace areas, except CFAs, are contained in FAA Order JO 7400.8, January 26, 2012, and are depicted on U.S. aeronautical charts. In addition, special use airspace, except CFAs, "are charted on IFR or visual charts and include the hours of operation, altitudes, and the controlling agency."[147]

a. *Prohibited Areas*

Prohibited areas are established for national security or other reasons associated with the national welfare. They include airspace of defined dimensions within which aircraft flight is prohibited. Prohibited areas are published in the *Federal Register* and are depicted on aeronautical charts.[148] Persons are prohibited from operating an aircraft within a prohibited area unless authorized by the using agency.[149] For example, a prohibited area has been established around certain areas in the District of Columbia, including the White House, the Naval Observatory, the Lincoln, Jefferson, and Washington Monuments, and other areas.[150]

b. *Restricted Areas*

Restricted areas contain airspace within which aircraft flight is subject to restrictions. They denote the "existence of unusual, often invisible, hazards to aircraft such as artillery firing, aerial gunnery, or guided missiles."[151] Entry into a restricted area "without authorization from the using or controlling agency may

---

[145] FAA AERONAUTICAL INFORMATION MANUAL (2010), Chap. 3, Sec. 4, sec. 3-4-1(a).
[146] 14 C.F.R. §§ 73.3(b)–(c).
[147] FAA AERONAUTICAL INFORMATION MANUAL, sec. 3-4-1(e).
[148] Id., sec. 3-4-2.
[149] 14 C.F.R. § 73.83.
[150] Federal Aviation Administration Order JO 7400.8U, Special Use Airspace, Jan. 26, 2012.
[151] FAA AERONAUTICAL INFORMATION MANUAL (2010), Chap. 3, Sec. 4, sec. 3-4-3(a).

be extremely hazardous to the aircraft and its occupants."[152] Aircraft may be restricted from an area between the designated altitudes and during the time of designation, unless that person has the advance permission of the using agency or the controlling agency.[153] When aircraft are operating on an IFR clearance via a route which lies within joint-use restricted airspace, the ATC facility will allow the aircraft to operate in the restricted airspace without issuing specific clearance for it to do so if the restricted area is not active and has been released to the controlling agency, which generally is the FAA. If the restricted area is active and has not been released to the FAA, the ATC will issue a clearance that ensures the aircraft avoids the restricted airspace, unless the aircraft is on an approved altitude reservation mission or has obtained its own permission to operate in the airspace and so informs the controlling facility.

For example, there is a restricted area designation for the Pacific Missile Range Facility in Hawaii. The boundaries of the designated airspace runs counterclockwise along the shoreline of Kauai clockwise along a line 3 nautical miles from the shoreline of Kauai. The designated altitudes are from the surface to unlimited and in effect from 0600–1800 local time Monday-Friday and during other times promulgated by NOTAM. The FAA, Honolulu Control Facility is the controlling agency, and Commanding Officer, Pacific Missile Range Facility, Hawaii is the using agency.[154]

c. *Warning Areas*

Warning areas are defined as "airspace of defined dimensions, extending from three nautical miles outward from the coast of the United States, that contains activity that may be hazardous to nonparticipating aircraft."[155] Warning areas may be established over domestic and/or international waters and are intended to warn nonparticipating pilots of the potential danger. For example, a warning area has been established for the U.S. Navy Fleet Area Control and Surveillance Facility off the Virginia coast along a line three nautical miles from and parallel to the shoreline, from the surface to a flight altitude of 750 feet. The using agency is the U.S. Navy, Fleet Area Control and Surveillance Facility, Virginia Capes, in Virginia Beach, Virginia.[156]

d. *Military Operation Areas*

Military Operation Areas (MOAs) consist of "airspace of defined vertical and lateral limits established for the purpose of separating certain military training

---

[152] Id.
[153] 14 C.F.R. § 73.13.
[154] Federal Aviation Administration Order JO 7400.8U, Special Use Airspace, Jan. 26, 2012.
[155] FAA AERONAUTICAL INFORMATION MANUAL (2010), Chap. 3, Sec. 4, sec. 3-4-4.
[156] Federal Aviation Administration Order JO 7400.8U, Special Use Airspace, Jan. 26, 2012.

activities from IFR traffic."[157] Nonparticipating IFR traffic may be cleared through a MOA if IFR separation can be provided by the ATC; if not, however, the ATC is required to reroute or restrict nonparticipating IFR traffic from the area. Activities that may be conducted in a MOA include: "air combat tactics, air intercepts, aerobatics, formation training, and low-altitude tactics."[158] Pilots operating under VFR should exercise extreme caution while flying within a MOA when military activity is being conducted and should contact the controlling agency for traffic advisories prior to entering an active MOA.[159] MOAs, for example, have been established in the vicinity of the U.S. Marine Corps Base in Quantico, Virginia.[160]

e. *Alert Areas*

Alert areas are depicted on aeronautical charts and are used to "inform nonparticipating pilots of areas that may contain a high volume of pilot training or an unusual type of aerial activity."[161] Accordingly, pilots should be particularly alert when flying in these areas. Pilots of participating aircraft as well as pilots transiting the area shall be equally responsible for collision avoidance. Naval Air Station Pensacola, Florida, for example, has an alert area established for operations in the vicinity of the surface to a height of 3,000 feet mean sea level within Federal airways. Commander, Training Wing 6, Naval Air Station, Pensacola, Florida is the using agency.[162]

f. *Controlled Firing Areas*

Controlled Firing Areas (CFAs) "contain activities which, if not conducted in a controlled environment, could be hazardous to nonparticipating aircraft."[163] CFAs differ from other special use airspace in that their "activities are suspended immediately when spotter aircraft, radar, or ground lookout positions indicate an aircraft might be approaching the area."[164] As a result, CFAs are not charted since they do not cause nonparticipating aircraft to change their flight path.

g. *National Security Areas*

National Security Area (NSAs) consist of airspace of defined vertical and lateral dimensions established at locations where there is a need for increased security of a ground facility. For example, NSAs have been established to provide enhanced

---

[157] FAA AERONAUTICAL INFORMATION MANUAL (2010), Chap. 3, Sec. 4, sec. 3-4-5(a).
[158] Id., sec. 3-4-5(b).
[159] Id., sec. 3-4-5(c).
[160] Federal Aviation Administration Order JO 7400.8U, Special Use Airspace, Jan. 26, 2012.
[161] FAA AERONAUTICAL INFORMATION MANUAL (2010), Chap. 3, Sec. 4, sec. 3-4-6.
[162] Federal Aviation Administration Order JO 7400.8U, Special Use Airspace, Jan. 26, 2012.
[163] FAA AERONAUTICAL INFORMATION MANUAL (2010), Chap. 3, Sec. 4, sec. 3-4-7.
[164] Id.

security for the U.S. Navy Bremerton Shipyard, Washington,[165] U.S. Navy Pearl Harbor, Hawaii,[166] and the U.S. Army, Bluegrass Army Depot munitions depot in Richmond, Kentucky.[167] These areas are established to request pilots to cooperate on a voluntarily basis to avoid flight through the NSA.

If there is a need for greater security, "flight in an NSA may be temporarily prohibited by regulation under the provisions of 14 CFR § 99.7, Special Security Instructions."[168] Prohibitions are issued by FAA Headquarters and disseminated via the U.S. NOTAM System.

---

[165] Federal Aviation Administration Order JO 7400.8U, Special Use Airspace, Jan. 26, 2012.
[166] Id.
[167] Id.
[168] Id.

SEVEN

SEA POWER, GRAND STRATEGY, AND FREEDOM OF THE SEAS

7.1 Seapower and Grand Strategy

The oceans are a continuous, global body of water comprising 71 percent of the surface of the Earth.[1] The unified world ocean has an area of more than 139 million square miles (361 million sq. km.) and a total volume of 322,280,000 cubic miles (1,347,000,000 cubic km.), comprising 97 percent of the water on the planet.[2] Frozen seawater trapped at the poles accounts for another 2.2 percent of the world's water.[3] Relatively little is known about seabed topography, as only ten percent of the seafloor has been mapped with seaborne instrumentation—mostly in the coastal zone.[4]

With relatively free interchange of water and aquatic life among the oceans, we should think in terms of the seas as being a single body of water. This interconnected quality has made the oceans an essential route for regional cabotage shipping and transcontinental voyages, including commercial trade, strategic mobility, and a vector for attack, as well as lawful and unlawful immigration, the transfer of cultures, and the transmission of disease.[5] As a domain principally useful for movement—shipping is still the most efficient method of transporting

---

[1] From the Greek word, 'Ὠκεανὸς, or "okeanos'" (Oceanus).
[2] Matthew A. Charette & Walter H. F. Smith, *The Volume of Earth's Ocean*, 23 Oceanography 112–114 (June 2010).
[3] Physics FactBook: An Encyclopedia of Scientific Essays Table 1 (Glen Elert ed.), http://hypertextbook.com/facts/2001/SyedQadri.shtml.
[4] Charette & Smith, *The Volume of Earth's Ocean*, at 112–114.
[5] The bubonic plague or "Black Death" is thought to have entered Venice via trading vessels from farther along the Eastern Mediterranean. Similarly, Europeans introduced smallpox and other infectious diseases into the Americas, devastating the native populations.

large quantities of heavy cargo and material long distances—the oceans have had a profound, indeed dispositive, effect on world politics.[6]

The oceans reflect the classic model of a global commons, and the term is a useful metaphor for thinking about shared space. In this respect, the oceans commons share both similarity and difference with other areas of shared space, such as airspace, cyberspace, and outer space. The benefits of operating in the oceans are diffuse and shared by all states; no nation may purport to establish exclusive control over the seas.

The unity of the oceans is the simple physical fact underlying the critical strategic value of sea power.[7] Throughout history, dominance of the oceans usually has been essential for command of the land. In 480 BC, for example, the ancient Greeks used an anti-access/area denial (A2/AD) strategy at Salamis, denying the invading Persians the ability to land a huge army on the Peloponnese.[8] If the Persians had gained a secure landing, there is little doubt they could have overrun the Greek world and changed the course of Western history.

7.1.1 *Littoral Regions*

The coastline and littoral regions have their own importance. Nearly all of the major global marketplaces are coastal regions of production and consumption, with international commerce feeding the global trading system. Nearly all of the major global marketplaces for international trade ring the ocean coastline. Because of the concentration of population, the diversity of ethnic groups, and the omnipresent competition for space, the shorelines are dynamic political centers susceptible to internal strife and international armed conflict.[9]

Politically, and therefore strategically, littoral seas are the seas that matter most, and maritime strategists are (or at least should be) more concerned with the littoral regions than anywhere else on the planet. The coastlines of Asia, Africa and Latin America teem with large numbers of idle adolescents growing up in unstable "feral" cities amidst rapid political and economic change. Non-traditional security threats are proliferating. While representing a relatively small portion of the world's surface, 70 percent of Earth's population lives within two

---

Jared Diamond, Guns, Germs and Steel: A Short History of Everybody for the Last 13,000 Years 195–215 (2005).
[6] James Kraska, Maritime Power and Law of the Sea (2011).
[7] John Halford Mackinder, Britain and the British Seas 12 (2d. ed., 1907).
[8] General Norton A. Schwartz and Admiral Jonathan W. Greenert, Air-Sea Battle: Promoting Stability in an Era of Uncertainty, Feb. 20, 2012.
[9] General C. Krulak, Commandant, U.S. Marine Corps, Operational Maneuver from the Sea: A Concept for the Projection of Naval Power Ashore 1 (1999).

hundred miles of the oceans; over 80 percent of the world's capital cities are located there.

7.1.2 Global System

Greek civilization, the Roman Empire, the Ottoman expansion, the Columbian Exchange, the rise of the Dutch Provinces and their separation from the Iberian powers, and British world hegemony all were made possible only by international sea transportation. Over the past five hundred years, the country to dominate the waves has also been dominant on land. This rule is so etched in the strategic psyche that by World War I the fulcrum of the conflict revolved around Germany's attempt to control the North Atlantic in order to keep U.S. supplies and troops from reaching Europe. World War II and the Cold War were both simply replays, demonstrating once again that sea power is the linchpin of world politics.

During the colonial era, the European countries were dominant because they could exert intercontinental power. Spain and Portugal divided a hemisphere on the other side of the world, tiny Dutch Republics controlled outposts across the globe. England controlled one quarter of the territory on Earth. The ability to wage intercontinental war over the waves was the key to European colonialism, with land powers such as France, enjoying imperial success for centuries, while Germany and Italy arrived too late to the table. During the Cold War, even as the United States was the dominant sea power, the Soviet Union aided North Korea by sea, and could ferry and sustain Cuban troops in a proxy war in Angola. Thus, Moscow's global reach was a function of its naval power. Today, however, the United States is the only nation with the power to launch and sustain a major intercontinental war, which it has done twice in Europe (World War I and II), twice in East Asia (the Korean peninsula and Indochina) and three times in Central Asia (Afghanistan once and Iraq twice).

The world political order largely has been an outgrowth of the sea as a means of military transit. With the arrival of reliable transcontinental travel and the emergence of Portuguese and Spanish empires in the New World, naval power permanently displaced land power as the strategic center of gravity in world war. After that point, the exercise of nearly all land power may be described as merely tactical; the only way for nations to achieve strategic supremacy—hegemony at the intercontinental or world system level—was through sea power. Dominance on land, no matter how decisive, whether it was the Ottoman Empire, the Nazi Reich, or the Soviet Army, could not maintain long-term strategic advantage without a first-rate maritime power.

Political science research bears out the historical relationship between dominant naval powers and their positions of global leadership, thus making access to the maritime domain the essential ingredient for status as a world power. When tested empirically, the theory is supported by the rise of naval power and assumption of leadership status for Portugal, The Netherlands, Great Britain and the United States.[10] Over the past five hundred years, all of the world's foremost powers achieved their position of world leadership through sea power. Even a traditional continental power such as Russia reached the zenith of its standing on the global stage through the use of naval power to expand its geographic reach and enhance its nuclear posture. As the Soviet fleet approached parity with the United States in the 1970s, the Soviet Union challenged the American position in virtually every corner of the world.[11] But the Soviet fleet faded with the dissolution of the Empire, and Soviet power evaporated with it.

The United States epitomizes the role of sea power in world politics. In six months of Operation Desert Shield in 1991, for example, the United States could move 500,000 troops and 540,000 tons of cargo by air into Kuwait and Saudi Arabia in response to Iraq's invasion of Kuwait.[12] At the same time, however, the Military Sealift Command moved five times that amount—2.4 million tons of equipment, vehicles, and ammunition—by sea. In comparison, it took the Allies two years to position forces for the D-Day invasion during World War II.[13] Indeed, the U.S. military's role as the steward of the global commons—and the oceans in particular—has facilitated an international system in which peace and prosperity can flourish.[14]

Ensuring maritime freedom of action is increasingly important.[15] During the Cold War, the epicenter of rivalry lay along the Fulda Gap and the Central Front, with Allies facing a numerically superior Warsaw Pact. Then, the United States developed land-oriented maneuver strategies to counter the Soviet Union— *Follow-On Forces Attack* and the Army's *AirLand Battle* concept. These operational concepts, just like *Blitzkrieg* during World War II, tried to emulate on land the three dimensional maneuver and mobility of the oceans and airspace. Strategic access to the oceans is most critical for maintaining national freedom of action, and the areas of the near-shore and inland coastal sea regions are the most important.

Since the beginning of the Republic, the United States has pursued a strategy of assured access to the global commons as an enduring American security interest.[16] Over the past century, freedom of the seas and unimpeded access to

---

[10] *See*, GEORGE MODELSKI & WILLIAM R. THOMPSON, SEA POWER IN GLOBAL POLITICS 1493–1993 (1988) (A global leader is present when the fleet of any single nation comprises 50 percent or more of the worldwide sea power assets).

[11] Sergei Chernyavskii, *The Era of Gorshkov: Triumph and Contradictions*, 28 J. OF STRATEGIC STUDIES 281, 282–84 (2005).

[12] SCHWARTZ & GREENERT, AIR-SEA BATTLE.

[13] Id.

[14] ANDREW F. KREPINEVICH, WHY AIR SEA BATTLE? 7 (2010).

[15] SCHWARTZ & GREENERT, AIR-SEA BATTLE.

[16] STEPHEN J. HADLEY, WILLIAM J. PERRY, ET AL., THE QDR IN PERSPECTIVE: MEETING AMERICA'S NATIONAL SECURITY NEEDS IN THE 21ST CENTURY: THE FINAL REPORT OF THE QUADRENNIAL DEFENSE REVIEW INDEPENDENT PANEL 25 and 48–49 (2010).

the associated aerospace have been prerequisites to freedom of action. The doctrine, force structure and capabilities of the U.S. Navy are designed to exploit the global commons as a maneuver space for power projection. For the United States, even the Army and Air Force are expeditionary forces designed for deployment abroad rather than combat at home. Still, the critical importance of strategic maritime mobility often is underappreciated.

Writing during World War I, British historian and Liberal Party politician Ramsay Muir stated, "In times of peace the freedom of the seas has been so long enjoyed by the whole world that men are apt to take it for granted; they do not consider how it came to be established, or what are the conditions necessary for its maintenance."[17] This sentiment is particularly apt today, when the United States fought two wars in Central Asia over the past decade. Reporters, scholars, and popular writers have become enamored with land warfare and counterinsurgency, failing to appreciate that the recent wars in Iraq and Afghanistan were tactical conflicts measured in years, rather than the far more critical strategic maritime competition measured in decades. The U.S. *National Military Strategy* suggests a broader vision, charging the sea services with taking the lead in "international efforts to safeguard access, sustain security ... and promote responsible norms in the global commons...."[18]

7.1.3 *Freedom of the Seas in the Early Modern Period*

As a physical domain of movement, the sea is governed by a juridical and political framework that developed over the past four hundred years. The governing regime is a product of the historic power relationships among coastal and maritime states. The relatively open or liberal legal order of the oceans derives from the policy preferences of rather liberally minded maritime states and their geopolitical position as an offshore balancing force in European politics. In particular, the maritime dominance of the Dutch Republic and England had a dispositive effect on the creation and maintenance of oceans governance. The United States has joined this Anglo-Saxon philosophical block, forming a trifecta for a liberal world order of the oceans.

Competition between the exercise of governmental authority over the sea and the opposing concept of freedom of the seas is the central and persistent theme in the history of the international law of the sea.[19] Extension of coastal state authority over the oceans was typically co-terminus with the military reach of the coastal state. Greek and Roman galleys, for example, rarely sailed beyond the horizon. Nights were spent on the beach, and endurance was limited to only

---

[17] Ramsay Muir, Mare Liberum: Freedom of the Seas 2 (London & New York: Hodder & Stoughton, 1917).
[18] Dep't of Defense, The National Military Strategy of the United States of America (2011).
[19] D. P. O'Connell, I The International Law of the Sea 1 (1982).

a few days journey from port due to the requirement for fresh water and food for the rowers. Ships of all nations freely used the littoral oceans. The early polities of the Mediterranean set aside exclusive state authority over only miniscule fisheries offshore. For the most part, however, the seas were regarded as under the ownership of no nation.

Cooperation among the cities and territories of the Hanseatic League, founded in 13th century German lands and the Italian city-republics, provided additional impetus for the development of international diplomacy. The rules concerning the oceans were a precursor to the 1648 Peace of Westphalia and subsequent development of *jus gentium* or the modern law of nations. Frederick III, who ruled from 1440–1483, was the last emperor crowned in Rome by the pope, and the weakening of the ecclesiastical order, which was accelerated by the Protestant Reformation, encouraged the development of a new source of authority to govern states that was based in law rather than papal decree.[20]

In the late 15th century, the Portuguese and Spanish empires asserted control over the vast and unexplored oceans of the Americas and Asia. The voyage of Christopher Columbus ignited a controversy over ownership of the newly discovered continents. The division of the world ocean into two spheres—one controlled by Castile (Spain) the other by Portugal—was memorialized by Pope Alexander VI in the papal Bull *Inter Caetera* in 1493, and adjusted slightly in favor of Portugal in the Treaty of Tordesillas the following year. Using a meridian located 370 leagues west of the Cape Verde Islands, which were owned by Portugal, the two powers laid claim to all of the New World. The agreement was extended to the East with the Treaty of Saragossa in 1529, which recognized Portuguese ownership of the Moluccan Islands, the modern day Strait of Malacca and Indonesia.

The devastation of the Thirty Years War—the Bourbon and Hapsburg rivalry that engulfed central Europe—inspired Italian theologian Alberico Gentili and Dutch jurist Hugo Grotius to collect and publish the laws of war and peace. The treatises these early masters produced reflected the accepted rules applicable in the global commons. In the early 17th century, Grotius penned the classic text animating the tradition of freedom of the seas, a doctrine that repudiated Portugal's claim of entitlement to the waters of Southeast Asia. Grotius' writing during the Dutch War of Independence or Eighty Years' War (1568–1648) championed access to the oceans for the United Provinces, and his work marked the rise of the first maritime power outside of Latin Europe. Although the concept of freedom of the seas was inherited from Rome and already was part of the lexicon, Grotius

---

[20] LORI F. DAMROSCH, ET AL., INTERNATIONAL LAW: CASES AND MATERIALS xxviii (4th ed. 2001).

and Gentili added a veneer of natural law theology, arguing that the sea was by nature open to all men and its use common to all.[21]

Spain and Portugal proved unable to obtain international acceptance for their claims over the sea. As the Iberian powers extracted vast hordes of gold and silver from the New World and began founding agricultural colonies, French, Dutch and British sea raiders disregarded the papal Bull and began targeting Spanish and Portuguese treasure fleets carrying specie back to Europe. Flouting the Treaty of Tordesillas, France, the nascent Dutch Republics, and eventually England, began to enter "Spanish" and "Portuguese" waters in the Americas and Asia, disrupting the carrying trade and developing their own colonies in the New World. Excluded from the original Iberian bargain, the emerging maritime states of The Netherlands and England adhered to a liberal view of the oceans based on freedom of the seas, a perspective that ignored the exclusive claims of Spain and Portugal.

The Anglo-Saxon-American tradition of liberty has infused oceans law and maritime governance. From the outset, the United States had two major planks of foreign policy. In the West, the country had to fulfill its manifest destiny and settle the Frontier. In the East, freedom of the seas in the Atlantic and Mediterranean were essential for American trade. Lacking the resources to pay tribute to the North African Barbary principalities to ensure its merchant ships were not attacked, for example, the United States fought two conflicts—one in 1802–04 and one in 1815—to ensure freedom of the seas.[22] Similarly, the issue of freedom of the seas was at the center of the Quasi-War with France from 1798–1800 and the War of 1812 with England.

7.1.4 *Freedom of the Seas in the World Wars and the Cold War*

One hundred years later, World War I produced a flurry of books on the importance of freedom of the seas.[23] The term "freedom of the seas" became synonymous with the British naval effort against the Germans during World War I.[24]

---

[21] Alberico Gentili, II DE IURE BELLI LIBRI TRES 24 (1612) (Oxford: Clarendon Press: John C. Rolfe, trans. 1933) and Theodor Meron, *Common Rights of Mankind in Gentili, Grotius and Suarez*, 85 AM. J. INT'L L. 110, 113–114 (1991).

[22] ROBERT C. GOLDSTON, THE BATTLES OF THE CONSTITUTION: OLD IRONSIDES AND FREEDOM OF THE SEAS (1969) (tracing the 170-year history of the famous ship, concentrating on the Barbary Wars and the War of 1812).

[23] *See, e.g.*, WILLIAM WOOD, FLAG AND FLEET: HOW THE BRITISH NAVY WON FREEDOM OF THE SEAS (1919), J. M. KENWORTHY & GEORGE YOUNG, FREEDOM OF THE SEAS (London: Hutchinson & Co. 1930), W.G. MACKENDRICK, GOD'S PLAN FOR FREEDOM OF THE SEAS (Toronto: Commonwealth Pub. Ltd. 1929).

[24] *See, e.g.*, BERNHARD RINGROSE WISE, THE FREEDOM OF THE SEAS (Darling & Sons, Ltd. 1915), RAMSAY MUIR, MARE LIBERUM: FREEDOM OF THE SEAS 2 (London & New York: Hodder & Stoughton 1917), and CHARLES STEWART DAVISON, FREEDOM OF THE SEAS: GERMANY'S INFRINGEMENTS OF MARITIME LAW (New York: Moffatt Yard & Co., 1918). German submarine warfare also inspired fiction oriented around freedom of navigation.

As freedom of the seas was essential for Allied strategy and maintenance of the "bridge" of supplies and troops flowing from North America to Western Europe, the doctrine became etched in the essential norms or mores of global governance. President Woodrow Wilson, for example, included the concept of free seas as one of the non-negotiable elements of his famous Fourteen Points, delivered to Congress on January 8, 1918. Point number two issued by President Wilson stated that the political and commercial provisions to be included in the Peace Treaty ending the war must include, "Absolute freedom of navigation upon seas, outside territorial waters, alike in peace and in war, except as the seas may be closed in whole or in part by international action for the enforcement of international covenants."[25]

One year before the address to Congress, while the nation was still neutral in the conflict, President Wilson stated in his "peace without victory" speech:

> And the paths of the sea must alike in law and in fact be free. The freedom of the seas is the *sine qua non* of peace, equality and cooperation. No doubt a somewhat radical reconsideration of many of the rules of international practice hitherto thought to be established may be necessary in order to make the seas indeed free and common in practically all circumstances for the use of mankind, but the motive for such changes is convincing and compelling. There can be no trust or intimacy between the people of the world without them. The free, constant, unthreatened intercourse of nations is an essential part of the process of peace and development. It need not be difficult to define or to secure the freedom of the seas if the governments of the world sincerely desire to come to an agreement concerning it.[26]

The Pope Benedict XV (1914–22) wrote in a peace message on August 1, 1917:

> First of all the fundamental points must be that for the material force of arms be substituted the moral force of right.... Once the supremacy of right has thus been established all obstacles to the means of communication of the peoples would disappear by assuring, by rules to be fixed later, the true liberty and community of the seas, which would contribute to ending the numerous causes of conflict and would also open to all, new sources of prosperity and progress.[27]

Similarly, freedom of the seas was championed by the Allied powers during World War II. Months before the Japanese attack on Pearl Harbor, President Roosevelt declared:

See, Ralph Henry Barbour, For Freedom of the Seas (New York: D. Appleton & Co. 1918).

[25] Woodrow Wilson & Howard Seavoy Leach, The Public Papers of Woodrow Wilson: War and Peace: Presidential Messages, Addresses, and Public Papers (1917–1924) 159 (Harper & Bros. 1927).

[26] *Address of the President to the Senate of the United States*, Jan. 22, 1917, 11 Am. J. Int'l L. Supp. 318, 322 (1917).

[27] Theodore Salisbury Woolsey, *Freedom of the Land and Freedom of the Seas*, 28 Yale L. J. 151, 151–52.

The Hitler Government, in defiance of the laws of the sea and of the recognized rights of all other nations, has presumed to declare, on paper, that great areas of the seas—even including a vast expanse lying in the Western Hemisphere—are to be closed, and that no ships may enter them for any purpose, except at peril of being sunk. Actually they are sinking ships at will and without warning in widely separated areas both within and far outside of these far-flung pretended zones.[28]

Later, freedom of the seas was included as a plank in the Atlantic Charter on war aims of the Allied powers that was fashioned by President Franklin D. Roosevelt and Prime Minister Winston Churchill at Placentia Bay off Newfoundland, Canada. The document outlined a plan for self-governance, international trade, and global governance in the postwar world. The Charter that emerged from the Placentia Bay conference formed the basis of all subsequent wartime discussions, including those at Yalta involving Joseph Stalin. The seventh tenet of the Atlantic Charter called for a peace that "should enable all men to traverse the high seas and oceans without hindrance."[29]

Yet, after the war, coastal states sought to internalize the benefits of offshore ocean space for themselves while externalizing the costs of their exclusive claims onto the international community. The difficulty in organizing a collective response among all of the nations of the world—each affected in a small way by the loss of part of the global commons—often means that excessive coastal state claims go unchallenged. The United States began to worry that acquiescence to excessive coastal state claims would impede U.S. naval and air forces, generating strategic follow-on effects, such as an inability to stay connected to allies in Europe and Asia. For sixty years the United States has pursued an active policy of arresting the spread of excessive maritime claims. After World War II, for example, the United States sought to preserve the three-mile territorial sea against expansion to 12 miles and beyond. In 1952, the Department of State circulated a memorandum to the Secretaries of Defense, Treasury, Interior, and Commerce, and to the Attorney General, concerning excessive maritime claims of other nations. The memorandum concluded:

> The immediate objective of the United States is to arrest, if possible, the present trend towards extension of the claims of coastal states over their adjacent seas. To this end, the United States should attempt to rally the active support of states which, like itself, have traditionally adhered to the principle of freedom of the seas based on a 3 mile limit of territorial waters.[30]

---

[28] *Radio Address Delivered by President Roosevelt from Washington*, V Dep't of State Bull., Sept. 11, 1941, p. 193.

[29] 2 The Papers of Robert A. Taft: 1939–1944, at 285–86 (Clarence E. Wunderlin, Jr., ed. 2001).

[30] Memorandum of the Legal Adviser (Phleger), Position of the United States concerning National Claims in Adjacent Seas, March 19, 1953, at 1674–1684, Dep't of State, Foreign Relations of the United States 1952–1954, I General Economic and Political Matters 1684 (1983).

In general, the other departments of the U.S. government concurred with the recommendations of the Department of State, although the Secretaries of Defense and Commerce, and the Attorney General, expressed reservations or offered specific suggestions for changing the wording or emphasis of some sections of the paper.[31]

The 1960s brought a wave of decolonization, however, with newly independent states less willing to support a free order of the oceans. The competition over how the law of the sea would be defined was summed up in 1964 by the Commander-in-Chief, U.S. Pacific Command, who wrote in a naval message to the Joint Chiefs of Staff:

> The principle that the free world is bound together in a loose oceanic confederation, which requires unimpeded sea lines of communication, is well recognized. However, since about the end of World War I there has been a progressive erosion of the universally accepted doctrine that the high seas were *res communis*, i.e. the community property of all. This doctrine required that the limits of national sovereignty over high seas areas be carefully and strictly regulated so as to prevent unreasonable interference with the rights of all nations to navigate without restriction on all the high seas of the word.
>
> During the period of *Pax Brittanica*, a few unilateral claims to large areas of the high seas were made, but they were ignored, strenuously opposed, and were soon abandoned. Since the Soviet Union attempted to gain international acceptance of a unilateral claim of a twelve-mile breadth of territorial sea, shortly after the end of World War I, numerous other claims have been made which, if permitted to stand, would encroach immeasurably upon the historic community property of all nations.[32]

Throughout the Cold War, freedom of navigation continued to serve as a basis for superpower competition, even leading to major theater war. The Suez Crisis of 1956, for example, came after eight years of Egyptian blockade of international shipping through the Strait of Tiran and in the Gulf of Aqaba. After the Crisis, Israel evacuated the Sinai Peninsula, except for a small strip along the coastline of the Gulf of Aqaba, which it temporarily retained until assurances for continued freedom of navigation were forthcoming.[33]

In November 1956, Israel sent a letter to UN Secretary-General Hammarskjold stating it would withdraw from Egyptian Sinai on condition of a declaration of an end to a state of belligerency with Egypt, and restoration of free transit though

---

[31] Id., at footnote 5, which states: "These replies are in Department of State file 711.022." See, http://history.state.gov/historicaldocuments/frus1952–54v01p2/d268.

[32] DEP'T OF DEFENSE, COMMANDER IN CHIEF, U.S. PACIFIC COMMAND, IMPLICATIONS [OF] INDONESIA'S MARE NOSTRUM, CINCPAC MESSAGE 102244Z OCT 64 Parts I & II (Secret; declassified), Oct. 22, 1964.

[33] Dep't of State Telegram from Ben Gurion, Tel Aviv to Secretary of State, No. 941, Feb. 10, 1957, in reply to President of the United States letter Feb. 3, (Marked "Presidential Handling," Confidential; declassified Apr. 16, 1990).

the Suez Canal and freedom of shipping in the Gulf of Aqaba. At the same time, Egypt insisted on unilateral control over the Suez Canal, which had been seized by military forces from the United Kingdom, France, and Israel.[34]

When Arabs and Israelis clashed again in 1967, the UN Security Council concluded that freedom of navigation was a key aspect of the Arab-Israeli conflicts—on par with settling the Palestinian refugee problem.[35] The Soviet Union agreed with that assessment, and Foreign Minister Dobrynin suggested in 1973 that, if Israel withdrew from Arab territories occupied in 1967, there would be "no special difficulties in solving other questions... [such as] ... providing for the freedom of navigation for Israeli ships through the Suez Canal and the Gulf of Aqaba."[36]

The result of the compromise depoliticized the Suez Canal in the same way that the United States allowed Soviet bloc ships to use the Panama Canal during the Cold War. The United States built the Panama Canal, finishing the project in 1914, and controlled it throughout the world wars and the Cold War. At the same time, however, the ships of all nations, including those carrying weapons to U.S. adversaries in Nicaragua during the 1980s, were permitted to freely transit the canal.

The Panama Canal is one of the most important pieces of global infrastructure, saving 13 days of transit time over the alternative route through the Strait of Magellan at the southern tip of Latin America.[37] Similarly, the Suez Canal is even more essential for commercial and military commerce, particularly for Euro-Asian trade. When the canal opened in 1869, it cut the distance between Europe and Asia by 6,400 nautical miles, or 14 days of travel over the route around the Cape of Good Hope off South Africa. Although the waterway is open to all nations under the Constantinople Convention, adopted by the major European powers in 1888, the British closed it to Axis vessels during World War II.

---

[34] Dep't of State Telegram from King Saud, Jeddah, to Secretary of State, No. 118, Sept. 4, 1956 (Marked "Presidential Handling, Secret; declassified Oct. 31, 1986).

[35] UN S/Res/242, Nov. 22, 1967.

[36] Message from the Soviet Ambassador (Dobrynin) to the President's Assistant for National Security Affairs (Kissinger) (undated), NAT'L ARCHIVES, NIXON PRESIDENTIAL MATERIALS, NSC FILES, KISSINGER OFFICE FILES, BOX 70, COUNTRY FILES, EUROPE, USSR, Exchange of Notes Between Dobrynin and Kissinger, Vol. 5. No classification marking. A handwritten notation at the top of the page reads: "Handed to HAK by Dobrynin 1/28/73," *reprinted in* DEP'T OF STATE, 25 FOREIGN RELATIONS OF THE UNITED STATES 1969–1976, ARAB-ISRAELI CRISIS AND WAR, 1973 19–21 (Nina Howland & Craig Daigle, eds. 2011).

[37] Captain R. S. Fahle, *The Panama Canal—An Auxiliary of the Fleet*, PROCEEDINGS OF THE U.S. NAVAL INSTITUTE, 1954, at pp. 495–503, at 497.

7.1.5 Freedom of the Seas, the Law of the Sea, and U.S. Policy

The United Nations Convention on the Law of the Sea (UNCLOS) was negotiated over a nine-year period between 1973 and 1982.[38] The impetus for the negotiations was two-fold. First, traditional maritime powers were concerned that the proliferation of excessive coastal state claims over the oceans would restrict fundamental navigational rights and freedoms. Second, developing countries wanted guaranteed access to living and non-living natural resources in their offshore waters, and they sought to share in the wealth extracted from the seabed in areas beyond national jurisdiction. At the same time, multinational conglomerates that could conduct seabed mining wanted an international convention that would provide legal certainty and secure tenure for mining sites.

The contending visions of the future shape of the world order in the oceans led American diplomat Lincoln P. Bloomfield to describe the negotiations for the Law of the Sea as the "most insanely complex global packages of rule making of all time, ranging through political, strategic, economic, commercial, and energy sectors all the way to full employment for lawyers." He stated the "smart money is quoting 50–50 odds on a favorable outcome in due time."[39] The negotiations were successful, resulting in UNCLOS, the most important treaty in existence after the UN Charter. At the end of the Conference in 1982, the United States did not sign the treaty, although the Reagan Administration issued an Oceans Policy Statement in 1983 that committed the United States to act in accordance with all parts of the treaty except for Part XI on seabed mining.[40]

The Convention was adopted by the Conference, and following more than a decade of renegotiation and the demise of the Soviet Union, Part XI was amended with the adoption of the 1994 Implementing Agreement. The Implementing Agreement transformed the rules on seabed mining from a socialist model to a market-oriented model, and made the treaty more attractive to the United States and other Western countries that had rejected the original Part XI framework.

The Convention is an epochal agreement on the order of the Treaty of Westphalia. As a constitution for the world's oceans,[41] the Convention's 320 articles and nine annexes, "...provide a framework for the allocation of jurisdiction, rights and duties among states that carefully balances the interests of States in

---

[38] United Nations Convention on the Law of the Sea, *opened for signature* Dec. 10, 1982, UN Doc. A/CONF.62/122 (1982), 1833 U.N.T.S. 3, 397, 21 I.L.M. 1261 (1982), *entered into force* Nov. 16, 1994 [Hereinafter, UNCLOS].

[39] Memorandum of Lincoln P. Bloomfield, National Security Council to Zbigniew Brzezinski, Visit to the [Law of the Sea] Conference, July 26, 1979, July 31, 1979 (Secret; declassified Aug. 22, 2000).

[40] Stmt. on U.S. Oceans Policy, Mar. 10, 1983, I PUBLIC PAPERS OF THE PRESIDENTS: RONALD REAGAN 1983, at 378–379, 22 I.L.M. 464; 77 AM. J. INT'L L. 619 (1983); DEP'T STATE BULL, June 1983, at 70–71.

[41] "Tommy" T. B. KOH, A CONSTITUTION FOR THE OCEANS (1982).

controlling activities off their own coasts and the interests of all states in protecting the freedom to use the ocean spaces without undue interference."[42] These globally accepted norms create stability and predictability in international affairs, and form a minimum basis for world public order.[43]

The commitment to preserving freedom of the seas explicitly within the text of UNCLOS was backed by the political power of the United States and was supported by the United Kingdom and the Soviet Union. Both superpowers made the issue a diplomatic priority during the negotiations for UNCLOS. The United States, fulfilling the historic British role of *Pax Brittanica*, sought to ensure that the treaty would codify essential freedom of movement throughout the globe. Walter Russell Mead observed, "As early as the time of the Stuarts, Anglo-American strategic thought grappled with questions of world order. As maritime trading peoples, the British and Americans were busy weaving webs of trade and investment covering whole continents and seas."[44] The United States and United Kingdom were principal developers of the international law of the sea, forming the core of the group of major maritime powers that coordinated UNCLOS negotiations. The Soviet Union, realizing that it lacked easy access to the high seas, also strongly supported freedom of navigation during the negotiations for UNCLOS, coordinating its positions on the major navigation issues, including transit passage throughout international straits, with France, the United Kingdom, Japan, and the United States.

The navigational provisions of the Convention represented a negotiating victory for the major maritime powers, but the downsides associated with the redistributionist scheme in Part XI on seabed mining limited the treaty's appeal. In July 1982, President Reagan announced that the United States would not sign UNCLOS "because several major problems in the Convention's deep seabed mining provisions are contrary to the interests and principles of industrialized nations and would not help attain the aspirations of developing countries." The president recognized that the treaty "contains provisions with respect to traditional uses of the oceans which generally confirms existing maritime law and practice and fairly balances the interests of all states." Accordingly, President Reagan directed:

> First, the United States is prepared to accept and act in accordance with the balance of interests relating to traditional uses of the oceans—such as navigation and overflight. In this respect the United States will recognize the rights of other states in

---

[42] COMMENTARY—THE 1982 UNITED NATIONS CONVENTION ON THE LAW OF THE SEA AND THE AGREEMENT ON IMPLEMENTATION OF PART XI, accompanying the Secretary of State Letter of Submittal in Senate Treaty Document 103–39, at p. 1, 6, U.S. DEP'T OF STATE DISPATCH, Supp. No. 1, Feb. 1995, at 5–52; 34 I.L.M. 1400–1447 (1995).

[43] MYRES S. MCDOUGAL & FLORENTINO P. FELICIANO, LAW AND MINIMUM WORLD PUBLIC ORDER 216, 297 (2d ed. 1967).

[44] WALTER RUSSELL MEAD, SPECIAL PROVIDENCE: AMERICAN FOREIGN POLICY AND HOW IT CHANGED THE WORLD 38 (2002).

the waters off their coasts, as reflected in the Convention, so long as the rights and freedoms of the United States and others under international law are recognized by such coastal states.

Second, the United States will exercise and assert its navigational and overflight rights and freedoms on a worldwide basis in a manner that is consistent with the balance of interests reflected in the Convention. The United States, will not, however, acquiesce in unilateral acts of other states designed to restrict the rights and freedoms of the international community in navigation and overflight and other related high seas uses.

Third, I am proclaiming today an Exclusive Economic Zone in which the United States will exercise sovereign rights in living and nonliving resources within 200 nautical miles of its coast.... Within this Zone all nations will continue to enjoy the high seas rights and freedoms that are not resource related, including the freedoms of navigation and overflight....[45]

The new policy was released on March 10, 1983, and more detailed guidance was set forth in a now partially declassified *National Security Decision Directive*.[46] The 1983 policy additionally claimed a 200-nm EEZ for the United States. The proclamation also made clear that, in accordance with international law, as reflected in UNLCOS, "the ships of all countries enjoy the right of innocent passage [within the territorial sea] and the ships and aircraft of all countries enjoy the right of transit passage through international straits."[47]

The EEZ proclamation asserts U.S. sovereign rights and jurisdiction over living and non-living resources within the zone while at the same time preserving for all nations high seas rights and freedoms that are not resource-related. Specifically, within the zone, the United States has:

(a) sovereign rights for the purpose of exploring, exploiting, conserving and managing natural resources, both living and non-living, of the seabed and subsoil and the superjacent waters and with regard to other activities for the economic exploitation and exploration of the zone, such as the production of energy from the water, currents and winds; and

(b) jurisdiction with regard to the establishment and use of artificial islands, and installations and structures having economic purposes, and the protection and preservation of the marine environment.

The 1983 presidential proclamation, however, recognizes that the EEZ "remains an area beyond the territory and territorial sea of the United States in which all States enjoy the high seas freedoms of navigation and overflight, the laying of submarine cables and pipelines, and other internationally lawful uses of the seas." The National Security Decision Directive is even broader, stating that within the

---

[45] President Ronald Reagan, Stmt. on United States Ocean Policy, 19 WEEKLY COMP. PRES. DOC. 383, Mar. 10, 1983.

[46] National Security Decision Directive 83, Mar. 10, 1983 (Confidential; partially declassified on Aug. 10, 1992).

[47] Pres. Proc. 5928, Territorial Sea of the United States of America, Dec. 27, 1988, 54 FR 777, Jan. 9, 1989.

U.S. EEZ, "all nations will continue to enjoy the high seas rights and freedoms that are not resource related...."[48]

Although UNCLOS allows coastal states to regulate marine scientific research (MSR) by other nations in the EEZ, the U.S. EEZ proclamation specifically excludes MSR from the scope of its application to avoid any unnecessary burdens on foreign states. Finally, nothing in the EEZ proclamation affects U.S. laws and policies concerning the continental shelf established by President Truman and codified by Congress.[49] The outer limits of the U.S. EEZ are published in the Federal Register.[50]

In 1988, the United States claimed a 12-nm territorial sea, and it claimed a 24-nm contiguous zone in 1999. The U.S. contiguous zone was established to "advance the law enforcement and public health interests of the United States," as well as prevent "the removal of cultural heritage found within 24 nautical miles of the baseline." Within the contiguous zone, the United States exercises control "necessary to prevent infringement of its customs, fiscal, immigration, or sanitary laws and regulations within its territory or territorial sea, and to punish infringement of the above laws and regulations committed within its territory or territorial sea." Again, the U.S. proclamation emphasized that in accordance with international law,

> within the contiguous zone of the United States the ships and aircraft of all countries enjoy the high seas freedoms of navigation and overflight and the laying of submarine cables and pipelines, and other internationally lawful uses of the sea related to those freedoms, such as those associated with the operation of ships, aircraft, and submarine cables and pipelines, and compatible with the other provisions of international law ... reflected in UNCLOS.[51]

Like all multilateral accords, UNCLOS reflects compromises inherent in obtaining broad agreement; there is a certain quality of constructive ambiguity in some of the terms. As a human undertaking, nine years of negotiations produced an imperfect document. The Law of the Sea Convention is not a panacea for rolling back excessive maritime claims or guaranteeing freedom of navigation, since many member States do not comply with the provisions of the treaty. As problematic as the treaty might be, it is the best—really the only—legal instrument that has proved effective at restraining the coastal state impulse to encroach on

---

[48] National Security Decision Directive 83, The White House, Mar. 10, 1983 (Confidential; partially declassified on August 10, 1992).

[49] Pres. Proc. 5030, Mar. 10, 1983, Exclusive Economic Zone of the United States, 48 FR 10605, Mar. 14, 1983) and President Ronald Reagan, Stmt. on United States Ocean Policy, 19 WEEKLY COMP. PRES. DOC. 383, Mar. 10, 1983.

[50] U.S. DEP'T OF STATE PUB. NOTICE 2237, Exclusive Economic Zone and Maritime Boundaries; Notice of Limits, 60 FR 43825, Aug. 23, 1995.

[51] Pres. Proc. 7219, Aug. 2, 1999, Contiguous Zone of the United States, 64 FR 48701, Aug. 8, 1999; Correction to Proc. 7219, 64 FR 49844, Sept. 14, 1999; Correction to Proc. 7219, 64 FR 49276, Sept. 10, 1999.

the global commons. Thus, the balance of U.S. interests falls decisively in favor of U.S. participation. If there is weakness in the Law of the Sea Convention, it lies in lackadaisical compliance and enforcement, rather than with any problems with the terms of the agreement.

The Convention helps to preserve the fundamental U.S. interest in global mobility and maneuverability, the pillar of American strategic interest in the oceans. Admiral Jay L. Johnson, who was serving as Chief of Naval Operations, underscored this point in a letter to the Senate Foreign Relations Committee on June 29, 2000:

> I would like to bring to your attention two alarming trends that adversely affect our navigational freedoms that are directly related to our failure to accede to the Convention. First, is the erosion of U.S. influence internationally in the development of the law of the sea. Secondly, and perhaps more alarming, is the emboldening of those who seek to fundamentally change the balance between our interests as a coastal nation and the role of the United States as the world's leading maritime nation and guarantor of freedom of the seas, to one of a coastal nation that places domestic and regional regulatory control first. These trends, which are closely interconnected, can be effectively curtailed if the United States accedes to the Convention.
>
> During my tenure, I have witnessed the jurisdictional creep of coastal states, often with the direct support of nongovernmental organizations (NGOs) Contrary to the law of the sea as codified in the Convention. These claims of regional and coastal state jurisdiction and authority are invoked to the detriment of navigational freedoms to further a wide range of special interests, including enhanced environmental protection, total nuclear disarmament, world health, limitations on measures to combat transnational crime and illegal migration, and management and allocation of the radio frequency spectrum.
>
> During the past decade, coastal states and regional groups of coastal states have continued their efforts to extend jurisdiction beyond that which is recognized and permitted under the Convention. Although the United States Navy does its best to counter those illegal extensions of jurisdiction by operationally challenging such claims and arguing that they are contrary to the principles of customary international law, we are increasingly being marginalized, both internationally and domestically, by the fact that the United States has not acceded to the Convention. In short, our failure to accede to the Convention permits domestic and international policymakers, foreign nations, and NGOs to increasingly pursue modifications to bedrock principles of customary international law, that affect our navigational freedoms over our most strenuous objection....[52]

At the bottom of the letter, Admiral Johnson penned a hand-written note that declared the treaty was his most important piece of "unfinished business." In 2007, the entire U.S. senor military leadership wrote a letter expressing strong support for the treaty. The letter included signatures by the Chairman and Vice Chairman of the Joint Chiefs of Staff, the Chief of Naval Operations, the

---

[52] Chief of Naval Operations Admiral Jay L. Johnson letter to the Hon. Sen. Jesse Helms (R-NC), Chairman, Senate Foreign Relations Committee, June 29, 2000.

Commandant of the Marine Corps, the Chief of Staff of the Army, the Chief of Staff of the Air Force, and the Commandant of the U.S. Coast Guard.[53]

7.2 U.S. Freedom of Navigation Program

The United States has worldwide security and economic interests, which are dependent on the transport of goods in international trade and the free movement of fleet submarines, surface ships and aircraft. Together with the U.S. Marine Corps and U.S. Coast Guard, as well as international partners and allies, the U.S. Navy is tasked with securing access to the world's oceans in order to retain global freedom of action to maintain international peace and security and facilitate and enhance global trade and commerce. The challenge for the sea services "is to apply seapower in a manner that protects U.S. vital interests" and "promotes greater collective security, stability and trust."[54] Because of the aforementioned leakage or slippage in compliance with UNCLOS, the United States maintains a freedom of navigation program, which is one of the most important ways to influence nations to either avoid new excessive maritime claims or renounce existing ones. The Freedom of Navigation program was initiated during the Carter presidency, an unsung political-military achievement of the administration.

In a July 1979 memorandum to National Security Adviser Zbigniew Brzesinski, Lincoln P. Bloomfield offered one of the first glimpses of what would become the U.S. Freedom of Navigation program:

> We also ought to be alerted to an issue brought to my attention by [the Navy]. I refer to the Navy's plans to make so-called 'protest sailings' through waters claimed by other states, in a staged series of maneuvers over the next few months. With respect specifically to Indonesia, on August 1st the American Embassy will shift from written notification to oral notification regarding American warships sailing through Indonesia-claimed waters; on September 1st no more advance notifications will be given. I gather this is within the framework of the policy agreed to by the [National Security Council (NSC)] Navigation and Overflight Committee.... [Department of Defense] is now composing a 'protest matrix,' and plans to report back to the NSC every six months on what has happened. Looking at some of the choke points around

---

[53] Chairman of the Joint Chiefs of Staff "24–star" letter to Hon. Joseph Biden, Jr., Chairman, Committee on Foreign Relations, U.S. Senate, June 26, 2007, signed by General Peter Pace, Chairman of the Joint Chiefs of Staff, Admiral E. P. Giambastiani, Vice Chairman, Joint Chiefs of Staff, Admiral M. G. Mullen, Chief of Naval Operations, T. Michael Mosely, Chief of Staff, U.S. Air Force, J. T. Conway, Commandant of the U.S. Marine Corps and George W. Casey, Chief of Staff, U.S. Army.

[54] Dep't of the U.S. Navy, A Cooperative Strategy for 21st Century Seapower (Oct. 2007).

the world that may be involved, I would think that this is something the NSC should monitor more closely than that.[55]

Between 1948 and 1979, the United States filed about 20 protests against excessive coastal state maritime claims. Seeing that simple diplomatic demarches were ineffective and that a tangible demonstration of U.S. resolve against excessive maritime claims was sorely needed, the Carter Administration launched the Freedom of Navigation (FON) program in March 1979.[56] The FON program uses U.S. warships and military aircraft to assert navigation and overflight rights and freedoms against excessive claims on a worldwide basis, and in a manner that is consistent with UNCLOS and the Chicago Convention on Civil Aviation.

The program is reflected in a series of classified White House directives prepared by the National Security Council and signed by subsequent presidents. National Security Decision Directive-20 (NSDD-20), United States Law of the Sea Policy, was signed on January 29, 1982, and is reproduced as Annex 1 to this chapter. National Security Decision Directive 265 (NSDD-265), Freedom of Navigation Program, March 16, 1987, is reproduced as Annex 2 to this chapter. National Security Directive 49 (NSD-49), Freedom of Navigation Program, was released on October 12, 1990 and is reprinted as Annex 3 to this chapter.

Presidential Decision Directive-32 (PDD-32), Freedom of Navigation, is the current version of U.S. Freedom of Navigation policy. President Clinton signed the policy on January 23, 1995. Like all presidential directives, it remains in effect unless cancelled by a subsequent presidential order. PDD-32 is a classified document, but redacted and unclassified excerpts have been released by the Joint Staff and are reprinted in Annex 4, U.S. Freedom of Navigation Policy. Finally, Annex 5 of this chapter displays nations subject to FON assertions or challenges by U.S. naval forces under PDD-32 for the period 1995–2003.

The FON Program challenges excessive maritime claims and demonstrates U.S. non-acquiescence in unilateral acts of other states that are designed to restrict navigation and overflight rights and freedoms of the international community and other lawful uses of the seas related to those rights and freedoms. Operating along three tracks, the FON program includes diplomatic protests or demarches and other communications by the Department of State, operational assertions by U.S. naval ships, aircraft and submarines, and U.S. bilateral and multilateral consultations with other governments.

Theoretically, the U.S. Air Force participates in challenging excessive coastal state claims over international airspace. In reality, however, the Air Force has not

---

[55] Lincoln P. Bloomfield, National Security Council Memorandum to Zbigniew Brzezinski, Visit to the [Law of the Sea] Conference, July 26, 1979, July 31, 1979 (Secret; declassified Aug. 22, 2000).
[56] *See*, William Aceves, *The Freedom of Navigation Program: A Study on the Relationship Between Law and Politics*, 19 HASTINGS INT'L & COMP. L. REV. 259 (1996).

been active in the program, to the detriment of the overall U.S. effort to resist excessive airspace claims.[57] The Coast Guard is also a potential player in FON assertions, but it has not conducted a pre-planned operational challenge against an excessive maritime claim in over forty years. Military-to-military contacts by the armed forces with their foreign counterparts promote maritime stability and consistency in applying the law of the sea.

In short, the FON program underscores American commitment to a stable legal regime for the world's oceans. Since its inception, hundreds of operational challenges and diplomatic protests have been conducted to demonstrate U.S. non-acquiescence in excessive maritime claims. A list of challenges and protests is contained in the individual country entries of the *Department of Defense Maritime Claims Reference Manual*.[58]

During the height of the Cold War when the U.S. Navy approached 600 ships, there were 35–40 ship and aircraft FON assertions per year. In recent years, however, the FON program has fallen on hard times. Downsizing of the U.S. fleet to below 300 ships and the drain of the ground wars in Iraq and Afghanistan have reduced both the ability and willingness of the country to maintain a robust program. With fewer ships and aircraft to challenge excessive maritime claims, today only about 5 to 8 surface ship and aircraft assertions are conducted each year. Furthermore, the Department of State has consistently and at a very high level pushed the Pentagon to limit the number and scope of challenges, since FON assertions may sour bilateral relationships. There is little evidence that the program will be reinvigorated with additional resources and a renewed commitment to challenge excessive maritime claims.

---

[57] Dale Cheney, *Freedom of Navigation*, THE MOBILITY FORUM, July/August 2003, at 30, 33.
[58] DEP'T OF DEFENSE, MARITIME CLAIMS REFERENCE MANUAL (MCRM), DOD 2005.1–M, June 2008.

ANNEX 1: NATIONAL SECURITY DECISION DIRECTIVE 20 (1982)

SECRET (DECLASSIFIED ON SEPT. 22, 2000)

THE WHITE HOUSE
WASHINGTON

NATIONAL SECURITY DECISION
DIRECTIVE NUMBER 20

January 29, 1982

United States Law of the Sea Policy

I have reviewed the interagency report on United States law of the Sea issues, along with the agencies' recommendations, and have decided that:

- The United States will continue to participate in the [Third United Nations Conference on the Law of the Sea] (U)
- The United States objectives in these negotiations will be a treaty that:
  (a) Will not deter development of any deep seabed mineral resources to meet national and world demand; (U)
  (b) Will assure national access to these resources by current and future qualified entities to enhance U.S. security of supply, to avoid monopolization of the resources by the operating arms of the International [Seabed] Authority and to promote the economic development of the resources; (U)
  (c) Will give the United States a decision-making role in the deep seabed regime that fairly reflects and effectively protects its political and economic interests and financial contributions; (U)
  (d) Will not allow for amendments to come into force without United States approval, including the advice and consent of the Senate; (U)
  (e) Will not set other undesirable precedents for international organizations; and (U)
  (f) Will be likely to receive the advice and consent of the Senate. (In this regard, the convention should not contain provisions creating serious political or commercial difficulties, including provisions for the mandatory transfer of private technology and participation by and funding for national liberation movements.)

- Fulfillment of these objectives shall be considered mandatory in the negotiations. It is understood that the United States negotiating effort will be based on the guidelines set forth in the interagency review. (S)
- United States negotiating strategy will make clear what aspects of the current draft convention are unacceptable to the United States and will be designed to achieve those changes necessary to fulfill all U.S. objectives and, pending that, to avoid a move by the conference to complete its work and open a convention for signature. (S)

Improvements consistent with United States interests in other areas shall be sought if opportunities arise and if this can be accomplished without risk to the military navigation and other important United States interests. (C) The United States will continue active negotiations with other countries interested in deep seabed mining with a view to concluding a reciprocating states agreement as early as possible on recognition of deep seabed mining licenses. (U)

The United States will also continue to exercise its rights with respect to navigation and overflight against claims that the United States does not recognize in accordance with established procedures and review for that program. (C)

The Senior Interdepartmental Group, including all relevant agencies, shall develop detailed instructions for achieving the objectives set forth above after immediate consultation with key allies and, as appropriate, other major participants in the conference. Any agency differences shall be forwarded for my consideration by February 15, 1982. The Senior Intergovernmental Group shall also oversee the Law of the Sea negotiations. The Delegation will not accept an ad referendum draft convention pending my decision on a report to be submitted by the Senior Interdepartmental Group on its acceptability in terms of satisfying United States objectives. (C)

/signed/
Ronald Reagan

Annex 2: National Security Decision Directive 265 (1987)

CONFIDENTIAL (DECLASSIFIED EXCERPTS)

THE WHITE HOUSE
WASHINGTON

NATIONAL SECURITY DECISION
DIRECTIVE NUMBER 265

March 16, 1987

Freedom of Navigation Program

Since March 1979, the United States has successfully conducted a Freedom of Navigation (FON) program to protect U.S. navigation, overflight, and related interests on and over the seas against excessive maritime claims.

Policy

In July 1982, the United States announced that it would not sign the Law of the Sea Convention because of several problems in the Convention's deep seabed mining provisions. The United States does, however, support the provisions of the Law of the Sea Convention governing traditional uses of the oceans which generally confirm existing maritime law and practice and fairly balance the interests of all states.

General U.S. policy on the Law of the Sea is contained in NSDD-83 (U.S. Oceans Policy, Law of the Sea, and Exclusive Economic Zone) and the public Presidential statement of March 10, 1983. Two important aspects of those documents pertain to U.S. policy on freedom of navigation and are reflected below.

First, the United States is prepared to accept and act in accordance with the balance of interests relating to traditional uses of the oceans—such as navigation and overflight. In this respect, the United States will recognize the rights of other states in waters off their coasts, as reflected in the Convention, so long as the right and freedoms of the United States and others under international law are recognized by such coastal states.

Second, the United States will exercise and assert its navigation and overflight rights and freedoms on a worldwide basis in a manner that is consistent with the balance of interests reflected in the Convention. The United States will not, however, acquiesce in unilateral acts of other states designed to restrict the rights and freedoms of the international community in navigation and overflight and other related high seas uses.

Categories of Excessive Maritime Claims

U.S. interests are to be protected against the following categories of excessive maritime claims:

1. Those historic bay/historic water claims not recognized by the United States.
2. Those territorial sea baseline claims not drawn in conformance with the customary international law reflected in the Law of the Sea (LOS) Convention.
3. Those territorial sea claims exceeding twelve nautical miles in breadth that:
   a. Overlap straits used for international navigation and do not permit transit passage in conformance with the customary international law reflected in the LOS Convention, including submerged transit of submarines, overflight of military aircraft, and surface transit of warships/naval auxiliaries, without prior notification or authorization, and including transit in a manner of deployment consistent with the security of the forces involved; or
   b. Contain requirements for advance notification or authorization for innocent passage of warships/naval auxiliaries or apply discriminatory requirements to such vessels; or
   c. Apply special requirements, not recognized by international law, for innocent passage of nuclear-powered warships (NPW) or warships/naval auxiliaries carrying nuclear weapons or special cargoes.
4. Territorial sea claims in excess of twelve nautical miles.
5. Other claims to jurisdiction over maritime areas in excess of twelve nautical miles, such as security zones, that purport to restrict non-resource related high seas freedoms.
6. Those archipelagic claims that either:
   a. Do not permit archipelagic sea lanes passage in conformance with customary international law reflected in the LOS Convention, including submerged passage of submarines, overflight of military aircraft, and surface transit of warships/naval auxiliaries, without prior notification or authorization, and including transit in a manner of deployment consistent with the security of the forces involved; or
   b. Are otherwise not in conformance with the customary international law reflected in the LOS Convention.

Program Guidance

The Department of Defense will plan and administer the program under the following procedures:

- [Redaction] U.S. rights against the following categories of excessive claims: unrecognized historic claims (paragraph 1 above), nonconforming baselines (paragraph 2 above), and territorial sea claims of twelve nautical miles or less which contain special requirements not recognized by international law (paragraphs 3.b and 3.c. above). [Redaction]
- [Redaction]
- International straits (paragraph 3.a above) and archipelagic sea lanes passage (paragraph 6.a above) will be used by both military ships and aircraft freely and frequently as directed by Department of Defense. [Redaction]
- The Department of Defense will routinely assert U.S. rights against territorial sea claims, other claims to jurisdiction over maritime areas in excess of twelve nautical

miles, and archipelagic claims not in conformance with the LOS Convention, (paragraphs 4, 5, and 6.b. above). [Redaction]
- A Table summarizing the above guidance is attached as Tab 1 to this NSDD [Table 1 is redacted in full].
- [Redaction]
- The Department of State will continue to protect in diplomatic channels the excessive claims of littoral countries.
- [Redaction]
- Where possible, we should strive for a balanced challenge program which contests the excessive claims or illegal regimes of allied or friendly states, inimical powers, and neutral states alike. [Redaction]
- Special emphasis should be given to challenging claims which have no record of prior challenge.

Annex 3: National Security Directive 49 (1990)

CONFIDENTIAL (DECLASSIFIED EXCERPTS)

THE WHITE HOUSE
WASHINGTON

October 12, 1990

NATIONAL SECURITY DIRECTIVE 49

MEMORANDUM FOR   THE VICE PRESIDENT
THE SECRETARY OF STATE
THE SECRETARY OF DEFENSE
THE SECRETARY OF TRANSPORTATION
THE CHIEF OF STAFF TO THE PRESIDENT
THE ASSISTANT TO THE PRESIDENT FOR NATIONAL
   SECURITY AFFAIRS
CHAIRMAN OF THE JOINT CHIEFS OF STAFF

SUBJECT: Freedom of Navigation Program (U)

United States security and commerce depend upon the internationally recognized freedoms of navigation and overflight of the seas. Since 1979, the United States has successfully conducted a Freedom of Navigation (FON) Program to protect U.S. navigation, overflight, and related interests on, under, and over the seas against excessive maritime claims. The purpose of the FON Program is to preserve the global mobility of U.S. forces by avoiding acquiescence in excessive maritime claims of other nations. (U)

This directive provides current guidance for the management and organization of the FON Program and supersedes National Security Decision Directive 265. (C)

Policy

While not a signatory to the 1982 Convention on the Law of the Sea (LOS Convention), the United States considered the Convention to accurately reflect the customary rules of international law concerning maritime navigation and overflight freedoms. (U)

General U.S. policy on the Law of the Sea is contained in NSDD-83 (U.S. Oceans Policy, Law of the Sea, and Exclusive Economic Zone) and the President's Oceans Policy statement of March 10, 1983. (C)

This policy provides that the United States will respect those maritime claims that are consistent with the navigational provisions of the LOS Convention.

Additionally, the United States will exercise and assert its navigation and overflight rights on a worldwide basis in a manner consistent with the LOS Convention. The United States will not acquiesce in unilateral acts of other states designed to restrict the rights and freedoms of the international community in navigation and overflight and other traditional uses of the high seas. (U)

The Freedom of Navigation Program combines diplomatic action and operational assertions of our navigation and overflight rights to encourage modification of, and to demonstrate non-acquiescence in, maritime claims that are inconsistent with the customary rules of international law pertaining to maritime navigation and overflight freedoms. (U)

Categories of Excessive Maritime Claims

U.S. interests are to be protected against the following categories of excessive maritime claims:

1. Historic bay/historic water claims not recognized by the United States. (U)
2. Territorial sea baseline claims not drawn in conformance with the customary international law reflected in the LOS Convention. (U)
3. Territorial sea claims not exceeding twelve nautical miles in breadth that:
    a. overlap straits used for international navigation and no not permit transit passage in conformance with the customary international law reflected in the LOS Convention, including submerged transit of submarines, overflight of military aircraft, and surface transit of warships/naval auxiliaries, without prior notification or authorization, and including transit in a manner of deployment consistent with the security of the forces involved; or
    b. contain requirements for advance notification or authorization for innocent passage of all vessels, including warships/naval auxiliaries, or apply discriminatory requirements to such vessels; or
    c. apply special requirements, not recognized by international law, for innocent passage based on means of propulsion, armament, or cargo. (U)
4. Territorial sea claims in excess of twelve nautical miles. (U)
5. Other claims to jurisdiction over maritime areas in excess of twelve nautical miles, such as security zones, that purport to restrict non-resource related high seas freedoms. (U)
6. Archipelagic claims that either:
    a. do not permit archipelagic sea lanes passage in conformance with customary international law reflected in the LOS Convention, including submerged transit of submarines, overflight of military aircraft, and surface transit of warships/naval auxiliaries, without prior notification or authorization, and including transit in a manner of deployment consistent with the security of the forces involved; or
    b. are otherwise not in conformance with customary international law reflected in the LOS Convention. (U)

Program Guidance

1. The Department of State shall act assertively to preserve U.S. navigation and overflight rights under international law. The Department of State shall use its facilities, here and abroad, to encourage each state with excessive maritime claims to conform its laws and/or conduct with customary international law concerning maritime navigation and overflight freedoms. The Department of State shall protest excessive maritime claims to avoid legal acquiescence. (C)
2. The Department of Defense will plan and administer the operational assertion portion of the FON Program under the following procedures:

    a. [Redacted] (C)

Criteria for the selection of an excessive maritime claim for the annual list will include, but are not limited to, the following:

   a. [Redacted] (C)
   b. Categories of excessive claims to be submitted for coordination include:
      – unrecognized historic bay/historic water claims (paragraph 1, above);
      – excessive straight baseline claims (paragraph 2, above);
      – territorial sea claims (of 12 nautical miles or less) that include unlawful restrictions or requirements relating to innocent passage (paragraph 3b, above); or that apply unlawful discriminatory restrictions or requirements based on means of propulsion, armament, or cargo (paragraph 3c, above);
      – territorial sea claims in excess of twelve nautical miles (paragraph 4, above) [Redacted] (C)
      – other claims to jurisdiction over maritime areas in excess of twelve nautical miles, such as security zones, that purport to restrict non-resource related high seas freedoms (paragraph 5, above) [Redacted] (C)

3. [Redacted] (C)
4. [Redacted] (C)
5. [Redacted] (C)
6. Military ships and aircraft will use international straits (paragraph 3a, above) and archipelagic sea lanes (paragraph 6l, above) freely and frequently [Redacted] (C)
7. Military ships and aircraft will routinely assert U.S. rights against territorial sea claims and other claims to jurisdiction over maritime areas in excess of twelve nautical miles that purport to restrict non-resource related high seas freedoms, and archipelagic claims not in conformance with the LOS Convention (paragraphs 4, 5, and 6b, above) [Redacted] (C)
8. [Redacted] (C)
9. [Redacted] (C)
10. [Redacted] (C)
11. The Department of Defense will provide to the Department of State and the National Security Advisor a semiannual list of operational assertions conducted under the FON Program. The Department of State shall, when appropriate,

use the semiannual list of operational assertions in its diplomatic efforts to preserve United States navigation and overflight rights under international law. The Department of State will publish an annual unclassified summary of the diplomatic activities under the FON Program. (U)
12. On an annual basis, the Department of Defense will incorporate into an already existing report an unclassified listing of FON operational assertions conducted during the previous year. The listing will specify the country and excessive claim, but not the date or frequency of the assertion. Assertions specified in the annual list will become unclassified upon incorporation into the report. (U)

ANNEX 4: PRESIDENTIAL DECISION DIRECTIVE 32 (1995)

CONFIDENTIAL (UNCLASSIFIED EXCERPTS)

January 23, 1995

PRESIDENTIAL DECISION DIRECTIVE/NSC-32

Subject: Freedom of Navigation (U)

This directive provides current guidance for protecting U.S. navigation, overflight rights and freedoms, and related interests on, under, and over the seas against excessive maritime claims. The purpose of this policy is to preserve the global mobility of U.S. forces by avoiding acquiescence in excessive maritime claims of other nations. (U)

This directive supersedes National Security Directive 49 dated October 12, 1990. (U)

Policy

The United States considers the 1982 Convention on the Law of the Sea (LOS Convention) to accurately reflect the customary rules of international law concerning maritime navigation and overflight rights and freedoms. (U)

It is U.S. policy to respect those maritime claims that are consistent with the navigational provisions of the LOS Convention. Additionally, the United States will exercise and assert its navigation and overflight rights on a worldwide basis in a manner consistent with the LOS Convention. The United States will not acquiesce in unilateral acts of other states designed to restrict the rights and freedoms of the international community in navigation and overflight and other traditional uses of the high seas. (U)

Annex 5: U.S. Freedom of Navigation Challenges 1995–2003

Albania	Iran	Sierra Leone
Algeria	Japan	Somalia
Angola	Kenya	Sri Lanka
Bangladesh	South Korea	Sudan
Burma	Liberia	Syria
Cambodia	Malaysia	Thailand
China	Maldives	Venezuela
Colombia	Malta	Vietnam
Croatia	Nicaragua	Yemen
Cuba	Oman	
Djibouti	Pakistan	
Ecuador	Philippines	
Egypt	Portugal	
El Salvador	Romania	
Greece	Saudi Arabia	
India	Seychelles	

EIGHT

FREEDOM OF NAVIGATION IN THE LAW OF THE SEA

The United Nations Convention on the Law of the Sea (UNCLOS)[1] is a comprehensive framework for the allocation of sovereignty, jurisdiction, and rights and duties among States, that carefully balances the interests of coastal States in exploiting the resources and controlling activities off their coasts with the interests of the international community in maintaining freedom of navigation and overflight and other lawful uses of the seas.

The Convention divides the seas into maritime zones—internal waters, archipelagic waters, territorial seas, contiguous zones, exclusive economic zones (EEZ), continental shelfs, high seas, and the Area—and establishes functional rights, obligations and jurisdiction over each zone related to navigation and overflight of the oceans, exploration, exploitation and conservation of ocean-based living and non-living resources, protection of the marine environment, and marine scientific research. Coastal State rights and jurisdiction in offshore areas diminish as the distance from the shoreline increases. Conversely, the rights and freedoms of the international community increase farther from land.

In short, the Convention protects critical freedoms of navigation and overflight and other internationally lawful uses of the sea, by establishing rules for the use of straight baselines and archipelagic baselines, prohibiting territorial sea claims in excess of 12 nm, accommodating passage rights through the territorial sea and archipelagic waters, including innocent passage, transit passage through international straits, and archipelagic sea lanes passage, and preserving high seas freedoms of navigation, overflight, laying of submarine cables and pipelines, and

---

[1] United Nations Convention on the Law of the Sea, Montego Bay Dec. 10, 1982, entered into force Nov. 10, 1994, UN Doc. A/CONF.62/122, 21 I.L.M. 1621–1354 (1982), 1833 U.N.T.S. 397 [Hereinafter UNCLOS].

related uses beyond the territorial sea, including the contiguous zone, the EEZ and the continental shelf.

8.1 Baselines

All maritime zones are measured from the baseline. The second Sub-committee of the 1930 Conference for the Codification of International Law adopted the historic rule of drawing the baseline from which the territorial sea is measured along the low water mark running along the entire coast.[2] The outcome reflected the American position that the territorial sea was measured from the low-water mark along the coast.[3] At the same conference, the three-mile limit for the territorial sea received the unconditional support of Canada, China, Great Britain, India, Japan, the Netherlands, South Africa, and the United States. Greece and Ireland were inclined to support the three-mile limit, as were Belgium, Egypt, France, Poland, and Germany, on the condition that the coastal State would have the right to exercise certain customs enforcement authorities in a zone contiguous to the territorial sea.[4]

The formula for determining normal baselines is to make observation of the low water mark running along the coast. Except as otherwise provided in UNCLOS, Article 5 specifies that "the normal baseline...is the low-water line along the coast as marked on large-scale charts officially recognized by the coastal State." Straight baselines may be used in very limited circumstances:

- "In localities where the coastline is deeply indented and cut into, or if there is a fringe of islands along the coast in its immediate vicinity...";[5]
- "Where because of the presence of a delta and other natural conditions the coastline is highly unstable...";[6]
- Across the mouth of a river that flows directly into the sea;[7] and
- To close the natural entrance of a bay, not to exceed 24 nm.[8]

---

[2] League of Nations: Acts of the Conference for the Codification of International Law, held at The Hague, March 13–April 12, 1930, III, Territorial Waters C.351(b) M.145(b), 1930, V, 206–207.
[3] S. Whittemore Boggs, *Delimitation of the Territorial Sea: The Method of Delimitation Proposed by the Delegation of the United States at the Hague Conference for the Codification of International Law*, 24 Am. J. Int'l L. 541–555, at 542 (July 1930).
[4] Memorandum of the Legal Adviser (Phleger), Position of the United States concerning National Claims in Adjacent Seas, Mar. 19, 1953, pp. 1674–1684, Foreign Relations of the United States 1952–1954 Vol. I General Economic and Political Matters at 1677 (Dep't of State 1983).
[5] UNCLOS, Article 7.1.
[6] Id., Article 7.2.
[7] Id., Article 9.
[8] Id., Article 10.4.

Improperly drawn straight baselines can significantly extend coastal State maritime jurisdiction seaward in a manner that prejudices navigational rights and freedoms and other lawful uses of the seas, infringing on the rights of the international community. It is therefore important that coastal States objectively apply the baseline rules contained in the Convention. It is especially important for the international community to challenge coastal States that elect to draw unlawful straight baselines or baselines otherwise inconsistent with international law. If challenges are not made against excessive straight baselines, they may, over time, acquire a stronger legal status. Furthermore, excessive baselines produced by one coastal State are a precedent that encourages other nations to do the same, generating a pernicious follow-on effect that threatens to undo the central bargain of the Law of the Sea Convention.

8.2 Internal Waters

Internal waters are defined in Article 8 of UNCLOS as all waters landward of the baseline along the coast. Lakes, rivers, some bays, roadsteads, harbors, canals, and lagoons are examples of internal waters, which lie landward of the baseline. Coastal nations exercise the same jurisdiction and control over their internal waters and superjacent airspace as they do over their land territory. Because ports and harbors are located landward of the baseline, entering a port ordinarily involves the consent of the port State and navigation through internal waters. There is no right of innocent passage by foreign vessels in internal waters.

Transit rights do not exist in internal waters except as authorized by the coastal State or, in some limited circumstances, as rendered necessary by force majeure or distress. Unless a ship or aircraft is in distress, however, it may not enter internal waters without the permission of the coastal state. In recent decades, coastal States have begun to narrow the rule on force majeure in an effort to keep vessels out of their ports and harbors for fear that they might produce harmful environmental spills. Thus, the extent of the classic right of force majeure, particularly when it is rejected explicitly by the coastal State, is not well settled. For example, the IMO *Guidelines on Places of Refuge for Ships in Need of Assistance* (IMO Resolution A.949(23), December 5, 2003) recognizes that the best way to prevent damage or pollution is to lighten a damaged ship's cargo and bunkers, and repair the damage, and that such operations are best carried out in a place of refuge. However, the Guidelines specifically provide that "when permission to access a place of refuge is requested, there is no obligation for the coastal State to grant it...." The coastal State need only weigh all the factors and risks in a balanced manner and "give shelter whenever reasonably possible."

In special circumstances, coastal states may be entitled to enclose limited parts of the oceans as "historic internal waters," but the test for doing so is notoriously difficult. The three-part test for historic waters claims emerged from customary international law and was explained by the UN Secretary-General in a 1962 United

Nations report. First, the coastal state has to exercise authority over the area. Second, the coastal state must demonstrate a continuity of the exercise of authority. Third, the coastal state bears the burden of showing the acquiescence of foreign nations.[9] Unfortunately, the rather strict rule for claiming historic internal waters is one of the most abused terms of the Convention, with nations in every region of the world asserting excessive claims that do not meet the test.

8.3 Territorial Sea

Under Part II of UNCLOS, all States may claim a 12 nm territorial sea.[10] Within the territorial sea, the coastal State exercises complete sovereignty over the water column, the seabed and subsoil, and the airspace above the territorial sea, subject to the right of innocent passage, transit passage, and archipelagic sea lanes passage.[11]

A fundamental tenet of international law is that all ships, including warships, enjoy the right of innocent passage through the territorial seas of coastal States.[12] Passage must be "continuous and expeditious," but may include stopping and anchoring if incidental to ordinary navigation or "rendered necessary by force majeure or distress or for the purpose of rendering assistance to persons, ships or aircraft in danger or distress."[13] Innocent passage does not, however, include a right of overflight over the territorial sea or submerged transit by submarines.[14] Article 20 requires submarines and other underwater craft engaged in innocent passage to "navigate on the surface and to show their flag."

Pursuant to Article 19, "passage is innocent so long as it is not prejudicial to the peace, good order or security of the coastal state." An inclusive list of activities considered to be non-innocent is contained in Article 19.2 and include:

> (a) any threat or use of force against the sovereignty, territorial integrity or political independence of the coastal State, or in any other manner in violation of the principles of international law embodied in the Charter of the United Nations;
> (b) any exercise or practice with weapons of any kind;
> (c) any act aimed at collecting information to the prejudice of the defense or security of the coastal State;
> (d) any act of propaganda aimed at affecting the defense or security of the coastal State;

---

[9] U.N. Doc A/CN.4/143, Juridical Regime of Historic Waters, Including Historic Bays, 1962, at 56.
[10] UNCLOS, Article 3.
[11] Id., Article 2.
[12] Id., Article 17.
[13] Id., Article 18.
[14] Id., Article 20.

(e) the launching, landing or taking on board of any aircraft;
(f) the launching, landing or taking on board of any military device;
(g) the loading or unloading of any commodity, currency or person contrary to the customs, fiscal, immigration or sanitary laws and regulations of the coastal State;
(h) any act of willful and serious pollution contrary to the Convention;
(i) any fishing activities;
(j) the carrying out of research or survey activities;
(k) any act aimed at interfering with any systems of communication or any other facilities or installations of the coastal State;
(l) any other activity not having a direct bearing on passage.

Equipment or anti-terrorism measures employed to protect the safety or security of the ship are not inconsistent with innocent passage. Additionally, vessel cargo, means of propulsion, flag or registry, origin, destination, or purpose of the voyage cannot be used as criteria by coastal States to inform a determination that the passage is not innocent.

8.4 Straits Used for International Navigation

Straits used for international navigation consist of overlapping territorial seas that connect one area of the high seas or exclusive economic zone (EEZ) to another area of the high seas or EEZ. With the expansion of the maximum breadth of the territorial sea from 3 to 12 nautical miles, more than 100 straits, which previously were separated by a high seas corridor, suddenly were overlapped by territorial sea. Without a right of transit passage, these straits would have been governed by the more restrictive regime of non-suspendable innocent passage.

The Law of the Sea Convention contains rules that guarantee the international community the right of navigation and overflight on, over, and under international straits. The rules governing the right of transit passage through international straits are fundamental to naval and air forces of all nations, as well as merchant vessels and civil aviation. Military and commercial ships and aircraft enjoy the right to transit these straits freely in their normal mode of operation as a matter of right and not based on the consent or at the whim of the bordering States.

8.4.1 Corfu Channel Case

The customary right of navigation through international straits was captured by the International Court of Justice (ICJ) judgment in the *Corfu Channel Case*. In the few years following World War II, the Royal Navy used the Corfu Channel, separating Albania and the Greek island of Corfu, to provide aid to the beleaguered Greeks, who were engaged in a struggle against a large communist insurgency. The People's Republic of Albania occupied the eastern side of the Corfu Channel; the Greek island of Corfu lies on the western side of the channel. At its narrowest point, the Channel closed to only three nautical miles, and Albania and Greece could claim a territorial sea out to the median line. Because of the rocky seabed of the Corfu Island side of the channel, however, ships using the route are forced to navigate within a mile of the Albanian coast as they negotiate the narrow channel off the port of Saranda in southeastern Albania.[15] Although the Corfu Channel is a strait used for international navigation, it also constitutes Albanian territorial seas.

The Royal Navy swept the Channel clear of mines in 1944 and 1945 and declared the waterway safe. The government in Tirana, however, had turned the tiny nation into a hard line communist enclave. There were three separate events involving Albanian attacks on Royal Navy ships using the Channel of Corfu.[16] During the first incident, Royal Navy ships came under fire from Albanian shore battery fortifications. In the second incident, Royal Navy ships struck mines while transiting the channel. The third incident, which gave rise to the ICJ case, occurred when the Royal Navy was conducting mine-clearing operations in the Corfu Channel, but in Albanian territorial waters, and Albania complained to the United Nations that the British mine countermeasure operations violated Albanian sovereignty over the territorial seas.

On May 15, 1946, two Royal Navy ships transited the Corfu Channel and came under fire from Albanian shore batteries, but the warships suffered no casualties. The British protested the attack, but Albania alleged that the warships violated Albanian sovereignty.[17] On October 22, 1946, another British Navy flotilla composed of the cruisers *HMS Mauritius* and *Leander* and the destroyers *HMS Saumarez* and *HMS Volage*, proceeded through the Medri channel. The narrow passage previously had been swept for mines. The *Saumarez* struck a mine at 14:53, however, and the blast caused severe damage to the ship and produced dozens of casualties. *Volage* closed on *Saumarez* and took her into tow, stern first. At 16:06 on the same day, a mine exploded near the *Volage*, severing the towline. While working damage control in the forward spaces, which were damaged by the mine, *Volage* reconnected the tow to *Saumarez* and both ships proceeded stern first, arriving at Corfu Roads at 03:10 the next morning. The Royal Navy suffered 44 dead and 42 injured in the mine strikes.

The British responded with naval operations, as well as diplomatic and legal action against Albania. Determined that it would re-sweep the Channel for mines in order to make the waterway safe and to obtain evidence of Albanian state responsibility, the Royal Navy began "Operation Retail" to clear mines from the strait.

---

[15] Stuart Thomson, *Maritime Jurisdiction and the Law of the Sea*, in THE ROYAL NAVY AND MARITIME POWER IN THE TWENTIETH CENTURY 148–49 (Ian Speller, ed. 2005).
[16] Id., at 149,154.
[17] *Corfu Channel Case* [Merits] 1949 I.C.J. 3, at 13–14.

The United Kingdom brought a case against Albania in the ICJ. Albania threw up numerous procedural maneuvers to delay the hearing, but ultimately the Court rendered a decision in 1949. The ICJ found that laying the minefield was the proximate cause of the explosions on October 22, 1946, and "could not have been accomplished without the knowledge of the Albanian Government."[18] The Court also noted Albania's "complete failure to carry out its [search and rescue] duties after the explosions," and the tribunal in the Netherlands was nonplussed at the "dilatory nature of [Albania] diplomatic notes" concerning the issue.[19] The Court ordered Albania to pay £875,000 in compensation to Great Britain, or the equivalent of more than £20 million today.[20]

The case is a classic restatement of the right of freedom of navigation through straits used for international navigation, and it informed the treaties governing the law of the sea that were produced in 1958 and 1982. But the decision was not entirely supportive of the British position, however. The World Court stated that in order to "ensure respect for international law," it "must declare that the [mine sweeping operation] of the British Navy constituted a violation of Albanian sovereignty." The Court rejected the United Kingdom's argument that Operation Retail was a method of self-protection or permissible self-help, because "respect for territorial sovereignty is an essential foundation of international relations." In other words, when balancing the norm against the use of force (laying mines) and the norm of sovereignty (Albania's territorial sea), the Court surprisingly chose sovereignty, ironically only four years after the end of the Second World War.

In further scolding the British government for demining the Corfu Channel, the judgment stated:

> The Court can only regard the alleged right of intervention as the manifestation of a policy of force, such as has, in the past, given rise to most serious abuses and such cannot, whatever be the present defects in international organization, find a place in international law. Intervention is perhaps still less admissible in the particular form it would take here; for, from the nature of things, it would be reserved for the most powerful States, and might easily lead to perverting the administration of international justice itself.[21]

The case is an early indication of the direction of the Court's jurisprudence on matters of aggression and self-defense in the setting of an international strait and is the first omen of disparate legal standards governing the use of force between wealthy and powerful states and impoverished and weak states.[22] Thus, the

---

[18] Id., at 22.
[19] Id., at 35.
[20] Id., at 11.
[21] Id., at 35.
[22] James Kraska, *A Social Justice Theory of Self-Defense of World Court Jurisprudence*, 9 LOY. U. CHI. INT'L L. REV. 25, 33–36 (2011) and John Norton Moore, *Jus ad Bellum Before the International Court of Justice*, 52 VA. J. INT'L L. 903, 916–19 (2012).

decision could presage the legal outcome of any Iranian-American litigation over freedom of navigation through the Strait of Hormuz.

With the *Corfu Channel* decision, the Court signaled an implicit soft-peddle of low-level aggression, which is the tool of weaker states, while at the same time strongly repudiating direct and robust measures taken in self-defense by a stronger nation. The measures in self-defense that the British took were both non-kinetic and offered a free public good to the international community, but the Court still condemned Operation Retail.

8.4.2 *The Straits Regime in UNCLOS*

Passage through international straits is governed by Part III of UNCLOS, which applies distinct legal regimes depending on the characteristics of straits used for international navigation.[23] The right of transit passage, for example, applies to straits used for international navigation that connect one part of the high seas or EEZ to another part of the high seas or EEZ, including strategic straits such as Gibraltar, Bab el Mandeb, Hormuz, Malacca and Singapore, Sunda, Lombok, and the Windward Passage.[24]

The decisive criterion for determining whether a strait is governed by the transit passage regime is not the history or volume of traffic traversing the strait, but rather whether the strait is (or can be) used for international navigation to or from the high seas or the EEZ. All ships and aircraft enjoy a right of unimpeded transit passage through such straits in the "normal mode of operation."[25]

The term "normal mode" means that submarines are entitled to transit submerged, military aircraft may overfly in combat formation and with normal equipment operation and surface ships may transit in a manner consistent with vessel security, to include formation steaming and launch and recovery of aircraft, if consistent with sound navigational practices. Article 44 prohibits States bordering an international strait from suspending transit passage for any purpose, including military exercises. In addition, Article 42(2) does not permit such States to adopt laws or regulations that have the practical effect of denying, hampering or impairing the right of transit passage.

---

[23] The terms "strait used for international navigation" and "international strait" are synonymous. The former term is used in UNCLOS, and is preferred by nations bordering Straits. The second term is a shorthand reference to straits that are used for international navigation. Although convenient (because it is shorter), it is disliked by some States bordering straits because they believe it implies that the strait is wholly an international area, deemphasizing the coastal State's overlapping territorial sea. We use the terms interchangeably, however, and do not imply an degradation in the rights of the coastal State or its sovereignty over territorial seas that form parts of a strait.
[24] UNCLOS, Article 37.
[25] Id., Articles 38 and 39.

A right of non-suspendable innocent passage applies in straits that connect a part of the high seas or EEZ with the territorial sea of a coastal State. These waterways are referred to as "dead-end straits," because they do not lead to the open sea, but rather form a *cul de sac*. The regime of non-suspendable innocent passage also applies to straits that connect one part of the high seas or EEZ and another part of the high seas or EEZ, where the strait is formed by an island of a State bordering the strait and its mainland, if there exists seaward of the island a route through the high seas or EEZ of similar convenience with regard to navigation and hydrographic characteristics.[26] There is, however, no right of overflight through such straits.

Coastal States that border international straits benefit from a number of provisions that help them to implement their responsibilities in the strait. The provisions of UNCLOS permit states bordering straits to exercise a degree of control over the waterway, with the important caveat that the rules implemented by the coastal State must be in accord with international standards and applied in a manner that is non-discriminatory. States bordering straits may designate sea lanes and prescribe traffic separation schemes for navigation in the straits when such regulations are necessary to promote the safe passage of ships.[27] Regulations must be in conformity with generally accepted international standards, so straits States may not impose unique, excessive or unreasonable requirements on international shipping.[28]

Before states bordering straits may designate or prescribe regulations, they are required to refer proposals to the IMO for adoption.[29] Once the Maritime Safety Committee has endorsed the proposal, it may be adopted by the IMO Assembly. The new rules should be duly designated and publicized by the State bordering the strait. Once designated by IMO, ships in transit passage have a duty to respect and observe approved sea lanes and traffic separation schemes.[30] Within specific limits, States bordering straits may adopt additional laws and regulations relating to transit passage through straits. Coastal States have authority to adopt laws relating to the safety of navigation and to institute IMO-approved traffic separation schemes.

Littoral State laws may be designed to prevent, reduce, and control pollution by giving effect to international regulations regarding "discharge of oil, oily waste and other noxious substances" in the strait.[31] The rule, however, does not entitle

---

[26] Id., Articles 45 and 38.
[27] Id., Art. 41(1).
[28] Id., Art. 41(3).
[29] Id., Art. 41(4). *See also*, Marion Llyod Nash, Digest of U.S. Practice in International Law 1979 at 1120–22. (Stmt. by Ambassador Elliot L. Richardson to Congressman Paul Findley (R-IL)).
[30] UNCLOS, Art. 41(7).
[31] Id., Art. 42(1)(b).

the littoral State to develop regulations that affect construction, design, equipping and manning (CDEM) of foreign-flagged ships.

States bordering straits also may adopt laws and regulations that relate to fishing, require the stowage of fishing gear during transit, and implement a wide range of customs, fiscal, immigration, and sanitary laws to protect the public health.[32] Foreign ships exercising the right of transit passage shall comply with the regulations, but the rules must not discriminate in form or in fact among foreign flagged vessels.[33] Moreover, UNCLOS does not welcome novel or outcome-based interpretations of the rules. Lastly, unlike innocent passage through territorial seas, states bordering international straits may not suspend transit passage.[34]

8.4.3 Types of Straits Used for International Navigation

There are six types of international straits: (1) geographic straits through which a high-seas corridor exists (such as the Taiwan Strait or some of the Japanese straits); (2) straits governed by long-standing conventions (such as the aforementioned Strait of Magellan and the Turkish Straits, as well as the Danish Straits); (3) straits with routes through the high seas or EEZ that are of similar convenience; (4) straits formed by islands (e.g. the Messina Strait); (5) archipelagic straits, governed by archipelagic sea lanes passage, and (6) dead end straits. Each archetype has unique characteristics.

8.4.3.1 Geographic Straits

Waterways that are greater than 24 nm wide, as measured from lawfully drawn baselines, may constitute a geographic but not a juridical international strait. In such cases, a corridor or route through the high seas or EEZ in that area creates an "exception" to the regime of transit passage in that complete high seas freedoms, rather than the more limited transit passage regime applies.[35]

Pursuant to Article 36 of UNCLOS, for example, ships and aircraft transiting through or above straits used for international navigation that have a high seas or EEZ corridor suitable for navigation, such as the Taiwan Strait, enjoy high seas freedoms of navigation and overflight and other lawful uses of the seas relating to such freedoms while operating in and over the high seas corridor. In adjacent areas constituting territorial seas, however, ships and aircraft enjoy only the right of innocent passage.

---

[32] Id., Art. 42(1)(c).
[33] Id., Art. 42(2) and (4).
[34] Id., Art. 44.
[35] Id., Art. 36.

Like the Taiwan Strait, many areas of the Northwest Passage are greater than 24 nautical miles in width and, therefore, consist of an EEZ or high seas corridor in the geographic strait. These cases obviate the need for applying the rules of transit passage regime in those areas in which the outer edges of the territorial seas on each side of the strait between the land areas do not overlap. High seas freedoms apply in such straits throughout the areas that lay beyond the territorial sea.

8.4.3.2 Long-standing Conventions

Second, transit passage does not affect the legal regime in straits in which passage is regulated by "long-standing international conventions in force" that specifically relate to such straits.[36] The navigational regime of transit passage in UNCLOS does not apply to straits regulated by long-standing international conventions in force specifically relating to such straits, such as the Turkish Straits (the Bosporus, the Sea of Marmara, and the Dardanelles) and the Strait of Magellan, which are both governed by treaties. Each strait under Article 35(c) of the Convention is *sui generis*, with the rules pertaining to the strait contained in a separate and pre-existing treaty.

The Montreux Convention of 1936 is an example of such a treaty.[37] The convention contains provisions governing the Bosporus, transit of the Sea of Marmara, and the Dardanelles, which form the Turkish Straits. By replacing the Lausanne Convention of July 24, 1923, the terms of the 1936 treaty prevail if there is a conflict between the Montreux treaty and UNCLOS.[38] During time of peace, merchant ships enjoy complete freedom of navigation through the Turkish Straits. Even in time of armed conflict, however, subject to specific provisions, warships of all nations not at war with Turkey are ensured freedom of navigation through the straits.[39]

Similarly, the Danish Great Belt Strait in the Baltic Sea is subject to the *Treaty for the Redemption of the Sound Dues* of March 14, 1857.[40] The parallel treaty, *Convention between the United States and Denmark for the Discontinuance of the Sound Dues*, April 11, 1857,[41] governs traffic through the strait. These treaties recognize

---

[36] Id., Art. 35(c).
[37] Convention Relating to the Regime of the Straits, July 20, 1936, 173 L.N.T.S. 213.
[38] Protocol Relating to Certain Concessions Granted in the Ottoman Empire, July 24, 1923, 28 L.N.T.S. 203.
[39] Convention Relating to the Regime of the Straits, Articles 10–12.
[40] Treaty between Great Britain, Austria, Belgium, France, Hanover, Mecklenburg-Schwerin, Oldenburg, the Netherlands, Prussia, Russia, Sweden, and Norway and the Hanse Towns, on the One Part and Denmark on the Other Part, for the Redemption of the Sound Dues, Copenhagen, Mar. 14, 1857, 116 CONSOLIDATED TREATY SERIES 357.
[41] Convention between the United States and Denmark for the Discontinuance of the Sound Dues, Apr. 11, 1857, U.S.-Den., 11 Stat. 719.

the "entire freedom of the navigation of the Sound and the Belts" and protection of "free and unencumbered navigation."[42]

The Åaland Strait and the Strait of Magellan are two other straits governed by long-standing international conventions. The *Convention on the Non-Fortification and Neutralization of the Åaland Islands* of October 21, 1921, provides that warships are prohibited except for innocent passage.[43] The Strait of Magellan is relevant to the law of the sea for two separate reasons. First, it is governed by a long-standing convention, rather than the terms of UNCLOS. Second, the Strait of Magellan is an international strait that penetrates the baselines and bisects the internal waters of the coastal State.

The Strait of Magellan is governed under the *Boundary Treaty between the Argentine Republic and Chile*, which was signed in Buenos Aires on July 23, 1881.[44] Article 5 of the treaty states that the Straits of Magellan are "neutralized forever, and free navigation is guaranteed to the flags of all nations."[45] Traversing the Strait of Magellan requires a voyage from east to west that penetrates the internal waters of Chile along the Southwestern Atlantic and emerges through the internal waters and into the territorial sea of Chile in the Southeastern Pacific.

8.4.3.3 Route of Similar Convenience

Third, no right of transit passage exists through a strait that contains a route through the high seas or EEZ that is of similar convenience as the strait, so long as the alternative route meets the test with respect to navigational and hydrographical characteristics.[46] This situation may arise if a coastal state chooses to maintain a high seas corridor between two land territories by not extending its territorial seas to 12 nautical miles.

During the negotiations for UNCLOS, Japan opposed any interpretation of the law regarding straits that would permit the Soviet Union to overfly the Tsugaru Strait.[47] But once the 12 nautical mile territorial sea and corresponding provisions

---

[42] Id. at Arts. I and II.
[43] Convention on the Non-Fortification and Neutralization of the Åaland Islands of October 21, 1921, 9 L.N.T.S. 211, *entered into force*, Apr. 6, 1922.
[44] Boundary Treaty between the Argentine Republic and Chile, done at Buenos Aires on July 23, 1881, 159 CONSOLIDATED TREATY SERIES 45 (Agreement between Argentina and Chile to neutralize the Straits of Magellan, place no fortifications along its shores, and open the Strait to shipping of all nations). The terms of the treaty were reaffirmed in Article 10 of the 1984 Treaty of Peace and Friendship between Argentina and Chile, resolving the Beagle Channel dispute. Hugo Caminos, THE LEGAL REGIME OF STRAITS IN THE 1982 UNITED NATIONS CONVENTION ON THE LAW OF THE SEA 131 (1987).
[45] Boundary Treaty between the Argentine Republic and Chile, July 23, 1881, 159 CTS 45, Article 5.
[46] UNCLOS, Art. 36.
[47] National Security Council Memorandum, Evening Report for Zbigniew Brzezinski, Aug. 1, 1978 (Secret/sensitive; declassified July 26, 2000).

of transit passage took hold at the negotiations, Japan elected to forgo claiming a 12 nautical mile territorial sea throughout four of its international straits.

The Soya Strait separates the northernmost part of Hokkaido and Russia's Sakhalin Island, the Tsugaru lies between Honshu and Hokkaido, the Osumi Strait is off the southern tip of Kyushu, and the Tsushima and Korea Straits separate Kyushu and South Korea. In each of these straits, Japan claims only a three nautical mile territorial sea, thus retaining an area of the EEZ through each strait in which high seas freedoms apply. In doing so, Japan deprived Soviet and North Korean surface ships, submarines and aircraft of the shoreline-to-shoreline right of navigation that comes with the regime of transit passage.

8.4.3.4 Island Forming a Strait (Route of Similar Convenience)

Fourth, transit passage does not apply in straits that are formed by an island of the state bordering the strait and its mainland and where there exists seaward of the island a route through the high seas or EEZ of similar convenience with respect to navigational and hydrographical characteristics.[48] The Strait of Messina, bordered by Sicily and Calabria, Italy, is the classic example of this type of strait regime.

The "Messina exception" to the general rule is identified in Article 38(1) of the Convention. Article 38(1) states that "transit passage shall not apply if there exists seaward of the island a route through the high seas or through the exclusive economic zone of similar convenience with respect to navigational and hydrographical characteristics."[49]

8.4.3.5 Archipelagic Straits

International straits that are located within archipelagic waters are subject to the navigational regime of archipelagic sea lanes passage (ASLP).[50] Article 53 defines ASLP as:

> The exercise in accordance with this Convention of the rights of navigation and overflight in the normal mode solely for the purpose of continuous, expeditious and unobstructed transit between one part of the high seas or an exclusive economic zone and another part of the high seas or an exclusive economic zone.[51]

The definition is nearly a verbatim replica of the regime of transit passage through international straits. The ASLP regime, unlike the regime of transit passage, does not permit passage throughout the entire strait (shoreline to shoreline). Instead, ships and aircraft may approach no closer to the land on either side of the strait

---

[48] UNCLOS, Art. 38(1).
[49] Id.
[50] Id., Arts. 46–47 and 53.
[51] Id., Art. 53.

than ten percent of the distance between island features. The regime applies to designated archipelagic sea lanes, and the coastal state has a duty to designate as sea lanes all routes normally used for international navigation and overflight.

An archipelagic state is not required to designate archipelagic sea lanes. However, if it elects to do so, it must first seek the approval of the International Maritime Organization. If the archipelagic state does not designate all routes normally used for international navigation, then vessels and aircraft of all nations are entitled nonetheless to utilize such routes in ASLP.

8.4.3.6   Dead-end Straits

Finally, the "dead end straits" exception applies to geographic circumstances in which high seas or the EEZ connects with the territorial seas of a state by means of a strait bordered by one or more states.[52] Ships entering the state located at the *cul de sac* end of the strait are entitled to non-suspendable innocent passage in order to ensure that the port state is not landlocked, with a territorial sea leading nowhere.[53] For example, if the regime of non-suspendable innocent passage was not recognized for Head Harbor Passage, international shipping would not have guaranteed access to U.S. ports in Maine that are situated at the end of a *cul de sac* consisting of a combination of Canadian internal waters and territorial seas.

The understanding that foreign-flagged vessels have access to dead-end straits is longstanding. The 1958 *Geneva Convention on the Territorial Sea and the Contiguous Zone*, for example, foresaw non-suspendable innocent passage in international straits, including dead-end straits. Article 16(4) of the 1958 Convention states that dead end straits are those "used for international navigation between one part of the high seas... and the territorial sea of a foreign state."[54]

The navigational regime of non-suspendable innocent passage for the Strait of Tiran, a prominent dead-end strait, was imported into the Israeli-Egyptian peace

---

[52]   Id., Art. 38(1) and 45(1)(b).
[53]   William L. Schachte, Jr. & J. Peter A. Bernhardt, *International Straits and Navigational Freedoms*, 33 Va. J. Int'l L. 534–535 (1992–93); *see also, e.g.*, Rear Admiral William L. Schachte, Jr., *International Straits and Navigational Freedoms*, Remarks prepared for presentation at the 26th Law of the Sea Institute Annual Conference, Genoa, Italy, June 22–26, 1992, at 12–13 and 18 (unpublished manuscript).
[54]   Convention on the Territorial Sea and the Contiguous Zone, 516 U.N.T.S. 205, 15 U.S.T. 1606, T.I.A.S. No. 5639, Geneva, Apr. 29, 1958, *entered into force* Sept. 10, 1964. The other 1958 treaties were: Convention on the High Seas, Geneva, 450 U.N.T.S. 11, 13 U.S.T. 2312, T.I.A.S. No. 5200, Apr. 29, 1958, *entered into force*, Sept. 1962; Convention on Fishing and Conservation of the Living Resources of the High Seas, Geneva, 559 U.N.T.S. 285, Apr. 29, 1958, *entered into force* Mar. 20, 1966; and Convention on the Continental Shelf, Geneva, 499 U.N.T.S. 311; 15 U.S.T. 417; T.I.A.S. No. 5578, Apr. 29, 1958, *entered into force* June 10, 1964.

treaty as a key pillar of stability for the two nations.[55] Article V of the treaty provides:

> Ships of Israel, and cargoes destined for or coming from Israel, shall enjoy the right of free passage through the Suez Canal and its approaches through the Gulf of Suez and the Mediterranean Sea on the basis of the Constantinople Convention of 1888, applying to all nations, Israeli nationals, vessels and cargoes, as well as persons, vessels and cargoes destined for or coming from Israel, shall be accorded non-discriminatory treatment in all matters connected with usage of the canal.
>
> The Parties consider the Strait of Tiran and the Gulf of Aqaba to be international waterways open to all nations for unimpeded and non-suspendable freedom of navigation and overflight. The parties will respect each other's right to navigation and overflight for access to either country through the Strait of Tiran and the Gulf of Aqaba.[56]

A similar provision is found in Article 14 of the Israel-Jordan peace treaty, which provides:

> 1. Without prejudice to the provisions of paragraph 3, each Party recognises the right of the vessels of the other Party to innocent passage through its territorial waters in accordance with the rules of international law.
> 2. Each Party will grant normal access to its ports for vessels and cargoes of the other, as well as vessels and cargoes destined for or coming from the other Party. Such access will be granted on the same conditions as generally applicable to vessels and cargoes of other nations.
> 3. The Parties consider the Strait of Tiran and the Gulf of Aqaba to be international waterways open to all nations for unimpeded and non-suspendable freedom of navigation and overflight. The Parties will respect each other's right to navigation and overflight for access to either Party through the Strait of Tiran and the Gulf of Aqaba.[57]

8.4.4 Transit Passage in the Approaches to the Strait

Transit passage also applies in the approaches to the strait that are comprised of the territorial seas of adjacent coastal States. Saudi Arabia, for example, clarified the rule in a 1996 declaration. Riyadh stated that

> ...the provisions of the [Law of the Sea] Convention relating to application of the system for transit passage through straits used for international navigation...apply to navigation between islands adjacent or contiguous to such straits, particularly

---

[55] Mohammed El Baradei, *The Egyptian-Israeli Peace Treaty and Access to the Gulf of Aqaba: A New Legal Regime*, 76 AM. J. INT'L L. 532, 534 (1982) and Ruth Lapidoth, *The Strait of Tiran, the Gulf of Aqaba, and the 1979 Treaty of Peace Between Egypt and Israel*, 77 AM. J. INT'L L. 84, 85 (1983).

[56] Treaty of Peace between the Arab Republic of Egypt and the State of Israel, *done at Washington*, Mar. 26, 1979, 18 I.L.M. 362 (1979).

[57] Treaty of Peace Between the State of Israel and the Hashemite Kingdom of Jordan, *done at Arava/Araba Crossing Point*, Oct. 26, 1994, 34 I.L.M. 43 (1994).

where the sea lanes used for entrance to or exit from the strait, as designated by the competent international organization [e.g. the International Maritime Organization], are situated near such islands.[58]

The U.S. official position is reproduced in Roach and Smith's authoritative volume, *Excessive Maritime Claims*:

> The geographics of straits vary. The areas of overlapping territorial seas in many cases do not encompass the entire area of the strait in which the transit passage regime applies. The regime applies not only in or over the waters overlapped by territorial seas but also throughout the strait and in its approaches, including areas of the territorial sea that are overlapped. The Strait of Hormuz provides a case in point: although the area of overlap of the territorial seas of Iran and Oman is relatively small, the regime of transit passage applies throughout the strait as well as in its approaches including areas of the Omani and Iranian territorial seas not overlapped by the other.[59]

Similarly, Charles H. Allen, Deputy General Counsel in the Department of Defense, explained:

> For transit passage... to have any meaning... surface, subsurface, and overflight navigation of waters constituting the approaches to the strait (including the territorial sea of adjacent coastal States) are also included within the scope of this important navigational right. If the right of overflight or submerged transit applied only within the geographical delineation of the strait, but not to areas leading into and out of the strait, it would effectively prevent the exercise of the right of transit passage in the normal overflight and submerged modes....
>
> Also, requiring ships and aircraft to converge at the hypothetical entrance to the strait would be inconsistent with sound navigational practices. That is why the United States has consistently maintained that the right of transit passage applies not only to the waters of the strait itself, but also to all approaches to the strait that are normally used.[60]

8.4.5 *Archipelagic Sea Lanes Passage*

Archipelagic sea lanes passage applies within archipelagic waters and the adjacent territorial sea where such waters have been established in accordance with Part IV of the Convention. The right of innocent passage applies in archipelagic waters not covered by the archipelagic sea lanes passage regime.

---

[58] UN Law of the Sea Bull. No. 31, at 10 (1996).
[59] J. Ashley Roach & Robert W. Smith, Excessive Maritime Claims 272 (3rd ed. 2012), excerpting Dep't of the U.S. Navy Judge Advocate General, Alexandria VA, Naval Message 061630Z Jun. 1988, State Dep't File No. P92 0140–0820/0822, Cumulative Digest of U.S. Practice in International Law 1981–88, at p. 2018.
[60] Charles A. Allen, *Persian Gulf Disputes*, 339, 340–41, *in* Security Flashpoints: Oil, Islands and Sea Access and Military Confrontations (Myron H. Nordquist & John Norton Moore, eds. 1988).

Article 46 of UNCLOS defines an archipelagic State as one "constituted wholly by one or more archipelagos and may include other islands." An archipelago is further defined as "a group of islands, including parts of islands, interconnecting waters and other natural features, which are so closely interrelated that such islands, waters and other natural features form an intrinsic geographical, economic and political entity, or which historically have been regarded as such."

Archipelagic sea lanes passage is virtually identical to transit passage. Article 53 defines archipelagic sea lanes passage as the exercise of the "rights of navigation and overflight in the normal mode solely for the purpose of continuous, expeditious and unobstructed transit" through archipelagic waters. All ships and aircraft enjoy the right of archipelagic sea lanes passage while transiting through, under, or over archipelagic waters and adjacent territorial seas via "all normal passage routes used as routes for international navigation or overflight..." whether or not sea lanes have been designated by the archipelagic State.[61] As is the case with transit passage, Article 54 provides that the right of archipelagic sea lanes passage cannot be impeded or suspended by the archipelagic State for any reason.

An archipelagic State may, but is not required to, designate sea lanes and air routes for the exercise of archipelagic sea lanes passage.[62] However, if sea lanes are designated, Article 53 requires that they include "all normal passage routes used as routes for international navigation or overflight through or over archipelagic waters...." Additionally, Article 53 requires that the sea lanes conform to generally accepted international regulations and that they be adopted by the IMO. When operating in designated sea lanes, Article 53 requires ships and aircraft to remain within 25 nautical miles to either side of the axis line and to navigate no closer to the coastline than 10 percent of the distance between the nearest islands.

The IMO reviews and adopts proposed ships routing measures and ships' routing systems, including mandatory ship reporting systems. IMO guidance also states "ships exercising the right of archipelagic sea lanes passage...must use applicable sea lanes (or normal passage routes if sea lanes have not been adopted or only a partial system of archipelagic sea lanes has been adopted)."[63]

8.4.5.1 Indonesia

Indonesia was the first nation to designate archipelagic sea lanes. The country did not, however, seek IMO approval of all normal routes used for international navigation, as required by Article 53 of UNCLOS. Most obviously, Indonesia has not sought IMO designation for an East-West lane through the archipelago. Thus, the

---

[61] UNCLOS, Article 53.
[62] Id.
[63] IMO Doc. SN/Circ.206/Corr.1, Guidance for Ships Transiting Archipelagic Waters, Mar. 1, 1999.

sea lanes resolution for Indonesia adopted by the IMO Maritime Safety Committee (MSC) is explicitly a "partial system."[64] Similarly, the IMO's *General Provisions on Ships' Routeing* (GPSR) refers to a "Partial System of Archipelagic Sea Lanes in Indonesian Archipelagic Waters."[65]

Consistent with Paragraph 6.7 of Part H of the GPSR, "where a partial archipelagic sea lanes proposal has come into effect, the right of archipelagic sea lanes passage may continue to be exercised through all normal passage routes used for international navigation or overflight in other parts of archipelagic waters in accordance with UNCLOS." Similarly, "if the IMO has adopted a sea lane proposal as a partial system of archipelagic sea lanes, the right of archipelagic sea lanes passage may continue to be exercised through all normal passage routes used as routes for international navigation in other parts of archipelagic waters."[66]

The GPSR requires the IMO to "determine if the proposal is a partial archipelagic sea lanes proposal."[67] The proposing State also has responsibility to clearly indicate if it seeks a full or partial archipelagic sea lane proposal."[68] The rules regarding "partial" designations and the preservation of archipelagic sea lanes passage in "all normal routes" are critical to preserve freedom of navigation and overflight through and over archipelagic waters.

By requiring designation of all normal routes, UNCLOS helps to preserve the critical balance between archipelagic State interests and maritime State interests reflected in the convention. Absent these rules, archipelagic States have greater temptation to restrict archipelagic sea lanes passage by seeking designation of only some of the routes normally used for international navigation.

8.5 Contiguous Zone

A single article in UNCLOS deals with a zone contiguous to the territorial sea, known as the "contiguous zone." Article 33 of UNCLOS authorizes the coastal State to claim a 24 nm contiguous zone in which the coastal State may exercise

---

[64] IMO Doc. MSC.72(69), Adoption, Designation, and Substitution of Archipelagic Sea Lanes, May 19, 1988. (The IMO "adopts... the Partial System of Archipelagic Sea Lanes in Indonesian Archipelagic Waters."). *See also*, IMO Doc. SN/Circ. 200, Adoption, Designation, and Substitution of Archipelagic Sea Lanes, May 26, 1998, IMO Doc. SN/Circ. 200/Add.1, Adoption, Designation, and Substitution of Archipelagic Sea Lanes, July 3, 2008, and IMO Doc. SN/Circ. 202, Adoption, Designation, and Substitution of Archipelagic Sea Lanes, July 31, 2008.
[65] IMO Doc. A.571(14), General Provisions on Ships' Routeing, Nov. 20, 1985, Part I.
[66] IMO Doc. SN/Circ. 206, Guidance for Ships Transiting Archipelagic Waters, Mar. 1, 1999, at para. 2.1.1.
[67] IMO Doc. A.571(14), General Provisions on Ships' Routeing, Nov. 20, 1985, Part H, para. 3.2.
[68] Id., at para. 3.9.

limited control necessary to prevent or punish infringement of its customs, fiscal, immigration, or sanitary laws and regulations in its territory or territorial sea. The objective of a contiguous zone is different than either the territorial sea or exclusive economic zone. The contiguous zone is not part of the territorial sea, and it is not subject to coastal State sovereignty. Vessels and aircraft of all States enjoy the same high seas freedom of navigation and overflight and other internationally lawful uses of the seas associated with those freedoms in the contiguous zone that apply in the EEZ and on the high seas.

The contiguous zone emerged from regulations concerning immigration at UNCLOS I. During negotiations at UNCLOS III, there was discussion about whether the contiguous zone was needed, since the territorial sea expanded from 3 to 12 nm. A majority of States supported retaining the concept of the contiguous zone in UNCLOS, however, since it related to specific coastal State powers that were not part of the regime of the exclusive economic zone.

8.6 Exclusive Economic Zone

UNCLOS created the exclusive economic zone (EEZ), a new coastal state zone cut from the high seas. Within this 200 nm zone, the coastal State enjoys sovereign rights for the purpose of "exploring, exploiting, conserving and managing" living and non-living natural resources, as well as jurisdiction over most off-shore installations and structures, marine scientific research, and the protection and preservation of the marine environment. Other activities related to the economic exploitation and exploration of the zone, such as the production of energy from the water, currents and winds, also fall under the control of the coastal State.[69]

Coastal States do not, however, exercise sovereignty over the EEZ. The term "sovereign rights" in Article 56 was deliberately chosen to clearly distinguish between coastal State resource rights and other limited jurisdiction in the EEZ, and coastal State authority in the territorial sea, where coastal States enjoy a much broader and more comprehensive right of "sovereignty."[70]

Accordingly, pursuant to Article 58.1, in the EEZ, all States enjoy high seas freedoms of navigation and overflight, laying of submarine cables and pipelines, and other internationally lawful uses of the seas related to those freedoms, such as those associated with the operation of ships, aircraft and submarine cables and pipelines, and which are compatible with the other provisions of the Convention.

---

[69] UNCLOS, Article 56.
[70] United Nations Convention on the Law of the Sea 1982: A Commentary II at 531–544 (Satya N. Nandan & Shabtai Rosenne, eds. 1993) [Hereinafter Virginia Commentary II].

8.6.1 Coastal State Competence in the EEZ

Even before the adoption of UNCLOS in 1982, there was ample concern that excessive coastal state environmental regulations might serve as a pretext to limit the right of warships to navigate offshore, particularly in innocent passage in the territorial sea. These concerns were amplified during the Third UN Conference debates over creation of the EEZ. The maritime powers feared that establishment of the new zone of the EEZ eventually would lead to an erosion of high seas freedoms in the zone.

The United States was not immune to the tendency of coastal States to maximize their offshore jurisdiction through an inflated sense of legal competence. During the negotiations of the Third UN Conference on the Law of the Sea, for example, Secretary of Defense Harold Brown sent a memorandum to President Carter, explaining that amendments to the new Federal Water Pollution Control Act (Clean Water Act), then under consideration by Congress, would undermine U.S. objectives in the negotiations and adversely affected U.S. national security interests.[71]

The amendments to section 311 of the law extended U.S. prescriptive and enforcement jurisdiction over offshore vessel source pollution and discharges. In general, however, States have no enforcement jurisdiction outside their own territory, i.e. beyond the territorial sea.[72] Nevertheless, the general rule against States exercising enforcement jurisdiction is militated or qualified by maritime law, which permits exceptions. The principle of freedom of navigation, however, requires that any deviation from the general rule be narrowly construed.

By enacting the CWA amendments, the United States risked retaliatory steps by other coastal States that might then try to assert jurisdiction over U.S. vessels transiting off their coasts. Secretary Brown told the President that he and the Joint Chiefs of Staff believed that the U.S. law "detrimentally affected our national security" in several ways:

> First, other countries will be encouraged to enact similar legislation, and may do so without the exemption for military vessels [found in the U.S. law]. Such legislation could be used to delay or deny the transit of United States warships. Nuclear-powered warships (now about one-third of our Naval vessels, most of them submarines) are particularly likely to be subjected to regulation in the form of pollution controls.
>
> Second, the amendments to Section 311 are a further step toward a worldwide creation of broad territorial seas through which warships would have only a right of "innocent" passage....[73]

---

[71] Secretary of Defense Harold Brown Memorandum For the President, Pollution Control Legislation and National Security Interests, Jan. 9 1978 (Released Aug. 16, 2000).

[72] *Case Concerning the Arrest Warrant of 11 April 2000* (Democratic Republic of the Congo v. Belgium, [Judgment] 2002 ICJ Reports 3, 169, at para. 49.

[73] Secretary of Defense Harold Brown Memorandum For the President, Pollution Control Legislation and National Security Interests, Jan. 9, 1978 (Declassified and released Aug. 16, 2000).

The memorandum also expressed worry that the draft treaty language for a new law of the sea was consistent with U.S. interests and would be "put at risk" by the U.S. lawmaking. Failure to revise the amendments prior to the next negotiating session threatened to reopen vessel source pollution control and concomitant navigational issues, namely whether coastal States could control navigation of foreign-flagged ships through anti-pollution laws.[74]

Article 58.2 of UNCLOS provides that "Articles 88 to 115 and other pertinent rules of international law apply to the EEZ in so far as they are not incompatible..." with Part V. All non-resource-related rights, duties and high seas freedoms and other internationally lawful uses of the sea, including not just navigation and overflight, but also laying of submarine cables and pipelines, hydrographic surveys, and military activities, may be conducted lawfully by all States in the EEZ without coastal State notice or consent.[75] Examples of lawful military activities that can be conducted in the EEZ of another nation are provided in Table 8.1.

Article 86 of the Convention confirms this broad interpretation. Although the first sentence of Article 86 establishes that the EEZ is *sui generis*, and that certain resource-related high seas freedoms (e.g., fishing and marine scientific research) do not apply in the EEZ, the second sentence of Article 86 makes clear that nothing in the Article abridges the high seas "freedoms enjoyed by all States in the EEZ in accordance with Article 58."

Some coastal States purport to expand their competence and jurisdiction in the EEZ, particularly by imposing restrictions on military activities. The zone, however, which comprises 38 percent of the world's oceans, was entirely high seas just three decades ago. The EEZ was created for the sole purpose of granting coastal states greater control over the resources adjacent to their coasts out to 200 nautical miles.[76] In particular, the exclusive right to fish and exploit the living resources of the zone was intended to benefit subsistence fishing communities lying along the coastlines.

Early efforts by a handful of nations, like El Salvador and Peru, to expand coastal state authority in the EEZ to include residual competences and rights in the zone were rejected by a majority of the State delegations at the Third UN Conference on the Law of the Sea.[77] The Conference negotiators finally agreed on

---

[74] Id.
[75] See Table 8.1. The list of non-resource related activities also includes intelligence, surveillance and reconnaissance (ISR), operations, oceanographic surveys, marine data collection, military exercises, use of weapons, flight operations, and actions taken to counter the slave trade or repress piracy, suppression of unauthorized broadcasting, suppression of narcotics trafficking, and the exercise of belligerent right of visit and search and the peacetime right of approach and visit, rending assistance, and hot pursuit.
[76] VIRGINIA COMMENTARY II, at 491–821.
[77] Id., at 529–530.

Table 8.1. Examples of Lawful Military Activities in the EEZ

Military marine data collection and naval oceanographic survey	Acoustic and sonar research and operations
Intelligence, surveillance, reconnaissance (ISR)	Sea-basing
Submarine support	Submarine navigation testing
Establishment and maintenance of military-related artificial installations	Ballistic missile defense operations and ballistic missile test support
Underway replenishment	Visit, board, search, and seizure and maritime interdiction operations
Bunkering	Naval control and protection of shipping
Conventional and ballistic missile testing and missile range instrumentation	Belligerent rights in naval warfare (e.g. right of visit and search)
Strategic arms control verification	Military surveys
War games and naval-air exercises	Deterrence patrols
Maritime forward presence operations	Freedom of navigation assertions
Humanitarian assistance and disaster relief operations	Maritime security operations (e.g., counter-terrorism and -proliferation)
Sea control	Power projection
Maritime law enforcement/constabulary operations (e.g. anti-piracy)	Aircraft carrier flight operations

Articles 55, 56, 58 and 86, all of which accommodate the various competing interests of coastal States and other States in the EEZ without diminishing freedom of navigation and other internationally lawful uses of the sea.

On the one hand, Articles 55 and 56 make clear that the EZZ is *sui generis* and that certain high seas freedoms relating to extraction of natural resources and conduct of marine scientific research (MSR) do not apply in the EEZ. On the other hand, Articles 58 and 86 make equally clear that all other high seas freedoms and other internationally lawful uses of the seas related to those freedoms apply seaward of the territorial sea and may be exercised by all states in a coastal State's EEZ without providing notice or seeking consent.[78]

Article 56 provides that coastal States have sovereign rights for the purpose of exploring, exploiting, conserving and managing the natural resources of the zone and with regard to other activities for the economic exploitation and exploration of the zone. The term "sovereign rights" was carefully chosen to make a clear distinction between coastal State rights and jurisdiction in the EEZ and coastal State authority in the territorial sea, where a much broader and more comprehensive right of "sovereignty" applies.[79]

The coastal State also has limited resource-related jurisdiction in the EEZ with regard to the establishment and use of artificial islands, installations and

---

[78] Id., at 60–71.
[79] UNCLOS, Article 2; VIRGINIA COMMENTARY II, at 531–544.

structures, marine scientific research (MSR), and the protection and preservation of the marine environment. The use of the term "marine scientific research" was used to distinguish MSR from other types of marine data collection that are not resource-related, such as hydrographic surveys and military oceanographic surveys.[80] The Convention treats MSR separate from surveys, for example, in Article 19(2)(j), where it refers to "research or survey activities" for ships engaged in innocent passage.

Article 40 applies a similar restriction to ships engaged in transit passage— "marine scientific research and hydrographic survey ships may not carry out any research or survey activities" without prior authorization of the states bordering the strait. The same restrictions apply to ships engaged in archipelagic sea lanes passage (Article 54) and ships transiting archipelagic waters in innocent passage (Article 52). Article 56 and Part XIII of the Convention, on the other hand, only refer to MSR, and not to other "survey" activities.[81] Thus, while the navigational regimes of innocent passage, transit passage through straits used for international navigation, archipelagic sea lanes passage, and non-suspendable innocent passage in archipelagic waters outside of sea lanes all permit the coastal State to regulate surveys and MSR, the regime of high seas freedoms that applies in the EEZ only references MSR and is silent on the issue of surveys.

The text of UNCLOS reflects state practice throughout the Cold War, when warships and merchant vessels from the Western alliance and the Soviet bloc enjoyed the right to conduct military surveys and intelligence collection beyond the territorial sea without interference. A handful of exceptions, such as the attack on the *USS Pueblo*, illuminate the rule.

After the Cold War, the United States continued to tolerate Russian naval vessels' exercise of freedom of navigation and other internationally lawful uses of the sea throughout its EEZs and the EEZs of its friends and treaty allies. In 1996, for example, the U.S. embassy in Vilnius, Lithuania, queried the Secretary of State on the U.S. government's view of Russian naval activities in Lithuania's EEZ.[82] Lithuania had joined NATO in 1991, so the inquiry from the U.S. embassy was particularly salient as an oceans law and maritime security issue. The Department of State's reply is instructive:

> . . .
> 2. Article 87 of the Law of the Sea Convention allows all ships and aircraft, including warships and military aircraft, freedom of movement and operation on and over

---

[80] UNCLOS, Article 19(2)(j), 40, 54, 87(1)(f) and Part XIII. *See*, ROACH & SMITH, EXCESSIVE MARITIME CLAIMS 413–450 (explaining types of marine data collection and applicable legal regimes).
[81] UNCLOS, Article 87(1)(f), also only refers to scientific research.
[82] SECRETARY OF STATE, U.S. DEP'T OF STATE, SECSTATE WASHDC 010044Z NOV 96 MSG to AMEMBASSY VILNIUS, Subject: Naval Vessels in Baltic Economic Zones, Nov. 1, 1996.

the high seas. With respect to the EEZ, Article 58 of the Convention allows all states to enjoy the high seas freedom of navigation and overflight, laying of submarine cables and pipelines, and other internationally lawful uses of the sea related to these freedoms and compatible with the other provisions of the Convention while operating in the EEZ. For warships and military aircraft, this includes task force maneuvering, flight operations, military exercises, surveillance, intelligence gathering activities, and ordnance testing and firing.

3. Although Article 58 allows traditional military activities within the EEZ, the state performing the activities must do so with due regard to the coastal state resources and other rights, as well as the rights of other states. It is the duty of the state conducting the military activity, not the coastal state, to exercise this "due regard" obligation. The due regard provision of Article 58 requires any state using the EEZ to be cognizant of the interests of others using the area, to balance those interests with its own, and to refrain from activities that unreasonably interfere with the rights and duties of other states.

4. With this legal basis in mind, it is the policy of the USG [U.S. Government] not to object to reasonable use of the Baltic Sea region by any naval power, including Russia, that is conducting traditional naval activities. These activities would include live missile firing conducted with due regard to the rights of the coastal and other states.

5. The United States Navy has frequently conducted naval activities, including live firing exercises, in the EEZ of other nations. Normally, the method of notification is by Notice to Mariners (NOTMAR).

6. The publication of a Notice to Mariners, however, does not relieve the state conducting potentially hazardous activities, from liability. Typically, when our government conducts these exercises, we assume responsibility for range clearance and if a possibility exists of interference with another vessel or aircraft, we suspend our exercises until they can be safety completed.

7. With the above in mind, the USG does not view with any special concern the naval activities of Russia in the Baltic Sea region. The USG would consider a formal NOTMAR as an appropriate method of notification of planned exercises. The USG, like the Russians, would object to a requirement to formally notify navies in the region of a live fire exercise beyond what was contained in a NOTMAR.[83]

Some states that were unable to achieve their objective to retain residual rights and competencies for the coastal State in the EEZ during the negotiations for UNCLOS have sought to unilaterally expand their control over lawful activities in the area since the treaty entered into force. In doing so, these States purport to assert offshore control over hydrographic surveys, military operations, and law enforcement operations—activities never included in the package deal.

By our count, 18 States purport to regulate or prohibit foreign military activities in the EEZ:[84]

---

[83] Id.
[84] Dep't of Defense, Maritime Claims Reference Manual (MCRM), DOD 2005.1-M, June 2008.

1. Bangladesh
2. Brazil
3. Burma (Myanmar)
4. Cape Verde
5. China
6. India
7. Indonesia
8. Iran
9. Kenya
10. Malaysia
11. Maldives
12. Mauritius
13. North Korea
14. Pakistan
15. Philippines
16. Portugal
17. Thailand
18. Uruguay

Furthermore, six coastal States, Benin, the Congo, Ecuador, Liberia, Peru, and Somalia claim a 200 nautical mile territorial sea that also purports to deny or restrict foreign-flagged military activities.[85]

Illegal coastal State restrictions over foreign-flagged ships and aircraft operating in the EEZ take a number of forms, but, for the most part, are directed at foreign military activities. Among all States, only Burma attempts to restrict freedom of navigation and overflight through the EEZ for all types of traffic, while Cape Verde imposes restrictions on "non-peaceful uses" of its EEZ. Of course, the Cape Verde rule begs the question of exactly what conduct it intends to regulate. If by forbidding "non-peaceful uses," Cape Verde simply implements the general rule that the oceans are reserved for peaceful purposes, similar to the principles of State conduct in the UN Charter and that are codified in Article 88 of UNCLOS, then its regulation is not inconsistent with international law. On the other hand, if the island nation purports to consider any or even some peacetime foreign-flagged naval operations as inconsistent with the "peaceful purposes" provisions, then it acts outside its competence as a coastal State.

India restricts military activities in the EEZ and purports to require 24 hours advance notice (but not permission) before ships carrying hazardous and dangerous goods, such as oil, chemicals, noxious liquids, and radioactive material, can transit through its EEZ.[86] The country also claims to limit the conduct of warships and sovereign immune vessels in its EEZ. In 2007, for example, Delhi protested the operation of the USNS *Mary Sears*, which was operating in its EEZ without

---

[85] Id. *See also*, JAMES KRASKA, MARITIME POWER AND THE LAW OF THE SEA: EXPEDITIONARY OPERATIONS IN WORLD POLITICS 291–330 (2011).

[86] Id.

having provided notice.[87] The ship was conducting military surveys, but India claimed that the vessel violated India's right to control marine scientific research in its economic zone.

Maldives takes the prior notice requirement one step further, requiring all ships to obtain prior permission to enter its EEZ.[88] North Korea purports to prohibit military surveys and photography in its EEZ, while Portugal, the only NATO member that restricts military activities in its EEZ, only permits innocent passage in the area.[89] Pakistan also restricts military activities in its EEZ, and Islamabad requires foreign State aircraft to file flight plans before transiting over the EEZ.[90]

Finally, while Indonesia and the Philippines have not officially enacted national regulations or made public statements restricting military activities in their EEZs, they have on a few occasions objected to foreign military activities in the area. For example, Malaysia joined Indonesia at a meeting of the ASEAN Regional Forum (ARF) in Manila in 2007 in objecting to proposed ASEAN military exercises in their respective EEZs.[91] The ARF had planned to conduct a military exercise, part of which would have taken place in the Malaysian and Indonesian EEZs, and the two coastal States objected.

Among all of the States that purport to limit military activities in the EEZ, however, China is an unfortunate stand out. China is the only nation in recent memory that has shown a willingness to use force to attempt to keep foreign warships from operating in its EEZ. Moreover, the government of China appears to purposefully aggravate the issue through denunciations in the state controlled media, while at the same time bringing intense pressure to bear on States exercising freedom of navigation and other internationally lawful uses of the sea in the area. For these reasons, China's excessive maritime claims deserve more thorough treatment, and are addressed in Chapter 10.[92]

---

[87] INTERNATIONAL LAW INSTITUTE, DIGEST OF UNITED STATES PRACTICE IN INTERNATIONAL LAW 648–50 (Sally J. Cummins, ed. 2007).
[88] DEP'T OF DEFENSE, MARITIME CLAIMS REFERENCE MANUAL, DOD 2005.1-M, June 2008.
[89] Id.
[90] Id.
[91] Raul (Pete) Pedrozo, *Military Activities In and Over the Exclusive Economic Zone*, 235, 237, in FREEDOM OF THE SEAS, PASSAGE RIGHTS, AND THE 1982 LAW OF THE SEA CONVENTION (Myron H. Nordquist, Tommy T. B. Koh, & John Norton Moore, eds. 2009).
[92] *See also*, Raul "Pete Pedrozo, *Preserving Navigational Rights and Freedom in the Exclusive Economic Zone*, 9 CHINESE J. INT'L L. 9–29 (2010), KRASKA, MARITIME POWER AND THE LAW OF THE SEA 312–330 (The 'special case' of China and excessive maritime claims), and ROACH & SMITH, EXCESSIVE MARITIME CLAIMS 384–90.

FREEDOM OF NAVIGATION IN THE LAW OF THE SEA 241

8.7 Continental Shelf

Coastal States also exercise sovereign rights over their continental shelf for the purpose of exploring and exploiting its natural resources, including "mineral and other non-living resources of the seabed and subsoil together with living organisms belonging to sedentary species."[93] Article 76 defines the continental shelf as "the seabed and subsoil of the submarine areas that extend beyond the territorial sea throughout the natural prolongation of its land territory to the outer edge of the continental margin," or to a distance of 200 nm from the baselines where the outer edge of the continental margin does not extend up to that distance.

The Convention established a Commission on the Limits of the Continental Shelf (CLCS), an independent technical international organization, to consider and make recommendations to coastal States on matters related to claims over the outer or extended continental shelf (ECS), i.e. the continental shelf that some coastal States may claim by virtue of geologic composition of the sea bed beyond 200 nm from the shore. The continental shelf regime preserves navigational freedoms in the zone by providing that coastal State rights over that part of the sea bed "do not affect the status of the superjacent waters or airspace above those waters."[94]

Since 1945, the United States has asserted jurisdiction and control over the continental shelf for the purpose of exploring and exploiting its resources. The Truman Proclamation placed all natural resources of the subsoil and sea bed of the continental shelf contiguous to the U.S. coast under the exclusive jurisdiction and control of the United States.[95] The Truman Proclamation on the continental shelf may be regarded as a classic example of the creation of "instant" customary international law.[96] The Truman Proclamation of 1945 was not challenged by governments and was followed by similar claims by other states.

The Proclamation was codified in statute in 1953 by the Outer Continental Shelf Lands Act (OCSLA), which affirmed U.S. exclusive jurisdiction over its continental shelf resources and created authority for the Department of the Interior to encourage offshore oil development through a leasing program. The Proclamation specifically preserves navigational freedoms, providing that "the character as high seas of the waters above the continental shelf and the right to their free and

---

[93] UNCLOS, Article 77.
[94] Id., Article 78.
[95] Pres. Proc. No. 2667, Policy of the United States with Respect to the Natural Resources of the Subsoil and Sea Bed of the Continental Shelf, 10 FR 12303, Sept. 28, 1945.
[96] RESTATEMENT (THIRD) FOREIGN RELATIONS LAW OF THE UNITED STATES § 102 (1987). The provisions of the Continental Shelf were included in the 1958 Convention on the Continental Shelf, and the doctrine was regarded as reflecting customary international law even for states that did not adhere to the Convention.

unimpeded navigation are in no way...affected" by the decree.[97] Unfortunately, although many States judiciously copied the Proclamation's claim over sea bed resources, they sometimes were less exacting in the nuances, often leaving out the provision protecting freedom of navigation.

8.8 High Seas

Beyond the 200 nm EEZ lies the high seas, which remain open to all States.[98] "No State may validly purport to subject any part of the high seas to its sovereignty."[99] Freedom of the high seas includes:

- Freedom of navigation and overflight;
- Freedom to lay submarine cables and pipelines;
- Freedom to construct artificial islands and other installations;
- Freedom of fishing;
- Freedom of scientific research; and
- Other internationally lawful uses of the sea.[100]

Pursuant to Article 87 of UNCLOS, warships and military aircraft enjoy freedom of movement and operation on and over the high seas, including task force maneuvering, flight operations, military exercises, surveillance, intelligence gathering activities, and ordnance testing and firing.

The mineral resources of the seabed beyond national jurisdiction, which includes both the EEZ and the ECS, comprises the Area. Resources of the Area are administered by the International Seabed Authority pursuant to Part XI of the Convention, as modified by the 1994 Agreement relating to the Implementation of Part XI.[101]

Navigational freedoms and other high seas freedoms (such as scientific research and telecommunications) in the Area are preserved by Article 135, which provides that neither Part XI "nor any rights granted or exercised pursuant thereto shall affect the legal status of the waters superjacent to the Area or that of the air space above those waters."

---

[97] Id.
[98] UNCLOS, Article 87.
[99] Id., Article 89.
[100] Id., Article 87.
[101] Id., Article 156.

NINE

EXCESSIVE MARITIME CLAIMS:
TERRITORIAL SEAS, STRAITS, AND ARCHIPELAGOS

9.1 INTRODUCTION

Since the end of the World War II, many coastal States have asserted maritime claims that are inconsistent with the international law of the sea, as embodied in the *United Nations Convention on the Law of the Sea* (UNCLOS).[1] In terms of international law, many of these claims are more accurately described as unlawful or illegal. Excessive maritime claims undermine the community rights of other States to freely navigate and use the world's oceans. The political, economic, and strategic implications for excessive maritime claims are enormous, weakening the global order by exacerbating regional tension, impairing maritime trade, and diminishing strategic mobility.

This chapter does not address all excessive or unlawful maritime claims, as that would require a complete volume focused solely on that issue (and for which we recommend Roach & Smith's *Excessive Maritime Claims* (3d ed. 2012). Instead, we have included representative case studies of excessive claims pertaining to territorial seas, straits used for international navigation, and archipelagic sea lanes passage.

Except for straight baseline claims that purport to close off the Strait of Hainan, we do not address China's numerous excessive maritime claims. Instead, those are covered in this volume separately in Chapter 10, *Security Claims in the EEZ*, and Chapter 11, *Flashpoint: South China Sea*.

Excessive maritime claims take many forms and may include:

---

[1] United Nations Convention on the Law of the Sea, Dec. 10, 1982, UN Doc. A/CONF.62/122 (1982), 1833 U.N.T.S. 3, 397, 21 I.L.M. 1261 (1982), *entered into force* Nov. 16, 1994.

- Improper use of straight baselines to measure coastal State maritime zones;
- Unrecognized historic water or historic bay claims;
- Territorial sea claims in excess of 12 nm;
- Restrictions on innocent passage in the territorial sea;
- Restrictions on transit passage in straits used for international navigation;
- Restrictions on archipelagic sea lanes passage through archipelagoes;
- Claims of security jurisdiction in the contiguous zone;
- Restrictions on military activities in the EEZ;
- Restrictions on other non-resource-related activities in the EEZ;
- Restrictions on ships based on cargo (e.g., hazardous material) or propulsion system (nuclear-powered vessels);
- Excessive continental shelf claims; and
- Environmental regulations inconsistent with international standards.[2]

Generally, illegal maritime claims may be divided into two types. First, claims that attempt to capture more area or water space represent a blatant policy of conversion of community property to the exclusive use of the coastal State. Second, perhaps now more insidious, are coastal State laws and regulations that exceed the lawful authority, jurisdiction, or competence in a lawfully drawn maritime zone. If left unchallenged, these claims may transform State practice and generate new legal norms, thereby limiting navigational rights and freedoms vital to global security and economic prosperity. In short, excessive maritime claims are one of the most critical issues in maritime security law because they heighten tension, fan nationalism, and risk conflict.

In the wake of the adoption and then entry into force of UNCLOS, some nations rescinded excessive maritime claims, particularly rolling back claims related to the width of the territorial sea. The trend in more recent years, however, has been moving in the opposite direction. International law is a necessary, but alone insufficient inducement for coastal States to roll back excessive maritime claims. The United States has championed UNCLOS as one element of a strategy to discourage coastal States from making and enforcing excessive maritime claims. The Law of the Sea Convention underpins all of the law and diplomacy directed at countering unlawful maritime claims. For this reason, the United States has strongly supported the treaty. The United States, however, is not a party to the Convention due to the opposition of Republican lawmakers in the U.S. Senate, who have declined to provide advice and consent for U.S. accession. Ironically, the political party with a strong reputation for supporting

---

[2] Letter from John H. McNeill, Senior Deputy General Counsel, Dep't of Defense and Chairman, Dep't of Defense Task Force on the Law of the Sea Convention to Ms. Ann Sauer, Office of Senator John McCain, Jan. 19, 1996. The landmark study on excessive maritime claims is J. ASHLEY ROACH & ROBERT W. SMITH, EXCESSIVE MARITIME CLAIMS (3rd ed. 2012). *See also*, John D. Negroponte, *Who Will Protect Freedom of the Seas?*, 86 DEP'T OF STATE BULL. 41 (Oct. 1986) and Ruth Lapidoth, *Freedom of Navigation—Its Legal History and Its Normative Basis*, 6 J. MAR. L. & COM. 259 (1974–75).

the military services has blocked the one treaty the Pentagon believes is most important to ensure freedom in the global commons.

In a letter to Senator Jesse Helms in 2000, for example, then Chief of Naval Operations (CNO) Admiral Jay L. Johnson advised that U.S. ratification of UNCLOS was a principal legal mechanism for strengthening international norms and countering excessive maritime claims. The Navy's top admiral sought U.S. action on the treaty to resist "alarming trends" that he described as "directly related to our failure to accede to the Convention."[3]

First, Admiral Johnson expressed concern that failure to become a party to UNCLOS relinquished U.S. influence internationally in development of the law of the sea. "Second, perhaps more disturbing," the admiral said, "is the emboldening of those who seek to fundamentally change our role as the world's leading maritime nation and guarantor of freedom of the seas to one of a coastal nation that places domestic and regional regulatory control first." Thus, the United States—like all coastal states—is not immune to what Professor Bernard H. Oxman separately has referred to as the "territorial temptation," or the incentive coastal States have to stake out grandiose offshore claims.[4]

The CNO recounted the "explosive growth" in the number and nature of claims of regulatory and jurisdictional authority by coastal States, often with the direct support of single-issue non-governmental organization (NGOs), contrary to the law of the sea as codified in UNCLOS. These excessive claims further a wide range of exclusive and special interests, including enhanced environmental protection. The claims also may make a political statement against the ships of a particular country or against warships or vessels performing certain functions, such as waste disposal, promote nuclear disarmament, limit measures to combat transnational crime and illegal migration, reduce the operating effectiveness of naval forces (particularly American and Western warships), appease domestic or coastal State political and economic constituencies, buttress psychological and emotional impulses, such as nativism and nationalism, and control management and allocation of radio frequency spectrum.

To counter the challenge of excessive maritime claims, the United States has used the Freedom of Navigation (FON) Program, which is discussed at greater length in Chapter 8. The FON Program consists of three elements: operational challenges by U.S. Navy ships and aircraft,[5] diplomatic demarches by the U.S.

---

[3] Letter from Admiral Jay L. Johnson, Chief of Naval Operations letter to The Hon. Jesse Helms, June 29, 2000.

[4] Bernard H. Oxman, *The Territorial Temptation: Siren Song at Sea*, 100 AM. J. INT'L L. 830 (2006).

[5] Theoretically, ships and aircraft of the other armed forces may also conduct FON assertions, but in reality it has been decades since another service has done so. The Coast Guard, for example, conducted FON challenges of Russia's excessive maritime claims in the Arctic more than forty years ago. DEP'T OF DEFENSE, MARITIME CLAIMS

Department of State, and military-to-military engagement by the U.S. armed forces.

The United Kingdom also incorporates promotion of freedom of navigation into its maritime doctrine. Under the heading of Freedom of Navigation Operations, U.K. maritime doctrine states that "[i]f a state's claim to territorial seas is not accepted or it attempts to restrict the use of the high seas or international straits, it may be necessary to use naval forces to demonstrate intent to use those waters."[6] The doctrine explains that "freedom of navigation operations are designed to persuade or dissuade a government and are therefore a form of naval diplomacy."[7] The United Kingdom files diplomatic demarches in protest of excessive maritime claims, but the Royal Navy does not routinely challenge such claims through operational assertions.

9.2 Illegal Straight Baselines

Article 7 of UNCLOS provides that coastal States may employ the use of straight baselines along their coasts in very limited circumstances to include "localities where the coastline is deeply indented and cut into, or if there is a fringe of islands along the coast in its immediate vicinity."[8] Furthermore, straight baselines "must not depart to any appreciable extent from the general direction of the coast," and the "sea areas lying within the lines must be sufficiently closely linked to the land domain to be subject to the regime of internal waters."[9]

Article 7 is perhaps the most abused provision of the entire Convention. Of the more than 70 nations that employ a system of straight baselines from which to measure the breadth of the territorial sea, the overwhelming majority of nations do so unlawfully. Vietnam's 1994 instrument of ratification to UNCLOS, for example, includes a statement that the National Assembly may review Vietnam's maritime claims to "consider the necessary amendments" to bring them into conformity the Convention.[10] Only two nations—Germany and Guinea—have ever rolled back their excessive straight baseline claims.[11]

Most nations' coastlines do not meet the geographic requirements of Article 7 for establishing straight baselines. Moreover, in many cases the waters enclosed by these baselines are not interrelated to the land. Although UNCLOS does not

---

Reference Manual, DOD 2005.1–M, June 2008 (Hereinafter Maritime Claims Reference Manual).

[6] Ian Speller, The Royal Navy and Maritime Power in the Twentieth Century 31 (2005).
[7] Id.
[8] UNCLOS, Article 7(1).
[9] Id., Article 7(3).
[10] Id.
[11] Roach & Smith, Excessive Maritime Claims at 133.

specify the maximum length of a straight baseline most experts would agree that a straight baseline should not exceed between 24 and 48 nm.[12] Accordingly, with a few exceptions, the baseline for most shorelines should be the low-water line as provided in Article 5 of UNCLOS.

Improperly drawn straight baselines significantly extend coastal State maritime jurisdiction seaward in a manner that prejudices community navigational rights and freedoms and other lawful uses of the seas. For example, on November 12, 1982, Vietnam issued a declaration establishing a straight baseline system along a significant portion of its coast. The 11 baseline points form a continuous system with 10 segments (totaling 846 nm). The mean distance between consecutive base points is 84.6 nm, although it ranges from 2.0 to 161.8 nm. Most of the base points are located nearly 40 nm out to sea, and one base point (A6) is 80.7 nm from the mainland at Hon Hai Islet.

The net effect of this system is to fence off 27,000 square nautical miles (93,000 square kilometers) of the South China Sea as internal waters; this area is properly viewed as consisting of Vietnam's territorial seas and EEZ, rather than enclosed within internal waters.[13] If the claim were to be regarded as valid, foreign flagged vessels would be precluded from transits through the area without Vietnamese consent. The cumulative effect of illegal straight baselines leads to a reduction in the area of the oceans open to the international community of States. It is therefore important for the international community to challenge coastal States that elect to draw straight baselines that are inconsistent with international law.

Historic waters are considered internal waters subject to exclusive coastal State sovereignty. Consequently, historic waters restrict freedom of navigation and overflight. Twenty nations claim historic title to bodies of water off their coasts. In order to substantiate a historic waters claim, a nation must demonstrate open, effective, long term and continuous exercise of authority over the body of water, coupled with acquiescence of the claim by foreign states.[14]

9.2.1 Libya's "Line of Death" in the Gulf of Sirte

Since October 1973, Libya has claimed the Gulf of Sirte (Sidra) as internal waters, drawing a 300 nm closing line across the mouth of the Gulf along 32°30'N latitude.[15] The closing line was referred to by Libya as a "line of death." In February 1974, the United States rejected the claim, and disagreement over the issue

---

[12] Dep't of State, Limits in the Sea No. 117, Straight Baseline Claim: China, July 9, 1996 [Hereinafter LIS]. See also, LIS No. 106, Developing Standard Guidelines for Evaluating Straight Baselines, Aug. 31, 1987, and Roach & Smith, Excessive Maritime Claims 64 (note 26).

[13] LIS No. 99, Straight Baselines: Vietnam, Dec. 12, 1983.

[14] UN Doc A/CN.4/143, Juridical Regime of Historic Waters, Including Historic Bays, 1962, at 56.

[15] Maritime Claims Reference Manual (Libya).

caused several military confrontations between Libyan and U.S. military forces. In mid-September 1980, a Libyan fighter jet aircraft fired at a U.S. EC-135 reconnaissance airplane that was conducting a sensitive reconnaissance operation (SRO) mission over the Mediterranean. The U.S. aircraft was not hit, so the United States did not respond militarily.

One year later, however, in August 1981, two U.S. F-14 fighter jet aircraft from the *USS Nimitz* (CVN 68) were flying a combat air patrol over the Gulf of Sidra when they were engaged by two Libyan SU-22 Fitter attack aircraft. Acting in self-defense, the F-14s shot down both Libyan fighters. The U.S. aircraft were part of a large naval force, including the *USS Nimitz* and *USS Forrestal* (CV 59) battle groups that had been deployed to the region to conduct Freedom of Navigation (FON) operations against Libya's excessive maritime claims.

In June 1983, two U.S. F-14 fighter jet aircraft intercepted two Libyan aircraft over the Gulf that were monitoring U.S. Airborne Warning and Control System (AWACS) airplanes; the AWACS were monitoring the border activity between Libya and Sudan. In July 1984, four U.S. Navy fighter jets conducted a FON challenge in the Gulf of Sidra without incident.[16] The operation was approved by officials at the Pentagon, the State Department, and the White House, underscoring the high level of support for such operations during the 1980s.[17] Libyan aircraft did not demonstrate hostile intent and were therefore not engaged by the U.S. fighter jets.

As in the days of the Barbary pirates, during the 1980s, freedom of navigation in the Mediterranean Sea was just one component of encounters by Westerners with Islamic militants. On June 14–15, 1985, Trans World Airlines (TWA) flight 847 was hijacked by members of Hezbollah and Islamic Jihad. The aircraft was held for three days, and a U.S. Navy diver on board was tortured and murdered, and his body dumped on the tarmac. On December 27 of that year, terrorists attacked targets in Rome and Vienna that left 20 civilians (including five Americans) dead.

In late January 1986, a large flotilla of U.S. warships, including ships from the *USS Saratoga* (CV 60), *USS Coral Sea* (CV 43) and *USS America* (CV 66) aircraft carrier battle groups, were deployed north of the "line of death." The ships conducted FON operations to demonstrate U.S. non-acceptance of the Libyan claim. The operations were planned to unfold in three phases: Phase I ran from January 26–30, Phase II from February 12–15, and Phase III from March 23–29, 1986. Phases I and II were completed without a major incident, although there were several non-hostile encounters between U.S. and Libyan military aircraft over the Gulf of Sidra in January and February.

---

[16] Fred Hiatt, *Flights Over the Gulf of Sidra; U.S. Navy Jets Challenge Libyan Sovereignty Claim*, WASH. POST, July 27, 1984, at A1.
[17] Id.

On March 24, however, after the *USS Ticonderoga* (CG-47), *USS Scott* (DDG 995) and *USS Caron* (DD 970) crossed the "line of death, Libyan shore-based surface-to-air (SAM) missile sites fired six SA-5 missiles and two SA-2 missiles at U.S. aircraft operating in support of the warships. In response, U.S. Navy A-6 Intruder attack aircraft from the *USS America* and the *USS Yorktown* (CG 48) destroyed the SA-5 ground sites and sank or damaged four Libyan attack boats, including a *Nanuchka*-class missile corvette and a *Combattante*-class missile attack boat, both of which had posed a threat to U.S. warships.[18] That same day, the White House issued the following media statement:

> U.S. naval aircraft and ships carrying out a peaceful freedom of navigation and overflight exercise in international waters and airspace in the Gulf of Sidra were fired on Monday by missile forces of Libya. This morning at 7:52 a.m. [Eastern Standard Time] Libyan forces without provocation fired two long-range SA-5 surface-to-air missiles from Sirte on the northern coast of Libya at U.S. aircraft operating in international waters in the Gulf of Sidra. U.S. forces had been operating in that area since Sunday afternoon. Two additional SA-5s and an SA-2 were launched from Sirte at 12:45 p.m. An additional SA-5 [Surface-to-Air missile] was fired at 1:14 p.m. At this point Libyan forces had fired a total of six surface-to-air missiles at U.S. forces.
> At approximately 2 p.m., a U.S. aircraft fired two Harpoon anti-ship missiles at a Libyan missile patrol boat which was located near the 32°30'N line and was a threat to U.S. naval forces. The Libyan fast-attack craft was hit. The ship is dead in the water, burning, and appears to be sinking. There are no apparent survivors. At approximately 3 p.m., U.S. forces operating south of the 32°30'N line responded to the missile attacks by launching two HARM (high-speed anti-radiation) missiles at the SA-5 site at Sirte. At that time the SA-5 complex was attempting to engage our aircraft. We are assessing the damage now.
> We have no reports of any U.S. casualties and no loss of U.S. aircraft or ships.
> This attack was entirely unprovoked and beyond the bounds of normal international conduct. U.S. forces were intent only upon making the legal point that, beyond the internationally recognized 12-mile limit, the Gulf of Sidra belongs to no one and that all nations are free to move through international waters and airspace. We deny Libya's claim, as do almost all other nations, and we condemn Libya's actions. They point out again for all to see the aggressive and unlawful nature of Colonel Qadhafi's regime.
> It should be noted that because of these numerous Libyan missile launches and indications that they intended to continue air and missile attacks on U.S. forces, we now consider all approaching Libyan forces to have hostile intent. We have taken appropriate measures to defend ourselves in this instance. We did not, of course, proceed into this area with our eyes closed. We reserve the right to take additional measures as events warrant.[19]

---

[18] CLYDE MARK, CONGRESSIONAL RESEARCH SERVICE ISSUE BRIEF FOR CONGRESS, LIBYA, Apr. 10, 2002 and *U.S. Resumes Retaliatory Attacks; Libya Guns Silent: 6th Fleet Knocks Out More Boats*, TIMES WIRE SERVICES, Mar. 25, 1986.

[19] Statement by Principal Deputy Press Secretary Speakes on the Gulf of Sidra Incident, Mar. 24, 1986. *See also*, Eleanor Clift and James Gerstenzang, *U.S. Warplanes Destroy*

Two days later, on March 26, 1986, the White House informed the Congress of the engagement:

> On March 23, United States forces in the Eastern Mediterranean began a peaceful exercise as part of a global Freedom of Navigation program by which the United States preserves its rights to use international waters and air space. This exercise is being conducted entirely in and over areas of the high seas, in accordance with international law and following aviation safety notification procedures.
>
> On March 24, our forces were attacked by Libya. In response, U.S. forces took limited measures of self-defense necessary to protect themselves from continued attack. In accordance with my desire that the Congress be informed on this matter, I am providing this report on the actions taken by United States Armed Forces during this incident.
>
> Shortly before 8:00 a.m. (EST) on March 24, two SA-5 surface-to-air missiles were fired at U.S. aircraft flying over the high seas in the Gulf of Sidra from a Libyan missile installation in the vicinity of Sirte on the northern Libyan coast.
>
> During the course of the next few hours, several surface-to-air missiles were fired at U.S. aircraft operating over the high seas. At approximately 3:00 p.m. (EST) these missile installations again activated their target-acquisition radars with the evident objective of firing upon U.S. aircraft. Two HARMs were thereupon fired by a U.S. Navy A-7 aircraft, apparently resulting in the destruction of the radars controlling the missile battery. After a short outage, the radar returned to active status and still posed a threat to U.S. forces. At 6:47 p.m., A-7 aircraft again fired two HARM missiles at the SA-5 radar at Sirte. After another short outage, the radar has returned to active status.
>
> Meanwhile, a Libyan missile patrol boat equipped with surface-to-surface missiles came within missile range of U.S. ships on the high seas well away from the Libyan coast. The U.S. commander determined, in light of the Libyan attacks on U.S. aircraft, that this vessel was hostile and therefore ordered U.S. aircraft to engage it. At approximately 2:00 p.m. (EST), U.S. Navy A-6 aircraft fired two Harpoon missiles, which struck and heavily damaged the Libyan vessel. At approximately 4:00 p.m. (EST), a second Libyan patrol boat approached U.S. forces, and was driven off by U.S. Navy aircraft.
>
> Shortly after 6:00 p.m. (EST), a third Libyan patrol boat approached the *USS Yorktown* at a high rate of speed; the *Yorktown* fired two Harpoon missiles, which hit the Libyan craft.
>
> Shortly after 12:20 a.m. (EST) on March 25, U.S. Navy A-6 aircraft armed with Harpoon missiles attacked another Libyan craft, apparently resulting in the sinking of that vessel.
>
> All U.S. aircraft returned safely to their carriers, and no casualties or damage [were] suffered by U.S. forces. The extent of Libyan casualties is not known.[20]

Secretary of Defense Caspar Weinberger wrote an open letter to Congress in an opinion editorial on March 30, 1986, in the *Los Angeles Times* titled, "Our One and Only Objective was Freedom of Navigation." He explained in the U.S. action:

Libya Missile Site, Sink Patrol Craft; Strike After Attack by Kadafi Forces; No American Losses, L.A. TIMES, Mar. 25, 1986, at 1.

[20] Letter from the President of the United States Ronald Reagan to Congress on the Gulf of Sidra Incident, Mar. 26, 1986.

[O]ur objective in this operation... [was] to maintain basic principles of freedom of navigation in international waters and airspace. We sought only to conduct a freedom-of-navigation exercise in waters universally recognized as international seas, more than 100 miles off the coast of a country whose government has made excessive claims to those waters and had militarily threatened any nation to defy them.

The significance of the freedom of navigation in international waters may not be fully understood or appreciated.

Freedom of navigation has been critically important to the world community since man began traveling the seas. Given that two-thirds of the world's surface is covered by water, this is not too surprising. Commercial vessels and warships have trafficked in international waters for centuries on strategic or economic missions—and sometimes just purely for pleasure. More recently, that same right was extended to commercial and military aircraft flying in international airspace.

For these reasons, the United States and most other countries must deny any excessive claims to waters made by any nation. This includes Libya, whose claims happen to be more excessive than most. Even the Soviets do not recognize Libya's claims to the Gulf of Sidra, only the 12-mile territorial sea limit.

To show that we do not recognize such claims, we have conducted freedom-of-navigation exercises many times in many places around the world—in international waters off countries both friendly and hostile. Since this program was instituted in 1979, many of the 90 countries with excessive claims have been challenged.[21]

National Security Council memoranda produced at the time and since declassified are consistent with Secretary Weinberger's public account.[22] It is also true, however, that privately the White House acknowledged that the operation was an opportunity to underscore President Reagan's fight against international terrorism.[23]

Then, on April 15, 1986, the LaBelle nightclub in Berlin was bombed. Three people, including two U.S. service members, were killed in the attack and over 200 people—including 60 Americans—were wounded. Evidence of culpability led to Libya. In response to the terrorist bombing, U.S. naval and air forces attacked a number of military targets in Libya.[24] The attacking bomber aircraft included 15 Navy A-6 Intruder and A-7 Corsair naval strike aircraft from the aircraft carriers *USS America* (CV 66) and *USS Coral Sea* (CV 43), as the ships were on patrol off the Libyan coast.

---

[21] Caspar W. Weinberger, *Our One and Only Objective was Freedom of Navigation*, L.A. TIMES, Mar. 30, 1986, part 5, at 5.

[22] Memorandum from Assistant Secretary of Defense Richard Armitage to John Poindexter regarding information on the 3/23–3/29/86 European Command (EUCOM) Military Maneuvers in the Gulf of Sidra, Mar. 21, 1986, Top Secret; declassified on May 30, 2001.

[23] David Hoffman & Lou Cannon, *Terrorism Provided Catalyst; Reagan Decided On "Get-Tough Attitude," Aide Says*, WASH. POST Mar. 25, 1986, at A1.

[24] George C. Wilson and David Hoffman, *U.S. Warplanes Bomb Targets in Libya As "Self-Defense" Against Terrorism*, WASH. POST, Apr. 15, 1986, at A1.

Eighteen U.S. Air Force F-111 Aardvark bomber aircraft based in the United Kingdom were also used in the attack. The F-111s flew a circuitous route around France and Spain and exercised transit passage through the Strait of Gibraltar. The longer route was selected because France had denied permission for the aircraft to overfly its territory. Although the 2,800 nautical mile trip included an additional 1,200 miles due to the diversion, the aircraft were refueled in the air several times by a fleet of aerial refueling tankers.[25] The flight through the Strait of Gibraltar underscored the strategic importance of the right of transit passage for overflying aircraft, without which the airplanes would not have been able to conduct the mission.

The last major incident over the "line of death" occurred on January 4, 1989, when two U.S. F-14 Tomcat fighter jets flying from the *USS John F. Kennedy* (CV 67) shot down two Libyan MiG-23 Flogger fighter jets 70 miles off the Libyan coast. The aircraft carrier *Kennedy* had been deployed to the region to monitor Libya's suspected efforts to build a large chemical weapons production facility near Rabta—the largest such facility in the developing world.[26] The two MiG-23s demonstrated "hostile intent" toward the U.S. fighters, triggering the right of self-defense under the American rules of engagement.[27]

9.3 Excessive Claims over the Territorial Sea and Contiguous Zone

Some States also claim authority to regulate innocent passage of warships in their territorial sea. These restrictions vary from State to State, but include:

- Requiring prior notice and/or consent before warships can enter the territorial sea;
- Limiting the number of foreign warships in the territorial sea; and
- Prohibiting transits by nuclear-powered ships or ships carrying hazardous or dangerous cargoes.[28]

UNCLOS allows coastal States to adopt laws and regulations relating to innocent passage through their territorial sea in respect of all of the following:

- Safety of navigation and regulation of maritime traffic;
- Protection of navigational aids and facilities;
- Protection of cables and pipelines;
- Conservation of living resources;
- Prevention of infringement of fisheries laws and regulations;

---

[25] Id.
[26] *Chemical Weapons Production Facility Pharma 150 (Rabta), Libya; Country Profile*, Nuclear Threat Initiative, Apr. 2012.
[27] Clyde Mark, Cong. Res. Service Issue Brief for Congress, Libya (Updated Apr. 10, 2002) and *U.S. Resumes Retaliatory Attacks; Libya Guns Silent: 6th Fleet Knocks Out More Boats*, Times Wire Services Mar. 25, 1986.
[28] Id.

- Preservation of the marine environment and reduction and control of pollution;
- Marine scientific research and hydrographic surveys; and
- Prevention of infringement of customs, fiscal, immigration or sanitary laws and regulations.[29]

The coastal State's laws and regulations, however, may not apply to design, construction, manning or equipping of foreign-flagged ships, unless the rules are consistent with generally accepted international standards adopted by the International Maritime Organization. Prohibiting transits based on the type of propulsion system or cargo on board, for example, is inconsistent with international law as embodied in UNCLOS. The coastal State may require nuclear-powered ships and ships carrying nuclear or other inherently dangerous or noxious substances or materials that lack sovereign immunity to use designated sea lanes and traffic separation schemes, as well as carry documents and observe special precautionary measures established for such ships by international agreements, but it may not prohibit transits by such ships.[30] Moreover, coastal State laws may not impose requirements on foreign ships that have the practical effect of denying, impairing or hampering the right of innocent passage.[31]

About one-fourth of the coastal States that are party to UNCLOS purport to condition the right of innocent passage of foreign-flagged warships in the territorial sea on provision of prior notice to the coastal State of the transit or consent by the coastal State for the transit.[32] China, for example, purports to require foreign warships and other government vessels operated for non-commercial purposes to obtain prior permission before engaging in innocent passage through the territorial sea.[33] China's requirement for prior permission does not comport with Article 17 of UNCLOS, which states, "ships of all States...enjoy the right of innocent passage through the territorial sea." On its face, Article 17 applies to all ships, including military and government vessels. This position is supported by Article 19 of the Convention, which contains a list of military activities that are prohibited when ships are engaged in innocent passage, such as weapons exercises, intelligence collection and launch or recovery aircraft or other military devices. The presumption is that warships not engaged in the prohibited activities automatically may enjoy the regime of innocent passage, as Article 19 would be unnecessary if warships did not have a right of innocent passage. A coastal state may, however, require a warship to leave its territorial sea immediately if

---

[29] UNCLOS, Article 21.
[30] Id., Articles 22 and 23.
[31] Id., Article 24.
[32] MARITIME CLAIMS REFERENCE MANUAL (review of coastal State laws).
[33] Order of the President of the People's Republic of China No. 55, The Standing Committee of the National People's Congress, Law of the Territorial Sea and the Contiguous Zone of Feb. 25 1992, Article 6, *reprinted in* LIS No. 117: STRAIGHT BASELINE CLAIM: CHINA, 11–14, July 9, 1996.

it engages in activities that are inconsistent with innocent passage or if it fails to comply with the coastal State's laws enacted pursuant to Article 21.[34]

During the UNCLOS negotiations, delegations from some States attempted (but failed) to achieve a majority of vote at the conference in favor of including prior notification or coastal State authorization in Article 21. The proponents of prior notice or prior consent requirements agreed not to press their proposed amendment of Article 21 to a vote at the conclusion of the negotiations, as it was clear that there was not sufficient support for the provisions to be adopted.[35] Shortly before the conclusion of the Third United Nations Conference on the Law of the Sea, the conference President, Ambassador Tommy Koh, confirmed the point. Ambassador Koh reiterated the understanding of the gathered delegations by stating on the record, "the Convention is quite clear on this point. Warships do, like other ships, have a right of innocent passage through the territorial sea, and there is no need for warships to acquire the prior consent or even notification of the coastal State."[36]

There are a number of nations that also claim authority over security-related matters in the contiguous zone. These countries include: Bangladesh, Burma (Myanmar), Cambodia, China, Egypt, Haiti, India, Iran, Pakistan, Saudi Arabia, Sri Lanka, Sudan, Syria, United Arab Emirates, Venezuela, Vietnam and Yemen.[37] These claims are not consistent with international law, including Article 33 of the Convention, which limits coastal State jurisdiction in the contiguous zone to that which is necessary to prevent or punish infringement of customs, fiscal, immigration, or sanitary (health and quarantine) laws in its territory or territorial sea. Efforts by a handful of nations to broaden the contiguous zone to include security jurisdiction in Article 33 also failed to garner majority support during the negotiations of the Convention.[38] Notably, similar efforts to include security jurisdiction in the 1958 Convention on the Territorial Sea and Contiguous Zone failed because it was feared that the "extreme vagueness" of the term "security" would lead to coastal State abuses.[39] The 1958 conference concluded that the enforcement of customs and sanitation laws would suffice to safeguard coastal State security interests.[40]

---

[34] UNCLOS, Article 30.
[35] UNITED NATIONS CONVENTION ON THE LAW OF THE SEA 1982: A COMMENTARY VOL. II 195–199. (Satya N. Nandan and Shabati Rosenne, eds. 1993) [Hereinafter VIRGINIA COMMENTARY II].
[36] Bernard H. Oxman, *The Regime of Warships Under the United Nations Convention on the Law of the Sea*, 24 VA. J. INT'L L. 809, at 854 (note 159) (1984).
[37] MARITIME CLAIMS REFERENCE MANUAL. (coastal State entries).
[38] VIRGINIA COMMENTARY II, at 272–274.
[39] Id.
[40] Id., at 274.

Most of these excessive claims have been challenged diplomatically and operationally by the United States under the FON Program. No other nation, however, conducts similar operational challenges.

9.3.1 Black Sea Bumping Incident

During the Cold War, the United States conducted FON operations more frequently than it does today. At the time, there was strong interagency support for freedom of navigation at the highest levels of the Department of State and Department of Defense, and the issue was made a priority by secretaries and assistant secretaries in the Pentagon and Foggy Bottom. The U.S. government viewed freedom of navigation with seriousness and energy that has been absent since the end of the Cold War. For example, in 1984, Bulgaria delivered a demarche to Washington after a U.S. warship steamed within 12 miles of its coast on the Black Sea. The United States responded by explaining the right of innocent passage, as reflected in UNCLOS. A Pentagon official recounted, "We came back to them and explained the correct view of international law."[41]

Similarly, during the U.S. challenge of Libya's excessive claims over the Gulf of Sidra in 1984, a U.S. Navy officer recalled another occasion when Albania ordered a U.S. cruiser to provide prior notification of its approach and transit of Albania's 15-mile territorial sea. Two Albanian hydrofoils approached to within about 1,000 yards of the U.S. warship and stopped, settling dead in the water. Eavesdropping on Albanian radio traffic, U.S. sailors on board the cruiser heard the Albanian ground radar station order the hydrofoils to approach the "target." The small attack craft lifted off the water and roared to within several hundred feet of the U.S. ship, and then settled into the water once again.[42] The ground station barked out the coordinates, demanding a response from the hydrofoils, and the captain of one of the craft replied, "We cannot locate any target."[43] The two hydrofoils turned and sped away.

The 1988 Black Sea bumping incident involving the United States and the Soviet Union is perhaps the most vivid example of how the FON Program helped preserve navigational rights and freedoms.[44] At the time, the Soviet Union

---

[41] Fred Hiatt, *Flights Over the Gulf of Sidra; U.S. Navy Jets Challenge Libyan Sovereignty Claim*, WASH. POST, July 27, 1984, at A1.
[42] Id.
[43] Id.
[44] DEP'T OF STATE, REPORT OF SOVIET WARSHIPS INTENTIONALLY COLLIDING WITH 2 U.S. WARSHIPS CONDUCTING FREEDOM OF NAVIGATION OPERATIONS IN BLACK SEA, Cable; For Official Use Only, Feb. 13, 1988. *See also*, William J. Aceves, *Diplomacy at Sea: U.S. Freedom of Navigation Operations in the Black Sea*, NAVAL WAR COLL. REV., Spring 1993, John Rolph, *Freedom of Navigation and the Black Sea Bumping Incident: How 'Innocent' Must Innocent Passage Be?*, 135 MILITARY L. REV. 137 (1992), and Richard J. Grunawalt, *Freedom of Navigation in the Post-Cold War Era*, 11, 18–19, *in* NAVIGATIONAL RIGHTS AND

recognized the right of innocent passage for warships in the territorial sea, but only in designated sea lanes. The United States challenged this position, arguing that there was no legal basis for a coastal State to limit warship transits to specified sea lanes. Two American warships had made a similar deployment in March 1986. The U.S.S.R. protested the 1986 transits, but did not try to physically interfere with the U.S. warships.[45]

On February 12, 1988, the *USS Caron* (DD 970) and *USS Yorktown* (CG 48) conducted a FON operation in the Black Sea, intentionally crossing the territorial sea of the U.S.S.R. The American warships were shadowed from their initial entry into the Black Sea, as three Soviet warships, supported by reconnaissance aircraft, followed the U.S. ships closely. The *Caron* and *Yorktown* were repeatedly warned away by Soviet naval vessels. Finally, as the U.S. warships clipped a corner of the Soviet territorial sea and transited through in innocent passage, the vessels were deliberately "shouldered" or bumped by two Soviet warships.

Sea lanes had not been designated by the Soviet Union in the Black Sea, but the U.S.S.R. insisted that the U.S. warships adhere to specified sea lanes. The U.S. ships countered that they were not required to do so.[46] As the *Caron* and *Yorktown* approached to within approximately 7 and 10 miles from the Crimean peninsula, however, the Russian ships moved much closer. The captain of one of the Soviet warships announced that "Soviets ships have orders to prevent a violation of territorial waters" and "I am authorized to strike your ship with one of ours."[47] The *USS Caron* responded: "I am engaged in innocent passage, consistent with international law."[48] Within moments, a Soviet *Mirka*-class patrol boat intentionally shouldered the *Caron*. Several minutes later a Soviet *Krivak*-class frigate bumped the *Yorktown*.[49] Both U.S. warships maintained even course after the bumping incident, eventually breaking from the Soviet coast and heading out to sea. Neither warship suffered major damage. In total, the two U.S. ships were within the territorial sea of the Soviet Union for about 75 minutes.[50]

In Moscow, the Defense Ministry issued a statement that blamed the U.S. warships for not reacting to "warning signals of Soviet border guard ships," and for "dangerously maneuvering in Soviet waters."[51] Although damage to the U.S.

FREEDOMS AND THE NEW LAW OF THE SEA (Donald R. Rothwell & Sam Bateman, eds. 2000).

[45] Id., and *U.S. Says Act was Unprovoked, Lodges Protest with Envoy, Law of the Sea*, LA TIMES (ASSOCIATED PRESS), Feb. 14, 1988, at p. 1.
[46] *Soviets Bump 2 U.S. Warships*, CHICAGO TRIB. (ASSOCIATED PRESS), Feb. 13, 1988, p. 1.
[47] Id.
[48] *U.S. Says Act was Unprovoked, Lodges Protest with Envoy, Law of the Sea*, LA TIMES (ASSOCIATED PRESS), Feb. 14, 1988, at p. 1.
[49] *Soviets Bump 2 Navy Ships in Black Sea; U.S. Says Act was Unprovoked, Lodges Protest with Envoy, Law of the Sea*, LA TIMES (ASSOCIATED PRESS), Feb. 14, 1988, at p. 1.
[50] *Soviets Bump 2 U.S. Warships*, CHICAGO TRIB. (ASSOCIATED PRESS), Feb. 13, 1988, p. 1.
[51] Id.

warships was slight and there were no injuries, the incident drew a sharp diplomatic protest from the U.S. Government.[52]

At the time of the incident, some analysts incorrectly suggested that because the purpose of the U.S. transit was merely to conduct a naval exercise or show the flag, it did not qualify as innocent passage.[53] Alfred P. Rubin of the Fletcher School of Law and Diplomacy argued, "[i]f the radio shacks of the U.S. warships were (passively) listening to anything from the coastal state not directly aimed at them, if the officers on the bridge were scanning the land..." then the ships were not in innocent passage. Rubin's rationale was that the activities he described constituted collection of intelligence that was to the detriment of the security of the coastal State, thereby making the passage not innocent. But it is hardly possible to expect any ship to transit within the territorial sea without scanning the land (and water) to maintain safe navigation. Furthermore, it is not practical for a radio shack to collect only radio transmissions purposefully aimed at them. Thus, Rubin's reading of the regime of innocent passage so narrowly defined the prohibition against "any other activity not having a direct bearing on passage," as to make the exception swallow the rule.[54] With less analysis and a dose of acrimony, *Washington Post* reporter and political activist William M. Arkin took to the pages of the *Bulletin of the Atomic Scientists*, blasting that "the [U.S.] Navy seems to have incompetent lawyers...."[55]

The Black Sea bumping incident was not the first time that the U.S. Navy had sent surface ships into the Black Sea. From January 10 to 13, 1966, for example, three Navy destroyers conducted operations to exercise freedom of the seas and collect intelligence.[56] The U.S. guided missile cruiser *Yarnell* (CG 17) and destroyer *Forrest Royal* (DD 872) were monitored with Soviet surface ships and aircraft from the time they entered the Black Sea until they exited the Bosporus. The *USS Corry* (DD 817) entered the Black Sea on February 9, 1966, and was overflown by Soviet Air Force surveillance aircraft. In each case, however, the U.S. ships were not harassed in a manner that was unsafe to navigation.

The Black Sea bumping incident reinvigorated bilateral discussions regarding the legal aspects of innocent passage—talks that had been ongoing between the United States and the Soviet Union since 1986. The discussions were viewed in the United States as a means to reconfirm a basic understanding of the content

---

[52] John Cushman, *2 Soviet Warships Reportedly Bump U.S. Navy Vessels*, N.Y. TIMES, Feb. 13, 1988.
[53] Alfred P. Rubin, *Innocent Passage in the Black Sea?*, CHRIST. SCI. MON., Mar. 1, 1988, p. 14 and William M. Arkin, *Spying in the Black Sea*, BULL. ATOMIC SCI. 5–6 (May 1988).
[54] Rubin, *Innocent Passage in the Black Sea?*
[55] Arkin, *Spying in the Black Sea.*
[56] W. W. Rostow, Memorandum for the President, Black Sea Operations by U.S. Naval Vessels, Feb. 16, 1967 (Secret; declassified Nov. 18, 1993).

of innocent passage. Both nations viewed UNCLOS as generally reflective of international law and practice, so the terms of the treaty were used as the point of departure for the talks.

Both superpowers also recognized the need to encourage all states to harmonize their domestic laws, regulations and practices with the provisions of UNCLOS. The discussions led to the signing of the *Uniform Interpretation of Rules of International Law Governing Innocent Passage* (*Jackson Hole Agreement*) in September 1989. In the end, the Soviet Union agreed with the U.S. position that "all ships, including warships, regardless of cargo, armament or means of propulsion, enjoy the right of innocent passage through the territorial sea in accordance with international law, for which neither prior notification nor authorization is required."[57] The Parties also agreed, *inter alia*, that Article 19 of UNCLOS contained an "exhaustive list of activities that would render passage not innocent."

9.3.2. *Jackson Hole Agreement*

JOINT STATEMENT
BY THE UNITED STATES OF AMERICA
AND THE UNION OF SOVIET SOCIALIST REPUBLICS

Since 1986, representatives of the United States of America and the Union of Soviet Socialist Republics have been conducting friendly and constructive discussions of certain international legal aspects of traditional uses of the oceans, in particular navigation.

The Governments are guided by the provisions of the 1982 United Nations Convention on the Law of the Sea, which, with respect to traditional uses of the oceans, generally constitute international law and practice and balance fairly the interests of all States. They recognize the need to encourage all States to harmonize their internal laws, regulations and practices, with those provisions.

The Governments consider it useful to issue the attached Uniform Interpretation of the Rules of International Law Governing Innocent Passage. Both Governments have agreed to take the necessary steps to conform their internal laws, regulations and practices with this understanding of the rules.

Jackson Hole, Wyoming
September 23, 1989

Attachment:
Uniform Interpretation of Rules of International Law Governing Innocent Passage

---

[57] Union of Soviet Socialist Republics-United States: Joint Statement with attached Uniform Interpretation of Rules of International Law Governing Innocent Passage, Jackson Hole, Wyoming, Sept. 23, 1989, 28 I.L.M. 1444 (1989).

UNIFORM INTERPRETATION OF RULES OF INTERNATIONAL LAW GOVERNING INNOCENT PASSAGE

1. The relevant rules of international law governing innocent passage of ships in the territorial sea are stated in the 1982 United Nations Convention on the Law of the Sea (Convention of 1982), particularly in Part II, Section 3.
2. All ships, including warships, regardless of cargo, armament or means of propulsion, enjoy the right of innocent passage through the territorial sea in accordance with international law, for which neither prior notification nor authorization is required.
3. Article 19 of the Convention of 1982 sets out in paragraph 2 an exhaustive list of activities that would render passage not innocent. A ship passing through the territorial sea that does not engage in any of those activities is in innocent passage.
4. A coastal State which questions whether the particular passage of a ship through its territorial sea is innocent shall inform the ship of the reason why it questions the innocence of the passage, and provide the ship an opportunity to clarify its intentions or correct its conduct in a reasonably short period of time.
5. Ships exercising the right of innocent passage shall comply with all laws and regulations of the coastal State adopted in conformity with relevant rules of international law as reflected in Articles 21, 22, 23 and 25 of the Convention of 1982. These include the laws and regulations requiring ships exercising the right of innocent passage through its territorial sea to use such sea lanes and traffic separation schemes as it may prescribe where needed to protect safety of navigation. In areas where no such sea lanes or traffic separation schemes have been prescribed, ships nevertheless enjoy the right of innocent passage.
6. Such laws and regulations of the coastal State may not have the practical effect of denying or impairing the exercise of the right of innocent passage as set forth in Article 24 of the Convention of 1982.
7. If a warship engages in conduct which violates such laws or regulations or renders its passage not innocent and does not take corrective action upon request, the coastal State may require it to leave the territorial sea, as set forth in Article 30 of the Convention of 1982. In such case the warship shall do so immediately.
8. Without prejudice to the exercise of rights of coastal and flag States, all differences which may arise regarding a particular case of passage of ships through the territorial sea shall be settled through diplomatic channels or other agreed means.

9.4 Excessive Claims over Straits Used for International Navigation

Restrictions on transit passage through international straits and associated waters are a particular security concern. A 1967 Top Secret memorandum from the Joint Chiefs of Staff to Secretary of Defense Robert McNamara, now declassified, underscores the strategic importance of international straits, using Asia as an example. Both in practice and principle, the Pentagon explained that the Malacca Strait and the Sunda Strait were key routes from East to West:

> The strategic importance of the Malacca Strait area from its controlling position with respect to passage between the Pacific and Indian Oceans and its proximity to the western approaches to Southeast Asia through Thailand. Freedom to transit

the Malacca and Sunda Straits, both of which can be controlled effectively from the Malaysian/Singapore area, is axiomatic in principle and necessary in practice. Continuation of the present high volume of military and commercial transits would require circumnavigation of the Indonesian Archipelago if control of the Straits areas were denied the United States or its allies. Such a detour of over 2,000 miles would be comparable to placing an additional ocean, the size of the Atlantic, in the path of seaborne traffic.[58]

Absent the right of transit passage, warships would only have a right of innocent passage (or at best, non-suspendable innocent passage) through straits used for international navigation. Submarines would be required to navigate on the surface, and overflight by aircraft would require coastal State consent. The same is true for transits through archipelagoes, since ships only enjoy a right of non-suspendable innocent passage in archipelagic waters, Overflight of archipelagic waters outside of archipelagic sea lanes requires the consent of the archipelagic State.

The uncertainty expressed by the Chairman of the Joint Chiefs of Staff in 1967 would not be resolved for another 15 years, but with the adoption of UNCLOS in 1982, the rules regarding transit passage through international straits were codified in a multilateral treaty. With the extension of the territorial sea from 3 to 12 nautical miles, most strategic straits—Hormuz, Gibraltar, Bab el Mandeb, Malacca, and many others—that traditionally had a high seas corridor to accommodate international shipping traffic became completely overlapped by coastal State territorial seas.

UNCLOS allows the bordering States to establish IMO-approved sea lanes and traffic separation schemes in straits used for international navigation, if necessary to promote safety of navigation.[59] Article 42 allows States bordering straits used for international navigation to adopt laws and regulations relating to transit passage with respect to:

- Safety of navigation and regulation of maritime traffic;
- Prevention, reduction and control of pollution by giving effect to applicable international regulations (i.e., 1973 International Convention for the Prevention of Pollution from Ships (MARPOL) as modified by the 1978 Protocol);
- Prevention of fishing, including the stowage of fishing gear; and
- Customs, fiscal, immigration or sanitary matters.

The laws and regulations may neither discriminate among foreign ships, nor have the practical effect of denying, hampering or impairing the right of transit

---

[58] Memorandum from the Joint Chiefs of Staff to Secretary of Defense McNamara, Australian Request for Consultations Regarding Future Security Arrangements in Malaysia/Singapore, Nov. 8, 1967, *reprinted in* 27 U.S. Dep't of State, Foreign Relations of the United States, 1964–1968, Mainland Southeast Asia; Regional Affairs, Document 33, at pp. 83–84.

[59] UNCLOS, Article 41.

passage. Moreover, with the limited exception of violations that may cause or threaten to cause major damage to the marine environment of the strait, a bordering State may not enforce its laws against foreign flag vessels transiting the strait.[60] Article 44 of UNCLOS specifically prohibits bordering States from hampering or suspending transit passage. Articles 39, 40, 42 and 44 apply *mutatis mutandis* to archipelagic sea lanes passage pursuant to Article 54.

9.4.1 Strait of Hainan

China claims the Strait of Hainan as internal waters, using straight baselines to close off its eastern and western approaches.[61] The strait is 19 miles wide and separates the Leizhou Peninsula in southern China from Hainan Island, connecting the Gulf of Tonkin to the James Shoal on the eastern edge of the South China Sea. From an historic perspective, China argues that the strait has always been subject to exclusive Chinese control and that a 1958 declaration reaffirmed that control.[62]

China's claim to the strait as internal waters has been protested by a number of nations, however.[63] Moreover, the strait qualifies as a strait used for international navigation in which the right of transit passage applies. China's claim is clearly inconsistent with UNCLOS Article 37, which provides that the transit passage regime applies to straits used for international navigation between one part of the high seas or an EEZ and another part of the high seas or an EEZ. Consequently, while China could, consistent with Article 41, designate IMO-approved sea lanes and traffic separation schemes in the strait if necessary to promote safe navigation, it may not close the Hainan Strait to international navigation merely by claiming that the strait constitutes internal waters.

Furthermore, even if China's new straight baselines closing off the strait were to be accepted by the international community, China would have a duty to recognize the right of non-suspendable innocent passage through the strait under Article 8(2) of UNCLOS.

9.4.2 Head Harbor Passage

Canada and the United States are at an impasse over the right of non-suspendable innocent passage in a "dead end" strait between the two countries, which runs between the Province of New Brunswick and the State of Maine. Ships bound for U.S. ports on the Maine side of the river may reach port only via transit through Canadian waters. Thus, without the cooperation or at least

---

[60] Virginia Commentary II, para. 42.10(g), at 377. *See also*, UNCLOS, Article 233.
[61] Maritime Claims Reference Manual (China).
[62] Zou Keyuan, *Historic Rights in International Law and in China's Practice*, 32 Ocean Development & Int'l Law 149–68 (2001).
[63] Id.

acquiescence of Canada, the terminals and ports of Maine along Passamaquoddy Bay, are entirely zone-locked—meaning that without access to the Canadian territorial sea (or internal waters) of Passamaquoddy Bay, the ports on the American side are blocked to maritime traffic. The St. Croix River and Passamaquoddy Bay constitute a "dead end" strait under Article 45 of UNCLOS. In such straits, the regime of non-suspendable innocent passage applies in accordance with Articles 17–19 of UNCLOS.[64]

The Canadian government has indicated obliquely but officially that it considers the area of the Bay of Fundy, and presumably Passamaquoddy Bay and the associated waterway of Head Harbor Passage to be within the internal waters of Canada.[65] There may be some good faith disagreement over the legal status of the Canadian waters. The waters are either Canadian territorial waters—that is, territorial seas—or Canadian internal waters. The question is not dispositive, or even necessarily relevant, however, to solving the legal questions concerning rights of transit by U.S.-bound shipping. Yet regardless of whether the Canadian waters are territorial seas or internal waters, there is no question that Canada exercises sovereignty over them. Whether the waters are internal waters or territorial seas, however, does not obviate the right of foreign-flagged ships to transit them, it merely changes the navigational regime that applies to such ships. As a dead-end strait, Head Harbor Passage is governed under the rules set forth in Article 45(1)(b) of UNCLOS, which addresses transits between "a part of the high seas or exclusive economic zone and the territorial sea of a foreign State." In such case, the regime of non-suspendable innocent passage applies in the Strait.[66]

9.4.3   *Northwest Passage*

Thirty-five years ago, Canada suggested that it had authority to assert sovereignty over regions of the Arctic Ocean, while the United States rejected Ottawa's claims that the waters constituted the internal waters of Canada.[67] The waterway has

---

[64] A dead-end strait is one of the six species of straits used for international navigation that are recognized in UNCLOS. William L. Schachte, Jr. & J. Peter A. Bernhardt, *International Straits and Navigational Freedoms*, 33 Va. J. Int'l L. 527 (1992–93).

[65] Letter from Government of Canada, Department of External Affairs, Bureau of Legal Affairs, Dec. 17, 1973, *reprinted in*, 12 Can. Y. B. Int'l L. 277, at p. 279 (1974).

[66] Message from the President of the United States Transmitting United Nations Convention on the Law of the Sea, with Annexes, done at Montego Bay, Jamaica, Dec. 10, 1982 and the Agreement Relating to the Implementation of Part XI of the United Nations Convention on the Law of the Sea of 10 Dec. 1982, with Annex, Adopted at New York, July 28, 1994, and signed by the United States, Subject to Ratification, on July 29, 1994, Treaty Doc. 103–39, Oct. 7, 1994, at p. 19.

[67] Memorandum from Theodore L. Eliot, Jr., United States Department of State, Information Memorandum for Mr. Kissinger—The White House, Mar. 12, 1970, *reprinted in* U.S. Dep't of State, Foreign Relations of the United States 1969–1976 Volume E-1, Documents on Global Issues 1969–1972.

been fully transited nearly 70 times by surface vessels belonging to Canada, the United States, Norway, the Netherlands, Japan, Bahamas, and Liberia, and transited numerous times by submarines of the United States and the United Kingdom and presumably, Russia. For decades, submarines from the U.S. Navy and the United Kingdom have conducted submerged transits throughout the Arctic region.

Canada exercises complete sovereignty over the islands of the North American Arctic. As a coastal State, however, Canada is not entitled to claim sovereignty over the waters lying beyond 12 nm from the low water mark running along the shore of the numerous islands. On September 10, 1985 "the Government of Canada claimed all the waters among its Arctic islands as internal waters, and drew straight baselines around its Arctic islands to establish its claim. The United States position is that there is no basis in international law to support the Canadian claim."[68] In 1997, Canada extended its territorial sea from 3 nm to 12 nm, aligning the outer limits of the Canadian territorial sea with the limit permitted under the Law of the Sea Convention.[69]

Three factors are to be considered in determining whether a body of water may be considered historic internal waters: (1) the exercise of authority over the area of the claiming nation; (2) the continuity of this exercise of authority; and, (3) the acquiescence of foreign nations.[70] This three-part test makes historic claims notoriously difficult to maintain. Donat Pharand, the dean of Canadian legal scholars on the Northwest Passage, conceded in an article in *Ocean Development and International Law* in 2007 that Canada could not meet the test.[71] Professor Pharand, however, concludes his analysis by reinforcing Canada's exclusive claim of internal waters, arguing that Ottawa's straight baseline claims were made prior to the country becoming a party to UNCLOS, and the Convention "cannot apply retroactively to change the established legal status."[72] Of course, the entire purpose of UNCLOS is to establish legal status, and it was negotiated in order to provide a common yardstick by which all States could adjust, revise, and correct erroneous claims.

The United States and the European Union have objected to Canadian internal waters claims over the Northwest Passage. The EU position is reflected in a British High Commission Note of 1986, which states, "The Member States acknowledge that elements other than purely geographical ones may be relevant for purposes

---

[68] Dep't of State, State Department File No. P86 0019–8641, Feb. 26, 1986.
[69] An Act Respecting the Oceans of Canada (Oceans Act), Jan., 1997, S.C. 1996, c. 31 (Assented to Dec. 18 1996).
[70] Juridical Regime of Historic Waters, Including Historic Bays, U.N Doc A/CN.4/143 (1962) at 56.
[71] Donat Pharand, *The Arctic Waters and the Northwest Passage: A Final Revisit*, 38 OCEAN DEVELOPMENT & INT'L L. 3, 13 (2007).
[72] Id., at 59.

of drawing baselines in particular circumstances but are not satisfied that the present baselines are justified in general. Moreover, the Member States cannot recognize the validity of a historic title as justification for the baselines drawn in accordance with the order."[73]

9.4.4 Torres Strait

The Torres Strait is a strait used for international navigation that separates Australia and Papua New Guinea (PNG). The waterway is about 90 nm wide and 150 nm long, and there is no doubt the area has a remarkable natural ecology. The land ringing the strait is home to over 10,000 indigenous Australians and 20,000 PNG indigenous inhabitants who depend heavily on the unique marine environment and abundant marine life found in the strait for subsistence and gathering. The shallow and fast moving waters feature 150 islands and numerous islets, coral reefs and cays. The complex and vulnerable ecosystem of the strait has extensive beds of sea grass, resident dugong and turtle populations, coral reefs, sand cays, mangrove islands, inactive volcanic islands and granite continental islands.[74] Larger commercial vessels are limited to using the Prince of Wales Channel and the Great North East Channel, which are only a few hundred meters wide in some places.

In 2003, Australia and PNG submitted a joint proposal to the IMO Marine Environment Protection Committee (MEPC) to designate the Torres Strait as a Particularly Sensitive Sea Area (PSSA) in order to protect the complex and vulnerable littoral ecosystem.[75] The proposal sought to extend the existing Great Barrier Reef region compulsory pilotage area to vessels navigating the Torres Strait and the Great North East Channel, a regime in effect since 1991.[76] The associated protective measure was deemed necessary to "improve safety of navigation in an area where freedom of movement of shipping is considerably inhibited by restricted sea-room, and where there are obstructions to navigation, limited depths and potentially unfavorable meteorological conditions."[77]

The proposal made compulsory the regime existing at the time for ships of 70 meters in length and over and for all loaded oil tankers, chemical tankers or

---

[73] British High Commission Note No. 90/86 of July 9, 1986, *reported in* American Embassy Paris telegram 33625, July 24, 1986, *as cited in* ROACH & SMITH, EXCESSIVE MARITIME CLAIMS, at 112 (note 121).
[74] IMO Doc. MEPC 49/8, Identification and Protection of Special Areas and Particularly Sensitive Sea Areas, Extension of Existing Great Barrier Reef PSSA to include the Torres Strait Region Submitted by Australia and Papua New Guinea, Apr. 10, 2003, para. 2.1–2.4.
[75] Id., para. 1.2.
[76] IMO Doc. A.710(17), Use of Pilotage Services in the Torres Strait and the Great North East Channel, Nov. 6, 1991 and IMO Doc. A 17/Res. 710, Use of Pilotage Services in the Torres Strait and the Great North East Channel, Nov. 29, 1991.
[77] IMO Doc. A.710(17), para. 1.3.

liquefied gas carriers, irrespective of size.[78] Reliance on the existing recommended pilotage regime was deemed unacceptable to Australia and Papua New Guinea because compliance had been declining over the years:

> Compliance with the existing recommended pilotage regime is declining and Resolution A.710(17) no longer provides an acceptable level of protection for Torres Strait. Data from shipping in Torres Strait in 1995 and 2001 showed compliance rates of 70 percent and 55 percent respectively.
>
> ... [A] detailed examination of data from September 2001 to August 2002 showed 840 transits through both the Prince of Wales and Great North East Channels and that compliance had further declined to 32 percent (139 out of 432) for vessels on eastbound voyages and 38.5 percent (157 out of 408) for west bound voyages. This amounts to over 500 unpiloted transits per year.... Australia and Papua New Guinea therefore consider that Resolution A.710(17) has proven to be inadequate to protect the Torres Strait.[79]

But Australian efforts to impose a mandatory pilotage regime for the Torres Strait were opposed by much of the international community as an illegal restriction on the right of transit passage. During a plenary session of the IMO's Maritime Environmental Protection Committee (MEPC), the United States and several other nations confirmed that the IMO could adopt a recommendatory, rather than compulsory, pilotage scheme in the strait. The Australian delegation indicated that it did not object to the U.S. statement.[80] The MEPC therefore noted the views expressed by the United States and other delegations and instructed "the PSSA Technical Group to prepare a draft MEPC resolution on the designation of the Torres Strait as an extension to the Great Barrier Reef PSSA and to report back to plenary."[81] Accordingly, member States adopted Resolution MEPC.133 at MEPC 53 on July 22, 2005:

> 1. DESIGNATES the Torres Strait, as defined in Annex 1 to this resolution, as an extension of the Great Barrier Reef Particularly Sensitive Sea Area...;
>
> 3. RECOMMENDS that Governments recognize the need for effective protection of the Great Barrier Reef and Torres Strait region and inform ships flying their flag that they should act in accordance with Australia's system of pilotage for merchant ships 70 m in length and over or oil tankers, chemical tankers, and gas carriers, irrespective of size....[82]

---

[78] MEPC 49/8, para. 5.7.
[79] Id., para. 5.9.
[80] Id., para. 8.6.
[81] Id., para. 8.7.
[82] IMO Doc. MEPC 53/24/Add.2, Report of the Marine Environment Protection Committee on its Fifty-Third Session, Annex 21, Aug. 21, 2005 and IMO Doc. MEPC.133(53), Designation of the Torres Strait as an Extension of the Great Barrier Reef Particularly Sensitive Sea Area, July 22, 2005.

Following MEPC, however, on May 16, 2006, the Australian Maritime Safety Authority (AMSA) issued Marine Notice 8/2006 "to advise ship-owners and operators of new requirements for pilotage in the Torres Strait to be introduced by the Australian and Papua-New Guinean governments in 2006."[83] Notwithstanding the language of Resolution MEPC.133(53) and the decision at MEPC 53 that the pilotage regime adopted for the Torres Strait was recommendatory rather than compulsory, the notice indicated that a new compulsory pilotage area for the Torres Strait would take effect on October 6, 2006.[84]

Following a series of diplomatic protests over the summer by the United States, Singapore, Japan, the International Chamber of Shipping (ICS), and other interested governments and entities, the AMSA issued Marine Notice 16/2006 on October 3, 2006.[85] The notice advised ship-owners, masters and operators "that, as a condition of entry into an Australian port, failure to carry a pilot as prescribed may result in a prosecution under Australian law."[86] The notice further advised that Australian authorities would "not suspend, deny, hamper or impair transit passage" and would "not stop, arrest or board ships that do not take on a pilot while transiting the Strait."[87] The notice provided that "the owner, master and/or operator of the ship may be prosecuted on the next entry into an Australian port..." if they did not take on a pilot as prescribed.[88]

Two weeks later, at MEPC 55, the matter was once again discussed in session in London. Singapore pointed out that reliance on Resolution MEPC.133(53) to support the compulsory pilotage system "was not in line with the outcome and understanding reached at MEPC 53."[89] Paragraphs 8.5 to 8.6 of Resolution MEPC.133(53) recorded that the IMO had approved recommendatory pilotage in the strait. There was no basis in international law for Australia to impose a scheme of mandatory pilotage for ships in transit in the Torres Strait or any other strait used for international navigation.[90] Singapore restated "its position that the imposition of compulsory pilotage for ships transiting a strait used for international navigation would have the practical effect of denying, hampering or impairing the right of transit passage, and thus be in contravention of Article 42(2) of UNCLOS"[91] Singapore's position was supported by "the Russian

---

[83] Marine Notice 8/2006, Revised Pilotage Requirements for Torres Strait, May 16, 2006.
[84] Id.
[85] Marine Notice 16/2006, Further Information on Revised Pilotage Requirements for Torres Strait, Oct. 3, 2006.
[86] Id.
[87] Id.
[88] Id.
[89] IMO Doc. MEPC 55/8/2/Add.1, Identification and Protection of Special Areas and Particularly Sensitive Sea Areas, Outcome of NAV 52 related to PSSAs, Note by the Secretariat, Sept. 7, 2006, para. 2.
[90] Id.
[91] Id.

Federation, Japan, the United States, Panama, China, Norway, Greece, Liberia, Brazil, United Kingdom, Ukraine, Cyprus, the Bahamas, South Africa [and]... the observers from ICS and the Baltic and International Maritime Council (BIMCO)."[92]

Representatives of the shipping industry, including ICS, BIMCO, INTERTANKO and INTERCARGO, likewise expressed concern over the publication of Marine Notice 8/2006. Highlighting the statement of the United States at MEPC 53 regarding the right of transit passage and the recommendatory nature of Resolution MEPC.133(53), the shipping representatives expressed the view "that the imposition of compulsory pilotage for ships transiting a strait used for international navigation would have the practical effect of denying, hampering or impairing the right of transit passage, and thus be in contravention of UNCLOS Article 42(2)."[93] Following the intervention of the shipping industry delivered at MEPC 55, the Chairman of MEPC "stated that historically, when the Committee adopts resolutions with an operative paragraph beginning with the word "RECOMMENDS," the content of that paragraph is of a recommendatory nature; therefore, any different interpretation would necessitate the revision of all resolutions adopted by the MEPC."[94]

Based on this discussion, Singapore "strongly urged Australia to review its positions in Marine Notices 8/2006 and 16/2006 to bring them in line with the understanding reached by the Committee."[95] The delegations of the Bahamas, Brazil, Chile, China, Cyprus, Finland, Ghana, Greece, India, Islamic Republic of Iran, Israel, Italy, Japan, Latvia, Liberia, Marshall Islands, Mexico, Nigeria, Norway, Panama, Republic of Korea, the Russian Federation, South Africa, Sri Lanka, Thailand, the United Kingdom, the United States, Vietnam and the United Arab Emirates associated themselves with the statement of the delegation from Singapore.[96] Cyprus (supported by Greece), in particular, stressed that "compulsory pilotage in straits used for international navigation was currently outside the legal framework of international law and, in addition, it was seriously concerned about the consequences that the introduction of such a system in the Torres Strait could have elsewhere."[97]

---

[92] Id., para. 3.
[93] IMO Doc. MEPC 55/8/3, Identification and Protection of Special Areas and Particularly Sensitive Sea Areas, Torres Strait (Submitted by ICS, BIMCO, INTERCARGO and INTERTANKO), Aug. 10, 2006, para. 4. The U.S. statement is contained in IMO Doc. MEPC 53/24, paras. 8.5 and 8.6.
[94] IMO Doc. MEPC 55/23, Report of the Marine Environment Protection Committee on its Fifty-fifth Session, Oct. 16, 2006, para. 8.10.
[95] Id., para. 8.12.
[96] IMO Doc. A 25/5(b)/2/Corr.1, Consideration of the Reports of the Committees of the Assembly, Reports of other committees, Report of the Technical Committee to the Plenary, Corrigendum, Nov. 29, 2007, para. 54.
[97] IMO Doc. MEPC 55/23, para. 8.15.

Australia defended AMSA regulations and was joined by the delegations of Germany, New Zealand and Papua New Guinea, who associated their positions with the Australian statement.[98] Denmark, bordering the Danish Straits, also supported Australia's efforts, indicating that the IMO "must shift [its] focus in order to adapt to the international opinion and current international priorities."[99] Denmark believed there was "a way to attain mandatory pilotage in an international strait," and stated that it would "continue to support any future efforts to get mandatory pilotage in the Torres Strait and similar exposed areas, at the IMO, or at any other competent level."[100]

Denmark's support for the Australian position may be viewed in light of international opposition against construction of the Great Belt Fixed Link and the Øresund Bridge-Tunnel across the Danish Straits (Great Belt, Little Belt and Øresund). The Link consists of a bridge and railway tunnel between Zealand Island and the Island of Sprogø and a second bridge between Sprogø and Funen Island. The Øresund Bridge-Tunnel connects Sweden and Denmark. Finland brought a case against Denmark over the issue at the International Court of Justice (ICJ) in 1991, claiming that construction of the Link would prevent the passage of Finnish-built mobile offshore drilling rigs through the Straits, and therefore was inconsistent with international law. The matter was never resolved by a decision of the Court, however, as the parties settled the case in 1992.[101]

The following month, in November 2007, the IMO Assembly "reaffirmed the decision reached at MEPC 55 that resolution MEPC.133(53) is recommendatory in nature."[102] Following additional diplomatic efforts in 2008 and 2009, Australia finally relented on the issue and it amended the mandatory pilotage requirement to apply only to vessels calling on Australian ports. On April 17, 2009, the AMSA issued Marine Notice 7/2009, which stated that "if a vessel passes through the Torres Strait and it does not comply with Australia's system of pilotage for merchant ships 70 meters in length and over or oil tankers, chemical tankers, and gas carriers, irrespective of size, the Government of Australia will notify the vessel's Flag State, Owner, Operator and Master that the vessel failed to take a pilot and henceforth cannot enter an Australian port without the risk of the Owner, Operator and/or Master of the vessel being subject to a non-custodial penalty under Australian law."[103]

---

[98] IMO Doc. A 25/5(b)/2/Corr.1, para. 5.
[99] IMO Doc. MEPC 55/23, para. 8.14 and Annex 24.
[100] Id. and IMO Doc. A 25/5(b)/2/Corr. para. 56.
[101] *Passage through the Great Belt* (Finland v. Denmark) Order of Sept. 10, 1992, I.C.J. Reports 1992, p. 348.
[102] IMO Doc. A 25/5(b)/2/Corr.1, para. 58.
[103] Marine Notice 7/2009: Bridge Resource Management (BRM) and Torres Strait Pilotage, Apr. 17, 2009.

Although the Torres Strait issue was successfully resolved in a manner that preserves, to some extent, freedom of transit passage through a strait used for international navigation, the case demonstrates the effort by coastal states to amend the navigational rules of UNCLOS without going through the formal amendment process contained in Part XVII. At MEPC 55, the delegation of Cyprus expressed serious concern "about the consequences that the introduction of such a system in the Torres Strait could have elsewhere."[104] This concern is not unfounded. In 2008, the Indonesian Transportation Ministry announced the implementation of a voluntary pilotage regime for the Strait of Malacca, with a plan to make it compulsory after an unspecified time period. The Transportation Ministry cited the "compulsory" Torres Strait regime as a precedent to support the proposal.[105]

9.4.5 *Strait of Hormuz*

For a distance of about 15 nautical miles, the Strait of Hormuz is less than 24 nautical miles wide. Both Iran and Oman claim a territorial sea of 12 nautical miles, so all ships passing through the Strait are in either Iranian or Omani waters. An IMO-approved routeing scheme is in place in the strait.[106]

On occasion Iran has threatened to close the strait to commercial and military traffic. In 2011, First Vice President Mohammad Reza Rahimi stated Tehran would close the strait to oil tanker traffic if U.S. and European Union sanctions were implemented against Iran for its nuclear program. Iranian Navy Admiral Habibollah Sayyari echoed the vice president's statement, indicating that it would be very easy for the Iranian navy to close the strait.[107] An average of 15 million barrels of oil passes through the strait each day.

In response to the threats, the Chairman of the Joint Chiefs of Staff and the Secretary of Defense warned that the United States was prepared to take action to reopen the strait should Iran follow through with its threats.[108] Great Britain has likewise indicated that it was prepared to use military force to keep the strait open. British Defense Secretary Philip Hammond told reporters that "any attempt

---

[104] IMO Doc. MEPC 55/23, para. 8.15.
[105] Dep't of State American Embassy Jakarta Cable, Demarche Response On Indonesia Scheme For Pilotage In The Strait Of Malacca, U.S. Cable 040058Z DEC 08, Dec. 4, 2008 and Y. Sulaiman, *Wake Up, Indonesia! Lessons From WikiLeaks*, Jakarta Globe, Sept. 02, 2011.
[106] Memorandum from the Legal Adviser, Department of State to Acting Secretary of State, Legal Rights of Passage Through the Strait of Hormuz and in the Persian Gulf in Light of the Hostilities Between Iran and Iraq. Sept. 26, 1980 (Confidential; declassified Oct. 22, 1998).
[107] Farnaz Fassihi, *U.S. Warns Tehran On Strait*, Wall St. J., Dec. 29, 2011.
[108] Elisabeth Bumiller, Eric Schmitt & Thom Shanker, *U.S. Sends Top Iranian Leader A Warning On Strait Threat*, N.Y. Times, Jan. 13, 2012.

270   CHAPTER NINE

to close the Strait of Hormuz would be illegal, and we need to send a very clear message to Iran that we are determined that the straits should remain open."[109]

9.5   Excessive Claims over Archipelagic Sea Lanes

During the negotiations for the Law of the Sea Convention, there were two sub-issues that were part of the deal-making on the navigational regime for transit passage through straits used for international navigation. The first challenge was overcoming what Ambassador John Norton Moore termed the "archipelagic problem." States such as Indonesia, Malaysia, the Philippines, and Fiji, opposed the notion of free transit through straits, because as archipelagos they feature numerous straits.[110] These states needed to maintain a sense of national unity, and they feared they could dissolve into disparate parts unless the oceans between the islands were integrated into the sovereignty of the country.

The United States conducted multiple negotiations on the question with Indonesia and the Philippines, as well as Fiji, which had some influence within the archipelago group. The United States sought to obtain unimpeded transit rights through archipelagic straits in return for U.S. support for recognition of the concept of archipelagic states.[111] The negotiations between the United States and the archipelagic states were carefully coordinated with the United Kingdom, France, Germany, the Soviet Union, and Japan—the other members of the major maritime powers.[112]

The negotiations ended with a trade-off: archipelagic states could draw straight baselines around their outermost islands and claim all the enclosed waters as archipelagic waters, while the international community would retain a right to transit through the archipelagos. All ships, submarines and aircraft enjoy a right of archipelagic sea lanes passage (ASLP) through designated sea lanes or routes normally used through archipelagic waters. The right may be exercised in the "normal mode of operation," meaning that submarines may transit submerged and aircraft may overfly the straits in ASLP.[113] Surface ships may transit in a manner

---

[109] Adrian Croft, U.K. *Signals Ready To Use Force To Keep Strait Open*, REUTERS, Jan. 5, 2012.
[110] Minutes of the Acting Secretary's Analytical Staff Meeting, Monday June 17, 1974— 3:00 P.M. (Secret document, declassified on Aug. 21, 2003, and as amended on Feb. 27, 2009), E-12 U.S. DEP'T OF STATE, FOREIGN RELATIONS OF THE UNITED STATES, DOCUMENT ON EAST AND SOUTHEAST ASIA, 1973–1976, Document 9.
[111] Id.
[112] In addition to unimpeded transit passage through straits, the Major Maritime Powers also sought to limit the number of nations that could claim archipelagic status to a small number of fix or six nations, including Indonesia. Id.
[113] UNCLOS, Articles 38, 39, 53 and 54.

consistent with self-defense, to include formation steaming and launching and recovery of aircraft, if doing so is consistent with sound navigational practices.

9.5.1 Indonesia's 1960s Archipelagic Claims

Before the meetings of the Third UN Conference on the Law of the Sea, Indonesia had attempted to close off the archipelago to foreign warships or at a minimum require prior notification of warship transits. On February 18, 1960, for example, Indonesia adopted into law Regulation No. 4, which abrogated a 3 mile territorial sea claim and instituted a 12 mile claim. The 12 mile territorial sea, measured from the outermost points of archipelagic straight baselines, was adopted before the juridical archipelago was accepted as a matter of international law.

Indonesia was also fairly testy over foreign-flagged ships transiting through the archipelago. On August 27, 1964, a British aircraft carrier task force steamed through the Sunda Strait, travelling toward Singapore. Indonesia and Malaysia were engaged in low-level hostilities, as Sukarno sought to break up Malaysia and oust the British from their military bases.[114] The conflict threatened to draw Britain, and perhaps even America, into the conflict. The British had three aircraft carriers in the Far East at that time. Indonesia threatened "retaliatory action" if the U.K. flotilla re-transited the strait on the return journey from Singapore. To avoid provocation, however, the British notified Indonesia of the return transit and conducted passage through the Lombok Strait rather than the Sunda Strait.[115]

Commander-in-Chief, U.S. Pacific Command (CINCPAC), the predecessor to today's Commander, U.S. Pacific Command (USPACOM), was the most active element of the Department of Defense in defending freedom of navigation in the oceans. In 1964, CINCPAC sent a secret message under the subject, "Implications [of] Indonesian Mare Nostrum," to the Joint Chiefs of Staff, with copies to the Chief of Naval Operations and the combatant commanders throughout the world, explaining the pressing need for both diplomacy and action to preserve navigational rights through Indonesia. The cable, which has since been declassified, provides a window into how the debates of 50 years ago still resonate today:

---

[114] Short-Term Prospects in the Malaysia/Indonesia, U.S. Special Intelligence Estimate, Sept. 16, 1964, SNIE 54/55–64, 26 U.S. DEP'T OF STATE, FOREIGN RELATIONS OF THE UNITED STATES 1964–1968, INDONESIA; MALAYSIA-SINGAPORE; PHILIPPINES, Document No. 75, pp. 158–160. *See also*, Note from Robert W. Komer of the National Security Council Staff to the President's Special Assistant for National Security Affairs (Bundy), Sept. 4, 1964, 26 U.S. DEP'T OF STATE, FOREIGN RELATIONS OF THE UNITED STATES 1964–1968, INDONESIA; MALAYSIA-SINGAPORE; PHILIPPINES, Document No. 71, at 153.

[115] Dep't of Defense, Commander in Chief, U.S. Pacific Commander, Implications [of] Indonesia's *Mare Nostrum*, CINCPAC MSG 102244Z OCT 64 Parts I and II, Oct. 19, 1964 (Secret; declassified).

The United States, since its inception, has been and is firmly committed to uphold the fundamental principle of freedom of the seas, which is for the general benefit and commerce of all nations, large and small. The United States regards as a wrongful and unacceptable appropriation of the high seas any claim more than three miles of territorial waters as well as any alleged right to convert into internal or territorial waters large areas of the high seas in and around island comprising [Indonesia] which have traditionally been used as high seas by vessels of all nations.

At the ANZUS Council meeting in Washington on July 18, 1964, the Secretary of State stated that the United States expected to move around international waters of the world as it wished.

While the stated policy has been clear and consistent, the United States has provided prior notification to Indonesia of intended transits [through the archipelago]. This advance notification on the part of the United States in essence acknowledges the existence of the Indonesian claim and is opposed to our previous effective doctrine of ignoring and strenuously opposing such claims. Indonesia, to the contrary, has taken positive action on many occasions to enforce her claim. Included [sic] were the arrest of a British ship for failure to fly British colors in claimed Indonesian waters; strafing of an Okinawan fishing boat; apprehension of two Japanese fishing boats; forcing a British Navy salvage ship to depart the area, which precluded rendering assistance to an Indian ship with several hundred passengers, which was grounded on a reef in the claimed waters.

Indonesia's claim of its nostrum precipitated as a result of the unannounced British transit of Sunda Strait with an aircraft carrier and several destroyers. As a resultant thereof [sic] the acting director of Indonesian naval intelligence informed the U.S. naval attaché that henceforth all repeat all [sic] ships would be required to provide written notification to and secure permission from the Indonesian foreign office prior to passing through Indonesian territorial waters.... [A]ny subsequent omission of stipulated procedures would be countered with military force.

The United States is contributing to the Indonesian position by helping to developing international custom that foreign warships must notify Indonesia before undertaking peaceful passage in her claimed territorial sea or inland waters. If the meaningful freedom of the seas concept developed during the period of *Pax Britannica* ... is to remain resolute and energetic, it follows that the actual policy of the United States as practiced today requires modification. All such invalid claims must be discredited by ignoring and opposing them on a world wide basis. The mere fact that the U.S. acknowledges the existence of these claims, coupled with the provision of prior notification and our reluctance to freely use such illegally claimed high seas tends to lend credence to their validity under international law.

It is essential that we reverse the tendency to habitually defer implementation [of freedom of the seas] because of the existence of other problems [in bilateral relations], which will usually be present.

If we continue to avoid transit or to notify the Government of Indonesia informally of USN transits, we set the stage for a future incident disadvantageous to the United States. It is recognized that insistence upon principle may result in some adverse effects. However, such effects would, in all probability, be no worse than have recently been evidenced in Indonesia, such as anti-U.S. charges, destruction of U.S. property, disrespect towards the U.S. flag and vilification of U.S. policies.... Historically, compromise of a principle has seldom accomplished its purpose. In the opinion of CINCPAC, the long-term importance of the principle of the freedom of the seas is so great that it must not be emasculated.

Inaction today will only more fully restrict the use of the high seas when needed tomorrow, not only in times of Cold War but more importantly in times of crisis and emergency. Accordingly, the [Commander in Chief, U.S. Pacific Command] recommends:

(a) the actual practice be modified to the end that the U.S. exercise its historic right to the free use of those waters of the Indonesian archipelago, and the claimed waters of all other countries, which it considered to be high seas, by the frequent and unannounced operation of its warships and aircraft therein;

(b) that the United States come out loud and clear in opposition to the mare nostrum edict of Indonesia by the execution within the time frame of the next two months, and at frequent intervals thereafter, of operations within these waters to include transits of the Sunda and/or Lombok straits with appropriate naval forces on an unannounced basis.[116]

9.5.2 *The Philippines*

In March 2009, the Philippines amended its archipelagic baselines to bring them into compliance with UNCLOS.[117] The Philippines Maritime Zones Act, adopted in December 2011, defines the archipelagic waters of the Philippines as "the waters on the landward side of the archipelagic baselines except as provided for under Section 3 hereof."[118] Section 4 states, "[w]ithin the archipelagic waters, closing lines for the delimitation of internal water shall be drawn pursuant to Article 50 of UNCLOS and other existing laws and treaties." While both of these rules appear consistent with the provisions of UNCLOS, the Philippines is also enacting legislation recognizing the right of foreign flagged ships to conduct archipelagic sea lanes passage through the archipelago. In January 2012 the Philippines House of Representatives approved a second reading of House Bill No. 4153, the Philippines Archipelagic Sea Lane Act, which was under consideration by the Senate.

House Bill No. 4153 would establish three archipelagic sea lanes (ASL) through the Philippine archipelago: ASL I connecting the Philippine Sea to the South China Sea through the Balintang Channel; ASL II connecting the Philippine Sea to the South China Sea through the Surigao Strait, the Bohol and Sulu Seas, the Nasubata Channel and the Balabac Strait; and ASL III connecting the Celebes Sea to the South China Sea through the Basilan Strait, the Sulu Sea and the Mindoro Strait.[119]

The legislation is problematic for several reasons. First, it appears that the Philippine government intends to unilaterally designate the three sea lanes. UNCLOS Article 53(9), however, requires archipelagic State to refer ASL proposals to the IMO for adoption. The *General Provisions on Ship's Routeing* (GPSR) similarly

---

[116] Id.
[117] Republic Act No. 9522, Mar. 10, 2009.
[118] Philippines Maritime Zones Act, Dec. 18, 2011, sec. 4.
[119] House Bill No. 4153, Feb. 8, 2011. *See also*, Ryan Ponce Pacpaco, Senate Urged to Fast-Track Bill Setting PH Sea Lanes, Journal Online (Manila), May 9, 2012.

provides that the "IMO is recognized as the competent international organization responsible for adopting archipelagic sea lanes...."[120]

Second, the bill fails to identify whether the designation is full or partial. UNCLOS Article 53(4) requires that ASLs "shall include all normal passage routes used as routes for international navigation or overflight through or over archipelagic waters...." Likewise, the GPSR requires that proposals for the adoption of ASLs include "all normal passage routes and navigational channels as required by UNCLOS."[121] The archipelagic State is to indicate if its proposal "is a partial archipelagic sea lane proposal,"[122] and the GPSR authorizes IMO to "determine if the proposal is a partial archipelagic sea lanes proposal."[123] There are more than three normal passage routes used as routes for international navigation and overflight through or over the Philippine archipelago, so the bill appears to have an incomplete or only partial designation of lanes.

Finally, section 3 of the draft law appears to limit the right of archipelagic sea lanes passage (ASLP) to only the three identified sea lanes. This limitation is inconsistent with UNCLOS Article 53, as well as various IMO instruments. Article 53 states that ships and aircraft enjoy a right of ASLP through all normal passage routes used as routes for international navigation or overflight through or over archipelagic waters. Similarly, Part H (paragraph 6.7) of the GPSR provides that "where a partial archipelagic sea lanes proposal has come into effect, the right of archipelagic sea lanes passage may continue to be exercised through all normal passage routes used as routes for international navigation or overflight in other parts of archipelagic waters in accordance with UNCLOS." Similar language is contained in *Safety of Navigation Circular* 206 (SN/Circ.206):

> ... if the IMO has adopted a sea lane proposal as a partial system of archipelagic sea lanes, the right of archipelagic sea lanes passage may continue to be exercised through all normal passage routes used as routes for international navigation in other parts of archipelagic waters.[124]

SN/Circ. 206 also states "ships exercising the right of archipelagic sea lanes passage ... must use applicable sea lanes (or normal passage routes, if sea lanes

---

[120] IMO Doc. MSC.71(69), Report of the Maritime Safety Committee on its Sixty-Ninth Session, May 19, 1998 *reprinted in* IMO Doc. MSC 69/22/Add.1, Annex 8, Adoption of Amendments to the General Provisions on Ships' Routeing (Resolution A.572(14) as amended), May 19, 1998, and IMO Doc. MSC 69/22, Report of the Maritime Safety Committee on its Sixty-Ninth Session, May 29, 1998. *See*, IMO Doc. A.571(14), General Provisions on Ships' Routeing, Nov. 20, 1985, Part H, para. 3.1, as amended.

[121] IMO Doc. A.571(14), General Provisions on Ships' Routeing, Nov. 20, 1985, Part H, para. 3.7.

[122] Id. para. 3.9.

[123] Id., at para. 3.2.

[124] IMO Doc. SN/Circ.206, Guidance for Ships Transiting Archipelagic Waters, Jan. 8, 1999, para. 2.1.1.

have not been adopted or only a partial system of archipelagic sea lanes has been adopted)."[125]

These rules regarding "partial" designations and the preservation of ASLP in "all normal routes" are critical to maintaining freedom of navigation and overflight through and over archipelagic waters and preserving the critical balance between archipelagic State interests and maritime State interests reflected in UNCLOS. Absent these rules, archipelagic States could restrict ASLP in a manner that is inconsistent with international law as reflected in UNCLOS. Perhaps the international community can convince the Philippines to submit its proposal to the IMO, as required by UNCLOS. At a time when Manila relies on UNCLOS in its EEZ dispute with China in the South China Sea, Manila's failure to submit the ASLP proposal to the IMO for adoption weakens the country's legal and diplomatic position.

9.5.3 *Maldives*

The Maldives purports to restrict ASLP through its archipelago without consent. It also limits ASLP to only three channels—the Equatorial, 1 ½ Degree, and Kaashidhoo Channels. Additionally, the Maldives does not recognize a right of innocent passage through archipelagic waters outside of sea lanes. The Maldives has not designated IMO-approved sea lanes or air routes through its archipelago. Consequently, pursuant to the IMO *Guidance for Ships Transiting Archipelagic Waters* and UNCLOS Article 52(12), all ships and aircraft enjoy the right of ASLP while transiting through, under, or over the Maldives archipelagic waters and adjacent territorial seas via all routes normally used for international navigation.

---

[125] Id., para. 4.

TEN

SECURITY CLAIMS IN THE EXCLUSIVE ECONOMIC ZONE

10.1 Security Claims in the Exclusive Economic Zone

Moving from West to East, virtually from Al Basrah, Iraq, next to Iran, to Vladivostok, Russia, just 30 miles from North Korea, there is a 7,000-mile unbroken line of States that purport to limit military activities in the EEZ that stretches from the Persian Gulf all the way to East Asia.[1] Thus, a warship traveling along the coast from the Northern Persian Gulf to the doorstep of Siberia would find itself in violation of the oceans laws of no less than 11 nations—every coastal State along the route. The "illegal" transit would encompass the length of the shorelines of Iran,[2] Pakistan,[3] India,[4] Bangladesh,[5] Myanmar,[6] Thailand,[7]

---

[1] Distances Between Ports (Publication 151) at 2, 120 (National Geospatial-Intelligence Agency, 11th ed. 2001).
[2] Act on the Marine Areas of the Islamic Republic of Iran, May 1993, Dep't of State, Limits in the Seas No. 114, Iran's Maritime Claims, Mar. 16, 1994, and, Dep't of Defense, Maritime Claims Reference Manual (DOD 2005.1-M) at 302–05 (Under Secretary of Defense for Policy, June 23, 2005). [Hereinafter, "MCRM"].
[3] Territorial Waters & Maritime Zones Act, Dec. 1976, Declaration upon Ratification of the Law of the Sea Convention, Feb. 1997, and MCRM, at 448–450.
[4] Declaration upon Ratification of the 1982 Law of the Sea Convention, June 1995, Naval Headquarters NAVAREA Notice, Jan. 1998, and MCRM, at 275–279.
[5] Declaration on Accession to the Law of the Sea Convention, July, 2001 and MCRM, at 68–70.
[6] Burma Law No. 3, Apr. 1977 and MCRM, at 84–89.
[7] Declaration on Accession to the Law of the Sea Convention, May 2011. The Declaration states that in the EEZ, "enjoyment of the freedom of navigation in accordance with the relevant provisions of the Convention excludes any non-peaceful use without the consent of the coastal State, in particular, military exercises or other activities which may affect the rights or interests of the coastal State." MCRM (Thailand Supplement), at 1–10 (Updated Apr. 2012).

Cambodia (contiguous zone),[8] Malaysia,[9] Vietnam[10] (contiguous zone), China,[11] and North Korea.[12] Furthermore, offshore states in South Asia and East Asia that assert excessive EEZ claims include Maldives,[13] Mauritius,[14] and Indonesia.[15] Thus, South Asia and East Asia contain more nations claiming a security interest in the EEZ than any other regions.

Worldwide, there are 18 nations that claim a security interest in the Exclusive Economic Zone (EEZ), typically by purporting to restrict foreign-flagged military activities. Among these nations, two are in South America (Brazil and Uruguay), two in Africa (Kenya and Cape Verde), one in the Middle East (Iran), and 13 are in Asia. Vietnam partially asserts an excessive EEZ claim by requiring warships that operate in its contiguous zone to seek and obtain permission 30 days in advance, and place weapons in an inoperative position during transit.

Portugal is the only State in Europe that asserts a security interest in the EEZ, and two States making such claims are former Portuguese colonies—Brazil in South America and Cape Verde in West Africa.

In addition, the seven nations that illegally claim territorial seas in excess of 12 nm include: Benin (200 nm), Republic of Congo (200 nm), Ecuador (200 nm), Liberia (200 nm), Peru (200 nm), Somalia (200 nm) and Togo (30 nm). And there are five nations that claim security jurisdiction in their 24 nm contiguous zone: Cambodia, China, Sudan, Syria, and Vietnam.

---

[8] MCRM, at 90–92 (purports to assert jurisdiction over security matters, including foreign warships, in the contiguous zone).

[9] Declaration upon Ratification of the Law of the Sea Convention, Oct. 1996 and MCRM, at 373–77.

[10] Statement, May 1977, Decree No. 30/C, Jan. 1980 (security authority in the contiguous zone), and MCRM, at 689–92. In the contiguous zone, submarines are required to navigate on the surface and show their flag. Aircraft are prohibited from being launched or recovered from ship, and ships must place weapons in an inoperative position prior to entry into the contiguous zone.

[11] EEZ and Continental Shelf Act, June 1988, Order No. 75, Surveying and Mapping Law, Dec. 2002 (President of the People's Republic of China, Aug. 29, 2002), and MCRM (China Supplement), at 1–6 (Updated Apr. 2011). China claims a security interest in the contiguous zone and claims that all surveying and mapping activities in sea area under Chinese jurisdiction is subject to approval.

[12] Decree Establishing the Economic Zone, Aug. 1977 and MCRM, at 346–48. (Prohibition against photography or survey activities in the EEZ). North Korea also maintains a 50 nm Military Zone, which went into effect on Aug. 1, 1977. *See*, MCRM, at 346.

[13] Maldives Act 6/96, June 1996 and MCRM, at 378–80. (Requires prior permission for entry into EEZ by "all foreign vessels.")

[14] Government of Mauritius Notice No. 199 (Maritime Zones Regulation—EEZ) and MCRM, at 386–90.

[15] Regulation No. 8, July 1962 and MCRM, at 280–303 (India Supplement, Aug. 30, 2010) (Restrictions on "stopping, dropping anchor, and/or cruising about without a legitimate reason" up to 100 miles seaward of territorial waters). Id., at 303.

Among all of these states, however, China is unique in its insistence that it has prescriptive and enforcement jurisdiction over foreign military activities in the EEZ. Since the end of the Cold War, China is alone in demonstrating a willingness to use force in pursuit of its excessive EEZ claims.

10.2 China's Oceans Law and the EEZ

Beijing has the most expansive security and sovereignty EEZ claim on the planet—a serial violator of the regime of high seas freedoms in the zone, China purports to regulate military activities, hydrographic surveys, and the laying of cables and pipelines.

China claimed a 200 nm EEZ in 1998.[16] Consistent with Article 56 of UNCLOS, Article 3 of the national law of China provides that the country exercises sovereign rights "for the purpose of exploring, exploiting, conserving and managing..." the living and non-living natural resources of the EEZ, "as well as for the purpose of other economic activities...such as utilization of seawater, sea current, and wind power to produce energy." Article 3 of the law further provides, consistent with UNCLOS, that China exercises "jurisdiction in relation to construction and exploitation of artificial islands, installations and structures as well as marine scientific research, [and] protection and conservation of [the] maritime environment...." Furthermore, Article 7 of the law requires Chinese approval for any exploration and exploitation of natural resources in the exclusive economic zone (EEZ).

Article 8 implements Article 60 of UNCLOS, relating to the right of coastal States to "construct, manage and authorize to construct, operate and utilize artificial islands, installations and structures in the EEZ." Whereas the article in the Chinese law appears to cover all structures and installations, however, the provision in UNCLOS is more narrowly drawn and refers specifically to installations and structures that relate to the competence of the coastal State in the EEZ, that is, sovereign rights over living and non-living resources in the zone. Article 8 also claims exclusive jurisdiction in the EEZ over "customs, finance, public health and entry and exit" matters—all of which are beyond the remit of the coastal State beyond the outer limits of the contiguous zone.

---

[16] Order No. 6 of the President of the People's Republic of China, Feb. 26, 1998, Law of the People's Republic of China on the Exclusive Economic Zone and the Continental Shelf, Adopted at the 3rd Meeting of the Standing Committee of the Ninth National People's Congress, June 26, 1998, Article 2. Likewise, China's law governing the territorial sea and contiguous zone is: Order No. 55 of the President of the People's Republic of China, The Standing Committee of the National People's Congress, Law of the People's Republic of China on the Territorial Sea and the Contiguous Zone of Feb. 25, 1992, Article 6, *reprinted in* U.S. Dep't of State, Limits in the Seas No. 117: Straight Baseline Claim: China, 11–14, July 9, 1996 (*See also*, Internet website of the Maritime Safety Administration of the People's Republic of China, http://en.msa.gov.cn/msa/).

Article 9 of China's law springs from Article 246 of UNCLOS, which grants coastal States authority to regulate and authorize marine scientific research (MSR) in the EEZ. China requires government approval in advance of the conduct of MSR in the EEZ. Similarly, Article 5 of the law requires Chinese approval for fishing activities in the EEZ. China has worked to establish conservation and management measures to ensure that fish stocks in its EEZ are protected from over-exploitation. Under Article 61, the coastal State has authority to determine allowable catch of the living resources, and China's law rests on this authority.

Although the general terms of the 1998 law appear to comport with UNCLOS, the actual text of the law is quite vague, and China often applies it inconsistently, both with its own prior practice and with UNCLOS. For example, the environmental provisions of the 1998 law are overly broad and have omitted the limitations that appear in UNCLOS on coastal State authority to enact and enforce domestic environmental laws and regulations.

Article 10 of the law provides that China "has the power to take necessary measures for preventing, eliminating and controlling pollution to [the] marine environment and protecting and conserving the marine environment..." of the EEZ. Although UNCLOS Article 56 grants the coastal state jurisdiction in the EEZ over the protection and preservation of the marine environment, Article 211(5) provides that any law adopted by the coastal State for the prevention or control of pollution from vessels must conform and give effect to "generally accepted international rules and standards established through the competent international organization—typically the International Maritime Organization—or a general diplomatic conference."

Moreover, coastal State authority to enforce environmental laws in domestic courts is limited to situations involving "clear objective evidence" that the vessel has committed a violation in the EEZ of applicable international rules for the prevention, reduction, and control of pollution from vessels that results in a discharge "causing major damage or threat of major damage to the coastline or related interests of the coastal state, or to any resources of its territorial sea or EEZ...."[17] The standards for vessel discharge are contained in instruments adopted by the IMO, such as the *International Convention for the Prevention of Pollution from Ships (MARPOL)*, the *Safety of Life at Sea Convention (SOLAS)*, the *International Convention on Standards of Training, Certification and Watchkeeping (STCW)* and the *International Convention on Oil Pollution Preparedness, Response, and Cooperation (OPRC)*.

The 1998 law also does not distinguish between China's jurisdictional reach over foreign commercial vessels on the one hand and foreign warships and other government operated, non-commercial vessels on the other. Similarly, China's Marine Environmental Protection Law and its implementing regulations purport

---

[17] UNCLOS, Article 220(6).

to apply to all vessels of Chinese or foreign registry operating in "sea areas under the jurisdiction" of China.[18] Consistent with UNCLOS Articles 211 and 220, however, China may apply its domestic environmental regulations only to the extent that they give effect to or implement IMO standards for commercial vessels transiting the EEZ. Furthermore, coastal States may not impose or enforce domestic laws on sovereign immune warships and other government, non-commercial vessels. UNCLOS specifically exempts from the environmental provisions of the Convention "warships, naval auxiliaries and other vessels or aircraft owned or operated by a state and used, for the time being, only on government non-commercial service...."[19] Therefore, China may not apply its domestic environmental laws to foreign-flagged sovereign immune ships and aircraft operating in its EEZ.

China's security-related claims over the EEZ are a major irritant to regional stability in the Western Pacific. While the People's Liberation Army-Navy (PLA-N) has taken advantage of navigational freedoms to operate throughout the EEZs of its neighbors, it has tacked decidedly toward an exclusive view of its own EEZ. China appears to believe that its rapid growth in stature over the past decade should translate into greater accommodation of its approach to its own EEZ, and China's legal overextension in the EEZ is backed by an ambitious maritime policy that is infused with nationalism and inflated security concerns.[20] But this perspective is at variance with state practice and customary law, most clearly illustrated by the experience of the Soviet Union and the United States during the Cold War.

At the height of the maritime competition between the superpower adversaries, the U.S.S.R. freely operated submarines between the United States and Hawaii and in the Florida straits without a provocative or dangerous response on the part of the United States.[21] The United States tolerated loitering Soviet signals intelligence trawlers near its coastline, and did not use force to eject them, even when they were discovered within the territorial sea. In one report, the Soviet trawler *Gidrofon*, for example, approached within five miles of Oahu. The United

---

[18] Order No. 26 of the President of the People's Republic of China, Marine Environment Protection Law of the People's Republic of China, Dec. 25, 1999, Article 2, adopted at the 24th Meeting of the Standing Committee of the Fifth National People's Congress, Aug. 23, 1982; revised at the 13th Meeting of the Standing Committee of the Ninth National People's Congress on Dec. 25, 1999, and Regulations of the People's Republic of China on the Control over Prevention of Pollution by Vessels in Sea Waters, Dec. 29, 1983.

[19] UNCLOS, Article 236.

[20] Robert S. Ross, *China's Naval Nationalism: Sources, Prospects, and the U.S. Response*, 34 INT'L SECURITY, Fall 2009, at 46, 60–68.

[21] Memorandum for the President's Files by the President's Deputy Assistant for National Security Affairs (Haig), Aug. 10, 1971, *reprinted in* DEP'T OF STATE, FOREIGN RELATIONS OF THE UNITED STATES 1969–1976, VOLUME XXXIV, NATIONAL SECURITY POLICY, Doc. No. 191, at pp. 818–819 (M. Todd Bennett, ed. 2011).

States merely monitored the ship and did not aggressively intercept it.[22] Thus, the aggressive intercepts that have become a feature of China's excessive EEZ claims are particularly vexing, being at odds with the U.S.-Soviet experience during the Cold War.

China's challenge to the right of foreign-flagged warships to exercise freedom of navigation and other internationally lawful uses of the sea in the EEZ has strategic implications for the U.S.-Japan alliance and the American-led security paradigm in Asia.[23] If China is successful at keeping foreign-flagged warships away from the continent of Asia, it will have effectively decoupled the United States from treaty allies in the region. The issue also reverberates beyond East Asia, however. Were China's restrictive view of military activities in the EEZ to prevail in other parts of the globe, and coastal States become entitled to assert a security interest in the zone, then U.S. strategic nuclear deterrence, and the extended deterrence umbrella that protects U.S. allies in Europe and Asia, will erode.

Strategic deterrence depends upon offensive nuclear forces, and ballistic missile submarines are the most survivable component of the traditional military force triad (the other two legs of the triad being land-based manned bombers and intercontinental ballistic missiles). Increasingly, deterrence also depends on missile defense, and a relatively small number of Aegis Ballistic Missile Defense (BMD) warships provide anti-missile defense for NATO countries and U.S. allies in Asia.[24] The warships protecting Europe operate in the Baltic Sea and Mediterranean Sea to deter Iranian attack, and the operating areas are entirely or almost entirely within coastal State EEZs. Similarly, U.S. warships in Asia conduct strategic BMD patrols in the EEZs of coastal states, ready to counter North Korea missiles. American and Japanese warships must be able to utilize the EEZs of nations near Japan, including China's economic zone, as maneuver space for BMD surface combatants in order to protect Japan from the threat of ballistic missiles. Japan also operates BMD-capable warships—the only nation besides the United States that possesses the capability. But if coastal states can dictate the scope of permissible military activities of foreign flagged warships in their EEZs, then the model of a sustainable at-sea missile defense in Europe and Asia disappears. Thus, the debate with China over military activities in the EEZ has wide-reaching strategic implications that are often unappreciated by legal scholars and policy analysts.[25]

---

[22] DEP'T OF DEFENSE, COMMANDER IN CHIEF, U.S. PACIFIC COMMAND USCINCPAC message to Joint Chiefs of Staff, Subject: Implications of Indonesian Mare Nostrum, 102244Z OCT 64, Oct. 10, 1964, para. 2.
[23] James Kraska, *Sovereignty at Sea*, 51 SURVIVAL 13, 16–18, June/July, 2009.
[24] Brooks Tigner, *NATO Missile Defence: Launch Control*, JANE'S DEFENCE WEEKLY, Feb. 8, 2012, at 24–29.
[25] JAMES KRASKA, MARITIME POWER AND LAW OF THE SEA: EXPEDITIONARY OPERATIONS IN WORLD POLITICS 179, 188 (2011).

Like all nations, China is a pluralistic country and civilization, so rather than having a single Chinese view of the law of the sea, there may be many. To be more accurate, there are many approaches used by Chinese scholars, policy makers, diplomats, military officers, and media bloggers and reporters, but their analysis universally leads in the same direction—justifying the Chinese government's position. Government and nationalist pressure on Chinese academics is intense, making it difficult for independent Chinese scholarship and analysis.

A deliberate and measured international response has developed among nations in the Indo-Pacific to counter China's "naval nationalism." Virtually every nation in Asia from India to Japan is acquiring submarines and surface combatants to balance a burgeoning Chinese navy. The United States can play an offshore role in the region as well by maintaining a naval force structure centered around major power projection assets, such as aircraft carriers and submarines. Intent on keeping a robust forward presence in the region, the United States continues deployment of naval platforms to the western Pacific Ocean, and is forging stronger ties with Japan and other treaty allies and new partners in the region. Time will tell whether these signals of resolve and the buildup in naval forces throughout the region will temper or inflame China's oceanic nationalism.[26]

10.3 NORTH KOREA'S MILITARY ZONE

North Korea also asserts a security interest in the EEZ—a claim the United States and South Korea have challenged on numerous occasions. On August 1, 1977, North Korea issued a surprise announcement proclaiming establishment of a 50 nm wide "military zone."[27]

The brevity of the proclamation for the zone raises questions about precisely how it applies in practice:

> Demanded by the situation prevailing in our country, the Supreme Command of the Korean People's Army establishes the military boundary to reliably safeguard the economic sea zone of the Democratic People's Republic of Korea and firmly defend militarily the nations interests and sovereignty of the country.
>
> The military boundary is up to 50 miles from the starting line of the territorial waters in the East Sea and to the boundary line of the economic sea zone in the West Sea.
>
> In the military boundary (on the sea, in the sea and in the sky) acts of foreigners, foreign military vessels, and foreign military planes are prohibited and civilian ships and civilian planes (excluding fishing boats) are allowed to navigate or fly only with appropriate prior agreement or approval.

---

[26] Ross, *China's Naval Nationalism: Sources, Prospects, and the U.S. Response*, at 78.
[27] DEP'T OF DEFENSE, MARITIME CLAIMS REFERENCE MANUAL, North Korea, DOD 2005.1-M, June 2008.

In the military boundary (on the sea, in the sea, and in the sky) civilian vessels and civilian planes shall not conduct acts for military purposes or acts infringing upon the economic interests.[28]

The military zone stretches 50 nm beyond the 12 nm territorial sea in the Sea of Japan on the east coast and to the outer limits of its EEZ in the Yellow Sea (abutting the Chinese EEZ) on the west coast.[29] Foreign warships and aircraft are forbidden from entry into the zone, and merchant ships and commercial airliners are required to seek permission from North Korea. Additionally, foreign ships and aircraft may not take photographs or collect marine data in the North Korean EEZ.[30]

10.4 Military Activities in the EEZ

During a conference in Singapore in 2008, Ambassador Tommy Koh, the President of UNCLOS III, discussed the legal status of the EEZ. He suggested that, "some coastal states would like the status of the EEZ to approximate the legal status of the territorial seas. Many other states held the view that the rights of the coastal States and EEZ are limited to the exploitation of living and non-living resources and that the water column should be treated much like the high seas."[31] Ambassador Koh went on to state, "I find a tendency on the part of some coastal States...to assert their sovereignty in the EEZ...[and doing so] is not consistent with the intention of those of us who negotiated this text, and is not consistent with the correct interpretation of this part [Part V] of the Convention."[32] Ambassador Koh's view reflects the understanding of the United States and the Soviet Union during the negotiations for UNCLOS. Along with the United States, Germany concluded that naval activities pursuant to self-defense were consistent with the Convention.[33] The Soviet Union also sought to fence off military activities from the purview of the Convention.[34]

---

[28] Korean Central News Agency, Aug. 1, 1977, in 4 Foreign Broadcast Information Service, Asia and Pacific, Aug. 1, 1977, at D6, and the People's Korea, Aug. 10, 1977, at 2, col. 1, *reprinted in* Choon-Ho Park, *The 50-mile Military Boundary Zone of North Korea*, 72 Am. J. Int'l L. 866, 866–67, note 1 (Oct. 1978).

[29] Id.

[30] Id. North Korea has not precisely delineated the coordinates of the military zone. A Japanese delegation that visited North Korea to conduct fishing negotiations obtained coordinates for zone in the Sea of Japan (eastern zone). Id.

[31] Tommy T.B. Koh, *Remarks on the Legal Status of the Exclusive Economic Zone*, in Freedom of Seas, Passage Rights and the 1982 Law of the Sea Convention 53 (Myron H. Nordquist, Tommy T.B. Koh & John Norton Moore, eds. 2009).

[32] Id., pp. 54–55.

[33] E. Rauch, *Military Uses of the Oceans*, 28 German Y.B. Int'l L. 241–42 (1985).

[34] Boleslaw Adam Bocek, *Peaceful Purposes Provisions of the United Nations Convention on the Law of the Sea*, 8 Ocean Y.B. 329, 363, 368 (1989).

Coastal States have used a variety of arguments to justify interference with foreign-flagged warships and aircraft patrolling their EEZ. These States seek to raise the political and operational military costs for such operations in order to pressure nations to remain outside the EEZ. Although the coastal States seek to raise the costs of such operations, they typically try to increase the credibility of their efforts by couching them in the terms of the law of the sea.

China has employed a handful of legal arguments to edge foreign flagged warships from its EEZ, and we cover the most prominent in this chapter. First, China has claimed that virtually any collection of information, data, or intelligence by warships and aircraft in the EEZ constitutes "marine scientific research," and is therefore subject to the prior consent of the coastal State. Second, China has asserted an ambiguous but insistent claim over the airspace above the EEZ. Third, pronouncement in UNCLOS that the seas are reserved solely for "peaceful purposes," has opened the door to specious claims that exercising freedom of navigation and other internationally lawful uses of the sea by naval forces is *a priori* conduct that is not peaceful (belligerent). Finally, China has become more nuanced in its employment of the law, most recently suggesting that marine environmental protection is the key to expanded coastal State competence and control offshore.

10.4.1 *Marine Data Collection*

Naval forces continually collect information and intelligence to ensure safety of navigation, to build oceanographic and meteorological profiles, to maintain antiterrorism and force protection, and to gather data to inform naval commanders, theater commanders, and national leaders. These military activities have been conducted since warships first went to sea. But only recently—since the end of the Cold War—have a few coastal States (most notably China) embarked on a serious effort to regulate such military activities under the provisions of the EEZ that govern the coastal State's authority over marine scientific research (MSR) in the zone.

The Law of the Sea Convention does not contain a definition of "marine scientific research," affording coastal States the opportunity to design their own definitions in national law. Although UNCLOS does not define MSR or hydrographic surveys, the Convention clearly distinguishes among MSR, surveys, and military activities in Parts II (Articles 19 and 21), III (Article 40), IV (Articles 52 and 54), V (Article 56) and VII (Article 87). For example, the treaty states that "ships engaged in innocent passage may not conduct "research *or* survey activities", and coastal states may adopt laws to regulate "marine scientific research *and* hydrograph surveys" in the territorial sea.[35] Similarly, ships in transit passage

---

[35] UNCLOS, Articles 19(2)(j), 21(1)(g) and 52(1) (our italics).

through international straits may not carry out any "research *or* survey" activities without the prior authorization of the bordering states.[36] The same rule applies to ships engaged in archipelagic sea lanes passage.[37]

Articles 56(1)(b)(ii) and 87(1)(f), as well as Part XIII, refer only to "marine scientific research" or "scientific research," not more generally to "surveys" or other military activities. Of note, even China recognizes the difference between these activities in its territorial sea law, clearly distinguishing between "scientific research" and "marine survey" in Article 11.[38] Consequently, the coastal State's right to regulate MSR does not cover separate and distinct activities, such as military surveys and intelligence gathering.

Coastal States may regulate MSR and surveys in the territorial sea, archipelagic waters, international straits, and archipelagic sea lanes, but they may not regulate surveys in the other maritime zones, to include the contiguous zone and the EEZ. Hydrographic surveys and other military marine data collection activities remain one element of high seas freedom of navigation and other internationally lawful uses of the sea, and they may be exercised in the contiguous zone and EEZ without notice to or consent of the coastal State.[39]

Article 8 of the 1998 *Law on the Exclusive Economic Zone and Continental Shelf* requires China's approval for foreign MSR in its EEZ, consistent with international law.[40] Implementing regulations for foreign-related MSR also appear, on their face, to generally comply with international law.[41] However, Beijing's application of the 1998 law, as well as its 2002 *Surveying and Mapping Law of the People's Republic of China*,[42] appears inconsistent with UNCLOS because they both purport to apply to hydrographic surveys and military marine data collection in the EEZ and thus are not solely limited to regulation of foreign MSR. To the extent the laws purport to regulate hydrographic surveys and military marine data collection activities, to include military oceanographic surveys and underwater, surface, and aviation surveillance and reconnaissance (spy) missions, they

---

[36] Id., Article 40 (our italics).
[37] Id., Article 54.
[38] Order No. 55 of the President of the People's Republic of China, The Standing Committee of the National People's Congress, Law of the People's Republic of China on the Territorial Sea and the Contiguous Zone of Feb. 25, 1992.
[39] UNCLOS, Articles 58, 86 and 87.
[40] Order No. 6 of the President of the People's Republic of China, Feb. 26, 1998, Law of the People's Republic of China on the Exclusive Economic Zone and the Continental Shelf, Adopted at the 3rd Meeting of the Standing Committee of the Ninth National People's Congress, June 26, 1998.
[41] Provisions on the Administration of Foreign-Related Maritime Scientific Research, June 18, 1996.
[42] 2002 Surveying and Mapping Law of the People's Republic of China.

are inconsistent with state practice and customary international law, as well as the plain language of UNCLOS.[43]

Beijing's broad application of MSR jurisdiction is illustrated by its interference with and harassment of U.S. military survey vessels operating in China's EEZ. There have been numerous confrontations between U.S. Navy survey ships and Chinese warships and other government vessels, but only a handful have been reported in the media. Therefore, States in the region and the American public are unaware of the scope of the problem. One of the most notable incidents that received widespread media coverage occurred in 2001, when the USNS *Bowditch* (T-AGS 62), a hydrographic survey ship, was involved in an encounter with a People's Liberation Army Navy (PLA-N) *Jianheu III*-class frigate.

On March 23, 2001, *Bowditch* was conducting routine military survey operations in China's EEZ in the Yellow Sea. The Chinese warship approached and ordered *Bowditch* to leave the area or "suffer the consequences." Being an unarmed vessel of the U.S. Naval Service, *Bowditch* complied with the order even though the ship is protected by sovereign immunity as a state vessel and naval ship. *Bowditch* returned to the area several days later with a destroyer escort to complete its mission. In response to the U.S. demarche protesting the incident, Beijing indicated that U.S. military survey operations in the EEZ posed a threat to its national security and required China's consent.[44]

China confirmed its approach the following year with the enactment of the 2002 *Surveying and Mapping Law*. Article 2 of the statute states that "all surveying and mapping activities in the domain of... China and other sea areas under the jurisdiction of... China shall comply with this law."[45] "Surveying and mapping" is defined as "the surveying, collection and presentation of the shape, size, spatial location and properties of the natural geographic factors or the man-made facilities on the surface, as well as the activities for processing and providing the obtained data, information and achievements."[46] Article 7 requires China's approval for any foreign surveying or mapping, which "must take the form of a joint venture... with the relevant departments or entities of... China, and may not deal with any state secret [or] harm the state security."[47]

---

[43] J. Ashley Roach & Robert W. Smith, Excessive Maritime Claims 413–450 (3rd ed. 2012) and Raul Pedrozo, *Coastal State Jurisdiction over Marine Data Collection in the Exclusive Economic Zone: U.S. Views*, in Military Activities in the EEZ: A U.S.-China Dialogue on Security and International Law in the Maritime Commons: China Maritime Study No. 7 23–26 (Peter Dutton, ed. 2010).

[44] Raul Pedrozo, *Close Encounters at Sea: The USNS Impeccable Incident*, 63 Naval War College Rev., Summer, 2009, at 101–111 [Hereinafter, Pedrozo, *Close Encounters*].

[45] 2002 Surveying and Mapping Law of the People's Republic of China, Article 2.

[46] Id.

[47] Id.

Commodore Sam Bateman, a prominent maritime security analyst based in Singapore and Australia, has suggested that maintaining the distinction between MSR and military surveys may be an anachronism because of technological developments since adoption of UNCLOS and the economic value of hydrographic survey data for resource exploitation.[48] While the distinction between MSR and surveys may (or may not) be an anachronism, the argument is irrelevant since the Convention clearly differentiates between the two activities. Moreover, the Law of the Sea Convention has a process for adoption of amendments. Coastal States may not, either individually or in a subset of States parties, amend the Convention without going through the elaborate amendment procedures set out in Part XVII. State practice, coupled with international acquiescence, may establish new customary norms over time, but until or unless that transpires, the clear distinction between the various types of marine data collection is a facet of the international law of the sea and embedded in UNCLOS.

On its face, Article 11 of the 1998 Chinese law appears to guarantee freedom of navigation and overflight of the EEZ: all nations "enjoy the freedom of navigating in and flying over the exclusive economic zone."[49] In practice, however, China claims the right to regulate foreign military activities in the EEZ based on a series of alternative legal arguments that have evolved over the past ten years, from an initial focus on national security and the "peaceful purposes" argument in 2001 to regulation of MSR in 2002 to arguments based on resource management and environmental protection in 2007.

The ships and aircraft used by China to challenge U.S. operations in the EEZ have likewise changed in accordance with the progressive transformation of Beijing's legal arguments. In the late-1990s and early-2000s, People's Liberation Army-Navy (PLA-N) ships and aircraft were most often used to intercept U.S. military surveys and surveillance flights in the EEZ. The interceptions gave way to Maritime Safety Administration (MSA) ships and aircraft interfering with U.S. naval vessels, and finally to State Oceanographic Administration (SOA) patrol vessels and Fisheries Law Enforcement Command (FLEC) vessels, now accompanied by civilian cargo ships and fishing trawlers surreptitiously manned by Chinese military or special forces. Thus, the ships operate in concert to dissuade U.S. presence in China's EEZ, with the softer or non-military elements increasingly taking the lead in order to avoid a direct military confrontation.

---

[48] Sam Bateman, *A Response to Pedrozo: The Wider Utility of Hydrographic Surveys*, 10 CHINESE J. INT'L L. 177–186 (2011).

[49] Order No. 6 of the President of the People's Republic of China, Feb. 26, 1998, Law of the People's Republic of China on the Exclusive Economic Zone and the Continental Shelf, Adopted at the 3rd Meeting of the Standing Committee of the Ninth National People's Congress, June 26, 1998.

10.4.2 International Airspace of the EEZ

Coastal States lack legal competence to regulate military activities in the airspace above the EEZ, particularly those activities that do not have an impact on the coastal State's rights over the resources of the water column or seabed below. UNCLOS Articles 2 and 49 provide that the airspace above the territorial sea and archipelagic waters is national airspace, subject to coastal State and archipelagic State sovereignty. Similar language is contained in Article 1 of the Convention on International Civil Aviation of 1944 (Chicago Convention) with regard to the airspace above the territorial sea.[50] The airspace above the EEZ, however, is international airspace. The coastal State does not have any right of sovereignty over the airspace above the EEZ.

Although several countries, such as Brazil, India, and Pakistan, have filed diplomatic protests with the U.S. State Department for "incursions" in the airspace of their respective EEZs by U.S. military aircraft, only Peru and China have taken aggressive action to enforce their claims. It has been more than 20 years since Peru shot at a U.S. aircraft flying over that country's EEZ.

10.4.2.1 Peruvian Attack on a U.S. C-130 State Aircraft (1992)

On April 25, 1992, Peruvian fighter jets shot at a U.S. propeller-driven C-130 aircraft that was conducting a routine counterdrug surveillance mission off the Peruvian coast, but outside of Peru's territorial sea and national airspace. One crewmember was killed; two were injured.[51] The U.S. airplane was forced to make an emergency landing at a small airstrip in Talara, Peru, near the border with Ecuador.

Although Peru expressed regret for the incident, Peruvian authorities justified their action by alleging that the U.S. aircraft was hundreds of miles off course and that it had failed to respond to several attempts to establish visual and radio warnings by the two fighter jets.[52] Similarly, in 1995, two C-130s were required to abort their mission after Peruvian refusal to permit entry into the Flight Information

---

[50] Convention on International Civil Aviation, 15 U.N.T.S. 295, 61 Stat. 1180, T.I.A.S. No. 1591, Dec. 7, 1944, *entered into force* Apr. 4, 1947, *as amended* 1175 U.N.T.S. 297, *entered into force* Oct. 1998. [Hereinafter CHICAGO CONVENTION]. The Chicago Convention was preceded by the Convention for the Unification of Certain Rules Relating to International Transportation by Air, Oct. 12, 1929, 137 L.N.T.S. 11, 2 BEVANS 983, 49 Stat. 3000, T.S. 876, *entered into force* Feb. 13, 1933 [Warsaw Convention].

[51] Dale Cheney, *Freedom of Navigation*, THE MOBILITY FORUM, July/August 2003, 30–33, at 33.

[52] Eric Schmitt, *U.S. Officials Say Mutual Errors May Have Led to Incident in Peru*, N.Y. TIMES, Apr. 27, 1992, N. Nash, *Peru Jets Attack U.S. Air Transport*, N.Y. TIMES, Apr. 26, 1992, and N. Nash, *U.S. Says a C-130 Was Hit by Gunfire From Peru*, N.Y. TIMES, Apr. 25, 1992.

Region (FIR) without diplomatic clearance.[53] The flight controllers demanded that the aircraft remain west of 90 degrees west longitude—650 nautical miles from the Peruvian coastline. As a sovereign immune aircraft, the C-130s were not required to observe directions from Peruvian authorities in the FIR.

As discussed in greater detail below, the Chicago Convention and ICAO rules and regulations authorize the establishment of FIRs. However, Article 3 of the Chicago Convention specifically exempts State aircraft, which includes aircraft used in military, customs, and police services, from compliance with the Convention. State aircraft are only required to exercise "due regard" for the safety of navigation of civil aircraft.

10.4.2.2 Chinese Collision with a U.S. EP-3 State Aircraft (2001)

China has been much more active in challenging U.S. military ships and aircraft operating within and over its EEZ. Although these air intercepts occur on a routine basis, the most notable incidents that received widespread media coverage occurred in 2001 and 2009. As discussed above, on March 23, 2001, the USNS *Bowditch* was intercepted and challenged by a Chinese frigate while the hydrographic survey ship was on a survey patrol in the Yellow Sea.[54] Eight days later, a much more significant incident would underscore two competing visions for the legal regime of the airspace above the EEZ.

Two People's Liberation Army Air Force (PLAAF) F-8 Finback fighter aircraft intercepted a U.S. EP-3 Orion propeller-driven aircraft conducting a routine sensitive reconnaissance operations (SRO) flight about 65 miles south-southwest of Hainan Island. One of the fighter jets edged too close to the U.S. aircraft, colliding with it. The pilot of the Finback ejected over the South China Sea after his plane was cut in half by the propeller of the Orion. The Chinese pilot was never recovered and presumed dead. The EP-3 suffered severe damage to its nosecone and number one propeller, and was forced to make an emergency landing at Lingshui airfield on Hainan Island.[55]

The U.S. crew was detained for ten days until the U.S. Ambassador to China negotiated their release. The EP-3 aircraft was seized and stripped of its hi-tech equipment. The aircraft was held by China for three months, despite its sovereign

---

[53] Cheney, *Freedom of Navigation*, The Mobility Forum.
[54] Shirley Kan, China-U.S. Aircraft Collision Incident of April 2001: Assessments and Policy Implications, Cong. Res. Service Report for Congress (Oct. 10, 2001); Chris Plante, *U.S. Quietly Resumes Surveillance Flights off China*, CNN.com, May 15, 2001; Mark Oliva, *Before EP-3, China Turned Away U.S. Research Ship in International Waters*, Stars & Stripes, May 20, 2001, at 101–111; Raul Pedrozo, *Beijing's Coastal Real Estate: A History of Chinese Naval Aggression*, ForeignAffairs.com, Nov. 15, 2010.
[55] Henry Chu & Paul Richter, L.A. Times, Apr. 4, 2001, at A1 and John Diamond, *U.S. Spy Plan in China's Hands; Beijing Urged to Return Crew of 24 After Collision*, Chicago Tribune, Apr. 2, 2001.

immune status. The airplane finally was returned to the United States in July 2001. Washington protested the incident as a violation of China's "due regard" obligation under international law. Beijing responded that U.S. military aircraft only had a right of overflight in the EEZ, but not intelligence collection. Intelligence collection posed a threat to China's national security interests, Beijing argued, and therefore was inconsistent with the "peaceful purposes" provisions of UNCLOS.[56]

10.4.2.2.1 *Law of the Sea*
The U.S. countered that China's security-related arguments were not supported by state practice, which has been tolerant of foreign intelligence collection outside of the land territory or territorial sea. Furthermore, nothing in either UNCLOS nor the Chicago Convention restricts intelligence collection or other military activities in the EEZ beyond 12 nm from the coastline. Furthermore, the aircraft was entitled to sovereign immunity, and China did not have a superior right to violate its status. Intelligence collection is addressed in only one article of UNCLOS. Article 19(2)(c) prohibits ships engaged in innocent passage in the territorial sea from collecting "information to the prejudice of the defense or security of the coastal state." Part V concerning the EEZ does not contain a similar restriction.

The negotiating history of the Convention also bears out the right of foreign-flagged ships and aircraft to conduct intelligence and reconnaissance missions beyond the territorial sea. At the Third UN Conference for the Law of the Sea, both China and Peru offered for consideration draft text that included security jurisdiction in the bundle of rights granted to the coastal State in the EEZ, but their proposals failed to achieve support from a majority of the delegations.[57] Most nations supported the position advocated by the major maritime powers, that:

> Military operations, exercises and activities have always been regarded as internationally lawful uses of the sea. The right to conduct such activities will continue to be enjoyed by all states in the exclusive economic zone. This is the import of Article 58 of the Convention.[58]

---

[56] UNCLOS, Articles 88, 141 and 301. *See also*, ROACH & SMITH, EXCESSIVE MARITIME CLAIMS, at 30–32, SHIRLEY KAN, U.S.-CHINA MILITARY CONTACTS: ISSUES FOR CONGRESS, CONG. RES. SERVICE REPORT FOR CONGRESS (RL32496), May 10, 2005, and KRASKA, MARITIME POWER AND LAW OF THE SEA at 253–262.

[57] II UNITED NATIONS CONVENTION ON THE LAW OF THE SEA 1982: A COMMENTARY (Satya N. Nandan & Shabati Rosenne, eds. 1993) [Hereinafter VIRGINIA COMMENTARY II], pp. 521–544, 553–565.

[58] 17 OFFICIAL RECORDS OF THE THIRD UN CONFERENCE ON THE LAW OF THE SEA, PLENARY MEETINGS 243, UN Doc.A/CONF.62/WS/37 and ADD.1 and 2 (New York: United Nations, undated).

10.4.2.2.2 *Aviation Law*

Activities in international airspace are regulated by the Chicago Convention, which was signed on December 7, 1944, and entered into force in April 1947. The Convention established the International Civil Aviation Organization (ICAO) as a specialized agency of the United Nations to promote the safe and orderly development of international civil aviation.

Article 3 exempts State aircraft from the rules of the Chicago Convention, including observance of Flight Information Regions (FIRs):

a. This Convention shall be applicable only to civil aircraft, and shall not be applicable to state aircraft.
b. Aircraft used in military, customs and police services shall be deemed to be state aircraft.
c. No state aircraft of a contracting State shall fly over the territory of another State or land thereon without authorization special agreement or otherwise, and in accordance with the terms thereof.
d. The contracting States undertake, when issuing regulations for their state aircraft, that they will have due regard for the safety of navigation of civil aircraft.[59]

Neither UNCLOS nor the Chicago Convention grant coastal States any authority over military aircraft operating in international airspace beyond the 12 nm territorial sea limit. Coastal State sovereign rights in the EEZ specifically are limited in Article 56 to the seabed, its subsoil and the waters superjacent to the seabed, with one exception. The ICAO Legal Committee has determined that the coastal State has sovereign rights with regard to the production of energy from the wind.[60] But the Committee rejected efforts by Brazil to designate the airspace above the EEZ as national airspace, calling the idea as "flagrantly contradicting the relevant provisions of UNCLOS which equate the EEZ...with the high seas as regards freedom of overflight."[61] This conclusion is confirmed by overwhelming State practice. Since the advent of aviation more than 100 years ago, military aircraft have flown countless missions beyond national airspace, to include intelligence collection missions and military exercises along the outer limits of the territorial sea.

Even on those rare occasions that a coastal State has objected to foreign surveillance or reconnaissance flights offshore and beyond the territorial sea, generally they have done so on the grounds that the aircraft intruded into "national"

---

[59] Id.
[60] Barbara Kwiatkowska, THE 200 MILE EXCLUSIVE ECONOMIC ZONE IN THE NEW LAW OF THE SEA 203 (1989).
[61] Id.

airspace, rather than questioning the legality of aerial surveillance missions generally.[62] We are unaware of any case in which a State intercepted and attacked an aircraft of another State collecting intelligence while flying in international airspace.

Several instances involving the United States and the Soviet Union during the Cold War gave rise to UN Security Council deliberations on this issue.[63] Each time, the Soviet delegation specifically rejected the position that a coastal State had a right to interfere with intelligence collection activities beyond national airspace.[64] The United Kingdom indicated without objection that aerial surveillance directed at a coastal State from international airspace was consistent with international law and the UN Charter.[65]

State practice since the end of the Cold War has continued to respect the distinction between national and international airspace with regard to aircraft spy missions. For example, in June 2012, Syrian forces shot down a Turkish RF-4E Phantom jet, an unarmed reconnaissance aircraft, operating off its coast. Turkey claimed the unarmed aircraft was flying in international airspace when it was engaged. Syria maintained that the Turkish spy plane was well within its national airspace when it was shot down.[66]

10.4.2.3 State Aircraft Sovereign Immunity

One of the major U.S. criticisms of China's response to the EP-3 case was the issue of sovereign immunity. In the aftermath of the incident, Beijing held the U.S. aircraft and its crew against their will and in contravention of international law. China's conduct was at odds with the practice of the United States and its NATO allies, who have responded to foreign aircraft intelligence missions beyond national airspace with great tolerance and respect for the sovereign immune status of the aircraft and the inviolability of the aircrews. For example, in February 1974, a Soviet reconnaissance aircraft flying a mission off the coast of Alaska ran low on fuel and made an emergency landing at Gambell Airfield in Alaska.[67] The Soviet crew remained overnight, and they were provisioned with space heaters and food

---

[62] Oliver J. Lissitzyn, *The Role of International Law and an Evolving Oceans Law*, *in*: ELECTRONIC RECONNAISSANCE FROM THE HIGH SEAS AND INTERNATIONAL LAW: 61 INTERNATIONAL LAW STUDIES 566–567, 574–575, and 578–579 (Lillich & Moore, eds. Naval War College, 1980).

[63] Id.

[64] Id.

[65] Id.

[66] Eric Schmitt & Sebnem Arsu, *Backed By NATO, Turkey Steps Up Warning To Syria*, N.Y. TIMES, June 27, 2012.

[67] DEP'T OF DEFENSE, NEWS TRANSCRIPT SECRETARY RUMSFELD BRIEFS ON EP-3 COLLISION, Apr. 13, 2001, 2:00 p.m. EDT, http://www.defenselink.mil/transcripts/transcript.aspx?transcriptid=1066.

by the U.S. armed forces. The plane was refueled the next day and allowed to depart without further incident. Similarly, in March 1994, a Russian surveillance aircraft monitoring a NATO anti-submarine warfare exercise ran low on fuel and made an emergency landing at Thule Air Base in Greenland.[68] Again, the crew was fed, and the aircraft was refueled and allowed to depart without delay.

Similar (but not analogous) facts arose between the United States and the Soviet Union during the Cold War. In 1976, a defecting Soviet pilot flew his MiG-25 Foxbat fighter jet to Japan. American officials thoroughly inspected the aircraft. The U.S.S.R. demanded that the fighter jet be returned, and the United States eventually complied, sending it back in parts. The distinction between the Soviet MiG-25 and the U.S. EP-3, however, was that the Soviet aircraft landed in Japan intentionally, whereas the U.S. aircraft entered China under exigency or duress.

More recently, from May 2007 to May 2008, Russian Tu-95 Bear bombers conducted operational flights just outside the 12-nm limit off Alaska and Canada. The surveillance flights in the Arctic were resumed in 2007 after a 15-year lapse—part of Russia's attempt to reenter great power politics. American and Canadian fighter jet aircraft intercepted and monitored the bombers, but in each instance the Russian aircraft were allowed to continue on their way when it was determined that they would not penetrate the airspace of the North American Aerospace Command (NORAD).[69] Similarly, in November 2007, British Typhoon fighter jets intercepted a Russian spy plane that was detected approaching British airspace.[70] In March and May 2008, U.S. F-15 jet aircraft intercepted Russian Tu-95 Bear heavy bombers off of Alaska.[71] And in February 2009, Canadian CF-18 fighters intercepted a Russian Tu-95 that was approaching Canadian airspace.[72] In each case, when it is determined that the intercepted aircraft were on a training mission or collecting intelligence and did not intend to enter national airspace, they were allowed to continue on their flight without harassment or interference.[73]

10.4.2.4 Schooner Exchange

The landmark case law on point is the U.S. Supreme Court decision, *Schooner Exchange v. M'Faddon, et al.*, of 1816.[74] The case stems from the 1812 detention

---

[68] Id.
[69] Rowan Scarborough, *Russian flights smack of Cold War*, WASH. TIMES, June 26, 2008.
[70] Hickley & Williams, *RAF Fighter Jets Scrambled to Intercept Russian Bombers*, MAIL ONLINE, Aug. 22, 2007.
[71] Erik Holmes, *More Russian Bombers Flying off Alaska*, AIR FORCE TIMES, Apr. 8 2008 and Scarborough, *Russian flights smack of Cold War*.
[72] *Russia Denies Plane Approached Canadian Airspace*, CANADIAN BROADCASTING CORP. NEWS, Feb. 27, 2009.
[73] Scarborough, *Russian flights smack of Cold War*.
[74] *Schooner Exchange v. M'Faddon, et al.*, 7 CRANCH, 116, 1812, *reprinted in* 3 AM. J. INT'L L. 227 (Jan. 1909).

of a French ship in the United States, but in the modern era the principal of sovereign immunity extends to warships and military aircraft as well. Americans John M'Faddon and William Gretham owned the Schooner *Exchange*. The ship sailed from Baltimore, Maryland, on October 27, 1809, bound for St. Sebastians, Spain. On December 30, 1810, however, the vessel was seized under authority of Napoleon Bonaparte's *Rambouillet Decree* against U.S. shipping. The *Exchange* was converted by the French Navy and armed and commissioned as the warship *Balaou*. Unlike the U.S. EP-3 aircraft two hundred years later, the ship was a civil or merchant vessel and was not involved in spying on the high seas. Subsequently, the *Balaou* was forced to enter a U.S. port due to dangerous weather, and M'Faddon and Gretham filed a claim against the ship, arguing that they were the proper owners of the vessel.

The two Americans charged France with illegally seizing the ship, but the U.S. district court ruled in favor of the French Government, finding that the two gentlemen had no right to the *Balaou* since it belonged to the State of France, which at the time was an ally of the United States against Britain in the War of 1812. (Had the ship belonged to a belligerent of the United States, it could have been seized as prize). The district court was reversed on appeal, and M'Faddon and Gretham were granted *in rem* property rights to the ship. The U.S. Supreme Court, however, reversed the circuit court decision, and affirmed the district court's dismissal of the case.

The Supreme Court held that the United States could not seize the French ship, even though two American citizens claimed it belonged to them and not Napoleon. The apparently inequitable ruling sprang from the fact that M'Faddon and his partner "were not subjects of rights in international law, but objects of them."[75] More importantly, however, the Court ruled, "A public vessel of war of a foreign sovereign at peace with the United States coming into our ports, and demeaning herself in a friendly manner, is exempt from the jurisdiction of our country." The United States simply had no jurisdiction over the warship *Balaou*, regardless of its prior status or ownership. The holding is even more compelling today, since the *Exchange* originally was a private vessel, and yet once converted into a warship by Napoleon, the ship was imbued with sovereign immune status and the court's *in rem* jurisdiction could not attach.

---

[75] J. S. Reeves, *A Note on Exchange v. M'Faddon*, 18 AM J. INT'L L. 320 (Apr. 1924). Years later, under the Treaty with France of 1831, French spoliation claims, including those under the *Rambouillet Decree*, were presented and paid. France paid over $5.5 million in compensation to owners of U.S. ships seized by the French government, and trustees and assignees of John M'Faddon and Gretham received $54,566.81 in compensation. Id.

10.4.2.5 Military Interception of Civil Aircraft in International Airspace

Coastal States may intercept foreign military aircraft that are operating offshore in order to determine their intentions or conduct a threat assessment. The interceptions, however, must be carried out in a safe and responsible manner consistent with ICAO guidelines, such as observance of due regard for the rights of other aircraft. Annex 2 contains explicit guidelines on the interception of civil aircraft that can be used as a guide for conducting air force intercepts. Section 3.8.1 provides that "interception of civil aircraft shall be governed by appropriate regulations and administrative directives issued by Contracting States in compliance with the..." Chicago Convention.[76] Particular emphasis is placed on Article 3(d) of the Convention, which requires Contracting States to "undertake, when issuing regulations for their State aircraft, to have due regard for the safety of navigation of civil aircraft."[77]

Accordingly, Contracting States are urged to give due regard to the provisions of Appendix 1, Section 2 and Appendix 2, Section 1 in their domestic intercept regulations and administrative directives. Attachment A to Annex 2 contains special recommendations that Contracting States are urged to apply to all intercepts of civil aircraft. When intercepted, Section 3.8.2 requires the pilot-in-command of the civil aircraft to comply with the Standards in Appendix 2, Sections 2 and 3, interpreting and responding to visual signals as specified in Appendix 1, Section 2.

Appendix 2 of Annex 2 contains principles to be observed by the Contracting States when developing regulations and administrative directives applicable to intercepts of civil aircraft. In this regard, Section 1.1 requires Contracting States to pay due regard to the following principles when developing domestic regulations and administrative directives:

a. interception of civil aircraft will be undertaken only as a last resort;
b. if undertaken, an interception will be limited to determining the identity of the aircraft, unless it is necessary to return the aircraft to its planned track, direct it beyond the boundaries of national airspace, guide it away from a prohibited, restricted or danger area or instruct it to effect a landing at a designated aerodrome;
c. practice interception of civil aircraft will not be undertaken;
d. navigational guidance and related information will be given to an intercepted aircraft by radiotelephony, whenever radio contact can be established; and

---

[76] RULES OF THE ROAD, CONVENTION ON INTERNATIONAL CIVIL AVIATION, Annex 2 (10th ed. July 2005).
[77] Id., sec. 3.8.1.

e. in the case where an intercepted civil aircraft is required to land in the territory overflown, the aerodrome designated for the landing is to be suitable for the safe landing of the aircraft type concerned.

Article 3*bis* of the Chicago Convention requires that "every State must refrain from resorting to the use of weapons against civil aircraft in flight." Section 1.2 requires Contracting States to publish a standard method for the maneuvering of aircraft intercepting a civil aircraft in order to "avoid any hazard for the intercepted aircraft." Special recommendations regarding a method for the maneuvering of the intercepting aircraft are contained in Section 3 of Attachment A to the Chicago Convention. In situations where communication in a common language is not possible between the intercepting and intercepted aircraft, standard radio-communication procedures (phrases and pronunciations) are provided.[78]

Recommended interception maneuvers contained in Attachment A to Annex 2 consist of special recommendations that Contracting States are urged to apply to all intercepts of civil aircraft. Contracting States also should establish a standard method for maneuver of the intercepting aircraft in order to avoid any hazard for the intercepted civil aircraft, taking "due account of the performance limitations of civil aircraft, the need to avoid flying in such proximity to the intercepted aircraft that a collision hazard may be created, and the need to avoid crossing the aircraft's flight path or to perform any other maneuver in such a manner that the wake turbulence may be hazardous, particularly if the intercepted aircraft is a light aircraft."[79]

An intercepted aircraft equipped with an airborne collision avoidance system (ACAS) "may perceive the interceptor as a collision threat and thus initiate an avoidance maneuver in response to an ACAS resolution advisory."[80] "Such a maneuver," however, "might be misinterpreted by the interceptor as an indication of unfriendly intentions."[81] Accordingly, pilots of intercepting aircraft equipped with a secondary surveillance radar (SSR) transponder to "suppress the transmission of pressure-altitude information (in Mode C replies or in the AC field of Mode S replies) within a range of at least 37 km (20 nm) of the aircraft being intercepted" should employ the SSR transponder in order to prevent "the ACAS in the intercepted aircraft from using resolution advisories in respect of the interceptor, while the ACAS traffic advisory information will remain available."[82]

There are three phases of maneuver for intercepting aircraft for the purpose of visually identifying a civil aircraft:

---

[78] Id., sec. 3 and Table A2-1.
[79] Id., sec. 3.1.
[80] Id., sec. 3.2.
[81] Id.
[82] Id.

Phase I

The intercepting aircraft should approach the intercepted aircraft from astern. The element leader, or the single intercepting aircraft, should normally take up a position on the left (port) side, slightly above and ahead of the intercepted aircraft, within the field of view of the pilot of the intercepted aircraft, and initially not closer to the aircraft than 300 meters. Any other participating aircraft should stay well clear of the intercepted aircraft, preferably above and behind. After speed and position have been established, the aircraft should, if necessary, proceed with Phase II of the procedure.

Phase II

The element leader, or the single intercepting aircraft, should begin closing in gently on the intercepted aircraft, at the same level, until no closer than absolutely necessary to obtain the information needed. The element leader, or the single intercepting aircraft, should use caution to avoid startling the flight crew or the passengers of the intercepted aircraft, keeping constantly in mind the fact that maneuvers considered normal to an intercepting aircraft may be considered hazardous to passengers and crews of civil aircraft. Any other participating aircraft should continue to stay well clear of the intercepted aircraft. Upon completion of identification, the intercepting aircraft should withdraw from the vicinity of the intercepted aircraft as outlined in Phase III.

Phase III

The element leader, or the single intercepting aircraft, should break gently away from the intercepted aircraft in a shallow dive. Any other participating aircraft should stay well clear of the intercepted aircraft and rejoin their leader.[83]

If it is necessary to intervene in the navigation of the intercepted aircraft after following the identification maneuvers in Phase I and II, the element leader or a single intercepting aircraft should "take up a position on the left (port) side, slightly above and ahead of the intercepted aircraft, to enable the pilot-in-command of the latter aircraft to see the visual signals given."[84] "It is indispensable that the pilot-in-command of the intercepting aircraft be satisfied that the pilot-in-command of the intercepted aircraft is aware of the interception and acknowledges the signals given."[85]

If repeated attempts are unsuccessful to attract the attention of the pilot-in-command of the intercepted aircraft using the Series 1 signal in Appendix 1, Section 2, other methods of signaling may be used for this purpose, including "as a last resort the visual effect of the reheat/afterburner, provided that no hazard is created for the intercepted aircraft."[86]

Section 3.5 of Annex 2 of the Chicago Convention recognizes that "meteorological conditions or terrain may occasionally make it necessary for the element

---

[83] Id., sec. 3.3.
[84] Id., sec. 3.4.1.
[85] Id., sec. 3.4.2.
[86] Id.

leader, or the single intercepting aircraft, to take up a position on the right (starboard) side, slightly above and ahead of the intercepted aircraft." In such case, the pilot-in-command of the intercepting aircraft should "take particular care that the intercepting aircraft is clearly visible at all times to the pilot-in-command of the intercepted aircraft."[87]

Visual signals for use by intercepting and intercepted aircraft are set forth in Appendix 1 to Annex 2 of the Chicago Convention. Section 6 of Attachment A specifies that "[i]t is essential that intercepting and intercepted aircraft adhere strictly to the signals and interpret correctly the signals given by the other aircraft, and that the intercepting aircraft pay particular attention to any signals given by the intercepted aircraft to indicate that it is in a state of distress or urgency."[88]

When an intercept occurs, it is recommended that the intercept control unit and the intercepting aircraft:

a) first attempt to establish two-way communication with the intercepted aircraft in a common language on the emergency frequency 121.5 MHz, using the call signs "INTERCEPT CONTROL," "INTERCEPTOR (call sign)," and "INTERCEPTED AIRCRAFT," respectively; and

b) failing this, attempt to establish two-way communication with the intercepted aircraft on such other frequency or frequencies as may have been prescribed by the appropriate ATS [Air Traffic Services] authority, or to establish contact through the appropriate ATS unit(s).[89]

If radio contact is established but communication in a common language is not possible, "attempts must be made to convey instructions, acknowledgement of instructions and essential information by using the phrases and pronunciations in [Section 9] Table A-1 and transmitting each phrase twice."[90] In all cases the intercepting aircraft must refrain from using weapons against a civil aircraft. In this regard, "[t]he use of tracer bullets to attract attention is hazardous," and it is therefore "expected that measures will be taken to avoid their use so that the lives of persons on board and the safety of aircraft will not be endangered."[91]

10.4.2.5.1 *U.S. Practice*

In conjunction with the U.S. Federal Aviation Administration (FAA), Air Defense Sectors monitor air traffic and can order an intercept in the interest of national security or defense. Intercepts during peacetime operations are vastly different than those conducted under increased states of readiness or warfare, but may still be conducted by fighter jet aircraft or rotary wing aircraft. The reasons for aircraft intercept include, but are not limited to, attempt to positively identify an aircraft;

---

[87] Id., sec. 3.5.
[88] Id., sec. 6.
[89] Id., sec. 7.1.
[90] Id., sec. 7.2.
[91] Id., sec. 8.

track an aircraft; inspect an aircraft; divert an aircraft; or establish communications with an aircraft.[92] U.S. intercept procedures, which were developed by the U.S. FAA and the Department of Defense, implement ICAO recommendations.[93] While these procedures apply to intercepts of civilian aircraft, they also can inform military intercepts. In all situations, however, the interceptor pilot will consider safety of flight for all concerned throughout the intercept procedure and will use caution to avoid startling the intercepted crew or passengers.

American fighter jet aircraft intercepts are conducted in three phases: Approach Phase, Identification Phase and Post-Intercept Phase:

1. Approach Phase

As standard procedure, intercepted aircraft are approached from behind. Typically, interceptor aircraft will be employed in a pair; however, it is not uncommon for a single aircraft to perform the intercept operation. Safe separation between interceptors and intercepted aircraft is the responsibility of the intercepting aircraft and will be maintained at all times.

2. Identification Phase

Interceptor aircraft will initiate a controlled closure toward the aircraft of interest, holding at a distance no closer than deemed necessary to establish positive identification and to gather the necessary information. The interceptor may also fly past the intercepted aircraft while gathering data at a distance considered safe based on aircraft performance characteristics.

3. Post-Intercept Phase

An interceptor may attempt to establish communications via standard ICAO signals. In time critical situations where the interceptor is seeking an immediate response from the intercepted aircraft or if the intercepted aircraft remains noncompliant to instruction, the interceptor pilot may initiate a divert maneuver. In this maneuver, the interceptor flies across the intercepted aircraft's flight path (minimum 500 feet separation and commencing from slightly below the intercepted aircraft altitude) in the general direction the intercepted aircraft is expected to turn. The interceptor will rock its wings (daytime) or flash external lights/select afterburners (night) while crossing the intercepted aircraft's flight path. The interceptor will roll out in the direction the intercepted aircraft is expected to turn before returning to verify the aircraft of interest is complying. The intercepted aircraft is expected to execute an immediate turn to the direction of the intercepting aircraft.

If the aircraft of interest does not comply, the interceptor may conduct a second climbing turn across the intercepted aircraft's flight path (minimum 500 feet separation and commencing from slightly below the intercepted aircraft altitude) while expending flares as a warning signal to the intercepted aircraft to comply immediately and to turn in the direction indicated and to leave the area. The interceptor is responsible to maintain safe separation during these and all intercept maneuvers. Flight safety is paramount.

---

[92] Id., sec. 5-6-2(a)(1).
[93] FEDERAL AVIATION ADMINISTRATION, AERONAUTICAL INFORMATION MANUAL, ch. 5, sec. 6, National Security and Interception Procedures.

Note

1. NORAD interceptors will take every precaution to preclude the possibility of the intercepted aircraft experiencing jet wash/wake turbulence; however, there is a potential that this condition could be encountered.
2. During Night/IMC [Instrument Meteorological Conditions], the intercept will be from below flight path.[94]

United States' interception Signals are contained in Tables 5-6-1 and 5-6-2 of the Federal Aviation Administration Aeronautical Information Manual, and reproduced as a combined two-part table, Table 10.1, in this chapter.

Table 10.1. Signals Initiated by Intercepting Aircraft and Responses by Intercepted Aircraft (United States)

Signals initiated by intercepting aircraft and responses by intercepted aircraft (ICAO Annex 2, Appendix 1, 2.1, Table 5-6-1)

Series	INTERCEPTING Aircraft Signals	Meaning	INTERCEPTED Aircraft Responds	Meaning
1	DAY-Rocking wings from a position slightly above and ahead of, and normally to the left of, the intercepted aircraft and, after acknowledgement, a slow level turn, normally to the left, on to the desired heading.	You have been intercepted. Follow me.	AEROPLANES: DAY-Rocking wings and following.	Understood, will comply.
	NIGHT-Same and, in addition, flashing navigational lights at irregular intervals.		NIGHT-Same and, in addition, flashing navigational lights at irregular intervals.	
	NOTE 1-Meteorological conditions or terrain may require the intercepting aircraft to take up a position slightly above and ahead of, and to the right of, the intercepted aircraft and to make the subsequent turn to the right.		HELICOPTERS: DAY or NIGHT- Rocking aircraft, flashing navigational lights at irregular intervals and following.	
	NOTE 2-If the intercepted aircraft is not able to keep pace with the intercepting aircraft, the latter is expected to fly a series of race-track patterns and to rock its wings each time it passes the intercepted aircraft.			

---

[94] Id., sec. 5-6-2(b).

Table 10.1 (*cont.*)

	Signals initiated by intercepting aircraft and responses by intercepted aircraft (ICAO Annex 2, Appendix 1, 2.1, Table 5-6-1)			
Series	INTERCEPTING Aircraft Signals	Meaning	INTERCEPTED Aircraft Responds	Meaning
2	DAY or NIGHT-An abrupt break-away maneuver from the intercepted aircraft consisting of a climbing turn of 90 degrees or more without crossing the line of flight of the intercepted aircraft.	You may proceed.	AEROPLANES: DAY or NIGHT- Rocking wings. HELICOPTERS: DAY or NIGHT- Rocking aircraft.	Understood, will comply.
3	DAY-Circling aerodrome, lowering landing gear and overflying runway in direction of landing or, if the intercepted aircraft is a helicopter, overflying the helicopter landing area.	Land at this aerodrome.	AEROPLANES: DAY-Lowering landing gear, following the intercepting aircraft and, if after overflying the runway landing is considered safe, proceeding to land.	Understood, will comply.
	NIGHT-Same and, in addition, showing steady landing lights.		NIGHT-Same and, in addition, showing steady landing lights (if carried).	
			HELICOPTERS: DAY or NIGHT- Following the intercepting aircraft and proceeding to land, showing a steady landing light (if carried).	

Table 10.1 (*cont.*)

Signals initiated by intercepted aircraft and responses by intercepting aircraft
(ICAO Annex 2, Appendix 1, 2.2, Table 5-6-2)

Series	INTERCEPTED Aircraft Signals	Meaning	INTERCEPTING Aircraft Responds	Meaning
4	DAY or NIGHT-Raising landing gear (if fitted) and flashing landing lights while passing over runway in use or helicopter landing area at a height exceeding 300m (1,000 ft) but not exceeding 600m (2,000 ft) (in the case of a helicopter, at a height exceeding 50m (170 ft) but not exceeding 100m (330 ft) above the aerodrome level, and continuing to circle runway in use or helicopter landing area. If unable to flash landing lights, flash any other lights available.	Aerodrome you have designated is inadequate.	DAY or NIGHT-If it is desired that the intercepted aircraft follow the intercepting aircraft to an alternate aerodrome, the intercepting aircraft raises its landing gear (if fitted) and uses the Series 1 signals prescribed for intercepting aircraft. If it is decided to release the intercepted aircraft, the intercepting aircraft uses the Series 2 signals prescribed for intercepting aircraft.	Understood, follow me. Understood, you may proceed.
5	DAY or NIGHT-Regular switching on and off of all available lights but in such a manner as to be distinct from flashing lights.	Cannot comply.	DAY or NIGHT- Use Series 2 signals prescribed for intercepting aircraft.	Understood.
6	DAY or NIGHT-Irregular flashing of all available lights.	In distress.	DAY or NIGHT- Use Series 2 signals prescribed for intercepting aircraft.	Understood.

10.4.3 *"Peaceful Purposes"*

One of the boldest efforts by coastal States to "territorialize" the EEZ is to suggest that foreign warships and state aircraft are not entitled to conduct intelligence collection in the zone, since doing so is tantamount to a violation of the "peaceful purposes" provision of Article 301 of UNCLOS. At times, China in particular, has asserted the "peaceful purposes" language of the Law of the Sea Convention authorizes coastal States to prohibit foreign military activities, to include intelligence collection, in the EEZ.

Article 301 of UNCLOS calls on states to "refrain from any threat or use of force against the territorial integrity or political independence of any state...." The language is identical to text in Article 2(4) of the UN Charter on the prohibition of armed aggression in the relations among states. UNCLOS, however, makes a clear distinction between "threat or use of force" on the one hand, and other military activities, including intelligence collection, on the other. Article 19(2)(a) governing innocent passage, for example, repeats the language of Article 301, that prohibits ships in innocent passage from engaging in "any threat or use of force against the sovereignty, territorial integrity or political independence of the coastal state...."

Subparagraphs 2(b)–(f) of Article 19 restrict other military activities in the territorial sea, including those found in subparagraph 2(c), which prohibit ships transiting the territorial sea in innocent passage from engaging in "any act aimed at collecting information to the prejudice of the defense or security of the coastal state." The separation of the two concepts—the use of force and intelligence collection—demonstrates that UNCLOS does not automatically equate one with the other. Intelligence collection, however else it may be characterized, is not necessarily a "threat or use of force" under UNCLOS or the UN Charter.

Intelligence collection does not violate Article 2(4) of the Charter and the prohibition on the use of "armed aggression" as a policy instrument, and therefore also is not inconsistent with the "peaceful purposes" concept in UNCLOS Article 301. Most commentators have agreed with the position that

> ...based on various provisions of the Convention...it is logical...to interpret the peaceful...purposes clauses as prohibiting only those activities which are not consistent with the UN Charter. It may be concluded accordingly that the peaceful purposes...clauses in Articles 88 and 301 do not prohibit all military activities on the high seas and in EEZs, but only those that threaten or use force in a manner inconsistent with the UN Charter.[95]

The determination of whether an activity is "peaceful" is made under Article 2(4) of the UN Charter, which states "All members shall refrain in their international

---

[95] Raul Pedrozo, *Responding to Ms. Zhang's Talking Points on the EEZ*, 10 Chinese J. Int'l L. 207–223 (2011) and Moritaka Hayashi, *Military and Intelligence Gathering Activities in the EEZ: Definition of Key Terms*, 29 Marine Pol'y 123–137 (2005).

relations from the threat or use of force against the territorial integrity or political independence of any state, or in any other manner inconsistent with the Purposes of the United Nations." Since the Convention is a peacetime agreement, it does not displace the body of the law of naval warfare and neutrality, which apply during time of armed conflict at sea.

The original version of Article 301 was proposed by a group of developing nations in 1980 as an additional provision to be included in Article 88. The language was not included in Article 88, however, and the text was reintroduced separately to read as a new article, "All states shall refrain from any threat or use of force against the sovereignty, territorial integrity or political independence of any state, or in any other manner inconsistent with the purpose of the United Nations and the principles of international law."[96] The phrase, "or in any manner..." was changed to, "or in any manner inconsistent with the principles of international law embodied in the Charter of the United Nations." The new language, supported by the United States, reflects broad principles of international law, including the threshold for the use of armed aggression in Article 2(4) and the inherent right of self-defense that is captured by Article 51.[97]

The final text of Article 301 of the Convention states, "States Parties shall refrain from any threat or use of force against the territorial integrity or political independence of any State." Regarding the placement of this article within the text of the Convention, one scholar commented, "[i]t is noteworthy that initially the intention had been to insert Article 301 in Part V [the EEZ section of the Convention]. This was [successfully] opposed by maritime States on the ground that security matters should not be considered within the EEZ regime."[98]

The term "peaceful purposes" is referenced in articles 88, 141, 143(1), 147(2)(d), 155(2), 240(a), 242(1) and 246(3) and 301 of the Convention. Marine scientific research, for example, should be conducted only for "peaceful purposes."[99] Article 88 of the Law of the Sea Convention reserves the high seas for "peaceful purposes" and requires states to refrain from the threat or use of force against the territorial integrity or political independence of another state.[100] This provision applies by extension throughout the EEZ in accordance with Article 58(2). The Preamble and Article 301 make reference to "peaceful uses" rather than "peaceful

---

[96] III UNITED NATIONS CONVENTION ON THE LAW OF THE SEA: A COMMENTARY ¶ 88.79(a), at 89, note 3 (Satya N. Nandan, C.B.E. & Shabtai Rosenne, eds. Center for Oceans Law & Policy, University of Virginia School of Law, 1995) (Hereinafter VIRGINIA COMMENTARY III).
[97] Id., at 54–55.
[98] DAVID J. ATTARD, THE EXCLUSIVE ECONOMIC ZONE 69 (1991).
[99] UNCLOS, Articles 240, 246.
[100] UNCLOS, Articles 88 and 58(2).

purposes," and the authoritative *III Virginia Commentary* suggests the two terms may be read as synonymous.[101]

With specific application to the oceans, the "peaceful purposes" language originally was derived from the text of UN General Assembly Resolution 2749 (1970), which declared that the high seas were to be open exclusively for peaceful purposes. Thereafter, the text gravitated to the Sea-Bed Committee in 1973, where Ecuador, Panama, and Peru proposed language for Article 88 of the draft Convention that read, "The international seas shall be open to all states...and their use shall be reserved for peaceful purposes."[102] Subsequently, the "peaceful purposes" text was imported into the *Informal Single Negotiating Text* (ISNT), which was issued by the President of the Conference at the end of the Third Session in 1975 as a basis for further negotiation.[103]

Consideration over the draft article continued at the Fourth Session in 1976, where states tended to align their views on the issue among three distinct groups. The first group, representing some of the developing states, maintained that the text would prohibit all military activities in the oceans. Ecuador represented this perspective, claiming "the use of the ocean space for exclusively peaceful purposes must mean complete demilitarization and the exclusion from it of all military activities."[104]

The second group suggested that the language prohibited only military activities that were conducted for purposes of aggression. Indeed, this is true, but many states argued the mere operation of a warship or spy plane—either on the high seas or in an EEZ—is not automatically an activity that might be characterized as "not peaceful." Consequently, the interpretation of the second group was too open to interpretive mischief. The third group, which included the United States and other maritime powers, argued that the test of whether an activity was considered "peaceful" was determined by the UN Charter and other obligations of international law.[105] In response to Ecuador's proposal at the Fourth Session, the U.S. delegate T. Vincent Learson declared,

> The term "peaceful purposes" did not, of course, preclude military activities generally. The United States has consistently held that the conduct of military activities for peaceful purposes was in full accord with the Charter of the United Nations and with the principles of international law. Any specific limitation on military activities would require the negotiation of a detailed arms control agreement. The Conference was not charged with such a purpose and was not prepared for such a negotiation.

---

[101] Virginia Commentary III, at 90.
[102] Id., at 88.
[103] The ISNT replaced the term, "international seas" with "high seas" in explaining the term, "peaceful purposes."
[104] Virginia Commentary III, at 88–89.
[105] Id., at 89–91.

Any attempt to turn the Conference's attention to such a complex task would quickly bring to an end current efforts to negotiate a law of the sea convention.[106]

Professor Moritaka Hayashi of Waseda University in Japan has divided application of the terms "peaceful purposes" and "peaceful uses" into four categories:

(1) Article 88, which reserves the high seas for peaceful purposes, and also applies to the EEZ though article 58(2);
(2) Article 141, 143(1), 147(2)(d) and 155(2), which relate to reservation of the Area, lying beyond the area of national jurisdiction, for use exclusively for peaceful purposes;
(3) Article 240(a) and 246(3) apply the principle of "peaceful purposes" to the conduct of marine scientific research;
(4) Article 301, widely applicable as a "constitutional" principle of the Law of the Sea, requires states to refrain from the threat or use of force against the territorial integrity or political independence of any other state, or act in a manner inconsistent with international law as reflected in the UN Charter.[107]

To accept that military activities were, by their nature, inconsistent with the "peaceful purposes," would mean that the high seas also were reserved only for identical "peaceful purposes." The same rules for the EEZ would apply throughout the high seas. This analysis leads to a point of *reductio ad absurdum* since it suggests that no State is permitted to operate military vessels or aircraft throughout not just the EEZ, but also the high seas. Such a conclusion is inconsistent with state practice, as well as the decisions reached by the UN Security Council. A 1985 report by the UN Secretary-General concluded, for example, that "military activities" consistent with the principles of international law embodied in the Charter of the United Nations, in particular with Article 2, paragraph 4, and Article 51, are not prohibited by the Convention on the Law of the Sea."[108]

The minimalist interpretation of the "peaceful purposes" provision that would exclude normal military activities was also rejected by the *San Remo Manual on the Law of Armed Conflicts at Sea*, which consolidates and serves as a restatement of the law of naval warfare. The *San Remo Manual* makes clear that armed conflict at sea can take place on the high seas and in the EEZ of a neutral state.[109]

If hostile actions are conducted within the EEZ of a neutral state, however, belligerents must "have due regard for the rights and duties of the coastal State," which are described as, *inter alia*, "the exploration and exploitation of the

---

[106] Id., ¶ 88.5, at 89 and V OFFICIAL RECORDS OF THE THIRD UNITED NATIONS CONFERENCE ON THE LAW OF THE SEA, ¶ 81, at 62. *See also*, Bernard H. Oxman, *The Regime of Warships under the United Nations Convention on the Law of the Sea*, 24 VA. J. INT'L L. 809, 829–832 (1984).
[107] Moritaka Hayashi, *Military and Intelligence Gathering Activities in the EEZ: Definition of Key Terms*, 29 MARINE POL'Y 123, 124 (2005).
[108] VIRGINIA COMMENTARY III, at 88–89.
[109] SAN REMO MANUAL ON THE LAW APPLICABLE TO ARMED CONFLICT AT SEA ¶ 10, at 8 (Louise Doswald-Beck, ed. 1995).

economic resources of the [EEZ] and the protection of the marine environment."[110] Belligerents are entitled to lay mines in the EEZ and on the continental shelf so long as the neutral state is notified of the danger and the size of the minefield and the type of mines laid do not endanger artificial islands, installations and structures used pursuant to the coastal State's authority in the EEZ. Additionally, mines in the EEZ "shall avoid so far as practicable interference with the exploration or exploitation of the zone by the neutral state."[111]

In the commentary accompanying the U.S. President's letter of transmittal of the Convention to the Senate in 1994, President Clinton stated:

> None of these provisions [article 88, 141, 143, 147, 155, 240, 242, 246 and 301] create new rights or obligations, imposes restraints upon military operations, or impairs the inherent right of self-defense.... More generally, military activities, which are consistent with the principles of international law, are not prohibited by these, or any other, provisions of the Convention.[112]

The United States retained this draft declaration concerning the meaning of the terms "peaceful uses" or "peaceful purposes" in President Bush's 2004 letter of transmittal of the Convention to the Senate: "The United States understands that nothing in the Convention, including any provisions referring to 'peaceful uses'[113] or 'peaceful purposes,'[114] impairs the inherent right of individual or collective self-defense or rights during armed conflict." This understanding of the term underscores the importance the United States attaches to the right of self-defense.[115] The interagency-cleared pronouncement accepts that the "peaceful purposes" provisions can only be read in conjunction with the general body of international law, including the inherent right of individual and collective self-defense, as reflected in the UN Charter in Article 51.[116]

Shortly after the 2004 transmittal, Ambassador John Norton Moore explained that the term, "peaceful purposes" was not intended to limit routine or customary military activities. Paradoxically, the assertion that Article 88 impedes naval forces has been resurrected by some opponents of the Convention in the United States, who are unwittingly recycling a shallow argument made by the U.S.S.R. in the 1970s:

> The critics evince little knowledge of international law or oceans law and as a result sometimes make arguments contrary to U.S. interests. For example, some have argued that the provision in Article 88 of the Convention limiting use of the high

---

[110] Id., ¶ 34, at 14.
[111] Id., ¶ 35, at 14.
[112] Senate Treaty Doc. 103–39, at iii and 94.
[113] UNCLOS, Article 301.
[114] UNCLOS, Articles 88 (reservation of high seas); 143(1), 147(2)(d), 240(a) and 246(3) (marine scientific research); and 141 and 155(2) (application to the Area).
[115] Senate Treaty Doc. 103–39, at 8.
[116] Id.

seas for "peaceful purposes" would constrain United States warships or prevent military activities on the high seas. But in making this argument they are unknowingly adopting the "old" Soviet line–no longer even embraced by Russia—and which was never supported by the United States.[117]

10.4.4 Offshore Environmental Regulation as Maritime Strategy

Beginning in the mid-2000s, as the argument that the coastal State had a national security interest in the EEZ gained little traction, Beijing searched for a new legal rationale to support its position that coastal States could regulate foreign military activities in the EEZ. The suggestion that mere military activities were inherently not peaceful had fallen flat. Furthermore, the claim that intelligence collection or military surveys on the water constituted MSR also was not widely accepted. Finally, the international community was similarly unwilling to recognize authority of coastal States to intercept foreign state aircraft in international airspace above the EEZ.

Thus, China turned toward new arguments rooted in the environmental provisions of the Convention in its quest to develop a convincing rationale that would support its claim to a security interest in the EEZ. Concomitantly, Beijing relied on new classes of ships and aircraft to enforce its excessive maritime claims in the EEZ. By 2005, harassment of U.S. Special Mission Ships by PLA-N warships and aircraft was the exception, not the rule, having been replaced by State Oceanographic Administration (SOA) and Maritime Safety Administration (MSA) patrol vessels and aircraft. The new approach, however, runs up against the fairly limited coastal State jurisdiction on issues of protection and preservation of the marine environment in the EEZ.

In 2007, Beijing amplified its environmental argument at meetings of the U.S.-China Military Maritime Consultative Agreement and Defense Policy Talks indicating that sonar use by U.S. SMSs was harming marine mammals and disrupting fish stocks in China's EEZ.[118] China had picked up on the popularity of coastal State assertions of "ecological protection," leveraging the trend for strategic military purposes.[119] In Europe, the idea that certain ocean space was deserving of

---

[117] John Norton Moore & Williams L. Schachte, Jr., *The Senate Should Give Immediate Advice and Consent to the Law of the Sea Convention: Why the Critics Are Wrong*, 59 COLUMBIA J. INT'L AFFAIRS 6 (2005).

[118] Captain Stacy A. Pedrozo, JAGC, USN, China's Active Defense Strategy and its Regional Impact, Prepared Statement by Jan. 27, 2011, Before the U.S.-China Economic & Security Review Commission, U.S. House of Representatives, First Session, 112th Congress, available at http://www.cfr.org.

[119] In the Mediterranean Sea, for example, a number of coastal states have opted for creation of "Ecological Protection Zones" (EPZs) in lieu of EEZs in those areas overlapped by conflicting claims. *See*, Angela Del Vecchio Capotosti, *In Maiore Stat Minus: A Note on the EEZ and the Zones of Ecological Protection in the Mediterranean Sea*, 39 OCEAN DEVELOPMENT & INT'L L. 287–297 (2008).

special rules that depart from ordinary law of the sea also had gained mainstream appeal, making many more sympathetic to China's claims. The Mediterranean Sea, for example, was regarded by many as "unlike any other geographical area," in its political, ethnic, economic, religious and social factors "stemming from temporal and cultural stratifications" [sic].[120] This new argument also coincided with a series of lawsuits filed by environmental groups in U.S. courts, including a 2007 ruling against the U.S. Navy in a lawsuit before the U.S. District Court in Southern California that challenged the Navy's use of mid-frequency active sonar during military exercises.

China also changed its operational approach to challenging U.S. military activities. Fisheries Law Enforcement Command (FLEC) vessels joined MSA and SOA vessels in interfering with U.S. military activities. China advanced this argument despite the fact that the environmental provisions of the Convention do not apply to sovereign immune vessels and even after the U.S. Supreme Court overturned the district court opinion and ruled in favor of the Navy in 2008. The U.S. high court ruled that there was no evidence that marine mammals were being harmed by the Navy's use of sonar in Southern California.[121]

In 2009, China once against changed its harassment tactics, this time relying on civilian proxies under the direction of the PLA-N to interfere with U.S. SMSs operating in the EEZ. On March 8, 2009, five Chinese vessels—a PLA-N intelligence ship, a FLEC patrol vessel, a SOA patrol vessel and two small civilian cargo vessels—surrounded and harassed the USNS *Impeccable* (T-AGOS 23) while she was conducting routine ocean surveillance activities approximately 75 miles south of Hainan Island. After making several close passes of the *Impeccable*, some within 25 feet in an effort to snag the towed sonar array cable protruding from the rear of the ship, the civilian merchant vessels stopped dead in the water before the U.S. ship, nearly causing a collision.

Although the PRC government vessels remained at a safe distance from the *Impeccable*, the video and subsequent photographs of the incident show that the merchant vessels were under the direction and control of the PLA-N. Washington immediately protested the Chinese actions as reckless, unprofessional and unlawful and vowed to continue deploying naval ships to the region.[122] Beijing responded that the presence of the U.S. SMSs in China's EEZ was a violation of

---

[120] Id. at 287. Spain Royal Decree 1315, Aug. 1, 1987, proclaimed a fisheries protection zone in the Mediterranean Sea; France created an EEZ in the Atlantic Ocean, but in 2003 created an EPZ off its Mediterranean coast by Law No. 2003–346 of Apr. 15, 2003; and, Croatia announced an EPZ and fisheries zone on Oct. 3, 2003. Id. at 292.

[121] *Winter, Secretary of the Navy, et al. v. Natural Resources Defense Council, Inc., et al.*, 555 U.S. 7, 129 S.Ct. 365, 172 L.Ed.2d 249 (2008).

[122] *United States Protests Chinese Interference with U.S. Naval Vessel, Vows to Continued Operations*, 103 Am. J. Int'l L. 349–351 (Apr. 2009).

Chinese domestic law and international law.[123] Two months later, a similar incident occurred when two Chinese fishing trawlers harassed the USNS *Victorious* (T-AGOS 19) while she was conducting a lawful military operation in the Yellow Sea, prompting the U.S. vessel to use its water hose to ward off the Chinese boats after they maneuvered within 90 feet of the SMS. The fishing vessels departed the area after a Chinese government vessel inexplicably arrived on scene. U.S. diplomatic protests were once again met with the worn argument that the SMS was violating Chinese domestic law and international law.[124]

China raised similar concerns in July 2010 following the announcement by the United States that the *USS George Washington* (CVN 73) would deploy to the Yellow Sea to participate in a joint military exercise (*Invincible Spirit*) with South Korean forces following the sinking of the South Korea warship *Cheonan* in March 2010 by a North Korean torpedo. China objected to the deployment, indicating that the presence of the carrier in the Yellow Sea would be provocative and a threat to Chinese national security. The U.S. carrier had conducted operations in the Yellow Sea earlier in the year without incident.

In an apparent effort to assuage Beijing's concerns, the *George Washington* participated in the exercise from the east side of the Korean peninsula.[125] A second and third round of what could be viewed as appeasement occurred in August 2010 and September 2010, when the UN Command in Seoul announced that *George Washington* would not participate in the military exercise *Ulchi Freedom Guardian*, an annual training event between U.S. and Republic of Korea military forces. *Ulchi Freedom Guardian* is held in mid-August. After Beijing repeated its objections to the presence of the U.S. carrier in the Yellow Sea, the U.S. also backed out of an anti-submarine exercise in the Yellow Sea scheduled for September 5–9.[126] Finally, in late November 2010, after Beijing filed a diplomatic protest to object to the participation of the aircraft carrier in a scheduled bilateral exercise with the South Korean Navy, the U.S. Seventh Fleet deployed the *George Washington* to the Yellow Sea.

Continuing efforts by China and others to impinge on traditional uses of the EEZ are inconsistent with international law and generally are opposed by sea-going nations. If China's position becomes the international standard, nearly 38 percent of the world's oceans that were once considered high seas and open to unfettered military use would come under coastal State regulation and control. Under such a regime, military forces could be denied access to all of the South China and East China Seas, the Sea of Japan and the Yellow Sea,

---

[123] Pedrozo, *Close Encounters*, at 101–111.
[124] *Pentagon Reports Naval Incident in Yellow Sea*, VOICE OF AMERICA NEWS.COM, May 5, 2009.
[125] Bill Gertz, *Inside the Ring: Chinese Carrier Pressure*, WASH. TIMES, July 21, 2010.
[126] DEP'T OF DEFENSE, NEWS BRIEFING WITH GEOFF MORRELL FROM THE PENTAGON, Aug. 5, 2010.

the Caribbean, the Sea of Okhotsk, the Mediterranean, the Baltic Sea, the Persian Gulf, the Red Sea and the Gulf of Aden; most of Oceania and the Bering Sea; and large swaths of the Arctic, Pacific and Indian Oceans. These waterways are home to most of the world's strategic sea lines of communication. This result was not envisioned during the negotiations during the Third UN Conference on the Law of the Sea, and would never have been accepted by the superpowers.

ELEVEN

FLASHPOINT: SOUTH CHINA SEA

11.1 The Political Seascape and Regional Stability

The South China Sea has resurfaced as a political and military flashpoint, coinciding with China's spectacular rise in economic and military might.[1] The waters are home to rich fishing grounds and, according to some estimates, the world's second largest oil reserves, containing as much as 213 billion barrels of oil worth over $18 trillion.[2] Today the South China Sea may be considered the "center of gravity for the global economy," with more than $5 trillion in commerce flowing through the region's sea lines of communication on an annual basis.[3]

The convergence of political, military, and economic interests among Vietnam, China, Malaysia, Indonesia, Brunei, Taiwan, and the Philippines makes the South China Sea the most volatile maritime flashpoint on earth. This is the only chapter in the book dedicated to examining maritime security in a single region, as we believe that tensions in the South China Sea could at any moment erupt into war. Furthermore, the international disputes in the region play out against the backdrop of law of the sea and the maritime rights and duties of States in the region.

China is at the center of the South China Sea controversy, and without Beijing's activism, the stage would be set for a rather drawn out but peaceful horse-trading among the littoral States to resolve conflicting claims. Capitalizing on Washington's preoccupation with the U.S. withdrawal from South Vietnam in late 1973,

---

[1] *South China Sea Flashpoint: As China Threats Grow, the U.S. Should Signal Support for ASEAN* (Op-ed.), Wall. St. J., July 2, 2011.
[2] Ray Kwong, *South China Sea: China Lays Claim to Every Inch That Matters*, Hsin Pao (Hong Kong Econ. J.), Oct. 19, 2011.
[3] Gidget Fuentes, *PACOM Boss: Fleet essential to protect commerce*, Navy Times, Oct. 25, 2011.

however, in January 1974 China invaded the Paracel Islands. Vietnam had inherited control and administration of the islands from colonial France (French Indochina) in 1956. The superior PRC expeditionary forces easily overwhelmed the smaller South Vietnamese garrison on Pattle Island, the largest feature in the Crescent Group of the archipelago. After a brief naval and island engagement, Chinese forces grabbed control of both the Amphitrite and Crescent Groups of the Paracel Islands. China has occupied the features since the invasion, drawing illegal straight baselines around the islands.[4] In April 2012, Beijing announced that it was considering opening the Paracel Islands to tourism in order to bolster its sovereignty claims.[5]

A second clash between China and Vietnam occurred in March 1988 as Vietnam's closest ally, the Soviet Union, was beginning to disintegrate. On March 14, the People's Liberation Army-Navy (PLA-N) marine forces attacked Vietnamese naval forces in the vicinity of Johnson South Reef, resulting in the sinking of several Vietnamese warships and the death of 72 Vietnamese sailors.[6] The skirmish extended over six atolls, all of which were then occupied by Beijing. Following this engagement, China occupied six additional key islets in the Spratly archipelago—Nanshan, Loaita Nan, Loaita Island, Namyit Island, Fiery Cross Reef, and Cuarteron Reef.[7]

On April 1, 2001, a Chinese People's Liberation Army Air Force F-8 Finback fighter aircraft collided with a U.S. EP-3 surveillance aircraft that was conducting a routine reconnaissance flight about 70 miles south-southwest of Hainan Island. The Chinese pilot was killed, the fighter jet lost at sea, and the damaged propeller-driven EP-3 aircraft made an emergency landing at Lingshui airfield on Hainan Island. The U.S. flight crew was illegally detained for over two weeks, and the aircraft was not returned until July 2001, by which time it had been dismantled and stripped. The Bush administration, which entered the White House just months before the incident, lodged a diplomatic protest with China, condemning the violation of the aircraft's sovereign immunity and illegal detention of the crew, and stating that U.S. surveillance activities and reconnaissance flights would continue.[8]

---

[4] ENERGY INFORMATION ADMINISTRATION, COUNTRY ANALYSIS BRIEFS—SOUTH CHINA SEA, Mar. 2008.
[5] Ben Blanchard & Chris Buckley, *China Stakes Claim To Islands With 'Princess Coconut' Voyage*, REUTERS, Apr. 10, 2012.
[6] *China's Syndrome: Ambiguity; What Seizing a Tiny Reef Says About Beijing's Soul*, WASH. POST, Mar. 19, 1995, A1.
[7] Id.
[8] SHIRLEY KAN, ET AL., CHINA-U.S. AIRCRAFT COLLISION INCIDENT OF APRIL 2001: ASSESSMENTS AND POLICY IMPLICATIONS, CONG. RES. SERVICE REPORT FOR CONGRESS, Oct. 10, 2001, C. Plante, *U.S. Quietly Resumes Surveillance Flights off China*, CNN.com, May 15,

Nearly eight years later to the day, the Obama Administration was similarly tested. In March 2009, two Chinese merchant vessels, apparently under the control of a PLA-N intelligence ship, harassed the U.S. special mission ship, USNS *Impeccable* (T-AGOS23), as it was conducting routine surveillance operations 75 nautical miles off the coastline of Hainan Island. Like the Bush administration, the Obama White House diplomatically protested the incident. A few days later, the Pentagon ordered the *Impeccable* back into the South China Sea to continue is surveillance mission with an armed warship escort.[9]

These two incidents, combined with many others that are not widely reported in the media, highlight a pattern of Chinese interference with the navigation and other internationally lawful uses of the sea in the region. Chinese ships and aircraft have harassed numerous U.S. naval ships and aircraft operating beyond the Chinese territorial sea and airspace in the East China Sea and South China Sea. Japanese, Australian, Malaysian, British, and Indian warships have been similarly harassed. Chinese government vessels also have interfered with Vietnamese and Filipino resource exploration and exploitation activities within their respective Exclusive Economic Zones (EEZs).

China claims sovereignty over all of the Spratly and Paracel Islands and their adjacent waters. Vietnam, Malaysia, Philippines, Brunei and Taiwan also claim some or all of the land features and surrounding waters—forming a milieu of overlapping maritime claims that undermine regional stability. Additionally, Indonesia has an EEZ claim that extends into the South China Sea. Brunei has not occupied any of land features in the South China Sea, but claims a continental shelf and EEZ that includes Louisa Reef, which is currently occupied by Malaysia. Malaysia occupies three islands in the South China Sea that the government of the Philippines considers to be within its EEZ and continental shelf.

11.1.1 *Chinese Maritime Claims*

China claims 80 percent of the South China Sea. With the exception of a high seas donut hole in the middle of the South China Sea, most of the sea area claimed by China is within 200 nm of the coasts of Vietnam, Malaysia, Brunei and the Philippines. China's claims are based on a handful of murky historical events, including the naval expeditions to the region by the Han Dynasty (110 AD) and the Ming Dynasty (1403–1433 AD).

Even if China were to exercise sovereignty over the South China Sea Islands, however, most of the features are shoals, low-tide elevations, and rocks that do

---

2001, M. Oliva, *Before EP-3, China Turned Away U.S. Research Ship in International Waters*, Stars and Stripes, May 20, 2001, and Raul Pedrozo, *Beijing's Coastal Real Estate: A History of Chinese Naval Aggression*, FOREIGNAFFAIRS.COM, Nov. 15, 2010.

[9] Raul Pedrozo, *Close Encounters at Sea: The USNS Impeccable Incident*, 63 NAVAL WAR COLL. REV. Summer 2009, at 101–111.

not generate an EEZ or continental shelf. Article 121(3) of the United Nations Convention on the Law of the Sea (UNCLOS) makes clear that "rocks which cannot sustain human habitation or economic life of their own shall have no exclusive economic zone or continental shelf."

Major General Luo Yuan, Director of the China Military Science Society, called for the establishment of a national coast guard, stationing PLA troops on more disputed land features in the Spratlys, and increased resource exploitation by Chinese fishermen and oil companies in and around those features to enforce China's territorial claims.[10] Chen Mingyi, a member of the Standing Committee of the Chinese People's Political Consultative Conference National Committee, called for the establishment of new Ministry of Oceans to enhance China's maritime law enforcement and resource exploration and exploitation on the high seas.[11]

When he opened the National People's Congress in March 2012, Chinese Premier Wen Jiabao stressed the need for China to "enhance the armed forces' capacity to accompllish a wide range of military tasks, the most important of which is to win local wars under information age conditions."[12] The reference to winning "local wars" could be seen as a veiled threat to the other South China Sea claimants. Previously, in a speech before the Central Military Commission (CMC) in December 2011, President Hu Jintao urged the PLA-N to "accelerate its transformation and modernization in a sturdy way, and make extended preparations for military combat in order to make greater contributions to safeguard national security and world peace."[13] One month earlier, Premier Wen, referring to the United States, "warned against interference by external forces in regional territorial disputes, including in the South China Sea."[14]

11.1.1.1 The U-Shaped Line (The "Cow Tongue")

In 1948, China issued a map that claimed the Pratas, Paracel, and Spratly Islands, as well as the Macclesfield Bank, as part of China, with the use of an 11-dashed or "U-shaped" dotted line (also referred to as the "Cow's Tongue"), which encircles 80 percent of the South China Sea. The southern-most point of China's claim extends to James Shoal at 4° North latitude. The 11-dotted line was reaffirmed by the newly established government of the People's Republic of China in 1949, but was subsequently replaced by a nine-dashed line in 1953 after Zhou Enlai

---

[10] Jeremy Page, *General Calls for New Coast Guard to Patrol South China Sea*, WALL ST. J. CHINA; REAL TIME REPORT, Mar. 7, 2012.
[11] *Call for Establishment of Ministry of Oceans in China*, CHINA DAILY, Mar. 5, 2012.
[12] *China Must Increase Ability to Win 'Local Wars:' Wen*, THE JAKARTA GLOBE, Mar. 5, 2012.
[13] Robert Saiget, *China's Hu urges Navy to Prepare for Combat*, AGENCE FRANCE-PRESSE, Dec. 7, 2011.
[14] Id.

authorized the elimination of two of the dots in the Gulf of Tonkin.[15] Taiwan's claims mirror those asserted by China.

China reaffirmed its claim of sovereignty over the islands and features of the South China Sea when it declared a 12-nautical mile territorial sea in 1958:

> The Government of the People's Republic of China declares:
>
> The breadth of the territorial sea of the People's Republic of China shall be twelve nautical miles. This provision applies to all territories of the People's Republic of China including the Chinese mainland and its coastal islands, as well as Taiwan and its surrounding islands, the Penghu Islands, the Dongsha Islands, the Xisha Islands, the Zhongsha Islands, the Nansha Islands and all other islands belonging to China which are separated from the mainland and its coastal islands by the high seas.[16]

Similar assertions were made in Article 2 of the 1992 territorial sea law of China,[17] in China's declaration upon ratifying the UNCLOS in 1996,[18] in Article 2 of the 1996 straight baseline law,[19] and in the 2009 *Law of the People's Republic of China on Island Protection*.[20] China reaffirmed its sovereignty claims over all of the South China Sea islands and their adjacent waters and continental shelves in a demarche filed with the United Nations in 2009, protesting Republic of the Philippines Act 9522, which defines the new Philippine archipelagic baselines and reasserts Filipino sovereignty over the Kalayaan Island Group (KIG) and Scarborough Shoal in the South China Sea.[21] Specifically, Beijing rejected the new Philippine law because it "illegally claims Huangyan Island... and some islands and reefs of the Nansha Islands... of China as areas over which the Philippines likewise exercises sovereignty and jurisdiction."[22] Beijing then reiterated that "Huangyan Island and Nansha Islands have been part of the territory of China since ancient time" and that China has "indisputable sovereignty" over them.[23]

---

[15] Li Jinming & Li Dexia, *The Dotted Line on the Chinese Map of the South China Sea: A Note*, 34 OCEAN DEVELOPMENT & INT'L L. 287–295 (2003).

[16] Declaration of the Government of the People's Republic of China on China's Territorial Sea, Sept. 4, 1958.

[17] People's Republic of China, Law of the Territorial Sea and the Contiguous Zone, Feb. 25, 1992.

[18] Declaration of the People's Republic of China upon ratifying the United Nations Convention on the Law of the Sea, June 7, 1996.

[19] Statement of the Chinese Government on the Baseline of the Territorial Sea of the People's Republic of China, May 15, 1996.

[20] People's Republic of China, Law of the People's Republic of China on Island Protection, Dec. 26, 2009.

[21] Republic of the Philippines Act No. 9522, An Act to Amend Certain Provisions of Republic Act No. 3046, as Amended by Republic Act No. 5446, to Define the Archipelagic Baselines of the Philippines and for Other Purposes, Mar. 10, 2009.

[22] The Permanent Mission of the People's Republic of China to the UN, Note CML/12/2009, Apr. 13, 2009.

[23] Id.

The U-shaped line appeared again in 2009 in Chinese protests to the submissions of Vietnam and Malaysia to the Commission on the Limits of the Continental Shelf (CLCS). Both claimed extended continental shelves in the South China Sea. In each of the demarches to its neighbors, Beijing asserted that it has "indisputable sovereignty over the islands in the South China Sea and the adjacent waters, and enjoys sovereign rights and jurisdiction over the relevant waters as well as the seabed and subsoil thereof [as depicted on the U-shaped map]."[24]

In March 2010, during private discussions with American diplomats, one official from the government in Beijing apparently took the unprecedented step of declaring that the South China Sea was a "core interest" of China, a description previously reserved only for China's most sensitive internal security concerns—Tibet, Xinjiang and Taiwan.[25] If China indeed elevated the South China Sea dispute to the level of a "core interest" it is a significant development, since China has not been reluctant to use force and coercive diplomacy to advance its position under those circumstances.

Chinese scholars and officials have said in confidence that the "core interest" statement may have been incorrectly reported and that the official actually suggested that it was in China's core interest to find a peaceful resolution to the disputes in the South China Sea. This more nuanced interpretation cannot be verified, however. Furthermore, if true, there has not been a public clarification of the statement. In any event, by the spring of 2011, having raised alarm bells in the halls of government from Delhi to D.C., China was easing away from the perception that it regarded the South China Sea as a core national interest.[26] But if Chinese officials genuinely regard the South China Sea as a core interest, it may suggest Beijing no longer sees room for compromise with the other South China Sea claimants and makes it more likely that China could resort to force.[27]

11.1.1.2 Sansha City

In June 2012, Beijing established a new prefecture level city (Sansha—the "city of three sands" in Chinese) to administer the Paracels (Xisha), Macclesfield Bank (Zhongsha) and the Spratlys (Nansha). The seat of government for the new city is

---

[24] Copies of China's protests to the Vietnamese and Malaysian submissions are available at http://www.un.org/Depts/los/clcs_new/submissions_files/mysvnm33_09/chn_2009re_mys_vnm_e.pdf and http://www.un.org/Depts/los/clcs_new/submissions_files/vnm37_09/chn_2009re_vnm.pdf.
[25] Peter Lee, *US Goes Fishing for Trouble*, ASIA TIMES, July 2010.
[26] Edward Wong, *China Hedges Over Whether South China Sea Is a 'Core Interest' Worth War*, N.Y. TIMES, Mar. 30, 2011, at A12.
[27] Greg Torode & Minnie Chan, *For China, War Games Are Steel Behind the Statements*, SOUTH CHINA MORNING POST, July 31, 2010.

on Woody Island (Yongxing) in the Paracels.[28] Woody Island, which is about half the size of New York City's Central Park, has a population of about 1,000 inhabitants (mostly Chinese fishermen).[29] There is little infrastructure on the island. The feature has a small airstrip, post office, bank, supermarket and hospital. The only fresh water on the island is shipped from mainland China.[30]

In July 2012, the PRC Central Military Commission issued a statement that it was establishing a military garrison at Sansha city on Woody Island. The new unit will be responsible for "national defense mobilization, guarding the city and supporting local emergency rescue and disaster relief, and carrying out military missions."[31] Senior Colonel Cai Xihong and Senior Colonel Liao Chaoyi have been named as the new garrison's commander and political commissar, respectively.[32] Hanoi and Manila have both protested the establishment of Sansha City and the garrison.

The U.S. Senate has also criticized China's behavior in the South China Sea, unanimously passing a resolution on August 2, 2012, condemning Beijing's unilateral action establishing Sansha city and stationing military forces on Woody Island.[33] The Senate Resolution was followed the next day by a press statement from the U.S. Department of State to express concern over the increased tensions in the South China Sea:

> ...We are concerned by the increase in tensions in the South China Sea and are monitoring the situation closely. Recent developments include an uptick in confrontational rhetoric, disagreements over resource exploitation, coercive economic actions, and the incidents around the Scarborough Reef, including the use of barriers to deny access. In particular, China's upgrading of the administrative level of Sansha City and establishment of a new military garrison there covering disputed areas of the South China Sea run counter to collaborative diplomatic efforts to resolve differences and risk further escalating tensions in the region.[34]

11.1.1.3 Regional Reaction to China's Claims

The body of statements and actions by China indicate the country claims sovereignty over all land features within the U-shaped map, as well as their adjacent territorial seas. It also appears from its 2009 protests to the CLCS that China is

---

[28] Pia Lee-Brago, *China Tightening Grip on Spratlys*, THE PHILIPPINE STAR, June 23, 2012.
[29] *China Dubs Tiny Island New City in Sea Claim Bid*, ASSOCIATED PRESS, July 24, 2012.
[30] Id.
[31] Ben Blanchard and Wan Xu, *China to formally garrison disputed South China Sea*, REUTERS, July 23, 2012.
[32] *China Appoints Officers To Sansha Garrison*, SOUTH CHINA MORNING POST, July 27, 2012.
[33] S. Res. 524, 112th Congress, 2d Session, Aug. 2, 2012.
[34] Press Statement on South China Sea by Patrick Ventrell, Acting Deputy Spokesperson, Office of Press Relations, U.S. Department of State, Washington, DC, August 3, 2012, http://www.state.gov/r/pa/prs/ps/2012/08/196022.htm.

claiming EEZ-like sovereign rights over the relevant waters, as well as the seabed and subsoil thereof, contained within the U-shaped line. Beijing's insistent but remarkably vague historic waters claims are dubious, since international law requires a State to demonstrate its open, effective, long-term, and continuous exercise of authority over the waters, coupled with an actual showing of acquiescence by other States in the exercise of that authority, in order to substantiate an historic waters claim.[35] Thus, historic waters claims are notoriously difficult to maintain, and the ephemeral nature of China's assertion makes it even more tenuous. Consequently, every other state that has expressed an opinion on the issue has openly challenged Beijing's position.

Vietnam, Malaysia, Indonesia and the Philippines have all rejected the U-shaped claim.[36] The Philippines challenged the claims by China on the relevant waters as well as the seabed and subsoil thereof that are reflected in the 9-dash line map attached to Notes Verbales CML/17/2009 and CML/18/2009.[37] Likewise, Vietnam asserted that "China's claim over the islands and adjacent waters in the Eastern Sea (South China Sea) as manifested in the map attached with Notes Verbale CLM/17/2009 and CLM/18/2009 has no legal, historical or factual basis, [and] therefore is null and void."[38]

Malaysia has indicated that its joint submission with Vietnam to the CLCS constitutes a "legitimate undertaking in implementation of the obligations of States Parties to...UNCLOS," and that the Government of Malaysia "has informed the People's Republic of China of its position prior to the submission...to the Commission on the Limits of the Continental Shelf."[39]

Similarly, even though it is not a party to the dispute, Indonesia has protested China's U-shaped claim to the UN Secretary General, indicating that the "so called nine-dotted-lines map as contained in... circular note Number CML/17/2009...clearly lacks international legal basis and is tantamount to

---

[35] Senate Treaty Doc. 103–39, Oct. 7, 1994.
[36] Note Verbale, Permanent Mission of the Socialist Republic of Vietnam to the United Nations, No. 86/HC-2009, May 8, 2009; Note Verbale, Permanent Mission of Malaysia to the United Nations, No. HA 24/09 May 20, 2009; Note Verbale, Philippine Mission to the United Nations, No. 000819, Aug. 4, 2009, and 000228, Apr. 5, 2011; and Note Verbale, Permanent Mission of the Republic of Indonesia, No. 480/POL-703/VII/10, July 8, 2010.
[37] Note Verbale, Philippine Mission to the United Nations, No. 000819, Aug. 4, 2009 and Permanent Mission of the Republic of the Philippines to the United Nations, No. 00228, in reply to People's Republic of China Notes Verbales CML/17/2009, May 7, 2009 and CML/18/2009, May 7, 2009, to the Secretary-General, Apr. 5, 2011.
[38] Note Verbale, Permanent Mission of the Socialist Republic of Vietnam to the United Nations, No. 86/HC-2009, May 8, 2009.
[39] Note Verbale, Permanent Mission of Malaysia to the United Nations, No. HA 24/09, May 20, 2009.

upset the UNCLOS 1982."[40] In addition, in September 2011, Indonesia and Vietnam agreed to institute joint patrols in the South China Sea to improve maritime security along their maritime border.[41]

On June 20, 2011, Singapore uncharacteristically called on China to clarify its claims in the South China Sea. The Foreign Ministry of Singapore stated, "It is in China's own interests to clarify its claims in the South China Sea with more precision as the current ambiguity as to their extent has caused serious concerns in the international community." The statement concluded by calling on the parties to the dispute to "act with restraint to create conditions conducive to the peaceful settlement of these disputes and the continuation of peace, stability and growth" in the region.[42]

India also questioned China's "U-shaped" claim after an unidentified PLA-N ship challenged the *INS Airavat* in July 2011, for "entering Chinese waters" 45 nm off the coast of Vietnam. Indian authorities downplayed the incident, but stated that all nations have "full freedom to transit through these waters or high seas" and that "for any country to proclaim ownership or question the right of passage by any other nation is unacceptable."[43]

11.1.2 *Vietnam's Maritime Claims*

Vietnam claims all of the Hoang Sa Islands (Paracel Islands) and Truong Sa Islands (Spratly Islands) as Vietnamese territory. It currently occupies over 20 islets in the Spratly Island chain. Hanoi's claims are generally based on historical grounds, including demonstrable French claims dating back to the 1930s, and the continental shelf principle—sovereignty derived from the extension of the continental shelf measured from the coastal landmass of Vietnam.

Vietnam is heavily dependent on the rich fishing grounds of the South China Sea as a primary source of protein for its population, and creation of the EEZ was originally tied to the subsistence fishing needs of coastal communities. Hanoi has also been actively exploring and exploiting the hydrocarbon reserves off its coast to sustain its economic growth. In response, China has taken a much more aggressive stance on what it sees as an infringement on its maritime claims in the South China Sea.

China has also threatened U.S. and international oil and gas companies, including British Petroleum in 2007 and Exxon/Mobil in 2008, with loss of business

---

[40] Note Verbale, Permanent Mission of the Republic of Indonesia, No. 480/POL-703/VII/10, July 8, 2010.
[41] *Indonesia, Vietnam Agree Joint Maritime Patrols*, CHANNEL NEWS ASIA, Sept. 14, 2011.
[42] Raju Gopalkrishnan, *Singapore Asks China to Clarify Claims on S. China Sea*, REUTERS, June 20, 2011.
[43] Ben Bland & Girija Shivakumar, *China confronts Indian Navy Vessel*, FINANCIAL TIMES, Aug. 31, 2011.

opportunities in China if they did not halt joint exploration ventures with Vietnam in the South China Sea.[44] China reacted similarly to an announced deal between India's state-owned Oil and Natural Gas Corporation (ONGC) Videsh Ltd. and PetroVietnam to explore and develop oil and gas blocks in the South China Sea within Vietnam's EEZ. On September 22, 2011, the Chinese Foreign Ministry condemned the deal, arguing any hydrocarbon exploration in the South China Sea was subject to Beijing's approval. Deals cut without Chinese consent were deemed an infringement on China's sovereignty and, therefore, illegal. New Delhi responded that the blocks in question were well within Vietnam's EEZ and that ONGC would continue its exploration activities.[45]

To further exacerbate the situation, on June 25, 2012, China National Offshore Oil Corp (CNOOC) announced that it was opening nine offshore oil blocks to joint exploration with foreign companies. Seven of these blocks are located in the Zhongjiannan Basin and two in the Wan'an and Nanweixi Basins. All of the blocks are on the western fringe of the U-shaped line and overlap with Vietnam's 200-nm EEZ. Hanoi condemned the announcement, noting that the offer violated Vietnam's sovereignty and called on CNOOC to immediately withdraw the solicitation.[46] PetroVietnam has also urged foreign companies to refrain from bidding on the CNOOC offer.[47]

Chinese activities in Vietnam's EEZ have not been limited to interference with resource exploration. For example, on July 22, 2011, an unidentified PLA-N warship and the Indian amphibious assault vessel, *INS Airavat*, were involved in a brief spat. The Indian warship departed the Vietnamese city of Nha Trang and was on its way to Hai Phong, approximately 45 nm off the Vietnamese coast, when it was hailed by a PLA-N warship. After identifying itself as the "Chinese Navy," the caller stated that the *Airavat* was "entering Chinese waters."[48] New Delhi responded by indicating that all nations have "full freedom to transit through these waters or high seas" and that "for any country to proclaim ownership or question the right to passage by any other nation is unacceptable."[49] Similarly, in June of 2012, four Indian Navy ships, including the *INS Shivalik* (F47), en route to South Korea from the Philippines were hailed by a PLA-N frigate. It was apparent from the tone of the transmission from the PLA-N ship—"welcome to the South China Sea,

---

[44] Peter Navarro, *China Stirs Over Offshore Oil Pact*, AsiaTimes.com, July 23, 2008.
[45] Michael Martina, *China paper condemns Vietnam-India Energy Cooperation*, Reuters, Sept. 22, 2011.
[46] *China's Energy Moves in the South China Sea*, Stratfor, June 29, 2012.
[47] *CNOOC Offers 26 Offshore Blocks to Foreign Partners*, Dow Jones Newswires, Aug. 28, 2012.
[48] Ben Bland & Girija Shivakumar, *China Confronts Indian Navy Vessel*, Financial Times, Aug. 31, 2011.
[49] Id.

Foxtrot-47"—that the Indian ships were entering "Chinese" waters.[50] The PLA-N frigate then shadowed the Indian vessels for 12 hours. Prior to the incident, the Indian warships had visited Singapore, Vietnam and the Philippines.[51]

On May 16, 2011, China instituted its annual four-month unilateral fishing ban for the northern part of the South China Sea, supposedly to conserve the region's depleted fish stocks. Similar bans in previous years have resulted in strong protests by Hanoi, as Vietnamese subsistence fishermen rely on the traditional fishing grounds. The ban has resulted in the arrest of hundreds of Vietnamese fishermen and confiscation of their vessels and fish catch by Chinese officials. In 2009, for example, Chinese authorities seized 33 Vietnamese fishing vessels, confiscated their catch and arrested 433 crewmembers.[52]

Ten days later, on May 26, 2011, three CMS patrol vessels harassed the *Binh Minh 02*, a survey ship operated by PetroVietnam approximately 116 nm off Dai Lanh, well within Vietnam's EEZ and some 600 km south of China's Hainan Island. The incident ended when one of the CMS patrol vessels intentionally cut the cable being towed by the survey ship.[53] Hanoi subsequently deployed eight ships to escort the *Binh Minh 02* so that it could complete its work. Then on June 9, 2011, a Chinese fishing vessel (No. *62226*) that was operating with two CMS patrol vessels rammed the survey cable of the *Viking 2*, as the PetroVietnam ship was conducting a seismic survey approximately 60 nm off the southern coast of Vietnam. The incident occurred over 1,000 km from Hainan Island, China. Both incidents took place within Vietnam's EEZ.

Hanoi immediately protested the incidents, claiming that the "premeditated attacks" had occurred within its EEZ. Beijing rejected the complaint and called on Vietnam to stop violating "Chinese sovereignty."[54] China's official response to the *Binh Minh 02* incident was posted on the Foreign Ministry's Internet homepage at the end of May, 2011:

> China holds a consistent and clear-cut position on the South China Sea issue. China opposes Vietnam's oil and gas exploration activities within the waters under the jurisdiction of China, which undermine China's rights and interests as well as jurisdiction over the South China Sea and violate the bilateral consensus on the South China Sea issue. Actions taken by China's competent authorities are regular maritime law enforcement and surveillance activities in the waters under the jurisdiction of China.
>
> China has been committed to peace and stability of the South China Sea. We stand ready to make joint efforts with relevant parties to seek proper solutions to relevant

---

[50] Ananth Krishnan, *In South China Sea, A Surprise Chinese Escort For Indian Ships*, THE HINDU, June 14, 2012.
[51] Id.
[52] *China Seizes Vietnamese Fishing Boat*, DEUTSCHE PRESSE-AGENTUR, Apr. 19, 2010.
[53] *VN Demands China Stop Sovereignty Violations*, VIETNAM PLUS, May 29, 2011.
[54] *Sea Spat Raises China-Vietnam Tensions*, NAMVIET NEWS, June 10, 2011.

disputes and conscientiously implement the Declaration on the Conduct of Parties in the South China Sea, with a view to safeguarding the stability of the South China Sea in real earnest.[55]

A few weeks later, without specifically referring to Vietnam, a spokesperson for the Chinese Foreign Ministry stated that "a country" had taken "unilateral actions to impair China's sovereignty and maritime rights and interests [and] released groundless and irresponsible remarks with the attempt to expand and complicate the dispute over the South China Sea."[56] Beijing also claimed that the *Viking 2* incident occurred when the net of a Chinese fishing boat that was being pursued by an armed Vietnamese patrol boat became entangled with the cable of the Vietnamese survey vessel.[57] Beijing's explanation is confusing, since the fishing boat incident took place in an area where the Chinese annual fishing ban was in effect—making it unlikely that fishing nets were in the water. Vietnam countered with an unprecedented live-fire exercise 20 nm off its coast.[58]

Then in July 2011, Vietnamese naval units participated in a bilateral exercise off Danang with units from the U.S. Seventh Fleet—*USS Chung-Hoon* (DDG-93), *USS Preble* (DDG-56) and a rescue and salvage ship. The exercise, which is designed to strengthen military ties between the two former enemies, included a number of non-combatant activities, including a search-and-rescue exercise, navigation training, and several community-service projects.[59] A similar exercise, involving the *USS John S. McCain* (DDG-56), was conducted in 2010 a few months before Vietnam's Prime Minister Nguyen Tan Dung announced at the closing of the 17th ASEAN summit that his country was reopening the sprawling naval complex at Cam Ranh Bay to foreign navies.[60]

The bilateral exchanges continued in April 2012 with a five-day exercise in Danang, including non-combatant events such as navigation and maintenance skills. This time, the U.S. Seventh Fleet flagship, *USS Blue Ridge* (LCC-19), and the *USS Chafee* (DDG-90), and the *USNS Safeguard* (T-ARS-50) participated in the event.[61] And in June 2012, U.S. Secretary of Defense Leon Panetta paid an official visit to Vietnam, stopping at the Cam Ranh Bay port facility where a U.S. supply ship, the *USNS Richard E. Byrd* (T-AKE-4), was undergoing repairs.[62]

---

[55] Peter Lee, *Southeast Asia Rises in US Reset*, ASIA TIMES ONLINE, June 4, 2011.
[56] Tania Branigan, *Vietnam Holds Live-fire Exercises as Territorial Dispute with China Escalates*, THE GUARDIAN, June 14, 2011.
[57] *Sea Spat Raises China-Vietnam Tensions*, NAMVIET NEWS, June 10, 2011.
[58] Branigan, *Vietnam Holds Live-fire Exercises.*
[59] Patrick Barta, *U.S., Vietnam in Exercises Amid Tensions With China*, WALL ST. J., July 16, 2011.
[60] *Vietnam to Reopen Cam Ranh Bay to Foreign Fleets: PM*, BANGKOK POST, Oct. 31, 2010.
[61] *Vietnam, U.S. To Hold Five Day Naval Exchange*, AGENCE FRANCE-PRESSE, Apr. 17, 2012.
[62] Gopal Ratnam, *Cam Ranh Bay Lures Panetta Seeking U.S. Return to Vietnam Port*, BLOOMBERG NEWS, June 4, 2012.

Vietnam has also embarked on a major naval expansion. In 2011, the Vietnam People's Navy purchased two Russian-built *Gepard*-class light frigates featuring the *Uran-E* missile system, also nicknamed the *Harpoonski* due to its similarity to the U.S. *Harpoon* anti-ship missile. Two additional frigates have been ordered from the Gorky Shipbuilding Plant. Vietnam has also purchased two *Molniya*-class corvettes from Russia armed with SS-N-25 *Switchblade* anti-ship missiles, which are augmented Uran-Es. In addition, Vietnam has acquired a license to indigenously build an additional ten corvettes. Vietnam finalized a contract to buy four Dutch *Sigma*-class corvettes. Of greater significance, however, is Hanoi's order for six diesel-powered *Kilo*-class submarines from Russia. One submarine will be delivered each year beginning in 2013, and it is expected that Vietnam will turn to India to provide training for Vietnamese crews. On the aviation side, Vietnam had at least 20 Su-30MK2 and 27 Su-27 fighter jet aircraft at the end of 2012. Additionally, six DHC-6 Twin Otter aircraft, purchased from Canada to improve Vietnam's naval surveillance capabilities, will be delivered between 2012 and 2014.[63]

Beijing, however, appears intent on establishing its sovereignty over the area, making the situation ripe for conflict. In February 2012, for example, China prevented 11 Vietnamese fishermen from taking safe harbor in the Paracel Islands after experiencing a violent storm at sea. Under general principles of international law reflected in Article 18 of UNCLOS, ships seeking shelter from a storm are normally allowed to enter a foreign port without notice or consent of the coastal State. A month later, Chinese officials detained two Vietnamese fishing vessels and their 21 crewmembers for illegally fishing near the Paracel Islands. Vietnam strongly protested the detentions, stating that China had seriously violated Vietnamese sovereignty and demanding the immediate and unconditional release of the fishermen. Chinese demands to pay a ¥ 70,000 ($11,000) fine were also rejected.[64]

11.1.3 *The Philippines' Maritime Claims*

The Philippines claims only a portion of the Spratly Islands, referred to by the Philippines as the Kalayaan Island Group (KIG). The Philippines occupies eight features within the KIG, and the Philippine government refers to its EEZ within the South China Sea as the West Philippine Sea. Manila's claims are based on the proximity principle, reinforced by the explorations of the Filipino explorer Tómas Cloma between 1947 and 1956. The KIG was officially claimed by the Philippines in 1971 on the grounds that the islands were *terra nullius* and not part of the

---

[63] *Vietnam Builds Naval Muscle*, ASIA TIMES, Mar. 28, 2012.
[64] *Vietnam, China in New Spat Over Fishermen Detentions*, AGENCE FRANCE-PRESSE, Mar. 22, 2012.

Spratly Islands. The KIG subsequently was designated as part of Palawan Province in 1972.[65]

Under the principle that land dominates the sea, the Philippines argues that it is exercising sovereignty and jurisdiction over the waters around the KIG or adjacent to each relevant geological feature of the Kalayaan Island, which is under the local government control of the Municipality of Kalayaan. Finally, the Republic of the Philippines regards all relevant waters, seabed and subsoil in KIG as part of Philippine territory, since the nation is an archipelagic state.

The Philippines' KIG claims have not, however, gone unchallenged by Beijing. In January 1995, several years after the U.S. base closures at Subic Bay and Clark Air Base, China secretly occupied Mischief Reef, an islet located within the Philippine EEZ, 130 miles from Palawan Island.[66] The reef is strategically situated astride one of Asia's most important sea lanes, the Palawan Strait. Despite repeated protests by Manila to withdraw from the islet, China has continued its military build-up on the reef.[67] Operating from the reef, PLA forces could use the facilities as a forward operating base to disrupt maritime traffic transiting the Malacca and Singapore Straits to the Philippines and Northern Asia.

The Philippines has similarly objected to claims by several of its neighbors that impinge on the KIG.[68] On April 5, 2011, the Philippine Mission to the United Nations issued a Note Verbale that states:

> FIRST, the Kalayaan Island Group (KIG) constitutes an integral part of the Philippines. The Republic of the Philippines has sovereignty and jurisdiction over the geological features in the KIG.
>
> SECOND, the Philippines, under the Roman notion of *dominium maris* and the international law principle of *la terre domine la mer*, which states that the land dominates the sea, necessarily exercises sovereignty and jurisdiction over the waters around or adjacent to each relevant geological feature of the KIG as provided for [in UNCLOS].
>
> At any rate, the extent of the waters that are "adjacent" to the relevant geological features are definite and determinable under UNCLOS, specifically under Article 121 (Regime of Islands), of the said Convention.
>
> THIRD, since the adjacent waters of the relevant geological features are definite and subject to legal and technical measurement, the claim as well by the People's Republic of China on the "relevant waters as well as the seabed and subsoil thereof" (as reflected in the so-called 9-dash line map attached to Notes Verbales CML/17/2009 dated 7 May 2009 and CML/18/2009 dated 7 May 2009) outside the aforementioned

---

[65] South China Sea Tables and Maps, Table 1, Territorial Claims in the Spratly and Paracel Islands, www.SouthChinaSea.org.

[66] *China's Syndrome: Ambiguity; What Seizing a Tiny Reef Says About Beijing's Soul*, WASH. POST, Mar. 19, 1995, at A1.

[67] THE INVENTORY OF CONFLICT & ENVIRONMENT (ICE). CASE STUDY NO. 21, SPRATLY ISLANDS DISPUTE, May 1997.

[68] Id.

relevant geological features in the KIG and their "adjacent waters" would have no basis under international law, specifically UNCLOS.

> With respect to these areas, sovereignty and jurisdiction or sovereign rights, as the case may be, necessarily appertain or belong to the appropriate coastal or archipelagic state—the Philippines—to which these bodies of waters as well as seabed and subsoil appurtenant, either in the nature of Territorial Sea, or 200 mile Exclusive Economic Zone, or Continental Shelf....[69]

In January 2012, Manila protested the presence of two Chinese vessels and a PLA-N warship that were spotted in the vicinity of Escoda (Sabina) Shoal, about 70 nm from Palawan.[70] Malacañang[71] indicated that the military airfield on Pag-asa (Hope) Island would be upgraded, and $283 million is earmarked to acquire new patrol ships, aircraft, and radars to protect Philippine interests in the South China Sea.[72] Refurbishment of the seaport and runway on Pag-asa began in April 2012—officially to attract commercial business and tourism to the island. Once the improvements are complete, however, some speculate Pag-asa Island could become a military outpost for U.S. and Philippine military forces.[73]

Beijing has expressed concern over the proposed improvements, indicating that Manila's actions would violate the spirit of the 2002 Declaration of Conduct and serve "no purpose but to undermine peace and stability in the region and sabotage China-Philippines relationship."[74] The Philippine Government, however, appears undeterred, particularly given that China has used the decade since the adoption of the Code of Conduct to strengthen its position throughout the South China Sea.

An editorial in the *Global Times* in late January 2012 criticized military ties between Washington and Manila and called for economic sanctions against the Philippines.[75] Subsequent statements have been somewhat more conciliatory, however. During a press interview in March 2012, Major General Jin Yinan indicated that China would not settle its disputes by pursuing "gunboat

---

[69] Id.
[70] Jerry Esplanada, *Philippines Protests Intrusion of 3 Chinese Vessels*, PHILIPPINE DAILY INQUIRER, Jan. 8, 2012.
[71] Malacañang Palace is the official residence and principle workplace of the President of the Philippines.
[72] Jaime Laude, *AFP to Maintain Presence in Spratlys*, PHILIPPINE STAR, Mar. 28, 2011, *Philippines to Bolster Watch in Disputed Spratlys*, BUSINESS WEEK, Mar. 28, 2011, and R. DE CASTRO & W. LOHMAN, U.S.–PHILIPPINES PARTNERSHIP IN THE CAUSE OF MARITIME DEFENSE, BACKGROUNDER # 2593, Aug. 8, 2011.
[73] Carlo Munoz, Reports, *US, Philippines Building New Naval Base in Spratlys*, THE HILL, Apr. 3, 2012 and Gerry Albert, *PH government now building Naval Base in Spratlys for US troops*, ALLVOICES.COM, Mar. 31, 2012.
[74] *Philippine lawmakers fly to Spratlys amid China warnings*, PHILIPPINE DAILY INQUIRER, July 20, 2011.
[75] *China Calls For Calm After Philippine Offer to U.S.*, AGENCE FRANCE-PRESSE, Jan. 29, 2012.

diplomacy."[76] The general is a member of the Chinese People's Political Consultative Conference and a professor at the National Defense University. Similarly, in her first press conference after assuming her post as the new Chinese ambassador to the Philippines, Ma Keqing reassured Malacañang that China had no intention of using force to interfere in the affairs of any of the South China Sea claimants. With regard to Reed Bank, the Ambassador stressed the need for both sides to focus on joint development of the Western Philippine Sea. Philippine Foreign Secretary Albert del Rosaria welcomed Chinese investment in developing areas under dispute in the region, but indicated joint development was not a viable option in areas like Reed Bank that are an integral part of the Philippines.[77]

Manila has sought assurances from the United States that it will provide military support to the Philippines in the event of conflict. Article IV of the U.S.-Philippines Mutual Defense Treaty (MDT) states that "[e]ach Party recognizes that an armed attack in the Pacific area on either of the Parties would be dangerous to its own peace and safety and declares that it would act to meet the common dangers in accordance with its constitutional processes." Article V defines an armed attack on either of the Parties "to include an armed attack on the metropolitan territory of either of the Parties, or on the island territories under its jurisdiction in the Pacific Ocean, its armed forces, public vessels or aircraft in the Pacific."[78]

Manila called for increased bilateral exercises with U.S. forces and has offered the United States greater access to civilian airfields throughout the Philippines for logistical support and temporary deployment of U.S. military aircraft, including surveillance aircraft.[79] The April 2012 *Balikatan* exercise, for example, included a combined U.S.-Filipino amphibious war game and an offshore oil platform defense exercise near Palawan. Perhaps of greater significance, Japanese, Australian, Malaysian, Indonesian, Singaporean and South Korean forces participated in the humanitarian assistance/disaster relief command post exercise at Camp Aguinaldo in in Quezon City, Manila.[80]

A few month later, on June 5, 2012, the Chairman of the U.S. Joint Chiefs of Staff, General Martin Dempsey, and Philippine Defense Undersecretary Honorio Azcueta met at Camp Aguinaldo to discuss ways to share information in real time

---

[76] Ma Haoliang & Jia Lei, *PRC Military Scholar Says China Will Not Settle Regional Disputes by Force*, HONG KONG TA KUNG PAO ONLINE, Mar. 16, 2012, http://www.takunpao.com.

[77] Jerry Esplanada, *China Will Not Use Force in Spratlys, Says New Envoy*, PHILIPPINE DAILY INQUIRER, Mar. 16, 2012.

[78] The Mutual Defense Treaty between the Philippines and the United States of America 3 U.S.T. 3947, T.I.A.S. 2529, 177 U.N.T.S. 77 (1951).

[79] Manuel Mogato & Rosemarie Francisco, *Manila Offers U.S. Wider Military Access, Seeks Weapons*, REUTERS, Mar. 29, 2012.

[80] *SDF [Japan Self-Defense Forces] To Join U.S.-Filipino Military Drill*, JAPAN TIMES, Mar. 5, 2012 and Xu Tianran, *War Games to Deter China*, GLOBAL TIMES (China), Apr. 7, 2012.

and to reaffirm their commitments under the MDT.[81] Two days later, following a state visit by President Benigno Aquino to the United States, Washington and Manila agreed to establish a National Coast Watch Center aimed at enhancing Manila's maritime domain awareness in the South China Sea.[82] The new surveillance system is used to detect unauthorized entry into Philippine waters, as well as guard against illegal fishing and other transnational threats, such as human trafficking, piracy, narcotics trafficking and maritime terrorism.[83]

An editorial in the *Liberation Army Daily* warned that the United States was "meddling" in the region, and that the Balikatan exercise, in particular, raised the risk of military confrontation in the South China Sea.[84] Lieutenant General Duane Thiessen, Commander of U.S. Marine Forces Pacific, however, reaffirmed U.S. defense obligations under the MDT. General Thiessen stated "[t]he United States and the Philippines have a mutual defense treaty which guarantees that we get involved in each other's defense and that is self-explanatory."[85]

As an additional hedge against possible Chinese aggression, the Philippines also sought to strengthen its defense ties with Vietnam. In 2011, the two Spratly claimants signed a memorandum of understanding (MOU) that called for joint patrols in the vicinity of Northeast Cay, which is occupied by the Philippines, and Southeast Cay, which is three kilometers away and occupied by Vietnam. A standard operating procedure to implement the Joint Patrol MOU was signed in March 2012 by Vice Admiral Alex Pama (Armed Forces Philippines Navy Flag Officer in Command) and Admiral Nguyen Van Hien (Vietnam's Navy Commander in Chief). At the same time, Pama and Hien signed a memorandum of understanding on the Enhancement of Mutual Cooperation and Information Sharing between the two navies.[86]

The Philippines and Vietnam have additionally agreed to establish a "hotline between their coast guards and maritime police to strengthen their capability to monitor maritime incidents, such as piracy and incursions into their territorial waters."[87] China has warned Manila and Hanoi that any joint military exercises or patrols in Chinese-claimed waters would complicate the ongoing territorial

---

[81] Alexis Romero, *PHL, US To Share Real-Time Info on Security Developments*, PHILIPPINE STAR, June 5, 2012.
[82] Barbara Dacanay, *Philippines, US erect National Coast Watch Centre*, GULF NEWS, June 17, 2012.
[83] Id.
[84] Chris Buckley, *China Military Warns Of Confrontation Over Seas*, REUTERS, Apr. 21, 2012.
[85] Alexis Romero, *U.S. Commander Reaffirms Defense Pact With Phl*, AGENCE FRANCE-PRESSE, Apr. 23, 2012.
[86] Rene Acosta, *PHL, Vietnam Navies Jointly Patrol Spratlys*, THE BUSINESS MIRROR (Philippines), Mar. 27, 2012.
[87] *Manila, Hanoi Try Football Diplomacy In Spratlys*, PHILIPPINE DAILY INQUIRER, Apr. 10, 2012.

dispute and damage peace and stability in the region.[88] But Vietnam and the Philippines appear not to be intimidated, agreeing to allow their sailors to play soccer matches and basketball games on the disputed features as a confidence building measure.[89]

11.1.4 ASEAN and the Declaration on the Conduct of Parties

From the time of its adoption, countries have questioned whether the 2002 *Declaration on the Conduct of Parties in the South China Sea* (DOC) between China and ten Southeast Asian nations was sufficient to avoid armed conflict.[90] The DOC was flawed from the beginning. Paragraph 5 of the draft declaration stated that parties to the agreement should not undertake activities that would escalate tension to affect stability in the region. The initial draft text prohibited the erection of new structures in the disputed areas. At the insistence of China, and with the reluctant acceptance of Vietnam, the term "erection of structures" was dropped from the text.[91] The parties reaffirmed, however, respect and commitment to the freedom of navigation and overflight of aircraft above the South China Sea as "provided for by the universally recognized principles of international law."[92]

During the first week of June 2011, CMS and PLA-N ships were observed unloading building material on Iroquois Reef and Amy Douglas Bank, which is approximately 125 nm from Palawan Island. Chinese military forces were observed erecting markers on the uninhabited feature.[93] If the report is true, it would indicate activity inconsistent with the DOC, which encourages the Parties "to exercise self-restraint in the conduct of activities that would complicate or escalate disputes and affect peace and stability including, among others, refraining from action of inhabiting on the presently uninhabited islands, reefs, shoals, cays, and other features and to handle their differences in a constructive manner."[94]

In a similar vein, in mid-June 2011, Beijing announced that Marine Oil 981, a massive new semi-submersible deepwater oil platform, would deploy to the South China Sea in July 2011. The massive rig is 114 meters long, 140 meters high,

---

[88] *China Warns Vietnam, Philippines Against Damaging Peace In Sea*, Kyodo News, Mar. 30, 2012.
[89] *Manila, Hanoi Try Football Diplomacy in Spratlys*, CBS News, Apr. 10, 2012.
[90] *Landmark Agreement on South China Sea*, Courier Mail (Queensland, Australia), Nov. 5, 2002, at 17.
[91] Hardev Kaur; Saiful Azhar Abdullah; Roziana Hamsawi, *Consensus reached on South China Se*, New Straits Times (Malaysia), Nov. 3, 2002, at 20.
[92] Id.
[93] Roel Landingin & Kathrin Hille, *China and Philippines Tensions Mount*, Financial Times, June 1, 2011.
[94] ASEAN Declaration on the Conduct of Parties in the South China Sea, Nov. 4, 2002, http://www.aseansec.org/13163.htm.

weighs 31,000 tons, can drill in waters up to 3,000 meters deep, and is capable of using a drill that can go as deep as 12,000 meters.[95] The Marine Oil 981 is China's latest strategic chess piece in the South China Sea. A few days later, the MSA's largest and most advanced patrol ship, the *Haixun-31*, set sail for a port call in Singapore via the Paracel and Spratly Islands. En route to its port visit, the 3,000-ton *Haixun-31* monitored shipping, conducted marine surveys, inspected oil wells, and completed a general mission to protect Chinese interests in the South China Sea.[96] In another show of force, Beijing announced that its new aircraft carrier would deploy to the South China Sea after its commissioning in September 2012.[97]

Chinese officials also issued a series of statements that will raise tensions. On June 9, 2011, China's ambassador in Manila, Liu Jianchao, warned the various claimants to stop searching for oil in the disputed region without Beijing's permission, indicating that China was "calling on other parties to stop searching for the possibility of exploiting resources in these areas where China has its claims."[98] Two weeks later, on June 21, 2011, the *People's Daily* ran a biting editorial that threatened Vietnam with armed intervention:

> If Vietnam wishes to create a war in the South China Sea, China will resolutely keep them company. China has the absolute might to crush the naval fleets sent from Vietnam. China will show no mercy to its rival due to 'global impact' concerns.[99]

The next day, China's Vice Foreign Minister Cui Tiankai warned the United States to stay out of the dispute. "The United States is not a claimant state to the dispute," Mr. Cui said, and he advised it would be "better for the United States to leave the dispute to be sorted out between the claimant states." In a somewhat more direct tone, he added: "I believe the individual countries are actually playing with fire, and I hope the fire will not be drawn to the United States." If the United States wants to play a role, Minister Cui suggested that Washington should "counsel restraint to those countries who've been frequently taking provocative action, and to ask them to be more responsible in their behavior."[100]

In August 2011, the *People's Daily* accused the Philippines of violating the DOC and re-affirmed that China would not "sit idly by while its territory is swallowed up by others." The editorial further warned, "Were there to be a serious strategic

---

[95] *Super Rig to Begin Testing this Week*, INVESTOR VILLAGE, June 14, 2011.
[96] *China Sends Patrol Ship into Disputed South China Sea*, BBC, June 16, 2011.
[97] *Chinese aircraft carrier to serve in South China Sea*, MARITIME SECURITY ASIA, Aug. 17, 2011.
[98] Jim Gomez, *China to Neighbors: Stop oil Search in Spratlys*, PHILIPPINE DAILY INQUIRER, June 9, 2011.
[99] Margie Mason, *Despite Dispute, Hanoi, Beijing Hold Exercises: Tempers Flare as Two Nations Spar over South China Sea*, WASH. TIMES, June 21, 2011.
[100] Edward Wong, *Beijing Warns U.S. About South China Sea Disputes*, N.Y. TIMES, June 22, 2011.

miscalculation on this matter, due consequences would have to be paid."[101] And an October 2011 editorial published in the *Global Times* cautioned that if the other South China Sea claimants do not "want to change their ways with China, they will need to prepare for the sounds of cannons."[102] Philippine Foreign Secretary del Rosario quickly condemned the editorial in the Chinese newspaper, which has close ties to the Chinese Communist Party, as "grossly irresponsible."[103]

In February 2012, the former Chinese Ambassador to the Philippines warned Manila that if the United States becomes involved in the South China Sea dispute, "there would be problems with China," and Beijing would certainly react.[104] The ambassador therefore advised that it would be unwise for the Philippines and other South China Sea claimants to "introduce Americans into the disputed waters."[105]

There may be little enthusiasm within ASEAN to directly challenge Chinese aggression in the South China Sea. All of the ASEAN member States are heavily dependent on China for their continued economic growth. However, that attitude may change over time as China becomes more intransigent and unwilling to resolve the dispute.

For instance, at the fifth meeting of the ASEAN Naval Chiefs (ANCM-5) in July, 2011, Vice Admiral Nguyen Van Hien, Deputy Defense Minister and Commander of the Vietnam People's Navy, called on the ASEAN navies to cooperate, indicating that "any violations of the national sovereignty of ASEAN countries [threatens peace and stability in the region and] would cause great concern inside and outside the region, especially with regards to any infringement of international laws...."[106]

Then in November 2011, ASEAN and Japan issued the Bali Declaration to enhance peace, stability and prosperity in the region through:

> Strategy 1: strengthening political-security cooperation in the region;
> Strategy 2: intensifying cooperation towards ASEAN community building;
> Strategy 3: enhancing ASEAN-Japan connectivity;
> Strategy 4: creating together a more disaster-resilient society; and
> Strategy 5: addressing together common regional and global challenges.[107]

---

[101] *China Lashes out at Philippines over Spratlys*, PHILIPPINE DAILY INQUIRER, Aug. 3, 2011.
[102] Estrella Torres, *DFA hits China over "Cannons" Statement*, ABS-CBN NEWS, Oct. 27, 2011.
[103] Id.
[104] Jerry Esplanada, *Ex-Chinese Envoys to Philippines: Keep US Out*, PHILIPPINE DAILY INQUIRER, Feb. 24, 2012.
[105] Id.
[106] *ASEAN Navy Chiefs Advance Cooperation*, VIET NAM NEWS, July 28, 2011.
[107] Joint Declaration for Enhancing ASEAN-Japan Strategic Partnership for Prospering Together (Bali Declaration), Nov. 18, 2011.

Under the first pillar of political-security cooperation, the declarants agreed on the need to resolve disputes peacefully, the significance of freedom of navigation and unimpeded commerce, the necessity to conclude a binding code of conduct for the South China Sea, and the importance of promoting regional defense and military cooperation:

I. Political-Security Cooperation

...

2. Continue to expand and deepen political and security cooperation at all levels in order to maintain regional peace and stability, to promote peaceful settlement of any disputes in the region in accordance with international law, to forge common vision and principles for the prosperity and stability in the region;

...

4. Promote and deepen ASEAN-Japan cooperation on maritime security and maritime safety in the region in accordance with universally-agreed principles of international law such as freedom of navigation, safety of navigation, unimpeded commerce and peaceful settlement of disputes, including the 1982 United Nations Convention on the Law of the Sea (UNCLOS) and other relevant international maritime law;

5. Welcome the adoption of the Guidelines for the implementation of the Declaration on the Conduct of Parties in the South China Sea and look forward to the eventual conclusion of a Code of Conduct in the South China Sea, so as to further contribute to peace, stability, respect of freedom and safety of navigation in and over-flight above the South China Sea, with adherence to international law;

...

12. Further promote defence and military cooperation and exchanges through bilateral and multilateral frameworks such as ADMM-Plus and the ARF....[108]

Finally, at the 20th ASEAN Summit in Phnom Penh on April 2, 2012, China motioned to eliminate a discussion of South China Sea issues from the Summit's agenda. The member States defeated the measure, however, embarrassing China and signaling solidarity against Beijing. China fears a combined effort by States in the region against it more than anything else. After a fruitful discussion on the issue, the ten ASEAN leaders agreed to draft a binding code of conduct for the South China Sea that would form the basis for further dialogue with Beijing.[109]

Even Myanmar, once thought to be solidly in China's camp, is reexamining its ties with Beijing as the government in Naypyidaw[110] prepares to assume the ASEAN Chair in 2014. Closer ties with the United States in early 2012 and suspension of a major dam project on the Irrawaddy River in Myitsone near the Chinese border have raised eyebrows in Beijing.[111]

---

[108] Id.
[109] *Summit a Success, But South China Sea Issue Remains: Analysts*, VOICE OF AMERICA/ KHMER, Apr. 5, 2012.
[110] Naypyidaw is the capital city of Myanmar.
[111] Yang Razali Kassim, *Myanmar's China Policy Shift: Preparing for ASEAN Chair?*, RSIS COMMENTARIES (RAJARATNAM SCHOOL OF INT'L STUDIES) No. 043/2012, Mar. 14, 2012.

11.2 American Security Relationships and the South China Sea

China's expansive maritime claims have led to greater U.S. attention in the region, just one example of how Beijing's touchy assertiveness undermines its own interests. Washington, however, has maintained its neutrality on the underlying legal merits of the competing claims to sovereignty over the South China Sea Islands. Nearly 20 years ago—on May 10, 1995—amid another period of rising tensions in the disputed region, the State Department issued an official statement on the Spratly Islands and the South China Sea:

> The United States is concerned that a pattern of unilateral actions and reactions in the South China Sea has increased tensions in that region. The United States strongly opposes the use or threat of force to resolve competing claims and urges all claimants to exercise restraint and to avoid destabilizing actions.
>
> The United States has an abiding interest in the maintenance of peace and stability in the South China Sea. The United States calls upon claimants to intensify diplomatic efforts which address issues related to competing claims, taking into account the interests of all parties, and which contribute to peace and prosperity in the region. The United States is willing to assist in any way that claimants deem helpful. The United States reaffirms its welcome of the 1992 ASEAN Declaration on the South China Sea.
>
> Maintaining freedom of navigation is a fundamental interest of the United States. Unhindered navigation by all ships and aircraft in the South China Sea is essential for the peace and prosperity of the entire Asia-Pacific region, including the United States.
>
> The United States takes no position on the legal merits of the competing claims to sovereignty over the various islands, reefs, atolls and cays in the South China Sea. The United States would, however, view with serious concern any maritime claim, or restriction on maritime activity, in the South China Sea that was not consistent with international law, including the 1982 United Nations Convention on the Law of the Sea.[112]

U.S. neutrality on the issue of sovereignty was reaffirmed on June 5, 2010, at the annual meeting of defense ministers in Singapore (Shangri-La Dialogue). In an address to his counterparts attending the meeting, U.S. Secretary of Defense Robert Gates indicated that the United States had a longstanding policy of defending freedom of navigation and that it would continue to do so. In response to China's "core interest" announcement, Secretary Gates stated that the South China Sea was an "area of growing concern" for the United States.[113] He emphasized that the South China Sea was "not only vital to those directly bordering it, but to

---

[112] U.S. Dep't of State, Daily Press Briefing, Office of the Spokesman, May 10, 1995.
[113] Remarks delivered by Secretary of Defense Robert M. Gates, Shangri-La Hotel, Singapore, June 5, 2010, http://www.defense.gov.

all nations with economic and security interests in Asia," and that U.S. policy was clear:

> ... [I]t is essential that stability, freedom of navigation, and free and unhindered economic development be maintained. We do not take sides on any competing sovereignty claims, but we do oppose the use of force and actions that hinder freedom of navigation. We object to any effort to intimidate U.S. corporations or those of any nation engaged in legitimate economic activity. All parties must work together to resolve differences through peaceful, multilateral efforts consistent with customary international law. The 2002 *Declaration of Conduct* was an important step in this direction, and we hope that concrete implementation of this agreement will continue.[114]

On July 23, 2010, at the 2010 ASEAN Regional Forum (ARF) in Vietnam, Secretary of State Hillary Clinton also took the opportunity to reemphasize the importance of the South China Sea, indicating that the "United States, like every nation, has a national interest in freedom of navigation, open access to Asia's maritime commons, and respect for international law in the South China Sea."[115] She elaborated that the United States supported a "collaborative diplomatic process by all claimants for resolving the various territorial disputes without coercion" and that the United States opposed "the use or threat of force by any claimant."[116] The United States, she said, "was neutral on the sovereignty issue, avoiding taking sides on the competing territorial disputes over land features in the South China Sea."[117]

She stressed, however, that the "claimants should pursue their territorial claims and the accompanying rights to maritime space" in accordance with UNCLOS and that "consistent with customary international law, legitimate claims to maritime space in the South China Sea should be derived solely from legitimate claims to land features."[118] The United States, she stated, was in support of the 2002 *ASEAN-China Declaration on the Conduct of Parties in the South China Sea (DOC)*, and she encouraged "the parties to reach agreement on a full code of conduct," and offered U.S. assistance "to facilitate initiatives and confidence building measures consistent with the declaration."[119] In conclusion, she stated that "it is in the interest of all claimants and the broader international community for unimpeded commerce to proceed under lawful conditions." Also, "respect for the interests of the international community and responsible efforts to address these unresolved claims will help create the conditions for resolution of the disputes

---

[114] Id.
[115] Remarks of Secretary of State Hillary Rodham Clinton at Press Availability of the Association of Southeast Asian Nations Regional Forum (ARF), National Convention Center, Hanoi, Vietnam, July 23, 2010.
[116] Id.
[117] Id.
[118] Id.
[119] Id.

and a lowering of regional tensions."[120] China responded to these statements with a renewed claim of "indisputable sovereignty" over the South China Sea.[121]

The Obama Administration's renewed emphasis on the South China Sea issue received strong support from the U.S. Senate. On June 27, 2011, the Senate passed Resolution 217 by unanimous consent. Noting that the South China Sea contains vital commercial shipping lines and points of access between the Indian Ocean and Pacific Ocean, the resolution calls for peaceful and multilateral resolution of the disputes in Southeast Asia. While recognizing that the United States is not a party to the disputes, the resolution reaffirmed "the United States has a national economic and a security interest in ensuring that no party uses force unilaterally to assert maritime territorial claims in East Asia."[122] The resolution also notes, that "like every nation, the United States has a national interest in freedom of navigation and open access to the maritime commons of Asia."[123] The United States "supports a collaborative diplomatic process by all claimants for resolving the various territorial disputes without coercion."[124] Accordingly, the resolution:

(1) reaffirms the strong support of the United States for the peaceful resolution of maritime territorial disputes in the South China Sea, and pledges continued efforts to facilitate a multilateral, peaceful process to resolve these disputes;
(2) deplores the use of force by naval and maritime security vessels from China in the South China Sea;
(3) calls on all parties to the territorial dispute to refrain from threatening force or using force to assert territorial claims; and
(4) supports the continuation of operations by the United States Armed Forces in support of freedom of navigation rights in international waters and air space in the South China Sea.[125]

Beijing immediately denounced the Senate action, indicating that, "freedom of shipping in the South China Sea has never been affected by the disputes...."[126] A Foreign Ministry representative added, "others without a direct stake should respect the efforts made by those directly concerned to resolve South China Sea disputes through dialogue and in a peaceful manner."[127] China's position misses an important point, however. When the United States and other maritime nations talk about "freedom of navigation," they are using the term in its broadest context, to include both navigation and overflight, and other internationally lawful

---

[120] Id.
[121] Greg Torode & Minnie Chan, *For China, War Games Are Steel Behind the Statements*, SOUTH MORNING CHINA POST, July 31, 2010.
[122] S. Res. 217, 112th Congress, 1st Session, June 27, 2011.
[123] Id.
[124] Id.
[125] Id.
[126] Ariel Zirulnick, *China rejects US involvement in South China Sea Disputes*, CHRISTIAN SCI. MON., June 28, 2011.
[127] Id.

uses of the sea. For example, there are a full range of high seas freedoms that apply in the EEZ that include military activities, operations, and exercises, which China does not recognize as lawful.

Admiral Mike Mullen, former Chairman of the U.S. Joint Chiefs of Staff and former Chief of Naval Operations, reemphasized these points in a series of speeches during and following his visit to China in July 2011. Admiral Mullen stated in a speech at Renmin University on July 10, 2011, that "now more than ever the United States is a Pacific nation and it is clear that our security interests and our economic well-being are tied to Asia's."[128] Mullen emphasized that the United States was "deepening its commitment to this region and the alliances and partnerships that define our presence here," and that the United States "will remain a Pacific power, just as China is a Pacific power."[129] More specifically, in response to a question regarding U.S. military exercises in the region, Admiral Mullen indicated that the United States has "had a presence in this region for decades and...certainly the intent is to broaden and deepen our interests here and our relationships here."[130] Finally, the Admiral repeated U.S. policy that the "United States doesn't take a position on resolution of the disputes between two countries, but is very focused on working towards solutions which are peaceful and don't result in conflict."[131]

At a joint press conference in Beijing, General Chen Bingde, Chief of the General Staff of the People's Liberation Army, responded that U.S. naval exercises with Vietnam and the Philippines were "extremely inappropriate."[132] Admiral Mullen replied that the United States would maintain its presence in the Pacific and emphasized that U.S. reconnaissance flights and other military operations and exercises "are all conducted in accordance with international norms, and essentially we will continue to comply with that in the future."[133] Rear Admiral Tom Carney, Commander, Logistics Group Western Pacific and Commander, Task Force 73, speaking in Danang, Vietnam later the same day, echoed Admiral Mullen's statement, indicating that the United States has "had a presence in the Western Pacific and the South China Sea for 50 to 60 years, even going back before World War II [and]...we have no intention of departing from that kind of activity."[134]

---

[128] Speech by Chairman, Joint Chiefs of Staff Admiral Mike Mullen on U.S.-China Relations at Renmin University on July 10, 2011, U.S. Embassy Beijing Press Office, July 11, 2011.
[129] Id.
[130] Id.
[131] Id.
[132] Michael Martina, *China raps U.S. over military drills in disputed seas*, REUTERS, July 11, 2011.
[133] Id.
[134] Patrick Barta, *U.S., Vietnam in Exercises Amid Tensions With China*, WALL ST. J., July 16, 2011.

Finally, on his return trip to Washington, Admiral Mullen told reporters at a media press conference in Tokyo on July 15 that "the United States is a Pacific power [and that]...we are not going away."[135] More specifically, in response to a question regarding Chinese persistence in the South China Sea, the Chairman re-stated that the United States does not take a position with respect to resolving the disputes. However, he stressed that the United States takes "a very strong position with respect to the international standard of freedom of navigation" and "it isn't whether or not the United States is involved in a freedom of navigation issue, because a violation of a freedom of navigation issue by anybody is of concern to many, many countries internationally."[136] Admiral Mullen concluded the press conference by stating that peace and stability in the Asia Pacific region "is critical to those who live here, but also to the United States," and that the United States has "operated in the South China Sea for many decades...[and] will continue to do that, and I'm sure other countries will as well."[137]

Secretary of Defense Leon Panetta echoed President Obama's sentiments on the U.S. presence in the Pacific during a visit to Hawaii in March 2012. Speaking to reporters on Oahu, Secretary Panetta stated that the United States was a Pacific power and was going to remain a Pacific power. In order to do that, the United States will need to have force projection in the region, and the Navy will maintain its fleet and aircraft carrier presence in the Pacific.[138] According to Secretary of the Navy Ray Mabus, within the next few years, 60 percent of the U.S. naval fleet will be based in the Pacific, up from the current 55 percent.[139]

Then in June 2012, while speaking before an audience at the 11th International Institute for Strategic Studies (IISS) Asia Security Summit (Shangri-Law Dialogue) in Singapore, Secretary of Defense Panetta outlined the new U.S. defense strategy for the Asia-Pacific region:

> ...The purpose of this trip, and of my remarks today, is to explain a new defense strategy that the United States has put in place and why the United States will play a deeper and more enduring partnership role in advancing the security and prosperity of the Asia-Pacific region, and how the United States military supports that goal by rebalancing towards this region.[140]

---

[135] Transcript of Remarks by Admiral Mike Mullen, Chairman of the Joint Chiefs of Staff, U.S. Embassy, Tokyo, Japan, July 15, 2011.
[136] Id.
[137] Id.
[138] William Cole, *Give Sanctions Time, Panetta Says*, HONOLULU STAR-ADVERTISER, Mar. 9, 2012.
[139] Mike McCarthy, *New Ships Will Account for Asia-Pacific Buildup, SECNAV Says*, DEFENSE DAILY, Mar. 9, 2012.
[140] The US Rebalance Towards the Asia-Pacific: Leon Panetta, Secretary of Defense, United States, First Plenary Session, The 11th IISS Asia Security Summit, The Shangri-La Dialogue, Singapore, June 2, 2012.

The Secretary also emphasized that the United States has been and will continue to be a Pacific nation in the 21st century:

> Since the United States grew westward in the 19th century, we have been a Pacific nation....
>
> I remember the fear that gripped our community during World War II, and later when war again broke out on the Korean Peninsula. Despite the geographic distance that separates us, I've always understood that America's fate is inexorably linked with this region.
>
> This reality has guided more than six decades of U.S. military presence and partnership in this region—a defense posture which, along with our trading relations, along with our diplomatic ties, along with our foreign assistance, helped usher in an unprecedented era of security and prosperity in the latter half of the 20th century.
>
> In this century, the 21st century, the United States recognizes that our prosperity and our security depend even more on the Asia-Pacific region. After all, this region is home to some of the world's fastest growing economies: China, India, and Indonesia to mention a few. At the same time, Asia-Pacific contains the world's largest populations, and the world's largest militaries. Defense spending in Asia is projected by... the IISS, to surpass that of Europe this year, and there is no doubt that it will continue to increase in the future.
>
> Given these trends, President Obama has stated the United States will play a larger role in this region over the decades to come. This effort will draw on the strengths of the entire United States government. We take on this role not as a distant power, but as part of the Pacific family of nations. Our goal is to work closely with all of the nations of this region to confront common challenges and to promote peace, prosperity, and security for all nations in the Asia-Pacific region.[141]

Secretary Panetta then outlined the approach to achieve America's long-term goal in the Asia-Pacific region, indicating that the United States must remain:

> firmly committed to a basic set of shared principles—principles that promote international rules and order to advance peace and security in the region, deepening and broadening our bilateral and multilateral partnerships, enhancing and adapting the U.S. military's enduring presence in this region, and to make new investments in the capabilities needed to project power and operate in Asia-Pacific.[142]

With respect to strengthening a rule-based order in the Asia-Pacific, Secretary Panetta emphasized the important role regional organizations, such as ASEAN, play in furthering such an order, a role the United States strongly supports:

> Last October, I had the opportunity to be the first U.S. secretary of defense to meet privately with all ASEAN defense ministers in Bali. We applaud the ASEAN Defense Ministers Meeting Plus for producing real action plans for multilateral military cooperation, and I strongly support the ASEAN decision to hold more frequent ADMM-Plus

---

[141] Id.
[142] Id.

discussions at the ministerial level. We think this is an important step for stability, real coordination, communication, and support between these nations.

> The United States believes it is critical for regional institutions to develop mutually agreed rules of the road that protect the rights of all nations to free and open access to the seas. We support the efforts of the ASEAN countries and China to develop a binding code of conduct that would create a rules-based framework for regulating the conduct of parties in the South China Sea, including the prevention and management of disputes.[143]

Secretary Panetta also took the opportunity to express concern over the situation in Scarborough Shoal in the South China Sea and restate the U.S. position concerning the ongoing dispute:

> The U.S. position is clear and consistent: we call for restraint and for diplomatic resolution; we oppose provocation; we oppose coercion; and we oppose the use of force. We do not take sides when it comes to competing territorial claims, but we do want this dispute resolved peacefully and in a manner consistent with international law. We have made our views known and very clear to our close treaty ally, the Philippines, and we have made those views clear to China and to other countries in the region.
>
> As a Pacific power, the United States has a national interest in freedom of navigation, in unimpeded economic development and commerce, and in a respect for the rule of law. Our alliances, our partnerships, and our enduring presence in this region all serve to support these important goals....[144]

In conclusion, Secretary Panetta stressed that:

> Over the course of history, the United States has fought wars, we have spilled blood, we have deployed our forces time and time again to defend our vital interests in the Asia-Pacific region. We owe it to all of those who have fought and died to build a better future for all nations in this region.
>
> The United States has long been deeply been involved in the Asia-Pacific: through times of war, times of peace, under Democratic and Republican leaders and administrations, through rancor and through comity in Washington, through surplus and through debt. We were there then, we are here now, and we will be here for the future.[145]

11.2.1 *U.S.-Philippine Cooperation*

On February 25, 2011, a PLA-N frigate *Dongguan 560* fired warning shots at three Filipino fishing vessels, F/V *Jaime DLC*, F/V *Mama Lydia DLS*, and F/V *Maricris 12*, as they were fishing in the vicinity of Jackson Atoll. The atoll lies within the Philippine EEZ, off Palawan Island.[146] The following week, on March 2, 2011, two

---

[143] Id.
[144] Id.
[145] Id.
[146] Tessa Jamandre, *China Fired at Filipino Fishermen in Jackson Atoll*, ABS-CBN News, June 3, 2011.

Chinese Maritime Surveillance (CMS) patrol boats, Nos. 71 and 75, threatened the civilian survey ship M/V *Veritas Voyager* as it was conducting an oil and gas survey on behalf of the Philippine Department of Energy (DOE) in the vicinity of Reed Bank. The ship was forced to withdraw from the area. The Chinese patrol boats departed as well after a Filipino Air Force OV-10 Bronco light attack/observation aircraft and a Navy reconnaissance plane arrived on the scene to investigate. Forum Energy, a U.K. company that had been awarded the contract to conduct seismic surveys in the Sampaguita gas field, completed the survey at the end of March, but under escort of a Philippine Coast Guard vessel.

Following completion of the survey, Malacañang invited foreign investors and oil companies to bid for the right to explore for oil and gas in 15 different blocks off the west coast of Palawan. Beijing protested Manila's actions on July 4, 2011, alleging that two areas (Blocks 3 and 4), which are 500 miles from the nearest Chinese coast, lie within China's area of "indisputable sovereignty."[147] The Philippines quickly dismissed the Chinese claim, and replied that Blocks 3 and 4 were within Philippine jurisdiction.

The Reed Bank oil and gas fields are located in the South China Sea within the Philippine EEZ, approximately 80 nm west of Palawan Island. Initial exploration by DOE of the Reed Bank in 2005 revealed that the area contains about 3.4 trillion cubic feet of natural gas and 440 million barrels of oil.[148] If confirmed, these figures indicate oil and gas fields that could provide much needed energy resources to fuel the burgeoning Philippine economy.[149]

On October 19, 2011, a Philippine patrol boat, *BRP Rizal* (PS-74), collided with a Chinese fishing vessel near Recto (Reed) Bank after the *Rizal* apparently experienced a steering casualty. The large Chinese mother ship was observed operating 80 nm off Palawan within the Philippine EEZ, towing 35 smaller fishing boats. When the *Rizal* investigated, it became entangled with one of the smaller boats and collided with the mother ship. The mother ship immediately fled the area, leaving the smaller fishing boats behind. The *Rizal* towed the Chinese boats to Hulugan Bay in Palawan, but no one was arrested. The Philippine Navy issued an apology to the Chinese Embassy in Manila following the incident.[150] Manila has refused, however, to unconditionally release the detained Chinese fishing vessels.

---

[147] *Manila Rejects New Chinese Claim to Territory Just 50 Miles Away From Philippine Province*, MARITIMESECURITY.ASIA, Nov. 14, 2011.

[148] Jaime Laude, *Spratlys: Chinese Jets Buzzed PAF Patrol Planes/Noy—No Hurry to Protest*, NEWSFLASH.COM, May 21, 2011.

[149] Al Labita, *Philippines Embraces U.S., Repels China*, ASIA TIMES, Mar. 22, 2011, Alena Mae S. Flores, *UK Oil Firm Completes South China Sea Survey*, MANILA STANDARD, Mar. 23, 2011, and IAN STOREY, CHINA AND THE PHILIPPINES: IMPLICATIONS OF THE REED BANK INCIDENT, 11 JAMESTOWN FOUNDATION CHINA BRIEF (May 6, 2011).

[150] Jaime Laude & Marichu Villanueva, *Navy Ship Scares Off Chinese Towing Boat*, THE PHILIPPINE STAR, Oct. 19, 2011 and *Philippines Apologizes To China Over Sea Accident*, THE PHILIPPINE STAR, Oct. 19, 2011.

The Department of Justice of the Republic of the Philippines advised the Department of Foreign Affairs not to return the vessels until the National Committee on Illegal Entrants completed its investigation of the incident.[151] A few months later, in December 2011, Malacañang announced the deployment of the *BRP Gregorio del Pilar* (PF-15), the Navy's largest warship, to the West Philippine Sea to protect ongoing offshore energy projects in the Malampaya oil and gas field near Palawan.[152]

Chinese interference with Philippine resource rights in its EEZ continued in 2012. For example, in April of 2012, two Chinese Maritime Safety Administration (MSA) surveillance ships, *Zhonggou Haijian 75* and *Zhonggou Haijian 84*, prevented *BRP Gregorio del Pilar* from arresting 15 Chinese fishing boats that were caught illegally fishing in the Philippine EEZ in the vicinity of Scarborough Shoal (also known as Panatag Shoal (Philippines) and Huangyan Island (China)).[153] Scarborough Shoal is approximately 120 nm west of the Philippines' main island of Luzon. Both sides exchanged diplomatic protests over the incident.[154] Manila dispatched a Philippine Coast Guard vessel to assist the Navy warship, which prompted Beijing to send a third MSA surveillance ship to the disputed shoal.[155] Beijing claims the area is an integral part of Chinese territory and a traditional Chinese fishing ground. Chinese boats had anchored at the shoal to seek shelter from a storm, China stated. Manila argued that the shoal is sovereign Filipino territory and vowed not to retreat on the issue.[156]

In an apparent effort to deescalate the impasse, however, both sides withdrew their diplomatic protests. The Philippines recalled its warship and replaced it with a coast guard vessel, which prompted China to withdraw one of its surveillance ships.[157] Manila also called on China to submit the dispute over Scarborough Shoal to the International Tribunal for the Law of the Sea (ITLOS) in Hamburg, Germany. The proposal was promptly ignored by Beijing.[158] A few days

---

[151] Ina Reformina, *DOJ Against Release of Chinese Fishing Vessels*, ABS-CBN News, Apr. 4, 2012.

[152] Alexis Romero, *Phl Navy: Deployment Of Warship To Spratlys Will Not Increase Tensions*, Philippine Star, Dec. 18, 2011.

[153] Priam Nepomuceno, *PHL Navy to Stand its Ground on Scarborough Shoal Stand-Off*, Zambo Times, Apr. 11, 2012.

[154] Roel Landingin & Kathrin Hille, *Philippines and China in Stand-Off*, Financial Times, Apr. 11, 2012.

[155] Jim Gomez, *China sends 3rd ship in standoff with Philippines*, Atlanta J. & Const., Apr. 12, 2012.

[156] James Hookway, *Philippine Warship In Standoff With China Vessels*, Wall St. J., Apr. 11, 2012.

[157] James Hookway, *Philippines, China Withdraw Protests On South China Sea Spat*, Wall St. J., Apr. 13, 2012.

[158] *Philippines Urges China to Bring Shoal Row to International Court*, Philippine Daily Inquirer, Apr. 17, 2012.

later, on April 23, 2012, a Chinese ship and aircraft confronted a Philippine-registered yacht, M/Y *Saranggani* that was conducting archaeological research near Scarborough Shoal.

In late May of 2012, two more Chinese ships were observed at Scarborough Shoal, bringing the total number of Chinese ships to 15—four China Maritime Surveillance (CMS) vessels (including Numbers *71, 75* and *81*), three Fisheries Law Enforcement Command (FLEC) ships and eight fishing boats.[159] Flag level officers from two countries in the region confirmed to us that when Chinese fishing boats are employed in this manner, they invariably are crewed by PLA special operations forces, and not fishermen. The Philippines had two ships in the area: a Coast Guard search and rescue vessel, *BRP*[160] *Edsa II SARV 002*, and a Bureau of Fisheries and Aquatic Resources ship, MCS *3008*.[161]

Neither State appeared willing to compromise on the sovereignty issue, but both sides exercised restraint in order to reduce tension. After meeting with his Chinese counterpart in Phnom Pehn on May 28, 2012, Philippine Defense Secretary Voltaire Gazmin stated that the two nations had agreed on three points: "to restrain our actions, to restrain our statements so that it does not escalate, and then we continue to open our line of communication until we come up with a peaceful resolution to the case."[162] In mid-June of 2012, both sides withdrew their vessels from the area after tropical storm Gutchol dumped heavy rains across the Philippines.[163] Both states stressed, however, that the pullout should not be interpreted as an abandonment of their respective claims, and it is certain that Philippine and Chinese vessels will return to the shoal.[164]

Manila intends to pursue a three-pronged approach to resolve the ongoing crisis. Briefing how he saw "the endgame of Scarborough being played out if China cannot be persuaded diplomatically to withdraw its vessels from the area," Secretary del Rosario stated in May 2012:

> ... We do have a three-track approach to endeavoring to solve the problem that we currently have with China in the Scarborough Shoal. It encompasses three tracks. The first track is the political track. We are pursuing the ASEAN as a framework for a solution to this problem through a code of conduct that we are trying to put together and ultimately approve. Hopefully that will quiet the situation.

---

[159] *More Chinese Ships Seen in Scarborough*, ABS-CBN NEWS.COM (Philippines), May 31, 2012.
[160] Commissioned vessels likewise carry the word *Bapor ng Republika ng Pilipinas* (BRP) before the name to identify them as ships owned by the government of the Republic of the Philippines.
[161] *More Chinese Ships Seen in Scarborough*, ABS-CBN NEWS.COM (Philippines), May 31, 2012.
[162] Id.
[163] *Philippine Ship Pull-Out Calms Tensions: China*, PHILIPPINE DAILY INQUIRER, June 18, 2012.
[164] Id.

344 CHAPTER ELEVEN

> Secondly, we are pursuing a legal track, and the legal track involves our pursuing a dispute settlement mechanism under UNCLOS. There are five [dispute settlement options under UNCLOS].... We think that we can avail of one or two of those mechanisms, even without the presence of China.
>
> Thirdly, we are pursuing a diplomatic approach, such as the one that we are undertaking, which is to have consultations with China in an attempt to defuse the situation.
>
> In terms of U.S. commitment, I think the U.S. has been very clear that they do not get involved in territorial disputes, but that they are firm in terms of taking a position for a—towards a peaceful settlement of the disputes in the South China Sea towards a multilateral approach and towards the use of a rules-based regime in accordance with international law, specifically UNCLOS. They have expressed that they will honor their obligations under the [U.S.-Philippine] Mutual Defense Treaty.[165]

American support for a rules-based order in the South China Sea is bipartisan. In 2011, for example, Senator John McCain called for greater U.S. assistance to ASEAN member states to include development of an early warning system in the South China Sea and deployment of coastal vessels to patrol the region. Speaking at the Center for Strategic and International Studies (CSIS) on June 20, 2011, the Senator emphasized that the best way to prevent conflict was to build capabilities and undertake joint operations. He also stressed the importance of a unified, multilateral ASEAN effort to address disputes with China, as well as the value of a binding Code of Conduct for the South China Sea. Finally, he reiterated Washington's support for its treaty ally, the Philippines.[166]

A few days after Senator McCain spoke at CSIS, Secretary Clinton met with Philippines Secretary of Foreign Affairs Albert del Rosario, who was in Washington to seek assurances that the United States would defend the Philippines against Chinese aggression in the South China Sea. At a joint press conference following the meeting, Secretary Clinton stated:

> The Philippines and the United States are longstanding allies, and we are committed to honoring our mutual obligations....
>
> ... We are concerned that recent incidents in the South China Sea could undermine peace and stability in the region. We urge all sides to exercise self-restraint, and we will continue to consult closely with all countries involved, including our treaty ally, the Philippines.
>
> ... [T]he United States has a national interest in freedom of navigation, respect for international law, and unimpeded, lawful commerce in the South China Sea. We

---

[165] Remarks with Secretary of Defense Leon Panetta, Philippines Foreign Secretary Albert del Rosario, and Philippines Defense Secretary Voltaire Gazmin After Their Meeting, Washington, D.C., May 2, 2012.

[166] Keynote Address by Senator John McCain, Center for Strategic & International Studies Conference, Maritime Security in the South China Sea, Washington, D.C., 20–21 June 2011.

share these interests not only with ASEAN members, but with other maritime nations in the broader international community. The United States does not take sides on territorial disputes over land features in the South China Sea, but we oppose the use of force or the threat of force to advance the claims of any party.

We support resolving disputes through a collaborative diplomatic presence and process without coercion. We believe governments should pursue their territorial claims and the accompanying rights to maritime space in accordance with customary international law, as reflected also in the Law of the Sea Convention. The United States supports the 2002 *ASEAN-China Declaration on the Conduct of Parties in the South China Sea*, and we encourage the parties to reach agreement on a full code of conduct. We look forward to having discussions on these issues at the upcoming ASEAN Regional Forum in July.[167]

Secretary del Rosario thanked the Secretary for her assurances that the U.S.-Philippine partnership "remains important to the United States and to the overall U.S. engagement in the Asia Pacific region."[168] He stressed that "[t]he United States remains the Philippines' most important strategic partner, and ... [that he welcomed] ... the opportunity to discuss ... new ways to strengthen our longstanding alliance."[169] With regard to the South China Sea, the Foreign Secretary stated that:

...while we are a small country, we are prepared to do what is necessary to stand up to any aggressive action in our backyard. The Philippines has made clear its position on the issue: to maintain peace while allowing for the economic development of the area. There is need to segregate the non-disputed areas from the disputed areas. What is ours is ours, and what is disputed can be shared.

He also emphasized the need for a rules-based regime based on UNCLOS and the need to eventually adopt a binding Code of Conduct for the South China Sea. Secretary del Rosario concluded by stating the Philippines' commitment to develop its own capabilities to protect its borders and "ensure freedom of navigation and the unimpeded flow of commerce" and he welcomed Secretary Clinton's assurances that the United States would honor its treaty obligations.[170]

In response to a specific question regarding China's recent aggressive actions against Vietnam and the Philippines and Chinese official statements that the United States did not have a role to play in helping to resolve the South China Sea disputes, Secretary Clinton responded that the U.S. position remained the same:

...We support a collaborative diplomatic process by all claimants to resolve their disputes without the use or threat of force. We're troubled by the recent incidents

---

[167] Remarks of Secretary of State Hillary Rodham Clinton with Philippines Foreign Secretary Albert del Rosario After Their Meeting, Treaty Room, Washington, D.C., June 23, 2011.
[168] Id.
[169] Id.
[170] Id.

in the South China Sea that have increased tensions and raised concerns about the peace and security of the region.

These reported incidents clearly present significant maritime security issues, including the freedom of navigation, respect for international law, and the lawful, unimpeded economic development and commerce that all nations are entitled to pursue. We support the ASEAN China declaration on the conduct of parties in the South China Sea. And... we encourage the parties to reach a full code of conduct.

... [T]he United States [does not] take a position on competing sovereignty claims over land features.... But the United States is prepared to support the initiatives led by ASEAN and work with the South China Sea's claimants to meet their concerns....[171]

More importantly, in response to a question regarding U.S. intentions under the Mutual Defense Treaty, Secretary Clinton responded that the United States would honor its commitments under the defense treaty. She added that the United States would do what it can "to support the Philippines in their desires for external support for maritime defense and the other issues..." and that the United States was "determined and committed to supporting the defense of the Philippines, and that means trying to find ways of providing affordable material and equipment that will assist the Philippine military to take the steps necessary to defend itself."[172]

Later that same week, Secretary del Rosario met with U.S. Defense Secretary Robert Gates at the Pentagon on June 23, 2011. Secretary Gates echoed Clinton's assurances that the United States was prepared to help the Philippines strengthen its capabilities to secure their maritime territory. The next day, the Foreign Secretary met with the Director for National Intelligence James Clapper, who pledged to enhance intelligence sharing with Manila to improve the Philippines' maritime domain awareness in the South China Sea.[173]

On August 17, 2011, the United States made good on its earlier promise to enhance Manila's military capabilities by delivering a *Hamilton*-class Coast Guard cutter to the Philippine Navy. A second cutter, *USCGC Dallas* (WHEC-716), was transferred to the Philippine Navy on May 25, 2012.[174] The Philippine Navy commissioned the ship *BRP Ramon Alcaraz* after the World War II hero.[175] The

---

[171] Id.
[172] Id.
[173] Embassy of the Philippines Washington, D.C. News Release, US Defense Secretary Gates Expresses Readiness to Strengthen PH's Capability on Maritime Security; National Intel Director Clapper Pledges Assistance in Maritime Surveillance, June 24, 2011.
[174] Embassy of the Philippines Washington, D.C. News Release, PH Navy Receives US Coast Guard Cutter Dallas, May 25, 2012.
[175] *BRP Ramon Alcaraz: The Next WHEC*, PH DEFENSE TODAY, May 6, 2012. During World War II, Alcaraz commanded one of the country's three motor torpedo boats, known as Q-boats.

United States also continues to support and finance the completion of the Coast Watch South (CWS) project, a multilateral maritime domain awareness system. Once finished, the network of 17 radar and communication stations will provide the AFP the ability to better monitor activities in the South China Sea and the Sulu Sea.[176]

In November 2011, the United States and the Philippines marked the 60th anniversary of the U.S.-Philippines Mutual Defense Treaty with the signing of the Manila Declaration on board the *USS Fitzgerald* (DDG 62) in Manila Bay. In the declaration, the Philippines and the United States reaffirm "the continuing relevance of the treaty for peace, security, and prosperity in the Asia-Pacific region...[and] reaffirm the treaty as the foundation of our relationship for the next 60 years and beyond."[177] In this regard both sides "expect to maintain a robust, balanced, and responsive security partnership including cooperating to enhance the defense, interdiction, and apprehension capabilities of the Armed Forces of the Philippines."[178] Both sides also indicated that they shared a "common interest in maintaining freedom of navigation, unimpeded lawful commerce, and transit of people across the seas and subscribe to a rules-based approach in resolving competing claims in maritime areas through peaceful, collaborative, multilateral, and diplomatic processes within the framework of international law."[179]

Three days later, at the East Asian Summit (EAS) in Bali, Indonesia, Asia-Pacific leaders stressed the importance of regional cooperation to address the region's political and security challenges, including maritime security. President Obama's participation in the event underscored the U.S. commitment to remain actively engaged in the region. With regard to maritime security issues, the President emphasized that:

> The Asia-Pacific region is home to some of the world's busiest ports and most critical lines of commerce and communication. Recent decades of broad regional economic success have been underpinned by a shared commitment to freedom of navigation and international law. At the same time, the region faces a host of maritime challenges, including territorial and maritime disputes, ongoing naval military modernization, trafficking of illicit materials, piracy, and natural disasters.[180]

---

[176] Renato De Castro & Walter Lohman, U.S.–PHILIPPINES PARTNERSHIP IN THE CAUSE OF MARITIME DEFENSE, BACKGROUNDER #2593, THE HERITAGE FOUNDATION BACKGROUNDER # 2593, Aug. 8, 2011.

[177] U.S. Dep't of State, Signing of the Manila Declaration on Board the *USS Fitzgerald* in Manila Bay, Manila, Philippines, Media Note, Office of the Spokesperson, U.S. Dep't of State, Nov. 16, 2011.

[178] Id.

[179] Id.

[180] The White House, Office of the Press Secretary, Briefing Sheet: East Asia Summit, Nov. 19, 2011.

The President reiterated a "principles-based U.S. approach to maritime security, including freedom of navigation and overflight and other internationally lawful uses of the seas, as well as use of collaborative diplomatic processes to address disputes."[181] He also "expressed strong opposition to the threat or use of force by any party to advance its territorial or maritime claims or interfere in legitimate economic activity" and reiterated U.S. support for the 2002 ASEAN DOC and encouraged all parties to conclude a binding code at the earliest opportunity.[182] The President further stated that the United States would continue to work with regional partners to build capacity and promote cooperation on maritime security issues, including by:

- Providing training, assistance, and equipment to regional maritime police and civil authorities to enhance their capabilities to secure the maritime space and address transnational security challenges such as piracy, illicit trafficking, and illegal fishing;
- Building facilities and providing equipment and technical support to enhance the ability of Southeast Asian nations to monitor the maritime domain and assess and share information;
- Hosting regional workshops to promote adherence to standard operating procedures and protocols that ensure safety at sea, help build a shared vision of international norms and behaviors in the maritime domain, and foster discussion of interpretations of customary international law; and
- Hosting and co-hosting multinational capacity-building exercises with regional military partners.[183]

Chinese Premier Wen Jiabao publicly criticized President Obama for raising the South China Sea issue at the EAS, indicating that the summit "was not a proper occasion to discuss the issue" and that the dispute must be resolved directly by the various claimants "through friendly consultation and negotiations."[184]

11.2.2　U.S.-Australian Cooperation

Australia has stepped up its activities in the region as well. The country participated in trilateral naval exercises with Japan and the United States off the coast of Okinawa in June 2010 and with Brunei in July 2011. Australia also completed

---

[181] Id.
[182] Id.
[183] Id.
[184] Ben Blanchard & Laura MacInnis, *China Rebuffs U.S., Asia Pressure in Sea Dispute*, REUTERS, Nov. 19, 2011.

the bilateral exercise *Semangat Bersatu* with Singapore in November 2011.[185] Two months earlier, in September 2011, Canberra and Washington issued a joint communiqué after the 2011 Australia-United States Ministerial Consultation (AUSMIN) that underscored the growing importance of the Asia-Pacific region and the alliance. The two allies stressed the importance of freedom of navigation in the South China Sea:

> We reaffirm our shared security obligations, underscore our common approach to regional developments and global security, and stress our resolve to increase future cooperation to address common strategic objectives.
>
> We underscore the growing importance of the Asia-Pacific region. The U.S.-Australia alliance is key to peace and security in the region, further fostering Asia's tremendous economic growth. We recognize the need to work together to shape the evolving strategic landscape that connects the Indian and the Pacific Oceans....[186]

The United States and Australia identified shared objectives to guide their ongoing cooperative and individual work in the Asia-Pacific, agreeing to:

- reiterate that the United States and Australia, along with the international community, have a national interest in freedom of navigation, the maintenance of peace and stability, respect for international law, and unimpeded lawful commerce in the South China Sea;
- reaffirm that we do not take a position on the competing territorial claims in the South China Sea and call on governments to clarify and pursue their territorial claims and accompanying maritime rights in accordance with international law, including the Law of the Sea Convention;
- reaffirm that the United States and Australia support the 2002 *ASEAN-China Declaration on the Conduct of Parties in the South China Sea* and encourage each of the parties to comply with their commitments, including exercising self-restraint and resolving their disputes through peaceful means, and to make progress towards a binding code of conduct; and,
- reiterate that we oppose the use of coercion or force to advance the claims of any party or interfere with legitimate economic activity.[187]

---

[185] *Days of Japan-US Joint Military Drills Increased in FY2010*, PAN ORIENT NEWS, Nov. 19, 2011, L. Xiaokun, *US 'won't take sides' in South China Sea*, CHINA DAILY, July 11, 2011, and *Singapore, Australia Conclude Bilateral Maritime Exercise*, CHANNEL NEWS ASIA (SINGAPORE), Nov. 17, 2011.
[186] Australia-United States Ministerial Consultation (AUSMIN) 2011 Joint Communiqué, Sept. 15, 2011.
[187] Id.

On November 16, 2011, the United States announced that it intended to increase its military presence in Australia beginning in 2012. Prime Minister Julia Gillard stated that the two long-time allies had agreed:

> to expand the existing collaboration between the Australian Defense Force and the U.S. Marine Corps and the U.S. Air Force... [Beginning in] mid-2012, Australia will welcome deployments of a company-size rotation of 200 to 250 Marines in the Northern Territory for around six months at a time.[188]

The total force is expected to grow to around 2,500 personnel over the next few years. In addition, she set forth a second component of the initiative, which grants:

> greater access by U.S. military aircraft to the Royal Australian Air Force facilities in our country's north. This will involve more frequent movements of U.S. military aircraft into and out of northern Australia. Now, taken together, these two initiatives make our alliance stronger, they strengthen our cooperation in our region.[189]

In concluding, Prime Minister Gillard emphasized that the U.S.-Australia alliance:

> ...has been a bedrock of stability in our region. So building on our alliance through this new initiative is about stability. It will be good for our Australian Defence Force to increase their capabilities by joint training, combined training, with the U.S. Marines and personnel. It will mean that we are postured to better respond together, along with other partners in the Asia Pacific, to any regional contingency, including the provision of humanitarian assistance and dealing with natural disasters.[190]

In response to a question regarding whether the increased U.S. presence in Australia was aimed at containing China's renewed assertiveness in the region, President Obama remarked that the United States welcomes

> ...a rising, peaceful China.... [However,] with their rise comes increased responsibilities. It's important for them to play by the rules of the road.... So where China is playing by those rules.... I think this is a win-win situation. There are going to be times where they're not, and we will send a clear message to them that we think that they need to be on track in terms of accepting the rules and responsibilities that come with being a world power.[191]

The first contingent of 180 U.S. Marines arrived in Darwin on April 4, 2012, for a six-month deployment.[192] The United States and Australia are also considering the possibility of using HMAS *Stirling*, the Royal Australian Navy's naval base south of Perth, as a future logistics base for U.S. warships, including aircraft carriers,

---

[188] Remarks by President Obama and Prime Minister Gillard of Australia in Joint Press Conference, Parliament House Canberra, Australia, Nov. 16, 2011.
[189] Id.
[190] Id.
[191] Id.
[192] Matt Siegel, *As Part of Pact, U.S. Marines Arrive in Australia, in China's Strategic Backyard*, N.Y. TIMES, Apr. 4, 2012.

and submarines. Washington and Canberra also have discussed the possibility of stationing unmanned and manned surveillance aircraft in the Cocos Islands that could carry out patrols over the Indian Ocean and the South China Sea.[193]

Interestingly, Indonesian Defense Minister Purnomo Yusgiantoro has stated that his government does not have a problem with the U.S. plan to rotate Marines through bases in northern Australia. The minister hinted at the possibility of conducting combined humanitarian assistance and disaster relief exercises with Australia and the United States.[194] One week later at the Jakarta International Defense Dialogue, Indonesian President Susilo Bambang Yudhoyono highlighted the importance of conducting more joint exercises in order to minimize the risk of conflict in the region.[195] Three months after his statement, the Indonesian Navy hosted the *USS Germantown* (LSD-42), *USS Vandegrift* (FFG-48) and *USCGC Waeshe* (WMSL-751) for the annual U.S.-Indonesia Cooperation Afloat Readiness and Training (CARAT) exercise off East Java.[196] CARAT consists of a series of bilateral military exercises between the U.S. Navy and the armed forces of Bangladesh, Brunei, Cambodia, Indonesia, Malaysia, the Philippines, Singapore, Thailand and Timor Leste (East Timor).

Singapore has also publicly welcomed a dominant U.S. presence in the Pacific, but also must figure out a way to get along with China.[197] On June 2, 212, the city-state approved a request from Washington to deploy up to four more Littoral Combat Ships (LCS), in addition to the two LCSs that will deploy to Singapore in 2013.[198] Canada has also expressed an interest in establishing a logistics facility in the city-state to support humanitarian assistance and disaster relief efforts.[199] However, Singaporean authorities have emphasized that the United States and China need to cooperate, not confront one another, if peace is to be maintained in the region.

11.2.3   U.S.-New Zealand Cooperation

For decades, New Zealand's anti-nuclear policy prevented visits by U.S. warships, which adhere to a strict policy to neither confirm or deny the presence of nuclear weapons on board. But recently, New Zealand is becoming more closely

---

[193] Brendan Nicholson, *U.S. Seeks Deeper Military Ties*, THE AUSTRALIAN, Mar. 27, 2012.
[194] *Indonesia Says "No Problem" With U.S. Marines Plan*, AGENCE FRANCE-PRESSE, Mar. 14, 2012.
[195] Zakir Hussain, *Indonesia Calls for More Joint Military Drills*, THE JAKARTA GLOBE, Mar. 22, 2012.
[196] Commander Naval Surface Force, U.S. Pacific Fleet, Press Release, CARAT 2012.
[197] Sydney Freedberg, Jr., *U.S. Should be Dominant In Pacific—But Must Make Nice With China, Says Singapore Defense Minister*, AOL DEFENSE, Apr. 4, 2012.
[198] Chua Chin Hon, *U.S., Singapore Defence Chiefs Reaffirm Strong Ties*, SINGAPORE STRAITS TIMES, Apr. 6, 2012.
[199] *Canada Eyes Singapore Hub As U.S. Shifts*, AGENCE FRANCE-PRESSE, June 3, 2012.

aligned with the United States on naval issues. New Zealand has joined Australia and the United States in stressing the need for the South China Sea claimants to abide by UNCLOS and adhere to the ASEAN DOC, stating that observance of the two instruments are essential "if peace and stability in the area are to be maintained."[200]

Another sign of closer association with the United States was the signing of a new defense cooperation agreement on June 19, 2012.[201] The Washington Declaration provides a new framework for cooperation to focus, strengthen and expand the U.S.-New Zealand defense relationship.[202] The participants intend to work towards greater bilateral cooperation by pursuing the following activities:

I. Defense Dialogues
   a. Exchange information and strategic perspectives; and
   b. Increase understanding of the respective defense policies of each Participant through, for example, personnel exchanges.

II. Security Cooperation
   a. Maritime Security Cooperation
      i. Share information and expertise;
      ii. Cooperate in maritime security and safety activities; and
      iii. Participate in bilateral and multilateral exercises, operations, and training opportunities, including those related to counter-proliferation, counter-terrorism, anti-piracy, addressing regional resource exploitation, and supporting freedom of commerce and navigation.
   b. Humanitarian Assistance and Disaster Relief (HA/DR) Cooperation with a focus on the Asia-Pacific and to
      i. Share information and expertise;
      ii. Plan for humanitarian assistance and disaster relief activities; and
      iii. Conduct bilateral and multilateral conferences, activities, and operational-level exercises to increase Participants' cross-domain interoperability.
   c. United Nations and other multi-national peacekeeping and peace support operations, which involve
      i. Sharing information and expertise; and
      ii. Exercises and training to maintain cross-domain interoperability both between the Participants as well as multilaterally.[203]

---

[200] DJ Yap, *New Zealand backs Philippine Position on Spratlys*, GLOBAL NATION INQUIRER, Aug. 12, 2011.
[201] DEP'T OF DEFENSE AND MIN. OF DEFENCE, WASHINGTON DECLARATION ON DEFENSE COOPERATION BETWEEN THE DEPARTMENT OF DEFENSE OF THE UNITED STATES OF AMERICA AND THE MINISTRY OF DEFENCE OF NEW ZEALAND AND THE NEW ZEALAND DEFENCE FORCE, June 19, 2012, http://www.defense.gov/news/WashingtonDeclaration.pdf.
[202] Id., para. 2.a.
[203] Id., Annex.

In September 2012, Secretary of Defense Panetta became the first defense secretary to visit New Zealand in 30 years. During the visit, Panetta announced that President Obama was revising U.S. policy to its once-ally, authorizing the Secretary of Defense to approve individual ship visits by the Royal New Zealand Navy to U.S. military and Coast Guard facilities.[204]

11.2.4 Trans-Pacific Partnership

On November 12, 2011, at a meeting in Honolulu, Hawaii, the leaders of Australia, Brunei Darussalam, Chile, Malaysia, New Zealand, Peru, Singapore, Vietnam, and the United States announced a broad outline for a 21st-century Trans-Pacific Partnership (TPP). The TPP is an economic compact that "will enhance trade and investment among the TPP partner countries, promote innovation, economic growth and development, and support the creation and retention of jobs."[205] The nine leaders hailed the agreement as "a model for ambition for other free trade agreements in the future, forging close linkages among our economies, enhancing our competitiveness, benefitting our consumers and supporting the creation and retention of jobs, higher living standards, and the reduction of poverty in our countries."[206]

The agreement reduces tariffs on goods as well as services, and includes:

- Core issues traditionally included in trade agreements, including industrial goods, agriculture, and textiles as well as rules on intellectual property, technical barriers to trade, labor, and environment.
- Cross-cutting issues not previously part of trade agreements, such as making the regulatory systems of TPP countries more compatible so companies from member States may operate more seamlessly in TPP markets, helping innovative, job-creating small- and medium-sized enterprises participate more actively in international trade.
- New emerging trade issues such as addressing trade and investment in innovative products and services, including information and digital technologies, and ensuring state-owned enterprises compete fairly with private companies and do not distort competition in ways that put U.S. companies and workers at a disadvantage.[207]

---

[204] Thom Shanker, *Panetta Announces Warmer Military Ties On New Zealand Trip*, THE NEW YORK TIMES, Sept. 21, 2012.
[205] Office of the United States Trade Representative, Trans-Pacific Partnership Fact Sheet, http://www.ustr.gov/tpp.
[206] Id.
[207] Id.

Washington's participation in the TPP process is a key element of a strategy to make engagement in the Asia-Pacific region a top national security and economic priority. In concluding the Hawaii meeting, President Obama made it clear that the United States is a Pacific nation that is deeply committed "to shaping the future security and prosperity of the Trans-Pacific region, the fastest-growing region in the world."[208] The TPP is envisioned as a future-oriented framework to tie together information-age economies on the Pacific Rim. But the compact excludes China and is viewed in Beijing as laden with political overtone and as a means of economically containing China and isolating it from other States in the region.

---

[208] Id.

TWELVE

SECURING THE MARINE TRANSPORTATION SYSTEM

12.1 THREATS TO INTERNATIONAL SHIP AND PORT FACILITY SECURITY

The world's sea lines of communication are the lifelines of today's global economy. According to the IMO, maritime transport is the "most cost-effective, fuel efficient, carbon friendly and fastest way" to move large quantities of goods around the world.[1] Therefore, it is no surprise that nearly 90 percent of world international trade and over two-thirds of petroleum are transported by sea.

In 2010, the United Nations Conference on Trade and Development (UNCTAD) reported that the operation of 50,000-plus ocean-going commercial ships, including bulk carriers, cargo ships, and oil tankers, contributed over $380 billion to the global economy.[2] The marine transportation network is massive in scale. Each year 15 million shipping containers make 230 million journeys, and although most are screened, only five percent are inspected.[3] The maritime transportation system and its related infrastructure ashore provide a significant source of income and jobs in many countries. Worldwide, more than 1.2 million people work directly for the shipping industry as seafarers and port workers. Other

---

[1] INT'L MARITIME ORG., IMO'S CONTRIBUTION TO SUSTAINABLE MARITIME DEVELOPMENT, INTERNATIONAL MARITIME ORGANIZATION, available at www.imo.org.
[2] The top 20 flag States with the greatest tonnage under registry include: Panama, Liberia, Marshall Islands, Hong Kong (China), Bahamas, Singapore, Greece, Malta, China, Cyprus, Italy, United Kingdom, Japan, Germany, Norway, South Korea, Isle of Man, Denmark, Antigua & Barbuda, and Bermuda. The ten largest container shipping companies in the world are based in Denmark, Switzerland, France, Taiwan, Germany, Singapore, South Korea/Germany, China and Japan. SHIPPING AND WORLD TRADE: KEY FACTS, http://www.marisec.org/shippingfacts/worldtrade/volume-world-trade-sea.php.
[3] Nicholas Fiorenza, Who Goes There? DEFENSE TECH. INT'L, Oct. 2009, 54–57, at 57.

shipping-related businesses, including cargo chain logistics, employ tens of millions more employees.[4]

Maritime transportation is the connective tissue of globalization, efficiently carrying a massive amount of international and transcontinental cargo, which has lifted hundreds of millions of workers out of poverty. Establishment and maintenance of security and good order at sea are a prerequisite for economic prosperity and for ensuring law and order on land. Yet, the worldwide marine transportation system is rife with regulatory seams, local and regional instability, persistent lapses in security, and endemic corruption. The Organization for Economic Cooperation and Development (OECD) described marine transportation as a system that involves "thousands of intermediaries, on vessels registered in dozens of countries that sometimes choose not to uphold their international responsibilities, and where some vessel owners can and do easily hide their true identities using a complex web of international corporate registration practices."[5]

Even ships in compliance with international standards face daily security risks. Threats fluctuate, depending on location, time of day, political events, the weather, type of vessel, speed of advance of the ship, and the skill and professionalism of the crew. Port facilities face uncertainty every time a new vessel pulls up to the pier, and persons and cargo are introduced into the area. After the attacks of 9/11 laid bare the risks to public infrastructure by non-state terrorist groups, the international community accelerated efforts to deter terrorism and the proliferation of weapons of mass destruction. Because the maritime transportation system is both a target and a conveyance for such threats, nations have heavily invested in maritime security.

There are an increasing variety of violent, non-state actors operating at sea. In the past two decades, sub-state criminal and terrorist organizations plying the oceans have multiplied. In March 1993, for example, Islamic terrorists clandestinely smuggled armaments, ammunition, and explosives by ship from Karachi, Pakistan, into the Indian state of Maharashtra. The armaments were used in devastating terrorist attacks. More recently, in December 2008, commandos from the Islamic terrorist group *Lashkar-e-taiba* traveled by sea on a hijacked Indian fishing vessel, infiltrating Mumbai. Once inside the country, the members of the radical group went on a murderous rampage, killing nearly two hundred people and bringing the nation's financial center to a standstill.

Across the forty-mile wide Palk Strait in South Asia, neighboring Sri Lanka recently ended a three-decades-long war of attrition against the *Liberation Tigers of Tamil Eelam* (LTTE). The small and fast suicide boats of the "Sea Tigers," the

---

[4] James Castonguay, *International Shipping: Globalization in Crisis*, WITNESS (online magazine), Vision Project Inc., http://www.visionproject.org/images/img_magazine/pdfs/international_shipping.pdf.

[5] Id.

maritime wing of the LTTE, were the most effective maritime terrorist organization in the world. Over the past three decades, the Sea Tigers sank dozens of Sri Lankan ships—claiming a higher tonnage of vessels destroyed than any conventional naval force of the contemporary era.

The group also engaged in numerous vessel hijackings, including the seizure of the *Irish Moa* in 1995, the *Princess Wave* in 1996, the *Athena, Misen, Morong Bon*, and the M/V *Cordiality* in 1997, and the *Princess Kash* in 1998. The group also hijacked the Malaysian-flagged M/V *Sik Yang* in 1999—neither the ship nor the sixty-three crew members were ever heard from again. In February 2008, the Sea Tigers sank a Sri Lankan fast attack craft in the sea of Thalaimannar, almost 200 nautical miles from Colombo. Before the defeat of the LTTE in 2009, the Sea Tigers were extraordinarily successful, sinking over 30 percent of the small boats in the Sri Lankan navy. Although the LTTE eventually was defeated on land, the Sea Tigers were never beaten at sea, and their success represents the specter of a new face of maritime terrorism.

In the intervening decades since the LTTE began its insurgency, other prominent maritime terrorist attacks have occurred throughout the world, including the bombing of Lord Mountbatten's private yacht in 1979 by the Provisional Irish Republican Army. In 2006, a Chinese-made C-802 cruise missile launched by Hezbollah struck the *Sa'ar 5*-class Israeli Navy corvette, *INS Hanit*, heavily damaging the ship and killing four crew members. Even more recently, on July 28, 2010, the Japanese oil tanker *M Star* was damaged by an attack while traveling from Qatar to Japan.[6] The mysterious explosion against the ship did not penetrate the hull, but the attack appears to have been detonated by *Abdullah Azzam Brigades*, an Al-Qaeda-linked terrorist group.[7]

Even more creative maritime dangers may be on the horizon. In the Gulf of Guinea, for example, guerillas from the Movement for the Emancipation of the Niger Delta (MEND) utilize small boat swarms to disrupt offshore oil infrastructure. Each day 150,000 barrels of oil is smuggled from Nigeria's energy production in the Gulf of Guinea. Nigeria is the second most dangerous country in the world for piracy, after only Somalia. Although the extent of the shadowy link between piracy in the Gulf of Guinea and MEND is unclear, in 2012 the group pledged to attack any ship in the region that refused to submit to boarding.[8]

Non-state groups operating at sea are particularly adept at leveraging new technologies. There is a renaissance underway in the development of unmanned aerial systems in conventional armed forces. As the technology becomes ubiquitous, it is being appropriated by insurgent groups and misused for water-borne

---

[6] *Mystery of Japanese Tanker Damage Probed*, BBC NEWS, July 29, 2010.
[7] *Japanese Tanker was Damaged in Terror Attack, UAE Says*, BBC NEWS, Aug. 6, 2010.
[8] Olawale Rasheed, *MEND Attacks Worsen Piracy in Gulf of Guinea*, SUNDAY TRIBUNE (Nigeria), Mar. 4, 2012.

improvised explosive devices. Commercial, off-the-shelf unmanned underwater vehicles used for oceanography, for example, may be converted into torpedoes or marine mines. Social media and cell phones were used to vector attacks against coalition forces in Iraq. Similarly, a network could agitate "flash mobs" embarked on swarms of shallow water speedboats to converge against merchant shipping or to block the passage of warships in littoral waters.

Thus, maritime threats range from the dramatic to the mundane and include piracy and armed robbery at sea; maritime terrorism; cargo tampering; sabotage or theft; smuggling of contraband, and particularly trafficking in weapons of mass destruction and their associated components; illegal migrants, stowaways, refugees and asylum seekers; environmental extremists; natural disasters and accidents; organized criminal gangs and militant organized labor; and errors and failures of the human element.

12.1.1 *Piracy and Armed Robbery at Sea*

Pirates are motivated by private interest to attack ships on the high seas or in territorial waters. (Private interest means that pirates are not acting as authorized agents of a government). Most instances of armed robbery at sea occur while vessels are at anchor in port. Ships are most vulnerable near land and while transiting choke points, as illustrated by the attacks against ships in the Gulf of Aden and Southeast Asia. But Somali pirates are adept at operating from large captured mother ships and may attack merchant shipping more than a thousand miles from their base on land. Southeast Asian pirates generally launch attacks against ships transiting in the vicinity of pirate bases hidden in coves and bays along the shoreline of small islands, but even Asian pirates have been known to conduct attacks far from land.

12.1.2 *Maritime Terrorism*

A ship may be used as a weapon or delivery vehicle to breach or penetrate the outer perimeter of a port to deposit a weapon. Since ships are capable of carrying such a large amount of cargo, they serve as an ideal platform for smuggling terrorists and weapons of mass destruction or for moving other illicit cargo. There have been only a few terrorist attacks against ocean-going merchant ships, but the determination and capability of Islamic extremists has been responsible for some of the most dramatic assaults at sea. In 1985, for example, Palestinian terrorists took control of the cruise ship *Achille Lauro*, murdering a passenger and holding the ship at gunpoint to secure the release of terrorists in Israeli prison.

In 2000, Al-Qaeda operatives attacked the *USS Cole* (DDG 67) in Aden, Yemen. The slow, low-tech suicide assault on the *Cole* killed 17 Navy sailors and nearly sank the powerful warship. The attack on the French oil tanker *Limburg*, also by members of Al-Qaeda, occurred off the coast of Yemen in October 2002, and exposed the vulnerability of the sea line of communication between the Strait of Hormuz and consumer markets in Europe and Asia. Two years later, the deadly bombing in the Philippines of *Super Ferry 14* by the Abu Sayyaf Islamist organization killed 116 people—the world's greatest and most costly maritime terrorist attack.

12.1.3 Cargo Tampering, Sabotage, or Theft

Cargo tampering can occur at any point throughout the marine transportation cargo chain, from on loading of ground transportation, point of embarkation, at sea during ship voyages, and point of debarkation at the pier. Although cargo theft can occur at sea, it is most often conducted in port, where ground transportation is positioned to fence stolen goods to market. Heavily taxed items, such as alcohol and cigarettes, as well as electronics, furs, and other low-density, high-value cargoes, are frequent targets of tampering and theft. Extreme and fairly rare cases of sabotage have involved the destruction of cargo or the sinking of a vessel in order to collect insurance proceeds.

12.1.4 Smuggling of Contraband

Although most international shipping container traffic undergoes some amount of screening, only a small number of containers in the stream of commerce are actually inspected. Smugglers seeking to introduce weapons or illegal drugs into an area often rely on international shipping to carry the cargo, secreting the contraband among legitimate commerce. Because containers are stacked aboard ship, they are literally impossible to inspect while a vessel is at sea, so the integrity of the marine transportation system is entirely dependent upon port security at point of on load and off load.

12.1.5 Illegal Migrants, Stowaways, Refugees, and Asylum Seekers

Unlawful travel of criminals and felons at large, undocumented displaced persons, and refugees and asylum seekers, presents a continuous challenge to the security of the marine transportation system. These individual persons may pose a direct danger to themselves, other crew and passengers, vessels, and cargos, and they may impose liability on the shipping company. Furthermore, migrants may be traveling with particularly vulnerable populations, including children, women, and the elderly.

12.1.6 Environmental Extremists

Environmental activist groups may be highly motivated to create disturbances or endanger ships or persons in order to gain attention for their causes, such as anti-whaling, protest of certain radiological or hazardous materials cargo, protests against the transportation of oil and related petroleum products, or attempts to stop the importation or export of certain natural resources, such as endangered forest products. Environmental extremists may threaten the safety of a vessel or its crew by interfering with normal shipboard operations, intentionally impeding a ship's passage (such as by disregard for the international rules of the road, chaining themselves to a vessel, or sabotaging a ship or its cargo). These antics also may elicit defensive action or over-reaction on the part of commercial vessels, resulting in the use of force.

12.1.7 Weather and Natural Disasters

The ocean may be a hostile and unforgiving operating environment, and natural disasters and violent weather, can endanger ship and port security. Earthquakes, tsunamis, storms, rogue waves, the presence of ice in the water, and high winds can imperil ship operations and slow down or halt port operations.

12.1.8 Accidents

There is no agreement on the extent that accidents impact the international shipping industry, but examples abound. In 2006, the Singaporean-flagged *Cougar Ace* nearly capsized during a ballast water accident, losing 4703 automobiles to damage from the shifting load, out of a total of 4,812 passenger vehicles on board the ship.[9] Similarly, although some reports suggest that 2,000 to 10,000 shipping containers are lost at sea every year, the World Shipping Council released a survey that indicates the real figure, even accounting for catastrophic events, is more likely to be about 700.[10]

These man-made casualties are the result of carelessness, poor training and lax crew discipline, unsafe operating practices, and failed lashing systems. In addition to the damage or loss of shipping containers, accidents may cause the release of liquid, solid or gaseous chemicals and hazardous materials, or the ignition of flammable materials and liquids. The result of accidents may damage the ship and cargo, port facilities and shore side communities, and cause personal injury or death.

12.1.9 Organized Labor Activities and Labor Violence

Control of waterfront activities through organized labor can be an effective means of disrupting international maritime trade. During the Cold War, for example, the Soviet Union had a dominant influence over organized labor in a number of

---

[9] Caren Silke Carty, *When Cargo Gets Lost at Sea Firms Can See Big Shortages*, USA TODAY, Aug. 4, 2006.
[10] *Study: 675 Containers a Year Lost at Sea*, AMERICAN SHIPPER, Aug. 11, 2011.

countries throughout the world, including major mining, fuel and power, overland and maritime transport, and waterfront and dockyard unions. These groups were used by Moscow to interfere with the shipment of strategic materials to the United States and its allies.[11] Ironically, however, the Polish trade union Solidarity was a key instrument in destabilizing the Warsaw Pact—eventually prompting the collapse of the Soviet Union. Lech Walesa, an electrician who worked at the Gdansk shipyard, became the leader of Solidarity and later won election to the presidency of Poland.

In recent time, labor unions and organizations representing (or purporting to represent) the interests of port facility operators and seafarers may disrupt or halt completely port or ship operations. In 2002, for example, a ten-day labor strike at the six largest container ports on the West Coast of the United States cost the U.S. economy $15 billion in lost trade.[12] At the time, the ports handled over half of all foreign origin or destination containers passing through American ports. A subsequent analysis done by the Congressional Budget Office concluded that a one week closure of the ports of Los Angeles and Long Beach would cost $125 to $200 million per day and that if the strike lasted for three years, the cost to the American economy would be about one-half of one percent of GDP, or $40 to $70 billion per year.[13]

The type of pressure brought to bear on ship owners and port management is limited only by the imagination of the labor organization. In the past, labor tactics have included mariners walking off ships, holding ships hostage, or refusing to load and offload cargo at the pier. Violence on board ship or in port can be associated with workplace grievances, organized crime, intimidation, and political activities wholly unrelated to the marine transportation system, such as the aforementioned case of Solidarity in Poland. Crew mutinies, although rare, usually occur at sea—especially among smaller crewed fishing boats—when all or part of the crew overtakes the master or lawful authority of a vessel.

States have banded together to address threats in a coordinated manner by implementing a range of ship, port, and coastal State measures. The common language and operational concepts for closer international cooperation is derived from the customary international law of the sea, associated treaties,

---

[11] CENTRAL INTELLIGENCE AGENCY, INTELLIGENCE MEMORANDUM NO. 272, THE PROBABILITY OF LOCAL INTERFERENCE WITH THE PRODUCTION AND MOVEMENT OF CERTAIN STRATEGIC MATERIALS IN THE EVENT OF WAR BEFORE 1954, Encl. A, at 1 (Central Intelligence Agency, Mar. 28, 1950) (Secret, declassified Apr. 1, 1976).

[12] The ports were Los Angeles, Long Beach, Oakland, Seattle, Tacoma, and Portland. The ports employ 16,000 longshoremen. Peter V. Hall, "We'd Have to Sink the Ships": Impact Studies and the 2002 West Coast Port Lockout, 18 ECON. DEVELOPMENT Q. 354, 355 (Nov. 2004).

[13] U.S. CONGRESSIONAL BUDGET OFFICE, THE ECONOMIC COSTS OF DISRUPTIONS IN CONTAINER SHIPMENTS, Mar. 29, 2006.

such as the *United Nations Convention on the Law of the Sea* (UNCLOS)[14] and the supplementary agreements, codes, and guidelines adopted by the member states of the International Maritime Organization (IMO).

12.2 The Law of the Sea and the IMO

As the specialized agency of the United Nations system for maritime matters, the IMO has a global mandate. Currently 170 sovereign states are members of the Organization. The predecessor institution, the International Maritime Consultative Organization, was established by the *Convention on the International Maritime Organization* and adopted by the United Nations Maritime Conference in Geneva on March 6, 1948.[15] The IMO is a consensus-based organization in which all member states may participate. Article 1 of the IMO Convention delineates the authority of the organization to develop governance regimes for the world's oceans.

The Organization has broad technical and operational competence for setting international standards for maritime safety and security, including design and equipment of ships, safety of navigation, radio communication, search and rescue, training and certification of mariners, carriage of cargoes, flag state responsibilities, port state control measures, and facilitation of international maritime traffic. These rules are set forth in over 50 international conventions and protocols as well as over 800 codes, recommendations, and guidelines.

The IMO is explicitly mentioned only in Article 2 of UNCLOS, but several additional provisions of the treaty refer to a "competent international organization" with authority to set additional standards and rules for international shipping. As an "umbrella convention," UNCLOS is a major feature of oceans law and policy, but many of its provisions for marine safety and security are broad or even aspirational in nature, requiring supplementary rule making by follow-on agreements and implementing legislation. The IMO serves as the principal means of developing more specific or detailed operative regulations than those that appear in UNCLOS. Contracting governments to the IMO Convention and subsequent maritime security conventions provide a roadmap for states to help ensure that ships that fly their flag and that ports and port facilities under their jurisdiction are protected from natural risks and man-made threats.

---

[14] United Nations Convention on the Law of the Sea, *opened for signature* Dec. 10, 1982, UN Doc. A/CONF.62/122 (1982), 1833 U.N.T.S. 3, 397, 21 ILM. 1261 (1982), *entered into force* Nov. 16, 1994 [hereinafter UNCLOS].

[15] The original name of the organization was the "Inter-Governmental Maritime Consultative Organization," but it was changed to "International Maritime Organization" by IMO Doc. A.358(IX), Amendments to the IMO Convention, Nov. 14, 1975 and IMO Doc. A.371(X), Correction of Assembly Resolution A.588(X), Nov. 9, 1977.

Numerous provisions in UNCLOS reference the work of the IMO, either explicitly or implicitly, through references to the "generally accepted international regulations," "recommendations of the competent international organization," or simple reference to the "competent international organization."[16] In such cases, parties to UNCLOS commit to "take account of," "conform to," "give effect to," or "implement,"[17] internationally recognized standards. The standards include:

- Rules for prevention of collisions at sea;[18]
- Designation of sea lanes;[19]
- Adoption of traffic separation schemes;[20]
- Requirements for foreign nuclear-powered ships and ships carrying nuclear or inherently dangerous or noxious substances;[21]
- Removal of abandoned installations or structures that pose navigational hazard;[22]
- Safety zones beyond a breadth of 500 meters;[23]
- Rules of navigation near artificial islands, installations, structures;[24]
- Duties of flag States in transit passage;[25]
- Rules for preventing marine pollution;[26] and
- Seaworthiness of vessels.[27]

The following IMO conventions may, on account of their worldwide acceptance, be considered as among the agreements reflecting internationally accepted standards:

- International Convention for the Safety of Life at Sea 1974;
- International Convention on Load Lines 1966;
- International Convention on Tonnage Measurement of Ships 1969;
- Convention on the International Regulations for Preventing Collisions at Sea, 1972;

---

[16] IMO Doc. LEG/MISC.6, Implications of the United Nations Convention on the Law of the Sea for the International Maritime Organization: Study by the Secretariat of the International Maritime Organization, Sept. 10, 2008, at 7.

[17] IMO Doc. LEG/MISC.6, Implications of the United Nations Convention on the Law of the Sea for the International Maritime Organization; Study by the Secretariat of the International Maritime Organization, Sept. 10, 2008, at 8. The UN Division for Ocean Affairs and Law of the Sea produced a table of subjects and articles in the sequence in which they appear in the Convention, together with the corresponding competent international organizations. *See*, LAW OF THE SEA BULL. NO. 31, at 79, 81–95 (1996).

[18] UNCLOS, Articles 21(4), 39(2), and (by reference) Article 54.

[19] Id., Article 22(3)(a).

[20] Id., Articles 41(4) and 53(9).

[21] Id., Article 23.

[22] Id., Articles 60 and 80, para. 3.

[23] Id., para. 5.

[24] Id., para. 6.

[25] Id., Articles 39(2) and 94(3)–(4).

[26] Id., Articles 210(4), 211 and (6), 216(1), Article 217(1)–(3), 218(1) and (3), and 220(1)–(3), and 226(1).

[27] Id., Articles 94(5), 219 and 226(1)(c).

- International Convention on Standards of Training, Certification and Watchkeeping for Seafarers 1978;
- International Convention on Maritime Search and Rescue 1979.[28]

Under Articles 60 to 62, the IMO may cooperate with governments and non-governmental organizations to accomplish its mission. The IMO uses two methods to advance and shape international maritime security law. First, recommendations and resolutions adopted by the IMO Assembly, and IMO committees, such as the IMO Maritime Safety Committee (MSC), IMO Legal Committee (LEG), and IMO Marine Environment Protection Committee (MEPC), may be adopted by states. Second, the IMO facilitates negotiation of treaties that become legally binding on States' parties. Through reciprocal recognition, national legislation implementing IMO recommendations can be applied with binding effect on foreign ships. IMO resolutions that include technical codes also may be made mandatory through national legislation.

The general obligations established by UNCLOS regarding compliance with IMO rules and standards should, in the case of IMO conventions and protocols, be assessed with reference to the specific operative features of each treaty. These features relate not only to the way in which the rules and standards regulate substantive matters, such as the construction, design, equipping and manning of ships, but also to the procedural rules governing the interrelations between flag and port State jurisdiction in everyday matters, such as certificate recognition and enforcement of sanctions.

Article 311 of UNCLOS regulates the relationship between the Convention and other conventions and international agreements. Article 311(2) provides that the Convention shall not alter the rights and obligations of States parties, which arise from other agreements, provided that they are compatible with the Convention and do not affect the application of its basic principles. Furthermore, several provisions of UNCLOS reflect principles that previously were features of IMO treaties adopted prior to the negotiation of the Law of the Sea Convention. In particular, UNCLOS amplifies duties by States on collisions at sea embedded in COLREGS 1972, search and rescue of persons in distress at sea (SAR Convention), traffic separation schemes, recognition of sovereignty over internal waters, and the exercise of port State jurisdiction.

---

[28] Id., at 16. *See also*, International Convention on Maritime Search and Rescue, Apr. 27, 1979, T.I.A.S. No. 11,093, 1405 U.N.T.S. 97 (with Annex), *entered into force* June 22, 1985 [Hereinafter IMO SAR Convention]; amendments to the International Convention on Maritime Search and Rescue of Apr. 27, 1979, May 18, 1998.

12.3 Exclusive Flag State Jurisdiction

Customary international law recognizes the plenary authority of the flag State over vessels flying its flag.[29] The authority includes corresponding obligations of the flag State, now reflected in Part VII of UNCLOS, in relation to safety of navigation, enforcement of international safety regulations, and the primacy of flag State jurisdiction. Flag State jurisdiction is the principle means for ensuring compliance with international standards, irrespective of where the ship is located.

Flag States have inherent authority to prescribe and enforce domestic laws and adopt and implement international rules for ships flying their flag. Normally vessels are subject to the exclusive jurisdiction of the flag State—the nation in which the ship is registered. A warship always may exercise enforcement jurisdiction over ships flying the same flag as a matter of international law. Generally, the flag State exercises exclusive enforcement jurisdiction over vessels flying its flag, although there are subtle signs that "exclusive" flag State jurisdiction is weakening from port state control, the usage of UN Security Council authority, and the law of self-defense.

Thus, increasingly there are exceptions to the universal rule of exclusive flag State jurisdiction. In contrast to the special ship boarding regimes applicable during times of war, the legal rationale for boarding foreign-flagged vessels in peacetime are more numerous and, in several respects, more complex. While the law of naval warfare is a rather discrete body of authority with well-developed ship boarding measures that apply during armed conflict, the rules for ship boarding during peacetime draw on a milieu of sources. Furthermore, peacetime boarding, often referred to as visit, board, search and seizure (VBSS), arises more often than the belligerent wartime right of visit and search. In both war and peace, however, only warships or government vessels on non-commercial service, such as marine law enforcement or coast guard ships, may exercise these rights.

Vessels on the high seas are subject to the norm of exclusive flag State jurisdiction, unless there is an exception or intervening rule. This principle means that the primary responsibility for the maintenance of security and law enforcement on ships in international waters falls on the flag State. States may provide permission or consent to outsource their responsibility, which may include negotiation of bilateral or multilateral agreements with other nations, but the flag State possesses authority as a matter of sovereignty.

Naval or maritime law enforcement authorities may seek consent from the flag State on an ad hoc basis to board a vessel. The request may be sent to the national-level authorities of the flag State or directly to the master of the vessel. Coordinating VBSS of a flag State's merchant ships with the authorities of another

---

[29] Lassa Oppenheim & Sir Ronald Roxburgh, International Law: Peace § 260–262 (Longmans, Green & Co., 3d ed., 1920).

country is an exercise, rather than a diminution, of flag State sovereignty. Permission granted to foreign police or military personnel to board a ship may be narrowly circumscribed, however, and does not necessarily entail consent to inspect, search or seize the vessel. Flag States cooperate to leverage the capabilities of other states to enforce international standards of safety and security.

Exceptions to exclusive flag State jurisdiction also exist in times of war or armed conflict, such as the belligerent right of visit and search of a vessel to determine the enemy character of the ship or its cargo.[30] The belligerent right of visit and search, which is a product of the law of naval warfare, is a separate legal right from peacetime maritime interception operations (MIO) and VBSS.[31] Belligerent parties to a conflict are entitled to board neutral ships anywhere in the oceans outside the territorial sea of a neutral state for the purpose of ascertaining the enemy character of the ship and its cargo. This wartime right is distinct from the aforementioned peacetime rule, in which the warship of one nation normally may not assert jurisdiction or control over a ship registered in another state. In times of peace, VBSS may only occur against a foreign-flagged ship subject to some other legal regime that serves as an exception to exclusive flag State jurisdiction.

Flag States are responsible for ensuring ships flying their flag comply with internationally accepted standards. The IMO has issued guidelines to member states on the implementation of SOLAS, MARPOL, Load Lines, and STCW.[32] In general, flag States have a legal duty to give effect in their national laws to international agreements to which they are party. Flag States are also required to enforce the requirements of the domestic laws that reflect the duties of international conventions. If a flag State authorizes third party organizations to act on its behalf, it must clearly delegate authority for doing so.[33] Some flag States have difficulty in implementing IMO instruments due to a lack of finances, shortcomings in technical expertise or trained personal, organization problems with delegation of authority or a lack of oversight over national agencies.[34]

---

[30] SAN REMO MANUAL ON INTERNATIONAL LAW APPLICABLE TO ARMED CONFLICTS AT SEA 25–29 (Louise Doswald-Beck ed., 1995).

[31] For a thorough treatment of the belligerent right of visit and search during time of armed conflict, see Wolff Heintschel von Heinegg, *Visit, Search, Diversion, and Capture in Naval Warfare: Part I, The Traditional Law*, 29 CAN. Y.B. INT'L L. 283 (1991) and Wolff Heintschel von Heinegg, *Visit, Search, Diversion, and Capture in Naval Warfare: Part II, Developments Since 1945*, 30 CAN. Y.B. INT'L L. 89 (1992).

[32] IMO Doc. A.847(20), Guidelines to Assist Flag States in the Implementation of IMO Instruments, Nov. 27, 1997.

[33] IMO Doc. Resolution A.739(18), Guidelines for the Authorization of Organizations Acting on Behalf of the Administration, Nov. 4, 1993 and IMO Doc. Resolution A.789(19), Specifications of the Survey and Certification Functions on Recognized Organizations Acting on Behalf of the Administration, Nov. 23, 1995.

[34] IMO Doc. Resolution A.847(20), Guidelines to Assist Flag States in the Implementation of IMO Instruments, Nov. 27, 1997, para. 1.4.

Subsequent IMO resolutions provides guidance to assist flag States in the self-assessment of their performance in implementing SOLAS,[35] MARPOL,[36] Load Lines,[37] STCW,[38] COLREGS,[39] and TONNAGE 69.[40] The resolutions contain templates for self-assessment of the conventions, which helps the Flag State Administration identify and correct deficiencies or weaknesses in fulfilling its obligations. The IMO guidance helps build a stronger culture of safety and security among seafarers and the shipping industry.

Another IMO Assembly resolution provides measures flag States may take to strengthen implementation of a variety of IMO instruments.[41] The IMO has provided a framework for national legislation that may be used by flag States to develop and enact legislation, assign responsibilities, and delegate authority within the Flag State Administration.[42]

Article 94 of UNCLOS requires flag States to conform to "generally accepted international regulations, procedures and practices" in the "construction, equipment and seaworthiness" of ships. Similarly, UNCLOS provides for enforcement by flag States of applicable international marine environmental laws.[43] Thus, compliance with IMO rules tends to be contingent upon how states interpret their obligation in UNCLOS to "give effect to," "implement," or "conform to" new standards.[44]

---

[35] International Convention for the Safety of Life at Sea reg. V/7, Nov. 1, 1974, 32 U.S.T. 47, T.I.A.S. 9700, 1184 U.N.T.S. 278, *entered into force* May 25, 1980, with protocols and regularly amended [Hereinafter SOLAS 1974].

[36] International Convention for the Prevention of Pollution from Ships, Nov. 2, 1973, 12 I.L.M. 1319 and Protocol of 1978 Relating to the International Convention for the Prevention of Pollution from Ships, done Feb. 17, 1978, 17 I.L.M. 546, *entered into force* Oct. 2, 1983) [Hereinafter MARPOL 73/78].

[37] International Convention on Load Lines 1966, Apr. 5, 1966, 18 U.S.T. 1857, T.I.A.S. No. 6331, 640 U.N.T.S. 133, *entered into force* July 21, 1968. [Hereinafter LOAD LINES 1966 or LL 66].

[38] International Convention on Standards of Training, Certification and Watchkeeping for Seafarers, Dec. 1, 1978, 1361 U.N.T.S. 2, *entered into force* Apr. 28, 1984, as amended and modified by the 1995 Protocol) [Hereinafter STCW 1995].

[39] Convention on International Regulations for Preventing Collisions at Sea, Oct. 20, 1972, *entered into force* July 15, 1977, 28 UST 3459, TIAS 8587, 1050 UNTS 17 [Hereinafter COLREGS 1972].

[40] International Convention on Tonnage Measurement of Ships, June 23, 1969, T.I.A.S. No 10,490, *entered into force* July 18, 1982 [Hereinafter TONNAGE 1969] and IMO Doc. Resolution A.912(22), Self-assessment of Flag State Performance, Nov. 29, 2001, Annex 1.

[41] IMO Doc. Resolution A.914(22), Measures to Strengthen Flag State Implementation, Nov. 29, 2001.

[42] IMO Doc. Resolution A.847(20), Guidelines to Assist Flag States in the Implementation of IMO Instruments, Nov. 27, 1997, Appendix.

[43] Id., Articles 217(1) and (2).

[44] IMO Doc. LEG/MISC.6, Implications of the United Nations Convention on the Law of the Sea for the International Maritime Organization: Study by the Secretariat of the International Maritime Organization, Sept. 10, 2008, at 12.

The IMO serves as the principal means of developing more specific or detailed operative regulations of the UNCLOS framework. When used in the singular, the term "competent international organization" in UNCLOS refers to the IMO.[45] Thus, UNCLOS requires states to "take account of," "conform to," "give effect to," or "implement" relevant internationally agreed or accepted regulations and standards developed by or through the "competent international organization"—typically, through the IMO. States have freedom, however, to devise the specific form of such application according to their individual interpretation of the regulations. Article 94 of UNCLOS regulates the duties of flag States and requires them to conform to "generally accepted international regulations, procedures and practices" in the "construction, equipment and seaworthiness" of ships.

The authority to conduct port state control inspections, although based on state sovereignty, is reflected in several IMO technical conventions and other international agreements. Some relevant agreements precede adoption of UNCLOS, and even the creation of International Maritime Consultative Organization (IMCO)—the predecessor of today's IMO—in 1959.[46]

12.3.1 *SOLAS*

The *International Convention for the Safety of Life at Sea* 1974 (SOLAS) is the bedrock IMO treaty for maritime safety and security. Today, SOLAS, with its 1978 protocol and many amendments, including the *International Safety Management (ISM) Code*[47] and the *International Ship and Port Facility Security (ISPS) Code* of 2002, contains comprehensive measures for securing ship and shore installations. The original version of the SOLAS Convention emerged in response to the Titanic disaster, and the treaty was adopted by a meeting of States in London on January 20, 1914. The first version of the treaty concerning the safety of merchant ships never entered into force, however, due to the intervention of World War I.[48]

---

[45] IMO Doc. LEG/MISC.6, Implications of the United Nations Convention on the Law of the Sea for the International Maritime Organization: Study by the Secretariat of the International Maritime Organization, Sept. 10, 2008, at 7.
[46] Convention on the Intergovernmental Maritime Consultative Organization (IMCO), Mar. 6, 1948, reprinted in 6C BENEDICT ON ADMIRALTY, Doc. 12-1A, at 12–23 (7th rev. ed. 1998).
[47] International Management Code for the Safe Operation of Ships and for Pollution Prevention 2010; IMO Doc. A.741(18), International Safety Management Code, Nov. 4, 1993, *reprinted in* 6D BENEDICT ON ADMIRALTY, Doc. 14-2, at 14-449 (7th rev. ed. 1998), *amended by* IMO Doc. MSC.104(73), Dec. 5, 2000, IMO Doc. MSC.179(79), Dec. 10, 2004, IMO Doc. MSC.195(80), May 20, 2005, and MSC.273(85), Dec. 4, 2008 [Hereinafter ISM Code].
[48] Arthur K. Kuhn, *The International Convention for Safety of Life at Sea*, 24 AM. J. INT'L L. 133, 135 (Jan. 1930).

The second iteration of SOLAS was adopted by a group of 18 nations meeting in London from April 16 to May 31, 1929.[49] Successive updates to SOLAS were produced in 1948, 1960, and 1974. There have been numerous revisions to the 1974 version under the tacit acceptance procedure that was built into the convention. Under tacit acceptance, all subsequent amendments automatically enter into force on a specified date unless, before that date, a specified number of states object to the amendment. Consequently, the 1974 SOLAS Convention has been updated numerous times and remains in force, as amended.

The 1974 SOLAS applies to 98 percent of world shipping, and it includes comprehensive safety standards for construction, design equipping and manning (CDEM) of vessels. Ship subdivision and stability, fire protection, life-saving appliances and arrangements, radio communications, safety of navigation, carriage of cargoes and dangerous goods, safe management and maritime security, are all part of the authoritative package. Flag States are responsible for ensuring that ships registered in the State comply with SOLAS, and vessels must retain on board the ship various certificates verifying compliance. State parties to SOLAS are authorized to inspect the ships of other flag States during a port visit, if there exist "clear grounds" for believing that the ship or its equipment are not in compliance with the Convention. The exercise of port state control is based on flag State consent to be bound by SOLAS and serves as an adjunct to the regime of exclusive flag State jurisdiction.

SOLAS now consists of general articles, with the main features included in an Annex comprised of 12 chapters, as follows:

Chapter I, General Provisions
Contains regulations concerning various types of ships, required documents and certifications, and provisions for port state control.

Chapter II-1, Construction, Subdivision and Stability, Machinery and Electrical Installations
Contains requirement that passenger ships be subdivided into watertight compartments, plus standards for machinery, electrical systems, watertight integrity, and stability. In 2010, "Goal-based standards" for new construction of oil tankers and bulk carriers were adopted.

Chapter II-2, Fire Protection, Fire Detection and Fire Extinction
Contains provisions on fire safety and firefighting, including division of ship into main and vertical zones separated by thermal and structural boundaries.

Chapter III, Life-saving Appliances and Arrangements
Contains requirements for lifeboats, rescue boats and life jackets, with technical requirements in the International Life-Saving Appliance (LSA) Code.

Chapter IV, Radio-communications
Contains the Global Maritime Distress and Safety System (GMDSS), which apply to passenger ships and all cargo ships of 300 gross tons on international voyages. Ships

---

[49] Id., at 133.

must carry distress radio beacons called emergency position-indicating radio beacons (EPIRBs) and search and rescue transponders (SARTs) to aid in search and rescue.

Chapter V, Safety of Navigation
Contains navigation safety services applicable to all ships on all voyages, such as meteorological, ice patrol service; ships' routeing, carriage of the automatic ship identification system (AIS) and voyage data recorders (VDRs), and search and rescue services. The chapter reiterates the legal duty of masters to provide assistance to mariners in distress.

Chapter VI, Carriage of Cargoes
Contains regulations concerning cargo ships (excepting liquids and gases in bulk).

Chapter VII, Carriage of Dangerous Goods
Part A contains special regulations on carriage of dangerous goods in packaged form, including labeling and storage, making mandatory the International Maritime Dangerous Goods (IMDG) Code, which came into effect on Jan. 1, 2004. Part B makes mandatory the International Bulk Chemical Code (IBC Code) for chemical carriers, and Part C promulgates International Gas Carrier Code (IGC Code) for gas carriers and ships carrying liquefied gases in bulk. Finally, Part D contains rules for the carriage of packaged irradiated nuclear fuel, plutonium and high-level radioactive wastes on board ships, which are set forth in the International Code for the Safe Carriage of Packaged Irradiated Nuclear Fuel, Plutonium and High-Level Radioactive Wastes on Board Ships (INF Code).

Chapter VIII, Nuclear Ships
Incorporates requirements for nuclear-powered ships in accordance with the Code of Safety for Nuclear Merchant Ships 1981.

Chapter IX, Management for the Safe Operation of Ships
Mandates shipowners adhere to the International Safety Management (ISM) Code.

Chapter X, Safety Measures for High-speed Craft
Mandates the International Code of Safety for High-Speed Craft (HSC Code).

Chapter XI-1, Special measures to enhance maritime safety
Contains responsibilities for ship surveys and inspections and port state control.

Chapter XI-2, Special Measures to Enhance Maritime Security
Contains Regulation XI-2/3 incorporating the International Ship and Port Facilities Security Code (ISPS Code). Part A of the Code is mandatory and Part B contains guidance for complying with Part A.

Chapter XII, Additional Safety Measures for Bulk Carriers
Contains structural requirements for bulk carriers greater than 150 meters in length.

Chapter XI-2 of the amended SOLAS constitutes the *International Code for the Security of Ships and Port Facilities* (ISPS Code). The ISPS Code contains detailed mandatory security-related requirements for governments, port authorities, and shipping companies, plus guidelines about how to implement the requirements. Generally the provisions apply to passenger ships and cargo ships of 500 gross tons or more, including high-speed craft, mobile offshore drilling units and port facilities serving such ships that are engaged on international voyages. States also may elect to impose the measures on their ships and port facilities that are not required to comply with the Code. The new regulations require states to set security levels and disseminate the information to ships entitled to fly their flag. When entering and while in a port, ships are required to observe the security level of the port.

Similarly, port States may board foreign ships at the pier under authority of SOLAS Chapter XI-2, Regulation 9, to determine the validity of vessel ISPS certificates. If "clear grounds" exist for believing that a ship is not in substantial compliance with the requirements of the ISPS Code, a port State may impose a number of control measures on the vessel. Control measures include inspection of the ship, delay or detention of the ship, restrictions on ship operations, expulsion from port, movement of the ship within the port, or denial of port entry. Port States are authorized to impose less severe administrative remedies to sanction noncompliance.

The international standards only apply as a matter of international law to specific vessels (e.g. ships of a certain size) and to vessels flying the flag of state parties. Port States may elect to apply the procedures to a greater population of visiting ships as a matter of port state control. For example, in cases in which vessels are not specifically subject to the security requirements imposed by SOLAS, the port State may still require adherence to the measures, either through unilateral authority of port state control or through bilateral agreement with other states, or both.

Administrations and their authorized Recognized Security Organizations (RSO) have sought to link the timing of verifications required by new maritime security measures with other verifications or inspections including, particularly, those required under the *International Safety Management* (ISM) Code. Combining inspections in this way can increase efficiency for flag States, port States and the shipping industry. In ports where ISM auditors are not always available, however, a combined approach may not be practicable and could unduly delay shipping. The training and experience required for those undertaking verifications and inspections under the maritime security measures of the ISPS Code may differ from those undertaking other forms of verification or inspection.[50]

In 1989, the IMO adopted initial guidelines on management of ships, and these guidelines later were reflected in the ISM Code. In 1994, the ISM Code was made mandatory by integrating it into the SOLAS Convention as chapter IX. The Code established international standards for the safe management and operation of vessels, which became compulsory for oil tankers, bulk carriers, and passenger ships in 1998 and for all other vessels in 2002.[51] These safety management systems are mostly in the form of checklists.

---

[50] ISM Code, para. 1.14.
[51] IMO Doc. MSC.99(73), Adoption of Amendments for the Convention on the Safety of Life at Sea, 1974, as amended, Dec. 5, 2000.

SOLAS illustrates how formerly non-mandatory rules were later incorporated into a legally binding IMO treaty. Following the adoption by the IMO Assembly of *Guidelines for Ships Operating in Polar Waters* in 2009, for example, the Sub-Committee on Ship Design and Equipment (DE) embarked on development of a mandatory Polar Code that is intended to supplement SOLAS and MARPOL.[52]

12.3.2 Load Lines

The *International Convention on Load Lines* (LOAD LINES 66) was adopted in April 1966 and entered into force in July 1968.[53] The 159 contracting state parties represent more than 99 percent of world shipping tonnage. LOAD LINES 66 established uniform standards for the safe loading of ships on international voyages. Regulations require vessels to have load line marks inscribed on the hull of the ship, to mark the point beyond which a vessel may not be safely loaded and hence submerged. Different load lines are observed during different seasons of the year and the geographic sea in which the ship sails. The regulations ensure ships are not over-loaded, based on the principle of reserve buoyancy, or the difference between the volume of a vessel below the waterline and the lowest opening that cannot be made watertight.[54]

Ships may not proceed to sea on an international voyage without having been surveyed and marked and carrying an appropriate certificate. Periodically, ships are surveyed to ensure they remain in compliance with the LOAD LINES standards, at which time its certificates are reissued. LOAD LINES was amended by a November 1988 Protocol, which entered into force in February 2000.[55] The 1988 Protocol synchronizes the treaty with SOLAS and MARPOL 73/78.

The LOAD LINES 66 Convention has strengthened port state control by recognizing the authority of Port State Control Officers (PSCOs) to board ships to verify the validity of ships' load certificates. Ships may not be loaded beyond allowable limits, and the position of the load must correspond with the certificate.[56] Port

---

[52] IMO Doc. A.1024(26), Guidelines for Ships Operating in Polar Waters, Dec. 2, 2009. The Polar Shipping Guidelines supplement the Guidelines for Ships Operating in Arctic Ice-Covered Waters, IMO Doc. MSC/Circ. 1056 and IMO Doc. MEPC/Circ. 399, Dec. 23, 2002.

[53] LOAD LINES 1966.

[54] Figuring reserve buoyancy considers the temperature and salinity and temperature of oceans in different regions to ensure that a vessel will remain watertight when sailing in those waters. The types of seawater represented by load lines are: tropical seawater (T); summer temperate seawater (S); winter temperate seawater (W); and winter North Atlantic (WNA).

[55] S. Treaty Doc. No. 2, 102d Cong., 1st Sess., at III (1991) and Marian Nash Leich, *Safety of Life at Sea and Load Lines Convention*, 85 AM J. INT'L L. 668, 671–73 (Oct. 1991).

[56] LOAD LINES 1966, Articles 21(1) and (2).

States may take control action against ships that have been materially altered in such a way that makes their cargo load manifestly unsafe to get underway.

12.3.3   MARPOL

The *International Convention for the Prevention of Pollution from Ships* (MARPOL 73/78) also includes provisions for port state vessel inspection.[57] Articles 5(2) and 6 provide port States with authority to verify the validity of MARPOL certificates. In cases in which "clear grounds" exist for believing that a vessel is not in "substantial compliance" with the Convention, the port State may take steps to stop the ship from getting underway.

Additional port state control measures are included in annexes to MARPOL, including regulation 8A of Annex I, regulation 15 of Annex II, regulation 8 of Annex III and regulation 8 of Annex V. Finally, article 5(4) of MARPOL provides that port States will not apply more favorable treatment to ships of countries that are not party to the Convention, avoiding the possibility that ships registered in non-MARPOL states would "benefit" from being outside of the regime.

12.3.4   STCW

Under the *International Convention on Standards of Training, Certification and Watchkeeping for Seafarers* (STCW), port States may detain ships that pose a danger to persons, property or the environment.[58] The original STCW was adopted in 1978, and major revisions were made in 1995 and July 2010 that bolstered port State authority. Revisions to the STCW are made under the IMO's tacit acceptance procedures.

STCW 1978 set forth standards on training, certification and watchkeeping for crews of merchant ships, such as deck officers, radio officers, and engineers. Today the STCW applies to 154 states representing more than 99 percent of the world's tonnage. The Convention also sets separate standards for crewing different classes of ships, including oil and chemical tankers, liquefied gas tankers, and cargo vessels carrying dangerous or hazardous cargoes.

Revised Chapter I of the STCW contains Regulation 1/4 that includes procedures for port state control in case of deficiencies that pose a danger to person, property or the environment. If a ship is involved in a collision, maneuvering in an erratic or unsafe manner, or if the ship illegally discharges pollution, port State authorities may detain the vessel.[59] Like MARPOL, article X(5) of the STCW states that no more favorable treatment will be given to the ships of countries

---

[57] MARPOL 73/78. Entry into force varies for each Annex. At the time of writing, Annexes I through VI were in force.
[58] STCW, Article X.
[59] Id. and STCW Regulation 1/4.

that are not party to the treaty.[60] The STCW Code stipulates that all Ship Security Officers (SSOs) and shipboard personnel should receive security-related familiarization training before taking up their duties.

The STCW and Code reflect a three-layer certification process. Flag State Administrations have authority for the first layer, which is issuance of Certificates of Competency. Administrations or approved training institutions may issue the second layer of certification, Certificates of Proficiency.[61] Documentary Evidence constitutes the third layer, and appropriate certificates may be issued by training institutions approved by Flag State Administrations.

In May 2006, STCW was amended, and the changes entered into force in January, 2008. The new provisions ensure merchant vessel crews are from nations that have fully implemented the Convention. Ships with crews with certificates from states not on the "white list" may be targeted for more rigorous inspection, while states that are on the "white list" may choose not to employ, on their own flagged vessels, mariners with certificates issued by non-white list countries.

Following amendments adopted at the 2010 Manila Diplomatic Conference, which entered into force on January 1, 2012,[62] the STCW Convention and related STCW Code recognized mandatory minimum requirements for security-related training and instruction for all SSOs and shipboard personnel serving on SOLAS ships. Although shipboard personnel are not security experts, they nonetheless are required to receive training and contribute to general awareness that enhances maritime security. In particular, the 2010 amendments include requirements that crews are proficient in anti-piracy measures. The STCW and associated Code, however, do not cover security-related requirements for Company Security Officers (CSOs).

12.3.5   *TONNAGE 69*

The *International Convention on Tonnage Measurement of Ships* 1969, provides a framework for states to enter into agreement to permit certain inspections of their vessels in the ports of other treaty partners. The treaty standardizes methods

---

[60] STCW, Article X(5).
[61] Certificates of Proficiency under regulations V/1-1 and V/1-2, however, may only be issued by Administrations and not approved training institutions.
[62] IMO Doc. A1/V/5.02 (NV.5), Notice of entry into force for all Parties, except Denmark, Finland, Ireland, Latvia, Lithuania, New Zealand, Portugal, Slovenia, and the United Kingdom, of the 2010 Manila Amendments to the Annex to the International Convention on Standards of Training, Certification and Watchkeeping for Seafarers (STCW), 1978, and the 2010 Manila Amendments to the Seafarers' Training, Certification and Watchkeeping Code, which were adopted by the Conference of Parties to the International Convention on Standards of Training, Certification and Watchkeeping for Seafarers (STCW), 1978, held in Manila, the Philippines, from June 21 to 25 2010, issued in London, March 19, 2012, Mar. 23, 2012.

for determining gross tonnage or overall size of a ship, as well as net tonnage, which is a measure of useful capacity.[63] Under article 12 of the Convention, a ship from one State party may be inspected by officials in the port of another State party for the purpose of verifying that the ship has a valid International Tonnage Certificate. If the characteristics of the ship differ from those on the International Tonnage Certificate, then the port State has a duty to inform the flag State.

12.3.6 IMO Member State Audit Scheme

After the guidelines on authorizing organizations to act on behalf of Flag Ftate Administrations became mandatory in SOLAS Chapter XI-1, *Special measures to enhance maritime safety*, the IMO sought methods to ensure better flag State compliance with obligations and duties of IMO mandatory instruments.[64] With the recognition that Flag State Administrations may designate organizations to act on their behalf, it became clear that there was not a universal and clear understanding of the roles, responsibilities, and authorities of such organizations.[65] Some of the recognized organizations have commercial interests in the ships registered by the Flag State Administration, creating a potential conflict of interest on their role as certifier and inspector on behalf of the Flag State Administration and their business relationship with shipowners and clients.[66]

With various actors involved in the global marine transportation system—IMO, State and their Administration, and Recognized Organizations, shipping companies and mariners—there was consensus for improving coordination to make sure that the system did not become disjointed, with each actor pursuing a separate course.[67] Consequently, the case for creation of a voluntary audit scheme was made to the member states, which accepted the idea.

Parties to SOLAS periodically provide information to the IMO on the authorization granted to Recognized Organizations (ROs) based on the aforementioned regulation. There is no independent mechanism to verify that state parties adhere to the provisions, however. As a result of this relationship, there is no clear universal understanding of the responsibilities of authorized ROs, the competence of such organizations and their representatives, and accountability to the international community.

---

[63] Id., Article 2.
[64] IMO Doc. A.789(19), Specifications on the Survey and Certification Functions of Recognized Organizations Acting on Behalf of the Administration, Nov. 23, 1995, *reprinted* Dec. 8, 1995.
[65] IMO Doc. A.739(18), Guidelines for the authorization of Organizations Acting on Behalf of the Administration, Nov. 4, 1993.
[66] L. D. Barchue, Sr., MAKING A CASE FOR THE IMO VOLUNTARY MEMBER STATE AUDIT SCHEME, at 1–2.
[67] Id.

The voluntary audit scheme is designed to promote universal implementation of IMO instruments relating to maritime safety and marine environmental protection by member States. At its twenty-third session held in November 2003, the IMO Assembly agreed to initiate voluntary IMO member state audits on the implementation of mandatory instruments.[68] The next year the IMO Assembly adopted a framework and code for the audit scheme.[69] Performance on implementation and enforcement of the following mandatory instruments may be the subject of a voluntary independent audit: SOLAS, MARPOL 73/78, STCW, LOAD LINES 1966, TONNAGE 1969, and COLREGS 1972.[70]

The 2005 Code helps states determine whether they are effectively implementing and enforcing IMO instruments, including enactment and enforcement of laws and regulations; delegations of authority; and monitoring of responsibilities by the member State. The audit provides a basis to assess the degree to which the member State conforms to IMO treaties made mandatory by acceptance and ratification by the state. The audits are sensitive to state sovereignty, and therefore the entire scheme is voluntary and intended to be a constructive, fair, and transparent means of assisting the audited states and the international maritime community in enhancing safety and effectiveness.

In June 2007, for example, Canada submitted to an audit by three outside experts (from Germany, Panama, and the United States). The audit report concluded that Canada substantially met its international obligations with regard to the mandatory IMO instruments to which it was a party and to the Code for the implementation of such instruments. The audit identified a number of areas of "good practice," as well as some relatively minor areas where "improvement was possible."[71]

12.3.7 ILO Instruments

Since its inception, the International Labor Organization (ILO) has exhibited a special concern for the work and welfare standards of mariners at sea.[72] Beginning with the First Maritime Session of the ILO in 1920 through to the present, the ILO has produced numerous instruments to advance the interests

---

[68] IMO Doc. Resolution A.946(23), Voluntary IMO Member State Audit Scheme, Nov. 27, 2003, *reprinted* Feb. 24, 2004.
[69] IMO Doc. A.974(24), Framework and Procedures for the Voluntary IMO Member State Audit Scheme, Dec. 1, 2005. The audit process is set forth in Appendices 1–4. See also, UN Doc. G.A. Res. 58/240, Oceans and Law of the Sea, Mar. 5, 2004, para. 30.
[70] IMO Doc. A.974(24), at 6–7.
[71] Voluntary Member State Audit Scheme, Audit of Canada 11–18 June 2007, Final Report, Oct. 2007.
[72] Frank L. Wiswall, Jr., *Uniformity in Maritime Law: The Domestic Impact of International Maritime Regulation*, 57 TUL. L. REV. 1208, 1222 (1982–83).

of seafarers. The ILO arose from the Labor Commission of the Versailles Peace Conference of 1919 and predates the creation of the League of Nations.[73]

As a precursor to organizations of the United Nations after World War II, the ILO has a general assembly called the International Labor Conference, which meets every June in Geneva, a Governing Body (comprised of 28 governments, plus 14 representatives from employers and 14 representatives from labor, both elected in their personal capacities), and a Secretariat, the International Labor Office. Among contemporary intergovernmental organizations, the ILO also has a most unique voting structure.[74] Article 3 of the ILO Constitution stipulates that States' parties are entitled to four votes at the annual meetings of the conference. Government representatives from each state cast two votes. A representative of the state's industrial management cast the third vote, and a representative from the state's organized labor casts the fourth vote.

The ILO has sponsored a number of treaties and recommendations related to maritime security as a way to protect seafarers. On February 23, 2006, the Tenth Maritime Session of the International Labor Conference of the ILO adopted the *Maritime Labor Convention* 2006 (MLC). The MLC is a comprehensive treaty for the protection of 1.2 million merchant mariners throughout the world. The treaty consolidates and updates more than 68 international standards (including 36 conventions and one protocol) developed by the ILO since its inception.[75] The most important among these agreements is the ILO *Merchant Shipping (Minimum Standards) Convention* No. 147, 1976.[76] Parties to Convention No. 147 commit to a series of safety and social security standards for mariners working on board ships registered to the State.[77] The standards cover shipboard conditions and living arrangements, mariner qualifications and training, and agreement to hold an official inquiry into any serious marine casualty, with the results of the investigation made public. The ILO has also adopted, in coordination with the IMO, a *Code of Practice for Security in Ports*.[78] The *Code of Practice* is designed to complement the ISPS Code by extending consideration of port security beyond the area of the fence line of the port facility and into the whole port area.[79]

---

[73] JAMES THOMSON SHOTWELL, I THE ORIGINS OF THE INTERNATIONAL LABOR ORGANIZATION 371 (1934).
[74] Wiswall, Jr., *Uniformity in Maritime Law*, at 1222.
[75] Article X, MLC 2006.
[76] International Labor Organization Merchant Shipping (Minimum Standards) Convention No. 147 1976, Oct. 29, 1976, *entered into force* Nov. 19, 1981, *reprinted in* 6A BENEDICT ON ADMIRALTY at 9–97 (M. Cohen rev. 7th ed. 1983).
[77] Id., Article 2.
[78] ILO SECURITY IN PORTS: ILO AND IMO CODE OF PRACTICE (2004).
[79] Id. at paras. 1.5.–1.6.

Table 12.1. Maritime Conventions and Protocols Revised by the Maritime Labor Convention, Feb. 23, 2006

Minimum Age (Sea) Convention, 1920 (No. 7)
Unemployment Indemnity (Shipwreck) Convention, 1920 (No. 8)
Placing of Seamen Convention, 1920 (No. 9)
Medical Examination of Young Persons (Sea) Convention, 1921 (No. 16)
Seamen's Articles of Agreement Convention, 1926 (No. 22)
Repatriation of Seamen Convention, 1926 (No. 23)
Officers' Competency Certificates Convention, 1936 (No. 53)
Holidays with Pay (Sea) Convention, 1936 (No. 54)
Shipowners' Liability (Sick and Injured Seamen) Convention, 1936 (No. 55)
Sickness Insurance (Sea) Convention, 1936 (No. 56)
Hours of Work and Manning (Sea) Convention, 1936 (No. 57)
Minimum Age (Sea) Convention (Revised), 1936 (No. 58)
Food and Catering (Ships' Crews) Convention, 1946 (No. 68)
Certification of Ships' Cooks Convention, 1946 (No. 69)
Social Security (Seafarers) Convention, 1946 (No. 70)
Paid Vacations (Seafarers) Convention, 1946 (No. 72)
Medical Examination (Seafarers) Convention, 1946 (No. 73)
Certification of Able Seamen Convention, 1946 (No. 74)
Accommodation of Crews Convention, 1946 (No. 75)
Wages, Hours of Work and Manning (Sea) Convention, 1946 (No. 76)
Paid Vacations (Seafarers) Convention (Revised), 1949 (No. 91)
Accommodation of Crews Convention (Revised), 1949 (No. 92)
Wages, Hours of Work and Manning (Sea) Convention (Revised), 1949 (No. 93)
Wages, Hours of Work and Manning (Sea) Convention (Revised), 1958 (No. 109)
Accommodation of Crews (Supplementary Provisions) Convention, 1970 (No. 133)
Prevention of Accidents (Seafarers) Convention, 1970 (No. 134)
Continuity of Employment (Seafarers) Convention, 1976 (No. 145)
Seafarers' Annual Leave with Pay Convention, 1976 (No. 146)
Merchant Shipping (Minimum Standards) Convention, 1976 (No. 147)
Protocol of 1996 to the Merchant Shipping (Minimum Standards) Convention, 1976 (No. 147)
Seafarers' Welfare Convention, 1987 (No. 163)
Health Protection and Medical Care (Seafarers) Convention, 1987 (No. 164)
Social Security (Seafarers) Convention (Revised), 1987 (No. 165)
Repatriation of Seafarers Convention (Revised), 1987 (No. 166)
Labour Inspection (Seafarers) Convention, 1996 (No. 178)
Recruitment and Placement of Seafarers Convention, 1996 (No. 179)
Seafarers' Hours of Work and the Manning of Ships Convention, 1996 (No. 180)

12.4   THE ISPS CODE

The most far-reaching maritime security instrument in decades—the *International Code for the Security of Ships and of Port Facilities*—emerged in the wake of the 9/11 terrorist attacks on the United States.[80] The abbreviated name is *ISPS*

---

[80] Resolutions of the Conference of Contracting Governments to the International Convention for the Safety of Life at Sea 1974, adopted Dec. 12, 2002, Conference resolution 2,

Code. The ISPS Code is the most comprehensive effort to institutionalize a global culture of maritime security.[81] The Code was incorporated into major amendments to the *International Convention for the Safety of Life at Sea Convention* 1974 (SOLAS 74) in December 2002.

Adopted by the Assembly and States' parties to the IMO, the Code incorporates international standards of maritime safety and security. Since its entry into force in July 2004, States' parties are obligated to establish security levels under the provisions of chapter XI-2 and Part A of the Code.[82] Flag State responsibilities normally are undertaken by the Administration for each country, which is responsible for verifying the compliance of ships with the provisions of chapter XI-2 and Part A of the ISPS Code applicable to ships. Thus, the Flag State Administration approves Ship Security Plans and issues International Ship Security Certificates.[83] Governments also are responsible for determining which of their port facilities require designation of a Port Facility Security Officer (PFSO), completion of Port Facility Security Assessments, and approval of port facility security plans (PFSP).[84]

Along with UNCLOS, the 1974 SOLAS Convention is one of the landmark treaties to form the global system of oceans governance. The SOLAS Convention sets forth the major provisions on ship and port security for ships on international voyages. The term "international voyage" means a voyage from a country to which the SOLAS Convention applies to a port outside such a country.[85]

The SOLAS Convention is the most comprehensive of the dozens of international treaties and agreements that have been negotiated at IMO, and it is the principal instrument for ship safety and security. Provisions governing ship construction, equipment, manning and operations are included in SOLAS through its numerous amendments. With the incorporation of the ISPS Code, SOLAS 74 established an international framework for cooperation among Flag State Administrations and the shipping and port industries to institute preventive security measures to protect global trade.[86] Roles and responsibilities among public and private actors were precisely defined, including rules for the efficient collection and exchange of security-related information.[87]

Historically, the port and shipping industries have suffered a high level of crime, particularly, pilferage and smuggling. If the security measures build greater

---

Annex: International Code for the Security of Ships and of Port Facilities [Hereinafter ISPS Code].

[81] *See generally*, Thomas A. Mensah, *The Place of the ISPS Code in the Legal International Regime for the Security of International Shipping*, 3 WMU. J. MARITIME AFF. 17 (2004).

[82] ISPS Code, para. A/7.1.

[83] Id., at paras. A/7.2 and B/1.6.

[84] Id. at para. B/1.6.

[85] SOLAS Chapter I "General provisions."

[86] ISPS Code, para. A/1.2.1.

[87] Id., at para. A/1.2.2 and 3.

confidence among port and ship users that their cargos will arrive safety, however, then a stronger culture of security in the shipping industry will generate positive externalities throughout the world economy. The costs of insurance and shipping will be reduced, cargo loss minimized, and injuries and deaths avoided. Thus, increased security can avoid both human tragedy and economic dislocation.

In 1996, the Maritime Safety Committee (MSC) broadened the rules for ship and port security to apply to international passenger ferry services and the ports that they use. The amendments recommended the use of three threat levels: (a) Background; (b) Moderate; and, (c) High. MSC's goal was to enhance confidence in the worldwide maritime transportation system by reducing security risks to vessel passengers, crews and port personnel and to better secure public and private property and cargos.[88]

The ISPS Code promulgated a standardized methodology for conducting security assessments on board ships and in port facilities, extending earlier work at the IMO to strengthen maritime security.[89] For example, greater guidance on the security of cruise ships and the ports that they use was issued by the IMO Maritime Safety Committee (MSC) in the wake of the 1985 attack on the *Achille Lauro*. This initial guidance covered the appointment of responsible officials within governments and in the private sector. Governments were required to appoint a Designated Authority (DA), who is responsible for cruise ship and port security. Shipping companies operating cruise ships must appointment a Company Security Officer (CSO) for the fleet, as well as individual Ship Security Officers (SSO) for every cruise ship. Commercial shipping firms also were required to undertake a Ship Security Survey (SSS) of each cruise ship and then prepare a Ship Security Plan (SSP) tailored to each vessel. The SSP is subject to approval by the Designated Authority within the flag State government. Similarly, Facility Security Officers (FSOs) are responsible for security at cruise ports, and they are required to conduct Facility Security Surveys (FSSs) for each one. The FSS are also subject to the approval of the Designated Authority.

In November 2001, only two months after the terrorist attacks of 9/11, the twenty-second session of the IMO Assembly adopted a resolution to obtain a review of measures and procedures to prevent acts of maritime terrorism.[90] An extraordinary meeting of the MSC, also held in November 2001, began work on amending SOLAS to address the threat of maritime terrorism. Work continued during an MSC Inter-sessional Working Group in February 2002, which reported findings of the gathering to a meeting of the seventy-fifth session of the MSC in May 2002, when an ad hoc MSC Working Group was established to further develop proposals. An Inter-sessional MSC Working Group met in September

---

[88] Id., at para. A/1.2.5.
[89] Id., at para. A/1.2.4.
[90] IMO Doc. A.924(22), Review of Measures and Procedures to Prevent Acts of Terrorism which Threaten the Security of Passengers and Crews and Safety of Ships, Nov. 20, 2001.

2002, and the results of the meeting were considered by the seventy-sixth session of the MSC in December 2002, immediately prior to the final text of the ISPS Code being sent to a Diplomatic Conference that same month.

The MSC and its associated Maritime Security Working Group led development of far-reaching amendments to the existing chapter XI of SOLAS. The amendments were adopted by the IMO Assembly and re-identified as chapter XI-1 of SOLAS. At the Conference of Contracting Governments to the *International Convention for the Safety of Life at Sea, 1974* (Diplomatic Conference on Maritime Security), from December 9 to 13, 2002, the member States of the IMO adopted a series of resolutions and measures amending SOLAS, which incorporated the new ISPS Code.

One hundred nine States' parties to the SOLAS Convention participated in the negotiations. The meeting included representatives from numerous international, intergovernmental, and non-governmental organizations. The ISPS Code, included as a new SOLAS chapter, XI-2 concerning special measures, was drafted at the same time. Chapter V of SOLAS was also amended. Due to the urgency and heightened sense of vulnerability on the waterfront and at sea, negotiations for the ISPS Code were completed in just over a year. The Diplomatic Conference also adopted resolutions to facilitate cooperation with the International Labor Organization (ILO) and the World Customs Organization (WCO).[91]

The new security measures created a framework for cooperation among governments and the shipping and port industries to deter and respond to security threats affecting international seaborne trade. States must provide updates to IMO on their security measures every five years with the last interval being July 1, 1999, and the next due on July 1, 2014. The ISPS Code focuses on the ship as a target, the potential use of the ship as a weapon, and the use of a ship as a means for transporting persons intending to cause a security incident. The use of ships in lawful trade to generate revenue to finance terrorist activities is not explicitly covered by the Code. SOLAS ships are required, however, to carry documentation concerning passengers and cargo that may be used to investigate terrorist finance. The respective roles and responsibilities of participants in the global marine transportation system were set forth, and a methodology was created for governments and the private sector to assess and react to a fluid threat environment. Designated governmental authorities, ship and port facility officers, and personnel on the shore and at sea each play an integral part in systemic security.

The ISPS Code applies to ships on international voyages (including passenger ships, cargo ships of 500 gross tons and upwards, and mobile offshore drilling

---

[91] Conference Resolution 8, Enhancement of Security in Cooperation with the International Labor Organization (Seafarer's Identity Documents and work on the wider issues of port security), including Annex, IMO/ILO work on port security, Dec. 12, 2002 and Conference Resolution 9, Enhancement of Security in Cooperation with the World Customs Organization (Closed cargo transportation units), Dec. 12, 2002.

units) and now, the port facilities serving such ships.[92] The SOLAS Convention previously did not apply to port facilities, but States parties at the IMO determined that inserting the ISPS Code into the multilateral treaty was the most expeditious method to establish new shore-side requirements. Under the ISPS Code, port facilities and ships are required to produce and implement security plans, which are reviewed by appropriate government agencies.

The ISPS Code entered into force on January 1, 2004. States' parties already should have made any necessary changes to national legislation, administrative processes, and governmental institutions to implement the Code. Many governments achieved compliance by the target date, although numerous interim arrangements were required to allow additional time for some nations.

The maritime security measures were adopted to deter and counter terrorist threats to the marine transportation system. But the provisions also proved helpful in reducing crime, accidents and stowaways, so some states expanded the application of the ISPS Code to port facilities and ships not covered under the terms of the actual SOLAS amendments. Ships operating in domestic service, for example, have been made subject to the security measures in some countries. In other cases, the IMO/ILO *Code of Practice on Port Security* has been applied to port areas that do not serve international shipping.

States' party to SOLAS committed to enact national legislation to implement the ISPS ship and port security regime. States have discretion to extend provisions to additional ships and port facilities that the measures do not apply to, but they have agreed not to adopt legislation that applies lower requirements or weaker standards to regulated ships and port facilities. Governments also may appoint Designated Authorities within the interagency community to implement the provisions or outsource the tasks to delegated private or non-governmental Recognized Security Organizations (RSOs).

The effectiveness of the new measures depends on the extent to which the provisions are universally implemented and enforced. The United States, for example, aligned the *Maritime Transportation Security Act of 2002* and its domestic regulations with the maritime security standards of SOLAS and the ISPS Code.[93] After a period of adjustment immediately following introduction of the Code, security-related deficiencies have declined in states that have implemented the new provisions. The success of the ISPS Code in reducing security problems on ships and in ports, however, is difficult to quantify. Most evidence remains anecdotal, although there appear to be fewer unauthorized entries into restricted areas and, most importantly, fewer deaths from accidents and crime.

---

[92] ISPS Code A/3.1.
[93] 33 C.F.R. Parts 101 through 107 (2011). Vessel security regulations are set forth in Part 104, some of which apply to foreign ships present in U.S. waters.

Still, for a variety of reasons, gaps in implementation and application of the security measures persist. States have taken a variety of approaches to implement the new maritime security measures tailored to the specific constitutional and legislative procedures in each country. Numerous states have yet to fully implement the measures. Generally, states have integrated the security measures into existing national law through amendments to legacy port and shipping legislation. In some cases, however, enactment of new legal instruments is necessary.

Obtaining full compliance among the world's port facilities is a significant challenge because of competing funding priorities, including maritime safety and marine environmental protection. High cost also serves as an impediment. A UN Conference on Trade and Development study found that the cost of implementing the provisions of the ISPS Code average $287,000 in initial investment costs and $105,000 in additional annual operating costs per port facility.

Since the requirements of Part A of the ISPS Code are mandatory, most of the legislative focus among States' parties has focused on rules to implement that part. Part B is non-mandatory. Numerous governments, however, have integrated provisions of Part B into their national legislation as well. Some states lack the legal and policy architecture needed to fully implement the measures, such as resolution of jurisdictional issues among government agencies. Resource constraints also limit the amount and quality of training for security officers, facility guards, and port managers. These factors have led to different levels of diligence, just as new threat patterns and incidents continually test the effectiveness of the present rules.

Comprehensive legislation to fully implement requirements in the security measures should include:

a. Definitions;
b. Application;
c. Designated Authority and Administration;
d. Security level;
e. Port facility;
f. Port facility security assessment;
g. Ship;
h. Port facility and ship security plans;
i. Retention of records and Declarations of Security;
j. Inspection of port facilities and ships;
k. Enforcement action;
l. Control and compliance measures; and
m. Criminal offenses relating to the Maritime Security Measures.[94]

---

[94] IMO Doc. MSC 89/WP.6/Add.1, Measures to Enhance Maritime Security: Piracy and Armed Robbery against Ships; Report of the Working Group, May 17, 2011, at para. 2.2.16, and IMO Doc. MSC 89/INF.13, Measures to Enhance Maritime Security, Maritime Security

The member states of the IMO balanced the risks with the costs of security. Besides the obvious financial burden of implementing the security measures, there are associated costs that are more difficult to quantify. For example, tight security still must accommodate reasonable access to shore and shore leave by seafarers and permit access to ships by persons representing organizations promoting seafarer welfare. The rules contained in the ISPS Code are integrated into other ongoing IMO initiatives and require a balance between the openness needed to facilitate trade and economic prosperity and security measures, such as effective screening of ships and cargo.

Because of the many different types and sizes of ships and facilities, the ISPS Code does not specify measures that each port and ship must take. Instead it outlines a standardized framework for evaluating and responding to risk. The risk assessment enables governments to offset changes in the threat condition with adjustments in the security measures. For ships, the new security measures include requirements for creation of Ship Security Plans (SSP), designation of Ship Security Officers (SSO) for each vessel, appointment of Company Security Officers (CSO) for each company, and requirements for certain equipment to be carried onboard ships. Similarly, port facilities are required to develop security plans, designate security officers, and install certain security equipment. Both ships and port facilities are required to monitor and control access, maintain awareness of the activities of surrounding people and cargo, and maintain viable communications.

Only one year after the attacks on the Pentagon and the World Trade Center, the ISPS Code launched a worldwide public-private partnership for maritime security that helps national governments develop better oversight of their commercial shipping and port facility industries. Chapter XI is divided into two parts: Chapter XI-1 is "Special Measures to Enhance Maritime *Safety*," and Chapter XI-2 is a new chapter titled "Special Measures to Enhance Maritime *Security*" (author's italics). The recent addition applies to passenger ships and cargo ships of 500 gross tons or greater, including high speed craft, mobile offshore drilling units and port facilities serving such ships engaged on international voyages. The ISPS Code stipulates a range of mandatory measures to enhance the security port facilities and ships engaged on international voyages. The provisions are focused on preventive action and do not extend to actual response to attack or consequence management. Combined, these measures are directed at protecting ships from being a target or being used as weapon or as a means of transport for persons intending to cause a security incident.

Manual—Guidance for Port Facilities, Ports and Ships, Mar. 5, 2011, at para. 2.2.16, *reproduced in* GUIDE TO MARITIME SECURITY AND THE ISPS CODE para. 2.2.16 (International Maritime Organization 2012 ed.), IMO Sales No. IA116E [Hereinafter Maritime Security Measures or MSM].

The requirements contained in the ISPS Code are in force for 158 states, which together constitute over 99 percent of the gross tonnage of the world's merchant fleet. Security is a risk management exercise and in order to determine appropriate security measures for ships and ports, an assessment of the risk must be made in each specific case. The Code sets forth a standardized and consistent formula for evaluating risk and to assist governments in synchronizing changes in the threat level with security measures in order to reduce vulnerability of the assets and infrastructure.

First, governments are required to conduct port facility assessments that identify and evaluate important shipping infrastructure that, if attacked, could cause significant loss of life or damage to the economy or the environment. Second, governments must identify actual threats to critical infrastructure and prioritize security measures. Finally, governments conduct vulnerability assessments to accurately gauge and evaluate risk. These comprehensive security assessments include physical security, structural integrity, utilities, communications, and port procedures. The complete implementation of the ISPS Code is unfolding—a work in progress—with some states struggling to enter into compliance. Application of the Code has been imperfect, but already it has had a global impact by linking ship and port facility security programs between government and commercial enterprise in a more integrated fashion.

The Code complements the World Customs Organization's (WCO) SAFE Framework of Standards that facilitate uniform rules for screening and inspection for national customs administrations, representing 99 percent of global trade. The International Labor Organization (ILO) works with the shipping industry to promulgate training and standards for seafarers whose job it is to implement security protocols. These three interlocking international organizations—IMO, WCO and ILO—create an institutional rule set for protecting the global cargo supply.

The ISPS Code contains a detailed mandatory section (Part A), which sets forth thirteen requirements for governments, port authorities and shipping companies. A second, non-mandatory section (Part B) provides guidance on how the measures might be implemented. Generally, the distinction between the mandatory provisions and supporting guidance may be discerned from the use of the term "must" or "is/are required" in mandatory provisions and "may," "could," or "should" in recommendatory guidance.

12.4.1 *Special Measures*

SOLAS Chapter XI-2 contains "special measures to enhance maritime security," which are included in ISPS Code Parts A and B. These Measures apply to port facilities within a State's jurisdiction, including a nation's overseas territories, to ships that fly the flag of a registering state and that are subject to SOLAS and ships operating in its territorial sea. Implementing legislation should specify which organization within government has authority for security in port facilities and on board ships that fly its flag.

The Maritime Security Measures (MSM) apply to ships that are subject to SOLAS and the ports that serve them. Port States also may extend the application of the measures to port facilities and ships not covered by SOLAS. Furthermore, although the MSM also do not apply to naval bases and ports primarily used for military purposes, Designated Authorities may apply the regulations to naval ports that routinely conduct commercial services. The Code does not apply to vessels entitled to sovereign immunity, however, including warships, naval auxiliaries or vessels owned or operated and used by a government on non-commercial service.[95]

Although SOLAS applies to passenger and cargo vessels on international voyages, for example, a flag State could choose to apply the rules to ships solely involved in cabotage or domestic voyages. Similarly, although the Maritime Security Measures do not extend to offshore activities or installations located on a coastal State's continental shelf, governments may adopt them or similar requirements for ships, mobile offshore drilling units on location, and fixed and floating platforms engaged in oil or gas production. When foreign flagged ships operate in support of these activities, they may be covered by both the security measures adopted by IMO, as well as additional coastal State regulations. Some coastal States have defined fixed platforms, or even floating production storage and offloading (FPSO) vessels used in oil and gas exploration and located on the continental shelf, as port facilities, which require appointment of a PFSO and preparation of a PFSP.[96]

Tug boats and other harbor craft, offshore supply and support ships, fishing vessels and recreational vessels and the facilities that serve these craft also may be regulated by the MSM through domestic legislation.[97] Notably, however, the security measures do not apply to the activities of foreign-flagged ships that operate off the shore of a coastal State in waters beyond the territorial sea. That is, the measures do not apply within a State's Exclusive Economic Zone (EEZ) or Continental Shelf, even though it is common for SOLAS ships to operate in these waters and interface with off-shore installations such as mobile offshore drilling units on location and FPSOs or other vessels, including non-SOLAS ships. Consequently, governments may develop bilateral or multilateral security regimes that regulate interaction in areas beyond the territorial sea. For example, states may agree that an interface between a SOLAS ship and an offshore installation or SOLAS or non-SOLAS vessel requires exchange of a Declaration of Security (DOS) or similar document.

---

[95] ISPS Code, para. A/3.3.
[96] Governments are required to provide an updated list of their ISPS Code-compliant port facilities at five yearly intervals. The next updated list has to be submitted by July 1, 2014. *See*, IMO Doc. MSC 89/INF.13, Maritime Security Measures, at para. 2.19.11.
[97] Id., at para. 2.2.52.

12.4.2 Security Levels

All officers, security officers, vessel crew and shipboard personnel should be trained in a security awareness program. It is incumbent on the various government agencies, port facility operators and administrators and industry shippers and carriers to maintain awareness of security in the supply chain. Core elements of security awareness include vigilance, information sharing, and training. Security drills or exercises help officers and crew acclimate to security issues. Local communities, land-holders, and small boat operators may be reached through general media concerning threats and countermeasures, whereas messages with greater fidelity, such as those targeted to mariners or the shipping industry, increase the effectiveness of law enforcement and enhance the vigilance of ships' crews.

Since individuals in the local community and small boat operators may have been accustomed to unrestricted access in port areas that now have more limited access, outreach to a wide audience by port officials and Designated Authorities is essential. Governments may deviate from the Maritime Security Measures by agreeing to separate procedures that may be included in Alternative Security Agreements (ASA). Generally covering short international voyages on fixed routes between dedicated ports, ASAs may be either bilateral or multilateral and reflect special requirements for specific routes.

Shipping companies must appoint at least one CSO for the company and a SSO for each of its vessels. Governments also are responsible for setting the security level for their ports and for ships that fly their flag.[98] Only government officials may set the applicable security level as well as approve port facility assessments and security plans, determine the ports that require a PFSO, exercise compliance measures pursuant to regulation XI-2/9, and establish requirements for a DOS.[99]

There are three levels of security in the ISPS Code: Level 1 (normal risk), Level 2 (heightened risk), and Level 3 (imminent risk). Ship and port facility security is an exercise in risk management to gauge the appropriate security level. The security measures put in place should match the risk presented by each particular level. The ISPS Code provides a standard framework for states to evaluate risk and it informs the setting or change of security levels based upon the vulnerability of ships and port facilities. Factors to be considered in setting security levels include the degree that the threat information is credible, corroborated, specific (or imminent), and the potential consequences of a security incident.[100]

Governments collect and assess information about potential threats to ports and ships flying their flag. Based on the threat information, the Designated Authority

---

[98] ISPS Code, para. A/4.1 and B/1.8.
[99] Id., at para. A/4.3.
[100] Id., at para. A/4.1.

(for ports) and the Administration (for ships) set a security level that reflects the degree of risk that a security incident, such as piracy, maritime terrorism, or sabotage, will occur or be attempted. Credible information that is corroborated and specific, or that poses greater risk of a higher potential consequence, such as an attack with weapons of mass destruction, is more apt to trigger an increase in the security level. There are three levels of risk commonly used:

- Security level 1—the minimum appropriate protective security measures are implemented at all times that are sufficient to counter most forms of criminality associated with ports and ships, such as trespass, cargo tampering and pilferage, and stowaways;
- Security level 2—additional protective security measures that are maintained for a period of time as a consequence of heightened risk. Generally, if a government sets a higher security for a reason other than the threat of terrorist attack, a brief statement describing the type of threat that caused the change may be published or transmitted to the commercial sector;
- Security level 3—is used in exceptional circumstances and establishes specific enhanced protective measures that are maintained for the duration of a period when a security incident is probable or imminent, and could even result in suspension of activities. Security level 3 normally is appropriate as a measure in response to information that a security incident is probable or imminent.

Governments may set a single security level for all ships registered to their flag and all of their ports and port facilities or differentiate levels among vessels and ports or between different parts of a port or port facility. Similarly, governments may apply a standardized security level throughout their territorial sea or set different security levels in different parts of their territorial sea.

Typically, the security level for port authorities is shared by the Designated Authority with the port or harbor security officer who transmits it to PFSOs and ship masters and SSOs of ships already in port or bound for port. Many Administrations transmit ship security level information via terrestrial or satellite-based facsimile or NAVTEX and Inmarsat-C SafetyNET directly to ships flying their flag, the latter of which are received through the ship's Global Maritime Distress Safety System (GMDSS). Other Administrations may alert CSOs of security levels and rely on them to forward the information to ships. Finally, Administrations will update ship security levels through general Notice to Mariners (NOTMARs).

Foreign-flagged ships traversing the territorial sea may be informed of the security level through NAVTEX, Inmarsat-C SafetyNET and SureFax. Changes to the security level in the territorial sea may be transmitted by Maritime Rescue Coordination Centers (MRCCs). Although foreign-flagged vessels in innocent passage (and not entering port) are not compelled by international law to adopt the security level set by the coastal State in the territorial sea, some Administrations have specified that ships flying their flag will apply the same security level as the coastal State when transiting the coastal State's territorial sea or even when operating within its EEZ. When a higher security level is set, ships should be able to communicate with a Contact Point ashore, who can accept security reports and advise ships. In some situations, the advice offered by the Contact Point may be sufficient to delay a transit or cause a change in course or speed or help the vessel to take advantage of the protection afforded by escort or patrol vessels.

12.4.3 Declaration of Security

A Declaration of Security (DOS) is an agreement between a ship and another ship or between a ship and a port facility with which it interfaces, specifying the security measures each will implement during the period of time they will interact. The DOS also specifies what security measures may be shared with the other party.[101] Governments are responsible for determining when a DOS is required for ships flying their flag and ports under their authority, depending upon the risk of the interaction between ships and ports to life or property.[102] The Designated Authority typically determines the circumstances requiring a DOS; Recognized Security Organizations (RSO) do not enjoy the same authority in this regard.[103]

DOS may be warranted in the following circumstances:

   a. A ship is operating at a higher security level than the port facility with which it is interfacing;[104]
   b. A security threat or incident has occurred that involves the port facility or another ship with which it is interfacing;[105]
   c. A port facility or ship is operating at Security level 3;
   d. The port facility or a ship with which it is interfacing has changed its security level;
   e. A specific ship to ship or ship to port interface that poses a danger to local facilities or residents, or presents a significant risk of marine environmental pollution;
   f. A ship or port interface involves embarkation or disembarkation of passengers or dangerous cargo, or transfer of passengers or dangerous cargo at sea;
   g. A ship is using a non-SOLAS port facility;[106]
   h. A ship is undertaking a ship-to-ship activity, such as taking on bunker fuel, and one ship is operating at a higher security level than the other vessel, or the ship is interacting with a non-SOLAS ship;
   i. Two governments have agreed that a DOS is required during a ship-to-ship interface;
   j. A non-SOLAS ship seeks to enter a port facility covered by SOLAS;
   k. The Designated Authority of the port facility or ship's Administration requires it;
   l. A ship is without a valid International Ship Security Certificate (ISSC).[107]

---

[101] Id., at para. A/5.5.
[102] Id., at para. A/5.
[103] Id., at para. A/4.3.6.
[104] Id., at para. A/5.2.1.
[105] Id., at para. A/5.2.3.
[106] Id., at para. A/5.2.4.
[107] Id., at para. A/19.

Table 12.2 identifies the circumstances when a port facility may require a DOS from a ship.[108] Security considerations drive the decision. When both the port facility and the ship are operating at security level 1, a DOS normally is not required, although a port facility can establish conditions for which a ship must produce a DOS. Similarly, a ship security assessment can set the precise conditions when a DOS is to be requested of another ship or port facility. Furthermore, some national authorities have imposed additional requirements concerning the period that the DOS must be retained; modifications to the model DOS Form issued by the IMO; and provisions to allow the use of a single DOS for multiple visits by a ship to the same port.

A government-to-government agreement generally covers specific voyages between two nations and specific passenger and cargo movements between the two states that pose a higher security risk. The agreement provides a mechanism for greater security without the burden of imposing a higher security level. In

Table 12.2. Declaration of Security Matrix for Port Facilities

Situation	Port Facility at Security Level 1	Port Facility at Security Level 2	Port Facility at Security Level 3
Non-SOLAS ship entering port facility (e.g. smaller craft)	Required / Not Required	Required / Not Required	Required / Not Required
Non-ISPS Code compliant ship entering port facility	Required / Not Required	Required / Not Required	Required / Not Required
Ship at Security Level 1	Required / Not Required	Required / Not Required	Required / Not Required
Ship at Security Level 2	Required / Not Required	Required / Not Required	Required / Not Required
Ship at Security Level 3	Required / Not Required	Required / Not Required	Required / Not Required
Following a security incident at port facility or on a ship	Required / Not Required	Required / Not Required	Required / Not Required
Following a threat to a port facility or a ship	Required / Not Required	Required / Not Required	Required / Not Required

---

[108] IMO Doc. MSC 89/INF.13, Maritime Security Measures, para. 2.7.5.

contrast, an Alternative Security Agreement (ASA) applies to shorter and regularized shipping between adjacent countries.

Typically, port facilities and ships retain a DOS for three to five years, although national authorities may set any period of time. But ships should have their DOS' available for inspection for the period covering the previous ten ports of call. A Continuous Declaration of Security (CDS) permits transit without a separate DOS for each port or ship interface encountered during either a specified time or under certain specified condition. The CDS remains in force under the terms of the port and flag State security conditions.

The Port Facility Security Plan (PFSP) promulgated by the Designated Authority sets forth the conditions under which a port facility will request ships to comply with a DOS. Similarly, a ship can request another ship or a port facility to agree to a DOS, and the circumstances under which such a request is made are specified in the Ship Security Plan (SSP). Port facilities are required to acknowledge request for a DOS made by a ship, but do not have to comply unless the request is consistent with the prescribed PFSP.

Security levels are set by the government, generally by the Designated Authority (DA). The DA is identified by each nation, usually in national legislation. Typically, the DA is the government official responsible for implementation of earlier provisions of the SOLAS Convention and other IMO legal instruments. DAs have plenary responsibility to designate port facilities that require appointment of a PFSO and preparation of a PFSP or to appoint a person ashore to be responsible for shore-side security. In the latter case, the DA must undertake a PFSA. The PFSA will involve entry of the land or premises of the port, inspection of the relevant documents, records and plans, and inspection of port security installations and equipment.

The Company Security Officer (CSO) is designated by a commercial shipping company to ensure that a Ship Security Assessment (SSA) is completed, that a Ship Security Plan is developed, approved and implemented, and to liaison with Port Facility Security Officers (PFSO) and the Ship Security Officer (SSO). The company has a duty to support the master, the CSO, and each SSO. The CSO also should designate a SSO for each ship, who is accountable to the master of the vessel in implementing the Ship Security Plan. Shipping companies are responsible for ensuring that each SSP "contains a clear statement emphasizing the master's authority" over the vessel.[109] The SSP should indicate that the master has "overriding authority" and responsibility to make decisions related to ship safety and security.[110]

---

[109] ISPS Code, para. A/6.1.
[110] Id.

392   CHAPTER TWELVE

Ships have an obligation to act under the security levels set by their flag State.[111] At security level 1, ships should carry out the following measures:

   a. ensure the performance of all ship security duties;
   b. control access to the ship;
   c. control embarkation of persons and baggage;
   d. monitor restricted areas inside and outside the ship;
   e. ensure security communications are readily available.[112]

At security levels 2 and 3, ships should add additional protective measures for each of the above activities as set forth in the SSP. Recommended measures for each security level are contained in Part B of the ISPS Code.[113]

12.4.4   *Security Plans for Port Facilities and Ships*

National law generally establishes rules applicable to industry for submission and approval of port facility and Ship Security Plans (SSP) and for amending approved plans. Municipal State law also authorizes Designated Authorities and Flag State Administrations, and any others who may undertake inspection duties on their behalf, authority to enter port facilities or board ships to assess compliance with the Maritime Security Measures (MSM). The powers include authority to inspect a port facility or ship to assess compliance, inspect security equipment, documents, records, and plans, conduct security-related interviews of port or ship personnel, and initiate and assess port facility or ship security drills.

Inspections may include examination of a port facility's Statement of Compliance or verification of a ship's International Ship Security Certificate (ISSC) or Interim ISSC, or any other activities to assess the compliance of a port facility or ship with the MSM. The ISSC is a Certificate issued by, or on behalf of, the ship's Administration, and attesting to the vessel's compliance with the MSM set forth in SOLAS Chapter XI-2 and the ISPS Code.

States may adopt legislation specifying enforcement actions that a Designated Authority and Administration can take against a deficient port facility or on a SOLAS ship. If the deficiency compromises the ability of a port facility or ship to operate at Security levels 1, 2, or 3, municipal law may authorize restriction or suspension notices that limit the operation of the port facility or ships until the deficiency is corrected. In such cases, port facilities and ships may be subject to administrative, civil, or criminal penalties, as set forth in domestic statute. Ships covered under SOLAS should appoint at least one Ship Security Officer (SSO) who

---

[111] Id., at para. A/7.1.
[112] Id., at para. A/7.2.
[113] Id., at para. B/9.14–9.49.

has authority to conduct a Ship Security Assessment (SSA) and prepare a Ship Security Plan (SSP) for each vessel.

Port States may establish control measures for foreign-flagged ships calling at their ports or indicating an intention to enter port. These measures include ship inspection, delay of entry into port or refusal of port entry, detention of the ship, restrictions on operations, and expulsion from port. Under some circumstances, foreign-flagged ships may claim compensation if they are unduly detained or delayed. The port State's criminal law or civil code may apply to foreign-flagged ships calling on ports of the state. Foreign-flagged ships are under obligation to provide information on the vessel, cargoes, and passengers, to the port state's Designated Authority or Administration.

12.4.5 Interagency Government Coordination

Individual governments delineate the roles of the Designated Authority, with regard to responsibilities for port facility security, and the Administration, which generally is responsible for ship security for vessels flying its flag. Some nations combine these two roles into one authority. Domestic law or regulation sets forth the division of labor and responsibility between the two entities. Typically, both entities are included in the Department or Ministry responsible for port and shipping matters, such as the Department of Transportation. Port and ship security also may be combined with security for other nodes of transportation, such as rail or aviation.

The Designated Authority may delegate maritime security responsibilities to a Recognized Security Organization (RSO) to undertake duties on its behalf for port facility security. The RSO may be authorized to approve SSPs, certify ship compliance with the measures, conduct PFSAs, and provide assistance on completion of PFSAs, PFSPs, SSAs, and SSPs. If the Designated Authority utilizes an RSO, it should inform the International Maritime Organization.[114]

Governments also may delegate responsibilities to off-shore international registries, which act subject to oversight of the granting Department or Ministry of Transportation. In other cases, Flag State Administrations may delegate ship security responsibilities to RSOs. But normally, the Administration retains authority to set security levels, establish requirements for a Declaration of Security, determine which port facilities should appoint a PFSO and prepare a PFSP, approve PFSAs and PFSPs and subsequent amendments, and exercise control over foreign-flagged SOLAS ships. The Administration also typically retains STCW Convention and STCW Code accreditation of seafarers.

Depending on the constitutional arrangement or federalist structure of governments, institutions or agencies involved in maritime security may be at the

---

[114] The Designated Authority may provide the information to the IMO via the Internet website: http://gisis.imo.org.

national, regional or prefectural, or local level of governance. Naval and Coast Guard forces conduct maritime security operations that include visit, board, search, and seizure (VBSS) of ships at sea. National customs and immigration forces adopt and implement practices drawn from the World Custom Organization's Framework of Standards to Secure and Facilitate Global Trade (SAFE Framework), which protects the global cargo supply chain. The foreign ministry is responsible for conducting international outreach and coordination. Intelligence agencies monitor maritime threats and provide information to decision makers. Local marine law enforcement organizations and harbor police patrol internal waters and roadsteads.

Ideally, the departments and ministries at the national level coordinate with organizations to develop integrated approaches to maritime security. Ensuring the cohesion of the disparate interagency community of departments, ministries, agencies and organizations is not an easy task. Institutional prerogatives, interagency politics, "stove-piped" authority, duplicate and overlapping authority (or a vacuum of authority) all impede unified action. To overcome these barriers, states may establish standing or ad hoc committees or offices that can serve as a fusion point for developing and implementing national maritime security policy. Often states establish a single National Maritime Security Committee that includes representatives from key agencies and departments, and it also may operate a maritime security operational response center to manage search and rescue (SAR), as well as the maritime interdiction of drug traffickers, migrant smugglers, and terrorists and weapons of mass destruction (WMD) at sea.

The ILO/IMO *Code of Practice on Port Security* suggests that states should develop a port security policy document. Generally, such a document will set forth the extent and significance of the country's maritime industries and infrastructure, identify key maritime threats, and specify the roles and responsibilities of the various security and law enforcement organizations, the application of national security policy to ports and ships, industry responsibilities, and the delineation of governmental authority.

The ISPS Code and Maritime Security Measures ensure that government and industry are effectively linked. At the same time, coordination across and throughout the levels of government enable effective, proportionate, and sustainable security procedures. Normally these functions are fulfilled by a National Maritime Security Committee, which includes representatives from the intelligence community, the merchant shipping industry, and the military. The interagency community generally has to work together to fashion a national concept of the security threats and vulnerabilities, national security priorities, developing maritime security initiatives based upon a national maritime security strategy or framework, developing coordinated positions on international treaties and commitments, resolving jurisdictional issues among departments and agencies, and executing national level policy.

12.4.6 Regional Organizations

Prominent regional organizations that can address issues related to implementing the Maritime Security Measures include:

- The Asia-Pacific Economic Cooperation (APEC), which has representation from 21 Contracting Governments in the APEC Region. The maritime security program is administered by the Transportation Working Group.[115]
- The Organization of American States (OAS), which has representation from 34 Contracting Governments throughout the Americas and the Caribbean. Maritime security functions of the OAS are administered by the Inter-American Committee for Counter-Terrorism and the Inter-American Committee for Ports.[116]
- The European Maritime Safety Agency (EMSA) has representation from 27 Contracting Governments.[117]
- The Secretariat of the Pacific Community (SPC) has 26 members including 22 Pacific Island countries and territories.[118]
- East African Community has six member nations—Burundi, Kenya, Rwanda, Tanzania, and Uganda.

Additionally, regional organizations are authorized to take action not rising to the level of UN Security Council enforcement action under chapter VIII, Article 52, of the UN Charter—Regional Arrangements. The U.S.-led invasion of Grenada in 1984 (codenamed Operation Urgent Fury), for example, was accomplished by the nations of the Organization of Eastern Caribbean States (OECS) and Barbados and Jamaica as a regional peace enforcement action in the context of the breakdown of order and civil strife.[119] Such actions may not usurp the authority of the Security Council to maintain international peace and security, but in the absence of Security Council enforcement action under chapter VII, regional organizations may take lesser action to ensure regional stability.

12.4.7 Recognized Security Organizations

Under a number of IMO conventions, governments may authorize certain nongovernmental organizations (recognized organizations) to act on their behalf in fulfilling some flag State responsibilities.[120] There are two types of such entities:

---

[115] The Internet website of the Transportation Working Group is located at www.apec-tptwg.org.cn.
[116] The Internet websites of the two committees are located at www.cicte.oas.org/Rev/En/Programs/Port.asp and www.safeports.org/.
[117] The Internet website is located at www.emsa.europa.eu.
[118] The Internet website is located at www.spc.int/maritime.
[119] John Norton Moore, *Grenada and the International Double Standard*, 78 AM. J. INT'L L. 145, 156 (Jan. 1984).
[120] IMO Doc. MSC/Circ.1074, Measures to Enhance Maritime Security, Interim Guidelines for the Authorization of Recognized Security Organizations Acting on Behalf of the

classifications societies and Recognized Security Organizations (RSOs). Classification societies are nongovernmental societies that establish technical standards in relation to the design, construction, and survey of marine related facilities, such as ships and offshore structures.[121] RSOs operate in accordance with a written agreement between the Administration and the recognized organization, with the recognized organization acting on behalf of the flag State. RSOs may implement a handful of selected state responsibilities under the Maritime Security Measures.

The Administration or the Delegated Authority may delegate the following functions, either in whole or in part, to an RSO:

a. approval of ship security plans;
b. verification for ships (such as inspections and audits);
c. issuance and endorsement of International Ship Security Certificates; and
d. development of port facility security assessments.[122]

Thus, if RSOs are used, the Designated Authority may delegate port security responsibility, whereas a Flag State Administration can delegate responsibility relating to ship security. Not every state utilizes RSOs, however.

Often a port authority or port facility operator serves as an RSO, but the scope of authority delegated to RSOs that undertake government responsibilities for Flag State Administrations is even broader. SOLAS and other IMO Conventions provide Administrations with a framework to empower RSOs to inspect, survey, verify and approve certificates for ships flying its flag. In each case, however, the RSO should have a record of organizational competency and technical proficiency, and the capabilities necessary to undertake the specific duties that may be delegated to them.[123] RSO duties may include the conduct of PFSAs, assisting ports in preparing PFSPs, training CSOs and SSOs, and training PFSOs and other port security personnel. Even as states use RSOs, the authorizing government retains oversight and ultimate responsibility for the work undertaken on its behalf.

Administration and/or Designated Authority of a Contracting Government, June 10, 2003. See also, SOLAS, Regulation I/6, LL Convention, Article 13, MARPOL Annex I, regulation 4, and Annex II, regulation 10, and TONNAGE 1969, regulation 6.

[121] See, e.g., IACS Explained—Members, at http://www.iacs.org.uk/Explained/members.aspx.

[122] IMO Doc. MSC/Circ.1074, Measures to Enhance Maritime Security, Interim Guidelines for the Authorization of Recognized Security Organizations Acting on Behalf of the Administration and/or Designated Authority of a Contracting Government, June 10, 2003, para. 1.

[123] These competencies are identified in IMO Doc. MSC 89/INF.13, Maritime Security Measures, Criteria for Selecting Recognized Security Organizations, Appendix 2.3, Maritime Security Measures.

In general, IMO guidelines pertaining to recognized organizations require that the size and capability of the organization be "commensurate with the type and degree of authority intended to be delegated."[124] The 13 largest marine focused classification societies are members of the International Association of Classification Societies (IACS).[125] The organization should be able to document experience in the area over which it exercises delegated authority, such as expertise in construction, design, and equipping of merchant ships.[126]

The IMO has offered guidance on criteria for selecting RSOs.[127] The organization should have demonstrated effectiveness, with clear lines of managerial oversight for the proposed delegation of authority, personnel with appropriate qualifications and experience, adherence to a company code of ethics or code of conduct, and an effective training and testing program. The RSO also should have procedures established to avoid unauthorized disclosure of, or access to, security sensitive material.

The work of RSOs is technical in nature, and requires knowledge of ship and port operations, including design and construction, knowledge of the Maritime Security Measures, and national regulations pertaining to security for installation, ships, and personnel. Finally, the RSO should be familiar with the most likely security threats. For these reasons, many RSOs are managed by or employ former military or intelligence officials.

12.4.8 Government Oversight and Enforcement

Governments should disseminate contact information for their national authorities responsible for ship security, port facility security, recipients of Ship Security Alert System (SSAS) alerts, and other maritime security related communications

---

[124] IMO Doc. A.739(18), Guidelines for the Authorization of Organizations Acting on Behalf of the Administration, Annex: Guidelines for the Authorization of Organizations Acting on Behalf of the Administration, Appendix, Minimum Standards for Recognized Organizations Acting on Behalf of the Administration, Nov. 4, 1993, para. 1.

[125] The Croatian Register of Shipping became a member on May 3, 2011. Other member societies include: American Bureau of Shipping, *Bureau Veritas*, China Classification Society, *Det Norske Veritas*, Germanische Lloyd, Indian Register of Shipping, Korean Register of Shipping, Lloyd's Register, *Nippon Kaji Kyokai*, Polish Register of Shipping, *Registro Italiano Naval*, and Russian Maritime Register of Shipping.

[126] IMO Doc. A.739(18), Guidelines for the Authorization of Organizations Acting on Behalf of the Administration, Annex: Guidelines for the Authorization of Organizations Acting on Behalf of the Administration, Appendix, Minimum Standards for Recognized Organizations Acting on Behalf of the Administration, Nov. 4, 1993, para. 2.

[127] IMO Doc. MSC/Circ.1074, Measures to Enhance Maritime Security, Interim Guidelines for the Authorization of Recognized Security Organizations Acting on Behalf of the Administration and/or Designated Authority of a Contracting Government, June 10, 2003.

and requests for assistance. The names and conditions of authority of RSOs should also be publicly available.[128]

Governments are responsible for inspecting and assessing the effectiveness of the Maritime Security Measures (MSM) required for their ships, port facilities, and shipping companies. RSOs are authorized to act on behalf of the government. Through control and compliance measures, governments also may assess the compliance of foreign flagged ships that use or intend to use, their ports. National oversight should be able to determine whether the government meets its obligations under the MSM.

Ultimately, governments are responsible for ensuring that their port facilities and SOLAS ships are in compliance with the MSM. National authorities may take enforcement action against ships and port facilities to ensure compliance. The MSM recommend governments use a stepped approach to enforcement, which follows distinct steps:

   a. Provide advice to the port facility or ship on correcting the deficiency;
   b. Persuade the port facility or ship of the need to correct the deficiency;
   c. Deliver formal notification of the requirement to correct the deficiency;
   d. Commence proceedings to impose sanctions for a failure to correct the deficiency; and
   e. Impose legal sanctions for failure to correct the deficiency.[129]

Sanctions against port facilities or ships may include counseling, a fine, suspension or restriction of activities, or withdrawal of certificates of compliance, such as a Ship Security Plan (SSP) or the International Ship Security Certificate (ISSC). Counseling normally is appropriate for recorded deficiencies and entails discussion with the PFSO or SSO, master of a vessel, or CSO. Discrepancies that remain uncorrected may be brought to the attention of senior management. In the most serious cases, the national authorities may suspend or restrict activities at a port facility or on a ship.[130]

Suspension or withdrawal of an approved PFSP or SSP may be taken in cases in which deficiencies persist. If activities at a port or on a ship are stopped or limited because of a security deficiency, the national authority may require completion of a PFSA or PFSP before operations can recommence.[131] Eventually, administrative or legal tribunals may take action against noncompliant ships or port facilities through civil or criminal proceedings.[132]

---

[128] IMO Doc. Circular Letter No. 2514, Information required from SOLAS Contracting Governments under the provisions of SOLAS regulation XI-2/13, Dec. 8, 2003.
[129] IMO Doc. MSC 89/INF.13, Maritime Security Measures, at 2.15.6.
[130] Id., at 2.15.18.
[131] Id., at para. 2.15.22.
[132] Id., at para. 2.15.26.

12.5 Maritime Domain Awareness

Maritime domain awareness (MDA), also known as, "maritime situational awareness," or even more recently, "maritime intelligence integration," is the process whereby governments and industry from flag States, port States and coastal States, collect and share information about activities occurring in maritime space. In a nutshell, MDA seeks to obtain, as far as possible, perfect information about the maritime environment in order to deter and suppress threats at sea. MDA serves three functions. First, it is an element of layered national or homeland security for coastal States. Second, it serves as an instrument to manage responsibilities of jurisdiction for flag States. Finally, it also is a means to enhance port state control for port States.

The following example illustrates how MDA contributes to maritime security. In May 2003, the freighter *Baltic Sky* loaded its cargo in Tunisia and got underway bound for the Sudan. Mysteriously, the ship zig-zagged through the Mediterranean Sea for more than six weeks and then unexpectedly made port in the small Greek city of Astakos. Tunisian authorities passed information to Greek port control officers, who boarded the 230-foot ship to discover it contained an undeclared cargo of more than 750 metric tons of ammonium nitrate explosive and 140,000 detonators.[133] In comparison, the domestic terrorist attack that struck the Oklahoma City Federal Building contained only 1.8 metric tons of a similar explosive.[134] The impact of 750 metric tons of ammonium nitrate may be likened to the power of an atomic bomb. The cargo was the greatest quantity of explosives ever seized from a ship.[135]

The difficulty is in finding illegal cargo among a vast fleet of legitimate fishing boats, commercial vessels, and pleasure craft. Using technical means, reporting requirements by vessels, and information-sharing and intelligence integration, authorities can more easily sort large numbers of ships to separate legitimate traffic from anomalous behavior at sea that might suggest the transit of illegal migrants or drug traffickers. By linking countries together, MDA is a force multiplier that affords a group of nations the benefits of shipping information collected by the rest of the partner states.

The terrestrial Long Range Navigation (LORAN) system was developed during World War II at the Massachusetts Institute of Technology Radiation Laboratory for the British Royal Navy and the U.S. Navy. The low frequency hyperbolic radio-navigation system is based on measuring the time difference between the receipt of signals from a pair of radio transmitted in order to determine fixed

---

[133] Andrew Chang, *Fearing Olympic Terror, Athens Gears Up*, ABC News, June 26, 2006.
[134] Commander Mike Holland, *Securing the Seas: The National Strategy for Maritime Security*, U.S. Coast Guard Proc., 9, at 9 (Fall 2006).
[135] Michael Richardson, A Time Bomb for Global Trade: Maritime-related Terrorism in an Age of Weapons of Mass Destruction 45–46 (2004).

positions of ships and aircraft. After the war, LORAN continued to be used throughout the world to aid navigation of commercial and military vessels and aircraft, assisting countless mariners in distress and supplementing aviation navigation during the Vietnam War.

During the 1980s, the United States established the Joint Maritime Information Element (JMIE). JMIE was an information-sharing consortium of Federal agencies with maritime security, safety, regulatory and enforcement responsibilities.[136] Information on merchant ships, cargoes, fishing and research vessels, and pleasure crafts was pooled to better conduct narcotics interdiction, arms smuggling, EEZ surveillance, search and rescue, alien migration interdiction, and other missions. JMIE was a joint U.S. Coast Guard Office of Intelligence (G-OCI) and Office of Naval Intelligence (ONI) program and passed legal reviews from both organizations for collection of information against vessels in U.S. territorial waters.[137] JMIE was replaced by MAGNET, the Maritime Awareness Global Network, which has worldwide application.

With the expansion of GPS in recent years, however, LORAN-C became outdated. Before LORAN sites closed in 2010, the U.S. Coast Guard operated only 18 LORAN Stations in the continental United States, six in Alaska, and 24 monitoring sites utilizing the final generation of the system, LORAN-C.[138] The sites in the higher latitudes were operated in conjunction with Canadian and Russian stations to provide coverage over Canadian waters and the Bering Sea, providing better than a 0.25 nautical mile absolute accuracy. On February 8, 2010, the U.S. Coast Guard terminated the transmission of the last U.S. LORAN-C signal. On August 1, 2010, the Russian-American signal was terminated, and two days later the Coast Guard transmission of Canadian LORAN-C signals was terminated.[139]

12.5.1 U.S. Maritime Domain Awareness Policy

Under the U.S. National Maritime Security Policy (NSPD-41), maritime domain awareness is defined as "the effective understanding of anything associated with the global maritime domain that could impact the security, safety, economy,

---

[136] JMIE organizations include U.S. Customs Service (USCS), Drug Enforcement Agency (DEA), Military Sealift Command (MSC), Department of Energy (DOE), Central Intelligence Agency (CIA) and the Maritime Administration (MARAD).

[137] Dep't of the Navy Office of the Judge Advocate General, Memorandum (Subject: Coordinated Legal Review of Joint Maritime Information Element), May 29, 1986, and Office of Intelligence Policy Review, Dep't of Justice, Memorandum for Stanley Sporkin, General Counsel, Central Intelligence Agency (Re: Joint Maritime Information Element), Dec. 12, 1985.

[138] 75 FED. REG. 997, Record of Decision (ROD) on the U.S. Coast Guard Long Range Aids to Navigation (Loran-C) Program, Jan. 7, 2010.

[139] 75 FED. REG. 998, Terminate Long Range Aids to Navigation (Loran-C), Jan. 7, 2010.

or environment of the United States."[140] The Maritime Security Policy seeks to integrate intelligence, surveillance, observation, and navigation systems into a common operating picture that can provide joint and interagency indications and warnings of gathering maritime threats before they materialize. The *National Plan to Achieve Maritime Domain Awareness* (MDA Plan) was one of the original eight supporting plans of the NSMS.[141] The MDA Plan set forth a unified U.S. approach to understanding the oceans environment and identifying threats as early and as far from American shores as possible.

Maritime domain awareness is an all-source activity in which information on the maritime environment is collected, fused, analyzed, and shared with multiple agencies, private industry, and foreign partners. Information is shared through a collaborative, network-centric common operating picture (COP) virtual information grid available to Federal, state, and local agencies with maritime security responsibilities.

The MDA Plan sought to simplify and integrate the complex and ambiguous marine environment through enhancing transparency at sea to detect, deter, and defeat threats. Marine threats arise from nations, terrorists, pirates, international criminal organizations, and other non-state actors, or from environmental or social catastrophes. The information should inform effective and confident decision-making in a dynamic environment. Ships, cargo, passenger and crew, and offshore installations are persistently monitored "anywhere on the globe," although not simultaneously over the entire globe.[142] The ultimate goal of MDA is to ensure freedom of navigation and the efficient flow of legitimate commerce.[143] Thus, MDA helps governments marshal and employ scarce resources.

The U.S. maritime security policy also directs the Secretaries of Defense and Homeland Security, working in conjunction with the Director of Central Intelligence, the Director of the National Counterterrorism Center (NCTC) and the Director of the Federal Bureau of Investigation (FBI), to integrate intelligence "on a global basis" and ascertain the "location, identity, and operational capabilities and intentions" of maritime threats. At the same time, the department principals were directed to prepare a national plan for *Global Maritime Intelligence Integration* (GMII), which was released in October 2005.[144]

The GMII Plan used existing or legacy capabilities to integrate all available data, information, and intelligence to support maritime security planning and operations. The Plan established a framework to ensure fusion of all source

---

[140] Id.
[141] UNITED STATES OF AMERICA, NATIONAL PLAN TO ACHIEVE MARITIME DOMAIN AWARENESS FOR THE NATIONAL STRATEGY FOR MARITIME SECURITY, Oct. 2005.
[142] Id., at 3.
[143] Id., at 2.
[144] UNITED STATES OF AMERICA, GLOBAL MARITIME INTELLIGENCE INTEGRATION PLAN, Oct. 2005.

information, and intelligence from a variety of U.S. government offices. The Office of Naval Intelligence (ONI) and the USCG Intelligence Coordination Center (ICC) constitute the core element. The core element serves as a center of strategic excellence for maritime intelligence analysis and integration.[145]

ONI and ICC, in turn, work with DHS Border & Transportation Security (BTS), DHS Transportation Security Administration (TSA), and intelligence analysts from the Department of Treasury, Department of Justice, the National Security Agency (NSA), and the National Geospatial-Intelligence Agency (NGA). A wider enterprise community is composed of the core element plus the intelligence community and the Homeland Security Operations Center, geographic combatant command Joint Intelligence Operations Centers (JIOCs) and Joint Interagency Task Forces (JIATFs), the Transportation Security Operational Center (TSOC), Navy numbered fleets and components, USCG Maritime Intelligence Fusion Centers (MIFCs), FBI Field Intelligence Groups, and the Department of Transportation Office of Intelligence and Security.[146] The enterprise members provide daily management and support to national and theater leadership.

The core element develops enterprise-wide tactics, techniques, and procedures for maritime intelligence sharing, conducts and disseminates strategic analysis and intelligence integration, and maintains a single integrated lookout (SILO) list of all ships of domestic or global intelligence interest.[147] Theater-level intelligence centers provide situational awareness within a specific geographic area of interest that supports a common operating picture (COP). The regional centers also maintain a 24-hour watch for indications and warning (I&W). Finally, the theater centers are especially focused on monitoring legal and political seams, such as international boundaries, zones in the oceans, such as territorial seas or exclusive economic zones, and lines separating geographic combatant commands or lines of authority separating captains of the port.[148] Local offices of the agencies with a stake in maritime security help to maximize all-source maritime intelligence sharing and provide on-scene support to Federal, state, and local law enforcement in domestic ports and internal waterways.[149]

Maritime domain awareness (MDA) is often viewed within the Pentagon as a tactical and technical challenge to be conquered rather than as an issue of global oceans policy and warfare strategy. On the Navy staff, the Deputy Chief of Naval Operations for Communication Networks (N6) assumed responsibility for MDA, after acquiring the lead from the Office of the Deputy Chief of Naval Operations for Information, Plans & Strategy (N3/N5). The Office of the Secretary of the Navy

---

[145] Id., at 10.
[146] Id., at 5 and 10.
[147] Id., at p. 9.
[148] Id., at 11.
[149] Id., at 12.

has been a zealous advocate for MDA, but it is unclear whether the resource sponsor is in sync with the global strategic priorities of the worldwide combatant commands.

Proponents maintain that MDA enables coastal States to fulfill their right to manage their EEZ and set conditions for offshore freedom of navigation.[150] But under article 87(1) of UNCLOS, flag States rather than coastal States are the appropriate authority for enforcing nearly all of the internationally accepted standards of safety, security and environmental protection in the EEZ. Coastal States step in, however, often because their unilateral rules are inconsistent with international standards. One Coast Guard lawyer argues advances in MDA are "merely the evolution of longstanding conditions placed on freedom of navigation [by the coastal State]."[151] Thus, some coastal nations have shown a willingness to use (or more accurately misuse) technical, legal and policy advances in maritime governance as opportunities to enforce excessive maritime boundary claims, market illegal claims of sovereignty or jurisdiction over the oceans, or impose unlawful restrictions on the rights and freedoms of navigation.

This argument suggests that it is easy to confuse MDA as a synonym for maritime security, rather than as one of a number of tools that can be used to enhance maritime security. MDA is not the tail wagging the dog of maritime security; rather, it is a single component supporting a constellation of efforts to enhance transparency and security in the maritime operating environment. Some suggest that the expansion of MDA should "make the oceans like the airspace," in which the location and course of every aircraft is carefully plotted by professional air traffic controllers.

After all, ships are both slower and larger than aircraft; if a global network of air traffic controllers can maintain real-time information on aircraft, then why not one for vessels? Certainly governments and the aviation industry benefit from decades of investment into air traffic control in a framework established under the *International Convention on Civil Aviation* (ICAO). Although MDA can be a valuable element of the overall approach to collaborative maritime security, it is not an unmitigated public good. Both coastal States and non-state maritime rogues, such as terrorists or pirates, may collect and misuse open source or freely available MDA data. Coastal States could utilize the information in order to impede freedom of navigation, and international criminal organizations could use the data to attack or disrupting legitimate shipping.

---

[150] Lieutenant Commander Jason M. Krajewski, USCG, *Out of Sight, Out of Mind? A Case for Long Range Identification and Tracking of Vessels on the High Seas*, 56 NAVAL L. REV. 219, 235 (2008).

[151] Id.

12.5.2 *Automatic Identification System*

The Automatic Identification System (AIS) was developed in the 1990s to make transit through the Panama Canal safer. Performance standards for AIS were adopted in 1998. The system is based on the VHF maritime band so the range generally only reaches to the horizon. After the attacks of 9/11, the United States led the way at the International Maritime Organization to amend the *Safety of Life at Sea Convention* (1974) so that all ships 300 gross tons or greater and that carry 12 or more passengers on international voyages are required to install AIS. In 2002, the forty-eighth session of the Sub-Committee on Safety of Navigation at the IMO agreed on guidelines for the installation of shipborne AIS. The seventy-sixth session of the Maritime Safety Committee concurred in the matter and approved the guidelines in 2003.[152] Today the system is used throughout the world and especially along chokepoints such as the Strait of Gibraltar.

Regulation 19 of SOLAS chapter V requires AIS to be fitted aboard all ships of 300 gross tons and upwards and engaged on international voyages, cargo ships of 500 gross tonnage and upwards not engaged on international voyages, and all passenger ships, irrespective of size. The requirement became effective for all ships on December 31, 2004.

The regulation mandates that AIS shall transmit vessel information, including the ship's identity, type, position, course, speed, navigational status and other safety-related information, automatically to shore stations and other appropriately equipped ships and aircraft. Ships also should be able to receive automatically such information from similarly fitted ships and be able to monitor and track ships and exchange data with shore-based facilities.

A ship intending to enter a port of another nation may be required to provide the following pre-arrival notification and information to port officials, and AIS can help the port state receive the information automatically:

- Confirmation of a valid ISSC and the name of its issuing authority;
- Security level at which it is currently operating;
- Security level at which it operated in the last 10 ports of call where it conducted a ship/port interface;
- Special security measures that were taken in the last 10 ports of call where it conducted a ship/port interface, e.g. Declarations of Security;
- Confirmation that the appropriate ship security procedures were maintained during any ship-to-ship activity during the last 10 ports of call, e.g. with ships that are not required to comply with the Maritime Security Measures or persons and goods rescued at sea;
- Any other practical security-related information, other than details of the Ship Security Plan. Examples of additional information include information contained in the Continuous Synopsis Record; the location of the ship at the time of reporting;

---

[152] IMO Doc. SN/Circ.227, Guidelines for the Installation of a Shipborne Automatic Identification System (AIS), Jan. 6, 2003.

SECURING THE MARINE TRANSPORTATION SYSTEM   405

the expected time of arrival; a list of crew and passengers; a general description of cargo being carried; identities of the persons responsible for appointing crew and other shipboard personnel; and, information on charter parties.[153]

Port States may require supplementary information as a condition of entry or, subsequent to entry, but a request for supplementary information may not include details of the SSP. Administrations establish standing requirements on the information to be provided and the time period required for submission of pre-arrival information. The IMO has promulgated a standard data set in this respect.[154]

Similarly, the ship operator has an obligation to comply with the LRIT requirements by providing onboard equipment for transmitting the identity of the ship, its position, and the date and time of the position to the Data Centre (DC) nominated by the ship's Administration. In exceptional circumstances and for the shortest duration possible, the LRIT system can be switched off if its operation is considered by the master to compromise the safety or security of the ship (e.g., transiting through pirate-infested waters). In such instances, the master is required to inform the Administration without undue delay and record the occurrence with the reason for the decision and duration of non-transmittal.

There are three types of AIS information. Static or fixed information is entered into AIS on installation and only has to be changed if the ship changes its name or undergoes a major conversion from one type of ship to another. Dynamic information is automatically updated from the ships sensors to AIS. Finally, voyage-related information may need to be entered manually and updated during a voyage. The AIS signal is transmitted at intervals that vary according to a ship's maneuvering status, signaling between every two seconds when it is exceeding 23 knots and changing course, to once every three minutes when it is at anchor.[155] The system transmits a variety of information. The most comprehensive policy analysis of AIS lists the full spectrum of data captured by AIS.

Static of fixed information is transmitted once every six minutes or upon request and includes:

- Maritime Mobile Service Identity (MMSI), which is set on installation, but may be changed if the ship changes ownership;
- Call sign and name—set on installation;
- IMO ship number—set on installation;
- Ship length and beam—set on installation (or if later changed);

---

[153] IMO Doc. MSC 89/INF.13, Maritime Security Measures, para. 2.12.20.
[154] Id., Appendix 4.6—Standard Data Set of Security-related Pre-Arrival Information.
[155] Brian Tetreault, *Automatic Identification System; The Use of AIS in Support of Maritime Domain Awareness*, US COAST GUARD PROC. 27, at 28 (Fall 2006).

- Location of position-fixing antenna—set on installation or may be changed for bi-directional vessels or vessels subsequently outfitted with additional antennae.[156]

Transmission of dynamic data includes:

- A unique maritime mobile service identity (MMSI) number;
- Ship's position with accuracy indication and integrity status, automatically updated from the position sensor connected to AIS. The accuracy indication is for better or worse than 10 m;
- Position time stamp in UTC: time stamp, accurate to nearest second and based on "Zulu" time (otherwise known as "Coordinated Universal Time" (UTC), automatically updated from ship's main position sensor connected to AIS;
- Course over ground (COG): automatically updated from ship's main position sensor connected to AIS, if that sensor calculates COG;
- Speed over ground (SOG): automatically updated from the position sensor connected to AIS;
- Heading: automatically updated from the position sensor connected to AIS;
- Navigational status: data must be entered manually by the officer of the watch and may include underway engines, at anchor, not under command (NUC), restricted in ability to maneuver (RIATM), moored, constrained by draught, aground, engaged in fishing, and underway by said. In practice, these elements relate to COLREGs and will be reflected in a change of lights and shapes;
- True heading at 0 to 359 degrees;
- Longitude and Latitude (to 1/10,000 minutes);
- Rate of return: automatically updated from the ship's ROT sensor or derived from the gyroscope, indicating port or starboard, in degrees per minute;
- Optional: angle of heel, pitch, and roll.[157]

Finally, transmission of voyage-related information includes ship's draught, hazardous cargo type and quantities, destination and ETA, and route plan, including waypoints.[158]

Ships fitted with AIS are expected to keep the system in operation at all times except where international agreements, rules or standards provide for the protection of navigational information. For example, under the amended SOLAS, if the master of a vessel believes that continual operation of AIS might compromise the safety of the ship, or where security incidents are imminent, the AIS may be switched off. In doing so, masters should bear in mind the possibility that attackers could be monitoring ship-to-shore communications and using intercepted information to select their targets.

---

[156] IMO Doc. A.22/Res.917, Guidelines for the Onboard Operational Use of Shipborne Automatic Identification Systems, Jan. 25, 2002. *See also*, Martin N. Murphy, *Lifeline or Pipedream? Origins, Purposes, and Benefits of Automatic Identification System, Long-Range Identification and Tracking, and Maritime Domain Awareness*, 13, 14–15, *in* LLOYD'S MIU HANDBOOK OF MARITIME SECURITY (Rupert Herbert-Burns, Same Bateman & Peter Lehr, eds. 2009).

[157] IMO Doc. A.22/Res.917, Guidelines for the Onboard Operational Use of Shipborne Automatic Identification Systems, Jan. 25, 2002.

[158] Id.

On the other hand, switching off AIS in high-risk areas reduces the ability of the patrolling naval vessels to track and trace commercial ships in need of assistance. The decision of whether to continue to transmit AIS information in high-risk areas is one of professional judgment in which the risks of exposure to piracy must be balanced against the need to maintain the safety of navigation. If AIS is turned off to avoid attracting unwanted attention of pirates, the device should be turned on again in the event the ship is actually faced with an imminent attack so that naval forces could be alerted and obtain position location for the victim ship.

The U.S. European Command has worked with the states of Africa and the Mediterranean basin to collect and fuse AIS data into a shared Internet-based application called the Maritime Safety & Security Information System (MSSIS). As a scalable and accessible web-based platform, MSSIS is called "wiki on the waves" and is a fusion point for AIS transmission from commercial vessels. The system provides an unclassified, near real-time view of vessel activity including speed and direction, cargo type, location of embarkation and destination, and ship type. All of this information is available over the Internet with a user name and password.

Similarly, the European Union is interested in a system by French military shipbuilder DCNS called Sismaris, which uses a combination of land-based radars, AIS receiving stations, and sophisticated mapping and intelligence to track ships up to 200 nautical miles from shore.[159] Sismaris can be used to ascertain illegal activities, such as transference of illegal drugs from one ship to another ship, or more mundane tasks, such as seeing if a vessel overshoots the speed limit. Sensor nets, electro-optical detectors and unmanned underwater vehicles lie on the horizon of MDA technology.

Operation of AIS both increases maritime security and at the same time raises security concerns because information is broadcast openly and made available to anyone, including persons planning acts of piracy or terrorism. For this reason, in November 2003, the IMO Assembly adopted a resolution that permits ship masters to switch off AIS in areas where they believe the ship may be in imminent danger from attack.[160] Some analysts suspect that Somali pirates used AIS to locate and hijack the 1,000-foot supertanker *Sirius Star*, which was transiting 450 miles off the coast of Kenya in November 2008 when it was hijacked and taken to Somalia. The Liberian-flagged vessel, which is owned by Aramco in Saudi Arabia, was carrying 25 seafarers and more than $100 million in oil cargo bound for the United States.

---

[159] Nicholas Fiorenza, *Who Goes There?* DEFENSE TECH. INT'L 54, 56 (Oct. 2009).
[160] IMO Doc. A.956(23), Amendments to the guidelines for the onboard operational use of shipboard automatic identification systems (AIS), Dec. 5, 2003, *amending* IMO Doc. A.917(22), Guidelines for the onboard operational use of ship borne automatic identification systems (AIS), Nov. 29, 2001.

For many areas, however, particularly near the restricted entrances to congested ports and harbors, the AIS provisions of SOLAS are an important component for strengthening maritime situational awareness. Furthermore, with the advent of the secure, satellite-based Long-Range Identification and Tracking of Ships, the protection afforded to merchant shipping by more secure methods of MDA is growing.[161]

12.5.3   Long-Range Identification and Tracking

AIS-generated ship data is not available on open source Internet sites as it is considered to be detrimental to the safety and security of ships and port facilities and undermines the efforts of the IMO and its Member States to enhance the safety of navigation and security in the international maritime transport sector. But virtually anyone can obtain password access to AIS data. Because of the limited range and open-access architecture of AIS, the United States led development of a follow-on satellite-based MDA system called Long-Range Identification and Tracking (LRIT). The IMO adopted LRIT in 2006. LRIT is a satellite-based tracking system designed to utilize existing shipboard equipment such as the Global Maritime Distress and Safety System (GMDSS) to track SOLAS-class vessels over 300 tons on international voyages. Ships are required to transmit LRIT information, which is comprised of the ship's identity, the ship's location (latitude and longitude), and the date and time of the position, four times daily and at six-hour intervals.

LRIT requirements are set forth in Chapter V, Regulation 19-1 of SOLAS and entered into force on January 1, 2008. Like AIS, LRIT requires ships 300 gross tons or greater and traveling on international voyages to transmit data. Fishing vessels are not covered by SOLAS and therefore are outside the scope of both AIS and LRIT.[162] From its beginning, however, there was controversy over how Contracting Governments—and in particular, coastal States—may use LRIT data. Originally, concept for LRIT was envisioned to enhance maritime security. It soon became evident, however, that such a system would be tremendously beneficial to search and rescue (SAR), and so the IMO agreed that LRIT data could be used for SAR purposes. Environmentalists salivated at the prospect of using LRIT to enforce vessel source pollution standards. In 2007, the IMO Assembly clarified

---

[161] IMO Doc. MSC.298(87), Establishment of a distribution facility for the provision of LRIT information to security forces operating in waters of the Gulf of Aden and the Western Indian Ocean to aid their work in the repression of piracy and armed robbery against ships (the distribution facility), May 21, 2010.

[162] UN Doc. A/63/174, Report on the work of the United Nations Open-ended Informal Consultative Process on Oceans and Law of the Sea at its ninth meeting, July 25, 2008, para. 43.

that LRIT data could be used for both maritime safety and marine environment protection purposes.[163]

Ships carrying AIS are required to be compliant with LRIT, with the exception of ships operating exclusively in coastal areas (defined by the Flag State Administration). The system is secure in that it is only available to coastal States, and the technology architecture permits flag and port States to collect information on vessels worldwide. As the LRIT system continues to be built, it is becoming a reliable, secure and persistent global surveillance of maritime traffic for the purposes of detecting, identifying and classifying vessels. The system can provide ship identity and current location information to allow governments to evaluate the security risk posed by ships off its coast.

Unlike AIS, LRIT communication is addressed, meaning that the system uses a secure point-to-point transmission of information, rather than an openly available broadcast. While routine tracking is every six hours, the performance standards stipulate that onboard terminals must be capable of being remotely reconfigured to transmit LRIT information as frequently as once every 15 minutes. Once communication has been established, the satellite terminal automatically responds to subsequent polling requests.[164]

Each Administration must have a Data Center (DC) to which its ships transmit the required information. The DC is the repository of all of the flag State's LRIT information and is connected to the wider International LRIT system via the International Data Exchange (IDE), through which all information is routed to other DCs. A Government not wishing to establish its own DC may utilize the services of another DC, although each Administration can associate itself with only a single DC. The majority of Administrations contract their DC services to third-party service providers.[165]

The DC collects data for each Administration and then shares it with requesting contracting governments that are entitled to the information under the SOLAS regulation. In addition to either establishing or joining a DC, each State party with covered vessels must appoint an Application Service Provider to conduct conformance tests on those ships, manage communications between the ships, the Communications Service Provider, and the DC.

States are entitled to request and receive LRIT data about ships that fly their flag, regardless of location of the ship. Port States are entitled to receive information about foreign-flagged ships that have expressed an intention to enter a port

---

[163] IMO Doc. MSC.243(83), Use of Long-Range Identification and Tracking Information for Maritime Safety and Marine Environment Protection Purposes, adopted Oct. 12, 2007, *reprinted in* IMO Doc. MSC 83/28/Add.2, Report of the Maritime Safety Committee on its Eighty-Third Session, Nov. 2, 2007, at Annex 6.

[164] IMO Doc. MSC.1/Circ.1298, Guidance on the Implementation of the LRIT System, Dec. 8, 2008.

[165] Id.

facility under the jurisdiction of the port State. Finally, coastal States are entitled to receive data on foreign-flagged ships navigating within 1000 nautical miles of their coastline. During the negotiations in 2006, Brazil and China sought to craft regulations that would entitle LRIT data to be made available to ships out to 200 nautical miles—coterminous with the EEZ. This effort was rejected by the United States, which was concerned that a 200-mile limit would strengthen the tendency of some coastal States to assert and enforce a security interest in the EEZ. The option for a 1,000-mile limit was supported by the United States, Australia, and Canada—nations that are faced with long, high seas approaches to their coastlines.

If an Administration has security concerns, it may at any time decide not to provide LRIT information about its ships to another state. In such case, however, the Administration must tell the IMO, which, in turn, is required to inform all other contracting governments.

The United States agreed to interim initial operation of the LRIT International Data Exchange beginning on December 16, 2008. The Ad Hoc LRIT Group is the IMO's LRIT governance body. During the 10th session of the Ad Hoc Group from October 31 to November 3, 2011, operation of the International Data Exchange for LRIT was transferred to the European Maritime Safety Agency (EMSA) in Lisbon, Portugal.[166] The transfer was completed on October 18, 2011, although the United States will continue to maintain a disaster recovery site for the system in case of a critical failure at the primary site in Portugal.

---

[166] *IMO Body Authorizes EMSA to Operate LRIT Data Exchange*, IMO NEWS 8 (2012).

THIRTEEN

PORT AND PORT FACILITY SECURITY

13.1 Ports in the Global Transportation System

Ports are windows to the world. As major transportation nodes in the global economy, ports are essential for the import and export of commodities and finished products through oceanic trade. The great empires of the past relied on ports to project power; the Persian, Ottoman, British, French, Dutch, Portuguese, and successive Chinese dynasties used ports as an avenue to join together distant regions, as well as a means to clash with their neighbors.[1] Myres S. McDougal and William T. Burke explain in their classic treatise, *The Public Order of the Oceans*:

> The chief function of ports for the coastal state is in provision of cheap and easy access to the oceans and to the rest of the world. Without suitable land-water conformations to serve as harbors a state may be largely isolated from the life of the community outside and even a plentiful resource base will be of greatly diminished value.[2]

The political and economic phenomenon of globalization that has so fundamentally transformed the world over the past three decades is dependent upon the flow of trade into ports. In reporting on a University of Maine School of Law symposium on marine port law, Charles H. Norchi describes how the attacks of 9/11,

---

[1] Charles H. Norchi, Public Order of Ports, 14 Ocean and Coastal L. J. 155, 155–56 (2009). See also, Charles H. Norchi, The Circum-Mediterranean: From Clashing Civilizations to Transnational Arbitration, in Naval Strategy and Policy in the Mediterranean: Past, Present and Future 301, 306 (John B. Hattendorf, ed., 2000).
[2] Myres S. McDougal & William T. Burke, The Public Order of the Oceans 90 (1962). (We thank Charles H. Norchi for bringing this section of McDougal & Burke's treatise to our attention).

however, changed the public order of maritime ports.[3] In the aftermath of the attacks, there was tremendous fear that a catastrophic terrorist attack against a major port in the United States, Europe, or Asia, not only could be locally devastating, but also generate massive follow-on effects throughout the global economy. Thus, strengthening port security acquired immediate urgency, and the principal means of doing so was to refurbish and update rules for port State control and port State security. The United States took the lead, enacting the *Maritime Transportation Security Act 2002* (MTSA).[4] The MTSA and the lessons learned from its implementation served as a guide for the international community to develop comprehensive mechanisms for port State control, a process pursued through the International Maritime Organization.

Port State control is predicated on the sovereignty and territorial jurisdiction of the port State. Traditionally, the flag State has been empowered to exercise jurisdiction and control in administrative, technical and social matters over ships flying its flag.[5] While this practice is reflected in Articles 92 and 94 of the 1982 United Nations Convention on the Law of the Sea (UNCLOS),[6] in recent years port States also have worked closely to expand their jurisdiction over vessels arriving in ports and at port facilities as a complement to exclusive flag State jurisdiction.

Most broadly, a port may be defined as an area where ships load or unload cargo, or embark or disembark passengers.[7] The *Maritime Ports Convention* 1923 committed member states to apply the principle of equal treatment to ships of other member states in "[a]ll ports which are normally frequented by sea-going

---

[3] Norchi, Public Order of Ports, at 159. Volume 14(2) of the Ocean and Coastal L. J. was dedicated to applying the New Haven School of jurisprudence in a comparative perspective to the notion of "port law," particularly as it relates to "incidents that implicate and spawn international law including custom, conventions, and agreements and national or municipal law including decisions, regulations, and statutes. Norchi, at 157, and note 10: "The incident method...takes a single critical event as a prism through which the reactions of elites to particular behavior may be examined and assessed as an indication of their views of law." International Incidents: The Law That Counts in World Politics 16 (W. Michael Reisman & Andrew Willard eds. 1988).

[4] Maritime Transportation Security Act of 2002, Pub. L. No. 107–295, 116 Stat. 2064 (2002).

[5] Convention on the High Seas, Geneva, Switzerland, concluded Apr. 29, 1958, entered into force Sept. 30, 1962, 13 UST 2312, 450 UNTS 11, Article 5.

[6] United Nations Convention on the Law of the Sea, opened for signature Dec. 10, 1982, UN Doc. A/CONF.62/122 (1982), 1833 U.N.T.S. 3, 397, 21 I.L.M. 1261 (1982), entered into force Nov. 16, 1994. [Hereinafter UNCLOS].

[7] C. John Colombos, The international Law of the Sea 175 (6th ed., 1967).

vessels and used for foreign trade...."[8] A port is an area of internal waters, along with lakes, rivers, bays, canals and waters landward of the territorial sea, under Article 5 of the 1958 Geneva Convention and Articles 8 and 11 of UNCLOS. Article 11 of UNCLOS regards harbor works as places sheltered from natural conditions, which protect ships from the weather so that they may facilitate the movement of cargoes or passengers in trade. The plenary authority of the port State applies throughout the port. Furthermore, both the 1958 High Seas Convention and UNCLOS Articles 218, 210, 220(1) and 226 contain provisions on port State control.

Port State control is also an element of numerous treaties and instruments that supplement or further develop the rules in UNCLOS, and include MARPOL Article 5(2) and (6),[9] Load Lines Convention Article 21,[10] COLREGS,[11] STCW,[12] and ILO Convention No. 147, Article 4.[13] The ISM Code, integrated into SOLAS as chapter IX in 1994, mandates that vessels carry a document of compliance from the Flag State Administration (or its designee) to attest that each ship's safety management system is in compliance with the Code.[14]

By voluntarily placing themselves in the port State, foreign-flagged ships fall under the territorial sovereignty of the port State.[15] Most scholars regard the authority of a port State over foreign-flagged vessels temporarily in the port to

---

[8] Convention on the International Regime of Maritime Ports, Dec. 9, 1923, Geneva Switzerland, entered into force July 26, 1926, 58 L.N.T.S. 285, 22 Am J. Int'l L. Supp. 69, Statute, Article I.

[9] International Convention for the Prevention of Pollution from Ships, Nov. 2, 1973, 12 I.L.M. 1319 and Protocol of 1978 Relating to the International Convention for the Prevention of Pollution from Ships, done Feb. 17, 1978, 17 I.L.M. 546 (entered into force Oct. 2, 1983).

[10] International Convention on Load Lines, Apr. 5, 1996, T.I.A.S. No. 6331, 640 U.N.T.S. 2, entered into force May 25, 1980.

[11] Convention on the International Regulations for Preventing Collisions at Sea, Oct. 20, 1972, T.I.A.S. No. 5857, 1050 U.N.T.S. 16, entered into force July 15, 1977 [Hereinafter COLREGs].

[12] International Convention on Standards of Training, Certification and Watchkeeping for Seafarers, Dec. 1, 1978, 1361 U.N.T.S. 2, entered into force April 28, 1984, as amended and modified by the 1995 Protocol [Hereinafter STCW].

[13] International Labor Organization Merchant Shipping (Minimum Standards) Convention No. 147 1976, Oct. 29, 1976, entered into force, Nov. 19, 1981, reprinted in 6A Benedict on Admiralty at 9–97 (M. Cohen 7th rev. ed. 1983).

[14] IMO Doc. A.741(18), International Management Code for the Safe Operation of Ships and Pollution Prevention (ISM Code) Annex to Nov. 4, 1993, reprinted in 6D Benedict on Admiralty, Doc. 14-2, at 14–449 (7th rev. ed. 1998) and International Convention for the Safety of Life at Sea, Nov. 1, 1974, 32 U.S.T. 47, T.I.A.S. 9700, 1184 U.N.T.S. 278, entered into force May 25, 1980, with protocols and regularly amended [Hereinafter SOLAS].

[15] R. R. Churchill and A. V. Lowe, The Law of the Sea 54 (3rd ed. 1999).

be superior to exclusive flag State jurisdiction, excepting certain cases involving force majeure or distress (UNCLOS Article 218),[16] warships or other sovereign immune vessels (UNCLOS Articles 32 and 95), or matters of diplomatic sovereign immunity.[17] Still, the preambles of many port State control memorandums of understanding recognize that the "principal responsibility" for implementing flag State standards on a vessel rests with the flag State and not the port State.

Flag States sometimes worry that port State control may impose inconsistent requirements on ships flying their flag because their vessels are subject to host nation laws only while in port. Consequently, flag State law should prevail in the case of contradictory requirements among different ports or port States.[18] General principles of international law and state sovereignty, however, mean that once a foreign ship voluntarily enters into a port of another country, the vessel becomes subject to the laws and regulations of the host nation irrespective of whether the host nation's rules are based on international treaties to which the flag State is a party.[19]

Port States may enforce certain laws against foreign flagged ships for activities that occur while the vessel is in port, including construction, design, safety, crewing and equipment standards.[20] The *Law of the Sea Convention* provides that a port State also has authority to enforce laws relating to some types of environmental protection and vessel source pollution activities of foreign vessels that occur in the waters of the host state prior to entry into port. To do so, however, the port State must be enforcing laws that were enacted "in accordance with" UNCLOS, or that reflect "applicable international rules and standards."[21]

At the port level, security coordination may be accomplished through establishment of a Port Security Committee (PSC). The PSC normally is comprised of representatives from the port or harbor authority, the port facilities within the port, government organizations operating in the port, first responders and local law enforcement agencies, and port employees and users. The Port Security Officer (PSO) and Port Facility Security Officers (PFSOs) from individual port facilities within a port complex typically are prominent members of the PSC. Generally, broader membership in the PSC is preferable and may include port managers and operators, customs and immigration representatives, organized labor, major commercial users of the port, the Designated Authority and

---

[16] Id. at 54–57.
[17] Ted L. McDorman, Regional Port State Control Agreements: Some Issues of International Law, 5 Ocean and Coastal L. J. 207, 210–11 (2000) and Ian Brownlie, Principles of Public International Law 315–317 (6th ed. 2003).
[18] McDorman, Regional Port State Control Agreements, at 210–11.
[19] Id.
[20] Ted L. McDorman, Port State Enforcement: A Comment on Article 218 of the Law of the Sea Convention, 28 J. Mar. L. & Com. 305, 311–12 (1997).
[21] UNCLOS, Article 220.

Administration assigned to the port, and municipal and regional governments. The chair of the PSC typically is the senior manager of the port operator who has overall responsibility for port security.

It is also helpful for the PSC to develop a common Terms of Reference, which may include relevant security threats, the process for reporting and assessing recent security incidents at the port, conducting exercises and drills, and enhancing coordination, such as synchronizing port facility security assessments with the overarching Port Security Assessment. This work also requires balancing the value of open and transparent consultation with the need to protect confidential security information and sensitive intelligence.

Port Security Officers (PSO) appointed by the PSC and endorsed by the Designated Authority usually serve as the initial point of contact for security matters for ships destined for the port. The PSOs are responsible for security of piers, anchorages, waiting berths and offloading berths, and warehouses operated by the Port Authority under the Port Facility Security Plan (PFSP), which is the template for security in the port area. The ILO/IMO *Code of Practice on Port Security* suggests that PSOs should conduct a security survey of the port, develop and maintain the port security plan, and undertake routine inspection of security and potential vulnerabilities.[22]

The ISPS Code does not require Port Security Assessments (PSAs) to be conducted and submitted for approval, although many Designated Authorities impose such a requirement anyway. Also, the rules do not require port authorities to develop Port Security Plans (PSPs), but nations still may require PSAs and the preparation, submission and approval of PSPs. (States in Europe, for example, have imposed such a requirement).

The IMO has promulgated advice on port facility security, and additional guidance on wider aspects of port security is contained in the ILO/IMO *Code of Practice on Port Security*. The IMO guidance on port facility security contained in the ISPS Code and the ILO/IMO *Code of Practice on Port Security* are mutually supportive.

Smaller marinas, ports and harbors that are not required to implement the Maritime Security Measures, but many consider their adoption appropriate.[23] Regular patrols, fencing and locked buildings, and other access controls are important physical security practices. Ports also may communicate current security information to users, including identification of any areas subject to special security conditions or restrictions. If non-SOLAS facilities are located in the vicinity of SOLAS port facilities, they may promulgate regulations governing interaction

---

[22] Int'l Labor Org., ILO/IMO Code of Practice: Security in Ports (2004).
[23] See, IMO Doc. MSC 89/INF.13, Measures to Enhance Maritime Security, Maritime Security Manual, Mar. 5, 2011, sec. 3, reproduced in Guide to Maritime Security and the ISPS Code paras. 3.1 to 3.10 (International Maritime Organization 2012 ed.), IMO Sales No. IA116E [Hereinafter Maritime Security Measures or MSM].

with SOLAS vessels and review their security arrangements in cooperation with the PFSOs.

Non-SOLAS facilities should implement security measures tailored to their size and complexity. Measures may include proper pier and water side illumination, passive monitoring, such as closed circuit television, visitor control procedures, diversion of transient vessels arriving at night to a specific area of the facility, installation of radio frequency identification devices to monitor ship entry and egress from the marina.

13.2 Port State Control

A State's sovereignty over its territory includes, with a very few caveats, absolute power to regulate civil or merchant maritime transportation and traffic in internal waters. A port State has virtually absolute discretion in admission of foreign vessels into its ports and internal waters, although all nations also have a duty to provide places of refuge for ships in need of assistance. The scope of force majeure, however, appears to be diminishing by state practice, as port States have become quite bold in refusing requests based on emergency circumstances. Port States also are entitled to establish and enforce conditions on entry, which may include actions to be taken before entry. Additionally, states may enter into agreements with other nations to limit this right, however, in order to facilitate traffic with neighboring nations.

In general, international law recognizes the authority of the port State to set conditions for the entry into internal waters or to call at ports. States may limit or suspend passage or movement of any vessels in internal waters. Nations also have responsibility to take action against unsafe, unsecure, or unseaworthy vessels. The overarching framework for oceans law and policy contains additional guidance. Article 25 of UNCLOS authorizes states to take action in the territorial sea as necessary to prevent any breach of conditions of port entry. Likewise, coastal States may temporarily suspend innocent passage in specified areas of the territorial sea for the purpose of protecting the nation's security. Suspension of innocent passage must be published and may not discriminate among foreign flag administrations. The authority of the port State to control foreign-flagged shipping extends throughout archipelagic waters. In archipelagic sea lanes and straits used for international navigation, however, port States may not enforce unilateral controls on shipping unless vessels are making port call.

A coastal State also has authority under international law to enact and enforce laws for the protection of certain installations and facilities that are located beyond its territorial sea in the exclusive economic zone (EEZ) or over or on its outer continental shelf. Under Articles 60 and 80 of UNCLOS, a state may regulate the operation and use of such facilities related to the coastal states jurisdiction over the EEZ, such as safety zones of up to 500 meters in width encircling such facilities. As part of its port State control program, a State may inspect a ship's papers and on board safety equipment, such as firefighting systems and lifeboats.

In rare circumstances, a port State has authority to detain a foreign-flagged vessel. Under Article 219 of UNCLOS, port States are authorized to prevent a vessel from sailing that may threaten the marine environment due to its failure to comply with internationally accepted rules of seaworthiness. Unseaworthy ships pose a risk of vessel source oil pollution. In taking action, the port State must act reasonably, in a transparent fashion, and not discriminate against or among ships of different flag State registries.

International standards for vessel safety and security flow from customary international law and UNCLOS, as well as a slate of additional multilateral and bilateral agreements. The standards contained in international law inform domestic rules and provide uniform benchmarks for implementation of port State control programs in municipal law. Shortcomings in safety standards often suggest the ships may present security risks to the port State. Port State controls help eliminate substandard vessels from the waters of the port state, enhancing general safety as well as security. Substandard vessels—those ships that have hull, machinery, equipment deficiencies or discrepancies, or crew qualifications that are below internationally accepted standards—pose the greatest safety risk to ports.[24]

Port State control measures are increasingly important for maintaining the overall security of the worldwide marine transportation system. Vulnerability at any point in the cargo chain—from on load and embarkation through open-ocean transit and then disembarkation at intermediate ports or the port of ultimate destination—poses a potential risk to maritime security. The United States, for example, had 76,372 port calls in 2010 by 9,620 ships from 90 different Flag State Administrations.[25] Each link in the cargo chain—including every load on every ship—increases systemic vulnerability. In order to reduce the risk, the U.S. Coast Guard conducted nearly 10,000 SOLAS safety exams and almost 9,000 ISPS exams on vessels in 2010.[26]

---

[24] U.S. Coast Guard, Dep't Homeland Security, Coast Guard Port State Control Targeting and Boarding Policy for Vessel Security and Safety, Navigation Vessel Inspection Circular (NVIC) No. 06–03, Change 2, Encl. (4), Mar. 27, 2007, at 1.

[25] U.S. Coast Guard, Dep't of Homeland Security, Port State Control in the United States Annual Report 2 (2010).

[26] Id. Among these ships, 17 were detained—compared to 18 ships detained in 2009.

13.2.1 *IMO Protocols*

Although the concept of port State jurisdiction is reflected in UNCLOS, the practical boundaries of the authority largely emanate from IMO treaties and protocols, and in particular safety and shipping anti-pollution regulations. The flag State has primary authority for enforcing IMO regulations against ships flying its flag. As the law of the sea has evolved over the past three decades, however, port States have acquired progressively greater authority to correct non-compliance of IMO rules and standards by foreign ships voluntarily in port.[27] By entering a foreign port voluntarily, it is implied that ships accept certain port State jurisdiction over issues of compliance with IMO regulations.[28]

The original 1995 IMO guidance in Assembly resolution A.787(19) provided the first comprehensive framework for port State control inspection and rules for detention.[29] IMO Assembly resolution A.787(19) of 1995, amended by resolution A.882(21) of 1999 and then replaced by resolution A.1052(27) of December 20, 2011, requires port States that initiate control actions to notify the Flag State Administration to which the vessel is registered. Notice to the flag State should be made as soon as possible in the case of security-related control actions against a vessel, such as ship inspection, delay or detention of a ship, restriction of operations, movement or expulsion from port.[30] Lesser penalties besides denial of entry, detention, or expulsion from port are available to port State control authorities and include civil penalties, letters of warning, and administrative or corrective measures.

The procedures applied to ships are subject to the provisions of a host of applicable international conventions.[31] The conventions were boot-strapped into port State control under specific provisions, including Regulation 19 of chapter I,

---

[27] IMO Doc. LEG/MISC.6, Implications of the United Nations Convention on the Law of the Sea for the International Maritime Organization: Study by the Secretariat of the International Maritime Organization, Sept. 10, 2008, at 13.
[28] Id.
[29] IMO Doc. A.787(19), Procedures for Port State Control, Nov. 23, 1995.
[30] SOLAS XI-2, Reg. 9.8.1.
[31] International Convention for the Safety of Life at Sea, 1974, as amended (SOLAS 74), the Protocol of 1988 relating to the International Convention for the Safety of Life at Sea, 1974 (SOLAS Protocol 1988), the International Convention on Load Lines, 1966 (Load Lines 66), the Protocol of 1988 relating to the International Convention on Load Lines, 1966 (Load Line Protocol 88), the International Convention for the Prevention of Pollution from Ships, 1973 as modified by the Protocol of 1978 relating thereto, as amended (MARPOL 73/78), the International Convention on Standards of Training, Certification and Watchkeeping for Seafarers, 1978, as amended (STCW 78), and the International Convention on Tonnage Measurement of Ships, 1969 (TONNAGE 69). IMO Doc. A.787(19), at para. 1.2.1 and Annex to IMO Doc. A.882(21), Amendments to the Procedures for Port State Control (Resolution A.787(19), Nov. 25, 1999).

regulation 6.2 of chapter IX and regulation 4 of chapter XI of SOLAS 74, as modified by SOLAS Protocol 88; article 21 of Load Lines 66, as modified by Load Line Protocol 88; articles 5 and 6, regulation 8A of Annex I, regulation 15 of Annex II, regulation 8 of Annex III and regulation 8 of Annex V of MARPOL 73/78; article X of STCW 78; and article 12 of TONONAGE 69.

In the original guidance port States were permitted to invoke the authorities for "the purposes of identifying deficiencies, if any, in such ship which may render them substandard, and ensuring that remedial measures are taken."[32] In the updated 1999 and 2011 guidance, however, the standard was strengthened so that port State control officers could "make effective use of these provisions for the purposes of identifying deficiencies, if any, in such ship which may render them substandard, and ensuring that remedial measures are taken."[33]

The procedures also reinforce provisions in SOLAS, MARPOL, and STCW that no more favorable treatment is to be given to ships of countries that are not party to the relevant convention.[34] Furthermore, even though ships of non-parties and ships below convention size are not provided with applicable SOLAS, Load Line or MARPOL certificates, port authorities should "take into account" the principles of the IMO procedures and be "satisfied that the ship and crew do not present a danger to those on board or an unreasonable threat of harm to the marine environment."[35] If such ships have some other documentation or certification, the Port State Control Officer (PSCO) may "take the form and content" of the documentation into account in evaluating the ship.[36]

Port State Control Officers are charged with securing the "rectification" of all deficiencies that are detected in ships in port. These officers are vested with authority to carry out port State control inspections, and they are responsible exclusively to the State party of the relevant conventions (e.g. SOLAS, STCW, TONNAGE, etc.).[37] In cases in which the deficiencies are "clearly hazardous to safety or the environment," the PSCO should "ensure that the hazard is removed before the ship is allowed to proceed to sea."[38] The PSCO is granted authority to take action, which may include "detention or a formal prohibition of a ship

---

[32] IMO Doc. A.787(19), at para. 1.4.
[33] IMO Doc. A.882 (21), at para. 1.4 and IMO Doc. A.1052(27), Procedures for Port State Control, 2011, Dec. 20, 2011, at para. 1.4.
[34] IMO Doc. A.1052(27), Procedures for Port State Control, 2011, Dec. 20, 2011, at para. 1.2.2. See, Article II(3) of the Protocol of 1978 to SOLAS 74, article 5(4) of MARPOL 73/78, and Article X(5) of STCW 78.
[35] IMO Doc. A.1052(27), Procedures for Port State Control, 2011, Dec. 20, 2011, at para. 1.5.2.
[36] Id., at para. 1.5.2 and para. 2.3.
[37] Id., at para. 1.7.7.
[38] IMO Doc. 882(21), at para. 4.72 and IMO Doc. A.1052(27), Procedures for Port State Control, 2011, Dec. 20, 2011, para. 3.7.2.

to continue" to operate.[39] If the deficiency cannot be remedied in port, the port authority may permit the ship to proceed to the nearest repair facility or shipyard available, and the destination is jointly decided by the master of the ship and the port authority and ratified by the port State and flag State. A deficient ship should not get underway unless it is able to proceed without risk to the safety of the passengers or crew, or risk to other ships or the marine environment.

Port State control is a key component of achieving maritime security, and control actions include denial of port entry or expulsion of a vessel from port, IMO reportable detentions, restriction of operations, direction of vessel movement, or delaying a vessel. With the consent of the Flag State Administration or master of the ship, a complete security evaluation may be conducted. The case of the M/S *Thor Liberty*, for example, illustrates how effective port State control can affect security in distant regions.

On December 21, 2011, Finnish port authorities impounded 160 tons of explosives and 69 Patriot surface-to-air missiles from the British Crown Dependency Isle of Man-flagged cargo ship *Thor Liberty*.[40] The ship sailed from the north German port of Emden on December 13, and arrived in Missalo harbor at the Finnish port of Kotka on December 15 in order to on load a cargo of anchor chains. The missiles and explosives appeared to be owned by a Danish company and to be lawful cargo, destined for South Korea via transshipment through Shanghai, China. But the explosives and missiles were marked improperly as "fireworks," and they were stored on open pallets rather than protective containers.

Port State control inspections may be conducted at the request or initiative of the port State administration, on the basis of information regarding a ship provided by another port State administration, or by information regarding a ship provided by a crewmember or any other individual with an interest in the safety of the ship, its crew and passengers. Thus, PSC inspections may be random, targeted or conducted on a periodic basis.

Port State control permits port States to detain ships for certain deficiencies in security and safety. A ship that does not possess documents required by widely accepted international conventions or that has deficient documents lacking key signatures or the name of the vessel or issuing authority may be detained by a port State. Under the ISPS Code, for example, port States may detain ships that lack or have an expired or invalid International Ship Security Certificate (ISSC) or interim certificate. In the United States, the decision to deny port entry or detain a vessel under port State control is made by the captain of the port (COTP) or officer in charge of marine inspection (OCMI).

---

[39] IMO Doc. 882(21), at para. 4.7.3 and IMO Doc. A.1052(27), Procedures for Port State Control, 2011, Dec. 20, 2011, para. 3.7.2.
[40] Finland Still Probing Patriot Missile Ship, CBS News/Associated Press, Dec. 22, 2011.

Ships in port may be subject to IMO reportable detentions if the PSCO believes, based on a PSC examination, that the ship poses an undue risk to the crew, vessel, or port. An IMO detention is appropriate when there are clear grounds that a ship subject to IMO instruments is substandard and corrective measures are necessary. Port States use IMO detention information to target vessels for closer scrutiny.

The current PSC procedures apply to ships falling under the provisions of a specific set of international agreements and standards, which include:

- International Convention for the Safety of Life at Sea, 1974, as amended (SOLAS);
- Protocol of 1988 relating to the International Convention for the Safety of Life at Sea, 1974 (SOLAS Protocol 1988);
- International Convention on Load Lines, 1966 (Load Lines);
- Protocol of 1988 relating to the International Convention on Load Lines, 1966 (Load Lines Protocol 1988);
- International Convention for the Prevention of Pollution from Ships, 1973, as modified by the Protocols of 1978 and 1997 relating thereto, as amended (MARPOL);
- International Convention on Standards of Training, Certification and Watchkeeping for Seafarers, 1978, as amended (STCW);
- International Convention on Tonnage Measurement of Ships, 1969 (TONNAGE 69); and
- International Convention on the Control of Harmful Anti-Fouling Systems on Ships (AFS).[41]

Some of the principal provisions of these instruments and their requirements are set forth below. The ISPS Code, for example, provides specific provisions that justify denial of port entry or IMO detention of ships already in port, including clear grounds related to:

- Documentary deficiencies. Lack of an assigned ships security officer (SSO), or the SSO cannot display the appropriate levels of training or certification;
- Crew anomalies. Crew anomalies may include gross incompetence, unaccounted or missing personnel, fraudulent document or other significant crew-related deficiencies;
- Security training. Glaring deficiencies in master, Ship Security Officer, or crew security training. The port state may not, however, require the SSO to have an encyclopedic knowledge of the ship security plan (SSP);
- Faulty Notice of Arrival. Inaccurate or incomplete notice of arrival information;[42]
- Security equipment. Deficient or nonexistent security equipment, such as an inoperable or missing ship security alert system;[43]
- Declaration of Security. Lack of a Declaration of Security, as required or previously agreed;
- Cargo handling. Suspicious cargo handling procedures; and

---

[41] IMO Doc. Res. 1052(27), Procedures for Port State Control, Dec. 20, 2011, para. 1.2.1.
[42] SOLAS Reg. XI-2/9.2.2.
[43] Id., XI-2/6.1.

- Access Control. Poor access control and screening procedures on passenger vessels (such as unmanned brow or gangway) or poor screening of unaccompanied baggage.

SOLAS also provides for detention of foreign-flagged vessels by port States in cases in which:

- Critical machinery is inoperable;
- Excessive oil in the engine room bilge or in the insulation of engine exhausts that creates a serious fire hazard;
- Certain equipment failures, including insufficient firefighting capacity, emergency systems, such as the generator or steering gear, absence of life-saving appliances, navigation equipment,[44] lights or sound signals; inoperable GMDSS; and
- Unsatisfactory drills or exercises, lack of a common crew language, improper manning documents.

Under the STCW, port State control measures include:

- Lack of appropriate seafarer certifications, certificates without a valid dispensation or proof of application for endorsement from a flag state administration; and
- Failure of safe manning requirements or proof of professional proficiency in the area of vessel source pollution, lack of navigational, radio-communications, or engineering watch program, inability to properly man watches, and inability to fulfill other rules promulgated by the flag state administration.

Finally, deficiencies in the Safety Management System (SMS) of the International Safety Management (ISM) Code may result in vessel detention under port State control authorities.[45] Vessels may be detained or expelled from port for major non-compliance with the ISM Code discovered during an expanded examination. The SMS documents each company's management of safety, security, and environmental protection on board the ship while the vessel is in port or at sea. The SMS contains information on preventive maintenance, navigation, bunkering operations, emergency preparedness, technical systems and communications, and pollution prevention. If failure to adhere to the SMS produces a serious and direct threat to personnel or ship safety and if there is evidence that the ship is not taking action to correct long-standing deficiencies, the vessel may be considered for detention. If a major deficiency is uncovered, the PSCO may request the Flag State Administration or an authorized recognized organization to perform an external audit of the vessel. However, a vessel should not be expelled solely for non-compliance with SOLAS IX and the ISM Code.

---

[44] Id., V/16.2.
[45] International Management Code for the Safe Operation of Ships and Pollution Prevention (ISM Code) Annex to IMO Doc. A.741(18), Nov. 4, 1993, reprinted in 6D Benedict on Admiralty, Doc. 14–2, at 14–449 (7th rev. ed. 1998) and Annex 8, IMO Doc. A.1052(27), Procedures for Port State Control, 2011, Dec. 20, 2011.

The Convention on the Facilitation of Maritime Traffic 1965, *as amended,* provides that foreign crew members shall be allowed ashore by the port State authorities while the ship on which they arrive is in port, provided that the formalities on arrival of the ship have been fulfilled and there is no reason based on public health, safety or public order, to deny the request to come ashore. In reviewing such requests, port State authorities should be sensitive to the welfare of ship's personnel, who live and work on the vessel. Shore leave and access to medical and welfare facilities improves the lives of seafarers.

Several initiatives from other international organizations have produced additional PSC agreements. The IMO is working with the World Customs Organization (WCO) to develop measures to enhance security throughout the cycle of the international movement of closed cargo transport units, which include transport vehicles, freight containers, or portable tanks in which the contents are totally enclosed by permanent structures. The revised *Seafarers' Identity Documents Convention* 2003 incorporates the use of biometric data, linked databases, and enhanced tamper resistant features to create uniform and verifiable credentials for mariners. But acceptance of mariner credentials in a port State depends on the domestic law of the port State.

The IMO is also providing technical assistance to developing countries, both individually and multilaterally, for improving PSC capacity. Funding for expansion of the Global Integrated Shipping Information System (GISIS), for example, promotes the transparency and exchange of maritime data.

13.2.2 Port State Regional MoUs

United Nations General Assembly Resolution 58/240 recognizes the importance of port State control for helping to ensure compliance with international standards of safety, security, labor, and pollution.[46] At the same time, the General Assembly invited the IMO to strengthen its approach to port State control related to maritime security. This function could be conducted in conjunction with the International Labor Organization and the Food and Agriculture Organization of the United Nations. As part of this effort, regional agreements have been negotiated to harmonize PSC inspections.

There are nine regional PSC regimes, covering virtually all of the world's oceans, and one major national regime, the program of the U.S. Coast Guard. Port State control measures are applied more diligently and effectively in the United States, Canada, and Europe, than in other regions of the world. Port authorities in North America and Europe use stringent U.S. Coast Guard or Paris MoU rules, which call for profiling visiting ships for inspection. Black lists of targeted, non-compliant flag States aid port security and inspection officials.

---

[46] UN Doc. A/Res/58/240, Oceans and Law of the Sea, Mar. 5, 2004, at para. 33.

13.2.2.1 Paris MoU

The Paris MoU arose from the disaster of the *Amoco Cadiz*. European states, the IMO and the ILO met in Paris in 1980 to eliminate substandard ships from "European waters." The existing Hague MoU of 1978 (also called the North Sea Agreement) was deemed to be ineffective for this purpose. The Paris Memorandum of Understanding on Port State Control (Paris MoU) was adopted in Paris at a second Ministerial conference on July 1, 1982.[47]

The Paris MoU has 27 member States: Belgium, Bulgaria, Canada, Croatia, Cyprus, Denmark, Estonia, Finland, France, Germany, Greece, Iceland, Ireland, Italy, Latvia, Lithuania, Malta, Netherlands, Norway, Poland, Portugal, Romania, the Russian Federation, Slovenia, Spain, Sweden, and the United Kingdom.[48] The regime has a target inspection rate based on ship risk profile and was formerly set at 25 percent of ships entering port.[49] The Paris MoU was the first major agreement to harmonize national inspection policies.[50]

13.2.2.2 Acuerdo de Viña del Mar

The Paris MoU was followed by the Latin American Agreement on Port State Control 1992, also called the *Acuerdo de Viña del Mar*. The Latin-American Agreement was signed in Viña del Mar, Chile on November 5, 1992, and has a target inspection rate of 20 percent of vessels entering port per flag State every three years. The Agreement has 13 members: Argentina, Bolivia, Brazil, Chile, Colombia, Cuba, Ecuador, Honduras, Mexico, Panama, Peru, Uruguay, and Venezuela. Dominican Republic and Guatemala are cooperating members.

During the 18th session in Montevideo, Uruguay from October 3–6, 2011, the Committee of the Latin American Agreement decided to submit details of its port State control activities to the IMO sub-committee on Flag State Implementation. The participating nations of Latin America conducted 8,584 PSC inspections in 2010, which resulted in 107 detentions, for a detention ratio of 1.25 percent.[51]

---

[47] Memorandum of Understanding on Port State Control in Implementing Agreements on Maritime Safety and Protection of the Marine Environment, 21 I.L.M. 1 (1982) [Hereinafter Paris MoU]. For an analysis of the Port State Control generally, and the Paris MOU, see, Z. Oya Özçayir, The Use of Port State Control in Maritime Industry and Application of the Paris MOU, 14 Ocean and Coastal L. J. 201 (2009).

[48] The Paris MoU originally was signed by 14 European states: Belgium, Denmark, Finland, France, Federal Republic of Germany, Greece, Ireland, Italy, the Netherlands, Norway, Portugal, Spain, Sweden, and the United Kingdom.

[49] Gerhard Kiehne, Investigation, Detention and Release of Ships Under the Paris MoU on Port State Control: A View from Practice, 11 Int'l J. Mar. & Coastal L. 217, 219 (1996).

[50] A. V. Lowe, A Move Against Substandard Shipping 6 Marine Pol'y 326, note 4 at 329 (1982).

[51] IMO Doc. FSI 20/INF.12, Harmonization of Port State Control Activities, 2010 Annual Statistical Report of the Viña del Mar Agreement, Jan. 10, 2012, Annex, pp. 1–3.

Liberia and Malta flagged ships each had seven detentions, and Honduras had five. There were also 20,941 deficiencies, and 49 percent of the inspections uncovered at least one deficiency—most of them minor.[52] Among these deficiencies, however, only 148 discrepancies dealt with a shortfall in areas relating to maritime security.

13.2.2.3 Tokyo MoU

The Memorandum of Understanding on Port State Control in the Asia-Pacific Region (Tokyo MoU) was signed in Tokyo on December 1, 1993.[53] The Tokyo MoU has a target inspection rate of 80% of the annual regional inspection rate. The 18 members, plus one cooperating member, are Australia, Canada, Chile, China, Fiji, Hong Kong, Indonesia, Japan, Republic of Korea, Malaysia, New Zealand, Papua New Guinea, the Philippines, the Russian Federation, Singapore, Thailand, Vanuatu, and Vietnam. The Republic of the Marshall Islands is the cooperating member.

Through the end of October 2011, the member authorities of the Tokyo MoU conducted 23,314 inspections and made 1,340 detentions as a result of serious deficiency found during PSC inspections.[54] These figures reflect a detention rate of 5.51 percent of ships arriving in port and inspected by Tokyo MoU nations.

13.2.2.4 Caribbean MoU

The Memorandum of Understanding on Port State Control in the Caribbean Region (Caribbean MoU) was signed in Christchurch, Barbados on February 9, 1996.[55] The Caribbean MoU has an annual inspection rate of 15 percent per country within three years of its entry into force. There are 15 member States: Aruba, Antigua and Barbuda, Bahamas, Barbados, Belize, Cayman Islands, Cuba, Curacao, Grenada, Guyana, Jamaica, The Netherlands, St. Christopher and Nevis, Suriname and Trinidad and Tobago.[56]

13.2.2.5 Mediterranean MoU

The Memorandum of Understanding on Port State Control in the Mediterranean Region (Mediterranean MoU) was signed in Valletta, Malta in July 1997. The

---

[52] Id.
[53] Memorandum of Understanding on Port State Control in the Asia-Pacific Region, Dec. 1, 1993, reprinted in New Directions in the Law of the Sea: Regional and National Developments (Roy S. Lee & Moritaka Hayashi, eds. 1997).
[54] IMO Doc. FSI 20/INF.10, Harmonization of Port State Control Activities, Summary of Tokyo MoU Activities in 2011, Jan. 10, 2012, at p. 3.
[55] Memorandum of Understanding on Port State Control in the Caribbean Region, 36 I.L.M. 231 (1997).
[56] IMO Doc. FSI 20/6/2, Harmonization of Port State Control Activities, Nov. 17, 2011.

European Commission financed development of the Mediterranean MoU, and it was co-sponsored by the IMO and ILO. The agreement was negotiated over two sessions—the first was held in Tunisia in March 1996, and the second meeting was conducted in Casablanca in December of the same year. There are ten port State authorities participating in the MoU: Algeria, Cyprus, Egypt, Israel, Jordan, Lebanon, Malta, Morocco, Tunisia and Turkey.

During the first three years of the agreement each State was required to maintain an inspection rate for foreign flagged ships of 15 percent per year. The port State authorities inspect for compliance with an entire menu of international standards reflected in relevant instruments, including the Load Lines 66, SOLAS 74, MARPOL 73/78, STCW 78, COLREGs, and ILO No. 147. Inspections consist of visit by port State authorities on board ships in order to check the validity of the certificates and other documents pertaining to the condition of the vessel, onboard equipment and crew, and living and working conditions.[57]

13.2.2.6 Indian Ocean MoU

The Indian Ocean Memorandum of Understanding on Port State Control (Indian Ocean MoU) was signed in Pretoria, South Africa on June 5, 1998 and it entered into force on April 1, 1999. During its first three years of operation, the MoU sought a ten percent inspection rate per country per year.

As of December 2011, the MoU had sixteen authorities: Australia, Bangladesh, Union of Comoros, Eritrea, France's La Réunion Island, India, Iran, Kenya, Maldives, Mauritius, Oman, South Africa, Sri Lanka, Sudan, Tanzania, and Yemen.[58] Djibouti, Mozambique, Myanmar, and Seychelles have pending acceptance of the MoU.[59]

The Indian Ocean MoU provides data to *Equasis*, *IHS Fairplay*, and *Lloyd's List Intelligence*, and a data exchange agreement was signed with the IMO during the 18th IMO Sub-committee on Flag State Implementation. During 2011, port State authorities conducted 5,537 inspections under the MoU, and 19,153 deficiencies were observed. More than 14 percent of deficiencies related to fire-fighting safety measures, nearly 9 percent concerned life-saving appliances, and the highest single category of deficiencies—safety of navigation—comprised nearly 15 percent.

Australia conducted 3,002 of the inspections under the MoU, with the balance divided among the other states. Tanzania was responsible for only 23 inspections. Australia was also the leading State concerning the number of deficiencies and

---

[57] The Memorandum of Understanding on Port State Control in the Mediterranean Region (Mediterranean MoU), was signed in Valletta (Malta), July 11, 1997, para. 3.1.2, http://www.medmou.org/.

[58] IMO Doc. FSI 20/INF.22, Harmonization of Port State Control Activities, Indian Ocean MoU PSC Activities in 2011, Jan. 20, 2012.

[59] IMO Doc. FSI 20/6/2, Harmonization of Port State Control Activities, Nov. 17, 2011.

number of detentions. There were 598 ships detained over the course of the year; Australia detained 275 of them.[60] Although Australia had a detention rate of 9.16 percent, it was not the highest detention rate among MoU states.[61] India had a detention rate of 22.89 percent based on 843 inspections, totaling 193 detentions.[62] Even Iran had a higher detention rate than Australia. Iran inspected 944 ships, and detained 115 of them, for a detention rate of 12.19 percent.[63]

13.2.2.7 Abuja MoU

The Memorandum of Understanding for the West and Central African Region (Abuja MoU) was signed in Abuja, Nigeria, on October 22, 1999.[64] The regime had the goal of reaching an inspection rate of 15 percent annually per country within three years. There are 22 members of the Abuja MoU: Angola* Benin, Cameroon*, Cape Verde*, Congo*, Côte d'Ivore, Democratic Republic of the Congo*, Equatorial Guinea*, Gabon, Ghana, Guinea, Guinea Bissau*, Liberia*, Mauritania*, Namibia*, Nigeria, Sao Tome & St. Principe*, Senegal, Sierra Leone, South Africa, The Gambia, and Togo.[65] (The symbol * denotes acceptance of membership was pending as of November 2011).

13.2.2.8 Black Sea MoU

The Memorandum of Understanding on Port State Control in the Black Sea Region (Black Sea MoU) was signed in Istanbul, Turkey on April 7, 2000. The regime has an inspection rate goal of 75 percent annual inspection rate per country within three years. There are six members: Bulgaria, Georgia, Romania, the Russian Federation, Turkey and Ukraine.

13.2.2.9 Riyadh MoU

The Riyadh Memorandum of Understanding on Port State Control (Riyadh MoU) was signed in Riyadh, Saudi Arabia, on June 30, 2004. The regime had the goal of a 15 percent annual inspection rate per country within the first three years. There are six members: Bahrain, Kuwait, Oman, Qatar, Saudi Arabia, and United Arab Emirates.

---

[60] IMO Doc. FSI 20/INF.22, Harmonization of Port State Control Activities, Indian Ocean MoU PSC Activities in 2011, Jan. 20, 2012.
[61] Id.
[62] Id.
[63] Id.
[64] See, West and Central African Nations Agree to Establish Port State Control Regime, IMO News 1998, at 31.
[65] IMO Doc. FSI 20/6/2, Harmonization of Port State Control Activities, Nov. 17, 2011.

Table 13.1. Applicability of Treaties in Port State Control

	LL 66	LL PROT 88	SOLAS 74	SOLAS PROT 88	MARPOL 73/78	STCW 76	COLREG 72	TONNAGE 69	ILO 147
Paris MoU	x	x	x	x	x	x	x	x	x
Acuero Viña del Mar	x	x	x	x	x	x		x	
Tokyo MoU	x	x	x	x	x	x	x	x	x
Caribbean MoU	x		x		x	x	x	x	x
Mediterranean MoU	x		x		x	x	x		x
Indian Ocean MoU	x	x	x	x	x	x	x	x	x
Abuja MoU	x		x		x	x	x	x	x
Black Sea MoU	x	x	x	x	x	x	x	x	x
Riyadh MoU	x		x		x	x	x	x	x
U.S. Coast Guard	x	x	x	x	x	x	x	x	x

Applicability of instruments under regional port state regimes in November 2011.[1521]

13.2.2.10 PERSGA

The Regional Organization for the Conservation of the Environment of the Red Sea and the Gulf of Aden (PERSGA) is an intergovernmental organization with observer status at the IMO. Seven states—Egypt, Djibouti, Jordan, Somalia, Saudi Arabia, Sudan and Yemen—are members of PERSGA. All of the members excepting Somalia are also party to one of the regional port state MoU regimes.[66] PERSGA is working with three member states—Jordan, Sudan, and Egypt. The three nations signed a port State control MoU for the Red Sea and the Gulf of Aden at a PERSGA workshop in Jeddah in April 2011.[68] The MoU will enter into force one month after it has been ratified by the three states.

Regional MoUs and U.S. security measures are used to help create a harmonized system of PSC to eliminate substandard vessels. A *Code of Good Practices for Port State Control Officers* has also helped to standardize professionalism and facilitate closer cooperation among the MoU regions.[69] The Code emphasizes integrity, professionalism, and transparency. PSCOs should conduct their work

---

[66] IMO Doc. FSI 20/6/2, Harmonization of Port State Control Activities, Nov. 17, 2011, Annex, p. 2.
[67] IMO Doc. FSI 20/6/2, Harmonization of Port State Control Activities, Nov. 17, 2011, at 2.
[68] Id.
[69] *See, Code of Good Practice for Port State Control Officers*, Code of Good Practice for Port State Control Officers Conducting Inspections within the Framework of the Memorandum of Understanding on Port State Control in the Asia Pacific Region (Tokyo MoU) and Annex I, Code of Good Practice for Port State Control Officers Conducting Inspections within the Framework of the Paris Memorandum of Understanding on Port State Control (undated).

with respect for the seafarers onboard ships and remember that the ship serves as a workplace as well as a home for ship personnel. Inspections should be carried out consistently, impartially, and professionally.

13.2.3 U.S. Port State Control

In the United States, port State control measures are well developed. The Secretary of Homeland Security is authorized to:

> order any vessel, in a port or place subject to the jurisdiction of the United States or in the navigable waters of the United States, to operate or anchor in a manner he directs if—
>
> (1) he has reasonable cause to believe such vessel does not comply with any regulation issued under [Ports and Waterways Safety Act] or any other applicable law or treaty; [or]
> (2) he determines that such vessel does not satisfy the conditions for port entry set forth in section 1228 of [Title 33, U.S. Code]....[70]

Alternatively, the Secretary may, consistent with recognized principles of international law, "deny entry into the navigable waters of the United States, to any port or place under the jurisdiction of the United States or to any vessel not in compliance with the provisions of this chapter or the regulations issued hereunder."[71] The Secretary also has authority to "carry out or require measures, including inspections...to prevent or respond to acts of terrorism...."[72]

The authority to enforce regulations issued by the Secretary under Title 33 is delegated to the U.S. Coast Guard and vested in the Captain of the Port (COTP).[73] The COTP may inspect and search any non-sovereign immune vessel or any person, article or thing thereon that is within the jurisdiction of the United States.[74] Furthermore, the COTP may "take full or partial possession or control of any vessel...within the territorial waters of the United States...whenever it appears...that such action is necessary in order to...prevent damage or injury to any vessel or waterfront facility...or to secure the observance of rights and obligations of the United States."[75] The COTP may also inspect, detain or deny port entry to any vessel that is not in compliance with regulations issued pursuant to the Maritime Security Transportation Act of 2002 (MTSA).[76]

---

[70] 33 U.S.C. § 1223(b).
[71] Id., § 1232(e).
[72] Id., § 1226(b).
[73] 33 C.F.R. § 6.04–1 and § 1.01–30.
[74] Id., § 6.04–7.
[75] Id., § 6.04–8.
[76] Id., § 101.410.

Alternatively, the MTSA authorizes the COTP to "deny entry into the navigable waters of the United States or to any port or place under the jurisdiction of the United States...to any vessel not in compliance with the provisions of the Port and Tanker Safety Act or the regulations issued thereunder."[77] COTP authority may be delegated to any commissioned, warrant or petty officer of the U.S. Coast Guard.[78]

Customs officers are likewise authorized to board "any vessel...at any place in the United States or within the customs waters...and examine the manifest and other documents and papers and examine, inspect and search the vessel... and any person, trunk, package, or cargo on board, and to this end may hail and stop such vessel...and use all necessary force to compel compliance."[79]

Similarly, U.S. Customs officers may also board and examine any "hovering vessel" within the customs waters of the United States, as well as "examine the master upon oath respecting the cargo and voyage of the vessel, and may also bring the vessel into the most convenient port of the United States to examine the cargo."[80] "Customs waters" are defined in Title 19 of the U.S. Code to include "the waters within four leagues of the coast of the United States."[81]

Similarly, 14 U.S.C. § 89 authorizes Coast Guard officials to make "inquiries, examinations, inspections, searches, seizures, and arrests upon the high seas and waters over which the United States has jurisdiction, for the prevention, detection, and suppression of violations of laws of the United States." Finally, Title 46 of the U.S. Code empowers the Secretary of Homeland Security to "prescribe and enforce regulations on the boarding of a vessel arriving at a port of the United States before the vessel has been inspected and secured."[82]

U.S. laws also allow the federal government to impose conditions on ships calling on U.S. ports:

(1) no vessel...shall operate in the navigable waters of the United States or transfer cargo or residue in any port or place under the jurisdiction of the United States, if such vessel...
(2) fails to comply with any applicable regulation issued under this chapter [the Ports and Waterways Safety Act], chapter 37 of title 46, or any other applicable law or treaty....[83]

---

[77] Id., § 160.107. See, The Port and Tanker Safety Act, 33 U.S.C. §§ 1221–1232.
[78] Id., § 1.01–90.
[79] 19 U.S.C. § 1581(a).
[80] Id., § 1587(a) and 33 C.F.R. § 162.3.
[81] 19 U.S.C. § 1401(j). A maritime league is 3 nautical miles.
[82] 46 U.S.C. § 60101.
[83] 33 U.S.C. § 1228.

In addition to these provisions, U.S. statute requires foreign-flagged vessels destined for U.S. ports to provide pre-arrival messages in sufficient time to permit advance vessel traffic planning prior to port entry.[84] Normally, a notice of arrival (NOA) must be submitted at least 96 hours before entering the port.[85] Certain ships not transporting dangerous cargo, vessels 300 gross tons or less, vessels arriving at a port under force majeure, and public vessels, are exempt from the pre-arrival notice requirements.[86] Information required in a NOA includes: vessel, voyage and cargo information; information for each crewmember and other persons onboard; operational condition of equipment;[87] International Safety Management (ISM) Code notice; cargo declaration (Customs Form 1302); and International Ship and Port Facility Code notice.

Thus, a foreign vessel that enters a U.S. port, whether suspect or not, may be boarded and searched upon its arrival to determine the nature of its cargo and its crew, as well as to review its compliance with other U.S. laws and regulations. Similarly, foreign vessels located within the U.S. territorial sea or contiguous zone may be boarded and searched if there is reason to believe that the vessels may be violating, *inter alia*, U.S. customs, sanitary (health), fiscal or immigration laws. Accordingly, if there are reasonable grounds to believe that a vessel is transporting prohibited items or persons in violation of U.S. customs and immigration laws, U.S. authorities may board and search it while it is present in the U.S. territorial sea or contiguous zone.

The U.S. Coast Guard regime has a 100 percent annual inspection rate per vessel under the safety risk and ISPS risk matrix, which is applied to all ships as a condition of port entry.[88] Data from the U.S. experience with port State control since the attacks of 9/11 suggest that the ISPS Code helps to reduce the number of unsecure and unsafe ships entering the country.[89]

The United States applies a five-pillar targeting matrix used to score and categorize vessels from all flag States. Vessels that score 17 points or higher are considered ISPS I vessels and are examined at sea prior to port entry. Vessels scoring between 7–16 points are classified as ISPS II vessels and are examined in port.

---

[84] 33 U.S.C. § 1223.
[85] 33 C.F.R. §§ 160.201–215.
[86] Id., § 160.203.
[87] Id., § 164.35.
[88] See, Table 3, ISPS/MTSA Security Compliance Targeting Matrix for Vessels Entering U.S. Ports, *infra*, Table 13.2.
[89] Some scholars, however, have formed a contrary impression; cf., Catherine Zara Raymond & Arthur Morriën, Security in the Maritime Domain and Its Evolution Since 9/11, in Lloyd's MIU Handbook of Maritime Security (Rupert Herbert-Burns, Sam Bateman, Peter Lehr, eds., 2008), pp. 3–12, at 6.

Table 13.2. The ISPS Code and U.S. Port State Control, 2004–2010

Calendar Year	Distinct Arrivals	Major ISPS Control Actions	Annual ISPS Control Action Ratio
2004	7,241	92	1.51%
2005	7,850	51	.65%
2006	8,178	35	.43%
2007	8,281	42	.51%
2008	8,661	27	.31%
2009	8,557	18	.21%
2010	9,260	17	.18%

The ISPS Code and U.S. Port State Control, 2004–2010[90]

Distinct arrivals: A vessel subject to the U.S. port security program, which called upon at least one U.S. port during the calendar year

Major ISPS control actions: A control measure—such as a detention, denial of entry, or expulsion—imposed on vessels that are not in compliance with SOLAS Chapter XI or part A of the ISPS Code

Annual ISPS control action ratio: Yearly sum of major ISPS control actions divided by the yearly sum of distinct arrivals (multiplied by one hundred)

Rolling average ISPS control action ratio: The average of the Annual ISPS Control Action ratio from 2008 to 2010

Vessels scoring 6 points or fewer are usually not selected for examination, but such vessels are subject to random examination.[91]

The criteria for determining vessel scores are set forth in Table 13.3, *ISPS/MTSA Security Compliance Targeting Matrix for Vessels Entering U.S. Ports*.[92] The U.S. Coast Guard focuses especially on ships from flag administrations that have Control Action Ratio (CAR) scores that are higher than the overall average for all flag States. Major CAR scores are based on three-year enforcement data (January 2008 to December 2010).[93] At the end of 2005, the targeting CAR for all administrations was fixed at 1.5%, and flags over this figure receive 2 points in the ISPS/MTSA targeting matrix, whereas ships from flag States that are more than twice the average among all countries are awarded 7 additional points on the ISPS/MTSA targeting matrix.[94] In 2010, Honduras, Lithuania, and Mexico received 7 points in column II of the ISPS/MTSA matrix, but Lithuania and Mexico had not been targeted in 2009.

---

[90] U.S. COAST GUARD, DEP'T OF HOMELAND SECURITY, PORT STATE CONTROL IN THE UNITED STATES ANNUAL REPORT 5 (2010).
[91] Id., at 19.
[92] Id.
[93] Id., at 20.
[94] Id.

Detected security deficiencies of all types declined for ships entering U.S. ports during 2006–2010. For example, the number of access control deficiencies was reduced from more than 25 in 2006 to 15 by 2010.[95] Declines were also recorded in deficiencies for controlled access to Restricted Areas, Ship Security Officer and Ship Security Plan deficiencies, as well as fewer deficiencies in training, screening process, and drills.[96] Bulk carriers and general dry cargo ships had the most control action over the period.

Table 13.3. Compliance Targeting Matrix for U.S. Ports

I Ship Management	II Flag State	III Recognized Security Organization	IV Security Compliance History	V Port of Call History
ISPS II Owner, if new owner since last ISPS exam 5 points Owner or operator or charterer associated with one ISPS related denial of entry or ISPS related expulsion from port in the past 12 months or 2 or more ISPS/MTSA control actions in a 12-month period	ISPS II If new flag since last ISPS examination 7 points SOLAS vessels Flag state has a CAR 2 or more time the overall CAR average for all flag states 2 points SOLAS vessels Flag has a CAR between the overall CAR average and up to 2 times overall CAR average for all flag states 7 points Non-SOLAS vessels Flag state has a CAR 2 or more times the overall CAR average for the flag states	ISPS I 3 or more RSO related major control actions in past 12 months 5 points 2 RSO related major control actions in the past 12 months 2 points 1 RSO related major control actions in the past 12 months	ISPS I Ship with ISPS denial of entry/ expulsion in past 12 months ISPS II If matrix score does not result in ISPS I priority and no ISPS compliance exam has been conducted in past 12 months 5 points Vessel with an ISPS/MTSA related detention in the past 12 months 2 points Vessel with 1 or more ISPS/MTSA control actions in past 12 months	ISPS I Vessels that have called upon non-ISPS compliant port in past 5 ports of call ISPS II If matrix score does not result in ISPS I priority and if the port or country is ISPS II under the monthly targeting update (CG-543) Conditions of Entry For last 5 ports— ports or countries specified by Federal Register as being without effective anti-terrorism measures

SPS/MTSA Security Compliance Targeting Matrix for Vessels Entering U.S. Ports

---

[95] Id., at 24.
[96] Id.

CHAPTER THIRTEEN

Table 13.4. Flag States Targeted by Port State Control

Paris MoU Blacklist		Tokyo MoU Blacklist		U.S. Coast Guard Blacklist (alphabetical order)
North Korea Libya Togo Sierra Leone Montenegro	Very high risk	Sierra Leone Georgia Cambodia		Bolivia Cook Islands Croatia Dominica Honduras
Albania Moldova Cambodia St. Kitts & Nevis	High risk	Papua New Guinea St. Kitts & Nevis North Korea Mongolia	Seven points	Lithuania Mexico St. Kitts & Nevis St. Vincent & the Grenadines
Comoros Georgia Bolivia Lebanon Syria	Medium to high risk	Indonesia Kiribati		Sierra Leone Venezuela Antigua and Barbuda Belgium Belize
Tanzania Ukraine St. Vincent & the Grenadines Azerbaijan	Medium risk	Bangladesh Tuvalu Thailand Belize Vietnam Turkey	Two points	Gribraltar (U.K.) India Italy South Korea Malta Panama Turkey

Targeted Flag State Administrations, 2008–2010[97]

Note: **Flag administrations appearing in bold are on all three lists.** *Flag administrations appearing in italics are on two lists.*

13.3 PORT FACILITY SECURITY

A "port facility," is a location where ship-port interface occurs. Each state is responsible for identifying port facilities that fall within the scope of the post-September 11, 2001, Maritime Security Measures.[98] States also have authority to

---

[97] IMO Doc. FSI 20/INF.5, Harmonization of Port State Control Activities: Flag Administrations Targeted by the Paris MoU, the Tokyo MoU, and the United States Coast Guard (Combined submission of the United States, the Paris MoU and the Tokyo MoU), Annex, Dec. 23, 2011.

[98] See, IMO Doc. MSC 89/INF.13, Measures to Enhance Maritime Security, Maritime Security Manual—Guidance for Port Facilities, Ports and Ships, Mar. 5, 2011, reproduced in Guide to Maritime Security and the ISPS Code para. 2.2.16 (International Maritime Organization 2012 ed.), IMO Sales No. IA116E [Hereinafter Maritime Security Measures or MSM].

consider and report the level of usage of the port facility by ships on international voyages. Port facility operators help to inform the government's decision by providing information on the types and frequency of ships using the facility, traffic and trading patterns, contents and types of cargoes handled, number and origins of passengers, and other information. Each designated port facility should be demarcated with a clear and secure geographic boundary.

A port facility may include areas of land or water, or land and water, used for embarkation of disembarkation of passengers or the loading or unloading of cargo. The port should be clearly delineated with a recognized boundary where special maritime security measures apply. Australia, for example, defines a port facility as "an area of land or water, or land and water, within a security regulated port (including any buildings, installations or equipment in or on the area) used either wholly or partly in connection with the loading or unloading of security regulated ships."[99]

The economic significance of the port facility and its proximity to populated areas of the country are key factors in fencing off the precise area of a port facility. The boundary should be inclusive of areas where passengers embark and disembark, locations where dangerous goods or high value cargoes are handled, or where containers are loaded, unloaded and stored. The boundary also should account for areas of heightened risk or vulnerability that have been identified by the Port Facility Security Assessment (PFSA). The boundary should enclose pipelines and related valves on the shore or on the waterside. Finally, natural features and barriers, such as heavy foliage, cliffs, drainage channels and inlets may provide some natural protection. Existing man-made barriers, such as fences, walls, roads, access gates and wide, empty approaches also can provide additional security. Once the boundaries of a port facility are determined, a clear map displaying the coordinates, routes, and directions should be inserted into the Port Facility Security Assessment and Port Facility Security Plan.[100]

Generally, the facility operator is responsible for managing the ship-port interface. An overall security manager should be designated in multiple-use facilities, and the position of security manager may be filled by the facility owner or the port authority or a port operator. At least once every five years, States provide notification to the IMO of the location of private and government port facilities within their territory that have an approved Port Facility Security Plan. The

---

[99] Dep't of Infrastructure and Transport, Government of Australia, Maritime Transport and Offshore Facilities Security Act 2003, §10.

[100] See, e.g., Mapping Standards for Port Facilities issued by the Australian Government Transport and Offshore Facilities Security Regulations 2003, 3.90, Sept. 11, 2011. The Ministry of Infrastructure and Transportation of the Government of Australia has produced guidance on developing a port facility map. See, Dep't of Infrastructure and Transport, Government of Australia Guidance Paper: Mapping Standards for Ports, Sept. 29, 2011.

next deadline for submission of information is July 1, 2014. The IMO inputs the data into its Global Integrated Shipping Information System (GISIS) database. Most ports maintain a Port Security Committee to oversee the security aspects of port policy and operations, and the Designated Authority should also appoint a port point of contact for use by SOLAS ships.

13.3.1 Designated Authority

The Designated Authority (DA) is responsible for identifying all of the port facilities within the nation's territory that are used by SOLAS ships. In each case, the DA determines whether a particular port facility is required to appoint a Port Facility Security Officer (PFSO) and submit a Port Facility Security Plan (PFSP). If a port facility is used only occasionally by SOLAS ships, the DA may determine that it does not have to appoint a PFSO. There is wide discretion in how port facilities are designated, and factors that may be considered include the frequency that the facility is used; the types of ships that use the facility, including vessels, such as cruise ships or ships carrying dangerous substances, that pose a heightened security risk, and proximity to populated areas.

The Designated Authority also may specify individual port facilities within a broad port area, or define the entire port area to capture the entire range of shipping activities, as a single port facility. Many Designated Authorities categorize port facilities based on the type of operation, such as cruise ships, roll-on/roll-off passenger ships, chemical, oil and gas shipments in bulk, container shipping and roll-on/roll-off carriers, and dry bulk cargo carriers.

States may elect to appoint well-qualified port authorities and port facility operators as Recognized Security Organizations (RSOs). In such cases, however, RSOs may not approve or certify work products that they developed or used subcontractors to develop on their behalf. National governments may enter into Alternative Security Agreements (ASAs) to implement maritime security measures involving ships such as ferries that conduct routine international voyages using fixed routes between the port state and another state.

13.3.2 Declaration of Security

A Declaration of Security (DOS) is a written agreement between a port facility and a ship visiting that facility setting forth the respective security responsibilities during the ship's port visit. The DOS includes the identity of the port facility and ship, the type of activity to be covered, its duration, and the appropriate security level that applies during the particular ship/port interface. If either a ship or port operates at a higher security level than the other, then the ship/port interface should take place at the higher of the two security levels. The Designated Authority determines the circumstance in which a port facility is required to initiate, complete and retain a DOS. Normally, the Port Facility Security Officer completes the DOS for the port, and the Ship Security Officer (SSO) or master of the vessel completes the DOS for the ship.

The Maritime Security Measures contain a model form for a Declaration of Security (DOS) between a port facility and a ship.[101] If a ship initiates a DOS, the port facility should acknowledge the request, although it is not required to comply with it. On the other hand, if a port facility initiates a DOS, the request should be acknowledged by the ship master or Ship Security Officer, and it must be completed if the ship intends to interface with the port facility. The circumstances or conditions under which a DOS may be requested include the following scenarios:

- A ship is operating at a higher security level than the port facility;
- There has been a recent security threat or a security incident involving either the port facility or the ship;
- The port facility or ship is operating at security level 3;
- There has been a recent adjustment in the security level of the port facility or the ship;
- The intended ship-port interface could endanger local facilities or residents;
- The intended ship-port interface could pose a significant risk of major pollution risk (although this must be weighed against considerations of *force majeure*);
- The intended ship-port interface involves embarking or disembarking passengers;
- The intended ship/port interface involves handling hazardous or dangerous cargo;
- The ship is intending to use a non-SOLAS port facility;
- A ship is undertaking a ship-to-ship interface, and it is at a higher security level than the other vessel;
- A ship is intending to interface with another ship for the transfer of passengers or hazardous or dangerous cargo at sea;
- There exists an agreement between the flag state of the vessel and the port state that requires a DOS under the circumstances;
- The port facility's Designated Authority or ship's Administration directs use of a DOS for the interface;
- The ship is not in compliance with the ISPS Code's Maritime Security Measures, such as a lack of ISSC.

The Port Facility Security Plan (PFSP) outlines procedures and appropriate security measures used in response to a request for a DOS or to initiate a request for a DOS. Special regulations to be observed during issuance of a DOS may include monitoring of restricted areas, controlling access to the port facility and ship, special regulations for cargo and unaccompanied baggage handling; and secure communications. Normally, if a ship refuses a request for a DOS, the Port Facility Security Officer (PFSO) would deny entry and notify the Designated Authority. In sum, a DOS should be completed before an interface between a port facility and a ship, or between two ships, when one of them operates at a different security level, if one of them does not have an approved security plan, if the interface

---

[101] See, IMO Doc. MSC 89/INF.13, Measures to Enhance Maritime Security, Maritime Security Manual—Guidance for port facilities, ports and ships, Mar. 5, 2011, Appendices 3.1 and 4.1.

involves a cruise ship or a ship carrying dangerous goods, or if either ship or port has security concerns about the interface.

13.3.3 *Port Facility Security Officer*

The Designated Authority (DA) determines which ports require appointment of a Port Facility Security Officer (PFSO). The PFSOs are appointed by, and report to, the management of a port facility. The PFSO serves as the link between the Company Security Officers (CSOs) and Ship Security Officers (SSOs) of ships that use the port facility. Because the PFSO is a sensitive security position, it may be subject to vetting for reliability and integrity and require the officer appointed to complete a training program approved by the DA.

A Port Facility Security Officer (PFSO) may be responsible for one or more port facilities.[102] Normally, the PFSO is responsible for conducting an initial survey of the security of the port facility, ensuring the development of the Port Facility Security Plan (PFSP), which is based in part upon consideration of past Port Facility Security Assessments.[103] The PFSO also is responsible for overseeing development and testing of the PFSP, regularly inspecting the port facility for security vulnerabilities, and fixing deficiencies in port facility security.[104] Finally, the PFSO has the lead in ensuring that all employees of the port facility understand the protocols for port security and are vigilant in their application.[105] The IMO has issued guidance concerning measurement of the competency of PFSOs,[106] port facility personnel with security duties,[107] and port facility personnel without security duties.[108] Training is key to ensuring that the human element is more effective.[109] The PFSO and other port facility security personnel should receive training, which takes into account the guidance set forth in Part B of the ISPS Code.

The Port Facility Security Officer (PFSO) implements the Port Facility Security Plan (PFSP) in coordination with appropriate CSOs and SSOs, and government or privately contracted armed security personnel.[110] Because of their interface with government personnel and sensitive commercial and government information, PFSOs should have a high degree of security training, appropriate security clearances and access to sensitive security information, and they should be actual port

---

[102] ISPS Code A/17.1.
[103] Id., at A/17.2.2.
[104] Id., at A/17.2.3–4.
[105] Id., at A/17.2.7.
[106] IMO Doc. MSC.1/Circ.188, Competency Matrix for Port Facility Security Officers, May 2006.
[107] Id.
[108] Id.
[109] ISPS Code A/18.
[110] Id., at A/17.2.9–10.

facility employees (rather than contracted from external companies or security firms). Furthermore, non-security duties should not interfere with the ability of seafarers to carry out their security duties. Other port facility personnel should be required to meet the same or similar requirements as PFSOs.

In 2007, the IMO invited member governments and regional port State control regimes to introduce a *Code of Good Practice* to officials exercising port and coastal State actions. Subsequently, a number of the port State control regional MoUs have adopted the Code as part of their regime.[111] The 28–point Code is based on three principles—integrity, professionalism, and transparency, meaning openness and accountability. The *Code of Practice*, for example, recommends that government officials carry appropriate identification documents to enter ports or board ships when acting in their official capacity. In case of emergency, first responders and pilots should also carry appropriate identification documents in order to gain quick access to port facilities.

13.3.4 Port Facility Security Plan

Port facilities are critical national infrastructure, which are protected by a variety of passive and active defenses. Clear approaches to the facility, fences, gates, vehicle barriers, closed circuit television (CCTV), motion detectors, and lighting along the perimeter help to identify and separate intruders from authorized persons and vehicles. Entrance points may feature archway metal detectors. Entry onto the installation or in controlled access areas may be regulated with automated access control equipment, such as identification readers or keypads. Cargo and vehicles may be subject to remote, canine, and human manual screening or inspection for explosives, poisonous gases, hazardous, flammable, or radiological material. The Port Facility Security Plan (PFSP) sets forth the security features for each individual port.

The Port Facility Security Plan (PFSP) is defined by the ISPS Code as "a plan developed to ensure the application of measures designed to protect the port facility and ships, persons, cargo, cargo transport units and ship's stores within the port facility from the risks of a security incident."[112] Based on the results of the approved Port Facility Security Assessment (PFSA), a PFSP is developed and maintained. The Designated Authority (DA) approves the Port Facility Security Plan. The DA will establish the requirements for preparation of the PFSP. The provisions on Declarations of Security in the Port Facility Security Plan will specify the type of security incidents that should be reported to the DA, as well as the frequency of reports. The DA reviews the PFSP and approves the Plan, subject to modifications or revisions. In some cases, the DA issues standard templates for development of the PFSP. There is a close inter-relationship between PFSAs and

---

[111] See, e.g., the Code of Good Practice, which is annexed to the Tokyo MoU.
[112] ISPS Code A/2.1.5.

PFSPs. The DA may not delegate approval authority for PFSPs to the Recognized Security Organization (RSO). However, the RSO (or PFSOs) may prepare the PFSP for approval by DAs. Thus, the plan must be approved by the state in which it is located.[113]

The Port Facility Security Officer (PFSO) is responsible for developing the PFSP in accordance with the approved port facility security assessment, although the PFSO does not have to personally undertake every duty associated with actually completion of the plan.[114] The security measures included in the security plan should be in place within a reasonable period of time following approval of the PFSP.[115]

At a minimum, the Port Facility Security Plan (PFSP) should establish procedures for changing the security level, specify the rules concerning use of armed security personnel, and contain essential records concerning Declarations of Security, security threats or incidents, training and exercises, maintenance of security infrastructure and equipment, reviews of port facility security assessments and plans. The use of firearms on or near ships and in port facilities poses significant safety risks for crew and passenger safety. The recommendations ISPS Code suggest governments consider the use of armed security very carefully.[116] In the event that a government uses either government or privately contracted armed security personnel, it should issue specific safety guidelines for their employment and ensure that all armed personnel are properly trained.

A complete Port Facility Security Plan (PFSP) should include at least the following elements:

- Measures to prevent unauthorized access into the port facility, or into restricted areas within the port facility. For each security level, the plan should specify the type of restriction or prohibition in place for each entry or exit point. Restrictions may include identification systems and segregation of general populations, such as ferry passengers, from restricted areas with limited access;
- Measures to prevent the introduction of unlawful or unauthorized weapons or dangerous substances and devices into the port facility;
- Procedures for responding to security threats or breaches of security, including provisions to maintain continuity of port operations during crisis;
- Procedures for responding to instructions from civil and military authorities in the country where the port is located;
- Procedures for interfacing with ship security activities;
- Identification of the port security officer, and a 24-hour contact, and more broadly, the organizational structure of the port facility security team and identification of contacts with local law enforcement or security forces;
- Procedures for responding in case of an activated ship security alarm system by a ship at the port facility;

---

[113] Id., at A/16.2 and Part B/16.5.
[114] Id., at B/16.1.
[115] Id., at B/16.6.
[116] Id., at B/16.7.

- Description of the security equipment for area monitoring, access control, system backup procedures and off-grid electric power capabilities, audible and visual alarms, and procedures for maintaining security and communication systems and equipment; and
- Procedures to facilitate shore leave of seafarers, and to provide for visitor access to ships using the facility.[117]

The Port Facility Security Plan (PFSP) should be exercised through scheduled drills. Security drills should be slated and conducted on a regular basis to test individual components of the PFSP. The exercises may be used to evaluate the effectiveness of electronic systems, identify gaps in training or policy, and ensure that equipment is working properly. Generally, security drills should occur quarterly and major security exercises should occur annually. The Plan is audited if a security incident involving the port facility has occurred, if the Port Facility Security Assessment (PFSA) is altered, or if an independent audit of the port facility security organization identifies shortcomings in the organization or questions the continuing relevance of significant elements of the approved PFSP.

The Port Facility Security Plan (PFSP) also should specify records to be kept, duration of their retention, and process for purging electronic and paper files. Records should capture past inspections, security personnel and their training (including participants and dates), drills and exercises (including outcomes and lessons learned), any real-world security incidents and responses, changes in the security level (including the time and date that the notification was received and the time that enhanced security measures went into effect), records of calibration and maintenance of security-related gear and equipment, Declarations of Security regarding the port facility, and associated amendments and records of inspections and patrols. Records generally are retained for two years.

The Port Facility Security Plan (PFSP) should ensure that measures for security level 1 are in place and that the additional measures under security levels 2 and 3 can be implemented quickly. The PFSP includes procedures for interacting with ships operating at higher security levels that apply for port entry, and for reporting incidents or threats to the government. PFSPs should detail:

- The introduction into the port of unauthorized weapons or any other dangerous substances;
- Measures to prevent unauthorized access to the port facility, to ships moored at the facility, and to especially to restricted areas of the facility;
- Procedures for the safe and secure handling of cargo;
- Procedures for responding to security threats or incidents;
- Procedures for being responsive to the directions of the Government of the territory in which the port is located;
- Procedures to maintain critical port operations;

---

[117] Id., at A/16.3 and Part B/16.3.

- Procedures for the independent audit of the Port Facility Security Plan;
- Procedures for the internal review and updating of the plan;
- Identification of the Port Facility Security Officer, port security organization, and emergency contact information;
- Information security, cyber security, and maintenance of confidential information, such as the Port Facility Security Plan;
- Procedures for responding to an activated ship security alert system of a ship moored at the port facility;
- Procedures for ensuring visitor access, and for enhancing the welfare of mariners, including access to shore side medical facilities and shore leave.

The Designated Authority (DA) must approve the measures in the Port Facility Security Plan (PFSP), and the DA should act prior to its implementation. Once the plan is implemented, exercises and drills should be conducted at between three and 18-month intervals. The exercises may be either full-scale or live, or notional simulations or seminars. To make exercises more efficient in the Asia-Pacific region, for example, the Asia-Pacific Economic Cooperation (APEC) forum's Transportation Working Group published a manual for planning, preparing, and conducting maritime security drills. Lessons learned from these drills and exercises may inform amendments to the approved PFSP, but significant amendments must be submitted to the DA for approval.

There are two types of actual security incidents. Those incidents involving unauthorized access to restricted areas within the port facility, bomb threats, and unauthorized disclosure of the Port Facility Security Plan (PFSP) must be reported to the authorities by the Port Facility Security Officer (PFSO). Typically Designated Authorities will require that port facilities report attacks and hijackings, armed robbery against ships, and the use of firearms or explosives in an attack or robbery. Less serious incidents may require investigation by the PFSO, but may not necessarily be reported. These include breaches of screening points, damage to security equipment through sabotage or vandalism, or suspicious behavior or suspicious packages.

PFSPs should include procedures for ensuring security information, including movement of ships and cargo. Sensitive information should be password-protected, and computer systems should be hardened against cyberattack and protected from unauthorized physical access.

13.3.5 *Port Facility Security Level*

The Port Facility Security Plan (PFSP) should establish measures for controlling access to the port facility. Each point of entry or egress should be specified, and the PFSP should include a means—such as issuance of identification badges and codes—to ensure that unauthorized persons cannot remain in the port facility without detection and challenge.[118] The PFSP also should identify areas of

---

[118] Id., at B/16.12.

screening and inspection of person, cargo, personal effects, and vehicles. Checked and unchecked persons, cargo, and vehicles, should be segregated.[119]

13.3.5.1 Port Access

There are three security levels for port security, and these have particular salience for controlling port access. Security procedures for controlling access to a port facility for the three security levels should be included in the Port Facility Security Plan (PFSP).

At security level 1, all persons entering the port facility should be subject to search. Measures may include:

- Control points for restricted access bounded by fencing or other barriers;
- Verification of the identity of every person entering a controlled access area;
- Verification of the reasons for which each entrant seeks to gain access;
- All persons, goods and vehicles are screened for weapons, explosives or incendiaries;
- Vehicles entering the port facility are checked;
- The identity of port facility personnel is verified;
- Closure of access points not in regular use;
- Search of persons, personal effects, vehicles and their contents; and
- Screen and searching unaccompanied baggage.[120]

The Port Facility Security Plan (PFSP) should adopt enhanced measures for security level 2, which may include:

- Increasing the frequency of searches of persons, personal effects and vehicles;
- X-ray screening of all unaccompanied baggage;
- Assignment of additional personnel to guard access points and to conduct perimeter patrols;
- Limiting the number of access points;
- Using patrols to enhance water-side security;
- Denying access to visitor unable to provide verifiable credentials;
- Impeding the movement through the remaining access points; and
- Coordination with the Designated Authority and law enforcement agencies.[121]

At security level 3, the port facility should comply with instructions issued by civil and military authorities. Measures at level 3 may include:

- Additional screening of unaccompanied baggage;
- Coordination with emergency response personnel and other port facilities;
- Plans to granting access to first responders;
- Suspension of all other access to the port facility;
- Suspension of cargo operations in all or part of the facility;
- Evacuation of the facility; and
- Increased monitoring and security patrols inside and outside the facility.[122]

---

[119] Id., at B/16.15.
[120] Id., at B/16.17.
[121] Id., at B/16.19.
[122] Id., at B/16.20.

13.3.5.2 Restricted Areas within the Port Facility

The Port Facility Security Plan (PFSP) should identify restricted areas within the port facility, and the enhanced security measures used to control activities within them. Restricted areas help to protect the port facility and ships using or serving the facility, and their related cargo and ship's stores, passengers, mariners, port facility personnel, and visitors.[123] All restricted areas should be clearly marked and may include shore- and water-side areas adjacent to ships, embarkation and disembarkation points, areas for the loading and unloading of cargo or storage, places where records are stored, areas where dangerous goods or hazardous cargos are held secure, vessel traffic management control rooms and security surveillance control rooms, and essential electrical and electronic functions and utilities.[124] Security procedures for restricted areas within the port facility should be adjusted depending upon the security level of the facility.[125]

Security measures for restricted areas at security level 1 may include:

- Permanent or temporary barriers to surround the restricted area;
- Procedures for securing all access points not actively used and providing physical barriers or security guards to impede movement through the remaining access points;
- Procedures for controlling access to restricted areas, such as a pass system that identifies an individual's entitlement to be within the restricted area;
- Procedures for examining the authorization passes and other identification of persons and vehicles seeking entry, and clearly marking vehicles allowed access to restricted areas;
- Procedures for patrolling or monitor the perimeter of restricted areas;
- Procedures for using security personnel, automatic intrusion detection devices or surveillance equipment/systems to detect unauthorized entry or movement in the restricted areas;
- Procedures for controlling the movement of vessels in the vicinity of ships using the port facility;
- Procedures for designating temporary restricted areas, if applicable, to accommodate port facility operations, including restricted areas for segregating unaccompanied baggage that has undergone authorized screening by a ship operator; and
- Procedures for conducting a security sweep, if a temporary restricted area is designated.[126]

Enhanced security measures for restricted areas at security level 2 may include:

- More effective physical barriers, use of patrols or intrusion detection devices
- Procedures for reducing the number of access points and enhancing controls applied at the remaining access points;
- Restricting parking of vehicles adjacent to ships;

---

[123] Id., at B/16.21.
[124] Id., at B/16.25.
[125] Id., at B/16.21–16.29.
[126] Id., at B/16.27.

PORT AND PORT FACILITY SECURITY 445

- Reducing access to restricted areas and movements and storage in them;
- Use of surveillance equipment that records and monitors continuously;
- Increasing the number and frequency of patrols, including the use of waterside patrols;
- Establishing and restricting access to areas adjacent to restricted areas; and
- Restrictions on access by unauthorized craft to the waters adjacent to ships using the port facility.[127]

At security level 3, ports should be ready to comply with instructions issued by first responders and national civil or military authorities. The PFSP should detail measures for restricted areas at security level 3, which may include:

- Procedures for designating additional restricted areas adjacent to the security incident or threat to which access is denied; and
- Procedures for searching restricted areas as part of a security sweep of all or part of a port facility.[128]

13.3.5.3 Cargo Handling

Port security measures include inventory control at access points to the port facility and within the port facility. Inside the port facility, cargo should be segregated and marked as having been screened, checked, or inspected, and accepted for loading onto a ship or placed in a storage area while awaiting transit. Cargo that does not have a confirmed shipping date may be restricted from the port facility.[129] Security procedures for handling cargo should be established in the Port Facility Security Plan (PFSP).

At security level 1, the PFSP should require examination of cargo using physical and visual means, as well as scanning and detection equipment, mechanical devices, and working dogs. Security level 1 examination may include:

- Verifying that cargo, containers and cargo transport units entering the port facility match the invoice or other cargo documentation;
- Routine inspection of cargo, containers, transport units and cargo storage areas before and during handling operations to detect evidence of tampering, unless unsafe to do so;
- Verifying that the cargo entering the facility matches the delivery documentation;
- Searching vehicles entering the port facility; and
- Examining seals and other methods used to detect evidence of tampering when cargo, containers or cargo transport units enter the port facility or are stored there.[130]

When there are routine cargo movements, the Company Security Officer or individual Ship Security Officers may agree to arrangements with shippers to include

---

[127] Id., at B/16.28.
[128] Id., at B/16.29.
[129] Id., at B/16.30–31.
[130] Id., at B/16.32.

advance or off-site screening, checking, sealing, or documenting cargo.[131] Such arrangements facilitate handling at the port.

Additional measures for cargo handling and control should be initiated at security level 2, and may include:

- Detailed checking of cargo, containers, and cargo transport units in or about to enter the port facility or cargo storage areas, for weapons, explosives and incendiaries;
- Intensified inspections to ensure that only documented cargo enters the port facility, is temporarily stored there and is then loaded onto the ship;
- Intensified search of vehicles for weapons, explosives and incendiaries;
- Increased frequency and detail of examinations of seals and other methods used to prevent tampering;
- Increased frequency and intensity of visual and physical inspections;
- Increased frequency of the use of scanning/detection equipment, mechanical devises or working dogs; and
- Enhanced security measures with shippers or those acting on their behalf in accordance with an established agreement and procedures.[132]

Finally, at security level 3, port facilities should be ready to comply with instructions issued by civil or military authorities. The Port Facility Security Plan (PFSP) should include measures that have been coordinated in advance with such authorities and may include:

- Restriction or suspension of cargo movements or operations in all or part of the port facility; and
- Confirmation of the safety and protection of special inventory and location of certain dangerous cargoes in the port facility.[133]

13.3.5.4 Delivery of Ships' Stores

Security procedures for delivery of ships' stores and bunkers should ensure checking package integrity. Stores should not be accepted without screening or inspection, and only packages that have been ordered should be accepted. Delivery vehicles should be inspected, and vehicles should offload at a safe setback distance from the ship.[134] Each of the three security levels requires progressively tighter controls for delivery of ships' stores.

13.3.5.4.1 *Security Level 1*

- Check ship stores—incoming goods should be inspected prior to placement on board the ship;

---

[131] Id., at B/16.34.
[132] Id., at B/16.35.
[133] Id., at B/16.37.
[134] Id., at B/16.38.

- Require advanced notification of the delivery of ships' stores or bunkers, including a list of stores, and driver and vehicle registration information in respect of delivery vehicles; and
- Inspect delivery vehicles at the rate specified in the Port Facility Security Plan.[135]

Checking ships' stores may be accomplished by visual and physical examination, as well as use of scanning or detection devices and working dogs.[136]

13.3.5.4.2 Security Level 2
At security level 2, the Port Facility Security Plan (PFSP) should apply enhanced measures to control the delivery of ships' stores, and these may include:

- Detailed or more thorough checks of ship's stores than under security level 1;
- Detailed searches of delivery vehicles;
- Coordination with ship personnel to check the order against the delivery note prior to entry to the port facility; and
- Escorting delivery vehicles in the port facility.[137]

13.3.5.4.3 Security Level 3
As with other port tasks, the port authorities should comply with the instructions issued by first responders to a security incident, including national civil and military authorities. Additional measures for security level 3 may include:

- Restricting or suspending the delivery of ships' stores and bunkers; and
- Refusing to accept ships' stores in the port facility.[138]

In response to specific incidents or threats, ports should initiate the following measures, which apply to all security levels:

- Responding to security threats, breaches of security and security incidents, including provisions to maintain critical port facility and interface operations;
- Evacuating the port facility in case of security threats and security incidents;
- Reporting security threats, breaches of security, and security incidents to the Designated Authority;
- Briefing port facility personnel on potential threats to security and the need for vigilance;
- Securing non-critical operations in order to focus response on critical operations; and
- Reporting security threats, breaches of security and security incidents to the appropriate law enforcement agencies, the Designated Authority and, if applicable, the port operator.

---

[135] Id., at B/16.40.
[136] Id., at B/16.41.
[137] Id., at B/16.42–43.
[138] Id., at B/16.44.

13.3.5.5 Monitoring the Port Facility

The Port Facility Security Officer (PFSO) oversees monitoring of the port facility and the land and water approaches to the facility.[139] Monitoring should be in place at all times—day and night—and during times of restricted visibility. The means of monitoring may include use of lighting, security guards (foot patrols, vehicles, or waterborne), and automatic intrusion and surveillance equipment. Specific measures available also include separate provisions for each of the three security levels.

Measures for monitoring port facilities at security level 1 may include:

- Observation of the general port facility area, including shore- and water-side accesses to it;
- Observation of access points, barriers and restricted areas; and
- Allow port facility security personnel to monitor areas and movements adjacent to ships, including augmentation of lighting provided by the ship itself.[140]

Monitoring measures at security level 2 may include:

- Increased coverage and intensity of lighting and surveillance equipment, including the provision of additional lighting and surveillance;
- Increased frequency of foot, vehicle or waterborne patrols; and
- Additional security personnel assigned to monitor and patrol.[141]

At security level 3, the port facility should comply with instructions issued by civil and military authorities, including first responders. The Port Facility Security Plan (PFSP) should detail measures at security level 3, which may include:

- Switching on all lighting in, or illuminating the vicinity of, the port facility;
- Switching on all surveillance equipment capable of recording activities in or adjacent to the port facility; and
- Maximizing the length of time that surveillance equipment can continue to record.[142]

Consistent with port security, shore leave for seafarers is a right, rather than being merely a privilege. Authorized persons are entitled to board a ship when necessary, and states should find practicable and uniform requirements and procedures for security measures that facilitate the movement of ships and goods, and that still preserves the rights of mariners. At the level of operations, PFSOs and PSOs can coordinate closely with Ship Security Officers well in advance of ship arrival to the port facility.

---

[139] Id., at B/16.49.
[140] Id., at B/16.52.
[141] Id., at B/16.53.
[142] Id., at B/16.54.

13.3.6 *Port Facility Security Assessment*

The ISPS Code requires governments in whose territory the port is located to undertake a Port Facility Security Assessment (PFSA) on each port facility subject to the Code.[143] The Assessment should be reviewed regularly, as it helps to determine which port facilities are required to appoint a Port Facility Security Officer (PFSO) and who receives a copy of the PFSA.

The Assessment should cover physical security, structural integrity, personnel protection systems, radio and telecommunications systems (including computer networks), and transportation infrastructure, such as piers and cranes, and utilities.[144] The PFSA also should cover any other area within the facility that, if damaged or used for illicit observation, poses a risk to persons, property, or operations in the port facility. The relative importance of port facility assets and infrastructure should be identified, taking into account the potential loss of life, economic significance, or symbolic value (such as government installations) of the port facility or selected areas inside the facility.[145]

The process of identifying critical infrastructure within the port helps to prioritize the relative importance of the entire port facility or individual areas within the facility for protection.[146] Generally, the most important infrastructure assets include entrances, approaches, anchorages, maneuvering, berthing areas, cargo facilities and terminals and cargo handling equipment, electrical and electronic systems and networks, port vessel traffic management, power plants, piping and utilities, port service vessels, such as tug boats, and connections to regional or national transportation networks, such as railroad lines.[147] Preventing or limiting the loss of life or injury is the greatest concern. States also may consider national economic and political effects of an attack, including the need to continue operations and reestablish normal functioning.

The Designated Authority (DA) is responsible for carrying out the PFSAs, which are essentially a multi-factor risk analysis of the port facility. The DA may delegate the responsibility for the PFSA to the Recognized Security Organization (RSO). The Port Facility Security Assessment (PFSA) is conducted by the DA or done by an RSO and then reviewed and approved on behalf of the DA for each port facility. The DA then transmits the Assessment to the Port Facility Security Officer (PFSO) so that it may be adopted and implemented in the Port Facility Security Plan (PFSP). The DA may use a PFSA for any period of time, but typically the Assessment will be reviewed annually or when there has been a significant security incident or change of operations or ownership at the port facility.

---

[143] Id., at A/15.2.
[144] Id., at B/15.3.
[145] Id., at B/15.5.
[146] Id., at B/15.6.
[147] Id., at B/15.7.

The Port Facility Security Assessment (PFSA) may involve one or more facilities, and it necessarily requires the participation of the port facility operators, who are experts in their facility's assets, infrastructure, vulnerabilities, and past security incidents. PFSAs include at least these four elements:

- Analysis of critical assets and infrastructure;
- Identification of potential threats and the likelihood of their occurrence;
- Development of countermeasures to reduce vulnerabilities; and
- Strengthening procedures and the human element in port security.[148]

Port facility vulnerabilities include water-side and shore-side access to ships and ground infrastructure, structural integrity of piers, warehouses, offloading equipment, and facilities, adjacent areas that may be exploited during or for an attack, the use of privately contracted armed security personnel, or deficiencies in training and skills, or shortcomings learned during exercises and drills.[149] The Port Facility Security Assessment (PFSA) typically will account for the most dangerous or likely forms of attack, identification of vulnerabilities, and allocation of scarce resources to defend the facility.[150] The Assessment should be based on the capability and intent of those likely to mount an attack, possible types of tactics or weapons used, and the likely consequences of an attack. All possible threats should be considered, however, and these may include the following types of security incidents:

- Damage to or destruction of the port facility or a ship moored at the pier;
- Vessel hijacking or seizure;
- Tampering with vessel cargo, essential ship equipment or systems, or ship's stores;
- Unauthorized access, including stowaways;
- Use of a ship with the intent to cause a security incident or use of a ship as a weapon or a means of delivering a weapon; and
- Attack by weapons of mass destruction, including nuclear, biological, chemical, radiological, and high explosives.[151]

Once the threats are better known, the Assessment can determine appropriate countermeasures. Countermeasures are employed to reduce the vulnerability of the port or interface between the port and a ship.[152] The written Port Facility Security Assessment (PFSA) describes how the Assessment was conducted,

---

[148] Id., at A/15.5.
[149] Id., at B/15.16.
[150] Id., at B/15.9.
[151] ISPS Code B/15.11.
[152] Countermeasures may be based on security surveys, inspections, audits, consultation with port facility owners and operators, historical information, and consideration of operations within the port facility, or operations at nearby port facilities. Id., at B/15.14.

PORT AND PORT FACILITY SECURITY   451

and it identifies each vulnerability and sets forth appropriate countermeasures.[153] The report is disseminated to the port facility to take corrective action, but it should be protected from unauthorized access or disclosure. The PFSA should be reviewed and updated on a periodic basis—once every 2 to 3 years for major port facilities and once every 5 years for smaller facilities. Within 6 weeks of a major security incident or a significant change in the security environment, however, the PFSA should be reviewed.

13.4 PORT STATE CONTROL CERTIFICATIONS AND DOCUMENTS

Port State Control Certifications and Documents[154]

1. International Tonnage Certificate (1969);
2. Passenger Ship Safety Certificate;[155]
3. Cargo Ship Safety Construction Certificate;[156]
4. Cargo Ship Safety Equipment Certificate;[157]
5. Cargo Ship Safety Radio Certificate;
6. Exemption Certificate;
7. Cargo Ship Safety Certificate;
8. Document of Compliance;[158]
9. Dangerous Goods Special List or Manifest, or Detailed Stowage Plan;
10. International Certificate of Fitness for the Carriage of Liquefied Gases in Bulk, or the Certificate of Fitness for the Carriage of Liquefied Gases in Bulk, whichever is appropriate;
11. International Certificate of Fitness for the Carriage of Dangerous Chemicals in Bulk, or the Certificate of Fitness for the Carriage of Dangerous Chemicals in Bulk, whichever is appropriate;
12. International Oil Pollution Prevention Certificate;
13. International Pollution Prevention Certificate for the Carriage of Noxious Liquid Substances in Bulk;
14. International Load Line Certificate (1966);
15. International Load Line Exemption Certificate;
16. Oil Record Book, parts I and II;
17. Shipboard Oil Pollution Emergency Plan;
18. Cargo Record Book;
19. Minimum Safe Manning Document;
20. Certificates of Competency;

---

[153] Id., at A/15.4.
[154] IMO Doc. 882(21), Amendments to the Procedures for Port State Control (Amending IMO Assembly Resolution A.787(19), Nov. 25, 1999), Feb. 4, 2000, Appendix 4. U.S. public vessel inspection certificates are set forth in 46 C.F.R. §§ 2.01–25.
[155] SOLAS regulation II-1(a), II-2/12, 14, II, IV and V. This provision is implemented in the United States by 46 U.S.C. § 176.910, Passenger Ship Safety Certificate.
[156] Implemented in the United States by 46 C.F.R. § 2.01–25.
[157] SOLAS regulation I-10 and 12.
[158] SOLAS regulation II-2/54.

21. Seafarers medical certificates;[159]
22. Stability information;
23. Safety Management Certificate and copy of Document of Compliance;[160]
24. Certificates as to the ship's hull strength and machinery installations issued by the classification society in question;
25. Survey Report Files;[161]
26. For roll-on/roll-off passenger ships and ferries, information on the A/A max ratio;[162]
27. Document of authorization for the carriage of grain;
28. Special Purpose Ship Safety Certificate;
29. High-Speed Craft Safety Certificate and Permit to Operate High-Speed Craft;
30. Mobile Offshore Drilling Unit Safety Certificate;
31. For oil tankers, the record of oil discharge monitoring and control system for the last ballast voyage;
32. The muster list, fire control plan and damage control plan;
33. Ship's log-book records of tests and drills and inspection and maintenance of life-saving appliances and arrangements;
34. Procedures and Arrangements Manual (chemical tankers);
35. Cargo Securing Manual;
36. Certificate of Registry or other document of nationality;
37. Garbage Management Plan;
38. Garbage Record Book;
39. Bulk carrier booklet;[163] and
40. Reports of previous port state control inspections.

13.5 Questionnaire for Designated Authorities

This questionnaire may be used by Designated Authorities to examine the status of implementation of the government's responsibilities for port facility security as specified in the Maritime Security Measures.[164]

---

[159] Convention concerning the Medical Examination of Seafarers, entry into force, Aug. 17, 1955, Adoption: Geneva, 28th ILC session, June 29, 1946 (ILO Convention No. 73).

[160] SOLAS Chapter IX.

[161] In case of bulk carriers or oil tankers, in accordance with IMO Doc. A.744(18), Guidelines on the Enhanced Program of Inspections During Surveys of Bulk Carriers and Oil Tankers, Nov. 4, 1993.

[162] The A/A max ratio is determined in accordance with a calculation procedure developed by the Maritime Safety Committee of IMO to assess the survivability characteristics of existing roll-on/roll-off (ro-ro) passenger ships. The IMO describes A/Amax as a simplified probabilistic approach attempting to assess the survivability standard of one ferry against another. The ratio is a rough guide that facilitates quick calculations on a representative number of ferries. Under April 1992 amendments to SOLAS, between October 1, 1994 and October 1, 2005, a slightly modified SOLAS 90 standard was phased in for existing ro-ro passenger ships based upon the A/A max.

[163] SOLAS Chapter VI regulation 7.

[164] IMO Doc. MSC.1/Circ.1192, May 2006. See also, IMO Doc. MSC 89/INF.13, Measures to Enhance Maritime Security, Maritime Security Manual—Guidance for port facilities, ports and ships, Mar. 5, 2011.

1. Who is the Designated Authority?[165]
2. What is the national legislative basis for the implementation of the International Ship and Port Facility Security Code?[166]
3. What guidance to industry was released to implement the International Ship and Port Facility Security Code?[167]
4. What are the means of communication with port facilities regarding International Ship and Port Facility Security Code implementation?[168]
5. What processes are in place to document initial and subsequent compliance with the International Ship and Port Facility Security Code?[169]
6. What is the Contracting Government's definition of a Port Facility?[170]
7. What are the procedures used to determine the extent to which port facilities are required to comply with the International Ship and Port Facility Security Code, with particular reference to those port facilities that occasionally serve ships on international voyages?[171]
8. Has the Contracting Government concluded in writing bi-lateral or multi-lateral agreements with other Contracting Governments on alternative security agreements?[172]
9. Has the Contracting Government allowed a port facility or group of port facilities to implement equivalent security arrangements?[173]

Port Facility Security Assessments

10. Who has the responsibility for notifying and updating the IMO with information in the Port Facility Security Assessment (PFSA) in accordance with SOLAS regulation XI-2/13?[174]
11. Who conducts Port Facility Security Assessments?[175]
12. How are Port Facility Security Assessments conducted and approved?[176]
13. What minimum skills are required for persons conducting Port Facility Security Assessment?[177]

---

[165] SOLAS regulation XI-2/1.11.
[166] Id., at XI-2/2 and XI-2/10.
[167] Id., at XI-2/2 and XI-2/10.
[168] Id., at XI-2/3 and XI-2/10.
[169] Id., at XI-2/10.2.
[170] Id., at XI-2/1.1.
[171] Id., at XI-2/1, XI 2/2.2.
[172] Id., at XI-2/11.1.
[173] Id., at XI-2/12.1.
[174] Id., at XI-2/13.
[175] Id., at XI-2/10.2.1, ISPS Code sections A/15.2 and 15.2.1.
[176] ISPS Code sections A/15.2 and 15.2.1.
[177] Id., at A/15.3.

14. Are Port Facility Security Assessments used for each Port Facility Security Plan?[178]
15. Do single Port Facility Security Assessments cover more than one port facility?[179]
16. Who is responsible for informing the IMO if the single Port Facility Security Assessment covers more than one port facility?[180]
17. What national guidance has been developed to assist with the completion of Port Facility Security Assessment?[181]
18. What procedures are in place for determining when re-assessment takes place?[182]
19. What procedures are in place for protecting the Port Facility Security Assessment from unauthorized access or disclosure?[183]

Port Facility Security Officers

20. How are Port Facility Security Officers designated?[184]
21. What are the minimum training requirements that have been set by the Contracting Government for Port Facility Security Officers?[185]

Port Facility Security Plans

22. Are procedures used to determine the individuals/organizations responsible for the preparation of the Port Facility Security Plan?
23. Are procedures in place to protect Port Facility Security Plans from unauthorized access?[186]
24. What procedures are in place for approval and subsequent amendments of the Port Facility Security Plans?[187]

Security Levels

25. Who is the authority responsible for setting the security level for port facilities?[188]

---

[178] Id., at A/15.1.
[179] Id., at A/15.6.
[180] Id., at A/15.6.
[181] SOLAS regulation XI-2/10.2.1.
[182] ISPS Code section A/15.4.
[183] Id., at A/15.7.
[184] Id., at A/17.1.
[185] Id., at A/18.1.
[186] Id., at A/16.7 and A/16.8.
[187] Id., at A/16.6.
[188] SOLAS regulation XI-2/3.2.

26. What are the procedures for communicating security levels to port facilities by the responsible authority?[189]
27. What are the procedures for communicating port facilities' security levels to ships?[190]
28. What are the contact points and procedures for receiving ships' security level information in the Contracting Government and for notifying ships of contact details?[191]

Declaration of Security

29. What procedures are used to determine when a Declaration of Security is required?[192]
30. What is the minimum timeframe that a Declaration of Security is required to be retained?[193]

Delegation of Tasks and Duties

31. What tasks and duties have the contracting government delegated to Recognized Security Organizations or others?[194]
32. To whom have these tasks and duties been delegated? What oversight procedures are in place?[195]

13.6 SECURITY CHECKLIST FOR PORT FACILITY OPERATORS

The IMO has provided a security checklist and guidance for port facility operators, which is reproduced in pertinent part, as set forth below.[196] The checklist includes mandatory provisions set forth in Part A of the International Ship and Port Facility Security Code and recommendatory guidance contained in Part B of the Code.

---

[189] Id., at XI-2/3.2.
[190] Id., at XI-2/4.3 and XI-2/7.1.
[191] Id., at XI-2/7.2.
[192] Id., at XI-2/10.3, ISPS Code section A/5.1.
[193] ISPS Code section A/5.6.
[194] Id., at A/4.3.
[195] SOLAS regulation XI-2/13.2.
[196] IMO Doc. MSC.1/Circ. 1192, Guidance on Voluntary Self-Assessment by SOLAS-Contracting Governments and Port Facilities, May 2006, Appendix 2, and ISPS Code A/14.2.

1. Port Facility Overview:

   - Name of port facility
   - Name of operator/authority
   - Name of Port Facility Security Officer
   - Average number of SOLAS ships handled per annum

2. Particular characteristics of the port facility and vessel traffic that increase security risk:

   - Passenger ships
   - Dangerous cargoes and goods
   - Ro-Ro and container terminal
   - Located near military installation
   - Explosives
   - Warships or other military vessels
   - Oil/gas refinery/terminal
   - Embarkation of military personnel or cargo
   - LPG, LNG or petrol storage

3. Security agreements and arrangements:

   .1 Is the port facility covered by an alternative security agreement?
   .2 Is the port facility operating under any temporary security measures?

13.6.1 *Guidance for Port Facility Operators*

13.6.1.1 Performance of Port Facility Security Duties

Part A

.1 Does the port facility's means of ensuring the performance of all security duties meet the requirements set out in the Port Facility Security Plan for security level 1 and 2?[197]
.2 Has the port facility established measures to prevent weapons or any other dangerous substances and devices intended for use against persons, ships, or the port, from entering the facility?[198]
.3 Has the port facility established evacuation procedures in case of security threats or breaches of security?[199]
.4 Has the port facility established procedures for response to an activation of a ship security alert system?[200]

---

[197] ISPS Code A/14.2.1.
[198] Id., at A/16.3.1.
[199] Id., at A/16.3.5.
[200] Id., at A/16.3.14.

Part B

Organization of Port Facility Security Duties[201]

.5 Has the port facility established the role and structure of the security organization?[202]

.6 Has the port facility established the duties and responsibilities for personnel with security roles?[203]

.7 Has the port facility established the training requirements for personnel with security roles?[204]

.8 Has the port facility established the performance measures needed to assess the individual effectiveness of personnel with security roles?[205]

.9 Has the port facility established their security organization's link with other national or local authorities with security responsibilities?[206]

.10 Has the port facility established procedures and practices to protect security sensitive information held in paper or electronic format?[207]

.11 Has the port facility established procedures to assess the continuing effectiveness of security measures and procedures?[208]

.12 Has the port facility established procedures to assess security equipment, to include identification of, and response to, equipment failure or malfunction?[209]

.13 Has the port facility established procedures governing submission and assessment of reports relating to possible breaches of security or security concerns?[210]

.14 Has the port facility established procedures to maintain and update records of dangerous goods and hazardous substances, including their location within the port facility?[211]

.15 Has the port facility established a means of alerting and obtaining the services of waterside patrols and search teams, to include bomb and underwater specialists?[212]

.16 Has the port facility established procedures for assisting, when requested, Ship Security Officers in confirming the identity of those seeking to board the ship?[213]

.17 Has the port facility established the procedures for facilitating shore leave for ship's crew members or personnel changes?[214]

.18 Has the port facility established the procedures for facilitating visitor access to the ship, to include representatives of seafarers' welfare and labor organizations?[215]

---

[201] Id., at B/16.8.
[202] Id., at B/16.8.1.
[203] Id., at B/16.8.2.
[204] Id., at A18.1, A/18.2, A/18.3 and B/16.8.2.
[205] Id., at B/16.8.2.
[206] Id., at B/16.8.3.
[207] Id., at B/16.8.6.
[208] Id., at B/16.8.7.
[209] Id., at B/16.8.7.
[210] Id., at B/16.8.8.
[211] Id., at B/16.8.11.
[212] Id., at B/16.8.12.
[213] Id., at B/16.8.13.
[214] Id., at B/16.8.14.
[215] Id., at B/16.8.14.

13.6.1.2 Controlling Access to the Port Facility

Part A

.1 Does the port facility's means of controlling access to the port facility meet the requirements set out in the Port Facility Security Plan for security level 1 and 2?[216]

Part B

Facility Security Measures[217]

.2 Has the port facility identified the appropriate location(s) where security measures can be applied to restrict or prohibit access. These should include all access points identified in the Port Facility Security Plan at security level 1 and 2?[218]
.3 Does the port facility specify the type of restrictions or prohibitions, and the means of enforcement to be applied at all access points identified in the Port Facility Security Plan at security level 1 and 2?[219]
.4 Has the port facility established measures to increase the frequency of searches of people, personal effects, and vehicles at security level 2?[220]
.5 Has the port facility established measures to deny access to visitors who are unable to provide verifiable justification for seeking access to the port facility at security level 2?[221]
.6 Has the port facility established the means of identification required to access and remain unchallenged within the port facility?[222]
.7 Does the port facility have the means to differentiate the identification of permanent, temporary, and visiting individuals?[223]
.8 Does the port facility have the means to verify the identity and legitimacy of passenger boarding passes, tickets, etc.?[224]
.9 Has the port facility established provisions to ensure that the identification systems are regularly updated?[225]
.10 Has the port facility established provisions to facilitate disciplinary action against those whom abuse the identification system procedures?[226]
.11 Has the port facility created procedures to deny access and report all individuals who are unwilling or unable to establish their identity or purpose for visit to the Port Facility Security Officer and to the national or local authorities?[227]
.12 Has the port facility identified a location(s) for searches of persons, personal effects, and vehicles that facilitates continuous operation, regardless of prevailing weather conditions?[228]

---

[216] Id., at A/14.2.2, A/14.2.1 and A/14.3.
[217] Id., at B/16.10, B16/12, B16/14, B16/17 and B/16.19.1.
[218] Id., at B/16.11, B/16.19.1.
[219] Id., at B/16.11 B/16.19.2, B/16.19.3.
[220] Id., at B/16.19.4.
[221] Id., at B/16.19.5.
[222] Id., at B/16.12.
[223] Id., at B/16.12.
[224] Id., at B/16.12.
[225] Id., at B/16.12.
[226] Id., at B/16.12.
[227] Id., at B/16.13.
[228] Id., at B/16.14.

PORT AND PORT FACILITY SECURITY 459

.13 Does the port facility have procedures established to directly transfer persons, personal effects, or vehicles subjected to search to the restricted holding, embarkation, or vehicle loading area?[229]

.14 Has the port facility established separate locations for embarking and disembarking passengers, ship's personnel, and their effects to ensure that unchecked persons do not come in contact with checked persons?[230]

.15 Does the Port Facility Security Plan establish the frequency of application of all access controls?[231]

.16 Does the Port Facility Security Plan establish control points for restricted areas bounded by fencing or other barriers to a standard, which is approved by the national government?[232]

.17 Does the Port Facility Security Plan establish the identification of and procedures to control access points not in regular use which should be permanently closed and locked?[233]

13.6.1.3 Monitoring of the Port Facility, Anchoring and Berthing Area

Part A

.1 Does the facility's means of monitoring the port facility, including berthing and anchorage area(s) meet the requirements set out in the Port Facility Security Plan for security level 1 and 2?[234]

Part B

Scope of Security Monitoring[235]

.2 Does the port facility have the capability to continuously monitor on land and water the port facility and its nearby approaches?[236]

.3 Which of the following means are employed to monitor the port facility and nearby approaches?[237]

- Patrols by security guards
- Patrols by security vehicles
- Patrols by watercraft
- Automatic intrusion-detection devices
- Surveillance equipment

.4 If automatic intrusion-detection devices are employed, do they activate an audible and/or visual alarm(s) at a location(s) that is continuously monitored?[238]

---

[229] Id., at B/16.14.
[230] Id., at B/16.15.
[231] Id., at B/16.16.
[232] Id., at B/16.17.1.
[233] Id., at B/16.17.7.
[234] Id., at A/14.2.3 and A/14.3.
[235] Id., B/16.49.
[236] Id., at B/16.49.
[237] Id., at B/16.49.
[238] Id., at B/16.50.

460   CHAPTER THIRTEEN

.5 Does the Port Facility Security Plan establish procedures and equipment needed at each security level?[239]

.6 Has the port facility established measures to increase the security measures at security level 1 and 2?[240]

- Increase intensity and coverage of lighting and surveillance equipment
- Increase frequency of foot, vehicle & waterborne patrols
- Assign additional personnel
- Surveillance

.7 Does the Port Facility Security Plan establish procedures and equipment necessary to ensure that monitoring equipment will be able to perform continually, including consideration of the possible effects of weather or power disruptions?[241]

Illumination at Port Facility[242]

.8 Does the port facility have adequate illumination, to allow for detection of unauthorized persons at or approaching access points, the perimeter, restricted areas and ships, at all times including the night hours and periods of limited visibility?[243]

13.6.1.4   Monitoring of Restricted Areas

Part A

.1 Does the port facility's means of limiting and monitoring access to restricted areas meet requirements of the Port Facility Security Plan for security level 1 and 2?[244]

Part B   Establishment of Restricted Areas

Establishment of Restricted Areas[245]

.2 Are restricted areas identified within the port facility?[246]

.3 Which of the following elements are identified for restricted areas in the Port Facility Security Plan?[247]

- Extent of area
- Times of application
- Security measures to control access to areas
- Security measures to control activities within areas
- Measures to ensure restricted areas are swept before and after establishment

---

[239] Id., at B/16.51.
[240] Id., at B/16.51, B/16.53.1, B/16.53.2 and B/16.53.3.
[241] Id., at B/16.51.
[242] Id., at A/14.3 and B/16.49.1.
[243] Id., at B/16.49.1.
[244] Id., at A/14.2.4 and A/14.3.
[245] Id., at B/16.21.
[246] Id., at B/16.21.
[247] Id., at B/16.21.

Part C Security Measures

Security Measures[248]

.4 Are restricted areas clearly marked, indicating that access to the area is restricted and that unauthorized presence constitutes a breach of security?[249]
.5 Are measures established to control access by individuals to restricted areas?[250]
.6 Does the port facility have the means to ensure that passengers do not have unsupervised access to restricted areas?[251]
.7 Are measures established to control the entry, parking, loading, and unloading of vehicles?[252]
.8 Are measures established to control movement and storage of cargo and ship's stores?[253]
.9 Are measures established to control unaccompanied baggage or personal effects?[254]
.10 If automatic intrusion-detection devices are installed, do they alert a control center capable of responding to the alarm?[255]
.11 Which of the following security measures are utilized to control access to restricted areas?[256]

- Permanent or temporary barriers to surround restricted area
- Access points controlled by security guards when in use
- Access points that can be locked or barred when not in use
- Use of passes to indicate a person's authorization for access
- Marking of vehicles that are allowed access
- Use of guards and patrols
- Use of automatic intrusion-detection devices or surveillance equipment and systems
- Control of vessel movement in vicinity of ships using port facility

.12 Has the port facility established measures to enhance the security of restricted areas for security level 2?[257]

- Enhance the effectiveness of barriers
- Reduce access points
- Enhance control of access points
- Restrict parking
- Control movement within
- Continuously monitor
- Enhance frequency of patrols
- Limiting access to spaces adjacent to ship

---

[248] Id., at B/16.22.
[249] Id., at B/16.23.
[250] Id., at B/16.22.1.
[251] Id., at B/16.12.
[252] Id., at B/16.22.2.
[253] Id., at B/16.22.3.
[254] Id., at B/16.22.4.
[255] Id., at B/16.24.
[256] Id., at B/16.27.
[257] Id., at B/16.28.

.13 Has the port facility established measures to enhance the effectiveness of barriers, reduce access points, and enhance access control for restricted areas at security level 2?[258]

13.6.1.5 Supervising the Handling of Cargo

Part A

.1 Does the port facility's means of supervising the handling of cargo meet the requirements identified in the Port Facility Security Plan for security level 1 and 2?[259]

Part B

Prevent Tampering, the Acceptance of Unauthorized Cargo, Inventory Control[260]

.2 Are measures employed to routinely monitor the integrity of cargo, including the checking of seals, upon entry to the port facility and whilst stored in the port facility at security levels 1 and 2?[261]
.3 Are measures employed to routinely monitor cargo transport units prior to and during cargo handling operations?[262]
.4 Which of the following means are employed to conduct cargo checking?[263] (e.g. visual or physical exams, scanning or detection equipment, working dogs).
.5 Are restricted areas designated to perform inspections of cargo transport units if a container seal appears to have been compromised?[264]
.6 Has the port facility established measures to intensity checks to ensure that only documented cargo enters the facility, and if necessary, is only stored on a temporary basis at security level 2?[265]
.7 Has the port facility established measures to intensify vehicle searches, the frequency and detail of examining cargo seals, and other tampering prevention methods at security level 2?[266]
.8 Are cargo delivery orders or equivalent cargo documentation verified before acceptance?[267]
.9 Are procedures utilized to randomly or selectively search vehicles at facility access points?[268]
.10 Are inventory control procedures employed at facility access points?[269]

---

[258] Id., at B/16.28.
[259] Id., at A/14.2.5 and A/14.3.
[260] Id., at B/16.30.1, B/16.30.2, and B/16.31.
[261] Id., at B/16.32.1.
[262] Id., at B/16.32.1.
[263] Id., at B/16.33.
[264] Id., at B/16.32.4.
[265] Id., at B/16.35.2.
[266] Id., at B/16.35.3.
[267] Id., at B/16.32.2.
[268] Id., at B/16.32.3.
[269] Id., at B/16.31.

.11 Are means of identification used to determine whether cargo inside the port facility awaiting loading has been either checked and accepted or temporarily stored in a restricted area?[270]

13.6.1.6 Supervising the Handling of Ship's Stores

Part A

.1 Does the port facility's means of supervising the handling of ship's stores meet the requirements identified in the Port Facility Security Plan at security level 1 and 2?[271]

Part B Ship's Stores Security Measures

Ship's Stores Security Measures[272]

.2 Are ship's stores examined to ensure package integrity at security level 1 and 2?[273]
.3 Are procedures established to ensure that no ship's stores are accepted into the port facility without checking at security level 1 and 2?[274]
.4 Which of the following means are employed to inspect ship's stores?[275] (e.g. visual and physical exams, scanning or detection equipment, working dogs).
.5 Are procedures established to prevent the tampering of ship's stores?[276]
.6 Are ship's stores deliveries preceded with an advanced notification of load composition, driver information, and vehicle registration?[277]
.7 Are unscheduled deliveries of ship's stores declined access to the port facility?[278]
.8 Are there procedures in place to prevent ships' stores being accepted unless ordered? Are manifests and order documentation validated prior to allowing then into the port facility at security level 1 and 2?[279]
.9 Are searches of vehicles delivering ship's stores performed prior to entry into the port facility?[280]
.10 Are escorts provided for ship's stores delivery vehicles within the port facility at security level 1 and 2?[281]
.11 Does the port facility increase the use of scanning/detection equipment mechanical devices, or dogs at security level 2?[282]

---

[270] Id., at B/16.31.
[271] Id., at A/14.2.6.
[272] Id., at B/16.38.
[273] Id., at B/16.38.1 and B/16.42.1.
[274] Id., at B/16.38.2 and B/16.42.2.
[275] Id., at B/16.41.
[276] Id., at B/16.38.3.
[277] Id., at B/16.40.2.
[278] Id., at B/16.38.4.
[279] Id., at B/16.38.4.
[280] Id., at B/16.38.5.
[281] Id., at B/16.38.6 and B/16.42.4.
[282] Id., at B/16.43.2.

13.6.1.7 Communications Security

Part A

    .1 Do the port facility's communication equipment and procedures meet the requirements identified in the Port Facility Security Plan at security level 1 and 2?[283]

Part B   Effectiveness and Protection of Communications

    Effectiveness and protection of Communication Equipment, Procedures and Facilities[284]

    .2 Is the port facility equipped with auxiliary communication systems for both internal and external communications that are readily available regardless of security level, weather conditions or power disruptions at security level 1 and 2?[285]

    .3 Are security personnel trained on communication equipment to ensure efficiency?[286]

    .4 Are telephone numbers for key personnel accurate and routinely validated?[287]

    .5 Are procedures in place to ensure that port facility communication systems and equipment are serviced and maintained?[288]

    .6 Has the port facility established procedures and means for the Port Facility Security Officer to effectively disseminate changes in the security level at the port facility or with a vessel interfacing with the port?[289]

    .7 Are security procedures established to protect radio, telecommunication equipment and infrastructure, and computer systems?[290]

    .8 Are entry control procedures established to restrict access of communication facilities and infrastructure?[291]

13.6.1.8 Training, Drills, and Exercises

Part A

    .1 Has the Port Facility Security Officer and appropriate port facility security personnel received sufficient training to perform their assigned duties as identified in the Port Facility Security Plan?[292]

    .2 Has the port facility implemented drills and exercises?[293]

---

[283] Id., at A/14.2.7 and A/14.3.
[284] Id., at B/16.8.4 and B/16.8.5.
[285] Id., at B/16.8.4.
[286] Id., at B/16.8.4.
[287] Id., at B/16.8.4.
[288] Id., at B/16.8.4.
[289] Id., at B/16.8.4.
[290] Id., at B/16.8.5.
[291] Id., at B/16.8.5.
[292] Id., at A/18.1 and A/18.2.
[293] Id., at A/18.3 and A/18.4.

Part B Training, Drills, and Exercises

Training, drills, and exercises on port facility security[294]

.3 Are the Port Facility Security Officer, personnel with security duties and all other port facility personnel familiar with the Port Facility Security Plan and have they received appropriate training?[295]

.4 Are security drills conducted at least every three months and security exercises conducted at least once each calendar year with no more than 18 months between the exercises?[296]

13.6.1.9 Miscellaneous

Part B

.1 Has the port facility established procedures and adopted measures with respect to ships operating at a higher security level than the port facility?[297]

.2 Has the port facility established procedures and adopted measures which can be applied when it is interfacing with:[298]

- a ship which has been at a port of a State which is not a Contracting Government;
- a ship to which the ISPS Code does not apply;
- service vessels covered by the Port Facility Security Plan are interfacing with fixed or floating platforms or mobile offshore drilling units on location.

---

[294] Id., at B/18.1, B/18.2, B/18.3, and B/18.6.
[295] Id., at B/18.1, B/18.2 and B/18.3.
[296] Id., at B/18.5 and B/18.6.
[297] Id., at B/16.55.
[298] Id., at B/16.56.

FOURTEEN

SHIP AND SHIP OPERATOR SECURITY

14.1 Shipping Company Responsibilities

14.1.1 *Applicability of IMO Maritime Security Measures*

The IMO Maritime Security Measures (MSM), which are based on SOLAS Convention chapter XI-2, "Special measures to enhance maritime security," entered into force on July 1, 2004. The Measures enshrined the ISPS Code Part A, which contains mandatory provisions, and Part B, which are advisory or recommendatory stipulations. The rules in both parts apply to States' parties, port authorities and operators, and commercial shipping carriers and operators with ships registered to the flag State.[1] The guidance set forth in the IMO authorities applies to government officials, port facility employees and shipping company employees and ship masters and crews.[2]

Many states that are party to SOLAS and that subsequently adopted the ISPS Code have overlaid the IMO rules on to substantive national requirements. The United States, for example, adopted the Maritime Transportation Security Act of 2002, which is implemented by the U.S. Coast Guard in the Code of Federal

---

[1] IMO Doc. MSC 89/INF.13, Measures to enhance Maritime Security, Maritime Security Manual—Guidance for port facilities, ports and ships, Mar. 5, 2011, para. 1.1.1, *reproduced in* Guide to Maritime Security and the ISPS Code para. 1.1.1 (International Maritime Organization 2012 ed.), IMO Sales No. IA116E [Hereinafter Maritime Security Measures or MSM]. The MSM are supplemented by IMO Doc. MSC 89/WP.6/Add.1, Measures to Enhance Maritime Security: Piracy and Armed Robbery against Ships; Report of the Working Group, May 17, 2011.
[2] MSM, 1.1.2.

Regulations.[3] Similarly, the European Union (EU) adopted regulations that made mandatory certain provisions of Part B of the ISPS Code.[4]

The security measures apply to passenger ships, including high-speed passenger craft, carrying 12 or more passengers, cargo ships of 500 gross tonnage and upwards, including high-speed craft, bulk carriers, chemical tankers, gas carriers and oil tankers, and mobile offshore drilling units, which are used to drill for resources beneath the sea-bed. The MSM also apply to special purpose ships over 500 gross tons that are not Government-owned and that have on board more than 12 personnel other than normal crew who are engaged in special duties, such as marine scientific research vessels, survey ships, training ships, fish processing and factory ships, salvage ships, cable and pipe laying ships, diving ships and floating cranes. However, the measures only apply to ships while they are underway.

The MSM do not apply to sovereign immune vessels, such as warships, naval auxiliaries or other ships operated by a government and used only on government non-commercial service. Bareboat charters, for example, that are wholly leased for government service, are not covered by the measures, although states may elect to apply some or all of the provisions to such ships. The measures also do not apply to ships engaged in domestic voyages or cabotage shipping among ports of a single State. Cargo ships of less than 500 gross tons, ships not propelled by mechanical means, wooden ships of primitive build, pleasure craft not engaged in trade and fishing vessels also are not covered by the measures, even though these craft may be engaged in international voyages. Sailing vessels fall into the category of special purpose ships, and normally are exempted by Flag State Administrations from the security measures. On the other hand, flag States have tended to apply some of the maritime security measures to certain categories of non-SOLAS vessels, such as ferries operating purely domestic services.

14.1.2 *Alternative Security Agreements*

Alternative Security Agreements (ASAs) are agreements between national governments on how to implement security measures that may deviate from the normal Maritime Security Measures (MSM). These special agreements may apply to "short international voyages" using fixed routes between port facilities

---

[3] 68 FR 60449–60472, General Provisions of Maritime Security, Oct. 22, 2003, 68 FR 60545–60559, Outer Continental Shelf Facility Security, Oct. 22, 2003, 68 FR 60483–60515, Vessels; Security Measures, Oct. 22, 2003, 68 FR 60472–60483, Area Maritime Security, Oct. 22, 2003, 68 FR 60559–60570, Automatic Identification System; Vessel Carriage Requirements, Oct. 22, 2003.

[4] Regulation (EC) No. 725/2004 of the European Parliament and of the Council, Mar. 31, 2004, on Enhancing Ship and Port Facility Security [2004] OFFICIAL J. OF THE EUROPEAN UNION L 129/6.

within their jurisdiction.[5] The SOLAS Convention defines a "short international voyage" within the context of life-saving appliances and arrangements as:

> ...[A]n international voyage in the course of which a ship is not more than 200 miles from a port or place in which the passengers and crew could be placed in safety. Neither distance between the last port of call in the country in which the voyage begins and the final port of destination nor the return voyage shall exceed 600 miles. The final port of destination is the last port of call in the scheduled voyage at which the ship commences its return voyage to the country in which the voyage began.[6]

Generally, ASAs cover international ferry services. The agreements address minor differences between the regulations of the two states from which the ferry operates. The agreements provide alternative provisions that may depart from those in the MSM. ASAs also contain guidance on required security assessments that apply in the absence of those in the MSM. For example, ASAs may specify how Declarations of Security and other pre-arrival matters are addressed by each state, when such provisions deviate from the procedures set forth in the MSM.

An ASA only covers ships and ports included in the agreement and does not apply to ship-to-ship activities of ships that are not covered by the Agreement. Generally Company Security Officers (CSOs) participate in the security assessments and in shaping ASAs. A Flag State Administration also may permit a ship or group of ships entitled to fly its flag to implement security measures different than but equivalent to those prescribed in the MSM. If ships incorporate equivalent security measures, such measures should be included in each Ship Security Plan (SSP).

Ships flying the flag of a State that is not party to the ASA may operate on the fixed routes covered by the agreement if their Administration agrees to apply the terms of the ASA to their ships.[7] Ships covered by the ASA may not conduct ship-to-ship interfaces with vessels that are not covered by the agreement. The firewall separating ships covered by the ASA and those outside of the agreement goes both ways. The ASA may not compromise the level of security of any other ship or port facility not covered by the agreement.[8] Under this regime, the agreement serves to insulate the ships making routine and short international voyages under an ASA from other ships. The segregation of the two classes of ships helps

---

[5] A "Short international voyage" is defined as "an international voyage in which a ship is not more than 200 miles for a port or a place in which the passenger and crew could be placed in safety. Neither the distance between the last port of call in the country in which the voyage begins and the final port of destination, nor the return voyage, shall exceed 600 miles. The final port of destination is the last port of call in the scheduled voyage at which the sip commences its return voyage to the country." Id., at 1.8.1.eee.

[6] The definition is imported from SOLAS into U.S. regulations at 46 CFR § 70.10–1.

[7] ISPS Code B/4.26.

[8] Id., B/4.26.

to protect those vessels covered by ASAs from contact with those that may have lower security standards.

The ASA is a shared framework in which the security assessments for the port facility and ship security assessment are undertaken by the flag State and the port State. Furthermore, the national authorities in both states should consult with counterparts in other nations that are likely to be affected by the operation of the proposed agreement.[9] Each government then is responsible for implementing the required control measures. Security procedures are applied and maintained at the port facilities and on the ships for the duration of the agreement.[10]

14.1.3 *Equivalent Security Agreements*

National authorities may permit port facilities and ships to implement Equivalent Security Arrangements (ESAs) that contain security measures substantially equivalent to those in the ISPS Code. Such measures have to be the functional equivalent of those prescribed in the Maritime Security Measures (MSM).[11] ESAs are not common, however, but they may be appropriate for specific ship or port facilities with limited or special operations, but more than occasional traffic.[12] ESAs may be used for facilities, such as terminals associated with factories or quaysides that do not have frequent operations.[13]

If a Flag State Administration permits ESAs to apply to one or more of its ships, those vessels should include the Arrangement in each Ship Security Plan.[14] The Designated Authorities may allow a port facility to implement security measures or procedures substantially equivalent to those in the MSM without having to appoint a Port Facility Security Officer or submit a Port Facility Security Plan.[15] ESAs are appropriate only for those ports with more than occasional use by SOLAS ships but without frequent services or that feature special operations, such as berths used by SOLAS ships at naval facilities with military security measures and procedures.[16]

The ESAs should not be used to allow SOLAS ships to avoid compliance with the requirements of the MSM.[17] If national authorities conclude ESAs, they should notify IMO through the GISIS portal, and give the name of the ships or port facili-

---

[9] MSM, 2.13.9.
[10] Id., 2.13.11.
[11] Id., 2.14.1.
[12] ISPS Code B/4.27.
[13] Id.
[14] MSM, 4.2.12.
[15] Id., 2.14.2.
[16] Id.
[17] Id., 2.14.5.

ties subject to the arrangement, the name of the arrangement, and a description of its terms.[18]

14.2 Checklist for Shipping Companies

This checklist is derived from IMO Maritime Safety Committee Circular 1217, released on December 14, 2006, which is used to help shipping companies and their Company Security Officers (CSOs) implement the maritime security requirements of SOLAS and the ISPS Code.[19]

Company Name, Address; Company Security Officer names, training certificates, Certificate submitted to the Administration for recognition?
Ship(s) names, IMO Number(s), Type(s), Flag state,
Ship security plan approved by (name) on (date)
International Ship Security Certificate (ISSC) issued by (name).

14.2.1 *Checklist*

14.2.1.1 Continuous Synopsis Record

Continuous Synopsis Record (CSR)[20]

.1 Has the Company ensured that all of its ships have been issued with an up-to date Continuous Synopsis Record?[21]
.2 Has the Company ensured that procedures are in place to notify the Administration when ships are transferred to the flag of another State?[22]

14.2.1.2 Ship Security Alert System

Ship Security Alert System (SSAS)[23]

.1 Has the Company ensured that an Ship Security Alert System has been installed and that it operates as required?[24]

---

[18] The GSIS portal is located at http://gisis.imo.org. See, MSM, 2.14.6.
[19] IMO Doc. MSC.1/Circ. 1217, Interim Guidance on Voluntary Self-Assessment by Companies and Company Security Officers, Dec. 14, 2006, and Appendix at Annex, Interim Guidance on Voluntary Self-Assessment by Companies and Company Security Officers (CSOs) for Ship Security. The annex guidance was adopted at the eighty-second session of the Maritime Safety Committee, Nov. 29–Dec. 8, 2006, and it is reproduced at Appendix 4.10, Implementation Checklist for Shipping Companies and their Company Security Officers, MSM.
[20] SOLAS regulation XI-1/5.
[21] Id., XI-1/5.
[22] Id., XI-1/5.7.
[23] Id., XI-2/6.
[24] Id., XI-2/6.1 and XI-2/6.3.

.2 Has the Company been designated by each ship's Administration to receive ship-to-shore security alerts (a separate answer should be given for each flag under which the Company's ships are flying)?[25]

.3 Does the Company Security Officer inform the Administration of Ship Security Alert System implementation details and alterations?[26]

.4 Does the Company have procedures in place to act upon receipt of a ship-to shore security alert, including notification of the Administration?[27]

14.2.1.3 Master's Discretion for Ship Safety and Security

Master's discretion for ship safety and security[28]

.1 Has the Company adopted a clearly stated policy that nothing constrains the master from taking or executing any decision which in his professional judgment is necessary to maintain the safety and security of the ship?[29]

14.2.1.4 Obligations of the Company

Obligations of the company[30]

Part A   Obligations of the Company

.1 Does the master have on board, at all times, information through which officers duly authorized by a Contracting Government can establish the following:
  .1 Who is responsible for appointing the members of the crew or other persons currently employed or engaged on board the ship in any capacity on the business of that ship?
  .2 Who is responsible for deciding the employment of the ship?
  .3 In cases where the ship is employed under the terms of charter party(ies), who are the parties to such charter party(ies)?[31]

.2 Has the Company established in the ship security plan that the master has the overriding authority and responsibility to make decisions with respect to the safety and the security of the ship and to request the assistance of the Company or of any Contracting Government as may be necessary?[32]

.3 Has the Company ensured that the Company Security Officer, the master and the Ship Security Officer are being given the necessary support to fulfill their duties and responsibilities in accordance with SOLAS chapter XI-2 and Part A of the Code?[33]

---

[25] Id., XI-2/6.2.1.
[26] Id.
[27] Id.
[28] Id., XI-2/8.1.
[29] Id.
[30] Id., XI-2/5, ISPS Code A/6.1, A/6.2 and B/6.1 to B/6.6.
[31] Id., XI-2/5.
[32] ISPS Code, A/6.1.
[33] Id., A/6.2.

Part B   Obligations of the Company

Obligations of the Company[34]

.4 Has the Company provided the master of each ship with information to meet the requirements of the Company under the provisions of SOLAS regulation XI-2/5, for each of the following:[35]
   .1 Parties responsible for appointing shipboard personnel, such as ship management companies, manning agents, contractors, and concessionaries (for example, retail sales outlets, casinos, etc.)?
   .2 Parties responsible for deciding the employment of the ship, including time or bareboat charterer(s) or any other entity acting in such capacity?
   .3 In cases when the ship is employed under the terms of a charter party, the contact details of those parties, including time or voyage charterers?
.5 Does the Company update and keep the information provided current and when changes occur?[36]
.6 Is the information provided in the English, French or Spanish language?[37]
.7 If the ships were constructed before 1 July 2004, does this information reflect the actual condition on that date?[38]
.8 If the ships were constructed on or after 1 July 2004, or the ships were constructed before 1 July 2004 but were out of service on 1 July 2004, was the information provided as from the date of entry of the ship into service and does it reflect the actual condition on that date?[39]
.9 When a ship is withdrawn from service, is the information provided as from the date of re-entry of the ship into service and does it reflect the actual condition on that date?[40]

14.2.1.5 Control and Compliance Measures

Control and compliance measures[41]

.1 Does the Company provide, or has it ensured that its ships provide, confirmation to a Contracting Government, on request, of the information required in SOLAS regulation XI-2/9.2.1.1 to 9.2.1.6, using the standard data set detailed in MSC/Circ.1305?[42]

---

[34] Id., B/6.1 to B/6.6.
[35] Id., B/6.1.
[36] Id., B/6.2.
[37] Id., B/6.3.
[38] Id., B/6.4.
[39] Id., B/6.5.
[40] Id., B/6.6.
[41] SOLAS regulation XI-2/9.2.1.
[42] Id., XI-2/9.2.1. *See also*, IMO Doc. MSC/Circ.1305, Revised Guidance to Masters, Companies and Duly Authorized Officers on the Requirements Relating to the Submission of Security-Related Information Prior to the Entry of a Ship Into Port, June 9, 2009.

14.2.1.6 Verification and Certification for Ships

Verification and certification for ships[43]

Part A   Verification and Certification for Ships

   .1 Does the Company ensure that each ship to which SOLAS chapter XI-2 and the ISPS Code apply is covered by a valid International Ship Security Certificate (ISSC)?[44]
   .2 Does the Company ensure that, when it assumes responsibility for a ship not previously operated by that Company, the existing International Ship Security Certificate is no longer used?[45]
   .3 Does the Company, when it ceases to be responsible for the operation of a ship, transmit to the receiving Company as soon as possible, copies of any information related to the or to facilitate the verifications required for an International Ship Security Certificate to be issued, as described in the ISPS Code A/19.4.2?[46]

14.2.1.7 Ship Security Assessment

Ship security assessment[47]

Part A   Ship Security Assessment

   .1 Does the Company Security Officer ensure that each ship security assessment is carried out by persons with appropriate skills to evaluate the security of a ship?[48]
   .2 Does the Company Security Officer ensure that the persons carrying out the ship security assessment take into account the guidance given in Part B of the ISPS Code and, in particular, paragraphs B/8.2 to B/8.13?[49]
   .3 Does the Company Security Officer ensure that ship security assessments include an on-scene security survey and at least the following elements:[50]
      .1 Identification of existing security measures, procedures and operations?
      .2 Identification and evaluation of key shipboard operations that it is important to protect?
      .3 Identification of possible threats to the key shipboard operations and the likelihood of their occurrence, in order to establish and prioritize security measures?
      .4 Identification of weaknesses, including human factors, in the infrastructure, policies and procedures?
   .4 Are ship security assessments documented, reviewed, accepted and retained by the Company?[51]

---

[43] ISPS Code A/19.
[44] Id., A/19.
[45] Id., A/19.3.9.2.
[46] Id., A/19.3.9.2.
[47] Id., A/8.1 to A/8.5.
[48] Id., A/2.1.7, A/8.2, B/8.1 and B/8.4.
[49] Id., A/8.2 and B/8.1.
[50] Id., A/8.4.
[51] Id., A/8.5.

Part B Company Security Officer Requirements to Conduct an Assessment

The Ship Security Assessment and the Company Security Officer[52]

.5 Has the Company Security Officer ensured that, prior to commencing the Ship Security Assessment, advantage was taken of information available on the assessment of threat for the ports at which the ship would call or at which passengers would embark or disembark and about the port facilities and their protective measures?[53]

.6 Has the Company Security Officer studied previous reports on similar security needs?[54]

.7 Has the Company Security Officer met with appropriate persons on the ship and in the port facilities to discuss the purpose and methodology of the assessment?[55]

.8 Has the Company Security Officer followed any specific guidance offered by the Contracting Governments?[56]

.9 Does the Company Security Officer obtain and record the information required to conduct an assessment, including the following:[57]

.1 The general layout of the ship?

.2 The location of areas which should have restricted access such as navigation bridge, machinery spaces of category A and other control stations as defined in chapter II-2?

.3 The location and function of each actual or potential access point to the ship?

.4 Changes in the tide which may have an impact on the vulnerability or security of the ship?

.5 The cargo spaces and stowage arrangements?

.6 The locations where ship's stores and essential maintenance equipment is stored?

.7 The locations where unaccompanied baggage is stored?

.8 The emergency and stand-by equipment available to maintain essential services?

.9 The number of ship's personnel and existing security duties and any existing training requirement practices of the Company?

.10 Existing security and safety equipment for the protection of passengers and ship's personnel?

.11 Escape and evacuation routes and assembly stations which have to be maintained to ensure the orderly and safe emergency evacuation of the ship?

.12 Existing agreements with private security companies providing ship/waterside security services?

.13 Existing security measures and procedures in effect, including inspection and control procedures, identification systems, surveillance and monitoring equipment, personnel identification documents and communication, alarms, lighting, access control and other appropriate systems?

---

[52] Id., B/8.2 and B/8.5.
[53] Id., B/8.2.
[54] Id.
[55] Id.
[56] Id.
[57] Id., B/8.5.

Part C   Content of the Ship Security Assessment

Content of the Ship Security Assessment[58]

.10 Does the Company Security Officer ensure that the ship security assessments address the following elements on board or within the ship:[59]
 .1 Physical security?
 .2 Structural integrity?
 .3 Personnel protection systems?
 .4 Procedural policies?
 .5 Radio and telecommunication and computer networks?
 .6 Other areas that may, if damaged or used for illicit observation, pose a risk to persons, property, or operations on board the ship or within a port facility?
.11 Does the Company Security Officer ensure those conducting a ship security assessment draw upon expert assistance in relation to the following:[60]
 .1 Knowledge of current security threats and patterns?
 .2 Recognition and detection of weapons, dangerous substances and devices?
 .3 Recognition of behavior patterns of persons who are likely to threaten security?
 .4 Techniques used to circumvent security measures?
 .5 Methods used to cause a security incident?
 .6 Effects of explosives on ship's structures and equipment?
 .7 Ship security?
 .8 Ship/port interface business practices?
 .9 Contingency planning, emergency preparedness and response?
 .10 Physical security?
 .11 Radio and telecommunication and computer networks?
 .12 Marine engineering?
 .13 Ship and port operations?
.12 Does the Company Security Officer ensure that ship security assessments examine each identified point of access, including open weather decks, and evaluate its potential for use by individuals who might seek to breach security? This question includes points of access as well as those who seek to obtain unauthorized entry.[61]
.13 Does the Company Security Officer ensure ship security assessments consider the continuing relevance of the existing security measures and have determined security guidance including the following:[62]
 .1 The restricted areas?
 .2 The response procedures to fire or other emergency conditions?
 .3 Supervision of passengers, visitors, vendors, repair technicians, etc.?
 .4 The frequency and effectiveness of security patrols?
 .5 The access control systems, including identification systems?
 .6 The security communications systems and procedures?
 .7 The security doors, barriers and lighting?
 .8 The security and surveillance equipment and systems, if any?

---

[58] Id., B/8.3, B/8.4, B/8.6 to B/8.13.
[59] Id., B/8.3.
[60] Id., B/8.4.
[61] Id., B/8.6.
[62] Id., B/8.7.

SHIP AND SHIP OPERATOR SECURITY

.14 Does the Company Security Officer ensure ship security assessments consider the persons, activities, services, and operations to be protected, including:[63]
  .1 The ship's personnel?
  .2 Passengers, visitors, vendors, repair technicians, port facility personnel, etc.?
  .3 The capacity to maintain safe navigation and emergency response?
  .4 The cargo, particularly dangerous goods or hazardous substances?
  .5 The ship's stores?
  .6 The ship's security communication equipment and systems, if any?
  .7 The ship's security surveillance equipment and systems, if any?
.15 Does the Company Security Officer ensure the ship security assessments considers all possible threats, including:[64]
  .1 Damage to, or destruction of, the ship or of a port facility (e.g. by explosive devices, arson or sabotage)?
  .2 Ship hijacking or kidnapping?
  .3 Tampering with cargo, essential ship equipment or systems or ship's stores?
  .4 Unauthorized access or use including presence of stowaways?
  .5 Smuggling weapons or equipment, including weapon of mass destruction?
  .6 Use of the ship to facilitate a security incident?
  .7 Use of the ship itself as a weapon?
  .8 Attacks from the sea while in port, at berth or at anchor?
  .9 Attacks at sea?
.16 Does the Company Security Officer ensure that ship security assessments take into account all possible vulnerabilities, including:[65]
  .1 Conflicts between safety and security measures?
  .2 Conflicts between shipboard duties and security assignments?
  .3 Watchkeeping duties and crew fatigue, alertness and performance?
  .4 Security training deficiencies?
  .5 Security equipment and systems, including communication systems?
.17 Do the Company Security Officer and the Ship Security Officer have regard for the effect of security measures on ship's personnel?[66]
.18 Does the Company Security Officer ensure that upon completion of the Ship Security Assessment, a summary report is prepared? Is the report protected from unauthorized access or disclosure?[67]
.19 Does the Company Security Officer review and accept the report of the Ship Security Assessment when the Ship Security Assessment has not been carried out by the Company?[68]

14.2.1.8 Ship Security Plan

Ship Security Plan[69]

---

[63] Id., B/8.8.
[64] Id., B/8.9.
[65] Id., B/8.10.
[66] Id., B/8.11.
[67] Id., B/8.12.
[68] Id., B/8.13.
[69] Id., A/9.1, A/9.4, A/9.4.1, A/9.6 and A/9.7.

Part A   Ship Security Plan

.1 Does the Company Security Officer ensure that a SSP is carried on board every ship for which he/she is the Company Security Officer?[70]
.2 Does the Ship Security Plan make provisions for the three security levels as defined in this Part of the Code?[71]
.3 Does the Company Security Officer ensure that the Ship Security Plan is written in the working language or languages of the ship?[72]
.4 Is an English, French or Spanish language version available?[73]
.5 Does the Ship Security Plan address the following:[74]
    .1 Measures designed to prevent weapons, dangerous substances and devices intended for use against persons, ships or ports and the carriage of which is not authorized from being taken on board the ship?
    .2 Identification of the restricted areas and measure for the prevention of unauthorized access to them?
    .3 Measures for the prevention of unauthorized access to the ship?
    .4 Procedures for responding to security threats or breaches of security, including provisions for maintaining critical operations of the ship or ship/port interface?
    .5 Procedures for responding to any security instructions Contracting Governments may give at security level 3?
    .6 Procedures for evacuation in case of security threats or breaches of security?
    .7 Duties of shipboard personnel assigned security responsibilities and of other shipboard personnel on security aspects?
    .8 Procedures for auditing the security activities?
    .9 Procedures for training, drills and exercises associated with the plan?
    .10 Procedures for interfacing with port facility security activities?
    .11 Procedures for the periodical review of the plan and for updating?
    .12 Procedures for reporting security incidents?
    .13 Identification of the ship security officer?
    .14 Identification of the Company Security Officer, including 24-hour contact details?
    .15 Procedures to ensure the inspection, testing, calibration, and maintenance of any security equipment provided on board?
    .16 Frequency for testing or calibration of any security equipment provided on board?
    .17 Identification of the locations where the ship security alert system activation points are provided?
    .18 Procedures, instructions and guidance on the use of the ship security alert system including the testing, activation, deactivation and resetting and to limit false alerts?

---

[70] Id., A/9.1.
[71] Id.
[72] Id., A/9.4.
[73] Id.
[74] Id.

SHIP AND SHIP OPERATOR SECURITY

.6 Has the Company ensured that the personnel conducting internal audits of the security activities specified in the Ship Security Plan, or evaluating its implementation, are independent of the activities being audited unless this is impracticable due to the size and the nature of the Company or of the ship?[75]

.7 Where the Ship Security Plan is kept in electronic format, has the Company established procedures aimed at preventing the unauthorized deletion, destruction or amendment or the Ship Security Plan?[76]

.8 Has the Company established procedures to ensure the Ship Security Plan is protected from unauthorized access or disclosure?[77]

Part B   Content of the Ship Security Plan

Content of Ship Security Plan[78]

.9 Has the Company Security Officer taken into account whether the Ship Security Plan is relevant for the ship it covers?[79]

.10 Has the Company Security Officer complied with advice on the preparation and content of Ship Security Plans issued by the ship's Administration?[80]

.11 Has the Company Security Officer taken into account that the Ship Security Plan details those items listed in ISPS Code B/9.2.1 to 9.2.7?

.12 Does the Company Security Officer consider that all Ship Security Plans have been prepared having undergone a thorough assessment of all the issues relating to the security of the ship, including in particular a thorough appreciation of the physical and operational characteristics?[81]

.13 Has the Company Security Officer developed the following procedures:[82]
   .1 To assess the continuing effectiveness of the Ship Security Plan?
   .2 To prepare amendments of the plan subsequent to its approval?

14.2.1.9   Records

Records[83]

Part A   Records

.1 Does the Company Security Officer ensure that records of the following activities addressed in the Ship Security Plan are kept on board for at least the minimum period specified by the Administration, bearing in mind the provisions of SOLAS regulation XI-2/9.2.3?[84]

---

[75] Id., A/9.4.1.
[76] Id., A/9.6.
[77] Id., A/9.7.
[78] Id., B/9.1 to B/9.5.
[79] Id., B/9.1.
[80] Id.
[81] Id., B/9.3.
[82] Id., B/9.5.
[83] Id., A/10.1 to A/10.4.
[84] Id., A/10.1.

.1 training, drills and exercises?;
.2 security threats and security incidents?;
.3 breaches of security?;
.4 changes in security level?;
.5 communications relating to the direct security of the ship such as specific threats to the ship or to port facilities the ship?;
.6 internal audits and reviews of security activities?;
.7 periodic review of the ship security assessment?;
.8 periodic review of the Ship Security Plan?;
.9 implementation of any amendments to the plan?; and
.10 maintenance, calibration and testing of any security equipment provided on board including testing of the ship security alert system?

.2 Does the Company Security Officer ensure that the records are kept in the working language or languages of the ship?[85]

.3 Records in English, French or Spanish also available?[86]

.4 Where the records are kept in electronic format, has the Company established procedures aimed at preventing their unauthorized deletion, destruction or amendment?[87]

14.2.1.10 Company Security Officer

Company security officer[88]

Part A   Company Security Officer

.1 Has the Company designated one or more Company Security Officer?[89]
.2 Where more than one Company Security Officer has been appointed, has it clearly been identified which ships each Company Security Officer is responsible for?[90]
.3 Do the Company Security Officer's duties and responsibilities include at least the following:[91]
　　.1 Advising the level of threats likely to be encountered by the ship, using appropriate security assessments and other relevant information?
　　.2 Ensuring that ship security assessments are carried out?
　　.3 Ensuring the development, the submission for approval, and thereafter the implementation and maintenance of the ship security plan?
　　.4 Ensuring that the ship security plan is modified, as appropriate, to correct deficiencies and satisfy the security requirements of the individual ship?
　　.5 Arranging for internal audits and reviews of security activities?
　　.6 Arranging for the initial and subsequent verifications of the ship by the Administration or the recognized security organization?

---

[85] Id., A/10.2.
[86] Id.
[87] Id., A/10.3.
[88] Id., A/11.1 to A/11.2, A/12.2.5.
[89] Id., A/11.1 and B/1.9.
[90] Id., A/11.1.
[91] Id., A/11.2.

.7 Ensuring that deficiencies identified in internal audits, periodic reviews, security inspections and verifications are addressed?
.8 Enhancing security awareness and vigilance?
.9 Ensuring adequate training for ship security personnel?
.10 Ensuring effective communication and co-operation between the Ship Security Officer and the relevant port security officers?
.11 Ensuring consistency between security requirements and safety requirements?
.12 Ensuring that, if sister-ship or fleet security plans are used, the plan for each ship reflects the ship-specific information accurately?
.4 Has the Company Security Officer implemented a mechanism for receiving from the Ship Security Officer, reports of any deficiencies and non-conformities identified during internal audits, periodic reviews, security inspections and verifications of compliance, and any corrective actions taken?[92]

14.2.1.11 Training, Drills, and Exercises on Ship Security

Training, Drills, and Exercises on Ship Security[93]

.1 Have the Company Security Officer and appropriate shore-based personnel received training, taking into account the guidance given in Part B of ISPS Code?[94]

Part A   Training, Drills, and Exercises

.2 Does the Company Security Officer ensure that drills are carried out at appropriate intervals, taking into account the ship type, ship personnel changes, port facilities to be visited and other relevant circumstances, and further taking into account the guidance in Part B of ISPS Code?[95]
.3 Does the Company Security Officer ensure the effective coordination and implementation of ship security plans by participating in exercises at appropriate intervals, taking into account the guidance given in Part B of ISPS Code?[96]

Part B   Training, Drills, and Exercises

Training, drills, and exercises[97]

.4 Have the Company Security Officer [and appropriate shore-based Company personnel] received training, in some or all of the following, as appropriate:[98]
.1 Security administrations?
.2 Relevant international conventions, codes and recommendations?
.3 Relevant Government legislation and regulations?
.4 Responsibilities and functions of other security organizations?
.5 Methodology of ship security assessment?

---

[92] Id., A/12.2.5.
[93] Id., A/13.1 to A/13.5.
[94] Id., A/13.1.
[95] Id., A/13.4.
[96] Id., A/13.5.
[97] Id., B/13.1 to B/13.4, B/13.6, and B/13.7.
[98] Id., B/13.1.

.6 Methods of ship security surveys and inspections?
.7 Ship and port operations and conditions?
.8 Ship and port facility security measures?
.9 Emergency preparedness and response and contingency planning?
.10 Instruction techniques for security training and education, including security measures and procedures?
.11 Handling sensitive security-related information?
.12 Knowledge of current security threats and patterns?
.13 Detection of weapons, dangerous substances and devices?
.14 Recognition of behavioral patterns of persons who are likely to threaten security?
.15 Techniques used to circumvent security measures?
.16 Security equipment and systems and their operational limitations?
.17 Methods of conducting audits, inspection, control and monitoring?
.18 Methods of physical searches and non-intrusive inspections?
.19 Security drills and exercises, including drills and exercises with port facilities?
.20 Assessment of security drills and exercises?

.5 Does the Company Security Officer ensure that drills are conducted at least once every three months with additional drills as recommended?[99]
.6 Does the Company Security Officer ensure that exercises are conducted at least once each calendar year with no more than 18 months between them?[100]
.7 Are these exercises:[101]
    .1 Full-scale or live?
    .2 tabletop simulation or seminar?
    .3 combined with other exercises held, such as search and rescue or emergency response exercises?
    .4 participated in by the Company Security Officer?
.8 Has the Company participated in exercises with another Contracting Government?[102]

14.2.1.12 Information and Cooperation (Best Practice)

.1 Is there a regular information exchange between the Company Security Officer and the Administration(s) responsible on best practices?

14.3 SHIP SECURITY

14.3.1 *Ship Security Levels*

Security levels for ships and port facilities are set at security level 1, 2, or 3. Governments, often through Flag State Administrations, set security levels, and they are responsible for disseminating changes to shipping companies. Ships bound for a port ascertain through contact with the port authority the security level in

---

[99] Id., B/13.6.
[100] Id., B/13.7.
[101] Id., B/13.7.
[102] Id., B/13.8.

force at the port or port facility. If a ship is operating at a higher security level than that covering the port or port facility, then it should convey that fact to the security officer of the port or port facility security officer prior to entry. A ship may not operate at a lower security level than the one in force at the port or port facility that it is visiting. (A ship may, however, operate at a higher security level than the port it is visiting).

Security plans should specify the security measures in place at each security level, including setting forth the appropriate measures to be implemented in the event that the ship is at a higher security level than the port that it is seeking to enter.

14.3.2 Declarations of Security

Flag State Administrations set standards for how ships are required to complete and retain a Declaration of Security (DOS). The DOS should include information on the name, port of registry and IMO number of both ships, as well as specify the types of activity it covers, the duration of the agreement, and the security level in effect for the ships. If the two vessels are at different security levels, the activity should take place at the higher security level.

The ship master or Ship Security Officer (acting on behalf of the master) normally completes the DOS, which is then signed and dated by both the master or Ship Security Officer (SSO), and the Designated Authority (DA) or Port Facility Security Officer (PFSO), if the interface is with a port facility, or the SSO, if the agreement is with another ship.

The DOS normally enters into force only after it has been signed by both parties. If a ship initiates a DOS, the port facility is required to acknowledge the request, but there is no requirement for a port facility to comply with the request. On the other hand, if a port facility initiates a DOS, the request must be acknowledged by the ship's master or SSO, and the ship may be required to comply as a condition of entry into or interface with the port.

The Ship Security Plan (SSP) should detail the security measures and procedures implemented in response to a request for a DOS or initiating a DOS. For a ship/port interface or a ship/ship interface, measures may include:

   a. ensure the performance of all security duties;
   b. monitor restricted areas to ensure that only authorized personnel have access;
   c. control access to the port facility and/or ship(s);
   d. monitor the port facility and/or ship(s), including berthing areas and areas surrounding the ship;
   e. monitor the port facility and/or ship(s), including berthing areas and areas surrounding the facility and/or ship(s);
   f. handle cargo and unaccompanied baggage;
   g. monitor the delivery of ship's stores;
   h. control the embarkation of persons and their effects;
   i. ensure that security communication is readily available between the ship(s) or between the ship and port facility.

If a Ship Security Officer (SSO) on a SOLAS ship is unable to contact a person ashore with responsibility for shore-side security, including completion of a DOS, the SSO may prepare the ship's DOS, setting forth the security measures and procedures to be applied during the ship/port interface. A SOLAS ship that intends to undertake ship-to-ship interface with a non-SOLAS ship normally is required to complete a DOS with the non-SOLAS ship. The SSO should notify the Designated Authority if a port facility refuses a request for a DOS or requests a DOS at security level 3. Normally, the DOS is kept on file for three years.

14.3.3 Model Declaration of Security for a Ship-to-Ship Interface

The following is a model declaration of Security for a Ship-to-Ship interface, derived from the Maritime Security Measures.[103]

This Declaration of Security is valid from _____ until _____, for the following activities: _____ (list the activities with relevant details) under the following Security levels:

Security level(s) for Ship A:
Security level(s) for Ship B:

Ship A	Ship B
Name	Name
Port of Registry	Port of Registry
IMO Number	IMO Number

Both ships agree to the following security measures and responsibilities to ensure compliance with the relevant requirements of their national maritime security legislation.[104]

The initials of each Ship Security Officer or Master in these columns indicates that the activity will be done, in accordance with their approved ship security plan, by Ship A and/or Ship B

---

[103] IMO Doc. MSC 89/INF.13, Measures to Enhance Maritime Security, Maritime Security Manual—Guidance for Port Facilities, Ports and Ships, Mar. 5, 2011, Appendix 4.1, *reproduced in* GUIDE TO MARITIME SECURITY AND THE ISPS CODE, Appendix 4.1.

[104] If no national legislation exists, then compliance with Chapter 5, Part A of the ISPS Code is required.

Activity	Ship A	Ship B
Ensuring the performance of all security duties		
Monitoring restricted areas to ensure that only authorized personnel have access		
Controlling access to ship A		
Controlling access to ship B		
Monitoring of ship A, including areas surrounding the ship		
Monitoring of ship B, including areas surrounding the ship		
Handling of cargo		
Delivery of ship's stores		
Handling unaccompanied baggage		
Control of embarkation of persons and their effects		
Ensuring that security communication is readily available between the ships		

The signatories certify that security measures for both ships meet the relevant provisions of their national maritime security legislation[105] and conform to their approved ship security plan or arrangements agreed to (as set out in the attached annex).

Date _____ Location _____

Signed for and on behalf of

Ship A: (Signature of Master or Ship Security Officer)
Name:
Title:
Contact Details:

---

[105] If no national legislation exists, then compliance with Chapter 5, Part A of the ISPS Code is required.

Ship B: (Signature of Master or Ship Security Officer)
Name:
Title:
Contact Details:

Telephone numbers, radio channels or frequencies	Ship A	Ship B
Master		
Ship Security Officer		
Company		
Company Security Officer		

14.3.4 *Ship Security Personnel*

Company Security Officers (CSOs) and Ship Security Officers (SSOs) are responsible for shipboard security. The shipping company is responsible for appointment of CSOs and SSOs. At times, however, all shipboard personnel, including the master and crew, may share some of the responsibility for implementing measures to enhance ship security.[106] Under the STCW Code, the Flag State Administration is responsible for properly issued certificates of proficiency to the SSOs and shipboard personnel, and such certificates should be available for inspection by officers undertaking control and compliance measures when the ship is in a foreign port.[107]

14.3.4.1 Company Security Officers

At the shipping company level, ship security falls within the authority of the Company Security Officer (CSO).[108] Each company is required to appoint one CSO. The Company Security Officer works in conjunction with their Ship Security Officers (SSOs) and Port Facility Security Officers (PFSOs) at the port facilities used by their ships. The CSOs are responsible for ensuring that each ship within the company meets the requirements of the Maritime Security Measures (MSM), and serve as the link between the ship and the Flag State Administration.[109]

---

[106] Shipboard personnel are defined as "masters and members of the crew or other persons employed or engaged in any capacity on board a ship in the business of that ship, including high-speed craft, special purpose ships and mobile offshore drilling units not on location." MSM, 1.8.1.uu.
[107] Id., 4.5.4.
[108] Id., 4.5.5.
[109] Id., 4.5.6.

Shipping companies must ensure the competency of the CSO.[110] The IMO has prepared a Competency Matrix for Company Security Officers.[111] Specific CSO responsibilities include identifying possible security threats, taking appropriate action to address security threats, and, maintaining effective security measures and procedures for ships.[112] The MSM sets forth a long list of duties for the CSO that includes:

a. Assess the level of likely threats to the ship;
b. Ensure that ship security assessments are conducted;
c. Ensure the development, approval, and implementation of Ship Security Plans, ASAs, and ESAs;
d. Modify and updating plans to correct deficiencies;
e. Arrange internal audits and reviews of security activities;
f. Arrange initial and subsequent verifications of ships by the flag state administration or RSOs acting on its behalf;
g. Address deficiencies and non-conformities identified during internal audits, periodic reviews, security inspections and verifications of compliance;
h. Ensure training and vigilance for the crew and those personnel responsible for ship security;
i. Ensure effective cooperation between Ship Security Officers and relevant PFSOs; and
j. Ensure consistency between security requirements and safety requirements.[113]

14.3.4.2 Ship Security Officers

Every SOLAS ship has a Ship Security Officer (SSO). The SSO is responsible for ship security, but he is subordinate to the master of the ship and reports to the CSO ashore.[114] The IMO has prepared a Competency Matrix for Ship Security Officers.[115] The SSO has authority over shipboard personnel with designated security responsibilities, and the SSO maintains contact with PSOs and PFSOs and port facilities that are used by the ship.[116]

The Ship Security Officer (SSO) ensures that the ship and its shipboard personnel operate in accordance with the approved Ship Security Plan (SSP), maintaining vessel security at all times. The SSO's duties include undertaking security inspections of the ship, developing, supervising, and implementing the SSP, taking care of ship board security equipment, and enhancing security awareness and

---

[110] IMO Doc. MSC/Circ.1154, Guidelines on Training and Certification for Company Security Officers, May 23, 2005, Annex, and reflected in MSM, Appendix 4.2, Competency Matrix for Company Security Officers.
[111] IMO Doc. MSC/Circ.1154, Guidelines on Training and Certification for Company Security Officers, May 23, 2005.
[112] MSM, 4.5.7.
[113] Id., 4.5.9.
[114] Id., 4.5.14.
[115] STCW Code A-VI/5, as amended.
[116] MSM, 4.5.15.

vigilance on-board the ship, including security-related training.[117] The SSO also reports security incidents.

Ship Security Officers (SSOs) are required to hold a certificate of proficiency of seagoing service of not less than 12 months (or otherwise appropriate seagoing service and knowledge of ship operations) and that confirms competency of relevant provisions of the STCW Code, including the 2006 amendments that entered into force in 2008, titled regulation VI/5 on "Mandatory minimum requirements for the issue of certificates of proficiency for ship security officers."[118] Part A of the STCW Code contains Knowledge, Understanding and Proficiency (KUP) requirements for certification of SSOs.[119]

The master is always considered to have overall security responsibility. Other shipboard personnel may be designated security duties, such as deck and gangway watch. If so designated, ship personnel, including privately contracted armed security personnel (PCASP), are required to earn a certificate of proficiency attesting to achievement of minimum standards of competency.[120] The shipboard personnel can acquire certification of their security duties through training from the SSO, including their collateral security positions in the Ship Security Plan. All shipboard personnel, regardless of specific duties, are required to receive approved security-related training that makes them competent to a report security incidents, such as a piracy attack, understand procedures to follow in the event of a security threat, and execute their role in security-related emergencies.[121] In order to clarify these responsibilities, the IMO has promulgated a Competency Matrix for Shipboard Personnel with Designated Security Duties[122] and a Competency Matrix on Security Awareness for all Shipboard Personnel.[123]

14.3.5 Ship Security Alert Systems

Generally, flag States require ships to report the presence of serious threats, such as bombings or bomb warnings, hijackings, discovery or use of illicit firearms, weapons or explosives, or unauthorized access to a restricted areas of the vessel.[124] Every SOLAS ship is required to have an operational Ship Security Alert System (SSAS) that is able to send a covert signal of distress that will not be obvious to

---

[117] Id., 4.5.17.
[118] Ship Security Officer competencies are reflected in MSM, Appendix 4.3, Competency Matrix for Ship Security Officers.
[119] Id.
[120] These obligations are set forth in the STCW and reflected in MSM, 4.5.21.
[121] MSM, 4.5.25. *See also,* Id., Appendix 4.5, Competency Matrix on Security Awareness for all Shipboard Personnel.
[122] STCW Code A-VI/6, as amended.
[123] Id.
[124] MSM, 4.8.37.

anyone on the ship who is unaware of the alert mechanism.[125] The alarm should be able to be activated from the navigation bridge and in at least one other location on the ship. The SSAS transmits a security alert to shore-based authorities designated by the Flag State Administration. The shipping company may fulfill this role, as it is best able to positively identify the ship and its location.

Flag States often designate the Company Security Officer (CSO) as the competent shore-based authority for receipt of SSAS alerts. In addition to designating CSOs as appropriate authorities, some nations operate Maritime Rescue Coordination Centers (MRCCs) that also have authority to receive SSAS alerts.[126] The shore-based authority should collect the name of ship, the IMO Ship Identification Number, the call sign of the vessel, Maritime Mobile Service Identity, and the GNSS position of the ship (at the time and date). The alert should indicate that the vessel is under imminent threat and it should not raise alarm on the ship. Separately, however the ship's master may initiate an overt alarm, such as VHF broadcast in the open, as a way to discourage would-be attackers.

The SSAS may be transmitted by radio to installations approved by the administration. Information on the SSAS, including activation points, procedures for testing, activation, deactivation and resetting the alarm, should be contained in the Ship Security Plan.

The designated competent authority should be able to alert the country's security forces responsible for protecting ships flying the flag of the state. Flag State Administrations also must be able to communicate with their nation's security forces and the competent authorities that receive SSAS alerts. Generally, however, the competent authority that receives an SSAS should not overtly acknowledge the message.

14.3.6 *Ship Security Assessments*

A Ship Security Assessment (SSA) must be conducted for each ship prior to crafting the Ship Security Plan.[127] The SSA is essentially a risk analysis of all aspects of a ship's operations in order to determine areas of greatest vulnerability.[128] The SSA must include the following elements:

---

[125] SOLAS, Chapter XI-2, regulation XI-2/5, and IMO Doc. MSC.147(77), Adoption of the Revised Performance Standards for a Ship Security Alert System, May 29, 2003, Annex, Revised Recommendation on Performance Standards for a Ship Security Alert System, at 1.1.
[126] MSM, 2.12.8.
[127] Id., 2.9.12–.2.9.14.
[128] Id., 4.3.2.

a. An on-scene security survey;[129]
b. Identification of existing security measures, procedures and operations;[130]
c. Identification of key shipboard operations and systems that must be protected;[131]
d. Identification and evaluation of important shipboard operations;[132]
e. Identification of possible threats to important shipboard operations and the likelihood of their occurrence in order to prioritize security measures; and
f. Identification of weaknesses including human factors in the infrastructure, policies and procedures.[133]

Company Security Officers (CSOs) are responsible for Ship Security Assessments (SSAs), including on-scene surveys. In this regard, Administrations set forth guidance to CSOs on the security risks facing their ships on voyages and in port. The Maritime Security Measures mandate that a current SSA should accompany, or be reflected in, Ship Security Plans before they are approved by the Flag State Administration.

The SSA is captured in a report that must be prepared after the assessment. The report summarizes how the assessment was conducted, describes each vulnerability found during the assessment, and specifies appropriate countermeasures to address each vulnerability. In order to ensure the integrity of the SSA, CSOs may distribute a limited run of numbered of copies of the SSA for initial evaluation. The SSA is updated after a significant security incident involving the ship, a change in the ship's schedule or routes, or a change in the owner or operator of the ship.[134]

14.3.7 Ship Security Plans

Each ship is required to carry a Ship Security Plan (SSP) approved by the Flag State Administration. The SSP should describe actions the crew will take in response to the threat of piracy and armed robbery at sea, maritime terrorism, or other maritime crime or violence. The SSP also should set forth measures based on three security levels designed to deter such attacks and specific steps that will be taken in reaction to an attack. If a SSP is submitted for approval, it must be accompanied by the Ship Security Assessment on which the plan or amendment was based.

Shipping companies bear responsibility for ensuring that each ship in their fleet has an SSP that clearly states the master's plenary authority over the vessel, including the authority to make decisions with respect to the safety and security of the ship, and to request assistance from the company or governments. Ship-

---

[129] Id., 4.7.5.
[130] ISPS Code A/8.4.1.
[131] Id., A/8.2.
[132] Id., A/8.4.3.
[133] Id., A/8.4.4.
[134] MSM, 4.7.12.

ping companies also have to support their Company Security Officers (CSOs), vessel masters and their Ship Security Officers (SSOs). Companies must ensure that each ship has a security assessment conducted and that documentation is retained on board the vessel.

The mandatory portion of the ISPS Code stipulates that shipping companies are required to ensure that the Ship Security Plan underscores the clear authority of the master of the vessel.[135] The master has "overriding authority and responsibility" to make decisions concerning safety and security of the ship and to request the assistance of governments.[136]

Furthermore, the company has a duty to ensure that the CSO, the master, and the SSO have the necessary support to fulfill their responsibilities under the ISPS Code.[137] Shipping companies must supply masters of ships in their fleet with information concerning appointment of crew members or other persons onboard their ship and their duties at sea, the party responsible for deciding on the employment and schedule of the ship, and identification of parties to any charter that the ship is employed under.[138] The company should keep such information current and make the information available in either English, French, or Spanish.[139] The Maritime Security Measures reflect the broad obligations for ships and companies relating to Ship Security Plans (SSPs).

SSPs include detail regarding the following issues:

a. measures designed to prevent weapons, dangerous substances and devices intended for use against persons, ships or ports from being taken on board;
b. restricted areas and access control measures;
c. measures and equipment to prevent unauthorized access to the ship while in port or at sea;
d. responses to security threats or breaches of security;
e. minimum operational and physical security measures for all security levels;
f. evacuation plan in case of security threats or breaches of security;
g. security-related duties of shipboard personnel;
h. procedures for auditing, training, drills, and exercises of the Ship Security Plan;
i. procedures for interfacing with port facilities and ships;
j. circumstances and procedures for admitting first responders and military or law enforcement boarding team on board the ship;
k. procedures and communications protocols, including 24-hour contact details for the Ship Security Officer and Company Security Officer and guidance on Ship Security Alert System usage; and
l. security-related equipment maintenance.[140]

---

[135] ISPS Code A/6.1.
[136] Id.
[137] Id., A/6.2.
[138] Id., B/6.1.
[139] Id., B/6.2–6.3 and SOLAS regulation XI-2/5.
[140] MSM, 4.8.5.

The SSP should set forth the organizational structure of the ship's security, and the vessel's relationship with the shipping company, port facilities, other ships and relevant authorities with security responsibility. The basic security measures at level 1—including operational and physical measures—should always be in place. The SSP should stipulate the circumstances that authorize movement to security level 2 or 3 (and back down). To avoid a conflict of interest, if the company is large enough, persons responsible for completing internal security audits should be different than those responsible for implementing the audits.[141]

The shipping company has an obligation to ensure that:

    a. Each ship security plan clearly states the master's overriding authority to:
       i. make decisions with respect to the safety and security of the ship;
       ii. request assistance from the company or Governments as may be necessary.
    b. Company Security Officers, ships' masters and their Ship Security Officers are given the necessary support to fulfill their duties and responsibilities.
    c. For each ship, a security assessment is conducted and its documentation retained.
    d. Masters have information on board that allows authorized government officials to establish:
       i. who is responsible for appointing crew members or other persons on-board their ship to duties on the ship;
       ii. who is responsible for deciding the employment of the ship;
       iii. who are the parties to any charter that the ship is employed under.[142]

Although shipping companies are not required to participate as members of port security committees, they often do so in order to facilitate ship-shore interface issues, such as shore leave for crew members and vessel access from the shore. The CSO is responsible for the development and revision of the SSP, which then is approved by the Flag State Administration and subsequently carried on board the ship.

Flag State Administrations should outline the parameters for preparing and submitting the SSP for approval and rules governing follow-on inspection of ships to assess compliance with approved plans. The Administration may propose, as part of the approval or renewal process, steps necessary for the modification or amendment of a SSP. Any modifications, however, should be taken in consultation with the CSO.

Administrations often issue guidance and detailed templates on the content and format of SSPs. SSPs typically include procedures for changing the ship's security level, security-related records that must be maintained on board the ship, and procedures for reporting security breaches and failures. The SSP also lays out the circumstances in which a DOS should be requested from a port facility or other ship, when the master of a vessel can decline an inspection prior to

---

[141] Id., 4.8.7.
[142] Id., 4.2.4.

the ship entering port, and appropriate responses to attempts at interdiction at sea. The SSP may provide guidance on the preservation of evidence following a security incident and the procedures for reporting security incidents to the Flag State Administration.

Generally, Administrations review SSPs once per year, taking into account drills or exercises, security breaches or actual security threat involving the ships, changes in shipping operations including the operator; completion of a SSA, and all of the likely security threats and the appropriate security measures to mitigate such threats. Specific guidance may be provided by the flag State to their CSOs concerning security for particular types of ships—cruise ships, Ro-Ro passenger or cargo ships, chemical, oil and gas tankers, container ships, and special purpose ships and mobile offshore drilling units. Typically, the annual review is sufficient, but the SSP may be reviewed more frequently in response to changes in ship operations, ownership and structure or as a consequence of failing a drill or exercise.

Administrations should notify CSOs of the type of amendments to an approved SSP that must be approved by the flag State. If the Administration permits a CSO or SSO to amend a SSP without flag State approval, the new provisions must be passed to the Administration.

Ship Security Plans (SSPs) should establish procedures for new security measures adopted based upon changes in the security level. If the flag State elects to permit the use of armed security on board ships, the Administration should ensure that security personnel are duly authorized and appropriately trained.

Finally, the SSP should specify the security records that a ship is required to keep and make available for inspection, including the Declarations of Security (DOS) with port facilities and other ships, security threats or incidents and breaches of security, issues or events that precipitate changes in the security level, communications protocols concerning threats to the ship, records of ship security training, drills and exercises, and reviews of the ship security assessments, SSPs and amendments thereto.[143] Security equipment should have appropriate records of maintenance.[144] SSPs also should establish internal audit procedures that companies and ships must follow.[145]

The SSP may be prepared by a Recognized Security Organization (RSO) on behalf of CSOs. RSOs also may review and even approve Ship Security Plans (SSPs) and their amendments, if so delegated by a Flag State Administration (and provided they were not involved in the preparation of the SSP under review or its related Ship Security Assessment).[146] Flag State Administrations may authorize

---

[143] Id., 2.9.38.
[144] Id., 2.9.41. Such equipment may include perimeter intruder detection systems (e.g., CCTV, lighting) and detection equipment (e.g., x-ray equipment, metal, explosive).
[145] Id., 2.9.39.
[146] Id., 4.8.2.

RSOs to act on their behalf to approve SSPs and to certify compliance of the commercial fleet with maritime security regulations. Shipping companies also may use RSOs to provide advice and assistance on Ship Security Assessments and SSPs, but RSOs should not approve SSPs if they were involved in conducting the underlying SSA.

The Flag State Administration may delegate responsibility for approving the SSP to the RSO so long as the RSO has not assisted in preparation of the Ship Security Plan. The SSP should provide for three security levels and corresponding security measures for each level. Flag State Administrations have responsibility for establishing the procedures for DOS that are in the Ship Security Plan.

14.3.8 Responding to Requests to Board the Ship in Port or at Sea

The Ship Security Officer (SSO) should contact the Port Facility Security Officer (PFSO) prior to arrival in port in order to coordinate shore access and on-board visit arrangements. Security is not an overriding consideration, but merely equally balanced with the needs of the ship and its crew. Ship visits by port authorities are required to "strike a balance" between the need for port security and the rights of seafarers to access the beach.[147]

Ship masters have plenary authority over their ships, and they may exercise discretion to allow foreign military and law enforcement forces to visit their ship when in international waters.[148] But even if the master consents to the visit and an inspection establishes that an offense has been committed, the flag State retains jurisdiction over the vessel. Of course, the flag State always may delegate authority or transfer jurisdiction to another State, but in such case the Flag State Administration should instruct their Company Security Officers of the actions that a master should take in response to a request to board and inspect from foreign security forces—and this contingency should be included in the Ship Security Plan.[149]

Flag State Administrations should provide guidance to CSOs on how ships flying their flag should respond to attempts to board and inspect vessels acting pursuant to UN Security Council enforcement action, multilateral agreements, such as the 2005 *Convention for the Suppression of Unlawful Acts Against the Safety of Maritime Navigation* (SUA) which entered into force in 2010, or bilateral arrangements, such as counterdrug or Proliferation Security Initiative ship boarding agreements.

Under the SUA Convention, for example, one contracting government may initiate a request to board a ship in international waters flying the flag of another contracting government if there are reasonable grounds for believing that a

---

[147] Id., 4.8.31.
[148] Id., 2.9.32.
[149] Id., 2.9.32.

terrorist-related offense has been or will be committed on board.[150] The legal procedure invokes the mechanism of prior flag State consent using the SUA Convention with jurisdiction retained by the flag State unless transferred.

During an emergency in response to an incident, only the person in charge of a team of first responders should be required to present identification prior to boarding the ship.[151] Furthermore, government officials and first responders should not be required to surrender their identification documents when boarding a ship during emergency response. Government personnel also are exempt from search by ship security personnel.[152]

Although the flag State exercises exclusive jurisdiction over the vessel, and the master of a merchant ship has plenary authority of his or her ship, SOLAS ships may be subject to specific port State control and compliance measures if they use or are bound for a foreign port. Thus, port State governments may mandate that foreign-flagged ships provide security-related information prior to entering port. Foreign-flagged ships also may be subject to inspection by port State authorities to ensure compliance with the security regulations. In fact, upon entry into a coastal State's territorial sea, the coastal State may seek to inspect the vessel, although the master has the right to refuse such an inspection. In either event, however, the port State may deny port entry or expel a ship from port. RSOs do not have authority to apply control and compliance measures on behalf of the port State government; such measures may be executed by duly authorized officers—usually through the Flag State Administration.

Ships should provide information as requested to port State authorities prior to port entry, generally between 24 and 96 hours prior to arrival. Although the IMO has suggested that port States request (and foreign-flagged ships provide) a standard data set of information about the ship prior to port entry, port States may require additional security-related information.[153]

Port State security officials are entitled to board a ship in port or intending to enter into port if they have clear grounds to believe that the ship may not be in compliance with the security regulations. The "clear grounds" evidentiary standard may be met by:

    a. evidence or reliable information that the ship has serious security deficiencies;
    b. receipt of a reliable report or complaint that the ship does not comply with the requirements of the MSM;
    c. evidence or reliable information that the ship had:
        a. a ship/port interface which did not comply (or did not have to comply) with the Maritime Security Measures and did not take either appropriate additional security measures or complete a DOS with the port facility; or

---

[150] Id., 2.9.35.
[151] Id., 4.8.26.
[152] Id., 4.8.28.
[153] Id., Appendix 4.6, Standard Data Set of Security-related Pre-Arrival Information.

b. a ship-to-ship activity with another ship which did not comply (or did not have to comply) with the Maritime Security Measures and did not take either appropriate security measures or complete a DOS with the other ship.
d. evidence that the ship holds a sequentially issued Interim International Ship Security Certificate contrary to the MSM; or
e. failure of the ship to provide requested security-related information.[154]

The ship's master or SSO should be given a report of the port State control and compliance measures, which sets forth a list of discrepancies and how the ship can rectify non-compliance.[155] While waiting for the ship to rectify the non-compliance, the port State authority may require it to proceed to a specified location within the territorial sea or internal waters of the port State. The port State also may conduct a detailed inspection of the ship, if it is within the territorial waters or internal waters.

Clear grounds that warrant a port State inspection include evidence that the ship's International Ship Security Certificate is not valid, evidence that the ship's crew are not familiar with essential shipboard security procedures, or evidence or observation that key members of the ship's crew are unable to communicate with crew members.[156] Denial of port entry or expulsion from port has major ramifications for international relations between the flag State and the port State. Denial of port entry or expulsion should be imposed only if a duly authorized port State officer believes that the ship poses an immediate security threat and that there is no other appropriate means of removing the threat.[157]

14.3.9 Vessel Pre-arrival Information

Suggested vessel pre-arrival information to convey to the port State is based on SOLAS and other authorities[158] and is provided in the Appendix to the Annex of IMO Maritime Safety Committee Circular MSC.1/Circ.1305, released on June 9, 2009.[159]

14.3.9.1 Ship and Contact Details

1.1 IMO Number:
1.2 Name of ship:
1.3 Port of registry:
1.4 Flag State:
1.5 Type of ship:

---

[154] Id., 2.11.10.
[155] Id., Appendix 2.14, Report of the Imposition of a Control and Compliance Measure.
[156] Id., 2.11.19.
[157] Id., 2.11.32.
[158] SOLAS regulation XI-2/9, and ISPS Code B/4.37 and B/4/40.
[159] IMO Doc. MSC.1/Circ.1305, Revised Guidance to Masters, Companies and Duly Authorized Officers on the Requirements Relating to the Submission of Security-related Information Prior to the Entry of a Ship into Port, June 9, 2009.

1.6 Call Sign:
1.7 Inmarsat call numbers:
1.8 Gross Tonnage:
1.9 Name of Company:
1.10 IMO Company identification number:
1.11 Name and 24–hour contact details of the Company Security Officer:

14.3.9.2 Port and Port Facility Information

2.1 Port of arrival and port facility where the ship is to berth:
2.2 Expected date and time of arrival of the ship in port:
2.3 Primary purpose of port call:

14.3.9.3 Information Required by SOLAS Regulation XI-2/9.2.1

3.1 The ship is provided with a valid:
  − International Ship Security Certificate Yes No
  − Interim International Ship Security Certificate Yes No
3.2 The certificate indicated in 3.1 has been issued by [enter Contracting Government or the Recognized Security Organization] and which expires on __[date]__.
3.3 If the ship is not provided with a valid International Ship Security Certificate or a valid Interim International Ship Security Certificate, explain why
3.4 Does the ship have an approved ship security plan on board? Yes No
3.5 Current security level:
3.6 Location of the ship at the time the report is made:
3.7 List the last ten ports of call, in chronological order with the most recent call first, at port facilities at which the ship conducted ship/port interface together with the security level at which the ship operated:

Table 14.1. Vessel Pre-Arrival Template for Last Ten Ports of Call

Level Number	Date	From/To	Port/Port Facility/ Country	UN/LOCODE[160]	Security level
10					
9					
8					
7					
6					
5					
4					
3					
2					
1					

---

[160] UN/LOCODE is the United Nations Code for Trade and Transport Locations. The 2011 version of UN/LOCODE contains codes for approximately 82,000 locations worldwide. TRADE DIVISION, UNITED NATIONS ECONOMIC COMMISSION FOR EUROPE, UN/LOCODE (CODE FOR TRADE AND TRANSPORT LOCATIONS), Aug. 8, 2011, updated Sept. 22, 2001.

3.8 Did the ship, during the period specified in 3.7, take any special or additional security measures, beyond those specified in the approved ship security plan?
Yes No

3.9 If the answer to 3.8 is Yes, for each of such occasions please indicate the special or additional security measures which were taken by the ship:
No. From To Special or additional security measures

3.10 List the ship-to-ship activities, in chronological order with the most recent ship-to-ship activity first, which have been carried out during the period specified in 3.7:
Not applicable
No. From To Location or Latitude and Longitude Ship-to-ship activity

3.11 Have the ship security procedures, specified in the approved ship security plan, been maintained during each of the ship-to-ship activities specified in 3.10?
Yes No

3.12 If the answer to 3.11 is No, identify the ship-to-ship activities for which the ship security procedures were not maintained and indicate, for each, the security measures which were applied in lieu:
No.
From
To
  Security measures applied
  Ship-to-ship activity

3.13 Provide a general description of cargo aboard the ship:

3.14 Is the ship carrying any dangerous substances (i.e. those covered by the International Maritime Dangerous Goods Code) as cargo?
Yes No

3.15 If the answer to 3.14 is Yes, provide details or attach a copy of the Dangerous Goods Manifest[161]

3.16 A copy of the ship's Crew List is attached[162]

3.17 A copy of the ship's Passenger List is attached[163]

14.3.9.4 Other Security-related Information

4.1 Is there any security-related matter you wish to report? Yes No

4.2 If the answer to 4.1 is Yes, provide details (e.g. carriage of stowaways or persons rescued at sea)

14.3.9.5 Agent of the Ship at the Intended Port of Arrival

5.1 Name and contact details (telephone number) of the agent of the ship at the intended port of arrival:

---

[161] INT'L MARITIME ORG. FACILITATION COMMITTEE (FAL) Form 7 (IMO Dangerous Goods Manifest). IMO FAL Form 7 is As required by SOLAS 74, chapter VII, regulations 4.5 and 7–2.2, MARPOL 73/78, Annex III, regulation 4.3 and chapter 5.4, paragraph 5.4.3.1 of the IMDG Code).

[162] INT'L MARITIME ORG. FACILITATION COMMITTEE (FAL) Form 5 (IMO Crew List).

[163] INT'L MARITIME ORG. FACILITATION COMMITTEE (FAL) Form 6 (IMO Passenger List).

14.3.9.6 Identification of the Person Providing the Information

6.1 Name:
6.2 Title or position (Master, Ship Security Officer, Company Security Officer or ship's Agent at intended port of arrival):
6.3 Signature:_____.
Date or report:_____.

14.3.10 *The International Ship Security Certificate*

Ships must carry either the International Ship Security Certificate (ISSC) or, in limited circumstances, the Interim ISSC, both of which are issued by their Flag State Administration.[164] For their part, Administrations should inspect ships entitled to fly their flag prior to the issuance or renewal of an ISSC.[165]

A ISSC must be issued by the Administration for a specific period of time not to exceed five years, with one exception. In cases in which a renewal verification is completed within three months of the expiration date of the existing ISSC, the new ISSC is valid from the date of completion of the renewal of verification to a date not exceeding five years from the expiry date of the existing ISSC.[166]

The ISSC should be issued only upon satisfaction by the Administration based upon objective evidence that the ship is compliant with the approved SSP. A certificate should not be issued even in cases in which the ship has only minor deviations from the SSP—and even if the ability of the ship to operate at security levels 1 to 3 is not compromised.[167]

A Certificate can be issued or endorsed by the Flag State Administration, an RSO that is authorized to act on behalf of the Administration, or another Administration acting on behalf of the Administration of the flag State. Ships subject to SOLAS may be checked to confirm compliance with the IMO's MSM. Verifications occur before a ship is put into service and before the ISSC is issued, at least once between the second and third anniversary of the issuance of the Certificate, and before the ISSC is renewed. Verification ensures the ship's security systems and any security equipment are operational. An intermediate verification is conducted in between initial verification and before renewal verification if the ISSC is valid for a period of five years.

To assist shipping companies, Administrations and their authorized RSOs have sought to link the timing of verifications required under the Maritime Security Measures with other verifications or inspections including, particularly, those

---

[164] A checklist for issuance of the ISSC is contained in MSM, Appendix 2.8, Sample of a Ship Security Inspection Check List.
[165] MSM, 2.10.2. The Maritime Security Measures contain a model ISSC at Appendix 2.6, Form of the International Ship Security Certificate.
[166] MSM, 2.10.4.
[167] Id., 2.10.6.

required under the ISM Code. Combining inspections in this way can significantly benefit the shipping industry. However, in ports where ISM auditors are not always available, this combined approach may not be practicable and could unduly delay shipping schedules.

SOLAS ships must carry the International Ship Security Certificate (or, in limited circumstances, the Interim ISSC). Prior to the Administration issuing an ISSC, the shipping company is required to verify compliance of the ship with the MSM. If compliance cannot be verified by the shipping company, then it must report the verification failure to the Administration.[168]

14.3.11 Checklist for Flag State Administrations

This questionnaire provides a framework for Flag State Administrations to implement the Maritime Security Measures, with the relevant sections of SOLAS regulations and the ISPS Code.[169]

1. What is the national legislative basis for the implementation of the ISPS Code?[170]
2. What guidance to industry was released to implement the ISPS Code?[171]
3. What are the means of communication developed by the Administration with (a) ships, and (b) companies, regarding ISPS Code implementation?[172]
4. What processes are in place to document verification and certification of initial and subsequent compliance with the ISPS Code?[173]
5. Has the Contracting Government nominated a point of contact for ships to request assistance or report security concerns? If yes, provide the name and contact details.[174]
6. Have officers been duly authorized to exercise control and compliance measures on security grounds and has guidance been issued to them?[175]
7. Has guidance been issued to companies and ships on the provision of information to other Contracting Governments when applying control and compliance measures, including the records to be retained by the ship in respect of the last ten calls at port facilities?[176]

---

[168] MSM, 4.9.2.
[169] IMO Doc. MSC.1/Circ.1193, Guidance on Voluntary Self-Assessments by Administrations and for Ship Security, May 30, 2006.
[170] SOLAS regulation XI-2/2 and XI-2/4.
[171] Id., XI-2/2, XI-2/4, XI-2/5 and XI-2/6.
[172] Id., XI-2/3 and XI-2/4.
[173] Id., XI-2/4.2.
[174] Id., XI-2/7.2.
[175] Id., XI-2/9.
[176] Id.

8. Has the Contracting Government concluded in writing bilateral or multilateral agreements with other Contracting Governments on alternative security agreements?[177]
9. Has the Administration allowed a ship or group of ships to implement equivalent security arrangements?[178]
10. Who has the responsibility for notifying and updating the IMO with information in accordance with SOLAS regulation XI-2/13?[179]

Ship Security Assessment (SSA)

11. Who conducts Ship Security Assessments?[180]
12. Has national guidance been developed to assist with the completion of the on-scene security survey?[181]

Ship Security Plans (SSPs)

13. Who approves Ship Security Plans?[182]
14. How are Company and Ship Security Officers designated?[183]
15. What are the minimum training requirements that have been set by the Administration for Company Security Officers and Ship Security Officers?[184]
16. Has guidance been issued on the development and approval of Ship Security Plans?[185]
17. Are procedures in place to protect Ship Security Plans from unauthorized access?[186]
18. What procedures are in place for approval and subsequent amendments of the Ship Security Plans?[187]
19. Do Ship Security Plans contain a clear statement emphasizing the master's authority?[188]
20. Is the original or a translation of the Ship Security Plan available in English, French or Spanish?[189]

---

[177] Id., XI-2/11.1.
[178] Id., XI-2/12.1.
[179] Id., XI-2/13.
[180] ISPS Code A/8.2 and 8.3.
[181] Id., A/8.4.
[182] Id., A/9.1 and 9.2.
[183] Id., A/11.1 and A/12.1.
[184] Id., A/13.1 and A/13.2.
[185] Id., A/9.2 and 9.4.
[186] Id., A/9.7.
[187] Id., A/9.5 and 9.5.1.
[188] Id., A/6.1.
[189] Id., A/9.4.

21. Who verifies Ship Security Plans?[190]
22. Has the Administration specified the periods when renewal, intermediate and additional verifications shall be carried out?[191]
23. Who issues the International Ship Security Certificate (ISSC)?[192]
24. Has the Administration specified the period of validity of International Ship Security Certificates?[193]
25. Does the Administration have procedures in place for the issue of Interim International Ship Security Certificates?[194]
26. Has the Administration specified the minimum period for which records of activities addressed in the Ship Security Plan shall be kept on board?[195]

Security Levels

27. Who is the authority responsible for setting the security level for ships? [196]
28. What are the procedures for communicating security levels to ships by the responsible authority?[197]
29. Have procedures been notified for a ship to comply with the security level set by the Contracting Government for a port facility whose security level is higher than set for the ship by the Administration?[198]
30. Are procedures in place to provide advice to ships in cases where a risk of attack has been identified?[199]

Declaration of Security

31. What procedures are used to determine when a Declaration of Security is required?[200]
32. What is the minimum time frame that a Declaration of Security is required to be retained?[201]

---

[190] Id., A/19.1.2.
[191] Id., A/19.1.1.
[192] Id., A/19.2.2.
[193] Id., A/19.3.1.
[194] Id., A/19.
[195] Id., A/10.1.
[196] SOLAS regulationXI-2/3.1.
[197] Id., XI-2/3.1.
[198] Id., XI-2/4.3 and XI-2/4.4.
[199] Id., XI-2/7.3.
[200] ISPS Code A/5.1.
[201] Id., A/5.7.

Delegation of Tasks and Duties

33. What tasks and duties, if any, have the Administration delegated to Recognized Security Organizations (RSOs)?[202]
34. To whom have these tasks and duties been delegated? Based on what criteria and under what conditions has the status of RSO been granted by the Administration to those organizations? What oversight procedures are in place?[203]
35. What procedures are in place to ensure that the RSO undertaking the review and approval process for an Ship Security Plan was not involved in the preparation of the Ship Security Assessment or Ship Security Plan?[204]

14.4 Checklist for Ship Security Personnel

This checklist for Ship Security Personnel may be used by ship security personnel to examine the status of implementation of the Special Measures.[205] The heading of each section are derived from the ISPS Code.[206] These provisions apply to the entire ships' company, and in particular, to Ship Security Officers and Company Security Officers.

14.4.1 *Basic Information for Ship Security Personnel*

Completion of the following section on basic information is recommended before using the checklist. It can be used to establish an overview of the ship's operations.

14.4.1.1 Company and Ship Overview

   a. Name of Administration
   b. Name of company
   c. Name of ship
   d. IMO Ship identification number
   e. Name of Company Security Officer
   f. Name of Ship Security Officer
   g. Number of ships operated by the company
   h. Number of ships for which the Company Security Officer is responsible

---

[202] Id., A/4.3.
[203] SOLAS regulation XI-2/13.2.
[204] ISPS Code, A/9.2.1.
[205] IMO Doc. MSC.1/Circ.1193, Guidance on Voluntary Self-assessment by Administrations and for Ship Security, May 30, 2006.
[206] ISPS Code, A/7.2.

14.4.1.2 Total Manning of the Ship and Crew with Security Duties on Board

a. Total number of crew members
b. Number of crew with security duties

14.4.1.3 Ship Security Information in the Last 12 Months

a. Number of crew members assigned on first time to the ship
b. Number of different Ship Security Officers
c. Number of changes in the security level
d. Number of security incidents
e. Number of breaches of security

14.4.1.4 Security Agreements and Arrangements

a. Is the ship operating between port facilities covered by an alternative security agreement?
b. Has the ship implemented any equivalent security arrangements allowed by the Maritime Administration?
c. Is the ship operating under any temporary security measures? Have these been approved or authorized by the Maritime Administration?

14.4.2 Checklist

The checklist is comprised of nine items. Each of the nine items (except for number seven) is divided into two parts, Part A and Part B. Part A reflects mandatory provisions of the ISPS Code. Part B contains the recommendatory stipulations of the ISPS Code.

14.4.2.1 Ensuring the Performance of All Ship Security Duties

Part A   Ensuring the Performance of All Ship Security Duties

.1 Does the ship's means of ensuring the performance of all security duties meet the requirements set out in the Ship Security Plan for security levels 1 and 2?[207]
.2 Has the ship established measures to prevent weapons, dangerous substances and devices intended for use against persons, ships or ports and the carriage of which is not authorized from being taken on board the ship?[208]
.3 Has the ship established procedures for responding to security threats or breaches of security, including provisions for maintaining critical operations of the ship or ship/port interface?[209]
.4 Has the ship established procedures for responding to any security instructions Contracting Governments may give at security level 3?[210]

---

[207] Id., A/7.2.1.
[208] Id., A/9.4.1.
[209] Id., A/9.4.4.
[210] Id., A/9.4.5.

.5 Has the ship established procedures for evacuation in case of security threats or breaches of security?[211]
.6 Have the duties of shipboard personnel assigned security responsibilities and other shipboard personnel on security aspects been specified?[212]
.7 Have procedures been established for auditing the security activities of the ship?[213]
.8 Has the ship established procedures for interfacing with port facility security activities?[214]
.9 Have procedures been established for the periodic review of the ship security plan and for its updating?[215]
.10 Has the ship established procedures for reporting security incidents?[216]

Part B   Organization and Performance of Ship Security Duties

.11 Has the ship implemented the organizational structure of security for the ships detailed in the Ship Security Plan?[217]
.12 Has the ship established the relationships with the Company, port facilities, other ships and relevant authorities with security responsibilities detailed in the Ship Security Plan?[218]
.13 Has the ship established the communication systems to allow effective continuous communication within the ship and between the ship and others, including port facilities, detailed in the Ship Security Plan?[219]
.14 Has the ship implemented the basic security measures for security level 1, both operational and physical, that will always been in place, detailed in the Ship Security Plan?[220]
.15 Has the ship implemented the additional security measures that will allow the ship to progress without delay to security level 2 and, when necessary, to security level 3 detailed in the Ship Security Plan?[221]
.16 Has the ship established procedures for regular review, or audit, of the Ship Security Plan and for its amendment in response to experience or changing circumstances?[222]
.17 Has the ship established reporting procedures to the appropriate Contracting Government's contact points?[223]
.18 Has the ship established the duties and responsibilities of all shipboard personnel with a security role?[224]

---

[211] Id., A/9.4.6.
[212] Id., A/9.4.7.
[213] Id., A/9.4.8.
[214] Id., A/9.4.10.
[215] Id., A/9.4.11.
[216] Id., A/9.4.12.
[217] Id., B/9.2.1.
[218] Id., B/9.2.2.
[219] Id., B/9.2.3.
[220] Id., B/9.2.4.
[221] Id., B/9.2.5.
[222] Id., B/9.2.6.
[223] Id., B/9.2.7.
[224] Id., B/9.7.1.

.19 Has the ship established the procedures or safeguards necessary to allow continuous communications to be maintained at all times?[225]

.20 Has the ship established the procedures needed to assess the continuing effectiveness of security procedures and any security and surveillance equipment and systems, including procedures for identifying and responding to equipment or systems failure or malfunction?[226]

.21 Has the ship established procedures and practices to protect security-sensitive information held in paper or electronic format?[227]

.22 Has the ship established the type and maintenance requirements of security and surveillance equipment and systems, if any?[228]

.23 Has the ship established the procedures to ensure timely submission and assessment of reports relating to possible breaches of security or security concerns?[229]

.24 Has the ship put in place procedures to establish, maintain and update an inventory of any dangerous goods or hazardous substances carried on board, including their location?[230]

14.4.2.2 Controlling Access to the Ship

Part A Access to the Ship

.1 Does the ship's means of controlling access to the ship meet the requirements set out in the Ship Security Plan for security levels 1 and 2?[231]

.2 Has the ship established measures to prevent unauthorized access?[232]

Part B Access to the Ship

.3 Has the ship established security measures covering all means of access to the ship identified in the Ship Security Assessment?[233]
   A. Access ladders
   B. Access gangways
   C. Access ramps
   D. Access doors, side scuttles, windows and ports
   E. Mooring lines and anchor chains
   F. Cranes and hoisting gear

.4 Has the ship identified appropriate locations where access restrictions or prohibitions should be applied for each of the security levels?[234]

.5 Has the ship established for each security level the means of identification required to allow access to the ship and for individuals to remain on the ship without challenge?[235]

---

[225] Id., B/9.7.2.
[226] Id., B/9.7.3.
[227] Id., B/9.7.4.
[228] Id., B/9.7.5.
[229] Id., B/9.7.6.
[230] Id., B/9.7.7.
[231] Id., A/7.2.2.
[232] Id., A/9.4.3.
[233] Id., B/9.9.
[234] Id., B/9.10.
[235] Id., B/9.11.

A. Security level 1
B. Security level 2
C. Security level 3

.6 Has the ship established the frequency of application of any access controls?[236]

Security level 1

.7 Has the ship established security measures to check the identity of all persons seeking to board the ship and confirming their reasons for doing so?[237]
.8 Has the ship established procedures to liaise with the port facility to ensure that designated secure areas are established in which inspections and searching of persons, baggage (including carry-on items), personal effects, vehicles and their contents can take place?[238]
.9 Has the ship identified access points that should be secured or attended to prevent unauthorized access?[239]
.10 Has the ship established security measures to secure, by locking or other means, access to unattended spaces, adjoining areas to which passengers and visitors have access?[240]
.11 Has the ship provided security briefings to all ship personnel on possible threats, the procedures for reporting suspicious persons, objects or activities and the need for vigilance?[241]
.12 Has the ship established the frequency of searches, including random searches, of all those seeking to board the ship?[242]

Security level 2

.13 Has the ship limited the number of access points to the ship, identifying those to be closed and the means for adequately securing them?[243]
.14 Has the ship established a restricted area on the shore side of the ship, in close cooperation with the port facility?[244]
.15 Has the ship arrangements to escort visitors on the ship?[245]
.16 Has the ship provided additional specific security briefings to all ship personnel on any identified threats, re-emphasizing the procedures for reporting suspicious persons, objects, or activities and stressing the need for increased vigilance?[246]
.17 Has the ship established procedures for carrying out a full or partial search of the ship?[247]

---

[236] Id., B/9.13.
[237] Id., B/9.14.1.
[238] Id., B/9.14.2.
[239] Id., B/9.14.6.
[240] Id., B/9.14.7.
[241] Id., B/9.14.8.
[242] Id., B/9.15.
[243] Id., B/9.16.2.
[244] Id., B/9.16.4.
[245] Id., B/9.16.6.
[246] Id., B/9.16.7.
[247] Id., B/9.16.8.

14.4.2.3 Controlling the Embarkation of Persons and Their Effects

Part A   Embarkation of Persons and Their Effects

> .1   Does the ship's measures for controlling the embarkation of persons and their effects meet the requirements set out in the Ship Security Plan for security levels 1 and 2?[248]

Part B.1   Embarkation of Persons and Their Effects

Security level 1

> .2   Has the ship established procedures to liaise with the port facility to ensure that vehicles destined to be loaded onboard car carriers, Ro-Ro and other passenger ships are subjected to search prior to loading?[249]
> .3   Has the ship established security measures to segregate checked persons and their personal effects from unchecked persons and their personal effects?[250]
> .4   Has the ship established security measures to segregate embarking from disembarking passengers?[251]

Security level 2

> .5   Has the ship increased the frequency and detail of searches of persons, personal effects, and vehicles being embarked or loaded onto the ship?[252]

Part B.2   Handling Unaccompanied Baggage

Handling unaccompanied baggage.[253]

> .6   Has the ship established security measures to be applied to ensure that unaccompanied baggage is identified and subject to appropriate screening, including searching, before it is accepted on board?[254]

Security level 1

> .7   Has the ship established security measures for screening and searching 100 percent, including x-ray screening?[255]

Security level 2

> .8   Are there additional security measures for handling unaccompanied baggage, including 100 percent x-ray screening?[256]

---

[248] Id., A/7.2.3.
[249] Id., B/9.14.3.
[250] Id., B/9.14.4.
[251] Id., B/9.14.5.
[252] Id., B/9.16.5.
[253] Id., B/9.38 to B/9.40.
[254] Id., B/9.38.
[255] Id., B/9.39.
[256] Id., B/9.40.

14.4.2.4 Monitoring of Restricted Areas

Part A   Restricted Areas on the Ship

.1 Does the ship's measures for monitoring access to restricted areas, to ensure that only authorized persons have access, meet the requirements set out in the Ship Security Plan for security levels 1 and 2?[257]

.2 Have restricted areas been identified and measures put in place to prevent unauthorized access to them?[258]

Part B   Restricted Areas on the Ship

.3 Has the ship clearly established policies and practices to control access to all restricted areas?[259]

.4 Has the ship clearly marked all restricted areas, indicating that access to the area is restricted and that unauthorized presence in the area constitutes a breach of security?[260]

.5 Which are identified as restricted areas?
  A. Navigation bridge, machinery spaces (category A), control stations;
  B. Spaces containing security and surveillance equipment and systems and their controls and lighting system controls;
  C. Ventilation and air-conditioning systems and other similar spaces;
  D. Spaces with access to potable water tanks, pumps and manifolds;
  E. Spaces containing dangerous goods or hazardous substances;
  F. Spaces containing cargo pumps and their controls;
  G. Cargo spaces and spaces containing ship's stores;
  H. Crew accommodation; and
  I. Any other areas.[261]

Security level 1

.6 Which of the following security measures have be applied to restricted areas on the ship?[262]
  A. Locking or securing access points;
  B. Using surveillance equipment to monitor the areas;
  C. Using guards or patrols; and
  D. Automatic intrusion-detection devices.

Security level 2

.7 Which of the following additional security measures have be applied to restricted areas on the ship?[263]
  A. Establishing restricted areas adjacent to access points;
  B. Continuously monitoring surveillance equipment; and
  C. Dedicating additional personnel to guard and patrol restricted areas.

---

[257] Id., A/7.2.4 and A/7.3.
[258] Id., A/9.4.2.
[259] Id., B/9.19.
[260] Id., B/9.20.
[261] Id., B/9.21.
[262] Id., B/9.22.
[263] Id., B/9.23.

14.4.2.5 Monitoring of Deck Areas and Areas Surrounding the Ship

Part A   Access to the Ship

.1 Does the ship's means of monitoring deck areas and areas surrounding the ship meet the requirements identified in the Ship Security Plan for security levels 1 and 2?[264]

Part B.1   Access to the Ship

Security level 2
.2 Has the ship assigned additional personnel to patrol deck areas during silent hours to deter unauthorized access?[265]
.3 Has the ship established security measures to deter waterside access to the ship including, for example, in liaison with the port facility, provision of boat patrols?[266]

Part B.2   Monitoring the Security of the Ship

Monitoring the security of the ship.[267]

.4 Which of the following monitoring capabilities have been established by the ship to monitor the ship, the restricted areas on board and areas surrounding the ship?[268]
   A. Lighting
   B. Watchkeepers, security guards and deck watches, including patrols
   C. Automatic intrusion-detection devices and surveillance equipment
.5 Do any automatic intrusion-detection devices on the ship activate an audible and/or visual alarm at a location that is continuously attended or monitored?[269]
.6 Has the ship established the procedures and equipment needed at each security level and the means of ensuring that monitoring equipment will be able to perform continually, including consideration of the possible effects of weather conditions or power disruptions?[270]

Security level 1

.7 Has the ship established the security measures to be applied, which may be a combination of lighting, watchkeepers, security guards or the use of security and surveillance equipment to allow ship's security personnel to observe the ship in general, and barriers and restricted areas in particular?[271]

---

[264] Id., A/7.2.5.
[265] Id., B/9.16.1.
[266] Id., B/9.16.3.
[267] Id., B/9.42 to B/9.48.
[268] Id., B/9.42.
[269] Id., B/9.43.
[270] Id., B/9.44.
[271] Id., B/9.45.

.8 Are the ship's deck and access points illuminated during hours of darkness and periods of low visibility while conducting ship/port interface activities or at a port facility or anchorage?[272]

Security level 2

.9 Which of the following additional security measures have been established to enhance monitoring and surveillance activities?[273]
   A. Increasing the frequency and detail of security patrols;
   B. Increasing the coverage and intensity of lighting or the use of security and surveillance equipment;
   C. Assigning additional personnel as security look-outs; and
   D. Ensuring co-ordination with water-side boat patrols, and foot or vehicle patrols on the shore side, when provided.

14.4.2.6 Supervising the Handling of Cargo and Ship's Stores

Part A Handling of Cargo

.1 Does the ship's means of supervising the handling of:
   A. cargo
   B. ship's stores[274]
      meet the requirements of the Ship Security Plan for security levels 1 and 2?

Part B.1 Handling of Cargo

Security level 1

.2 Are measures employed to routinely check the integrity of cargo, including the checking of seals, during cargo handling?[275]
.3 Are measures employed to routinely check cargo being loaded matches the cargo documentation?[276]
.4 Does the ship ensure, in liaison with the port facility, that vehicles to be loaded on car carriers, ro-ro and passenger ships are searched prior to loading, in accordance with the frequency required in the Ship Security Plan?[277]
.5 Which of the following security measures are employed during cargo checking?[278]
   A. Visual examination;
   B. Physical examination;
   C. Scanning or detection equipment;
   D. Other mechanical devices; and
   E. Dogs.

---

[272] Id., B/9.46.
[273] Id., B/9.47.
[274] Id., A/7.2.6.
[275] Id., B/9.27.1 and B/9.27.4.
[276] Id., B/9.27.2.
[277] Id., B/9.27.3.
[278] Id., B/9.28.

Security level 2

.6 Which of the following additional security measures are applied during cargo handling?[279]
   A. Detailed checking of cargo, cargo transport units and cargo spaces;
   B. Intensified checks to ensure that only the intended cargo is loaded;
   C. Intensified searching of vehicles; and
   D. Increased frequency and detail in checking of seals or other methods used to prevent tampering.

Part B.2   Delivery of Ship's Stores

Delivery of ship's stores.[280]

.7 Has the ship established security measures to ensure stores being delivered match the order, prior to being loaded on board and to ensure their immediate secure stowage at security level 1?[281]
.8 Has the ship established additional security measures at security level 2 by exercising checks prior to receiving stores on board and intensifying inspections?[282]

14.4.2.7 Ensuring Security Communication is Readily Available

Part A   Ensuring Security Communication

.1 Do the ship's communication equipment and procedures meet the requirements identified in the Ship Security Plan at security levels 1 and 2?[283]
.2 Has the ship security officer been identified?[284]
.3 Has the company security officer been identified and 24 hour contact details been provided?[285]
.4 Has the ship established procedures to ensure the inspection, testing, calibration and maintenance of any security equipment provided on board?[286]
.5 Has the frequency for testing or calibration of any security equipment provided on board been specified?[287]
.6 Have the locations on the ship where the ship security alert system activation points are provided been identified?[288]
.7 Have procedures, instructions and guidance been established and communicated on the use of the ship security alert system, including the testing, activation, deactivation and resetting and to limit false alerts?[289]

---

[279] Id., B/9.30.
[280] Id., B/9.33 to B/9.36.
[281] Id., B/9.35.
[282] Id., B/9.36.
[283] Id., A/7.2.7.
[284] Id., A/9.4.13.
[285] Id., A/9.4.14.
[286] Id., A/9.4.15.
[287] Id., A/9.4.16.
[288] Id., A/9.4.17.
[289] Id., A/9.4.18.

14.4.2.8 Training, Drills, and Exercises

Part A   Training, Drills, and Exercises

.1 Have the:
   A. Company Security Officer and appropriate shore-based personnel security personnel received sufficient training to perform their assigned duties?[290]
   B. Ship Security Officer received sufficient training to perform their assigned duties?[291]

.2 Do shipboard personnel having specific security duties and responsibilities understand their responsibilities for ship security and have sufficient knowledge and ability to perform their assigned duties?[292]

.3 Has the company and ship implemented drills and participated in exercises?[293]

.4 Has the ship established procedures for training, drills and exercises associated with the ship security plan?[294]

Part B   Training, Drills, and Exercises

.5 Have the Company Security Officer, appropriate shore-based Company personnel and the Ship Security Officer received the appropriate levels of training?[295]

.6 Do shipboard personnel with security responsibilities have sufficient knowledge and ability to perform their duties?[296]

.7 Are security drills conducted:
   A. at least every three months?
   B. in cases where more than 25 percent of the ship's personnel has been changed, at any one time, with personnel that have not previously participated in any drill on that ship within the last three months?[297]
   C. to test individual elements of the ship security plan such as those security threats listed in ISPS Code B/8.9?[298]

14.4.2.9 Miscellaneous

Part A   Miscellaneous

.1 Have different RSOs undertaken (a) the preparation of the Ship Security Assessment and Ship Security Plan and (b) the review and approval of the Ship Security Plan?[299]

---

[290] Id., A.13.1.
[291] Id., A/13.2.
[292] Id., A/13.3.
[293] Id., A/13.4 and A/13.5.
[294] Id., A/9.4.9.
[295] Id., B/13.1 and B/13.2.
[296] Id., B/13.3.
[297] Id., B/13.6.
[298] Id., B/13.6.
[299] Id., A/9.2.1.

.2 Does the Master have a contact point in the Administration to seek consent for the inspection of those provisions in the Ship Security Plan that are considered confidential information, when access to them is requested by a duly authorized officer of another Contracting Government?[300]

.3 Has the ship established procedures to protect from unauthorized access or disclosure the records of activities addressed in the Ship Security Plan which are required to be kept on board?[301]

.4 In which of the following circumstances does the ship request completion of a Declaration of Security?[302]
   A. When the ship is operating at a higher security level than the port facility or another ship it is interfacing with;
   B. The ship is covered by an agreement on a Declaration of Security between Contracting Governments;
   C. When there has been a security threat or a security incident involving the ship or port facility it is calling at;
   D. When the ship is at a port which is not required to have and implement an approved port facility security plan;
   E. When the ship is conducting ship-to-ship activities with another ship not required to have and implement an approved Ship Security Plan.

.5 Does the Company Security Officer or Ship Security Officer periodically review the Ship Security Assessment for accuracy as part of the Ship Security Plan review process? [303]

.6 Does the ship adequately maintain the required security records and are they sufficiently detailed to allow the Company Security Officer and Ship Security Officer to identify areas for improvement or change in the current security procedures and measures?[304]
   A. Training, drills and exercises;[305]
   B. Security threats and security incidents;[306]
   C. Breaches of security;[307]
   D. Periodic review of the Ship Security Plan.[308]

.7 Is the ship adequately manned and does its complement include the grades/capacities and number of persons required for the safe operation and the security of the ship and for the protection of the marine environment?[309]
   A. When the ship is operating at security level 1;
   B. When the ship is operating at security level 2.

---

[300] Id., A/9.8.1.
[301] Id., A/10.4.
[302] Id., A/5.2.
[303] Id., A/10.1.7.
[304] Id., A/10.1.
[305] Id., A/10.1.1.
[306] Id., A/10.1.2.
[307] Id., A/10.1.3.
[308] Id., A/10.1.8.
[309] Id., B/4.28. *See also*, IMO Doc. A.890(21), Principles of Safe Manning, Nov. 25, 1999, *reprinted in* IMO Doc. A 21/RES 890, Feb. 4, 2000, as amended by IMO Doc. A.955(23), Amendments to the Principles of Safe Manning, Dec. 5, 2003, *reprinted in* IMO Doc. A 23/RES 955, Feb. 26, 2004, and SOLAS regulation V/14.1.

Part B Miscellaneous

.8 Has the ship established procedures on handling requests for a Declaration of Security from a port facility?[310]

.9 Have procedures been established in the Ship Security Plan as to how the Company Security Officer and Ship Security Officer intend to audit the continued effectiveness of the Ship Security Plan and to review, update or amend the Ship Security Plan?[311]

.10 Has the ship established additional security procedures to be implemented when calling into a port facility which is not required to comply with the requirements of SOLAS chapter XI-2 and the ISPS Code?[312]

Findings and Recommendations identified by the assessor.

Name, date of completion and signature of assessor.

14.5 Yachts and Other Non-SOLAS Vessels

There are four major classes of non-SOLAS vessels: commercial non-passenger and special purpose vessels; passenger vessels; fishing vessels; and, pleasure craft.[313]

There are a vast—probably innumerable—number of smaller vessels included in these four categories that lie outside of regulation under the SOLAS-ISPS regime. These small ships are not required to comply with SOLAS chapter XI-2 and the ISPS Code, but the IMO has endorsed non-mandatory guidelines that may be applied by states to such ships.[314] The guidelines contains information for member states and authorities responsible for administering non-SOLAS vessels, as well as information that may be used by owners and operators of non-SOLAS ships and facilities. Furthermore, in some cases, SOLAS contracting governments extend some or all of the provisions of the treaty to non-SOLAS vessels. For example, flag States may require automated tracking equipment or ships security alert systems installed on non-SOLAS ships to enhance safety and security or facilitate a more rapid emergency response to maritime accidents or casualties.

But Non-SOLAS vessels on international voyages, however, may be required to declare arrival and departure information to obtain permission to enter or leave port.[315] Such a declaration may be required by local authorities before arrival or

---

[310] ISPS Code B/9.52.
[311] Id., B/9.53.
[312] Id., B/4.20.
[313] MSM, 4.11.2.
[314] IMO Doc. MSC.1/Circ.1283, Draft MSC Circular—Non-Mandatory Guidelines on Security Aspects of the Operation of Vessels which do not Fall Within the Scope of SOLAS Chapter XI-2 and the ISPS Code, Dec. 22, 2008.
[315] Information delivered to port facility authorities may include the name of the vessel, date/time of arrival, position in port, particulars of Master/owner/shipping line/agent,

prior to departure from port. If a non-SOLAS vessel operator completes a Declaration of Security (DOS) with a PFSO or Ship Security Officer, the Ship Security Officer or PFSO should detail via the appropriate DOS form the security measures with which the non-SOLAS vessel is being asked to comply. Both parties should complete and sign a DOS.[316]

As with SOLAS vessels, non-SOLAS ships should control access to operational areas of the vessel or maintenance/storage facilities, such as crew rest rooms, store rooms, hatches and lockers. Ships may consider measures, such as over-the-side lighting, which gives an even distribution of light on the whole hull and waterline, maintaining a deck watch and challenging and stopping approaching boats. Prior to a ship getting underway, it should be thoroughly inspected so that cargo and persons on board the vessel are properly identified. All visitors should be identified and present valid documentation to board the ship, such as a ticket. Passengers and visitors should be briefed on ship security procedures, including how to report suspicious persons, activity, or packages.

Security incidents that occur while a vessel is at sea should be reported to the Master or Ship Security Officer. The Master may activate a ship alert to the nearest coastal state authorities or vessels in the vicinity. Some of the activities that may constitute suspicious behavior include:

   a. Unknown persons photographing vessels or facilities;
   b. Unknown persons inquiring about ship or facility security operating procedures;
   c. Theft or loss of security procedures or related documents;
   d. Unauthorized persons, such as workmen, trying to gain access to facilities;
   e. Inappropriate or unauthorized attempts to gain access to vessels or facilities;
   f. Theft of facility vehicles;
   g. Theft of personnel passes or personnel uniforms;
   h. Inappropriate use of Global Maritime Distress Safety and Security procedures;
   i. Suspicious persons loitering in the proximity of port facilities.

Because of their relatively small size and crew, yachts are particularly vulnerable to threat at sea. The case of the S/V *Quest* illustrates how exposed and defenseless a small pleasure craft can be against violent attack. On a crystal clear February 18, 2011, Somali pirates hijacked the yacht *Quest* as it sailed 240 miles west of Oman. The boat was registered in Marina del Ray, California, and the four Americans on board were taken hostage as the tiny craft bobbed in the Arabian Sea.

The next day U.S. warships began to shadow the yacht as it headed toward the Somali Basin under an impossibly bright sky. The naval flotilla was comprised of the aircraft carrier *USS Enterprise*, the guided-missile cruiser *USS Leyte Gulf*, and the guided-missile destroyers *USS Sterett* and *USS Bulkeley*. After two weeks

---

purpose of call, amount of cargo on board, a passenger and crew list, and emergency contact numbers.

[316] MSM, 4.11.9.

monitoring the sailing vessel, the standoff developed into a routine. Thus, the sailors on watch onboard *USS Sterett* on March 3, 2011, did not expect that the pirates would launch a rocket-propelled grenade (RPG) at them.

The *Sterett* had been trailing the *Quest* at 600 yards, and after the RPG round went wide of its target, the sounds of gunfire from on board the *Quest* penetrated the early morning. President Obama already had authorized the use of deadly force by naval forces in the event that the lives of the hostages were believed to be in danger, so a team of SEAL commandos quickly left the *Sterett* in a rigid-hull inflatable boat and headed toward the sailing vessel.

Two pirates were killed during the boarding process, including one was stabbed with a knife by a SEAL team member acting in self-defense. The remaining pirates surrendered. The boarding party detained 13 Somalis and one Yemeni national. The pirates were armed with AK-47 *Kalashnikov* and FN *Fabrique Nationale de Hersta* automatic assault rifles. The four American crewmembers were found dead or near death from gunshot wounds. The pirates were removed from the yacht and taken to the aircraft carrier, and later the suspects were flown by U.S. Marshalls to Norfolk, Virginia, for trial in U.S. Federal court. But the greatest lesson of the misadventure of the *Quest* is that the yacht was on a pleasure cruise, with little pressing need to transit the dangerous high risk area of the Western Indian Ocean—an intentional and seemingly unnecessary frolic into a dangerous "maritime neighborhood."

In an effort to improve safety of yachts and pleasure craft, some national Flag State Administrations have issued special rules applicable to such vessels. The International Merchant Marine Registry of Belize (IMMARBE), for example, released guidelines to strengthen security for yachts and pleasure craft that are not subject to SOLAS and ISPS Code certification. On April 30, 2004, IMMARBE issued regulations that give legal effect to the ISPS Code for all Belize-registered vessels, *mutatis mutandis*.[317] The Regulations apply to commercial yachts of 24 meters in length or 500 gross tons or larger, which are engaged on international voyages. Perhaps most importantly, yachts should avoid high risk areas that are more susceptible to attack by pirates.

The Belize guidelines warn yachtsmen of common security threats to smaller craft. Pirates, for example, frequently use the ploy of feigning distress as a trick to get close to the yacht. Any ship, including junks, fishing vessels, dhows, and other yachts, are a potential threat to yachts. Additional advice includes limiting (and searching) the number of persons invited on board the vessel. The yacht should maintain lookouts on both sides of the vessel and be vigilant in piracy-prone areas. Prior to getting underway, all crewmembers should be briefed on the risks of attack by pirates and armed robbers. The spaces on board the ship, such

---

[317] Registration of Merchant Ships (Ship Security) Regulations 2004, Stat. Instr. No. 90 of 2004 Regulations, www.immarbe.com/maritimesecurity.htm.

as the bridge, engine room, steering gear compartments, officer's cabins and crew quarters, should be secured.

Yachts should plan a response to an apparent attack so they will be prepared if the ship is in danger. The crew should be trained properly. Most importantly, high-risk areas and bottlenecks should be avoided. Yachts are also more vulnerable if they are awaiting a berth in port. If a berth is not immediately available, the yacht should consider delaying the trip to minimize the ship's vulnerability.

While transiting high-risk areas, yachts should augment bridge watches and lookouts, and add additional watches on the stern—a visual and radar "blind spot" that is often exploited by pirates. Watches should be equipped with low-light binoculars and night-vision goggles. Radio communication with shore and naval authorities should be maintained throughout the transit.

If a suspicious ship approaches, the yacht should increase speed and alter course. During nighttime, the yacht should darken itself and direct searchlights toward any oncoming ship. Finally, if the yacht is seized by armed pirates, most Administrations recommend that the crew not attempt to resist, unless there is a clear situation that threatens human life. A security alarm should be initiated and a distress message broadcasted. As is common in any hostage situation, the victims should attempt to establish a reasonable rapport with the pirates by determining and cooperating with reasonable demands.

FIFTEEN

GLOBAL AUTHORITIES TO COUNTER DRUG TRAFFICKING

15.1 INTERNATIONAL LAW AND THE TRADE IN ILLEGAL DRUGS

The international trade in illegal drugs ranks third in value among global commodity flows, after the international trade in oil and agriculture.[1] During the early-1990s, much of the illegal traffic in drugs flowing into the United States came from the Andean Ridge of South America, which moved northward via open-air fast boats transiting through the Eastern Pacific or the Caribbean Sea. By the end of the 1990s, the increased volume of international trade in legitimate goods associated with globalization provided opportunities to comingle licit and illicit cargoes. The greater quantity of cargoes also made it more difficult for customs services to screen—let alone inspect—goods being shipped.[2]

After marijuana, cocaine is the second most common illegal drug entering the United States. The illicit cocaine market funnels vast sums of cash to criminal gangs throughout the Americas, including Mexican drug cartels and the terrorist organization *Fuerzas Armadas Revolucionarias de Colombia* or Revolutionary Armed Forces of Columbia (FARC). Illegal drugs travel by sea from the coca-producing region of Bolivia, Colombia, and Peru, to isolated beaches along the coasts of Mexico, where the contraband is loaded onto trucks and driven across the Southwest border. Peru has surpassed Colombia as the world's greatest cocaine producer, whereas cocaine production in Colombia decreased 60 percent from 2000 to 2010 due to the successful effort to suppress the FARC.[3]

---

[1] Chiefs of European Navies Maritime Operational Concept (CHENS MOC), p. 5.
[2] DIRECTOR OF CENTRAL INTELLIGENCE, CRIME AND NARCOTICS CENTER, GLOBALIZATION OF THE COCAINE TRADE, INTELLIGENCE REPORT, Dec. 28, 1999, p. 7 (Secret, declassified May 2004).
[3] Jeanna Cullinin, *How Peru Beat Colombia to be the World's Biggest Cocaine Producer*, IN SIGHT: ORGANIZED CRIME IN THE AMERICAS, Oct. 28, 2011.

In addition to cocaine and marijuana, hashish from Morocco and North Africa and heroin poppy from Afghanistan and South America also enter the stream of world commerce, bound primarily for lucrative markets in North America and Europe. Since most of the drugs travel by sea, international cooperation has coalesced around efforts to enhance maritime security. Furthermore, the interrelationship between drug trafficking and insurgency in Colombia underscores the hybrid nature of the threat to maritime security.

Treaties to suppress international drug trafficking constitute some of the most mature maritime agreements. One point of nomenclature arises in the context of counterdrug treaties and deserves some clarification before proceeding. Although the pharmacological term "narcotics" includes popular substances such as cocaine, opium, and heroin, other illegal drugs, for example stimulants, such as methamphetamines, technically are not "narcotics." This chapter, however, uses the term "illicit drugs" or "narcotics" interchangeably, following popular convention.

In Europe, economic and political integration permits travelers to avoid customs and immigration checks, facilitating an expansion of cocaine trafficking on the continent. The 1985 *Schengen Accord*, which was implemented in Europe between 1995 and 1997, abolished most of the internal border controls within the European Union among 23 nations. The agreement also includes non-EU states Iceland and Norway.

The entire Accord does not, however, apply to Ireland and the United Kingdom. Nonetheless, a protocol to the *Treaty of Amsterdam* allows Ireland and the United Kingdom to take part in some or all of the Schengen arrangements, if the Schengen member States and the government representatives of the country in question vote unanimously in favor within the Council of the EU. In March 1999, for example, the United Kingdom asked to cooperate in some aspects of Schengen, namely police and judicial cooperation for criminal law enforcement matters, the fight against illegal drugs, and the Schengen Information System. The Council approved the request on May 29, 2000 (Decision 2000/365/EC). In June 2000, Ireland made a similar request to take part in some parts of Schengen, roughly corresponding to the aspects covered by the United Kingdom's request. Ireland's request was adopted by the Council on February 28, 2002 (Decision 2002/192/EC). On December 22, 2004, the Council voted to allow the United Kingdom to implement the provisions of the Schengen *acquis* governing police and judicial cooperation (Decision 2004/926/EC).

Borderless Europe now facilitates both legitimate and illicit movement of goods and people, leading some countries to question the long-term wisdom of the entire project.[4] Outside of Europe, closer transcontinental trade links tend to make port and customs officials more reluctant to institute aggressive cargo

---

[4] *Sarkozy Threatens to Withdraw from Schengen Accord*, BBC NEWS, Mar. 11, 2012, http://www.bbc.co.uk/news/business-17332458.

inspections without specific intelligence about drug caches, for fear of provoking retaliatory delays of their nation's exports arriving in foreign ports.

Furthermore, cooperation between drug traffickers and terrorists has increased in Latin America, Asia, Africa, and the Middle East. The well-organized separatist group Liberation Tigers of Tamil Eelam (LTTE) of Sri Lanka was deeply involved in maritime drug trafficking using an extensive "phantom fleet" of unregistered ships, which helped to fund its three-decade insurgency. During this period, the group integrated drug trafficking into its normal maritime transport of commerce, such as timber and sugar. The LTTE earned proceeds from drugs sold as close as Burma and as far away as Turkey. The insurgency also provided protection and courier services to the sea-borne drug shipments from Burma to Europe and the United States—using the payoff to fund its separatist campaign.[5]

The corrosive effect of drug trafficking on economic prosperity and political stability has been evident since the early 1900s. Nations realized that since drug trafficking was by nature an international problem, cross-border cooperation was essential. Two major conferences on the threat of opium were held in The Hague during the winter of 1911–12.[6] The effort was launched in the interest of China by the United States in consultation with a handful of other Western nations.[7] The *International Opium Convention* was signed by 12 States, including the United Kingdom, on January 23, 1912.[8] Switzerland joined two years later.[9] The Opium Convention aimed at controlling various forms of opium, morphine, heroin and cocaine. The treaty was folded into the terms of the League of Nations after World War I, and by the mid-1920s, already had 60 States' parties. Later, the international effort was taken over by the United Nations, and the Opium Convention was superseded by the *Single Convention on Narcotic Drugs* in 1961. The 1961 Convention was followed by two more major multilateral counter-drug treaties—the *Convention on Psychotropic Substances* 1971 and the *UN Convention on Illicit Traffic of Narcotics and Psychotropic Drugs* 1988, as well as the *United Nations Convention on the Law of the Sea* 1982.

---

[5] Cdr. P. K. Ghosh, *Maritime Security Challenges in South Asia and the Indian Ocean: Response Strategies*, A paper prepared for the Center for Strategic and International Studies—American-Pacific Sealanes Security Institute conference on Maritime Security in Asia. January 18–20, 2004, Honolulu, Hawaii, p. 6, http://tamilnation.co/intframe/indian_ocean/pk_ghosh.pdf.

[6] *Suppression of Opium Traffic*, 7 AM. J. INT'L L. SUPP. 353 (Apr. 1913).

[7] Id., 353–54.

[8] International Opium Convention, *signed at The Hague*, Jan. 23, 1912, *reprinted in* 6 AM. J. INT'L L. SUPP. 177 (July 1912).

[9] Traffic in Opium and Other Dangerous Drugs—Ratification by Switzerland of the Opium Convention of 1912, Letter from the Swiss Government to the Secretary-General of the League, Berne, June 16, 1924, 5 LEAGUE OF NATIONS OFFICIAL J. 1117 (1924).

15.2 The Multilateral Treaty Framework

The *United Nations Convention on the Law of the Sea* is the bedrock authority in international law for conducting maritime counter drug operations.

15.2.1 United Nations Convention on the Law of the Sea

The *United Nations Convention on the Law of the Sea* (UNCLOS) contains rules applicable to activity on, over and under the sea.[10] Article 108 of UNCLOS reflects the duty of all states to cooperate in the suppression of illicit drug trafficking by ships on the high seas.

Article 108

1. All States shall cooperate in the suppression of illicit traffic in narcotic drugs and psychotropic substances engaged in by ships on the high seas contrary to international conventions.
2. Any State which has reasonable grounds for believing that a ship flying its flag is engaged in illicit traffic in narcotics drugs or psychotropic substances may request the cooperation of other States to suppress such traffic.

The obligations in Article 108 apply by extension of Article 58(2) to the Exclusive Economic Zone (EEZ).[11] "Therefore, the obligation to cooperate in suppressing illicit traffic in narcotic drugs and psychotropic substances applies in the exclusive economic zone as well as on the high seas."[12] Under Article 27 of UNCLOS, a coastal State may assert criminal jurisdiction over foreign-flagged ships in innocent passage, but Article 58(2) recognizes that in the area beyond the territorial sea, international cooperation is essential for effective counter-drug efforts.[13]

The 1971 Sea-Bed Committee was the genesis for Article 108. Malta proposed text for its draft ocean space treaty, which read: "Every State has the obligation to adopt effective measures to prevent and punish the illicit transport of narcotic drugs in vessels authorized to fly its flag."[14] The next year, the Sea-Bed Committee added narcotics trafficking to its list of issues to be addressed by a proposed Third UN Conference on the Law of the Sea.[15] During the second session of the Conference, nine Western European States proposed draft text that stated that all

---

[10] United Nations Convention on the Law of the Sea, *opened for signature* Dec. 10, 1982, UN Doc. A/CONF.62/122 (1982), 1833 U.N.T.S. 3, 397, 21 I.L.M. 1261 (1982) (*entered into force* Nov. 16, 1994) [Hereinafter UNCLOS].

[11] United Nations Convention on the Law of the Sea: A Commentary III 230 (Satya N. Nandan, Shabtai Rosenne, & Neal R. Grandy, eds. 1995).

[12] Id.

[13] Id.

[14] A/AC.138/53, Article 16, *reprinted in* Sea-Bed Committee Report 1971, p. 105, 123.

[15] Sea-Bed Committee Report 1972, p. 5. The issue of illegal drugs was mentioned along with piracy and slavery.

States should cooperate against the suppression of illicit traffic in narcotic drugs by ships on the high seas. Furthermore,

> Any State which has reasonable grounds for believing that a vessel is engaged in illicit traffic in narcotic drugs may, whatever the nationality of the vessel but provided that its tonnage is less than 500 tons, seize the illicit cargo. The State which carried out this seizure shall inform the State of nationality of the vessel in order that the latter State may institute proceedings against those responsible for the illicit traffic.[16]

By the third session in 1974, a draft Article 94 appeared in the Integrated Single Negotiating Text (ISNT) Part II, which read:

1. All States shall cooperate in the suppression of illicit traffic in narcotics drugs and psychotropic substances by ships on the high seas contrary to international conventions.
2. Any State which has reasonable grounds for believing that a vessel flying its flag is engaged in illicit traffic in narcotics drugs and psychotropic substances may request the cooperation of other States to suppress such traffic.[17]

The fourth session in 1976 closely followed the ISNT draft Article 94, but added the phrase "narcotic drugs and psychotropic substances," and the sixth session renumbered the provision as Article 108 in the Informal Composite Negotiating Text (ICNT).[18] Minor changes were made to the text at the tenth session in 1981, but the basic authority remained unchanged through to adoption of the treaty in 1982. The Convention does not provide any enforcement mechanism, but rather sets out a basic obligation to cooperate against trafficking that is "contrary to international conventions." Thus, UNCLOS, as an umbrella agreement, draws additional multilateral treaties into the law of the sea framework, and nowhere is this better illustrated than in the area of counter-drug cooperation.

There are a number of additional international and regional agreements that can be used in conjunction with UNCLOS to strengthen cooperation and build partnerships to combat illicit drug trafficking. Three widely accepted multilateral drug trafficking treaties have near universal acceptance and therefore great authority. Building networks for time-sensitive coordination, increasing political will and operational capability among states will further enhance these efforts. The principal treaties in this realm are the *Single Convention on Narcotic Drugs*

---

[16] UN Doc. A/CONF.62/C.2/L.54, Article 21*bis*, III OFFICIAL RECORDS OF THE THIRD UNITED NATIONS CONFERENCE ON THE LAW OF THE SEA 229, 230 (1974) (Belgium, Denmark, France, Federal Republic of Germany, Ireland, Italy, Luxembourg, Netherlands, and United Kingdom) [Hereinafter OFFICIAL RECORDS].

[17] UN Doc. A/CONF.62/WP.8/Part II (ISNT 1975), IV OFFICIAL RECORDS 137, 166 (1975).

[18] UN Doc. A/CONF.62/WP.10 (ICNT 1977), Article 108, VIII OFFICIAL RECORDS 1, 19 (1977).

(1961),[19] the *Convention on Psychotropic Substances* (1971),[20] and the *UN Convention on Illicit Traffic of Narcotics and Psychotropic Drugs* (1988),[21] also called the Vienna Convention. These three major international drug control treaties are mutually supportive and complementary.

An important purpose of the first two treaties is to codify internationally applicable control measures in order to ensure the availability of lawful narcotic drugs and psychotropic substances for medical and scientific purposes while preventing their diversion into unlawful channels. They also include general provisions on criminal trafficking and drug abuse. The third treaty regulates precursor chemicals used in manufacturing drugs controlled by the *Single Convention* and the *Convention on Psychotropic Substances*, and it also strengthens provisions against money laundering and other drug-related crimes.

15.2.2 *1961 Single Convention on Narcotic Drugs, As Amended*

In 1958, the UN Economic and Social Council convened a conference for the purpose of adopting a single convention to replace the existing multilateral narcotic drug treaties, to reduce the number of international treaty organs exclusively concerned with the control of narcotic drugs, and to make provision for the control of the production of raw materials of narcotic drugs. The United Nations Conference for the Adoption of a Single Convention on Narcotic Drugs met in New York from January 24 to March 25, 1961, and it adopted the *Single Convention on Narcotic Drugs* (1961). The convention was subsequently amended by the adoption of a Protocol in 1972. The 1972 Protocol added provisions on technical and financial assistance[22] and created regional centers for scientific research and education to combat the use of illegal drugs.[23] Article 22(2) of the 1972 Protocol permits seizure and destruction of illegally cultivated opium poppies and cannabis. Finally, the Protocol modified the penal provisions of the 1971 Convention. The *Single Convention on Narcotic Drugs* has been in force since 1964 and has 180 state parties.

---

[19] Single Convention on Narcotic Drugs (1961 New York, 30 Mar. 1961) 520 U.N.T.S. 151, entered into force 13 Dec. 1964, as amended by the Protocol amending the Single Convention on Narcotic Drugs, 1961 (Geneva, 25 Mar. 1972) 976 U.N.T.S. 3, entered into force 8 Aug. 1975 and Single Convention on Narcotic Drugs, 1961, as amended by the Protocol amending the Single Convention on Narcotic Drugs, 1961, New York, Aug. 8, 1975, 976 U.N.T.S. 105, *entered into force* Aug. 8, 1975 [Hereinafter 1961 Convention].

[20] Convention on Psychotropic Substances, Vienna, Feb. 21, 1971, 32 U.S.T. 543, 1019 U.N.T.S. 175, entered into force Aug. 16, 1976 [Hereinafter 1971 Convention].

[21] United Nations Convention against Illicit Traffic in Narcotic Drugs and Psychotropic Substances, Vienna, Dec. 20, 1988, UN Doc. E/CONF.82/15/Corr.1 and Corr.2, 1582 U.N.T.S. 164, 28 I.L.M. 493 (1989) *entered into force* Nov. 11, 1990, [Hereinafter 1988 Vienna Convention].

[22] 1971 Convention, Article 14.

[23] Id., Article 38.

The 1961 Single Convention achieved its stated goals of consolidating and replacing ten existing international narcotic drug treaties. Second, it combined the Permanent Central Board and the Drug Supervisory Board into the International Narcotics Control Board, thereby simplifying the international drug control framework. Finally, it provided increased controls over the cultivation of plants grown for narcotics, provisions on medical treatment and rehabilitation of drug addicts, prohibited use of narcotic drugs for nonmedical purposes, required States' parties to regulate particularly dangerous drugs, such as heroin, included measures to regulate the export and import of narcotic drugs, and reinforced pre-existing controls on the manufacture and trade and distribution of narcotic substances, including measures to regulate new synthetic drugs.

Pursuant to Article 4 of the convention, the Parties agree to cooperate with other States in implementing the convention and to adopt domestic laws and administrative measures necessary to, *inter alia*, "limit exclusively to medical and scientific purposes the production, manufacture, export, import, distribution of, trade in, use and possession of drugs." Article 21 limits the manufacture and importation of drugs by any country or territory in any one year to the sum of the following:

   a) The quantity consumed, within the limit of the relevant estimate, for medical and scientific purposes;
   b) The quantity used, within the limit of the relevant estimate, for the manufacture of other drugs, of preparations in Schedule III, and of substances not covered by this Convention;
   c) The quantity exported;
   d) The quantity added to the stock for the purpose of bringing that stock up to the level specified in the relevant estimate; and
   e) The quantity acquired within the limit of the relevant estimate for special purposes.

Article 21*bis* further limits the production of opium, while Article 24(1)(b) prohibits a State Party from producing opium or increasing its existing production of opium for export if "in its opinion such production or increased production . . . may result in illicit traffic in opium." Additionally, States that were not previously producing opium for export prior to 1961, but subsequently desire to export opium in amounts not exceeding five tons annually, are required by Article 24(2)(a) to provide the following information to the International Narcotics Control Board:

   i) The controls in force as required by this Convention respecting the opium to be produced and exported; and
   ii) The name of the country or countries to which it expects to export such opium.

The Board may either approve the notification or may recommend to the State Party that it not engage in the production of opium for export. Similarly, States wishing to produce opium for export in excess of five tons annually are required by Article 24(2)(b) to provide the UN Economic and Social Council with the following information:

i) The estimated amounts to be produced for export;
ii) The controls existing or proposed respecting the opium to be produced;
iii) The name of the country or countries to which it expects to export such opium.

The Council shall either approve the notification or may recommend to the Party that it not engage in the production of opium for export. These requirements, however, do not apply to States that were exporting opium during the ten years immediately prior to January 1, 1961.[24] The same system of controls applicable to the opium poppy shall be applied to the coca bush and coca leaves pursuant to Article 26(1) and to the cannabis plant pursuant to Article 28.

Article 24(4)(a) prohibits States from importing opium from any country or territory, except opium that is produced by a State authorized by Article 24 to export the drug. This prohibition, however, does not apply to opium imported from a country that produced and exported opium during the ten years prior to January 1, 1961, "if such country has established and maintains a national control organ or agency for the purposes set out in Article 23 and has in force an effective means of ensuring that the opium it produces is not diverted into the illicit traffic."[25] In addition, pursuant to Article 24(5), nothing prohibits a State Party from producing opium sufficient for its own requirements or from exporting opium seized in the illicit traffic to another Party in accordance with the provisions of the convention.

States that allow for the cultivation of the opium poppy for purposes other than the production of opium are required by Article 25 to take the necessary measures to ensure that opium is not produced from such opium poppies and that the manufacture of drugs from poppy straw is adequately controlled.

Article 27 also allows States to use coca leaves for the preparation of as a flavoring agent, which shall not contain any alkaloids. And Article 28 permits States to cultivate cannabis plants exclusively for industrial purposes (fiber and seed) or horticultural purposes. However, States shall adopt necessary measures to "prevent the misuse of, and illicit traffic in, the leaves of the cannabis plant."[26]

Under Article 22, States that elect to prohibit the cultivation of opium poppy, the coca bush or the cannabis plant to protect the public health and welfare, as well as prevent the diversion of drugs into the illicit drug trade, are required to take appropriate measures to seize any plants illicitly cultivated and destroy them. Additionally, Article 26(2) requires States to uproot all coca bushes that grow wild and destroy bushes that are illegally cultivated.

Article 29(1) requires that the manufacture of drugs be under license "except where such manufacture is carried out by a State enterprise or State enterprises." Similarly, Article 30(1)(a) requires that the trade in and distribution of drugs be

---

[24] 1961 Convention, Article 24(3).
[25] Id., Article 24(4)(b).
[26] Id., Article 28(3).

under license, "except where such trade or distribution is carried out by a State enterprise or State enterprises" and Article 30(2)(b)(i) requires the use of medical prescriptions for the supply or dispensation of drugs to individuals.

Regarding international trade, Article 31(1) prohibits States from exporting drugs to any country or territory except:

　　a) In accordance with the laws and regulations of that country or territory; and
　　b) Within the limits of the total of the estimates for that country or territory..., with the addition of the amounts intended to be re-exported.

In addition, Article 31(3) requires States to:

　　a) Control under license the import and export of drugs except where such import or export is carried out by a State enterprise or enterprises;
　　b) Control all persons and enterprises carrying on or engaged in such import or export.

Moreover, a separate import or export authorization is required for each import or export of drugs, whether it consists of one or more drugs.[27]

Article 35 requires States, consistent with their constitutional, legal and administrative systems, to take actions against the illicit trade, including:

　　a) Make arrangements at the national level for co-ordination of preventive and repressive action against the illicit traffic; to this end they may usefully designate an appropriate agency responsible for such coordination;
　　b) Assist each other in the campaign against the illicit traffic in narcotic drugs;
　　c) Cooperate closely with each other and with the competent international organizations of which they are members with a view to maintaining a coordinated campaign against the illicit traffic;
　　d) Ensure that international cooperation between the appropriate agencies be conducted in an expeditious manner; and
　　e) Ensure that where legal papers are transmitted internationally for the purposes of a prosecution, the transmittal be effected in an expeditious manner to the bodies designated by the Parties; this requirement shall be without prejudice to the right of a Party to require that legal papers be sent to it through the diplomatic channel;
　　f) Furnish, if they deem it appropriate, to the Board and the Commission through the Secretary-General, in addition to information required by article 18, information relating to illicit drug activity within their borders, including information on illicit cultivation, production, manufacture and use of, and on illicit trafficking in, drugs; and
　　g) Furnish the information referred to in the preceding paragraph as far as possible in such manner, and by such dates as the Board may request; if requested by a Party, the Board may offer its advice to it in furnishing the information and in endeavoring to reduce the illicit drug activity within the borders of that Party.

---

[27] Id., Article 31(4).

Under Article 36(1)(a) States' parties must adopt, consistent within their constitutional limitations, such measures that

> will ensure that cultivation, production, manufacture, extraction, preparation, possession, offering, offering for sale, distribution, purchase, sale, delivery on any terms whatsoever, brokerage, dispatch, dispatch in transit, transport, importation and exportation of drugs contrary to the provisions of this Convention, and any other action which in the opinion of such Party may be contrary to the provisions of this Convention, [are made]... punishable offenses when committed intentionally, and that serious offenses shall be liable to adequate punishment particularly by imprisonment or other penalties of deprivation of liberty.

This provision includes, subject to the constitutional limitations of a State Party, "intentional participation in, conspiracy to commit and attempts to commit, any of such offenses, and preparatory acts and financial operations in connection..." with such offenses.[28] Any drugs, substances and equipment used in or intended for the commission of any of the offenses referred to in Article 36 are subject to seizure and confiscation.[29] Additionally, as an alternative to conviction or punishment, or in addition to conviction or punishment, drug abusers that commit such offenses may be required under Article 36(1)(b) to undergo treatment, education, after-care, rehabilitation and social reintegration.

Offenses enumerated in Article 36 "shall be deemed to be included as an extraditable offense in any extradition treaty existing between Parties," and the "Parties undertake to include such offenses as extraditable offenses in every extradition treaty to be concluded between them."[30] Moreover, Article 36(2)(b)(ii) provides that

> ... [i]f a Party which makes extradition conditional on the existence of a treaty receives a request for extradition from another Party with which it has no extradition treaty it may at its option consider this Convention as the legal basis for extradition in respect of the offenses enumerated in [Article 36]....

In cases where States do not make extradition conditional on the existence of a treaty, Article 36(2)(b)(iii) allows those States to recognize the offenses enumerated in Article 36 "as extraditable offenses between themselves, subject to the conditions provided by the law of the requested Party." A State may, however, refuse to grant extradition "in cases where the competent authorities consider that the offense is not sufficiently serious."[31]

---

[28] Id., Article 36(2)(a)(ii).
[29] Id., Article 37.
[30] Id., Article 36(2)(b)(i).
[31] Id., Article 36(2)(b)(iv).

15.2.3 1971 Convention on Psychotropic Substances

Increasing concern over the harmful effects of psychotropic substances, such as barbiturates, amphetamines, LSD[32] and tranquilizers, prompted the UN Economic and Social Council to convene a conference to adopt a Protocol on Psychotropic Substances to supplement the 1961 Single Convention. The UN Conference for the Adoption of a Protocol on Psychotropic Substances met in Vienna from January 11 to February 21, 1971 and adopted the *Convention on Psychotropic Substances* (1971). The *Convention on Psychotropic Substances* entered into force in 1976 and has 175 States parties.

The new convention significantly enhanced international drug controls by providing prohibitive measures for hallucinogens, such as LSD, that present a high risk of abuse, have no therapeutic application, and the treaty requires licenses for the manufacture, trade and distribution of all of the drugs listed in the text. Psychotropic drugs with great potential for abuse that have therapeutic value (e.g., sleeping pills) and international trade in amphetamines and other dangerous stimulants are also strictly regulated.

Pursuant to Articles 5 and 7, the Parties are required to limit the use of substances in Schedule I. Article 7 requires the Parties to:

a) Prohibit all use except for scientific and very limited medical purposes by duly authorized persons, in medical or scientific establishments, which are directly under the control of their Governments or specifically approved by them;
b) Require that manufacture, trade, distribution and possession be under a special license or prior authorization;
c) Provide for close supervision of the activities and acts mentioned in paragraphs *a*) and *b*);
d) Restrict the amount supplied to a duly authorized person to the quantity required for his authorized purpose;
e) Require that persons performing medical or scientific functions keep records concerning the acquisition of the substances and the details of their use, such records to be preserved for at least two years after the last use recorded therein; and
f) Prohibit export and import except when both the exporter and importer are the competent authorities or agencies of the exporting and importing country or region, respectively, or other persons or enterprises which are specifically authorized by the competent authorities of their country or region for the purpose. The requirements of paragraph 1 of article 12 for export and import authorizations for substances in Schedule II shall also apply to substances in Schedule I.

With regard to substances in Schedules II, III and IV, Article 5(2) requires the Parties to "limit by such measures as it considers appropriate the manufacture, export, import, distribution and stocks of, trade in, and use and possession of, substances in Schedules II, III and IV to medical and scientific purposes." In

---

[32] Lysergic acid diethylamide is a semi-synthetic psychedelic drug, which was developed in 1938.

addition, Article 5(3) encourages the Parties to limit the "possession of substances in Schedules II, III and IV except under legal authority." Article 8(1) also requires that "the manufacture of, trade (including export and import trade) in, and distribution of substances listed in Schedules II, III and IV be under license or other similar control measure." Additionally, Schedule II, III and IV substances shall only be supplied or dispensed for use by individuals pursuant to a medical prescription.[33]

The treaty controls the international trade of Schedule I and II substances. Article 12(1) requires a separate import or export authorization for each import or export of a Schedule I or II substance whether it consists of one or more substances. Exports of Schedule III substances require a declaration in triplicate containing the following information:

> i) The name and address of the exporter and importer;
> ii) The international non-proprietary name, or, failing such a name, the designation of the substance in the Schedule;
> iii) The quantity and pharmaceutical form in which the substance is exported, and, if in the form of a preparation, the name of the preparation, if any; and
> iv) The date of dispatch.[34]

A State Party may, however, notify all other Parties through the Secretary-General "that it prohibits the import into its country or into one of its regions of one or more substances in Schedule II, III or IV, specified in its notification."[35] Upon receipt of such a notification, a Party "shall take measures to ensure that none of the substances specified in the notification is exported to the country or one of the regions of the notifying Party."[36]

Regarding illicit trafficking, Article 21 requires the Parties, subject to their constitutional, legal and administrative systems, to:

> a) Make arrangements at the national level for the co-ordination of preventive and repressive action against the illicit traffic; to this end they may usefully designate an appropriate agency responsible for such co-ordination;
> b) Assist each other in the campaign against the illicit traffic in psychotropic substances, and in particular immediately transmit, through the diplomatic channel or the competent authorities designated by the Parties for this purpose, to the other Parties directly concerned, a copy of any report addressed to the Secretary-General under Article 16 in connection with the discovery of a case of illicit traffic or a seizure;
> c) Co-operate closely with each other and with the competent international organizations of which they are members with a view to maintaining a coordinated campaign against the illicit traffic;

---

[33] 1971 Convention, Article 9.
[34] Id., Article 12(2).
[35] Id., Article 13(1).
[36] Id., Article 13(2).

d) Ensure that international co-operation between the appropriate agencies be conducted in an expeditious manner; and
   e) Ensure that, where legal papers are transmitted internationally for the purpose of judicial proceedings, the transmittal be effected in an expeditious manner to the bodies designated by the Parties; this requirement shall be without prejudice to the right of a Party to require that legal papers be sent to it through the diplomatic channel.

Article 22(1) requires the Parties, subject to their constitutional limitations, to "treat as a punishable offense, when committed intentionally, any action contrary to a law or regulation adopted in pursuance of its obligations under this Convention, and shall ensure that serious offenses shall be liable to adequate punishment, particularly by imprisonment or other penalty of deprivation of liberty." Punishable offenses shall include, subject to the constitutional limitations of a Party, "intentional participation in, conspiracy to commit and attempts to commit, any of such offenses, and preparatory acts and financial operations in connection with the offenses…" referred to in Article 22.[37] Any psychotropic substance or other substance, as well as equipment, used in or intended for the commission of any of the offenses referred to in Article 22 are subject to seizure and confiscation.[38] As an alternative to conviction or punishment, or in addition to conviction or punishment, drug abusers that commit such offenses may be required by States under Article 22(1)(b) to undergo treatment, education, aftercare, rehabilitation and social reintegration.

Article 22(2)(b) recommends that offenses referred to in Article 22 be included as extradition crimes in any extradition treaty that has been or may be later concluded between any of the Parties. In cases where States do not make extradition conditional on the existence of a treaty or reciprocity, Article 22(2)(b) allows those States to recognize the offenses referred to in Article 22 as extradition crimes, provided extradition shall be granted in conformity with the law of the requested Party. The requested State may, however, refuse to grant extradition "in cases where the competent authorities consider that the offense is not sufficiently serious."[39]

15.2.4   *1988 Vienna Drug Convention*

Growing economic and social threats associated with the expanding illicit drug trade led the UN General Assembly in 1984 to request the UN Economic and Social Council to invite the Commission on Narcotic Drugs to prepare, as a matter of priority, a comprehensive draft convention against illicit traffic in narcotic drugs to fill any gaps not envisaged in the 1961 Single Convention and 1971

---

[37] Id., Article 22(2)(a)(ii).
[38] Id., Article 22(3).
[39] Id., Article 22(2)(b).

Convention. An initial draft text was prepared by the UN Secretary-General and circulated to all Governments in 1987.

Preparatory work on the draft convention occurred at two sessions of an open-ended intergovernmental expert group in April 1987 and at a special session of the Commission on Narcotic Drugs in February 1988. In May 1988, the Economic and Social Council decided to convene a conference in Vienna to adopt a convention against illicit traffic in narcotic drugs and psychotropic substances. The United Nations Conference for the Adoption of a Convention against Illicit Traffic in Narcotic Drugs and Psychotropic Substances met in Vienna from November 25 to December 20, 1988, and adopted the Convention on December 19, 1988.

The *UN Convention on Illicit Traffic of Narcotics and Psychotropic Drugs* (1988) has been in force since 1990 and has 170 States parties. The treaty has a specific maritime dimension. Articles 17(3)–(4) and (7)–(11) urge states to cooperate and provide consent in the boarding of their ships engaged in international drug trafficking.[40]

The Convention takes a comprehensive approach to deal with the illicit drug trade, addressing issues such as: tracing, freezing and confiscating proceeds and property derived from illegal drug trafficking; the extradition of drug traffickers; mutual legal assistance between the Parties on drug-related investigations; the elimination or reduction of the demand for illicit drugs and substances; and controls on chemicals used to manufacture illicit drugs.

The purpose of the 1988 Convention "is to promote co-operation among the Parties so that they may address more effectively the various aspects of illicit traffic in narcotic drugs and psychotropic substances having an international dimension."[41] Article 2 further requires the Parties to "take necessary measures, including legislative and administrative measures, in conformity with the fundamental provisions of their respective domestic legislative systems."

In this regard, Article 3(1) requires each Party to adopt measures necessary to establish as criminal offenses under its domestic law the following acts, when committed intentionally:

i) The production, manufacture, extraction; preparation, offering, offering for sale, distribution, sale, delivery on any terms whatsoever, brokerage, dispatch, dispatch in transit, transport, importation or exportation of any narcotic drug or any psychotropic substance contrary to the provisions of the 1961 Convention, the 1961 Convention as amended or the 1971 Convention;
ii) The cultivation of opium poppy, coca bush or cannabis plant for the purpose of the production of narcotic drugs contrary to the provisions of the 1961 Convention and the 1961 Convention as amended;

---

[40] *See also,* Eur. Consult. Ass., Agreement by Illicit Traffic by Sea, Implementing Article 17 of the United Nations Convention Against Illicit Traffic in Narcotic Drugs and Pyschotropic Substances, Doc. No. 156 (1995).
[41] 1988 Convention, Article 2.

iii) The possession or purchase of any narcotic drug or psychotropic substance for the purpose of any of the activities enumerated in i) above;
iv) The manufacture, transport or distribution of equipment, materials or of substances listed in Table I and Table II, knowing that they are to be used in or for the illicit cultivation, production or manufacture of narcotic drugs or psychotropic substances;
v) The organization, management or financing of any of the offenses enumerated in i), ii), iii) or iv) above.

Crimes also must be established against the conversion or transfer of property, knowing that such property is derived from any offense or offenses established in accordance with or from an act of participation in them, for the purpose of concealing or disguising the illicit origin of the property or of assisting any person who is involved in the commission of such an offense or offenses to evade the legal consequences of his actions.

Article 3(1)(c) additionally requires a Party, subject to its constitutional principles and the basic concepts of its legal system, to criminalize:

i) The acquisition, possession or use of property, knowing, at the time of receipt, that such property was derived from an offense or offenses established in accordance with subparagraph a) of this paragraph or from an act of participation in such offense or offenses;
ii) The possession of equipment or materials or substances listed in Table I and Table II, knowing that they are being or are to be used in or for the illicit cultivation, production; or
iii) Publicly inciting or inducing others, by any means, to commit any of the offenses established in accordance with this article or to use narcotic drugs or psychotropic substances illicitly;
iv) Participating in, association or conspiracy to commit, attempts to commit, and aiding, abetting, facilitating and counseling the commission of any of the offenses established in accordance with this article.

Each Party shall also, subject to its constitutional principles and the basic concepts of its legal system, "adopt such measures as may be necessary to establish as a criminal offense under its domestic law, when committed intentionally, the possession, purchase or cultivation of narcotic drugs or psychotropic substances for personal consumption contrary to the provisions of the 1961 Convention, the 1961 Convention as amended or the 1971 Convention."[42]

Offenses established by States pursuant to the Convention shall be subject to sanctions that take into consideration the grave nature of the offense, to include "imprisonment or other forms of deprivation of liberty, pecuniary sanctions and confiscation."[43] In addition to conviction or punishment for an offense, a Party may also require an offender to "undergo measures such as treatment, education,

---

[42] Id., Article 3(2).
[43] Id., Article 3(4)(a).

aftercare, rehabilitation or social reintegration."[44] For minor offenses, Article 3(4)(c) allows States to provide "measures such as education, rehabilitation, or social integration..." as an alternative to conviction or punishment, and in the case of drug abusers, "treatment and aftercare."

Aggravating factors that should be taken into consideration by national courts include:

a) The involvement in the offense of an organized criminal group to which the offender belongs;
b) The involvement of the offender in other international organized criminal activities;
c) The involvement of the offender in other illegal activities facilitated by commission of the offense;
d) The use of violence or arms by the offender;
e) The fact that the offender holds a public office and that the offense is connected with the office in question;
f) The victimization or use of minors;
g) The fact that the offense is committed in a penal institution or in an educational institution or social service facility or in their immediate vicinity or in other places to which school children and students resort for educational, sports and social activities;
h) Prior conviction, particularly for similar offenses, whether foreign or domestic, to the extent permitted under the domestic law of a Party.[45]

The seriousness of the offense also should be taken into consideration when considering the early release or parole of a person convicted of an offense established pursuant to the Convention.[46]

Article 5(1) requires each Party to adopt necessary measures to enable confiscation of:

a) Proceeds derived from offenses established in accordance with Article 3, paragraph 1, or property the value of which corresponds to that of such proceeds;
b) Narcotic drugs and psychotropic substances, materials and equipment or other instrumentalities used in or intended for use in any manner in offenses established in accordance with article 3, paragraph 1.

Furthermore, Article 5(2) requires each Party to adopt necessary measures "to enable its competent authorities to identify, trace, and freeze or seize proceeds, property, instrumentalities or any other things referred to in paragraph 1 of this article, for the purpose of eventual confiscation."

Article 6(2) provides with regard to extradition that:

Each of the offenses to which this article applies shall be deemed to be included as an extraditable offense in any extradition treaty existing between Parties. The Parties

---

[44] Id., Article 3(4)(b).
[45] Id., Article 3(5).
[46] Id., Article 3(7).

undertake to include such offenses as extraditable offenses in every extradition treaty to be concluded between them.

Moreover, if a Party that "makes extradition conditional on the existence of a treaty receives a request for extradition from another Party with which it has no extradition treaty," it may consider the Vienna Convention as the legal basis for extradition in respect of any offense to which Article 6 applies.[47] Parties that "do not make extradition conditional on the existence of a treaty shall recognize offenses to which...[article 6] applies as extraditable offenses between themselves."[48]

Extradition may be denied when a requested State has substantial grounds "to believe that compliance would facilitate the prosecution or punishment of any person on account of his race, religion, nationality or political opinions, or would cause prejudice for any of those reasons to any person affected by the request."[49] A Party that refuses to extradite an alleged offender is required by Article 6(9) to submit the case to its competent authorities for the purpose of prosecution, unless otherwise agreed with the requesting Party."

Requirements for mutual legal assistance with regard to investigations, prosecutions and judicial proceedings are provided for in Article 7. If requested, Parties shall afford one another the widest measure of mutual legal assistance for any of the following purposes:

a) Taking evidence or statements from persons;
b) Effecting service of judicial documents;
c) Executing searches and seizures;
d) Examining objects and sites;
e) Providing information and evidentiary items;
f) Providing originals or certified copies of relevant documents and records, including bank, financial, corporate or business records;
g) Identifying or tracing proceeds, property, instrumentalities or other things for evidentiary purposes.

Paragraphs 8 through 19 of Article 7 provide procedures for handling requests for assistance in cases where the Parties in question are not bound by a treaty of mutual legal assistance. Requests for mutual legal assistance may be refused in the following circumstances:

a) If the request is not made in conformity with the provisions of this article;
b) If the requested Party considers that execution of the request is likely to prejudice its sovereignty, security, order public or other essential interests;
c) If the authorities of the requested Party would be prohibited by its domestic law from carrying out the action requested with regard to any similar offense,

---

[47] Id., Article 6(3).
[48] Id., Article 6(4).
[49] Id., Article 6(6).

had it been subject to investigation, prosecution or proceedings under their own jurisdiction;

d) If it would be contrary to the legal system of the requested Party relating to mutual legal assistance for the request to be granted.[50]

In addition to mutual legal assistance, Article 9 provides for other forms of cooperation and training to enhance the effectiveness of law enforcement action to suppress the illicit drug trade. Some of these other forms of cooperation include:

a) Establish and maintain channels of communication between their competent agencies and services to facilitate the secure and rapid exchange of information concerning all aspects of offenses established in accordance with article 3, paragraph 1, including, if the Parties concerned deem it appropriate, links with other criminal activities;

b) Co-operate with one another in conducting enquiries, with respect to offenses established in accordance with article 3, paragraph 1, having an international character, concerning:
   i) The identity, whereabouts and activities of persons suspected of being involved in offenses established in accordance with article 3, paragraph 1;
   ii) The movement of proceeds or property derived from the commission of such offenses;
   iii) The movement of narcotic drugs, psychotropic substances, substances in Table I and Table II of this Convention and instrumentalities used or intended for use in the commission of such offenses;

c) In appropriate cases and if not contrary to domestic law, establish joint teams, taking into account the need to protect the security of persons and of operations, to carry out the provisions of this paragraph. Officials of any Party taking part in such teams shall act as authorized by the appropriate authorities of the Party in whose territory the operation is to take place; in all such cases, the Parties involved shall ensure that the sovereignty of the Party on whose territory the operation is to take place is fully respected;

d) Provide, when appropriate, necessary quantities of substances for analytical or investigative purposes;

e) Facilitate effective co-ordination between their competent agencies and services and promote the exchange of personnel and other experts, including the posting of liaison officers.[51]

Article 9(3) further requires the Parties to assist one another to plan and implement research and training programs for law enforcement and other personnel (e.g., customs officials) in the following areas:

a) Methods used in the detection and suppression of offenses established in accordance with article 3, paragraph 1;

b) Routes and techniques used by persons suspected of being involved in offenses established in accordance with article 3, paragraph 1, particularly in transit States, and appropriate countermeasures;

---

[50] Id., Article 7(15).
[51] Id., Article 9(1).

c) Monitoring of the import and export of narcotic drugs, psychotropic substances and substances in Table I and Table II;
d) Detection and monitoring of the movement of proceeds and property derived from, and narcotic drugs, psychotropic substances and substances in Table I and Table II, and instrumentalities used or intended for use in, the commission of offenses established in accordance with article 3, paragraph 1;
e) Methods used for the transfer, concealment or disguise of such proceeds, property and instrumentalities;
f) Collection of evidence;
g) Control techniques in free trade zones and free ports;
h) Modem law enforcement techniques.

In addition to controlling the illicit traffic in narcotic drugs and psychotropic substances, Article 12(1) requires the Parties to take necessary measures and to cooperate to prevent the diversion of substances that can be used to illicitly manufacture illegal drugs and substances. In this regard, Article 12(9) requires the Parties to take the following measures with respect to the substances listed in the Annex to the convention:

a) Establish and maintain a system to monitor international trade in substances in Table I and Table II in order to facilitate the identification of suspicious transactions. Such monitoring systems shall be applied in close co-operation with manufacturers, importers, exporters, wholesalers and retailers, who shall inform the competent authorities of suspicious orders and transactions.
b) Provide for the seizure of any substance in Table I or Table II if there is sufficient evidence that it is for use in the illicit manufacture of a narcotic drug or psychotropic substance.
c) Notify, as soon as possible, the competent authorities and services of the Parties concerned if there is reason to believe that the import, export or transit of a substance in Table I or Table II is destined for the illicit manufacture of narcotic drugs or psychotropic substances, including in particular information about the means of payment and any other essential elements which led to that belief.
d) Require that imports and exports be properly labeled and documented. Commercial documents such as invoices, cargo manifests, customs, transport and other shipping documents shall include the names, as stated in Table I or Table II, of the substances being imported or exported, the quantity being imported or exported, and the name and address of the exporter, the importer and, when available, the consignee.
e) Ensure that documents referred to in subparagraph d) of this paragraph are maintained for a period of not less than two years and may be made available for inspection by the competent authorities.

Similarly, Article 13 requires the Parties to take appropriate measures and cooperate "to prevent trade in and the diversion of materials and equipment for illicit production or manufacture of narcotic drugs and psychotropic substances...."

Guidance on the eradication of illicit cultivation of narcotic plants and measures to reduce the demand for illicit drugs and substances is provided in Article 14. Appropriate measures shall be taken by each Party "to prevent illicit cultivation of and to eradicate plants containing narcotic or psychotropic substances, such as opium poppy, coca bush and cannabis plants...."[52] Cooperation between the Parties in this regard may include support "for integrated rural development leading to economically viable alternatives to illicit cultivation..." taking into consideration "[f]actors such as access to markets, the availability of resources and prevailing socio-economic conditions...."[53] Article 14(3)(b) calls on the Parties to "facilitate the exchange of scientific and technical information and the conduct of research concerning eradication." Neighboring States are also encouraged to cooperate in eradication programs in their respective areas along their borders.[54] And Article 14(4) calls of States to adopt appropriate measures to eliminate or reduce illicit demand for narcotic drugs and psychotropic substances.

In light of the threat posed by the use of commercial carriers to transport illicit drugs and substances, Article 15(1) requires the Parties to take appropriate measures to ensure that commercial means of transport are not used in the commission of offenses established by the Convention, to include special arrangements with commercial carriers. In this regard, each Party shall require commercial carriers to take reasonable precautions to prevent the use of their means of transport for the commission of offenses established by the Convention, to include:

a) If the principal place of business of a commercial carrier is within the territory of the Party:
   i) Training of personnel to identify suspicious consignments or persons;
   ii) Promotion of integrity of personnel;
b) If a commercial carrier is operating within the territory of the Party:
   i) Submission of cargo manifests in advance, whenever possible;
   ii) Use of tamper-resistant, individually verifiable seals on containers;
   iii) Reporting to the appropriate authorities at the earliest opportunity all suspicious circumstances that may be related to the commission of offenses established in accordance with article 3, paragraph 1.[55]

Additionally, Article 15(3) calls on the Parties to encourage commercial carriers to cooperate with government authorities at points of entry and exit and other customs control areas in order to prevent unauthorized access to means of transport and cargo and to implement appropriate security measures.

15.2.4.1 Illicit Traffic by Sea

Article 17 establishes an elaborate process to suppress illicit drug traffic by sea, to include provisions that allow for the boarding of vessels suspected of engaging in illicit trafficking.

---

[52] Id., Article 14(2).
[53] Id., Article 14(3)(a).
[54] Id., Article 14(3)(c).
[55] Id., Article 15(2).

Article 17
Illicit Traffic by Sea

1. The Parties shall cooperate to the fullest extent possible to suppress illicit traffic by sea, in conformity with international law of the sea.
2. A Party which has reasonable grounds to suspect that a vessel flying its flag or not displaying a flag or marks of registry is engaged in illicit traffic may request the assistance of other Parties in suppressing its use for that purpose. The Parties so requested shall render such assistance within the means available to them.
3. A Party which has reasonable grounds to suspect that a vessel exercising freedom of navigation in accordance with international law and flying the flag or displaying marks of registry of another Party is engaged in illicit traffic may so notify the flag State, request confirmation of registry and, if confirmed, request authorization from the flag State to take appropriate measures in regard to that vessel.

The provisions, however, are unclear on particular points. If a Party has reasonable grounds to suspect that a vessel flying its flag or a stateless vessel is engaged in illicit traffic, it "may request the assistance of other Parties in suppressing its use for that purpose" and "Parties so requested shall render such assistance within the means available to them."[56] Article 17(3) specifies the type of assistance that may be requested or rendered. Additionally, a Party that has reasonable grounds to suspect that a foreign flag vessel is engaged in illicit traffic "may so notify the flag State, request confirmation of registry and, if confirmed, request authorization from the flag State to take appropriate measures in regard to that vessel."[57] If so requested, the flag State may authorize (with or without mutually agreed conditions) the requesting State to:

a) Board the vessel;
b) Search the vessel;
c) If evidence of involvement in illicit traffic is found, take appropriate action with respect to the vessel, persons and cargo on board.[58]

Furthermore, Article 17 also specifies that

5. Where action is taken pursuance to [Article 17], the Parties concerned shall take due account of the need not to endanger the safety of life at sea, the security of the vessel and the cargo or to prejudice the commercial and legal interests of the flag State or any other interested State.
6. The flag State may, consistent with its obligation in paragraph 1 of this article, subject its authorization to conditions to be mutually agreed between it and the requesting Party, including conditions relating to responsibility.[59]

---

[56] Id., Article 17(2).
[57] Id., Article 17(3).
[58] Id., Article 17(4).
[59] Id., Article 17(5)–(6).

Flag States are expected to respond expeditiously to requests from other Parties to verify a vessel's nationality or to authorize its boarding.[60] The requesting State shall promptly inform the flag State of the results of any action taken against the vessel, its crew and any cargo on board.[61] Parties are encouraged to enter into bilateral or regional agreements or arrangements to enhance the effectiveness of the Convention.[62] Consistent with this provision, the United States and other nations have entered into a series of bilateral and multilateral agreements and arrangements to facilitate the interception and boarding of vessels that are suspected of being engaged in the illicit drug trade.

Actions under Article 17(4) may be carried out only by warships and military aircraft, and other ships and aircraft "clearly marked and identifiable as being on government service and authorized to that effect."[63] Additionally, any action taken pursuant to Article 17 "shall take due account of the need not to endanger the safety of life at sea, the security of the vessel and the cargo or to prejudice the commercial and legal interests of the flag State or any other interested State." Such actions shall likewise "take due account of the need not to interfere with or affect the rights and obligations and the exercise of jurisdiction of coastal States in accordance with the international law of the sea."[64]

Article 17 is consistent with Article 108(1) of the United Nations Convention on the Law of the Sea (UNLCOS), which requires States to "cooperate in the suppression of illicit traffic in narcotic drugs and psychotropic substances engaged in by ships on the high seas contrary to international conventions." Article 108(2) further provides that "any State which has reasonable grounds for believing that a ship flying its flag is engaged in illicit traffic in narcotic drugs or psychotropic substances may request the cooperation of other States to suppress such traffic."

The major drawback of Article 17 is that it is based on the flag State consent provisions of UNCLOS. Article 92(1) specifically provides that "ships shall sail under the flag of one State only and, save in exceptional cases expressly provided for in international treaties or in this Convention, shall be subject to its exclusive jurisdiction on the high seas." Counter-narcotics, however, is not one of the exceptional cases provided for in UNCLOS. Non-consensual boardings are only permitted under Article 110 of UNCLOS for ships engaged in piracy, slave trade or unauthorized broadcasting, as well as ships without nationality or ships assimilated to a ship without nationality under Article 92(2).

---

[60] Id., Article 17(7).
[61] Id., Article 17(8).
[62] Id., Article 17(9).
[63] Id., Article 17(10).
[64] Id., Article 17(11).

15.3 INTERNATIONAL MARITIME ORGANIZATION

The International Maritime Organization has been active in developing guidelines to prevent and suppress the smuggling of illicit drugs and precursor chemicals on ships engaged in international trade. These efforts are consistent with and complement Article 15 of the 1988 Vienna Convention, which requires Parties to take appropriate measures to ensure that commercial carriers are not used to transport illicit drugs and substances.

15.3.1 *IMO Guidelines*

In 1997, the IMO Assembly adopted *Guidelines for the Prevention and Suppression of the Smuggling of Drugs, Psychotropic Substances, and Precursor Chemicals on Ships Engaged in International Traffic*.[65] In 2005, the Assembly authorized the Facilitation Committee and the Maritime Safety Committee to adopt jointly the necessary amendments to align the Guidelines with the provisions of SOLAS Chapter XI-2 and the ISPS Code and to revise them in a manner that reflects developments to prevent and combat the smuggling of illicit substances and precursor chemicals.[66] Accordingly, the Maritime Safety Committee and the Facilitation Committee adopted a set of *Revised Guidelines for the Prevention and Suppression of the Smuggling of Drugs, Psychotropic Substances and Precursor Chemicals on Ships Engaged in International Maritime Traffic* in 2006 and 2007, respectively.[67]

Illicit drug trafficking can negatively affect international shipping in two ways. First, because illegal drugs can be concealed on board vessels, law enforcement efforts to inspect those vessels can result in long delays to the departure of ships,

---

[65] IMO Doc. A.872(20), Guidelines for the Prevention and Suppression of the Smuggling of Drugs, Psychotropic Substances and Precursor Chemicals on Ships Engaged in International Maritime Traffic, Nov. 27, 1997 and IMO Doc. A/Res.872, Guidelines for the Prevention and Suppression of the Smuggling of Drugs, Psychotropic Substances and Precursor Chemicals on Ships Engaged in International Maritime Traffic, Dec. 5, 1997.

[66] IMO Doc. A.985(24), Revision of the Guidelines for the Prevention and Suppression of the Smuggling of Drugs, Psychotropic Substances and Precursor Chemicals on Ships Engaged in International Maritime Traffic, Dec. 1, 2005 and IMO Doc. A24/Res.985/Rev.1, Revision of the Guidelines for the Prevention and Suppression of the Smuggling of Drugs, Psychotropic Substances and Precursor Chemicals on Ships Engaged in International Maritime Traffic (Resolution A.872(20)), Feb. 6, 2006.

[67] IMO Doc. MSC.228(82), Revised Guidelines for the Prevention and Suppression of the Smuggling of Drugs, Psychotropic Substances and Precursor Chemicals on Ships Engaged in International Maritime Traffic, Dec. 7, 2006, IMO Doc. MSC 82/24/Add.2, Report of the Maritime Safety Committee on its Eighty-Second Session, Dec. 22, 2006, Annex 14; IMO Res. FAL.9(34), Revised Guidelines for the Prevention and Suppression of the Smuggling of Drugs, Psychotropic Substances and Precursor Chemicals on Ships Engaged in International Maritime Traffic, Mar. 30, 2007, and IMO Doc. FAL34/19, Report on the Facilitation Committee on its Thirty-Fourth Session, May 15, 2007, Annex 2.

particularly cargo ships. Secondly, crew members that use drugs threaten the safety of the vessel. The revised guidelines therefore attempt to strike a balance between the facilitation of international trade and management of security in order to prevent drug-trafficking activities. However, it is important to strike the right balance—too much control hampers international trade by causing unnecessary delays for both ships and port facilities, while inadequate control leads to increased risks of drug trafficking.

Prevention is one of the most important aspects of combating illicit drug trafficking and should include all persons who are associated with the maritime sector. Part of prevention includes "enhancing the safety and security arrangements for boarding points, ports, port facilities and ships, and supporting coordinated action among the competent authorities in port, particularly those operating at the ship-port interface."[68] It additionally includes increasing the awareness of all persons who are involved with the maritime sector of the "scale of the global drug trafficking problem and encouraging them to contribute to the international efforts to detect and eliminate..." the illicit drug trade.[69]

Measures to enhance port facility security are contained in Section 1.5 of the Revised Guidelines. Locations covered by "approved port facility security plans should implement security procedures in accordance with the provisions of the ISPS [International Ship and Port Facility Security] Code." Port facilities and other locations that are not covered by an approved port facility security plan should establish appropriate measures to enhance the security of ships interfacing with them, including:

.1 The control of access by private vehicles to cargo stores and loading services.
.2 Having a list of all vehicles and persons with regular authorized access to cargo stores and port services, and making this list available to the competent Authorities.
.3 Restricting parking of all vehicles to a designated area, remote from the active loading areas.
.4 Any vehicle authorized to enter at one time to cargo stores or loading services must be issued with a dated entry pass and parking should be restricted to designated areas. The pass numbers should be recorded and made available to the competent Authorities if required.
.5 When the port facility or ship has electronic security systems, such as closed circuit television covering the cargo holding or loading area, the systems must be accessible to the competent Authorities, if they so request.
.6 Access to cargo and loading areas should only be permitted to authorized persons and vehicles showing the correct identification.
.7 All these precautions and actions should be harmonized, to the extent possible, with the relevant measures in the ship security plan.

---

[68] IMO Doc. MSC 82/24/Add.2.
[69] IMO Res. MSC.228(82).

Drug traffickers routinely transship drugs several times in order to conceal country of origin. As a result, "few ports can now be considered safe from attempts to place drugs and other illicit substances on board...," particularly ports in drug producing countries.[70] In assessing the possibility that illicit drugs may be concealed on board a vessel, carriers should take the following factors into consideration:

    .1 ports of call and routes taken by the vessel;
    .2 the origin and routeing of the cargo;
    .3 the level of control exercised at port facilities;
    .4 the degree of control exercised regarding access to the ship; and
    .5 the vulnerability of the crew to pressure by drug traffickers.[71]

15.3.2 Maritime Trafficking

Carriers must also take into consideration that ships are particularly vulnerable to being used as a conduit for the movement of drugs:

    .1 in cars, freight vehicles, trailers, etc.;
    .2 by visitors to the vessel;
    .3 in luggage placed in a baggage trolley;
    .4 in ships' stores;
    .5 by contractors' personnel (for example repair or cleaning gangs);
    .6 as part of crew effects;
    .7 concealed on or in the vessel's machinery or hull; and
    .8 in cargo or in the structure of cargo containers or packing.[72]

As a result, trafficking on commercial vessels can be conducted by:

    2.1 Overt or covert entry and concealment of drugs within the ship...
    2.2 Indirect entry and concealment of drugs within the ship [e.g., in cargo, crew baggage, etc.]...
    2.3 Conspiracy to insert and conceal drugs within the ship [e.g., crew member and dock worker]...
    2.4 Concealment of drugs on the outside of the ship [e.g., securing package to ship's hull].[73]

The key is, therefore, to implement measures to control access to the ship and its cargo to prevent drugs from getting on board. Controlling access can be enhanced by:

- Educating and training the crew on the risks associated with becoming involved in drug trafficking or abuse.

---

[70] Id.
[71] Id.
[72] Id.
[73] Id.

- Good communication and liaison between the company and port authorities to provide local intelligence and assist in threat assessments.
- Awareness of the risk of illicit trafficking in each port of call.
- Continuous review of the ship's security plan.
- A vigilant shore-based and seagoing staff.
- Sharing information with port authorities to establish container-risk profiles, such as consignee companies, owners, source, market history, form of payment, ports of call, etc.[74]

Traffickers will normally look for easy targets to carry out their illicit smuggling activities. An unsecured vessel or cargo compound is much more likely to be targeted than a vessel or compound that has visible security arrangements.

If shore-side security measures are inadequate, the ship's master or Ship Security Officer should implement additional shipboard security measures to maintain the integrity of the vessel. Access control through crew awareness and control of entry to the vessel are therefore key features in any in-port shipboard security plan. If persons other than crew members are going to be permitted on board, Section 4.2.3 of the Guidelines suggests that the following precautions should be observed:

.1 access may be authorized to specific departments but should not be granted to restricted areas, engine rooms, holds, stores, etc.;
.2 any package or bag brought on board or removed from the ship should be examined;
.3 in the case of shore personnel working on board, for maintenance, loading, unloading, stowing or unstowing the ship, etc., the ship security officer should ensure that access to restricted and unauthorized areas is controlled; and
.4 access control at the ship's access ladder or gangway while at the port facility.

The ship's hull creates a natural boundary for keeping would-be traffickers from gaining access to the ship. Section 4.3 of the Guidelines therefore recommends taking the following measures to protect the hull's integrity:

.1 Access points to the vessel should be kept to a minimum, ideally a single controlled gangway, ramp or companionway. When regulations demand a second emergency ladder, consideration should be given to keeping it rolled up or lifted clear of the water.
.2 If the risk warrants it, access points should be manned. In certain circumstances two members of the crew or supplementary security staff may be required. They should be fully briefed on their duties and the action to take in the event of an incident or emergency. They need to be provided with a flash light, a means of summoning assistance and communications equipment to remain in touch with the duty officer. A means of discreet communications by radio, direct-line facilities or other reliable means should be provided at each access point for use by security or operating personnel to contact the port facility security officer in the event that assistance is required.

---

[74] Id., 3.1–3.6.

.3 Gangway duty personnel need to hold a list of crew members, shore officials and expected visitors. Security alarms and devices may be appropriate in certain ports, as a complement to guards and patrols. Immediate and appropriate response to alarms is important if they are to be effective.
.4 Packages, spares, and stores should be carefully scrutinized when being taken on board.
.5 Random, frequent, and thorough searches should be made if it is impractical to search every item. Items sent ashore for repair, inspection or replenishment, such as fire extinguishers, gas bottles, etc., should be closely examined on return to the vessel.

In high-risk ports, it may be necessary to search and photograph persons coming on board, as well as escort such persons while on board. Any person coming on board, including port facility employees, vendors, and port authorities, should also be required to properly identify themselves with appropriate credentials. Any stranger should be challenged and unexpected visitors should be watched at all times. In addition, visitors should be denied unescorted access to areas of the ship that are more susceptible to drug smuggling, such as infrequently used compartments and unmanned machinery spaces. Alternatively, such areas should be locked and randomly inspected for signs of tampering. Watch standers should be vigilant for suspicious objects or packages found on board the ship. Additionally, crew members should be instructed to not accept packages from strangers.[75]

Traffickers may attempt to conceal illicit drugs externally on the ship's hull. Measures to deter against external concealment efforts include illumination of the ship's deck and overside during periods of darkness and posting lookouts to watch for divers and small boats. Any small boat in the vicinity of the ship should be challenged and kept under surveillance, particularly at night. If a breach of security occurs, a search should be conducted below the waterline by qualified divers.[76]

There are countless places on board a ship where drugs can be concealed, including accommodation spaces (e.g., cabins, lavatories, game rooms, etc.), machinery, unmanned spaces and little-used compartments. Additionally, the cargo, particularly containerized cargo, provides ample opportunities for concealment of illicit substances. Section 6.2 of the Guidelines provides a list of some of the more common places where drugs can be hidden:

.1 where it is unlikely that anyone will enter or where searches are rarely made, whether due to respect (for example master's cabin, the sofa in his day room), awkwardness (for example propeller shaft tunnel) or danger (for example behind electrical panels and in inert cargo spaces); near the funnel where fumes may disguise distinctive smells such as cannabis; passenger cabins;
.2 store rooms (flour bins, refrigerators, freezers for provisions such as fish and meat, sacks of vegetables or inside canned goods);

---

[75] Id., 4.3.
[76] Id., 4.4.

546   CHAPTER FIFTEEN

- .3 deposited provisions (wardrobes);
- .4 paint stores (paint lockers);
- .5 in crew quarters (for example behind or in radiators or toilet fittings, behind pictures or skirting boards, in porthole paneling, in cabin, ceiling and wall paneling, in false compartments in the bases of wardrobes and in coat hangers, under lockers and drawers, beneath bunks and mattresses and other cabin furniture);
- .6 places where access is prohibited to unauthorized personnel;
- .7 inside lubricating oil tanks or cargo tanks; in companionway ducts, floor, wall and ceiling panels, inside ventilation pipes and shaft tunnels or cable ducts in the deck or inside engine-room machinery, in computer rooms, control panels, sumps, bilges and funnel shafts;
- .8 crates or containers with false bottoms; double-bottomed oil drums, cylinders and paint drums;
- .9 places where the substances may not seem out of place (for example medical stores, lifeboat stores); inside fire extinguishers, hoses and their storage spaces;
- .10 inside recent structural alterations; in freight containers or in hollow spaces in their construction;
- .11 inside false floors and/or ceilings in cabins and companionways;
- .12 in oil or water tanks false probes or visual indicators and falsely calibrated gauges may be fitted.

A vigilant and well-trained crew is critical to the success of any shipboard security plan. Suspicious circumstances must be reported immediately to the Ship's Security Officer. Some examples of suspicious circumstances that warrant further investigation include:

- .1 strangers found in unusual places while the ship is in port;
- .2 strangers carrying parcels and seeking access to the vessel;
- .3 shore gangs or contractors' staff working unsupervised on apparently unnecessary work or outside normal hours without good reason;
- .4 unanticipated work, especially structural adaptations of alterations (for example closed off spaces);
- .5 crew members found in strange places without reason (for example, catering crew in the hold or engine room), loitering in unusual places during the voyage or showing undue interest or unease during officers' inspections;
- .6 passengers found outside passenger or public areas;
- .7 unexpected occurrences (for example, a supposedly full ballast tank found empty) or things out of place (for example, sacks of flour in the paint store);
- .8 evidence that packages, tanks or containers have been opened;
- .9 disturbed stowage, closed off spaces, pipes going nowhere;
- .10 missing keys;
- .11 unexplained failure of electrics or mechanics, for however short a period; and
- .12 evidence of tampering with welded tank tops, primed gauges, insecure boat covers, unlocked "secure places".[77]

A security checklist for masters and ships' officers is included at Section 6.4 of the Guidelines:

---

[77] Id., 6.3.

.1 know your crew's usual habits and study any unease or departure from routine, such as unusual places for routine jobs on board or any uncharacteristic behavior;
.2 maintain proper gangway watch at all times in port and forbid unauthorized access;
.3 conduct regular inspections of varied nature, place and duration and log them;
.4 question all strange persons in an unusual place on board while the ship is in port;
.5 take into consideration the possible significance of finding things out of place; for example, a supposedly full ballast tank found empty, or sacks of flour in the paint store;
.6 inspect all disturbed stowage, closed off spaces, pipes going nowhere;
.7 seek evidence of tampering with the ship's fittings, for example, welded tank tops, insecure boat covers, equipment which does not work;
.8 where possible, arrange supervision of shore gangs; and
.9 lock all spaces and access points to, for example, cargo spaces not regularly in use and control access to keys.

Crew members and passengers should be observed for any indications that they might be involved in illicit drug smuggling. Some behavior patterns that should raise concerns include:

.1 nervous or suspicious behavior;
.2 unusually large amounts of money;
.3 unusually large local purchases;
.4 expensive clothing;
.5 lists containing names, dates or places and references to money, weights or other units;
.6 unusual clothing when going ashore or returning to the vessel (for example, bulky or out-of-season clothing, conspicuous bulges on the body);
.7 unusual interest in a particular area of the vessel, consignment or container;
.8 possession of unusual tools not connected to the job; and
.9 possession of drug paraphernalia.[78]

Ship owners and shipping companies also have a role to play in preventing the illegal transport of drugs and other substances by sea. In particular, Company Security Officers should determine the drug trafficking threat for each port of call, taking into consideration whether:

.1 the person making the cargo booking is familiar;
.2 the shipper/consignee is a regular customer or a first-time client;
.3 the article involved is consistent with the client's business;
.4 the shippers'/consignees' addresses are incomplete, misspelt, vague or inappropriate;
.5 the "notify party" is difficult to contact;
.6 it is a last minute booking;
.7 the charges are prepaid and in cash;
.8 any attempt has been made to hide the name/address of the payer of freight;
.9 the shipment originates in a known drug source or transit country;

---

[78] Id., 6.5.

.10 the consignment appears to be normal bearing in mind the origin and routeing of the cargo, commodity, country of origin and destination and the value of the goods;
.11 the cargo is properly described on the documentation; and
.12 the size/weight ratio is commensurate with the commodity.[79]

In addition, cargo handlers should be instructed to watch for:

.1 broken seals on containers;
.2 false floors in containers (not flush with the door frame) or false ceilings (roof above the corner blocks or changes in height of internal ceiling);
.3 blocked cavities in the frame of containers or trailers;
.4 evidence of drilling in the frame of a container or chassis;
.5 evidence of fresh paint or new welding, or variations in wall, floor or ceiling texture, which may indicate a structural alteration designed to conceal drugs or other contraband.[80]

The Guidelines additionally contain provisions to control the transport of precursors and other chemical products that can be used to manufacture illegal drugs and psychotropic substances. Table 15.1 summarizes the chemicals used to manufacture various narcotic drugs:

In addition, the Guidelines call on ships and port facilities to "formulate and implement plans to prevent and control the illegal diversion of chemical substances in order to restrict illicit drug production."[81]

Table 15.1. Chemical Processing in Manufacture of Illegal Drugs

INDUSTRIAL CHEMICALS	DRUGS PRODUCED
acetone	heroin, morphine, cocaine
ethyl acetate	heroin, cocaine
butyl acetate	Cocaine
hydrochloric acid	heroin, morphine, cocaine
sulphuric acid	cocaine, marijuana oil
butyl alcohol	morphine, cocaine paste
acid anhydride	heroin, methaqualone
chloroform	heroin, morphine, cocaine
sodium carbonate	heroin, morphine, cocaine
methanol	Cocaine
ethyl ether	heroin, cocaine

---

[79] Id., 6.7.
[80] Id.
[81] Id., Chapter 2, Section 1.

15.4 UN BASIC PRINCIPLES ON THE USE OF FORCE

Counter-narcotics operations may, in appropriate circumstances, involve the use of force by law enforcement officials. The UN has developed a set of principles to guide law enforcement officials when using force in the execution of their duties. Consistent with Article 3 of the *Code of Conduct for Law Enforcement Officials*, the basic principles emphasize that deadly force should be used by law enforcement personnel only when strictly necessary and to the extent required for the performance of their duty. The underlying premise of the guidelines is that "law enforcement officials have a vital role in the protection of the right to life, liberty and security of the person, as guaranteed in the Universal Declaration of Human Rights and reaffirmed in the International Covenant on Civil and Political Rights" and that the "use of force and firearms by law enforcement officials should be commensurate with due respect for human rights."[82] States are encouraged to take the principles into account to ensure and promote the proper role of law enforcement officials within the framework of their national laws and practices.

15.4.1 *Basic Principles on the Use of Force and Firearms*

General provisions on the use of force and firearms are fairly restrictive and include the following guidelines:

1. Governments and law enforcement agencies shall adopt and implement rules and regulations on the use of force and firearms against persons by law enforcement officials. In developing such rules and regulations, Governments and law enforcement agencies shall keep the ethical issues associated with the use of force and firearms constantly under review.
2. Governments and law enforcement agencies should develop a range of means as broad as possible and equip law enforcement officials with various types of weapons and ammunition that would allow for a differentiated use of force and firearms. These should include the development of non-lethal incapacitating weapons for use in appropriate situations, with a view to increasingly restraining the application of means capable of causing death or injury to persons. For the same purpose, it should also be possible for law enforcement officials to be equipped with self-defensive equipment such as shields, helmets, bullet-proof vests and bullet-proof means of transportation, in order to decrease the need to use weapons of any kind.
3. The development and deployment of non-lethal incapacitating weapons should be carefully evaluated in order to minimize the risk of endangering uninvolved persons, and the use of such weapons should be carefully controlled.

---

[82] Basic Principles on the Use of Force and Firearms by Law Enforcement Officials, adopted by the Eighth United Nations Congress on the Prevention of Crime and the Treatment of Offenders, Havana, Cuba, Aug. 27 to Sept. 7, 1990, http://www2.ohchr.org/english/law/firearms.htm.

4. Law enforcement officials, in carrying out their duty, shall, as far as possible, apply non-violent means before resorting to the use of force and firearms. They may use force and firearms only if other means remain ineffective or without any promise of achieving the intended result.
5. Whenever the lawful use of force and firearms is unavoidable, law enforcement officials shall:
   (a) Exercise restraint in such use and act in proportion to the seriousness of the offense and the legitimate objective to be achieved;
   (b) Minimize damage and injury, and respect and preserve human life;
   (c) Ensure that assistance and medical aid are rendered to any injured or affected persons at the earliest possible moment;
   (d) Ensure that relatives or close friends of the injured or affected person are notified at the earliest possible moment.
6. Where injury or death is caused by the use of force and firearms by law enforcement officials, they shall report the incident promptly to their superiors, in accordance with principle 22.
7. Governments shall ensure that arbitrary or abusive use of force and firearms by law enforcement officials is punished as a criminal offense under their law.
8. Exceptional circumstances such as internal political instability or any other public emergency may not be invoked to justify any departure from these basic principles.[83]

More specific guidance, which is equally restrictive, is provided in Principles 9–11:

9. Law enforcement officials shall not use firearms against persons except in self-defense or defense of others against the imminent threat of death or serious injury, to prevent the perpetration of a particularly serious crime involving grave threat to life, to arrest a person presenting such a danger and resisting their authority, or to prevent his or her escape, and only when less extreme means are insufficient to achieve these objectives. In any event, intentional lethal use of firearms may only be made when strictly unavoidable in order to protect life.
10. In the circumstances provided for under principle 9, law enforcement officials shall identify themselves as such and give a clear warning of their intent to use firearms, with sufficient time for the warning to be observed, unless to do so would unduly place the law enforcement officials at risk or would create a risk of death or serious harm to other persons, or would be clearly inappropriate or pointless in the circumstances of the incident.
11. Rules and regulations on the use of firearms by law enforcement officials should include guidelines that:
    (a) Specify the circumstances under which law enforcement officials are authorized to carry firearms and prescribe the types of firearms and ammunition permitted;
    (b) Ensure that firearms are used only in appropriate circumstances and in a manner likely to decrease the risk of unnecessary harm;
    (c) Prohibit the use of those firearms and ammunition that cause unwarranted injury or present an unwarranted risk;
    (d) Regulate the control, storage and issuing of firearms, including procedures for ensuring that law enforcement officials are accountable for the firearms and ammunition issued to them;

---

[83] Id.

(e) Provide for warnings to be given, if appropriate, when firearms are to be discharged;
(f) Provide for a system of reporting whenever law enforcement officials use firearms in the performance of their duty.[84]

Guidelines for policing unlawful assemblies and persons in custody or detention are contained in Principles 12–14 and Principles 15–17, respectively. Guidance regarding qualification, training and counseling of law enforcement officials is also provided in Principles 18–21. With regard to training, Principle 20 provides that:

20. In the training of law enforcement officials, Governments and law enforcement agencies shall give special attention to issues of police ethics and human rights, especially in the investigative process, to alternatives to the use of force and firearms, including the peaceful settlement of conflicts, the understanding of crowd behavior, and the methods of persuasion, negotiation and mediation, as well as to technical means, with a view to limiting the use of force and firearms. Law enforcement agencies should review their training programs and operational procedures in the light of particular incidents.[85]

Reporting and review procedures are outlined in Principles 22–26. In cases where death, serious injury or other grave consequences have occurred, Principle 22 requires that a detailed report "be sent promptly to the competent authorities responsible for administrative review and judicial control."[86] Pursuant to Principle 23, persons (including dependents in case of death) affected by the use of force or firearms "shall have access to an independent process, including a judicial process."[87]

Principle 24 applies the concept of command responsibility, providing that superior officers should be "held responsible if they know, or should have known, that law enforcement officials under their command are resorting, or have resorted, to the unlawful use of force and firearms, and they did not take all measures in their power to prevent, suppress or report such use."[88] Additionally, obedience to superior orders is not a defense "if law enforcement officials knew that an order to use force and firearms resulting in the death or serious injury of a person was manifestly unlawful and had a reasonable opportunity to refuse to follow it."[89] However, refusal to obey an unlawful order to use force and firearms is a defense.[90]

---

[84] Id.
[85] Id.
[86] Id.
[87] Id.
[88] Id.
[89] Id., Principle 26.
[90] Id., Principle 25.

15.4.2 Use of Force in the Case of the M/V Saiga

Standards similar to the UN Basic Principles were applied by the International Tribunal for the Law of the Sea (ITLOS) in the M/V *Saiga Case*, decided by the Tribunal in 1999.[91] The *Saiga* was an oil tanker owned by Tabona Shipping Company Ltd. of Nicosia, Cyprus, managed by Seascot Shipmanagement Ltd. of Glasgow, Scotland, chartered to Lemania Shipping Group Ltd. of Geneva, Switzerland, provisionally registered in Saint Vincent and the Grenadines, and manned by a Ukrainian master and crew. The *Saiga* was engaged in selling gas oil as bunker and occasionally water to vessels off the coast of West Africa.

On October 28, 1997, the *Saiga* was attacked by a Guinean patrol boat south of the southern limit of the Guinean EEZ. Guinean officials subsequently boarded the *Saiga* and arrested it. The ship and its crew were brought to Conakry, Guinea, where the master was detained. Two crew members were injured during the attack. The cargo of 4,941.322 metric tons of gas oil on board the ship was subsequently discharged by order of the Guinean authorities. The ship was ultimately released on February 28, 1998.

In considering the force used by Guinean authorities to arrest the *Saiga*, ITLOS determined that it "must take into account the circumstances of the arrest in the context of the applicable rules of international law...," which require "that the use of force must be avoided as far as possible and, where force is unavoidable, it must not go beyond what is reasonable and necessary in the circumstances."[92] According to the Tribunal, these principles have been followed over the years in law enforcement operations at sea:

> The normal practice used to stop a ship at sea is first to give an auditory or visual signal to stop, using internationally recognized signals. Where this does not succeed, a variety of actions may be taken, including the firing of shots across the bows of the ship. It is only after the appropriate actions fail that the pursuing vessel may, as a last resort, use force. Even then, appropriate warning must be issued to the ship and all efforts should be made to ensure that life is not endangered....[93]

After noting that the *Saiga's* maximum speed was 10 knots and that the vessel was almost fully laden and low in the water at the time it was approached by the Guinean patrol vessel, ITLOS determined that the ship could have been "boarded without much difficulty by the Guinean officers."[94] Consequently, there was no excuse for firing at the ship with live ammunition "without issuing any of the

---

[91] The M/V *Saiga* (No. 2) Case (Saint Vincent and the Grenadines v. Guinea), July 1, 1999.
[92] Id., para. 155.
[93] Id., para. 156. *See*, S.S. *"I'm Alone"* (Canada/United States, 1935), U.N.R.I.A.A., Vol. III, p. 1609; *The Red Crusader* (*Commission of Enquiry*, Denmark/United Kingdom, 1962), I.L.R., Vol. 35, p. 485.
[94] Id., para. 157.

signals and warnings required by international law and practice."[95] ITLOS additionally found that the Guinean officials had used excessive force after boarding the *Saiga*:

> Having boarded the ship without resistance, and although there is no evidence of the use or threat of force from the crew, they fired indiscriminately while on the deck and used gunfire to stop the engine of the ship. In using firearms in this way, the Guinean officers appeared to have attached little or no importance to the safety of the ship and the persons on board. In the process, considerable damage was done to the ship and to vital equipment in the engine and radio rooms. And, more seriously, the indiscriminate use of gunfire caused severe injuries to two of the persons on board.[96]

For these reasons, the Tribunal found that Guinea had "used excessive force and endangered human life before and after boarding the *Saiga*, and thereby violated the rights of Saint Vincent and the Grenadines under international law."[97]

---

[95] Id.
[96] Id., para. 158.
[97] Id., para. 159.

SIXTEEN

REGIONAL AUTHORITIES TO COUNTER DRUG TRAFFICKING

16.1 Regional Cooperation in Countering Maritime Drug Trafficking

A number or regional, bilateral and domestic measures have been adopted to supplement and implement the requirements of the various international counter-narcotics treaties discussed in Chapter 15 of this volume. There are a wide range of measures at the regional level, and these include the *Caribbean Regional Maritime Agreement* (CRMA), the *Paris Pact Initiative*, and the Organization of American States (OAS) *Model Procedures for Counter-drug Operations*.

Bilateral cooperation—such as the U.S.-Mexico Mérida Initiative—has been effective in providing financial and technical assistance to the Mexican Government's efforts to combat organized criminal groups engaged in the illicit drug trade. The United States has also entered into a series of bilateral maritime counter-narcotics agreements that have enhanced combined efforts with regional partners to interdict illicit drugs at sea before they reach drug markets in the United States. In Asia, Coast Watch South, an inter-agency mechanism implemented in the Philippines, is intended to enhance maritime domain awareness and to protect the Philippines and its people from maritime threats, and it helps reduce drug trafficking by ship.

16.2 Caribbean Regional Maritime Agreement

The *Agreement Concerning Cooperation in Suppressing Illicit Maritime and Air Trafficking in Narcotic Drugs and Psychotropic Substances in the Caribbean Area* was adopted in 2003 by the Caribbean nations to supplement the 1988 Vienna Convention. The Agreement entered into force in 2008. By July 14, 2010, States' parties to the Agreement included: Belize, Costa Rica, Dominican Republic, France, Guatemala, the Netherlands, and the United States. Haiti, Honduras,

Jamaica, Nicaragua and the United Kingdom also have signed the Agreement, but have not yet ratified it.[1] Under the agreement, the "Caribbean area", as defined in Article 1(j), includes "the Gulf of Mexico, the Caribbean Sea and the Atlantic Ocean west of longitude 45° West, north of latitude 0° (the Equator) and south of latitude 30° North with the exception of the territorial sea" of States not party to the agreement.

Recognizing that the nature of the illicit drug trade requires regional and subregional cooperation, the Agreement seeks to increase cooperation between the Caribbean nations in order to enhance their effectiveness in suppressing illicit traffic in narcotic drugs and psychotropic substances by sea.[2] Accordingly, the Convention commits the States' parties to:

> ...cooperate to the fullest extent possible in combating illicit maritime and air traffic in and over the waters of the Caribbean area, consistent with available law enforcement resources of the Parties and related priorities, in conformity with the international law of the sea and applicable agreements, with a view to ensuring that suspect vessels and suspect aircraft are detected, identified, continuously monitored, and where evidence of involvement in illicit traffic is found, suspect vessels are detained for appropriate law enforcement action by the responsible law enforcement authorities.[3]

Expeditious handling of requests from other States' parties to take appropriate law enforcement actions against suspect vessels and aircraft can greatly enhance regional efforts to combat illicit drug trafficking. Article 4(1), therefore, encourages each Party "to accelerate the authorizations for law enforcement vessels and aircraft, aircraft in support of law enforcement operations, and law enforcement officials of the other Parties to enter its waters, air space, ports and airports in order to carry out the objectives of this Agreement...."

Likewise, Article 6(4) requires requests for verification of nationality of a vessel to be answered expeditiously—that is, an answer shall be provided "as soon as possible, but in any event within four (4) hours."[4] Furthermore, Article 4(3) requires effective coordination between "civil aviation and law enforcement authorities to enable rapid verification of aircraft registrations and flight plans."[5]

Other measures to enhance law enforcement efforts against the illicit drug trade include: posting of liaison officers; exchanging law enforcement officials

---

[1] Agreement Concerning Cooperation in Suppressing Illicit Maritime and Air Trafficking in Narcotic Drugs and Psychotropic Substances in the Caribbean Area Digest of United States Practice in International Law 2005 (not yet in force) [Hereinafter Caribbean Regional Maritime Agreement].
[2] J. Ashley Roach, *Initiatives to Enhance Maritime Security*, 28 MARINE POL'Y 41, 64 (2004) (describing ship boarding provisions).
[3] Caribbean Regional Maritime Agreement, Article 2.
[4] Id., Article 6(4).
[5] Id., Article 4(3).

and other experts; training of law enforcement officials in combined maritime law enforcement operations (e.g., boarding, search and detention of vessels); and embarkation of law enforcement officials on another Party's law enforcement vessels.[6]

In order to discharge their obligations under the Agreement, each Party is required to establish the capability to:

   a. respond to requests for verification of nationality;
   b. authorize the boarding and search of suspect vessels;
   c. provide expeditious disposition instructions for vessels detained on its behalf;
   d. authorize the entry into its waters and air space of law enforcement vessels and aircraft and aircraft in support of law enforcement operations of the other Parties.[7]

The agreement further requires the Parties to authorize their law enforcement and aviation officials, or other competent national authority, "to permit the entry of law enforcement vessels, law enforcement aircraft and aircraft in support of law enforcement operations... into their waters and air space."[8] The Parties are required to "notify the Depositary of the authority or authorities... to whom requests should be directed under paragraph 1" of the Article.[9]

The Parties are also obligated by Article 9(1) to designate qualified law enforcement officials to act as embarked law enforcement officials on vessels of the other Parties. When embarked on vessels of another Party, these officials may, subject to the domestic laws and regulations of the designating Party:

   a. embark on law enforcement vessels of any of the Parties;
   b. enforce the laws of the designating Party to suppress illicit traffic in the waters of the designating Party, or seaward of its territorial sea in the exercise of the right of hot pursuit or otherwise in accordance with international law;
   c. authorize the entry of the law enforcement vessels on which they are embarked into and navigation within the waters of the designating Party;
   d. authorize the law enforcement vessels on which they are embarked to conduct counter-drug patrols in the waters of the designating Party;
   e. authorize law enforcement officials of the vessel on which the law enforcement officials of the designating Party are embarked to assist in the enforcement of the laws of the designating Party to suppress illicit traffic; and
   f. advise and assist law enforcement officials of other Parties in the conduct of boardings of vessels to enforce the laws of those Parties to suppress illicit traffic.[10]

---

[6] Id., Articles 4(2), 4(4) and 9.
[7] Id., Article 7.
[8] Id., Article 8(2).
[9] Id., Article 7(2).
[10] Id., Article 9(3).

Search and seizure of property, detention of persons and any use of force during an enforcement action being carried out pursuant to the authority of an embarked law enforcement official shall be carried out only by such officials, except that:

> a. crew members of the other Party's vessel may assist in any such action if expressly requested to do so by the law enforcement officials and only to the extent and in the manner requested. Such a request may only be made, agreed to, and acted upon if the action is consistent with the applicable laws and procedures of both Parties; and
> b. such crew members may use force in accordance with Article 22 and their domestic laws and regulations.[11]

Article 22(10) provides that "[n]othing in this Agreement shall impair the exercise of the inherent right of self-defense by law enforcement or other officials of any Party."

Law enforcement operations to suppress illicit traffic of drugs and other substances in and over a State Party's territorial waters shall be conducted in accordance with UNCLOS Article 2, which recognizes that coastal State sovereignty extends throughout the territorial sea (and archipelagic waters) and the air space above it. Accordingly, such operations in and over the territorial sea of a Party are prohibited unless authorized by the coastal State.[12] Consistent with Article 4, requests from another Party to conduct operations in and over the territorial sea shall be decided upon expeditiously by the coastal State.[13] States' Parties may elect to extend application of the Agreement to some or all of its internal waters adjacent to its territorial sea or archipelagic waters upon signing or ratifying the Agreement, or at any time thereafter.[14] Additionally, the convention provides that "[n]othing in this Agreement shall preclude any Party from otherwise expressly authorizing law enforcement operations by any other Party to suppress illicit traffic in its territory, waters or air space, or involving vessels or aircraft of its nationality suspected of illicit traffic."[15]

If a coastal State law enforcement official is not embarked or a coastal State law enforcement vessel is not immediately available to investigate, coastal States may elect to allow law enforcement vessels of another Party to follow a suspect vessel into the territorial sea of the coastal State, take actions to prevent the escape of the vessel, board the vessel and secure the vessel and persons on board while awaiting a response from the coastal State to enter its territorial sea by providing prior notice to the coastal State.[16] If evidence of illicit trafficking is found on board the vessel, the coastal State "shall be promptly informed of the

---

[11] Id., Article 9(4).
[12] Id., Article 11(2).
[13] Id.
[14] Id., Article 15.
[15] Id., Article 14(1).
[16] Id., Article 12(1)(b).

results of the search" and "[t]he suspect vessel, cargo and persons on board shall be detained and taken to a designated port..." unless otherwise directed by the coastal State.[17] The same procedures apply to suspect aircraft.[18]

A State Party also may request aircraft support from another Party "for assistance, including monitoring and surveillance, in suppressing illicit traffic."[19] To ensure safety of air navigation, the requested Party shall observe the following procedures:

    a. In the event of planned bilateral or multilateral law enforcement operations, the requested Party shall provide reasonable notice and communications frequencies to the appropriate authorities, including authorities responsible for air traffic control, of each Party of planned flights by participating aircraft in the air space of that Party.
    b. In the event of unplanned law enforcement operations, which may include the pursuit of suspect aircraft into another Party's air space, the law enforcement and appropriate civil aviation authorities of the Parties concerned shall exchange information concerning the appropriate communications frequencies and other information pertinent to the safety of air navigation.
    c. Any aircraft engaged in law enforcement operations or operations in support of law enforcement activities shall comply with such air navigation and flight safety directions as may be required by each concerned Party's aviation authorities, in the measure in which it is going across the airspace of those Parties.[20]

These provisions are consistent with Article 3(d) of the *Chicago Convention on International Civil Aviation*, which requires State aircraft to operate with due regard for the safety of civil aviation, and Article 13(11), which provides that "the Parties shall not endanger the lives of persons on board or the safety of civil aviation..." while conducting air activities pursuant to the Agreement.[21]

In addition, Article 13(5) requires the requested Party to "maintain contact with the designated law enforcement officials of the requesting Party and keep them informed of the results of such operations so as to enable them to take such action as they may deem appropriate." Moreover, "the requesting Party shall authorize aircraft of a requested Party, when engaged in law enforcement operations or activities in support of law enforcement operations, to fly over its territory and waters; and,... to relay to suspect aircraft, upon the request of the

---

[17] Id., Article 12(3).
[18] Id., Article 12(4) and (5).
[19] Id., Article 13(1).
[20] Id., Article 13(4).
[21] Convention on International Civil Aviation, 15 U.N.T.S. 295, 61 Stat. 1180, T.I.A.S. No. 1591, Dec. 7, 1944, *entered into force* Apr. 4, 1947, *as amended* 1175 U.N.T.S. 297, *entered into force* Oct. 1998 [Hereinafter Chicago Convention]. The Chicago Convention was preceded by the Convention for the Unification of Certain Rules Relating to International Transportation by Air Oct. 12, 1929, 137 L.N.T.S. 11, 2 Bevans 983, 49 Stat. 3000, T.S. 876, *entered into force* Feb. 13, 1933 [Warsaw Convention].

authorizing Party, orders to comply with the instructions and directions from its air traffic control and law enforcement authority...," if either:

a. authorization has been granted by the authority or authorities of the Party requesting assistance...; or
b. advance authorization has been granted by the Party requesting assistance.[22]

Boarding of suspect foreign flag vessels seaward of any State's territorial sea is greatly facilitated by Article 16 of the Agreement, which states that it constitutes flag State authorization to board and search the suspect vessel, its cargo and question the person on board in order to determine if the vessel is engaged in illicit drug trafficking, unless a Party notifies the Depository:

2. upon signing, ratification, acceptance or approval of this Agreement,... that vessels claiming the nationality of that Party... may only be boarded upon express consent of that Party; or
3. upon signing, ratification, acceptance or approval of this Agreement, or at any time thereafter,... that Parties shall be deemed to be granted authorization to board a suspect vessel... that flies its flag or claims its nationality and to search the suspect vessel, its cargo and question the persons found on board in order to determine if the vessel is engaged in illicit traffic, if there is no response or the requested Party can neither confirm nor deny nationality within four (4) hours following receipt of an oral request....[23]

Notwithstanding these foregoing procedures, law enforcement officials of one Party may board a suspect vessel claiming the nationality of another Party in order to examine the vessel's documents when:

a. it is not flying the flag of that other Party;
b. it is not displaying any marks of its registration;
c. it is claiming to have no documentation regarding its nationality on board; and
d. there is no other information evidencing nationality.[24]

If documentation or evidence of nationality is found on board the vessel, the procedures outlined in Article 16(1)–(3) shall apply. On the other hand, if no evidence of nationality is found on board the vessel, "the boarding Party may assimilate the vessel to a ship without nationality in accordance with international law."[25] Similarly, if the claimed flag State Party refutes the claim of nationality made by the suspect vessel, the vessel can be assimilated to be a ship without nationality.[26]

Nothing in the Agreement, however, should be interpreted to limit boarding of vessels by a state Party in accordance with international law, whether based on

---

[22] Chicago Convention, Article 13(6).
[23] Id., Article 16(2) and (3).
[24] Id., Article 16(6).
[25] Id., Article 16(7).
[26] Id., Article 6(5).

the right of visit (consistent with Article 110 of UNCLOS, for example), the duty to render assistance to persons, vessels, and property in distress or peril of being lost at sea (as reflected in Article 98 of UNCLOS), or on flag State consent to take enforcement action (consistent with Article 92 of UNCLOS).[27]

In those cases in which the boarding officials uncover evidence of illicit trafficking, the vessel, cargo and persons on board may be detained pending expeditious disposition instructions from the flag State. Articles 16(5) and 26(1) further require the boarding Party to promptly inform the flag State of the results of any boarding or search conducted pursuant to the Agreement.

In additional to authorizing law enforcement officials of another State to board its vessels, a Party may also request that State to make available one or more of its law enforcement vessels to assist the requesting Party in maritime patrol and surveillance in order to detect and prevent the illicit traffic of drugs by sea and air. If the requested Party has forces available and is willing to provide such assistance, it should provide the requesting Party with the following information via secure communications channels:

    a. the name and description of its law enforcement vessels;
    b. the dates at which, and the periods for which, they will be available;
    c. the names of the Commanding Officers of the vessels; and
    d. any other relevant information.[28]

When boarding a vessel at sea, law enforcement officials "shall take due account of the need not to endanger the safety of life at sea, the security of the vessel and cargo, and not to prejudice any commercial or legal interest...," in particular:

    a. the dangers involved in boarding a vessel at sea, and give consideration as to whether it could be more safely done in port; and
    b. the need to avoid unduly detaining or delaying a vessel.[29]

Any claims against a Party for damages, injury or loss resulting from an interdiction operation, including claims against law enforcement personnel, shall be settled in accordance with international law.[30]

Force may be used to interdict a suspect vessel, but may not be used against civil aircraft in flight.[31] In addition, force should only be used if there is no other feasible means of resolving the situation. Any force used must, however, be "proportional to the objective for which it is employed" and "shall in all cases be the minimum reasonably necessary under the circumstances."[32] Additionally,

---

[27] Id., Article 17.
[28] Id., Article 21.
[29] Id., Article 20(4).
[30] Id., Article 28.
[31] Id., Article 22(1) and (8).
[32] Id., Article 22(2)–(3).

the convention requires that "a warning shall be issued prior to any use of force except when force is being used in self-defense."[33] Nonetheless, nothing in the Agreement impairs the exercise of the inherent right of self-defense by law enforcement or other officials of any States' Party.[34] If force is used against a suspect vessel, the flag State should be informed as soon as practicable. Claims against law enforcement officials will be resolved in accordance with Article 28, as noted above.

To complement the boarding provisions of the Agreement, Parties are required to take the necessary measures to establish its jurisdiction over the offenses it has established in accordance with Article 3(1) of the 1988 Vienna Convention, when:

   a. the offence is committed in waters under its sovereignty or where applicable in its contiguous zone;
   b. the offence is committed on board a vessel flying its flag or an aircraft which is registered under its laws at the time the offence is committed;
   c. the offence is committed on board a vessel without nationality or assimilated to a ship without nationality under international law, which is located seaward of the territorial sea of any State;
   d. the offence is committed on board a vessel flying the flag or displaying the marks of registry or bearing any other indication of nationality of another Party, which is located seaward of the territorial sea of any State.[35]

In addition, Article 24 recognizes that States Parties may consent to the exercise of jurisdiction by another State over their flag vessels interdicted seaward of any State's territorial sea. Information regarding the results of any prosecution or judicial proceeding shall be provided to the flag State.[36]

Assets seized, confiscated or forfeited as a result of any law enforcement operation shall be disposed of by the coastal State, the flag State or the boarding State in accordance with Article 27. "To the extent permitted by its laws and upon such terms as it deems appropriate, a Party may ... transfer forfeited property or proceeds of their sale to another Party or intergovernmental bodies specializing in the fight against illicit traffic in and abuse of narcotic drugs and psychotropic substances."[37]

When signing, ratifying, accepting or approving the Agreement, Article 38 allows States to make declarations or statements "with a view, *inter alia*, to the harmonization of its laws and regulations with the provisions of this Agreement,

---

[33] Id., Article 22(4).
[34] Id., Article 22(10).
[35] Id., Article 23. *See,* United Nations Convention against Illicit Traffic in Narcotic Drugs and Psychotropic Substances, Vienna, Dec. 20, 1988, UN Doc. E/CONF.82/15/Corr.1 and Corr.2, 1582 U.N.T.S. 164, 28 I.L.M. 493 (1989) *entered into force* Nov. 11, 1990, [Hereinafter Vienna Convention].
[36] Chicago Convention, Article 26(2).
[37] Id., Article 27(3).

provided that such declarations or statements do not purport to exclude or to modify the legal effect of the provisions of this Agreement in their application to that State." Consistent with this provision, the United States signed the Agreement without reservation, but has filed the following declaration:

16.2.1 U.S. Declaration of the Agreement

> Declaration of the United States of America Upon Signature of the *Agreement Concerning Cooperation in Suppressing Illicit Maritime and Air Trafficking in Narcotic Drugs and Psychotropic Substances in the Caribbean Area*, April 10, 2003
>
> Regarding the *Agreement Concerning Cooperation in Suppressing Illicit Maritime and Air Trafficking in Narcotic Drugs and Psychotropic Substances in the Caribbean Area* (hereinafter "the Agreement"), the Government of the United States hereby notifies the Depositary that, pursuant to Article 36 (a) of the Agreement, the United States signs the Agreement without reservation as to ratification, acceptance or approval, subject to the following declarations:
>
> 1. Pursuant to paragraph (b) of Article 1 of the Agreement . . . the "competent national authority" of the United States for purposes of the implementation of this Agreement is the United States Coast Guard.
> 2. Pursuant to paragraph (c) of Article 1 of the Agreement, the "law enforcement authorities" for the United States for purposes of this Agreement are the Department of Homeland Security and the Department of Justice.
> 3. Pursuant to paragraph (d) of Article 1 of the Agreement, the law enforcement officials for the United States for purposes of this Agreement are uniformed and other clearly identifiable members of the law enforcement authorities of the United States and may be assisted, on occasion, by uniformed members of the Department of Defense.
> 4. Pursuant to paragraph 5 of Article 9 of the Agreement, the Commander, Seventh Coast Guard District, is the authority responsible for the designation of embarked law enforcement officials.
> 5. Pursuant to paragraph 2 of Article 12 of the Agreement, the United States elects the procedures set forth in paragraph 1(a) of Article 12. Accordingly, the United States understands that a law enforcement vessel of a Party may follow a suspect vessel into the waters of the United States in the Caribbean area and take actions to prevent the escape of the vessel, board the vessel and secure the vessel and persons on board awaiting an expeditious response from the United States once the Party has received authorization from the Commander, Seventh Coast Guard District.
> 6. Pursuant to paragraph 5 of Article 12 of the Agreement, the United States elects the procedures set forth in paragraph 4(a) of Article 12. Accordingly, the United States understands that a law enforcement vessel of a Party may follow a suspect aircraft into the waters of the United States in the Caribbean area in order to maintain contact with the suspected aircraft once the Party has received authorization from the Commander, Seventh Coast Guard District.
> 7. Pursuant to paragraph 7 of Article 13 of the Agreement, the United States elects the procedures set forth in paragraph 6(a) of Article 13. Accordingly, the United States understands that it may authorize aircraft of a Party, when engaged in law enforcement operations or activities in support of law enforcement operations, to fly over United States territory and waters when authorization has been granted

by the Commander, Seventh Coast Guard District. The United States understands further that, subject to the laws of the United States and of the requested Party, the requested Party may, upon the request of the Commander, Seventh Coast Guard District, relay to suspect aircraft orders to comply with the instructions and directions from air traffic control and law enforcement authorities of the United States.
8. Pursuant to paragraph 2 of Article 16 of the Agreement, the United States elects the procedures set forth in paragraph 3 of Article 13. Accordingly, the United States understands that Parties shall be deemed to be granted authorization to board a suspect vessel located seaward of the territorial sea of any State that flies its flag or claims its nationality and to search the suspect vessel, its cargo and question the persons found on board in order to determine if the vessel is engaged in illicit traffic, if there is no response or the United States can neither confirm nor deny nationality within four (4) hours following receipt of an oral request pursuant to Article 6 of the Agreement.
9. Pursuant to Articles 7 and 18 of the Agreement, the single point of contact for the United States with the capability to receive, process and respond to requests and reports at any time is the (Commander, Seventh Coast Guard District, Miami, Florida)....
10. Pursuant to paragraph 1 of Article 19 of the Agreement, the United States designates Commander, Joint Interagency Task Force East (JIATF-East)[38] [note: JIATF-East was a standing joint task force under Commander, U.S. Southern Command] as the United States coordinator to organize its participation and to identify the vessels, aircraft and law enforcement officials involved in any regional and sub-regional maritime law enforcement co-operation and co-ordination programs among the law enforcement authorities of the Parties.
11. Pursuant to paragraph 1 of Article 25 of the Agreement, the United States has established an Internet web page [maintained by the U.S. Coast Guard], to keep Parties fully informed of its applicable laws and procedures, particularly those pertaining to use of force.
12. With reference to paragraph 2 of Article 31 of the Agreement, which provides that nothing in the Agreement shall alter or affect in any way the rights and obligations of a Party which arise from agreements between it and United States on the same subject, it is the understanding of the United States that, in any given operation to suppress illicit traffic, the Parties engaged in the operation may mutually agree to proceed under provisions of both this Agreement and other applicable agreements in force between it and the United States.... [T]he United States understands that a Party with whom the United States also has a bilateral agreement in force on the same subject as this Agreement should specify under which agreement it desires to proceed at the time of making any request to the United States that would be potentially actionable under both this Agreement and the applicable bilateral agreement.... [S]uch specification is made without prejudice to any subsequent request in the same or future operation. The United States of America declares that it shall specify under which agreement it desires to proceed at the time of making any request to a Party with whom the United

---

[38] JIATF-East is now designated "JIATF South," having been merged with a Joint Interagency Task Force known by that name that was closed pursuant to requirements of the Panama Canal Treaty stipulation that U.S. forces would evacuate Panama.

States also has an applicable bilateral agreement in force on the same subject as this Agreement.
13. With reference to paragraph 2 of Article 33 of the Agreement, the United States understands the term "consensus" means adoption of a decision without voting and without the expression of any stated objection.
14. It is the view of the United States that, although paragraph 1 of Article 10 of the Agreement provides that boardings and searches pursuant to the Agreement shall be carried out only by teams of authorized law enforcement officials from law enforcement vessels, paragraph 2 of Article 10 makes clear that such boarding and search teams may also operate from law enforcement aircraft of any of the Parties, and from law enforcement vessels and law enforcement aircraft of other States as agreed among the Parties.
15. The United States understand that completion of a registry check by the claimed flag State is not a prerequisite for the claimed flag State to grant permission to take appropriate actions based on the claim of nationality made by a vessel, whether verbally, by flying a flag, presentation of a document, or other external indicia of nationality. While granting permission to board and search based on provisional or presumptive flag State authority provides a useful means for expediting the authorization process, it does not prevent the boarding State from making the determination, upon discovery of applicable conditions, that the vessel is assimilated under international law to a ship without nationality. Accordingly, the United States understands that paragraph 3 of Article 16 of the Agreement permits the boarding and search of a suspect vessel if the claimed flag State reports that it can neither confirm nor deny nationality within four hours following receipt of an oral request pursuant to Article 6. Although paragraph 5 of Article 16 of the Agreement addresses the effect of such a response on a request for boarding and search, the United States notes that the Agreement is silent on the effect of such a response with respect to the exercise of jurisdiction following the discovery of evidence of illicit traffic, and understands the exercise of jurisdiction over such a vessel should be predicated on an unequivocal confirmation or refutation of nationality by the claimed flag State. Consequently, ... if a claimed flag State does not affirmatively and unequivocally assert that the vessel is of its nationality upon receiving a report on the results of enforcement action pursuant to paragraph 1 of Article 26, the United States reserves the right to assimilate the vessel to a ship without nationality and subject the vessel, cargo, and persons on board to the exercise of the jurisdiction of the United States.[39]

Maritime law enforcement efforts to combat illicit drug trafficking can also be enhanced through the establishment of regional and sub-regional cooperation and coordination programs. This can include assigning personnel to regional and sub-regional coordination centers, as well as developing standard operating procedures for conducting joint law enforcement operations. Article 19 of the Agreement additionally encourages the Parties to conduct bilateral or multilateral exercises to enhance interoperability between law enforcement officials responsible for maritime law enforcement operations.

---

[39] Declaration of the United States of America upon Signature of the Agreement Concerning Co-operation in Suppressing Illicit Maritime and Air Trafficking in Narcotic Drugs and Psychotropic Substances in the Caribbean Area, Apr. 10, 2003.

16.3 Caribbean Basin Security Initiative

Consistent with Article 19 of the Caribbean Regional Maritime Agreement, the United States launched the *Caribbean Basin Security Initiative* (CBSI) to bring together the nations of the Caribbean to combat the illicit drug trade and other transnational crimes that threaten regional security.

This shared partnership deepens regional security cooperation between the United States, the Caribbean Community (CARICOM) nations[40] and the Dominican Republic, while complementing other Western Hemisphere security initiatives, such as the *Mérida Initiative* in Mexico, the *Central America Regional Security Initiative*, and the *Colombia Strategic Development Initiative*. The three core objectives identified by the participants to deal with the threats facing the Caribbean include:

- Reduce Illicit Trafficking: through programs ranging from counter-narcotics to reducing the flow of illegal arms/light weapons.
- Advance Public Safety and Security: through programs ranging from reducing crime and violence to improving border security.
- Promote Social Justice: through programs designed to promote justice sector reform, combat government corruption, and assist vulnerable populations at risk of recruitment into criminal organizations.[41]

The CBSI partner nations have identified several priority areas to achieve these objectives, to include "building a regional information sharing network, improving maritime interdiction coordination, developing regional training capacity, implementing corrections reforms, improving asset sustainment and maintenance practices, and addressing illicit firearms trafficking."[42]

Over the past two years, the United States has contributed $139 million to provide assistance in the following areas:

> *Maritime and Aerial Security Cooperation.* Supporting regional maritime and aerial coordination by improving radar coverage in strategic locations and sharing radar information. Providing equipment and training that will enable Caribbean governments to carry out maritime and aerial operations to identify and respond to threats,

---

[40] CARICOM is a common market organization that includes the following member states: Antigua and Barbuda, The Bahamas, Barbados, Belize, Dominica, Grenada, Guyana, Haiti, Jamaica, Montserrat, Saint Lucia, St. Kitts and Nevis, St. Vincent and the Grenadines, Suriname, and Trinidad and Tobago. CARICOM associate members are: Anguilla, Bermuda, the British Virgin Islands, Cayman Islands, and Turks and Caicos islands. The Treaty establishing the Caribbean Community was signed at Chaguaramas on July 4, 1973. Since 1973, the Treaty has been revised. *See,* Revised Treaty of Chaguaramas Establishing the Caribbean Community including the CARICOM Single Market and Economy (2001).
[41] Dep't of State, Caribbean Basin Security Initiative Brief, Nov. 2, 2011.
[42] Id.

engage in effective end game operations, and sustain those capabilities with reliability and regularity.

Law Enforcement Capacity Building. Enhancing law enforcement effectiveness through police professionalization, anti-corruption training, community-based policing, and sharing regional ballistics and fingerprint information. Equipment and training will enhance the region's polygraph capacity, cultivate expertise in the delivery of specialized law enforcement training, and support vetted units in conducting complex investigations, anti-gang initiatives, and combating money laundering and other financial crimes.

Border/Port Security and Firearms Interdiction. Providing technical support, technology upgrades, and training on techniques for intercepting smuggled narcotics, weapons, bulk cash, and other contraband at commercial airports and seaports, to include the enhancement of strategic trade controls through training to strengthen border security capabilities. Funding will also support the interdiction of firearms and secure management of weapons and ammunition stockpiles.

Justice Sector Reform. Reforming and strengthening juvenile justice systems through alternative sentencing and rehabilitation services. Regional justice advisors are providing technical assistance to judges and prosecutors, advising on legal reform, and developing a task force to address critical crime issues. Funding will support prison assessments and training to assist host governments in alleviating overcrowding and improving prison conditions.

Crime Prevention and At-Risk Youth. Increasing educational opportunities and providing workforce development and entrepreneurship training for at-risk youth as an alternative to crime and other harmful behavior. Funding also will support drug demand reduction through the training of treatment and rehabilitation professionals.[43]

The CBSI, however, is not only about drug interdiction. It emphasizes a whole-of-government approach to citizen safety that focuses on:

Partnerships. A defining purpose of U.S. policy in the Western Hemisphere is to build effective partnerships to advance our common strategic interests—partnerships that can better develop, mobilize and apply the capacity of the region toward accomplishing shared objectives.

The Personal Element. Our commitment to broad partnerships that advance citizen safety signals that the U.S. understands that while security is a key priority throughout the region, people often understand security in a personal way on their street corners, on a bus to and from work, or in their markets.

Crime Linkages. Forging effective partnerships requires an understanding of and an ability to address fundamental links between local, transnational and "white collar" crime (e.g., corruption), and the nexus between these threats and the big social and economic challenges the region faces. We seek to improve public safety, improving security for each and every citizen through these partnerships.[44]

---

[43] Id.
[44] Id.

Drug trafficking is one important element of an entire constellation of threats to national and human security, and the Caribbean nations are lacking in sufficient government and societal capacity. The United States has provided funding to assist in "HIV/AIDs prevention, military education and training, advancing economic development and trade, and promoting social inclusion for marginalized groups."[45]

Following the second Caribbean-United States Security Cooperation Dialogue in November 2011, the participating governments issued the following joint statement:

16.3.1 *CBSI Joint Statement*

Caribbean Basin Security Initiative Joint Statement
Second Caribbean-United States Security Cooperation Dialogue
November 10, 2011, Nassau, The Bahamas

> We, the Governments of Antigua and Barbuda; The Bahamas; Barbados; Belize; the Commonwealth of Dominica; the Dominican Republic; Grenada; the Co-operative Republic of Guyana; the Republic of Haiti; Jamaica; St. Kitts and Nevis; Saint Lucia; St. Vincent and the Grenadines; the Republic of Suriname; the Republic of Trinidad and Tobago; and the United States of America,
>
> REAFFIRMING our commitment to the Caribbean Basin Security Initiative (CBSI) Partnership launched on 27 May 2010, at the Inaugural Caribbean-U.S. Security Cooperation Dialogue in Washington, DC;
>
> REAFFIRMING also our keen interest in advancing our commitments stated in the *Caribbean-United States Declaration of Principles*; the *Caribbean-United States Plan of Action on Security Cooperation*; and the *Joint Caribbean-United States Framework for Security Cooperation Engagement*;
>
> RECALLING the 2010 Commitment of Bridgetown and the 2011 Joint Press Release on the U.S.-Caribbean Ministerial Meeting, which celebrated the strong spirit of cooperation underlying the CBSI Partnership;
>
> . . . .
>
> JOINTLY PLEDGE to work together in a spirit of partnership and mutual respect to—
>
> - Strengthen the Caribbean Community (CARICOM) security structure and institutions, such as the CARICOM Implementation Agency for Crime and Security (IMPACS), and improve ties between CARICOM and the Dominican Republic, in order to more effectively promote regional and international coordination, the sharing of best practices, and the implementation of the CBSI to address the security challenges facing the Caribbean.
> - Develop and implement sustainable programs to address the security challenges in the Caribbean region.

---

[45] Id.

- Adopt policy and legislative reforms, as appropriate, in accordance with national laws to implement information sharing mechanisms on a region-wide basis, including the sharing of—
  - radar and sensor data for the purpose of detecting, monitoring, and interdicting illicit activities in the Caribbean; and
  - law enforcement information such as fingerprint and ballistics data in order to strengthen the fight against crime.
- Develop a common strategy, as well as standard operating procedures or other measures including, as appropriate, those provided in the *Caribbean Regional Maritime Agreement* and the *CARICOM Maritime and Airspace Security Cooperation Agreement*, that allow for the coordination of maritime interdiction efforts between and among Caribbean countries, to include regional security institutions such as the Regional Security System (RSS).
- Adopt a sustained approach to citizen safety in the Caribbean by strengthening budgetary measures to meet recurring security costs.
- Develop a sustainable regional defense, maritime and security training capacity in the Caribbean that utilizes existing national and regional training facilities and expertise to establish and maintain standards for regional training.
- Enact, as necessary, and harmonize legislation in the Caribbean that allows for the seizure of assets used in illicit activity and, in turn, makes these assets available to support law enforcement and crime prevention initiatives as a means to strengthen national and regional security capabilities.
- Adopt a coordinated approach for engaging development partners in the implementation of social development and crime prevention initiatives.
- Establish a regional repository of best practices in the areas of crime prevention and social justice to facilitate networking, policy development, and programming.
- Develop a regional juvenile justice policy and harmonized legislation promoting community intervention and alternatives to sentencing and incarceration.
- Create a mechanism for dissemination of information on CBSI and national efforts to address crime and violence in the Caribbean.[46]

16.4 Organization of American States Model Operating Procedure

The Organization of American States (OAS) Model Operating Procedure for Combined Maritime Drug Operations (Model SOP) is another cooperative effort that has emerged from Article 19 of the Caribbean Regional Maritime Agreement.[47] The Model SOP is the product of a group of experts tasked by the XXXIV Regular Session of the Inter-American Drug Abuse Control Commission (CICAD) in November 2003 to develop a *Model Guide for Maritime Operating Procedures*.

---

[46] Caribbean Basin Security Initiative, Joint Statement Second Caribbean—United States Security Cooperation Dialogue, Nov. 10, 2011.

[47] Model Operating Procedure for Combined Maritime Drug Operations, (undated document), http://cicad.oas.org/Reduccion_Oferta/ENG/Resources/Maritime/model_op_proc_eng.pdf. The Inter-American Drug Abuse Control Commission (CICAD) has issued a parallel Best Practices Guide for Developing Procedures Applicable to Combined Maritime Counterdrug Operations.

The Model SOP recognizes that "predefined operational procedures that can be activated by the participating countries when suspect vessels or aircraft are identified..." can save time and expedite the planning and organizational phases of joint counter-narcotics operations.[48] The SOP therefore "provides a framework for establishing procedures that will be implemented during joint and combined bilateral/multilateral counterdrug operations."[49] It additionally "identifies various elements that should be included in such procedures and some of the issues that the procedures need to address."[50]

Combined operations can be either planned or unplanned. Planned operations include predefined plans of action "to conduct operational activities within specific parameters such as geographical area, time period, frequency or potential targets or suspects."[51] Operational activities may include "conducting intelligence or monitoring patrols, taking enforcement actions, enforcing international conventions, or enforcing bilateral/multilateral agreements with respect to counterdrug situations."[52] Unplanned operations are "conducted in response to immediate, unanticipated counterdrug situations within the limits of each country's capability and jurisdiction" and may "include detection, monitoring and interdiction of vessels or aircraft."[53]

The Model SOP contains a number of procedures that can be used to facilitate the planning of cooperative counterdrug operations and coordinate effective responses to unplanned events, such as the detection of targets of mutual interest. These cooperative procedures address a wide-spectrum of activities, including training and exercises; logistical and technical support; designation of on-scene commanders; development of an action plan; rules for the use of force (RUF) and rules of engagement (ROE); boarding policies; hot pursuit; law enforcement actions; communications procedures; debriefing operations; and jurisdiction over offenses.

States are encouraged to train and exercise their forces to ensure preparedness for operations and improve tactics, techniques and procedures. Host nations should also consider entering into arrangements that will facilitate support to participating States during combined counterdrug operations. Member States are encouraged to establish procedures to designate an on-scene commander/coordinator as early in the operation as possible. This person will be responsible for directing the activities of the joint, bilateral or multilateral operation.[54] In addition, States participating in a combined operation should identify on-sight liaison officers to assist in the proper flow of intelligence and information.

---

[48] Model Operating Procedure for Combined Maritime Drug Operations.
[49] Id.
[50] Id.
[51] Id.
[52] Id.
[53] Id.
[54] Id.

An action plan, including the following elements, should be developed when States conduct combined operations:

- an operations order when applicable,
- joint review of intelligence /information,
- aircraft coordination,
- personnel exchange,
- reporting requirements,
- rendezvous times, and
- command & control.[55]

When conducting combined operations, it is essential that all States understand their own laws and policies regarding the Rules for the Use of Force and Rules of Engagement (RUF/ROE) of the other States participating in the operation. More importantly, prior to the start of an operation, all States must agree on the RUF/ROE, and these rules should be reflected in the operational procedures established for the operation. RUF/ROE provisions must be sufficiently clear, comprehensive and detailed on "when and under what circumstances force may be used, the nature of such force, responsibilities for decisions related to the use of force, and ... all other relevant issues related to the use of force."[56]

It is equally important that participating States are aware of their domestic laws and policies, as well as their international authorities, which apply during boarding operations. When and how a boarding will take place must be clearly identified and agreed to by the participating States. Similarly, all States must understand their domestic and international legal authorities regarding the right of hot pursuit of suspect vessels.

Formal requests from one State to another to support a law enforcement action should clearly state the type of assistance required. Prior to the commencement of the operation, all involved States must agree on the type of action that will be provided. It is also important for the requesting State to share all pertinent information concerning the proposed operation. Important details that should be shared include:

- vessel name,
- vessel type,
- nationality,
- vessel position,
- suspected activity,
- type of drug/quantity (known or suspected),
- number of people on board, and
- known or suspected weapons.[57]

---

[55] Id.
[56] Id.
[57] Id.

Clear and concise objectives, as well as how these objectives will be accomplished, must be identified and included in the operational plan.

Prior to conducting a combined operation, all participating States must agree on the following evidence gathering, evidence seizure and evidence handling procedures:

- what evidence is being sought,
- who will seize the evidence,
- how evidence will be handled and stored,
- where it will be stored,
- how evidence will be inventoried,
- if evidence can be turned over to another jurisdiction, and
- other issues.[58]

Similarly, with regard to arrest and prosecution of suspected drug traffickers, the Model SOP specifies that all States participating in a combined operation should agree on:

- who will be responsible for making arrests,
- who will secure prisoners,
- where prisoners will be secured, and
- who will prosecute.[59]

A detailed report of any enforcement action taken during a combined operation should be provided to all participating States. Reporting procedures should identify:

- who is responsible for completing the report,
- what format should the report take,
- what details need to be covered in the report, and
- who will receive the report.[60]

Additionally, a debriefing should be conducted to assess:

- actions taken,
- information/intelligence sharing,
- logistical issues, and
- legal issues.[61]

These assessments should be shared with the other States involved in the operation in an effort to establish lessons learned and improve future operations.

The Model SOP additionally calls on States to establish national communication protocols, as well as test communication links and procedures with neighboring States, which address the following areas:

---

[58] Id.
[59] Id.
[60] Id.
[61] Id.

- establish protocols at a national level,
- communication security,
- operational security,
- comparable methods of communications, and
- establishing agreed codes/geographical points.[62]

16.5 THE PARIS PACT INITIATIVE

Illicit production of opiates represents a severe threat to Afghanistan, neighboring States, and to transit and consumption countries along the trafficking routes. To address this danger, the UN Office of Drugs and Crime launched the *Paris Pact Initiative* (PPI) following a Ministerial Conference held in Paris in May 2003. At that meeting, 55 affected States "committed themselves to increase action and support throughout the region in order to combat the growing drug trafficking and related problems and proposed a coordinated response."[63] The ministers stressed that it was important "to find a comprehensive, balanced and coordinated national and international response to the threat that this scourge represents for all their societies" and committed "to combine their wills and their countries' efforts to step up national capabilities, develop regional partnerships and hence tackle all the aspects of this problem."[64]

To address this national security imperative, the partnership of nations and 23 international organizations focuses on enhanced border control and law enforcement cooperation in order to combat Afghan opiates trafficking, consumption and related problems along the trafficking routes.[65]

A second ministerial was held in Moscow in June 2006 to further promote the Paris Pact process and recommend effective countermeasures against drug trafficking from Afghanistan. At that meeting, the participants recognized that "the spread in the use and trafficking of illicit drugs and the risk that narco-business may become fused with terrorist and extremist activities... makes it urgent to intensify joint efforts to address this global threat."[66] It was therefore decided that participating States should continue to undertake activities that target drug

---

[62] Id.
[63] Paris Pact Initiative—Statement of the Ministerial Conference, May, 2003, https://www.paris-pact.net/index.php?action=cms_render&section=50&mm=mm3.
[64] Conference on Drug Routes from Central Asia to Europe, Paris Statement, May 21–22, 2003.
[65] UNITED NATIONS OFFICE OF DRUGS AND CRIME, COUNTRY OFFICE, PAKISTAN, THE PARIS PACT INITIATIVE: A PARTNERSHIP TO COUNTER TRAFFICKING AND CONSUMPTION OF AFGHAN OPIATES, ILLICIT DRUG TRENDS IN PAKISTAN 21–23 (Apr. 2008).
[66] Second Ministerial Conference on Drug Trafficking Routes from Afghanistan, Moscow Declaration, June 26–28, 2006.

traffickers, and "strengthen and diversity rural livelihoods, reduce domestic demand, treat drug users and build efficient counter narcotics institutions."[67]

The ministers also noted, "it was imperative to strengthen cooperation between Afghanistan and its neighbors with a view to achieving a modern and effective border management system."[68] Additionally, the need to conduct "law enforcement and special services operations to suppress the channels of illicit trafficking in drugs and precursors was reaffirmed."[69] With regard to precursors, in particular, it was decided that "more attention should be paid to the issue of the diversion of chemical precursors used to produce heroin."[70]

The ministers also agreed on the need to "strengthen interaction among justice, judicial and supervising bodies..." of the participating States, improve "informational and operational interaction among law enforcement agencies and special services of the States concerned...," and "strengthen the fight against money laundering from criminal activities...."[71] Moreover, due attention must be paid to the health aspects of drug trafficking, "in particular the prevention and treatment of drug addiction and diseases transmitted through intravenous injection, such as HIV/AIDS and hepatitis."[72]

Despite these international efforts, the threat of drug trafficking from Afghanistan continues to be of serious concern. Accordingly, the Paris Pact participants held a third ministerial in Vienna on February 16, 2012. The goal of the third ministerial was "to reaffirm the commitments of members of the international community towards the fight against illicit traffic in opiates, to strengthen cooperation among Paris Pact partners and to urge them to achieve substantial practical results in reducing illicit opiates trafficked from Afghanistan."[73]

The 2012 meeting had in attendance 12 Ministers, including the Minster of Foreign Affairs of the Russian Federation, Sergey Lavrov, and the UN Secretary-General, as participants. The ministers determined that efforts to reduce illicit traffic in opiates, in order to enhance international peace and stability, should focus on the following areas:

1. Strengthening the capacity of... Afghanistan in combating illicit opium poppy cultivation and illicit opiates production, including through law enforcement and socio-economic measures, such as alternative livelihoods, and in fighting trafficking as a contribution to international endeavors to improve stability in the region and beyond and tackle terrorism, organized crime and corruption;

---

[67] Id.
[68] Id.
[69] Id.
[70] Id.
[71] Id.
[72] Id.
[73] Third Ministerial Conference of the Paris Pact Partners on Combating Illicit Traffic in Opiates Originating in Afghanistan, Vienna Declaration, Feb. 16, 2012.

2. Continuing to assist... Afghanistan... in implementing its national Drug Control Strategy, aimed at eliminating, significantly and measurably, the illicit traffic in opiates, including through increased support for relevant Afghan institutions;
3. Providing urgent and appropriate technical assistance and support to the most affected transit States, based on the principle of common and shared responsibility, in order to promote the capacities of such States to counter the flow of illicit drugs;
4. Taking measures to stem the illicit traffic in opiates and to stop the diversion of precursor chemicals used for the illicit manufacturing of heroin and other opiates between Afghanistan, Paris Pact partners and other countries in the region and beyond, and to eliminate illicit heroin production facilities and their spread;
5. Providing further training to assist... Afghanistan and other relevant Paris Pact partners to effectively implement the applicable international conventions including through relevant programs and projects;
6. Facilitating cross-border operations between law enforcement agencies, including the planning of joint operations and in this respect appreciating joint operations by the members of the Triangular Initiative and supporting coordination of border management activities in the region, including the coordination of donor assistance to the region's border management programs;
7. Supporting... [the United Nations Office of Drugs and Crime—UNODC] in its efforts to coordinate effective and result-oriented assistance to... Afghanistan and neighboring countries in countering illicit traffic in opiates, including through the UNODC Regional Program for Afghanistan and Neighboring Countries;
8. Commending the work of UNODC to collect and analyze data on illicit traffic in opiates and trends regarding the global Afghan opiate trade, encouraging the utilization of such analyses, as appropriate, while formulating and implementing regional and country programs to support and assist States affected by opiates originating in Afghanistan, and encouraging Paris Pact partners to collect and share relevant data with UNODC;
9. Elaborating and implementing comprehensive regional programs, to effectively counteract the challenges and threat of illicit traffic in opiates, in particular, the UNODC Regional Program for Afghanistan and Neighboring Countries, including:
    (a) Supporting trans-regional cooperation;
    (b) Enhancing counter-drug and related anti-crime cooperation and coordination efforts among regional and international organizations, including through controlled deliveries and joint operations, to interdict illegal shipments of opiates and precursors, such as the law enforcement operation Channel, the operations TARCET and TOPAZ and the operations conducted in the framework of the Triangular Initiative;
    (c) Encouraging and supporting Paris Pact partners to coordinate initiatives to promote health and welfare of human beings, social and economic development, including trade capacity-building and job creation, crop substitution and alternative development programs in Afghanistan in collaboration with the international organizations concerned.[74]

In addition to these areas of action, the ministers identified the need to develop practical cooperation to undermine organized crime networks involved in illicit traffic in opiates by:

---

[74] Id.

1. Enhancing the exchange of information on financial flows, linked to illicit traffic in opiates, including bank deposits, investments and property, using the existing mechanisms to the fullest extent possible;
2. Providing effective mutual legal assistance in a timely manner to tackle illicit financial flows in compliance with the [1988 Vienna Convention], the 2000 [UN] *Convention against Transnational Organized Crime*, and the 2003 [UN] *Convention against Corruption*;
3. Providing support in developing national legislation, expertise, enforcement and administrative procedures consistent with established international standards to combat money laundering and to train personnel in relevant fields;
4. Exchanging best practices in detection and suppression of financial flows linked to illicit traffic in opiates, including by inviting Paris Pact partners to continue and enhance cooperation with the private sector as appropriate;
5. Encouraging studies by relevant international and regional organizations and mechanisms in cooperation with UNODC, to determine the most effective ways and means to detect and block financial flows linked to the illicit traffic in opiates;
6. Encouraging UNODC, with due regard to its mandate, to consult with the Paris Pact partners, and while respecting national legislation, to explore with relevant international financial institutions the feasibility of new and innovative approaches to financing the prevention and the fight against illicit traffic in opiates, including consideration of whether and how confiscated proceeds of crime might be further mobilized.[75]

It was also decided that the Paris Pact partners should enhance cooperation to prevent the supply of precursor chemicals to Afghanistan in order to stop the illicit manufacturing and traffic in opiates, to include:

1. Exchanging data on suspicious transactions involving precursor chemicals among law enforcement and customs authorities, particularly through efforts to prevent diversion of legal dual-use chemicals, such as acetic anhydride, paying regard, as appropriate, to existing initiatives such as joint initiatives of UNODC, the World Customs Organization (WCO), the International Criminal Police Organization (INTERPOL), the Container Control Program and Program Global Shield;
2. Strengthening the capacity of law enforcement and customs authorities in Afghanistan and its neighboring countries, including by training their specialists in special investigative techniques, such as controlled deliveries, related to the diversion of precursor chemicals;
3. Assisting concerned Paris Pact partners in preventing and detecting illicit operations involving precursor chemicals as requested;
4. Providing forensic support to criminal justice entities of the Islamic Republic of Afghanistan and Paris Pact partners concerned when investigating crimes linked to the diversion of and illicit traffic in precursor chemicals;
5. Building capacities and exchanging best practices on the methodology for investigating cases of illicit diversion and traffic in precursor chemicals in order to detect and dismantle organized crime networks involved in illicit traffic in opiates;

---

[75] Id.

6. Reinvigorating international and regional initiatives to combat the flow of precursor chemicals, including by cooperation with the International Narcotics Control Board (INCB);
7. Encouraging Operation TARCET to set specific objectives to allow measurable outcomes in the light of latest findings on emerging trends;
8. Involving countries in the above-mentioned activities, together with INCB and in accordance with the three drug control conventions and the principle of common and shared responsibility, including, as appropriate, countries which are not Paris Pact partners, in particular those where chemicals used in illicit production of heroin and other opiates are manufactured;
9. Urging Paris Pact partners that have not yet requested pre-export notification for shipments of precursor chemicals in accordance with article 12 of the [1988 Vienna Convention] and relevant United Nations resolutions, to do so and report it to the INCB and encourages all countries where precursor chemicals are produced to cooperate closely with ... Afghanistan and its neighboring countries to continue the tracking of shipments of precursor chemicals and to prevent their diversion into illicit networks;
10. Enhancing public/private partnerships to detect and prevent the illicit export and diversion of precursor chemicals used in manufacturing heroin and other illicit opiates to Afghanistan in line with the INCB Guidelines for a voluntary code of practice for the chemical industry.[76]

Finally, the ministers identified the need to decrease the abuse of drugs and the number of drug addicts through an effective drug demand reduction policy. To this end, the ministers agreed to intensify cooperation in the following ways:

1. Ensuring that drug demand reduction policies are balanced and comprehensive and in full compliance with the three international drug control conventions, as well as fundamental human rights and freedoms, and based on scientific evidence;
2. Stressing an effective, balanced and comprehensive approach to reducing demand for and supply of illicit drugs;
3. Promoting short-term, mid-term and long-term planning and implementation of drug demand reduction programs and measures, including those aimed at reducing the spread of blood borne diseases in particular HIV/AIDS;
4. Promoting collaboration among governments and civil society including non-governmental organizations and the private sector on drug demand reduction measures;
5. Engaging civil society and mass media, including to discourage the abuse of opiates;
6. Elaborating targeted drug addiction prevention, treatment, care, rehabilitation and reintegration programs on this basis in families and households, schools and other educational institutions, health and social service settings, workplaces, in prisons, including through the use of media, including for groups most at risk;
7. Improving specialized training systems for drug treatment professionals with regard to the abuse of opiates in all Paris Pact partners, particularly ... Afghanistan.[77]

---

[76] Id.
[77] Id.

Today, the *Paris Pact Initiative* consists of three main components:

1. A two-pronged Consultative Mechanism that facilitates periodical consultations at the expert and policy level between partners, in order to jointly discuss, identify and set in motion concrete measures to stem the increasing level of opiates trafficked from Afghanistan;
2. The Automated Donor Assistance Mechanism (ADAM), an internet-based tool which provides Paris Pact partners with essential information to coordinate counter narcotics technical assistance in countries along the main opium trafficking routes from Afghanistan; and
3. To further strengthen counter narcotics data collection and analytical capacity, a network of 10 National Strategic Analysts cover key Paris Pact partner countries in their work, such as the Islamic Republics of Afghanistan, Iran, Pakistan, the Central Asian Republics of Kazakhstan, Kyrgyzstan, Tajikistan, Turkmenistan and Uzbekistan, the Russian Federation, Serbia and the Former Yugoslav Republic of Macedonia.

Despites the efforts of the Paris Pact partners, UNODC has determined that the problem of opiate trafficking from Afghanistan has not been abated and actually is getting worse. Afghanistan is now the leading poppy cultivating country in the world, having overtaken Myanmar in 2003. By 2009, Afghanistan was producing 89 percent of the opiates on the world market, with an export value of approximately $64 billion. Between 2006 and 2009, poppy production levels increased 50 percent. Since 2007, more land is being used for opium production in Afghanistan than for cocoa cultivation in Latin America. It is therefore apparent that the work of the Paris Pact partners is far from complete.[78]

16.6 Republic of the Philippines National Coast Watch System

The Celebes and Sulu Seas and their adjacent land territories have long been considered "as a major source of instability within Southeast Asia."[79] Poor policing, lack of capacity and highly porous maritime borders has "made the area extremely vulnerable to infiltration and penetration by criminals, pirates, militias, separatist groups, terrorists, [drug smugglers,] and illegal migrants."[80] In an effort to address these non-traditional security threats, the Republic of the Philippines launched a new initiative in 2011—the National Coast Watch System (NCWS).

---

[78] The Paris Pact Initiative—Achievement Since 2006, Discussion Paper, Jan. 2011.
[79] Peter Chalk, *Sealing the "Back Door" in the Philippines, Second Line of Defense* STRATEGIC INSIGHTS, No. 26, Aug. 2010.
[80] Id.

16.6.1 *Executive Order 57*

Established by Executive Order 57, the Initiative expands the scope of Coast Watch South and provides for enhanced maritime domain awareness and a coordinated approach to maritime security operations:

> Malacañang Palace, Manila by the President of the Philippines
>
> Executive Order No. 57, Sept. 6, 2011, Establishing a National Coast Watch System ...
>
> ... [I]t is the policy of the State to safeguard national sovereignty, territorial integrity, national interest, and the right to self-determination;
>
> ...
>
> ... [T]he Philippines faces serious maritime security challenges threatening not only its territorial integrity but the peaceful existence of the Filipinos and their inherent rights to be free from such threats as piracy, armed robbery, terrorism, proliferation of weapons of mass destruction, trafficking in persons, drugs and firearms trafficking, smuggling, illegal fishing, transnational crimes, national disasters, climate change, and marine environment degradation;
>
> ... [T]here is pressing need for the government to address maritime security challenges in the Philippines ...;
>
> ...
>
> ... [T]he Philippine Navy forged the establishment of an infrastructure for a national coast watch system, the Coast Watch South, which has the primary objective of providing maritime domain awareness in support of security operations in Southern Philippines;
>
> ...
>
> ... [E]nhancing maritime security in the seas ... promotes our national interest;
>
> ...
>
> ... [I]t is imperative for the government to integrate and strengthen its maritime security initiatives through effective inter-agency cooperation, collaboration, and coordination to bring about efficient and effective maritime security policy; and
>
> ...
>
> ... Benigno S. Aquino, President of the Philippines ... do hereby order:
>
> Section 1. Establishment of the National Coast Watch System. There is hereby established a National Coast Watch System (NCWS) as the central inter-agency mechanism for a coordinated and coherent approach on maritime issues and maritime security operations towards enhancing governance in the country's maritime domain.
>
> Section 2. Establishment of the National Coast Watch Council. There is hereby established a National Coast Watch Council ... which shall be composed of [and Executive Secretary serving as a Chairperson, and the Secretaries of Transportation and Communications, National Defense, Foreign Affairs, Interior and Local Government, Justice, Energy, Finance, Environment and Natural Resources, and Agriculture].
>
> ...

Section 3. Powers and Functions of the Council. The Council shall be the central inter-agency body, which shall be in charge of formulating strategic direction and policy guidance for the NCWS. The Council shall further have the following powers and functions:

a) Provide strategic direction and policy guidelines for NCWS maritime security operations, and multinational and cross-border cooperation on maritime security;
b) Conduct periodic review of maritime security operations and render periodic reports to the President and the National Security Council (NSC);
c) Recommend to the President policies and procedures in managing and securing the country's maritime domain...;
d) Harmonize capability plans and fund requirements...;
e) Harmonize and coordinate the roles and relationships of different government agencies...;
f) Convene or dissolve...interagency committees and/or working groups to assist the Council...;
g) Exercise overall jurisdiction and direction over policy-formulation, implementation and coordination with other government agencies, experts and organizations, both foreign and local, on all maritime issues affecting the country;
h) Enlist and/or require the support and/or assistance of any department, bureau or agency of the government in the pursuit of its mandates and functions;
i) Promulgate rules and regulations...for the Council to perform its mandate under this Executive Order; and

...

Section 4. The Coast Watch Council Secretariat. The Coast Watch Council Secretariat, hereinafter referred to as the "Secretariat," is hereby established to provide technical and administrative support to the Council. The Secretariat shall also have the following functions:

a) Provide consultative research and administrative services to the Council;
b) Assist the Council in proposing and reviewing legislative and administrative issuances on maritime security;
c) Assist inter-agency committees and working groups created by the Council in the performance of their respective mandates, including the provision of administrative, technical and secretariat support; and
d) Perform such other functions and tasks as the Council may direct.

...

Section 5. National Coast Watch Center. The National Coast Watch Center...in accordance with the strategic direction and policy guidance issued by the Council, shall implement and coordinate maritime security operations. It shall further have the following functions:

a) Gather, consolidate, synthesize and disseminate information...;
b) Develop and maintain effective communications and information systems to enhance interagency coordination...;
c) Coordinate the conduct of maritime surveillance or response operations upon the request of a member agency or when an exigency arises;
d) Plan, coordinate, monitor, evaluate, document and report on the conduct of maritime security operations;
e) When so authorized by the Council, coordinate cross-border and multinational maritime security cooperation;
f) Coordinate support for the prosecution of apprehended violators;

g) Develop a common operating picture to enhance maritime situational awareness;
h) Conduct periodic assessments on maritime security;
i) When so authorized by the Council, and in coordination with the Department of Foreign Affairs, initiate cross-border and multinational maritime security cooperation.

The Center shall be established in and headed by the Philippine Coast Guard (PCG).

Section 6. Support Agencies. Subject to such rules and regulations, which the Council shall promulgate, the following agencies shall provide manpower, equipment and material support to the Center and its operations:

a) Philippine Navy;
b) Philippine Coast Guard;
c) Philippine National Police Maritime Group;
d) National Prosecution Service of the Department of Justice;
e) Bureau of Customs;
f) Bureau of Immigration;
g) National Bureau of Investigation;
h) Bureau of Fisheries and Aquatic Resources; and
i) Philippine Center on Transnational Crime.

The roles and responsibilities of each of the support agencies . . . shall be set forth in the rules and regulations to be promulgated by the Council. All other government agencies are hereby directed to actively coordinate and cooperate with the Council and support the maritime security operations of the government. . . .[81]

Executive Secretary Paquito Ochoa Jr., tasked with heading the newly established National Coast Watch Council, believes that it will allow the Philippines to "prioritize maritime security in the country, especially in the face of maritime challenges and threats such as terrorism, transnational crimes, drug and firearms trafficking, smuggling, human trafficking, climate change, illegal fishing, marine environment degradation and other security concerns."[82] Ochoa states that NCWS allows the government to harmonize its "policies, programs and activities on intelligence work, border control, interdiction and law enforcement of several government agencies . . . for better maritime governance."[83] Vice Admiral Alexander Pama, head of the Philippine Navy, also welcomed the creation of the new inter-agency organization.

NCWS replaces the current Coast Watch South (CWS) concept that brought the Philippine Navy, Philippine National Policy, Philippine Coast Guard and the

---

[81] Executive Order No. 57, Establishing a National Coast Watch System, Providing for its Structure and Defining the Roles and Responsibilities of Member Agencies in Providing Coordinated Inter-agency Maritime Security Operations and for Other Purposes, Sept. 26, 2011.
[82] Delon Porcalla, *Aquino forms National Coast Watch System*, THE PHILIPPINE STAR, Sept. 12, 2011.
[83] Id.

Departments of Immigration, Customs and Environment together to enhance the nation's maritime domain awareness in the Sulu and Celebes Seas. The main functions of CWS included:

- Develop a common operating picture of the maritime domain in western and southern Philippines;
- Collect, consolidate and integrate information relevant to maritime security;
- Provide real-time information for the purposes of securing the maritime environment in the area.[84]

CWS, which is headquartered at Western Mindanao Command in Zamboanga, consists of monitoring platforms at eight stations strategically located in Mindanao that have both surveillance and interdiction capabilities. An integrated Data Management System allows the collection, synthesis and dissemination of information, which provides government authorities the ability to monitor and interdict suspicious ships, as well as "establish trends that can then be used to develop tactical and strategic threat forecasts."[85] The ultimate objective is to integrate NCWS with other regional maritime security systems in Malaysia and Indonesia to further enhance maritime security in the region.

16.7 Mérida Initiative

The *Mérida Initiative* is one of a number of regional U.S. initiatives to combat transnational crime in the Western Hemisphere. Based on principles of shared responsibility, mutual trust and respect for national sovereignty, the initiative involves a partnership between the United States and Mexico designed to "fight organized crime and associated violence while furthering respect for human rights and the rule of law."[86] The four pillars of the initiative include:

1. *Disrupt Organized Criminal Groups*. This includes increasing coordination and information sharing to fight drug trafficking organizations (DTO) by focusing on intelligence collection and analysis, training and equipping special units, enhancing police and prosecutors' investigative capacity, conducting targeted investigation against money laundering, improving interdiction capability, and by supporting effective command and control centers across Mexico.

2. *Institutionalize Reforms to Sustain Rule of Law and Respect for Human Rights*. This involves continuing to build security and justice sector institutions at the federal level and expanding these efforts to additional federal, state, and local institutions.

---

[84] Chalk, *Sealing the "Back Door" in the Philippines.*
[85] Id.
[86] Bureau of Western Hemisphere Affairs, Dep't of State, Mérida Initiative: Expanding the U.S./Mexico Partnership, Mar. 29, 2012.

3. *Create a 21st Century Border.* This involves advancing citizen safety while increasing global competitiveness through efficient and secure flows of two-way commerce and travel.

4. *Build Strong and Resilient Communities.* This includes programs that will leverage support for greater community involvement in developing a culture of lawfulness, as well as addressing socio-economic challenges in the community, including stemming the flow of potential recruits for the cartels by helping to promote constructive, legal alternatives for young people.[87]

Since 2008, the U.S. Congress has appropriated $1.6 billion to fund a number of activities. First, the United States is supporting Mexico's implementation of comprehensive justice sector reforms through the training of justice sector personnel including police, prosecutors, and defenders, correction systems development, judicial exchanges, and partnerships between Mexican and U.S. law schools. The Agency for International Development (USAID) is working with the Government of Mexico and civil society to promote the rule of law and build strong and resilient communities by supporting the implementation of Mexico's new justice system; increasing knowledge of, and respect for, human rights, and by strengthening social networks and community cohesion, addressing the needs of vulnerable populations (youth and victims of crime), and increasing community and government cooperation.

Air mobility has been increased through the delivery of eight Bell helicopters to the Mexican Army/Air Force, three UH-60M Black Hawk helicopters to the Federal Police, and three UH-60M Black Hawk helicopters to the Mexican Navy to provide for rapid transport of personnel for counter-narcotics and other security operations. The U.S. also has provided scanners, X-ray machines, and other non-intrusive inspection equipment to enhance Mexican authorities' ability to detect illicit goods at key checkpoints at land and air ports of entry. Finally, the Mexican government has established a corrections academy to train Mexican federal correctional staff at Xalapa in Mexico's Veracruz state.[88]

The United States also assisted in training over 4,000 Mexican police officers at the Federal police training facility in San Luis Potosí. By March 31, 2010, 46 percent of the $1.6 billion had been obligated and approximately 9 percent was expended. In fiscal year 2011, the Obama Administration asked for an additional $310 million in assistance for the *Mérida Initiative* in Mexico, $100 million for *Central America Regional Security Initiative* (CARSI), and $79 million for CBSI.[89]

---

[87] GOVERNMENT ACCOUNTABILITY OFFICE, REPORT TO CONGRESSIONAL REQUESTERS, MÉRIDA INITIATIVE: THE UNITED STATES HAS PROVIDED COUNTER-NARCOTICS AND ANTICRIME SUPPORT BUT NEEDS BETTER PERFORMANCE MEASURES, July 2010, GAO-10-837 [Hereinafter GAO MÉRIDA INITIATIVE].

[88] BUREAU OF WESTERN HEMISPHERE AFFAIRS, DEP'T OF STATE, MÉRIDA INITIATIVE: EXPANDING THE U.S./MEXICO PARTNERSHIP, Mar. 29, 2012.

[89] GAO MÉRIDA INITIATIVE.

The *Mérida Initiative* has also contributed to enhanced anti-crime information sharing and collaboration, including the placement of Mexican law enforcement personnel within the El Paso Intelligence Center and the Air and Marine Operations Center. The benefits of increased information exchange and expedited operational communications between the two partners has enhanced interdiction efforts and enabled more complex and effective investigations, and more kingpin arrests. For example, between 2007 and 2010, the U.S. Customs and Border Protection (CBP) and U.S. Immigration and Customs Enforcement (ICE) increased the number of seizures of southbound illegal currency and enhanced efforts to disrupt the flow of weapons into Mexico.[90]

Similarly, the Southwest Border Initiative, a cooperative effort by the Drug Enforcement Agency (DEA), the Federal Bureau of Investigation (FBI), Customs and Border Protection (CBP), Immigration and Customs Enforcement (ICE), and U.S. Attorney's offices, combats the threat posed by Mexico-based drug trafficking groups operating along the Southwest Border. The Bureau of Alcohol, Tobacco, Firearms and Explosives (ATF) of the Department of Justice manages Project Gunrunner, which focuses on stemming the flow of firearms into Mexico, and it has deployed a Spanish-language version of eTrace, a firearms tracking technology, in Mexico City and five Central American countries.

The Department of Treasury is taking a comprehensive approach to countering the illicit financial activities that fuels the drug trade, and since 2000, Department of Defense (DOD) initiatives have facilitated occasional maritime operations between Mexico and the United States that has spurred greater cooperation between the two countries, particularly with respect to boarding, searching, and seizing suspected vessels transiting Mexican waters.

The Department of Defense provides support to U.S. and foreign agencies in Mexico and Central America, which has increased in recent years and is separate from that provided under Mérida. The Pentagon's effort includes training, equipment, information sharing, technical advice, and related support. In Mexico, for example, DOD support includes pilot and maintenance training, surveillance aircraft, and various other training activities. In Central America, DOD support includes training and equipment for maritime communications and intelligence sharing, boats, and spare parts.

Under the *Mérida Initiative*, pre-planned U.S.-Mexico combined maritime counter-narcotics operations have increased from 4 in 2008 to 10 in 2009 to 24 in 2010. In addition, a liaison officer from *la Secretaría de la Defensa Nacional* (SEDENA)—the Mexican Secretariat of National Defense—was posted at

---

[90] Testimony of Commissioner Alan D. Bersin, U.S. Customs and Border Protection, Before the Senate Caucus on International Narcotics Control, Money Laundering and Bulk Cash Smuggling Along the Southwest Border, Mar. 9, 2011. *See also*, U.S. NATIONAL SECURITY STRATEGY (May 2010).

U.S. Northern Command in 2009. Liaison officers from *la Armada de México* (SEMAR)—the Mexican Navy—have been assigned to JIATF-South, U.S. Fleet Forces Command, and U.S. Northern Command.

16.8 THE CENTRAL AMERICA REGIONAL SECURITY INITIATIVE

Finally, the *Central America Regional Security Initiative* (CARSI) seeks to address the corrosive impact of narcotics and weapons trafficking, gangs, organized crime, porous borders, public safety, and rule of law issues that exist in many Central American countries. The initiative also facilitates further regional security cooperation among the Central American nations in coordination within the *Mérida Initiative* and CBSI.[91]

Trafficking in drugs, persons and firearms continues to be a pervasive problem in Central America. The expansion of national and transnational organized criminal groups and trafficking routes, as well as the widespread availability of firearms throughout the region has led to a dramatic increase in violent crime and corruption in many Central American nations. CARSI is designed to respond to "the region's threats and [build] upon existing strategies and programs, both on a bilateral and regional basis..." by stopping "the flow of narcotics, arms, weapons, and bulk cash generated by illicit drug sales, and to confront gangs and criminal organizations."[92]

By strengthening and integrating security efforts from the United States to Panama and the littoral waters of the Caribbean, CARSI strives "to produce a safer and more secure region where criminal organizations no longer wield the power to destabilize governments or threaten national and regional security and public safety, as well as to prevent the entry and spread of illicit drugs, violence, and transnational threats to countries throughout the region and to the United States."[93]

The Five Goals of CARSI in Central America are to:

1. Create safe streets for the citizens in the region.
2. Disrupt the movement of criminals and contraband within and between the nations of Central America.
3. Support the development of strong, capable and accountable Central American Governments.

---

[91] GAO MÉRIDA INITIATIVE.
[92] DEP'T OF STATE FACT SHEET: THE CENTRAL AMERICA REGIONAL SECURITY INITIATIVE, www.state.gov.
[93] Id.

4. Re-establish effective state presence and security in communities at risk.
5. Foster enhanced levels of security and rule of law coordination and cooperation between the nations of the region.[94]

The $165 million in U.S. CARSI assistance committed to date seeks to support the following programming in Central America:

- Law enforcement and security force assistance to confront narcotics and arms trafficking, gangs, organized crime, border security deficiencies, as well as to disrupt criminal infrastructure, such as money laundering and trafficking routes and networks;
- Capacity enhancements for public security, law enforcement and justice sector actors and institutions, and rule of law agencies and personnel to provide the skills, technology and systems expertise to address the threats of the region; and
- Community policing, gang prevention and economic and social programming for at risk youth in areas adversely impacted by crime.[95]

---

[94] Id.
[95] Id.

SEVENTEEN

U.S. MARITIME COUNTERDRUG LAW

17.1 Maritime Drug Law Enforcement Act

The U.S. Coast Guard (USCG) is the lead federal agency for maritime law enforcement, including drug interdiction, and the co-lead for air interdiction operations with the U.S. Customs and Border Protection (CBP) Agency. Although the Department of Defense (DOD) is the single lead agency for detection and monitoring of illegal drugs under Title 10 of the U.S. Code, the actual maritime interdiction and seizure of illicit drugs at sea is a law enforcement function authorized by several authorities, including the Maritime Drug Law Enforcement Act (MDLEA).[1] Originally the statute was enacted to address the increased use of boats to smuggle illicit drugs into the United States. But with the growing threat posed by the use of self-propelled semi-submersible (SPSS) vessels by drug traffickers, the MDLEA was amended in 2008.

17.1.1 Jurisdiction under MDLEA

The U.S. Congress determined that: "(1) trafficking in controlled substances aboard vessels is a serious international problem, is universally condemned, and presents a specific threat to the security and societal well-being of the United States...."[2] Vessels subject to the jurisdiction of the United States under the Act include:

(A) a vessel without nationality;
(B) a vessel assimilated to a vessel without nationality under paragraph (2) of article 6 of the 1958 Convention on the High Seas;
(C) a vessel registered in a foreign nation if that nation has consented or waived objection to the enforcement of United States law by the United States;

---

[1] 46 U.S.C. §§ 70501–70508.
[2] 46 U.S.C. § 70501(1).

(D) a vessel in the customs waters of the United States;
(E) a vessel in the territorial waters of a foreign nation if the nation consents to the enforcement of United States law by the United States; and
(F) a vessel in the contiguous zone of the United States...,[3] that—
   i. is entering the United States;
   ii. has departed the United States; or
   iii. is a hovering vessel.[4]

Vessels that are considered to be without nationality, and therefore subject to U.S. jurisdiction, include:

(A) a vessel aboard which the master or individual in charge makes a claim of registry that is denied by the nation whose registry is claimed;
(B) a vessel aboard which the master or individual in charge fails, on request of an officer of the United States authorized to enforce applicable provisions of United States law, to make a claim of nationality or registry for that vessel; and
(C) a vessel aboard which the master or individual in charge makes a claim of registry and for which the claimed nation of registry does not affirmatively and unequivocally assert that the vessel is of its nationality.[5]

A "claim of nationality or registry" by a ship is normally demonstrated by "possession on board the vessel and production of documents evidencing the vessel's nationality" in accordance with Article 5 of the 1958 Convention on the High Seas, flying the flag of the registering or flag State, or making a verbal claim of nationality or registry by the master of the vessel.[6]

17.1.2 Offenses under MDLEA

The MDLEA prohibits the manufacture, distribution, or possession of controlled substances on board vessels subject to U.S. jurisdiction.[7] A "vessel of the United States" for example, is defined in the MDLEA to include ships "owned in any part by an individual who is a citizen of the United States, the United States Government, the government of a State or political subdivision of a State, or a corporation incorporated under the laws of the United States or of a State...."[8] The MDLEA prohibitions apply extraterritorially, as though the offenses were committed inside the United States.[9]

---

[3] The "contiguous zone of the United States" is defined in Pres. Proc. 7219, Sept. 2, 1999 (43 U.S.C. § 1331 note).
[4] 46 U.S.C. § 70502(c)(1). A "hovering vessel" is defined in sec. 401 of the Tariff Act of 1930 (19 § U.S.C. 1401).
[5] 46 U.S.C. § 70502(d)(1).
[6] Id., at § 70502(e).
[7] Id., at § 70503(a).
[8] Id., at § 70502(b).
[9] Id., at § 70503(a) and (b).

A failure on the part of the United States to comply with international law while conducting an interdiction of a drug trafficker cannot be asserted as a legal defense to criminal prosecution or civil action under the Act.

> A person charged with violating [the MDLEA] does not have standing to raise a claim of failure to comply with international law as a basis for a defense. A claim of failure to comply with international law in the enforcement of this chapter may be made only by a foreign nation. A failure to comply with international law does not divest a court of jurisdiction and is not a defense to a proceeding under this chapter.[10]

However, the statute does not apply to:

> (A) a common or contract carrier or an employee of the carrier who possesses or distributes a controlled substance in the lawful and usual course of the carrier's business; or
> (B) a public vessel of the United States or an individual [person] on board the vessel who possesses or distributes a controlled substance in the lawful course [of duty ... or] if the controlled substance is part of the cargo entered in the vessel's manifest and is intended to be imported lawfully [for scientific, medical, or other lawful purpose].[11]

Property that is used or intended for use to commit or facilitate the commission of an offense under § 70502 may be seized and forfeited.[12]

17.1.3 Intent to Commit an Offense under MDLEA

Evidence based upon practices commonly recognized as "smuggling tactics may provide prima facie evidence of intent to use a vessel to commit" or facilitate an offense, and therefore support the legal seizure and forfeiture of the vessel, even if there are no controlled substances aboard the ship.[13]

Finally, the statute contains a non-exhaustive list of indicia that may be considered, in the totality of the circumstances, to be prima facie evidence that a vessel is intended to be used to commit, or to facilitate the commission of a drug trafficking an offense. The list includes features such as low observable design to avoid detection, hidden compartments, non-standard auxiliary fuel tanks, engines that are "excessively over-powered," camouflage paint schemes, and marks of false registry.

> (1) The construction or adaptation of the vessel in a manner that facilitates smuggling, including—
>   (A) the configuration of the vessel to ride low in the water or present a low hull profile to avoid being detected visually or by radar;

---

[10] Id., at § 70505.
[11] Id., at § 70503(c).
[12] Id., at § 70507(a). Property is described in 21 U.S.C. § 881(a).
[13] Id., at § 70507(b).

(B) the presence of any compartment or equipment that is built or fitted out for smuggling, not including items such as a safe or lock-box reasonably used for the storage of personal valuables;
(C) the presence of an auxiliary tank not installed in accordance with applicable law or installed in such a manner as to enhance the vessel's smuggling capability;
(D) the presence of engines that are excessively over-powered in relation to the design and size of the vessel;
(E) the presence of materials used to reduce or alter the heat or radar signature of the vessel and avoid detection;
(F) the presence of a camouflaging paint scheme, or of materials used to camouflage the vessel, to avoid detection; or
(G) the display of false vessel registration numbers, false indicia of vessel nationality, false vessel name, or false vessel homeport.
(2) The presence or absence of equipment, personnel, or cargo inconsistent with the type or declared purpose of the vessel.
(3) The presence of excessive fuel, lube oil, food, water, or spare parts, inconsistent with legitimate vessel operation, inconsistent with the construction or equipment of the vessel, or inconsistent with the character of the vessel's stated purpose.
(4) The operation of the vessel without lights during times lights are required ... in a manner of navigation consistent with smuggling tactics used to avoid detection by law enforcement authorities.
(5) The failure of the vessel to stop or respond or heave to when hailed by government authority, especially where the vessel conducts evasive maneuvering when hailed.
(6) The declaration to government authority of apparently false information about the vessel, crew, or voyage or the failure to identify the vessel by name or country of registration....
(7) The presence of controlled substance residue on the vessel, on an item aboard the vessel, or on an individual aboard the vessel, of a quantity or other nature that reasonably indicates manufacturing or distribution activity.
(8) The use of petroleum products or other substances on the vessel to foil the detection of [the residue] of a controlled substance (e.g. in an effort to defeat ion swipes).
(9) The presence of a controlled substance in the water in the vicinity of the vessel, where given the currents, weather conditions, and course and speed of the vessel, the quantity or other nature is such that it reasonably indicates manufacturing or distribution activity.[14]

17.2 Drug Trafficking Vessel Interdiction Act

Over the past decade, U.S. authorities have witnessed the development of a new technique for smuggling illicit drugs into the United States, as drug traffickers adapt their operations and routes to counter effective drug interdiction efforts by law enforcement and intelligence agencies. Traditionally, Colombian drug

---

[14] Id., at 70507(b).

traffickers moved cocaine from the Andean Ridge to North America on "go fast" boats—sleek, open-air speedboats capable of slicing through the water at up to 80 miles per hour in calm seas. Go-fast boats are fiberglass watercraft that can carry two tons of drugs, and often have 55-gallon drums of fuel visible on deck, peeking above the gunwale. But at high speed, the craft leave huge wakes, making them easily detectable from the air. Brian Wilson of the U.S. Global Maritime Operational Threat Response Coordination Center (GMCC) suggests that as anti-drug agents using helicopters have become more adept at spotting and interdicting go-fasts, drug traffickers are switching to semi-submersible craft.[15]

Over the past 15 years interdiction against go-fasts has become more robust. In the mid-1990s, the Coast Guard began arming helicopters and employing over-the-horizon cutters. Non-lethal methods of stopping the vessels, such as entanglement nets, engine disablement using specialized small arms technologies, and specialized rubber bullets to disable go-fast boat operators have also been employed. Advanced technologies are being developed, and include shooting deployable drogue chutes into a fleeing vessel. In response to these advancements, drug trafficking organizations, particularly in the Eastern Pacific, have increasingly turned toward a new and highly mobile, asymmetrical method of transport, the self-propelled semi-submersible (SPSS) watercraft.

17.2.1 *Self-propelled Semi-submersible (SPSS) Watercraft*

A "semi-submersible vessel" is defined to include "any watercraft constructed or adapted to be capable of operating with most of its hull and bulk under the surface of the water, including both manned and unmanned watercraft."[16] A "submersible vessel" is defined as "a vessel that is capable of operating completely below the surface of the water, including both manned and unmanned watercraft."[17] The semi-submersible is, in essence, a go-fast boat with a fiberglass top fitted with air vents that stick out of the water. Resting low in the water, the SPSS is difficult to detect visually or by radar. By 2008, it was estimated that over 33 percent of all cocaine entering the United States from the Eastern Pacific was being shipped in SPSSs.[18]

Instead of high-speed engines, the semi-submersibles are powered by a 200 or 300 horsepower diesel motor, allowing the vessel to move about 10 miles per hour. The resulting wake is so small that anti-drug agents must get within 3,000 yards of the vessels to spot them. Most semi-submersibles are built along the

---

[15] Brian Wilson, *Submersibles and Transnational Criminal Organizations*, 17 OCEAN & COASTAL L. J. 1, at 1–2.
[16] 46 U.S.C. § 70502(f)(1).
[17] Id., at § 70502(f)(2).
[18] Douglas A. Kash & Eli White, *A New Law Counters the Semisubmersible Smuggling Threat*, FBI LAW ENFORCEMENT BULL., Mar. 2010.

rivers, estuaries, and mangrove swamps of Colombia's Pacific coast, and at a minimum cost of between $500,000 and $1 million per vessel.

Although drug traffickers have experimented with the use of semi-submersibles to smuggle drugs since the early 1990s, a new generation of SPSS watercraft, with greater cargo capacity and range, poses a significant challenge for law enforcement to interdict drugs in the transit zone. Initially constructed of fiberglass and wood, the new SPSS vessels are now built of steel and additional features have raised the cost to as much as $2 million per craft. But the new SPSS can carry larger loads and travel long distances, so the increased costs are insignificant to trafficking organizations.

SPSS vessels normally range from 40 to 80 feet in length, carry a crew of four (or may be remotely controlled) and are capable of transporting up to 12 metric tons of drugs. A 10-ton SPSS therefore may carry as much as $20 million worth of cocaine, assuming one kilogram is worth $20,000 wholesale. The crew is paid between $10,000 and $100,000 per person for a single delivery. AN SPSS can travel up to 2,500 nautical miles without refueling, and they normally plod through the water at a speed of no more than 13 knots. Because of their low-signature design and low freeboard (one foot above water), SPSSs are extremely difficult to detect or identify. The SPSS structure is designed to minimize the vessel's wake. The engine is covered, and exhaust pipes are installed to minimize the engine's thermal signature. The SPSS normally will deliver its cargo to other vessels at sea for transport ashore and shipment via land routes to the United States. After the delivery is made, the crew will scuttle the ship.[19]

In July 2011, U.S. Coast Guard Cutter *Seneca* conducted the first recorded interdiction of an SPSS in the Caribbean.[20] *Seneca* intercepted a SPSS off the coast of Honduras carrying seven tons of cocaine. The Coast Guard interdicted two more SPSSs in 2011, one in August (CGC *Oak*) and another in September (CGC *Mohawk* and CGC *Cypress*).[21]

17.2.2 *Criminal and Civil Penalties for Operation of SPSS*

In the early- and mid-2000s, loopholes in the U.S. law allowed traffickers who successfully scuttled their SPSSs (and its cargo) to escape criminal prosecution because the government lacked tangible evidence of any criminal wrongdoing. Congress responded in 2008 by enacting the Drug Trafficking Vessel Interdiction Act (DTVIA), which provides new legal tools to go after SPSSs.[22] The new law imposed criminal and civil penalties for simply operating or embarking in a

---

[19] Kash & White, *A New Law Counters the Semisubmersible Smuggling Threat*.
[20] J. R. Wilson, *From Georgia to the Caribbean Basin: Future Challenges Today*, U.S. COAST GUARD DISTRICT 7, Feb. 26, 2012.
[21] Id.
[22] 18 U.S.C. § 2285.

stateless SPSS in international waters with the intent to evade detection, regardless of whether drugs are found on the vessel.

> Whoever knowingly operates, or attempts or conspires to operate, by any means, or embarks in any submersible vessel or semi-submersible vessel that is without nationality and that is navigating or has navigated into, through, or from waters beyond the outer limit of the territorial sea of a single country or a lateral limit of that country's territorial sea with an adjacent country, with the intent to evade detection, shall be fined under this title, imprisoned not more than 15 years, or both.[23]

The presence of any of the indicia in 46 U.S.C. § 70507(b)(1)(A), (E), (F), and (G) or in § 70507(b)(4)–(6) may be considered to be prima facie evidence by an SPSS crew of "intent to evade detection."

> (1) The construction or adaptation of the vessel in a manner that facilitates smuggling, including—
>
>   (A) the configuration of the vessel to ride low in the water or present a low hull profile to avoid being detected visually or by radar;
>   (B) the presence of any compartment or equipment that is built or fitted out for smuggling, not including items such as a safe or lock-box reasonably used for the storage of personal valuables;
>   (C) the presence of an auxiliary tank not installed in accordance with applicable law or installed in such a manner as to enhance the vessel's smuggling capability;
>   (D) the presence of engines that are excessively over-powered in relation to the design and size of the vessel;
>   (E) the presence of materials used to reduce or alter the heat or radar signature of the vessel and avoid detection;
>   (F) the presence of a camouflaging paint scheme, or of materials used to camouflage the vessel, to avoid detection; or
>   (G) the display of false vessel registration numbers, false indicia of vessel nationality, false vessel name, or false vessel homeport.
>
> (2) The presence or absence of equipment, personnel, or cargo inconsistent with the type or declared purpose of the vessel.
> (3) The presence of excessive fuel, lube oil, food, water, or spare parts, inconsistent with legitimate vessel operation, inconsistent with the construction or equipment of the vessel, or inconsistent with the character of the vessel's stated purpose.
> (4) The operation of the vessel without lights during times lights are required ... in a manner of navigation consistent with smuggling tactics used to avoid detection by law enforcement authorities.
> (5) The failure of the vessel to stop or respond or heave to when hailed by government authority, especially where the vessel conducts evasive maneuvering when hailed.
> (6) The declaration to government authority of apparently false information about the vessel, crew, or voyage or the failure to identify the vessel by name or country of registration. . . .[24]

---

[23] 18 U.S.C. § 2285(a). Similar language is found in 46 U.S.C. § 70508(a).
[24] 18 U.S.C. § 2285(b); 46 U.S.C. §§ 70507(b) and 70508(b).

The DTVIA also may be applied extraterritorially.[25] Claims of nationality or registry under the statute include possession on board the vessel and production of documents evidencing the vessel's nationality; flying the flag or ensign of a nation; or a verbal claim of nationality or registry by the master of the vessel.[26] There are, however, a number of affirmative defenses under the statute. In this regard, the burden is on the defendant to prove by a preponderance of the evidence that the submersible or SPSS involved was at the time of the offense:

(A) a vessel of the United States or lawfully registered in a foreign nation as claimed by the master . . .;
(B) classed by and designed in accordance with the rules of a classification society;
(C) lawfully operated in government-regulated or licensed activity, including commerce, research, or exploration; or
(D) outfitted with an operable automatic identification system, vessel monitoring system, or long range identification and tracking system.[27]

The affirmative defenses may be proved conclusively by the production of government documents that show the vessel's nationality at the time of the offense, a certificate of classification issued by the vessel's classification society upon completion of relevant classification surveys and valid at the time of the offense, or government documents evidencing licensure, regulation, or registration for commerce, research, or exploration.[28] The law does not apply to "lawfully authorized activities carried out by or at the direction of the United States Government."[29] Failure on the part of the United States to comply with international law, however, is not a defense to a criminal or civil enforcement proceeding.[30] Furthermore, assertion of appropriate jurisdiction over the craft by the United States is not an element of the offense.[31]

17.2.3 Legal Challenges to DTVIA

Challenges as to the constitutionality of the DTVIA have been unsuccessful. The first legal test of the Act occurred in 2009 in the case of *United States v. Ibarguen-Mosquera*. On January 8, 2009, the U.S. Coast Guard Cutter *Alert* received a report from a maritime patrol aircraft (MPA) that an unmarked SPSS was spotted in the Eastern Pacific Ocean, approximately 163 nm off the coast of Colombia. The SPSS was ocean blue in color, 50 to 60 feet in length, and sat very low in the water. The *Alert* immediately proceeded to the location and arrived around 12 hours later.

---

[25] 18 U.S.C. § 2285(c).
[26] Id., at § 2285(d).
[27] 18 U.S.C. § 2285(e)(1); 46 U.S.C. § 70508(c)(1).
[28] 18 U.S.C. § 2285(e)(2); 46 U.S.C. § 70508(c)(2).
[29] 18 U.S.C. § 2285(f).
[30] 18 U.S.C. § 2285(g); 46 U.S.C. § 70505.
[31] 18 U.S.C. § 2285(g); 46 U.S.C. § 70504.

Before the *Alert* arrived, the MPA crew observed four men exit the cabin, don life-vests, inflate life rafts, and jump into the water. After a short period of time, the defendants deflated the rafts and resumed their travel. When *Alert* arrived on scene, it dispatched a helicopter to covertly observe the craft. On two occasions, the vessel stopped and the crew exited the forward hatch and scanned the area before returning below deck. After observing the SPSS for about an hour, the *Alert's* helicopter illuminated the vessel and announced its presence. At the same time, the *Alert* dispatched a rigid-hull inflatable boat to interdict the vessel. After being illuminated, the defendants exited the SPSS, donned life jackets, and inflated the life rafts. One of the defendants then returned below deck, at which time the helicopter crew observed a flash of light and smoke or steam emit from the vessel. The defendants then jumped into the water and the SPSS sank.

After being retrieved from the water, the defendants were subsequently flown to Tampa, Florida, where they were arrested and charged with violating the DTVIA. On January 13, 2009, a Federal grand jury returned a two-count indictment charging the defendants with conspiring to operate or embark in a semi-submersible vessel in international waters, without nationality and with the intent to evade detection.[32] The defendants were aiding and abetting in the operation of a semi-submersible vessel in international waters, without nationality and with the intent to evade detection, in violation of 18 U.S.C. § 2285 and 18 U.S.C. § 2. The District Court found the defendants guilty and sentenced each to 108 months imprisonment and three years supervised release. Each count ran concurrently.

The defendants appealed their convictions to the 11th Circuit Court of Appeals on five grounds. First, the appellants contended that the DTVIA was unconstitutional on various grounds. Second, they argued that convicting them of both conspiracy to violate and a substantive violation of a single statute runs afoul of the Constitution's prohibition against double jeopardy. Third, the appellants argued that the government's demonstration of statelessness of the craft and navigation of the craft in international waters bear on culpability and thus should be considered elements of the crime requiring proof beyond a reasonable doubt and proof of *mens rea*. Fourth, appellants argued that, even if the court found that the district court applied the elements of the DTVIA correctly, there was insufficient evidence to find them guilty of violating the statute. Finally, the traffickers argued that the district court erred when it excluded certain favorable expert witness testimony. After a review of the case and oral argument, however, the Court of Appeals found that the appellants' arguments lacked merit. The convictions were affirmed.[33]

---

[32] 18 U.S.C. § 2285.
[33] *U.S. v. Ibarguen-Mosquera*, 634 F.3d 1370 (11th Cir. 2011).

A second challenge to the DTVIA occurred several months after *United States v. Ibarguen-Mosquera*. The cases *United States v. Valarezo-Orobio* and *United States v. Palomino-Moreno* were consolidated for appeal at the 11th Circuit Court of Appeals after the defendants were convicted in separate actions before the District Court for violation of 18 U.S.C. § 2285. Both defendants were crewmembers on a 35-foot, aqua blue SPSS that was apprehended by the U.S. Coast Guard on July 27, 2009. The vessel did not display a flag and had no visible markings of registry.

The SPSS was operating in international waters in the vicinity of Malpelo Island, Colombia, en route to Ecuador to pick up a cargo of illicit drugs. While at sea, Valarezo spotted a Coast Guard helicopter and notified the captain, who immediately ordered Valarezo to scuttle the vessel. By the time a Coast Guard cutter arrived on scene, the SPSS had sunk. Valarezo and Palomino were transported to the United States for criminal prosecution and at trial were charged in a two-count indictment for conspiracy and substantive violations of the DTVIA. The defendants moved to dismiss the indictment on the grounds that 18 U.S.C. § 2285 was unconstitutional, but the motion was denied by the District Court.

Valarezo and Palomino then pleaded guilty to the charges without any plea agreement, preserving the right to appeal the district court's ruling about the statute's constitutionality. The District Court sentenced the defendants to 108 months of imprisonment on each count, to run concurrently, followed by 36 months of supervised release. Both Valarezo and Palomino appealed the District Court's order denying their motion to dismiss the indictment. The 11th Circuit Court of Appeals, however, determined that the appellants' constitutional challenges to the DTVIA were foreclosed by the Court's earlier decisions in *United States v. Ibarguen-Mosquera* and *United States v. Saac*, and therefore affirmed the District Court's order denying the motion to dismiss.[34]

The United States is developing and deploying new technologies to defeat SPSS traffickers, including "advanced radar technology, unmanned aerial vehicles that can loiter for long periods of time, remote laser infrared detection, acoustic sensors, and satellites...."[35] Top tier technology, however, is insufficient to counter illicit SPSS trafficking. The United States therefore has led an effort to develop new Federal criminal laws against SPSS. Regional states and organizations are beginning to contribute to the campaign.

Colombia, for example, passed an SPSS law on July 9, 2009, that criminalizes the finance, construction, storage, commercialization, transport, procurement or use of a SPSS or submersible vessel with illicit intent. Penalties under the Colom-

---

[34] *United States v. Valarezo-Orobio* and *United States v. Palomino-Moreno*, 635 F.3d 1261 (11th Cir. 2011).
[35] Kash & White, *A New Law Counters the Semisubmersible Smuggling Threat*.

bian law include fines between $246,340 up to more than $17 million and incarceration from six to 14 years.[36]

17.2.4 *SPSS Model Law of the Organization of American States*

The Organization of American States (OAS) has also developed model legislation on submersible and semi-submersible vessels to assist member States to enact domestic legislation to criminalize the construction and operation of, as well as embarkation upon, such vessels. The Model OAS legislation provides model text for countries to consider in drafting new legislation to suppress the threat of "submersible vessels and semisubmersible vessels without nationality."[37] By criminalizing the construction, operation of, and embarkation upon stateless submersible and semi-submersible vessels, the model law seeks to deter the use of the inherently unsafe vessels and facilitate criminal prosecution of those involved in criminal activities.

> Model Law of the Organization of American States
>
> Article 1. Findings and recommendations.
>
> [Parliament/Congress/Legislature/Government of (Country)] finds and declares that constructing, embarking upon, utilizing, or operating a submersible vessel or semi-submersible vessel without nationality is a serious international problem, facilitates transnational crime, including drug trafficking... and presents a specific threat to the safety of maritime navigation and the security of (country). This law applies to any type of artifact that is not destined to be used as touristic, scientific, or for any other legal activity.
>
> Definition: Applicable to this Law, a submersible vessel or semisubmersible vessel is a vessel capable of moving in the water with or without self-propulsion, and whose characteristics or design allow for total or partial immersion for the purpose of avoiding detection.[38]
>
> Article 2. Operation of Submersible or semisubmersible vessel without nationality.
>
> A. Offense: Whoever, without permission from a competent authority, operates or embarks in a submersible vessel or semi-submersible vessel that is without

---

[36] *Colombian, U.S. Laws fight Semi-submersible Threat*, U.S. COAST GUARD NEWS, July 16, 2009.

[37] Organization of American States, Inter-American Drug Abuse Control Commission (CICAD) Model Legislation on Self-Propelled Submersible and Semi-Submersible Vessels, OEA/Ser.L/XIV.2.49, CICAD/doc.1891/11—corr. 2, 30 June 2011.

[38] The Agreement notes:
The definitions needed of terms used in the Articles will vary by country; it is important to define any term that is unusual, ambiguous or may be interpreted in different ways.
   In countries where there are potential legitimate uses for the type of vessel that would fall within the definition of a submersible or semisubmersible vessel, such as for artesian or hand fishing, a narrowly defined exception for those legitimate uses may be desired. Id.

nationality shall be [fined and/or imprisoned, as specified]. Whoever attempts or conspires to commit any of the acts described in this section shall be [fined and/or imprisoned, as specified]. Penalties should be commensurate with other drug trafficking penalties.

B. Aggravating Circumstances: Whoever utilizes a submersible vessel or semisubmersible vessel to store, transport, or sell narcotic substances or consumables required to manufacture narcotic substances shall be [fined and/or imprisoned, as specified]. The penalty shall be increased by (fill in details) when the illegal actions are facilitated by a [government official or a current or former member of law enforcement or the military].

Article 3 sets forth supporting offenses. "Whoever... finances, constructs, or purchases a submersible vessel or semi-submersible vessel shall be [subject to fine and/or imprisoned, as specified]." Like Article 2, this Article also contains an inchoate offense of conspiracy to commit the proscribed acts; merely the construction or financing of an illegal SPSS is subject to punishment. Article 3 additionally contains aggravating circumstances that increase the punishment if someone provides "conditions for usage and operation" of an SPSS in an illegal activity.

Article 4 recognizes extraterritorial jurisdiction over an offense under the agreement, including the attempt or conspiracy offenses. The Article states that the "scope of the extraterritorial jurisdiction may be limited by international law; however, a broadly defined scope of extraterritorial jurisdiction allows application to the fullest extent permitted under international law."

Finally, Article 5 stipulates legitimate claims of nationality or registry for an SPSS. Such claims are valid only if they are supported by possession

> ... on board the vessel and production of documents evidencing the vessel's nationality as provided in Article 91 of the 1982 United Nations Convention on the Law of the Sea (UNCLOS); Flying its nation's ensign or flag; or a verbal claim of nationality or registry by the master or individual in charge of the vessel.[39]

17.3 Foreign Narcotics Kingpin Designation Act

One of the primary tools available to disrupt and dismantle transnational organized crime (TOC) networks is the "continued use of economic sanctions under the Foreign Narcotics Kingpin Designation Act (Kingpin Act) to pursue transnational drug organizations...."[40] The Kingpin Act facilitates the prosecution of "persons involved in illegal activities linked to drug trafficking, such as arms trafficking, bulk cash smuggling, or gang activity."[41]

---

[39] Countries that are not party to UNCLOS may substitute Article 5 of the 1958 Convention on the High Seas in place of Article 91 of UNCLOS.
[40] 21 U.S.C. § 1901–1908, 8 U.S.C. § 1182, Pub. L. 106–120, Dec. 3, 1999.
[41] Strategy to Combat Transnational Organized Crime 24 (July 2011).

17.3.1 *Executive Order 12978*

Executive Order 12978, signed by President William Clinton on October 21, 1995, was the genesis for The Kingpin Act.[42] The presidential order declared a national emergency to deal with the threat to the national security, foreign policy and economy of the United States resulting from "the actions of significant foreign narcotics traffickers centered in Colombia, and the unparalleled violence, corruption, and harm that they cause in the United States and abroad...."[43] To counter the threat, Section 1 of the order blocks:

> ... all property and interests in property that are or hereafter come within the United States, or that are or hereafter come within the possession or control of United States persons, of:
>
> (a) the foreign persons listed in [an Annex to the order, including Gilberto Rodriguez Orejuela, Miguel Angel Rodriguez Orejuela, José Santacruz Londoño, and Helmer Herrera Buitrago];
> (b) foreign persons determined by the Secretary of the Treasury, in consultation with the Attorney General and the Secretary of State:
>   (i) to play a significant role in international narcotics trafficking centered in Colombia; or
>   (ii) materially to assist in, or provide financial or technological support for or goods or services in support of, the narcotics trafficking activities of persons designated in or pursuant to this order; and
> (c) persons determined by the Secretary of the Treasury, in consultation with the Attorney General and the Secretary of State, to be owned or controlled by, or to act for or on behalf of, persons designated in or pursuant to this order.[44]

Section 2 of the Order prohibits:

> (a) any transaction or dealing by United States persons or within the United States in property or interests in property of the persons designated in or pursuant to this order;
> (b) any transaction by any United States person or within the United States that evades or avoids, or has the purpose of evading or avoiding, or attempts to violate, any of the prohibitions set forth in this order.[45]

17.3.2 *Purpose of the Kingpin Act*

The Kingpin Act addresses the continuing "national emergency resulting from the activities of international narcotics traffickers and their organizations that threatens the national security, foreign policy, and economy of the United States."[46]

---

[42] Executive Order 12978, Blocking Assets and Prohibiting Transactions with Significant Narcotics Traffickers, Oct. 21, 1995, FR Vol. 60, No. 205, Oct. 24, 1995.
[43] Id.
[44] Id.
[45] Id.
[46] 21 U.S.C. § 1901(a)(4).

The purpose of the Act is to deny access to the U.S. financial system to significant foreign narcotics traffickers, their related businesses, and their operatives, and to prohibit all trade and transactions between the traffickers and U.S. companies and individuals:

> The purpose of this chapter is to provide authority for the identification of, and application of sanctions on a worldwide basis to, significant foreign narcotics traffickers, their organizations, and the foreign persons who provide support to those significant foreign narcotics traffickers and their organizations, whose activities threaten the national security, foreign policy, and economy of the United States.[47]

Title 21 of the U.S. Code defines a "significant foreign narcotics trafficker" as "any foreign person that plays a significant role in international narcotics trafficking...."[48] The Secretary of the Treasury, the Attorney General, the Secretary of State, the Secretary of Defense, and the Director of the Central Intelligence Agency are required to coordinate and identify significant foreign narcotics traffickers and propose them to the President for economic and other financial sanctions.[49] Based on their recommendation, the President is required by statute to submit a report to specified congressional committees that publicly identifies significant foreign narcotics traffickers that he determines are appropriate for sanctions and expresses his intent to impose such sanctions.[50]

> (b) Public identification and sanctioning of significant foreign narcotics traffickers
>
> Not later than June 1, 2000, and not later than June 1 of each year thereafter, the President shall submit a report to the Permanent Select Committee on Intelligence, and the Committees on the Judiciary, International Relations, Armed Services, and Ways and Means of the House of Representatives; and to the Select Committee on Intelligence, and the Committees on the Judiciary, Foreign Relations, Armed Services, and Finance of the Senate—
>
>> (1) identifying publicly the foreign persons that the President determines are appropriate for sanctions pursuant to this chapter; and
>> (2) detailing publicly the President's intent to impose sanctions upon these significant foreign narcotics traffickers pursuant to this chapter. The report required in this subsection shall not include information on persons upon which United States sanctions imposed under this chapter, or otherwise on account of narcotics trafficking, are already in effect.
>
> The president is authorized by statute to make out-of-cycle determinations.
> (h) Changes in determinations to impose sanctions
> (1) Additional determinations
>> (A) If at any time after the report required under subsection (b) of this section the President finds that a foreign person is a significant foreign narcotics

---

[47] Id., at § 1902.
[48] Id., at § 1907(7).
[49] Id., at § 1903(a).
[50] Id., at § 1903(b).

trafficker and such foreign person has not been publicly identified [in an earlier report submitted under the Act] the President shall submit an additional public report... with respect to such foreign person to the Permanent Select Committee on Intelligence, and the Committees on the Judiciary, International Relations, Armed Services, and Ways and Means of the House of Representatives, and the Select Committee on Intelligence, and the Committees on the Judiciary, Foreign Relations, Armed Services, and Finance of the Senate.

(B) The President may apply sanctions authorized under this chapter to the significant foreign narcotics trafficker identified in the report submitted under subparagraph (A) as if the trafficker were originally included in the report submitted pursuant to subsection (b) of this section.

(C) The President shall notify the Secretary of the Treasury of any determination made under this paragraph.[51]

The Kingpin Act is not limited to individual persons. For purposes of the Act, a "person" is defined as "an individual or entity,"[52] and may include a corporation or non-state armed group. Furthermore, a "foreign person" is defined as "any citizen or national of a foreign state or any entity not organized under the laws of the United States, but does not include a foreign state."[53] Under the statute, an "entity" includes any "partnership, joint venture, association, corporation, organization, network, group, or subgroup, or any form of business collaboration."[54]

Foreign persons publicly identified in the President's report or designated by the Secretary of the Treasury as significant foreign narcotics traffickers are subject to the sanctions.[55] The law may be used to block assets that include

... property and interests in property within the United States, or within the possession or control of any United States person, which are owned or controlled by—

1. any significant foreign narcotics trafficker publicly identified by the President in the report....;
2. any foreign person that the Secretary of the Treasury[56]... designates as materially assisting in, or providing [support to] a significant foreign narcotics trafficker so identified in the report....;
3. any foreign person that the Secretary of the Treasury... designates as owned, controlled, or directed by, or acting for or on behalf of, a significant foreign narcotics trafficker so identified in the report...;[57] and

---

[51] Id., at § 1903(h)(1).
[52] Id., at §1907(5).
[53] Id., at § 1907(2).
[54] Id., at §1907(1).
[55] Id., at § 1904.
[56] The Secretary of the Treasury makes such designation in consultation with the Attorney General, the Director of Central Intelligence, the Director of the Federal Bureau of Investigation, Administrator of the Drug Enforcement Administration, the Secretary of Defense, and the Secretary of State. Id., at § 1904(b).
[57] The Secretary of the Treasury makes such designation in consultation with the Attorney General, the Director of Central Intelligence, Director of the Federal Bureau of

4. any foreign person that the Secretary of the Treasury... designates as playing a significant role in international narcotics trafficking.[58]

The following transactions also may be prohibited under the statute:

(1) Any transaction or dealing by a United States person, or within the United States, in property or interests in property of any significant foreign narcotics trafficker so identified in the report [... and] foreign persons designated by the Secretary of the Treasury....[59]

(2) Any transaction or dealing by a U.S. person, or within the United States, that evades or avoids, or has the effect of evading or avoiding, and any endeavor, attempt, or conspiracy to violate, any of the prohibitions contained in this chapter.[60]

Criminal penalties for individuals who violate the act include up to 10 years in prison and/or fines in the amount provided for in Title 18 of the U.S. Code, while entities that violate the Act may be fined up to $10,000.[61] Any officer, director, or agent of an entity who knowingly violates the Act may be imprisoned up to 30 years and/or fined $5 million.[62] Civil penalties up to $1.075 million may be imposed by the Secretary of the Treasury on any individual or entity who violates any license, order, rule, or regulation issued in compliance with the provisions of the statute.[63]

Between 2000 and 2009, the President identified 78 significant foreign narcotics traffickers and the Department of the Treasury's Office of Foreign Assets Control issued a total of 496 derivative designations pursuant to its authorities under Title 21 U.S.C. § 1904(b)(2)–(4). The Sinaloa Cartel, Los Zetas and La Familia Michoacana were added to the list in April 2009.[64]

17.4 U.S. Coast Guard Authorities

The U.S. Coast Guard is the primary maritime law enforcement service of the United States. The Coast Guard is part of the Department of Homeland Security

---

Investigation, Administrator of the Drug Enforcement Administration, the Secretary of Defense, and the Secretary of State. Id.

[58] The Secretary of the Treasury makes such designation in consultation with the Attorney General, the Director of Central Intelligence, Director of the Federal Bureau of Investigation, Administrator of the Drug Enforcement Administration, the Secretary of Defense, and the Secretary of State. Id.

[59] Id., at § 1904(c).

[60] Id.

[61] Id., at § 1906(a)(1).

[62] Id., at § 1906(a)(2).

[63] Id., at § 1906(b).

[64] Office of the White House Press Sec'y, Overview of the Foreign Narcotics Kingpin Designation Act, April 15, 2009. A complete list of individuals and entities sanctioned under the Act may be found at www.treasury.gov/ofac.

and is the lead federal agency for maritime drug interdiction and the co-lead for air interdiction operations (with Customs and Border Patrol). The challenge is great, and the Coast Guard deploys ships and aircraft throughout a six million square mile area that includes the Caribbean Sea, Gulf of Mexico and an enormous swath of the Eastern Pacific. Operational interdictions have seized 800,000 pounds of cocaine and over 300,000 pounds of marijuana since 1997. Fifty-one percent of all U.S. government seizures of cocaine each year are attributed to the Coast Guard.

17.4.1 *Plenary U.S. Maritime Law Enforcement Authority*

The Coast Guard has authority to enforce or assist in the enforcement of "all applicable Federal laws on, under, and over the high seas and waters subject to the jurisdiction of the United States...."[65] This statutory grant of plenary authority means the Coast Guard may enforce all U.S. laws and treaty obligations at sea, to include that authority to board, inspect, search, inquire and arrest any vessel subject to U.S. jurisdiction. To carry out these missions, the Coast Guard is authorized to "make inquiries, examinations, inspections, searches, seizures, and arrests upon the high seas and waters over which the United States has jurisdiction, for the prevention, detection, and suppression of violations of laws of the United States."[66] Commissioned, warrant or petty officers of the Coast Guard are authorized to "go on board of any vessel subject to the jurisdiction, or to the operation of any law, of the United States, address inquiries to those on board, examine the ship's documents and papers, and examine, inspect, and search the vessel and use all necessary force to compel compliance."[67]

If a violation of U.S. law is discovered on board a vessel during a Coast Guard boarding, 14 U.S.C. § 89(a) authorizes the arrest of the person(s) responsible and seizure of the vessel and its cargo.

U.S. Coast Guard officers engaged in enforcing the laws of the United States shall:

(1) be deemed to be acting as agents of the particular executive department or independent establishment charged with the administration of the particular law; and
(2) be subject to all the rules and regulations promulgated by such department or independent establishment with respect to the enforcement of that law.[68]

---

[65] 14 U.S.C. § 2.
[66] 14 U.S.C. § 89(a).
[67] Id.
[68] 14 U.S.C. § 89(b).

17.4.2   *Use of Force*

The use of force to compel a suspect vessel to stop is authorized by federal statute.

> ...Whenever any vessel liable to seizure or examination does not stop on being ordered to do so or on being pursued by an authorized vessel or authorized aircraft which has displayed the ensign, pennant, or other identifying insignia prescribed for an authorized vessel or authorized aircraft, the person in command or in charge of the authorized vessel or authorized aircraft may...fire at or into the vessel which does not stop.[69]

The use of force, however, is conditioned on first employing warning shots. Under the subsequent paragraph of 14 U.S.C. § 637, the Coast Guard is required to "fire a gun as a warning signal" before firing into a vessel. No warning shot is required, however, if the Coast Guard official determines that it would "unreasonably endanger persons or property in the vicinity of the vessel to be stopped."[70]

Coast Guard personnel operating under the authority of § 637 "shall be indemnified from any penalties or actions for damages for firing at or into a vessel."[71] Additionally, "if any person is killed or wounded by the firing, and the person in command of the authorized vessel or authorized aircraft or any person acting pursuant to their orders is prosecuted or arrested therefor, they shall be forthwith admitted to bail."[72]

The following ships and aircraft may use force in maritime counter drug interdiction:

- Coast Guard ships and aircraft;[73]
- U.S. naval vessels or U.S. military aircraft on which one or more USCG members are assigned;[74] and
- [A]ny other vessel or aircraft on government noncommercial service under the tactical control of a member of the Coast Guard.[75]

The Coast Guard implements the statutory provisions on the use of force in the *Maritime Law Enforcement Manual* (MLEM), a publication that is marked "For Official Use Only," and therefore not publicly available.[76] The MLEM contains guidance on the use of force against suspected persons and non-compliant vessels. An example of how force is employed by Coast Guard during an interdiction

---

[69] 14 U.S.C. § 637.
[70] Id.
[71] Id.
[72] Id.
[73] Id.
[74] 10 U.S.C. § 379.
[75] 14 U.S.C. § 637(b).
[76] Commandant, U.S. Coast Guard, Maritime Law Enforcement Manual (COMDTINST M16247.1 (series).

at sea that involves aircraft, however, may be gleaned from the following official narrative media release by the U.S. Coast Guard 7th District in Miami.

17.4.3 Airborne Use of Force

The storyline below is excerpted at some length because it is rare in providing an official, yet publicly available narrative of the interaction between the legal authorities of the Department of Defense and the Coast Guard in an operational interdiction, and between the airborne use of force and surface maritime narcotics interdiction.

> [... In 2006] the U.S. Navy and U.S. Coast Guard reached a significant milestone in the war on drugs.... The *USS John L. Hall* [(FFG 32)] was assigned with Law Enforcement Detachment (LEDET) 408 from the U.S. Coast Guard Tactical Law Enforcement Team in Miami to patrol the Caribbean Sea for detection and monitoring of suspected narcotics smugglers. The [Navy ship and the embarked Coast Guard LEDET], working together, successfully completed the first joint service airborne use of force involving Coast Guard and Navy assets.
>
> During the early hours of September 10, 2006, a Navy helicopter operating from the *USS Hall* was on routine patrol north of the coast of Colombia [under the operational control of Department of Defense Joint Interagency Task Force South—JIATF South—located in Key West, Florida]. [The helicopter] spotted a fast moving, surface contact on its radar. As the helicopter closed on the radar contact, the crew noticed the vessel was on a northerly course at approximately 30 mph. The radar operator on the helicopter relayed the developing situation to the *Hall*, [alerting the embarked] Coast Guard LEDET Officer in Charge.... As [JIATF South] was informed of the situation, the *Hall* made best speed to intercept the suspicious contact. Upon recommendation from the Coast Guard officer in charge, tactical control was shifted from the task force in Key West to Coast Guard District Seven headquartered in Miami and the Coast Guard Ensign was hoisted on the *Hall*. [At this point, the *USS Hall* was under operational control of JIATF South and under Tactical Control of the Officer in Charge of [the embarked] Coast Guard LEDET].
>
> Once tactical control was shifted to the Coast Guard, law enforcement actions were enabled. The helicopter was able to track the suspect vessel using both radar and their infrared camera, which was able to display video to the *Hall*. The video was real time and could be seen by the crew of the *Hall* coordinating the interdiction efforts. As the crew of the helicopter reported its observations of the go-fast vessel, it was being relayed through the Coast Guard officer in charge to the law enforcement duty Officer at [Coast Guard] District Seven in Miami.
>
> The helicopter reported that the contact was approximately 30 to 40 feet in length, two outboard engines, four persons on board and numerous fuel drums located on deck. Additionally, the vessel had no name painted on its hull, no flag was being flown to indicate nationality of the vessel, and there was no registry to identify the vessel in any way. With this information, District Seven granted permission from the District Seven commander to stop the vessel including the use of warning shots and disabling fire to conduct a right of visit boarding.
>
> The helicopter was informed that they were granted permission to stop the vessel including the use of warning shots and disabling fire. Before proceeding with warning shots and disabling fire, the helicopter must first proceed with the signaling phase of

the interdiction process. During the signaling phase, the vessel is contacted via VHF radio in both English and Spanish to stop and prepare to be boarded. The helicopter also maneuvers close to the vessel in an effort to stop the vessel before employing warning shots and disabling fire. The helicopter proceeded through the parts of the signaling phase, and the vessel proceeded at a high rate of speed away from the helicopter. Assessing the signals, maneuvering and ineffective radio calls, the helicopter crew prepared to employ warning shots.

Under the agreement between the Navy and Coast Guard, all warning shots and disabling fire must come from a qualified Coast Guard aerial gunner and observer. Once the observer verifies that all parts of the signaling phase checklist have been completed, he or she coordinates with the aircraft commander that they are ready to proceed with warning shots.

Once ready to employ the warning shots, the aerial gunner aims the shots just in front of the vessel's bow using the mounted M240 machine gun. During this instance, warning shots were fired across the go-fast's bow and immediately the go-fast stopped and became dead in the water. With the vessel stopped, the helicopter relayed its current position and the *Hall* adjusted course to the new location of the go-fast vessel.

As the helicopter was continuing to monitor the vessel, some of the [go-fast] crew moved forward in the vessel, opened a compartment and proceeded to throw large objects overboard, which appeared to be bales of narcotics. On board the *Hall*, all this was being viewed on monitors and was all being recorded on videotape. This was relayed immediately back to District Seven and the *Hall* continued to close on the position. The helicopter flew over the debris field and dropped a Coast Guard datum marker buoy, which is normally used to mark the position of search and rescue victims and emits a radio signal, which can be heard by nearby aircraft and vessels. The helicopter continued to mark the position of the go-fast vessel and debris field until it had to return to the ship and refuel. Shortly thereafter, the *Hall* arrived on scene, and a Coast Guard team boarded the vessel and took control of it and its crew.

The initial purpose of the boarding was to identify nationality of the vessel and crew in order to establish authority and jurisdiction for the Coast Guard boarding team to be legally present on the vessel. The master of the vessel failed to provide any documentation for the vessel to identify his claim that the vessel was Colombian flagged. This was relayed to District Seven, who later assimilated the vessel to stateless status and U.S. law [could be enforced against the crew] for suspicion of smuggling narcotics. The crew was detained and 1,465 kilograms of narcotics were recovered from the sea.[77]

In 2008, the U.S. Coast Guard established a Helicopter Interdiction Tactical Squadron (HITRON) as the only U.S. airborne law enforcement unit trained and authorized to employ the Airborne Use of Force. HITRON aircraft and crews are forward deployed on U.S. Coast Guard cutters. When a go-fast craft is detected, the HITRON crew will launch and intercept the boat. The checklist outlined above is followed in such cases. First, the helicopter crew confirms the nationality

---

[77] LT(jg) Ronald D. Bledsoe, *Joint Service Airborne Use of Force*, Dep't of Homeland Security, U.S. Coast Guard, District 7 News (2006).

or lack of national registry or status and determines whether the vessel is a suspected drug smuggling vessel.

The aircrew will use sirens, loud speakers, visual hand signals, and radio communications in both English and Spanish in order to convince the vessel to stop on its own accord. If the go-fast continues at speed after numerous visual and verbal warnings, the helicopter will maneuver to a firing position alongside the fleeing boat and fire warning shots to further compel it to stop. If the warning shots are not effective, then the helicopter may use .50 caliber rifles to disable the engines of the go-fast. Since most go-fast vessels have more than one engine, the helicopter will methodically destroy each one in order or continue to fire until the vessel stops.

17.4.4 *Maritime Enforcement of U.S. Immigration Law*

Immigration laws may also be used to exclude aliens suspected of engaging in illicit trafficking of narcotic drugs and psychotropic substances from entering the United States. Federal statute prohibits the issuance of a visa or admission of entry into the United States to any alien who the consular officer or Attorney General knows or has reason to believe "is or has been an illicit trafficker in any controlled substance" or federally listed chemical.[78] Persons who are believed to be "a knowing aider, abettor, assister, conspirator, or colluder with others in the illicit trafficking" may also be prevented from entry.[79] Even the spouse or children of an alien inadmissible under the immigration law due to suspicion of a drug offense may be denied entry if they have, within the past five years, "obtained any financial or other benefit from the illicit activity of that alien, and knew or reasonably should have known" that the financial or other benefits were from a criminal activity.[80]

17.5 DEPARTMENT OF DEFENSE LEGAL AUTHORITIES

As a general rule, Department of Defense (DOD) personnel may not engage in law enforcement activity. Unless otherwise authorized by the Constitution or an Act of Congress, officials of the U.S. government are barred by the Posse Comitatus Act from using Army and Air Force personnel as a "posse comitatus or otherwise to execute the laws...."[81] Similar restrictions are imposed on the use of the Navy and Marine Corps by Federal law, which requires the Secretary of Defense to

---

[78] 8 U.S.C. § 1182(a)(2)(C). *See also,* 21 U.S.C. § 802.
[79] Id.
[80] Id.
[81] 18 U.S.C. § 1385.

... prescribe such regulations as may be necessary to ensure that any activity (including the provision of any equipment or facility or the assignment or detail of any personnel) under this chapter does not include or permit direct participation by a member of the Army, Navy, Air Force, or Marine Corps in a search, seizure, arrest, or other similar activity unless participation in such activity by such member is otherwise authorized by law.[82]

Over the years, however, a number of exceptions have been enacted by Congress to allow civilian authorities to utilize DOD forces in support of Coast Guard and other law enforcement agencies in the execution of its counter-drug mission.

17.5.1 Lead Agency for Detection and Monitoring

The Department of Defense (DOD) is the single lead federal agency "for the detection and monitoring of aerial and maritime transit of illegal drugs into the United States" in order to support "the counter-drug activities of Federal, State, local, and foreign law enforcement agencies." In carrying out this mission, 10 U.S.C. §124(b) authorizes DOD personnel to operate DOD equipment to intercept a vessel or an aircraft detected outside the land area of the United States for the purposes of:

(A) identifying and communicating with that vessel or aircraft; and
(B) directing that vessel or aircraft to go to a location designated by appropriate civilian officials.[83]

The Pentagon uses airborne assets, such as Airborne Warning and Control (AWAC) aircraft and aerostats, Navy surface warfare ships, and land-based radar, including Remote Over the Horizon (ROTHR) sites, to fulfill this mission.

Pursuit of a vessel or aircraft by the military forces may continue over the land area of the United States in cases where the vessel or aircraft was first detected outside the land area of the United States. Interestingly, unlike typical DOD support to other Federal, state, or local agencies, counterdrug support is not reimbursable.

17.5.2 Military Support for Civilian Law Enforcement

Chapter 18 of Title 10 of the U.S. Code contains additional exceptions allowing for Department of Defense (DOD) support to civilian law enforcement.[84] DOD

---

[82] 10 U.S.C. § 375.
[83] 10 U.S.C. § 124 (Detection and monitoring of aerial and maritime transit of illegal drugs; Department of Defense to be lead agency). Current through P.L. 112–123, May 31, 2012. A prior section 124, added Pub. L. 87–651, title II, Sec. 201(a), Sept. 7, 1962, 76 Stat. 514; amended Pub. L. 98–525, title XIII, Sec. 1301(a), Oct. 19, 1984, 98 Stat. 2611; Pub. L. 99–145, title XIII, Sec. 1303(a)(1), Nov. 8, 1985, 99 Stat. 738, related to establishment, composition, and functions of combatant commands, prior to repeal by Pub. L. 99–433, Sec. 211(c)(1). *Also see* section 161 *et seq.* of the title.
[84] Id., at §§ 371–382.

may provide "civilian law enforcement officials any information collected during the normal course of military training or operations that may be relevant to a violation of any Federal or State law within the jurisdiction of such officials."[85] Moreover, § 371(b) provides that "[t]he needs of civilian law enforcement officials for information shall, to the maximum extent practicable, be taken into account in the planning and execution of military training or operations." This proviso includes the prompt release of intelligence information held by DOD, "to the extent consistent with national security... and relevant to drug interdiction or other civilian law enforcement matters...."[86]

Public Law 108–136, as amended by Public Law 109–163, authorizes DOD standing Joint Interagency Task Forces providing support to civilian law enforcement agencies conducting counter-drug activities (e.g. JIATF South and JIATF West) to provide similar support to law enforcement agencies conducting counter-terrorism activities within their geographic area of responsibility.

The Secretary of Defense is authorized to make available any DOD "equipment (including associated supplies or spare parts), base facility, or research facility... to any Federal, State, or local civilian law enforcement official for law enforcement purposes."[87] Furthermore, § 373 allows SECDEF to make DOD personnel available:

(1) to train Federal, State, and local civilian law enforcement officials in the operation and maintenance of equipment, including equipment made available under section 372 of this title; and
(2) to provide such law enforcement officials with expert advice relevant to the purposes of this chapter.[88]

The Secretary of Defense also may "make DOD personnel available for the maintenance of equipment for Federal, State, and local civilian law enforcement officials, including equipment made available under section 372 of this title."[89] The provision permits skilled DOD maintenance personnel to work on helicopters, radar, and other high value equipment for civilian law enforcement—including equipment provided to law enforcement from DOD stocks.

If requested by the head of a federal law enforcement agency, the Secretary of Defense may "make DOD personnel available to operate equipment... with respect to," *inter alia*, a criminal violation of The Controlled Substances Act[90] or the Controlled Substances Import and Export Act[91] or "assistance that such agency is authorized to furnish to a State, local, or foreign government which is

---

[85] Id., at § 371(a).
[86] Id., at § 371(c).
[87] Id., at § 372.
[88] Id., at § 373.
[89] Id., at § 374(a).
[90] 21 U.S.C. § 801, *et seq.*
[91] Id., at § 951, *et seq.*

involved in the enforcement of similar laws...."[92] Department of Defense personnel may be made available to operate equipment under authority of 10 U.S.C. § 374(b)(2) for the following purposes:

- (A) Detection, monitoring, and communication of the movement of air and sea traffic.
- (B) Detection, monitoring, and communication of the movement of surface traffic outside of the geographic boundary of the United States and within the United States not to exceed 25 miles of the boundary if the initial detection occurred outside of the boundary.

    [Note: This provision permits sufficient time for Department of Defense assets to "hand off" tracking of a suspected ship, aircraft, or ground vehicle, to civil law enforcement authorities.]

- (C) Aerial reconnaissance.
- (D) Interception of vessels or aircraft detected outside the land area of the United States for the purposes of communicating with such vessels and aircraft to direct such vessels and aircraft to go to a location designated by appropriate civilian officials.
- (E) Operation of equipment to facilitate communications in connection with law enforcement programs specified in paragraph (4)(A) [of the section].
- (F) Subject to joint approval by the Secretary of Defense and the Attorney General (and the Secretary of State in the case of a law enforcement operation outside of the land area of the United States)—
    - (i) the transportation of civilian law enforcement personnel along with any other civilian or military personnel who are supporting, or conducting, a joint operation with civilian law enforcement personnel;

        [Note: the authority to provide transportation of civilian law enforcement personnel covers tactical and operational requirements, such as movement to international waters to conduct a law enforcement operation. The authority does not include routine or non-operational transportation.]

    - (ii) the operation of a base of operations for civilian law enforcement and supporting personnel; and
    - (iii) the transportation of suspected terrorists from foreign countries to the United States for trial (so long as the requesting Federal law enforcement agency provides all security for such transportation and maintains custody over the suspect through the duration of the transportation).[93]

Department of Defense (DOD) personnel made available to operate equipment for the purpose intercepting vessels or aircraft detected outside the land area of the United States "may continue to operate such equipment into the land area of the United States in cases involving the pursuit of vessels or aircraft where the detection began outside such land area."[94] This provision ensures the smooth

---

[92] 10 U.S.C. § 374(b). The provision includes equipment support made available under authority of 10 U.S.C. § 372.
[93] 10 U.S.C. § 374(b)(2).
[94] Id., at § 374(b)(3).

handover of suspicious contacts during a tracking operation. Additionally, the Secretary of Defense may make available DOD personnel to any Federal, State or local civilian law enforcement agency to operate equipment for other purposes, but only to the extent that DOD personnel do not participate directly in a civilian law enforcement operation (unless otherwise authorized by law).[95] It should be noted, however, that Public Law 103–337 prohibits DOD personnel from being "detailed to another department or agency in order to implement the *National Drug Control Strategy* unless the Secretary of Defense certifies to Congress that the detail of such personnel is in the national security interest of the United States."

For Fiscal Years 2002–2011,[96] DOD could provide additional support for counter-drug activities of any other department or agency of the Federal Government or of any State, local or foreign law enforcement agency if requested by such agencies for the following purposes:

(1) The maintenance and repair of equipment that has been made available to any department or agency of the Federal Government or to any State or local government by the Department of Defense for the purposes of—
   (A) preserving the potential future utility of such equipment for the Department of Defense; and
   (B) upgrading such equipment to ensure compatibility of that equipment with other equipment used by the Department of Defense.
(2) The maintenance, repair, or upgrading of equipment (including computer software), other than equipment referred to in paragraph (1) for the purpose of—
   (A) ensuring that the equipment being maintained or repaired is compatible with equipment used by the Department of Defense; and
   (B) upgrading such equipment to ensure the compatibility of that equipment with equipment used by the Department of Defense.
(3) The transportation of personnel of the United States and foreign countries (including per diem expenses associated with such transportation), and the transportation of supplies and equipment, for the purpose of facilitating counter-drug activities within or outside the United States.
(4) The establishment (including an unspecified minor military construction project) and operation of bases of operations or training facilities for the purpose of facilitating counter-drug activities of the Department of Defense or any Federal, State, or local law enforcement agency within or outside the United States or counter-drug activities of a foreign law enforcement agency outside the United States.
(5) Counter-drug related training of law enforcement personnel of the Federal Government, of State and local governments, and of foreign countries, including associated support expenses for trainees and the provision of materials necessary to carry out such training.
(6) The detection, monitoring, and communication of the movement of—

---

[95] Id., at § 374(c).
[96] Public Law 101–510, *as amended by* Public Laws 102–190, 102–484, 103–160, 103–337, 105–261, 107–107 and 109–364.

(A) air and sea traffic within 25 miles of and outside the geographic boundaries of the United States; and
(B) surface traffic outside the geographic boundary of the United States and within the United States not to exceed 25 miles of the boundary if the initial detection occurred outside of the boundary.
(7) Construction of roads and fences and installation of lighting to block drug smuggling corridors across international boundaries of the United States.
(8) Establishment of command, control, communications, and computer networks for improved integration of law enforcement, active military, and National Guard activities.
(9) The provision of linguist and intelligence analysis services.
(10) Aerial and ground reconnaissance.

Support provided under these Public Laws is subject to the restrictions in 10 U.S.C. § 375, which prohibits DOD personnel from engaging in a search, seizure, arrest, or other similar activity unless otherwise authorized by law. Furthermore, support or equipment provided to civilian law enforcement officials under Chapter 18 of Title 10 may not affect adversely the military preparedness of the United States.[97] In addition, to the extent required by the Economy Act or other applicable law, the Secretary of Defense "shall require a civilian law enforcement agency to which support is provided under this chapter to reimburse the Department of Defense for that support"[98] unless such support:

(1) is provided in the normal course of military training or operations; or
(2) results in a benefit to the element of the Department of Defense providing the support that is substantially equivalent to that which would otherwise be obtained from military operations or training.[99]

DOD is authorized to sell law enforcement equipment suitable for counter-drug activities to States and units of local government.[100] In order to enhance U.S. drug interdiction efforts, federal law also requires "that there be assigned on board every appropriate surface naval vessel at sea in a drug-interdiction area members of the Coast Guard who are trained in law enforcement and have powers of the Coast Guard under title 14, including the power to make arrests and to carry out searches and seizures."[101] No fewer than 500 USCG active duty personnel "shall be assigned each fiscal year to duty under this section" unless there are insufficient naval vessels available for use in drug interdiction missions.[102]

Chapter 18 of Title 10 provides policy guidance for implementing the statutory authority for DOD support. Pentagon implementation guidance is contained

---

[97] 10 U.S.C. § 376.
[98] 31 U.S.C. § 1535.
[99] 10 U.S.C. § 377.
[100] Id., § 381.
[101] Id., § 379(a).
[102] Id., § 379(c).

primarily in *Department of Defense Directive* (DODD) 5525.5, *Chairman of the Joint Chiefs of Staff Instruction* (CJCSI) 3710.01 (series) and *Joint Publication* (JP) 3-07.4.

17.5.2.1 Department of Defense Directive 5525.5

Subject to the limitations in Title 10 and Title 18, "it is Department of Defense policy to cooperate with civilian law enforcement officials to the extent practical."[103] However, any cooperation provided "shall be consistent with the needs of national security and military preparedness, the historic tradition of limiting direct military involvement in civilian law enforcement activities, and the requirements of applicable law...."[104] The Secretary and Deputy Secretary of Defense are authorized to waive the policy restriction against direct assistance by military personnel to execute the laws if the military actions are conducted outside the territorial jurisdiction of the United States and the case under consideration presents "compelling and extraordinary circumstances to justify..." an exception to policy.[105]

Consistent with Title 10 U.S.C. § 371, *Department of Defense Directive* 5525.5 encourages the military departments and defense agencies "to provide to Federal, State, or local civilian law enforcement officials any information collected during the normal course of military operations that may be relevant to a violation of any Federal or State law within the jurisdiction of such officials."[106] This authority includes passing information concerning illegal drugs to the interagency El Paso Intelligence Center (EPIC), located on the Southwest Border.[107] Information acquired in the normal course of military operations also may be transferred to other departments and agencies within the United States.[108]

Pentagon missions or training may not be planned or created, however, for "the primary purpose of aiding civilian law enforcement officials," nor may such missions or training be conducted "for the purpose of routinely collecting information about U.S. citizens."[109] "[T]he planning and execution of compatible military training and operations may take into account the needs of civilian law enforcement officials for information when the collection of the information is an incident aspect of training performed for a military purpose."[110]

---

[103] DEP'T OF DEFENSE, DEP'T OF DEFENSE DIRECTIVE 5525.5, DOD COOPERATION WITH CIVILIAN LAW ENFORCEMENT OFFICIALS, Jan. 15, 1986, Change 1, Dec. 20, 1989, para. 4.
[104] Id., at para. 4, Encl. 2, para. 2.2, Encl. 3, para. 3.3, and Encl. 4, para. 4.4; *See also*, 10 U.S.C. §§ 375–76.
[105] DEP'T OF DEFENSE DIRECTIVE 5525.5, para. 8.1.
[106] Id., Encl. 2, para. 1.
[107] Id., Encl. 2, para. 1.5.
[108] Id., Encl. 4, para. 1.7.1.
[109] Id., Encl. 2, para. 1.4.
[110] Id.

In addition, "local law enforcement agents may accompany routinely scheduled training flights as observers for the purpose of collecting law enforcement information."[111]

Military aircraft may be used to provide point-to-point transportation and training flights for civilian law enforcement officials consistent with the regulations concerning eligibility for DOD air transportation.[112] The acquisition and dissemination of information by DOD shall also comply with the requirements of other DOD directives, including directives concerning collection and retention of U.S. person information by the military forces.[113]

Enclosure 3 of DOD Directive 5525.5 contains guidance to military forces in implementing 10 U.S.C. § 372, which authorizes DOD to make equipment, base facilities, or research facilities available to civilian law enforcement officials for a law enforcement purpose. Military personnel also may be made available to operate or maintain, or assist in operating and maintaining, equipment provided under Enclosure 3, but only if the "training of non-DOD personnel would be unfeasible or impractical from a cost or time perspective and would not otherwise compromise national security or military preparedness concerns."[114] If provided, such assistance shall be limited as follows:

> Such assistance may not involve DOD personnel in a direct role in a law enforcement operation . . . except as provided in paragraph E4.1.6.3 . . . or as otherwise authorized by law.[115]
>
> Except as otherwise authorized by law, the performance of such assistance by DOD personnel shall be at a location where there is not a reasonable likelihood of a law enforcement confrontation.[116]
>
> The use of military aircraft to provide point-to-point transportation and training flights for civilian law enforcement officials may be provided only in accordance with DoD 4515.13-R. . . .[117]

"DOD personnel may be assigned to operate or assist in operating equipment to the extent the equipment is used for monitoring and communicating to civilian

---

[111] Id.
[112] Id. *See also*, Dep't of Defense, Dep't of Defense Directive 4515.13-R, Air Transportation Eligibility, Nov. 1994.
[113] Dep't of Defense Directive 5525.5, Encl. 2, para. 1.2 and 1.3. *See also*, Dep't of Defense Directive 5200.27, Acquisition of Information Concerning Persons and Organizations not Affiliated with the Department of Defense, Jan. 7, 1980; Dep't of Defense Directive 5240.1, DOD Intelligence Activities, Aug. 27, 2007; Dep't of Defense Directive 5240.1-R, Procedures Governing the Activities of DOD Intelligence Components that Affect United States Persons, Dec. 1982, and Dep't of Defense Directive 5400.11. DOD Privacy Program, May 8, 2007, updated Sept. 1, 2011.
[114] Dep't of Defense Directive 5525.5, Encl. 4, para. 1.6.
[115] Id., Encl. 4, para. 1.6.1.1.
[116] Id., Encl. 4, para. 1.6.1.2.
[117] Id., Encl. 4, para. 1.6.1.3.

law enforcement officials the movement of air and sea traffic with respect to any criminal violation of..." the Controlled Substances Act or the Controlled Substances Import and Export Act, to include the communication of "information concerning the relative position of civilian law enforcement officials and other air and sea traffic."[118] Moreover, in an emergency situation, "equipment operated by or with the assistance of DOD personnel may be used outside the land area of the United States... as a base of operations by Federal law enforcement officials to facilitate the enforcement of..." the Controlled Substances Act or the Controlled Substances Import and Export Act.[119] This stipulation includes the transportation of law enforcement officials connected with such an operation, subject to the following limitations:

> Equipment operated by or with the assistance of DOD personnel may not be used to interdict or interrupt the passage of vessels or aircraft, except when DOD personnel are otherwise authorized to take such action with respect to a civilian law enforcement operation.[120]
>
> There must be a joint determination by the Secretary of Defense and the Attorney General that an emergency circumstance exists under 10 U.S.C. §374(c) (2).... An emergency circumstance may be determined to exist for purposes of this subparagraph only when the size and scope of the suspected criminal activity in a given situation poses a serious threat to the interests of the United States... would be impaired seriously if the assistance described in this subparagraph were not provided.[121]
>
> The emergency authority in this subparagraph may be used only with respect to large-scale criminal activity at a particular point in time or over a fixed period. It does not permit use of this authority on a routine or extended basis.[122]
>
> Nothing in this subparagraph restricts the authority of military personnel to take immediate action to save life or property or to protect a Federal function....[123]

Pentagon guidance also allows military personnel to provide training and expert advice to civilian law enforcement officials.[124] Training assistance is subject to the following guidance:

> This assistance shall be limited to situations when the use of non-DOD personnel would be unfeasible or impractical from a cost or time perspective and would not otherwise compromise national security or military preparedness concerns.[125]

---

[118] Id., Encl. 4, para. 1.6.2.4.1.
[119] Id., Encl. 4, para. 1.6.2.4.2.
[120] Id., Encl. 4, para. 1.6.2.4.2.1.
[121] Id., Encl. 4, para. 1.6.2.4.2.2.
[122] Id., Encl. 4, para. 1.6.2.4.3.
[123] Id., Encl. 4, para. 1.6.2.4.4.
[124] 10 U.S.C. § 373.
[125] DEP'T OF DEFENSE DIRECTIVE 5525.5, Encl. 4, para. 1.4.2.1.

> Such assistance may not involve DOD personnel in a direct role in a law enforcement operation, except as otherwise authorized by law.[126]
>
> Except as otherwise authorized by law, the performance of such assistance by DOD personnel shall be at a location where there is not a reasonable likelihood of a law enforcement confrontation.[127]

Department of Defense persons may not, however, provide large scale or elaborate training. Moreover, DOD personnel may not engage in training events that would regularly or directly involve them in activities that are fundamentally civilian law enforcement operations, unless otherwise authorized by law or DOD policy.[128]

Department of Defense assistance provided under Enclosure 4 of DOD Directive 5525.5 also must comply with the Posse Comitatus Act (PCA). Unless otherwise authorized by law or DOD policy, the prohibition on the use of military personnel "as a posse comitatus or otherwise to execute the laws" prohibits the direct assistance by DOD personnel in interdiction of a vehicle, vessel, aircraft,[129] search or seizure,[130] arrest, apprehension, stop and frisk of suspected persons,[131] the use of military personnel for surveillance or pursuit of individuals, or as undercover agents, informants, investigators, or interrogators.[132]

Because the Posse Comitatus Act only applies to the Navy and Marine Corps as a matter of policy rather than law, the Secretary of the Navy may grant exceptions on a case-by-case basis to allow naval personnel to provide direct assistance to civilian law enforcement agencies.[133] Such exceptions include requests from the Attorney General.

> When requested by the Attorney General, it shall be the duty of any agency or instrumentality of the Federal Government to furnish assistance, including technical advice, to him for carrying out his functions under this subchapter; except that no such agency or instrumentality shall be required to furnish the name of, or other identifying information about, a patient or research subject whose identity it has undertaken to keep confidential.[134]

Any exception granted under this provision that is likely to involve naval personnel in the "interdiction of a vessel or aircraft, a law enforcement search or seizure, an arrest, apprehension, or other activity that is likely to subject civilians to the use of military power that is regulatory, prescriptive, or compulsory," requires

---

[126] Id., Encl. 4, para. 1.4.2.2.
[127] Id., Encl. 4, para. 1.4.2.3.
[128] Id., Encl. 4, para. 1.4.1.
[129] Id., Encl. 4, para. 1.3.1.
[130] Id., Encl. 4, para. 1.3.2.
[131] Id., Encl. 4, para. 1.3.3.
[132] Id., Encl. 4, para. 1.3.4.
[133] Id., Encl. 4, para. 3.2.
[134] 21 U.S.C. § 873(b).

prior approval by the Secretary of Defense.[135] Such approval will only be granted if the head of the civilian agency concerned verifies that

> ... the size or scope of the suspected criminal activity poses a serious threat to the interests of the United States and enforcement of a law within the jurisdiction of the civilian agency would be impaired seriously if the assistance were not provided because civilian assets are not available to perform the missions;[136] or
>
> Civilian law enforcement assets are not available to perform the mission and temporary assistance is required on an emergency basis to prevent loss of life or wanton destruction of property.[137]

Consistent with 10 U.S.C. § 377, the Economy Act, and the Leasing Statute,[138] any services or equipment provided by DOD personnel to civilian law enforcement will normally be reimbursed.[139] Waivers may be granted if reimbursement is not otherwise required by law and

> ... [the military support is] provided as an incidental aspect of the activity that is conducted for military purposes.[140]
>
> ... [the military support involves DOD] personnel in an activity that provides DOD training operational benefits that are substantially equivalent to the benefit of DOD training or operations.[141] [Note: For example, training of foreign governmental agencies with a counterdrug responsibility may provide a cultural or linguistic familiarity to U.S. trainers, such as U.S. special forces, who benefit from increased awareness and knowledge of that specific foreign language and national or regional culture.]

Budgetary resources available to the civilian law enforcement agency shall also be taken into consideration.[142] Reimbursement may not be waived, however, "if deletion of such funds from a DOD account could adversely affect the national security or military preparedness of the United States."[143]

17.5.2.2 Chairman of the Joint Chiefs of Staff Instruction 3710.01B

The Chairman of the Joint Chiefs of Staff has approved more detailed guidance for military counterdrug operational support. The specific guidance is contained in Enclosure A of *Chairman of the Joint Chiefs of Staff Instruction (CJCSI)* 3710.01 (series). The Instruction establishes policies and guidelines for international counterdrug policy implementation, criteria for approval of requests for international

---

[135] Id., Encl. 4, para. 3.
[136] Id., Encl. 4, para. 3.2.1.
[137] Id., Encl. 4, para. 3.2.2.
[138] 10 U.S.C. § 2667.
[139] DEP'T OF DEFENSE DIRECTIVE 5525.5, Encl. 5, para. 2.1.
[140] Id., Encl. 5, para. 2.2.1.
[141] Id., Encl. 5, para. 2.2.2.
[142] Id., Encl. 5, para. 2.4.
[143] Id., Encl. 5, para. 3.

support, and approval procedures for departmental international counterdrug support. CJCSI 3710.01 does not restrict detection and monitoring operations "conducted to detect and track the aerial and maritime transit of illegal drugs into the United States," since the Department of Defense is the lead or supported (rather than supporting) department or agency for those operations.[144]

The Secretary of Defense has delegated approval authority for Department of Defense counterdrug support to the four-star Geographic Combatant Commanders (GCC). In this regard, GCCs may approve requests for DOD counterdrug support from domestic law enforcement agencies (LEAs), including U.S. Federal, state, territorial, tribal, and local agencies; other U.S. government departments or agencies with counterdrug responsibilities, such as U.S. Customs Services; and foreign law enforcement agencies with counterdrug responsibilities, including foreign military forces with counterdrug responsibilities that request DOD support through counterpart U.S. Federal LEAs or other U.S. government agencies with counterdrug responsibilities.

Paragraph 3 of the Chairman of the Joint Chiefs of Staff Instruction permits the military forces to provide the following types of counterdrug support to civilian agencies:

   a. Maintenance and repair of loaned defense equipment to preserve the potential future utility or to upgrade to ensure compatibility of that equipment[145]
   b. Transportation support[146]
   c. Establish and/or operate bases or training facilities (includes engineer support)[147]
   d. Counterdrug-related training of law enforcement personnel[148]
   e. Detection, monitoring, and communication of the movement of air and sea traffic within 25 miles of ... United States borders[149]
   f. Detection, monitoring, and communication of the movement of surface traffic detected outside US borders for up to 25 miles within the United States[150]
   g. Engineering support (roads, fences, and lights) at US borders[151]
   h. Command, control, communications, computer, and intelligence (C^4I)[152]
   i. Linguist support[153]
   j. Intelligence analyst support[154]

---

[144] CHAIRMAN OF THE JOINT CHIEFS OF STAFF, CHAIRMAN OF THE JOINT CHIEFS OF STAFF INSTRUCTION 3710.01B, DOD Counterdrug Support, Jan. 26, 2007 (current as of Jan. 28, 2008), Encl. A, para. 2. See, 10 U.S.C. § 124.
[145] National Defense Authorization Act Fiscal Year 1991 (P.L. 101–510), as amended, Additional Support to Counterdrug Activities, Section 1004(b)(1)–(2).
[146] CJCSI 3710.01B, at (B)(3).
[147] Id., at (B)(4).
[148] Id., at (B)(5).
[149] Id., at (B)(6)(A).
[150] Id., at (B)(6)(B).
[151] Id., at (B)(7).
[152] Id., at (B)(8).
[153] Id., at (B)(9).
[154] Id.

    k. Aerial reconnaissance support[155]
    l. Ground reconnaissance support[156]
   m. Diver support[157]
    n. Tunnel detection support[158]
    o. Use of military vessels for LEA operating bases by Coast Guard personnel[159]
    p. Technology demonstrations.[160]

Paragraph 4.a of Enclosure A to CJCSI 3710.01B authorizes aerial reconnaissance support using radar and sensors, including synthetic aperture radar, forward-looking infrared, and electro-optic device, unmanned aerial vehicles, and aerial visual and photographic reconnaissance, and national overhead and aerial imagery. Ground reconnaissance support may include the use of unattended ground sensors and ground surveillance radar. This provision includes the "initial detection and reporting of the presence or movement of buildings, vehicles, vessels, or persons within surface areas...."[161]

Department of Defense (DOD) personnel also may be made available to provide tunnel detection support; however, DOD personnel "may not search, enter, or otherwise participate directly in law enforcement operations."[162] Aquatic diver support can be provided "to conduct subsurface hull inspections and training...."[163] During such missions, DOD divers may visually inspect and report to law enforcement officials any unusual physical hull configurations, but they "may not attempt entry or search, or alter features detected."[164]

Geographic Combatant Commanders (GCCs) also have the authority under paragraph 4.e to approve requests for linguist and intelligence analyst support. But this authority does not include the "authority to approve cryptologic support, real-time translation of oral or wire intercepts, direct participation in interrogation activities, or the use of counterintelligence assets for ... [counterdrug] purposes."[165]

Equipment maintenance and operation support may be approved, but it does not include the cost of parts or equipment.[166] The Pentagon forces also may assist in establishing and maintaining a Command, Control, Communications,

---

[155] Id., at (B)(10).
[156] Id.
[157] 10 U.S.C. § 371.
[158] Id.
[159] Id., at § 379.
[160] 10 U.S.C. § 380.
[161] CJCSI 3710.01B, Encl. A, para. 4.b.
[162] Id., Encl. A, para. 4.c.
[163] Id., Encl. A, para. 4.d.
[164] Id.
[165] Id., Encl. A, para. 4.e.
[166] Id., Encl. A, para. 4.h. Approval must be in accordance with Public Law 107–107 (§ 1021) and Chapter 18 of Title 10 (10 U.S.C. §§ 371–374, 377 and 379).

Computer, and Intelligence (C4I) networks to improve integration of law enforcement, active military, and National Guard counterdrug activities.[167] Finally, the military may conduct technology demonstrations with the DOD Counter-Narco-terrorism Technology Program Office, and the technology requirements for the demonstrations may be based on the input and needs of civilian law enforcement.[168]

Transportation support may also be provided subject to the requirements of paragraph 4.f of Enclosure A to CJCSI 3710.01B. The GCCs are not, however, "authorized to approve transportation support in direct tactical support of the operational portions of ongoing...[U.S. law enforcement] or foreign...[law enforcement] operations, or of any activities where...[counterdrug]-related hostilities are imminent."[169] In order to preserve the chain-of-custody of evidence collected in tactical operations, any criminal evidence or prisoners seized by civilian law enforcement agents that "are brought aboard DOD aircraft, vehicles, or vessels being used to provide transportation" must remain within the control and custody of the civilian law enforcement authorities.[170] The use of military vessels as a base of operations by civilian law enforcement agencies requires the approval of the Secretary of Defense and the Attorney General.[171] Use of military vessels as civilian law enforcement operating bases in territorial waters of another nation also requires SECDEF approval.[172]

17.5.2.3 Geographic Combatant Commander Counterdrug Authority

Commander, U.S. Northern Command, Commander U.S. Southern Command, and Commander, U.S. Pacific Command are authorized to approve training, not to include advanced military training, for civilian law enforcement personnel in the United States.[173] Commander, U.S. Special Operations Command also may approve such training by special operations forces in exceptional cases. The U.S. Army Military Police may train LEA personnel in the Counterdrug Special Reaction Team Course, Counterdrug Field Tactical Police Operations Training, and Counterdrug Marksman/Observer Course. Commanders of Northern Command and Pacific Command may approve engineering support in the United States. Such support is limited, however, to the Southwest border and to mobility and counter-mobility programs, such as fencing, lighting, and road improvement.

---

[167] CJCSI 3710.01B, Encl. A, para. 4.i. Approval must be in accordance with Public Law 107–107, as amended.
[168] Id., Encl. A, para. 4.j. *See also*, 10 U.S.C. § 380.
[169] CJCSI 3710.01B, Encl. A, para. 4.f.(4).
[170] Id.
[171] Note: unless otherwise authorized by § 1021 of Public Law 107–107, as amended.
[172] CJCSI 3710.01B, Encl. A, para. 4.g.
[173] Id., Encl. A, para. 5.b.

The Geographic Combatant Commanders may also approve the following types of DOD counterdrug support to civil LEAs:

1. Planning and Coordination Visits at U.S. embassies abroad, contingent on Embassy approval. These visited are conducted with theater-assigned forces and may help to coordinate maritime and ground interdiction intelligence, operations, and training.[174]
2. Intelligence Analyst Support. Intelligence analyst support may be provided to US Ambassadors using theater-assigned forces.[175]
3. Planning and Coordination Visits. Planning and coordination visits of ten personnel or less for 60 days or less to ... [Host Nation] headquarters (contingent on American Embassy approval) may be conducted with theater-assigned or allocated forces to accomplish the GCCs ... [detection and monitoring] mission or to support the US Ambassador's ... [counterdrug] effort with expert advice or assistance to the US Country Team.
4. Linguist Support. Includes translator and interpreter support.... This delegation [of authority] does not include authority to approve cryptologic support, real-time translation of oral or wire intercepts, direct participation in interrogation activities, or the use of counterintelligence assets for ... [counterdrug] purposes. Linguist missions to locations outside American Embassies will be limited to short-duration visits (not to exceed 30 days) of no more than ten persons to primary ... [Host Nation] and US C⁴I headquarters for the express purpose of accomplishing the mission of supporting the Ambassador's ... [counterdrug] effort.
5. Counterdrug-Related Training of Law Enforcement Personnel
   a. GCCs may approve CD-related training of foreign law enforcement personnel requiring no more than 50 theater-assigned personnel for no more than 45 days with ... [Host Nation] and Country Team approval and notification.
   b. GCCs may approve ... [counterdrug]-related technical and administrative support team deployments requiring no more than 25 personnel for no more than 179 days with ... [Host Nation] and [U.S. embassy] Country Team approval and notification.[176]

17.5.2.4 Maritime Counterdrug Rules of Engagement

Military personnel providing assistance to civilian law enforcement agencies are required to use force only in accordance with the Standing Rules of Engagement (SROE), which are contained in the Chairman of the Joint Chiefs of Staff Instruction 3121.01B (CJCSI 3121.01B).[177] SROE apply to U.S. forces during all military operations and contingencies outside of the territory of the United States, unless otherwise directed. (The rules also apply in certain narrowly prescribed cases inside the United States, such as protection of U.S. airspace).

---

[174] Note: In accordance with DOD 5240-1R and 50 U.S.C. §§ 413 and 413a.
[175] Note: In accordance with DOD 5240-1R and 50 U.S.C. §§ 413 and 413a.
[176] CJCSI 3710.01B, Encl. A, para. 6.
[177] Chairman of the Joint Chiefs of Staff Instruction 3121.01B, Standing Rules of Engagement Standing Rules for the Use of Force (SROE/SRUF) for US Forces, June 13, 2005 (CJCSI 3121.01B).

The SROE contain rules of engagement specifically for counterdrug support operations that are conducted outside the territory of the United States. During counterdrug support missions in the United States, separate Standing Rules for the Use of Force (SRUF) are used, and those are also contained in CJCSI 3121.01B.[178] However, DOD personnel will not accompany civilian law enforcement authorities on actual counterdrug field operations, and military personnel cannot participate in activities where counterdrug-related hostilities are imminent.[179]

17.5.3 *Joint Publication 3-07.4, Counterdrug Operations*

Joint Publication 3-07.4, *Counterdrug Operations*, sets forth doctrine for the planning and execution of U.S. military support to counterdrug operations. The joint doctrine governs the activities and performance of DOD personnel in joint operations (i.e. those operations involving any two of the three military departments) and provides the doctrinal basis for interagency coordination and for U.S. military involvement in combined, coalition, or multinational counterdrug operations. The publication also provides guidance for the exercise of authority by Geographic Combatant Commanders and other joint force commanders and prescribes joint doctrine for operations, education, and training. Appendix G of the publication describes procedures for the use of USCG Law Enforcement Detachments (LEDETs) on board U.S. Navy ships to perform law enforcement activities, as prescribed in 10 U.S.C. § 379.

17.5.3.1 Coast Guard Law Enforcement Detachments

The Navy contributes significantly to the detection and monitoring phase of international counterdrug trafficking operations. Because they are forward deployed, U.S. Navy ships are in a position to intercept and apprehend drug traffickers at sea that are crossing the oceans heading toward entry points in the United States or in neighboring countries. In light of the restrictions placed on DOD personnel regarding direct participation in search, seizure, arrest and other similar activities, however, U.S. Coast Guard personnel are normally embarked as Law Enforcement Detachments (LEDETs) on U.S. and allied ships to perform these criminal law enforcement functions.

A LEDET is normally composed of seven U.S. Coast Guard personnel that are assigned on a temporary basis to U.S. or foreign warships. Detachments are led by an officer in charge in the pay grade of Chief Petty Officer (E-7) through the rank of Lieutenant (O-3).[180] The detachment also includes a boarding officer

---

[178] CJCSI 3710.01B, Encl. A, para. 8.q.
[179] Id., Encl. A, para. 5.a(3).
[180] CHAIRMAN OF THE JOINT CHIEFS OF STAFF, JOINT PUBLICATION 3-07.4, COUNTERDRUG OPERATIONS, June 13, 2007, Appendix G.

in the pay grade of Petty Officer First Class (E-6) or above, and five additional boarding team members. The officer in charge (OIC) is responsible for advising the commanding officer of the ship about Coast Guard policies, maritime law enforcement procedures, and monitoring and interdiction maneuvering.[181] The OIC will also determine which vessels to board, make law enforcement decisions and coordinate Navy vessel support for the boarding party during the boarding phase of the operation. The OIC is additionally tasked with providing guidance to the boarding officer and will direct all searches and make all enforcement decisions. The JIATF has an in-house lawyer of the armed services (judge advocate) who coordinates with USCG lawyers during boarding.

Law enforcement boarding parties consist of at least two members, at least one of which will be a qualified boarding officer. The boarding party is armed and equipped as necessary. The boarding party typically will approach a vessel of interest and note its location, activities, and identifying characteristics. While maintaining continuous surveillance of the vessel and in an enhanced state of readiness, the boarding party will hail the vessel.

If the LEDET decides to board the vessel, the master of the ship being boarded will be instructed on how to prepare for the operation. In cases in which illegal activity is suspected, or when it is believed that there is a potential threat to the safety of the boarding party, the vessel's crew may be instructed to move to a single open location, such as the vessel's fantail.[182]

> Upon boarding, the boarding party will conduct an initial safety inspection, which is a quick and limited protective sweep of the vessel, for any hazards to the boarding party. The inspection will include securing any weapons found on board, identifying and securing hidden crew members or passengers, and assessing the basic stability of the vessel to determine if it is safe to remain on board. An extended initial safety inspection may be conducted only when reasonable suspicion exists that there is a particular hazard that may threaten the boarding team's safety to include known weapons onboard, an unaccounted for person(s), and a known safety hazard.

> Once the boarding party's safety is assured, the accuracy of any information provided by the vessel's crew will be verified. The vessel will be inspected and arrests or seizures will be made, as necessary. After the boarding party debarks, briefings and documentation of the boarding will be completed. The boarding party will prepare and deliver a case package to support any subsequent U.S. or Partner Nation penalty or prosecution action.[183]

17.5.3.2 Department of Defense Joint Interagency Task Forces

The Navy and Coast Guard have drafted memorandums of agreement (MOA) that govern USCG LEDET procedures. Pursuant to these MOAs, the Navy and Coast

---

[181] Id.
[182] Id.
[183] Id.

Guard provide ships and cutters to operate under the tactical control (TACON) of a Joint Interagency Task Force (JIATF) when engaged in detection and monitoring missions. The JIATFs are Department of Defense standing joint task forces assigned to the Geographic Combatant Commanders (GCCs), although only two GCCs actually have JIATFs—Commander, U.S. Southern Command (JIATF South) and Commander, U.S. Pacific Command (JIATF West). Joint Interagency Task Force South (JIATF South) and JIATF West spearhead DOD counterdrug operations, intelligence activities, and training.

The JIATFs began to leverage Pentagon resources as part of President George H. W. Bush's "war on drugs." In 1989, Joint Task Force FIVE (JTF-5) was established in Alameda, California, as a standing joint task force under U.S. Pacific Command. The command was assigned the task of carrying out DOD's (then new) mission of detection and monitoring aerial and maritime illicit drug shipments bound for the United States. Joint Task Force 5 used the full range of national assets to interdict the flow of drugs emanating from the Andean Ridge and up through the Eastern Pacific and into Mexico for follow-on ground transportation across the land border into the United States.[184] Similarly, Joint Task Force SIX (JTF-6) was created in November 1989. The Task Force was renamed JTF North in 2004, when it acquired counter-terrorism responsibilities.

By 1994, there were three JIATFs (East, West and South) established under the National Interdiction Command and Control Plan to coordinate and direct the detection, monitoring, and sorting of suspect drug-trafficking aircraft and vessels for turn over to appropriate U.S. law enforcement authorities for apprehension. In 1999, JIATF East merged with JIATF South, which is located in Key West, Florida.

In 2004, JIATF West relocated to Honolulu, Hawaii, from Alameda, California. In doing so, JIATF West lost its operational interdiction role in the Eastern Pacific and turned its attention exclusively toward suppression of international drug trafficking activities and intelligence operation in the Indo-Pacific region. JIATF South acquired the maritime interdiction mission for the Eastern Pacific as well as the Caribbean Sea and Gulf of Mexico.

The JIATFs maintain a 24-hour watch floor that coordinates the shift of tactical control (TACON) of Navy ships to the Coast Guard prior to actual ship boarding and arrest of suspected drug traffickers. In addition, the Navy ship will display the U.S. Coast Guard ensign before engaging in a law enforcement operation under TACON of the Coast Guard. The Coast Guard LEDETs riding on board Navy ships employ the practices and rules, including the use of force policy, contained in the U.S. Coast Guard *Maritime Law Enforcement Manual*.

---

[184] *See generally*, James C. Kraska, *Counterdrug Operations in US Pacific Command*, JOINT FORCE Q. 81–85 (Autumn-Winter 1997–98).

U.S. Navy ships made available by the combatant commanders to support USCG law enforcement operations are categorized as either "specially designated" vessels or "ships of opportunity." Specially designated ships are specifically dedicated to support counterdrug operations, and they may be under the tactical control (TACON) of a JIATF for a period of several weeks or months. These ships are under TACON of the Director of the JIATF—typically a two-star U.S. Coast Guard admiral—and shift TACON from the Department of Defense to the U.S. Coast Guard when conducting law enforcement operations against suspect vessels. Ships of opportunity, on the other hand, are not pre-designated to support counterdrug operations and are therefore not under the control of a JIATF or the Coast Guard. These ships operate under the operational control (OPCON) of the Geographic Combatant Commander, but due to their capabilities or proximity, may be called upon on short notice to participate in a counterdrug operation. These ships also may switch TACON to the Coast Guard to conduct intelligence and analysis of drug trafficking.

JIATF-South's primary mission is to detect, monitor, and handoff suspected illicit trafficking targets to appropriate law enforcement agencies, promote security cooperation, and coordinate country team and partner nation initiatives in order to defeat the flow of illicit traffic. JIATF-West's primary mission is to detect, disrupt, and dismantle drug-related threats in Asia and the Pacific by providing interagency intelligence fusion, supporting U.S. law enforcement, and developing partner nation capacity in order to protect U.S. security interests at home and abroad.[185]

The JIATFs work with partner nations and U.S. law enforcement agencies to interdict illicit drugs and other narco-terrorist threats in support of U.S. and partner nation security. JIATF-West partners, for example, include: Australian Customs Service, Australian Federal Police, U.S. Defense Intelligence Agency, U.S. Drug Enforcement Administration, U.S. Federal Bureau of Investigation, U.S. National Geospatial Intelligence Agency, U.S. Naval Criminal Investigative Service, New Zealand Police, U.S. Army, U.S. Air Force, U.S. Coast Guard, U.S. Customs and Border Protection, U.S. Navy, U.S. Marine Corps, and U.S. Immigration and Customs Enforcement. By joining forces with U.S. and foreign law enforcement agencies, the JIATFs enhance international efforts to disrupt and dismantle transnational criminal organizations and their networks.

JIATF South plays a key role in Operation *Martillo* (Hammer), a combined U.S., European, and Western Hemisphere effort aimed at targeting illicit trafficking routes in coastal waters along the Central American isthmus. More than 80 percent of the cocaine coming to the United States is transported via these sea lanes. The operation's objective is to limit the ability of drug traffickers to use Central

---

[185] JOINT PUBLICATION 3-07.4, Counterdrug Operations, Chapter I, para. 2.d.

America as a transit zone for the movement of drugs, precursor chemicals, cash and weapons.

A total of 13 countries are currently contributing military forces and law enforcement personnel to conduct detection, monitoring and interdiction operations as part of Operation *Martillo*. These countries include: Belize, Canada, Colombia, El Salvador, France, Guatemala, Honduras, the Netherlands, Nicaragua, Panama, Spain, the United Kingdom and the United States. The U.S. contribution includes Navy and Coast Guard vessels, as well as aircraft from various U.S. Federal law enforcement agencies. In 2012, Operation *Martillo* resulted in the interdiction of 119 metric tons of cocaine, valued at $2.35 billion.

EIGHTEEN

U.S. INTERNATIONAL MARITIME COUNTERDRUG POLICY

18.1 THE U.S. POLICY AND OPERATIONAL FRAMEWORK

Since the late-1990s, the availability of illicit drugs and the total number of drug users has increased dramatically. In 2010, the U.N. Office of Drugs and Crime (UNODC) estimated that over 230 million people—or 5 percent of the world's adult population—have used illicit substances at least once. There are 27 million problem drug users. Worldwide, about 200,000 drug users died from a fatal overdose or some other associated side effect (for example, HIV or hepatitis from sharing needles, suicide, etc.). Cannabis is the most widely used type of illegal drug, followed by amphetamine-type stimulants (ATS) (e.g., crystal methamphetamine and ecstasy), opioids (e.g., opium and heroin) and cocaine.[1]

Trafficking patterns vary according to drug type, but are directed primarily toward the vast market in North America, although no region of the world is immune. Although cannabis is the largest illicit drug product, it is normally produced and consumed locally. International trafficking is therefore limited. The second largest illicit drug product is cocaine, followed by heroin. Both drug types are trafficked intra-regionally and internationally. ATS are also manufactured in the region of consumption; however, ATS precursor chemicals are widely trafficked across regions. Although illegal drugs are trafficked by land, sea and air, the use of the maritime transportation system to move illicit substances has been identified as the key emerging threat by UNODC.[2]

Illegal drug flows vary based upon countries of origin and destination. Europe and Asia are the primary global consumption markets for opiates supplied from Afghanistan and Myanmar. Afghanistan (75 percent) and Myanmar (24 percent)

---

[1] UNITED NATIONS OFFICE OF DRUG AND CRIME, WORLD DRUG REPORT 59 (2012).
[2] Id.

account for over 99 percent of the world total export of opiates. The largest cocaine market is the United States, followed closely by Europe. The cocaine for these markets is supplied mostly by Colombia, Peru and Bolivia, and is transported to the destination countries primarily by sea. There is a large concentration of ATS laboratories located in North America (Canada, Mexico and the United States), which produce methamphetamines for intra-regional trafficking and consumption. ATS markets have expanded, and now include East and South-East Asia, with West Africa emerging as a new trans-shipment source of ATS drugs and precursors for the Asian markets. Africa is also used as a trans-shipment point for Afghan heroin and South American cocaine bound for Europe, while South Asia has become a major procurement location for legal ephedrine and pseudoephedrine used in the illicit production of methamphetamine. In 2009, cannabis markets increased in the Americas, Africa and Asia, but were stable or have declined in Western Europe and Oceania.[3]

Like other forms of transnational crime, illicit drug trafficking, and the global criminal enterprise that it supports, presents significant and diverse challenges to the international community. Valued in the hundreds of billions of dollars, the illicit drug trade not only affects international peace and security, but also subverts the social and economic fabric of nations. Drug traffickers corrupt government officials, engage in acts of violence against the communities, and support terrorist activities that destabilize legitimate governments, especially in South America and Asia. Moreover, drug-related crime and other social problems associated with drug use, such as the spread of infectious diseases, place an enormous drain on local law enforcement and healthcare resources, affecting the well being of entire communities.[4]

18.1.1 U.S. National Drug Threat Assessment

Consistent with the UNODC *World Drug Report*, the 2009 U.S. National Survey on Drug Use and Health (NSDUH) found that the demand for illicit drugs in the United States is rising, particularly among young people. The National Drug Intelligence Center (NDIC) estimates that the cost of illicit drug use to American society in 2007 was $193 billion, including direct and indirect costs associated with drug-related crime ($61 billion), drug-related health care costs ($11 billion), and lost productivity ($120 billion). Statistics collected by the Arrestee Drug Abuse Monitoring Program (ADAM II) demonstrate a direct correlation between drug abuse and criminal activity. Data from a 2010 study indicate that a majority of arrestees in ten major U.S. cities test positive for an illegal substance at the time of their arrest.[5]

---

[3] Id.
[4] Id.
[5] U.S. Dep't of Justice, National Drug Intelligence Center, National Drug Threat Assessment (Aug. 2011).

The production, transportation and distribution of most illicit drugs in the United States are controlled by seven Mexican-based transnational criminal organizations: the *Sinaloa* Cartel, *Los Zetas*, the Gulf Cartel, the *Juárez* Cartel, *Beltrán-Leyva* Organization, *La Familia Michoacana*, and the *Tijuana* Cartel. Of these groups, the *Sinaloa* Cartel is the dominant organization, with an extensive distribution network that is capable of providing all the major illicit drugs to all regions of the United States. Access to and control of the smuggling routes along the Southwest border of the United States afford Mexican-based groups a competitive advantage over other transnational groups. As a result of proximity to markets, most of the heroin, marijuana and methamphetamine available in the United States are distributed by these organizations. Furthermore, collaboration with U.S. criminal gangs along the U.S.-Mexican border facilitates drug trafficking into and within the United States.[6]

Table 18.1. Mexican-based Transnational Criminal Organizations

TCOs[7]	Primary Drugs	Primary Regions
Sinaloa Cartel	Cocaine Heroin Marijuana MDMA (ecstasy) Methamphetamine	Florida/Caribbean Great Lakes Mid-Atlantic New England New York/New Jersey Pacific Southeast Southwest West Central
Los Zetas	Cocaine Marijuana	Florida/Caribbean Great Lakes Southeast Southwest
Gulf Cartel	Cocaine Marijuana	Florida/Caribbean Mid-Atlantic New England New York/New Jersey Southeast Southwest
Juárez Cartel	Cocaine Marijuana	Great Lakes New York/New Jersey Pacific Southeast Southwest West Central

---

[6] Id.
[7] Concentrated Activity by Mexican-Based Transnational Criminal Organizations in the Nine Organized Crime Drug Enforcement Task Force (OCDETF) Regions, Id.

Table 18.1 (cont.)

TCOs	Primary Drugs	Primary Regions
BLO	Cocaine Heroin Marijuana	Southeast Southwest
LFM	Cocaine Heroin Marijuana Methamphetamine	Southeast Southwest
Tijuana Cartel	Cocaine Heroin Marijuana Methamphetamine	Great Lakes Pacific Southwest

Other transnational criminal organizations are also active in the North American illicit drug trade. Although trafficking by Colombian-based organizations has declined over the past several years, these groups remain active in the production and smuggling of cocaine and heroin into eastern U.S. markets (primarily New York and South Florida). Colombian organizations primarily use commercial airlines and maritime vessels to smuggle drugs into the United States, often transiting Caribbean island countries, such as the Dominican Republic. Alternatively, Dominican criminal groups obtain cocaine and heroin from Colombian gangs and smuggle the drugs into the United States for distribution in Northeastern markets (primarily New York, New Jersey, and Boston) and the Southeast region (Charlotte, Atlanta, and other cities).

Ethnic Asian (primarily Vietnamese) Canadian-based transnational criminal organizations are active along the Northern border, producing and smuggling large quantities of ecstasy (MDMA) and high-potency marijuana into the United States for distribution to U.S. markets. West African transnational criminal organizations have begun smuggling limited quantities of Asian heroin into U.S. cities, including New York, Baltimore, Washington D.C., Atlanta, Detroit, Chicago, and Houston, using mail parcel and air freight, as well as human couriers.[8]

With the exception of cocaine, the availability of illicit drugs is also increasing in the United States. Increased heroin production in Mexico and increased trafficking of South American heroin by Mexican-based groups has resulted in an increased availability of heroin in most U.S. drug markets. Similarly, increased cannabis cultivation in Mexico boosted availability of marijuana in the United

[8] Id.

States. Ecstasy (MDMA) is also more prevalent in U.S. markets, as Canadian-based Asian groups have increased their production of the drug, and Mexican-based organizations have increased MDMA trafficking operations. Methamphetamine availability is likewise increasing following high levels of production in Mexico.[9]

The primary gateway for illicit drug smuggling into the United States is the southwest border region, including Arizona, California, New Mexico and Texas. Although the use of land routes and noncommercial vehicles is the preferred method of entry, enhanced U.S. border control and countermeasures have forced Mexican-based traffickers to rely on alternative smuggling conveyances, such as non-commercial maritime vessels and stealthy, ultra-light aircraft. Ultra-light aircraft are relatively inexpensive and are difficult to interdict. Freight trains and tunnels under the southwest border have also been used to smuggle drugs from Mexico into the United States. Ultimately, the route, conveyance, and type of drug selected for smuggling depend on the organization in local control, access to a particular type of drug, demands of the U.S. market, and the terrain of the Southwest border. These factors combine to form an overall picture of smuggling along a north-south axis.

- Cocaine is smuggled across the border primarily in areas of Southern California and South Texas.
- Heroin is smuggled across the border primarily in southern California, Arizona and South Texas.
- Marijuana is smuggled primarily through ports of entry in Arizona.
- Ecstasy is not smuggled across the Southwest border in large quantities.
- Methamphetamine is primarily smuggled across the Southwest border in Southern California.[10]

Ecstasy and marijuana are the primary drug threats along the U.S. border with Canada. Although air and sea routes along northwestern Washington and British Colombia are used to some extent, smugglers prefer to use land routes along the border at ports of entry in Washington, Michigan, New York, Vermont, and the Akwesasne Indian Reservation, New York.[11]

Maritime drug smuggling by South American and Caribbean transnational criminal organizations will continue to pose a threat to the United States and Puerto Rico, but it is not expected to increase dramatically in volume, since the market is fairly stable. These organizations normally use cargo ships and maritime shipping containers to smuggle cocaine and marijuana into Atlantic and Gulf Coast ports in Florida, and ports of entry in New Jersey and New York.

---

[9] Id.
[10] Id.
[11] Id.

Passengers and crew on board commercial vessels, including holiday cruise ships, are used to traffic heroin into South Florida. Cocaine and heroin are smuggled into Puerto Rico on ferries from the Dominican Republic, for example. Non-commercial vessels are used to smuggle cocaine and marijuana into South Florida from the Bahamas and into Puerto Rico from the Dominican Republic and the Lesser Antilles. Mexican-based traffickers are also increasing use of non-commercial vessels (called *lanchas* or *pangas*) to smuggle marijuana into South Texas and Southern California to avoid stronger security elsewhere along the U.S.-Mexican border.[12]

The primary threat of drug trafficking by air is from South American and Caribbean transnational criminal organizations smuggling cocaine and heroin into East Coast airports (e.g., New York and Miami) on board commercial flights. Drugs are normally concealed in passenger luggage, mail parcels transported by the airlines, or in air cargo. Non-commercial aircraft are used on a limited basis by Caribbean organizations to smuggle cocaine from the Dominican Republic to the Bahamas and into south Florida.[13]

18.1.2 U.S. National Drug Control Strategy

According to the 2010 U.S. *National Security Strategy*, transnational criminal organizations and illicit trafficking networks pose a significant national security challenge for the United States and its partner nations:

> Transnational Criminal Threats and Threats to Governance: Transnational criminal threats and illicit trafficking networks continue to expand dramatically in size, scope, and influence—posing significant national security challenges for the United States and our partner countries. These threats cross borders and continents and undermine the stability of nations, subverting government institutions through corruption and harming citizens worldwide.
>
> Transnational criminal organizations have accumulated unprecedented wealth and power through trafficking and other illicit activities, penetrating legitimate financial systems and destabilizing commercial markets. They extend their reach by forming alliances with government officials and some state security services. The crime-terror nexus is a serious concern as terrorists use criminal networks for logistical support and funding. Increasingly, these networks are involved in cybercrime, which cost consumers billions of dollars annually, while undermining global confidence in the international financial system.
>
> Combating transnational criminal and trafficking networks requires a multidimensional strategy that safeguards citizens, breaks the financial strength of criminal and terrorist networks, disrupts illicit trafficking networks, defeats transnational criminal organizations, fights government corruption, strengthens the rule of law,

---

[12] Id.
[13] Id.

bolsters judicial systems, and improves transparency. While these are major challenges, the United States will be able to devise and execute a collective strategy with other nations facing the same threats.[14]

To address this challenge, the Obama Administration issued a *National Drug Control Strategy* in 2011 that adopts a government-wide public health approach to reduce drug use and its negative consequences in the United States, while maintaining strong support for law enforcement efforts to combat illicit trafficking. Law enforcement efforts emphasize the need to share law enforcement and intelligence information to reduce illicit drug trafficking, as well as enhance international partnerships to "strengthen economic development, the rule of law, government institutions, and local communities seeking to reduce their own internal drug consumption."[15]

Efforts to strengthen international partnerships focus on three principles.

- Principle 1: Collaborate with International Partners to Disrupt the Drug Trade.

The first principle recognizes that major drug trafficking organizations are sophisticated and transnational in character. International cooperation and flexibility is therefore necessary to effectively disrupt these networks by reducing the quantity of drugs being trafficked. This reduction in trafficking will, in turn, reduce the amount of illegal proceeds available to these organizations that can be used to finance further illegal activities. Sharing best practices and the latest research on demand reduction strategies can help partner nations address their own drug consumption problems.[16]

- Principle 2: Support is provided to the Drug Control Efforts of Major Drug Source and Transit Countries.

The second principle looks to expand on successful U.S. and partner nation efforts in recent years to reduce drug use and distribution. Combined efforts in support of Colombia's *Strategic Development Initiative*, for example, have significantly reduced the international market for cocaine. The initiative focuses on expanding government presence, control and development opportunities in zones previously controlled by drug traffickers and illegal armed groups, like the *Fuerzas Armadas Revolucionarias de Colombia* (FARC). Cocaine production has been significantly reduced as a result of sustained aerial spraying and manual coca crop reduction. In other areas, one of the focal points for global cocaine trafficking—the San Martin area of Peru's Upper Huallaga valley—has been replaced

---

[14] NATIONAL SECURITY STRATEGY OF THE UNITED STATES Ch. 6 (May 2010).
[15] OFFICE OF NAT'L DRUG CONTROL POLICY, NATIONAL DRUG CONTROL STRATEGY (2011).
[16] Id.

by a thriving agricultural economy as a result of mandatory coca elimination and alternative development programs that strengthen economic and social stability in coca growing areas.[17]

The United States also provides equipment, training and technical assistance to support law enforcement and interdiction operations, as well as strengthen the capacities of Central American governmental institutions to address security challenges, and the underlying economic and social conditions that contribute to them, through the *Central American Regional Security Initiative* (CARSI). Likewise, in cooperation with its Caribbean partners, the United States has also developed a political framework through the *Caribbean Basin Security Initiative* (CBSI) that focuses on improving citizen safety by reducing drug smuggling, increasing public safety and security, and promoting social justice. Four working groups have also been established under the CBSI to address maritime security, information sharing, law enforcement strengthening, and crime prevention.[18]

- Principle 3: Attacks are conducted against Key Vulnerabilities of Drug Trafficking Organizations.

The third principle is aimed at attacking key vulnerabilities of drug trafficking organizations. These efforts include increasing the number of illicit drug shipment seizures in the transit zone and implementing supply and demand reduction strategies tailored to meet the specific needs of partner nations. In fiscal year 2010, for example, U.S. and partner nations' interdiction forces successfully intercepted over 30 percent (244 metric tons) of the 804 metric tons of total documented cocaine movement through the Western Hemisphere transit zone.

18.1.3 *Strategy to Combat Transnational Organized Crime*

In July 2011, the U.S. drug control strategy was augmented by a new initiative to address the increasing involvement of transnational organized criminal groups in the drug trade. The new *Strategy to Combat Transnational Organized Crime* recognizes that "the demand for illicit drugs, both in the United States and abroad, fuels the power, impunity, and violence of criminal organizations around the globe," and that a number of "well-established organized criminal groups that had not been involved in drug trafficking—including those in Russia, China, Italy, and the Balkans—are now establishing ties to drug producers to develop their own distribution networks and markets."[19]

To reduce the increasing threat from illicit trafficking by transnational groups, the United States "will continue ongoing efforts to identify and disrupt the

---

[17] Id.
[18] Id.
[19] STRATEGY TO COMBAT TRANSNATIONAL ORGANIZED CRIME: ADDRESSING CONVERGING THREATS TO NATIONAL SECURITY (July 2011).

leadership, production, intelligence gathering, transportation, and financial infrastructure of major Transnational Organizes Crime (TOC) networks."[20] These efforts will focus on "targeting the human, technology, travel, and communications aspects of these networks... [in order] to monitor and gather intelligence to identify the full scope of the TOC networks, their members, financial assets, and criminal activities."[21] Additionally, the United States "will continue ongoing efforts to enhance collaboration among domestic law enforcement agencies and our foreign counterparts in order to strengthen our ability to coordinate investigations and share intelligence to combat drug trafficking and TOC."[22] This includes "enhanced intelligence sharing and coordination among law enforcement and intelligence agencies, the military, and... [the] diplomatic community [that] will enable the interagency community to develop aggressive, multi-jurisdictional approaches to dismantle TOC networks involved in drug trafficking."[23]

The strategy is premised on the assumption that disrupting and dismantling the major TOC networks involved in drug trafficking will enable the United States "to reduce the availability of illicit drugs, inhibit terrorist funding, improve national and international security, and bring TOC networks to justice." Key actions to accomplish this goal include:

> A. Work with international partners to reduce the global supply of and demand for illegal drugs and thereby deny funding to TOC networks.
> B. Sever the links between the international illicit drug and arms trades, especially in strategic regions that are at risk of being destabilized by these interconnected threats.
> C. Sustain pressure to disrupt Consolidated Priority Organization Targets, as they often have a particularly corrupting influence or provide support to terrorism.
> D. Maximize use of the Kingpin Act to pursue transnational drug organizations.
> E. Develop a comprehensive approach to dismantle DTOs with connections to terrorist organizations.
> F. Work with international partners to shut down emerging drug transit routes and associated corruption in West Africa.
> G. Coordinate with international partners to prevent synthetic drug production, trafficking, and precursor chemical diversion.[24]

A key aspect of the strategy is "to aggressively target the nexus among TOC networks involved in drug trafficking, terrorist groups, piracy on the high seas, and arms traffickers."[25] In this regard, in 2002 the U.S. Drug Enforcement Agency (DEA) established the Counter-narco-terrorism Operations Center (CNTOC) within the Special Operations Division (SOD). The SOD is a "multi-agency

---

[20] Id.
[21] Id.
[22] Id.
[23] Id.
[24] Id.
[25] Id.

operations coordination center with participation from Federal law enforcement agencies, the Department of Defense, the Intelligence Community, and international law enforcement partners."[26] The SOD's mission "is to establish strategies and operations to dismantle national and international trafficking organizations by attacking their command and control communications," with special emphasis "on those major drug trafficking and narco-terrorism organizations that operate across jurisdictional boundaries on a regional, national, and international level."[27] By coordinating overlapping foreign and domestic investigations, the SOD ensures "that tactical and operational intelligence is shared among law enforcement agencies."[28]

18.1.4 *Department of Defense U.S. Southern Command*

The major focus of the U.S. interagency effort against narcotics is on disrupting the flow of illegal narcotics from South America, Central America, and the Caribbean Sea into the United States. Central America is the key transshipment zone for illicit trafficking in the Western hemisphere, and the Department of Defense serves as the "single lead agency" for the detection and monitoring of illegal drugs entering the United States.[29]

In March 2012, the Commander of the U.S. Southern Command (SOUTHCOM), General Douglas Fraser, testified that "90 percent of cocaine destined for the United States now transits the sub-region [of Central America]."[30] The rising level of violence associated with illicit trafficking, "coupled with the expansive resources of transnational organized crime, is challenging the law enforcement capacities of some Central American governments."[31] The UN Office of Drugs and Crime estimates that transnational organized crime generates over $84 billion in annual global gross profits from cocaine sales. Of that figure, $35 billion—over 41 percent—comes from retail and wholesale profits in the North American market.[32] Mexican-based transnational criminal organizations alone operate in over 1,000 U.S. cities, working in conjunction with local and nationally branded U.S. gangs to distribute and traffic illicit drugs.[33] General Fraser stressed that the illicit organizations

---

[26] Id.
[27] Id.
[28] Id.
[29] 10 U.S.C. §124(a).
[30] Posture Statement of General Douglas M. Fraser, United States Air Force, Commander, United States Southern Command, before the 112th Congress, House Armed Services Committee, Mar. 6, 2012.
[31] Id.
[32] Id.
[33] Id.

... operate with impressive acumen, employing an interconnected network of operational enablers: brokers who negotiate with coca growers in South America; *transportistas* who act as sub-contractors to coordinate cocaine shipments through the transit zone; specialists who construct sophisticated submersible vessels capable of transporting 8–10 metric tons of cocaine in one trip; hitmen or *sicarios* whose violent services ensure compliance and territorial protection through coercion and intimidation; wholesalers and retailers in the U.S. who distribute illicit products; and attorneys, bankers, and accountants who help launder illicit proceeds that can be used for corruption of police and border officials to ensure freedom of movement.[34]

The General further testified that lucrative profits from cocaine sales, estimated at over $18 billion per year, enable drug traffickers and organized criminal groups in South America, Central America and the Caribbean to overpower law enforcement.

[The profits enable these groups] to increase operational capacity at a rate that far outpaces that of regional law enforcement and militaries, purchasing sophisticated, military-grade weapons, investing in semi and fully submersible vessels to improve transportation, corrupting and coercing government officials to ensure freedom of movement, and recruiting and bankrolling highly trained specialists, many with military backgrounds.[35]

Moreover, there is growing evidence that terrorist groups throughout the region, like the FARC in Colombia and *Sendero Luminoso* in Peru, fund their insurgencies and other illegal activities through the proceeds wrought from illicit drug trafficking.[36]

SOUTHCOM's first line of defense against organized criminal groups is Joint Interagency Task Force South (JIATF South), headquartered in Key West, Florida. JIATF South is a Department of Defense interagency standing task force under the authority of Commander, U.S. Southern Command. With a Coast Guard admiral as director and a staff that includes all five armed services of the United States, JIATF South conducts detection, monitoring, and interdiction of multi-ton loads of cocaine from South America. The task force uses the full range of national assets, including Coast Guard and Navy ships and aircraft, to disrupt the flow of drugs. In 2011, for example, JIATF South participated in the seizure or destruction of 119 metric tons of cocaine with a street value of over $7 billion. These efforts resulted in the arrest of 355 traffickers and the seizure of 70 aircraft and vessels.[37]

JIATF South is also responsible for planning, coordinating, and synchronizing the major elements of Operation *Martillo*. General Fraser described the operation as support for a "whole-of-government approach to countering the spread of

---

[34] Id.
[35] Id.
[36] Id.
[37] Id.

transnational organized crime in Central America by denying the use of the Central American littorals as transshipment routes for illicit drugs, weapons, people, and bulk cash."[38] Operational *Martillo* is "designed to foster capacity building to enable partner nation successes within their own sovereign responsibilities," thereby enhancing regional stability and ultimately reducing the flow of cocaine to the United States.[39]

Congressional leaders have generously funded narcotics interdiction. While acknowledging that there is no traditional military threat emanating from the SOUTHCOM Area of Responsibility, for example, Senator Carl Levin (D-MI), Chairman of the Senate Armed Services Committee (SASC), indicated that the United States must be prepared to contend with the "increasingly powerful and capable threat in the form of Transnational Organized Crime."[40] After highlighting the threat to national and international security posed by these criminal organizations, the Senator pledged his committee's support for considering ways to enable the Pentagon "to provide its unique capabilities to American law enforcement, as well as foreign law enforcement and militaries. . . ."[41]

Similarly, Senator John McCain (R-AZ) stated that "the horrific violence attributed to transnational criminal organizations and cartels continues to threaten the United States and erode governance and security across the region."[42] Lucrative profits have allowed these organizations to accumulate large cash reserves that are used to acquire military-grade weapons. By being better equipped and more capable than government forces in several countries, international criminal organizations have eroded the government's monopoly on the use of force.[43] In Mexico, for example, McCain said nearly 50,000 Mexicans have been killed as a result of drug-related violence since 2006. The threat of violence, however, does not end at the Southwest border.

Despite JIATF South's successes and Congressional support for counterdrug operations, there is growing evidence that the United States and its regional partners are losing the war against drugs. Due to the limited number of ships and aircraft available to SOUTHCOM to interdict drug smugglers, U.S. authorities intercept only one-third of all drugs bound for the United States.[44] The shortage of assets can only get worse. The Department of Defense faces mandatory budget

---

[38] Id.
[39] Id.
[40] Opening Statement by Senator Carl Levin at the Senate Armed Services Committee Hearing on U.S. Southern Command and U.S. Northern Command, Mar. 13, 2012.
[41] Id.
[42] Opening Statement by Senator John McCain at the Senate Armed Services Committee Northern Command/NORAD and Southern Command Posture Hearing, Mar. 13, 2012.
[43] Id.
[44] *General: Increasing Number of Drugs and Guns Moving Into U.S.*, U.S. NEWS, Mar. 13, 2012 and Sydney J. Freedberg, Jr., *US Intercepts Only 1 of 3 Drug Smugglers It Tracks, Says General*, DEFENSEAOL.COM, Mar. 7, 2012.

cuts in the out-years due to the Nation's woeful fiscal situation.[45] Meanwhile a greater share of U.S. naval and air forces are being sent to the Asia-Pacific region as a hedge against China.[46] Amidst these conditions, the Navy and Air Force are retiring older ships and aircraft to limit maintenance costs, and these assets are not being replaced.[47]

18.2 U.S. Bilateral Maritime Counterdrug Instruments

International cooperation is essential to the successful suppression of drug smuggling at sea. To facilitate that cooperation, the United States relies extensively on over 30 bilateral maritime counterdrug agreements, memorandums of understanding, and operational procedures that have been negotiated with regional partners. A list of U.S. maritime law enforcement agreements, understandings and operational procedures begins at section 18.4 of this chapter.

These instruments have proven to be an "extremely effective tool of international cooperation in maritime drug interdiction."[48] Leveraging foreign law enforcement and military assets through these cooperative arrangements is a force multiplier for U.S. efforts, increasing the "business risk" to smugglers by denying favored maritime smuggling routes.[49]

The agreements and procedures are based on Article 17 of the 1988 Vienna Drug Convention, which urges nations to enter into bilateral and regional agreements to facilitate and enhance cooperation to suppress illicit traffic by sea. The operational goal of the agreements "is to streamline the lengthy diplomatic process required to obtain flag state authority for law enforcement actions against foreign suspect vessels on the high seas."[50] Some of the agreements allow foreign counterdrug operations to be conducted within another nation's territorial sea and national airspace, or they may provide expedited and streamlined decision making processes that facilitate real time or near real time communication between two countries during a counterdrug operation. Consequently, territorial boundaries are more transparent to law enforcement authorities from different countries who are conducting operations against international narcotics traffickers.[51]

---

[45] *General: Increasing Number of Drugs and Guns Moving Into U.S.*, U.S. News, Mar. 13, 2012.
[46] Id.
[47] Id.
[48] Statement of Rear Admiral Ernest R. Riutta on Maritime Bilateral Counterdrug Agreements, Before the House Subcommittee on Criminal Justice, Drug Policy, and Human Resources Committee on Government Reform, May 13, 1999.
[49] Id.
[50] Id.
[51] Id.

Case-by-case authorization to interdict suspect vessels and engage in law enforcement action at sea can be extremely time-consuming. Normally, once a suspect vessel is detected, it may take several hours before the flag State is contacted and is able to grant authorization to board and search the vessel. The wait can be even longer if the request to board is made after normal working hours or on weekends and holidays. Suspect vessels often exploit these operational delays by fleeing into the territorial sea of a nearby country.[52] Unless authorized by the affected coastal State, hot pursuit of the suspect vessel into the territorial sea of another nation is not permitted. Advance authorization provided in a bilateral agreement is therefore invaluable to ensure law enforcement officials can intervene before the traffickers are able to "jettison contraband, destroy evidence, or evade apprehension."[53]

The bilateral counterdrug agreements are not identical. Some instruments are more limited in scope than others, depending on the threat, the views or concerns of sovereignty by the partner nation, and the operational imperative to reach agreement. The comprehensive model agreement developed by the United States, however, seeks to include standing authority for U.S. maritime forces to have or quickly obtain authority for the following actions:

1. Board and search vessels claiming the flag of a signatory nation;
2. Embarkation of a coastal State shiprider empowered to authorize patrols, boardings, searches, seizures, and arrests in sovereign waters;
3. Pursuit of suspect vessels into sovereign waters with permission to stop, board, and search;
4. Entry into sovereign waters to investigate suspect vessels and aircraft, also with permission to stop, board, and search;
5. Overflight by state aircraft of sovereign airspace in support of counterdrug operations; and
6. Authority to relay an order-to-land in the territory of a signatory nation.[54]

The model agreement also contains provisions that allow the flag or coastal State to exercise or waive prosecutorial jurisdiction over a suspected vessel or persons if drugs are found on board, as well as "provisions for disposition of seized assets, including transfer of forfeited assets or proceeds of their sale as a consequence of any interdictions."[55] The agreements also provide the basis for professional education and training for partner nations, fusing capacity building with operational collaboration.

---

[52] Id.
[53] Id.
[54] Id.
[55] Id.

18.2.1 Agreement to Suppress Illicit Traffic by Sea (U.S.-Colombia)

Agreement between the Government of the Republic of Colombia and the Government of the United States of America to Suppress Illicit Traffic by Sea[56]

The United States and Colombia have two bilateral counterdrug agreements focusing on suppression of traffic in illicit drugs in the transit zone. The *Agreement to Suppress Illicit Traffic by Sea* is the centerpiece agreement for U.S. and Colombian maritime interdiction. Article 2 of the Agreement stipulates that the two Parties "shall cooperate in combating illicit traffic by sea to the fullest extent possible consistent," within their available resources. Cooperation is based on "application of procedures for boarding and search of private or commercial vessels of the nationality of one of the Parties and which meet the conditions set forth in this Agreement."

Article 6 makes clear, however, that the agreement only applies to "the boarding and search of private or commercial vessels of the nationality or registry of one of the Parties, which are found seaward of the territorial sea of any State, and which either of the Parties has reasonable grounds to suspect are involved in illicit traffic." Moreover, unlike many other bilateral counterdrug agreements, Article 4 prohibits the Parties from undertaking operations to suppress illicit traffic in and over the territorial sea and internal waters of the other Party.

Compare this provision with Article 5 of the *Agreement Between the Government and the United States of America and the Government of Barbados Concerning Cooperation in Suppressing Illicit Maritime Drug Trafficking*, which limits, but does not prohibit counterdrug operations in the territorial sea or internal waters of the other Party:

1. Operations to suppress illicit traffic in or over the waters within which a Party exercises sovereignty shall be carried out by, or under the direction of, the law enforcement authorities of that Party.
2. Neither Party shall conduct operations to suppress illicit traffic in or over the waters of the other Party without the permission of the Government of the other Party, granted pursuant to this Agreement.
3. Nothing in this Agreement shall be construed to permit a law enforcement vessel, or aircraft of one Party, to randomly patrol within the waters or airspace of the other Party.[57]

---

[56] Agreement Between the Government of the Republic of Colombia and the Government of the United States of America to Suppress Illicit Traffic by Sea (1997), U.N.T.S. 2348 (2005), No. 42099.
[57] Agreement between the Government and the United States of America and the Government of Barbados Concerning Cooperation in Suppressing Illicit Maritime Drug Trafficking (1997).

Boarding procedures are outlined in Articles 7 to 15 of the U.S.-Colombian agreement. Article 7 provides that "[w]henever law enforcement officials of one Party find a vessel... claiming registration in the other Party, competent authority of the former Party may request the competent authority of the other Party to verify the vessel's registry, and in case it is confirmed, its authorization to board and search the vessel." Article 8 requires the Parties to expeditiously respond to requests from the other Party to verify registry and to board and search a suspect vessel. If the requested Party does not respond within three hours, authorization to board and search the suspect vessel is presumed. When responding to a request to board and search, "the requested Party may take into account whether it has a unit available to carry out the boarding and search in a timely and effective manner." If the requested Party cannot or does not confirm registry, the requesting Party may assimilate the vessel to be stateless and proceed to board the vessel in accordance with international law.

To carry out the above requirements, Article 9 identifies the competent authority for Colombia as the Ministry of National Defense, through the Colombian Navy Operations Center, and, for the United States, the U.S. Coast Guard Operations Center. In accordance with Article 10, a boarding and search under the agreement may be conducted only by law enforcement officials embarked in law enforcement vessels, warships or other ships clearly marked and identifiable as being on government service. Moreover, Article 11 requires that boarding parties act in accordance with international law and internationally accepted practices. In addition, "when conducting a boarding and search, law enforcement officials shall take due account of the need not to endanger the safety of life at sea, the security of the suspect vessel and its cargo, or to prejudice the commercial and legal interests of the flag State or any other interested State." Furthermore, Article 11 requires that boarding officials "bear in mind the need to observe norms of courtesy, respect, and consideration for the persons on board the suspect vessel."

With regard to the use of force, Article 12 states that "law enforcement officials shall avoid the use of force in any way, including the use of firearms, except in the exercise of the right of self-defense. . . ." Article 12 also allows the use of force in the following cases:

(a) To compel the suspect vessel to stop when the vessel has ignored the respective Party's standard warnings to stop;
(b) To maintain order on board the suspect vessel during the boarding and search or while the vessel is preventively held, when the crew or persons on board resist, impede the boarding and search or try to destroy evidence of illicit traffic or the vessel, or when the vessel attempts to flee during the boarding and search or while the vessel is preventively held.

Article 12 also states that boarding parties may be armed with conventional small arms. However, law enforcement officials will only discharge a firearm "when it is not possible to apply less extreme measures." Moreover, if the discharge of a firearm is required, prior authorization from the flag State is required "except when indirect warning shots are required as a signal for the vessel to stop, or in the exercise of the right of self-defense." If force is used, "it shall be the minimum reasonably necessary and proportional under the circumstances."

After an operation is completed, regardless of the results, Article 13 requires that the Party conducting the boarding and search to "immediately submit a detailed report to the other Party of what happened...." In addition, if requested by a Party, the other Party shall, consistent with its laws, report "on the status of all investigations, prosecutions and judicial proceedings resulting from boarding and searches conducted in accordance with this Agreement where evidence of illicit traffic was found." The Parties are required to "provide each other the assistance provided for in Article 7 of the 1988 [Vienna Drug] Convention relating to investigations, prosecutions, and judicial proceedings which result from boarding and searches conducted in accordance with [the] Agreement where evidence of illicit traffic is found." Pursuant to Article 18, any claim for damages, injury or loss resulting from an operation carried out under the Agreement "shall be processed, considered, and, if merited, resolved in favor of the claimant by the Party whose authorities conducted the operation, in accordance with the domestic law of that Party, and in a manner consistent with international law." Claims between the Parties may be raised through diplomatic channels.

In cases where evidence of illicit traffic is found on board a Colombian flag vessel, Article 16 provides that Colombia will exercise criminal jurisdiction if the vessel is located outside the Colombian EEZ or seaward of the territorial sea of any other State, unless otherwise provided for in Colombian law. In those cases in which evidence of illicit traffic is found in U.S. territory, waters, or airspace, or concerning U.S. flag vessels seaward of any nation's territorial sea, the United States "shall have the right to exercise jurisdiction over the ... vessel, the persons on board and cargo, provided however, that the Government of the United States may, subject to its constitution and laws, authorize the enforcement of Colombian law against the vessel, persons on board and cargo." Regardless of which Party exercises jurisdiction, Article 17 allows either state, "to the extent permitted by their laws and regulations, and taking into consideration agreements in force between them, ... [to] share those forfeited assets which result from boarding and searches conducted in accordance with this Agreement where evidence of illicit traffic is found, or the proceeds of their sale."

18.2.2 *Air Bridge Denial Agreement (U.S.-Colombia)*

> *Agreement Between the Government of the United States of America and the Government of the Republic of Colombia Concerning the Program for the Suppression of Illicit Aerial Traffic in Narcotic Drugs and Psychotropic Substances*[58]

---

[58] Agreement between the Government of the United States of America and the Government of the Republic of Colombia Concerning the Program for the Suppression of

Combined air interdiction operations between Colombia and the United States are governed by the bilateral *Air Bridge Denial Agreement*. The agreement established the Air Bridge Denial (ABD) Program, which strengthens the capability of the Government of Colombia to eliminate illicit aerial trafficking in narcotic drugs and psychotropic substances in Colombian airspace. The Colombian Air Force (FAC) is responsible for implementing the ABD Program. The United States, through JIATF-South, may provide aerial assets to the ABD Program, but will retain tactical control of them at all times.

Pursuant to Article II.A, non-commercial aircraft flying in Special Zones of Air Control are "subject to special surveillance by ground and aerial detection assets to determine whether the aircraft is reasonably suspected to be primarily engaged in illicit drug trafficking...." An aircraft is reasonably suspected of being "primarily engaged in illicit drug trafficking" under Article II.F when a sufficient basis exists to reasonably suspect that the primary purpose of the operation of the aircraft is:

(1) The illicit transport of narcotic drugs or psychotropic substances (as defined in the 1988 Convention), or the travel of the aircraft to the place where it illicitly receives narcotic drugs or psychotropic substances or the return of the aircraft after illicitly moving narcotic drugs or psychotropic substances, or
(2) The transport of proceeds that directly result from an illicit transaction in such narcotic drugs or psychotropic substances (or the travel of the aircraft to the place where it delivers or receives the proceeds).

Factors that should be considered in determining whether the aircraft is reasonably suspected of being "primarily engaged in illicit drug trafficking" are set out in the Appendix to Annex A of the agreement and include:

(1) Did the aircraft fail to file a required flight plan?
(2) Is it inexplicably flying outside the route designated in its approved flight plan?
(3) Is it not using the assigned transponder code?
(4) Is it flying at an inexplicably low altitude?
(5) Is it flying at night with its lights out?
(6) Does the aircraft have false (or no) tail numbers?
(7) Are the windows blacked out?
(8) Does the physical description of the aircraft match the description of an aircraft previously used in illicit drug trafficking?
(9) Is there signal or human intelligence indicating that the aircraft is primarily engaged in illicit drug trafficking?
(10) Is the aircraft flying without permission over a FAC restricted area in a ZECA?
(11) Is the aircraft parked at night at a non-monitored airfield in a ZECA (in which overnight stays are prohibited) without permission?
(12) Have all attempts to identify the aircraft failed?

Illicit Aerial Traffic in Narcotic Drugs and Psychotropic Substances, signed in Bogota on Apr. 28, 2003.

(13) Has the aircraft failed to respond to all attempts to communicate?
(14) Has the aircraft ignored the FAC's orders?
(15) Have any objects been jettisoned from the aircraft?
(16) Is there any other information suggesting that the aircraft is primarily engaged in illicit drug trafficking?
(17) Is there any information suggesting that the aircraft is not primarily engaged in illicit drug trafficking?

According to Article II.H, the "highest priority for the ABD Program is to have the intercepted aircraft land safely at the nearest . . . [Colombian]-controlled landing strip, where law enforcement personnel may take control of the aircraft." Accordingly, safety procedures set out in Annex A to the agreement provide implementation guidance for the ABD Program. In this regard, Article II.B provides that air and ground safety monitors, as well as JIATF-South, will verify compliance with the safety procedures contained in Annex A. Additionally, Article II.G provides that "[i]f any . . . [Colombian or U.S. individual] participant in the ABD Program has reason to believe that persons not willfully engaged in illicit drug trafficking are on board an aircraft, that aircraft shall not be considered to have a primary purpose of illicit drug trafficking." Moreover, pursuant to Article II.H, "[t]he pilot, crew, and passengers of all aircraft subject to action under the ABD program are presumed not to be engaged in illicit drug trafficking."

The Government of Colombia (FAC in coordination with the Special Administrative Unit of the Civil Aviation Agency) is responsible under Article III.B(2) for designating Special Zones of Air Control (ZECA) in their national airspace. The Colombian Government shall clearly define the ZECAs and clearly and widely disseminate throughout the civil aviation community, via the Aeronautical Information Publication of Colombia, Notice to Airmen (NOTAM), their existence prior to the commencement of activities under the ABD Program. Intercept procedures, including the consequences of noncompliance, shall also be widely promulgated.[59] ZECAs are designated in areas "where there is sufficient basis to reasonably suspect that there are routes used for illicit trafficking in narcotic drugs or psychotropic substances and may not be designated over areas that are heavily populated." The Government of Colombia provides U.S. authorities 30 days advance notice of any changes to the ZECAs.[60]

The Colombian Government shall ensure that its pilots, Mission Commanding Officers, and Air and Ground Safety Monitors are proficient in English and are familiar with common-use and specialized aviation terminology, as well as with "agreed-upon communication protocols for the operational implementation of

---

[59] Agreement Between the Government of the United States of America and the Government of the Republic of Colombia Concerning the Program for the Suppression of Illicit Aerial Traffic in Narcotic Drugs and Psychotropic Substances (2009), Article III.B(4).
[60] Id., Article III.B(3).

the ABD Program."[61] In addition, Colombia is responsible under Article III.B(8) for publishing pertinent documents and information so that owners and pilots of civil aircraft are aware of the following requirements when operating aircraft in Colombian airspace:

(a) File a flight plan before taking off (or if filing before takeoff is not possible, as soon as possible after taking off);
(b) Contact the nearest air traffic service as soon as possible after takeoff;
(c) Continuously monitor the proper air traffic service radio frequency and, where necessary, establish two-way communications with the air traffic service. In cases where it is impossible to make contact with the proper air traffic service, maintain an open channel on ICAO emergency frequencies;
(d) Be familiar with aerial intercept and radio and visual communication procedures promulgated by ICAO in Annex 2 to the Chicago Convention;
(e) Keep activated the transponder equipment with the code assigned by the Special Administrative Unit of the Civil Aeronautics;
(f) Obtain permission before flying over FAC restricted areas; and
(g) Refrain from staying overnight at non-controlled airfields in which the FAC has prohibited overnight stays.

Article IV.A authorizes the U.S. Government to provide training, cryptographic equipment, aerial and maritime interdiction information, and other support to the FAC to support the ABD Program. However, prior to providing support, the U.S. Government ensures that an annual certification of the ABD Program is conducted in accordance with 22 U.S.C. § 2291–4(a), which provides that:

> Notwithstanding any other provision of law, it shall not be unlawful for authorized employees or agents of a foreign country (including members of the armed forces of that country) to interdict or attempt to interdict an aircraft in that country's territory or airspace if—
>
> (1) that aircraft is reasonably suspected to be primarily engaged in illicit drug trafficking; and
> (2) the President of the United States has, during the 12-month period ending on the date of the interdiction, certified to Congress with respect to that country that
>   (A) interdiction is necessary because of the extraordinary threat posed by illicit drug trafficking to the national security of that country; and
>   (B) the country has appropriate procedures in place to protect against innocent loss of life in the air and on the ground in connection with interdiction, which shall at a minimum include effective means to identify and warn an aircraft before the use of force directed against the aircraft.

Air interdiction procedures, designed to protect against loss of life in connection with the ABD Program, are contained in Annex A to the agreement. In general, aircraft may be damaged, rendered inoperative, or destroyed only if (1) they are reasonably suspected of being primarily engaged in illicit drug trafficking, as determined using the factors set forth in the Appendix as well as other rel-

---

[61] Id., Article III.B(6).

evant information gathered before and during the detection, sorting, identification, monitoring, and interception phases of each ABD event, and (2) they fail to comply with instructions from the FAC.[62]

When a track of interest is detected in a ZECA, the Colombian Battle Commander Officer (OCB) in the Colombian Air Force Command and Control Center (CCOFA) use all available resources to gather information on the aircraft, including radar systems, radio and visual contact with the aircraft, electronic systems, and relevant air traffic control centers, "to determine whether the aircraft is reasonably suspected to be a primarily engaged in illicit drug trafficking."[63] If the OCB reasonably suspects that an aircraft is primarily engaged in illicit drug trafficking, that aircraft is tracked and monitored. If Colombian authorities are unable to identify the aircraft as a legitimate track, the aircraft is considered suspect and may be intercepted by the FAC.[64]

Air intercepts occur in three phases. Phase I (interception phase) includes attempts to contact the suspect aircraft by radio and/or visual signals in order to determine the identity of the pilot or suspect aircraft. During the interception phase, Colombian authorities attempt to:

(1) determine with greater certainty the identity of the intercepted aircraft. The tracker or interceptor aircraft shall take all reasonable measures, including the use of night vision devices, to identify the intercepted aircraft by visual or electronic observation of the nationality markings, registration number, and any other license number or identifying features or markings on the intercepted aircraft;
(2) gather any further information regarding the intercepted aircraft that may help determine whether the intercepted aircraft is reasonably suspected to be primarily engaged in illicit drug trafficking . . .;
(3) establish communications with the intercepted aircraft through the use of radio communications or visual signals; and
(4) order the intercepted aircraft to land at the nearest suitable airfield, if factors continue to support a determination that the aircraft is primarily engaged in illicit drug trafficking.[65]

In addition, the interceptor aircraft maneuver in accordance with the ICAO interception maneuver procedures contained in Annex 2 to the Chicago Convention in order to:

(1) avoid endangering the lives of persons on board the intercepted aircraft;
(2) permit the unimpeded and continuous visual observation of the intercepted aircraft; and
(3) allow communications to be established with the intercepted aircraft through the use of radio communications or visual signals.[66]

---

[62] Id., Annex A, para. I.A.
[63] Id., Annex A, para. II.
[64] Id., Annex A, para. III.
[65] Id., Annex A, para. IV.A.
[66] Id., Annex A, para. IV.B.

Interceptor aircraft attempt to establish contact in English and Spanish with the intercepted aircraft using the ICAO radio communications procedures contained in Annex 2 to the Chicago Convention. If radio contact is established, "the interceptor aircraft shall interrogate the pilot of the intercepted aircraft to determine its status."[67] If radio contact is not established, the interceptor aircraft use the ICAO visual signals for interception found in Annex 2 to the Chicago Convention to attempt to establish communication. If a reasonable suspicion continues to exist that the aircraft is primarily engaged in illicit drug trafficking, the interceptor aircraft order the suspect aircraft to land, using ICAO radio or visual signals, at a designated place suitable for a safe landing. If the aircraft fails to comply with the procedures and instructions given by the FAC interceptor aircraft, the suspect aircraft "shall be classified as hostile by the FAC under FAC procedures. . . ."[68]

If a suspect aircraft fails to comply with an interceptor's order to land, Colombian authorities may move into Phase II. This phase involves the use of warning shots (tracer rounds) "in order to demonstrate to the pilot of the intercepted aircraft that he must comply with the interceptor's order."[69] Warning shots may not be used, however, until the interceptor aircraft requests and receives authorization from the Commander of the Colombian Air Force (COFAC). In addition, the interceptor aircraft shall be warned in advance (using ICAO radio procedures) "that warning shots shall be used if the intercepted aircraft refuses to comply."[70] Warning shots "shall be fired from a position slightly ahead of the wing line and parallel to the course of the intercepted aircraft to ensure that the intercepted aircraft is not in the line of fire," unless the safety of flight prevents it.[71] Reasonable efforts are taken to ensure that the warning shots are visible to the pilot of the intercepted aircraft.

If the suspect aircraft does not respond appropriately to the use of warning shots, the interceptor aircraft may fire weapons at the aircraft if authorized by the COFAC. In any event, the suspect aircraft is not engaged in Phase III if:

(1) the aircraft has met one or more of the conditions contained in section I.H [state or commercial aircraft, operating in accordance with a filed flight plan, pilot is reasonably believed to be incapacitated, or pilot appears to be under duress];
(2) the tracking of the intercepted aircraft has been intermittent and positive re-identification has not been made with reasonable certainty; or
(3) the aircraft is operating in proximity to a populated area or the action being taken could reasonably be expected to result in loss of innocent life in the air or on the ground.[72]

---

[67] Id., Annex A, para. IV.D.
[68] Id., Annex A, para. IV.G.
[69] Id., Annex A, para. V.
[70] Id., Annex A, para. V.B.
[71] Id.
[72] Id., Annex A, para. VI.A.

Interceptor aircraft are warned in advance (using ICAO radio procedures) "that it shall be fired upon if it refuses to comply."[73] If force is used against the suspect aircraft, it "shall not be in excess of the minimum necessary to disable it, starting with a minimum level of fire in an attempt to persuade the intercepted aircraft to land as directed."[74] After being given a reasonable opportunity to obey any previously issued orders to land, the suspect aircraft may be engaged using increasing levels of force. Any ABD event that moves into Phase II or III is jointly reviewed by JIATF-South and the Chief of Air Operations of the FAC.

Annex B to the Agreement governs the use of ABD assets in support of suppression of illicit maritime trafficking in narcotic drugs and psychotropic substances (SSIMT). SSIMT missions are executed under three categories: scheduled/pre-planned missions, alert-launched/ad hoc missions, and transition missions. For each surface track, paragraph II.B(1) of Annex B requires the Air Safety Monitor to provide as much of the following information as possible:

(a) Vessel Name;
(b) Vessel Length;
(c) Vessel Flag;
(d) Vessel Type;
(e) Vessel Position;
(f) Vessel Course;
(g) Vessel Speed; and
(h) Suspect activities in which vessel or crew members are engaged, if any.

(2) Suspicious activity may include, but is not limited to, the following:

(a) An unusual number of antennae;
(b) No radar reflectors (especially on sailboats);
(c) Equipment missing or in disrepair (especially on fishing vessels);
(d) Covered or blackened windows;
(e) An unusual amount of fuel drums or containers on deck;
(f) Water containers or bladders on deck;
(g) Vessel name painted over or on a plaque;
(h) Missing or conflicting registration numbers;
(i) No flag or too many flags displayed;
(j) An unusual attitude displayed by crew (ignoring presence);
(k) An excessive number of people on board for type of vessel;
(l) New paint or patch work visible;
(m) Crew jettisons material;
(n) A false waterline;
(o) Failure of vessel to respond when called/signaled via normal methods;
(p) Unusual maneuvering or positioning; e.g. fishing vessel not on fishing grounds, change in speed/course upon detection;
(q) Hull scratches or damage (indicating alongside/transfer ops w/other vessel); and
(r) Low profile vessel (LPV) characteristics.

---

[73] Id., Annex A, para. VI.C.
[74] Id.

If a surface track of interest is detected, FAC aircraft should maneuver and attempt to establish radio communications with the suspect vessel. Once communications are established, "right of approach" questions should be used to determine the following:

(1) Name of the vessel;
(2) Nationality of the vessel;
(3) Home port;
(4) Official registration number;
(5) Last port of call;
(6) Next port of call; and
(7) Purpose of voyage.[75]

18.3 Conclusion

Drug trafficking organizations operate using the full range of air, land, and maritime modes of transport. New developments in technology and communications equipment allow these groups, as well as other transnational criminal organizations to plan, coordinate and execute their operations with increased mobility and anonymity. Weak border security controls and ill-equipped law enforcement agencies further facilitate their operations. Moreover, the huge profits generated from smuggling activities allow criminal organizations to exploit political and legal limitations by bribing government officials in various countries, undermining fledgling democratic institutions and moving illicit drugs with impunity. These huge profits allow these organizations to develop and exploit more sophisticated vessels and modes of conveyance, as well as multiple contingency logistics chains that further degrade the ability of law enforcement to effectively detect, monitor and interdict their activities. These interdiction challenges will become even more acute as drug traffickers continue to develop more clandestine means, methods and modes of conveyance.

18.4 U.S. International Maritime Law Enforcement Instruments

18.4.1 *Bilateral Maritime Counterdrug Agreements*

1. Agreement between the Government of the United States of America and the Government of **Antigua and Barbuda** concerning maritime counterdrug operations, signed at St. John's April 19, 1995; entered into force April 19, 1995. Amended by exchange of notes at St. John's June 3, 1996; entered into force June 3, 1996. TIAS 12763. Further amended by Protocol signed at Washington

---

[75] Id., Annex B, para. II.C.

September 30, 2003, entered into force September 30, 2003. TIAS 12763, 2003 U.S.T. LEXIS 84.

2. Agreement between the Government of the United States of America and the Government of **The Bahamas** concerning cooperation in maritime law enforcement, signed at Nassau June 29, 2004; entered into force June 29, 2004.

> Understanding between the Governor of **The Bahamas** and the United States Coast Guard effected by exchange of letters dated December 4 and 11, 1964. *Provisions pertaining to maritime law enforcement terminated June 29, 2004.*
>
> Agreement on the Continuance of United States Military Rights and Maritime Practices in the **Bahamas** effected by exchange of notes dated July 10 and 20, 1973. TIAS 7688, 24 UST 1783. *Provisions pertaining to maritime law enforcement terminated June 29, 2004.*
>
> Understanding concerning military operating rights and maritime practices effected by exchange of notes dated April 5, 1984. TIAS 11058, 2034 U.N.T.S. 189. *Provisions pertaining to maritime law enforcement terminated June 29, 2004.*
>
> Understanding concerning drug interdiction and other operations effected by exchange of notes dated May 22 and 28, 1992. *Terminated June 29, 2004.*
>
> Agreement between the Government of the United States of America and the Government of **Bahamas** concerning a cooperative shiprider and overflight drug interdiction program, effected by exchange of notes at Nassau May 1 and 6, 1996, entered into force May 6, 1996. TIAS 12750. *Terminated June 29, 2004.*

3. Agreement between the Government of the United States of America and the Government of **Barbados** concerning cooperation in the suppressing illicit maritime drug trafficking, signed at Bridgetown June 25, 1997, entered into force October 11, 1998. TIAS 12872, 1997 U.S.T. LEXIS 5.
4. Agreement between the Government of the United States of America and the Government of **Belize** concerning maritime counterdrug operations, signed at Belmopan December 23, 1992; entered into force December 23, 1992. TIAS 11914, 2231 U.N.T.S. 511. Amended by a Protocol signed at Belmopan April 25, 2000, entered into force April 25, 2000.
5. Agreement between the Government of the United States of America and the Government of **Colombia** to suppress illicit traffic by sea, signed at Bogota February 20, 1997, entered into force February 20, 1997. TIAS 12835, 2348 U.N.T.S. 195.
6. Agreement between the Government of the United States of America and the Government of the Republic of the **Cook Islands** concerning cooperation to suppress illicit traffic in narcotic substances and psychotropic substances by sea, signed at Rarotonga, November 8, 2007; entered into force November 8, 2007.
7. Agreement between the Government of the United States of America and the Government of the Republic of **Costa Rica** concerning cooperation to suppress illicit traffic, signed at San Jose December 1, 1998; entered into force November 19, 1999. TIAS 13005. Amended by the Protocol signed at San Jose July 2, 1999, entered into force on November 19, 1999. TIAS 13005.

8. Agreement between the Government of the United States of America and the Government of **Dominica** concerning maritime counterdrug operations, signed at Roseau April 19, 1995, entered into force April 19, 1995. TIAS 12630, UN Reg. I-44176.
9. Agreement between the Government of the United States of America and the Government of the **Dominican Republic** concerning maritime counterdrug operations, signed at Santo Domingo March 23, 1995; entered into force March 23, 1995. TIAS 12620, UN reg. I-44184. Amended by the Protocol signed at Washington May 20, 2003, entered into force May 20, 2003. 2003 U.S.T. LEXIS 31.
10. Agreement between the Government of the United States of America and the Government of **Grenada** concerning maritime counterdrug operations, signed at St George's May 16, 1995; entered into force May 16, 1995. TIAS 12648, UN reg. I-44177. Amended by exchange of notes at St. George's November 26, 1996, entered into force November 26, 1996. TIAS 12648.
11. Agreement between the Government of the United States of America and the Government of the Republic of **Guatemala** concerning cooperation to suppress illicit traffic in narcotic drugs and psychotropic substances by sea and air, signed at Guatemala City June 19, 2003, entered into force October 10, 2003.
12. Agreement between the Government of the United States of America and the Government of the Co-operative Republic of **Guyana** concerning cooperation to suppress illicit traffic by sea and air, signed at Georgetown April 10, 2001, enters into force upon exchange of notes indicating all necessary domestic requirements of each Party have been completed.
13. Agreement between the United States of America and the Republic of **Haiti** concerning cooperation to suppress illicit maritime drug traffic, signed at Port au Prince October 17, 1997, entered into force September 5, 2002. 1997 U.S.T. LEXIS 128.
14. Agreement between the United States of America and the Republic of **Honduras** concerning cooperation for the suppression of illicit maritime traffic in narcotic drugs and psychotropic substances, signed at Tegucigalpa March 29, 2000, entered into force January 30, 2001. TIAS 13088.

    Implementing agreement between the United States of America and the Republic of **Honduras** concerning cooperation for the suppression of illicit maritime traffic in narcotic drugs and psychotropic substances, signed at Tegucigalpa March 29, 2000, entered into force January 30, 2001. TIAS 13088, 2000 U.S.T. LEXIS 159.

15. Agreement between the Government of the United States of America and the Government of **Jamaica** concerning cooperation in suppressing illicit maritime drug trafficking, signed at Kingston May 6, 1997; entered into force March 10, 1998. 1997 U.S.T. LEXIS 21. Amended by Protocol signed at Kingston February 6, 2004, entered into force February 6, 2004. 2004 U.S.T. LEXIS 1.

16. Agreement between the Government of the United States of America and the Government of the Republic of **Malta** concerning cooperation to suppress illicit traffic in narcotic substances and psychotropic substances by sea, signed at Valletta June 16, 2004, entered into force January 24, 2008.
17. Agreement between the Government of the United States of America and the Government of **Nicaragua** concerning cooperation to suppress illicit traffic by sea and air, signed at Managua June 1, 2001, entered into force November 15, 2001. 2001 U.S.T. LEXIS 63.
18. Arrangement between the Government of the United States and the Government of **Panama** for Support and Assistance from the U.S. Coast Guard for the National Maritime Service of the Ministry of Government and Justice, signed at Panama March 18, 1991, entered into force March 18, 1991. TIAS 11833, 2212 U.N.T.S. 7.

    Supplementary Arrangement between the Government of the United States of America and the Government of Panama to the Arrangement between the Government of the United States and the Government of **Panama** for Support and Assistance from the U.S. Coast Guard for the National Maritime Service of the Ministry of Government and Justice, signed at Panama February 5, 2002, entered into force February 5, 2002. 2002 U.S.T. LEXIS 51.

19. Agreement between the Government of the United States of America and the Government of **St. Kitts and Nevis** concerning maritime counterdrug operations, signed at Basseterre April 13, 1995; entered into force April 13, 1995. TIAS 12775. Amended by exchange of notes at Bridgetown and Basseterre June 27, 1996, entered into force June 27, 1996. TIAS 12775.
20. Agreement between the Government of the United States of America and the Government of **St. Lucia** concerning maritime counterdrug operations, signed at Castries April 20, 1995; entered into force April 20, 1995. TIAS 12764. Amended by exchange of notes at Bridgetown and Castries June 5, 1996, entered into force June 5, 1996. TIAS 12764.
21. Agreement between the Government of the United States of America and the Government of **St. Vincent and the Grenadines** concerning maritime counterdrug operations, signed at Kingstown and Bridgetown June 29 and July 4, 1995, entered into force July 4, 1995. TIAS 12676.
22. Agreement between the Government of the United States of America and the Government of **Suriname** concerning cooperation in maritime law enforcement, signed at Paramaribo December 1, 1998, entered into force August 26, 1999. 1998 U.S.T. LEXIS 166.
23. Agreement between the Government of the United States of America and the Government of **Trinidad and Tobago** concerning maritime counterdrug operations, signed at Port of Spain March 4, 1996, entered into force March 4, 1996. TIAS 12732, 1996 U.S.T. LEXIS 59, UN reg. I-44046.
24. Agreement between the Government of the United States of America and the Government of the **United Kingdom of Great Britain and Northern Ireland**

to facilitate the interdiction by the United States of vessels of the United Kingdom which are suspected of being engaged in trafficking in drugs, effected by exchange of notes at London November 13, 1981, entered into force November 13, 1981. TIAS 10296. 33 UST 4224; 1285 U.N.T.S. 197.

> Agreement between the Government of the United States of America and the Government of the **United Kingdom of Great Britain and Northern Ireland** concerning maritime and aerial operations to suppress illicit trafficking by sea in waters of the Caribbean and Bermuda, signed at Washington July 13, 1998, entered into force October 30, 2000.

25. Agreement between the Government of the United States of America and the Government of **Venezuela** to suppress illicit traffic in narcotic drugs and psychotropic substances by sea, signed at Caracas November 9, 1991; entered into force upon signature. TIAS 11827; 2211 U.N.T.S. 387. Amended by the Protocol signed at Caracas July 23, 1997, entered into force July 23, 1997. TIAS 12876.

18.4.2 *Memorandums of Understanding and Operational Procedures*

1. Memorandum of Understanding between the Government of the United States of America and the Government of Great Britain and Northern Ireland, on behalf of the Government of the **British Virgin Islands**, concerning maritime narcotics interdiction operations, signed at Tortola February 6, 1990. Amended by exchange of notes on December 2 and 10, 1992. *Terminated October 30, 2000.*
2. Memorandum of Understanding between the Government of the **United Kingdom** of Great Britain and Northern Ireland including the Government of the **Turks & Caicos Islands** (the Government of the United Kingdom), the Government of the **Bahamas** (the Government of the Bahamas) and the Government of the United States of America (the Government of the United States), signed at Washington July 12, 1990.
3. Memorandum of Understanding between the Government of the United States of America and the Government of the **United Kingdom** of Great Britain and Northern Ireland concerning the deployment of United States Coast Guard Law Enforcement Detachments on Royal Navy and Royal Fleet Auxiliary Ships in the waters of the Caribbean and Bermuda, signed at Washington June 23, 1999; amended by exchange of notes signed in London and Washington October 29, 2004; modified by exchange of notes signed in Key West May 9, 2008.
4. Memorandum of Understanding between the Government of the United States of America and the Government of the Kingdom of **Belgium** concerning the deployment of United States Coast Guard Law Enforcement Detachments on

Belgian Navy vessels in the waters of the Caribbean Sea, signed at Washington March 1, 2001.
5. U.S. Coast Guard and Colombian Navy Combined Boardings Standard Operating Procedures implementing the Agreement between the Government of the United States of America and the Government of **Colombia** to suppress illicit traffic by sea, 1997, signed at Bogota and Washington April 20, 2006.
6. **Ecuador**—U.S. Operational procedures for boarding and inspecting vessels suspected of illicit traffic in narcotic drugs and psychotropic substances and of smuggling migrants by sea, signed at Quito, August 30, 2006.
7. **Mexico**—Letter of Intent to strengthen the exchange of information and cooperation among the Mexican Navy, U.S. Coast Guard, and U.S. Northern Command in matters of safety and maritime security in order to improve mutual capacity for operational coordination, signed April 15, May 12 and May 16, 2008.
8. **Peru**—Operational Procedures for Boarding and Inspecting Vessels Suspected of Illicit Traffic in Narcotic Drugs and Psychotropic Substances between the Peruvian National Maritime Authority and the United States Coast Guard, signed Mar. 24, 2010 (Spanish and English). Annex 2 form was subsequently modified (by informal mutual agreement, April 2010).

18.4.3 Forward Operating Location/Cooperative Security Location Agreements

1. Supplemental Agreement for Cooperation and Technical Assistance in Defense and Security between the Governments of the United States of America and the Republic of **Columbia**, signed at Bogota October 30, 2009, entered into force October 30, 2009.
2. Agreement of Cooperation between the Government of the United States of America and the Government of the Republic of **Ecuador** concerning United States access to and use of installations at the Ecuadorian Air Force Base in Manta for aerial counter-narcotics activities, signed at Quito November 12, 1999, entered into force November 17, 1999, expired November 11, 2009.
3. Agreement of Cooperation between the Government of the United States of America and the Government of the Republic of **El Salvador** concerning United States access to and use of facilities at the International Airport of El Salvador for aerial counter-narcotics activities, signed at San Salvador March 31, 2000, entered into force August 23, 2000, 2000 U.S.T. LEXIS 134.
4. Agreement of Cooperation between the Government of the United States of America and the Kingdom of **the Netherlands** concerning access to and use of facilities in the Netherlands Antilles and Aruba for aerial counter-narcotics activities, signed at Oranjestad, Aruba, March 2, 2000. Provisionally applied from April 1, 2000, entered into force November 2, 2001, 2000 U.S.T. LEXIS 157.

18.4.4 *Multilateral Counterdrug Agreements*

1. United Nations Convention Against Illicit Traffic in Narcotic Drugs and Psychotropic Substances, done at Vienna December 20, 1988, entered into force November 11, 1990. 1582 UNTS 165 (1990).
2. Agreement Concerning Co-operation in Suppressing Illicit Maritime and Air Trafficking in Narcotics and Psychotropic Substances in **the Caribbean Area**, opened for signature at San Jose April 10, 2003, entered into force September 18, 2008. The United States signed the Agreement definitively, with a declaration, on April 10, 2003.

NINETEEN

MIGRANT SMUGGLING AT SEA

19.1 Transnational Threat of Irregular Migration

Transnational migration has existed since the beginning of time. Threats today have dramatically increased the impetus for oppressed segments of society to migrate, legally or illegally, in search of a better life. Individuals and groups are motivated by the difference in economic opportunity between industrialized and developing countries. Many migrants flee racial, ethnic and religious persecution; war and armed conflict; spiraling population growth in Third World nations; poverty and severe unemployment; natural disasters, environmental degradation and climate change; and regional social and political unrest. Furthermore, globalization has increased awareness in less developed countries of the disparity in quality of life in wealthier nations, while plummeting costs of transportation and information have made travel easier. Thus, migration is booming, and no small part of it is unlawful and moves by sea. In response, governments have turned to improved and more robust border control to stem the influx of irregular or illegal migrants. Unfortunately, these enhanced border controls have forced migrants to rely unwittingly on the assistance of organized criminal groups to gain access to destination countries, such as the United States and other industrialized nations.

The UN Office on Drugs and Crime (UNODC) estimates there are "50 million irregular international migrants in the world today...."[1] Many of these people have paid traffickers for assistance to illegally enter another state. Increased success rates fuel demand, allowing smugglers to strengthen their control over the

---

[1] United Nations Office of Drugs and Crime, The Globalization of Crime: A Transnational Organized Crime Threat Assessment (2010) United Nations publication, Sales No. E.10.IV.6.

market in humans as more migrants seek assistance to illegally cross international borders. For example, 97 percent of all irregular migrants entering The Netherlands in 2005 from Africa were assisted by professional smugglers, while irregular Asian migrants seeking entry into the United States or Europe rely almost exclusively on international criminal organizations for their travel arrangements.[2] American officials estimate that over 30,000 irregular Chinese migrants enter the United States each year, with each migrant paying as much as $30,000 to transnational organized crime (TOC) groups to facilitate their travel.[3]

The International Organization for Migration (IOM) defines unlawful migrant smuggling as the "... facilitation of movement of people across international borders, in violation of laws or regulations, for the purpose of financial or other gain to the smuggler."[4] Human trafficking ranges from simple, small scale, and occasional smuggling operations to highly sophisticated, organized enterprises that provide irregular migrants with a wide range of services, to include complex travel itineraries and false travel documents such as passports, visas and entry permits. Factors that affect the degree of organization include "the distance to be travelled, the degree of cultural isolation of the migrants and the difficulties of evading law enforcement."[5]

Smugglers charge a fee of $1,500 to $40,000, depending on the circumstances, including the length of the journey, mode of conveyance (land, air or sea), accommodations provided, additional services provided (e.g., forged travel documents) and risk to the smugglers.[6] A single boatload of 300 illegal migrants can generate a profit of $12 million. Migrants that cannot afford to pay the fees upfront enter into contracts with the smugglers and incur large debts that are paid off in the country of destination by working as prostitutes or domestic servants, engaging in other criminal activities such as drug smuggling, or working in sweat shops or restaurants for little or no pay. Indentured servitude can last for years until the debt is repaid.

The risk of detection and criminal prosecution is low and sunk costs for the smugglers are minimal. Smuggling operations into the United States appear to be the most lucrative. Of the nearly three million migrants that enter the United States illegally each year, most of the persons are assisted by transnational orga-

---

[2] UNITED NATIONS OFFICE OF DRUGS AND CRIME, THE ROLE OF ORGANIZED CRIME IN THE SMUGGLING OF MIGRANTS FROM WEST AFRICA TO THE EUROPEAN UNION (2011).

[3] International Organization of Migration (IOM), The Criminalization of Migrant Smuggling, IMO Internet Website, http://www.iom.int/jahia/jsp/index.jsp.

[4] Id.

[5] Id.

[6] UNITED NATIONS OFFICE OF DRUGS AND CRIME, THE GLOBALIZATION OF CRIME: A TRANSNATIONAL ORGANIZED CRIME THREAT ASSESSMENT (2010). *See also*, UNDOC Report: The role of organized crime in the smuggling of migrants from West Africa to the European Union (2011).

nized crime (TOC). There is over $6.6 billion annually in net income generated by the operations.[7] Increased profits lead to more sophisticated and capable criminal networks that threaten local governments and undercut the rule of law. There are links between migrant smuggling operations and other forms of organized crime, including trafficking in drugs and weapons.

There are many more people lining up to take the trip than can be accommodated, so smugglers are busy and they have little concern for the safety or basic human rights of the migrants. Each year thousands of irregular migrants die during the smuggling process. Transported in deplorable conditions without adequate food, water, or sanitary facilities, often spending months on end in unseaworthy vessels, many migrants never reach their destination. Cause of death can vary, and include dehydration, suffocation in shipping containers, drowning at sea, and murder at the hands of their smugglers or other migrants. The international community has responded to the threat to domestic, social, and economic development, as well as government institutions, by leveraging a number of old and new multilateral and bilateral initiatives that strengthen collaborative approaches to combating smuggling of migrants by sea.

19.2 Law of the Sea Convention

The customary international law norm of providing assistance to person in distress at sea is codified in Article 12 of the 1958 *Convention on the High Seas*. Article 12 states:

1. Every State shall require the master of a ship sailing under its flag, insofar as he can do so without serious danger to the ship, the crew or the passengers;
   a. To render assistance to any person found at sea in danger of being lost;
   b. To proceed with all possible speed to the rescue of persons in distress if informed of their need of assistance, insofar as such action may reasonably be expected of him;
   c. After a collision, to render assistance to the other ship, her crew and her passengers and, where possible, to inform the other ship of the name of his own ship, her port of registry and the nearest port at which she will call.
2. Every coastal State shall promote the establishment and maintenance of an adequate and effective search and rescue service regarding safety on and over the sea and—where circumstances so require—by way of mutual regional arrangements cooperate with neighboring States for this purpose.[8]

The obligation to provide assistance to persons in distress is repeated in the 1982 *United Nations Convention on the Law of the Sea* (UNCLOS). Article 98 states:

---

[7] United Nations Office of Drugs and Crime, The Role of Organized Crime in the Smuggling of Migrants from West Africa to the European Union (2011).
[8] Convention on the High Seas (1958), 13 U.S.T. 2312, T.I.A.S. No. 5200, 450 U.N.T.S. 82.

1. Every State shall require the master of a ship flying its flag, in so far as he can do so without serious danger to the ship, the crew or the passengers;
    a. to render assistance to any person found at sea in danger of being lost;
    b. to proceed with all possible speed to the rescue of persons in distress, if informed of their need of assistance, in so far as such action may reasonably be expected of him;
    c. after a collision, to render assistance to the other ship, its crew and its passengers and, where possible, to inform the other ship of the name of his own ship, its port of registry and the nearest port at which it will call.
2. Every coastal State shall promote the establishment, operation and maintenance of an adequate and effective search and rescue service regarding safety on and over the sea and, where circumstances so require, by way of mutual regional arrangements co-operate with neighboring States for this purpose.[9]

The duty applies equally in the 200 nautical mile exclusive economic zone (EEZ) pursuant to Article 58(2), which provides that "Articles 88 to 115 and other pertinent rules of international law apply to the exclusive economic zone in so far as they are not incompatible with this Part."[10]

19.3 Transnational Organized Crime Convention

The *United Nations Convention against Transnational Organized Crime* (TOCC) was adopted by the General Assembly on November 15, 2000, and it entered into force on September 29, 2003.[11] The TOCC is the main international instrument to bring states together in the fight against transnational organized crime. It is supplemented by three Protocols: the *Protocol to Prevent, Suppress and Punish Trafficking in Persons, Especially Women and Children*; the *Protocol against the Smuggling of Migrants by Land, Sea and Air* (Migrant Smuggling Protocol); and the *Protocol against the Illicit Manufacturing of and Trafficking in Firearms, their Parts and Components and Ammunition*. However, before a country can become a party to any of the Protocols, it must first become a party to the Convention.

The Convention reflects a major effort by the international community in the fight against transnational organized crime and the serious problems associated with it. Close international cooperation is necessary to address the threat, and the 172 States Parties to the Convention commit to taking numerous measures against transnational organized crime. Some of these measures include:

---

[9] United Nations Convention on the Law of the Sea, *opened for signature* Dec. 10, 1982, UN Doc. A/CONF.62/122 (1982), 1833 U.N.T.S. 3, 397, 21 I.L.M. 1261 (1982), *entered into force* Nov. 16, 1994, [Hereinafter UNCLOS] Article 98.
[10] Id., at Articles 58(2) and 87.
[11] UN Doc. A/RES/55/25, United Nations Convention against Transnational Organized Crime, Nov. 15, 2000.

the creation of domestic criminal offences (participation in an organized criminal group, money laundering, corruption and obstruction of justice); the adoption of new and sweeping frameworks for extradition, mutual legal assistance and law enforcement cooperation; and the promotion of training and technical assistance for building or upgrading the necessary capacity of national authorities.[12]

19.3.1 Executive Order 13581

The United States signed the Transnational Organized Crime Convention when it was opened for signature on December 13, 2000, and ratified the Convention on November 3, 2005. Executive Order 13581 is one of the tools used by the United States to implement its obligations under the Convention, and it was signed by President Barack Obama on July 25, 2011.

Executive Order 13581 blocks property of certain transnational criminal organizations. The President noted that these organizations meet certain criteria that make them especially dangerous:

- [...They] have reached such scope and gravity that they threaten the stability of international political and economic systems;
- ... such organizations are increasingly entrenched in the operations of foreign governments and the international financial system, thereby weakening democratic institutions, degrading the rule of law, and undermining economic markets;" and
- [they...] organizations facilitate and aggravate violent civil conflicts and increasingly facilitate the activities of other dangerous persons.[13]

The qualities outlined by the President mean that the organizations pose "an unusual and extraordinary threat to the national security, foreign policy, and economy of the United States."[14] The President declared a national emergency to address the threat.[15]

Section 1(a) of the executive order blocks and prohibits the transfer, payment, exportation, withdrawal of or other dealing in "all property and interests in property that are in the United States, that hereafter come within the United States, or that are or hereafter come within the possession or control of any United States person... including any overseas branch," of a class of identified indivudal persons, that includes:

  (i) [those persons specifically listed in the Annex to the order] and
  (ii) any person determined by the Secretary of the Treasury, in consultation with the Attorney General and the Secretary of State:

---

[12] United Nations Office on Drugs and Crime, United Nations Convention against Transnational Organized Crime and the Protocols Thereto, http://www.unodc.org/unodc/en/treaties/CTOC/.
[13] Executive Order13581, Blocking Property of Transnational Criminal Organizations, July 25, 2011.
[14] Id.
[15] Id.

(A) to be a foreign person that constitutes a significant transnational criminal organization;
(B) to have materially assisted, sponsored, or provided financial, material, or technological support for, or goods or services to or in support of, any person whose property and interests in property are blocked pursuant to this order; or
(C) to be owned or controlled by, or to have acted or purported to act for or on behalf of, directly or indirectly, any person whose property and interests in property are blocked pursuant to this order.[16]

In Section 1(c), the executive order provides that the prohibitions include, but are not limited to:

(i) the making of any contribution or provision of funds, goods, or services by, to, or for the benefit of any person whose property and interests in property are blocked pursuant to this order; and
(ii) the receipt of any contribution or provision of funds, goods, or services from any such person.

Furthermore, Section 2 provides that:

(a) Any transaction by a United States person or within the United States that evades or avoids, has the purpose of evading or avoiding, causes a violation of, or attempts to violate any of the prohibitions set forth in this order is prohibited.
(b) Any conspiracy formed to violate any of the prohibitions set forth in this order is prohibited.[17]

The Annex identifies the following groups as subject to the order: *The Brothers' Circle* (also known as *Family of Eleven* or *The Twenty*), *Camorra*, *Yakuza* (a.k.a. *Boryokudan* or *Gokudo*) and *Los Zetas*.[18]

19.4 MIGRANT SMUGGLING PROTOCOL

The Migrant Smuggling Protocol addresses the growing problem of organized criminal groups who smuggle migrants for profit, often at high risk to the migrants. Its stated purpose is "to prevent and combat the smuggling of migrants, as well as to promote cooperation among States Parties to that end, while protecting the rights of smuggled migrants."[19]

Migrant smuggling is defined in Article 3 of the Protocol as "the procurement, in order to obtain, directly or indirectly, a financial or other material benefit,

---

[16] Id.
[17] Id.
[18] Id.
[19] UN Doc. A/RES/55/25, Protocol against the Smuggling of Migrants by Land, Sea and Air, supplementing the United Nations Convention against Transnational Organized Crime, Nov. 15, 2000, Article 2 [Hereinafter Migrant Smuggling Protocol].

of the illegal entry of a person into a State Party of which the person is not a national or a permanent resident."[20] However, the Protocol does not apply to all migrant smuggling operations. Article 4 limits application of the Protocol to "the prevention, investigation and prosecution of offenses established in accordance with article 6 of [the] Protocol, where the offenses are transnational in nature and involve an organized criminal group, as well as to the protection of the rights of persons who have been the object of such offenses."[21] The prohibited activity therefore must be transnational in character and involve an organized criminal group. Ad hoc, small scale operations by family members or larger events involving international human rights groups, like the Mariel boatlift in 1980, are excluded.

Smuggling of migrants and related activities that enable a migrant to circumvent national migratory laws constitute criminal offenses under the Protocol:

(a) The smuggling of migrants;
(b) When committed for the purpose of enabling the smuggling of migrants:
   (i) Producing a fraudulent travel or identity document;
   (ii) Procuring, providing or possessing such a document;
(c) Enabling a person who is not a national or a permanent resident to remain in the State concerned without complying with the necessary requirements for legally remaining in the State by the means mentioned in subparagraph (b) of this paragraph or any other illegal means; when committed intentionally and in order to obtain, directly or indirectly, a financial or other material benefit. Aggravating factors to these offenses can include circumstances
   (i) That endanger, or are likely to endanger, the lives or safety of the migrants concerned; or
   (ii) That entails inhuman or degrading treatment, including exploitation, of such migrants.[22]

The Protocol makes clear, however, that migrants cannot be criminally prosecuted for the simple act of having been smuggled.[23] Nonetheless, smuggled migrants may be prosecuted for violation of immigration laws of the nation concerned.[24] The smugglers are the primary targets of the Protocol, rather than the migrants.

Chapter II of the Protocol focuses on suppression of specific acts or criminal enterprise involved with smuggling of migrants by sea, and it requires States to "cooperate to the fullest extent possible to prevent and suppress the smuggling of migrants by sea, in accordance with the international law of the sea."[25] To facilitate cooperation, Article 8 sets out measures that can be implement by the

---

[20] Id., at Article 3.
[21] Id., at Article 4.
[22] Id., at Article 6.
[23] Id., at Article 5.
[24] Id., at Article 6.4.
[25] Id., at Article 7.

States Parties to prevent the smuggling of migrants by sea, including an elaborate regime to allow the boarding and inspection of ships that are suspected of engaging in migrant smuggling operations. Flag States may request assistance from other States to prevent the use of its vessels for the smuggling of migrants if the flag State has reasonable grounds to believe one of its ships is either flying its flag or claiming its registry without authority, and is involved in smuggling.[26] If requested, other States are required to render assistance to the extent possible.

In circumstances where a State Party has reasonable grounds to suspect that a vessel it has encountered is flying the flag of another State Party is engaged in the smuggling of migrants, the State may notify the flag State and request confirmation of registry. If registry is confirmed, the State may seek authorization from the flag State to take appropriate measures with regard to the suspicious vessel."[27] Under such conditions, the flag State may authorize the requesting State to take any of the following actions:

(a) To board the vessel;
(b) To search the vessel; and
(c) If evidence is found that the vessel is engaged in the smuggling of migrants by sea, to take appropriate measures with respect to the vessel and persons and cargo on board, as authorized by the flag State.[28]

If authority is granted to board and search the vessel, the State taking any measure against the ship "shall promptly inform the flag State concerned of the results of that measure."[29]

State Parties are required to "respond expeditiously to a request from another State Party to determine whether a vessel that is claiming its registry or flying its flag is entitled to do so and to a request for authorization made in accordance with paragraph 2 of [Article 8]."[30] While the Protocol is designed to facilitate cooperation among flag States and boarding States, however, it does not alter the flag State's role in exercise exclusive flag State jurisdiction over ships flying its flag under Articles 92 and 94 of UNCLOS. Even when consenting to enforcement measures on board a ship flying its flag, the flag State may "subject its authorization to conditions ... including conditions relating to responsibility and the extent of effective measures to be taken."[31] The requesting State shall not take "additional measures without the express authorization of the flag State, except those necessary to relieve imminent danger to the lives of persons or those which derive from relevant bilateral or multilateral agreements."[32]

---

[26] Id., at Article 8.1.
[27] Id., at Article 8(2).
[28] Id.
[29] Id., at Article 8(3).
[30] Id., at Article 8(4).
[31] Id., at Article 8(5).
[32] Id.

Consistent with Articles 92(2) and 110 of UNCLOS, the Protocol authorizes any State to board and search a stateless vessel if the State concerned "has reasonable grounds to suspect that a vessel is engaged in the smuggling of migrants by sea and is without nationality or may be assimilated to a vessel without nationality...."[33] If evidence of smuggling is found during the boarding process, the State interdicting the suspect vessel may also "take appropriate measures in accordance with relevant domestic and international law."[34]

When taking action pursuant to Article 8, State authorities shall:

(a) Ensure the safety and humane treatment of the persons on board;
(b) Take due account of the need not to endanger the security of the vessel or its cargo;
(c) Take due account of the need not to prejudice the commercial or legal interests of the flag State or any other interested State;
(d) Ensure, within available means, that any measure taken with regard to the vessel is environmentally sound.[35]

If no evidence of smuggling is found, then the vessel shall be compensated for any loss or damage resulting from the action, so long it has not committed "any act justifying the measures taken."[36] In addition, Article 9(3) requires that any measure taken, adopted or implemented in accordance with Chapter II shall not interfere with or affect:

(a) The rights and obligations and the exercise of jurisdiction of coastal States in accordance with the international law of the sea; or
(b) The authority of the flag State to exercise jurisdiction and control in administrative, technical and social matters involving the vessel.

Finally, enforcement actions under Chapter II are limited to warships or military aircraft, or "other ships or aircraft clearly marked and identifiable as being on government service and authorized to that effect."[37]

In circumstances where irregular migrants are interdicted by government authorities of a destination or transit State, Article 18 of the Protocol requires the State of origin "to facilitate and accept, without undue or unreasonable delay,"[38] the return of migrants who are its nationals or permanent residents. Return of migrants to their State of origin shall be carried out "in an orderly manner and with due regard for the safety and dignity of the person."[39] However, nothing in the provisions on return affects any obligation "entered into under any other

---

[33] Id., Article 8(7).
[34] Id.
[35] Id., at Article 9(1).
[36] Id., at Article 9(2).
[37] Id., at Article 8(4).
[38] Id., at Article 18.
[39] Id., at Article 18(5).

applicable treaty, bilateral or multilateral, or any other applicable operational agreement or arrangement that governs... the return of persons..." who have been smuggled.[40] That is, States may make bilateral agreements to further implement Article 18. Italy and Libya, for example, completed an agreement that provides that the "Parties will exchange information on the flows of illegal migrants, on criminal organizations that promote them, on modus operandi and the routes taken and the specialized agencies in forging documents and passports, and the reciprocal assistance and cooperation in combating illegal migration, including the repatriation of illegal immigrants."[41]

The United States has similar agreements with The Bahamas, the Dominican Republic and Ecuador. For example, the U.S.-Bahamas Agreement provides that "The Bahamas agrees... to facilitate and accept without under or unreasonable delay the return... of migrants" that have Bahamian nationality, citizenship, or permanent residence.[42] Regardless of the citizenship status or nationality of the migrants, The Bahamas also agrees to give "due consideration" to requests made by U.S. law enforcement authorities to accept the return of migrants found on board ships registered in The Bahamas, vessels subject to the jurisdiction of The Bahamas or vessels operated by Bahamian nationals.[43]

19.5 IMO Initiatives

In the early-1990s, a string of tragic deaths of hundreds of irregular seaborne migrants prompted the International Maritime Organization (IMO) to explore the issue of migrant smuggling from the perspective of safety of life at sea. Working in the IMO's Maritime Safety Committee, the member States focused on developing standardized rules for addressing the problem, which culminated in the adoption of the *Interim Guidelines for Combating Unsafe Practices Associated with the Trafficking or Transport of Migrants by Sea* in December 1998. The guidelines were subsequently amended in 2001, and now request IMO Contracting Governments to accept a reporting requirement to generate better data on the scope of the problem and better inform decisions pertaining to humanitarian response and law enforcement.

---

[40] Id., at Article 18(8).
[41] Agreement between the Italian Government and the Transitional National Council of Libya, done at Rome, June 17, 2011, http://download.repubblica.it/pdf/2011/migrazione.pdf.
[42] Agreement between the Government of the United States of American and the Government of the Commonwealth of the Bahamas concerning Cooperation in Maritime Law Enforcement, done at Nassau, June 29, 2004, Article 11, http://www.state.gov/documents/organization/108940.pdf.
[43] Id.

19.5.1 Assembly Resolution A.773(18)

The incident involving the *Golden Venture* highlighted the unsafe conditions associated with the smuggling of migrants by sea. On June 6, 1993, the M/V *Golden Venture*, a Honduran-registered cargo ship carrying 300 illegal Chinese migrants ran aground off the coast of New York. Many of the undocumented aliens were forced by their smugglers to jump overboard into the water to evade apprehension by local authorities. Ten of the migrants died trying to reach the shore.

Five months later, the International Maritime Organization (IMO) took the first step in addressing the issue of unsafe practices associated with the smuggling of migrants by sea. The IMO Assembly adopted Resolution A.773(18), which constructed an overarching framework for states to work together to avoid maritime migrant smuggling tragedies.[44] The IMO noted with great concern that "incidents involving the smuggling of aliens on board ships and the serious problems associated with such activities for safety of life at sea" and the "numerous incidents involving the smuggling of aliens aboard ships have resulted in sickness, disease and death of the individuals concern."[45] Member Governments were called upon to, *inter alia*:

- cooperate to suppress unsafe practices associated with alien smuggling by sea;
- develop agreements and procedures to facilitate this cooperation;
- share information on ships believed to be engaged in such unsafe practices;
- authorize other States to conduct safety examinations on their behalf of ships entitled to fly their flag that are suspected of engaging in unsafe practices associated with alien smuggling; and
- take appropriate action against stateless vessels engage in alien smuggling.[46]

Clearly, however, the machinery of law and policy was moving too slowly. In 1996, 280 irregular South Asian migrants drowned when the M/V *Yioham*, a grossly overloaded Honduran-registered tramp steamer, collided with a smaller boat onto which they were being transferred, and which sank.[47] The smaller vessel had been stolen in Malta on December 24. The calamity occurred on Christmas Day in the waters between Sicily and Malta. Survivors arrived in Napflion, Greece, on December 29, 1996, and were placed in a warehouse and abandoned by their smugglers. Looking for food, many of the migrants wandered the local area until they were arrested by Greek law enforcement officials.

---

[44] IMO Doc. A.773(18), Enhancement of the Safety of Life at Sea by the Prevention and Suppression of Unsafe Practices Associated with the Smuggling of Aliens by Ships, Nov. 4, 1993.
[45] Id.
[46] Id.
[47] Raul Pedrozo, *International Initiatives to Combat Trafficking of Migrants by Sea*, in CURRENT MARITIME ISSUES AND THE INTERNATIONAL MARITIME ORGANIZATION (Myron H. Nordquist & John Norton Moore, eds. 1999).

19.5.2 Assembly Resolution A.867(20)

Following a request by Italy to reconsider the issue of unsafe practices associated with the smuggling of migrants on board M/V *Yioham*, the IMO Assembly revisited the issue in 1997 and adopted Resolution A.867(20).[48] The Resolution noted with concern that the use of substandard ships to traffic and transport irregular migrants had resulted in heavy loss of life. Resolution A.773(18) was renewed, and the appeal to member Governments to cooperate and develop agreements and procedures to suppress unsafe practices associated with migrant trafficking by sea was amplified. The UN Commission on Crime Prevention and Criminal Justice also had reviewed the issue of migrant smuggling in the context of a new international instrument to combat transnational organized crime. Similarly, IMO Resolution A.867(20) directed consideration of the issue of migrant smuggling as another key dimension of safety of life at sea. The Resolution recommended that the IMO Secretary-General:

> 7. ...ensure participation by IMO in the preparation of any draft convention or other instrument intended to combat the trafficking or transport of migrants by sea...;
> 8. ...bring...the outcome of the work of...[the IMO] on the matter, to the attention of the United Nations and other international organizations...with the recommendation that an international convention be concluded aiming at combating the trafficking or transport of migrants by sea.

Based on these recommendations, the issue of migrant smuggling was taken up at the 69th meeting of IMO Maritime Safety Committee (MSC 69) in May 1998. Italy proposed the adoption of an MSC Circular, *Guidelines for the Prevention and Suppression of Unsafe Practices Associated with the Trafficking or Transport of Migrants by Sea.*

19.5.3 Maritime Safety Committee Circular 896

The loss of life associated with migrant smuggling and the increase in the number of persons illegally coming ashore along the Italian coast led the Rome delegation to urge the IMO to consider a new "imperative that effective international measures be adopted urgently" to address the problem. After considerable debate in plenary session 69 of the Maritime Safety Committee on May 11–20, 1998, an informal group under U.S. leadership was created to offer a preliminary consideration of the Italian proposal. Although progress was made at MSC 69, the informal group was unable to complete its work. Therefore, MSC established a

---

[48] IMO Doc. A.867(20), Combating Unsafe Practices Associated with the Trafficking or Transport of Migrants by Sea, Nov. 27, 1997.

correspondence group, again under U.S. leadership, to work between sessions to further develop guidelines and to report back to MSC 70.[49]

Numerous States participated in the inter-sessional working group, including Denmark, France, Germany, Italy, Japan, the Russian Federation, Tunisia, the United Kingdom and the United States. In recognition that it would take time for the United Nations to negotiate the TOCC, the correspondence group agreed with a French proposal that MSC embark on a two-track approach to deal with the issue of migrant smuggling. The seventieth session of the MSC continued to work on preparing elements for consideration by the United Nations in development of the TOCC. While completion of the TOCC was pending, MSC 70 considered adoption of a non-binding circular to provide member Governments with interim measures to prevent and suppress unsafe practices associated with the trafficking and transport of irregular migrants by sea. MSC 70 agreed to this two-track approach and established a Drafting Group to finalize a non-binding circular in compliance with international law. MSC 70 also developed the elements of IMO's contribution to the UN's work on the TOCC.

MSC met again from December 7–11, 1998. Representatives from 20 nations, the UN Division for Ocean Affairs and the Law of the Sea, UN High Commissioner for Refugees (UNHCR), and the International Confederation of Free Trade Unions (ICFTU) participated in the Drafting Group. The group finalized the draft MSC circular and agreed that, rather than prepare a separate document, the entire circular would be forwarded to the United Nations for consideration at the first negotiating session of the TOCC in January 1999. MSC 70 approved draft Circular MSC/Circ.896 on December 16, 1998.[50]

The Circular provides non-binding measures for the prevention and suppression of unsafe practices associated with the trafficking and transport of migrants by sea, and it was adopted as an interim measure pending entry into force of the Migrant Smuggling Protocol to the TOCC.[51] MSC 73, which met from May 30 to June 8, 2001, amended the Circular.[52] The purpose of the circular is "to promote awareness and co-operation among Contracting Governments... so that they may address more effectively unsafe practices associated with the trafficking or transport of migrants by sea which have an international dimension."[53]

---

[49] Pedrozo, *International Initiatives to Combat Trafficking of Migrants by Sea*, in CURRENT MARITIME ISSUES AND THE INTERNATIONAL MARITIME ORGANIZATION (Nordquist & Moore, eds. 1999).

[50] Id.

[51] IMO Doc. MSC/Circ.896, Interim Measures for Combating Unsafe Practices Associated with the Trafficking or Transport of Migrants by Sea, Dec. 16, 1998.

[52] MSC/Circ.896/Rev.1, Interim Measures for Combating Unsafe Practices Associated with the Trafficking or Transport of Migrants by Sea, June 12, 2001.

[53] Id., para. 3.

The revised Circular defines "unsafe practices" as "any practice, which involves operating a ship that is obviously in conditions which violate fundamental principles of safety at sea, in particular those of the SOLAS Convention; or not properly manned, equipped or licensed for carrying passengers on international voyages, and thereby constitute a serious danger for the lives or the health of the persons on board, including the conditions for embarkation and disembarkation."[54] States are called on to take steps relating to maritime safety, in accordance with domestic and international law, to eliminate unsafe practices associated with the trafficking or transport of migrants by sea. State obligations include:

> .1 ensuring compliance with the International Convention for the Safety of Life at Sea, 1974, *as amended* (SOLAS);
> .2 collecting and disseminating information on ships believed to be engaged in unsafe practices associated with trafficking or transporting migrants;
> .3 taking appropriate action against masters, officers and crew members engaged in such unsafe practices; and
> .4 preventing any such ship:
> .1 from again engaging in unsafe practices; and
> .2 if in port, from sailing.[55]

Measures taken that are adopted or implemented pursuant to the Circular "should be in conformity with the international law of the sea and all generally accepted relevant international instruments, such as the United Nations 1951 Convention and the 1967 *Protocol Relating to the Status of Refugees*."[56] Through their activities that implement the measures, States should give due regard to:

> .1 the authority of the flag State to exercise jurisdiction and control in administrative, technical and social matters involving the ship; and
> .2 the rights and obligations of the coastal State.[57]

When taking measures against a ship, States are required to "take into account the need not to endanger the safety of human life at sea and the security of the ship and the cargo, or to prejudice the commercial and/or legal interests of the flag State or any other interested State."[58] Furthermore, States are called upon to cooperate to the fullest extent possible in the prevention and suppression of unsafe practices associated with the trafficking or transport of migrants by sea,

---

[54] Id., para. 2.3.
[55] Id., para. 4.
[56] Id., para. 5. *See also,* Convention Relating to the Status of Refugees, *opened for signature* July 28, 1951, 19 U.S.T. 6259, 189 U.N.T.S. 137; Protocol Relating to the Status of Refugees, *opened for signature* Jan. 31, 1967, *entered into force,* Oct. 4, 1967, 19 U.S.T. 6223,T.I.A.S. No. 6577, 606 U.N.T.S. 267, *reprinted in* 6 I.L.M. 78 (1967).
[57] MSC/Circ.896/Rev.1, para. 6.
[58] Id., para. 7.

in conformity with international law.[59] In particular, the Circular states that "it is consistent with international law for a flag State to authorize a vessel flying its flag to be boarded and inspected by a warship of another State" in accordance with the boarding procedures set out in the Circular. To facilitate ship boarding, information sharing and other cooperation, States may elect to enter into bilateral or regional agreements.[60]

The Circular also sets forth model boarding procedures based on historic principles of flag State jurisdiction on the high seas, universal jurisdiction over ships without flag registry (nationality), and the right of approach and visit.[61] Paragraph 11 authorizes a State to act if it has "reasonable grounds" to suspect that a ship:

    .1 is flying its flag or claiming its registry, or
    .2 is without nationality, or
    .3 though flying a foreign flag or refusing to show its flag is, in reality, of the same nationality as the State concerned,

is engaged in unsafe practices associated with the trafficking or transport of migrants by sea, ... [to] request the assistance of other States.... The States so requested should render such assistance as is reasonable under these circumstances.[62]

Paragraph 16 recognizes the assertion of universal jurisdiction over stateless vessels. The paragraph authorizes States to conduct a safety examination of any ship "when there are reasonable grounds to suspect [it] is engaged in unsafe practices associated with trafficking or transport of migrants by sea," and the intercepting vessel concludes in accordance with the international law of the sea that the ship is "without nationality, or has been assimilated to a ship without nationality."[63] If it is discovered that the ship has been engaged in unsafe practices, paragraph 16 also allows the boarding State to "take appropriate measures in accordance with relevant domestic and international law."[64]

The guidelines also recognize authority to board of foreign flagged vessels based on flag State consent. A State that has reasonable grounds to suspect that a ship "... flying the flag or displaying marks of registry of another State is engaged in unsafe practices associated with the trafficking or transport of migrants by sea may so notify the flag State, request confirmation of registry and, if confirmed, request authorization from the flag State to take appropriate measures in regard to that ship."[65] The flag State may authorize the requesting State to, *inter alia*:

---

[59] Id., para. 8.
[60] Id., paras. 9 and 10.
[61] Id., paras. 11–20. *See also*, UNCLOS, Articles 92 and 110.
[62] Id., para. 11.
[63] Id., para. 16.
[64] Id.
[65] Id., para. 12.

.1 board the ship;
.2 inspect and carry out a safety examination of the ship, and
.3 if evidence is found that the ship is engaged in unsafe practices, take appropriate action with respect to the ship, persons and cargo on board, as authorized by the flag State.

"A State which has taken any action in accordance with this paragraph should promptly inform the flag State concerned of the results of that action." If the ship is found to have been "engaged in unsafe practices associated with the trafficking or transport of migrants by sea," the boarding State should:

.1 immediately report the findings of the safety examinations... to the administration of the State whose flag the ship is entitled to fly or in which it is registered; and
.2 immediately consult on the further actions to be taken after giving or receiving reports on the ship involved.[66]

In situations where flag State consent is required, flag States also have a responsibility to "respond expeditiously to a request from another State to determine whether a ship that is claiming its registry or flying its flag is entitled to do so," as well as to any request to board the vessel.[67] However, paragraph 13 authorizes the flag State to "subject its authorization to conditions to be mutually agreed between it and the requesting State, including conditions relating to responsibility and to the extent of effective measures to be taken including the use of force." If limitations are placed on the boarding, the requesting "State shall take no additional actions without the express authorization of the flag State, except those necessary to relieve imminent danger or those that follow from relevant bilateral or multilateral agreements."[68]

Pursuant to paragraph 17, any action taken by the boarding State should:

.1 ensure the safety and the humanitarian handling of the persons on board and that any actions taken with regard to the ship are environmentally sound; and
.2 take appropriate action in accordance with relevant domestic and international law.[69]

Consistent with international law and SOLAS regulation I/19(c), port States are also required "to ensure that a ship involved in unsafe practices associated with the trafficking or transport of migrants by sea does not sail until it can proceed to sea without endangering the ship or persons on board, and to report promptly to the State whose flag the ship is entitled to fly, or in which it is registered, all incidents concerning such unsafe practices which come to their attention."[70] In

---

[66] Id., para. 15.
[67] Id., para. 14.
[68] Id., para. 13.
[69] Id., para. 17.
[70] Id., para. 18.

addition, the guidelines require that actions taken at sea pursuant to the Circular "be carried out only by warships or military aircraft, or other ships or aircraft clearly marked and identifiable as being on government service and authorized to that effect."[71]

The guidelines impose on Contracting Governments a reporting requirement. Paragraph 23 requires States to provide reports to the IMO on incidents and the measures taken against ships engaged in unsafe practices, as soon as possible, using the form provided in the Appendix to the guidelines. On a biannual basis, IMO disseminates the data provided by Contracting Governments. The First Biannual Report, which was released in February 2010, recorded 2,030, incidents since 1998, involving 77,853 migrants.[72] The Second Biannual report tabulated 103 incidents involving 12,661 migrants.[73] In 2011, there were 189 incidents involving 14,985 migrants.[74] These figures are likely to be inaccurate, however, due to rampant underreporting, as only Canada, Greece, Italy, and Turkey, provided data.

19.5.4 *Guidelines on the Treatment of Persons Rescued at Sea*

The IMO crafted *Guidelines on the Treatment of Persons Rescued at Sea* in 2004, and this development is indicated in the amendments to the Search and Rescue (SAR) Convention. The purpose of the guidelines is "to provide guidance to Governments and to shipmasters with regard to humanitarian obligations and obligations under the relevant international law relating to treatment of persons rescued at sea."[75] Specifically, the guidelines make clear that vessel Masters and Member States have corresponding obligations under international law in distress situations. In this regard, the Guidelines specify that "the obligation of the master to render assistance should complement the corresponding obligation of IMO Member Governments to co-ordinate and co-operate in relieving the master of the responsibility to provide follow up care of survivors and to deliver the persons retrieved at sea to a place of safety."[76]

---

[71] Id., para. 20.
[72] IMO Doc. MSC.3/Circ.18, Unsafe Practices Associated with the Trafficking or Transport of Migrants by Sea: First Biannual Report, Feb. 18, 2010.
[73] IMO Doc. MSC.3/Circ.20, Unsafe Practices Associated with the Trafficking or Transport of Migrants by Sea: Second Biannual Report, Dec. 16, 2011.
[74] IMO Doc. MSC.3/Circ.21, Unsafe Practices Associated with the Trafficking or Transport of Migrants by Sea: Annual Statistics for 2011, Jan. 5, 2012.
[75] IMO Doc. MSC.167(78), Guidelines on the Treatment of Persons Rescued at Sea, May 20, 2004, para. 1.1, *reprinted in* IMO Doc. MSC 78/26/Add.2, Annex 34, May 28, 2004.
[76] Id., para. 1.2.

The Government in control of the SAR region in which survivors are recovered is primarily responsible "to provide a place of safety, or to ensure that a place of safety is provided" for them within a reasonable time.[77]

Shipmasters are encouraged to:

> .1 understand and heed obligations under international law to assist persons in distress at sea (such assistance should always be carried out without regard to the nationality or status of the persons in distress, or to the circumstances in which they are found);
>
> .2 do everything possible, within the capabilities and limitations of the ship, to treat the survivors humanely and to meet their immediate needs . . .;
>
> .6 seek to ensure that survivors are not disembarked to a place where their safety would be further jeopardized; and
>
> .7 comply with any relevant requirements of the Government responsible for the SAR region where the survivors were recovered, or of another responding coastal State, and seek additional guidance from those authorities where difficulties arise in complying with such requirements.[78]

The guidelines also make clear, however, that "a ship should not be subject to undue delay, financial burden or other related difficulties after assisting persons at sea; therefore coastal States should relieve the ship as soon as practicable."[79] Prior to disembarkation, several factors should be taken into account, including "the situation on board the assisting ship, on scene conditions, medical needs, and availability of transportation or other rescue units."[80] Additionally, asylum-seekers and refugees recovered at sea should not be disembarked in territory where their lives or freedoms are threatened by a well-founded fear of persecution.[81]

Migrants should be disembarked at a "place of safety," which is defined as "a location where rescue operations are considered to terminate" and includes "a place where the survivors' safety of life is no longer threatened and where their basic human needs (such as food, shelter and medical needs) can be met."[82] A place of safety is also the "place from which transportation arrangements can be made for the survivors' next or final destination."[83] A place of safety may be on land or on board a "suitable vessel or facility at sea."[84] However, while the assisting ship may serve as a temporary place of safety, it should be relieved of the responsibility once alternative arrangements are made.[85]

---

[77] Id., para. 2.5.
[78] Id., para. 5.1.
[79] Id., para. 6.3.
[80] Id., para. 6.15.
[81] Id., para. 6.17.
[82] Id., para. 6.12.
[83] Id.
[84] Id., para. 6.14.
[85] Id., para. 6.13.

19.6 Duty to Assist

The human cost of migrant smuggling is staggering. Considered by their smugglers as a commodity, migrants are treated with little respect for human dignity. Forced to travel long distances in rough seas in over-crowded, unseaworthy vessels with insufficient food and water and poor sanitation, many migrants do not survive the journey. For example, the United Nations High Commissioner on Refugees (UNHCR) estimates that between 250,000–500,000 Vietnamese boat people died at sea as they fled North Vietnamese aggression at the end of the Vietnam War.[86]

Likewise, thousands of Cuban, Haitian and Dominican migrants have been lost at sea trying to reach South Florida or Puerto Rico. In 1994, an estimated 75 percent of Cuban immigrants died at sea as they attempted to cross the Florida Strait in makeshift rafts during the *Balsero* Crisis.[87] Each year nearly 2,000 African migrants die in the Mediterranean Sea while bound for Southern Europe.[88] In April 2011, 250 migrants died when their boat capsized in the Mediterranean after departing Libya en route to Italy. Another 25 Africans were found dead in August 2011 by the Italian Coast Guard in the hold of small ship that was crammed with nearly 300 migrants.[89] Interdiction of these unsafe vessels is justified on law enforcement grounds as well as humanitarian grounds.

The obligation to render assistance to those in peril or lost at sea is one of the oldest and most deeply-rooted maritime traditions. For centuries, seafarers have considered it a duty to assist fellow mariners in peril on the high seas. The moral obligation is codified in a several international agreements, as well as national laws and regulations, and it is considered to form part of customary international law.

19.7 Salvage Conventions

The duty to assist mariners in distress was recognized long before the adoption of the 1958 *High Seas Convention*. The obligation first appeared in a multilateral treaty in the 1910 *Convention for the Unification of Certain Rules of Law*

---

[86] R. J. Rummel, Death by Government 287 (1997).
[87] Ray Walser, Jena Baker McNeill & Jessica Zuckerman, The Human Tragedy of Illegal Immigration: Greater Efforts Needed to Combat Smuggling and Violence, The Heritage Foundation Backgrounder, No. 2568, June 22, 2011.
[88] United Nations Office of Drugs and Crime (UNODC) Report: The Role of Organized Crime in the Smuggling of Migrants from West Africa to the European Union (2011).
[89] Alessandra Rizzo, *25 migrants found dead on boat traveling to Italy*, Associated Press, Aug. 1, 2011 (25 African migrants died in the hold of a boat bound for Libya).

Respecting Assistance and Salvage at Sea.[90] Article 11 of the Convention provides that "every master is bound, so far as he can do so without serious danger to his vessel, her crew and her passengers, to render assistance to everybody, even though an enemy, found at sea in danger of being lost."[91] Article 11 also states that "the owner of a vessel incurs no liability by reason of contravention of the above provision."[92] Similar language was also included in Article 10 of the 1989 *International Convention on Salvage*:

> 1. Every master is bound, so far as he can do so without serious danger to his vessel and persons thereon, to render assistance to any person in danger of being lost at sea.
>
> * * *
>
> 3. The owner of the vessel shall incur no liability for a breach of the duty of the master under paragraph 1.

Subsection 2 of Article 10 imposes an obligation on State Parties to "adopt the measures necessary to enforce the duty set out in paragraph 1." In addition, although sovereign immune vessels are exempt from mandatory compliance with the Convention, Article 4 allows State Parties to voluntarily apply it to its warships and other non-commercial vessels owned or operated by the State. If a State decides to apply it to its sovereign immune vessels, Article 4(2) requires the Government to "notify the Secretary-General thereof specifying the terms and conditions of such application."[93] For example, pursuant to U.S. Navy Regulations (1990) and U.S. Coast Guard Regulations (1992), the U.S. Government imposes the obligation on its warships and other government non-commercial vessels.

19.8 International Convention for the Safety of Life at Sea

Among all of the international treaties concerning the safety of commercial ships, the SOLAS Convention is the most important. Initially adopted in 1914 in response to the *Titanic* disaster, subsequent versions of the treaty in 1929, 1948, 1960 and 1974 address virtually every aspect of safety of life at sea, including the duty to assist mariners in distress.

The obligation to provide assistance was originally contained in Article 45 of the 1929 Convention. Article 45 was replaced in 1948 with Regulation V/10, which remained in the 1960 and 1974 editions of the Convention. However, amend-

---

[90] Lassa Oppenheim, Ronald Francis Roxburgh & Sir Ronald Roxburgh, International Law: A Treatise § 271, at p. 432 (Longmans, Green & Co. 1920).

[91] 1910 Convention for the Unification of Certain Rules of Law relating to Assistance and Salvage at Sea, 212 CTS 178, U.S.T.S. 576, 37 Stat. 1658, U.K.T.S. No. 4 (1913).

[92] Id.

[93] International Convention on Salvage, Apr. 28, 1989, *entered into force* Sept. 6, 1991, IMO Doc. LEG/Conf.7/27, *reproduced in* 14 Law of the Sea Bull. 77 (Dec. 1989).

ments to the 1974 Convention in 2004 replaced Regulation V/10 with Regulation V/33.[94] Regulation V/33 establishes several new obligations and procedures that apply during distress situations. These provisions are fairly comprehensive. The authoritative nature of SOLAS means the core text is worth reproducing with only light edits:

1. The master of a ship at sea which is in a position to be able to provide assistance on receiving information from any source that persons are in distress at sea, is bound to proceed with all speed to their assistance, if possible informing them or the search and rescue service that the ship is doing so. This obligation to provide assistance applies regardless of the nationality or status of such persons or the circumstances in which they are found. If the ship receiving the distress alert is unable or, in the special circumstances of the case, considers it unreasonable or unnecessary to proceed to their assistance, the master must enter in the log-book the reason for failing to proceed to the assistance of the persons in distress, taking into account the recommendation of the Organization, to inform the appropriate search and rescue service accordingly.
    1.1. Contracting Governments shall coordinate and cooperate to ensure that masters of ships providing assistance by embarking persons in distress at sea are released from their obligations with minimum further deviation from the ships' intended voyage, provided that releasing the master of the ship from the obligations under the current regulation does not further endanger the safety of life at sea. The Contracting Government responsible for the search and rescue region in which such assistance is rendered shall exercise primary responsibility for ensuring such coordination and cooperation occurs, so that survivors assisted are disembarked from the assisting ship and delivered to a place of safety, taking into account the particular circumstances of the case and guidelines developed by the Organization. In these cases the relevant Contracting Governments shall arrange for such disembarkation to be effected as soon as reasonably practicable.
2. The master of a ship in distress or the search and rescue service concerned ... has the right to requisition one or more of those ships as the master of the ship in distress or the search and rescue service considers best able to render assistance, and it shall be the duty of the master or masters of the ship or ships requisitioned to comply with the requisition by continuing to proceed with all speed to the assistance of persons in distress.
3. Masters of ships shall be released from the obligation imposed by paragraph 1 on learning that their ships have not been requisitioned and that one or more other ships have been requisitioned and are complying with the requisition. This decision shall, if possible, be communicated to the other requisitioned ships and to the search and rescue service.
4. The master of a ship shall be released from the obligation ... on being informed ... that assistance is no longer necessary.

---

[94] MSC 78/26/Add.1, Annex 3, Resolution MSC.153(78), Adoption of Amendments to the International Convention for the Safety of Life at Sea, as amended, 1974, May 20, 2004.

5. The provisions of this regulation do not prejudice the Convention for the Unification of Certain Rules of Law Relating to Assistance and Salvage at Sea... particularly the obligation to render assistance imposed by article 11 of that Convention.
6. Masters of ships who have embarked persons in distress at sea shall treat them with humanity, within the capabilities and limitations of the ship.[95]

Paragraphs 1.1 and 6 were added as a result of the M/V *Tampa* incident, which occurred in August 2001. On August 24, 2001, the Norwegian freighter M/V *Tampa*, commanded by Captain Arne Rinnan, rescued 438 refugees, mostly Afghan nationals, from a 20-meter Indonesian fishing boat, the *Palapa 1*, about 140 kilometers north of Christmas Island. The *Palapa 1* was in extremis, as the ship was sinking. Indonesian authorities advised Captain Rinnan to disembark the refugees at Merak, the closest suitable port for disembarkation.

A delegation of five refugees, however, aggressively approached the master of the vessel and demanded that he alter course to Christmas Island, a non-self-governing territory of Australia. The Australian Government, however, denied a request to disembark the asylum seekers at Christmas Island. The Government of Australia stated that it did not have an obligation under international law to accept persons rescued at sea. Fearing that the refugees would harm his crew, the master repeated his request to disembark the refugees on Christmas Island. Although local Australian authorities provided food and medical assistance to the refugees, Rinnan's request was denied.

On August 29, Captain Rinnan declared an emergency and entered Australian territorial waters without permission. Canberra responded by deploying a detachment of commandos to prevent the ship from reaching land.[96] The refugees were subsequently transferred to the HMAS *Manoora* and transported to Nauru. Norway strongly protested the incident and argued that Australia had failed to comply with its international obligations. Oslo reported its complaint to the United Nations, United Nations High Commission for Refugees (UNHCR), and the IMO. The master was awarded Norway's highest civil honor and the crew of the M/V *Tampa* received the 2002 Nansen Refugee Award from the UNHCR.[97]

The incident served as the basis for amendments to SOLAS. The amended regulation requires governments to coordinate and cooperate "to ensure that masters

---

[95] SOLAS Regulation V/33.
[96] Vanda Carson & Natalie O'Brien, *The Storming of the Tampa*, THE AUSTRALIAN, Aug. 30, 2001, at 3 and ANDREAS SCHLOENHARDT, MIGRANT SMUGGLING: ILLEGAL MIGRATION AND ORGANIZED CRIME IN AUSTRALIA AND THE ASIA-PACIFIC REGION 84–89 (2003).
[97] Nansen Refugee Award Ceremony: Statement by Mr. Ruud Lubbers, United Nations High Commissioner for Refugees, on the occasion of the award of the Nansen Refugee Award for 2002 to Captain Arne F. Rinnan and the Crew of the M/V *Tampa* vessel, Oslo, June 20, 2002, http://www.unhcr.org/3d1732b14.html.

of ships providing assistance by embarking persons in distress at sea are released from their obligations with minimum further deviation from the ships' intended voyage...."[98] Ships that provide assistance also have an obligation to disembark persons rescued at sea to a place of safety "as soon as reasonably practicable."[99]

Like the 1989 Salvage Convention, however, SOLAS requirements do not apply to sovereign immune vessels. Regulation I/3 indicates that "the present Regulations, unless expressly provided otherwise, do not apply to: (i) Ships of war and troopships...."[100] Additionally, Regulation V/1 exempts "warships, naval auxiliaries or other ships owned or operated by a Contracting Government and used only on government non-commercial service" from the requirements of Chapter V. Such vessels, however, "are encouraged to act in a manner consistent, so far as reasonable and practicable, with this chapter."[101]

19.9 International Convention on Maritime Search and Rescue

The requirement to provide assistance to mariners in distress is also found in the 1979 *International Convention on Maritime Search and Rescue* (SAR Convention). Chapter 2 requires parties to ensure that assistance is "provided to any person in distress at sea ... regardless of the nationality or status of such a person or the circumstances in which the person is found."[102] "Rescue" is defined in the 1998 amendments to the Convention as "an operation to retrieve persons in distress, provide for their initial medical or other needs, and deliver them to a place of safety."[103]

Like SOLAS, the Annex to the SAR Convention was also amended after the M/V *Tampa* incident by adding a new paragraph to Chapter 3, which now provides:

> Parties shall coordinate and cooperate to ensure that masters of ships providing assistance by embarking persons in distress at sea are released from their obligations with minimum further deviation from the ships' intended voyage, provided that releasing the master of the ship from these obligations does not further endanger the safety of life at sea.[104]

The State Party responsible for SAR responsibilities in the region in which assistance is rendered has primary responsibility for coordination and cooperation so

---

[98] SOLAS Regulation V/33, para. 1.1.
[99] Id.
[100] SOLAS Regulation I/3.
[101] SOLAS Regulation V/1.
[102] International Convention on Maritime Search and Rescue, Apr. 27, 1979, 405 U.N.T.S. 97, para. 2.1.10 [Hereinafter SAR Convention].
[103] Id., at Annex, Chapter 1, para. 1.3.2.
[104] Id., at Paragraph 3.1.9.

that survivors are properly assisted and disembarked to a place of safety. Furthermore, rescued persons are assured quick transportation to safety, as "the relevant Parties shall arrange for such disembarkation to be effected as soon as reasonably practicable."[105]

19.10 Refugee Convention

The Migrant Smuggling Protocol provides that "nothing in this Protocol shall affect the other rights, obligations and responsibilities of States and individuals under international law, including international humanitarian law and international human rights law and, in particular, where applicable, the 1951 Convention and the 1967 Protocol relating to the Status of Refugees and the principle of *non-refoulement* as contained therein."[106] Similarly, paragraph 5 of the IMO Interim Guidelines requires that any measures taken "should be in conformity with the international law of the sea and all generally accepted relevant international instruments, such as the United Nations 1951 Convention and the 1967 *Protocol Relating to the Status of Refugees*."

The 1951 Refugee Convention defines the term "refugee" as a person who:

(1) Has been considered a refugee under the Arrangements of 12 May 1926 and 30 June 1928 or under the Conventions of 28 October 1933 and 10 February 1938, the Protocol of 14 September 1939 or the Constitution of the International Refugee Organization;
(2) Decisions of non-eligibility taken by the International Refugee Organization during the period of its activities shall not prevent the status of refugee being accorded to persons who fulfill the conditions of paragraph 2 of this section;
(3) As a result of events occurring before 1 January 1951 and owing to well-founded fear of being persecuted for reasons of race, religion, nationality, membership of a particular social group or political opinion, is outside the country of his nationality and is unable or, owing to such fear, is unwilling to avail himself of the protection of that country; or who, not having a nationality and being outside the country of his former habitual residence as a result of such events, is unable or, owing to such fear, is unwilling to return to it.[107]

If a person has more than one nationality, then the term "country of his nationality shall mean each of the countries of which he is a national, and a person shall not be deemed to be lacking the protection of the country of his nationality if,

---

[105] IMO Doc. MSC.155(78), Adoption of Amendments to the International Convention on Maritime Search and Rescue, 1979, as amended, May 20, 2004, MSC 78/26/Add.1 Annex 5.
[106] Migrant Smuggling Protocol, Article 19.
[107] Convention Relating to the Status of Refugees, July 28, 1951, 189 U.N.T.S. 150, Article 1 [Hereinafter 1951 Refugee Convention].

without any valid reason based on well-founded fear, he has not availed himself of the protection of one of the countries of which he is a national."[108] The 1967 Protocol slightly modifies this rule as follows:

> 2. For the purpose of the present Protocol, the term "refugee" shall, except as regards the application of paragraph 3 of this article, mean any person within the definition of article 1 of the Convention as if the words "As a result of events occurring before 1 January 1951" [and the words] "... as a result of such events," in article 1... were omitted.[109]

The Convention also prohibits States from imposing "penalties, on account of their illegal entry or presence, on refugees who, coming directly from a territory where their life or freedom was threatened in the sense of article 1, enter or are present in their territory without authorization, provided they present themselves without delay to the authorities and show good cause for their illegal entry or presence."[110] States may not apply restrictions "to the movements of such refugees... other than those which are necessary and such restrictions shall only be applied until their status in the country is regularized or they obtain admission into another country."[111] Finally, States "shall allow such refugees a reasonable period and all the necessary facilities to obtain admission into another country."[112]

Article 32 of the Convention restricts States from expelling a refugee lawfully in their territory, except on "grounds of national security or public order." In this regard, expulsions "shall be only in pursuance of a decision reached in accordance with due process of law."[113] Furthermore, unless required by compelling reasons of national security, "the refugee shall be allowed to submit evidence to clear himself," and to effect an appeal.[114] States are also required to "allow such a refugee a reasonable period within which to seek legal admission into another country."[115] However, States may "reserve the right to apply during that period such internal measures as they may deem necessary."[116]

Article 33 prohibits *refoulement* (return) of a refugee to areas "where his life or freedom would be threatened on account of his race, religion, nationality, membership of a particular social group or political opinion." The prohibition

---

[108] Id., at Article 1.
[109] Protocol relating to the Status of Refugees, Dec. 16, 1967, 606 U.N.T.S. 267 [Hereinafter 1967 Refugee Protocol].
[110] 1951 Refugee Convention, Article 31.
[111] Id.
[112] Id.
[113] Id., at Article 32.
[114] Id.
[115] Id.
[116] Id.

on *refoulement*, however, does not apply to refugees for whom there are "reasonable grounds for regarding as a danger" to public security, such as having been convicted of a "serious crime."

19.11 The U.S. Experience in Law and Practice

The U.S. Code codifies the duty in international law to provide assistance to persons in distress at sea:

> A master or individual in charge of a vessel shall render assistance to any individual found at sea in danger of being lost, so far as the master or individual in charge can do so without serious danger to the master's or individual's vessel or individuals on board.[117]

Failure to provide the required assistance is a criminal offense, subjecting the master or other person in charge to a maximum penalty of two years in prison and a fine of $1,000.[118] The legal sanctions for failure to act, however, do "not apply to a vessel of war or a vessel owned by the United States Government appropriated only to a public service." Nonetheless, Department of Defense and U.S. Coast Guard regulations impose a similar obligation on commanding officers of U.S. warships, naval auxiliaries or other U.S. public vessels. For example, U.S. Navy Regulations provide that:

> insofar as can be done without serious danger to the ship or crew, the commanding officer or the senior officer present as appropriate shall
>
> a. proceed with all possible speed to the rescue of persons in distress if informed of their need for assistance, insofar as such action may reasonably be expected of him or her;
> b. render assistance to any person found at sea in danger of being lost;
> c. afford all reasonable assistance to distressed ships and aircraft; and
> d. render assistance to the other ship, after a collision, to her crew and passengers and, where possible, inform the other ship of his or her identity.[119]

Coast Guard commanders have a similar obligation:

> * * *
>
> B. Upon receiving information that a vessel or aircraft is in distress within the area of operation of the unit, the commanding officer shall, whenever it is appropriate to do so, assist such vessel or aircraft as soon as possible....
> C. In rendering assistance during any distress case, the commanding officer shall aid the distressed vessel or aircraft and its passengers and crew until such time as it

---

[117] 46 U.S.C. § 2304(a)(1).
[118] 46 U.S.C. § 2406.
[119] Dep't of the Navy, U.S. Navy Regulations, Article 0925(1) (1990).

is able to proceed safely, or until such time as further Coast Guard assistance is no longer required.[120]

* * *

A. Unless other directed, the commanding officer of a ship under way shall proceed immediately toward the scene of any reported distress within the range of operation....
B. ...Except when ordered or authorized not to proceed, the commanding officer [of a ship in port] shall proceed, as soon as possible, to the scene of any reported distress within that area of operation....
C. In rendering aid, the commanding officer shall use sound discretion and shall not unnecessarily jeopardize the vessel or the lives of the personnel assigned to it.
D. Emergency assistance shall be rendered to vessels or aircraft of a foreign state at peace with the United States.
E. In giving assistance, the commanding officer shall not interfere with private enterprise, though assistance may be given to private efforts, and shall do so when necessary....
F. Having due regard for the health of personnel in the command, the commanding officer shall take on board distressed seamen of the United States, shipwrecked persons, and persons requiring medical care. The assisted persons shall be furnished rations and may be transported to the nearest or most convenient port of the United States.... The commanding officer shall assist distressed vessels and seamen of countries with which the United States is at peace.[121]

Two incidents from the 1980s involving Vietnamese boat people illustrate the importance that the United States places on this long-standing humanitarian requirement to provide assistance to people in distress at sea and obligations under the international law of the sea.

19.11.1 *USS Morton* (DD 948)

On June 9, 1982, the U.S. Navy destroyer *USS Morton* (DD 948) encountered a 25-foot open sampan as it bobbed in the South China Sea, about 100 nautical miles from Thailand. Eighteen Vietnamese men were crammed on board the small, wooden, flat-bottomed boat. Prior to the ship's deployment to participate in a naval exercise with the Royal Thai Navy, the commanding officer had received verbal instructions from his squadron commander that he was not to pick up any Vietnamese boat people.

Commanding officers were only authorized to provide food, fuel, water, and directions to the nearest land. The rationale for the orders was that picking up refugees would handicap the warships in the accomplishment of their operational tasking. The refugee camps in Southeast Asia, and especially in Thailand, Hong Kong, and the Philippines, were already overflowing with Vietnamese "boat people." Rescuing boat people was thought to only encourage even more refugees

---

[120] U.S. Coast Guard, Commandant Instruction (COMDTINST) M5000.3B, para. 4-1-7.
[121] U.S. Coast Guard Regulations 4-2-5 (1992).

to take to the sea in dangerous craft. Many of the boat people were victims of pirates who believed the refugees were carrying gold, cash, or jewelry.

Despite orders from the squadron commander, the commanding officer of the ship, Commander Corwin "Al" Bell, decided to take on board the *Morton* the Vietnamese, as they appeared to be in declining health. One day later, the warship encountered a second boatload of Vietnamese refugees in the South China Sea, this time in a 35-foot wooden fishing boat. The fishing vessel was packed with 52 men, women and children.[122] The small boat was taking on water in rough seas and the weather was worsening due to an impending storm, so the commanding officer had all of the refugees brought on board the ship. Three days later the *Morton* arrived in Subic Bay, Philippines where the refugees were turned over to Philippine authorities and placed in a refugee camp on Bataan. For their compassionate action, the crew of the *Morton* were awarded the Humanitarian Service Medal.

19.11.2   USS Dubuque (LPD 8)

Compare the case of the *USS Morton* rescue with the incident involving the *USS Dubuque* (LPD 8) six years later.[123] On June 10, 1988, the *Dubuque* came across a boatload of 80 Vietnamese refugees adrift in a Chinese-style junk in the South China Sea. The *Dubuque* was en route to the Persian Gulf to assume minesweeping duties, a high priority mission at the time in light of the fact that the *USS Roberts* (FFG 58) had struck an Iranian mine in the Gulf in April 1988 during the "tanker war" and the subsequent U.S. action, *Operation Praying Mantis*. The *Dubuque* was also carrying a contingent of 900 Marines bound for the Persian Gulf, as the prospect of a U.S.-Iran naval war loomed.

Unknown to Captain Alexander Balian, the commanding officer of the U.S. warship, the junk had been adrift for 19 days due to engine failure. The vessel originally carried 110 passengers, 30 of whom already had died before the *Dubuque* encountered the vessel.

Standing orders for U.S. warships operating in the Pacific Fleet at the time included:

- U.S. Navy Regulation article 0925—A commanding officer must render assistance to any person found at sea in danger of being lost.
- Commander, U.S. Seventh Fleet Operations Order (COMSEVENTHFLT OPORDER) 201—The natural inclination of mariners, the customs and traditions of the sea,

---

[122] Tara Bahrampour, *Emotional Rescue, Emotional Reunion*, WASH. POST, May 15, 2011, at C1.

[123] Jon Swain, *Boat People Kill and Eat Children to Survive; Vietnamese Refugees Turned to Murder after being Left at Sea by US Navy*, The Sunday Times (London), Nov. 20, 1988, at 27.

and Navy Regulations require U.S. Navy ships to render aid to vessels and persons found in distress. In those instances wherein relief of persons in life endangering circumstances cannot be accomplished, by repair to boats, re-provisioning or navigational assistance, rescue is normally by means of embarkation.

As the *Dubuque* approached the junk, the Officer of the Deck (OOD) and the Junior Officer of the Deck (JOOD) observed the people on the boat waving pieces of white cloth. One of the boat people jumped into the water. The OOD immediately notified the captain. The warship approached the junk. When the *Dubuque* was within 500 yards of the craft, more than ten refugees jumped into the water, which prompted several of the crew members on board the *Dubuque* to throw life jackets into the water. The captain immediately ordered the crew to stop throwing life jackets into the water and instructed them to prevent the refugees from boarding the ship.

Captain Balian ordered his executive officer (XO) to take a small team in the ship's motor whaleboat to check out the situation on the junk. One of the members of the team spoke Vietnamese, but very poorly. The XO reported back to the captain that the vessel had a makeshift sail, but that it did not have an engine. The ship appeared to be seaworthy. The XO also reported that the junk had left Vietnam seven days ago, that 20 people had already died on the voyage, and that the remaining 60 persons on board the boat looked emaciated and distressed.

The captain reasoned that embarking the refugees on board *Dubuque* would endanger his mission by adding considerable delay to his arrival in the Persian Gulf. He was concerned that the refugees might infect the crew with communicable disease or threaten their physical security. Finally, he also believed that the refugees would be able to travel the remaining 200 miles to the Philippines in seven days, since they had been at sea for seven days and had already travelled 200 miles. The Captain was no stranger to such encounters at sea, as he had rescued Vietnamese boat people on two previous occasions. After evaluating his options, Captain Balian elected to provide the Vietnamese refugees with sufficient supplies rather than bring them aboard the warship. The *Dubuque* transferred to the junk 300 pounds of fruit, 107 pounds of canned food, 60 pounds of uncooked rice and 50 gallons of fresh water, and a navigational chart with coordinates plotted for the Philippines.

As a result of a series of miscommunications between the U.S. interpreter and the refugees, however, Captain Balian was unaware of several significant factors that may have affected his decision. The boat had an operational engine during the first few days of the trip, and the vessel had been adrift for 17 days, not seven. As a result of these errors, the captain miscalculated the distance the junk travelled by sail alone. This fatal error led the captain to miscalculate how long it would take the boat people to reach the Philippines, and therefore the amount of food they would need for the journey was incorrectly figured. Finally, there were still 80 refugees on board the junk, rather than 60—again affecting the critical calculation of food and water.

After the *Dubuque* left the scene, the junk drifted for 19 more days. Finally, a Filipino fishing vessel rescued the junk. Of the original 110 refugees that left Vietnam, only 52 survived. The food that had been provided by the *Dubuque* lasted for only a few days. Those that lived resorted to cannibalism to survive.

As a result of his failure to act to rescue the refugees, Captain Balian was held responsible for the tragedy and faced criminal charges at General Courts-Martial. The military court found Captain Balian guilty of dereliction of duty for failure to give adequate assistance to the refugees. The officer was awarded a career-ending letter of reprimand, and he was relieved of command.

19.11.3   *U.S. Counter-Migrant Smuggling Initiatives*

As a preferred destination country for undocumented migrants, the United States has considerable experience dealing with irregular migration. Thousands of irregular migrants, primarily from Cuba, Haiti, Mexico, China, Ecuador and the Dominican Republic, attempt to enter the United States illegally each year by sea. The majority of these migrants rely on organized criminal groups to arrange their entry. Billions of dollars are spent each year in law enforcement operations and social services.

As the primary maritime law enforcement agency, the U.S. Coast Guard is tasked with interdicting irregular migrants at sea. Migrants that are interdicted at sea are quickly returned to their countries of origin without incurring all of the procedural time and expense associated with repatriating a foreign national that successfully enters the United States. Between 1982 and 2011, the U.S. Coast Guard interdicted 240,000 illegal migrants at sea.

The Coast Guard's migrant interdiction mission gained high visibility in 1980 when Fidel Castro announced that anyone that wanted to leave Cuba was free to do so. During the *Mariel Boatlift*, over 124,000 undocumented Cuban immigrants entered the United States by sea. In response to the Boatlift and the growing number of Haitian migrants attempting to enter the United States by sea, President Reagan issued Presidential Proclamation 4865 on September 29, 1981, which suspended the entry of undocumented aliens traveling into the United States from the high seas, and he ordered the interdiction of all vessels carrying such aliens.[124]

Executive Order 12324 was issued the same day, and it provided instructions to the Coast Guard to interdict vessels engaged in "irregular transportation of persons or violations of United States law or the law of a country with which the United States has an arrangement authorizing such action."[125] Interdiction

---

[124] Pres. Proc. 4865, High Seas Interdiction of Illegal Aliens, Sept. 29, 1981, 46 FR 48107, 3 C.F.R., 1981 Comp., p. 50.
[125] Executive Order 12324, Interdiction of Illegal Aliens, Sept. 29, 1981, 46 FR 48109, 3 C.F.R., 1981 Comp., p. 180.

authority was limited to vessels of the United States, stateless vessels and vessels of foreign nations with whom the United States had arrangements that gave U.S. authority to stop and board such ships. In addition, a bilateral agreement between the United States and Haiti allowed the U.S. Coast Guard to board and inspect Haitian-flagged vessels on the high seas. Between 1982 and 1991, the Coast Guard interdicted nearly 32,000 illegal migrants.

In 1991, President Jean-Bertrand Aristide was ousted from power by a military coup. The increase in illegal Haitian migration to the United States convinced President Bush to issue Executive Order 12807, which revoked Executive Order 12324.[126] The new order directed the Coast Guard to interdict undocumented migrants at sea and return them to their country of origin. Again, maritime interdiction authority was limited to vessels of the United States, stateless vessels, and vessels of foreign nations with whom the United States had arrangements and delegated authority by the flag State to stop and board such vessels.

The following year Operation *Able Manner* was launched to interdict migrants fleeing Haiti. Between 1991 and 1994, when the operation was terminated, the Coast Guard interdicted nearly 70,000 Haitian migrants in the Windward Passage between Haiti and Cuba. Haitian migrants interdicted at sea were also automatically repatriated to Port-au-Prince unless they qualified for refugee status.

In 1994, Operation *Able Vigil* commenced to stop a second mass migration from Cuba—the *Balsero* Crisis—after Castro announced that Cuban authorities would not prevent Cubans from leaving the country by sea. Prior to 1994, any Cuban refugees picked up at sea were brought to the United States and allowed to remain. Beginning in 1995, however, Cubans interdicted at sea were returned to Cuba unless they already qualified for asylum.[127] Under the *Cuba-U.S. Migration Accord*, Cuba agreed not to take adverse action against returnees as a consequence of their attempt to emigrate illegally. The U.S. Coast Guard interdicted nearly 39,000 Cuban rafters during the operation.

With the implementation of the "wet foot, dry foot" policy in 1995, Cuban migrants have relied on the assistance of organized smugglers to reach U.S. soil. In many cases, the $10,000 fee for transport to the United States is paid on behalf of the immigrants by relatives already living in the United States. Smugglers have also changed their *modus operandi*, island hopping from the Dominican Republic to Puerto Rico and then into the continental United States, to avoid Coast Guard patrols in the Florida Strait.

The Dominican Republic is also a major source country for irregular migration to the United States. Thousands of Dominicans have attempted to cross the

---

[126] Exec. Ord. 12807, Interdiction of Illegal Aliens, May 24, 1992 and Exec. Ord. 12807 was amended in 2003 by Exec. Ord. 13287, 68 FR 10619 Feb. 28, 2003.
[127] R. WALSER, J. MCNEILL & J. ZUCKERMAN, THE HUMAN TRAGEDY OF ILLEGAL IMMIGRATION: GREATER EFFORTS NEEDED TO COMBAT SMUGGLING AND VIOLENCE, THE HERITAGE FOUNDATION BACKGROUNDER, No. 2568, June 22, 2011.

Mona Passage between the Dominican Republic and Puerto Rico on homemade boats known as *Yolas*. Most of these migrants are assisted by organized criminal trafficking organizations.

Between April 1, 1995 and October 1, 1997, the Coast Guard conducted Operation *Able Response* to interdict irregular migrants from the Dominican Republic. During this period, the Coast Guard intercepted over 9,500 migrants at sea. Like Haitian migrants, illegal aliens from the Dominican Republic were automatically repatriated to the Dominican Republic unless they qualified for refugee status.

In addition to the large influx of illegal migrants from Caribbean countries and Mexico, irregular migration from Asia, particularly China, also poses a significant challenge for the United States. Chinese migrants, in particular, rely on well-organized, extremely violent, smugglers known as "Snakeheads" to gain illegal entry into the United States. After the long sea journey across the Pacific to the United States in over-crowded, unsafe boats, the migrants are transferred to smaller vessels for the final leg of the journey to shore. Alternatively, the migrants may disembark in a Central American country, where they are turned over to other organized smuggling groups that facilitate their entry into the United States via Mexico. Chinese migrants have also attempted to enter the United States via Guam. Since 1990, the Coast Guard has interdicted nearly 7,000 illegal Chinese migrants at sea.

The United States has bilateral maritime migrant agreements with The Bahamas (2004), the Dominican Republic (2003) and Ecuador (2006). The agreements are similar in nature and contain provisions to facilitate the boarding and inspection of vessels suspected of engaging in the smuggling of migrants by sea. For example, if a suspect vessel encountered seaward of the territorial sea of another nation claims U.S. or Bahamian nationality, Article 8(1) of the U.S.-Bahamas agreement authorizes one Party to request that the other Party:

> a. confirm the claim of nationality ... and
> b. if such claim is confirmed, the requested Party may:
>   i. authorize the boarding and search of the suspect vessel, cargo and the persons found on board by law enforcement officials of the requesting Party; and
>   ii. if evidence of illicit traffic, the unsafe transport of migrants, or the smuggling of migrants is found, authorize the law enforcement officials of the requesting Party to detain the vessel, cargo and persons on board pending instructions from the law enforcement authorities of the requested Party as to the exercise of jurisdiction in accordance with Article 10 of this Agreement.

Additionally, Article 8(3) requires that the requested Party "make best efforts to respond to requests ... as expeditiously as possible, and in any case shall confirm or refute the claim of nationality within four (4) hours of the initial request."[128]

---

[128] Agreement between the Government of the United States of American and the Government of the Commonwealth of the Bahamas concerning Cooperation in Maritime Law Enforcement, June 29, 2004.

Migrant smuggling by sea continues to pose a serious threat to the United States. Additionally, the human tragedy associated with these illicit operations is overwhelming when one considers the significant loss of life at sea, the appalling conditions in which migrants are smuggled, and their eventual exploitation by criminal organizations once they reach their destination country.

19.12 Conclusion

Smuggling of migrants by organized criminal groups presents the international community with one of its most critical challenges. Widespread economic and social disparity in the developing nations will continue to provide a strong incentive for irregular migrants to solicit the assistance of transnational criminal organizations to facilitate their illegal entry into the industrialized States. Moreover, huge profits generated from these operations provide a strong incentive for smugglers to continue to provide this service.

Thousands of lives are placed at risk each day governments fail to act to suppress maritime human trafficking. Much to their credit, the IMO and UNODC have taken concrete steps to combat this new form of slave trade by adopting the *Guidelines to Combat Unsafe Practices Associated with the Trafficking or Transport of Migrants by Sea* and the *Migrant Smuggling Protocols*. More needs to be done by individual States to implement these instruments. In this regard, UNODC has developed a *Model Law against the Smuggling of Migrants* to "promote and assist the efforts of Member States to become party to and implement the United Nations Convention against Transnational Organized Crime and the Protocols thereto ..., in particular ... the Protocol against the Smuggling of Migrants by Land, Sea and Air, supplementing the Convention."[129] All of the provisions required or recommended by the Protocol to be included in national legislation are contained in the Model Law. National laws also may include requirements from international human rights law, international humanitarian law, and refugee law.

The Model Law cautions, however, that the provisions of the *Migrant Smuggling Protocol* "be read and applied together with the provisions of the Convention and that domestic legislation be developed to implement not only the Protocol but also the Convention."[130] Many of the crimes, which include participation in an organized criminal group, corruption, obstruction of justice and money laundering, are contained in the TOCC. Additionally, the Model Law is not intended to be a stand-alone instrument. Stronger national legislation to implement the TOCC and its Protocols is necessary for it to become more effective.

---

[129] United Nations Office on Drugs and Crime, Model Law against the Smuggling of Migrants (2010).
[130] Id.

TWENTY

MARITIME PIRACY AND ARMED ROBBERY AT SEA

The International Maritime Organization (IMO) reports that in 2012, there were 297 attempted or successful acts of piracy and armed robbery against ships, decrease of 142 over the figure for 2011.[1] East Africa and the South China Sea were the areas most affected in 2010 and 2011, followed by the Indian Ocean and West Africa (principally the Gulf of Guinea). Somalia has been a hotbed of piracy, and incidents off the coast of East Africa increased from 172 in 2010 to 223 in 2011, returning to the same level as in 2009 (222 incidents).[2] In 2012, however, the incidence of piracy off the coast of Somalia plummeted to just 49 attacks.

Since 2005, when Somali piracy emerged as an issue affecting international freedom of navigation, gangs operating from Puntland increased their operational range each year. Mother ships are used to stage attacks farther out to sea, which has helped pirates expand their range nearly to the coast of India. The number of attacks in the Arabian Sea increased from 16 in 2010 to 28 in 2011.[3] The number of incidents in the Indian Ocean decreased from 77 to 63 in 2011, although the reduction mostly was a consequence of three factors: greater implementation by the shipping industry of self-protective measures ("Best Management Practices"), air and naval patrols conducted by the North Atlantic Treaty Organization, the U.S.-sponsored Combined Maritime Force, and the European Union, and the increased use of privately contracted armed security on board ships. Thus, while the number of attacks against maritime shipping off East Africa remains stubbornly high, the success rate has been significantly reduced. In 2010, Somali pirates had a 29 percent success rated. Out of a total of 172 ships

---

[1] IMO Doc. MSC.4/Circ.180, Reports on Acts of Piracy and Armed Robbery against Ships, Annual Report, 2011, Mar. 1, 2012 and Int'l Maritime Bureau 2012 Annual Report.
[2] IMO Doc. MSC. 4/Circ. 180, para. 6.
[3] Id.

that were attacked, 50 were successfully hijacked. By 2011, however, there were 286 attacks, but only 33 resulted in a successful hijacking—a success ratio of just 11.5 percent.[4] In 2012, only 11 ships were successfully attacked.

Maritime security law has been a key enabler of the regional and global effort to suppress international piracy. In particular, the threat of piracy off the coast of East Africa and in Southeast Asia has galvanized the international community to develop more effective responses. One important element of this struggle is to understand—and build upon—the international law of piracy.

20.1 The Historical Roots of the Law of Piracy

Alfred P. Rubin's venerable study of the historic law of piracy, published by the Naval War College in 1988, is still the best single volume on the subject.[5] Rubin's magisterial book traces the meaning of the word "piracy" from its Indo-European root (*per*, which means "risk," and from which comes the modern English word, "peril"), through Latin (*pirata*) and Greek (*peirato*).[6] In its early conception in the Roman world, *peirato* was applied to "freebooters," although the term was not restricted to brigands. Piracy often was a way of warfare conducted by commerce raiding communities.[7] The word *peirato* was applied to littoral Mediterranean societies "operating in ways that had been accepted as a legitimate for at least a millennium."[8] The rise of Roman hegemony, however, and the monopoly on the use of force by the state made the continued existence of seaside pirate communities unacceptable.[9] Roman sovereignty swallowed up the independent pirate states of the Eastern Mediterranean, including the Aegean islands, Crete, the Dodecanese, and much of Asia Minor.

The legal concept of piracy emerged from some of the early jurist opinions appearing in the Justinian Digest of 534 A.D. Paulus, for example, wrote *circa* 230 A.D. that "persons who have been captured by pirates or robbers remain [legally] free."[10] The classical Roman conception of piracy did not originally carry the implication of criminality or violation of international law, as it was related

---

[4] Id., Annex 5.
[5] ALFRED P. RUBIN, THE LAW OF PIRACY (International Law Studies No. 63, U.S. Naval War College, 1988), *reprinted as*, ALFRED P. RUBIN, THE LAW OF PIRACY (2d. ed. 1998). *See also*, JAMES KRASKA, CONTEMPORARY MARITIME PIRACY: INTERNATIONAL LAW, STRATEGY, AND DIPLOMACY AT SEA (2011).
[6] RUBIN, at 1–4.
[7] Id., at 5–6.
[8] Id., at 6.
[9] Id., at 6–7.
[10] Id., at 11, note 56, *citing Corpus Juris Civilis* (Mommsen & Krueger text, Kunkel ed., 1954), XLIX.15.19.2, Paulus, *On Sabinus*, Bk. Xvi: "*A piratis aut latronibus capti liberi permant.*" *See also*, J. B. SCOTT, THE CIVIL LAW 184 (1932).

more to a way of life and a method of warfare—much as we use the word "Viking" or "Norsemen" to describe Nordic raiding civilizations of the early-Middle Ages. This usage carried into the Mediterranean, where the Barbary corsairs along the North Africa Maghreb—Algiers, Rabat, Tripoli and Tunis—were considered warring states rather than criminal enclaves. By the end of the sixteenth century, Muslim raiders and Christian orders of knighthood operated flourishing slave markets in Malta, Italy, and North Africa.

20.1.1 *Mediterranean Sea and the Rise of the Nation State*

For five hundred years, Christian and Islamic soldiers, sailors, and galley slaves, fought a protracted maritime war throughout the Mediterranean Sea from the era of the Crusades in the eleventh century to the sixteenth century. Piracy was a major element of the warfare, and the rowed, oared galley the principal war-fighting platform. In 1291, the Christians lost their last major foothold on the Levant when Acre fell to Islam. Mehmet II conquered Byzantium in 1453. The Catholic Hapsburgs in Spain and a collection of Venetian traders, Franks, and Italian principalities fought a series of epic battles against the Ottoman Turks for the control of the Eastern Mediterranean. The contest culminated in the Siege of Malta in 1565 and the naval battle of Lepanto in 1571.[11]

The Christian victories presaged the shift from rowed galleys to wind driven sailing ships and the introduction of dozens of crew-served guns on board large *galleasses*—an intermediate warship between a rowed galley and the later full-fledged man of war, the precursor to the galleon, which became the ship of the line. The new warships were more revolutionary than the Dreadnought-class of British battleships on the eve of the First World War and were used with dispositive effect at the Battle of Lepanto to route the Ottoman fleet. With the emergence of the sail-driven galleon, the Portuguese and Spanish discovered and exploited the New World, and they were followed and challenged for maritime supremacy by the Dutch and then the English. These European fleets came to dominate the globe, and piracy was separated into two categories: lawful privateering under license, a supplementary form of naval warfare, and illegal, unlicensed crime.[12]

20.1.2 *Renaissance Scholars Shape the Law*

By 1588 and the defeat of the Spanish Armada, the Royal Navy dominated the seas. The term "pirates" began to displace "Spaniards" as the villain in popular English imagination, much as "terrorists" displaced "Soviets" as the focus of fear in the United States between the end of the Cold War and the attacks of 9/11. The

---

[11] Roger Crowley, Empires of the Sea: The Siege of Malta, the Battle of Lepanto, and the Contest for the Center of the World, parts II & III (2008).
[12] Rubin, at 15.

Italian legal scholar Alberico Gentili, while teaching at Oxford, wrote in 1598 that only states have the legal right to resort to war. Therefore, a state of war cannot exist merely as a result of rampage by individual pirates and robbers. Piracy was a crime, not an act of war—an unauthorized taking of foreign life or property not authorized by a sovereign, and synonymous with brigandage or robbery on land.[13] Proceedings in admiralty were conducted under prize law because within his domain only the sovereign could adjudicate property rights.

Gentili suggested that each sovereign was free to classify belligerent maritime behavior as "piracy," when conducted by a non-sovereign (or unrecognized sovereign). Privateers of recognized belligerent sovereigns were subjected to the laws of war (international law), whereas individual freelance pirates, freebooters, brigands, or privateers working for unrecognized sovereigns, were subject to municipal (domestic law) criminal law.[14] This rule was attractive both to sovereigns, who could leverage the merchant fleet as a force multiplier, and the commercial shipping interests, who stood to earn prizes from the capture of enemy ships.

Dutch prodigy Hugo Grotius also took up the issue of a legal definition of piracy. Rather than the status-based definition advocated by Gentili, Grotius developed an objective test based upon conduct. For Grotius, piracy was committed by those who banded together to commit crime, but not by other societies that formed for other reasons, even if they also committed illegal acts.[15] Pirates were robber bands that plied the seas. But even Grotius saw that the distinction was without a difference to those on the receiving end. The practical difference was also difficult to determine. Were the Barbary principalities, for example, engaged in a lawful maritime war against European merchants, or were they instead pirates who could never obtain legal title to their booty? He cited without comment a judgment of the highest court in Paris:

> The decision held that goods which had belonged to French citizens, and had been captured by Algerians, a people accustomed in their maritime depredations to attack all others, had changed ownership by the law of war, and therefore, when recaptured by others, became the property of those who had recovered them.[16]

Both Gentili and Grotius, however, agreed that robber bands that did not possess a license or letter of *marque* from a sovereign were pirates. Brigands could be dealt with by the municipal law of the state in which they were found. With the rise of English sea power and growing sophistication of English courts in the sixteenth century, England has had the greatest impact on the formation of the modern law of piracy. In 1535 and 1536, England adopted a statute that

---

[13] Id., at 20.
[14] Id., at 25.
[15] Id., at 27, note 115, *citing*, Hugo Grotius, 2 On the Law of War and Peace Book III, Chs. I and ii, pp. 630–31.
[16] Rubin, at 28.

established tribunals to try in court under common law "pirates, thieves, robbers and murders upon the sea."[17]

With the rise of nation states, Dutch and English fleets kept piracy in check. Composed of fast sailing ships and eventually, steam-powered vessels, the seafaring states began to establish and maintain control of maritime commerce.[18] In 1569 Queen Elizabeth proclaimed "all *pyrats* and rovers upon the seas" that operate without a license or commission were deemed beyond her protection and "lawfully to be by any person taken, punished, and suppressed with extremity."[19] Assertion of English jurisdiction, however, was not based on universal jurisdiction over foreigners engaged in piratical conduct, but rather that one of the ships involved in an incident—either a victim ship or a pirate ship—flew the English flag. For the crime of piracy, however, two ships had to be involved.[20] In addition to common law crime, piracy was also evolving in the civil law, as courts struggled with assigning ownership over captured pirate ships and goods and the rights of unwary downstream purchasers of them.

Thus, the early law of piracy arose in the West from three sources. Gentili and Grotius developed conceptions of piracy within the milieu of emerging international law, analogous to a world system during the time of the Roman Empire. The English derived laws against piracy from municipal or domestic civil and common law. Special courts in admiralty were established to address the crime. The English approach asserted jurisdiction over piracy based upon the legal authority of the sovereign of England over his or her subjects and territory.

20.1.3 *Anglo-American Law of Piracy*

English courts also resurrected the Latin phrase *hostes humani generis*—enemies of all mankind—to describe piracy. As Rubin explains:—"*Pirata* were *hostes* in a permanent belligerent relationship to all communities, because they did not declare war before their attack...."[21] The term *hostes* distinguishes rebels fighting without a declaration of war against legitimate governments from mere criminal robbers.

The United States inherited the tradition of English law and with it the early concept of piracy as "a kind of public war and special sort of crime."[22] The English view of piracy as either an unlicensed belligerency or as a municipal crime persisted in American courts. Article 1, section 8 of the U.S. Constitution granted

---

[17] Id., at 36, note 160, *citing*, 27 Hen. VIII c.4 (1535), in 4 PICKERING, THE STATUTES AT LARGE 348–349 (1763).
[18] John L. Anderson, *Piracy and World History in* BANDITS AT SEA: A PIRATES READER 90 (C. R. Pennell, ed. 2001).
[19] RUBIN, at 40.
[20] Id., at 48.
[21] Id., at 83.
[22] Id., at 122.

Congress the power "to define and punish Piracies and Felonies committed on the high Seas, and Offences against the Law of Nations."[23] In his 1833 *Commentaries on the Constitution*, Joseph Story explained:

> By the law of nations, robbery or forcible depredation upon the sea, *animo furandi*, is piracy. The common law, too, recognizes, and punishes piracy as an offence, not against its own municipal code, but as an offence against the universal law of nations; a pirate being deemed an enemy of the human race. The common law, therefore, deems piracy to be robbery on the sea; that is, the same crime, which it denominates robbery, when committed on land.[24]

Similarly, the English jurist Blackstone wrote, "[p]iracy consists of the common law, of those acts of depredation and robbery committed on the high seas, which if committed upon the land, would amount to felony there."[25] The next clause of the same article sets forth the authority of Congress "to declare War, grant Letters of Marque and Reprisal, and make Rules concerning Captures on Land and Water."[26] The right of the sovereign to issue letters of *marque* and reprisal to privateers was a way for the government to supplement the naval power of the state, at least for such time as was needed to grow the armed forces. In addition to buttressing the navy during time of conflict, letters of *marque* and reprisal were granted to merchant shipping that was wrongfully harmed by foreign naval forces, such as a wrongful seizure of neutral cargo. As Blackstone explained:

> But, as the delay of making war may sometimes be detrimental to [persons] who have suffered by depredations from foreign potentates, our laws have in some respect armed the subject with powers to impel the prerogative; by directing the ministers of the crown to issue letters of *marque* and reprisal upon due demand: the prerogative of granting which is nearly related to, and plainly derived from, that other of making war; this being indeed only an incomplete state of hostilities, and generally ending in a formal denunciation of war. These letters are grantable by the law of nations, whenever the subjects of one state are oppressed and injured by those of another; and justice is denied by that state to which the oppressor belongs. In this case letters of *marque* and reprisal ... may be obtained, in order to seize the bodies or goods of the subjects of the offending state, until satisfaction be made, wherever they happen to be found....
>
> But here the necessity is obvious of calling in the sovereign power, to determine when reprisals may be made; else every private sufferer would be a judge in his own cause. And, in pursuance of this principle ... if any subjects of the realm are oppressed in time of truce by any foreigners, the king will grant *marque* in due form, to all that

---

[23] U.S. Const. Art. 1, sec. 8, cl. 10.
[24] Joseph Story, 3 Commentaries on the Constitution § 1154, pp. 89–90 (Boston: Univ. of Chicago, 1833) *See also*, Eugene Kontorovich, *The "Define and Punish" Clause and the Limits of Universal Jurisdiction*, 103 Nw. U.L. Rev. 149 (2009).
[25] William Blackstone, 4 Commentaries on the Laws of England 499 (London: Saunder & Bayly, John Bethune Bayly, ed. 1840).
[26] U.S. Const., Art. 1, sec. 8, cl. 11.

feel themselves grieved. Which form is thus directed to be observed: the sufferer must first apply to the lord privy-seal, and he shall make out letters of request under the privy seal; and, if, after such request of satisfaction made, the party required do not within convenient time make due satisfaction or restitution to the party grieved, the lord chancellor shall make him out letters of *marque* under the great seal; and by virtue of these he may attack and seize the property of the aggressor nation, without hazard of being condemned as a robber or pirate.[27]

The early American Republic also addressed the civil law issue of jurisdiction and title over merchant ships that had been captured and converted to state vessels by foreign sovereigns. The case of the schooner *Exchange* is a landmark judgment concerning foreign sovereign immunity. The schooner *Exchange* was owned by a U.S. citizen. The ship embarked on a voyage to Spain in October 1809. On December 30, 1810, the ship was forcibly seized by the French Navy on order of Napoleon Bonaparte and converted to a vessel of the state. Thereafter, the ship entered into a Philadelphia port seeking refuge from a storm, and the former owners, M'Faddon and Greetham, filed a claim in district court to reclaim title to the ship. The district court denied the claim, but the appellate court reversed the decision.

The Supreme Court affirmed the district court. Finding that the United States was at peace with France, the Court held that U.S. courts do not have jurisdiction over a public vessel in the service of a foreign sovereign. Regardless of how the ship came into the possession of the Emperor of France, it entered the U.S. port under an implied promise of sovereign immunity:

> ... [T]he Exchange, being a public armed ship, in the service of a foreign sovereign, with whom the government of the United States is at peace, and having entered an American port open for her reception, on the terms on which ships of war are generally permitted to enter the ports of a friendly power, must be considered as having come into the American territory, under an implied promise, that while necessarily within it, and demeaning herself in a friendly manner, she should be exempt from the jurisdiction of the country.[28]

20.2 Contemporary Law of Maritime Piracy

Maritime piracy is a violation of international law and a universal crime. The *United Nations Convention on the Law of the Sea* (UNCLOS) defines maritime piracy as an illegal act of violence or detention committed for private ends, and on the high seas or in any other place outside the jurisdiction of a state, such as an ungoverned area like Somalia's territorial sea. Customary international law provides that any nation may assert jurisdiction over piracy, including the State

---

[27] William Blackstone, 1 Commentaries on the Laws of England: A Facsimile of the First Edition of 1765–1769 at 249–251 (Chicago: University of Chicago Press, 1979).
[28] *The Schooner Exchange v. M'Faddon*, (1812) 11 U.S. (7 Cranch) 116, 3 L. Ed. 287.

of registry or flag of the attacked vessel, the nationality of any of the victims and in some cases coastal and port States. This long-standing norm is reflected in UNCLOS, and Article 100 requires States to cooperate in the repression of piracy outside of any State's territorial seas.

20.2.1 UN Convention on the Law of the Sea

Piracy affects the entire international community, and therefore is a classic collective action problem. States have tried to spur collective action through development of a uniform set of rules aimed at suppressing piracy. The *United Nations Convention on the Law of the Sea* (UNCLOS) serves as the omnibus, umbrella treaty for essentially all activities occurring on the oceans.[29] The treaty represents the fruition of four multilateral efforts over the past century to codify the laws applicable to the oceans. Major multilateral conferences in 1930, 1958 and 1960 were unsuccessful in adopting a major restatement of the international law of the sea. The Third UN Conference on the Law of the Sea, however, which met from 1973–1982, codified the essential provisions of anti-piracy law.

UNCLOS restates much of the international law of the sea, but by recognition of a 12 nautical mile territorial sea and creation of an exclusive economic zone (EEZ), the treaty transforms the nature of the relationship between coastal States and the international community. Upon its adoption in 1982, and certainly after its entry into force in 1994, UNCLOS was recognized, in the words of Singaporean ambassador "Tommy" Koh, as the constitution for the world's oceans. As a package deal that captures the most salient oceans interests, the Convention reflects customary international law and is binding on all nations.

The first successful attempt to codify universal jurisdiction over piracy emerged from the 1958 First UN Conference on the Law of the Sea. Article 15 of the *Convention on the High Seas* advanced the formula reached at the 1930 conference and was informed by earlier text developed at Harvard in 1932.[30]

Articles 100–107 of UNCLOS contain both broad philosophy and specific mandates concerning maritime piracy. In its contemporary form, maritime piracy is any illegal act of violence, detention or depredation committed for private (unauthorized by a sovereign) ends by crew or passengers of a private ship or aircraft against another ship, persons or crew and committed outside of a State's territorial waters. Armed robbery at sea typically involves an act of violence or detention occurring within the jurisdiction of a State inside the territorial sea and generally is the enforcement responsibility of a coastal State.

---

[29] United Nations Convention on the Law of the Sea, *opened for signature* Dec. 10, 1982, UN Doc. A/CONF.62/122 (1982), 1833 U.N.T.S. 3, 397, 21 I.L.M. 1261 (1982) (*entered into force* Nov. 16, 1994) [Hereinafter UNCLOS].

[30] Convention on the High Seas, Apr. 29, 1958, 13 U.S.T. 2312, 450 U.N.T.S. 82.

The rising tide of Somali piracy attacks has renewed an interest in Articles 100–107 and associated legal measures, such as UN Security Council enforcement action, supplementary treaties, including the *Convention on the Suppression of Unlawful Acts against the Safety of Maritime Navigation*, and new intergovernmental coordination through the Contact Group on Piracy off the Coast of Somalia (CGPCS).[31] This chapter reflects the work of Kraska and Wilson that suggests that contemporary law against maritime piracy is formed from a web of legal and institutional responses with UNCLOS at its core.[32]

Article 101 of UNCLOS defines piracy as consisting of the following acts:

(a) any illegal acts of violence or detention, or any act of depredation, committed for private ends by the crew or the passengers of a private ship or private aircraft, and directed—
   i. on the high seas, against another ship or aircraft, or against persons or property on board such ship or aircraft;
   ii. against a ship, aircraft, persons or property in a place outside the jurisdiction of any State;
(b) any act of voluntary participation in the operation of a ship or of an aircraft with knowledge of the facts making it a pirate ship or aircraft;
(c) any act of inciting or intentionally facilitating an act described in subparagraph (a) or (b).

Under Article 100 of UNCLOS, all nations have a general duty to cooperate against maritime piracy, and other provisions immediately following Article 100 specify authority for nations to act against piracy. First, naval warships or law enforcement vessels of any nation may interdict pirate ships. Ordinarily, jurisdiction may be asserted over a ship at sea only by the flag State, or in special cases, by a port or coastal State. In the case of piracy, however, there is no requirement for a jurisdictional link to the flag State—any nations may exercise jurisdiction over pirates, which are considered the "enemy of all mankind." Piracy occurs in any waters beyond the 12-nautical mile territorial sea; inside the territorial sea, the crime is called "armed robbery at sea," and it is the sole responsibility of the coastal State.

The generalized authority of all nations to assert universal jurisdiction over pirate ships is set forth in Article 105 of UNCLOS: "On the high seas [or exclusive economic zone], or in any other place outside the jurisdiction of any State, every

---

[31] *See, e.g.*, J. Ashley Roach, *Countering Piracy Off the Coast of Somalia: International Law and International Institutions*, 104 AM. J. INT'L L. 397 (2010).

[32] *See, e.g.*, James Kraska & Brian Wilson, *Countering Maritime Piracy: The Coalition is the Strategy*, 45 STAN. J. INT'L L. 241 (2009); James Kraska, *Coalition Strategy and the Pirates of the Gulf of Aden and the Red Sea*, 28 COMPARATIVE STRATEGY 197–216 (2009); Kraska & Wilson, *The Global Maritime Partnership and Somali Piracy*, 25 DEFENSE & SECURITY ANALYSIS, 222–234 (Sept. 2009); Kraska & Wilson, *Somali Piracy: A Nasty Problem, a Web of Responses*, CURRENT HISTORY (April 2009); and, Kraska & Wilson, *Fighting Piracy: The Pen and the Sword*, THE WORLD POLICY JOURNAL (Winter 2008/09).

State may seize a pirate ship [or ship] taken by piracy and under the control of pirates, and arrest the persons and seize the property on board."

Naval forces may board merchant vessels under the right of approach and visit pursuant to Article 110 of UNCLOS, if reasonable grounds exist to suspect the vessel is engaged in piracy. In some cases, the extension of port state control authority may be used to board a vessel that has declared an intention to enter port. Pirate ships, however, may not be seized in the 12-nautical mile territorial seas, archipelagic waters (such as Indonesian), and internal waters (such as harbors), without the consent of the coastal State, even for criminal acts of piracy committed on the high seas. In areas that have national waters in close proximity to other nations, fleeing pirate vessels can escape into the territorial sea of a neighboring state and avoid capture if the adjoining state is unable to act. States may reach agreement to cooperate in such cases.

A coastal State may lawfully pursue a ship from the territorial sea, archipelagic waters, or the contiguous zone onto the high seas when it believes the vessel violated the law of that State. If the pursuit begins within the contiguous zone, however, it may be conducted only for violations of the rules pertaining to the contiguous zone, such as customs-related offenses. Likewise, if a foreign ship violates the lawful regulations of the coastal State pertaining to the exclusive economic zone, such as state fisheries laws, the coastal State may initiate pursuit of the vessel from the EEZ into the high seas. Hot pursuit may not extend into the territorial sea of another state, however, without the permission of the other State.

The articles on piracy relate to the high seas, but they are operative throughout the EEZ beyond the territorial sea of coastal states. Article 58(2) imports virtually the entire high seas regime of Part VI into the EEZ, so long as those provisions are not inconsistent with the enumerated economic and tertiary coastal State rights in the EEZ. Moreover, although Article 86 of UNCLOS recognizes that the EEZ is a *sui generis* zone, it also clarifies that Part V does not abridge the high seas freedoms enjoyed by all States in the EEZ.

> The provisions of this Part apply to all parts of the sea that are not included in the exclusive economic zone, in the territorial sea or in the internal waters of a State, or in the archipelagic waters of an archipelagic State. This article does not entail any abridgement of the freedoms enjoyed by all States in the exclusive economic zone in accordance with article 58.

Under Article 56(2), the coastal State has a duty to observe "due regard" for the rights of other nations in the EEZ. Thus, all states may conduct counter-piracy operations in the EEZ beyond the territorial sea of any state, or on the high seas. Actual counter-piracy operations or patrols by foreign flagged ships, however, require the consent or permission of the coastal State if they are conducted in straits used for international navigation or archipelagic sea lanes. In such cases, the former category constitutes territorial seas; the latter category constitutes internal archipelagic waters.

20.2.2 UN Security Council

20.2.2.1 Somalia

In the summer of 2008, at the prompting of the IMO, the UN Security Council turned its attention toward combating piracy. Resolution 1816 was adopted on June 2, 2008 at the 5902nd meeting of the Security Council. Acting under Chapter VII of the UN Charter, the Security Council called on states to repress Somalia piracy and armed robbery. The Security Council stated it

> Decides... States cooperating with the Transitional Federal Government (TFG) in the fight against piracy and armed robbery at sea... may:
>
> (a) Enter the territorial waters of Somalia for the purpose of repressing acts of piracy and armed robbery at sea....
> (b) Use, within the territorial waters of Somalia... all necessary means to repress acts of piracy and armed robbery....[33]

Resolution 1816 encouraged States to increase and coordinate their efforts to deter acts of piracy with the Somali TFG, Somalia's troubled coalition governing authority.[34] The Somali TFG must provide notification to the UN Secretary General of States that exercise the authority. In short, the Security Council decided the situation in Somalia constituted a threat to international peace and security in the region and acted under Chapter VII to address the threat. Paragraph 7(a) of UN Security Council Resolution 1816 authorized all nations in cooperation with the Transitional Federal Government, to conduct anti-piracy naval and air maritime security operations within and beyond the territorial sea of Somalia to repress Somali piracy. Naval forces may, "in a manner consistent with action permitted on the high seas with respect to piracy under relevant international law," utilize "all necessary means to repress acts of piracy and armed robbery."[35]

The counter-piracy authorities contained in the resolution (and follow-on resolutions) apply only to the situation of Somali piracy and do not automatically apply to piracy in other regions of the world, such as Southeast Asia. This point was particularly sensitive for Indonesia, which grapples with maritime security throughout its 18,000-island archipelago. With occasional ruminations, particularly from Australia, that the vast maritime space of Indonesia may be characterized as "ungoverned," Jakarta wanted to be sure that the Somali piracy resolution was explicit in that it did not provide a precedent for application to other areas of the oceans.

---

[33] S/RES/1816 (2008), para. 7.
[34] Bronwyn Bruton & J. Peter Pham, *The Splintering of Al Shabaab: A Rough Road from War to Peace*, Foreign Affairs, Feb. 2, 2012.
[35] S/RES 1816, June 2 (2008), para. 7(b).

States also were called upon to cooperate in determining jurisdiction and in the investigation and prosecution of pirates. It is especially important that once a piracy attack is disrupted at sea that States coordinate to provide real-time disposition and logistics assistance with respect to the suspected pirates, victims and witnesses. The Security Council resolution did not compel any State to accept suspected pirates, victims or witnesses, but instead served as a reservoir of political legitimacy that helped increase participation in collective action. Resolution 1816 also solved one of the most difficult issues associated with counter-piracy in the Horn of Africa by recognizing a mechanism whereby naval forces could enter Somalia's territorial seas in order to pursue pirates who hijack vessels and flee toward shallow water to evade capture. The authority deprived Somali pirates of the "safe haven" of Somalia's territorial sea. In order to develop a long-term solution, Resolution 1816 also sought to bring together individual nations, the IMO and other international organizations to build partnership capacity in the East coast of Africa to develop a regional counter-piracy architecture.

The hijacking of the roll-on/roll-off (RO/RO) M/V *Faina* in September 2008 prompted the UN Security Council to consider greater action. Next, in Resolution 1838 on October 7, 2008, the Security Council expressed that it was "gravely concerned" by the increased frequency and audacity of Somali acts of piracy and armed robbery at sea against vessels off the coast.[36] The Security Council called on Member States to deploy naval surface and air forces to the western Indian Ocean to suppress Somali piracy. Maritime piracy in the Somali Basin was recognized particularly as a threat to the prompt, safe and effective delivery of humanitarian aid to Somalia by vessels under contract with the World Food Program, as well as to freedom of navigation and commercial shipping and fishing activities. Reiterating the authorization under Chapter VII of the Charter of the United Nations, Resolution 1838 condemned acts of piracy in the region and called upon states to participate in fighting piracy by sending naval vessels and aircraft to the region. The Security Council also reaffirmed that the laws reflected in UNCLOS embody the rule set applicable to countering piracy and armed robbery at sea.

Security Council Resolution 1844 imposed measures against individuals or entities that have been designated as engaging in or providing support for acts that threaten the peace, security or stability of Somalia, acting in violation of the arms embargo, or obstructing humanitarian assistance to Somalia. Finally, the Security Council supported targeted financial sanctions against individuals and entities involved in promoting Somali piracy.[37]

---

[36] S/RES/1838 (2008).
[37] S/RES 1844, para. 8 (2008).

On December 2, 2008, the Security Council adopted Resolution 1846.[38] The Resolution welcomed the naval patrols by Canada, Denmark, France, India, the Netherlands, the Russian Federation, Spain, the United Kingdom, and the United States to suppress piracy off the coast of Somalia.[39] The Resolution also extended the authority to enter into the territorial waters of Somalia for an additional year.[40] For the first time, the Security Council attempted to leverage the *Convention on the Suppression of Unlawful Acts against the Safety of Maritime Navigation* (SUA Convention) in order to facilitate greater end-game cooperation with criminal prosecution. The Resolution states that the Security Council

> *Notes* that the 1988 [SUA Convention] provides for parties to create criminal offences, establish jurisdiction, and accept delivery of persons responsible for or suspected of seizing or exercising control over a ship by force or threat thereof or any other form of intimidation....[41]

Unfortunately, although the 1988 SUA Convention was in force in 2008 with nearly 150 States' parties, it was underutilized. The greatest hurdle continued to be that States were reluctant to criminally prosecute detained Somali pirates, leading to the most common response of "catch and release" for 90% of captured pirates.

Resolution 1851 is significant because it ramped up the operational authority of naval forces involved in counter-piracy off the coast of Somalia. Also adopted under Chapter VII of the UN Charter, Resolution 1851 calls on States to

> take part actively in the fight against piracy and armed robbery at sea off the coast of Somalia ... by deploying naval vessels and military aircraft and through seizure and disposition of boats, vessels, arms and other related equipment used in the commission of piracy and armed robbery at sea off the coast of Somalia, or for which there are reasonable grounds for suspecting such use....;[42]

Resolution 1851 employs a law enforcement standard of reasonable suspicion for seizure of piracy-related boats and weapons. Perhaps more significantly, the Resolution

> *notes* the primary role of the TFG in rooting out piracy and armed robbery at sea, and *decides* ... States and regional organizations cooperating in the fight against piracy and armed robbery at sea off the coast of Somalia for which advance notification has been provided by the TFG to the Secretary-General may undertake all necessary measures that are appropriate in Somalia, for the purpose of suppressing acts of piracy and

---

[38] S/RES/1846 (2008), Dec. 2, 2008.
[39] Id., para. 6.
[40] Id., para. 10(a).
[41] Id., para. 15.
[42] S/RES/1851 (2008), Dec. 16, 2008, para. 2.

armed robbery at sea... consistent with applicable international humanitarian and human rights law;[43]

This provision is also important, as it opened up the land territory of Somalia to counter-piracy operations. The authority is especially interesting in that it stresses that such operations shall be consistent with both international humanitarian law (law of armed conflict, which applies during time of armed conflict), and human rights law, which applies during peacetime. Placing the limitation of international humanitarian law on the naval response restricted the options of operational commanders. Under the law of armed conflict, civilians may not be targeted except in self-defense or if they are directly participating in hostilities.[44] Resolution 1851 also encourages states to

> conclude special agreements or arrangements with countries willing to take custody of pirates in order to embark law enforcement officials ("shipriders") from the latter countries, in particular countries in the region, to facilitate the investigation and prosecution of persons detained as a result of operations conducted under this resolution for acts of piracy and armed robbery....[45]

Nearly one year after Resolution 1851 was adopted, the Security Council followed with adoption of Resolution 1897, which renewed the authorities in previous resolutions for a period of twelve months.[46] In the intervening year, the Contact Group on Piracy off the Coast of Somali was established, and the forum brought together about fifty nations and numerous other stakeholders to plan better international cooperation in the campaign against Somali piracy.

The phenomenon of "catch and release" persisted throughout 2009–2011, however, as States struggled to ensure that suspected pirates captured at sea were properly subject to criminal prosecution. Resolution 1918 requested that the Secretary-General of the United Nations report on possible options available for criminal prosecution and imprisonment of Somali pirates.[47]

The Security Council wanted an analysis of all of the options available for prosecuting the crime of maritime piracy, including an assessment of the option of creating special domestic chambers, possibly with international components, a regional tribunal or an international tribunal, and corresponding imprisonment arrangements. In reply, in July 2010, the Secretary-General issued a report that identified seven options for consideration: (1) build regional capacity; (2) cre-

---

[43] Id., at para. 6. Colum Lynch, *U.N. Authorizes Land, Air Attacks on Somali Pirates*, WASH. POST, Dec. 17, 2008, at A14.
[44] Geneva Conventions on the Laws of War, Common Article 3(1) (1949); Protocol Additional to the Geneva Conventions of Aug. 12, 1949, and relating to the Protection of Victims of Non-International Armed Conflicts [Protocol II], June 8, 1977, Article 13.
[45] S/RES/1851 (2008), Dec. 16, 2008, para. 3.
[46] S/RES/1897 (2009), Nov. 30, 2009.
[47] S/RES/1918 (2010), Apr. 27, 2010, para. 4.

ate a Somali court in a regional state; (3) create a special tribunal in a regional state without UN support; (4) create a special tribunal in a regional state with UN support; (5) create a regional tribunal; (6) establish an international tribunal; and, (7) create an UN Security Council piracy court.[48] The July 2010 report did not advocate any single approach, but rather was a neutral compendium of the options available and the advantages/disadvantages of each.[49]

The extraordinary time and costs in establishment and operation of international courts, however, and the small volume of suspects they would prosecute, augurs in favor of national courts as a more efficient option. The author of the study, Special Adviser to the Secretary-General Jack Lang, advocated a combination of domestic courts and international courts. Lang's study recommended establishment of specialized Somali courts to try suspected pirates in Somalia and in another country in the region.[50]

United Nations Security Council Resolution 1950 extended the counter-piracy authorities in earlier resolutions by a period of twelve months.[51] Resolution 1976 began a shift in emphasis away from the maritime threat of piracy and back toward the problems of instability and lack of governance and absence of the rule of law endemic in Somalia as a failed State. Four years of counter-piracy naval operations had dented the Somali piracy business model, but warships did not stop the ship hijackings. By 2011, pirates from East Africa were found as far as the shores of India, so the extent of their operations had vastly expanded from 2005. Although the incidence of successful attacks declined due to enhanced ship security and implementation of shipping industry *Best Management Practices for Protection against Somalia Based Piracy*, ransoms were going up and ships were still at risk.[52]

---

[48] S/2010/394, Report of the Secretary-General on possible options to further the aim of prosecuting and imprisoning persons responsible for acts of piracy and armed robbery at sea off the coast of Somalia, including, in particular, options for creating special domestic chambers possibly with international components, a regional tribunal or an international tribunal and corresponding imprisonment arrangements, taking into account the work of the Contact Group on Piracy off the Coast of Somalia, the existing practice in establishing international and mixed tribunals, and the time and resources necessary to achieve and sustain substantive results, July 26, 2010.
[49] Id.
[50] S/2011/30, Report of the Special Adviser to the Secretary-General on Legal Issues Related to Piracy off the Coast of Somalia, Annex, Jan. 24, 2011.
[51] S/RES/1950 (2010), Nov. 23, 2010, para. 7.
[52] INT'L CHAMBER OF SHIPPING, ET AL., BEST MANAGEMENT PRACTICES FOR PROTECTION AGAINST SOMALI BASED PIRACY: SUGGESTED PLANNING AND OPERATIONAL PRACTICES FOR SHIP OPERATORS, AND THE MASTERS OF SHIPS TRANSITING THE HIGH RISK AREA (4th ed. Aug. 2011), *distributed via* IMO Doc. MSC.1/Circ.1339, Piracy and Armed Robbery against Ships in Waters off the Coast of Somalia: Best Management Practices for Protection against Somali Based Piracy, Sept. 14, 2011.

The Security Council stated that piracy and armed robbery at sea off the coast of Somalia exacerbates the situation in Somalia, which "continues to constitute a threat to international peace and security in the region."[53] The Security Council requested "States, UNODC, the United Nations Development Program, the United Nations Political Office for Somalia (UNPOS) and regional organizations to assist the TFG and regional authorities in Somalia in establishing a system of governance, rule of law and police control in lawless areas where land-based activities related to piracy are taking place...."[54]

The Security Council adopted Resolution 2015 on October 24, 2011, at its 6635th meeting.[55] The Resolution reemphasized a finding of the *Lang Report* that the international community shared "the ultimate goal of enhancing Somali responsibility and active involvement in efforts to prosecute suspected pirates...."[56] This perspective reflects a weariness on the part of the international community, and a growing sense that there should occur a "Somaliazation" of the response to maritime piracy. Despite its gross corruption and weakness, the TFG was still recognized as the relevant regional authority for eradicating piracy from Somalia.[57] The Resolution also promoted the Lang recommendation aimed at

> establishment of specialized anti-piracy courts in Somalia and other States in the region with substantial international participation and/or support, and *requests* that the Secretary-General, in conjunction with UNODC and UNDP, further consult with Somalia and regional States willing to establish such anti-piracy courts on the kind of international assistance, including the provision of international personnel, that would be required to help make such courts operational; the procedural arrangements required for transfer of apprehended pirates and related evidence; the projected case capacity of such courts; and the projected timeline and costs for such courts....[58]

Stressing a comprehensive approach to Somali piracy, Resolution 2020 of November 2011 recognized the need

> to investigate and prosecute not only suspects captured at sea, but also anyone who incites or intentionally facilitates piracy operations, including key figures of criminal networks involved in piracy who illicitly plan, organize, facilitate, or finance and profit from such attacks....[59]

In sum, the UN Security Council resolutions against piracy off the coast of Somalia have captured a number of recurring themes over the past five years:

---

[53] S/RES/1976 (2011), Apr. 11, 2011.
[54] Id., para. 4.
[55] S/RES/2015 (2011), Oct. 24, 2011.
[56] Id., para. 1.
[57] Id., para. 2.
[58] Id., para. 16.
[59] S/RES/2020, Nov. 22, 2011, paras. 3–4.

maritime piracy is a threat to international peace and security; the solution ultimately resides on land; the international community should conduct naval and aviation military operations in support of World Food Program shipments and in defense of international shipping and freedom of navigation, and against Somali pirates. States should conduct law enforcement operations against Somali pirates, suspected Somali pirates should be criminally prosecuted in domestic courts, financiers and logistics supporters of Somali piracy should be individually and collectively targeted, Flag State Administrations should ensure that ships that fly their flag implement industry *Best Management Practices*, lack of rule of law and political stability in Somalia is breeding piracy and international crime, and, all activities to suppress piracy should be conducted in accordance with the international law of the sea, international humanitarian law, and human rights law.

20.2.2.2 African Union Mission to Somalia

The fight against piracy begins and ends in Somalia. Although much of the country has been cast into political chaos since the early-1990s, other parts are relatively stable and secure, and governed by responsible authorities. Somaliland, for example, has maintained a piracy-free coastline and authorities are consolidating a nascent democracy after the free and fair presidential election of June 2010. The trend in Southern Somalia is less promising.

In 2007, the UN Security Council voted to authorize African states to intervene in Somalia on behalf of the TFG in order to try to bring stability to the failed state. Armed groups operate with impunity in much of the country and control key towns and population centers in the central and southern region. The PKO in Somalia wants and needs equipment and training to facilitate the mission and assist the TFG in stabilizing the country, which everyone agrees is the only long-term solution to the problem of Somali piracy. Some African states, such as Djibouti and Sierra Leone, have indicated a desire to expand participation in Somali peacekeeping operations, but lack the resources to do so. General officers from East African states complain that the naval mission is merely "swatting bees." These motivated indigenous forces seek the resources to "go after the beehive."

The Security Council stated that the establishment of the African Union Mission to Somalia (AMISOM), and particularly the major commitment of troops by Uganda and Burundi, is an essential part of bringing stability to the country.[60] AMISOM has 7,000 Ugandan military forces and 2,000 from Burundi. There are sixty staff members from African countries—for example, Kenya has sent four advisers. The United States is training troops from Djibouti to participate in the mission. But the East African states envision a force of 20,000. Nigeria and Sierra Leone have declined to participate due to a lack of resources, and provisioning

---

[60] S/RES 1772, (2007), para. 9 and S/RES 1863 (2009).

and training their forces for Peacekeeping Operations (PKO) duty in Somalia is among the most cost effective measures that could be undertaken. The TFG, allied militias and AMISOM are engaged in a war against *Harakat al-Shabaab al-Mujaahidiin*, commonly known as Al Shabaab. The TFG security forces are largely devoid of a sense of patriotic nationalism, and instead retain clan-based loyalties to individual commanders who look to AMISOM rather than the Government for leadership and support.[61] Unlike Al Shabaab, the TFG relies on external forces for security.

Al Shabaab is the principal impediment to peace and security in Somalia.[62] The Islamist group is not unstoppable. Even after conducting several spectacular suicide attacks in 2010—one on August 24 at the Muna Hotel that killed four members of Parliament and another on September 9 at Mogadishu International Airport coinciding with the arrival of a high-level international delegation—Al Shabaab has experienced hard setbacks. In 2010, the influx of 2,000 Ugandan peacekeepers and an aggressive counter-offensive by TFG forces reversed the gains made by Al Shabaab.

Beginning with an offensive by the AMISOM Burundi detachment complemented by TFG forces in 2011, Al Shabaab was kicked out of Mogadishu altogether. In September 2012, Kenyan forces that were part of AMISOM ejected Al Shabaab from Kismayo, a seaside port and Al Shabaab stronghold. These defeats, possibly exacerbated by a reliance on inexperienced conscripted child soldiers, have forced the extremist group to focus on nurturing clan alliances rather than relying on ideology to attract supporters.[63]

The United Nations Monitoring Group reports that Al Shabaab generates $70 to $100 million per year in duties and fees levied at airport, seaports, local sales taxes, and ad hoc "jihad contributions," and checkpoint extortions justified in terms of religious obligation or *zakat*.[64] The Uganda forces that participate in Peacekeeping in Somalia have observed that Al Shabaab is also being financed from the ransom proceeds obtained in piracy. When large ransoms are paid there is an increase in Al Shabaab activity, including noticeable increases in the expenditure of ammunition. Al Shabaab is reliant on the use of improvised explosive devices (IEDs), grenades, and small arms sniper fire to create havoc, so a small amount of money from piracy goes a long way.

Al Shabaab, not piracy, is the most acute threat to security and stability in East Africa. The group already has conducted attacks in Addis Ababa, Ethiopia and coordinated double suicide bombings at two nightclubs in Kampala on July 11, 2010. The nightclub attacks were committed by non-Somalis from Uganda

---

[61] S/2011/433, para. 15.
[62] Id., paras. 17–18.
[63] Id., paras. 19–24.
[64] Id., para. 60.

and Kenya; 79 people died and scores were injured.[65] Indigenous populations inside Kenya are now involved in recruiting, radicalizing, and training for Al Shabaab, and the group has links to jihadist groups in northern and western Africa and the middle East.

Leveraging the PKO in the fight against piracy treats the maritime threat at sea more like a war than a law enforcement operation. East African military forces understand that piracy is regarded as a crime of universal jurisdiction and not generally considered armed conflict. While the threat of piracy poses a relatively minor inconvenience to most states, J. Peter Pham—dean of African politics and director of the Michael S. Ansari Africa Center at the Atlantic Council in the United States—has reported that the effect on East Africa has been devastating—tantamount to a blockade.[66] From the perspective of the United States and Europe, piracy looks like a crime spree, but on the ground in East Africa, it is war. Under this theory, pirates are acting in sustainment of Al Shabaab, and therefore become lawful targets under international humanitarian law (if one accepts that there is a "war" being conducted against Al Shabaab).

In private conversations, African military leaders describe the naval coalition on patrol in the Indian Ocean as ineffective and inefficient. The East African armed forces have suggested that they could use assistance to solve the threat of piracy "in a few months." Not only is this approach the humane and efficient method of addressing the threat of Somali piracy, it is also the most prudent. General officers in East Africa want to get the job done now before the disrupting effect of piracy ransoms, powerful criminal organizations, and an even a wealthier and more powerful Al Shabaab throw the country into worse condition than it already is. Al Shabaab is evolving into a powerful pseudo-political criminal cartel with a religious message that reverberates throughout the Muslim communities of East Africa—if it successfully makes the transition into the mainstream, the threat will dwarf the rag-tag pirates.

The naval coalition, being relatively cost-ineffective, is the wrong tool for the job of suppressing piracy, even at sea. Warships patrolling the Internationally Recognized Transit Corridor in the Gulf of Aden have helped to reduce piracy attacks by 50 percent in that area. But implementation of the *Best Management Practices* by merchant ships and use of private security companies have also had an impact on reducing piracy in the Gulf of Aden—perhaps even a larger impact than naval patrols. In any event, attacks have increased significantly in

---

[65] Id., para. 46.
[66] J. Peter Pham, *Putting Somali Piracy in Context*, 28 J. CONTEMP. AFRICAN STUDIES, 325 at 330–335 (July 2010) and J. Peter Pham, Somalia: Insurgency and Legitimacy in the Context of State Collapse, at 277, 283–288, *in* VICTORY AMONG PEOPLE: LESSONS FROM COUNTERING INSURGENCY AND STABILIZING FRAGILE STATES (David Richards & Greg Mills eds., 2011).

areas where there are fewer naval patrols, such as the Red Sea and the Western Indian Ocean.[67]

The answer is not to concentrate high-end warships, but rather to create a diffuse network consisting of private security and small boat coastal security and naval forces. The fleet commander of Kenya, for example, has indicated that his naval force consists of two fast attack ships and two offshore patrol vessels (OPVs). The OPVs are 70-meters in length and weigh about 700 tons, a much more precise and cost-effective solution to piracy than billion-dollar capital warships. The versatile boats have a 14-day endurance. The Kenyan naval base at Manda Bay sits on the northern edge of Kenya, next to the Somali coast. If the Kenyan Navy had four additional OPVs and additional training, it could divide its existing crews among the new platforms and completely control piracy along the Somali coast as far north as Kismayo.

The West has waffled on whether to commit to the long-term viability of the TFG. While multiple UN Security Council resolutions, binding on all nations under Chapter VII, have called on the international community to back the TFG, actual support has been tepid. The reason that States are relatively reticent about the future of the TFG is that at times, the organization has been remarkably incompetent, suffers from rampant corruption, and is woefully lacking in vision and capability. But the TFG has hung on—long after many Africa observers thought it would fall. In early August 2011, TFG forces with the great assistance of AMISOM ejected Al Shabaab out of Mogadishu in a show of strength that provides a glimpse of promise for its future. Perhaps most importantly, there is no other option than the TFG. For all its faults, the TFG may be the only viable choice, and the UN Security Council and our East African partners have put their eggs in the same basket with the TFG.

By 2011, 12,000 troops from Burundi, Uganda, and Djibouti were engaged in operations inside Somalia as UN peacekeepers under AMISOM. The AMISOM operation inevitably began to affect the entire security situation in Somalia, as its main strategic objective is to diminish the capacity of armed groups in the failed state so that Somali National Forces can assume control of security. Once security is established and maintained, there is greater space for a legitimate government to thrive. In order to accomplish its mission, AMISOM must preserve the support of the local population and maintain protected lines of communication throughout the area in which it operates. Finally, AMISOM is dependent upon substantial support from the international community.

On October 16, 2011, 4,000 Kenyan troops supported by helicopter gunships launched Operation *Linda Nchi* ("Protect the Nation") to secure the border area,

---

[67] S/2011/433, para. 88.

including the port town of Kismayo, an Al Shabaab stronghold.[68] One month later, Kenya also committed three army battalions of 1,000 troops each to operate with AMISOM peacekeepers. On February 3, 2012, two Kenyan helicopter gunships hit an Al Shabaab convoy, killing about 100 members of the terrorist group. Similarly, on January 21, 2012, a U.S. drone flying on the outskirts of Mogadishu killed Bilal al-Barjawi, an Al Qaeda member assisting Al Shabaab.

In February 2012, the Security Council agreed to increase the number of AMISOM forces to 17,731 troops. At the same time, Kenya began to have notable success in southern Somalia in defeating pockets of Al Shabaab militants. Once the process of integrating Kenyan and Sierra Leonean units in south Somalia was completed, the force expanded its presence in the regions of Bay, Gedo and Lower Juba in addition to Banadir and Middle and Lower Shabelle.

J. Peter Pham has written eloquently of his visits to the region and the evidently severe—perhaps fatal—problems that exist with the TFG.[69] The transitional government is a skeleton organization, lacking capability and capacity. Even more importantly, it is, in the words of Africa specialists at the Atlantic Council of the United States, "corrupt to the core," with 96 percent of foreign aid during 2009–2010 siphoned off by the TFG leadership.[70] The lack of stability along the northern border with Somalia also impedes Kenya's application for an extended continental shelf claim beyond 200 nautical miles from the shore.[71]

The Djibouti Agreement of June 9, 2008, between the TFG and the Alliance for the Re-liberation of Somalia (ARS), may serve as the most feasible basis to unwind the two-decade war in the country and restore peace. The Security Council and African Union apparently still believe that the best hope for establishment of stability and security in Somali lies with the troubled Transitional Federal Government (TFG).[72] The Kamapala Accord (*Agreement between the President of the TFG and the Speaker of the Transitional Federal Parliament*), made on June 9, 2011, provides a milestone for ending the transitional phase of Somali government on August 20, 2011, a date selected to begin a one year process toward a power

---

[68] Russell Jones, *Kenya Agrees to Join AMISOM to fight Al-Shabab*, JANE'S DEFENCE WEEKLY, Dec. 14, 2011, at 15.

[69] J. Peter Pham, *Putting Somali Piracy in Context*, 28 J. CONTEMP. AFRICAN STUDIES, 325 at 330–335 (July 2010) and J. Peter Pham, Somalia: Insurgency and Legitimacy in the Context of State Collapse, at 277, 283–288, *in* VICTORY AMONG PEOPLE: LESSONS FROM COUNTERING INSURGENCY AND STABILIZING FRAGILE STATES (David Richards & Greg Mills eds. 2011).

[70] Bronwyn Bruton & J. Peter Pham, *The Splintering of Al Shabaab: A Rough Road from War to Peace*, FOREIGN AFFAIRS, Feb. 2, 2012, ("Corruption is rampant with the TFG ... a confidential donor-supported audit showed that 96 percent of bilateral aid awarded between 2009–2010 simply disappeared."), http://www.foreignaffairs.com.

[71] *War Hits Kenya Bid to Expand Waters*, THE EAST AFRICAN, theeastafrican.co.ke, Jan. 29, 2012.

[72] S/2009/210.

sharing formula and free elections for Somali leaders in August, 2012.[73] But, as is often the case in Somalia, the deadline came and went, without adding clarity to the future of Somali governance.

20.2.2.3   Gulf of Guinea

Piracy in West Africa, principally the Gulf of Guinea area, has increased dramatically since 2009. The model for piracy in West African waters is different than in East Africa. The attacks in the Gulf of Guinea tend to be more violent than those off the Horn of Africa and many robberies likely go unreported due to the high frequency of illegal oil bunkering in the Niger Delta.

The Joint War Committee (JWC) is comprised of underwriting representatives that write marine hull insurance. The JWC added the exclusive economic zones (EEZs) of Nigeria and Benin north of Latitude 3° North to its list of areas severely affected piracy and terrorism.[74] The Gulf of Guinea also suffers from a prevalence of Illegal, Unreported, and Unregulated (IUU) fishing. London-based MRAG Limited, a maritime consultancy, estimates the illegal catch to be 40 percent higher than reported legal catch.[75] Finally, there is convergence of human trafficking, weapons smuggling, and narcotics trafficking in the region.

The November 2010 report by the Atlantic Council of the United States on *Security and Stability in the West African Maritime Domain* underscores that high levels of violence in largely ungoverned offshore areas of Central and West Africa is creating insecurity and instability on land. In particular, the security in the Gulf of Guinea is key to ensuring the unimpeded flow of oil from West Africa. The security of energy related infrastructure and assets, the safe and efficient flow of vessels, cargo, and people bound to or from foreign ports, the absence of a safehaven for transnational terrorist and criminal organizations, and, promotion of political development, sustainable economic growth, and enduring stability in the region can avert state failure and violent extremism.

Beginning in 2011, the UN Security Council began to be deeply concerned about the threat of piracy and armed robbery in the Gulf of Guinea, and the dangers posed to international navigation, regional security, and economic development. The Security Council has sought to supplement or empower regional international organizations to fight piracy in the Gulf of Guinea. The Economic

---

[73] Agreement between the President of the Transitional Federal Government HE Sharif Sheikh Ahmed and the Speaker of the Transitional Federal Parliament Honorable Shariff Hassan Sheikh Aden, (Kamapala Accord), June 9, 2011.

[74] Joint War Committee, Lloyd's, Hull War, Piracy, Terrorism, and Related Perils: Listed Areas, JWLA/020, Mar. 28, 2012.

[75] MRAG LIMITED AND FISHERIES ECOSYSTEMS RESTORATION RESEARCH, FISHERIES CENTRE, UNIVERSITY OF BRITISH COLUMBIA, THE GLOBAL EXTENT OF ILLEGAL FISHING at 9–10 and 16 (Apr. 2008).

Community of Central African States (ECCAS), the Economic Community of West African States (ECOWAS), the Gulf of Guinea Commission (GGC) and the Maritime Organization for West and Central Africa (MOWCA), work to enhance maritime safety and security in the Gulf of Guinea.[76] These regional organizations can have the greatest impact through "development of laws and regulations ... criminalizing piracy," development of a regional operational framework, that includes information sharing and coordination of patrols, and implementation of international agreements concerning maritime safety and security. The Security Council also urges Flag State Administrations to issue to ships flying their flag "appropriate advice and guidance," on self-protection techniques, such as avoidance, evasion, and defensive measures to thwart an attack in the waters of the Gulf of Guinea.[77]

In 2012, the UN Security Council envisioned an even broader role for regional organizations in West Africa. For example, ECCAS completed the maritime security architecture to counter piracy in the Central African sub-region.[78] The effort includes a strategy adopted by the ECCAS Peace and Security Council in February 2008 and establishment of the Regional Centre for Maritime Security in Central Africa (CRESMAC) in Pointe-Noire, Congo.

20.2.3 *International Maritime Organization*

On November 17, 1983, the IMO adopted Resolution A.545(13), aimed at preventing piracy and armed robbery at sea.[79] The Resolution cited article 15(j) of the IMO Convention concerning the functions of the Assembly in relation to establishing regulations for maritime safety. As a "matter of the highest priority," Member States were urged to take "all measures necessary to prevent and suppress acts of piracy and armed robbery against ships in or adjacent to their waters...."[80] The IMO Assembly also for the first time asked States to inform the organization of acts of piracy and armed robbery as a way to gain a better understanding of the frequency of the threat.[81]

In 1986 the Maritime Safety Committee at IMO adopted circular 443, concerning measures to prevent unlawful acts against passengers and crew on board ships.[82] The circular applied to passenger ships on voyages of 24 hours or more and the port facilities that service those vessels. A few years later, in 1991, the IMO

---

[76] S/RES/2018 (2011), Oct. 31, 2011.
[77] Id., para. 4.
[78] S/RES/2039 (2012), Feb. 29, 2012.
[79] IMO Doc. A13/Res.545, Feb. 29, 1984 and IMO Doc. Resolution A.545(13), Nov. 17, 1983.
[80] Id., para. 1.
[81] Id., para. 4.
[82] IMO Doc. MSC/Circ.443, Measures to Prevent Unlawful Acts against Passengers and Crew on Board Ships, Sept. 26, 1986, para. 3.3.

once again requested governments to report "promptly and in detail" all incidents of maritime piracy.[83] States were also invited to coordinate their actions against pirates and armed robbers "operating in areas within or adjacent to their waters."[84]

Further guidance from IMO includes a resolution to urge states to recommend "precautionary measures for the avoidance" of piracy attacks, and "procedures to be followed if they occur...."[85] Flag States should ensure that ships that fly their flags report maritime piracy attacks immediately to the nearest Rescue Coordination Center (RCC), which are normally used to manage search and rescue (SAR). Governments also were asked to ensure the RCCs were linked with local security forces "so that contingency plans may be implemented and to warn shipping in the immediate area of the attack...."[86]

During the 1990s, Southeast Asia suffered from a wave of piracy attacks that resulted in the taking and conversion of vessels and reregistering them under a new name. Often the entire crew was thrown overboard, and the ship and its cargo were then sold on the black market. These stolen "phantom ships" took advantage of lax registration procedures to reenter the stream of commerce as legitimate carriers. The IMO fought to stem the threat by inviting Governments to tighten ship registration procedures and to assist in obtaining evidence against ships previously registered under a different name and flag. The IMO adopted a resolution concerning "phantom ships" on November 29, 2001, which

> Invites also Governments to exhaust all means available to them to obtain evidence that a ship previously registered under another State's flag has been deleted, or that consent to the transfer of the ship has been obtained from that State's register. Registration of a ship, which has previously not been registered should not take place until sufficient evidence of it not being registered has been received. Prior to registration of any ship, Governments should verify its identity, including the IMO Ship Identification Number, where appropriate, and other records of the ship, so that the ship does not fly the flags of two or more States simultaneously.[87]

After a surge in piracy in the early 1990s, two circulars were issued by IMO.[88] The first document contained detailed recommendations to governments for

---

[83] IMO Doc. Res. A.638.17, Prevention and Suppression of Piracy and Armed Robbery against Ships, Nov. 6, 1991, para. 6.
[84] Id., para. 2.
[85] IMO Doc. A.738(18), Measures to Prevent and Suppress Piracy and Armed Robbery against Ships, Nov. 4, 1993, *reprinted* A 18/Res.738, Nov. 17, 1993.
[86] Id., para. 7.
[87] IMO Doc. A.923(22), Measures to Prevent the Registration of "Phantom Ships," Nov. 29, 2001, *reprinted* A 22/Res. 923, Jan. 22, 2002.
[88] IMO Doc. MSC/Circ.622, Recommendations to Government for preventing and suppressing piracy and armed robbery against ships, June 16, 1999 and IMO Doc. MSC/Circ. 623, Guidance to shipowners and ship operators, shipmasters and crews on preventing and suppressing acts of piracy armed robbery against ships.

preventing and suppressing piracy, and the second document focused on providing guidance to the maritime commercial sector. In 1999 both circulars were revised.[89]

The revision to MSC/Circ.622 recommended that states work with seafarers and shipowners as part of the process of crafting action plans for preventing piracy and responding to piracy attacks. The document also set forth investigative protocols for use after a pirate attack.[90] Finally, the circular contains a draft regional agreement on cooperation for the prevention and suppression of acts of piracy and armed robbery against ships. Provisions of the draft agreement include procedures for each country to conduct boarding and search of suspect vessels, and provisions for criminal enforcement and determining choice of jurisdiction among coastal and flag states.[91] The second revised circular, MSC/Circ.623.rev.1, provided guidance on measures for the shipping industry to reduce vulnerability to piracy, such as enhanced lighting and detection, and it set forth additional steps that states could take during and after an attack, such as enhanced alarm procedures and reporting.[92] In light of the rapid increase in piracy attacks off the coast of Somali in 2006, MSC Circular 622/Rev.1, *Recommendations to Governments*, and MSC Circular 623/Rev.3, *Guidance to Shipowners*, were redistributed by the IMO to Member States on June 15, 2007.[93]

In issuing MSC Circular 1233 on piracy off the coast of Somalia, the IMO noted that most attacks occurred within 200 nautical miles from the shore of East Africa.[94] By the next year, however, the organization reported that, "there has been a worrying increase in the number of attacks off the east coast of Somalia in the Western Indian Ocean, some taking place over 500 nautical miles off that coast."[95] The expansion in areas vulnerable to Somali pirates caused the International Chamber of Shipping to advise its members on April 15, 2009, that the Maritime Safety Centre Horn of Africa (MSCHOA) advised shipmasters not to plan their passage within 600 nautical miles of the Somali coast. The IMO distributed the advice to Member States.[96]

---

[89] IMO Doc. MSC/Circ. 622/Rev. 1 and MSC/Circ. 623/Rev. 1. were revised based upon recommendations that came out of regional seminars in Brazil and Singapore in 1998.

[90] IMO Doc. MSC/Circ. 622/Rev. 1 (protective measures at paras. 3–15 and investigative protocols at paras. 16–20).

[91] IMO Doc. MSC/Circ. 622/Rev. 1, Appendix 5.

[92] IMO Doc. MSC/Circ. 623/Rev. 1, Jun. 29, 1999. The Circular has undergone Revision 2, Oct. 6, 2001 and Revision 3, Oct. 7, 2001.

[93] IMO Doc. MSC.1/Circ.1233, Piracy and Armed Robbery against Ships in Waters off the Coast of Somalia, June 15, 2007.

[94] Id., para. 3.

[95] IMO Doc. MSC.1/Circ.1302, Piracy and Armed Robbery against Ships in Waters off the Coast of Somalia, Apr. 16, 2009, para. 1.

[96] Id., para. 3.

The IMO also recommended that Governments should inform ship operators and managers, shipping companies, and ship masters that vessels should report their navigation route through the Gulf of Aden and/or Western Indian Ocean to the United Kingdom Maritime Trade Operations (UKMTO) in Dubai.[97] In 2008, Denmark's delegation at the IMO proposed that both MSC/Circ.622/Rev.1 and MSC/Circ.623/Rev.3 series circulars should be reviewed and updated. On June 23, 2009, the eighty-sixth session of the Maritime Safety Committee adopted MSC.1/Circ.1334, *Guidance to Shipowners and Ship Operators* (revoking MSC/Circ.623/Rev.3).

Circular 1334 issues guidance to "shipowners, companies, ship operators, masters and ship operators to take seamanlike precautions when their ships navigate in areas where the threat of piracy and armed robbery exists."[98] The IMO warns ships and companies to:

- avoid carrying large sums of cash on board the ship;[99]
- be aware that attackers may be monitoring ship-to-shore communications and using intercepted information, such as the Automatic Identification System, to select their targets;[100]
- maintain vigilance in watchkeeping to ensure early detection of pirates and armed robbers approaching the ship;[101]
- route ships away from bottlenecks and areas where attacks are known to have occurred;[102]
- practice the implementation of the ship security plan;[103]
- maintain communications security and vigilance, and transmit a distress signal in case of imminent danger;[104]
- use maximum lighting available consistent with safe navigation, and in compliance with the 1972 Collision Regulations;[105]
- maintain physical security of ship spaces, and especially securing doors to limit access to access to the bridge, engine-room, steering gear compartments, officers' cabins and crew accommodations;[106]
- understand how to employ alarm signals, distress flares, defensive measures and maneuvers, and non-lethal devices, to repel pirate attacks;[107]

---

[97] Id., para. 5.4.
[98] IMO Doc. MSC.1/Circ.1334, Piracy and Armed Robbery Against Ships, Guidance to Shipowners and Ship Operators, Shipmasters and Crews on Preventing and Suppressing Acts of Piracy and Armed Robbery Against Ships, Annex, Guidance to Shipowners, Companies, Ship Operators, Shipmasters and Crews on Preventing and Suppressing Acts of Piracy and Armed Robbery Against Ships, June 23, 2009.
[99] Id., para. 5.
[100] Id., paras. 6–8.
[101] Id., paras. 13–19 and 27–31.
[102] Id., para. 20.
[103] Id., paras. 21–23.
[104] Id., paras. 32–44, and Appendix 4.
[105] Id., paras. 45–46.
[106] Id., paras. 47–51.
[107] Id., paras. 51–58.

- utilize unarmed and armed security personnel and interact with privately contracted armed security and military teams or law enforcement officers;[108] and
- be familiar with the phases of a piracy attack, from early detection, attempted boarding, entry of pirates onto the ship, to disembarkation from the ship and reporting the attack and post-incident follow-up, such as seafarer assistance.[109]

Similarly, on June 26, 2009, the MSC adopted MSC.1/Circ.1333, *Recommendations to Governments for Preventing and Suppressing Piracy and Armed Robbery against Ships* (revoking MSC/Circ.622.Rev.1). The Circular issues recommendations to Flag State Governments, including:

- discouraging the carriage of firearms by seafarers for person protection or protection of the ship;[110]
- considerations for the use of privately contracted armed security personnel or armed military or law enforcement security teams;[111]
- creation of action plans for reporting and responding to piracy;[112]
- matters of criminal jurisdiction over pirates;[113]
- coastal state responses to piracy in offshore waters;[114]
- flow diagram demonstrating connections among Flag States, Coastal States, RCCs, and the shipping industry;[115]
- flow diagram for reporting piracy incidents in Asia;[116]
- phases related to voyages in areas threatened by piracy;[117]
- ships' message formats for reporting piracy;[118]
- a format for reporting piracy and armed robbery at sea to the IMO through Flag State Administrations or international organizations;[119]
- a draft regional agreement for enhancing cooperation against piracy.[120]

On December 2, 2009, the IMO also issued a *Code of Practice for the Investigation of Crimes of Piracy and Armed Robbery against Ships*.[121] The Code serves as an "*aide-mémoire* to facilitate the investigation of the crimes of piracy and armed

---

[108] Id., paras. 59–64.
[109] Id., paras. 65–94.
[110] IMO Doc. MSC.1/Circ.1333, Recommendations to Governments for Preventing and Suppressing Piracy and Armed Robbery against Ships, June 26, 2009, para. 5.
[111] Id., paras. 6–8.
[112] Id., paras. 9–25.
[113] Id., paras. 26–31.
[114] Id., paras. 32–39.
[115] Id., Appendix 1.
[116] Id., Appendix 2.
[117] Id., Appendix 3.
[118] Id., Appendix 4.
[119] Id., Appendix 5.
[120] Id., Appendix 6.
[121] IMO Doc. A.1025(26), Code of Practice for the Investigation of Crimes of Piracy and Armed Robbery Against Ships, Dec. 2, 2009, *reprinted in*, IMO Doc. A 26/Res.1025, Jan. 18, 2010.

robbery against ships."[122] The Code provides information on criminal investigation and prosecution of suspected pirates at trial. Investigators should be properly trained, and the involvement of intergovernmental organizations can serve as a force multiplier against transnational criminal enterprises. The key tasks set forth in the *Code of Practice* include:

- Addressing the initial report, including preservation of life, prevention of escape of the offenders, warnings to other ships at risk, protection of crime scenes, and security evidence;[123]
- Investigation of the crimes, including proportionality (an investigation commensurate with the seriousness of the offense), establishing and recording relevant facts, recording individual witness accounts, conducting a detailed forensic examination of the crime scene, searching intelligence databases and distributing information and intelligence to international law enforcement and industry.[124]

The *Code of Practice* is supplemented by IMO *Guidelines for the Investigation of the Crimes of Piracy and Armed Robbery at Sea*.[125] The Guidelines state that "capture, prosecution and sentencing of pirates and armed robbers is probably the most appropriate deterrent action available to Governments." Given that regional courts are saturated with piracy cases, and the general reluctance by naval powers to criminally prosecute pirates, the threat of prosecution may not be a strong deterrent. Certainly the seemingly lackadaisical approach to criminal prosecution by many states, particularly in Europe, has not served to promote the optics of law and order.

Finally, the IMO has issued omnibus Assembly resolutions concerning piracy and armed robbery in waters off the coast of Somalia. The November 30, 2011, iteration of the resolution captures the spectrum of counter piracy activities, from stability operations and capacity building inside Somalia to warship patrols and shipping industry best practices.[126]

20.2.4 Djibouti Code of Conduct

The *Djibouti Code of Conduct* is one of the most significant efforts of the IMO in recent years. The *Code of Conduct concerning the Repression of Piracy and Armed Robbery against Ships in the Western Indian Ocean and the Gulf of Aden* is the first regional agreement between Arab and African countries to address

---

[122] Id., Annex, para. 1.
[123] Id., Annex, para. 6.
[124] Id., Annex, para. 7.
[125] IMO Doc. MSC.1/Circ.1404, Guidelines to Assist in the Investigation of the Crimes of Piracy and Armed Robbery against Ships, May 23, 2011.
[126] IMO Doc. A.1044(27), Piracy and Armed Robbery against Ships in Waters off the Coast of Somalia, Nov. 30, 2011, *reprinted in* IMO Doc. A 27/Res.1044, Dec. 20, 2011 (revoking IMO Doc. A.1026(26), Piracy and Armed Robbery against Ships in Waters off the Coast of Somalia, Dec. 2, 2009, *reprinted in* IMO Doc. A 26/Res.1026, Dec. 3, 2009.

maritime piracy. The Djibouti code sprang from IMO Resolution A.1002 (25) of November 29, 2007, which called upon regional states in East Africa to conclude an international agreement to prevent, deter and suppress piracy.[127]

Seeking to replicate the success of counter-piracy agreements in Asia, the IMO sponsored meetings from 2005–2008 in Yemen (Sana'a Seminar), Oman (the Oman Workshop), and Tanzania (Dar es Salaam), to facilitate negotiation of an anti-piracy agreement among regional states. Djibouti, Egypt, Eritrea, Jordan, Oman, Somalia, and Yemen endorsed the *Sana'a-Muscat Memorandum of Understanding* in January 2006 at the Oman Workshop.[128] A final meeting in Djibouti in January 2009 produced an agreement among 17 regional states to enhance cooperation in the prosecution and repatriation of captured Somali pirates.

Djibouti, Ethiopia, Kenya, Madagascar, Maldives, Seychelles, Somalia, the United Republic of Tanzania and Yemen signed the original agreement, which remains open for signature by other countries in the region. Comoros, Egypt, Eritrea, Jordan, Mauritius, Oman, Saudi Arabia and Sudan have since signed the Code. Twenty countries have signed the agreement out of 21 eligible states. Because of the limited capacity of the countries involved, however, the Code of Conduct is not legally binding. Participating nations are expected only to act only in accordance with available resources, and in accordance with international law, and their respective national laws.

The signatories to the Code agreed to cooperate in conducting a number of counter piracy activities, which are based on four broad pillars: information sharing, updating legislation, regional training and capacity building (particularly for maritime security). First, the States involved are establishing reliable maritime domain awareness networks in the region, including sharing information from the Automatic Identification System (AIS) and radar networks, in order to be able to locate and track merchant shipping. The IMO is working with regional States to identify bilateral technical projects to fit AIS and radar sites along the periphery of the western Indian Ocean. By capitalizing on existing infrastructure, the IMO is fusing information collection and sharing protocols and agreements to establish a common regional operating "picture." In Tanzania, for example, the IMO and the United States have improved the nation's national maritime domain awareness architecture by connecting X-band radar at Tanga with AIS stations at Pemba, Kilwa, Ungujia and Mtwara with a maritime center and a base station in Dar es Salaam. The World Bank has funded a complementary effort to develop a data link from the Maritime Electronic Highway in the Mozambique Channel.

---

[127] IMO Doc. A.1002(25), Piracy and Armed Robbery against Ships in the Waters off the Coast of Somalia, Nov. 29, 2007, para. 7.
[128] IMO Doc. MSC 85/9, Draft Report of the Maritime Safety Committee on its Eighty-Fifth Session, Dec. 1, 2008, p. 89 and IMO Doc. C 105/12/Add.1, Oct. 8, 2010.

Second, States also are developing coastal security and naval forces, including boats, equipment, facilities, and maritime technical training, to be able to conduct constabulary patrols in the region. Finally, the States are establishing long-term infrastructure in the region to support maritime safely, security, and environmental resource management. The Republic of Korea is providing funds for linking Vessel Tracking Services (VTS) and AIS in the headquarters of the Yemen Coast Guard with the ISC in Sana'a, Djibouti and Oman. Once a common operating picture is fully operational, the IMO is exploring the concept of creating an East Africa Standby Force Maritime Forces (EASF MARFOR) to maintain maritime security as a strategic, regional objective under a single and unified command structure.

Additional efforts include construction of new port facilities, aids to navigation and drafting regulatory codes that preserve freedom of navigation, while also supporting port and coastal state authorities. The overall effort is comprehensive, and the Code provides the framework for assistance to regional states. Increasingly, donors are channelling funding for individual projects through the Djibouti Code framework, with the goal of enhancing the ability of states in the region to accomplish the range of anti-piracy tasks:

(a) the investigation, arrest and prosecution of persons, who are reasonably suspected of having committed acts of piracy and armed robbery against ships, including those inciting or intentionally facilitating such acts;
(b) the interdiction and seizure of suspect ships and property on board such ships;
(c) the rescue of ships, persons and property subject to piracy and armed robbery and the facilitation of proper care, treatment and repatriation of seafarers, fishermen, other shipboard personnel and passengers subject to such acts, particularly those who have been subjected to violence; and
(d) the conduct of shared operations—both among signatory States and with navies from countries outside the region—such as nominating law enforcement or other authorized officials to embark on patrol ships or aircraft of another signatory.

Participating states also agree to apprehend and prosecute persons. Pirates that are prosecuted, convicted at trial and imprisoned are entitled to proper care and treatment, and the agreement calls for states to repatriate seafarers, fishermen, and other shipboard passengers and victims of piracy. The signatories also undertook to review their national legislation with a view to ensuring that there are laws in place to criminalize piracy and armed robbery against ships and to make adequate provision for the exercise of jurisdiction, conduct of investigations and prosecution of alleged offenders.

Signatory States express a commitment to report relevant information through a system of national focal points and information centers, and to interdict ships suspected of engaging in acts of piracy or armed robbery against ships. The Code provides for sharing information through tactical maritime security centers, which were established through the support of the IMO. In April 2010, the secretariat of the IMO in London developed a menu of projects to promote the Code of Conduct regionally. A new Project Implementation Unit (PIU) within the Maritime Safety Division of IMO is the lead institution for the effort. The PIU is funded through the Djibouti Code Trust Fund, and is helping to establish a training center in Djibouti (Regional Training Center Djibouti—DRTC) and three regional counter-piracy information-sharing centers (ISCs).

The first of three information-sharing centers (ISCs) pursuant to the Djibouti Code of Conduct opened in Mombasa, Kenya, in early 2011. The Mombasa ISC is co-located with the Regional Maritime Rescue Coordination Center, which operates around-the-clock.[129] The Maldives, Seychelles, Mauritius, Kenya, and eventually, Somalia, will be linked with the Mombasa ISC. The Mombasa MRCC was established in 2006 and covers a vast area of the Western Indian Ocean extending to the Seychelles. The Mombasa MRCC is linked with the Dar es Salaam MRCC sub-center, which was commissioned in 2009. The ISC also shares information with the Sana'a ISC and Dar es Salaam ISCs to form a three-ISC network, as envisioned under the Djibouti Code.[130] The centers receive and respond to piracy alerts and requests for information or assistance. Each center is also designed to share information with maritime authorities and the international coalition of warships.

The infrastructure for information-sharing leverages existing facilities, such as the Regional Maritime Rescue Coordination Centre in Mombasa, Kenya and the Rescue Coordination Sub-Centre in Dar es Salaam, Tanzania. A third regional maritime information center is being constructed in Sana'a, Yemen. The Sana'a ISC likely will use Vessel Traffic Services (VTS) and AIS in the Gulf of Aden. The information fusion centers will disseminate alerts regarding imminent threats or incidents to ships, and collect and analyze information, which can be transmitted as actionable intelligence, or be used to prepare statistics on threat trends.

The DRTC training center in Djibouti will be used to train staff watch officers in the three centers. The DRTC is intended to become the single point of contact for maritime training in the region, including maritime authorities and law enforcement agencies. The IMO has funded the construction of the DRTC with a grant to the government of Djibouti of up to $2.5 million. Djibouti is responsible for clearing the site, and providing services and road access to the site. Curriculum will be developed by the government of Djibouti, acting in conjunction with IMO and European Union. As an initial step, all countries were asked to complete a needs assessment in order to establish a training matrix. The final workshop in Djibouti in May 2011 developed the finalized training plan. Training in Djibouti will be developed in coordination with the European Commission (EC) team in the country.

---

[129] *Piracy Information-Sharing Centre in Mombasa Commissioned*, IMO NEWS, Issue 2, 2011, at p. 9.
[130] Id.

Table 20.1. Djibouti Code of Conduct Information Sharing Network

Mombasa ISC	Sana'a ISC	Dar es Salaam ISC
Kenya	Yemen	Kenya
Mauritius	Egypt	Tanzania
Maldives	U.A.E.	Comoros
Seychelles	Djibouti	Reunion (France)
Somalia (South Central)	Ethiopia	Madagascar
	Jordan	Mozambique
	Oman	South Africa
	Saudi Arabia	
	Somalia (Puntland)	
	Sudan	

Each ISC integrates law enforcement agencies with the maritime industry and naval forces under a national focal point. The focal point should coordinate among the marine police, port authorities, seafarers, ship owners, shipping agencies, ship registry, insurance companies and P&I clubs, fishery agency, coast guard and naval authorities. (In the United States, broad maritime security crisis coordination is done through the Global Maritime Operational Threat Response (MOTR) Coordination Center, which is located in Washington, D.C.).

The ISCs should facilitate closer cooperation among states and build confidence in addressing the threat of piracy. By linking stakeholders and issuing warning throughout a network of responders, the focal points can better alert national and coastal shipping. The focal points link tactical maritime law enforcement officials to ministry-level decision makers within each State. Developing these communications nodes is especially helpful in the Horn of Africa, where many countries have adequate law on the books to deal with piracy, but find that the maritime forces work for a separate ministry and may not have a mandate or authority to take action or arrest pirates. Perhaps the best way to close this gap is to require that government patrol vessels carry on board law enforcement personnel who have authority to make arrests in cases of piracy. This approach is essentially a domestic ship-rider concept, and it is used by a number of States.

Japan is a major contributor to the IMO's technical cooperation programs, and Tokyo pledged $13.5 million to initiate the Djibouti Code Trust Fund. A handful of prominent international organizations are involved in the effort, supporting the IMO. The European Commission (EC), Regional Agreement on Combating Piracy and Armed Robbery against ships in Asia (ReCAAP), United Nations Political Office for Somalia (UNPOS), the United Nations Office on Drugs and Crime (UNODC), and the International Criminal Police Organization (INTERPOL), are working to implement a broad maritime security capacity-building program for the states that have signed the Code. For example, counter-piracy officials from signatory States are receiving training by ReCAAP's Information

Sharing Centre in Singapore, which promotes harmonization of State practice in Africa and Asia.[131]

Maritime and port authority officials from Djibouti, Egypt, Eritrea, Ethiopia, Jordan, Oman, Saudi Arabia, Somalia, Sudan, and Yemen have been trained at the ISC.[132] A combined IMO/UNODC workshop was held in Djibouti from March 1 to 3, 2011, for regional ministries of transport, police, and justice, to develop crime-scene methods and protocols for arrest. The IMO in conjunction with UNODC and the EU seeks to connect anti-piracy efforts to the Eastern and Southern Africa and Indian Ocean (ESA-IO) initiative, which was devised at a meeting in Mauritius in October 2010.[133] At the tactical level, sea-going law enforcement needs an adequate domestic legal framework to arrest and prosecute suspected pirates.

20.3 Counter-piracy Operations

In the early-2000s, Somali pirates rarely strayed far out to sea, and transit beyond 200 miles from the shore was a virtual guarantee of safety. Because the Somali Basin—the wide strip of water running along a north-south axis adjacent to the coastline of East Africa—lies near busy shipping lanes, the attack on the *Seaborne Spirit* marked a turning point in how Somali pirates operated their "business." The pirates learned that rather than awaiting targets of opportunity near the coast, there were larger ships vulnerable to attack located farther from shore. Bigger ships and larger crews meant a potentially much higher ransom payoff could be extracted as tribute from the owners in order to free the vessel.

Major intercontinental shipping lanes, such as the Gulf of Aden, also had a much larger number of vessels than could be found in the Somali Basin. Each year, thirty thousand ships ply the strategically important but vast maritime space that includes the Gulf of Aden, the Red Sea, the Arabian Sea and the western Indian Ocean. In retrospect, the combination of large, vulnerable ships and exposed, busy shipping lanes made the shift from localized maritime piracy from open-air skiffs to coordinated and extended operations conducted from mother ships virtually inevitable. The lack of governance inside Somalia and the chal-

---

[131] IMO Doc. A.1002 (25) para. 7.
[132] IMO Doc. C 102/14, Protection of Vital Shipping Lanes, Sub-regional meeting to conclude agreements on maritime security, piracy and armed robbery against ships for States from the Western Indian Ocean, Gulf of Aden and Red Sea areas, Apr. 3, 2009. *See also*, IMO Doc. C/ES.25/12, Nov. 5, 2009, IMO Doc. C 102/14/1, Protection of Vital Shipping Lanes, Project Profile for the Implementation of the Djibouti Code of Conduct, May 5, 2009.
[133] Joint Communiqué from the Eastern and Southern Africa—Indian Ocean Ministers and European Union High Representative at the 2nd Regional Ministerial Meeting on Piracy and Maritime Security in the Eastern and Southern Africa and Indian Ocean Region, Oct. 7, 2010, Grand Bay, Republic of Mauritius.

lenges of imposing order at sea through warships from distant countries inures to the benefit of the pirates.

In September 2008, the Ukrainian ship *Faina*, was seized by Somali pirate raiders, as it transported armored battle tanks and associated equipment and ammunition to South Sudan. The day after the *Faina* was captured, Russia sent the Baltic fleet missile frigate *Neustrashimy* (Fearless) to the Horn of Africa to fight piracy.[134] Two months later, Somali pirates captured the very large crude carrier *Sirius Star*, a Saudi tanker carrying oil valued at over $ 100 million—one-fourth of Saudi Arabia's daily production. The ship was taken at a point 450 miles southeast of Kenya, underscoring the greatly expanded reach of Somali pirates.[135] The ship was freed in January 2009 after payment of $3 million was parachuted to the pirates from a privately contracted intermediary in a light aircraft.

These attacks presaged others, as Somali pirates swarmed throughout the Gulf of Aden and the western Indian Ocean. Gradually the shipping lanes of the Arabian Sea and the western Indian Ocean—virtually to the coast of India—were placed at risk. The costs of Somali piracy were ballooning. Ransoms were going up. From 2009 to 2011, the average ransom paid to release a hijacked ship and captured crew has almost doubled, from $1 million to $3.5–4 million per year, and now ransoms in excess of $10 million have been reported.

Despite the efforts to contain the threat, the costs to industry from piracy are climbing, and reach an estimated $7 to $12 billion per year.[136] Ransoms and insurance (war risk, kidnap and ransom or "K&R," cargo and hull insurance) have increased steadily. Costs of re-routing ships around the Cape of Good Hope are estimated to be $2.4 to $3 billion per year.[137] Security costs for ship owners and carriers have reached as much as $2.5 billion per year, and this does not include the cost of warship sorties and patrols.[138] Secondary costs have been imposed on nations in the region, and include the government of Egypt losing revenue from Suez Canal operations ($642 million per year), a reduction in commercial trade by Kenya and Yemen ($564 million per year), and losses in fisheries and tourism for the tiny small island state of Seychelles ($6 million per year).[139]

20.3.1 *Combined Maritime Force—Task Force 151*

Based in Bahrain, Combined Maritime Forces (CMF) is an international naval partnership headed by the U.S. Navy Vice Admiral serving as Commander, Naval Forces, U.S. Central Command and Commander, U.S. Fifth Fleet. The three-star admiral separately exercises authority as Commander, Combined Maritime Force.

---

[134] *Russia Sends Warship to Fight Piracy Near Somalia*, RIA NOVOSTI, Sept. 26, 2008.
[135] *Saudi Tanker Freed off Somalia*, REUTERS, Jan. 9, 2009.
[136] OCEANS BEYOND PIRACY, THE ECONOMIC COSTS OF PIRACY (2010).
[137] Id.
[138] Id.
[139] Id.

The CMF consists of warships and aircraft from 26 navies. The Force conducts maritime security operations throughout 2.5 million square miles of ocean space, targeting terrorism, piracy, illegal human trafficking and marine drug trafficking. Nations as far as Australia, Canada, France, Turkey, Pakistan, South Korea and Thailand participate.

The CMF commander also leads three subordinate task forces that are focused on separate missions and which have rotating multinational leadership. CTF-150 focuses on maritime security and anti-terrorism throughout the Gulf of Aden, Gulf of Oman, Arabian Sea, the Red Sea, and the Indian Ocean, as part of Operation Enduring Freedom. CTF-151 is responsible for conducting counter-piracy operations, primarily against Somali pirates operating in the western Indian Ocean. CTF-151 has been under command of officers of the Royal Thai Navy, the Denmark Navy, the Republic of Korea Navy, the Pakistan Navy, the Turkish Navy, and the U.S. Navy. Counter-piracy operations are managed from a flagship, such as the RFA *Fort Victoria*, a Royal Fleet Auxiliary of the United Kingdom. The Maritime Liaison Office Bahrain (MARLO) is associated with CTF-151 and links CMF, Naval Forces U.S. Central Command, and the commercial shipping industry. MARLO is led by a U.S. Coast Guard commander and serves as a conduit for exchanging information among naval and civil maritime authorities. Finally, CTF-152, established in March 2004, coordinates Theater Security Cooperation (TSC) activities in the Arabian Gulf.

CTF 151 was established in January 2009, assuming counter-piracy duties as a dedicated, standing task force from CTF 150. Leadership of CTF 151 rotates among participating naval forces on a four- to six-month basis. Under the authority of Commander, U.S. Fifth Fleet, the U.S. Navy maintains a number of operational task forces, such as Combined Task Force Iraqi Maritime (CTF-IM). CTF-IM supports Iraq in protecting the offshore *Al Basrah* oil terminal (ABOT) and *Khawr Al Amaya* oil terminal (KAAOT), which account for about 90 percent of the Iraq's gross domestic product.

20.3.2 *North Atlantic Treaty Organization—Operation Ocean Shield*

NATO's contribution to international efforts to combat piracy off the Horn of Africa—*Operation Ocean Shield*—is directed from NATO's Maritime Command Headquarters, based in Northwood. In addition to patrols at sea, NATO is assisting regional countries to develop their own ability to ensure security at sea.

NATO consists of 28 nations, but not all are involved in the counter-piracy effort. For a decade, the North Atlantic Treaty Organization (NATO) has been conducting a maritime anti-terrorism operation in the Mediterranean named *Active Endeavour*.[140] The objective of *Active Endeavour* is to target terrorists involved in

---

[140] NATO also used maritime forces in support of policing the arms embargo against the toppled regime of Muammar Qaddafi in Libya under authority of UN Security Council Resolutions 1970 and 1973.

the conflicts in Afghanistan, the Balkans, and Iraq. NATO warships have boarded thousands of ships in the Mediterranean Sea, and provided technical and legal experience for the more recent counter-piracy operations.

The NATO Shipping Centre (NSC) operates within the NATO Maritime Command Headquarters Northwood, UK as a permanently established point of contact between naval forces and the merchant shipping industry. The effort provides a liaison between NATO, the European Union (EU) and multi-national naval forces, including CTF-151, and the international shipping industry.

Operation Ocean Shield maintains a current plot of merchant ships in the region. Guidance is provided to the international merchant shipping community. Warships and aircraft patrol the waters of the western Indian Ocean and are situated to respond to piracy incidents as they occur. The NSC works cooperatively with UKMTO Dubai, the EU's MSCHOA and U.S. MARLO to ensure synchronization of databases, accurate tracking of merchant shipping in the region, and share responsibility for sea lines of communication.

Even before the EU became involved in counter-piracy, NATO responded to the threat with its first out-of-area maritime mission. In a September 25, 2008 letter, UN Secretary-General Ban Ki-moon asked NATO to provide warship escorts to World Food Program (WFP) vessels transiting through the waters of the Horn of Africa, bound for Kenyan ports. The request was intended to fill a gap in security escorts until the EU could pick up the mission. In response, NATO's *Operation Allied Provider* conducted its first escorts from October to December 2008, utilizing a deployed Standing NATO Maritime Group (SNMG).

From March to August 2009, NATO continued the more modest *Operation Allied Protector*, but then transitioned to *Operation Ocean Shield*. The North Atlantic Council approved Operation Ocean Shield on August 17, 2009, and the effort expands *Operation Allied Protector*, which ended the day before. *Ocean Shield* entails the following military missions:

- Deter and disrupt pirate attacks and come to the aid of ships *in extremis*.
- Search for suspected pirates, detaining them and seizing their vessels—delivering both to law enforcement authorities.
- Build local and regional maritime security capacity.
- Collaborate with EU NAVFOR and other international organizations conducting counter-piracy operations.

On March 19, 2012, *Operation Ocean Shield* was extended through the end of 2014.

NATO has two principal maritime groups, which are multinational, scalable and flexible, integrated maritime forces comprised of warships from member nations that train and operate as a single unit. Under the command of a commodore or rear admiral, the SNMGs can perform the gamut of missions, from peacekeeping exercises, maritime security operations and major combat operations. From March to June 2009, NATO deployed five warships of the SNMG1 as part of *Operation Allied Provider*. Since then, the counter-piracy mission has rotated between SNMG1 and SNMG2. Command of the SNMGs periodically rotates among NATO nations, but the command element for *Operation Ocean Shield* is located in Northwood Middlesex, United Kingdom. The NATO Shipping Centre also is located at the Allied Maritime Command Headquarters Northwood.

Operation Ocean Shield also operates an Internet website that includes emergency contact telephone numbers for the NATO Shipping Centre, MSCHOA and the International Maritime Bureau (IMB) Piracy Reporting Centre (PRC), the last of which is operated by the International Chamber of Commerce (ICC). The NATO website also maintains a daily piracy overview, weekly assessments, updated advice on vessel safety precautions, information on use of onboard citadels, and locations of suspected pirate action groups (PAGs) stalking merchant ships. *Ocean Shield* is also contributing to public diplomacy by broadcasting on Somali radio to correct disinformation that the pirates pass on to the Somali population. The NATO force operates beyond the Gulf of Aden and the International Recognized Transit Corridor (IRTC),[141] sending forces to patrol the Somali Basin.

Portugal, for example, operates a P-3 Orion Maritime Patrol and Reconnaissance Aircraft from the Seychelles. While at-sea counter-piracy operations and aerial surveillance will continue to be the focus, a new element of regional-state counter-piracy capacity building has been developed for *Operation Ocean Shield*. NATO's capacity building effort will aim to assist East African states in developing local and regional capabilities to combat piracy activities.

20.3.3 *European Union Naval Force Somalia—Operation Atalanta*

European Union Naval Force (EU NAVFOR) Somalia launched *Operation Atalanta* on December 8, 2008, as part of the European Common Security and Defense Policy (CSDP). Based out of Northwood in Middlesex, and commanded by a Royal Navy Rear Admiral or a Royal Marine Major General, the EU's first naval operation conducts counter-piracy operations and has the specific remit of protecting shipping.

Operation Atalanta grew out of the EU mission to escort shipments for the World Food Program (WFP) and the African Union Mission on Somalia (AMISOM). The Operation typically consists of five to ten surface combat vessels, one or two auxiliary naval ships, and four maritime patrol and reconnaissance aircraft. Since its establishment, the operation periodically has been extended, and participation has expanded to include non-EU member states of Croatia, Montenegro, Norway, and Ukraine. The Maritime Security Centre—Horn of Africa (MSCHOA) in Dubai is the planning and coordination authority that connects EU NAVFOR *Operation Atalanta* to merchant ships transiting the western Indian Ocean.

---

[141] IMO Doc. SN.1/Circ.281, Information on the Internationally Recommended Transit Corridor (IRTC) for Ships Transiting the Gulf of Aden, Aug. 3, 2009.

The European Union and the United Kingdom Maritime Transportation Office (UKMTO) established a maritime security patrol area (MSPA) effective on February 1, 2009. The MSPA includes a 12-nautical mile wide Internationally Recognized Transit Corridor (IRTC) akin to a traffic separation scheme for traffic in the Gulf of Aden and heading to or from the Strait of Bab el Mandeb.[142] The corridor has two lanes, each five miles wide, running parallel, separated by a two-mile wide lane. The IRTC helps to reduce collision risk and provides standard grid geo-reference coordinates for warship zone coverage of the IRTC.

European nations contribute a large number of international coalition warships to patrol the western Indian Ocean to deter and disrupt piracy. European Union states have contributed to the U.S.-fashioned counter-piracy Coalition Task Force 151 (CTF 151), which reports to U.S. Central Command's three-star Navy component commander forward deployed to Bahrain. The EU Joint Strategy Paper for Somalia for 2008–2013 allocates €215.8 million under the 10th European Development Fund (EDF). With characteristic multilateralism, European states are most likely to conduct counter-piracy operations under the aegis of a broad international effort.

European interest in the threat of Somali piracy emerged in 2005–06 out of concern over the vulnerability of WFP shipments to Somali pirates. For 3.2 million people in Somalia—43 percent of the population—humanitarian assistance is necessary to meet basic human needs. In many areas of south and central Somalia, 15 to 20 percent of the population suffers from acute child malnutrition. Ninety percent of the WFP aid into Somalia is carried by sea. Because of the general state of disrepair of the Somali road infrastructure and the relative efficiency of moving bulk goods by ship, food from donor nations outside East Africa arrives by port into Somalia.

In order to husband scarce funds, the WFP typically leases older, smaller vessels to carry humanitarian aid. These ships are particularly vulnerable to Somali piracy since they lack speed and sit low in the water. In a country where food security is at risk for millions of people, the WFP shipments are attractive targets for Somali pirate gangs operating from the beach in Puntland. Somali pirates began attacking WFP shipments in 2006. If the shipments are seized, the pirates use the food as a weapon, withholding it from needy populations and dispensing it to enforce political patronage. Furthermore, the ransom to free the ship and crew constitute a nice bonus.

Thus, the initial impetus for EU involvement in counter-piracy operations was to protect the vulnerable WFP ships from Somali pirates. France, the Netherlands, Canada and Denmark offered naval escorts to ensure that humanitarian food aid reached Somalia. By November 2007, naval escorts began to accompany

---

[142] Id., at Annex.

WFP food shipments to Somalia, and these missions were formalized in December 2008 with the inception of *Operation Atalanta*.[143]

Operation Atalanta is conducted within the framework of the Common Security and Defence Policy (CSDP). The 27 countries of the EU are working to establish a single voice on security issues. The CSDP is managed through a handful of permanent EU politico-military bodies based in Brussels, including the ambassadorial-level Political and Security Committee, which monitors threats and develops integrated responses. The EU Military Committee is the high military body within the Council of the European Union and consists of chiefs of defense of the various states. Finally, two additional bodies—Civilian Aspects of Crisis Management and the EU Military Staff—play a role in integrating the variety of national responses into a cohesive effort under the EU banner.

In 1999 the EU dispatched its first peacekeepers—helping to stabilize in Bosnia and Herzegovina. The deployment in Bosnia was followed by a peacekeeping effort in Macedonia, *Operation Concordia*. In 2005, a rule of law mission was established in Iraq, and a EU police mission was set up in Afghanistan in 2007. Further peacekeeping involvement in Chad and the Central African Republic was followed in August 2008 by a brokered ceasefire and deployment of observers to stop hostilities between Russia and Georgia.

The EU counter-piracy effort began in December 2008. Since its origin, the scope of *Operation Atalanta* has expanded from protecting WFP ships delivering humanitarian aid to Somalia to broader support for the African Union Mission in Somalia (AMISOM). The resolution under which EU NAVFOR operates sets forth a commitment to conduct operations in accordance with relevant UN Security Council Resolutions (UNSCR) and international law:

> The European Union shall conduct a military operation in support of [UNSCRs] ... consistent with action permitted with respect to piracy under Article 100 *et seq*. of the United Nations Convention on the Law of the Sea...., hereinafter called "Atalanta" in order to contribute to:
>
> - the protection of vessels of the WFP delivering food aid to displaced persons in Somalia, in accordance with the mandate laid down in [UNSCR] 1814 (2008);
> - the protection of vulnerable vessels cruising off the Somali coast, and the deterrence, prevention and repression of acts of piracy and armed robbery off the Somali coast, in accordance with the mandate laid down in [UNSCR] 1816 (2008).[144]

Adhering to the Security Council mandates, *Operation Atalanta* conducts patrols to protect both WFP and AMISOM shipping. While this sort of mission creep

---

[143] Acts Adopted Under Title V of the EU Treaty, Council Decision of 2008/918/CFSP, Dec. 8, 2008, OFFICIAL J. OF THE EUROPEAN UNION, Sept. 12, 2008, at L 330/19.

[144] European Union Council Joint Acton 2008/851/CFSP of Nov. 10, 2008 on a European Union military operation to contribute to the deterrence, prevention and repression of acts of piracy and armed robbery off the Somali coast, Nov. 11, 2008, OFFICIAL J. OF THE EUROPEAN UNION, at L 31/304.

is perhaps inevitable in order to defeat pirates, it begins to place EU forces on one side of a multi-dimensional internal struggle for power inside Somalia. Other nations—Uganda, which has provided the bulk of troops in support of AMISOM—have paid a price for disrupting the operations of the Somali Islamic terrorist organization, *Harakaat al-Shabaab al-Mujaahidiin*, which is also known as "Al Shabaab." Al Shabaab claims responsibility for a 2010 bombing in Kampala that killed 76 people—an attack that was in retaliation for Uganda's leadership in AMISOM. There is still uncertainty over whether the kidnappings and murders of European tourists that occurred in coastal resort areas in Kenya in September and October 2011 are related to Somali piracy, or even more ominously, the Al Shabaab Islamic terrorist organization.[145] In response to the violence inside Kenya, two battalions of Kenyan Army troops supported by helicopter gunships crossed into Somalia on October 16, 2011, to conduct a pincer maneuver against the Shabaab stronghold at Kismayo.[146]

The EU NAVFOR also monitors fishing activities off the coast of Somalia to ensure that foreign-flagged ships from distant water states are not poaching Somalia's fish stocks. Some Somali pirates, especially in the "early" years of 2004–2006, claim that they were operating as an informal coast guard to suppress illegal, unreported, and unregulated (IUU) fishing.

The force elements of EU NAVFOR consist of surface navy vessels and auxiliary ships, such as oilers, manned Maritime Patrol and Reconnaissance Aircrafts (MPRA), and individual Vessel Protection Detachment (VPD) teams embarked on commercial ships transiting the area.[147] The air and sea forces are orchestrated out of the EU NAVFOR Operational Headquarters in Northwood, United Kingdom and through members of the armed forces serving on board ships in theater.

The EU NAVFOR totaled € 8.4 million in 2010, € 8.05 million in 2011, and € 8.3 million in 2012. Financing is derived from a formula based on the Athena

---

[145] Four European women were kidnapped in the span of less than a month. One United Kingdom national was kidnapped in Kenya in September, and her husband was murdered during the abduction. A French national was seized from her coastal home only two weeks later, and she was confirmed dead on Oct. 19, 2011. Two Spanish aid workers from the humanitarian group *Médecins Sans Frontiéres* were kidnapped from the Dadaab refugee camp on Oct. 13, 2011. Lauren Gelfand, Kenya Opens Ground War in Somalia against Shabab, Jane's Defence Weekly, Oct. 26, 2011, at p. 5.

[146] Id.

[147] Council Joint Acton 2008/851/CFSP of Nov. 10, 2008 on a European Union military operation to contribute to the deterrence, prevention and repression of acts of piracy and armed robbery off the Somali coast, OFFICIAL J. OF THE EUROPEAN UNION, L 31/304, Nov. 11, 2008, Council Decision 2009/907/CFSP of Dec. 8, 2009 amending Joint Action 2008/851/CFSP on a European Union military operation to contribute to the deterrence, prevention and repression of acts of piracy and armed robbery off the Somali coast, OFFICIAL J. OF THE EUROPEAN UNION, L 322/27, Sept. 12, 2009.

Mechanism, which distributes assessments among the EU member states based upon their gross domestic product. Common costs are shared among the participating states and include the operation of the Northwood command center and embarked NAVFOR headquarters located aboard a flagship. Medical services and transportation are also shared expenses. Each individual state, however, shoulders the cost of deployment of its own ships, aircraft and military personnel.

The size of EU naval forces on station in the western Indian Ocean varies according to the threat level. The cyclical ebb of the monsoon seasons affects the prevalence of piracy. Generally, *Operation Atalanta* consists of five to ten surface combat vessels, one or two auxiliary ships, and as many as four Maritime Patrol and Reconnaissance Aircraft (MPRA). Including those based on land, approximately 2,000 military personnel are assigned to EU NAVFOR. Since its inception, more than 20 vessels and aircraft have participated in the effort.

EU NAVFOR patrols an area that stretches from the south of the Red Sea and the Gulf of Aden to the western part of the Indian Ocean extending to the Seychelles. This region is comparable in size to the Mediterranean Sea and is 2 million square nautical miles (almost 4 million square kilometers), or the equivalent of 30 times the size of England, ten times the size of Germany, or seven times the area of France or Spain. Since the launch of the initiative, EU NAVFOR has had a 100 percent success rate with its escorts of WFP vessels delivering over 520,000 tons of food that has fed 1.13 million Somalis per day. The force has also participated in protecting the Internationally Recommended Transit Corridor through the Gulf of Aden, ensuring safe passage to and from the Suez Canal. The EU also operates Maritime Safety Center—Horn of Africa (MSCHOA) to help to coordinate international merchant shipping through the region.

Any long-term solution will have to involve the African states, and the EU is heavily involved in developing regional capacity to counter Somali piracy. The mission has broadened to include land-based programs designed to build state institutions and broaden the rule of law in Somalia and the surrounding states. After adoption of UNSCR 1872 in 2009, for example, the EU began a program for training of Somali security forces in Uganda.[148] The Political and Security Committee decided on April 21, 2009, to accept contributions of third states to EU NAVFOR[149] and established a Committee of Contributors.[150] Norway was the first non-EU country to contribute to the operation. Croatia and Ukraine provided

---

[148] S/RES 1872 (2009), May 26, 2009.
[149] Political and security Committee decision Atalanta 1/2010, Mar. 5, 2010 amending Political and Security Committee Decision Atalanta 2/2009 on the acceptance of third States' contributions to the European Union military operation to contribute to the deterrence, prevention and repression of acts of piracy and armed robbery off the Somali coast (Atalanta).
[150] EU Political and Security Committee Decision ATALANTA/3/2009 on the setting up of the Committee of Contributors for the European Union military operation to

staff officers to the headquarters, and Montenegro entered into a Participation Agreement with the EU on March 22, 2010.[151]

On January 25, 2010, the EU Council approved a programmed military mission to help train Somali security forces. This decision resulted in establishment of the EU training mission (EUTM) on April, 7, 2010, as part of the overall effort to strengthen the Transitional Federal Government (TFG) and governmental authority and institutions of Somalia. The actual training, which takes place in Uganda, began in May 2010, and includes coordination with AMISOM, the TFG, Uganda, the African Union, the United Nations and the United States. Training has been provided to 3,000 Somali recruits up to and including the platoon level, including appropriate modular and specialized training for officers and non-commissioned officers. On January 22, 2013, the EU Council agreed to extend its military mission in Somalia until March 31, 2015.[152]

The EU also signed an agreement to assist the Seychelles.[153] The comprehensive Status of Forces Agreement specifies that EU personnel, ships, and aircraft may be used in Seychelles and throughout the territorial sea of the country against pirate ships.[154] Seychelles grants "EUNAVFOR personnel freedom of movement and freedom to travel within its territory, including its waters and its air space."[155] "Freedom of movement" for EU forces includes "stopping and anchoring under any circumstances."[156] EU forces also have permission to use any "military device" on land or at sea, but subject to host nation rules on flight safety.[157] The agreement also contains standards privileges and immunities from Seychelles' civil law process.

---

contribute to the deterrence, prevention and repression of acts of piracy and armed robbery off the Somali coast (Atalanta).

[151] EU Council Decision 2010/199/CFSP, Mar. 22, 2010, on the signing and conclusion of the Agreement between the European Union and Montenegro on the participation of Montenegro in the European Union military operation to contribute to the deterrence, prevention and repression of acts of piracy and armed robbery off the Somali coast (Operation Atalanta), Official Journal of the European Union, Aug. 4, 2010, at L 88/1-/2.

[152] EU Council Decision 2010/766/CFSP of Dec. 7, 2010, amending Joint Action 2008/851/CFSP on a European Union military operation to contribute to the deterrence, prevention and repression of acts of piracy and armed robbery off the Somali coast, OFFICIAL J. OF THE EUROPEAN UNION, Nov. 12, 2010, L 327/49–50.

[153] Council Decision 2009/916/CFSP of Oct. 23, 2009 concerning the signing and conclusion of the Agreement between the European Union and the Republic of Seychelles on the status of the European Union-led force in the Republic of Seychelles in the framework of the EU military operation Atalanta, OFFICIAL J. OF THE EUROPEAN UNION, L 323/12–13.

[154] Id.
[155] Id.
[156] Id.
[157] Id.

NATO, EU and CTF-151 share responsibility for patrolling the MSPA and IRTC.[158] Each command element cannot control units from other task forces, but recommendations may be made in order to synchronize deterrence and response. The task forces may communicate with each other over unclassified Mercury circuits and other communications systems. Beyond the efforts of the three multinational task forces, however, the naval units of some nations operate in the region independently to escort merchant shipping.

20.3.4 *Japan Maritime Self-Defense Force*

In 2008, Japan made the decision to provide assistance in the fight against Somali piracy, and sent aircraft and warships to the area beginning in 2009. In March 2009, the Japan Maritime Self-Defense Force (JMSDF) deployed two destroyers into the Gulf of Aden to protect ships from pirates carrying Japanese cargo. The ships were supplemented with the addition of two P-3C maritime patrol aircraft in June 2009. The next month, the adoption of a June 19 law provided authority for Japan to escort foreign-flagged ships at risk of piracy attack. The law also provides authority for JMSDF ships to fire on suspicious ships as a last resort to prevent piracy.[159]

Each year about 2,000 ships flagged in Japan or owned by Japanese corporations transit the Gulf of Aden and coast of Somalia. The Gulf of Aden is a particularly important sea lane, connecting Japan to Europe. Responding to an urgent need to protect the lives and property of Japanese nationals, the Prime Minister, acting upon Cabinet decision, approved a maritime security order on March 13, 2009, to deploy Self-Defense Forces to the region.[160] The destroyers *Sazanami* and the *Samidare* departed Japan on March 14 and began escort operations in the Gulf of Aden on March 30.[161] A detachment of Japan Coast Guard officers was embarked on each warship. During their first 90 days on station, the ships escorted 100 ships, including Japanese-flagged ships, foreign-flagged ships with Japanese crew or operated by Japanese carriers, or vessels that transport important Japanese cargo.

Japan opened its first overseas base since World War II on June 1, 2011, as part of that country's contribution to the fight against piracy. The Japan Self-Defense Forces (SDF) established a 12-hectare base northwest of Djibouti International Airport to support the anti-piracy mission in the Horn of Africa. Defense Ministry

---

[158] IMO Doc. SN.1/Circ.281, Information on the Internationally Recommended Transit Corridor (IRTC) for Ships Transiting the Gulf of Aden, Aug. 3, 2009.
[159] ASAHI SHIMBUN, June 3, 2011, KYODO NEWS SERVICE, June 1, 2011 and JIJI, July 2009.
[160] The measure was issued under Article 82 of the Self-Defense Forces Law, providing stopgap authority until a law was enacted. MINISTRY OF DEFENSE, GOVERNMENT OF JAPAN, DEFENSE OF JAPAN 2009, at 128–29 (2009).
[161] Id., at 129.

officials stated to Japanese media that they expect piracy to persist for the foreseeable future—and may continue for a decade.[162] The full-scale facility has a gymnasium, dining and dormitory buildings, an aircraft tarmac capable of handling three aircraft, and an aircraft maintenance hangar that can accommodate P-3C maritime patrol aircraft.[163] Approximately 150 Maritime SDF and Ground SDF members are stationed at the base.[164] Public broadcaster NHK stated that the facility reflects Japan's long-term commitment to stabilize the Horn of Africa, although the Maritime SDF Chief of Staff Admiral Masahiko Sugimoto suggested that the facility was not an "outlying base" where Japanese forces would be permanently stationed.[165]

It is no accident that once China succeeded in deploying to the region Japan was close behind. For Japan, which has long operated a highly advanced and well-maintained naval force, the counter-piracy operations have less to do with exercising the operational effectiveness of the force than with signaling a political maturation inside the Government of Japan. Inhibited by its constitution from assuming a political role commensurate with its economic and military capacity, Japan's counter-piracy deployment constitutes another toe in the water, testing the boundaries of the concept of "self-defense." Japan is furthermore deeply concerned about promoting rule of law in the oceans and preserving the concept of freedom of the seas. As the leader in counter-piracy cooperation in Asia during the early- and mid-2000s, no nation has done more to suppress piracy than Japan. An island nation wholly dependent on Persian Gulf oil and international maritime trade, Japan is a reliable leader for developing new approaches to maritime security.

The Japanese public has supported the deployments by a ratio of about two-to-one, and the missions resulted in more than 800 messages of gratitude by ship masters and ship owners who have been escorted.[166] On November 23, 2010, the IMO conferred a bravery award for Japanese successes—a testament to the high degree of professionalization of the Japan Maritime Self-Defense Force. The counter-piracy mission has drawn the attention of the international community, and already there is an expectation that Japan Self-Defense Forces may play a greater role in maintaining regional political stability. Whispers suggest that the Japan Self-Defense Forces, for example, might deploy next to South Sudan to help stabilize that war-torn country.

---

[162] ASAHI SHIMBUN, June 3, 2011.
[163] NHK, KYODO, June 1, 2011 and THE DAILY YOMIURI, May 28, 2011.
[164] ASAHI SHIMBUN, June 3, 2011.
[165] KYODO NEWS SERVICE, June 1, 2011.
[166] MINISTRY OF DEFENSE, GOVERNMENT OF JAPAN, DEFENSE OF JAPAN 2010, at 252 (2010).

Table 20.2. Japanese Counter-piracy Legal Authorities[167]

Activity	Maritime Patrol Activities	Counter-piracy Operations
Issuance of instructions and orders	In cases necessary to protect lives and property and maintain security at sea	When necessary to combat acts of maritime piracy
Interagency procedure	Minister of Defense issues order upon approval of the Prime Minister	Minister of Defense submits an outline of operations to the Prime Minister; upon approval, the Minister of Defense issues an order, also subject to approval of the Prime Minister
Report at the Diet	No provisions	Prime Minister reports to the Diet when he has approved counter-piracy operations, or when a mission has been completed
Ships and vessels that may be protected	Japan-affiliated ships, including ships flagged in Japan, owned by Japanese corporations, or carrying Japanese crews or significant cargoes	All ships and vessels
Legal authority for the Self-Defense Forces to Act	Japan Coast Guard Law (Article 93 of the Self-Defense Forces Law), specifically, Article 16 (a request for cooperation to ships in the vicinity); Article 17(1) (on-scene inspection and questioning crew); Article 18 (route change, spotting the ship)	Article 16 (a request for cooperation to ships in the vicinity); Article 18 (route change, spotting the ship), Article 8 of the Anti-piracy Law
Use of force	Article 7 of the Act concerning the Execution of Official Police Duties, the use of armed force is permitted when used for self-protection, the protection of others, or for the prevention of interference in official duties, to the extent reasonably necessary under the circumstances.	Article 7 of the Act concerning the Execution of Official Police Duties, the use of armed force is permitted when used for self-protection, the protection of others, or for the prevention of interference in official duties, to the extent reasonably necessary under the circumstances.

---

[167] Id., at 246 (2010).

20.3.5 *Flag State Administrations and Best Management Practices*

Primary responsibility to protect ships from piratical acts rests with the flag State. Accordingly, flag States should promulgate to their ships detailed guidance on how to implement industry best practices to deter and defeat pirate attack. Flag States should have a program to implement the framework, which was developed by the shipping community. The program implements avoidance, evasion, and defensive best practices to prevent and suppress piracy, and is tailored to suit the respective risk profiles and resource portfolios of ships conducting voyages in High Risk Areas.[168]

Vessels that are slower—transiting at 14 knots are less—and have a lower freeboard, are at greater risk. Ships that are not in in conformity with the fourth edition of the international shipping industry's *Best Management Practices* (BMP4) are also more vulnerable. BMP4 measures include:

- maintaining a proactive 24 hour lookout;
- reporting suspicious activities to authorities;
- removing access ladders;
- protecting the lowest points of access;
- employing passive anti-access measures, such as use of deck lighting, netting, razor wire, electrical fencing, fire hoses and surveillance and detection equipment;
- engaging in evasive maneuvering and speed during a pirate attacks; and
- joining convoy transits.[169]

An individual risk assessment is required for each ship because not all security measures or best practices are appropriate for each type of vessel. The assessment should account for crew safety, freeboard, maximum speed of the ship under conditions of sea state, and prevalence of pirate activity in the area to be transited.

Shipping companies and the Flag State Administration complete risk assessments, periodic review of vessel Safety Management Systems or Ship Security Plans (SSP) for countering maritime piracy, and test communication requirements with UKMTO and MSCHOA prior to and during transit of the High Risk Area. Training oversight, consistent with the requirements of the STCW, are a major feature of the BMP4. If the administration permits the option of ship borne government or privately contracted armed security personnel (PCASP), it should promulgate guidance on their use.

The Administration should establish a coordinated contingency and emergency communication plan for travel through the High Risk Area designated off

---

[168] IMO Doc. MSC.324 (89) and IMO Doc. A.1044(27).
[169] INT'L CHAMBER OF SHIPPING, ET AL., BEST MANAGEMENT PRACTICES FOR PROTECTION AGAINST SOMALI BASED PIRACY: SUGGESTED PLANNING AND OPERATIONAL PRACTICES FOR SHIP OPERATORS, AND THE MASTERS OF SHIPS TRANSITING THE HIGH RISK AREA (4th ed. Aug. 2011), *distributed via* IMO Doc. MSC.1/Circ.1339, Piracy and Armed Robbery against Ships in Waters off the Coast of Somalia: Best Management Practices for Protection against Somali Based Piracy, Sept. 14, 2011.

the coast of East Africa, and during a piracy attack. Procedures also should be produced for liaison with friendly naval forces. Administrations ensure that vessels exercise and implement an effective program of Self-Protection Measures (SPMs).[170] The SPMs may include, but are not limited to, the following:

(a) Watchkeeping and Enhanced Vigilance;
(b) Effective use of monitoring and/or surveillance equipment;
(c) Maneuvering practice;
(d) Alert systems to demonstrate awareness to any potential attacker;
(e) Use of deck lighting and illumination to demonstrate awareness to any potential attacker;
(f) Denial of use of ship's tools and equipment, and protection of equipment stored on the upper deck;
(g) Protection of navigation and engineering control spaces and erection of physical barriers;
(h) Other equipment used for self-defense; and
(i) Safe-muster points and Citadels, if determined appropriate.[171]

Flag State Administrations promote the use of avoidance, evasion, and defensive best practices against piracy. Ship owners should also provide to ship Masters regularly updated piracy-related threat information before and during sailing through High Risk Areas. The anti-piracy measures contained in BMP4 should be understood by ship owners and ship operators. Flag State Administrations should ensure oversight for its implementation on ships flying their flag.[172] Unfortunately, accelerating attacks in 2011 and lax application of the BMP4 by many ships prompted the IMO to issue Circular Letter 3164, which warned

> Naval forces operating in the region off the coast of Somalia have reported that an unacceptably high proportion of the ships transiting the Gulf of Aden are not registered with the Maritime Security Centre Horn of Africa1; are not reporting to UKMTO Dubai2; show no visible deterrent measures and are not acting upon the navigational warnings to shipping promulgating details of pirate attacks and suspect vessels.
>
> **Failure to implement fully the best management practice guidance significantly increases the risk of successful pirate attacks.**
>
> All those concerned, particularly Administrations, industry representative bodies, seafarer associations, shipowners and companies are, therefore, **strongly urged to take action to ensure that ships' masters receive updated information unfailingly**

---

[170] IMO Doc. MSC Circ. 1390, Guidance for Company Security Officers (CSOs)—Preparation of a Company and Crew for the Contingency of Hijack by Pirates in the Western Indian Ocean and the Gulf of Aden, Dec. 9, 2010.
[171] Id., at Annex.
[172] IMO Doc. MSC.324(89), Implementation of the Best Management Practice Guidance, May 20, 2011, *reprinted in* IMO Doc. MSC 89/25/Add.4.

and that all the recommended preventive, evasive and defensive measures are fully and effectively implemented.[173]

The warning was included as part of an "action plan" issued by a letter from the IMO Secretariat. The letter stated,

> Member Governments, industry organizations, seafarer representative bodies and shipmasters are invited, as the case may be:
>
> .1 to consider participating in the anti-piracy campaign launched by IMO by providing naval, aerial and other resources to join those already deployed in the waters off the coast of Somalia and in the Gulf of Aden;
> .2 to promulgate, as widely as possible, the IMO and industry recommended measures and best management practices;
> .3 to provide LRIT information to security forces operating in the Gulf of Aden and the Western Indian Ocean;
> .4 to register their ships, before entering areas known as piracy affected, with the established operational centers; and
> .5 while sailing through piracy-infested areas, to comply with and implement [the Best Management Practices and industry recommended measures].[174]

In 2012, although the BMP4 remained essential for effective deterrence against piracy, the precipitous drop in the number of attempted and actual piracy attacks off the coast of Somalia may be attributed to the generous use of armed security on board ships.

---

[173] IMO Doc. Circular Letter No. 3164, Responding to the Scourge of Piracy, Feb. 14, 2011, at p. 3 (bold in original).
[174] Id. (bold in original).

TWENTY-ONE

MARITIME TERRORISM AND WEAPONS OF MASS DESTRUCTION AT SEA

21.1 Prevalence of Maritime Terrorism

There are about 500 terrorist organizations in the world—100 of them are large groups, and about 100 are active at sea. The most dangerous groups include Al Qaeda in the Islamic Maghreb (AQIM), Al Qaeda in the Arabian Peninsula (AQAP), the Revolutionary Armed Forces of Colombia (FARC), Hamas, Hezbollah, Boko Haram, and the Movement for the Emancipation of the Niger Delta (MEND). Their combined budget varies from $5 billion to $20 billion and annual losses from maritime crime are around $16 billion.[1] Between 1968 and 2000, these organizations committed about 7,900 acts of terrorism, which resulted in over 10,000 deaths and 53,000 injuries.[2] Al Qaeda, Abu Sayyaf, Hezbollah, Hamas, Irish Republican Army (IRA), Palestinian Islamic Jihad, Palestine Liberation Front (PLF), and the Liberation Tigers of Tamil Eelam (LTTE or Tamil Tigers) have carried out numerous maritime attacks. Maritime terrorists use small boat suicide attacks, lay mines and explosives against ships and port facilities, conduct stealth approaches by underwater demolition teams, engage in raids against onshore targets (launched from mother ships), and conduct missile and rocket attacks against civilian and military vessels.

The list of potential maritime targets extends beyond passenger ships and tankers containing crude oil, liquefied natural gas, or chemical compounds and vessels freighting nuclear waste, weapons, or explosive and combustible agents. High-value

---

[1] Volodymyr Bezkorovainiy and Sergiy Sokolyuk, Piracy, Maritime Terrorism and Disorder at Sea: The View from the Ukraine, Corbett Paper No. Feb. 8, 2012, at p. 2.
[2] Id.

and high-risk infrastructure such as gas and oil platforms (GOPLATs), refineries and port facilities are also key targets of maritime terrorism.

Between 1971 and 1990, the Provisional Irish Republican Army (PIRA) attacked nine civilian and military ships. Eight of the vessels sank, and the ninth—the RFA *Fort Victoria* was severely damaged. On August 27, 1979, PIRA terrorists assassinated Lord Louis Mountbatten, Admiral of the Fleet and member of the House of Lords, by detonating a radio-controlled explosive device hidden aboard his yacht. The attack killed Lord Mountbatten and three other persons.

21.1.1 *Palestine Liberation Front and the Achille Lauro*

On October 7, 1985, four terrorists tied to the Palestine Liberation Front (PLF) hijacked the cruise ship *Achille Lauro* as it sailed Egyptian waters. The ship was headed from Alexandria to Port Said, Egypt. The terrorists diverted the ship to Syria while holding the crew and passengers hostage, and demanded the release of 50 Palestinians imprisoned in Israel. When the vessel was refused permission to enter port at Tartus, Syria, the hijackers murdered 69-year old disabled Jewish-American passenger Leon Klinghoffer and threw his body into the ocean. The ship then sailed back to Port Said, and after two days of negotiations, the terrorists surrendered to Egyptian authorities in exchange for safe passage to Tunisia.

But the bargain with the Egyptian government apparently was based upon the proviso that the terrorists had not injured any of the passengers, and it was unknown at the time of Klinghoffer's murder. Once the murder was discovered, however, the deal was nixed. On October 10, 1985, U.S. Navy aircraft from the aircraft carrier *USS Saratoga* operating in the Mediterranean Sea intercepted the airliner carrying the terrorists and forced it to land at a U.S. airbase at Sigonella, Sicily. The aircraft landed at the U.S. base, and was surrounded by U.S. Navy SEALs, who arrived in two C-141 transport aircraft. Italian Prime Minister Bettino Craxi claimed that Italian territorial sovereignty had been violated over the use of the NATO base, however, and Italian Air Force personnel and *Carabinieri* surrounded the SEALs and the aircraft. After a five-hour standoff between U.S. and Italian soldiers, the terrorists were taken into custody by Italian authorities.

An Italian court convicted 11 of 15 persons on board the aircraft associated with the hijacking. Inexplicably, PLF leader and mastermind Mohammad Abbas and a PLO political officer on board the aircraft were placed on another flight in Rome bound for Belgrade, Yugoslavia. From Belgrade, Abbas wound up in Baghdad, where he remained as a guest of Saddam Hussein. Abbas was tried in absentia by an Italian court and convicted to five terms of life imprisonment for his role in the hijacking, but Iraq shielded him from extradition to Italy (or the United States). In 1990, Abbas launched an abortive speedboat attack on sunbathers on a beach near Tel Aviv.

Abbas carried an Iraqi passport and floated through Tunisia and lived for a time in the Gaza Strip. As a result of the 1995 Israeli Palestinian interim peace agreement, Abbas and other PLO members were granted criminal immunity for their violent crimes committed before the Oslo agreement was signed in October 1993. Thereafter, it appears Abbas was a courier for Saddam Hussein, carrying payments to families of suicide bombers. On April 15 2003, Abbas died of natural causes during his detention by American forces during Operation Iraqi Freedom.

Less than three years after the attack on *Achille Lauro*, on July 11, 1988, another passenger ship, *City of Poros*, was attacked while transiting three miles off Aegina, Greece by terrorists from the Abu Nidal Palestinian terrorist organization. Once again posing as passengers, the terrorists, armed with machine guns and grenades, gained access to the ship. Nine tourists were killed and 98 injured. The terrorists then fled the ship by speedboat.

21.1.2 Sri Lanka and the Tamil Tigers

Across the 40-mile wide Palk Strait separating India and Sri Lanka, the Liberation Tigers of Tamil Eelam (LTTE) waged a three-decade war against Sri Lanka to create a separate and sovereign Tamil state. The LTTE emerged from humble beginnings to operate a sophisticated network of maritime commercial infrastructure and attack craft based in Tamil Nadu. The organization used commercial vessels to transport weapons and smuggle illegal drugs, weapons, LTTE fighters, and other contraband—some ships were large enough to carry one or two shipping containers.[3] The LTTE, along with the Irish Republican Army and the Palestine Liberation Organization, are the only insurgent organizations believed to have a fleet of deep sea-going vessels, although Hezbollah and Hamas appear to have state sponsors, such as Iran and in the latter case, Turkey, that may make vessels available to the terrorist groups.

The LTTE's transport ships were wired with explosives so they could be scuttled if they were interdicted. This was the case with the M/V *Ahat*, which was interdicted by the Indian Navy on January 14, 1993. The ship was headed toward Thailand. Accounts vary as to how it went to the bottom. It was either towed to Madras Port, but sank after catching fire, or exploded at sea, before it could be boarded.[4] The entire fleet of LTTE ships was believed to number 12 to 15, generally displacing 1,000 to 1,500 tons each.[5]

The small and fast suicide boats of the Sea Tigers, the maritime wing of the LTTE, were the most effective maritime terrorist platforms in the world. The LTTE's insurgency began in 1983 and ended in 2009, when the group was dismantled by the Sri Lankan armed forces. During the intervening decades, the

---

[3] VIJAY SAKHUJA, THE DYNAMICS OF LTTE'S COMMERCIAL MARITIME SHIPPING INFRASTRUCTURE, ORF OCCASIONAL PAPER 1 (Observer Research Foundation, Apr. 2006).
[4] JANE'S WORLD INSURGENCY AND TERRORISM (2004) (Subscription online).
[5] SAKHUJA, THE DYNAMICS OF LTTE'S COMMERCIAL MARITIME SHIPPING INFRASTRUCTURE, at 2.

LTTE Sea Tigers conducted two-dozen hijackings and suicide attacks with waterborne improvised explosive devices (IEDs).

Over the years, the Sea Tigers killed 270 civilians and members of the armed forces, as well as sank or damaged 20 ships. The group engaged in numerous vessel hijackings, including assaults on the *Irish Mona* in August 1995, *Princess Wave* in August 1996, *Athena*, May 1997, *Misen*, July 1997, *Morong Bon*, July 1997, M/V *Cordiality* in September 1997, and the *Princess Kash* in August 1998. The group also is believed to have hijacked the 2,818-ton Malaysian-flagged M/V *Sik Yang* in 1999. The ship sailed from India to the Malaysia port of Malacca, but apparently was intercepted by the LTTE—neither the ship nor its 63 crew members were ever heard from again.[6]

Operation *Cactus*, undertaken in 1988 by India in the Maldives, was one of the most remarkable naval operations to counter maritime terrorism.[7] The Indian Navy was invited to defend the democratic government of President Maumoon Abdul Gayoom of the Maldives against the November 1988 coup d'état. The coup was led by a small coterie of Maldivians under Abudllah Luthufi and supported by 80 Sri Lankan secessionist militants from the People's Liberation Organization of Tamil Eelam (PLOTE). When the plot was foiled, a group of 47 mercenaries attempted to escape by sea, hijacking the M/V *Progress Light*, with 23 hostages. The frigate *INS Betwa* and *INS Godavari*, a frigate carrying Sea King helicopters, tracked the ship in conjunction with Alize maritime patrol aircraft operating out of Kochi. Gunfire from the *Godavari* and two depth charges dropped by the Alize aircraft convinced the mercenaries to surrender. The vessel was boarded and secured by marine commandoes operating out of Ratmalana Airfield on the outskirts of Colombo. In July 1989, India repatriated the mercenaries to the Maldives to stand trial. President Gayoom commuted the death sentences passed against them to life imprisonment.

In another case still clouded in mystery, a consignment of 32,000 mortar shells produced by the Zimbabwe Defense Industries (ZDI) was loaded on a ship at the Mozambican port of Beira on May 23, 1997. The ammunition cache was bound for the Sri Lankan government, but it never reached its destination. Instead, the mortar shells appear to have been transferred at sea onto an LTTE ship, *Limassol*.[8]

On October 23, 2000, the "Black Tigers," a unit of the Sea Tigers brigade, used two small boats packed with explosives to attack two Sri Lankan ferries. One ferry was destroyed and the other damaged. Two hundred fifty people were killed and 300 wounded in the attack. The next year, LTTE suicide bombers struck the

---

[6] Id., at 3–4.
[7] Admiral Sureesh Mehta, Chief of the Naval Staff, Freedom to Use the Seas: India's Maritime Military Strategy 22 (Integrated Headquarters Ministry of Defence (Navy) 2007).
[8] Raymond Bonner, *Tamil Guerillas in Sri Lanka: Deadly and Armed to the Teeth*, N.Y. Times, Mar. 7, 1998.

Silk Pride tanker in Sri Lankan coastal waters, sending the ship to the bottom. In February 2008, the LTTE Sea Tigers sank a Sri Lankan fast attack craft in the Sea of Thalaimannar, almost 200 nautical miles from Colombo. The "sea tigers" have been extraordinarily successful, having sunk over 30 percent of the small boats in the Sri Lankan navy—the new face of maritime terrorism. Over years of fighting, the Sri Lankan Navy lost about half its force to LTTE attacks, leading the insurgent group at one point to boldly propose maritime zones and distinct sea lanes to separate the LTTE and the Sri Lankan Navy.[9] Sri Lanka rejected the idea.

India also has been the victim of an amphibious type of maritime terrorism. Islamic terrorists from neighboring Pakistan have used the ocean to strike the world's largest democracy. Mumbai suffered devastating terrorist attacks in March 1993 and again in December 2008; both assaults emerged from the sea. In 1993, terrorists clandestinely smuggled arms, ammunition and explosives by ship from Karachi into the Indian state of Maharashtra. More recently, in December 2008, terrorist commandos traveled by sea from Karachi across the Arabian Sea, entering India from speedboats launched from trawlers. Once in India the group went on a rampage throughout Mumbai, murdering nearly two hundred people and bringing the financial center to a standstill. Ships were also used to transport the explosives that bombed the U.S. embassies in Dar es Salaam and in 1998.

21.1.3 *Al Qaeda and the* USS Cole

For more than a decade, Al Qaeda and associated extremist groups have conducted a campaign of maritime terrorism. On January 3, 2000, members of Al-Qaeda tried to attack the *USS The Sullivans*, a guided-missile destroyer, as it lay in port at Aden, Yemen. A small boat, loaded with a large amount of explosives, was preparing to get near the ship and explode. But the boat was so overloaded that it sank and the attack was abandoned. The attempt against *The Sullivans*, however, provided practice for the successful attack on the *USS Cole* (DDG-67). The October 12, 2000, slow, low-tech assault against the *USS Cole* nearly sunk the powerful warship. Al-Qaeda suicide bombers attacked the guided-missile destroyer with a small boat carrying more than 1,000 pounds of explosives as the warship lay at anchor in Aden, Yemen. The explosion tore a gaping hole 40 feet (12 meters) in diameter on the port side of the ship, killing 17 crewmembers and injuring 39. In February of that same year, the Moro Islamic Liberation Front, an Al Qaeda affiliate, carried out a bomb attack against the ship *Our Lady of Mediatrix*, killing more than 40 crew members.[10]

---

[9] Vijay Sakhuja, The Dynamics of LTTE's Commercial Maritime Shipping Infrastructure, ORF Occasional Paper 4 (Observer Research Foundation, Apr. 2006).

[10] Philippe Migauz, *The Future of the Islamist Movement, in* THE HISTORY OF TERRORISM: FROM ANTIQUITY TO AL QAEDA 349, 353 (Gérard Chaliand & Arnaud Blin, eds., 2007).

On October 6, 2002, members of al Qaeda rammed a small boat filled with explosives into the French oil tanker *Limburg* as it transited off the coast of Yemen from Iran to Malaysia. The attack exposed the vulnerability of the oil transshipment route through the Strait of Hormuz. Four hundred thousand barrels of oil spilled into the ocean. One crewmember was killed, and 12 were injured. Another Islamic terrorist cell, the Abu Sayyaf organization in the Philippines, struck next. On February 27, 2004, the passenger ship *SuperFerry 14* sank in Manila Bay from the detonation of a bomb planted on board by members of Abu Sayyaf. Of the 899 passengers on board the ship, 116 were killed in the attack. In March 2004, Hamas conducted a double suicide bombing of the port of Ashdod, Israel.[11] Ashdod is one of the most sensitive infrastructure complexes in the entire country, containing a number of bromine tanks and other hazardous chemical storage facilities. Two Palestinian terrorists infiltrated the port by hiding behind a false wall in a 15-meter shipping container. The container had been inspected at the Karni crossing in Gaza and also at Ashdod, but inspectors failed to detect the bombers.[12] The next year, on August 19, 2005, Al Qaeda terrorists fired rockets at *USS Kearsarge* (LHD 3) and *USS Ashland* (LSD 48) as they moored in Jordan's Red Sea port of Aqaba.[13] The ships avoided damage, but the port facilities were slightly damaged, and 10 security guards were killed. The Israeli port of Eliat was also hit.

On April 24, 2004, Al Qaeda suicide bombers in an explosives-laden dhow approached Khawr Al Amaya Oil Terminal (KAOT) 15 miles off the port of Basra, Iraq. The Iraqi terminal, which is 15 miles off the port of Basra, is one of two terminals that pipe about 90 percent of the oil produced by Iraq to oil tankers lying offshore. A rigid-hull inflatable boat (RHIB) from the U.S. Cyclone-class patrol boat *USS Firebolt* approached the dhow to conduct a boarding of the vessel. The RHIB had a boarding team of seven persons. When the dhow exploded, two U.S. service members were killed in the attack, including Coast Guardsman Petty Officer Third Class Nathan Bruckenthal, the first Coast Guardsman to die in action since the Vietnam War. The RHIB was flipped by the explosion, and the remaining crew was rescued by an SH-60 Seahawk helicopter from the Australian frigate *HMAS Stuart*. The *Firebolt* avoided damage. The oil terminal was closed for two days at a cost of $40 million. The attack on KAOT illustrates how "soft" economic targets are easily damaged or destroyed by waterborne IEDs, rocket-propelled grenades, and big-bore sniper rifles with high explosive or armor-piercing incendiary ammunition.

---

[11] Nicholas Fiorenza, *Who Goes There?* DEFENSE TECHNOLOGY INT'L, Oct. 2009, 54–57, at 57.

[12] Id.

[13] *Al-Zarqawi Group Claims Attack on U.S. Ships: Jordan Arrests Syrian Allegedly Part of Iraq-based Terrorist Group*, MSNBC.COM, Aug. 23, 2005.

More recently, on July 27, 2010, the oil tanker *M. Star* was attacked by a suicide bomber in a speedboat as it transited Omani waters. The attack, presumably by Al Qaeda in the Arabian Peninsula, damaged the hull of the ship and killed one crewmember, but there was no oil spill. The evidence of trace explosives on the hull of the ship and record of a small boat radar contact before the attack provides circumstantial evidence of an Al Qaeda-affiliated attack.

Another Al Qaeda plot against U.S. or European ships in the Mediterranean Sea was foiled in February 2012 when Algerian police arrested three members of a cell that apparently was connected to Al Qaeda in the Islamic Maghreb.[14] Members of the terrorist cell planned to ram merchant ships with an explosive-laden boat, but the plot was disrupted in the planning stage. Similarly, Al Shabaab fighters fled Puntland in at least 10 skiffs bound for Zinjabar, an Al Qaeda held port in Yemen.[15] The movement followed an earlier outflow of 14 speedboats ferrying Al Qaeda and Al Shabaab militia across the Gulf of Aden to Yemen after African peacekeepers routed them from Somalia in December 2011 and January 2012.

The evidence linking Al Qaeda to attacks on international shipping and the maritime domain is particularly worrisome in light of efforts by the organization and other extremist groups to obtain weapons of mass destruction (WMD). The seas are susceptible to being used both as a method of transportation as well as a vector for delivery of WMD. To counter these threats, the international community has developed a broad legal regime. Although the framework is becoming stronger, it nonetheless reveals major flaws.

Just as the Al Qaeda, Abu Sayyaf group, and other Islamic extremist organizations have used maritime terrorism as a component of irregular warfare, so too has Hezbollah. On July 24, 2006, a C-802 anti-ship cruise missile hit the Israeli Navy corvette *Ahi Hanit* in Lebanese waters, resulting in major damage to the ship. Hezbollah fired the shore-to-ship missile at the Corvette, killing four crew members. The warship was demobilized and towed to Ashdod for repair.

21.2 Non-Proliferation Treaty

The *Nuclear Non-Proliferation Treaty* (NPT) was originally negotiated and designed to prevent the spread of nuclear weapons beyond the five-recognized nuclear-weapon states—China, France, Russia, United Kingdom and the United States.[16] Although there were some initial setbacks when India, Israel, Pakistan

---

[14] Lee Ferran & Pierre Thomas, *A Qaeda Affiliate Targets U.S. Ships: Report*, ABC News, Jan. 24, 2012.
[15] Jama Deberani & Robert Young, *Qandala: Al Shabaab Fighters on the Run: Fighters Spotted Fleeing to Yemen*, Puntland Press, Jan. 8, 2012.
[16] Nuclear Non-Proliferation Treaty, 729 U.N.T.S. 161 (No. 10485), July 1, 1968; I.L.M. (1968) 809; U.K.T.S. (1970) 88; T.I.A.S. 6839.

and South Africa did not sign the NPT in 1968 and subsequently acquired nuclear weapons, the treaty entered into force in March 1970, and the agreement has been generally successful in limiting the spread of nuclear weapons beyond the five permanent members of the UN Security Council.

Belarus (1993), Kazakhstan (1994) and Ukraine (1994) acceded to the NPT and returned the nuclear weapons they had inherited from the former Soviet Union to the Russian Federation. Although India, Israel and Pakistan remain outside the treaty and continue to possess nuclear arsenals, South Africa abandoned its nuclear weapons program and joined the NPT in 1991, as did Argentina (1995), Brazil (1998), Libya (1975), South Korea (1975) and Taiwan (1970). The two Gulf Wars and United Nations inspections effectively ended Iraq's nuclear ambitions.[17]

21.2.1 North Korea

However, there is a growing concern in recent years that the NPT regime may be unraveling. In January 2003, North Korea (DPRK) withdrew from the NPT citing national security concerns. The government of North Korea issued this statement:

> Under the grave situation where our state's supreme interests are most seriously threatened, the DPRK government adopts the following decisions to protect the sovereignty of the country and the nation and their right to existence and dignity: firstly, the DPRK government declares an automatic and immediate effectuation of its withdrawal from the NPT....
>
> Secondly, it declares that the DPRK withdrawing from the NPT is totally free from the binding force of the safeguards accord with the IAEA under its Article 3. The withdrawal from the NPT is a legitimate self-defensive measure taken against the US moves to stifle the DPRK and the unreasonable behavior of the IAEA following the US. [T]hough we pull out of the NPT, we have no intention to produce nuclear weapons and our nuclear activities at this stage will be confined only to peaceful purposes such as the production of electricity.[18]

Three years later, in October 2006, the DPRK successfully conducted a nuclear test at its Phunggye-ri facility. This test, which broke a decade-long de-facto global moratorium on nuclear explosive testing, was viewed by the IAEA as a threat to the NPT regime, "a clear setback to international commitments to move towards nuclear disarmament," and a serious security challenge for the international community. A second successful test was conducted by the DPRK in May 2009 at the Kilju test site.[19]

---

[17] DARYL KIMBALL, ET AL., NUCLEAR WEAPONS: WHO HAS WHAT AT A GLANCE (Arms Control Association, May 2010).

[18] GOVERNMENT OF THE DEMOCRATIC REPUBLIC OF NORTH KOREA, STATEMENT ON NPT WITHDRAWAL, Jan. 10, 2003.

[19] INT'L ATOMIC ENERGY AGENCY MEDIA RELEASES 2006/17, DEMOCRATIC REPUBLIC OF NORTH KOREA NUCLEAR TEST, Oct. 9, 2006.

A report by the IAEA Director General released in August 2010 stated that "the DPRK has not permitted the Agency to implement safeguards in the country [since December 2002] and, therefore, the Agency cannot draw any safeguards conclusion regarding the DPRK."[20] Additionally, the report indicates that the DPRK has not "implemented the relevant measures called for in United Nations Security Council Resolutions 1718 (2006) and 1874 (2009)" and that, since April 15, 2009, the IAEA "has not been able to carry out any monitoring and verification activities in the DPRK and thus cannot provide any conclusions regarding the DPRK's nuclear activities."[21] Similarly, a report issued by a UN panel of experts in May 2011 revealed that the DPRK and Iran were routinely sharing ballistic missile-related items and technology in violation of UN sanctions. The report implicated China as a possible transshipment source.[22]

21.2.2 Iran

Iran's fledgling nuclear weapons program is of equal concern. Fear over Tehran's nuclear ambitions increased in 2002 when the IAEA discovered a number of on-going activities that had not been previously reported by Iran, including the importation of 1,800 kg of natural uranium, a uranium enrichment program, a heavy water reactor program, and the existence of centrifuge and laser enrichment activities and facilities.[23]

Although Iran signed an Additional Protocol to its nuclear safeguards agreement in December 2003 that would allow IAEA inspectors greater authority to verify Iran's nuclear program and agreed to suspend all uranium enrichment-related and reprocessing activities, in September 2005, the IAEA determined that Iran had violated its safeguards agreement.[24] In March 2006, Iran announced its intentions to resume its enrichment-related activities and suspended cooperation with the IAEA. The Security Council responded with Resolution 1696 (2006)

---

[20] INT'L ATOMIC ENERGY AGENCY, REPORT OF THE DIRECTOR GENERAL, APPLICATION OF SAFEGUARDS IN THE DEMOCRATIC PEOPLE'S REPUBLIC OF KOREA, GOV/2010/45-GC(54)/12, Aug. 31, 2010 and GOV/2010/45/Corr.1-GC(54)/12/Corr.1, Sept. 1, 2010, para. 9.

[21] Id. Applicable IAEA resolutions concerning Implementation of the NPT Safeguards Agreement with the DPRK are available at http://www.iaea.org/newscenter/focus/iaeadprk/iaea_resolutions.shtml.

[22] Dan Bilefsky, *China Delays Report Suggesting North Korea Violated Sanctions*, N.Y. TIMES, May 14, 2011.

[23] INT'L ATOMIC ENERGY AGENCY, REPORT OF THE DIRECTOR GENERAL, IMPLEMENTATION OF THE NPT SAFEGUARDS AGREEMENT IN THE ISLAMIC REPUBLIC OF IRAN, GOV/2003/40, June 6, 2003.

[24] INT'L ATOMIC ENERGY AGENCY, REPORT OF THE DIRECTOR GENERAL, IMPLEMENTATION OF THE NPT SAFEGUARDS AGREEMENT IN THE ISLAMIC REPUBLIC OF IRAN, GOV/2005/67, Sept. 2, 2005.

demanding that Iran suspend all enrichment-related and reprocessing activities, including research and development.[25]

Five subsequent UN Security Council Resolutions and a series of IAEA resolution have failed to bring Iran into compliance with its international obligations. In particular, in May 2011, the IAEA found that Iran was not implementing the provisions of its Additional Protocol or its Safeguards Agreement and had not suspended its enrichment-related or heavy water-related activities. The IAEA also sought clarification on a number of issues that raised concern that Iran's nuclear program has military dimensions, including a neutron generator and associated diagnostics; uranium conversion and metallurgy; high explosives manufacture and testing; exploding bridge wire detonator studies; multipoint explosive initiation and hemispherical detonation studies involving highly instrumented experiments; high voltage firing equipment and instrumentation for explosives testing over long distances and possibly underground, and missile re-entry vehicle redesign activities for a new payload assessed as being nuclear in nature.[26] These programs "weaponize" a nuclear capability.

Six months later, the IAEA issued a report with a detailed analysis of the information available to the Agency that credibly suggests possible military dimensions to Iran's nuclear program. The information, contained in the Annex to the report, indicates that Iran has carried out the following activities that are relevant to the development of a nuclear explosive device:

- Efforts, some successful, to procure nuclear related and dual use equipment and materials by military related individuals and entities (Annex, Sections C.1 and C.2);
- Efforts to develop undeclared pathways for the production of nuclear material (Annex, Section C.3);
- The acquisition of nuclear weapons development information and documentation from a clandestine nuclear supply network (Annex, Section C.4); and
- Work on the development of an indigenous design of a nuclear weapon including the testing of components (Annex, Sections C.5–C.12).[27]

Based on this information, the Agency determined that Iran has carried out activities relevant to the development of a nuclear explosive device and that some of these activities still may be ongoing. The Agency therefore was unable to provide credible assurances that Iran's nuclear program was solely for peaceful purposes.

---

[25] S/RES/1696 (2006), July 31, 2006.
[26] INT'L ATOMIC ENERGY AGENCY, REPORT OF THE DIRECTOR GENERAL, IMPLEMENTATION OF THE NPT SAFEGUARDS AGREEMENT IN THE ISLAMIC REPUBLIC OF IRAN, GOV/2011/29, May 24, 2011.
[27] INT'L ATOMIC ENERGY AGENCY, REPORT OF THE DIRECTOR GENERAL, IMPLEMENTATION OF THE NPT SAFEGUARDS AGREEMENT IN THE ISLAMIC REPUBLIC OF IRAN, GOV/2011/65, Nov. 8, 2011.

Efforts by the IAEA to resolve these outstanding issues in January and February, 2012, failed to clarify Iran's intentions. During the first round of discussions between January 29 and 31:

- The Agency explained its concerns and identified the clarification of possible military dimensions to Iran's nuclear program as the top priority.
- The Agency requested access to the Parchin site, but Iran did not grant access to the site at that time.
- The Agency and Iran had an initial discussion on the approach to clarifying all outstanding issues in connection with Iran's nuclear program, including issues to be addressed, initial actions and modalities.
- A draft discussion paper on a structured approach to the clarification of all outstanding issues in connection with Iran's nuclear program was prepared for further consideration.[28]

A second round of talks took place on February 20 and 21 to further elaborate the Agency's concerns and obtain Iran's cooperation:

- The Agency reiterated its request for access to Parchin. Iran still declined to grant access to that site.
- An intensive discussion was held on the structured approach to the clarification of all outstanding issues related to Iran's nuclear program. No agreement was reached between Iran and the Agency, as major differences existed with respect to the approach.
- In response to the Agency's request, Iran provided the Agency with an initial declaration in connection with the issues identified in Section C of the Annex to the Director General's November 2011 report to the Board of Governors (GOV/2011/65). Iran's declaration dismissed the Agency's concerns in relation to the aforementioned issues, largely on the grounds that Iran considered them to be based on unfounded allegations.
- The Agency gave a presentation to Iran on the Agency's initial questions on Parchin and the foreign expert, and provided clarification of the nature of the Agency's concerns and the information available to it, in this regard.[29]

Despite these efforts, Iran failed to provide the necessary cooperation to enable the Agency to provide credible assurances about the absence of undeclared nuclear material and activities in Iran, and therefore to conclude that all nuclear material in Iran is in peaceful activities. The IAEA, therefore, expressed continued concern regarding the possible dimensions of Iran's nuclear program. The IAEA report further highlights that Iran did not provide access to Parchin, as requested, and that no agreement was reached on a structured approach to resolving all outstanding issues in connection with Iran's nuclear program.[30]

---

[28] Report of the Director General, Implementation of the NPT Safeguards Agreement in the Islamic Republic of Iran, GOV/2012/9, Feb. 24, 2011.
[29] Id.
[30] Id.

Iran has been particularly effective at waging a public diplomacy campaign to disguise its weapons program as an exercise of its right to enrich uranium as part of its peaceful pursuit of nuclear power and technology. Enrichment can produce fuel for nuclear power reactors, but highly enriched uranium can be used to construct an atomic bomb. Uranium for power generation is enriched at 3.5 percent; nuclear medicine requires 20 percent enriched uranium. Weapons-grade uranium is at 90 percent enriched, or higher. At talks in Moscow in June 2012, the Iranian delegate stated that the minimum demand from Tehran was that the world powers recognize its right under the NPT to enrich uranium. But the NPT grants no such right.[31]

Article IV of the NPT merely states:

> [N]othing in this Treaty shall be interpreted as affecting the inalienable right of all Parties to the Treaty to develop, research, production, and use of nuclear energy for peaceful purposes without discrimination and in conformity with Articles I and II of this Treaty.

Thus, there is no right of enrichment specifically enumerated in Article IV. Furthermore, the right to develop nuclear energy is based on compliance with Article II, which requires non-nuclear weapons States to "[undertake] ... not to manufacture or otherwise acquire nuclear weapons." Article III requires such States to accept IAEA "verification of the fulfillment of its obligations."

21.2.3 Is the NPT Viable?

The actions by the DPRK and Iran in defiance of the Security Council and IAEA draw into serious question the continued viability of the NPT to stop the spread of nuclear weapons and related technology in the 21st Century. Coupled with their unpredictable political regimes, growing ballistic missile programs, and the possibility that nuclear devices and related technology from these countries could find their way into the hands of terrorist groups or rogue states, such as Burma and Syria, both clandestine nuclear programs pose a serious threat to international peace and security.

The U.S. Secretary of Defense, the Director of the Central Intelligence Agency and the Chairman of the Joint Chiefs of Staff have all indicated that the DPRK's expanding ballistic missile and nuclear programs may become a direct threat to the United States. Intelligence estimates indicate that the DPRK will have the capability to strike the continental United States with an intercontinental ballistic missile within the next five years. And the DPRK has, on more than one occasion, threatened South Korea with nuclear war. Similarly, successive Iranian presidents have made it quite clear that Israel should be "wiped off the map"

---

[31] Michael Makovsky & Blaise Misztal, *Iran Has No 'Right' to Enrich Uranium* (Op-ed), WALL ST. J., July 9, 2012, at A15.

and that nuclear weapons developed by a Muslim state might be used to destroy Israel. To address this growing challenge, the international community has responded with a series of UN Security Council and IAEA resolutions, multilateral and bilateral agreements, and non-binding initiatives and arrangements to stem the proliferation of nuclear weapons and their related technology.

The NPT defines nuclear-weapon states in Article IX to include those states that had "manufactured and exploded a nuclear weapon or other nuclear explosive device prior to January 1, 1967." These states include the United States (1945), Soviet Union (1949), United Kingdom (1952), France (1960) and China (1964). India and Pakistan did not test their nuclear weapons until 1974 and 1998, respectively. Israel and South Africa have not publicly conducted nuclear tests.[32]

Pursuant to Article II of the NPT, the 184 non-nuclear-weapon State Parties agree "not to receive the transfer... of nuclear weapons or other nuclear explosive devices... not to manufacture or otherwise acquire nuclear weapons or other nuclear explosive devices; and not to seek or receive any assistance in the manufacture of nuclear weapons or other nuclear explosive devices." To ensure peaceful nuclear material is not diverted for illegal weapons purposes, the non-nuclear-weapon states also agree under Article III to "accept safeguards... for the exclusive purpose of verification of... its obligations assumed under this Treaty with a view to preventing diversion of nuclear energy from peaceful uses to nuclear weapons or other nuclear explosive devices" and to "conclude agreements with the International Atomic Energy Agency to meet [these] requirements...." North Korea detonated nuclear devices in 2006 and 2009.

Pursuant to Article III, both Iran and the DPRK entered into safeguard agreements with the IAEA in 1974[33] and 1992,[34] respectively. In Article 1 of the respective agreements, both governments agree to "accept safeguards... on all source or special fissionable material in all peaceful nuclear activities within its territory, under its jurisdiction or carried out under its control anywhere, for the exclusive purpose of verifying that such material is not diverted to nuclear weapons or other nuclear explosive devices." They further agreed in Article III to "co-operate to facilitate the implementation of the safeguards provided for in this Agreement." Despite these undertakings, neither Iran nor the DPRK have complied with their legal obligations under the NPT or their safeguard agreements.

---

[32] KIMBALL, ET AL., NUCLEAR WEAPONS: WHO HAS WHAT AT A GLANCE.
[33] Agreement of January 30, 1992, between the Government of the Democratic People's Republic of Korea and the International Atomic Energy Agency for the Application of Safeguards in Connection with the Treaty on the Non-Proliferation of Nuclear Weapons, INFCIRC/402, May 1992.
[34] Agreement between Iran and the Agency for the Application of Safeguards in Connection with the Treaty on the Non-Proliferation of Nuclear Weapons, INFCIRC/214, Dec. 13, 1974.

21.3 COASTAL STATE AND FLAG STATE JURISDICTION

Unlike land territory, which rarely gives rise to questions of state jurisdiction, assertion of jurisdiction over vessels at sea opens a milieu of applicable—and sometimes conflicting—laws regarding jurisdiction. In general, international law recognizes that states have "a wide measure of discretion" to extend their laws and the jurisdiction of their courts to "persons, property, or acts outside their territory."[35]

The interdiction of weapons of mass destruction (WMD) and related systems and materials is governed by a panoply of international and domestic laws and regulations. These rules are grounded in the principles of international maritime law reflected in the *United Nations Convention on the Law of the Sea* (UNCLOS) and associated international agreements and arrangements.[36] In general, a vessel's state of registry or flag State, has exclusive authority over matters that occur on board ships flying their flag.[37] Jurisdiction to board and inspect foreign flag vessels also may flow from the location of the vessel (*i.e.*, internal waters, territorial sea, contiguous zone, exclusive economic zone (EEZ) or high seas), the vessel's status (*i.e.*, public or commercial) and the vessel's conduct (*i.e.*, legal or illegal).

21.3.1 *Coastal State Authorities*

Coastal States enjoy complete sovereignty over their internal waters, as well as their territorial sea and archipelagic waters, subject to the right of innocent passage by foreign-flagged ships.[38] The balance between the right of the coastal State to ensure reasonable safety and security of its land and sea territory and airspace is balanced with the presumption of exclusive flag State jurisdiction over ships flying its flag. Accordingly, coastal States may adopt laws and regulations consistent with international law relating to innocent passage through the territorial sea in respect of, *inter alia*, the prevention of infringement of the customs, fiscal, immigration or sanitary laws and regulations of the coastal state.[39]

The concept of passage that is not innocent has its roots in the 1930 Hague Conference, which defined it as "when a vessel makes use of the territorial sea of a Coastal State for the purpose of doing any act prejudicial to the security, to

---

[35] *The Lotus*, P.C.I.J., SERIES A, No. 10, 1927, p. 4, 19.
[36] United Nations Convention on the Law of the Sea, *opened for signature* Dec. 10, 1982, UN Doc. A/CONF.62/122 (1982), 1833 U.N.T.S. 3, 397, 21 I.L.M. 1261 (1982), *entered into force* Nov. 16, 1994. [Hereinafter UNCLOS.]
[37] *Wildenhus' Case*, 120 U.S. 1, 12 (1887).
[38] UNCLOS, Articles 2 and 49.
[39] Id., Articles 21(1)(h) and 52.

the public policy, or to the fiscal interests of the coastal State."[40] Article 14 of the 1958 *Convention on the Territorial Sea and Contiguous Zone* states:

4. Passage is innocent so long as it is not prejudicial to the peace, good order or security of the coastal State. Such passage shall take place in conformity with these articles and with other rules of international law.
5. Passage of foreign fishing vessels shall not be considered innocent if they do not observe such laws and regulations as the coastal State may make and publish in order to prevent these vessels from fishing in the territorial sea.[41]

The terms "peace, good order or security of the coastal State," were not defined, however, which appeared to leave determination to the discretion of the coastal State.[42] During the negotiations for UNCLOS, the provision on innocent passage emerged from Article 19 with an attached, exhaustive list of items that rendered passage not innocent:

Article 19
Meaning of innocent passage

1. Passage is innocent so long as it is not prejudicial to the peace, good order or security of the coastal State. Such passage shall take place in conformity with this Convention and with other rules of international law.
2. Passage of a foreign ship shall be considered to be prejudicial to the peace, good order or security of the coastal State if in the territorial sea it engages in any of the following activities:
   a. any threat or use of force against the sovereignty, territorial integrity or political independence of the coastal State, or in any other manner in violation of the principles of international law embodied in the Charter of the United Nations;
   b. any exercise or practice with weapons of any kind;
   c. any act aimed at collecting information to the prejudice of the defense or security of the coastal State;
   d. any act of propaganda aimed at affecting the defense or security of the coastal State;
   e. the launching, landing or taking on board of any aircraft;
   f. the launching, landing or taking on board of any military device;
   g. the loading or unloading of any commodity, currency or person contrary to the customs, fiscal, immigration or sanitary laws and regulations of the coastal State;
   h. any act of willful and serious pollution contrary to this Convention;
   i. any fishing activities;

---

[40] League of Nations, I Acts of the Conference for the Codification of International Law, LN Doc. C.351.M.145, 1930.V, Annex 10, App. I, Article 3, at 123, 127, *reproduced in* 3 League of Nations Conference for the Codification of International Law [1930] 829 (Shabtai Rosenne ed., 1975).
[41] Convention on the Territorial Sea and Contiguous Zone (1958), Articles 3 and 4. *See*, UN Doc. Report of the First Committee, A/CONF.13/L28/Rev.1 (1958), para. 63, United Nations Conference on the Law of the Sea I (1958), OFFICIAL RECORDS 115, 120.
[42] UNITED NATIONS CONVENTION ON THE LAW OF THE SEA 1982: A COMMENTARY, VOL. II at 167 (Satya N. Nandan, Shabtai Rosenne & Neal Grandy eds., 1993).

j. the carrying out of research or survey activities;
k. any act aimed at interfering with any systems of communication or any other facilities or installations of the coastal State;
l. any other activity not having a direct bearing on passage.

Paragraph 2(a) merely restates the fundamental proscription of international law reflected in article 2(4) of the *Charter of the United Nations* that the aggressive use of force may not be used as an instrument of state policy. Within the contiguous zone, a coastal State may also exercise the control necessary to prevent infringement of its customs, fiscal, immigration or sanitary laws and regulations within its territory or territorial sea, and punish infringement of these laws and regulations committed within its territory or territorial sea.[43] Additionally, in the case of ships proceeding to internal waters, the coastal State may also take the necessary steps to prevent any breach of the conditions to which admission of those ships is subject.[44]

21.3.2 *Exclusive Flag State Jurisdiction*

As a general rule, ships shall sail under the flag of only one state and, with limited exceptions, are subject to the exclusive jurisdiction of the flag State on the high seas.[45] Typically, flag State or master consent is therefore required before a warship can stop and board a foreign flag vessel on the high seas. States may grant the right of any ship to fly their flag, and often neither the ships nor their owners have significant contacts with the state with which they register.[46] Under Article 5 of the 1958 *Convention on the High Seas* and Article 91 of UNCLOS, there must be a "genuine link" between the ship and the state conferring nationality on the ship. The scope of the "genuine link" is uncertain.

The concept of a genuine link was reflected in the *Nottebohm Case* of 1955. The *Nottebohm Case* arose over whether Liechtenstein could make a claim on behalf of Frederic Nottebohm against Guatemala for seizing his property without compensation. Nottebohm had resided in Guatemala from 1905 to 1939, and then subsequently left the country and was granted citizenship by Liechtenstein in October 1939. Traveling under a Liechtenstein passport, Nottebohm returned to Guatemala during World War II. The government of Guatemala seized his property as a war measure aimed at persons believed to be Nazi sympathizers.[47] Liechtenstein made a claim against Guatemala for the seizure of the property contrary to the principles of international law of a citizen of the country. The ICJ,

---

[43] UNCLOS, Article 33.
[44] Id., Articles 25(2) and 52.
[45] Id., Article 92.
[46] *See, e.g.*, BOLESLAW ADAM BOCZEK, FLAGS OF CONVENIENCE: AN INTERNATIONAL LEGAL STUDY 2 (1962).
[47] *Liechtenstein v. Guatemala*, 1955 I.C.J. 4, 18 (*Nottebohm Case*).

however, sided with Guatemala in a vote of 11 to 3, dismissed the claim by Liechtenstein. The Court found the link between Nottebohm and Liechtenstein as rather tenuous, whereas his connection to Guatemala was strong and enduring. The Court ruled that "[n]ationality is a legal bond having as its basis a social fact of attachment, a genuine connection of existence, interests, sentiments, together with the existence of reciprocal rights and duties."[48]

The *Nottebohm* decision clarified the question of whether a state was required to recognize the nationality of an individual person in the absence of a "genuine link." The principle has carried over to the international law of the sea, where it became a feature of both the 1958 *Convention on the High Seas* and UNCLOS.[49] Although states embarked on a quest to more precisely define the "genuine link" requirements, the *Nottebohm* test may be regarded as overly restrictive. In a 1960 advisory opinion to the International Maritime Consultative Organization, the predecessor of the International Maritime Organization, the International Court of Justice declined to apply the *Nottebohm* genuine link test against Panama and Liberia. The two open registry states had applied for membership on the Maritime Safety Committee of IMCO, but France, Norway, the Netherlands, and the United Kingdom sought to apply *Nottebohm* to deny the admission because the open registries were not "legitimate" ship owning states. The ICJ rejected the application, however, and refused to apply a strict test of genuine link to the ships registered by Liberia and Panama.[50]

Thus, the actual content of the genuine link is elusive. One thing is certain, however. The mere fact of ship registration does not create such a link. The Convention does not specify precisely what a genuine link must entail, or the consequences (if any) that follow from its absence.[51] There is general agreement, however, that the link must be real and independent of the act of registration.

> Although it is not an obligatory criterion for establishing the genuineness of a link the effective exercise of jurisdiction and control over its ships is one of the principal ways in which a flag State may demonstrate that the link between itself and its ships is genuine. To demonstrate that it is able effectively to exercise its jurisdiction and

---

[48] Id., at 23.
[49] Report of the International Law Commission Covering the Work of its Eighth Session (A/3159), Article 29 Commentary, para. 3 at 2790, *cited in* III UNITED NATIONS CONVENTION ON THE LAW OF THE SEA: A COMMENTARY 104 (Satya N. Nandan & Shabtai Rosenne eds., 1995).
[50] *Constitution of the Maritime Safety Committee of the International Maritime Consultative Organization* (Adv. Op.) 1960 I.C.J. 150, 171 (June 8, 1960).
[51] Moria L. McConnell, *Darkening Confusion Mounted Upon Darkening Confusion: The Elusive Quest for the Genuine Link*, 16 J. MAR L. & COM. 366, 367 (1985).

21.3.3 Stateless Vessels

control over a ship, a State must be able to show that the necessary mechanisms for such exercise are in place at the time when the ship is granted its nationality.[52]

The United States, the United Kingdom and other nations authorize seizure of stateless vessels by any nation, as they enjoy the protection of no flag State.[53] Common indicia of statelessness include no claim of nationality, multiple claims or conflicting claims of nationality, and a change of flags during a voyage.

To illustrate this point, in November 2002, U.S. intelligence sources began to track the M/V *So San* after it departed Nampo, North Korea, with a suspected cargo of missiles bound for the Middle East. The *So San* was registered in Cambodia, but was sailing without a flag. In addition, the ship's name and identification number had been painted over.

Efforts to verify the flag State of the vessel were unsuccessful, and the ship was therefore assimilated to be stateless. At the request of the United States, Spanish warships *Navarra* (F-85) and *Patino* (A-14) in the vicinity of the *So San* were requested to stop and inspect the vessel on the high seas, about 600 miles off the Yemeni coast. On December 9, 2002, after the *So San* failed to respond to requests to heave to and failed to respond to warning shots from *Navarra* and *Patino* and attempted to escape, Spanish Special Forces conducted a nonconsensual boarding by helicopter and small boat. The ship's manifest indicated that the freighter carried a cargo of cement to Yemen.

A subsequent search of the cargo hold by Spanish and U.S. naval personnel, however, discovered 15 SCUD ballistic missiles, 15 conventional warheads and 85 drums of inhibited red fuming nitric acid used as rocket propellant hidden under 40,000 bags of cement.[54] Although the vessel and its cargo were subsequently released and allowed to proceed to Yemen, the incident illustrates how nations can cooperate to interdict WMD and related materials on the high seas. However, it also served as a wake-up call for states of proliferation concern such as Iran and the DPRK—it is unlikely these states will ever use a stateless vessel to transport prohibited cargo.

Another example, which occurred in October 2003, involved the interdiction of the *BBC China*, a German-owned merchant vessel suspected by U.S. and British intelligence of carrying an illegal cargo of uranium centrifuge enrichment

---

[52] Robin R. Churchill, The Meaning of the "Genuine Link" in Relation to the Nationality of Ships 5 (A Study Prepared for the International Transport Worker's Federation, Oct. 2000.
[53] Malcolm Shaw, International Law 547 (5th ed. 2003).
[54] Brian Knowlton, *Ship allowed to take North Korea Scuds on to Yemeni Port: U.S. Freed Freighter Carrying Missiles*, N. Y. Times, Dec. 12, 2002 and Amitai Etzioni, *Tomorrow's Institution Today: The Promise of the Proliferation Security Initiative*, ForeignAffairs. Com Comment, May/June 2009.

parts from Malaysia to Libya. Based on a request by the U.S. Government, German authorities directed the ship's owner to divert the vessel to Taranto. Upon arrival, Italian authorities searched the vessel and discovered the nuclear centrifuge parts.[55]

21.3.4 Consent of the Master

International law provides a number of exceptions to the principle of exclusive flag State jurisdiction on the high seas. For instance, the flag State or the Master may give consent to authorities of another state to board and inspect one of its vessels on the high seas. Obviously, from a practical standpoint, as well as the safety of the boarding party, flag State and/or Master consent are the preferred methods to gain access to a ship. The Master of the ship has plenary authority and "final responsibility" for the vessel.[56] Accordingly, as a matter of State practice, U.S. warships routinely request and receive permission from the Master and/or the flag State to board vessels suspected of engaging in illegal activities, such as narcotics trafficking, migrant smuggling, counter-proliferation and terrorist-related activities.[57]

Not all nations agree, however, with the U.S. view that the Master can legally give consent to foreign authorities to board his or her vessel. Nonetheless, the U.S. takes the position that, as the official representative of the flag State, the Master has plenary authority over all activities on board the vessel while in international waters, including authority over all personnel on board. Under the U.S. position the scope of Master's consent is fairly circumscribed, and reflected in a September 15, 1990, cable, which states:

> Consent by the master of a foreign vessel to boarding by law enforcement officials of another state in international waters, for the purpose of gathering information. The master determines the scope, conduct and duration of the boarding. Flag state authorities are not contacted before the boarding. No enforcement jurisdiction, such as arrest or seizure, may be exercised during a consensual boarding of a foreign flag vessel without the permission of the flag state (whether or not the master consents), even if evidence of illegal activity is discovered.[58]

---

[55] Mary Beth Nikitin, PROLIFERATION SECURITY INITIATIVE (PSI), CONGRESSIONAL RESEARCH SERVICE, Jan. 18, 2011.
[56] MARTIN DAVIES & ANTHONY DICKEY, SHIPPING LAW 303 (1990) and ROBERT P. GRIMES, SHIPPING LAW 99 (1991). See also, PROFESSOR CAPTAIN EDGAR GOLD, COMMAND: PRIVILEGE OR PERIL: THE SHIPMASTER'S LEGAL RIGHTS AND RESPONSIBILITIES, BACKGROUND PAPER FOR THE 12TH INTERNATIONAL COMMAND SEMINAR, RESTORING CONFIDENCE IN COMMAND, LONDON, 21–23 May 2003.
[57] Sandra L. Hodgkinson, et al., Challenges to Maritime Interception Operations in the War on Terror: Bridging the Gap, 22 AM. U. INT'L L. REV. 583, 591–608 (2007).
[58] DEP'T OF STATE, DIGEST OF UNITED STATES PRACTICE IN INTERNATIONAL LAW 1989–1990 at 449 (Margaret S. Pickering et al. eds., 2003).

The U.S. position is supported by Article 27(1)(c) of UNCLOS, which recognizes the authority of the Master to request the assistance of local authorities to exercise criminal jurisdiction on board his or her vessel. Similarly, Article 8(1) of the 2005 *Protocol to the Convention for the Suppression of Unlawful Acts of Violence Against the Safety of Maritime Navigation* (2005 SUA Convention) provides that "the master of a ship of a State Party (the "flag State") may deliver to the authorities of any other State Party (the "receiving State") any person who the master has reasonable grounds to believe has committed an offense set forth in article 3, 3*bis*, 3*ter*, or 3*quater*."

It should be noted, however, that Master's consent only permits the boarding and search of the vessel. It does not allow the assertion of additional law enforcement authority, such as arrest of persons or seizure of cargo or arrest of the vessel. Even under the U.S. view, flag State consent would be required to take these additional law enforcement measures against the vessel, unless unilateral action was required in self-defense.

Nonconsensual ship boarding can also be conducted if the foreign flag vessel is engaged in universally condemned activities. Pursuant to the right of visit, reflected in Article 110 of UNCLOS, a warship that encounters a foreign ship (except sovereign immune vessels) beyond the territorial sea of another nation may board the ship if there are reasonable grounds to suspect that the ship is engaged in piracy, slave trade or unauthorized broadcasting. After inspecting the ship's papers, if suspicion remains that the ships is engaged in one of the prohibited activities, the boarding officer may proceed with a further examination of the ship. The right of visit does not apply to ships engaged in proliferation-related or terrorist-related activities, or to drug interdiction.

21.4 Cases on the Use of Force in Shipboarding

21.4.1 *The Caroline*

The law governing the use of force in maritime security operations is merely an outgrowth of the law controlling the use of force generally. The international law of self-defense and "self-preservation" crystallized in the case of *The Caroline*, a product of the Canadian rebellion of 1837. Americans living along the border were actively sympathetic toward the Canadian rebels, although the government of the United States took steps to restrain their support. The main force of rebels was defeated, and many rebels fled south to the United States. In Buffalo, New York, rebel leaders McKenzie and Rolfe conducted large public meetings to solicit a force to assist them against the British Crown authority in Canada.[59]

---

[59] R. Y. Jennings, *The Caroline and McLeod Cases*, 32 Am. J. Int'l L. 82, at 82 (1938).

Under the leadership of an American named Van Rausselear, the armed force composed mostly of Americans, invaded and took possession of Canada's Navy Island from December 13 to 29. The small island belonged to Britain, but was to be used as a staging area for insurrection on the Canadian side of the river. On December 29, *The Caroline* went down the Niagara River from Buffalo past Grand Island, owned by the United States, and landed at Navy Island. It was evident to British observers at Chippewa that the ship ferried armaments to the rebels. The ship made several trips to Fort Schlosser and Navy Island, transporting a six-pound cannon and other "warlike stores." The Lieutenant Governor appraised the Governor of the State of New York, but received no answer to his communication.[60]

Fearing the Caroline would be used to ferry additional supplies to Navy Island, and also prove a means for the rebels to attack Canada, Colonel McNab, commanding British forces assembled across the river at Chippewa, set out to destroy the American ship.[61] The operation was conducted under the leadership of Captain Drew on the night of December 29. Seventy to 80 armed men stormed the ship during the middle of the night, as the vessel lay moored at Fort Schlosser. The ship was abandoned without resistance, and the Canadians set it on fire, cut it adrift, and the burning vessel went over the falls at Niagara.

The British defended their action based upon three arguments: (1) that the ship had a "piratical character;" (2) the area of Fort Schlosser was lawless, and public authority "overborne;" and (3) self-defense. The United States and Britain ultimately focused their diplomatic exchanges principally on the third issue of self-defense, in which the ship was treated by Britain as a "belligerent vessel" and the United States was alleged to have abandoned its duties as a "neutral." Britain dispatched Lord Ashburton to Washington, D.C. to consider the U.S. complaint over *The Caroline* in conjunction with further negotiations concerning settlement of a northeastern boundary dispute. In the meantime, William Henry Harrison was sworn into office as president on March 4, 1841; he died 32 days later and was replaced by John Tyler, who was sworn into office as president on April 4, 1841. Tyler sought a quick resolution to the dispute.

On July 27, 1842, Secretary of State Daniel Webster sent a note to Lord Ashburton, enclosing a copy of a letter dated April 24, 1841, which had been addressed to Fox. Webster called upon the British to bear the burden of proof to demonstrate there was a

> ... necessity of self–defense, instant, overwhelming, leaving no choice of means and no moment of deliberation. It will be for it to show, also, that the local authorities of Canada, even supposing the necessity of the moment authorized them to enter the territories of the United States at all, did nothing unreasonable or excessive; since the act, justified by the necessity of self-defense, must be limited by that necessity,

---

[60] Id., at 83.
[61] Id.

and kept clearly within it. It must be shown that admonition or remonstrance to the persons on board the Caroline was impracticable, or would have been unavailing; it must be shown that day-light could not be waited for; that there could be no attempt at discrimination between the innocent and the guilty; that it would not have been enough to seize and detain the vessel; but that there was a necessity, present and inevitable, for attacking her in the darkness of night, while moored to the shore, and while unarmed men were asleep on board, killing some and wounding others, and then drawing here into the current, above the cataract, setting her on fire, and, carless to know whether there might not be in her the innocent with the guilty, or the living with the dead, committing her to a fate which fills the imagination with horror. A necessity for all this, the Government of The United States cannot believe to have existed."[62]

The Webster letter also used the terms "self-defense" and "self-preservation" synonymously, with the declaration that "a just right of self-defense attaches to nations as well as to individuals, and is equally necessary for the preservation of both." The ingenious reply by Lord Ashburton fits the narrative into the model for lawful self-defense erected by Mr. Webster, along with an apology. While not ever admitting that the action was justified, Webster accepted the apology in a letter of August 6, 1842. The restrictive formula offered by Webster and adopted by Ashburton vitiated the Naturalist notion of "an absolute primordial right of self-preservation" with the limiting condition of necessity.[63]

21.4.2 *I'm Alone*

The 1929 arbitration commission involving the sinking of the British-flagged, Canadian-registered schooner *I'm Alone* is one of the key cases concerning the use of force against foreign-flagged ships navigating beyond the territorial sea of the United States.[64] The commission was unable to determine the precise location of *I'm Alone* when the incident began, but conflicting evidence suggests the ship was anchored between 8 and 15 miles off the coast of Louisiana on March 22, 1929. Coast Guard cutter *Wolcott* initiated pursuit of *I'm Alone*, suspecting the ship was involved in smuggling alcoholic liquor into the United States.

There was no dispute that the ship was a smuggling vessel transporting liquor from Belize and the Bahamas to smaller boats waiting offshore beyond the

---

[62] Letter from Mr. Webster to Lord Ashburton, July 27, 1842, Enclosure, Letter from Mr. Webster to Mr. Fox, April 24, 1841, *reprinted in* 29 BRITISH AND FOREIGN STATE PAPERS 1129, 1138 (1840–41).

[63] R. Y. Jennings, *The Caroline and McLeod Cases*, 32 AM. J. INT'L L. 82, at 92 (1938).

[64] *I'm Alone*, 3 REP. INT'L ARBITRAL. AWARDS 1611 (1935), and Claim of the British Ship "I'm Alone" v. United States: Reports of the Commissioners, 29 AM. J. INT'L L. 326 (Apr. 1935). *See also*, G. G. Fitzmaurice, The Case of the *I'm Alone*, 17 BRIT. Y.B. INT'L L. 82 (1937), Charles Cheney Hyde, The Adjustment of the *I'm Alone* Case, 29 AM. J. INT'L L. 296 (Apr. 1935), and William C. Dennis, *The Sinking of the I'm Alone*, 23 AM. J. INT'L L. 351 (Apr. 1929).

3 nautical mile territorial sea, which would deliver the goods into the land territory of the United States in violation of the National Prohibition Act. The U.S. position was that *I'm Alone* had a constructive presence in the territorial waters of the United States through the intermediary boats.[65]

Article II of the bilateral treaty Liquor Convention of January 23, 1924, stated that the U.S. Coast Guard could board Canadian ships to inspect the vessel's "papers for the purpose of ascertaining whether the vessel or those on board [were] endeavoring to import ... alcoholic beverages into the United States.... When such enquiries and examination show reasonable grounds for suspicion, a search of the vessel may be instituted."[66] If the search confirms the suspicions, the ship may be seized and taken to a U.S. port "for adjudication in accordance with such laws."[67] One important caveat, however, specified that "the rights conferred by this article shall not be exercised at a greater distance from the coast of the United States, its territories or possessions than can be traversed in one hour by the vessel suspected of endeavoring to commit the offense."[68]

Pursuit by the cutter *Wolcott* began beyond the limit of the 3 nautical mile territorial waters of the United States. As *I'm Alone* fled toward the open ocean, Coast Guard cutter *Dexter* joined *Wolcott*. Two days later, on March 22, 1929, after the chase had covered a distance of more than 200 miles from the shore of the United States, *Dexter* fired upon *I'm Alone*. First *Dexter* shot across the bow of *I'm Alone* and into the sails and rigging. The fleeing ship was ordered to stop under threat that it would be sunk, but the master of *I'm Alone* displayed a handgun and promised to forcibly repel any attempt to board the ship. Dexter once again began to fire into *I'm Alone*—this time into the hull. As a result of the attack, *I'm Alone* was struck by gunfire and sank to the bottom within 30 minutes. The captain and crew were rescued, although one crew member drowned. The ship, cargo and personal effects of the crew were a total loss.

In August of that year, the United States and Canada agreed to assemble a commission under Article IV of the Convention. The commission was comprised of two members, who considered a claim by Canada against the United States in respect to the sinking of the ship. On the question of whether the sinking of the vessel was legally justified, the Commissioners stated:

> [The] United States might, consistently with the Convention, use necessary and reasonable force for the purpose of effecting the objects of boarding, searching, seizing and brining into port the suspected vessel; and if sinking should occur accidentally, as the result of the exercise of necessary and reasonable force for such purpose, the pursuing vessel might be entirely blameless. But the Commissioners think that, in

---

[65] MYRES MCDOUGAL & WILLIAM T. BURKE, PUBLIC ORDER OF THE OCEANS 909–911 (1962, rev. ed. 1987).
[66] *I'm Alone*, 3 REP. INT'L ARBITRAL. AWARDS 1611 (1935).
[67] Id.
[68] Id., at 1612.

the circumstances stated ... the admittedly intentional sinking of the suspected vessel was not justified by anything in the Convention.[69]

The commission applied the standard of "reasonable and necessary" use of force to all phases of visit, board, search, and seizure.

21.4.3 Red Crusader

Another maritime use of force case, the *Red Crusader*, involved a British fishing vessel interdicted by the Danish frigate *Niels Ebbesen* near the Danish Faeroe islands on May 21, 1961.[70] The *Niels Ebbesen* suspected *Red Crusader* was engaged in illegal fishing. Whether the ship actually was fishing and the precise location of the ship was in dispute. Using siren and signal searchlight, the *Niels Ebbesen* ordered the ship to stop. When *Red Crusader* did not comply, *Niels Ebbesen* fired a blank 40 mm warning shot across the bow of the fishing vessel. The warning shot caused the ship to heave to in order to accept a two-man custody crew that would pilot the ship into port behind *Niels Ebbesen*.

Once the custody crew was on board, however, the master of *Red Crusader* locked up the boarding party and began to flee. *Niels Ebbesen* fired two 127 mm warning shots and transmitted a Morse code "K" signal, "stop." Two more warning shots were fired in conjunction with a whistle signal to stop. Finally, *Niels Ebbesen* fired a solid shot at the fishing vessel's scanner, mast, hull, and stem, all while continuing to hail the ship to stop. *Red Crusader* suffered damage from this gunfire, although no one on board the ship was injured.

The Commission of Enquiry later determined:

> In opening fire at 03.22 hours up to 03.53 hours, the Commanding Office of the *Niels Ebbesen* exceeded legitimate use of armed force on two counts: (a) firing without warning of a solid gun-shot; (b) creating danger to human life on board the *Red Crusader* without proved necessity, by the effective firing at the *Red Crusader* after 03.40.[71]

The Commission also found that the attempt by the *Red Crusader* to escape was in "flagrant violation" of the order to heave to, but those circumstances "cannot justify such violent action."[72] The Commission concluded with the opinion that "other means should have been attempted," which might have convinced the master of the *Red Crusader* to stop and comply with directions issued by the *Niels Ebbesen*.[73] The Commission stated that the use of force that endangers human

---

[69] Id., 1617 (1935) and *Claim of the British Ship 'I'm Alone' v. United States: Reports of the Commissioners*, 29 AM. J. INT'L L. 326, 328 (Apr. 1935).
[70] *The Red Crusader* (U.K. v. Den.), *Comm'n of Enquiry*, Mar. 23, 1962, 35 INT'L REP. 485 (1962).
[71] Id., at 499.
[72] Id.
[73] Id.

life could be permissible in cases of "proved necessity," but it did not provide any fidelity on what such circumstances would entail.

If the Danish action in the case were excessive, however, there is no indication by the Commission how good order at sea can be maintained against a determined lawbreaker. Professor Myres McDougal, for example, suggested:

> The authority to prescribe law, to make law, if it is to have any meaning must carry with it the authority to apply the law, decide what it is in particular instances, and to enforce it ... Mr. Burke and I have collected the authorities on this for every type of area. It is our conclusion that you can be reasonably sure that States are authorized by international law to employ force when it is necessary to apply any law which they are authorized to make for the protection of their various exclusive interests. A comparable competence is established for the protection of the inclusive interests.... The principal point ... is that, by and large, the maintenance of order upon the oceans is a function of the application of force by the ship of nation-States.[74]

The decision of the *Red Crusader* is narrower than both the preceding *I'm Alone* and the subsequent ruling by the International Tribunal of the Law of the Sea in the case of the M/V *Saiga*.

21.4.4 M/V Saiga

The next paradigmatic case on the use of force during maritime security operations arose from the arrest of the M/V *Saiga*. The *Saiga* was a St. Vincent and the Grenadines-registered oil tanker supplying bunkering services—fuel oil and water—to fishing vessels and other ships in the Gulf of Guinea. The vessel was owned by a company in Cyprus, but managed by another firm in Scotland and chartered by yet a third corporation based in Geneva, Switzerland. The crew of *Saiga* was comprised of Ukrainians and three painters from Senegal.

In October 1997, the ship left Senegal to supply fuel oil to fishing vessels and serviced three ships licensed by Guinea to fish in the EEZ. Just days later, the ship was intercepted by *P35*, a Guinean customs patrol boat. The patrol boat fired on the *Saiga*, damaging the ship and critically wounding two crew members. The ship was arrested by Guinean officials and brought to the port of Conarky. As the ship and crew were held in detention, St. Vincent initiated proceedings for prompt release of the vessel under Article 292 of UNCLOS at the International Tribunal for the Law of the Sea (ITLOS).

On December 4, 1997, ITLOS ordered the release of the ship and its crew upon posting of a financial security. On December 17, 1997, the Master of the *Saiga* was convicted in a Guinea court of importing diesel oil into Guinean territory and disobeying the lawful commands of the Guinean navy. A majority of the judges decided in favor of St. Vincent and the Grenadines in the first proceedings (*Saiga* No. 1) concerning the issue of prompt release. Ignoring the Guinean claim that it

---

[74] McDougal & Burke, Public Order of the Oceans, at 557–58.

acted to enforce its customs laws, the Tribunal instead based its decision upon a rather convoluted extrapolation of bunkering as an activity related to fishing under Article 73 of UNCLOS.

As the bond was being negotiated, St. Vincent and the Grenadines pursued a second claim relating to the merits of the case (*Saiga* No. 2) concerning the legality of the arrest. Further issues of jurisdiction of the Tribunal over the case and admissibility of the complaint by St. Vincent were conjoined. But the principle question resolved by ITLOS was whether Guinea had grounds for the arrest.

St Vincent and the Grenadines argued two propositions. First, *Saiga* had not breached any Guinean law. Second, if the laws cited by Guinea did apply to the activities of *Saiga*, those laws were in violation of UNCLOS.[75] The law in Guinea claimed as the basis for the arrest was aimed at fighting the unlawful import, purchase, and sale of fuel, but it only prohibited the unauthorized distribution of fuel *in* the Republic of Guinea.[76] Since the EEZ was not *in* the Republic of Guinea, the law against smuggling of gas oil did not apply. Thus, by providing bunkering services in the EEZ, the *Saiga* was not in violation of Guinean law, since the EEZ is not *in* Guinea.[77]

Guinea also argued, however, that the bunkering activities of the *Saiga* violated the Customs Code of Guinea and the anti-smuggling law.[78] Bunkering services constituted an economic or commercial activity in the EEZ, and could be regulated by the coastal State. The *Saiga* was arrested for "engaging in unwarranted commercial activities" in the EEZ, not for navigating in the EEZ.[79] But St. Vincent responded that Guinea could not extend its customs laws into a purported 250 kilometer "customs radius," which overlapped the EEZ, as the only rights the coastal State could exercise in the zone were set forth in Articles 56 and 58 of UNCLOS. The Guinean interdiction interfered with the right of St. Vincent to exercise freedom of navigation in the EEZ, and the supply of fuel oil by *Saiga* to other vessels in the EEZ constituted "other internationally lawful uses of the sea" associated with the operation of ships.[80]

---

[75] M/V *Saiga* No. 2 (*Saint Vincent and the Grenadines v. Guinea*) (Merits) (Judgment) ITLOS Case No. 2 (July 1, 1999) 1999 ITLOS REPORTS 10–25, 38 I.L.M. 1323–1442 (1999), para. 110. *See also*, Louise Angélique de La Fayette, The M/V *Saiga* (No. 2) Case (*St. Vincent and the Grenadines v. Guinea*) Judgment, 49 INT'L & COMP. L. Q. 467 (2000) and Barbara Kwiatkowska, *Inauguration of the ITLOS Jurisprudence: The Saint Vincent and the Grenadines v. Guinea and M/V Saiga Cases*, 30 OCEAN DEV. & INTL L. 355 (2000).

[76] Guinean Law No. L/94/007/CTRN, March 15, 1994, *reprinted in* JOURNAL OFFICIEL DE LA RÉPUBLIQUE DE GUINÉE, Mar. 25, 1994.

[77] *Saiga* No. 2, paras. 111–18.

[78] Customs Code of Guinea, Nov. 28, 1990, *reprinted in* JOURNAL OFFICIEL DE LA RÉPUBLIQUE DE GUINÉE, Apr. 20, 1997.

[79] *Saiga* No. 2, paras. 124–25 and 128.

[80] Id., para. 124 (*citing*, UNCLOS, Article 58).

On the questions of freedom of navigation and "other internationally lawful uses of the sea," associated with the operation of ships, the Tribunal sided with St. Vincent by a vote of 18 to 2.[81] The idea was roundly rejected that Guinea could exercise customs jurisdiction in the EEZ. Judge Zhao from China, however, dissented on this issue. Although Zhou voted in favor of the Judgment, he issued a separate opinion much more circumspect on the issue of bunkering in the EEZ. He concluded that bunkering did not fall within the ambit of freedom of navigation or other internationally lawful uses of the sea. For Zhou, uses of the sea that were not specifically attributable to the coastal State under UNCLOS did not automatically or necessarily revert to being within the scope of freedom of navigation or other lawful uses associated with freedom of navigation.

St. Vincent also claimed that the Guinean patrol boat used excessive and unreasonable force to stop and subdue *Saiga*. The ship was unarmed, and fully laden with oil, and could manage a top speed of only 10 knots. The ship had a low freeboard, so it was easy to board. Despite these circumstances, however, *P35* discharged into the ship live ammunition from large caliber automatic weapons, even though there was no resistance from the unarmed crew of *Saiga*. Guinea claimed that the level of force had been necessary because the ship had refused to stop after repeated demands over the radio. The Law of the Sea Convention is silent on the use of force, although Article 293 of UNCLOS requires application of "other rules of international law not incompatible with" the Convention. Under general international law, the use of force must be both reasonable and necessary and requires observance of the rule of humanity. By a vote of 18 to 2, ITLOS ruled that in stopping and arresting *Saiga*, Guinea used excessive force contrary to international law and in violation of the rights of the flag State:

> Although the (Law of the Sea) Convention does not contain express provisions on the use of force in the arrest of ship, international law, which is applicable by virtue of article 293 of the (Law of the Sea) Convention, requires that the use of force must be avoided as far as possible and, where force is unavoidable, it must not go beyond what is reasonable and necessary in the circumstances. Considerations of humanity must apply in the law of the sea, just as they do in other areas of international law.[82]

St. Vincent had a more persuasive account of the facts, and ITLOS drew upon *I'm Alone* and *Red Crusader* in determining that Guinea should have exercised greater precaution.[83] The accepted practice for using force against a civilian ship at sea was first to give internationally recognized visual and auditory signals to heave to. If the signals failed, then warships may climb an escalatory ladder that first includes non-damaging measures, such as the use of warning shots across the bow. Only after these steps prove futile may force be used as a

---

[81] Id., para. 136.
[82] Id., para. 155.
[83] Id., para. 153.

last resort.[84] Even then, however, care should be taken to avoid endangering human life. Guinean officers acted unreasonably in firing live ammunition at the ship without first giving any of the recognized international signals. ITLOS also ruled that Guinean officers used excessive force and had endangered life both before and after boarding the *Saiga*.[85]

21.5 UN Security Council

It has been more than 100 years since the international community became keenly aware of the strategic impact of anarchy and terrorism. From the excesses of the French Revolution through the revolutions of 1848, the assassination of President William McKinley by anarchist Leon Czolgosz in September 1901, the assassination of Serbian Archduke Ferdinand on the eve of the First World War to the Bolshevik Revolution at the end of the war, nations have struggled with how to control terrorism and anarchy. During the Interwar period, the League of Nations observed that "the rules of international law concerning the repression of terrorist activity are not at present sufficiently precise to guarantee efficiently international cooperation . . .," and the international body established a group of experts to develop a draft international convention to "assure the repression of conspiracies or crimes committed with a political and terrorist purpose."[86]

In 1972, the UN General Assembly followed in the footsteps of the League and established an Ad Hoc Committee on International Terrorism,[87] which, with little fanfare and even less effect, issued a report in 1979.[88] But the creation of the Security Council has always provided the best hope of creating authoritative anti-terrorism policy at the global level. Pursuant to Article 39 of the Charter, the Security Council has the authority to "determine the existence of any threat to the peace, breach of the peace, or act of aggression . . ." and "decide what measures shall be taken in accordance with Articles 41 and 42, to maintain or restore international peace and security."

Measures adopted under Article 41 do not include the use of "armed force" and "may include complete or partial interruption of economic relations and of rail, sea, air, postal, telegraphic, radio, and other means of communication, and the severance of diplomatic relations." But there may be levels of force that fall under the threshold of "armed force," and therefore could be authorized by a UNSC Resolution adopted under Article 41. Such forceful measures that may not

---

[84] Id., para. 156.
[85] Id., para. 157–59.
[86] *Draft Convention on Jurisdiction with Respect to Crime*, 29 Am. J. Int'l L. Supp. 435, 554 (1935).
[87] UNGA Res. 3034 (XXVII), Dec. 18, 1972.
[88] 34 UN GAOR Supp. (No. 37), UN Doc A/34/37 (1979).

rise to the level of armed force may include maritime interception operations or visit, board, search and seizure.

In accordance with Article 42, if the Security Council determines that measures not involving the use of armed force will not be adequate "or have proved to be inadequate, it may take such action by air, sea, or land forces as may be necessary to maintain or restore international peace and security...," to include "demonstrations, blockade, and other operations by air, sea, or land forces...." Prior to adopting measures under Articles 41 or 42, the Security Council may "call upon the parties concerned to comply with such provisional measures as it deems necessary or desirable."[89] Furthermore, the Security Council often adopts a resolution without specifying whether the authority is cast under Article 41 or 42—perhaps a form of constructive ambiguity that helps the States reach agreement under Chapter VII. But such ambiguity also leaves room for disagreement, and not every observer would assume that citing authority under Chapter VII of the UN Charter thereby permits any use of force, let alone "armed force." A more convincing view, however, is that while the level of force authorized by Articles 41 and 42 are separate and distinct, with Article 42 only serving to authorize "armed force," Article 41 opens the door for lesser forms of force, which may manifest in ship boarding or maritime interception operations.

21.5.1 *Resolution 1540*

On January 31, 1992, the Security Council found that the "proliferation of all WMD" constitutes a threat to international peace and security.[90] It was not until more than a decade later—April 28, 2004—however, that the Security Council acted under Chapter VII to adopt Resolution 1540.[91] After acknowledging that the proliferation of weapons of mass destruction (WMD) and their delivery systems constitutes a threat to international peace and security and expressing grave concern posed by the risk that non-State actors may acquire, develop, traffic in or use WMD-related materials, the Security Council called upon all States:

> 1. ... [to] refrain from providing any form of support to non-State actors that attempt to develop, acquire, manufacture, possess, transport, transfer or use nuclear, chemical or biological weapons and their means of delivery; ...
>
> * * *
>
> 10. ... in accordance with their national legal authorities and legislation and consistent with international law, to take cooperative action to prevent illicit trafficking in nuclear, chemical or biological weapons, their means of delivery, and related materials; ....

---

[89] Charter of the United Nations, Oct. 24, 1945, 1 UNTS XVI, Art. 40.
[90] S/23500, Statement by the President of the Security Council, Jan. 31, 1992.
[91] S/RES/1540 (2004), Apr. 28, 2004.

Just as the terrorist attacks of 9/11 served as the political backdrop for Resolution 1540, there is little doubt that the *Kananaskis Principles* were also a progenitor of its development. Analysis by Douglas Guilfoyle has shed light on some of the genealogy of Resolution 1540.[92] Operative paragraph 3 of the resolution imports text—some of it verbatim—from *Kananaskis Principles* 2–5, and Paragraph 8 of the resolution is "substantially reproduced" from *Kananaskis Principle* 1.[93] Besides these parallels, Guilfoyle uncovers some rather interesting context for the negotiations for Resolution 1540.

First, at China's request, the importation of *Kananaskis Principle* 4 into operative Paragraph 3(c) of the Security Council Resolution dropped all references to "interdiction."[94] Second, Resolution 1540 does not contain text concerning disposal of fissile material, elimination of chemical weapons, or reduction of stocks of dangerous biological toxins "based on the recognition that the threat of terrorist acquisition is reduced as the overall quantity of such items is reduced," even though this is mentioned in *Kananaskis Principle* 6.[95] This omission strikes smaller, non-proliferating nations such as the Philippines as unfair because it shifts obligations onto them to "police leakages from states with larger militaries," without any corresponding recognition that the major military powers with large inventories of WMD have created much of the risk.[96]

Resolution 1540 was adopted amidst two decades of Security Council efforts to control WMD from specific threats—namely, the resolutions adopted against North Korea beginning in 1993, and then Iran, in 2006.

21.5.2 *North Korea*

On February 19, 1992, Republic of Korea (ROK) and the DPRK issued a joint declaration to renounce the test, manufacture, production, receipt, possession, storage, deployment or use of nuclear weapons. Additionally, both parties agreed to "use nuclear energy solely for peaceful purposes" and not to "possess nuclear reprocessing and uranium enrichment facilities. . . ."[97] A year later, in March 1993, the DPRK sent a letter to the President of the Security Council stating its intent to withdraw from the NPT.

The Security Council responded with the adoption of Resolution 825 on May 11, 1993, in which it called on North Korea to reconsider its decision, reaffirm its commitment to the NPT and honor its non-proliferation obligations under the

---

[92] Douglas Guilfoyle, Shipping Interdiction and International Law 239–40 (2009).
[93] Id.
[94] Id. Guilfoyle *cites* to S/PV.4950, Apr. 22, 2006, at 6.
[95] Guilfoyle, Shipping Interdiction, at 239–340.
[96] Id. Guilfoyle *cites* to S/PV.4950, Apr. 22, 2006, at 2.
[97] Joint Declaration of South and North Korea on the Denuclearization of the Korean Peninsula, Feb. 19, 1992.

NPT and its safeguards agreement with the IAEA.[98] In response, the DPRK suspended its withdrawal from the NPT on June 9, 1993. Thus began the saga of broken promises, non-compliance with numerous United Nations Security Council resolutions (UNSCRs) and IAEA resolutions, and other unsuccessful and frustrating efforts to convince the DPRK to abandon its nuclear ambitions.

Ten years later, in January 2003, the DPRK revoked its previously announced suspension and formally withdrew from the NPT. Citing serious threats to its national security brought about by a "hostile" U.S. policy and "unreasonable" behavior of the IAEA, Pyongyang declared it could "no longer remain bound to the NPT" and was "totally free from the binding force of the safeguards accord with the IAEA...."[99]

Notwithstanding its withdrawal, however, Pyongyang pledged that it had "no intention to produce nuclear weapons and our nuclear activities at this stage will be confined only to peaceful purposes such as the production of electricity."[100] In September 2005, following the fourth round of the Six-Party Talks in Beijing, the DPRK re-affirmed this pledge, and indicated that it was committed to abandoning all nuclear weapons and its existing nuclear programs and that it would return to the NPT and IAEA safeguards.[101]

International expectations for a more stable Korean Peninsula were shattered, however, on July 5, 2006, when the DPRK launched a number of ballistic missiles that landed in the Sea of Japan in violation of its self-proclaimed moratorium on missile launching. The Security Council reacted 10 days later by condemning the multiple launches and demanding that the DPRK suspend all activities related to its ballistic missile program.[102] UN Security Council Resolution 1695 additionally required "all Member States, in accordance with their national legal authorities and legislation and consistent with international law," to prevent:

- the transfer of missile and missile-related items, materials, goods and technology to the DPRK's missile or WMD programs;
- the procurement of missile and missile-related items, materials, goods and technology from the DPRK; and
- the transfer of any financial resources in relation to the DPRK's missile or WMD programs.

The DPRK responded to UN Security Council Resolution 1695 with a nuclear weapon test on October 9, 2006, in flagrant disregard for the Security Council's demands. Recognizing that this test had increased tensions in the region and was a "clear threat to international peace and security," the Council condemned

---

[98] S/RES/825 (1993), May 11, 1993.
[99] North Korea's Statement on NPT Withdrawal, Jan. 10, 2003.
[100] Id.
[101] Joint Statement of the Fourth Round of the Six-Party Talks, Beijing, People's Republic of China, Sept. 19, 2005.
[102] S/RES/1695 (2006), July 16, 2006.

it and demanded that the DPRK not conduct any further tests or ballistic missile launches.[103]

Acting under Chapter VII (Article 41) of the Charter, UN Security Council Resolution 1718 further directed the DPRK to abandon all nuclear weapons and nuclear programs, and other existing WMD and ballistic missiles programs, in a complete, verifiable and irreversible manner. Furthermore, UN Security Council Resolution 1718 imposed sanctions on the DPRK that directs all Member States to prevent the supply, sale or transfer to the DPRK, through their territories or by their nationals, or using their flag vessels or aircraft, of:

- any battle tanks, armored combat vehicles, large caliber artillery systems, combat aircraft, attack helicopters, warships, missiles or missile systems, or related materials including spare parts;
- items, materials, equipment, goods and technology that could contribute to the DPRK's nuclear-related, ballistic missile-related or other WMD-related programs; and
- luxury goods.

The DPRK was also prohibited from export of such items. In addition, Member States were directed to:

- prohibit the procurement of these items from the DPRK by their nationals or using their flagged vessels or aircraft;
- prevent any transfers to or from the DPRK by their nationals or from their territories, of technical training, advice, services or assistance related to these items;
- freeze financial assets located in their territories used to support the DPRK's nuclear-related, other WMD-related and ballistic missile-related programs; and,
- impose travel restrictions on designated persons responsible for the DPRK's nuclear-related, ballistic missile-related and other WMD-related programs polices.

Finally, Member States were urged to "take, in accordance with their national authorities and legislation, and consistent with international law, cooperative action including through inspection of cargo to and from the DPRK."

Three years later, the DPRK reacted to the stricter sanctions in UN Security Council Resolution 1718 with a second nuclear test on May 25, 2009. The Security Council responded with UN Security Council Resolution 1874, which reiterated the condemnations, demands and economic sanctions of UN Security Council Resolution 1718, prohibited all weapons exports by the DPRK and expanded the arms embargo to the DPRK to include all arms (except small arms and light weapons).[104] Security Council Resolution 1874 also established an inspection regime that required all states to inspect:

- in accordance with their national authorities and legislation, and consistent with international law, all cargo to and from the DPRK, in their territory, including

---

[103] S/RES/1718 (2006), Oct. 14, 2006.
[104] S/RES/1874 (2009), June 12, 2009.

- seaports and airports, if they have reasonable grounds to believe the cargo contains items prohibited by Security Council Resolution 1718 or 1874 (i.e., port state control or jurisdiction); and
- vessels, with the consent of the flag state, on the high seas, if they have reasonable grounds to believe that the vessel's cargo contains items prohibited by Security Council Resolutions 1718 or 1874 (i.e., flag State jurisdiction or consent).

With regard to the latter point, if the flag State does not consent to the inspection on the high seas, it shall direct the vessel to proceed to an appropriate and convenient port for the required inspection by local authorities. If an inspection discovers prohibited items, Member States are further authorized to seize and dispose of them.

The "diversion" provision of the resolution is an interesting, but irrelevant, new development. While responsible flag States will, in all probability, observe this requirement and divert their vessels to a convenient port for inspection, it is highly unlikely that rogue states such as Syria, Iran, and the DPRK will comply with the mandate.

The "no bunkering" provision in Security Council Resolution 1874 is rather novel and warrants special mention. Operative paragraph 17 of the resolution prohibits Member States from providing "bunkering services, such as provision of fuel or supplies, or other servicing of vessels, to DPRK vessels if they have ... reasonable grounds to believe they are carrying items ... prohibited by ... resolution 1718 (2006) or ... resolution [1874]...." This provision was instrumental in preventing a suspected weapons shipment from finding its way from the DPRK to Myanmar in July 2009. In June 2009, satellites detected that the DPRK was loading the tramp steamer *Kang Nam 1* with a cache of weapons bound for Myanmar.

The vessel got underway and was shadowed by USS *John S. McCain* (DDG 56) over the course of several days. When it became apparent to the ship's Master that he would not be able to refuel in Singapore as originally planned, the *Kang Nam 1* reversed course and returned to the DPRK.[105] The "bunkering" provision was again used in May 2011 to prevent a suspected transshipment of prohibited military-related items from the DPRK to Myanmar on board the M/V *Light*, which also appeared intent on violation of Security Council Resolution 1874.

The ship was Chinese owned and operated, but was registered in Belize and manned by a North Korean crew. Pursuant to the *U.S.-Belize Proliferation Security Initiative* (PSI) boarding agreement, Belizean authorities granted permission for U.S. naval personnel to board and inspect the vessel. At the same time, Washington received assurances from Singapore and Malaysia that the vessel would not be allowed into port, consistent with Security Council Resolution 1874. On May 26, USS *McCampbell* (DDG 85) intercepted the cargo vessel south of Shanghai

---

[105] *A Victory for UN Sanctions*, BANGKOK POST (Op-ed) July 10, 2009.

and requested permission to board. The North Korean Master, however, refused to authorize the boarding, claiming the vessel carried industrial chemicals to Bangladesh.[106]

Despite having received permission to board from Belize, in an effort to minimize risk to the crew and de-escalate the situation, U.S. authorities did not board the vessel. The ship remained under surveillance by the *USS McCampbell* and U.S. military aircraft for several days. Fearing that he would not be able to secure fuel for the ship in Singapore or Malaysia, the Master reversed course on May 29 and returned to port in North Korea.[107] Assuming regional coastal nations such as China, Indonesia, Malaysia and Singapore continue to comply with the prohibition, it will be extremely difficult, if not impossible, for vessels carrying prohibited cargoes to make the long voyage from the DPRK to Myanmar or Iran without a brief stop for fuel along the route.

In an apparent breakthrough in February 2012, Pyongyang agreed to suspend its uranium enrichment activities at the Yongbyon facility, and stop nuclear tests and the long-range missile program in exchange for 240,000 metric tons of food aid from the United States.[108] Washington additionally issued a public statement that the United States "reaffirms that it does not have hostile intent toward [North Korea] and is prepared to take steps to improve our bilateral relationship in the spirit of mutual respect for sovereignty and equality."[109]

Although the agreement was met with some skepticism in the international community based on the DPRK's past practices, it was hailed as a major first step in dismantling North Korea's nuclear weapons program.[110] However, the deal quickly fell apart after North Korea announced in mid-March that it was going to launch an earth observation satellite (*Kwangmyongsong*-3) on board an *Unha*-3 long-range rocket in April 2012. Despite intense international criticism concerning the DPRK's announcement, Pyongyang launched the rocket on April 13. Although the launch failed, it was quickly condemned by the United States, Russia, Japan and South Korea as a violation of UNSCRs 1718 and 1874.[111]

Three days later, the Security Council also strongly condemned the launch:

---

[106] Euan Graham, *Maritime Counter-proliferation: The Case of MV Light*, RSIS Commentaries, No. 96/2011, June 29, 2011.

[107] *U.S. Denied Request to Board N. Korean Ship Suspected of Carrying Illegal Weapons*, Maritime Executive, June 14, 2011.

[108] Jay Solomon & Evan Ramstad, *North Korea Pledges New Nuke Freeze*, Wall St. J., Mar. 1, 2012.

[109] Id.

[110] Id.

[111] Maxim Duncan & Ju-min Park, *Embarrassed by Rocket Crash, North Korea May Try Nuclear Test*, Reuters, Apr. 13, 2012.

Statement by the President of the Security Council

At the 6752nd meeting of the Security Council, held on Monday, 16 April 2012, in connection with the Council's consideration of the item entitled "Non-proliferation / Democratic People's Republic of Korea," the President of the Security Council made the following statement on behalf of the Council:

The Security Council strongly condemns the 13 April 2012 (local time) launch by the Democratic People's Republic of Korea (DPRK).

The Security Council underscores that this satellite launch, as well as any launch that uses ballistic missile technology, even if characterized as a satellite launch or space launch vehicle, is a serious violation of Security Council Resolutions 1718 (2006) and 1874 (2009).

The Security Council deplores that such a launch has caused grave security concerns in the region.

The Security Council demands that the DPRK not proceed with any further launches using ballistic missile technology and comply with resolutions 1718 (2006) and 1874 (2009) by suspending all activities related to its ballistic missile program and in this context re-establish its pre-existing commitments to a moratorium on missile launches.

The Security Council agrees to adjust the measures imposed by paragraph 8 of resolution 1718 (2006), as modified by resolution 1874 (2009).

The Security Council directs the Committee established pursuant to resolution 1718 (2006) to undertake the following tasks and to report to the Security Council within fifteen days:

(a) Designate additional entities and items;
(b) Update the information contained on the Committee's list of individuals, entities, and items (S/2009/205 and INFCIRC/254/Rev.9/Part.1), and update on an annual basis thereafter;
(c) Update the Committee's annual work plan.

The Security Council further agrees that, if the Committee has not acted pursuant to the paragraph above within fifteen days, then the Security Council will complete action to adjust these measures within an additional five days.

The Security Council demands that the DPRK immediately comply fully with its obligations under Security Council Resolutions 1718 (2006) and 1874 (2009), including that it: abandon all nuclear weapons and existing nuclear programs in a complete, verifiable and irreversible manner; immediately cease all related activities; and not conduct any further launches that use ballistic missile technology, nuclear tests or any further provocation.

The Security Council calls upon all Member States to implement fully their obligations pursuant to resolutions 1718 (2006) and 1874 (2009).

The Security Council expresses its determination to take action accordingly in the event of a further DPRK launch or nuclear test.[112]

---

[112] S/PRST/2012/13, Statement by the President of the Security Council, Apr. 16, 2012.

To further complicate matters on the Korean Peninsula, *IHS*[113] *Jane's* reported that North Korea included a mobile ballistic missile launcher in a military parade on April 15, 2011. The April 16, 2012, revelation suggests that China either sold the design or a manufactured 16-wheeled transporter-erector-launcher (TEL) for long-range missiles, since the equipment appears to be remarkably similar to the WS2600 Chinese design from the 9th Academy of the China Aerospace Science and Industry Corporation (CASIC).[114] If Beijing did provide a TEL to North Korea, it would have been a violation of UN Security Council Resolution 1874, which bans provision of "any arms" to the reclusive state.

21.5.3 Iran

In March 2006, Iran announced its intentions to resume its enrichment-related activities and Tehran suspended cooperation with the IAEA. The Security Council responded with a weak resolution, adopted under Article 40 of the Charter, demanding Iran suspend all enrichment-related and reprocessing activities, including research and development.[115] Security Council Resolution 1696 additionally called on all States, "in accordance with their national legal authorities and legislation and consistent with international law, to . . . prevent the transfer of any items, materials, goods and technology that could contribute to Iran's enrichment-related and reprocessing activities and ballistic missile programs."

It is unclear why this resolution did not mirror the language in Security Council Resolution 1695 regarding the DPRK's proliferation activities, which prevented the procurement of missile and missile-related items, from the DPRK and the transfer of any financial resources related to the DPRK's missile or WMD programs. Perhaps sensitivity to the role of Iran in the world's oil markets was a factor, but by watering down Security Council Resolution 1696 the Security Council missed an opportunity to send a stronger message to Tehran.

As was the case with the DPRK, Iran ignored the Council's demands in Security Council Resolution 1696. In response, the Security Council adopted enhanced measures under article 41 of the Charter to demand that Iran suspend all enrichment-related and reprocessing activities, including research and development, and all work on heavy water-related projects, including construction of a research reactor moderated by heavy water.[116]

---

[113] Information Handling Services, Jane's Information Group.
[114] CASIC is also known as *Hubei Sanjiang Space Wanshan Special Vehicle Co. Ltd*, which produces a series of ballistic missile Transporter Erector Launchers (TELs). *See*, James Hardy, *UNSC Investigates Chinese Link to North Korean TEL*, JANE'S DEFENCE WEEKLY, Apr. 25, 2012, at 6.
[115] S/RES/1696 (2006), July 31, 2006.
[116] S/RES/1737 (2006), Dec. 27, 2006.

On December 23, 2006, Security Council Resolution 1737 provided that all Member States prevent the supply, sale or transfer to Iran, from their territories or by their nationals or using their flag vessels or aircraft, of all items, materials, equipment, goods and technology that could contribute to Iran's enrichment-related, reprocessing or heavy water-related activities, or to the development of nuclear weapon delivery systems.[117]

Member States are also required to "prevent the provision to Iran of any technical assistance or training, financial assistance, investment, brokering or other services, and the transfer of financial resources or services, related to the supply, sale, transfer, manufacture or use of the prohibited items, materials, equipment, goods and technology..." specified in the resolution. Additionally, Member States are required to prevent the "specialized teaching or training of Iranian nationals" of disciplines that would contribute to Iran's proliferation sensitive nuclear activities and development of nuclear weapon delivery systems. Security Council Resolution 1737 also prohibits Iran from exporting, and Member States were prohibited (or allowing their nationals or use of their flag vessels or aircraft) from procuring from Iran, any of the items listed in documents S/2006/814 (nuclear program-related materials) and S/2006/815 (ballistic missile program-related materials).

Finally Member States were directed to freeze financial assets located in their territories that were owned or controlled by persons identified by the Security Council as being engaged in, directly associated with or providing support for Iran's proliferation sensitive nuclear activities or the development of nuclear weapon delivery systems. Unlike Security Council Resolution 1718, however, which imposed travel restrictions on certain individuals responsible for the DPRK's nuclear and ballistic missile programs, Security Council Resolution 1737 only requires states to exercise "vigilance" regarding the entry or transit of their territories of individuals involved in Iran's proliferation sensitive nuclear activities or the development of nuclear weapon delivery systems. It is unclear why the Security Council would elect to impose lesser restrictions on Iran when it was apparent that enhanced sanctions had failed to convince the DPRK to abandon its nuclear weapons program.

When Iran failed to comply with the requirements of Security Council Resolution 1737, the Security Council imposed new measures under article 41 of the Charter on March 24, 2007. The resolution was aimed at encouraging Iran to comply with its previous resolutions and the requirements of the IAEA.[118] The Security Council decided that Iran "shall not supply, sell or transfer directly or

---

[117] Prohibited items were contained in S/2006/814, Nuclear Program List Pursuant to Resolution 1718, Oct. 13, 2006 (nuclear program-related materials) and S/2006/815, Ballistic Missile Program List Pursuant to Resolution 1718, Oct. 13, 2006 (ballistic missile program-related materials).
[118] S/RES/1747 (2007), Mar. 24, 2007.

indirectly from its territory or by its nationals or using its flag vessels or aircraft any arms or related material, and that all States shall prohibit the procurement of such items from Iran by their nationals, or using their flag vessels or aircraft, and whether or not originating in the territory of Iran." The new measures in resolution 1747 include a prohibition on:

- the supply, sale or transfer by Iran (or its nationals or use of its flag vessels or aircraft) of any arms or related materials; and
- the procurement of such items from Iran by any State (or its nationals or use of its flag vessels or aircraft).

All states are urged, but not required, to:

> exercise vigilance and restraint in the supply, sale or transfer directly or indirectly from their territories or by their nationals or using their flag vessels or aircraft of any battle tanks, armored combat vehicles, large caliber artillery systems, combat aircraft, attack helicopters, warships, missiles or missile systems... and in the provision to Iran of any technical assistance or training, financial assistance, investment, brokering or other services, and the transfer of financial resources or services, related to the supply, sale, transfer, manufacture or use of such items....

Similarly, states and international financial institutions are urged, but not required, not to "enter into new commitments for grants, financial assistance, and concessional loans..." to Iran. The failure to impose a mandatory arms embargo on major weapons systems and mandatory economic sanctions on Iran sends the wrong signal to Iran and other states of proliferation concern and demonstrates a lack of resolve on the part of the Security Council to adequately curtail Iran's nuclear ambitions.

Less than one year later, the Director General of the IAEA issued a report indicating that Iran had not suspended its enrichment-related and reprocessing activities and heavy water-related projects as required by UNSCRs 1696, 1737 and 1747.[119] The report further suggested that Iran had not resumed its cooperation with the IAEA and had taken issue with the IAEA's right to verify design information in accordance with article 39 of Iran's Safeguards Agreement.

In an effort to persuade Iran to comply with resolutions 1696, 1737, and 1747 and IAEA requirements, the Security Council adopted additional measures under article 41 of the Charter.[120] On March 24 2008, Security Council Resolution 1803 imposed new travel restrictions, directing all States to prevent the entry into or transit through their territories of designed individuals that were engaged in, directly associated with or providing support for Iran's proliferation

---

[119] Report of the Director General, Implementation of the NPT Safeguards Agreement and relevant provisions of Security Council Resolutions 1737 (2006) and 1747 (2007) in the Islamic Republic of Iran, GOV/2008/4, Feb. 28, 2008.
[120] S/RES/1803 (2008), Mar. 3, 2008.

sensitive nuclear activities or development of nuclear weapon delivery systems. The resolution additionally requires all states to take the necessary measures to prevent the supply, sale or transfer from their territories or by their nationals or using their flag vessels or aircraft to Iran of:

- all items, materials, equipment, goods and technology associated with Iran's nuclear program, as set out in relevant Security Council documents (except for use in light water reactors), and
- all items, materials, equipment, goods and technology associated with Iran's ballistic missile program, as set out in relevant Security Council documents.

Resolution 1803 calls upon states to act "consistent with international law, in particular the law of the sea and relevant international civil aviation agreements, to conduct inspections of vessel and aircraft cargoes to and from Iran, or owned or operated by Iran Air Cargo and Islamic Republic of Iran Shipping Lines," when there exists "reasonable grounds to believe that the aircraft or vessel is transporting" goods prohibited under Resolutions 1737 (2006), 1747 (2007) or 1803 (2008). States are urged, but not required, to exercise vigilance in entering into new commitments for financial support for trade with Iran and over the activities of financial institutions in their territories with all banks in Iran in order to avoid such activities contributing to Iran's nuclear activities or the development of nuclear weapon delivery systems. Finally, states are urged, but not required, to exercise port State jurisdiction in accordance with their national legal authorities and legislation and consistent with international law, in particular the law of the sea and relevant international civil aviation agreements. Specifically, states are requested to inspect the cargoes at their airports and seaports located on board aircraft and vessels owned or operated by Iran Air Cargo and Islamic Republic of Iran Shipping Line, if the state concerned has reasonable grounds to believe that the aircraft or vessel was transporting goods prohibited under the relevant UNSCRs to or from Iran.

Like Resolution 1540, Resolution 1803 raises the issue of whether a coastal State would be entitled to board a foreign-flagged ship or Iranian ship claiming to exercise the right of innocent passage in its territorial sea because such transit is per se inconsistent with innocent passage since it violates one of the two Security Council Resolutions and may be regarded as a threat to international peace and security. But UN Security Council language has to be specific in order to overcome the principle of non-interference of innocent passage embodied in article 19 of UNCLOS. For example, operative paragraph 8 of Security Council Resolution 1803 states that the Council "[d]ecides that all States shall take the necessary measures to prevent the supply, sale or transfer directly or indirectly from their territories...." The phrase "from their territories" is sufficient to trump the principle of non-interference in article 19. The farther argument, however, that transport of WMD on board a vessel exercising innocent passage in the territorial sea violates Security Council Resolution 1540 because the conduct is per se not innocent, or because the conduct is recognized as a threat to the peace and security of the coastal state, is less well settled.[121]

Despite numerous political and diplomatic efforts over the next 15 months to bring Iran into compliance with its obligations under the NPT and relevant UNSCRs, including an offer by Russia and France to have Iran swap its low-enriched uranium for higher-grade fuel rods for use in its nuclear reactors, Iran was not dissuaded from pursuing its nuclear ambitions.[122] The Security Council adopted yet another resolution on September 27, 2008, that reaffirmed the earlier resolutions.[123]

Then, in mid-May 2010, a trilateral agreement was concluded between Iran, Turkey, and Brazil to send low-enriched uranium abroad for enrichment.[124] The Joint Declaration issued by the parties on May 17 reaffirmed the parties' commitment to the NPT, as well as Iran's right to engage in peaceful nuclear activities and indicated that Iran would:

> 5. ... deposit 1200 kg LEU in Turkey. While in Turkey this LEU will continue to be the property of Iran. Iran and the IAEA may station observers to monitor the safekeeping of the LEU in Turkey.
> 6. Iran will notify the IAEA in writing through official channels of its agreement with [Brazil and Turkey] ... within seven days following the date of this declaration. Upon positive response of the Vienna Group (US, Russia, France and the IAEA) further details of the exchange will be elaborated through a written agreement and proper arrangement between Iran and the Vienna Group that specifically committed themselves to deliver 1200 kg of fuel needed for the Tehran Research Reactor (TRR).
> 7. When the Vienna Group declares its commitment to this provision, then both parties would commit themselves to the implementation of the agreement.... Iran expressed its readiness to deposit its LEU (1200kg) within one month. On the basis of the same agreement the Vienna Group should deliver 1200 kg fuel required for TRR in no later than one year....[125]

Notwithstanding these various efforts, in May 2010, an IAEA report indicated that Iran was not cooperating with the IAEA and had not suspended its enrichment-related and reprocessing activities and heavy water-related projects as required

---

[121] James Kraska, *Broken Taillight at Sea; The Peacetime Law of Visit, Board, Search and Seizure*, 16 OCEAN & COASTAL L. J. 1, 22 (2010).

[122] Lara Setrakian, *Iran Agrees to Draft of a Nuclear Deal—Again*, ABC NEWS, Oct. 21, 2009.

[123] S/RES/1835 (2008), Sept. 27, 2008.

[124] Joint Declaration by Iran, Turkey and Brazil, May 17, 2010 (signed by Manucher Mottaki, Minister of External Relations of the Islamic Republic of Iran, Ahmet Davutoğlu, Minister of Foreign Affairs of the Republic of Turkey, and Celso Amorim, Minister of Foreign Affairs of the Federative Republic of Brazil).

[125] Id.

by UN Security Council Resolutions 1696, 1737, 1747 and 1803.[126] The finding that Iran constructed an enrichment facility at Qom and had enriched uranium to 20 percent without notifying the IAEA was of greater concern, as these steps violated Tehran's obligations under its Safeguards Agreement.

In response to the report, the Security Council directed that Iran not begin construction on any new uranium-enrichment, reprocessing, or heavy water-related facility and discontinue any ongoing construction of any such facility.[127] Security Council Resolution 1929 further provides that all states prohibit Iran, its nationals and entities incorporated in (or acting on behalf of) Iran from acquiring an interest in any commercial activity in their territories involving uranium mining, production or use of nuclear materials and technology. Additionally, all states are directed to "prevent the ... supply, sale or transfer to Iran, from or through their territories or by their nationals ... or using their flag vessels or aircraft ... of any battle tanks, armored combat vehicles, large caliber artillery systems, combat aircraft, attack helicopters, warships, missiles or missile systems ... or related material, including spare parts...."[128]

States are directed to prevent the provision to Iran of technical training, financial resources or services, advice, other services or assistance related to the supply, sale, transfer, provision, manufacture, maintenance or use of such arms and related materials. Similarly, Iran is directed not to undertake any activity related to ballistic missiles capable of delivering nuclear weapons, including launches using ballistic missile technology, and states are directed to take the necessary measures to prevent the transfer of technology or technical assistance to Iran related to such activities.[129]

Unlike the limited travel restrictions imposed by Security Council Resolution 1737, Security Council Resolution 1929 imposes a strict travel ban on certain designated individuals, similar to the travel restrictions imposed by Security Council Resolution 1718 on individuals responsible for the DPRK's nuclear and ballistic missile programs. States are also urged to exercise vigilance over transactions involving the Islamic Revolutionary Guard Corps that could contribute to Iran's proliferation-sensitive nuclear activities or the development of nuclear weapons. Additional economic sanctions regarding banking and financial services are also now in place.

With regard to cargo inspections, Security Council Resolution 1929 calls upon all states to exercise port state jurisdiction by inspecting, "in accordance with their national authorities and legislation and consistent with international law, in

---

[126] Report of the Director General, Implementation of the NPT Safeguards Agreement and relevant provisions of Security Council Resolutions 1737 (2006), 1747 (2007), 1803 (2008), and 1835 (2008) in the Islamic Republic of Iran, GOV/2010/8, May 31, 2010.
[127] S/RES/1929 (2010), June 9, 2010.
[128] Id.
[129] Id.

particular the law of the sea and relevant international civil aviation agreements, all cargo to and from Iran, in their territory, including seaports and airports, if the state concerned has ... reasonable grounds to believe the cargo contains items ..." prohibited by UN Security Council resolutions 1737, 1747, 1803 or 1929.

All states are urged to, "consistent with international law, in particular the law of the sea, ... request inspections of vessels on the high seas with the consent of the flag State ..." and to "cooperate in such inspections if there is information that provides reasonable grounds to believe the vessel is carrying items ..." prohibited by Resolutions 1737, 1747, 1803 or 1929. If prohibited items are discovered during an inspection, states are authorized to seize and dispose of the items. Bunkering services to Iranian-owned or contracted vessels are also prohibited, and this provision mirrors similar restrictions imposed on DPRK ships under Security Council Resolution 1874.

Unlike Security Council Resolution 1874, however, Security Council Resolution 1929 did not contain a "diversion" provision that requires a flag State that does not consent to an inspection on the high seas of one of its vessels to direct the vessel to proceed to an appropriate port for inspection.

In November 2011, the IAEA Director General issued a new report that the IAEA had determined that Iran had not yet suspended its enrichment related activities at the Natanz Fuel Enrichment Plant, the Natanz Pilot Fuel Enrichment Plant, and the Fordo Fuel Enrichment Plant.[130] In addition, the report indicated that Iran had failed to provide information requested by the IAEA regarding the announced construction of 10 new uranium enrichment facilities or Tehran's announcement that it possessed laser enrichment technology. Furthermore, contrary to IAEA and UNSC resolutions, Iran has not suspended work on the heavy water moderated research reactor (Iran Nuclear Research Reactor (IR-40 Reactor)) and the Heavy Water Production Plant, which appears from satellite imagery to be in operation, and Tehran has not granted IAEA inspectors access to the heavy water stored at the Uranium Conversion Facility in order to take samples. The report further indicates that although it is obliged to suspend all enrichment related activities and heavy water related projects, Iran continues to conduct a number of activities at the Uranium Conversion Facility and the Fuel Manufacturing Plant at Esfahan. More importantly, contrary to Security Council Resolution 1929 (2010), the IAEA believes Iran has carried out the following activities relevant to the development of a nuclear explosive device:

- Efforts, some successful, to procure nuclear related and dual use equipment and materials by military related individuals and entities (Annex, Sections C.1 and C.2);
- Efforts to develop undeclared pathways for the production of nuclear material (Annex, Section C.3);

---

[130] Implementation of the NPT Safeguards Agreement and relevant provisions of Security Council Resolutions in the Islamic Republic of Iran, GOV/2011/65, Nov. 8, 2011.

- The acquisition of nuclear weapons development information and documentation from a clandestine nuclear supply network (Annex, Section C.4); and
- Work on the development of an indigenous design of a nuclear weapon including the testing of components (Annex, Sections C.5–C.12).

The Annex to the report provides a detailed analysis of the information available to the IAEA that gives rise to serious concerns about the military dimensions to Iran's nuclear program.

Iran's representative to the IAEA, Ali Asghar Soltanieh, immediately dismissed the IAEA's findings, alleging that the report was "unbalanced, unprofessional and politically motivated."[131] In January 2012, the IAEA confirmed Iran's announcement that it had commenced enriching uranium up to 20 percent at the Fordo Fuel Enrichment Plant, a hardened underground bunker near the city of Qom that is defended by Revolutionary Guard air defense missile batteries.[132]

Iran had constructed a large explosive containment chamber at the Parchin military complex, which apparently was designed to conduct hydrodynamic experiments. An IAEA team visited Iran in January and February 2012 in order to, *inter alia*, gain access to the complex. Iran, however, did not grant access to the site.[133] Satellite imagery of the Parchin complex reveals that Iran may be attempting to clean up radioactive traces from the facility.[134] Satellite images published in late May 2012 reveal that two small buildings at the Parchin site had been removed, raising suspicions that Iran is removing evidence of its nuclear weapons program before access is granted to the IAEA.[135] Hydrodynamic experiments that involve high explosives in conjunction with nuclear material or nuclear material surrogates strongly indicate weapons development.[136] Access to the Parchin facility was a topic of discussion when the Permanent Five plus Germany met with Iranian officials in Baghdad in April and May 2012.[137] The nuclear talks with Iran, however, failed to reach an agreement on this issue, despite the fact that Iran

---

[131] David Sanger & William Broad, *U.N. Agency Says Iran Data Points to A-Bomb Work*, N.Y. TIMES, Nov. 8, 2011.
[132] George Jahn, *UN Agency Confirms Iran Nuke Work at Bunker*, YAHOO NEWS, Jan. 9, 2012.
[133] Implementation of the NPT Safeguards Agreement and relevant provisions of Security Council Resolutions in the Islamic Republic of Iran, GOV/2012/9, Feb. 24, 2012.
[134] George Jahn, *Iran may be Cleaning up Nuke Work*, ASSOCIATED PRESS, Mar. 7, 2012.
[135] Fredrick Dahl, *Iran Site Buildings "Completely Razed": U.S. Think-tank*, REUTERS, May 31, 2012.
[136] Implementation of the NPT Safeguards Agreement and relevant provisions of Security Council Resolutions in the Islamic Republic of Iran, GOV/2011/65, Nov. 8, 2011, Annex, para. 51.
[137] Fredrik Dahl, *Powers Urge Iran to Open Army Site to IAEA Inspectors*, REUTERS, Mar. 9, 2012; Nicholas Kulish & James Kanter, *World Powers Agree to Resume Nuclear Talks With Iran*, N. Y. TIMES, Mar. 6, 2012 and Steven Erlanger, *As Nuclear Talks With Iran Restart, New Hopes for Deal*, N. Y. TIMES, Apr. 13, 2012.

earlier agreed to allow some IAEA inspections of its nuclear research facilities.[138] The parties reconvened in mid-June 2012 in Moscow to continue the talks, but again failed to reach a acceptable solution.[139]

Despite the IAEA and UN Security Council actions, Iran has been a serial proliferator of weapons. In January 2009, an arms shipment from Iran was seized in Cyprus. The shipment had been loaded on to a Cypriot-flagged, Russian vessel, *Monchegorsk*, which had been leased by an Islamic Republic of Iran Shipping Lines (IRISL), and previously had been intercepted in the Red Sea by warships of the U.S. Fifth Fleet. The *Monchegorsk* was found to be carrying tank, artillery, mortar shells, and material for producing rockets.

In early November 2009, Israeli commandoes boarded the *Francop*, a merchant ship flagged in Antigua. The vessel was traveling about 100 miles off the coast, west of the state of Israel. The ship was found to be carrying a significant cache of 500 tons of weapons from Iran to Hezbollah, disguised as civilian cargo in violation of Security Council Resolutions 1701 and 1747 that prohibited Iran from exporting or trading in any form of weapons.[140] The illicit cargo was unloaded at the Israeli port of Ashdod by the Israeli military. Many of the shipping containers on board the vessel were marked "IRISL." The master of the vessel consented to the boarding, which was conducted without the use of force.

The weapons cache included 122 mm Katyusha rockets, and 9,000 M48 120 mm mortar shells (also bearing markings of Iranian production). Three thousand recoilless gun shells and 20,000 hand grenades and over a half million rounds of small arms ammunition were also secreted in mismarked containers. One month later—in October 2009—the German-flagged *Hansa India* was found carrying a cargo of eight containers, which it attempted to unload in Egypt. Denied permission to offload the containers, the ship got underway to Malta, where officials seized the vessel at the request of the United States. Containers were found stuffed with ammunition and industrial supplies for the production of weapons bound for Syria. At the end of October, the government in Sana'a, Yemen seized the Iranian ship *Mahan 1*, carrying a cache of weapons and ammunition intended for Shi'ite insurgents in the northwest of the country.

The *Francop* interdiction was the largest since Israel intercepted the *Karine A* near Sharm a-Sheikh on January 3, 2002. In December 2001, *Karine A* was loaded with weapons in Iran and was bound for the Gaza strip. The vessel set sail for Egypt, where it would offload its cargo onto small fishing vessels for transport into Gaza. A team of Israeli naval commandoes seized the ship, however. These

---

[138] Joby Warrick, *Iran, U.N. Reach Deal on Tehran's Nuclear Program before Key Talks*, WASH. POST, May 22, 2012.

[139] Steven Erlanger & Rick Gladstone, Iran Nuclear Talks End with No Deal, N.Y. TIMES, May 24, 2012.

[140] The Ministry of Foreign Affairs has made public several videos of the *Francop* interdiction, http://www.mfa.gov.il/.

incidents of weapons trafficking demonstrate Iran's use of the marine transportation system to broaden its influence in the region. Iran has constructed a seaport on the Eritrean coast in the port city of Assab for use by the Revolutionary Guards to help foment further instability in the region.[141]

21.5.4 Ineffectiveness of the Security Council

Despite years of economic sanctions and arms embargoes, both the DPRK and Iran appear unwilling to abandon their nuclear weapons and ballistic missile programs. Not only have they disregarded their obligations under the NPT, their respective IAEA Safeguard Agreements and numerous Security Council resolutions, neither the DPRK nor Iran participate in any of the relevant counter-proliferation initiatives established to curtail the spread of MWD and ballistic missile technology, including the *Australia Group, Missile Technology Control Regime, Nuclear Suppliers Group, Wassenaar Arrangement, Global Initiative to Combat Nuclear Terrorism, Hague Code of Conduct against Ballistic Missile Proliferation* and the *Proliferation Security Initiative*. Nor have the two emerging nuclear-armed powers filed the reports required by Security Council Resolutions 1540 and 1673.

Most experts would agree with former IAEA Director General Mohamed ElBaradei that the DPRK has become a "fully fledge nuclear power." Having conducted successful nuclear tests in 2006 and 2009, the Arms Control Agency now estimates that the DPRK has separated enough plutonium for up to 12 nuclear warheads. Moreover, in November 2010, the DPRK announced that it could produce uranium hexafluoride (raw material for uranium enrichment) and had constructed a uranium-enrichment plant at Yongbyon that could be easily converted to produce highly enriched uranium for weapons.

American officials have indicated that the DPRK has at least one other uranium-enrichment facility apart from the Yongbyon plant. When fully operational, the Arms Control Agency estimates that the new plant could produce enough material for one to two bombs each year. The DPRK also has an active ballistic missile program and is in the process of developing intercontinental ballistic missiles, which pose a direct threat to the United States and other Asia-Pacific nations. The DPRK remains a major exporter of ballistic missile technology to the Middle East, South Asia and North Africa.

Iran continues to insist that it does not have nuclear weapons ambitions and that its peaceful nuclear efforts are purely for energy production and medical research, but remains defiant of Security Council and IAEA demands for transparency. In late January 2011, nuclear talks between Iran and the P5+1 (Britain, China, France, Russia, the United States and Germany) collapsed after Iran refused to

---

[141] Yoel Guzansky, *The Naval Arena in the Struggle against Iran*, INSS INSIGHT No. 146 (Institute for National Security Studies, Tel Aviv, Israel, Dec. 3, 2009).

allow increased IAEA scrutiny of its nuclear program.[142] Ali Asghar Soltaneih, Iran's representative to the IAEA, stated, "resolutions, sanctions, threats, computer virus [sic] or even a military attack will not stop uranium enrichment in Iran."[143] This statement is consistent with Iranian practice.

Two secret nuclear facilities—a heavy-water production plant near Arak (that could be used to produce plutonium) and a gas centrifuge uranium-enrichment facility near Natanz (that could be used to produce fissile materials for weapons)—were discovered by the IAEA in 2002. A number of additional clandestine nuclear activities have been discovered since that time, including a secret facility near Qom.

Uranium extracted from a mine in southern Iran, near Bandar Abbas, and considerable amounts of yellowcake (uranium concentrate) acquired from South Africa in the 1970s and China before UN sanctions were imposed, could be used to offset UN sanctions that ban Iran from importing nuclear material. Additionally, Iran continues to develop and refine its ballistic missile forces, one of the largest in the Middle East. Reported ranges for these missiles vary from 1,000 to 2,000 kilometers, some of which could be used to attack targets in Israel. These activities have prompted Israel to call for concerted action by the international community to eliminate the Iranian threat, including the use of a pre-emptive military strike if Iran does not abandon its nuclear ambitions.[144] Iran announced it had started enriching uranium at the Fordo underground nuclear facility near Qom, but the site suffered a mysterious and massive explosion on January 21, 2013.[145]

While the United States has warned Israel not to act unilaterally, the Obama Administration has indicated that it will use force as a last resort to prevent Iran from developing nuclear weapons.[146] In mid-May 2012, speaking before the Israeli Bar Association, Daniel Shapiro, the American ambassador to Israel, stated that the United States was prepared to use military force to stop Iran from developing nuclear weapons, although it would be "preferable to solve this diplomatically and through the use of pressure, than to use military force." However, the ambassador added: "But that doesn't mean that option isn't fully available. Not just available, it's ready. The necessary planning has been done to ensure that it's ready."[147]

---

[142] *EU Lawmakers Seek to Extend Iran Sanctions*, YAHOO NEWS, Jan. 25, 2011.

[143] George Jahn, Iran sees progress at talks, other demur, YAHOO News, Jan. 21, 2011.

[144] ISRAEL MINISTER: STRIKE ON IRAN COULD BE NECESSARY, YAHOO NEWS, May 30, 2011.

[145] Yoel Goldman, *Israeli Sources Reportedly Confirm Blast at Iranian Nuclear Facility*, TIMES OF ISRAEL, Jan. 28, 2013.

[146] Mark Landler, *Obama Says Iran Strike Is an Option, but Warns Israel*, N.Y. TIMES, Mar. 2, 2012.

[147] *U.S. Military Prepared for Iran Strike, Ambassador Says*, UNITED PRESS INTERNATIONAL, May 17, 2012.

21.6 Proliferation Security Initiative

In December 2002, President George W. Bush unveiled a new, more robust strategy to combat WMD proliferation that went beyond the traditional methods of dealing with proliferation—diplomacy, arms control, threat reduction assistance and export controls—by placing greater emphasis on the need to interdict WMD and related materials. The 2002 *National Strategy to Combat Weapons of Mass Destruction* identified effective interdiction as "a critical part of the U.S. strategy to combat WMD and their delivery means." In this regard, the new strategy calls for enhanced "capabilities of our military, intelligence, technical, and law enforcement communities to prevent the movement of WMD materials, technology, and expertise to hostile states and terrorist organizations."[148]

Just a few months later, in the spring of 2003, President Bush announced the establishment of the *Proliferation Security Initiative* (PSI) during a speech in Krakow, Poland. Initial supporters of the initiative included Australia, France, Germany, Italy, Japan, the Netherlands, Poland, Portugal, Spain and the United Kingdom. This core group was responsible for drafting a *Statement of Interdiction Principles* that relies on voluntary actions by states that are consistent with their national legal authorities and relevant international law and frameworks in order to prevent the proliferation of WMD and related materials.[149]

Support for the initiative has grown from its original 11 members to over 100 participating countries, although the level of active participation varies from country to country.[150] It has also garnered the support of the Obama Administration, which entered its second term with continued strong support for the Bush-era counter-proliferation efforts. At a speech at Hradčany Square in Prague on April 5, 2009, President Obama reaffirmed "America's commitment to seek the peace and security of the world without nuclear weapons." The President announced that the United States would take "concrete steps toward a world without nuclear weapons," strengthen the NPT, and, "ensure that terrorists never acquire a nuclear weapon."[151] One year later the White House released the 2010 *National Security Strategy*, which emphasizes that the Administration will "work to turn programs

---

[148] The White House, National Strategy to Combat Weapons of Mass Destruction (Dec. 2002).
[149] Mary Beth Nikitin, Proliferation Security Initiative (PSI), Cong. Res. Service CRS Report for Congress (Jan. 18, 2011).
[150] Proliferation Security Initiative Participants, U.S. Dep't of State, http://www.state.gov/t/isn/c27732.htm.
[151] Remarks Prior to a Meeting With President Vaclav Klaus and Prime Minister Mirek Topolanek by President Barack Obama, Prague, Czech Republic, Apr. 5, 2009, Administration of Barack Obama 439–444 (U.S. Gov't Printing Office, 2009).

such as the *Proliferation Security Initiative* and the *Global Initiative to Combat Nuclear Terrorism* into durable international efforts."[152]

Of course, states of proliferation concern, like the DPRK, Iran, and Syria, have not signed up to the initiative. Additionally, there are some notable countries that have rejected PSI as contrary to international law, including Brazil, China, Bangladesh, India, Indonesia, Malaysia and Pakistan. Unfortunately, many of these states are strategically situated along the sea routes leading to states of proliferation concern. Their lack of participation could significantly diminish the effectiveness of the interdiction regime envisioned by the initiative, in particular port State and coastal State interdiction efforts.

Recognizing that the spread of WMD, their delivery systems and related materials represent a fundamental threat to global peace and security, PSI is designed to prevent trafficking in WMD and related materials to and from states and non-state actors of proliferation concern. PSI does not, however, create a new international organization with formal membership and a secretariat to run day-to-day operations. Rather, it is an operationally focused activity that relies on the voluntary participation of states with common interests, using existing national and international legal authorities and frameworks, to stem the growing threat of WMD proliferation by air, land and sea.

PSI, moreover, is not intended as a replacement for other nonproliferation mechanisms such as SUA, the UN Security Council sanctions regime, IAEA oversight, the NPT, and the *Missile Technology Control Regime*. It is designed to reinforce and compliment these mechanisms. Since its inception in 2002, dozens of exercises, aimed at enhancing counter-proliferation cooperation, have been conducted by the participating nations.

21.6.1 *Statement of Interdiction Principles*

States that endorse PSI commit themselves to follow the *Statement of Interdiction Principles* (SIP). These principles establish a more coordinated and effective basis through which to disrupt trafficking in WMD, their delivery systems, and related items consistent with national and international legal authorities and nonproliferation frameworks. In particular, the SIP encourage supporting states to commit to:

- Undertake effective measures, either alone or in concert with other states, for interdicting the transfer or transport of WMD, their delivery systems, and related materials to and from states and non-state actors of proliferation concern....
- Adopt streamlined procedures for rapid exchange of relevant information concerning suspected proliferation activity,... dedicate appropriate resources and efforts

---

[152] THE WHITE HOUSE, NATIONAL SECURITY STRATEGY OF THE UNITED STATES OF AMERICA 24 (May 2010).

to interdiction operations and capabilities, and maximize coordination among participants in interdiction efforts.
- Review and work to strengthen their relevant national legal authorities where necessary to accomplish these objectives, and work to strengthen when necessary relevant international law and frameworks in appropriate ways to support these commitments.
- Take specific actions in support of interdiction efforts regarding cargoes of WMD, their delivery systems, or related materials, to the extent their national legal authorities permit and consistent with their obligations under international law and frameworks....[153]

Interdiction efforts contained in the SIP are based on the existing legal principles of port State control, coastal State jurisdiction and exclusive flag State jurisdiction, and include:

- Not to transport or assist in the transport of MWD-related cargoes to or from states or non-state actors of proliferation concern, and not to allow any persons subject to their jurisdiction to do so.
- At their own initiative or at the request by another state, to take action to board and search any vessel flying their flag in their internal waters or territorial seas, or areas beyond the territorial seas of any other state, that is reasonably suspected of transporting such WMD-related cargoes, and to seize such cargoes that are identified.
- To seriously consider providing consent to other states to board and search its flag vessels, and to seize WMD-related cargoes in such vessels.
- To take appropriate actions to stop and/or search in their internal waters, territorial seas, or contiguous zones vessels that reasonably are suspected of carrying WMD-related cargoes and to seize such cargoes.
- To take appropriate actions to enforce conditions on vessels entering or leaving their ports, internal waters or territorial seas, such as requiring vessels to be subject to boarding and search prior to entry.
- At their own initiative or upon the request by another state, to (a) require aircraft that are reasonably suspected of carrying MWD-related cargoes and that are transiting their airspace to land for inspection and seize any such cargoes that are identified; and/or (b) deny aircraft reasonably suspected of carrying such cargoes transit rights through their airspace in advance of such flights.
- If their ports, airfields, or other facilities are used as transshipment points for shipment of WMD-related cargoes, to inspect vessels, aircraft, or other modes of transport reasonably suspected of carrying such cargoes, and to seize such cargoes that are identified.[154]

21.6.2 *Bilateral Shipboarding Agreements*

Consistent with UN Security Council Resolution 1540 and SUA, PSI encourages states to enter into bilateral agreements or operational arrangements to enhance

---

[153] DEP'T OF STATE, STATEMENT OF INTERDICTION PRINCIPLES FOR THE PROLIFERATION SECURITY INITIATIVE, Sept. 4, 2003.
[154] Id.

cooperation and facilitate authorized ship boarding by participating flag States. In this regard, the United States has entered into a number of bilateral boarding agreements with key flag States, including the major flags of convenience, to allow for boarding and inspecting of suspect ships seaward of the territorial sea of other nations. Under these agreements, if a vessel registered in the U.S. or the partner country is suspected of carrying WMD-related cargo, either Party can request the other to confirm the nationality of the ship and authorize the boarding, search, and detention of the vessel and its cargo.

The boarding provisions vary from agreement-to-agreement, and specify either that flag State consent is required under all circumstances (*i.e.*, Bahamas and Croatia), or that boarding authority is presumed if the flag State does not respond within a certain timeframe (*i.e.*, Belize, Liberia, Marshall Islands, Mongolia and Panama), or that authority to board within a certain period of time is presumed only if registry cannot be confirmed (*i.e.*, Cyprus, Liberia, Malta, Marshall Islands, Mongolia, and Panama). This third model is useful if national authorities lack around-the-clock access to their registry to confirm ship registration. Furthermore, confirmation of registry may be complicated if a vessel is registered in one state, but flies the flag of another state independent of that registry, as is permitted under Article 91 of UNCLOS. Under the doctrine of presumptive flag State authority, however, the United States accepts at face value ostensible claims of nationality of a vessel. Thus, ship markings or registry, the flag flying on the mast, or statements by the Master of the ship each serve as presumptive indication that the ship is under the jurisdiction of the state as represented.[155]

The United States has concluded 11 such agreements with Antigua & Barbuda, the Bahamas, Belize, Croatia, Cyprus, Liberia, Malta, Marshall Islands, Mongolia, Panama, and St. Vincent and the Grenadines. These countries account for over 60 percent of the world's shipping in terms of deadweight tonnage.[156]

The U.S.-Belize agreement is the only one that has been publicly acknowledged to support an actual interdiction operation. In late May 2011, intelligence sources revealed that the M/V *Light* was illegally transporting prohibited military items from the DPRK to Myanmar in violation of UN Security Council Resolution 1874. Although the ship was Chinese owned and manned by a North Korean crew, it was registered in Belize. American authorities requested permission from the Government of Belize to board the vessel pursuant to the U.S.-Belize PSI ship boarding agreement.[157]

Belize authorities quickly granted permission for U.S. naval personnel to board and inspect the vessel, and an American destroyer was dispatched to intercept

---

[155] *R. V. Dean and Bolden*, 2 Cr. App. R. 171, 173–74 (1998).
[156] Flags of Convenience Countries, International Transport Workers' Federation, http://www.itfglobal.org/.
[157] David Sanger, *U.S. Said to Turn Back North Korea Missile Shipment*, N.Y. Times, June 13, 2011, at A4.

the illicit cargo. On May 26, the USS McCampbell (DDG 85) caught up with the M/V *Light* south of Shanghai and requested permission to board on four separate occasions. The North Korean Master, however, refused to authorize the boarding. He claimed the vessel was carrying industrial chemicals to Bangladesh, not military equipment.[158]

Despite having received permission from the Government of Belize to board, U.S. authorities did not board the vessel in order to de-escalate the situation. The ship was, however, kept under surveillance for several days by the *McCampbell* and U.S. military aircraft. Afraid that he would not be able to secure fuel in Singapore or Malaysia after both of those governments gave assurances to the United States that they would inspect the vessel if it came into port, the *Light's* Master reversed course on May 29 and returned to port in North Korea.[159]

The U.S.-Belize agreement was signed on August 4, 2005, and entered into force on October 19 of the same year.[160] Consistent with 2005 SUA, Article 1(1) of the agreement defines "proliferation by sea" to include, not only illicit transportation by ship of WMD, but also the illicit transport of "their delivery systems, and related materials." "Related materials" are defined in article 1(3) as "materials, equipment and technology, of whatever nature or type that are related to and destined for use in the development, production, utilization or delivery of WMD."

Operations to suppress proliferation by sea under article 3 of the agreement shall be carried out in accordance with the principle of exclusive flag State jurisdiction embodied in Article 92 of UNCLOS:

> Operations to suppress proliferation by sea pursuant to this Agreement shall be carried out only against suspect ships having or otherwise claiming the nationality of one of the Parties, suspect ships without nationality, and suspect ships assimilated to ships without nationality, but not against a ship registered under the law of one of the Parties while bareboat chartered in another State not party to this Agreement.

Pursuant to Article 4 of the bilateral agreement, interdiction operations are limited to international waters seaward of the territorial sea of any nation. "International waters" are defined in Article 1(8) as "all parts of the sea not included in the territorial sea, internal waters and archipelagic waters of a State, consistent with . . . the United Nations Convention on the Law of the Sea."

---

[158] Euan Graham, MARITIME COUNTER-PROLIFERATION: THE CASE OF MV LIGHT, RSIS COMMENTARIES, No. 96/2011, June 29, 2011.
[159] *U.S. Denied Request to Board N. Korean Ship Suspected of Carrying Illegal Weapons*, MARITIME EXECUTIVE, June 14, 2011.
[160] Agreement Between the Government of the United States of America and the Government of Belize Concerning Cooperation to Suppress the Proliferation of Weapons of Mass Destruction, Their Delivery Systems, and Related Materials By Sea, Aug. 4, 2005.

Consistent with the boarding regime set out in the 2005 SUA, if security officials of one Party ("the requesting Party") suspect that a ship located in international waters is a suspect ship that claims nationality of the other Party ("the requested Party"), the requesting Party may ask the requested Party to:

    a. confirm the claim of nationality of the suspect ship; and
    b. if such claim is confirmed:
        i. authorize the boarding and search of the suspect ship, cargo and the persons found on board by Security Force Officials of the requesting Party; and
        ii. if items of proliferation concern are found,
        authorize the Security Force Officials of the requesting Party to exercise control over the movement of the ship, as well as items and persons on board, pending instructions conveyed through the Competent Authority of the requested Party as to the actions the requesting Party is permitted to take concerning such items, persons and ships.[161]

"Suspect ship" is defined in article 1(7) as "a ship used for commercial or private purposes in respect of which there are reasonable grounds to suspect it is engaged in proliferation by sea."

When responding to a request to confirm a claim of nationality, the requested state may either refuse the claim of the suspect ship to its nationality or verify its nationality. If the nationality is verified, the requested Party may, if satisfied that the vessel is a suspect ship:

    i. decide to conduct the boarding and search with its own Security Force Officials;
    ii. authorize the boarding and search by the Security Force Officials of the requesting Party;
    iii. decide to conduct the boarding and search together with the requesting Party; or
    iv. deny permission to board and search.[162]

The agreement recognizes that time is of the essence in any interdiction operation. Accordingly, requests for verification of nationality and authority to board shall be answered within two hours of receipt of the request.[163] If the requested Party does not respond within the two-hour window and has not requested additional time in which to respond, the requesting Party shall contact the requested Party to verify the reasons for the non-reply. If contact cannot be established with the requested Party, the requesting Party may "board the suspect vessel for the purpose of inspecting the vessel's documents in order to verify the said vessel's nationality."[164] If the requesting Party "is satisfied that the ship has the nationality of the Requested Party, the Requesting Party will be deemed to have been

---

[161] Id., Article 4(1).
[162] Id., Article 4(3)(b).
[163] Id., Article 4(3)(c).
[164] Id., Article 4(3)(e)(2).

authorized by the Requested Party to question persons on board and to search the vessel to determine if it is so engaged in proliferation by sea."[165]

Consistent with Article 110 of UNCLOS, nothing in the agreement prohibits security force officials of one Party to board suspect ships

> ... claiming nationality in the other Party that are not flying the flag of the other Party, not displaying any marks of its registration or nationality, and claiming to have no documentation on board the ship, for the purpose of locating and examining the ship's documentation. Provided that:
> a. If documentation or other physical evidence of nationality is located, the foregoing paragraphs of this Article apply.
> b. If no documentation or other physical evidence of nationality is available, the requesting Party may assimilate the ship to a ship without nationality in accordance with international law.[166]

Nothing in the agreement limits the right of either Party to board a vessel in accordance with international law "whether based, *inter alia*, on the right of visit, the rendering of assistance to persons, ships and property in distress or peril, or an authorization from the Flag or Coastal State, or other appropriate bases in international law."[167]

Pursuant to article 4(5), the authority to "board, search and detain includes the authority to use force...." Article 9 provides that:

> 1. All uses of force pursuant to this Agreement shall be in strict accordance with this Agreement, the applicable laws and policies of the Parties and applicable international law.
> 2. Each Party shall avoid the use of force except when and to the degree necessary to ensure the safety of Security Force Officials and ships, and of persons on board the suspect ship, and where Security Force Officials are obstructed in the execution of their duties.
> 3. Only that force reasonably necessary under the circumstances may be used.
> 4. Boarding and search teams and Security Force ships have the inherent right to use all available means to apply that force reasonably necessary to defend themselves or others from physical harm.

When conducting a boarding and search pursuant to the agreement, security force officials shall comply with their respective national laws and policies and act consistent with international law and accepted international practices.[168] Article 8 requires that the Parties apply certain safeguards when conducting counter-proliferation activities at sea:

---

[165] Id., Article 4(3)(e)(3).
[166] Id., Article 4(4).
[167] Id., Article 4(6).
[168] Id., Article 7(1).

1. Where a Party boards, searches, detains, seizes, arrests, forfeits, or takes other measures against a suspect ship, or persons on board, or an item of proliferation concern on a suspect ship, in accordance with this Agreement, that Party shall:
   a. take due account of the need not to endanger the safety of life at sea;
   b. take due account of the security of the ship and its cargo;
   c. not prejudice the commercial or legal interests of the Flag State;
   d. ensure within available means, that any measure taken with regard to the suspect ship is environmentally sound under the circumstances;
   e. ensure that persons on board are afforded the protections, rights and guarantees provided by international law and the boarding State's law and regulations;
   f. ensure the master of the suspect ship is, or has been, afforded the opportunity to contact the ship's owner, manager or Flag State at the earliest opportunity.
2. Reasonable efforts shall be taken to avoid a suspect ship from being unduly detained or delayed.

Any claim "for damage, harm, injury, death or loss resulting from an operation carried out by a Party... shall be resolved by that Party in accordance with the domestic law of that Party, and in a manner consistent with international law."[169]

Under article 5(1), if a vessel is boarded in international waters, the flag State retains the primary right to exercise jurisdiction "over a detained ship, cargo or other items and persons on board (including seizure, forfeiture, arrest, and prosecution)." In the event the interdiction occurs in the contiguous zone of a Party, both Parties retain the authority to board and exercise jurisdiction to prosecute the vessel, except "in cases involving suspect ships fleeing from the territorial sea of a Party in which that Party has the authority to board and to exercise jurisdiction...," in which case that Party shall have the right to exercise jurisdiction.[170] In any event, the Party conducting the boarding and search is required by article 6(2) to "promptly notify the other Party of the results thereof... and... make full disclosure and submit a comprehensive report in respect of the boarding, search and results of the investigation." Periodic status reports are required under article 6(3).

Unless otherwise agreed, "cargo and other items seized in consequence of operations undertaken onboard ships subject to the jurisdiction of a Party pursuant to this Agreement shall be disposed of by that Party in accordance with its laws."[171] In addition, article 12(2) allows the Party that exercises jurisdiction to "transfer forfeited cargo, assets and other items or proceeds of their sale to the other Party."

In order to facilitate counter-proliferation operations, article 6(1) encourages the Parties "to exchange operational information on the detection and location of suspect ships...." Each Party is also encouraged by article 10(1) to keep the

---

[169] Id., Article 13(2).
[170] Id., Article 5(2).
[171] Id., Article 12(1).

other Party informed "of its respective applicable laws and policies, particularly those pertaining to the use of force." Article 11(1) likewise requires each Party to inform the other Party "the points of contact for communication, decision and instructions under Articles 4 and 5, and notifications under Articles 6 and 10 of this Agreement." Additionally, one Party may request the other Party "to provide technical assistance, such as specialized assistance in the conduct of search of suspect ships or other facilities, for the search of suspect ships or other facilities located in the territory or waters of the requesting Party."[172]

While PSI has enhanced international cooperation to prevent the spread of WMD through operational exercises and information sharing, there are still few concrete examples of successful interdiction efforts. One such success story—the interdiction of the *BBC China*—occurred in October 2003, one month after the SIP was adopted by the PSI core group. The *BBC China* was a German-owned ship registered in Antigua and Barbuda, and en route to Libya with a suspected load of centrifuge components for the Khadafy regime.

At the request of Washington and Berlin, the ship owner directed the ship to proceed to Taranto, where Italian officials inspected the vessel and seized the cargo.[173] The interdiction of an *Ilyushin* cargo plane by Thai authorities in 2009 constitutes another success attributed to the initiative. In December 2009, Thai officials seized a Georgian-registered airplane and its cargo when it landed at Don Muang airport in Bangkok to refuel. The inspection of the aircraft by Thai authorities revealed 35 tons of explosives, rocket-propelled grenades and surface-to-surface missile components in violation of the UN arms embargo against the DPRK.[174]

Although there have been successes along the way—some unacknowledged by the states involved—PSI suffers from some of the same defects as other counter-proliferation regimes. Generally, PSI interdiction is based upon flag State consent, although port State control authorities are increasing the options for States to disrupt WMD flows. States of proliferation concern and key States that have refused to participate in the initiative (e.g., Brazil, China, India, Indonesia, Malaysia, and Pakistan) can operate their ships and aircraft on the high seas or disregard their port State/coastal State responsibilities with impunity.

---

[172] Id., Article 16(1).
[173] Jeffrey Lewis & Philip Maxon, *The Proliferation Security Initiative*, DISARMAMENT FORUM 2010, 35–43, at 37.
[174] *Crew of N. Korean Weapons Plan in Thai Court*, WORLDNEWS, Dec. 14, 2009.

Table 21.1. U.S. Bilateral PSI Shipboarding Agreements

1. Agreement between the Government of the United States of America and the Government of the Antigua & Barbuda Concerning Cooperation to Suppress the Proliferation of Weapons of Mass Destruction, Their Delivery Systems, and Related Materials by Sea, signed at St. John's, Antigua, April 26, 2010; *entered into force* September 27, 2010.
2. Agreement between the Government of the United States of America and the Government of the Commonwealth of the Bahamas Concerning Cooperation to Suppress the Proliferation of Weapons of Mass Destruction, Their Delivery Systems, and Related Materials by Sea, signed at Nassau, August 11, 2008; *enters into force upon an exchange of notes indicating that the necessary internal procedures of each Party have been completed.*
3. Agreement between the Government of the United States of America and the Government of Belize Concerning Cooperation to Suppress the Proliferation of Weapons of Mass Destruction, Their Delivery Systems, and Related Materials by Sea, and note, signed at Washington, August 4, 2005, *entered into force* October 19, 2005.
4. Agreement between the Government of the United States of America and the Government of Croatia Concerning Cooperation to Suppress the Proliferation of Weapons of Mass Destruction, Their Delivery Systems, and Related Materials by Sea, signed at Washington, June 1, 2005, *entered into force* March 6, 2007.
5. Agreement between the Government of the United States of America and the Government of Cyprus Concerning Cooperation to Suppress the Proliferation of Weapons of Mass Destruction, Their Delivery Systems, and Related Materials by Sea, signed at Washington, July 25, 2005, *entered into force* January 12, 2006.
6. Agreement between the Government of the United States of America and the Government of the Republic of Liberia Concerning Cooperation to Suppress the Proliferation of Weapons of Mass Destruction, Their Delivery Systems, and Related Materials by Sea, signed at Washington February 11, 2004, applied provisionally from February 11, 2004; *entered into force* December 8, 2004.
7. Agreement between the Government of the United States of America and the Government of the Republic of the Malta Concerning Cooperation to Suppress the Proliferation of Weapons of Mass Destruction, Their Delivery Systems, and Related Materials by Sea, signed at Washington March 15, 2007; *entered into force* December 19, 2007.
8. Agreement between the Government of the United States of America and the Government of the Republic of the Marshall Islands Concerning Cooperation to Suppress the Proliferation of Weapons of Mass Destruction, Their Delivery Systems, and Related Materials by Sea, signed at Honolulu August 13, 2004, applied provisionally from August 13, 2004; *entered into force* November 24, 2004.
9. Agreement between the Government of the United States of America and the Government of Mongolia Concerning Cooperation to Suppress the Proliferation of Weapons of Mass Destruction, Their Delivery Systems, and Related Materials by Sea, signed at Washington October 23, 2007; *entered into force* February 20, 2008.
10. Amendment to the Supplementary Arrangement between the Government of the United States of America and the Government of the Republic of Panama to the Arrangement between the Government of the United States of America and the Government of Panama for Support and Assistance from the United States Coast Guard for the National Maritime Service of the Ministry of Government and Justice, signed at Washington, May 12, 2004, applied provisionally from May 12, 2004; *entered into force* December 1, 2004.
11. Agreement between the Government of the United States of America and the Government of Saint Vincent and the Grenadines Concerning Cooperation to Suppress the Proliferation of Weapons of Mass Destruction, Their Delivery Systems, and Related Materials by Sea, signed at Kingstown, May 11, 2010; *entered into force* May 11, 2010.

21.7 CAN THE NPT SURVIVE?

Although the NPT has been widely accepted and offers a framework for preventing the spread of nuclear weapons and related materials, it lacks the necessary "teeth" to keep rogue nations in line. Moreover, the IAEA, the Security Council and the international community have been reluctant to use robust measures to enforce its provisions. As a result of this state of affairs, a regime that envisioned a world with only five nuclear weapons states is now faced with the realization that India, Israel, Pakistan and the DPRK possess nuclear weapons in flagrant disregard of the NPT structure.

Depending on which report is accurate, Iran could have enough enriched uranium to produce nuclear weapons as early as 2013, though most analysts believe that 2015 is a more realistic date. The British Defense Secretary told Parliament in January 2011 that Iran could produce such weapons as early as 2012, an assessment that proved false.[175] This British assessment was in line with a study by the Federation of American Scientists that indicates Iran is not slowing down its nuclear ambitions and could produce a simple nuclear warhead.[176] Iran remains openly defiant of UN sanctions and IAEA inspectors—speaking on Iranian state television, Iran's envoy to the IAEA indicated that UN sanctions and threats by the international community would not stop Iran's uranium enrichment program.[177] Iranian officials have accused the Western powers of "nuclear terrorism," blaming Israel and the United States for the assassination of Iran's leading nuclear scientists, including Majid Shahriariwas.[178] Another scientist—Mostafa Ahmadi Roshan—was killed by a car bomb in January 2012. Roshan was the director of the Natanz uranium enrichment facility.[179]

United Nations sanctions have been ineffective in preventing the development of nuclear weapons by the DPRK. Yet, sanctions imposed on Iran have followed the exact same stepped-approach, and in some cases have been less stringent than those imposed on the DPRK. More importantly, whereas DPRK sanctions focused on, *inter alia*, "luxury goods" to encourage North Korean leaders to return to the NPT and abandon their nuclear weapons program, an obvious omission from UN sanctions is a limitation on Iran's oil exports.

Loss of oil revenues would cripple Iran's economy and would undoubtedly have a lasting, detrimental effect on Tehran's nuclear ambitions. Although such

---

[175] DIRECTOR OF NAT'L INTELLIGENCE, UNITED STATES OF AMERICA, IRAN: NUCLEAR INTENTIONS AND CAPABILITIES, NATIONAL INTELLIGENCE ESTIMATE, Nov. 2007.
[176] Ali Akbar Dareini & George Jahn, *Iran's Nuke Program—How Much Time for Diplomacy?*, YAHOO NEWS, Jan. 20, 2011.
[177] George Jahn, *Iran Sees Progress at Talks, Others Demur*, YAHOO NEWS, Jan. 21, 2011.
[178] George Jahn, *Iran Accuses West of 'Nuclear Terrorism'*, YAHOO NEWS, Jan. 25, 2011.
[179] Mark Whittington, *Covert War in Iran Heats Up with Execution of Nuclear Scientist*, YAHOO NEWS, Jan. 11, 2012.

a measure would adversely affect the price of energy and the world economy, oil prices would also skyrocket if a nuclear-armed Iran attacks Israel or one of its neighbors. The question is—does the world deal with the rise of oil prices now with a non-nuclear Iran, or does it wait and deal with the inevitable rise in oil prices after Iran acquires and uses nuclear weapons? Dealing directly and harshly with a non-nuclear Iran is preferred, a course of action recognized by Spain's Member of the European Parliament, Alejo Vidal-Quadras. Vidal-Quadras argues the current "soft" approach used by the Western powers to deal with Iran has proven futile.[180] Consistent with Vidal-Quadras' "tough" approach, the United States[181] and the European Union imposed additional sanctions on Iran in December 2011 and January 2012, respectively, aimed at crippling the nation's oil exports.[182] In February 2012, the Obama Administration tightened sanctions by issuing Executive Order 13599, which freezes all property of the Government of Iran and Iranian financial institutions in the United States:

> Section 1. (a) All property and interests in property of the Government of Iran, including the Central Bank of Iran, that are in the United States, that hereafter come within the United States, or that are or hereafter come within the possession or control of any United States person, including any foreign branch, are blocked and may not be transferred, paid, exported, withdrawn, or otherwise dealt in.
>
> (b) All property and interests in property of any Iranian financial institution, including the Central Bank of Iran, that are in the United States, that hereafter come within the United States, or that are or hereafter come within the possession or control of any United States person, including any foreign branch, are blocked and may not be transferred, paid, exported, withdrawn, or otherwise dealt in.
>
> (c) All property and interests in property that are in the United States, that hereafter come within the United States, or that are or hereafter come within the possession or control of any United States person, including any foreign branch, of the following persons are blocked and may not be transferred, paid, exported, withdrawn, or otherwise dealt in: any person determined by the Secretary of the Treasury, in consultation with the Secretary of State, to be owned or controlled by, or to have acted or purported to act for or on behalf of, directly or indirectly, any person whose property and interests in property are blocked pursuant to this order.

* * *

> Sec. 5. (a) Any transaction by a United States person or within the United States that evades or avoids, has the purpose of evading or avoiding, causes a violation of, or attempts to violate any of the prohibitions set forth in this order is prohibited.

---

[180] *EU Lawmakers Seek to Extend Iran Sanctions*, YAHOO NEWS, Jan. 25, 2011.
[181] National Defense Authorization Act for Fiscal Year 2012, § 1245.
[182] Hossein Jaseb & Justyna Pawlak, *Iran Slams EU Oil Embargo, Warns Could Hit U.S.*, REUTERS, Jan. 23, 2012.

(b) Any conspiracy formed to violate any of the prohibitions set forth in this order is prohibited.[183]

Despite international sanctions and diplomatic efforts to curb Iran's and North Korea's nuclear ambitions, all of the maritime interdiction regimes currently in existence, including UN Security Council Resolutions and PSI, fail to prevent rogue states from transporting WMD-related material by sea. All of these regimes suffer from the same fatal defect—they are based on exclusive flag State jurisdiction on the high seas. One would expect a responsible state to consent to a boarding of one of its flag vessels on the high seas if there were reasonable grounds to believe that the ship is transporting prohibited goods. However, in most cases, ships registered in responsible states will not be used by proliferators of WMD. Rather, these states will use their own flag vessels to transport material to support their nuclear and ballistic missile programs. If a request is made to board one of these vessels, the answer will undoubtedly be "no." The only way to get on board one of these suspect ships to inspect its cargo is through a nonconsensual boarding.

Speaking on the issue of nonproliferation, the commander of the U.S. Pacific Command observed, "[H]ow do you leverage with a regime [such as the DPRK] that does not care how it is viewed by the rest of the world, and does not care how it treats its own people?"[184] The same observation could be made regarding Iran's insensitivity to world opinion. One option is to replace the current "sanctions and diplomacy" approach with more forceful measures, such as nonconsensual vessel boarding. Because of decades of dithering, the international community will soon be faced with the prospect that armed force alone is the only effective recourse to stop WMD proliferation.

The only UN sanction regimes that have worked in recent memory were the sanctions imposed on Iraq and the Former Republic of Yugoslavia (FRY). They were effective because the Security Council authorized the use of "all necessary means," to include the use of force and nonconsensual ship boarding, to interdict all shipping entering or departing Iraqi and FRY ports. Iraq, for example, was subjected to a total embargo (except medical and humanitarian foodstuffs) and severe economic sanctions for over a decade.[185]

United Nations Security Council Resolution 665 authorized a maritime blockade of Iraq, including the use of such "measures commensurate to the ... circumstances as may be necessary ... to halt all inward and outward maritime shipping, in order to inspect and verify their cargoes and destinations and to ensure strict

---

[183] Exec. Ord. 13599, Blocking the Property of the Government of Iran, Feb. 5, 2012, Fed. Reg. Vol. 77, No. 26, Feb. 8, 2012.
[184] RSN Singh, *India and the US-China Great Game*, 25 INDIAN DEFENCE REVIEW, Dec. 20, 2010.
[185] S/RES/662 (1990), Aug. 9, 1990.

implementation of the provisions related to such shipping laid down in resolution 661 (1990)."[186] These sanctions, coupled with the maritime blockade and U.S.-led invasion of Iraq, later authorized by Security Council Resolution 1441 in 2003, put an end to Saddam Hussein's nuclear ambitions.[187]

The Security Council adopted similar measures with regard to the Federal Republic of Yugoslavia in resolutions 713 (1991), 724 (1991), 757 (1992), 787 (1992), 820 (1993), 942 (1994), 943 (1994), and 1015 (1995). Security Council Resolution 787 called on "states, acting nationally or through regional agencies or arrangements, to use such measures commensurate with the specific circumstances as may be necessary... to halt all inward and outward maritime shipping in order to inspect and verify their cargoes and destinations and to ensure strict implementation of the provisions of resolutions 713 (1991) and 757 (1992)."[188] Security Council Resolution 713 required all States to "immediately implement a general and complete embargo on all deliveries of weapons and military equipment to Yugoslavia...."[189] Security Council Resolution 757 extended the sanctions to "all commodities and products originating in the Federal Republic of Yugoslavia (Serbia and Montenegro)."[190] Finally, Security Council Resolution 820 reaffirmed the authority of States acting under UN Security Council Resolution 787 "to use such measures commensurate with the specific circumstances as may be necessary... to enforce the present resolution and its other relevant resolutions, including in the territorial sea of the Federal Republic of Yugoslavia (Serbia and Montenegro)."[191]

Absent more effective sanctions enforcement and authority for nonconsensual boarding, Israel may have to once again intervene, as it did in 1981 and 2007, to ensure that nuclear weapons do not fall into the hands of erratic Middle Eastern states. On June 7, 1981, Israeli aircraft destroyed the Iraqi nuclear reactor under construction in Osirak, Iraq.[192]

Two decades later, on September 6, 2007, Israeli aircraft destroyed a possible undeclared nuclear reactor in the Deir ez-Zor region of Syria.[193] Although condemned by many nations, Operations *Opera* and *Orchard* effectively prevented Iraq and Syria from advancing their respective nuclear weapons programs. Alternatively, continued cyber attacks like the Stuxnet malware virus can be used to significantly damage and delay Iran's enrichment program. Iran has acknowl-

---

[186] S/RES/665 (1990), Aug. 25, 1990.
[187] S/RES/1441 (2003), Nov. 8, 2003.
[188] S/RES/787 (1992), Nov. 16, 1992.
[189] S/RES/713 (1991), Sept. 25, 1991.
[190] S/RES/757 (1992), May 30, 1992.
[191] S/RES/820 (1993), Apr. 17, 1993.
[192] A discussion of Operation Opera is available at http://www.absoluteastronomy.com/topics/Operation_Opera.
[193] Id.

edged that Stuxnet disrupted uranium enrichment at Natanz in November 2010 by crippling thousands of centrifuges.[194] An article in the *New York Times* on June 1, 2012, attributes the Stuxnet cyber attack to the United States.[195] Similarly, the catastrophic explosion on January 21, 2013, at the deep underground Fordo nuclear enrichment facility suggests States are taking preemptive action.

---

[194] Ali Akbar Dareini & George Jahn, *Iran's Nuke Program—How Much Time for Diplomacy?*, YAHOO NEWS, Jan. 20, 2011; William Broad, John Markoff & David Sanger, *Israeli Test on Worm Called Crucial in Iran Nuclear Delay*, N.Y. TIMES, Jan. 15, 2011; Ed Barnes, *Mystery Surrounds Cyber Missile that Crippled Iran's Nuclear Weapons Ambitions*, FOX NEWS, Nov. 26, 2010; Ken Dilanian, *Iran's Nuclear Program and a New Era of Cyber War*, L.A. TIMES, Jan. 17, 2011.

[195] David Sanger, *Obama Order Sped Up Wave of Cyberattacks Against Iran*, N.Y. TIMES, June 1, 2012.

TWENTY-TWO

COMMENTARY FOR THE CONVENTION ON THE SUPPRESSION
OF UNLAWFUL ACTS AGAINST THE SAFETY OF MARITIME NAVIGATION

22.1 Convention for the Suppression of Unlawful Acts (SUA)

Concern about unlawful acts that threaten the safety of ships and the security of their passengers and crews grew during the 1980s, with reports of crews kidnapped, ships hi-jacked, and vessels deliberately run aground or blown up by explosives. Passengers were threatened and sometimes killed. On October 7, 1985, Palestinian terrorists hijacked the Italian cruise ship *Achille Lauro* while the ship was sailing from Alexandria to Port Said, off the coast of Egypt.[1]

The hijackers demanded the release of 50 Palestinian prisoners from Israel in exchange for the 400 passengers and crew on board the vessel, and threatened to blow up the ship if a rescue attempt was attempted.[2] When their demands were not met, the terrorists killed Leon Klinghoffer, a 69-year-old disabled Jewish-American tourist, and threw his body over the side with his wheelchair. The hijackers ultimately surrendered to Egyptian authorities in exchange for a pledge of safe passage by aircraft out of the country. However, while the Egyptian aircraft was en-route to Tunisia, it was intercepted by U.S. Navy fighter jets over the Mediterranean Sea, and forced to land in Sicily, where the terrorists were

---

[1] John Tagliabue, *Ship Carrying 400 Seized; Hijackers Demand Release Of 50 Palestinians In Israel*, N.Y. Times, Oct. 8, 1985 at A1.
[2] Judith Miller, *Hijackers Yield Ship In Egypt; Passenger Slain, 400 Are Safe; U.S. Assails Deal With Captors*, N.Y. Times, Oct. 10, 1985, at A1, and Thomas L. Friedman, *Port Of Israel Described As Target Of Terrorists Who Seized Vessel*, N.Y. Times, Oct. 11, 1985, at A1.

taken into custody.[3] Thereafter, there ensued a diplomatic row among the United States, Italy, and Egypt, over custody of the accused terrorists.

In November, 1985 the problem of extradition or prosecution was considered by the fourteenth session of the IMO Assembly, and a proposal by the United States that measures to prevent such unlawful acts should be developed by IMO was supported. The next year the Maritime Safety Committee (MSC) issued a circular titled *Measures to prevent unlawful acts against passengers and crews on board ships*.[4] The IMO Assembly also adopted a resolution that called for development of measures to prevent unlawful acts that threaten the safety of ships, and their passengers and crew.[5] Member States of the IMO sought to strengthen the legal regime applicable to international seagoing vessels.

In November 1986, the Governments of Austria, Egypt, and Italy proposed that IMO prepare a convention on the subject of maritime terrorism "to provide for a comprehensive suppression of unlawful acts committed against the safety of maritime navigation, which endanger innocent human lives, jeopardize the safety of persons and property, seriously affect the operation of maritime services and thus are of grave concern to the international community as a whole." Under the convention, an act is "unlawful" if it is conducted without authority, and the exemption of warships and maritime law enforcement vessels from the terms of the treaty in article 2 suggests that constabulary or naval action is presumptively lawful.

The three states prepared draft text based on the Hostage Convention, and the Hague and Montreal Conventions against airplane hijacking and hostage taking, and submitted it to the IMO.[6] The Hague and Montreal Conventions established what has become a "familiar and reliable formula" for multilateral conventions against terrorism.[7] State Parties agree that certain specific heinous conduct constitutes an offense, regardless of the motivation of the offender. The conduct

---

[3] *American Killed as Terrorists Capture Cruise Ship*, CNN INTERACTIVE VIDEO ALMANAC, Oct. 7, 1985 and *Terrorism: The Price of Success*, TIME MAGAZINE, Oct. 28, 1985, at 32–33.
[4] IMO Doc. MSC/Circ.443, Measures to Prevent Unlawful Acts Against Passengers and Crews on Board Ships, Sept. 26, 1986.
[5] IMO Doc. A.584(14), Measures to Prevent Unlawful Acts Which Threaten the Safety of Ships and the Security of Their Passengers and Crew, Nov. 20, 1985.
[6] Hague Convention on Suppression of Unlawful Seizure of Aircraft, Dec. 16, 1970, 22 U.S.T. 1641, T.I.A.S. No. 7192, 860 U.N.T.S. 105 [Hague Convention] (addressing aircraft hijacking); Convention for the Suppression of Unlawful Acts Against the Safety of Civil Aviation, Sept. 23, 1971, 24 U.S.T. 564, T.I.A.S. No. 7570 (Montreal Convention; addressing sabotage of aircraft); and, Convention Against the Taking of Hostages, Dec. 17, 1979, *reprinted in* 18 I.L.M. 1456 (1979) (addressing hostage taking).
[7] Samuel M. Witten, *Introductory Note, Convention on the Suppression of Unlawful Acts Relating to International Civil Aviation and Protocol Supplementary to the Convention for the Suppression of Unlawful Seizure of Aircraft*, 50 I.L.M. 141–159 (2011).

is criminalized within the territory of each State Party, and jurisdiction is created over the offenders. Mutual legal assistance relating to the covered offenses requires States to extradite or prosecute alleged offenders (*aut dedere aut judicare*). The general formula surfaced in agreements for international cooperation on attacks on diplomats[8] and bombings of public places and infrastructure,[9] and also became a feature of the draft text of the SUA Convention.

The IMO Council unanimously agreed the issue required urgent attention.[10] The Council established the Ad Hoc Preparatory Committee on the Suppression of Unlawful Acts against the Safety of Maritime Navigation, which finished two draft texts based upon the convention prepared by Egypt, Austria, and Italy—one dealing with ships and the other with fixed platforms on the continental shelf.[11] The Preparatory Committee met twice, once in March 1987 in London and again in May 1987 in Rome, to work on the proposed Convention. Acting under article 2(b) of the *Convention on the International Maritime Organization*, the Council of the IMO decided at its fifty-eighth session in June 1987 to convene an international conference on the suppression of unlawful acts against the safety of maritime navigation. The decision was furthered at the fifteenth regular session of the IMO on November 20, 1987, when the Assembly endorsed the decision, and added the conference to its work program for 1988.[12]

Italy offered to serve as the venue for the conference, which was held in Rome at the headquarters of the Food and Agriculture Organization of the United Nations from March 1–10, 1988. Representatives from 76 nations participated in the conference; observers from Cuba, Guinea, the Holy See, Panama, Qatar, Tunisia, and the Palestine Liberation Organization also attended, along with representatives of the United Nations, and intergovernmental and non-governmental organizations. Professor L. Ferrari Bravo of the Italian delegation was elected to serve as president of the Conference.

The Conference established a Committee of the Whole to consider two draft instruments: the draft *Convention for the Suppression of Unlawful Act against the Safety of Maritime Navigation* (1988 SUA Convention) and the draft *Protocol for the Suppression of Unlawful Acts against the Safety of Fixed Platforms located on the Continental Shelf* (1988 SUA Protocol). The Conference also created a Drafting Committee and a Credentials Committee, the latter of which had a purely

---

[8] United Nations Convention on the Prevention and Punishment of Crimes Against Internationally Protected Persons, Dec. 14, 1973, 3166 U.N.T.S. 1035.
[9] United Nations Convention for the Suppression of Terrorist Bombings, Dec. 15, 1997, 37 I.L.M. 249.
[10] IMO Doc. C 57/25, Oct. 1, 1986.
[11] IMO Doc. C 57/WP.1, Nov. 12, 1986, para. 25(a)(2).
[12] IMO Doc. A.633(15), Work Program and Budget for the Fifteenth Financial Period 1988–1989, Nov. 20, 1987.

administrative function to examine the credentials of the representatives to the Conference.

The Convention and Protocol were negotiated successfully, and their terms help advance the rule of law in maritime counter-terrorism. The 1988 Convention managed to avoid the thicket of defining terrorism, bypassing the politically charged issue and instead focusing on specific, discrete acts of human conduct that do injury to international governance and stability. The 1988 Convention and associated commentary are included in this section, but not the 1988 Protocol. The consolidated 2005 Protocol, however, appears in section 22.1.3, after the 2005 Convention.

Only 52 states became parties to the 1988 Convention in its first 13 years. After the terrorist attacks of 9/11, however, the IMO Assembly passed resolution A.924(22) calling on governments to consider ratifying the treaty "at the earliest opportunity."[13] Since its entry into force on March 1, 1992, the 1988 Convention has attracted 160 States parties as of January 2, 2013. Despite widespread subscription by the international community, however, every aspect of the Convention is underutilized. While the treaty is a potentially strong instrument against international piracy and maritime terrorism, it must be exercised in order to have a beneficial effect. With the creation of the 2005 Convention, the international community has a renewed opportunity to solidify the treaty in State practice.

22.1.1 *1988 Convention*

The SUA Convention was adopted by the IMO on March 10, 1988, and it entered into force on March 1, 1992.[14] The main purpose of the Convention is to ensure that appropriate action is taken against persons who commit unlawful acts against ships. These crimes include the seizure of ships by force, acts of violence against persons on board ships, and the placing of devices on board a ship, which are likely to destroy or damage it.

The preamble to the Convention illuminates some of the international law authorities considered in drafting the text, such as the *Charter of the United Nations*, the *Universal Declaration of Human Rights* and the *International Covenant on Civil and Political Rights*. The treaty also acknowledges UN General Assembly resolution 40/61 of December 9, 1985, which "unequivocally condemns, as criminal, all acts, methods and practices of terrorism wherever and by whomever

---

[13] IMO Doc. A.924(22), Review of Measures and Procedures to Prevent Acts of Terrorism Which Threaten the Security of Passengers and Crews and the Safety of Ships, Nov. 20, 2001.

[14] Convention for the Suppression of Unlawful Acts Against the Safety of Maritime Navigation, Rome Mar. 10, 1988, entered into force Mar. 1, 1992, 27 I.L.M. 672 (1988), UN LAW OF THE SEA BULL. NO. 11, July 1988, at 14, 1678 U.N.T.S. 221 [Hereinafter SUA Convention].

committed...." The same UNGA resolution invited the IMO to "study the problem of terrorism aboard or against ships with a view to making recommendations on appropriate measures."

The 1988 Convention applies to ships navigating (or scheduled to navigate) beyond the territorial sea. Interestingly, the treaty was deemed to apply within straits used for international navigation, notwithstanding the legal status of the waters forming such straits.[15] The linchpin of the treaty, however, is the article 6 obligation among States' Parties to prosecute or extradite criminals who are suspected of committing an offense under article 3.[16] The offenses in article 3 also are deemed as covered by any extradition treaty in force between the States Parties.[17]

The Master of a ship of a State Party may deliver to the authorities of another state (the receiving state) any person who he has "reasonable grounds" to believe has committed an offense under the Convention.[18] While making such delivery, the Master shall give notification of his intention to do so, "if possible before entering the territorial sea of the receiving State."[19] The receiving state is required to accept delivery, but there is a rather wide exception that applies. In cases in which the receiving state has "grounds" to believe the Convention does not apply, it may refuse to accept the suspect. The standard for developing "grounds" is undefined; there is no qualification that the grounds must be reasonable or made in good faith, although general principles of law suggest they apply.

Although the 1988 SUA Convention includes a duty among States Parties to cooperate in the prevention of the offenses set forth in article 3, the treaty was primarily an instrument to ensure the prosecution or extradition of suspected offenders.[20] Article 13 also includes the obligation to take "practicable measures to prevent the preparations" of SUA offenses committed inside or outside their territories. Still, the SUA Convention has not been effective at preventing maritime terrorism or WMD proliferation at sea. Even the mandate to prosecute or extradite such suspects or fugitives has not been widely followed, although there are 160 States Parties to the 1988 Convention.

Article 1

Article 1 is short, containing just a single definition. The article defines a "ship" as "a vessel of any type whatsoever not permanently attached to the sea-bed,

---

[15] Id., article 4.
[16] Id., article 6(4).
[17] Id., article 11.
[18] Id., article 8.
[19] Id., article 8I(1).
[20] Id., article 13.

including dynamically supported craft (e.g. hydrofoils), submersibles, or any other floating craft."

> Article 1
>
> For the purposes of this Convention, "ship" means a vessel of any type whatsoever not permanently attached to the sea-bed, including dynamically supported craft (e.g. hydrofoils), submersibles, or any other floating craft.

Article 2

Article 2 exempts from the Convention sovereign immune warships and other government ships in state service operated for non-commercial service (such as a naval auxiliary, customs cutter, or police boat), and ships that are "withdrawn from navigation or laid up."

The limitation on the treaty not applying to ships "withdrawn from navigation or laid up" was adopted into the text by the Preparatory Committee instead of competing language requiring the ship be "in service." There were concerns over when a ship could be considered "in service."

"Is a ship from which all passengers and crew have disembarked that is being cleaned and readied for the next trip 'in service'? What about a ship temporarily in port because it is undergoing repairs? A cruise ship whose next voyage has not yet been set?"[21]

To avert confusion, the "in service" limitation was dropped in the final text.

> Article 2
>
> 1. This Convention does not apply to:
>   (a) a warship; or
>   (b) a ship owned or operated by a State when being used as a naval auxiliary or for customs or police purposes; or
>   (c) a ship which has been withdrawn from navigation or laid up.
> 2. Nothing in this Convention affects the immunities of warships and other Government ships operated for non-commercial purposes.

Article 3

Article 3 establishes a list of new criminal offenses, which States Parties are required to implement through national legislation. These offenses require mental culpability on the part of the offender who must act "unlawfully" (not conforming to law or acting without authority) and "intentionally" (deliberately or purposefully). Neither the 1988 Convention (nor, for that matter, the 2005 Protocol) delve into the thorny questions of who constitutes a terrorist. Instead, the text focuses on proscribing specific conduct.

---

[21] Malvina Halberstam, *Terrorism on the High Seas: The Achille Lauro, Piracy, and the IMO Convention on Maritime Safety*, 82 Am. J. Int'l L. 269, 303–304 (1988).

Acts prohibited under article 3 of the Convention include seizing or exercising control over a ship by force, performing acts of violence against a person on board a ship that is likely to endanger navigation of the vessel, destroying a ship or causing damage to the ship or its cargo, placing a device or substance on the ship that is likely to destroy the ship or cause damage to it or its cargo and which endangers (or is likely to endanger) the navigation of the vessel, destroying or damaging maritime navigational facilities or seriously interfering with their operation, communicating information which is known to be false that endangers the safe navigation of the ship, or injuring or killing any person in connection with the commission of any of the offenses.

The last crime in the list above, that of taking action that "injures or kills a person," was included in the original draft submitted to IMO by the co-sponsors, but was subject to an effort by several other states at the Preparatory Committee to eliminate it from the text.[22] Since the Convention was designed to suppress acts against the safety of maritime navigation, critics of the crime in article 3, paragraph 1(g) suggested that injuring or killing of a passenger on a seized vessel that did not endanger the ship's navigation should not be included in the treaty, whereas injury or killing that does endanger the ship's navigation is already covered under paragraph 1(b) (an act of violence likely to endanger the ship's navigation).[23] The provision was retained, however, on the basis that the deliberate injury or murder of a person on board the ship was a separate and distinct offense, not merely an aggravating circumstance of seizing the ship.[24]

Furthermore, failure to include injury or murder as a separate criminal offense, as opposed to an aggravating circumstance of another crime, might foreclose using it as the basis for extradition under the Convention, weakening the entire structure of "extradite and prosecute." Malvina Halberstam explains that if the offender was extradited to another state for other offenses under the Convention, that state normally would not have jurisdiction over the defendant for the separate crime of injury or murder, since extradition law typically precludes trial in the receiving state for any offenses other than those for which he was extradited.[25] Halberstam also cites J. B. Moore, whose 1891 *Treatise on Extradition and Interstate Rendition* states:

> Among writers on international law there is almost uniform concurrence in the opinion that a person surrendered for one offense should not be tried for another until

---

[22] IMO Doc. PCUA 1/4, Ad Hoc Preparatory Committee on the Suppression of Unlawful Acts against the Safety of Maritime Navigation, Report of the First Session, Mar. 16, 1987, para. 30.
[23] Id.
[24] Halberstam, *Terrorism on the High Seas* at 294.
[25] Id.

he shall have been replaced in the jurisdiction of the surrendering state or had an opportunity to return thereto.[26]

Thus, while killing a passenger does not necessarily endanger the safety of the vessel, the principle reason for protecting the ship is to secure the persons onboard.

The requisite *mens rea* in the chapeau for offenses in article 3 is intent and that is combined with a second mental element in the provision that could be either one of general intent (for example, in 1(c), the offender damages a ship, which is *likely to endanger* safe navigation) or specific intent (for example, in 1(f), the offender communicates information, *knowing* it to be false).

> Article 3
>
> 1. Any person commits an offense within the meaning of this Convention if that person unlawfully and intentionally:
>   (a) seizes or exercises control over a ship by force or threat thereof or any other form of intimidation; or
>   (b) performs an act of violence against a person on board a ship if that act is likely to endanger the safe navigation of that ship; or
>   (c) destroys a ship or causes damage to a ship or its cargo which is likely to endanger the safe navigation of that ship; or
>   (d) places or causes to be placed on a ship, by any means whatsoever, a device or substance which is likely to destroy that ship, or cause damage to that ship or its cargo which endangers or is likely to endanger the safe navigation of that ship; or
>   (e) destroys or seriously damages maritime navigational facilities or seriously interferes with their operation, if any such act is likely to endanger the safe navigation of a ship; or
>   (f) communicates information which that person knows to be false, thereby endangering the safe navigation of a ship; or
>   (g) injures or kills any person, in connection with the commission or the attempted commission of any of the offenses set forth in subparagraphs (a) to (f).
> 2. Any person also commits an offense if that person:
>   (a) Attempts to commit any of the offenses set forth in paragraph 1; or
>   (b) Abets the commission of any of the offenses set forth in paragraph 1 perpetrated by any person or is otherwise an accomplice of a person who commits such an offense; or
>   (c) threatens, with or without condition, as is provided for under national law, aimed at compelling a physical or juridical person to do or refrain from doing any act, to commit any of the offenses set forth in paragraph 1, subparagraph (b), (c), and (e), if that threat is likely to endanger the safe navigation of the ship in question.

The Diplomatic conference resolved several outstanding textual issues concerning article 3 that were considered political in nature. First, the government of

---

[26] JOHN BASSETT MOORE, I TREATISE ON EXTRADITION AND INTERSTATE RENDITION 217 (1891) and M. WHITEMAN, 6 DIGEST OF INTERNATIONAL LAW 728 (1968), *as cited in* Halberstam, *Terrorism on the High Seas*, note 104, pp. 294–95.

Kuwait introduced a proposal to insert the phrase "whether acting on his own initiative or on behalf of a government" following "any person" in the beginning of article 3(1), so that it would read: "Any person, whether acting on his own initiative or on behalf of a government, commits an offense if that person unlawfully and intentionally" commits one of the proscribed acts (literally, "prohibited actions").[27] The Kuwaiti proposal was intended to prevent an alleged offender from being shielded by a claim of state immunity, but the liability ran to the offender and not the state.[28] On the other hand, the words "any person" appear on their face to apply to all individuals, acting either in their personal capacity or on behalf of a government. The language was rejected at the Diplomatic conference and not included in the final text, however.

Saudi Arabia proposed that the language in article 3 read: "Any ordinary person or government commits an offense...."[29] The Saudi proposal would have made the state itself liable for the covered conduct of its agents. The greatest problem with the proposal was that the use of force by states is a question of *jus ad bellum* and controlled by customary international law and article 2(4) of the UN Charter. Furthermore, the provision has no application to states—states cannot be prosecuted or extradited, and the draft text was dropped.

Article 4

The 1988 Convention applies to ships navigating (or scheduled to navigate) into, through, or from waters beyond the territorial sea of a State Party, or if the suspect offender is present in the State.

An earlier draft circulated by the co-sponsors proposed that the treaty should apply only if "the place of departure or the place of arrival" of the vessel "lie[s] outside the territory of the flag state."[30] This limitation would have avoided application of the Convention regarding offenses against or on board ships navigating between two ports of the flag State, even if a short portion of the route juts into

---

[27] IMO Doc. PCUA 2/4, Ad Hoc Preparatory Committee on the Suppression of Unlawful Acts against the Safety of Maritime Navigation, May 8, 1987. *See also*, IMO Doc. PCUA 2/5, Ad Hoc Preparatory Committee on the Suppression of Unlawful Acts against the Safety of Maritime Navigation, Report of the 2nd Session, 18–22 May, 1987, June 2, 1987 and IMO Doc. SUA/CONF/RD/6, International Conference on the Suppression of Unlawful Acts against the Safety of Maritime Navigation, Sixth Committee, Record of Decisions, Mar. 10, 1988 (1989).

[28] IMO Doc. PCUA 2/5, Report of the Ad Hoc Preparatory Committee on the Suppression of Unlawful Acts against the Safety of Maritime Navigation, 2nd Session, 18–22 May 1987, June 2, 1987, para. 65. *See also*, JAVAID REHMAN, ISLAMIC STATE PRACTICES, INTERNATIONAL LAW AND THE THREAT FROM TERRORISM: A CRITIQUE OF THE 'CLASH OF CIVILIZATIONS' IN THE NEW WORLD ORDER 160–61 (2005).

[29] IMO Doc. PCUA 1/3/3, Ad Hoc Preparatory Committee on the Suppression of Unlawful Acts against the Safety of Maritime Navigation, Feb. 26, 1987.

[30] Halberstam, *Terrorism on the High Seas*, at 304.

the high seas. The formula, however, would have prevented application of the Convention even for a voyage in which most of the trip involved the high seas, such as a voyage from San Diego to Honolulu. Unable to find a rule that would exclude from the Convention those transits involving only brief passage on the high seas, the proposal was scrapped.

The text that was adopted includes offenses committed on the high seas, as well as those committed in the territorial waters, if the ship is scheduled to navigate on the high seas.

> Article 4
> 1. This Convention applies if the ship is navigating or is scheduled to navigate into, through or from waters beyond the outer limit of the territorial sea of a single State, or the lateral limits of its territorial sea with adjacent States.
> 2. In cases where the Convention does not apply pursuant to paragraph 1, it nevertheless applies when the offender or alleged offender is found in the territory of a State Party other than the State referred to in paragraph 1.

Article 5

Article 5 requires State Parties to make offenses in article 3 punishable by "appropriate penalties," which take into account their "grave nature."

> Article 5
> Each State Party shall make the offenses set forth in article 3 punishable by appropriate penalties, which take into account the grave nature of those offenses.

Article 6

International law generally recognizes five basis of jurisdiction: nationality, territoriality, passive personality (nationality of the victim), the protective principle (threat to the State), and universality. In UNCLOS, flag State jurisdiction is an expression of the territoriality principle or as an application of the nationality principle, and is reflected in articles 91 and 92.[31]

At the time of adoption of the 1988 SUA Convention, the passive personality principle was emerging as a valid basis for jurisdiction over offenders. The principle had not been accepted for ordinary torts or crimes, but was starting to be applied to terrorist attacks. As organized attacks on a state's nationals by reason of their nationality increased, however, the passive personality approach became more widely accepted. Several multilateral conventions already had offered jurisdiction based upon the nationality of the victim, including the Hostage Convention (article 5(d)) and the *Convention Against Torture and Other Cruel and Inhuman or Degrading Treatment or Punishment* (article 5(1)(c)).

---

[31] *See* Restatement (Third) of Foreign Relations Law of the United States § 402 (1988).

Similarly, the protective principle—that the state has a legitimate basis of jurisdiction over offenses that undermine its governmental functions, such as printing counterfeit currency—justified jurisdiction in paragraph 2(c) of article 6 in cases in which a terrorist attack seeks to compel or restrain some state action. The Restatement (Third) on Foreign Relations Law, for example, provides that a state may exercise jurisdiction to prescribe and apply its law with respect to "certain conduct" outside its territory or committed by nationals of another state, but that is directed against the security of the state or its interests.[32]

There are two types of jurisdiction under the 1988 SUA Convention: obligatory and discretionary. Under article 6(1) states are obligated to assert jurisdiction. The provision states that each State Party "shall take measures as may be necessary to establish its jurisdiction over the offenses set forth in article 3," when the offense is committed against or on board a ship flying its flag, in its territory, or by one of its nationals. Thus, when the State Party is the flag State, the nationality of the offender, or the offense is committed on the territory of the State, it is required to establish jurisdiction.

Under paragraph (2), States Parties may establish jurisdiction over an offense when:

(a) it is committed by a stateless person whose habitual residence is in that State; or
(b) during its commission a national of that State is seized, threatened, injured or killed; or
(c) it is committed in an attempt to compel that State to do or abstain from doing any act.

Thus, if the State Party is only the habitual residence of the offender, the state of nationality of the victim, or a state being pressured to change its conduct by an offender terrorist, then that state has the option of establishing jurisdiction. During the negotiations, there was some measure of opposition among member States over the provision permitting the state of nationality of the victim to assert jurisdiction. The matter was put to a vote in the session and 32 nations supported the provision, four states opposed the provision, and three abstained.[33]

Eight states also opposed the provision allowing a State Party to establish jurisdiction in cases in which the nation is being targeted by a terrorist to take or refrain from taking some action. In the case of the *Achille Lauro* hijacking, for example, the vessel was flagged in Italy and the murdered victim was American, but the demand made by the terrorists was for Israel to release Palestinian prisoners. Similarly, American hostages were taken in Lebanon, and the captors demanded that Kuwait release prisoners. In the end, 16 states supported the measure allowing for jurisdiction on the part of the targeted state. Fourteen

---

[32] RESTATEMENT (THIRD) OF FOREIGN RELATIONS LAW OF THE UNITED STATES § 402 (1988).
[33] IMO Doc. PCUA 2/5, June 2, 1987 at 18, para. 89.

nations abstained, and the measure ultimately was retained in the treaty text in paragraph (2)(c).[34] The provision is particularly important for the United States, which often is the target of terrorist attack, but rarely the flag State of the vessel or the state of nationality of the offender.

Opponents of the provisions allowing States to establish jurisdiction over the offender based upon the nationality of the victim or the state whose policy or conduct the terrorists are trying to compel, argued that the nationality and territoriality principles were generally accepted and should not be expanded. Expanding jurisdiction might vest jurisdiction in a large number of states whose nationals are victims, creating situations of competing jurisdiction among states. The idea prevailed, however, that it is better to have potentially conflicting jurisdiction than cases of no jurisdiction at all, and the measures were retained in the text.[35] Reliance on nationality or territoriality likely would create gaps in jurisdiction, since the state of nationality of the offender may decide not to prosecute, and some of the numerous small state flags of convenience may be unable or unwilling to do so.

The universality principle of jurisdiction permits all states to assert jurisdiction over offenses that are a common among nations. The crime of maritime piracy, for example, which is addressed in chapter 20, arose from the concern that pirates were *hostis humani generis*—enemies of all mankind.[36] Likewise, the *Draft Convention on Jurisdiction with Respect to Crime* permits States to assert jurisdiction over "any crime committed outside its territory by an alien," if the offense injures the state and yet occurred outside the "authority of any state."[37]

> Article 6
>
> 1. Each State Party shall take measures as may be necessary to establish its jurisdiction over the offenses set forth in article 3 when the offense is committed:
>   (a) against or on board a ship flying the flag of the State at the time the offense is committed; or
>   (b) in the territory of that State, including its territorial sea; or
>   (c) by a national of that State.
> 2. A State Party may also establish it jurisdiction over any such offense when:
>   (a) it is committed by a stateless person whose habitual residence is in that State; or
>   (b) during its commission a national of that State is seized, threatened, injured or killed; or

---

[34] Id. at 18, para. 94.
[35] Halberstam, *Terrorism on the High Seas*, at 296.
[36] *See*, Edward Coke, 3 Institutes on the Laws of England 113 (1797); Lassa Oppenheim, International Law: A Treatise § 272, at 325–26 (1905); and Restatement (Second) of Foreign Relations Law of the United States § 34 cmt. b (1965).
[37] *Draft Convention on Jurisdiction with Respect to Crime*, 29 Am. J. Int'l L. Supp. 439, 440–41 (1935), article 10(c).

(c) it is committed in an attempt to compel that State to do or abstain from doing any act.
3. Any State Party which has established jurisdiction mentioned in paragraph 2 shall notify the Secretary-General of the International Maritime Organization. If such State Party subsequently rescinds that jurisdiction, it shall notify the Secretary-General.
4. Each State Party shall take such measures as may be necessary to establish its jurisdiction over the offenses set forth in articles 3 in cases where the alleged offender is present in its territory and it does not extradite the alleged offender to any of the States Parties which have established their jurisdiction in accordance with paragraphs 1 and 2 of this article.
5. This Convention does not exclude any criminal jurisdiction exercised in accordance with national law.

Article 7

A state in whose territory the offender is present is obligated to "take him into custody" or take other measures to "ensure his presence" at trial. In this case, the State should conduct a "preliminary inquiry" of the facts surrounding the case. The suspected offender retains the right to communicate with a consular official or other representative of his state of nationality.

Article 7
1. Upon being satisfied that the circumstances so warrant, any State Party in the territory of which the offender or the alleged offender is present shall, in accordance with its law, take him into custody or take other measures to ensure his presence for such time as it is necessary to enable any criminal or extradition proceedings to be instituted.
2. Such State shall immediately make a preliminary inquiry into the facts, in accordance with its own legislation.
3. Any person regarding whom the measures referred to in paragraph 1 are being taken shall be entitled to:
   (a) communicate without delay with the nearest appropriate representative of the State of which he is a national or which is otherwise entitled to establish such communication or, if he is a stateless person, the State in the territory of which he has habitual residence;
   (b) be visited by a representative of that State.
4. The rights referred to in paragraph 3 shall be exercised in conformity with the laws and regulations of the State in the territory of which the offender or the alleged offender is present, subject to the proviso that the said laws and regulations must enable full effect to be given to the purposes for which the rights accorded under paragraph 3 are intended.
5. When a State Party, pursuant to this article, has taken a person into custody, it shall immediately notify the States which have established jurisdiction in accordance with article 6, paragraph 1, and if it considers it advisable, any other interested States, of the fact that such person is in custody and of the circumstances which warrant his detention. The State which makes the preliminary inquiry contemplated in paragraph 2 of this article shall promptly report its findings to the said States and shall indicate whether it intends to exercise jurisdiction.

Article 8

Article 8 covers the responsibilities and roles of the master of the ship, flag State and receiving state in delivering to the authorities of any State Party any person believed to have committed an offense under the Convention, including the furnishing of evidence pertaining to the alleged offense.

> Article 8
>
> 1. The master of a ship of a State Party (the "flag State") may deliver to the authorities of any other State Party (the "receiving State") any person who the master has reasonable grounds to believe has committed an offense set forth in article 3.
> 2. The flag State shall ensure that the master of its ship is obliged, whenever practicable, and if possible before entering the territorial sea of the receiving State carrying on board any person whom the master intends to deliver in accordance with paragraph 1, to give notification to the authorities of the receiving State of his intention to deliver such person and the reasons therefor.
> 3. The receiving State shall accept the delivery, except where it has grounds to consider that the Convention is not applicable to the acts giving rise to the delivery, and shall proceed in accordance with the provisions of article 7. Any refusal to accept a delivery shall be accompanied by a statement of the reason for refusal.
> 4. The Flag State shall ensure that the master of its ship is obliged to furnish the authorities of the receiving State with the evidence in the master's possession, which pertains to the alleged offense.
> 5. A receiving State which has accepted the delivery of a person in accordance with paragraph 3 may, in turn, request the flag State to accept delivery of that person. The flag State shall consider any such request, and if it accedes to the request it shall proceed in accordance with article 7. If the flag State declines a request, it shall furnish the receiving State with a statement of the reasons therefor.

Article 9

> Article 9
>
> Nothing in this Convention shall affect in any way the rules of international law pertaining to the competence of States to exercise investigative or enforcement jurisdiction on board ships not flying their flying their flag.

Article 10

Much like some other anti-terrorism conventions, including the Hague Convention, the Montreal Convention, the Hostage Convention and the Internationally Protected Persons Convention, the entire 1988 SUA Convention is structured around the requirement for States Parties to either "extradite or prosecute" suspected offenders, which is contained in article 10.[38]

---

[38] Hague Convention, article 7, Montreal Convention, article 7, Hostage Convention, article 8, and the Convention on the Prevention and Punishment of Crimes Against

Article 10 requires a State Party in whose territory the offender is found, to initiate criminal prosecution if it does not extradite him. Some states interpret the provision as meaning that the State Party in such a situation has an obligation to prosecute only if a request for extradition is received—a reading inconsistent with the legislative history of identical provisions of the Hostage Taking Convention.[39] Other nations argued that they are unable to prosecute without a request for extradition.[40] Thus, if jurisdiction in articles 6 and 10 were limited to the nationality and territoriality principles (rather than having been expanded in article 6(2)), and the offender is in a state that does not receive a request for extradition from either the state of nationality or territory on which the offense occurred, the offender might escape justice.

Article 10

1. The State Party in the territory of which the offender or the alleged offender is found shall, in cases to which article 6 applies, if it does not extradite him, be obliged, without exception whatsoever and whether or not the offense was committed in its territory, to submit the case without delay to its competent authorities for the purpose of prosecution, through proceedings in accordance with the law of the State. Those authorities shall take their decision in the same manner as in the case of any other offense of a grave nature under the law of that state.
2. Any person who is taken into custody or regarding whom any other measures are taken or proceedings are being carried out pursuant to this Convention, shall be guaranteed fair treatment, including enjoyment of all rights and guarantees in conformity with the law of the State in the territory of which that person is present.

Article 11

Article 11 covers extradition procedures, which were amended by article 10 of the 2005 SUA Protocol. The first four paragraphs of article 11 were revised by article 10(1) of the 2005 SUA Protocol to incorporate into the extradition regime the offenses set forth in articles 3, 3*bis*, 3*ter* or 3*quarter*.

Article 11

1. The offenses set forth in article 3 shall be deemed to be included as extraditable offenses in any extradition treaty existing between any of the States Parties. States Parties undertake to include such offenses as extraditable offenses in every extradition treaty to be concluded between them.
2. If a State Party which makes extradition conditional on the existence of a treaty receives a request for extradition from another State Party with which it has no extradition treaty, the requested State may, at its option, consider this Convention

---

Internationally Protected Persons, Including Diplomatic Agents, Dec. 14, 1973, 28 UST 1975, TIAS No. 8532 (Internationally Protected Persons Convention), article 7.

[39] Robert Rosenstock, *International Convention Against the Taking of Hostages: Another Community Step Against Terrorism*, 9 DEN. J. INT'L L & POL'Y 169, 181 (1980).

[40] Halberstam, *Terrorism on the High Seas*, at 297.

as a legal basis for extradition in respect to the offenses set forth in articles 3. Extradition shall be subject to the other conditions provided by the law of the requested State Party.
3. States Parties which do not make extradition conditional on the existence of a treaty shall recognize the offenses set forth in article 3 as extraditable offenses between themselves, subject to the conditions provided by the law of the requested State Party.
4. If necessary, the offenses set forth in articles 3 shall be treated, for the purposes of extradition between States Parties, as if they had been committed not only in the place in which they occurred but also in a place within the jurisdiction of the State Party requesting extradition.
5. A State Party which receives more than one request for extradition from States which have established jurisdiction in accordance with article 6 and which decides not to prosecute shall, in selecting the State to which the offender or alleged offenders is to be extradited, pay due regard to the interests and responsibilities of the State Party whose flag the ship was flying at the time of the commission of the offense.
6. In considering a request for the extradition of an alleged offender pursuant to this Convention, the requested States shall pay due regard to whether his rights as set forth in article 7, paragraph 3, can be effected in the requesting State.
7. With respect to the offenses defined in this Convention, the provisions of all extradition treaties and arrangements applicable between States Parties are modified as between States Parties to the extent that they are incompatible with this Convention.

Article 12

Article 12

1. States Parties shall afford one another the greatest measure of assistance in connection with criminal proceedings brought in respect of the offenses set forth in article 3, including assistance in obtaining evidence at their disposal necessary for the proceedings.
2. States Parties shall carry out their obligations under paragraph 1 in conformity with any treaties on mutual assistance that may exist between them. In the absence of such treaties, States Parties shall afford each other assistance in accordance with their national law.

Article 13

Article 13

1. States Parties shall cooperate in the prevention of offenses set forth in articles 3, particularly by:
    (a) taking all practicable measures to prevent preparation in their respective territories for the commission of those offenses within or outside their territories;
    (b) exchanging information in accordance with their national law, and coordinating administrative and other measures taken as appropriate to prevent the commission of offenses set forth in articles 3.
2. When, due to the commission of an offense set forth in 3, the passage of a ship has been delayed or interrupted, any State Party in whose territory the ship or

passengers or crew are present shall be bound to exercise all possible effort to avoid a ship, its passengers, crew or cargo begin unduly detained or delayed.

Article 14

Article 14

Any State Party having reason to believe that an offense set forth in article 3 will be committed shall, in accordance with its national law, furnish as promptly as possible any relevant information in its possession to those States which it believes would be the States having established jurisdiction in accordance with article 6.

Article 15

Article 15

1. Each State Party shall, in accordance with its national law, provide to the Secretary-General, as promptly as possible, any relevant information in its possession concerning:
   (a) the circumstances of the offense;
   (b) the action taken pursuant to article 13, paragraph 2;
   (c) the measures taken in relation to the offender or the alleged offender and, in particular, the results of any extradition proceedings or other legal proceedings.
2. The State Party where the alleged offender is prosecuted shall, in accordance with its national law, communicate the final outcome of the proceedings to the Secretary-General.
3. The information transmitted in accordance with paragraphs 1 and 2 shall be communicated by the Secretary-General to all States Parties, to Member of the International Maritime Organization, to other States concerned, and to the appropriate international intergovernmental organizations.

Article 16

Article 16

1. Any dispute between two or more States Parties concerning the interpretation or application of this Convention which cannot be settled through negotiation within a reasonable time shall, at the request of one of them, be submitted to arbitration. If, within six months from the date of the request for arbitration, the parties are unable to agree on the organization of the arbitration any one of those parties may refer the dispute to the International Court of Justice by request in conformity with the Statute of the Court.
2. Each State may at the time of signature or ratification, acceptance or approval of this Convention or accession thereto, declare that it does not consider itself bound by any or all of the provisions of paragraph 1. The other States Parties shall not be bound by those provisions with respect to any State Party which has made such a reservation.
3. Any State which has made a reservation in accordance with paragraph 2 may, at any time, withdraw that reservation by notification to the Secretary-General.

Article 17

Article 17

1. This Protocol shall be open for signature at Rome on 10 March 1988 by States participating in the International Conference on the Suppression of Unlawful Acts against the Safety of Maritime Navigation and at the Headquarters of the Organization by all States from 14 March 1988 to 9 March 1989. It shall thereafter remain open for accession.
2. States may express their consent to be bound by this Protocol by:
   (a) signature without reservation as to ratification, acceptance or approval; or
   (b) signature subject to ratification, acceptance or approval; or
   (c) accession.
3. Ratification, acceptance, approval or accession shall be effected by the deposit of an instrument to that effect with the Secretary-General.

Article 18

Fifteen States must either sign the Convention without reservation as to ratification, acceptance or approval, or deposit an instrument of ratification, acceptance, approval, or accession before the Convention can enter into force.

Article 18

1. This Protocol shall enter into force ninety days following the date on which fifteen States have either signed it without reservation as to ratification, acceptance or approval, or have deposited an instrument of ratification, acceptance, approval or accession with the Secretary-General.
2. For a State which deposits an instrument of ratification, acceptance, approval or accession in respect of this Convention after the condition for entry into force thereof have been met, the ratification, acceptance, approval or accession shall take effect ninety days after the date of such deposit.

Article 19

Article 19
Denunciation

1. This Protocol may be denounced by any State Party at any time after the expiry of one year from the date on which this Convention enters into force for that State.
2. Denunciation shall be effected by the deposition of an instrument of denunciation with the Secretary-General.
3. A denunciation shall take effect one year, or such longer period as may be specified in the instrument of denunciation, after the deposit of the instrument with the Secretary-General.

Article 20

Article 20

1. A Conference for the purpose of revising or amending this Protocol may be convened by the Organization.

2. The Secretary-General shall convene a conference of States Parties to this Protocol for revising or amending the Protocol, at the request of one third of the States Parties, or ten States Parties, whichever is the higher figure.
3. Any instrument of ratification, acceptance, approval or accession deposited after the date of entry into force of an amendment to this Convention shall be deemed to apply to the Convention as amended.

Article 21

Article 21

1. This Convention shall be deposited with the Secretary-General.
2. The Secretary-General shall:
   (a) inform all States which have signed this Convention or acceded thereto, and all Members of the [International Maritime] Organization of:
      (i) each new signature or deposit of instrument of ratification, acceptance, approval or accession together with the date thereof;
      (ii) the date of entry into force of this Protocol;
      (iii) the deposit of any instrument of denunciation of this Protocol together with the date on which it is received and the date on which the denunciation takes effect;
      (iv) the receipt of any declaration or notification made under this Convention;
   (b) transmit certified true copies of this Convention to all States which have sign this Convention or acceded thereto.
3. As soon as this Convention enters into force, a certified true copy of the text shall be transmitted by the Depositary to the Secretary-General of the United Nations for registration and publication in accordance with article 102 of the Charter of the United Nations.

Article 22

The text of the 1988 SUA Convention was produced in six languages, all of which are equally valid.

Article 24
Languages

This Protocol is established in a single original in the Arabic, Chinese, English, French, Russian and Spanish languages, each text being equally authentic.

IN WITNESS WHEREOF the undersigned, being duly authorized by their respective Governments for that purpose, have signed this Convention.[41]

DONE AT ROME this tenth day of March one thousand nine hundred and eighty-eight.

---

[41] Signature pages omitted in the original published text.

22.1.2 *2005 Convention*

The 1988 Convention and its related Protocol were amended in 2005 following the terrorist attacks against the United States in September 2001.[42] The member States of the IMO negotiated the new convention within the context of Assembly resolution A.924(22). Several UN General Assembly documents also inspired action by the IMO. In the *Declaration on Measures to Eliminate International Terrorism*, annexed to UN General Assembly resolution 49/60 of December 9, 1994, States reaffirmed an unequivocal condemnation of all acts, methods and practices of terrorism as criminal and unjustifiable, wherever and by whomever committed. The 1994 Declaration was supplemented by General Assembly resolution 51/210 of December 17, 1996. After the attacks of 9/11, the UN Security Council adopted resolution 1368 and 1373, committing states to combat terrorism "in all its forms and manifestations."

The 2005 Convention is one of the strongest instruments to stop the scourge of international terrorism. The preamble to the treaty references "terrorism," and "terrorist attacks," and "terrorist acts," and article 3*ter* incorporates by reference nine other anti-terrorism conventions.[43] The 2005 Protocols, which entered into force in July 2010, add a number of new offenses directly related to terrorism and the proliferation of weapons of mass destruction. Both the 1988 Convention and the 2005 Protocol to the Convention are to be read as a single, integrated treaty called the 2005 SUA Convention, and which consists of the consolidated text of the *Convention for the Suppression of Unlawful Acts against the Safety of Maritime Navigation* and of the Protocol of 2005 to the Convention.[44] Article 15 of the

---

[42] IMO Doc. LEG/CONF. 15/21, Adoption of the Final Act and Any Instruments, Recommendations and Resolutions Resulting from the Work of the Conference, Protocol of 2005 to the Convention for the Suppression of Unlawful Acts against the Safety of Maritime Navigation, Nov. 1, 2005.

[43] Convention on Offenses and Certain Other Acts Committed on Board Aircraft, Tokyo, Sept. 14, 1963, 704 U.N.T.S. 219; Convention for the Suppression of Unlawful Seizure of Aircraft (Hijacking), The Hague, Dec. 16, 1970, 860 U.N.T.S. 105; Convention for the Suppression of Unlawful Acts against the Safety of Civil Aviation (Sabotage), Montreal, Sept. 23, 1971, 974 U.N.T.S. 178, and its Protocol on the Suppression of Unlawful Acts of Violence at Airports Serving International Civil Aviation, Montreal, Feb. 24, 1988, 1589 U.N.T.S. 474; Convention on the Prevention and Punishment of Crimes against Internationally Protected Persons, including Diplomatic Agents, New York, Dec. 14, 1973, 1035 U.N.T.S. 167; International Convention against the Taking of Hostages, New York, Dec. 17, 1979, 1316 U.N.T.S. 206; Convention on the Physical Protection of Nuclear Material, Vienna, Mar. 3, 1980; International Convention on the Marking of Plastic Explosives for the Purpose of Detection, Montreal, Mar. 1, 1991; International Convention for the Suppression of Terrorist Bombings, New York, Dec. 15, 1997; and, International Convention for the Suppression of the Financing of Terrorism, adopted by the UN General Assembly, Dec. 9, 1999.

[44] Article 15, 2005 SUA Protocol, IMO Doc. LEG/CONF. 15/21, Adoption of the Final Act and Any Instruments, Recommendations and Resolutions Resulting from the Work of

2005 SUA Protocol provides the basic structure for the new 2005 SUA Convention: article 1 to 16 of the Convention, as amended by the 2005 SUA Protocol, together with articles 17 to 24 of the 2005 SUA Protocol and the Annex, "shall constitute and be called together the Convention for the Suppression of Unlawful Acts against the Safety of Maritime Navigation, 2005 (2005 SUA Convention)." The same nomenclature applies to the treaty concerning fixed platforms on the continental shelf, which is referred to as the 2005 Protocol. The amendments to the 1988 *Protocol for the Suppression of Unlawful Acts against the Safety of Fixed Platforms Located on the Continental Shelf* reflect those in the 2005 Protocol to the SUA Convention.

Major amendments to the 1988 Convention and its related Protocol were adopted by the Diplomatic Conference on the Revision of the SUA Treaties held from October 10 to 14, 2005. The amendments were crafted in the form of Protocols to the SUA treaties (the 2005 Protocols); the 2005 Protocols were adopted by a Diplomatic Conference of the IMO on October 14, 2005, and entered into force on July 28, 2010. The amended treaty is called the 2005 SUA Convention and reflects the 2005 Protocol amendments to the 1988 Convention.

The new convention greatly expands the list of criminal offenses, which are set out in article 3 and now include unlawful acts that are motivated by an intent on the part of the offender to intimidate a population or compel a government to do or refrain from doing any act. The treaty also contains inchoate offenses or crimes of accessory, such as attempting, abetting, being an accomplice, directing, or assisting or aiding the offender. Finally, the new convention contains a comprehensive shipboarding regime that provides a template for how flag State governments may cooperate in granting permission to foreign-flagged warships to board vessels flying their flag.

Some believe the 2005 SUA Convention may end up eclipsing the informal, but highly successful Proliferation Security Initiative (PSI). First, the era of the "coalition of the willing" may be coming to a close, the concept having been badly bruised by the experience of Iraq. For all the groundbreaking and frankly astonishing success of PSI, some countries are wary of its informal nature and process. Second, shipping commerce is a global industry—the basis for which is international conventions and treaties. The industry can only operate efficiently when regulations applicable to a particular ship are identical in the port of departure, on the high seas and in the port of arrival.

Since PSI focuses on enlarging national authorities rather than global rules, it is more likely to inadvertently create a web of asynchronized national laws. Many in the shipping industry are hopeful that the 2005 Convention will attract widespread support and enter into force quickly. This does not diminish the fairly

---

the Conference, Protocol of 2005 to the Convention for the Suppression of Unlawful Acts against the Safety of Maritime Navigation, Nov. 1, 2005.

grand success of nations coming together as an informal coalition to participate in PSI or in the nascent 2005 SUA Convention, to address the threat of terrorism and WMD.

Article 1

Article 2 of the 2005 SUA Protocol amends the original article 1 of the 1988 Convention, creating a new article 1 for the 2005 Convention. Article 1 of the 2005 SUA Convention either imports from the 1988 Convention definitions of terms, or sets forth entirely new definitions. "Organization," for example, is defined in amended article 1(g) as the International Maritime Organization, and the term Secretary-General is defined in amended article 1(f) to mean the Secretary-General of the IMO. Both terms appeared at article 1 of the 1988 Convention.

Article 1 also includes additional definitions, such as "Transport," which means "to initiate, arrange, or exercise effective control, including decision-making authority, over the movement of a person or item." This term is used in relation to the movement of terrorist fugitives or WMD and WMD-related components aboard ships. "Serious injury" means "serious bodily injury; extensive destruction of a place of public use, state, or government facility, infrastructure facility, or public transportation system, resulting in major economic loss; or substantial damage to the environment, including air, soil, water, fauna, or flora."

Article 1 also adds extensive definitions for "BCN weapons" to include biological weapons, chemical weapons, and nuclear weapons and other nuclear explosive devices. Confusingly, article 1(d) of the 1988 Convention was amended by article 2 of the 2005 Protocol, producing an amended article 1 of the 2005 Convention, which defines a "BCN weapon" as including:

> Article 1
> . . .
>
> (i) "biological weapons"... are:
>   1. microbial or other biological agents, or toxins whatever their origin or method of production, of types and in quantities that have no justification for prophylactic, protective, or other peaceful purposes; or
>   2. weapons, equipment or means of delivery designed to use such agents or toxins for hostile purposes or in armed conflict.
> (ii) "chemical weapons"... are, together or separately:
>   1. toxic chemicals and their precursors, except where intended for:
>   A. industrial, agricultural, research, medical, pharmaceutical or other peaceful purposes; or
>   B. protective purposes, namely those purposes directly related to protection against toxic chemicals and to protection against chemical weapons; or
>   C. military purposes not connected with the use of chemical weapons and not dependent on the use of the toxic properties of chemicals as a method of warfare; or
>   D. law enforcement including domestic riot control purposes as long as the types and quantities are consistent with such purposes;

2. munitions and devices specifically designed to cause death or harm through the toxic properties of those toxic chemicals specified in subparagraph (ii)(1), which would be released as a result of the employment of such munitions and devices;
3. any equipment specifically designed for the use directly in connection with the employment of munitions and devices specified in paragraph (ii)(2).
(xii) Nuclear weapons and other nuclear explosive devices.

Furthermore, amended article 1 adheres to the definitions of the Convention on the Prohibition of the Development, Production, Stockpiling, and Use of Chemical Weapons and their Destruction (CWC) terms "toxic chemical" and "precursor." These terms are defined as:

(e) "toxic chemical" means any chemical which through its chemical action on life processes can cause death, temporary incapacitation or permanent harm to humans and animals. This includes all such chemicals, regardless of their origin or their method of production, and regardless of whether they are produced in facilities, in munitions or elsewhere.

(f) "precursor" means any chemical reactant which takes part at any stage in the production by whatever method of a toxic chemical. This [definition] included any key component of a binary or multicomponent chemical system.

These terms have the same meaning as their use in the Biological Weapons Convention[45] and the Chemical Weapons Convention.[46]

The terms "place of public use," "State or government facility," "infrastructure facility," and "public transportation system," are drawn from the Terrorist Bombing Convention. Similarly, the terms "source material" and "special fissionable material" have the same meaning as those terms in article 2(2)(b) of the 2005 Protocol as they have in the *Statute of the International Atomic Energy Agency*, done at New York on 26 October 1956.[47]

Article 2

The original article 2 of the 1988 Convention is preserved as article 2 of the 2005 Convention, and it provides an exemption for sovereign immune warships and ships that are withdrawn from navigation.

---

[45] Convention on the Prohibition of the Development, Production, and Stockpiling of Bacteriological (Biological) and Toxin Weapons and Their Destruction (Biological Weapons Convention), *done at* Washington, London, and Moscow on April 10, 1972.
[46] Convention on the Prohibition of the Development, Production, and Stockpiling, and Use Chemical Weapons and on Their Destruction (Chemical Weapons Convention), done at Paris on January 13, 1993.
[47] OFF. REC. OF THE 1956 CONFERENCE ON THE STATUTE OF THE INTERNATIONAL ATOMIC ENERGY AGENCY, IAEA/CS/OR.39, for the unanimous adoption of the Statute and *see* IAEA/CS/OR.40, pp. 11–15, T.I.A.S. 3873, for the text of the Statute.

Article 2

1. This Convention does not apply to:
   a. a warship; or
   b. a ship owned or operated by a State when being used as a naval auxiliary or for customs or police purposes; or
   c. a ship which has been withdrawn from navigation or laid up.
2. Nothing in this Convention affects the immunities of warships and other Government ships operated for non-commercial purposes.

Article 2*bis*

Article 2*bis* was added to the Convention by the 2005 Protocol. Paragraph 1 contains a boilerplate statement that the Convention does not affect rights, obligations, or responsibilities of states or individuals under international law, and in particular, the UN Charter, international human rights law, and refugee and international humanitarian law (also known as the law of armed conflict).

Paragraph 2 of article 2*bis* identifies two exceptions to the 2005 Convention concerning applicability to armed forces covering "armed forces during armed conflict" and "activities undertaken by a State." Paragraph 2*bis*, article 2 states:

> This Convention does not apply to the activities of armed forces during an armed conflict, as those terms are understood under international humanitarian law, which are governed by that law, and the activities undertaken by military forces of a State in the exercise of their official duties, inasmuch as they are governed by other rules of international law.

The exceptions are designed to exclude from the scope of the Convention the activities of state military forces, as well as those of sub-national or non-state armed forces so long as those activities are in the course of an "armed conflict." A similar exception is contained in article 19(2) of the Terrorist Bombings Convention. The exceptions may exempt groups such as Al-Qaeda from coverage by the conventions during time of armed conflict—the exceptions appearing to swallow the rule. For this reason, the United States articulated in its instrument of ratification a clarifying understanding regarding the similar provisions in the Terrorist Bombings Convention. The term "armed conflict" also reflects language contained in article 2(1)(b) the Terrorism Financing Convention. The United States also submitted an understanding in its instrument of ratification for that convention as well. Both U.S. understandings reject the application of an exemption for sub-national groups or non-state groups engaged in armed conflict since it likely would be exploited by terrorist organizations to avoid jurisdiction under the Convention.

The definition of "armed conflict" in the 2005 Convention may be interpreted to be at variance with how that term is defined in *Protocol II Additional to the Geneva Conventions* of August 12, 1949 (APII). Paragraph 2 of article 1 of APII states that "armed conflict" does not include "internal disturbances and tensions such as riots, isolated and sporadic acts of violence and other acts of a similar nature."[48] The U.S. Department of State recommends in its transmittal package to the president for the 2005 Convention that the United States include an understanding that the term "armed conflict" in the 2005 SUA Convention be read in a manner consistent with how the terms is used in APII to "help counter attempts by terrorists to claim protection from [the] exception in circumstances for which it is not intended."[49]

Furthermore, the exception in Paragraph 2 of article 2*bis* of the 2005 Convention does not cover activities of "armed forces" during an "armed conflict" as "those terms are understood under international humanitarian law" and governed by that law. The term "international humanitarian law" might be mistaken for "human rights law." For this reason, the U.S. transmittal package to the president recommends that the U.S. submit an understanding for the term "international humanitarian law" indicating that the United States understands the term to be synonymous with "law of war."[50]

Finally, the exemption above applies to the "armed forces" during conflict, and "military forces of a State." It is unclear on its face, however, if the exemption covers civilians who are directing or supporting the military forces, such as civilian staff—from the Secretary of Defense to civilian logisticians at a service component command. The United States proposed a curative understanding for this issue as well, and included the following clarification in its 2007 transmittal package that indicates the 2005 Convention does not apply to:

a. the military forces of a State, which are the armed forces of a State organized, trained and equipped under its internal law for the primary purpose of national defense or security, in the exercise of their official duties;
b. civilians who direct or organize the official activities of military forces of a State; or
c. civilians acting in support of the official activities of the military forces of a State, if the civilians are under the formal command, control, and responsibility of those forces.[51]

Paragraph 3 of article 2*bis* is boilerplate text stating that the 2005 Convention does not affect rights, obligations, or responsibilities concerning the Non Proliferation Treaty (NPT), done at Washington and Moscow on 1 July 1968, the BWC, or the CWC.

---

[48] Protocol II Additional to the Geneva Conventions of August 12, 1949, and Relating to the Protections of Victims of Non-International Conflicts, *opened for signature*, Dec. 12, 1977, *reprinted in* 16 I.L.M. 1442 (1977).
[49] Protocols of 2005 to the Convention Concerning Safety of Maritime Navigation and to the Protocol Concerning Safety of Fixed Platforms on the Continental Shelf, Senate Treaty Doc. 110-8, at IX (2007).
[50] Id. at X.
[51] Id. at XI.

Article 3

Article 3 is wholesale imported from the 1988 Convention to form the basis of the substantive criminal framework of the 2005 Convention.

> Article 3
> 1. Any person commits an offense within the meaning of this Convention if that person unlawfully and intentionally:
>   (a) seizes or exercises control over a ship by force or threat thereof or any other form of intimidation; or
>   (b) performs an act of violence against a person on board a ship if that act is likely to endanger the safe navigation of that ship; or
>   (c) destroys a ship or causes damage to a ship or its cargo which is likely to endanger the safe navigation of that ship; or
>   (d) places or causes to be placed on a ship, by any means whatsoever, a device or substance which is likely to destroy that ship, or cause damage to that ship or its cargo which endangers or is likely to endanger the safe navigation of that ship; or
>   (e) destroys or seriously damages maritime navigational facilities or seriously interferes with their operation, if any such act is likely to endanger the safe navigation of a ship; or
>   (f) communicates information which that person knows to be false, thereby endangering the safe navigation of a ship.
> 2. Any person also commits an offense if that person threatens, with or without condition, as is provided for under national law, aimed at compelling a physical or juridical person to do or refrain from doing any act, to commit any of the offenses set forth in paragraphs 1(b), (c), and (e), if that threat is likely to endanger the safe navigation of the ship in question.

Article 3*bis*

Paragraphs 5–7 of article 4 of the 2005 Protocol create four new types of offenses under the Convention: (1) using a ship in a terrorist offense; (2) transportation of Weapons of Mass Destruction or their delivery systems, and related materials or items; (3) transportation of a terrorist fugitive; and (4) inchoate offenses. Article 4(5) of the 2005 Protocol forms article 3*bis* of the amended 1988 Convention (now known as the 2005 Convention).

In general terms, article 3*bis*(1)(a) contains counterterrorism offenses, including using a ship or discharge from a ship as a weapon in a manner that causes or is likely to cause death or serious injury or damage. Article 3*bis*(1)(b) contains counter-proliferation offenses, including transport on a ship any explosive or other WMD, such as BCN weapons or materials, or related materials, equipment, or software. Specifically, the provision covers explosives and radioactive material, "special fissionable" material, and "source material." "Special fissionable material" is defined in the IAEA Statute to include plutonium-239, uranium enriched isotopes 235 or 233, and any other fissionable material, as declared by the IAEA

Board of Governors.[52] The term "source material" is also defined in the IAEA Statute, and it means "uranium containing a mixture of isotopes occurring in nature," and other sources, such as thorium, as determined by the Board of Governors of the *International Atomic Energy Agency*.[53]

Each of the aforementioned offenses are recognized as crimes, subject to the persons involved having formed the *mens rea* of acting "unlawfully and intentionally" and "with the purpose to intimidate" a population or compel a government from taking or not taking any action.

Article 3*bis*

1. Any person commits an offense within the meaning of this Convention if that person unlawfully and intentionally:
   (a) when the purpose of the act, by its nature or context, is to intimidate a population, or to compel a Government or an international organization to do or to abstain from any act:
      (i) uses against or on a ship or discharges from a ship any explosive, radioactive material or BCN (biological, chemical, nuclear) weapon in a manner that causes or is likely to cause death or serious injury or damage; or
      (ii) discharges, from a ship, oil, liquefied natural gas, or other hazardous or noxious substance, which is not covered by subparagraph (a)(i), in such quantity or concentration that causes or is likely to cause death or serious injury or damage; or
      (iii) uses a ship in a manner that causes death or serious injury or damage; or
      (iv) threatens with or without a condition, as is provided for under national law, to commit an offense set forth in subparagraph (a)(i), (ii) or (iii); or
   (b) transports on board a ship:
      (i) any explosive or radioactive material, knowing that it is intended to be used to cause, or in a threat to cause, with or without condition, as is provided for under national law, death or serious injury or damage for the purpose of intimidating a population, or compelling a Government or an international organization to do or to abstain from doing any act; or
      (ii) any BCN weapon, knowing it to be a BCN weapon as defined in article 1; or
      (iii) any source material, special fissionable material, or equipment or material especially designed or prepared for the processing, use or production of special fissionable material, knowing that it is intended to be used in a nuclear explosive activity or in any other nuclear activity not under safeguards pursuant to an IAEA comprehensive safeguards agreement; or
      (iv) any equipment, materials or software or related technology that significantly contributes to the design, manufacture or delivery of a BCN weapon, with the intention that it will be used for such purpose.
2. It shall not be an offense within the meaning of this Convention to transport an item or material covered by paragraph 1(b)(iii) or, insofar as it related to a

---

[52] IAEA Statute, article XX(1).
[53] Id. at XX(3).

nuclear weapons or other nuclear explosive devices, paragraph 1(b)(iv), if such item or material is transported to or from the territory of, or is otherwise transported under the control of, a State Party to the Treaty on the Non Proliferation of Nuclear Weapons (NPT) where:
(a) the resulting transfer or receipt, including internal to a State, of the item or material is not contrary to such State Party's obligations under the [NPT]; and
(b) if the item or material is intended for the delivery system of a nuclear weapon or other nuclear explosive device of a State Party to the [NPT], the holding of such weapon or device is not contrary to the State Party's obligations under that Treaty.

The dual *mens rea* requirement for article 3*bis* (and the triple requirement in 3*quarter*) contain both the element of general intent and a specific intent and are illustrative of the carefully constructed protections that ensure innocent seafarers are not subject to criminal prosecution under the Convention merely because a ship was being used for illegal purposes. The mariner could avoid prosecution under the Convention even with simple knowledge of the criminal activity. For example, under 3*bis*(1)(b)(iv), a seafarer transporting a dual use item that is destined as a component in a WMD must have the general intention that the device can be used as part of a WMD, and the specific intent that in fact the particular component will be used in the design, manufacture, or delivery of a weapon.

By criminalizing the transportation of fissionable material, the nonproliferation offenses complement the NPT framework, adding an additional enforcement mechanism. The amendments to article 3 also promote UN Security Council objectives to stop WMD proliferation, which were laid out in Resolution 1540 (2004) and 1673 (2006). Finally, article 3*bis*(1)(b)(iii) provides a "savings clause" to preserve the right of nuclear powers to move or deliver nuclear weapons or other explosive devices to or from the territory of or under the control of an NPT State Party. Thus, nuclear material may be transported by sea from an NPT State Party or a non-NPT party to an NPT nuclear weapon State Party, regardless of whether it is under safeguards in the NPT.[54]

Article 3*ter*

Article 4(6) of the 2005 Protocol adds article 3*ter* to the Convention, which criminalizes the transport of terrorist fugitives. Just as the new offenses in 3*bis* have a substantial *mens rea* element, so too, does the proscription against aiding terrorist fugitives. The offense under this article is performed to aid a fugitive after a crime already has been completed, whereas some of the other counterterrorism treaties criminalize assisting a fugitive as an accessory before the crime has occurred. It is an offense for a person to "unlawfully and intentionally" transport another person

---

[54] Protocols of 2005 to the Convention Concerning Safety of Maritime Navigation and to the Protocol Concerning Safety of Fixed Platforms on the Continental Shelf, SENATE TREATY DOC. 110-8, at XIV (2007).

on a ship, "knowing that the person has committed an act" that constitutes an offense under articles 3, 3*bis*, 3*ter* or 3*quarter*, and then "intending to assist that person to evade criminal prosecution." Thus, there are three prongs for mental culpability that must be met in article 3*ter*.

> 3*ter*
>
> Any person commits an offense within the meaning of this Convention if that person unlawfully and intentionally transports another person on board a ship knowing that the person has committed an act that constitutes an offense set forth in article 3, 3*bis* or 3*quarter* or an offense set forth in any treaty listed in the Annex, and intending to assist that person to evade criminal prosecution.

Therefore, article 3*ter* prohibits the transportation of a person on board a ship knowing that the person has committed an act that constitutes an offence under the 2005 SUA Convention *or* any other offense that is a feature of any one of the nine counterterrorism treaties listed in the Annex, which was formed by Article 7 of the 2005 Protocol. The treaties listed in the Annex are:

(1) Convention for the Suppression of Unlawful Seizure of Aircraft, done at The Hague on 16 December 1970;
(2) Convention for the Suppression of Unlawful Acts against the Safety of Civil Aviation, done at Montreal on 23 September 1971;
(3) Convention on the Prevention and Punishment of Crimes against Internationally Protected Persons, including Diplomatic Agents, adopted by the General Assembly of the United Nations on 14 December 1973;
(4) International Convention against the Taking of Hostages, adopted by the General Assembly of the United Nations on 17 December 1979;
(5) Convention on the Physical Protection of Nuclear Material, done at Vienna on 26 October 1979;
(6) Protocol for the Suppression of Unlawful Acts of Violence at Airports Serving International Civil Aviation, supplementary to the Convention for the Suppression of Unlawful Acts against the Safety of Civil Aviation, done at Montreal on 24 February 1988;
(7) Protocol for the Suppression of Unlawful Acts against the Safety of Fixed Platforms Located on the Continental Shelf, done at Rome, 10 March 1988;
(8) International Convention for the Suppression of Terrorist Bombings, adopted by the General Assembly of the United Nations on 15 December 1997;
(9) International Convention for the Suppression of the Financing of Terrorism, adopted by the General Assembly of the United Nations on 9 December 1999.

Article 3*quater*

The last part of amended article 3 includes a bevy of inchoate crimes, including attempt, accomplice, criminal organization or leadership in a criminal enterprise, or making a contribution to the commission of one of the offenses. Following in the footsteps of the original 1988 article 3 and some of the 2005 provision in article 3*bis* and 3*ter*, these offenses also contain multiple *mens rea* elements. The provision of article 3quarter (a)(ii), for example, requires that an offense is committed if the offender serves as an accomplice with the knowledge that the group in which he participates is violating an offense in one of the nine anti-terrorism conventions identified in article 3*ter*.

Some offenses naturally fall within the ambit of the listed anti-terrorism conventions, so that if a person were smuggling a bomb on board a ship in order to later place it aboard an airliner, a prosecutor might argue that it is only common sense that the offender knew the action violated the *Convention for the Suppression of Unlawful Seizure of Aircraft*. On the other hand, what person other than an expert in public international law, has actually read, let alone can say for certain, that bombing a civilian aircraft is included in the terms of the convention? Thus, the layers of intent create a fairly high burden on the part of prosecuting governments, as it may be impossible to demonstrate specific knowledge.

> Article 3*quarter*
>
> Any person also commits and offense within the meaning of this Convention if that person:
>
> (a) unlawfully and intentionally injures or kills any person in connection with the commission of [any offense in article]; or
> (b) attempts to commit an offense set forth in article 3, paragraph 1, article 3*bis*, paragraph 1(a)(i), (ii) or (iii), or subparagraph of this article; or
> (c) participates as an accomplice in an offense set forth in article 3, article 3*bis*, article 3*ter* or subparagraph (a) or (b) of this article, by a group of persons acting with a common purpose, intentionally and either:
> (i) with the aim of furthering the criminal activity or criminal purpose of the group, where such activity or purpose involves the commission of an offense set forth in articles 3, 3*bis*, 3*ter*, or
> (ii) in the knowledge of the intention of the group to commit an offense set forth in articles 3, 3*bis*, or 3*ter*.

The accessory offenses in 3*quarter* are similar to the ones provided in the Terrorist Bombings Convention and the Terrorist Financing Convention. The provisions open the possibility of criminal cases for conspiracy offenses, permitting investigation, prosecution, and extradition of suspected offenders even before one of the underlying offenses have been completed.

Article 4

The Convention applies to ships in the territory—including the territorial sea—of a State Party. The Convention applies to ships navigating into the State Party's territorial sea, scheduled to navigate through the State Party's territorial sea or from waters beyond the territorial sea, that is, from the territorial sea of an adjacent state or the exclusive economic zone (EEZ) of the State Party. Thus, the Convention does not apply through the jurisdiction of a coastal State Party to foreign-flagged ships conducting high seas freedoms or other internationally lawful uses of the sea in the EEZ or on the high seas, without some other jurisdictional hook, such as having expressed an intention to enter the territorial sea or port of a State Party.

Article 4

1. This Convention applies if the ship is navigating or is scheduled to navigate into, through or from waters beyond the outer limit of the territorial sea of a single State, or the lateral limits of its territorial sea with adjacent States.
2. In cases where the Convention does not apply pursuant to paragraph 1, it nevertheless applies when the offender or alleged offender is found in the territory of a State Party other than the State referred to in paragraph 1.

Article 5 and Article 5*bis*

Article 5(1) of the 2005 Protocol adds the offenses enumerated in article 3 to the list of crimes that states must make punishable by "appropriate penalties that take into account their grave nature."[55] Article 5(2) of the 2005 Protocol creates a new provision, article 5*bis* to the 2005 Convention that adds liability for legal entities such as corporations, in addition to persons. Furthermore, the legal sanctions against such corporate entities may be criminal, civil, or administrative in nature, and may include monetary sanctions. This liability is separate and distinct from exposure to legal liability that might be faced by the individual(s) controlling or managing the entity.

Article 5

Each State Party shall make the offenses set forth in [article 3] punishable by appropriate penalties that take into account the grave nature of those offenses.

Article 5*bis*

1. Each State Party, in accordance with its domestic legal principles, shall take the necessary measures to enable a legal entity located in its territory or organized under its laws to be held liable when a person responsible for management or control of that legal entity has, in that capacity, committed an offense set forth in this Convention. Such liability may be criminal, civil, or administrative.
2. Such liability is incurred without prejudice to the criminal liability of individuals having committed the offenses.
3. Each State Party shall ensure, in particular, that legal entities liable in accordance with paragraph 1 are subject to effective, proportionate and dissuasive criminal, civil, or administrative sanctions. Such sanctions may include monetary sanctions.

Article 5*bis* requires State Parties to enact, within their domestic laws, statutes that hold both persons and legal or corporate entities liable for offenses under the Convention. Legal entities located in the territory of a State Party, or organized under its laws or having a corporate charter under its laws, are subject to the provision when a person who has management or control of the entity has committed an offense under the Convention. The relevant domestic laws must be

---

[55] Id., at XVI.

"effective, proportionate, and dissuasive." The terms of article 5*bis* mirror the text in Article 5 of the Terrorism Financing Convention.

Article 6

Article 6

1. Each State Party shall take measures as may be necessary to establish its jurisdiction over the offenses set forth in articles 3, 3*bis*, 3*ter* or 3*quarter* when the offense is committed:
   (a) against or on board a ship flying the flag of the State at the time the offense is committed, or
   (b) in the territory of that State, including its territorial sea; or
   (c) by a national of that State.
2. A State Party may also establish it jurisdiction over any such offense when:
   (a) it is committed by a stateless person whose habitual residence is in that State; or
   (b) during its commission a national of that State is seized, threatened, injured or killed; or
   (c) it is committed in an attempt to compel that State to do or abstain from doing any act.
3. Any State Party which has established jurisdiction mentioned in paragraph 2 shall notify the Secretary-General. If such State Party subsequently rescinds that jurisdiction, it shall notify the Secretary-General.
4. Each State Party shall take such measures as may be necessary to establish its jurisdiction over the offenses set forth in articles 3, 3*bis*, 3*ter* or 3*quarter* in cases where the alleged offender is present in its territory and it does not extradite the alleged offender to any of the States Parties which have established their jurisdiction in accordance with paragraphs 1 and 2 of this article.
5. This Convention does not exclude any criminal jurisdiction exercised in accordance with national law.

Article 7

Article 7

1. Upon being satisfied that the circumstances so warrant, any State Party in the territory of which the offender or the alleged offender is present shall, in accordance with its law, take him into custody or take other measures to ensure his presence for such time as it is necessary to enable any criminal or extradition proceedings to be instituted.
2. Such State shall immediately make a preliminary inquiry into the facts, in accordance with its own legislation.
3. Any person regarding whom the measures referred to in paragraph 1 are being taken shall be entitled to:
   (a) communicate without delay with the nearest appropriate representative of the State of which he is a national or which is otherwise entitled to establish such communication or, if he is a stateless person, the State in the territory of which he has habitual residence;
   (b) be visited by a representative of that State.
4. The rights referred to in paragraph 3 shall be exercised in conformity with the laws and regulations of the State in the territory of which the offender or the alleged

COMMENTARY FOR THE CONVENTION ON THE SUPPRESSION   833

offender is present, subject to the proviso that the said laws and regulations must enable full effect to be given to the purposes for which the rights accorded under paragraph 3 are intended.

5. When a State Party, pursuant to this article, has taken a person into custody, it shall immediately notify the States which have established jurisdiction in accordance with article 6, paragraph 1, and if it considers it advisable, any other interested States, of the fact that such person is in custody and of the circumstances which warrant his detention. The State which makes the preliminary inquiry contemplated in paragraph 2 of this article shall promptly report its findings to the said States and shall indicate whether it intends to exercise jurisdiction.

Article 8

Article 8 covers the responsibilities and roles of the master of the ship, flag State and receiving state in delivering to the authorities of any State Party any person believed to have committed an offense under the Convention, including the furnishing of evidence pertaining to the alleged offense.

Article 8

1. The master of a ship of a State Party (the "flag State") may deliver to the authorities of any other State Party (the "receiving State") any person who the master has reasonable grounds to believe has committed an offense set forth in article 3, 3*bis*, 3*ter* or 3*quarter*.
2. The flag State shall ensure that the master of its ship is obliged, whenever practicable, and if possible before entering the territorial sea of the receiving State carrying on board any person whom the master intends to deliver in accordance with paragraph 1, to give notification to the authorities of the receiving State of his intention to deliver such person and the reasons therefor.
3. The receiving State shall accept the delivery, except where it has grounds to consider that the Convention is not applicable to the acts giving rise to the delivery, and shall proceed in accordance with the provisions of article 7. Any refusal to accept a delivery shall be accompanied by a statement of the reason for refusal.
4. The Flag State shall ensure that the master of its ship is obliged to furnish the authorities of the receiving State with the evidence in the master's possession, which pertains to the alleged offense.
5. A receiving State which has accepted the delivery of a person in accordance with paragraph 3 may, in turn, request the flag State to accept delivery of that person. The flag State shall consider any such request, and if it accedes to the request it shall proceed in accordance with article 7. If the flag State declines a request, it shall furnish the receiving State with a statement of the reasons therefor.

Article 8*bis*

Article 8*bis* of the Protocol includes a comprehensive framework to facilitate boarding of suspect vessels at sea and requires States Parties to "cooperate to the fullest extent possible to prevent and suppress unlawful acts covered by the Convention...and...respond to [boarding] requests...as expeditiously as possible." This new article was created by article 8(2) of the 2005 SUA Protocol and establishes a comprehensive shipboarding regime for adoption by the States Parties. It is the longest article in the amended Convention, with 15 paragraphs.

The boarding regime does not change existing international law of the sea or infringe upon traditional rights and freedoms of navigation, and flag States maintain their traditional exclusive authority over ships flying their flag. The boarding regime provides a framework, however, for expedited decision-making that State Parties may elect to be bound to and that facilitates coordination. In short, the article delineates a process for cooperation and procedures to be followed if a State Party desires to board a ship flying the flag of another State Party, when the requesting Party has "reasonable grounds" to suspect that the ship or a person on board the ship is, has been, or is about to be involved in, the commission of an offense under the Convention. Thus, the flag State may request and leverage the assistance of other States Parties in preventing or suppressing offenses set forth in article 3, 3*bis*, 3*ter*, or 3*quarter*.

First, 8*bis*(1) sets forth the general obligation to cooperate "to the fullest extent possible" among the State Parties, and to respond to requests from other State Parties "as expeditiously as possible." This general obligation is reflected in and derived from article 17(1) of the 1988 UN *Convention against Illicit Traffic in Narcotic Drugs and Psychotropic Substances* (1988 Vienna Narcotic Drug Convention) and article 7 of the *Protocol against Smuggling of Migrants by Land, Sea and Air,* supplementing the UN *Convention against Transnational Organized Crime* (Migrant Smuggling Protocol).

Second, article 8*bis*(2) sets forth the type of information that should accompany any request to board a ship, including, *inter alia,* the name of the vessel, its IMO ship identification number, and port of registry. Third, article 8*bis*(3) is a reminder that it is often impossible to conduct a thorough inspection of either a small craft or large commercial vessel at sea, and often the best course of action is to bring the ship into port to facilitate the inspection. This provision requires the boarding state to consider the particular "dangers and difficulties" involved in boarding a ship underway.

Fourth, article 8*bis*(4) provides a mechanism whereby a State Party with reasonable grounds to suspect that an offense delineated in articles 3, 3*bis*, 3*ter*, or 3*quarter* has been, is being, or is about to be committed "involving a ship flying its flag," may request the assistance of other States Parties. This provision is derived from article 17(2) of the 1988 Vienna Narcotic Drug Convention and article 8(1) of the Migrant Smuggling Protocol.

Fifth, article 8*bis*(5) contains procedures for shipboarding. Officials from one State Party ("the requesting Party"), encountering beyond the territorial sea of any state a ship flying the flag or registered with another State Party, and suspecting the ship has been, is or is about to be involved in an offense in article 3, 3*bis*, 3*ter*, or 3*quarter*, and desiring to board the ship, must adhere to the steps set forth in the new article. The first Party—the flag State—should confirm the nationality of the vessel. If nationality is confirmed, the flag State may authorize boarding or appropriate measures, such as stopping the ship, searching the vessel, its cargo, and persons on board, and questioning the persons on board. In such case, the flag State has four options: it may authorize the requesting State authority to board; it may conduct a boarding and search with its own forces; it may conduct a boarding with its forces working in tandem with the boarding forces of the requesting State, or it may decline the requesting State permission to board. In this regard, if a boarding request is received by the flag State, it must:

- authorize the requesting party to board and take appropriate measures, which may include stopping, boarding and searching the ship, its cargo and person on board, and questioning the persons on board in order to determine if an offense has been committed under the Convention;
- conduct the boarding and search with its own officials;
- conduct the boarding and search with the requesting party; or
- decline to authorize the boarding and search.

The flag State may place limitations or conditions on its approval if it grants the request. Thus, the flag State controls how the boarding is conducted, if at all.

A State Party has the option of notifying the IMO Secretary-General that it would allow authorization to board and search a ship flying its flag, its cargo, and persons on board if there is no response from the flag State within four hours. This four-hour rule, however, is optional for the flag State. A State Party also may notify the IMO Secretary-General that it authorizes a requesting Party to board and search a ship flying its flag, onboard cargo and persons, and to question the persons on board if the requesting state has reasonable grounds that an offense is being, has been, or is about to be, committed. Alternatively, States Parties may also notify the IMO Secretary-General in advance that any other State Party may board and search one of their vessels if they do not respond to a boarding request within four hours of acknowledgement of receipt of a request to confirm the ship's nationality. In either case, once such notification is made to the Secretary-General, that information is promulgated by the IMO to other States Parties.

Under subparagraphs 8*bis*(5)(d) and (e), a flag State may provide pre-approval or advance consent to board some or all of the ships flying its flag to certain requesting states, if the rest of the criteria have been met (e.g., reasonable suspicion) and the requesting state has not received a substantive response from the flag State Party within four hours of acknowledgment of receipt of a request to confirm nationality.

More robust than any other multilateral agreement, the 2005 SUA framework still is weakened by some of the same drawbacks as other counterterrorism and counter-proliferation initiatives in that it is based on flag State consent. Article 8*bis* specifically provides that "the requesting Party shall not board the ship or take measures...without the express authorization of the flag State." This provision likely will prevent boarding by requesting States of ships registered or flagged in States of proliferation concern, such as North Korea or Iran, even if those nations become a State Party to the 2005 Convention.

Paragraph 6 of article 8*bis* stipulates that when the requesting Party boards a foreign flagged ship and finds evidence of offenses under articles 3, 3*bis*, 3*ter*, or 3*quarter*, the flag State may (but is not required to) authorize the requesting Party temporarily to detain the ship, cargo and persons on board, pending receipt of further instructions from the flag State. In any case, the requesting Party must inform the flag State of the results of the boarding, search, and detention, including discovery of evidence of a violation of articles 3, 3*bis*, 3*ter*, or 3*quarter* or illegal conduct that is not a subject of the Convention. The remit in paragraph 6 would appear to require the requesting State to produce to the flag State any evidence discovered of any crime, including evidence of a crime in a third state or non-State Party.

Paragraph 7 of article 8*bis* provides that a flag State may craft its authorization under paragraphs 5 and 6 to a requesting State to include caveats or conditions. For example, the flag State may request that the requesting state obtain additional information, such as its willingness to assume responsibility for certain and the extent of measures to be taken during the boarding process or during detention. This provision relates back to similar text in article 17(6) of the 1988 *Vienna Narcotic Drug Convention* and article 8(5) of the Migrant Smuggling Protocol. The requesting state is protected, however, by a related provision that permits the requesting state to take additional measures *sua sponte* in order to "relieve imminent danger to the lives of persons." Since the word "measures" is not defined, they may be broadly understood to include action as disparate as emergency medical intervention or the use of force. Finally, the requesting Party also may take measures derived from "relevant bilateral or multilateral agreements," and such measures might include activities authorized by a PSI Shipboarding Agreement, an existing counterdrug agreement, or a broader mandate under a regional security framework or even a UN Security Council resolution.

Paragraph 8 reaffirms in accordance with articles 91 and 92 of UNCLOS and articles 5 and 6 of the 1958 Convention on the High Seas that the flag State does not relinquish its right to exercise jurisdiction over a ship flying its flag, or its cargo or persons on board, regardless of whether that ship is detained by a requesting state. This means the flag State may assert seizure, forfeiture, arrest, and prosecution of the vessel or persons on board. At its option, however, the flag Sate may consent to the exercise of jurisdiction by the requesting state or another State Party that has jurisdiction in its domestic laws in accordance with article 6 of the 2005 Convention.

Paragraph 9 mandates that the use of force should be avoided "except when necessary to ensure the safety of its officials and persons on board," or in cases in which "officials are obstructed in the execution of the authorized actions." Furthermore, any use of force "pursuant to this article shall not exceed the minimum degree of force which is necessary and reasonable in the circumstances." The text concerning necessary and reasonable force under the circumstances is similar to the provisions regarding the use of force in fisheries enforcement reflected in article 22(1)(f) of the *Agreement for the Implementation of the Provisions of the United Nations Convention on the Law of the Sea of 10 December 1982 Relating to the Conservation and Management of Straddling Fish Stocks and Highly Migratory Fish Stocks*. Likewise, the United States and other nations have implemented similar text in numerous counterdrug maritime interdiction agreements.

Paragraph 10 of article 8*bis* includes safeguards that apply when a State Party takes measures against a foreign-flagged ship of another State Party to the 2005 Convention, including shipboarding. These safeguards require the requesting State that conducts a boarding to take "due account of the need not to endanger the safety of life at sea," act in a manner that preserves the basic human dignity of all persons on board the ship and that complies with international human rights law; ensure that a boarding and search is conducted in accordance with international law, take "due account" of the safety and security of the ship and its cargo; take "due account" of the need not to prejudice the commercial or legal interests of the flag State, and, ensure, "within available means" that its actions concerning the ship or its cargo are "environmentally sound under the circumstances."

Furthermore, additional safeguards required by the requesting State include ensuring that persons suspected of having committed the offenses set forth in articles 3, 3*bis*, 3*ter* or 3*quarter* are afforded the protections, regardless of location, of paragraph 3 of article 10 of the 2005 SUA Protocol, which are codified in the 2005 SUA Convention at article 11*ter*. These rights relate to protection from prosecution or punishment of a person on account of that person's race, religion, nationality, ethnic origin, political opinion or gender. Finally, the requesting Party must ensure that the Master is advised that his ship will be boarded, that he has the opportunity to contact the ship's owner and the flag State "at the earliest opportunity," and that the State Party conducting the ship boarding will take "reasonable efforts" to avoid unduly detaining or delaying the ship. These safeguards extend those already contained in the 1988 Vienna Narcotic Drug Convention and Article 9 of the Migrant Smuggling Protocol.

Article 8*bis* paragraph 10(b) sets forth a framework for considering liability under the shipboarding regime. First, the mere grant of authorization to board by a flag State does not *per se* "give rise to its liability." States Parties, however, incur liability under two circumstances. Second, they "shall be liable for any damage, harm or loss attributable to them arising from measures" taken under article 8*bis*, in the event that the "grounds for such measures prove to be unfounded," so long as the ship has not committed any act justifying the measures taken; and second, if "such measures are unlawful or exceed those reasonably required in light of available information to implement the provisions" of the shipboarding regime. Third, the article asserts that States Parties shall provide "effective recourse" in respect of such damage, harm or loss, although that term is undefined, and there is no specific remedy or arbitral tribunal forum required to litigate questions of liability. The provisions concerning liability reflect the framework contained in article 22(3) of the High Seas Convention and article 9(2) of the Migrant Smuggling Protocol.

Paragraph 10(c) of article 8*bis* requires states that take measures against a ship under the Convention to take "due account" of the need not to interfere with the rights and obligations and exercise of jurisdiction by coastal States, or the authority of flag States to exercise jurisdiction in administrative, technical, or social matters involving the ship. UNCLOS is specified as the template or metric against which both the rights of coastal States and the rights of flag States are understood. Rights of flag States are specified in article 94(1) of UNCLOS, and the provision in the 2005 SUA Convention also amplifies article 17(11) of the 1988 Vienna Drug Convention and article 9(3) of the Migrant Smuggling Protocol.

Under the rule in paragraph 10(d) and (e), shipboarding must be carried out by "law enforcement or other authorized officials" operating from warships or military aircraft clearly marked and identifiable on government service. The term "law enforcement or other authorized officials" is defined as "uniformed or otherwise clearly identifiable members of law enforcement or other government authorities duly authorized by their government." Such individuals may include civil and military authorities, including special operations forces (SOF). Interestingly, the persons conducting the boarding must present to the Master of the ship for examination appropriate government-issued identification documents. The paragraph, however, does not stipulate at what point in the boarding process such identification must be presented, although normally it would be presented as soon as the boarding party sets foot on the ship. On the other hand, boarding in a non-permissive or hostile environment would preclude presentation of such identification until after the vessel is secured. The sovereign immune exemptions and special status of warships in articles 2 and 2*bis* enable rather than conflict with this provision.

Paragraph 11 of article 8*bis* recognizes that there are sundry additional basis outside of the 2005 Convention in which law enforcement or armed forces of one state may be authorized to board a ship flying the flag or registered in another state. The 2005 SUA Convention does not limit or otherwise affect other lawful boarding measures conducted beyond the territorial sea of any coastal State, such as the right of approach and visit under article 110 of UNCLOS, the exercise of the inherent right of self-defense under article 51 of the UN Charter, the exercise of the belligerent right of visit and search under the law of war, measures taken under regional arrangements in accordance with Chapter VIII of the UN Charter, enforcement of UN Security Council resolutions authorizing such action under Chapter VII of the UN Charter, or pursuant to some other bilateral or multilateral agreement between the state boarding the ship and the state in which the ship is registered.

Paragraph 12 simply encourages states to develop even more detailed operating procedures for combined operations, in order to harmonize tactics, techniques, and procedures. Similarly, paragraph 13 encourages States Parties to reach agreements or arrangements between them to implement the article. The provision replicates similar text in article 17(9) of the 1988 Vienna Narcotic Drug Convention and article 17 of the Migrant Smuggling Protocol. Paragraph 14 requires State Parties to take "appropriate measures" to ensure that its law enforcement or other authorized officials, are "empowered to act" pursuant to the shipboarding regime. Thus, law enforcement or other officials must have the legal capacity under domestic law to carry out shipboarding.

Upon becoming a State Party, paragraph 15 requires each nation to designate within one month an authority (or authorities) who can serve as a liaison with other nations on time-sensitive issues arising under the treaty, such as receiving and responding to for assistance, confirming vessel nationality, and for authorizing appropriate measures. The designation is made to the Secretary-General, who promulgates it among IMO Member States. The provision is similar to article 17(7) of the 1988 Vienna Narcotic Drug Convention and article 8(6) of the Migrant Smuggling Protocol. The United States typically designates the Commandant of the U.S. Coast Guard, via the interagency watch floor stood up by the *Maritime Operational Threat Response Plan.*

Article 8*bis* and the shipboarding regime is reproduced:

Article 8*bis*

1. State Parties shall cooperate to the fullest extent possible to prevent and suppress unlawful acts covered by this Convention, in conformity with international law, and shall respond to requests pursuant to this article as expeditiously as possible.
2. Each request pursuant to this article should, if possible, contain the name of the suspect ship, the IMO ship identification number, the port of registry, the ports of origin and destination, and any other relevant information. If a request is conveyed orally, the requesting Party shall confirm the request in writing as soon as possible. The request Party shall acknowledge its receipt of any written or oral request immediately.
3. States Parties shall take into account the dangers and difficulties involved in boarding a ship at sea and searching its cargo, and give consideration to whether other appropriate measures agreed between the States concerned could be more safely taken in the next port of call or elsewhere.
4. A State Part that has a reasonable grounds to suspect that an offense set forth in article 3, 3*bis*, 3*ter*, or 3*quarter* has been, is being or is about to be committed involving a ship flying its flag, may request the assistance of other States Parties in preventing or suppressing that offense. The States Parties so requested shall use their best endeavors to render such assistance within the means available to them.
5. Whenever law enforcement or other authorized officials of a State Party ("the requesting Party") encounter a ship flying the flag or displaying marks of registry of another State Party ("the first Party") located seaward of any State's territorial sea, and the requesting Party has reasonable grounds to suspect that the ship or a person on board the ship has been, is or is about to be involved in the commission of an offense set forth in article 3, 3*bis*, 3*ter* or 3*quarter*, and the requesting Party desires to board,

(a) it shall request, in accordance with paragraphs 1 and 2 that the first Party confirm the claim of nationality, and
(b) if nationality is confirmed, the requesting Party shall ask the first Party (hereinafter referred to as "the flag State") for authorization to board and to take appropriate measures with regard to that ship which may include stopping, boarding, and searching the ship, its cargo, and persons on board, and questioning the persons on board in order to determine if an offense set forth in article 3, 3*bis*, 3*ter* or 3*quarter* has been, is being or is about to be committed, and
(c) the flag State shall either:
   (i) authorize the requesting Party to board and to take appropriate measures set out in subparagraph (b), subject to any conditions it may impose in accordance with paragraph 7; or
   (ii) conduct the boarding and search with its own law enforcement officials; or
   (iii) conduct the boarding and search together with the requesting Party, subject to any conditions it may impose in accordance with paragraph 7; or
   (iv) decline to authorize a boarding and search.

The requesting Party shall not board the ship or take measures set out in subparagraph (b) without the express authorization of the flag State.

(d) Upon or after depositing its instrument of ratification, acceptance, approval, or accession, a State Party may notify the Secretary-General that, with respect to ships flying its flag or displaying its mark of registry, the requesting Party is granted authorization to board and search the ship, its cargo and persons on board, and to question the nationality and determine if an offense set forth in article 3, 3*bis*, 3*ter* or 3*quarter* has been, is being or is about to be committed, if there is no response from the first Party within four hours of acknowledgement of receipt of a request to confirm nationality.
(e) Upon or after depositing its instrument of ratification, acceptance, approval or accession, a State Party may notify the Secretary-General that, with respect to ships flying its flag or displaying its mark of registry, the requesting Party is authorized to board and search a ship, its cargo and persons on board, and to question the persons on board in order to determine if an offense set forth in article 3, 3*bis*, 3*ter* or 3*quarter* has been, is being or is about to be committed.

The notification made pursuant to this paragraph can be withdrawn at any time.

6. When evidence of conduct described in article 3, 3*bis*, 3*ter* or 3*quarter* is found as the result of any boarding conducted pursuant to this article, the flag State may authorize the requesting Party to detain the ship, cargo and persons on board pending receipt of disposition instructions from the flag State. The requesting Party shall promptly inform the flag State of the results of a boarding, search, and detention conducted pursuant to this article. The requesting Party shall also promptly inform the flag State of the discovery of evidence of illegal conduct that is not subject to this Convention.
7. The flag State, consistent with the other provisions of this Convention, may subject its authorization under paragraph 5 or 6 to conditions, including obtaining additional information from the requesting Party, and conditions relating to responsibility for and the extent of measures to be taken. No additional measures may be taken without the express authorization of the flag State, except when necessary

to relieve imminent danger to the lives of persons or where those measures derive from relevant bilateral or multilateral agreements.
8. For all boardings pursuant to this article, the flag State has the right to exercise jurisdiction over a detained ship, cargo or other items and persons on board, including seizure, forfeiture, arrest and prosecution. However, the flag State may, subject to its constitution and laws, consent to the exercise of jurisdiction by another State having jurisdiction under article. 6.
9. When carrying out the authorized actions under this article, the use of force shall be avoided except when necessary to ensure the safety of its officials and persons on board, or where the officials are obstructed in the execution of the authorized actions. Any use of force pursuant to this article shall not exceed the minimum degree of force which is necessary and reasonable in the circumstances.
10. Safeguards:
    (a) Where a State Party takes measures against a ship in accordance within this article, it shall:
        (i) take due account of the need not to endanger the safety of life at sea;
        (ii) ensure that all persons on board are treated in a manner which preserves their basic human dignity, and in compliance with the applicable provisions of international law, including international human rights law;
        (iii) ensure that a boarding and search pursuant to this article shall be conducted in accordance with applicable international law;
        (iv) take due account of the safety and security of the ship and its cargo;
        (v) take due account of the need not to prejudice the commercial or legal interests of the flag State;
        (vi) ensure, within available means that any measure taken with regard to the ship or its cargo is environmentally sound under the circumstances;
        (vii) ensure that persons on board against whom proceedings may be commenced in connection with any of the offences set forth in article 3, 3*bis*, 3*ter* or 3*quarter* are afforded the protections of paragraph 3 of article 10 regardless of location;
        (viii) ensure that the master of a ship is advised of its intention to board, and is, or has been, afforded the opportunity to contact the ship's owner and the flag State at the earliest opportunity; and
        (ix) take reasonable efforts to avoid a ship being unduly detained or delayed.
    (b) Provided that authorization to board by a flag State shall not per se give rise to its liability, States Parties shall be liable for any damage, harm or loss attributable to them arising from measures taken pursuant to this article when:
        (i) the grounds for such measures prove to be unfounded, provided that the ship has not committed any act justifying the measures taken; or
        (ii) such measures are unlawful or exceed those reasonably required in light of available information to implement the provisions of this article.

States Parties shall provide effective recourse in respect of such damage, harm or loss.

    (c) Where a State Party takes measures against a ship in accordance with this Convention, it shall take due account of the need not to interfere with or to affect:

(i) the rights and obligations and the exercise of jurisdiction of coastal States in accordance with the international law of the sea;

(ii) the authority of the flag State to exercise jurisdiction and control in administrative, technical and social matters involving the ship.

(d) Any measure taken pursuant to this article shall be carried out by law enforcement or other authorized officials from warships or military aircraft, or from other ships or aircraft clearly marked and identifiable as being on Government service, and authorized to that effect and, notwithstanding articles 2 and 2*bis*, the provisions of this article shall apply.

(e) For the purposes of this article "law enforcement or other authorized officials" means uniformed or otherwise clearly identifiable members of law enforcement or other government authorities duly authorized by their Government. For the specific purpose of law enforcement under this Convention, law enforcement or other authorized officials shall provide appropriate government-issued identification documents for examination by the master of the ship upon boarding.

11. This article does not apply to or limit boarding of ships conducted by any State Party in accordance with international law, seaward of any State's territorial sea, including boardings based upon the right of visit, the rendering of assistance to person, ships and property in distress or peril, or an authorization from the flag State to take law enforcement or other action.

12. State Parties are encouraged to develop standard operating procedures for joint operations pursuant to this article and consult, as appropriate, with other States Parties with a view to harmonizing such standard operating procedures for the conduct of operations.

13. States Parties may conclude agreements or arrangements between them to facilitate law enforcement operations carried out in accordance with this article.

14. Each State Party shall take appropriate measures to ensure that its law enforcement or other authorized officials, and law enforcement and other authorized officials of other States Parties acting on its behalf, are empowered to act pursuant to this article.

15. Upon or after depositing its instrument of ratification, acceptance, approval or accession, each State Party shall designate the authority, or where necessary, authorities, to receive and respond to requests for assistance, for confirmation of nationality, and for authorization to take appropriate measures. Such designation, including contact information, shall be notified to the Secretary-General within one month of becoming a Party, who shall inform all other States Parties within one month of the designation. Each State Party is responsible for providing prompt notice through the Secretary-General of any changes in the designation or contact information.

Article 9

Article 9 contains boilerplate language preserving existing international law, which tends to limit the rights of states to exercise investigative or enforcement jurisdiction on foreign-flagged ships. The rule reflects the concept of exclusive flag State jurisdiction codified in articles 92 and 94 of UNCLOS.

> Article 9
>
> Nothing in this Convention shall affect in any way the rules of international law pertaining to the competence of States to exercise investigative or enforcement jurisdiction on board ships not flying their flying their flag.

Article 10

Article 10(2) of the 2005 SUA Convention was amended by article 9 of the 2005 SUA Protocol. The amendment adds specific text on top of the same article in the 1988 SUA Convention that requires treatment of alleged offenders to be in accord with not only the law of the State Party, but also that of "applicable provisions of international law, including international human rights law." The provision is designed to strengthen protections for international seafarers. Any person taken into custody or subject to legal or administrative proceedings pursuant to measures conducted under the 2005 Convention is guaranteed "fair treatment." Protections under the law of the state taking action, as well as "applicable provisions" of international law and international human rights law apply. The amendment reflects similar text in article 17 of the Terrorism Financing Convention and article 14 of the Terrorist Bombings Convention.

> Article 10
> 1. The State Party in the territory of which the offender or the alleged offender is found shall, in cases to which article 6 applies, if it does not extradite him, be obliged, without exception whatsoever and whether or not the offense was committed in its territory, to submit the case without delay to its competent authorities for the purpose of prosecution, through proceedings in accordance with the law of the State. Those authorities shall take their decision in the same manner as in the case of any other offense of a grave nature under the law of that state.
> 2. Any person who is taken into custody or regarding whom any other measures are taken or proceedings are being carried out pursuant to this Convention, shall be guaranteed fair treatment, including enjoyment of all rights and guarantees in conformity with the law of the State in the territory of which that person is present and applicable provisions of international law, including international human rights law.

Article 11

Article 11 covers extradition procedures, which were amended by article 10 of the 2005 SUA Protocol. The first four paragraphs of article 11 were revised by article 10(1) of the 2005 SUA Protocol to incorporate into the extradition regime the offenses set forth in articles 3, 3*bis*, 3*ter* or 3*quarter*.

> Article 11
> 1. The offenses set forth in articles 3, 3*bis*, 3*ter* or 3*quarter* shall be deemed to be included as extraditable offenses in any extradition treaty existing between any of the States Parties. States Parties undertake to include such offenses as extraditable offenses in every extradition treaty to be concluded between them.
> 2. If a State Party which makes extradition conditional on the existence of a treaty receives a request for extradition from another State Party with which it has no extradition treaty, the requested State may, at its option, consider this Convention as a legal basis for extradition in respect to the offenses set forth in articles 3, 3*bis*, 3*ter* or 3*quarter*. Extradition shall be subject to the other conditions provided by the law of the requested State Party.

3. States Parties which do not make extradition conditional on the existence of a treaty shall recognize the offenses set forth in article 3, 3*bis*, 3*ter* or 3*quarter* as extraditable offenses between themselves, subject to the conditions provided by the law of the requested State Party.
4. If necessary, the offenses set forth in articles 3, 3*bis*, 3*ter* or 3*quarter* shall be treated, for the purposes of extradition between States Parties, as if they had been committed not only in the place in which they occurred but also in a place within the jurisdiction of the State Party requesting extradition.
5. A State Party which receives more than one request for extradition from States which have established jurisdiction in accordance with article 6 and which decides not to prosecute shall, in selecting the State to which the offender or alleged offenders is to be extradited, pay due regard to the interests and responsibilities of the State Party whose flag the ship was flying at the time of the commission of the offense.
6. In considering a request for the extradition of an alleged offender pursuant to this Convention, the requested States shall pay due regard to whether his rights as set forth in article 7, paragraph 3, can be effected in the requesting State.
7. With respect to the offenses defined in this Convention, the provisions of all extradition treaties and arrangements applicable between States Parties are modified as between States Parties to the extent that they are incompatible with this Convention.

Article 11*bis*

Article 10(2) of the 2005 SUA Protocol adds article 11*bis* to the 2005 SUA Convention. The new article 11*bis* states that none of the offenses should be considered for the purposes of extradition or mutual legal assistance as a political offense. Requests for extradition or mutual legal assistance based on any of the set forth in articles 3, 3*bis*, 3*ter* or 3*quarter* may not be denied solely because the act constituted a political offense in the view of the state receiving the request. There is a similar provision in article 14 of the Terrorism Financing Convention and article 11 of the Terrorist Bombing Convention. By eliminating the political offense as the sole basis for extradition or assistance, the 2005 Convention narrows the grounds for denying such a request.

> Article 11*bis*
>
> None of the offenses set forth in article 3, 3*bis*, 3*ter* or 3*quarter* shall be regarded for the purposes of extradition or mutual legal assistance as a political offense or as an offense connected with a political offense or an offense inspired by political motives. Accordingly, a request for extradition or for mutual legal assistance based on such an offense may not be refused on the sole ground that it concerns a political offense or an offense connected with a political offense or an offense inspired by political motives.

Article 11*ter*

The new article 11*ter* was created by article 10(3) of the 2005 Protocol and has been added to the Convention. It states that the obligation to extradite or afford mutual legal assistance need not apply if the request for extradition is believed to have been made for the repugnant purpose of prosecuting or punishing a person on account of that person's race, religion, nationality, ethnic origin, political opinion or gender, or that compliance with the request would cause prejudice to that person's position for any of these reasons.

> Article 11*ter*
>
> Nothing in this Convention shall be interpreted as imposing an obligation to extradite or to afford mutual legal assistance, if the requested State Party has substantial grounds for believing that the request for extradition for offenses set forth in article 3, 3*bis*, 3*ter* or 3*quarter* or for mutual legal assistance with respect to such offenses has been made for the purpose of prosecuting or punishing a person on account of that person's race, religion, nationality, ethnic origin, political opinion or gender, or that compliance with the request would cause prejudice to that person's position for any of these reasons.

Article 12

Article 11(1) of the 2005 SUA Protocol amended article 12(1) of the Convention to require States Parties to afford one another assistance in connection with criminal proceedings brought in respect of the new offenses from article 3, 3*bis*, 3*ter* or 3*quarter*. States Parties shall carry out their existing obligations under any other mutual assistance treaties that exist, and the 2005 Convention does not change the terms of those treaties.

> Article 12
>
> 1. States Parties shall afford one another the greatest measure of assistance in connection with criminal proceedings brought in respect of the offenses set forth in article 3, 3*bis*, 3*ter* or 3*quarter*, including assistance in obtaining evidence at their disposal necessary for the proceedings.
> 2. States Parties shall carry out their obligations under paragraph 1 in conformity with any treaties on mutual assistance that may exist between them. In the absence of such treaties, States Parties shall afford each other assistance in accordance with their national law.

Article 12*bis*

A new article 12*bis* covers the conditions under which a person who is being detained or is serving a sentence in the territory of one State Party may be transferred to another State Party for purposes of identification, testimony, or to provide some other assistance in obtaining evidence for the investigation or prosecution of any of the new offenses. Two conditions must be met before a person can be transferred. First, the person in custody must freely give his informed consent to the transfer. Second, the competent authorities in both States must agree upon the transfer. The text replicates similar language in article 16 of the Terrorism Financing Convention and article 13 of the Terrorist Bombings Convention. The return of a transferred individual does not trigger extradition proceedings to send the person in custody back to the sending state.

Article 12*bis*

1. A person who is being detained or is serving a sentence in the territory of one State Party whose presence in another State Party is requested for purposes of identification, testimony or otherwise providing assistance in obtaining evidence for the investigation or prosecution of offenses set forth in article 3, 3*bis*, 3*ter* or 3*quarter* may be transferred if the following conditions are met:
   (a) the person freely gives informed consent; and
   (b) the competent authorities of both States agree, subject to such conditions as those States may deem appropriate.
2. For the purposes of this article:
   (a) the State to which the person is transferred shall have the authority and obligation to keep the person transferred in custody, unless otherwise requested or authorized by the State from which the person was transferred;
   (b) the State to which the person is transferred shall without delay implement its obligation to return the person to the custody of the State from which the person was transferred as agreed beforehand, or as otherwise agreed, by the competent authorities of both States;
   (c) the State to which the person is transferred shall not require the State from which the person was transferred to initiate extradition proceedings for the return of the person;
   (d) the person transferred shall receive credit for service of the sentence being served in the State from which the person was transferred for time spent in the custody of the State to which the person was transferred.
3. Unless the State Party from which a person is to be transferred... so agrees, that person, whatever that person's nationality, shall not be prosecuted or detained or subjected to any other restriction of personal liberty in the territory of the State to which that person is transferred in respect of acts or convictions anterior to that person's departure from the territory of the State from which such person was transferred.

Article 13

Article 13 contains conforming changes to the 2005 SUA Convention created to reference the new offenses set forth in articles 3, 3*bis*, 3*ter* or 3*quarter*, reflecting text adopted in article 12 of the 2005 SUA Protocol. States must take all "practicable measures" to prevent commission of the covered offenses. Since reasonable people can differ on whether something is extremely essential or simply impracticable, the new standard in article 13 provides at least some metric for vigilance, albeit a very low one, below which States may not dip. Similarly, States Parties are committed to exercise "all possible effort" to avoid "unduly" delaying ships, cargo, or passengers due to criminal investigation or prosecution of one of the crimes in articles 3, 3*bis*, 3*ter* or 3*quarter*.

Article 13

1. States Parties shall cooperate in the prevention of offenses set forth in articles 3, 3*bis*, 3*ter* or 3*quarter*, particularly by:
   (a) taking all practicable measures to prevent preparation in their respective territories for the commission of those offenses within or outside their territories;

(b) exchanging information in accordance with their national law, and coordinating administrative and other measures taken as appropriate to prevent the commission of offenses set forth in articles 3, 3*bis*, 3*ter* or 3*quarter*.
2. When, due to the commission of an offense set forth in 3, 3*bis*, 3*ter* or 3*quarter*, the passage of a ship has been delayed or interrupted, any State Party in whose territory the ship or passengers or crew are present shall be bound to exercise all possible effort to avoid a ship, its passengers, crew or cargo begin unduly detained or delayed.

Article 14

Article 14 reflects conforming amendments concerning information sharing among States Parties under the Convention.

Article 14

Any State Party having reason to believe that an offense set forth in article 3, 3*bis*, 3*ter* or 3*quarter* will be committed shall, in accordance with its national law, furnish as promptly as possible any relevant information in its possession to those States which it believes would be the States having established jurisdiction in accordance with article 6.

Article 15

Article 15(3) is updated by article 14 of the 2005 SUA Protocol.

Article 15

1. Each State Party shall, in accordance with its national law, provide to the Secretary-General, as promptly as possible, any relevant information in its possession concerning:
   (a) the circumstances of the offense;
   (b) the action taken pursuant to article 13, paragraph 2;
   (c) the measures taken in relation to the offender or the alleged offender and, in particular, the results of any extradition proceedings or other legal proceedings.
2. The State Party where the alleged offender is prosecuted shall, in accordance with its national law, communicate the final outcome of the proceedings to the Secretary-General.
3. The information transmitted in accordance with paragraphs 1 and 2 shall be communicated by the Secretary-General to all States Parties, to Member of the Organization, to other States concerned, and to the appropriate international intergovernmental organizations.

Article 16

Article 16

1. Any dispute between two or more States Parties concerning the interpretation or application of this Convention, which cannot be settled through negotiation within a reasonable time shall, at the request of one of them, be submitted to arbitration. If, within six months from the date of the request for arbitration, the parties are unable to agree on the organization of the arbitration any one of those

parties may refer the dispute to the International Court of Justice by request in conformity with the Statute of the Court.
2. Each State may at the time of signature or ratification, acceptance or approval of this Convention or accession thereto, declare that it does not consider itself bound by any or all of the provisions of paragraph 1. The other States Parties shall not be bound by those provisions with respect to any State Party which has made such a reservation.
3. Any State which has made a reservation in accordance with paragraph 2 may, at any time, withdraw that reservation by notification to the Secretary-General.

Article 16*bis*

Article 16 of the 2005 SUA Protocol adds the new article 16*bis* to the Convention, identifying that the final clauses of the Convention are in articles 17 to 24. References in the 2005 SUA Convention to States Parties refers to States Parties to the 2005 SUA Protocol.

> Article 16*bis*
>
> Final clauses of the Convention
>
> The final clauses of this Convention shall be articles 17 to 24 of the Protocol of 2005 to the Convention for the Suppression of Unlawful Acts against the Safety of Maritime Navigation. References in this Convention to States Parties shall be taken to mean references to States Parties to that Protocol.

Article 17

Article 17 provides that the 2005 SUA Convention shall be open for signature on February 14, 2006, to February 13, 2007; thereafter, the Convention remains open to accession. There are three paths a state may take to becoming a State Party to the Convention: signature, signature plus some additional step, such as ratification, acceptance or approval through a domestic legal or constitutional process, or accession. Only a Party that has gone through one of these three steps may become a Party to the Convention.

> Article 17
> *Signature, ratification, acceptance, approval and accession*
>
> 1. This Protocol shall be open for signature at the Headquarters of the Organization from 14 February 2006 to 13 February 2007 and shall thereafter remain open for accession.
> 2. States may express their consent to be bound by this Protocol by:
>   (a) signature without reservation as to ratification, acceptance or approval; or
>   (b) signature subject to ratification, acceptance or approval; or
>   (c) signature subject to ratification, acceptance or approval, followed by ratification, acceptance or approval; or
>   (d) accession.
> 3. Ratification, acceptance, approval or accession shall be effected by the deposit of an instrument to that effect with the Secretary-General.

> 4. Only a State which has signed the Convention without reservation as to ratification, acceptance or approval, or has ratified, accepted, or approved or acceded to the Convention, may become a Party to this Protocol.

Article 18

The 2005 SUA Convention entered into force on July 28, 2010. Going forward, the Convention enters into force 90 days after the deposit of the instrument of accession for States that accede to the Convention.

> Article 18
> *Entry into force*
>
> 1. This Protocol shall enter into force ninety days following the date on which twelve States have either signed it without reservation as to ratification, acceptance or approval, or have deposited an instrument of ratification, acceptance approval or accession with the Secretary-General.
> 2. For a State which deposits an instrument of ratification, acceptance, approval or accession in respect of this Protocol after the conditions in paragraph 1 for entry into force thereof have been met, the ratification, acceptance, approval or accession shall take effect ninety days after the date of such deposit.

Article 19

Any State Party may denounce the 2005 SUA Protocol any time after it enters into force for the State. Denunciation is effected through deposit of an instrument of denunciation with the Secretary-General.

> Article 19
> *Denunciation*
>
> 1. This Protocol may be denounced by any State Party at any time after the date on which this Protocol enters into force for that State.
> 2. Denunciation shall be effected by the deposition of an instrument of denunciation with the Secretary-General.
> 3. A denunciation shall take effect one year, or such longer period as may be specified in the instrument of denunciation, after the deposit of the instrument with the Secretary-General.

Article 20

Article 20 contains provisions for revising and amending the 2005 SUA Protocol. The IMO Secretary-General will convene a special conference to revise or amend the treaty at the request of one third of the States Parties or 10 States Parties, whichever figure is higher. Any subsequent instrument of ratification, acceptance, approval or accession deposited after entry into force of an amendment to the 2005 SUA Protocol is considered to apply to the 2005 SUA Convention under the terms of article 16 of the 2005 SUA Convention.

Article 20
Revision and amendment
1. A Conference for the purpose of revising or amending this Protocol may be convened by the Organization.
2. The Secretary-General shall convene a conference of States Parties to this Protocol for revising or amending the Protocol, at the request of one third of the States Parties, or ten States Parties, whichever is the higher figure.
3. Any instrument of ratification, acceptance, approval or accession deposited after the date of entry into force of an amendment to this Protocol shall be deemed to apply to the Protocol as amended.

Article 21

Article 21 permits States Parties to the Convention to make declarations with respect to any of the treaties listed in the Annex (and in this volume reproduced in the discussion for article 3*ter, supra*) to which it is not a party, to the effect that the treaty is deemed not to be included in article 3*ter* for that State Party. The declaration shall cease to have effect as soon as such treaty enters into force for the State Party. Finally, article 21(3) makes allowance for the domestic laws of some states that offer defenses for criminal prosecution for family members, such as spousal immunity, who otherwise might be charged with aiding or abetting fugitive terrorists.

Article 21
Declarations
1. Upon deposition its instrument of ratification, acceptance, approval or accession, a State Party which is not a party to a treaty listed in the Annex may declare that, in the application of this Protocol to the State Party, the treaty shall be deemed not to be included in article 3*ter*. The declaration shall cease to have effect as soon as the treaty enters into force for the State Party, which shall notify the Secretary-General of this fact.
2. When a State Party ceases to be a party to a treaty listed in the Annex, it may make a declaration as provided for in this article, with respect to that treaty.
3. Upon depositing its instrument of ratification, acceptance, approval or accession, a State Party may declare that it will apply the provisions of article 3*ter* in accordance with the principles of its criminal law concerning family exemptions of liability.

Article 22

Article 22 contains a mechanism whereby States Parties may add new treaties to the list of treaties in the Annex to the 2005 SUA Convention (and that is reproduced at Table 22.1 and in the discussion accompanying article 3*ter, supra*). Any State Party may make a recommendation for a treaty to be added to the Annex by requesting that the Secretary-General distribute among the Member States of the IMO as an amendment under the terms of article 22(1).

Under article 22(4), however, each State Party is not bound to any additional treaty unless it deposits an instrument of ratification, acceptance or approval for that amendment with the Secretary-General. The new treaty added to the Annex enters into force for those States Parties that have consented to be bound 30 days after deposit with the Secretary-General the twelfth instrument of ratification, acceptance, or approval of the amendment.

Article 22
Amendments to the Annex

1. The Annex may be amended by the addition of relevant treaties that:
   (a) are open to the participation of all States;
   (b) have entered into force; and
   (c) have been ratified, accepted, approved or acceded to by at least twelve States Parties to this Protocol.
2. After the entry into force of this Protocol, any State Party thereto may propose such an amendment to the Annex. Any proposal for an amendment shall be communicated to the Secretary-General in written form. The Secretary-General shall circulate any proposed amendment that meets the requirements of paragraph 1 to all members of the Organization and seek from States Parties to this Protocol their consent to the adoption of the proposed amendment.
3. The proposed amendment to the Annex shall be deemed adopted after more than twelve of the States Parties to this Protocol consent to it by written notification to the Secretary-General.
4. The adopted amendment to the Annex shall enter into force thirty days after the deposit with the Secretary-General of the twelfth instrument of ratification, acceptance or approval of such amendment for those States Parties to this Protocol ratifying accepting or approving the amendment after the deposit by such State party of its instrument of ratification, acceptance, or approval.

Article 23

The IMO Secretary-General is the depositary for the 2005 SUA Convention.

Article 23
Depositary

1. This Protocol and any amendments adopted under articles 20 and 22 shall be deposited with the Secretary-General.
2. The Secretary-General shall:
   (a) inform all States which have signed this Protocol or acceded to this Protocol of:
      (i) each new signature or deposit of instrument of ratification, acceptance, approval or accession together with the date thereof;
      (ii) the date of entry into force of this Protocol;
      (iii) the deposit of any instrument of denunciation of this Protocol together with the date on which it is received and the date on which the denunciation takes effect;
      (iv) any communication called for any article of this Protocol;
      (v) any amendment deemed to have been adopted in accordance with article 22, paragraph 2;
      (vi) any amendment deemed to have been adopted in accordance with article 22, paragraph 3;
      (vii) any amendment ratified, accepted or approved in accordance with article 22, paragraph 4, together with the date on which that amendment shall enter into force; and

(b) transmit certified true copies of this Protocol to all States which have signed or acceded to this Protocol.

3. As soon as this Protocol enters into force, a certified true copy of the text shall be transmitted by the Secretary-General to the Secretary-General of the United Nations for registration and publication in accordance with article 102 of the Charter of the United Nations.

Article 24

The text of the 2005 SUA Protocol was produced in six languages, all of which are equally valid.

> Article 24
> *Languages*
>
> This Protocol is established in a single original in the Arabic, Chinese, English, French, Russian and Spanish languages, each text being equally authentic.
>
> DONE AT LONDON this fourteenth day of October two thousand and five.
>
> IN WITNESS WHEREOF the undersigned, being duly authorized by their respective Governments for that purpose, have signed this Protocol.[56]

Table 22.1. United Nations Terrorism Conventions

(1) Convention for the Suppression of Unlawful Seizure of Aircraft, done at The Hague on 16 December 1970;
(2) Convention for the Suppression of Unlawful Acts against the Safety of Civil Aviation, done at Montreal on 23 September 1971;
(3) Convention on the Prevention and Punishment of Crimes against Internationally Protected Persons, including Diplomatic Agents, adopted by the General Assembly of the United Nations on 14 December 1973;
(4) International Convention against the Taking of Hostages, adopted by the General Assembly of the United Nations on 17 December 1979;
(5) Convention on the Physical Protection of Nuclear Material, done at Vienna on 26 October 1979;
(6) Protocol for the Suppression of Unlawful Acts of Violence at Airports Serving International Civil Aviation, supplementary to the Convention for the Suppression of Unlawful Acts against the Safety of Civil Aviation, done at Montreal on 24 February 1988;
(7) Protocol for the Suppression of Unlawful Acts against the Safety of Fixed Platforms Located on the Continental Shelf, done at Rome, 10 March 1988;
(8) International Convention for the Suppression of Terrorist Bombings, adopted by the General Assembly of the United Nations on 15 December 1997;
(9) International Convention for the Suppression of the Financing of Terrorism, adopted by the General Assembly of the United Nations on 9 December 1999.

---

[56] Signature pages omitted in the original published text.

Table 22.2. Original Contracting States for the 2005 SUA Protocol

Original Contracting states for the Protocol of 2005 to the Convention for the Suppression of Unlawful Acts Against the Safety of Maritime Navigation (SUA 2005), done at London, 14 October 2005, entered into force 28 July 2010.[57]

Country	Date of signature or deposit of instrument
Cook Islands (accession)	12 March 2007
Dominican Republic (accession)	9 March 2010
Estonia (ratification)	16 May 2008
Fiji (accession)	21 May 2008
Latvia (accession)	16 November 2009
Liechtenstein (accession)	28 August 2009
Marshall Islands (accession)	9 May 2008
Nauru (accession)	29 April 2010
Saint Kitts and Nevis (accession)	29 March 2007
Spain (ratification)	16 April 2008
Switzerland (accession)	15 October 2008
Vanuatu (accession)	20 August 2008

22.1.3 *2005 Protocol (Safety of Fixed Platforms)*

This section contains text and analysis of the *Protocol for the Suppression of Unlawful Acts against the Safety of Fixed Platforms located on the Continental Shelf, 2005* (SUA PROT 2005) (Consolidated text of the Protocol for the Suppression of Unlawful Acts against the Safety of Fixed Platforms located on the Continental Shelf and of the Protocol of 2005 to the Protocol).

Article 1

Article 1

1. The provisions of article 1, paragraphs 9(c), (d), (e), (f), (g), (h) and 2(a) of articles 2*bis*, 5, 5*bis* and 7, and of articles 10 to 16, including articles 11*bis*, 11*ter* and 12*bis*, of the Convention for the Suppression of Unlawful Acts against the Safety of Maritime Navigation, as amended by the Protocol of 2005 to the Convention for the Suppression of Unlawful Acts against the Safety of Maritime Navigation, shall also apply mutatis mutandis to the offenses set forth in articles 2, 2*bis*, and 2*ter* of this Protocol where such offenses are committed on board or against fixed platforms on the continental shelf.

2. In cases where this Protocol does not apply pursuant to paragraph 1, it nevertheless applies when the offender or alleged offender is found in the territory of a

---

[57] IMO Doc. SUA.3/Circ.11, Original contracting states for the Protocol of 2005 to the Convention for the Suppression of Unlawful Acts Against the Safety of Maritime Navigation (SUA 2005), done at London, 14 October 2005, entered into force 28 July 2010, May 4, 2010.

State party other than the State in whose internal waters or territorial sea the fixed platform is located.
3. For purposes of this Protocol, fixed platform means an artificial island, installation or structure permanently attached to the sea-bed for the purpose of exploration or exploitation of resources or for other economic purposes.

Article 2

Article 2

1. Any person commits an offense if that person unlawfully and intentionally:
    (a) seizes or exercises control over a fixed platform by force or threat thereof or any other form of intimidation; or
    (b) performs an act of violence against a person on board a fixed platform if that act is likely to endanger its safety; or
    (c) destroys a fixed platform or cause damage to it which is likely to endanger its safety; or
    (d) places or causes to be placed on a fixed platform, by any means whatsoever, a device or substance which is likely to destroy that fixed platform or likely to endanger its safety.
2. Any person who commits an offense if that person threatens, with or without condition, as is provided for under national law, aimed at compelling a physical or judicial person to do or refrain from doing any act, to commit any of the offenses set forth in paragraphs 1(b) and (c), if that threat is likely to endanger the safety of the fixed platform.

Article 2*bis*

Article 2*bis*

Any person commits an offense within the meaning of this Protocol if that person unlawfully and intentionally, when the purpose of the act, by its nature or context, is to intimidate a population, or to compel a Government or an international organization to do or to abstain from doing any act:

   (a) uses against or on a fixed platform or discharges from a fixed platform any explosive, radioactive material or BCN weapons in a manner that causes or is likely to cause death or serious injury or damage; or
   (b) discharges, from a fixed platform, oil, liquefied natural gas, or other hazardous or noxious substance, which is not covered by subparagraph (a), in such quantity or concentration that causes or is likely to cause death or serious injury or damage; or
   (c) threatens, with or without a condition, as is provided for under national law, to commit an offense set forth in subparagraph (a) or (b).

Article 2*ter*

Article 2*ter*

Any person also commits an offense within the meaning of this Protocol if that person:

(a) unlawfully and intentionally injures or kills any person in connection with the commission of any of the offenses set forth in article 2, paragraph 1 or article 2*bis*; or
(b) attempts to commit an offense set forth in article 2, paragraph 1, article 2*bis*, subparagraph (a) or (b), or subparagraph (a) of this article; or
(c) participates as an accomplice in an offense set forth in article 2, article 2*bis* or subparagraph (a) or (b) of this article; or
(d) organizes or directs others to commit an offense set forth in article 2, article 2*bis* or subparagraph (a) or (b) of this article; or
(e) contributes to the commission of one or more offenses set forth in article 2, article 2*bis* or subparagraph (a) or (b) of this article, by a group of persons acting with a common purpose, intentionally and either:
   (i) with the aim of furthering the criminal activity or criminal purpose of the group, where such activity or purpose involves the commission of an offense set forth in article 2 or 2*bis*; or
   (ii) in the knowledge of the intention of the group to commit an offense set forth in article 2 or 2*bis*.

Article 3

Article 3

1. Each State Party shall take such measures as may be necessary to establish its jurisdiction over the offenses set forth in article 2, 2*bis* and 2*ter* when the offense is committed:
   (a) against or on board a fixed platform while it is located on the continental shelf of that State; or
   (b) by a national of that State.
2. A State Party may also establish its jurisdiction over any such offense when:
   (a) it is committed by a stateless person whose habitual residence is in that State;
   (b) during its commission a national of that State is seized, threatened, injured or killed; or
   (c) it is committed in an attempt to compel that State to do or abstain from doing any act.
3. Any State Party which has established jurisdiction mentioned in paragraph 2 shall notify the Secretary-General. If such State Party subsequently rescinds that jurisdiction, it shall notify the Secretary-General.
4. Each State Party shall take such measures as may be necessary to establish its jurisdiction over the offenses set forth in articles 2, 2*bis* and 2*ter* in cases where the alleged offender is present in its territory and it does not extradite the alleged offender to any of the States Parties which have established their jurisdiction in accordance with paragraphs 1 and 2.
5. This Protocol does not exclude any criminal jurisdiction exercised in accordance with national law.

Article 4

Article 4

Nothing in this Protocol shall affect in any way the rules of international law pertaining to fixed platforms located on the continental shelf.

Article 4*bis*

Article 4*bis*
Final clauses of the Protocol

The final clauses of this Protocol shall be articles 8 to 13 of the *Protocol of 2005 to the Protocol for the Suppression of Unlawful Acts against the Safety of Fixed Platforms Located on the Continental Shelf*. References in this Protocol to States Parties shall be taken to mean references to States Parties to the 2005 Protocol.

FINAL CLAUSES

[Articles 8 to 13 of the Protocol to the Protocol of 2005 to the Protocol for the Suppression of Unlawful Acts against the Safety of Fixed Platforms Located on the Continental Shelf.]

[Note: articles 5, 6 and 7 of the Protocol of 2005 to the *Protocol for the Suppression of Unlawful Acts against the Safety of Fixed Platforms Located on the Continental Shelf* notate deletions and edits to the original 1988 Protocol and are omitted in the consolidated version presented here.]

Article 8

Article 8
Signature, ratification, acceptance and accession

1. This Protocol shall be open for signature at the Headquarters of the Organization from 14 February 2006 to 13 February 2007 and shall thereafter remain open for accession.
2. States may express their consent to be bound by this Protocol by:
    (a) signature without reservation as to ratification, acceptance or approval; or
    (b) signature subject to ratification, acceptance or approval, followed by ratification, acceptance or approval; or
    (c) accession.
3. Ratification, acceptance, approval or accession shall be effected by the deposit of an instrument to that effect with the Secretary-General.
4. Only a State which has signed the 1988 Protocol without reservation as to ratification, acceptance or approval, or has ratified, accepted, approved or acceded to the 1988 Protocol may become a Party to this Protocol.

Article 9

Article 6 of the Protocol now comprises article 9 of the SUA PROT 2005, and pertains to the entry into force of the Protocol of 2005 to the SUA Protocol of 1988.

Article 9
Entry into force

1. This Protocol shall enter into force ninety days following the date on which three States have either signed it without reservation as to ratification, acceptance or approval, or have deposited an instrument of ratification, acceptance, approval or accession with the Secretary-General. However, this Protocol shall not enter into force before the Protocol of 2005 to the Convention for the Suppression of Unlawful Acts against the Safety of Maritime Navigation has entered into force.

2. For a State which deposits an instrument of ratification, acceptance, approval or accession in respect of this Protocol after the conditions in paragraph 1 for entry into force thereof have been met, the ratification, acceptance, approval or accession shall take effect ninety days after the date of such deposit.

Article 10

Article 10
Denunciation

1. This Protocol may be denounced by any State Party at any time after the date on which this Protocol enters into force for that State.
2. Denunciation shall be effected by the deposit of an instrument of denunciation with the Secretary-General.
3. A denunciation shall take effect one year, or such longer period as may be specified in the instrument of denunciation, after the deposit of the instrument with the Secretary-General.

Article 11

Article 11
Revision and amendment

1. A conference for the purpose of revising or amending this Protocol may be convened by the Organization.
2. The Secretary-General shall convene a conference of States Parties to this Protocol for revising or amending the Protocol, at the request of one third of the States Parties, or five States Parties, whichever is the higher figure.
3. Any instrument of ratification, acceptance, approval or accession deposited after the date of entry into force of an amendment to this Protocol shall be deemed to apply to the Protocol as amended.

Article 12

Article 12
Depositary

1. This Protocol and any amendments adopted under article 11 shall be deposited with the Secretary-General.
2. The Secretary-General Shall:
   (a) inform all States which have signed this Protocol or acceded to this Protocol of:
      (i) each new signature or deposit of an instrument of ratification, acceptance, approval or accession together with the date thereof;
      (ii) the date of the entry into force of this Protocol;
      (iii) the deposit of any instrument of denunciation of this Protocol together with the date on which it is received and the date on which the denunciation takes effect;
      (iv) any communication called for by any article of this Protocol; and
   (b) transmit certified true copies of this Protocol to all States which have signed or acceded to this Protocol.
3. As soon as this Protocol enters into force, a certified true copy of the text shall be transmitted by the Secretary-General to the Secretary-General of the United Nations for registration and publication in accordance with Article 102 of the Charter of the United Nations.

Article 13

Article 13
Languages

This Protocol is established in a single original in the Arabic, Chinese, English, French, Russian and Spanish languages, each text being equally authentic.

DONE AT LONDON this fourteenth day of October two thousand and five.

IN WITNESS WHEREOF the undersigned, being duly authorized by their respective Governments for that purpose, have signed this Protocol.[58]

The 2005 Protocol to the *Protocol for the Suppression of Unlawful Acts against the Safety of Fixed Platforms Located on the Continental Shelf* (SUA PROT 2005), entered into force on July 28, 2010.[59]

Table 22.3. Original Contracting States for the Fixed Platforms Protocol of 2005

Original Contracting states for the Protocol of 2005 to the Convention for the Suppression of Unlawful Acts Against the Safety of Maritime Navigation (SUA 2005), done at London, 14 October 2005, entered into force 28 July 2010.[60]

Country	Date of signature or deposit of instrument
Dominican Republic (accession)	9 March 2010
Estonia (ratification)	16 May 2008
Fiji (accession)	21 May 2008
Latvia (accession)	16 November 2009
Liechtenstein (accession)	28 August 2009
Marshall Islands (accession)	9 May 2008
Nauru (accession)	29 April 2010
Spain (ratification)	16 April 2008
Switzerland (accession)	15 October 2008
Vanuatu (accession)	20 August 2008

---

[58] Signature pages omitted in the original published text.
[59] IMO Doc. SUA.4/Circ.10, The 2005 Protocol to the Protocol for the Suppression of Unlawful Acts against the Safety of Fixed Platforms Located on the Continental Shelf (SUA PROT 2005), May 4, 2010.
[60] IMO Doc. SUA.3/Circ.11, Original contracting states for the Protocol of 2005 to the Convention for the Suppression of Unlawful Acts Against the Safety of Maritime Navigation (SUA 2005), done at London, 14 October 2005, entered into force 28 July 2010, May 4, 2010.

TWENTY-THREE

IRREGULAR NAVAL WARFARE AND BLOCKADE

The law of naval warfare is a subset of the law of armed conflict, and it consists mostly of *jus in bello*, or the conduct of hostilities during a state of war. The law of naval warfare still reflects a great dose of customary international law, although much of it has been codified in treaty. The contemporary law of naval warfare was developed largely through customary international law from the time of the age of sail through the end of World War I, and it was largely codified by the Hague Conventions of 1907. The 1995 *San Remo Manual on International Law Applicable to Armed Conflicts at Sea*, which was developed in the aftermath of the Iran-Iraq "tanker war" of the 1980s, contains a restatement of current practice in the law of naval warfare.[1]

23.1 Irregular Naval Warfare

Before we discuss the law, it is useful to scope out the nature of the new face of irregular naval warfare, which is a function of changing tactics and doctrine and the emergence of new technologies. The combination of small, organized armed groups able to inflict devastation previously reserved only for nation-states is symptomatic of the contemporary international security system. Advances in information technology, communications, and kinetic warheads have transformed war at sea. First, perhaps the greatest change in naval warfare over the past 30 years is the revolution in precision-guided munitions (PGMs). PGMs were once

---

[1] San Remo Manual on International Law Applicable to Armed Conflicts at Sea (Louise Doswald-Beck ed., 1995) [Hereinafter San Remo Manual]. *See also*, Louise Doswald-Beck, *The San Remo Manual on International Law Applicable to Armed Conflicts at Sea*, 89 Am. J. Int'l L. 192 (1995).

considered purely an advanced and top-tier capability—the preserve of only a few of the most advanced naval forces.

Now PGMs are ubiquitous, a pervasive presence in Asia, Africa, and the Middle East—a proliferating maritime capability that even terrorist groups are acquiring. Emerging technologies and the downward curve in acquisition costs have stripped developed nations of their monopoly on higher end naval weapons. These changes have had a profound effect on maritime security. For the first time in recent memory, if not the first time in history, the maritime commons is no longer a permissive operating environment for the most powerful navies.

Second, the end of the Cold War brought a return of the historic truism that instability on land produces disorder at sea. In this regard, the present is no different than the past. During the era of the Barbary pirates, for example, the power of despots and absence of rule of law in North Africa made the entire Mediterranean Sea and part of the Atlantic Ocean a danger zone. Today, organized gangs of Somali pirates roam throughout the western Indian Ocean, threatening shipping traffic and extracting ransom booty that flows into the failed state, propping up militias. The political turbulence that emanates from parts of the developing world since the implosion of the bipolar political order in 1989 has fueled the emergence of large, well organized non-state organizations such as Hezbollah, that are able to project force far out to sea. This element represents the maritime dimension of the "return of history."[2]

The irregular or asymmetric threats emerging in the maritime domain belie the state-centered, indeed in many ways anachronistic character of the law of naval warfare. Many aspects of the law of naval warfare were codified at the Hague Conference of 1907—the first successful effort at defining in a treaty specific rules of international humanitarian law (IHL). The Hague law is supplemented by custom and state practice honed by two world wars, which cemented norms governing new technologies, including poisonous gas, effective naval mines, the submarine and torpedoes, and the atomic bomb.

Likewise, the law of naval warfare was shaped by changes in public international law after World War II. Two transformational strands of international law—entry into force of the UN Charter and entry into force of the *United Nations Convention on the Law of the Sea* (UNCLOS)—have brought further changes to how the law of naval warfare applies in practice, particularly to irregular conflicts at sea.[3] Today naval warfare most likely means hybrid conflict—set at the

---

[2] Robert Kagan, The Return of History and the End of Dreams 102–03 (2009) and Louise Oswald-Beck, *Vessels, Aircraft, and Persons Entitled to Protection During Armed Conflicts at Sea*, 1994 Brit. Y.B. Int'l L. 211.

[3] United Nations Convention on the Law of the Sea, *opened for signature* Dec. 10, 1982, UN Doc. A/CONF.62/122 (1982), 1833 U.N.T.S. 3, 397, 21 I.L.M. 1261 (1982), *entered into force* Nov. 16, 1994 [Hereinafter UNCLOS].

nexus of peacetime and armed conflict. In just over 100 years, the law of naval warfare now must account for issues entirely foreign to the Victorian world of the Royal Navy. International regulation of the marine environment, the spread of submarine cables and their renewed importance as conduits for nearly all Internet traffic, and the protected status of enemy-flagged coastal fishing vessels must be taken into account.

After 2001, the conflicts in Iraq and Afghanistan underscore the concept of irregular warfare as a regular feature of world politics. The laws and policies regarding the interface of law enforcement, conventional armed forces, and the intelligence community have given rise to vexing issues of detention, interrogation, collateral damage and targeting, and the whole realm of counterinsurgency, stability, and capacity-building operations. For the most part, these are lessons relearned, not only from the French and U.S. experiences in Indochina, but also from post-colonial wars in Africa, Latin America, the Philippines, and elsewhere. Likewise, the maritime variant of irregular warfare has posed a mortal threat to nations as different as Colombia and Sri Lanka, and it was a major focus of Israel's war with Lebanon in 2006 and *Operation Cast Lead* in Gaza. Finally, irregular maritime operations are an ongoing element of *Operation Enduring Freedom* in the Philippines, fighting insurgency[4] in the Indonesian archipelago, where pirates and ethnic groups endanger legitimate commerce, and in the South China Sea, where China uses fishing vessels and marine law enforcement in an attempt to pry away the exclusive economic zones of Vietnam, the Philippines, and Malaysia.[5]

A comparative study on irregular maritime warfare conducted by the RAND Corporation concluded that maritime operations help governments fighting insurgencies to scale and economize their ground involvement in ways that promote both military and political goals.[6] Coastal maritime interdiction, for example, can be effective at cutting the lines of supply that sustain rebellion, and deny insurgent fighters a critical sanctuary.[7] Basing forces at sea provides operational mobility while also reducing presence ashore, ameliorating political backlash among local populations.

Unlike much of warfare on land, war at sea (or in the air) mostly is fought from platforms, such as ships or aircraft, rather than by individual soldiers. Traditional naval warfare is fought from warships and is governed by conventional law of

---

[4] The U.S. maritime counter-terrorism and counter-insurgency assistance in the Philippines informed the major RAND Corp. study. MOLLY DUNIGAN, ET AL., CHARACTERIZING AND EXPLORING THE IMPLICATIONS OF MARITIME IRREGULAR WARFARE 19–34 (2012).
[5] BONNIE S. GLASER, ARMED CLASH IN THE SOUTH CHINA SEA: CONTINGENCY PLANNING MEMORANDUM NO. 14, Council on Foreign Relations, Apr. 2012 at 1–3.
[6] DUNIGAN, ET AL., CHARACTERIZING AND EXPLORING THE IMPLICATIONS OF MARITIME IRREGULAR WARFARE, at xvii–xviii.
[7] Id.

armed conflict. But having a strong navy is no longer a guarantee for maintaining sea control, and the wartime laws that applied during the First and Second World Wars no longer offer a complete rulebook for management of today's irregular, asymmetric or hybrid warfare at sea.[8]

The German invasion of Poland in 1939 was a classic violation of the proscription against armed aggression as a modality of political change. Since the end of World War II, however, such cases of clear-cut aggression have yielded to much more ambiguous conflicts, typically involving attacks by irregular forces, armed non-state groups and sundry militant and terrorist organizations against a government. The Vietnamese National Liberation Front or *Việt cộng* in Indochina, the *Fuerzas Armadas Revolucionarias de Colombia* or Revolutionary Armed Forces of Colombia (FARC) in South America, Iranian Revolutionary Guard Corps (IRGC) in the Persian Gulf, the Liberation Tigers of Tamil Eelam (LTTE) in Sri Lanka, the Party of God or Hezbollah in Lebanon and the *Ḥarakat al-Muqāwamat al-Islāmiyyah* or Islamic Resistance Movement (Hamas) in Gaza are just several of the powerful sub-state groups capable of concerted low-intensity warfare against member States of the United Nations.

Since 1979, Iran has employed guerilla and terrorist groups for operations in neighboring States and in homeland security. The Iranian Revolutionary Guard Corps, which has been preferred over the regular armed forces as a means of power projection abroad, maintains close links with groups such as Hezbollah in Lebanon. The Russian incursion into Grozny against Chechen paramilitary fighters in 1994–95, and the Slovenian, Bosnia, Serbian, and Croatian engagements in the 1990s—are all hybrid wars—and they model the sort of full-spectrum and asymmetric conflict of the future.[9] Likewise, the Israeli experience against Hezbollah does not conform to the classical guerilla war or approximate challenge by a pure conventional force. The conflict will be the archetype of a future with less clarity and more diversity on the battlefield.[10]

The term "hybrid warfare" captures the "blurring and blending of previously separate categorizations of different modes of conflict."[11] Today maritime threats surface from traditional wartime systems, such as submarines and missiles, alongside law enforcement or terrorist threats, such as booby-trapped fishing boats, suicide bombers in speedboats, and improvised explosive devices on

---

[8] GENERAL NORTON A. SCHWARTZ AND ADMIRAL JONATHAN W. GREENERT, AIR-SEA BATTLE: PROMOTING STABILITY IN AN ERA OF UNCERTAINTY, Feb. 20, 2012.

[9] STEPHEN BIDDLE AND JEFFREY A. FRIEDMAN, THE 2006 LEBANON CAMPAIGN AND THE FUTURE OF WARFARE: IMPLICATIONS FOR ARMY AND DEFENSE POLICY 74–79 (Sept. 2008).

[10] Id. at 73 and 87.

[11] F. G. Hoffman, *"Hybrid Threats": Neither Omnipotent Nor Unbeatable*, ORBIS, Summer 2010, at 441, 443. *See also*, John J. McCuen, *Hybrid Wars*, MILITARY REVIEW, April–May 2008, at 107–113, and *see generally*, DAVID KILCULLEN, ACCIDENTAL GUERILLA (2009).

garbage barges. Disguised as a husbanding agent in the port of Aden, Al Qaeda saddled up to the USS Cole in 2000 and detonated a high explosive improvised device that nearly sank the warship. Thus, hybrid threats may be defined as: "any adversary that simultaneously and adaptively employs a fused mix of conventional weapons, irregular tactics, terrorism, and criminal behavior in the battle space to obtain their political objectives."[12]

In early May 2012, for example, a drone strike in Yemen killed Sheikh Fahd al-Quso, who was connected to the bombing of the USS Cole. In retaliation, al-Qaeda in the Arabian Peninsula conducted a surprise attack on a military base in southern Yemen. The strike consisted of simultaneous coordinated attacks from the land and sea and resulted in the death of at least 20 Yemeni soldiers and another 25 taken hostage.[13]

In hybrid war, different modes of warfare, including conventional capabilities, irregular tactics and formations, terrorist acts and criminal disorder, are fused into a comprehensive approach to undermine the government. Addressing the panoply of threats within hybrid warfare at sea or irregular naval warfare requires application of the law of naval warfare, but done in deft combination with other rules derived from peacetime law of the sea and maritime law enforcement. International humanitarian law, national constitutional and statutory law, and an array of international regulations, work in combination. Thus, conventional law of naval warfare is supplemented with new legal authorities to deal with lower order threats. These bodies of law comprise a single law of irregular or hybrid naval warfare to regulate conflict that is a mixture of violence qualitatively different than that found solely during peacetime, but lower than the threshold of violence that typifies wartime.

A host of states and non-state actors are acquiring and fielding a range of sophisticated weapons designed to preclude access to the oceans and deny portions of the maritime commons to naval forces. The hallmark of hybrid naval warfare is the combination of high technology with insurgent methods. Hybrid war is illustrated most vividly by the attack on the *INS Hanit* in 2006. On July 14, 2006, Hezbollah struck the Israeli frigate *INS Hanit* with an anti-ship cruise missile, while the *Sar*-class vessel was patrolling ten miles off the coast of Lebanon.

Hezbollah fighters fired two missiles. The first missile missed the *Hanit* and struck an Egyptian freighter 37 miles out to sea. The second missile—believed to be a Chinese electro-optically guided C-701—burst into the flight deck of the 1,200-ton warship, killing four sailors and setting the ship ablaze. The ship limped into Ashdod, delivering a major propaganda coup for Hezbollah.

---

[12] Hoffman, *Hybrid Threats*, at 443.
[13] *Mujahideen attack by sea and by land, defeating three brigades of puppets in Yemen*, KAVKAZ CENTRE, May 8, 2012. (www.kavkazcenter.com is self-described as "a Chechen Internet agency which is independent, international and Islamic").

The Al Qaeda attacks against the *USS Cole* at Aden, Yemen and the oil tanker *Limburg* as it transited near the Strait of Hormuz, represent the new vulnerability of warships and commercial vessels alike. More recently, Russia developed the Club K, a system of four cruise missiles that can be hidden and launched from a standard freight container aboard a merchant ship.[14] Cruise missiles, sea mines, ballistic missiles, and even maritime improvised explosive devices, place sea power at risk, blurring the distinction between peace and war.

Hybrid rules have evolved to deal with hybrid war. Lying at the intersection of war and peace, irregular naval warfare raises a host of legal issues, much as counter-insurgency and counter-terrorism have done so for post-modern or Fourth Generation ground warfare.[15] Most importantly, what rule set (or sets) pertains to irregular naval warfare? Some of the rules and norms are familiar, whereas others are just now emerging.

The rules that apply to irregular naval warfare are a combination of peacetime and wartime norms, and the mixture of rules makes the setting more complex than law governing naval warfare of the past. The law of naval warfare is properly understood as a subset of international humanitarian law, also called the law of armed conflict, rather than being part of the international law of the sea. Supplementary rules also apply, however, including the peacetime international law of the sea, the UN Charter governing the use of force, anti-terrorist conventions, and international trafficking in arms regulations.

23.1.1 *Law of the Sea during Armed Conflict*

The peacetime rules reflected in UNCLOS continue to apply to conditions of war at sea for neutral states and in some cases, to belligerent states, but they share the stage with the law of naval warfare, which is a subset of international humanitarian law (IHL). Naval warfare may be conducted anywhere on the high seas or in the territorial sea or internal waters of an enemy state. Belligerents may not

---

[14] Thomas Harding, *A Cruise Missile in a Shipping Box on Sale to Rogue Bidders*, THE TELEGRAPH (London), Apr. 25, 2010.

[15] "Fourth Generation warfare" is a term developed by William S. Lind in 1989 to describe. *See*, William S. Lind, et al., *The Changing Face of War: Into the Fourth Generation*, MARINE CORPS GAZETTE pp. 22–26 (Oct. 1989). The First Generation of Warfare began with the Peace of Westphalia in 1648, the treaties that ended the Thirty Years War and established the state monopoly on war. The Second Generation of Warfare focused on massed firepower—artillery—and war of attrition, and was developed during World War I. Third Generation warfare broke massed firepower through maneuver, and is reflected in the German Blitzkrieg and the NATO strategy of Follow-on Forces Attack and deep strike to circumvent enemy strongholds. The Fourth Generation of warfare marks a return to pre-Westphalian fighting—a political order in which tribes, armed groups, and international networks once again challenge state-centric military forces.

conduct naval warfare in neutralized waters, such as those around Antarctica, the territorial waters of the Aäland Islands, or the waters of the Strait of Magellan. Artificial waterways, such as the Kiel and Panama canals, are regulated by treaty. The Suez Canal, for example, is to remain open to all maritime traffic in peacetime and war, except for the warships of a State at war with Egypt.

The Law of the Sea Convention, however, changed the conduct of naval warfare in three important ways, all of which curtailed the available operational space for belligerent ships and aircraft. First, the expansion of the territorial sea from three to twelve nautical miles increased the area under neutral sovereignty—barring most belligerent activity in those areas. Second, the creation of the exclusive economic zone (EEZ) imposed new duties on the part of belligerents to exercise due regard for newly-created coastal State sovereign rights and jurisdiction over the living and nonliving resources, associated artificial islands, installations, and structures, and marine scientific research and protection and preservation of the marine environment in areas previously regarded as the high seas.

Third, creation of archipelagic states—and corresponding sovereign archipelagic waters throughout vast areas of the oceans—further restricted the available space for belligerent naval operations. With UNCLOS, nearly 40 percent of the ocean surface came under some type of coastal state jurisdiction. Most of the areas over which coastal states now exercise jurisdiction once was subject only to the regime of the high seas. To a varying extent, these areas now have restrictions on freedom of action—naval mobility and maneuverability—that apply in peacetime, during periods of crisis, and time of war.[16]

Among these changes, perhaps the greatest new restriction on belligerents is the expansion of coastal state sovereignty over a larger territorial sea. Horace B. Robertson's analysis of the impact of the expanded territorial sea on the law of naval warfare in a *Naval War College Newport Paper* concludes:

> Massive expansions of waters that are denied to belligerents for hostile operations and for which neutral States have burdensome duties of surveillance and control are likely to increase beyond belligerents' power to resist the temptation to violate such waters and to overtax the capabilities of neutral States to enforce their duties within them. The result may well be increased tension between neutral and belligerent States with the consequent danger of widening the area of conflict and drawing neutral States into it.[17]

---

[16] A. L. Morgan, *The New Law of the Sea: Rethinking the Implications for Sovereign Jurisdiction and Freedom of Action*, OCEAN DEV. & INT'L L. 5, 22 (1996) (assessment of UNCLOS restrictions on freedom of action for maritime states at the expense of greater sovereignty, rights, and jurisdiction for coastal states).

[17] HORACE B. ROBERTSON, NEWPORT PAPER NO. 3: THE "NEW" LAW OF THE SEA AND THE LAW OF ARMED CONFLICT AT SEA, 41 (Oct. 1992).

Belligerents enjoy the right of transit passage through neutral straits used for international navigation or non-suspendable innocent passage in several types of straits in which that navigational regime applies.[18] During transit passage, submarines may transit undersea, and warships may steam in formation, launch and recover aircraft and other military devices, and take measures in force protection to ensure continuous and expeditious transit. Warships also enjoy the right of archipelagic sea lanes passage through designated routes or, in the alternative, all routes normally used to transit through archipelagic waters of neutral states.

Furthermore, UNCLOS massively expanded the area in which the coastal State may exercise functional rights and sovereign jurisdiction by creating the exclusive economic zone (EEZ) and recognition of the continental shelf. In accordance with Articles 58 and 87 of UNCLOS, all ships enjoy the peacetime right of freedom of navigation on the high seas and throughout the EEZ.

At the same time, however, peacetime or belligerent naval operations in the EEZ must observe due regard for the economic and resource rights of the coastal State. Consequently, a belligerent would be barred from using a fixed oil platform in the EEZ of a neutral nation to aid the war effort, although it may elect to destroy an artificial installation being used by the enemy as a base of hostile operations.

The continental shelf, that is, the seabed beneath the EEZ or its natural prolongation under parts of the high seas, may become an area of hostilities. Just as the water column of the EEZ and high seas are areas open to naval warfare, so too is the seabed beyond the territorial sea. Belligerents lawfully may affix artificial installations and devices to the seabed of the EEZ, so long as they do not unreasonably infringe upon the coastal State's exclusive sovereign rights and jurisdiction. In doing so, however, belligerents should exercise due regard to avoid damaging submarine cables and pipelines that do not exclusively serve them.[19] Belligerents also may emplace artificial installations or devices on the seabed of a neutral state so long as the installations and devices are not related

---

[18] SAN REMO MANUAL ON INTERNATIONAL LAW APPLICABLE TO ARMED CONFLICT AT SEA paras. 27–30 (Louise Doswald-Beck, ed. 1995).

[19] The actual operative term is contained in Article II of the 1884 International Convention For The Protection Of Submarine Cables (Cable Convention): "It is a punishable offense to break or injure a submarine cable, willfully or by culpable negligence, in such manner as might interrupt or obstruct telegraphic communication...." The treaty is considered customary international law and was adopted by United States and Germany, Argentine Confederation, Austria-Hungary, Belgium, Brazil, Costa Rica, Denmark, Dominican Republic, Spain, United States of Columbia, France, Great Britain, Guatemala, Greece, Italy, Turkey, Netherlands, Persia, Portugal, Romania, Russia, Salvador, Serbia, Sweden and Norway, Uruguay, and the British Colonies. It was concluded Mar. 14, 1884, *ratified* Jan. 26, 1885, *ratifications exchanged* Apr. 16, 1885, proclaimed May 22, 1885, and entered into force for the United States May 1, 1888. The United States set forth provisions of the Cable Convention at 24 Stat. 989 to 1000.

to the economic prerogatives of the coastal State and have due regard for the rights of the coastal State in the zone. That is, the exercise of belligerent rights may not unreasonably infringe upon or diminish the rights of the coastal State over artificial islands, installations, and structures that serve the sovereign rights of the coastal State to explore and exploit living and nonliving resources, and to oversee marine scientific research and marine environmental protection. Although the right to emplace non-resource related devices on the continental shelf or on the seabed below the EEZ of a coastal State is fairly read as a reflection of the customary law restated in UNCLOS, there is no doubt that many coastal States would challenge a belligerent's right to do so, particularly on the continental shelf beneath the EEZ.

23.1.2 *Combatants at Sea*

Only warships may engage in lawful belligerency. A warship must be registered in the list of national warships of the state whose flag it flies. The 1856 *Declaration of Paris* abolished privateering, and the agreement established basic rules governing the law of blockade and the capture of prizes.[20] The Declaration has entered into state practice and acquired the status of *opinio juris*, and thus is an element of customary international law of armed conflict at sea. Thus, after the abolition of privateering, only warships may participate in hostilities.

A warship is defined as a ship belonging to the armed forces of a nation bearing external markings distinguishing the character and nationality of such ships, under the command of an officer duly commissioned by the government of that nation, whose name appears in the appropriate service list of officers, and manned by a crew that is under regular armed forces discipline.[21] The rule has been further extended with the development of international humanitarian principles. Only those vessels entitled to carry arms and take part in hostilities are lawful belligerents. Thus, merchant ships may not conduct military operations or provide intelligence or support as part of naval warfare.

Naval auxiliaries are those vessels employed in non-commercial government service, such as transporting war materiel or military cargo. Although protected with sovereign immune status, auxiliaries may not take part in hostilities. Even though they are owned or operated exclusively for the military forces or government of a belligerent, auxiliaries are often manned by a civilian crew and therefore do not meet the requirements of the 1907 *Hague Convention VII*.

---

[20] *Declaration of Paris*, 1 Am. J. Int'l L. Supp. 89 (Apr. 1907), Article 1 and Charles H. Stockton, *The Declaration of Paris*, 14 Am. J. Int'l L. 356–368 (July 1920). At the outbreak of the Spanish-American War, the United States was not a party to the Declaration of Paris, but both belligerents adhered to the treaty. Frederick Pollock, *The Sources of International Law*, 2 Col. L. Rev. 511, 512 (Dec. 1902).

[21] Robert W. Tucker, The Law of War and Neutrality at Sea 39 (1957).

Just as irregular warfare and insurgency on land create confusion and debate over the status of belligerents, warfare at sea has experienced similar controversy. Over the past thirty years, for example, the irregular naval forces of the Iranian Revolutionary Guards Corps Navy (IRGCN) have maintained a low-level guerilla war in the Persian Gulf. During the 1980–88 Iran-Iraq War, the group operated against Iraq and neutral shipping in the Gulf. Since then, the IRGCN has been a powerful force that is integrated into Iranian strategic planning. The small, fast Boston whalers and rigid hull inflatable boats or "RHIBS" operated by the IRGCN have conducted strike exercises in the Persian Gulf and the approaches to the Strait of Hormuz against both warships and oil tankers of other nations.

Merchant vessels are not entitled to participate in hostilities. As civilian objects, if merchant ships enter the conflict and engage in hostilities, they lose their special protected status. The 1907 *Hague Convention VII* on the transformation of merchantmen into warships states that in order for merchant ships to be lawfully converted into warships, they should bear the external marks denoting the nationality of the nation's warships, be commanded by a naval officer, be crewed by a force under military discipline, and observe the laws and customs of war. In such case, however, the ship's civilian crew may be treated as criminals rather than as privileged combatants because they are civilians fighting on behalf of a belligerent. Enemy ships are subject to capture in time of war.

Similarly, civilian fixed installations on the enemy's continental shelf are not lawful military targets *per se*, although they may be engaged if they are being used for military purposes, or if they contribute to the enemy's war-fighting or war-sustaining capability. In 1988, for example, during *Operation Praying Mantis*, the United States attacked derelict Iranian oil platforms located on Iran's continental shelf. The platforms were being used by the IRGCN to collect intelligence and target Western warships and merchant tanker vessels transiting the Gulf.

Merchant ships have an obligation to submit to the lawful exercise of the belligerent right of visit and search. Belligerents are entitled to determine or confirm the enemy character of ships and cargoes during time of war. Merchant ships that resist or refuse to submit to the belligerent right of visit and search may be forcibly compelled.

In sum, merchant ships may be attacked during periods of armed conflict if they:

- Take part in hostilities;
- Resist the belligerent right of visit and search;
- Resist capture (if an enemy flagged ship);
- Fail to stop or divert after being ordered by a belligerent warship to do so;
- Sail under enemy convoy, escorted by warships or military aircraft of a belligerent State;
- Integrate into the enemy's war-fighting effort (or war-sustaining effort under farther-reaching U.S. doctrine);
- Serve an intelligence or communications function for enemy military forces;
- Act as an auxiliary naval vessel for enemy military forces.

During World War I, Germany considered merchant vessels that attempted to ram U-boats before or during a torpedo attack to be acting unlawfully. In some cases, the commanders of the ramming vessels were executed because they were considered unprivileged combatants. On the other hand, others regard the actions of such merchant ships as a lawful countermeasure against the practice of unrestricted submarine warfare.[22] Either way, the practice reflects disagreement over the extent that merchant ships can take measures in self-defense against belligerent attack without losing their protected status.

The fundamental rule of submarines is that they should observe the same rules as surface vessels, and this basic tenet is a feature of the 1936 *London Protocol*. On the other hand, the impracticality of the rule is self-evident. Submarines on the surface of the ocean are especially at risk of destruction by aircraft or warships. Thus, it is particularly difficult for a submarine to surface and provide a targeted merchant ship with the opportunity to surrender, when doing so will expose the submarine to defensive response. This predicament is no excuse, however, to derogate from the *London Protocol*.

The Nuremberg Tribunal stated that naval commanders are not authorized to destroy a merchant vessel on sight, even if the exercise of visit and search exposes the submarine to heightened risk or outright danger. But both the Allies and Axis powers conducted unrestricted submarine warfare during World War II. The Nuremburg Tribunal found German U-boat Admiral Doenitz not guilty of unrestricted U-boat warfare, since Germany's illegal operations were deemed to be response to the Allied policy of integrating merchant ships into the war effort. Allied merchant ships conducted military surveillance, reporting the position of German submarines to Allied naval and air forces, and in doing so, they surrendered the special protections afforded in the law of naval warfare.[23]

23.2 Quarantine

Blockade was a feature of the world wars, but its practice involved unrestricted submarine warfare, and it is often viewed as an historical artifact. Contemporary blockade is less of a strategic factor than in the past, and the use of blockade has acquired greater nuance after adoption of the *Charter of the United Nations*, and the adoption of the 1949 Geneva Conventions.

The end of the Second World War ushered in an era of persistent confrontation between democracy and communism. The bipolar period never erupted into

---

[22] L. F. Openheim, II Oppenheim's International Law: Disputes, War and Neutrality 467–68 (H. Lauterpacht ed, 7th ed., Longman, London, 1952).
[23] *The United States of America et al. v. Göring et al.* (Judgment and Sentences of the International Military Tribunal) (Nuremberg) (1 October 1946), *reprinted in* 41 Am. J. Int'l L. 172, at 303–6 (1947).

open warfare between the two superpowers, but instead it simmered throughout decades of proxy wars. During the Berlin Crisis and the Cuban Missile Crisis, political maneuvers and oblique military confrontation raised the level of tension between the two superpowers nearly to the breaking point. During this period, the United States was faced with Soviet activity in Cuba—a policy that was regarded in Washington, D.C. as the first real challenge to the 1823 Monroe Doctrine. In response, the United States used naval power in a traditional way to intercept naval shipping.

Blockade meant war, however, so the Kennedy Administration called the action a new concept in naval competition—quarantine. The term implies a non-violent, but enforced isolation in order to further a community interest, particularly in prevention of the spread of disease. Naval quarantine manages shipping and air traffic during a period of heightened tensions without resort to armed conflict. Peacetime quarantine was similar to, but more limited and less provocative than, traditional wartime blockade, and it was used only once.

23.2.1 *Cuban Missile Crisis*

On October 14, 1962, a CIA-modified U-2 spy airplane flying from Edwards Air Force Base in California conducted a high altitude mission over Cuba. The special aircraft did not encounter surface-to-air (SAM) missiles or interceptor jets over Cuba; when the aircraft landed, the pilot, Major Richard S. Heyser, described the mission as a "milk run."[24] Once the film from his onboard camera was examined, however, it became evident that medium-range ballistic nuclear missile sites were being constructed near San Cristobal.

The Soviet Union was in the process of installing nuclear missiles just 90 miles from Florida. Photographs taken by the U-2 conclusively showed the presence of intermediate-range and medium-range missiles, as well as mobile missile launchers. Sixteen of the SS-4 "Shyster" missiles were believed to be operational and could be fired within 18 hours after a decision to launch was taken. The missiles had a range of 1020 nautical miles. The threat arc included Oklahoma City, Dallas-Fort Worth, San Antonio, the Panama Canal, every capital in Central America, and the Venezuelan oil fields.[25]

On October 16, President John F. Kennedy met with his national security staff to discuss the situation. Two courses of action were presented: a U.S. air strike

---

[24] Curtis Utz, Cordon of Steel: The U.S. Navy and the Cuban Missile Crisis 18–21 (1993).

[25] Colonel John R. Wright, Jr., U.S. Army, Cuba Intelligence Memorandum, prepared for a briefing given on September 28 (material from the paper was included in the briefing given the Secretary of Defense and the Joint Chiefs of Staff on October 1), Top Secret declassified, *reprinted in* U.S. Dep't of State, Foreign Relations of the United States, 1961–1963 Vol. XI, Cuban Missile Crisis and Aftermath, Doc. 1 (Edward C. Keefer, et al. eds. 1996).

and invasion to eliminate the threat, or a naval quarantine, with the threat of further military action. Additional photos taken by a second U-2 flight on October 17 revealed several more missiles on the ground, with a total count believed to be between 16 to 32 missiles.

The next day, President Kennedy met with Soviet Foreign Minister Andrei Gromyko in Berlin. After a preliminary conference on other matters, the issue of Cuba came up. Not knowing that the United States had photographs of the missile sites, the Soviet Foreign Minister indicated that Soviet aid to Castro was purely defensive and did not pose a threat to the United States.

Without revealing the existence of the U-2 photographs, President Kennedy warned Gromyko that the "gravest consequences would follow if significant Soviet offensive weapons were introduced into Cuba."[26] A presidential memorandum summarized the meeting, and Kennedy assured Gromyko that the United States had "no intention" to invade Cuba.[27]

Meanwhile, White House advisers refined the two major courses of action in response to the missiles: military or political. Political options included whether to provide a warning to Moscow prior to military action. The two sets of questions revolved around military action and political action:

1. Military action:
   a. Limited air strike: supported by Secretary of State Dean Rusk, probably Under Secretary of State George Ball and Vice President Lyndon Johnson; favored originally by former Secretary of State Dean Acheson;[28]
   b. Full air strike: supported by Secretary of Defense Robert McNamara and Chairman of the Joint Chiefs of Staff General Maxwell Taylor (who convinced Acheson). The full air strike was Charles E. Bohlen's 2nd choice;[29]
   c. Blockade: Promoted by Bohlen and Ambassador "Tommy" Thompson[30]; probably SECDEF McNamara and CJCS General Maxwell Taylor's 2nd choice.
2. Political action—preceding military action with a letter of warning to Khrushchev?
   a. If blockade or invasion: everyone says yes;
   b. If air strike—yes: Amb. Bohlen and Amb. Thompson;
   c. If airstrike—no: CJCS Maxwell Taylor, SecDef McNamara, and presumably Acheson;

---

[26] DEP'T OF THE U.S. NAVY, REPORT ON THE NAVAL QUARANTINE OF CUBA (Chief of Naval Operations 1963).
[27] Memorandum of Conversation with Andrei Gromyko, Oct. 18, 1962, 5 p.m., *reprinted in* Id.
[28] Secretary of State Dean Acheson (Apr. 11, 1893–Oct. 12, 1971) served under President Harry Truman, and was called upon by President John F. Kennedy to be part of the ExComm during the Cuban Missile Crisis.
[29] Charles E. Bohlen (Aug. 30, 1904–Jan. 1, 1974) was a prominent U.S. diplomat and relieved George Kennan as U.S. ambassador to the Soviet Union in 1953.
[30] Llewellyn E. "Tommy" Thompson (Aug. 24, 1904–Feb. 6, 1972) was a former U.S. ambassador to the Soviet Union, preceded in that position by Charles E. Bohlen. Thompson had lived with Khruschev, and understood the Soviet leader.

d. Undecided: SecState Dean Rusk and Bohlen divided over the two approaches.
   i. Secretary of State Rusk favored limited or surgical air strikes without prior political action or warning. This course of action was opposed by 3 groups—diplomats, military, and blockade advocates. The diplomats (Bohlen, Thompson, probably Martin) insist that prior political action is essential and not harmful. The military leaders (McNamara, Taylor, McCone) insist that the air strike could not be limited.
   ii. Amb. Bohlen favored a blockade, with a prompt letter dispatched to Khrushchev. After a reply from Moscow, they would decide whether to use air strikes or conduct a blockade. All blockade advocates would support this final course of action, and some of the air strike advocate, although Taylor would oppose this, unless the decision had already been made to go the blockade route.[31]

McGeorge Bundy, Special Assistant for National Security Affairs, General Maxwell Taylor, Chairman of the Joint Chiefs of Staff, the other members of the Joint Chiefs of Staff, John McCone, the Director of the Central Intelligence Agency, and Secretary of the Treasury Douglas Dillon, all supported air strikes. The air strike option came to be known as the "Bundy Plan," and was based on the premise that an attack was necessary immediately, as it was the last chance for the United States to destroy the missiles. Bundy also emphasized that the air strike could be expanded to destroy Soviet Ilyushin IL-28 medium bombers stationed in Cuba.

The blockade option also had merit. The United States did not believe that the Soviet Union would use force to breach a blockade. There were disadvantages of imposing a blockade, however. First, it required a long time to achieve the objective. Second, a blockade would produce serious political trouble at home and could signal weakness abroad. On the other hand, a blockade was likely to cause the least trouble with U.S. allies. A surprise air attack was considered contrary to American traditions and certainly was more provocative than a blockade. Airstrikes were more likely than a blockade to escalate to general war.

Secretary McNamara also warned that "an air strike would not destroy all the missiles and launchers in Cuba, and ... [that] those missiles not destroyed could be fired from mobile launchers...."[32] An effective air strike would involve over 800 sorties, and likely produce a large number of Russian casualties. Secretary Rusk added that an air strike as a first option had no support in law or morality.

The Attorney General suggested a two pronged strategy. First, the United States would institute a blockade. If the Soviets did not react favorably to the blockade and continued to build up their missile capabilities in Cuba, the United States would conduct an air strike to destroy the missiles, the launchers, and the missile sites. Ambassador-at-Large Llewellyn Thompson agreed with this course of action, as did CIA Director McCone. This alternative plan suggested that the United States should give the Russians 72 hours to dismantle their missiles.

---

[31] REPORT ON THE NAVAL QUARANTINE OF CUBA.
[32] Id.

To avoid negative connotation from using the term "blockade," which would be construed as an act of war, Secretary Rusk recommended calling the measure "quarantine." The United States distinguished between the quarantine and the Soviet blockade of Berlin by emphasizing that U.S. action was not preventing shipments of food and medicine. The President, however, authorized the Chairman to prepare the military forces for an air strike on the missiles if necessary, as well as to have ready a force capable of conducting a military invasion of Cuba within seven days after the air strike.

By October 21, the U.S. Navy had 40 ships in position or en route to the Caribbean to implement the quarantine.[33] The Navy was tracking 27 to 30 Soviet ships that were bound for Cuba. Commander Anti-submarine Western Force, Atlantic, was ordered to position aircraft at the U.S. Naval Stations at Roosevelt Roads, Puerto Rico, and Bermuda, to enhance U.S. air surveillance over the region.[34] Simultaneously, Commander Amphibious Squadron 8 was directed to reinforce Guantanamo Bay's 8,000 personnel with an additional 5,200 marines.[35]

The Joint Chiefs of Staff issued a detailed order providing a list of prohibited items subject to the quarantine order. A concept of operations for the quarantine, including rules of engagement for conducting visit and search of ships, was developed, as well as a plan for the defense of the U.S. installations in Guantanamo Bay.[36] Interception of Soviet bloc and non-Soviet bloc ships would follow accepted international rules for boarding.

Warships would use all available communications, including international code signals, flag hoists, blinking lights, radio, and loud speakers, to hail the Russian ships. Russian linguists would be used. If the ship failed to heed the communication, the ship could utilize warning shots fired across the bow. If warning shots failed to halt the ship, then additional options could be implemented further up the escalation of force ladder. Use of force could be used to damage non-vital parts of the ship—refraining insofar as possible from inflicting personal injury or loss of life. Admiral George Anderson, the Chief of Naval Operations, estimated that it would take the Soviet Union at least 10 days to deploy surface ships to the area and 10 to 14 days to deploy submarines.[37]

Once a ship was stopped, a boarding party, which included Russian linguists, would conduct visit and search to inspect the vessel's manifest and cargo. If the ship resisted visit and search, it would be seized or destroyed. Commander,

---

[33] The force included ships assigned to Commander Task Force 136, Commander Cruiser-Destroyer Flotilla Six, Commander Destroyer Squadron 25, Commander Destroyer Squadron 16, Commander Carrier Division 18, and Commander Destroyer Squadron 24.
[34] REPORT ON THE NAVAL QUARANTINE OF CUBA.
[35] Id.
[36] Id.
[37] DEP'T OF STATE, 47 DEP'T STATE BULL. 715, 716 (1962).

Quarantine Force included Coast Guard boarding specialists, engineers, and force protection elements. If a ship were taken into custody, it would be escorted to a U.S. port, where Coast Guard units were standing by to assume control over the ship from the Navy prize master.[38]

President Kennedy informed Premier Nikita Khrushchev by letter of the impending U.S. action around Cuba and demanded that the Soviet Union immediately remove the missiles and destroy their launch sites.[39] Kennedy informed British Prime Minister Harold Macmillan, emphasizing that Soviet missiles could overwhelm the U.S. warning system, which did not face south. The short distance of the Cuban missiles to the United States compressed missile flight times that might facilitate a Soviet first strike.[40] French President Charles de Gaulle and German Chancellor Konrad Adenauer were also briefed, as were the ambassadors from NATO and other alliance partners.

At a meeting of the NSC later that day, Secretary Rusk "stated that the best legal basis for our blockade action was the Rio Treaty" and that "[t]he use of force would be justified on the ground of support for the principles of the UN Charter, not on the basis of Article 51, which might give the Russians an excuse for attacking Turkey."[41] Bobby Kennedy also emphasized the importance of getting the Organization of American States (OAS) support for the U.S. action.

In a telecast on October 22, President Kennedy declared a quarantine would be imposed, and the situation would be brought before the OAS and the United Nations. One hour before the televised speech, Secretary Rusk notified the Soviet Ambassador to the United States, Anatoly Dobrynin, of the contents of the President's speech.

The following day, in reply, Khrushchev accused the United States of violating the UN Charter and international norms of freedom of navigation on the high seas. The United States, he charged, did not have a right to inspect foreign-flag shipping in international waters. Khrushchev reaffirmed that the Soviet weapons in Cuba were purely defensive in nature and urged the President to renounce his decision or risk catastrophic consequences for world peace:

---

[38] Id.
[39] Letter From President Kennedy to Chairman Khrushchev, Oct. 22, 1962, Dep't of State *reprinted in* FOREIGN RELATIONS OF THE UNITED STATES, 1961–1963, VOLUME VI, KENNEDY-KHRUSHCHEV EXCHANGES, Document 60, pp. 165–66 (Charles s. Sampson, ed. 1996) and DEP'T OF STATE BULL., Nov. 19, 1973, pp. 635–636.
[40] Id.
[41] Id. Inter-American Treaty of Reciprocal Assistance (Rio Treaty), signed at Ri de Janeiro, Sept. 2, 1947, *entered into force* Dec. 3, 1948, 43 AM. J. INT'L L. 53 (1949). The Rio Treaty was ratified by all 21 American republics. Under the terms of the treaty, an armed attack or threat of aggression against any signatory nation is considered an attack against all. *See*, Article 31.

I must say frankly that measures indicated in your statement constitute a serious threat to peace and to the security of nations... [and violate] international norms of freedom of navigation on the high seas.... The United Nations Charter and international norms give no right to any state to institute in international waters the inspection of vessels bound for the shores of the Republic of Cuba.[42]

The OAS Council adopted a resolution by a vote of 19 to 0 (with one abstention),[43] which called for the "immediate dismantling and withdrawal from Cuba of all missiles and other weapons with any offensive capability...." Furthermore, the OAS resolution recommended that member states "take all measures, individually and collectively, including the use of armed force, which they may deem necessary, to ensure that Cuba cannot continue to receive military armaments and related supplies, which may threaten the peace and security of the Continent, and to prevent the missiles in Cuba with offensive capability from ever becoming an active threat to the peace and security of the Continent...." A draft resolution was introduced at the UN Security Council, which called for the immediate dismantlement and removal of offensive missiles from Cuba.[44]

Citing OAS support, President Kennedy issued the Proclamation of Interdiction on the evening of October 23, to take effect the following morning:

...

WHEREAS by a Joint Resolution passed by the Congress of the United States and approved on October 3, 1962, it was declared that the United States is determined to prevent by whatever means may be necessary, including the use of arms, the Marxist-Leninist regime in Cuba from extending, by force or the threat of force, its aggressive or subversive activities to any part of this hemisphere....

...

NOW, THEREFORE, I, JOHN F, KENNEDY... in accordance with the aforementioned resolutions... proclaim that the forces under my command are ordered... [beginning] October 24, 1962, to interdict... the delivery of offensive weapons and associated materiel to Cuba.

...the following are declared to be prohibited materiel: ... Surface-to-surface missiles; bomber aircraft; bombs, air-to-surface rockets and guided missiles; warheads for any of the above weapons....

...

Any vessel or craft which may be proceeding toward Cuba may be intercepted and may be directed to identify itself, its cargo, equipment and stores and its ports of call, to stop, to lie to, to submit to visit and search, or to proceed as directed. Any vessel

---

[42] Chairman Khrushchev Letter to President Kennedy, Oct. 23, 1962 (Department of State Division of Language Services (Translation), LS NO. 45989, T-85/T-94, *reprinted in* FOREIGN RELATIONS OF THE UNITED STATES, 1961–1963, VOLUME VI, KENNEDY-KHRUSHCHEV EXCHANGES, Document 61, pp. 166–67 (Charles S. Sampson, ed. 1996).

[43] The Uruguayan delegate abstained on the 23rd because he had not received instructions from his Government on how to vote. On October 24, however, Uruguay cast an affirmative vote making approval of the resolution unanimous.

[44] S/5182, United States of America: Draft Resolution, Oct. 22, 1962.

> or craft which fails or refuses to respond to or comply with directions shall be subject to being taken into custody. Any vessel or craft which it is believed is en route to Cuba and may be carrying prohibited materiel or may itself constitute such materiel shall, wherever possible, be directed to proceed to another destination of its own choice and shall be taken into custody if it fails or refuses to obey such directions. All vessels or craft taken into custody shall be sent into a port of the United States for appropriate disposition.
>
> ...[F]orce shall not be used except in case of failure or refusal to comply with directions, ... after reasonable efforts have been made to communicate them to the vessel or craft, or in case of self-defense. In any case, force shall be used only to the extent necessary.[45]

Chairman Khrushchev sent correspondence to President Kennedy challenging the legality of the quarantine and the OAS resolution.

> ...[Q]uarantine may be established, according to accepted international practice, only by agreement of states between themselves, and not by some third party. Quarantines exist, for example, on agricultural goods and products.
>
> ...
>
> Reference to the decision of the Organization of American States cannot in any way substantiate the demands now advanced by the United States. This Organization has absolutely no authority or basis for adopting decisions such as the one you speak of in your letter. Therefore, we do not recognize these decisions. International law exists and universally recognized norms of conduct exist. We firmly adhere to the principles of international law and observe strictly the norms which regulate navigation on the high seas, in international waters....
>
> ...[T]he violation of the freedom to use international waters and international air space is an act of aggression, which pushes mankind toward the abyss of a nuclear-missile war. Therefore, the Soviet Government cannot instruct the captains of Soviet vessels bound for Cuba to observe the orders of American naval forces blockading that Island. Our instructions to Soviet mariners are to observe strictly the universally accepted norms of navigation in international waters and not to retreat one step from them.... Naturally we will not simply be bystanders with regard to piratical acts by American ships on the high seas. We will then be forced on our part to take the measures we consider necessary and adequate in order to protect our rights....[46]

Commander in Chief, Atlantic established a surface warship quarantine line, which was held by 12 destroyers from Task Force 136. The flotilla patrolled on an arc 500 miles from Cape Maysi, out of range of Soviet IL-28 bombers based in Cuba. Orders were issued to prepare to intercept any ship that crossed the quarantine line bound for Cuba. By October 25, 16 Soviet ships that were en route

---

[45] Pres. Proc. Interdiction of the Delivery of Offensive Weapons to Cuba by the President of the United States of America, Oct. 23, 1962.
[46] Letter From Chairman Khrushchev to President Kennedy, Oct. 24, 1962, *reprinted in* FOREIGN RELATIONS OF THE UNITED STATES, 1961–1963, VOLUME VI, KENNEDY-KHRUSHCHEV EXCHANGES, Document 63, pp. 169–170 (Charles S. Sampson, ed. 1996).

to Cuba had reversed or altered course to avoid the quarantine area. Another 15 vessels, however, remained on their course toward Cuba.

The first interception operation occurred in the early morning hours of the 25th after the USS *Essex* made contact with the M/V *Bucharest*, a Russian ship bound from the Black Sea for Cuba. The interception was conducted with the utmost professionalism and, after *Essex* determined that the *Bucharest* was loaded with petroleum and was not carrying prohibited items, the Soviet tanker was allowed to continue on its course to Cuba.

23.2.2 *Legality of Quarantine*

The USS *Pierce* and USS *Joseph P. Kennedy* stopped and boarded a Lebanese cargo ship, M/V *Marucla*, in the early morning of October 26. After inspecting the ship's papers and confirming that the ship was carrying a cargo of sulphur, asbestos, news-print, emery paper, lathes, automotive parts, and 12 trucks, the *Marucla* was released and allowed to proceed to Havana. Three more Russian merchant ships headed for Cuba—the *Vishnevsky*, the *Okhotsk* and the *Sergev Botkin*—reversed course and returned to their ports of departure. Photographic evidence, however, revealed that construction of the missile sites had been accelerated, and Soviet IL-28 bomber aircraft were being uncrated at Cuban airfields.

Subsequently, the Soviet Union demanded removal of U.S. Jupiter missiles from Turkey in exchange for the withdrawal of Soviet strategic missiles in Cuba.[47] On October 27, the President ultimate decided that removal of the Jupiter missiles would be part of the overall bargain. Later that night, Robert Kennedy met secretly with Ambassador Dobrynin and reached a basic understanding. The Soviet Union would withdraw the missiles from Cuba under United Nations supervision in exchange for an American pledge not to invade Cuba. Under a separate agreement to remain secret for 25 years, the United States would remove the Jupiter missiles from Turkey. Khrushchev accepted the terms in a letter to the President signed on October 28.[48]

The aftermath of the crisis produced discussion among international law scholars concerning the legality of the U.S. quarantine. Writing in the *American Journal of International Law*, Quincy Wright concluded that it was "difficult" to find that the Soviet Union had violated any duty in international law by shipping missiles to Cuba, and installing them less than 100 miles from the United States.[49]

---

[47] Letter From Chairman Khrushchev to President Kennedy, Oct. 27, 1962, Dep't of State Div. Language Serv. (Trans.) LS NO. 46236 T-94/T-24, *reprinted in* FOREIGN RELATIONS OF THE UNITED STATES, 1961–1963, VOLUME VI, KENNEDY-KHRUSHCHEV EXCHANGES, Document 66, pp. 178–81 (Charles S. Sampson, ed. 1996).

[48] Letter From Chairman Khrushchev to President Kennedy, Oct. 28, 1962, *reprinted in* FOREIGN RELATIONS OF THE UNITED STATES, 1961–1963, VOLUME VI, KENNEDY-KHRUSHCHEV EXCHANGES, Document 68, pp. 183–87 (Charles S. Sampson, ed. 1996).

[49] Quincy Wright, *The Cuban Quarantine*, 57 AM. J. INT'L L. 546, 548–49 (July 1963).

The missiles could not be considered a "threat of force" or "threat to peace" under Articles 2(4) or 39 of the UN Charter, Wright stated. He suggested that generally, "defensive" displays of armament do not constitute a "threat of force," "so long as they remained on the high seas or on the state's own territory, unless there was some evidence of an immediate intention to use them for attack."[50] Because the United States already had invaded Cuba at the Bay of Pigs and continued to apply economic sanctions against the island nation, there appeared justification for accepting Soviet missiles to deter attack and ensure self-defense.[51] "In principle, a sovereign state is free to take, within its territory, measures which it deems necessary for its defense...."[52]

On the other hand, the deceptive program to install the missiles, which included Soviet denials, and the inherently offensive character of the weapons systems, were certain to offend the traditional U.S. policy enounced by the 1823 Monroe Doctrine.[53] The deception and denials by Soviet officials inured against the weapons being defensive in nature. The Monroe Doctrine is political, rather than legal in character, however, and cannot legally bind the U.S.S.R.

The maritime interception measures declared on October 22, 1962, were justified as a quarantine, rather than a blockade. Akin to a "pacific blockade," it might be argued that quarantine constitutes a "peaceful method" for settling disputes under Article 2(3) of the UN Charter.[54] Similarly, like the British and French invasion of Egypt during the Suez Crisis of 1956, the United States also might argue that the quarantine was not a violation of Article 2(4) because it was not directed against the territorial integrity or political independence of any state, nor contrary to the purpose of the United Nations.[55] Wright suggests, however, that the quarantine fails on this account because the threat of military forces against a state's vessels on the high seas to "induce its government to change its policy or to abandon its rights," constitutes a *per se* violation of Article 2(4).[56]

Finally, both the Rio Treaty and Article 51 of the UN Charter, permit measures for individual and collective self-defense. Thus, Quincy Wright concludes that quarantine, "in addition to being a non-peaceful means forbidden by Article 2(3),

---

[50] Id., at 549.
[51] Id., at 549–50.
[52] Id., at 550.
[53] Id. Secretary Dean Rusk testified before the Senate Foreign Relations Committee on September 17, 1962, that the Monroe Doctrine was "altered, perhaps both by circumstance and by agreement [such as the Rio Treaty, but was] still an elementary part of our whole national security interests." Id. (citing Senate Hrgs.).
[54] Wright, *The Cuban Quarantine*, at 553. President Franklin D. Roosevelt used the same argument in his Chicago Bridge speech in 1937 to outline possible responses to Japanese aggression against China. Id., at note 32.
[55] Id., at 553–54, and note 38.
[56] Id., at 557.

was a 'threat of force' forbidden by Article 2(4)...."[57] In extenuation, Wright also notes, however, that few ships were actually boarded, and no force was used by U.S. warships.[58] The quarantine was lifted on November 21, 1962, even though Cuba had violated it, since Castro refused to permit UN inspectors into Cuba.

The United States asserts that the quarantine of Cuba was designed as a self-defense measure of limited scope, authorized by the OAS as a lawful action under Chapter VIII of the *Charter of the United Nations*, and implemented utilizing the minimum force required to achieve its purpose, while at the same time preserving navigational rights and freedoms for the international community.[59] Great efforts were taken by the Administration to distinguish the quarantine from a traditional wartime blockade. The U.S. Navy's *Commander's Handbook on the Law of Naval Operations* recognizes quarantine as a legitimate peacetime military action that can be distinguished from a true blockade, in that:

1. Quarantine is a measured response to a threat to national security or an international crisis; blockade is an act of war against an identified belligerent;
2. The goal of quarantine is de-escalation and return to the *status quo ante* or other stabilizing arrangement; the goal of a blockade is denial and degradation of an enemy's capability with the ultimate end-state being capitulation in armed conflict;
3. Quarantine is selective in proportional response to the perceived threat; blockade requires impartial application to all nations—discrimination by a blockading belligerent renders the blockade legally invalid.[60]

The *Maritime Operational Zones Manual*, also published by the U.S. Naval War College, suggests the following factors should be taken into consideration before implementing quarantine measures to stabilize an international crisis:

1. The existence of an international crisis (a destabilizing departure from the security *status quo*) or extreme threat to the nation, allies, or regional security.
2. The assertion of the state's right to:
   a. act in individual or collective self-defense in response to the threat; or
   b. act pursuant to a collective security agreement in the absence of UN action or as an alternative to ineffective action; or
   c. act anticipatorily in response to an unacceptable risk to security interests (necessity).
3. An order by the President, Secretary of Defense, or responsible combatant commander (most likely in the United States to be directed by the President).
4. Notice to the international community of the actions to be taken and areas where forces would establish the zone of control (Notice to Mariners or Special Warning).

---

[57] Id., at 558 and 562.
[58] Id., at 562.
[59] John M. Raymond, *Legal Implications of the Cuban Crisis*, 3 SANTA CLARA LAWYER 126, 128–132 (1963).
[60] DEP'T OF THE NAVY, COMMANDER'S HANDBOOK ON THE LAW OF NAVAL OPERATIONS, Naval Warfare Publication 1–14M, July 2007.

5. Creation of mission-specific rules of engagement (ROE), which:
    a. Identify hostile forces or objects of attack;
    b. Identify actions considered hostile; and
    c. Establish effective warning procedures.[61]

23.3 Cordon Sanitaire

A *cordon sanitaire* is a French phrase that means a "sanitary cordon" that is similar to quarantine in that it is a self-defense measure by a state to stabilize a crisis situation at a tactical level. Although the term originally meant a buffer zone to prevent the spread of disease, it is used as a metaphor in international law and politics to refer to a separation between two states or groups in order to maintain stability. The term was reportedly first used in this context in March 1918 by French prime minister Georges Clemenceau to describe the newly independent states that seceded from the Russian Empire and Soviet Russia after World War I.[62] With Poland as the linchpin, the states between Germany and Russia served as a *cordon sanitaire* or firewall, protecting Europe from the spread of Bolshevism. The U.S. Naval War College *Maritime Operational Zones Manual*, for example, defines *cordon sanitaire* as an area "in which the presence of units of a potential enemy would be considered a hostile act, making such units subject to military action."[63]

In the 1960s, the U.S. Navy considered the concept as a possible measure to counter Soviet Auxiliary General Intelligence (AGI) spy ships (referred to as "tattletales"), but it was not implemented. During the Cold War, Soviet AGIs routinely shadowed U.S. carrier battle groups. The "tattletales" had the ability to provide the Soviet forces with real time targeting data that could be used to carry out a pre-emptive strike against U.S. aircraft carriers during the initial stage of conflict. Recognizing that the AGIs posed a threat to aircraft carrier battle groups, the Navy explored the possibility of establishing a *cordon sanitaire* around carriers.

The Naval War College compilation, *Maritime Operational Zones Manual*, describes *cordon sanitaire* as a self-defense mechanism "…established as a response to deteriorating conditions between potential political or military adversaries…. [C]ordon sanitaire requires the complete removal of all designated hostile forces within the zone but permits the presence of neutrals and friendly forces." *Cordon sanitaire* is a tactical measure to protect high value units in crisis situations where the inherent right of individual or collective self-defense exists.

---

[61] Dep't of the Navy, Maritime Operational Zones Ch. 3 (Richard Jacques ed. U.S. Naval War College, International Law Department, Center for Naval Warfare Studies 2006) [Hereinafter Maritime Operational Zones].
[62] *See generally,* Lyman William Priest, The Cordon Sanitaire: 1918–1922 at Ch. V (1954).
[63] Maritime Operational Zones, Ch. 3.

It is selectively applied in order to minimize interference with internationally recognized freedoms of navigation and overflight during times of peace.

Although the concept of *cordon sanitaire* was never implemented by the United States during the Cold War, a similar concept, the "defensive bubble," was established in the 1980s to protect U.S. ships and aircraft operating in the Persian Gulf. In January 1984, U.S. Central Command issued a notice to airmen (NOTAM) requesting aircraft operating at less than 2,000 feet above-ground-level (AGL) that had not been cleared for approach or departure to or from a regional airport to avoid approaching closer than five nautical miles to U.S. naval forces. The NOTAM additionally requested that aircraft approaching within five nautical miles establish and maintain radio contact with U.S. naval forces and warned that aircraft operating within five nautical miles at altitudes less than 2,000 AGL whose intentions were unclear could be subject to U.S. self-defense measures.

The combined U.S. Central Command and U.S. Pacific Command NOTAM made clear, however, that it was not intended to interfere with internationally recognized freedoms of navigation and overflight of any nation.

> A. US Naval forces operating in international waters within the Persian Gulf, Strait of Hormuz, and the Gulf of Oman are taking additional defensive precautions against terrorist threats. Aircraft at altitudes less than 2000 feet AGL, which are not cleared for approach/departure to or from a regional airport are requested to avoid approaching closer than five nautical miles to US Naval forces. It is also request that aircraft approaching within five nautical miles establish and maintain radio contact... aircraft which approach within five nautical miles at altitudes less than 2000 feet AGL whose intentions are unclear to US Naval forces may be held at risk by US defensive measures.
> B. This notice is published solely to advise that hazardous operations are being conducted on an unscheduled basis; it does not affect the freedom of navigation of any individual or state.[64]

A similar notice to mariners (NOTMAR) was promulgated the following day to warn surface ships and subsurface craft to avoid closing on U.S. forces closer than five nautical miles without first identifying themselves and maintaining radio contact:

> A. US Naval forces operating in international waters within the Persian Gulf, Strait of Hormuz, and the Gulf of Oman and the Arabian Sea north of twenty degrees North are taking additional defensive precautions against terrorist threats. All surface and subsurface ships and craft are requested to avoid closing US forces closer than five nautical miles without previously identifying themselves. US forces, especially when operating in confined waters, shall remain mindful of navigational consideration of ships and craft in their immediate vicinity. It is request that radio contact with US Naval forces be maintained on Channel 16... when approaching within

---

[64] COMMANDER IN CHIEF, U.S. CENTRAL COMMAND, USCINCCENT MACDILL MSG Subject: NOTAM for Persian Gulf, Strait of Hormuz, Gulf of Oman, and North Arabian Sea, 202222Z JAN 84 (Jan. 20, 1984, at 2222 "Zulu" time). Id., Appendix C.

five nautical miles of US Naval forces. Surface and subsurface ships and craft that close US Naval forces within five nautical miles without making prior contact and/ or whose intentions are unclear to such forces may be held at risk by US defensive measures.

B. These measures will also apply when US forces are engage in transit passage through the Strait of Hormuz or when in innocent passage through foreign territorial waters and when operating in such waters with the approval of the coastal state.

C. ...The measures will be implemented in a manner that does not impede the freedom of navigation of any vessel or state.[65]

23.4 Neutrality and Maritime Blockade

The law of neutrality and blockade—a subset of the law of armed conflict that has major implications for war at sea—is a fulcrum of the law of naval warfare. The law of naval warfare helps to regulate relations between neutral states and belligerent states, and the law of blockade is an important element of IHL.[66] Consequently, in some circumstances the law of blockade and the complementary provision for the belligerent right of visit and search provide fidelity to the peacetime framework of navigational freedom during periods of armed conflict.[67]

The *Charter of the United Nations* includes the concept of naval blockade as a legitimate instrument for the use of force by the UN Security Council. Importantly, the concept of blockade in the Charter appears in Article 42 (military sanctions) rather than in Article 41 (economic sanction). Likewise, scholars and practitioners in naval warfare similarly have accepted blockade as a legal mechanism during armed conflict. For example, article 97 of the 1993 *San Remo Manual of International Law Applicable to Armed Conflicts at Sea* also accepts blockade as a lawful tool of naval warfare.[68]

23.4.1 *Blockade in History*

The roots of legal blockade date to the early modern period of the Westphalian state system. From the 15th to the 18th centuries, belligerent powers frequently

---

[65] DMAHTC WASHINGTON DC MSG Subject HYDROPAC 78/84 (62) Persian Gulf, Strait of Hormuz, and Gulf of Oman, 210100Z JAN 84 (Jan. 21, 0100 "Zulu" time), at Id.

[66] Helsinki Principles on the Law of Maritime Neutrality, adopted by the International law Association, Taipei, Taiwan, May 30, 1998, Helsinki Principles on the Law of Maritime Neutrality, 68 Int'l L. Assoc. Conf. Rep. 497 (1998), *reprinted in* The Laws of Armed Conflicts: A collection of Conventions, Resolutions and Other Documents, Doc. 115, at pp. 1425–1430 para. 1.3 (Dietrich Schindler & Jiri Toman eds., 2004).

[67] L. Oppenheim, International Law 768–769 (Vol. II, H. Lauterpacht ed., 7th ed. 1969).

[68] San Remo Manual, para. 97.

would grant letters of *marque* to private ships authorizing them to conduct hostilities at sea against enemy-flagged commerce. Blockade became a routine belligerent practice in European conflicts. The *Consolato del Mare*, for example, regulated maritime practice throughout the middle ages, and it contained provisions that permitted private enemy vessels and private enemy property to be seized and appropriated by licensed privateers. Merchant ships and goods disassociated from a conflict were considered inviolate.

During the 17th and 18th centuries, sovereignties commonly declared blockades against enemy ports, often without the warships to enforce them. But the difficulty of blockading long coastlines soon gave rise to the "paper blockade," in which a nation might declare a blockade, but lack the naval force to effectively maintain it. The early Dutch blockades of England (1662) and France (1672–73) and the Dutch-English blockade against France (1689) were regarded as paper blockades.[69] Likewise, the Napoleonic wars that pitted France against Great Britain from 1793 to 1815 included a continental decree issued by Paris on November 21, 1806, with the goal of closing off Europe to British goods. The project proved too ambitious, however, and it was not well enforced. The practice of paper blockades inspired the *Agreement among Armed Neutralities* in 1778 and 1800 that amplified the rule that blockades must be physically effective in order to be legally binding.[70]

British and French navies blockaded Russia during the Crimean War from 1854–1856 in order to coerce Moscow to abandon its aspirations in Turkey. The Treaty of Paris ended the Crimean War on March 30, 1856. Soon after, however, on April 16, 1856, at the urging of Count Walewski, the French representative to the peace negotiations, the plenipotentiaries also signed the *Paris Declaration Respecting Maritime Law* (Paris Declaration).[71] The "effectiveness" criterion entered into the law as a requirement in paragraph 4 of the 1856 Paris Declaration.

In the open salvo of the Spanish-American War on April 21, 1898, Secretary of the Navy John Long directed U.S. warships of the North Atlantic Squadron to blockade Cuba to wrest control of the island from Madrid. Spain was ill prepared to defend its possession, and within days the island was locked in a vice grip.[72] Blockade also was an enduring feature of the First and Second World Wars. With

---

[69] MICHAEL N. SCHMITT ESSAYS ON LAW AND WAR AT THE FAULT LINES 220–222 (2012).
[70] NATALINO RONZITTI, THE LAW OF NAVAL WARFARE: A COLLECTION OF AGREEMENTS AND DOCUMENTS WITH COMMENTARIES 66 (1988).
[71] Id., 64–65. *See also, Declaration of Paris, reprinted in* 1 AM. J. INT'L L. SUPP. 89–90 (1907) and Charles H. Stockton, *The Declaration of Paris*, 14 AM. J. INT'L L. 356–368 (July 1920).
[72] Mark L. Hayes, *The Naval Blockade of Cuba during the Spanish-American War, in* NAVAL BLOCKADES AND SEAPOWER: STRATEGIES AND COUNTER-STRATEGIES, 1805–2005 80–90 at 81–85 (Bruce A. Elleman and S. C. M. Paine eds., 2006).

the Orders-in-Council of March 11, 1915, London instituted a blockade "to prevent vessels carrying goods for or coming from Germany." Britain also blockaded the Russian port of Petrograd on October 10, 1919, as part of their intervention in the Russian revolution. In the case of the Petrograd blockade, the British government acted even though it was uncertain whether a "state of war" existed between the two nations—a precedent for emplacement of a blockade against unfriendly adversaries even in time of peace.[73]

Blockade was employed as a method of war by Axis and Allied powers during World War II, and naval blockades devastated the economies of Nazi Germany and Imperial Japan. Following the two world wars, war zones and exclusion zones have been justified by belligerents "as reasonable...measures to contain the geographic area of the conflict or to keep neutral shipping at a safe distance from areas of actual or potential hostilities."[74] The establishment of such zones does not, however, create a free fire zone or relieve belligerents of the legal obligation under the law of armed conflict to attack only lawful military targets. In other words, a protected platform, such as a civilian passenger liner, may not be engaged simply because it enters a declared zone of blockade.

In the 1950s, the French Navy blockaded Algeria during its struggle with the rebellious colony. The United States conducted naval blockades during the Korean War[75] and the Vietnam War (Haiphong Harbor), and Moscow protested the latter as interference with freedom of navigation.[76] The act of initiating a blockade is tantamount to war, and it is one of the enumerated acts of aggression that appear in the consensus Definition of Aggression adopted by the UN General Assembly on December 14, 1974.[77]

Iran and Iraq blockaded each other's ports during their war in the 1980s, with Tehran's order of October 1, 1980, initiating a tit-for-tat tanker war that endangered oil shipping. Iran boarded 1,200 foreign-flagged merchant ships during the early-1980s, and that figure includes U.S.-flagged vessels. Tehran boarded the ships in a manner that for the most part was professional. On the other hand, Iran covertly laid mines in the shipping channels of the Gulf and launched numerous cruise missiles, conducted aviation and small boat attacks against civil neutral

---

[73] JAMES CABLE, GUNBOAT DIPLOMACY 1919–1979 at 70 (1981).
[74] NWP 1–14M/MCWP 5–12.1/COMDTPUB P5800.7A, THE COMMANDER'S HANDBOOK ON THE LAW OF NAVAL OPERATIONS, July 2007, para. 7.9.
[75] Blockade during the Korean War is discussed in RUSSELL F. WEIGLEY, THE AMERICAN WAY OF WAR: A HISTORY OF UNITED STATES MILITARY STRATEGY AND POLICY 388–389 (1973).
[76] MYRES S. MCDOUGAL AND FLORENTINO P. FELICIANO, LAW AND MINIMUM WORLD PUBLIC ORDER: THE LEGAL REGULATION OF INTERNATIONAL COERCION 493–495 (1961) and F. B. Swayze, *Traditional Principles of Blockade in Modern Practice: united States Mining of Internal and territorial Waters of North Vietnam*, 29 JAG J.143 (1977).
[77] UNGA Res. 3314, Dec. 14, 1974, Article 3(c).

shipping, and on numerous occasions abrogated its responsibilities under the law of armed conflict.

Although much of the law of naval warfare is rather antiquated, the law surrounding naval blockades still has currency. Following the 1980–1988 Iran-Iraq War, the International Law Association (ILA) formed a Committee on Maritime Neutrality to consider the rules affecting neutral ships, which had suffered heavily during the conflict. Throughout the war, the UN Security Council called on states to respect the right of neutral shipping to freedom of navigation, but often with little effect.[78] In order to strengthen recognition of these rights, the law of blockade was reflected in the *Helsinki Principles on the Law of Maritime Neutrality*, which were adopted by the ILA at its Taipei Conference on May 20, 1998.

During the NATO intervention against the Federal Republic of Yugoslavia in 1999, the United States proposed the blockade of the port of Bar, but the idea was not endorsed by France and Italy, as they deemed it would have required authorization by the UN Security Council. In 2006, Israel blockaded the coast of Lebanon as part of its war against Hezbollah. Blockade is an example of asymmetric warfare in that it is not easy to enforce a blockade against a powerful adversary, with the blockading force running the risk of being exposed to missile fire and air strikes from the coastal State.

23.4.2 Law of Blockade

Maritime blockade may be analogized to land-based siege warfare. The law concerning siege on land, and by implication naval blockade, implicate the principles of distinction and proportionality. Consequently, siege and blockade often give rise to criticism that the measures are inconsistent with the duty of belligerents to protect civilian populations.

The contemporary conception of the international law of blockade emerged from a lack of consensus over the customary international law of prize, which was to be applied by an International Prize Court established by *Hague Convention XII* of 1907.[79] In an effort to clarify the customary law relative to prize, ten powers met at a conference in London beginning on December 4, 1908 to determine and codify the rules.[80] The negotiators produced the 1909 *London Declaration Concerning the Laws of Naval War* (the London Declaration). The London Declaration contains 21 provisions concerning Blockade in Time of War.[81] States

---

[78] S/RES/540 (1983), S/RES/552 (1984), S/RES/582 (1986), and S/RES/598 (1987).
[79] International Prize Court, Hague Convention XII (1907), *reprinted in* THE LAWS OF ARMED CONFLICTS: A COLLECTION OF CONVENTIONS, RESOLUTIONS AND OTHER DOCUMENTS, Doc. 81 (Dietrich Schindler and Jiri Toman eds., 2004).
[80] Austria-Hungary, France, Germany, Great Britain, Italy, Japan, Netherlands, Russia, Spain and the United States participated in the conference.
[81] Naval Conference of London, Declaration Concerning the Laws of Naval Warfare, *signed at London* Feb. 26, 1909, *reprinted in* THE LAWS OF ARMED CONFLICTS: A

never ratified the Declaration, but it is accepted as an expression of the customary international law of blockade.

23.4.2.1 Object of Blockade

The object of the blockade must be to prohibit war-sustaining goods. Blockades aimed at starving the civilian population of the blockaded coast are forbidden, which is a stricter standard than siege, which may not be aimed "solely" at the starvation of the civilian population.[82]

23.4.2.2 Geographic Scope

It is incumbent upon a nation conducting an effective blockade to employ "force sufficient really to prevent access to the enemy coastline."[83] The date of beginning, the duration of the blockade and the specific geographic boundaries must be published to the international community. Although a blockade is declared within a defined area, it may be applied virtually worldwide outside of the territorial seas of neutral states. The prohibition against visit and search in neutral territorial waters also applies in archipelagic sea lanes of neutral states and straits used for international navigation that are overlapped by the territorial seas of a neutral state.

Blockade also may not bar access to neutral coastlines or ports.[84] Furthermore, blockade must be applied against ships of all nations in a manner that is impartial, and the belligerent may not discriminate among nations in the enforcement of the blockade.[85] The 1909 London Declaration preserved the rule that, in order to be lawful, a blockade must be effective. Neutral vessels must be given a reasonable period of advance warning so as to avoid the blockade, typically between two and 30 days. Failure to provide safe passage from a blockaded coast before initiation of a blockade renders the declaration unlawful.[86] Merchant vessels in breach of blockade may be captured and adjudicated as a prize.

COLLECTION OF CONVENTIONS, RESOLUTIONS AND OTHER DOCUMENTS, Doc. 83, at pp. 1111–1122 (Dietrich Schindler & Jiri Toman eds., 2004).

[82] Article 54 (1), Geneva Additional Protocol I (1977) and Article 33, Geneva Convention IV. The more permissive scope of the law of siege, however, has not aged well. With the growth in international humanitarian law since World War II, a siege that had starvation of civilians as one of its goals would be unlawful.

[83] London Declaration, Article 2.

[84] Id., Article 18.

[85] Id., Article 5.

[86] Id., Article 10.

23.4.2.3 Absolute and Conditional Contraband

Classic blockade does not target any specific cargo, but rather constitutes a total exclusion of transit into and out of the area or location.[87] The original categories of contraband and free goods set forth in the 1909 London Declaration are obsolete. Belligerents today tend to compile very broad contraband lists. Since naval blockade is imposed for security purposes and not to punish the civilian population, humanitarian material must be separated from contraband. The blockading force may prescribe technical enforcement arrangements, including visit and search, under which the passage is permitted, in order to ensure that no aid inures to the benefit of enemy armed forces.

Contraband includes goods destined for the enemy, while goods coming from enemy territory and destined for neutral States cannot be considered contraband, otherwise the right of neutrals to trade with belligerents would be undermined. The doctrine according to which goods destined for a neutral country may be captured since they produce revenues that contribute to the war effort is controversial, giving rise to the "war fighting" or "war sustaining" dichotomy.

The London Declaration distinguishes between absolute contraband, conditional contraband, and goods, which should not be considered contraband, such as free goods. Weapons, ammunition and other items of military utility constitute "absolute contraband," and may be seized.[88] Other goods and material, such as medicine and religious objects, constitute "free goods" and may not be seized as contraband.[89] Clothing, bedding, and essential foodstuffs and means of shelter for the civilian population generally are considered free goods, provided "there is not serious reason to believe that such goods will be diverted to other purpose," or accrue a "definite military advantage" to the enemy.[90]

Some scholars retain a third category of "conditional goods," which are those goods that are considered contraband under the circumstances of the conflict. Even though not patently military goods, conditional goods are susceptible to being used for a military purpose. In order to consider enumerated conditional goods as contraband, the blockading state must designate them on a published list.[91] For example, building materials such as concrete and steel beams have both civilian and belligerent uses, as they may be used to build homes or underground bunkers. Fuel oil is also considered conditional contraband. Legally, however, the "war-sustaining" element of blockade is actually quite minimal. Geneva Convention IV, for example, states that blockade must allow "free passage of all

---

[87] Michael N. Schmitt, Blockade Law: Research Design and Sources at 3 (1991).
[88] London Declaration, Article 22.
[89] Article 38, GC II and article 23(1), 59 and 61, GC IV. *See also*, San Remo Manual, para. 150.
[90] GC III and Article 59, GC IV. *See also*, San Remo Manual, para. 150.
[91] San Remo Manual, para. 149.

consignments of foodstuffs, clothing and tonics intended for children under fifteen, expectant mothers, and maternity cases," and then only on condition that there be "no reason for fearing...that a definite advantage may accrue to the military efforts or economy of the enemy."[92]

23.4.2.4 Belligerent Right of Visit and Search

Belligerents may enforce blockade against an enemy coastline or port through the belligerent right of visit and search. The right of visit and search is the means by which a belligerent warship or military aircraft may enforce a blockade against an enemy for the purpose of inspecting commercial shipping in order to ascertain the enemy character of the ship and its cargo. This rule reflects a wartime right and a lawful basis for compliant, noncompliant or opposed boarding of foreign-flagged merchant ships at sea.

Visit and search is the process whereby a warship summons to a neutral ship to lie to, using the international flag signal (SN or SQ)[93] or firing a blank charge, in order that the warship may determine the enemy character and destination of the ship or its cargo.[94] The summoned neutral merchant ship is required to stop and display her colors and submit to boarding and inspection of the vessel. As a wartime right, visit and search is entirely separate and distinct from other lawful bases for boarding foreign-flagged ships at sea, including self-defense, authorization by the UN Security Council, boarding as a condition of port entry or boarding under authority of flag State consent via direct permission, procedures exercised under a bilateral or multilateral maritime security agreement or, in the view of the United States and other States, the consent of the Master of the vessel.

Belligerent right of visit and search in time of war is an entirely different concept than the peacetime right of approach and visit under article 110 of UNCLOS. Whereas the right of approach is intended to authorize all States to assert jurisdiction over vessels suspected of piracy, slave trafficking, illegal broadcast, or that are stateless, the belligerent right of visit and search is used to determine the enemy character of cargoes and ships. Visit and search may be conducted on the high seas, in any nation's EEZ, and in the territorial sea of a belligerent (but not a neutral) state. These rules makes logical sense, because if a blockading belligerent were forbidden from conducting visit and search in enforcement of a blockade in international waters, then the only place that such activity could occur would be within 12 nautical miles of the shoreline of the enemy—inside the enemy's territorial sea. This interpretation would require an impossibly large force lay

---

[92] GC IV, Article 23.
[93] International maritime signal flags for "SN" are as follows: "S" is a white flag with a blue square in the center; "N" is a blue and white checkerboard pattern. "Q" is a solid yellow flag.
[94] Helsinki Principles, para. 5.2.1.

down to cover a coastline of any size, as well as compel the blockading belligerent naval force to operate exposed in dangerous littoral waters to try to enforce a blockade under the nose of visual coastal surveillance and vulnerable land-based attack. In this case, operational prerogatives of naval forces have shaped the law of blockade, and provide illustration of the balance in the law of naval warfare between permissive rules that license belligerent conduct even while other provisions ameliorate the effects on the civilian population.

If a shipboarding visit to enforce blockade cannot be carried out on the high seas or in belligerent waters, the vessel should be diverted to a belligerent port and submitted for adjudication by a prize tribunal. The neutral prize may be destroyed rather than diverted, however, if diversion would constitutes a danger to the warship. The prize may be destroyed in such case only after the passengers and crew have been made safe.

The *Commander's Handbook on the Law of Naval Operations*, a manual published by the U.S. Navy, Coast Guard and Marine Corps, reflects U.S. practice on the law of blockade.[95] The *Commander's Handbook* indicates "[a]ttempted breach of blockade occurs from the time a vessel or aircraft leaves a port or airfield with the intention of evading the blockade.... It is immaterial that the vessel or aircraft is at the time of interception bound for neutral territory, if its ultimate destination is the blockaded area."[96] Yoram Dinstein and Wolff Heintschel von Heinegg agree that neutral merchant ships outside neutral waters are subject to visit and search by belligerent warships in order to determine the enemy character of the cargo and vessel, unless such ships are traveling under convoy of neutral warships.[97]

23.4.2.5 Attempted Breach

The blockading state enjoys the belligerent right to capture and condemn neutral or enemy merchant vessels and cargo as prize if they constitute contraband, attempt to breach a blockade, if ships are fraudulently documented, they operate under the control of the enemy, they transport enemy troops or they violate regulations in the immediate area of naval operations.[98] Neutral ships also may be attacked if they engage in belligerent acts on behalf of the enemy or are assimilated into the enemy's intelligence system, such as merchant ships that report the movement of belligerent ships or aid the enemy in targeting of belligerent

---

[95] Declaration concerning the Laws of Naval War, 208 Consol. T.S. 338 (1909).
[96] COMMANDER'S HANDBOOK ON THE LAW OF NAVAL OPERATIONS, at para. 7.7.4.
[97] YORAM DINSTEIN, THE CONDUCT OF HOSTILITIES UNDER THE LAW OF INTERNATIONAL ARMED CONFLICT 217 (2004). *See also*, W. Heintschel von Heinegg, *Visit, Search, Diversion and Capture in Naval Warfare, Part I: The Traditional Law*, 29 CAN. Y. B. INT'L L. 283, 299 (1991) and *Part II Developments Since 1945*, 30 CAN. Y. B. INT'L L 89, 115 (1992).
[98] SAN REMO MANUAL, 212–216 paras. 141–148.

ships.[99] A merchant vessel also may be attacked if it "otherwise makes an effective contribution to the enemy's military action."

A warship may direct the neutral merchant to a belligerent port to conduct a shore-side inspection of the ship and cargo. If passengers leave the ship, they are not to be regarded as prisoners of war, but instead should be repatriated as quickly as feasible. The officers and crews of captured neutral merchant vessels who are nationals of a neutral nation do not become prisoners of war and must be repatriated "as soon as circumstances reasonably permit."[100] The U.S. Navy has issued additional guidance to its forces to conduct visit and for search, boarding and salvage, and prize crew bill, including a checklist of information that the boarding officer should obtain, such as the enemy character of the vessel, the ports of departure and destination, nature of cargo, manner of employment, and crew list and other information.[101]

Ordinarily, merchant ships are warned by belligerents so that they may re-route or off-load belligerent cargo. If neutral flagged merchant ships ignore the warning, the Helsinki Principles set forth that:

> Merchant ships flying the flag of a neutral State may be attacked if they are believed on reasonable grounds to be carrying contraband or breaching a blockade, and after prior warning they intentionally and clearly refuse to stop, or intentionally and clearly resist visit, search, capture or diversion.[102]

The 1999 *Model Manual of the Law of Armed Conflict for Armed Forces*, published by the International Committee of the Red Cross (ICRC) indicates "Merchant vessels believed on reasonable ground to be breaching a blockade may be captured and those which, after prior warning, clearly resist capture may be attacked."[103] Similarly, the neutral merchant vessels that attempt to breach a blockade or resist attempts to conduct visit and search may be treated as enemy ships.[104] Thus, failure of a neutral ship to submit to visit and search is an assumption of risk for damage or loss of the ship. Naval forces that conduct visit and search may use force to compel compliance, including deadly force that leads to personal injury or death, and destruction of the vessel.

---

[99] Helsinki Principles, para., 5.1.2(4).
[100] *Commander's Handbook on the Law of Naval Operations*, para. 7.10.2.
[101] Normally, the following papers will be examined: the certificate of national registry, crew list, passenger list, logbook, bill of health clearances, charter party (if chartered), invoices or manifests of cargo, bills of lading, and on occasion, a consular declaration or other certificate of non-contraband carriage certifying the innocence of the cargo. *See*, OPNAVINST 3120.32C CH-6, May 26, 2005, para. 630.23.
[102] Helsinki Principles, para., 5.1.2(3) and London Declaration, Article 20.
[103] INTERNATIONAL COMMITTEE OF THE RED CROSS, MODEL MANUAL OF THE LAW OF ARMED CONFLICT FOR ARMED FORCES, Rule 1710.4 (1999).
[104] DEP'T OF THE NAVY, COMMANDER'S HANDBOOK ON THE LAW OF NAVAL OPERATIONS (NWP 1–14M), (U.S. Navy, U.S. Coast Guard and U.S. Marine Corps doctrine publication), para. 7.5.2.

23.4.3 Law of Neutrality

Belligerents engaged in armed conflict are not entitled to disrupt the commerce and friendly relations among neutral States. Warfare may not be conducted in neutral waters, which encompass internal waters, territorial waters, and archipelagic waters of neutral States. The contiguous zone and the exclusive economic zone of all States are considered high seas for the purposes of navigation and other internationally lawful uses of the sea, and thus they are lawful areas for belligerent operations.

Neutral States are inviolable and their land territory, airspace, internal waters and territorial seas may not be used to wage naval warfare or used as a sanctuary by belligerent armed forces. Belligerents may conduct naval operations in neutral territorial seas, however, if enemy forces are using them as a sanctuary or to launch attacks. To retain their inviolable status, neutral States have an affirmative duty to prevent belligerent warships from violating their neutral waters. If a belligerent State conducts operations in neutral waters, the neutral State must take steps, including the use of force, to stop the violation.[105] Neutral States also must enforce their rights without discriminating among flag States.[106]

Neutral nations can condition, restrict, or prohibit belligerent warships from entering their internal waters and territorial sea and archipelagic waters.[107] Belligerent warships may exercise innocent passage in the territorial sea of a neutral State, but they may not extend passage for more than 24 hours, unless delayed due to ship damage or harsh weather.[108] Belligerent warships may be permitted to remain for a period of no more than 24 hours in the internal waters, ports, roadsteads, or territorial waters of a neutral power. Neutral States may permit belligerent warships within their internal waters and their territorial sea to transit the territorial sea[109] and replenish food, water, and fuel on board a warship in order to reach a friendly port, but not to repair damage to combat systems or enhance its fighting ability.[110] During World War II, for example, the German pocket battleship *Graf Spee* was damaged in battle and permitted to make repairs to become seaworthy, but not to restore or increase its fighting strength.[111]

Enemy merchant vessels may be captured as a prize, after adjudication by a prize tribunal. This adjudication stage is deemed necessary, even though the current edition of the UK Manual states the contrary and affirms that captured

---

[105] San Remo Manual, para. 22.
[106] Id., para. 19.
[107] Convention concerning the Rights and Duties of Neutral Powers in Naval War, Articles, 1–2 (1907 Hague Convention XIII), Oct. 18 1907, *entered into force* Jan. 26, 1910, 1 Bevans 723. *See also*, Helsinki Principles, para. 1.4 and San Remo Manual, para. 15.
[108] 1907 Hague Convention XIII, Articles 9 and 12; Helsinki Principles para. 2.2, and San Remo Manual, para. 21.
[109] 1907 Hague Convention XIII, Article 10.
[110] Id., Article 19.
[111] Id., Article 17.

enemy vessels automatically become the property of Her Majesty's government. Neutral goods on enemy merchant ships may be seized if they constitute contraband of war. Commander and crew are entitled to prisoners of war status unless a more favorable treatment is accorded. Neutral ships in a neutral convoy are exempt from visit, unless the convoy commander allows it on the request of the belligerent. However, the right of convoy, which is admitted by the 1909 London Declaration, is not recognized by all maritime powers, for instance, the UK.

23.5   Blockade in Non-International Armed Conflict

23.5.1   U.S. Civil War

During the U.S. Civil War, the Union conducted a strangling blockade against the Confederacy. The Northern blockade was initiated only days after the war with the South began. At 0430 on April 12, 1861, 43 Confederate guns situated in a ring around Fort Sumter in Charleston Harbor began a bombardment that thrust America into its bloodiest war ever. President Lincoln declared a blockade against Confederate ports seven days later—on April 19, 1861.[112] The blockade was the most ambitious undertaken by any nation, stretching 3,549 miles along a complex coastal zone featuring of 180 bays, rivers and harbors.[113]

The rather novel application of the law of blockade against one's own nation required all of the legal and political skills of the president and Secretary of State William H. Seward. Because of the dismal condition of the U.S. Navy, the blockade served more to put foreign nations on notice not to conduct maritime trade with the South than to actually stop all traffic in and out of the Confederacy. The paucity of Union naval forces and the challenges posed by the extensive coastline called into question the effectiveness of the blockade. Of the 1,300 attempts to break the blockade, 1,000 of were successful.[114]

The Union argued that the Confederate States of America did not form a legitimate sovereign, but rather should be characterized as an insurrection.[115] At the same time, however, the Union boarded and captured Southern merchant ships

---

[112] Proclamation of President Abraham Lincoln, Apr. 19 1861, V Official Records of the Union and Confederate Navies in the War of Rebellion at 620 (Richard Rush et al. eds., Ser. I, 27 vols, 1903).

[113] To make matters worse, nearly one-quarter of U.S. naval officers resigned their commissions and offered their services to the Confederacy. Civil War Desk Reference 547 (Margaret E. Wagner, Gary W. Gallagher & Paul Finkelman eds., 2002).

[114] Id., at 548.

[115] Greater than a riot, which is a "minor disturbance of the peace...perpetrated by a mob," an insurrection was regarded as an "organized armed uprising which seriously threatens the stability of government and endangers social order." There is no recognition of belligerency, and combatants have no immunity for their actions on the field of battle. Insurrection was distinguished from rebellion, which was regarded as

in international waters. The Confederate commercial ships protested their capture, arguing that since war can only be conducted between two or more sovereign nations, the Union blockade of the South was unlawful. Initially, European states also questioned the legality of the blockade, echoing the concerns of the Confederacy that Union action was an unlawful impairment of the right of all nations to exercise freedom of the seas during peacetime. *British Law Officers* stated:

> For the United States to demand the exercise of these belligerent rights, and at the same time to refuse a belligerent status to the enemy was plainly contradictory. In truth the position is as novel and unsound in international law and clearly propounded for the first time for the obvious purpose of giving the United States the advantage of being exclusively recognized by the Neutral State as Belligerent.[116]

Over time, neutral European states began to comply out of practical reasons with the terms of the blockade, submitting their merchant ships to inspection by Union naval forces. At the same time, however, the Europeans argued that acceptance of the belligerent right of the Union to impose a blockade against the South also triggered for the Confederacy enjoyment of the entire menu of belligerent rights in time of war. The Confederacy was entitled to formal belligerent status, which would have the effect of converting a non-international armed conflict (NIAC) into an international armed conflict (IAC).

In addition to the dilemma posed in the law of armed conflict, there was a related constitutional problem. Blockade is an act of belligerency, yet it was Congress that held the power to declare war. Finessing this point, Lincoln's proclamation included a savings clause, making the blockade operative only "until Congress shall have assembled and deliberated" on the issue, thereby giving the legislative branch the ultimate authority over whether to maintain the blockade. Eventually, Congress approved the blockade, but that still left the complaint of the English and other neutral nations and the status of the Confederacy as a lawful belligerency.

> According to English reasoning, although Lincoln proclaimed the rebels to be insurrectionists and thus not recognizable under international law as a belligerent power engaged in war, his declared blockade was an act of war, which would have to be conducted against a sovereign state. Thus, Lincoln had actually granted belligerency status to the Confederacy and thereby forced foreign powers to do the same. By proclaiming neutrality, England afforded the Confederacy the status of a belligerent power.[117]

---

a less extensive form of conflict. JAMES RANDALL, CONSTITUTIONAL PROBLEMS UNDER LINCOLN 59–60 (1926).

[116] F.O. 83,2225, *reproduced in* Herbert A. SMITH, LAW OF NATIONS, 309–310 (1932).

[117] Abraham Lincoln: American President; An Online Reference Source, Miller Center of Public Affairs, University of Virginia, http://millercenter.org.

The English position—that the blockade converted a NIAC into an IAC—came to be validated by the U.S. Supreme Court. In the 1863 *Prize Cases*, the Court held that a state of armed conflict existed between the North and the South, even though the Confederacy was not a sovereign state.[118] Owners of seized Confederate merchant vessels sought to have the court recognize that only an insurrection existed between the North and the South, and therefore seizure of their private property was invalid. The Court rejected this argument, however, and held that whether a state of war existed, as opposed to a state of insurrection, was determined by the magnitude of the violence attendant to the conflict and not by the language contained in formal declarations.[119] The Northern blockade and the subsequent British proclamation of neutrality meant that there existed a war between two belligerents. Therefore the law of blockade applied to the conflict, and President Lincoln's blockade strategy was upheld as lawful.[120]

Washington's interest was to deny the Confederacy status as a belligerent, because doing so opened the door to a host of belligerent rights and privileges that the South would enjoy. As a belligerent party, the naval forces of the Confederacy stood to benefit from safe harbor, secure credit and contract for warships and other weapons from neutral states. The English Parliament could take up the merits of more active or formal intervention in the war in support of the South. These issues were only the tip of the iceberg, as belligerent status implicated almost every aspect of the conflict, including:

> ... [t]he treatment of captured "insurgents" as criminals instead of prisoners of war; the possible punishment of such "insurgents" as traitors, and the confiscation of their property; the use of the municipal power over the territory claimed by the insurgents when such territory should be captured; the legality of Confederate captures at sea, and the disposition to be made of the crews of Confederate warships and privateers.[121]

Inevitably, some hybridization of the conflict slowly evolved. Throughout the war, for example, the Union government often afforded Confederate forces belligerent status, particularly when they were captured while in uniform, even though the South was never formally recognized as a belligerent party. On the other hand, captured Southern privateers were hanged as pirates early in the war. The death penalty was imposed on the crews and officers of Confederate naval vessels and privateers operating under letters of *marque* issued by the Confederate government, in strict accord with Lincoln's blockade proclamation. Later, however, the

---

[118] *The Prize Cases*, 67 U.S. 635, 2 Black 635, 17 L 459, 477 (1863).
[119] Id., at 670.
[120] Leslie C. Green, The Contemporary Law of Armed Conflict 303 (1993).
[121] James Randall, Constitutional Problems under Lincoln 59–60 (1926).

Union changed this practice as it found it impolitic to punish Confederate sailors as pirates.[122]

23.5.2 *Spanish Civil War*

The concept of blockade was a feature of the interwar period. On March 8, 1936, the United Kingdom, France, Italy and Germany established a four-power Non-Intervention Patrol to prevent outside involvement in the Spanish Civil War. The Patrol maintained a blockade of the Spanish coastline, with France and Great Britain participating in the Patrol after Italy and Germany dropped out.[123] Spanish Nationalists proclaimed a blockade of Republican ports on November 17, 1936. The Nationalists announced that they would attack international shipping bound for these ports. The blockade was somewhat effective.

On December 3, 1936, Britain (really the only major nation genuinely neutral in the conflict) prohibited the export of arms to Spain in British-flagged vessels. Meanwhile, Stalin was supplying war materiel to the Spanish Republic, and the Soviet merchant freighter *Komsomol* was the first Soviet ship to transport armored battle tanks, armored cars and artillery into the country. Eighty-four Soviet ships were stopped and searched by Spanish Nationalists from October 1936 to April 1937. The *Canarias*, the flagship of the Nationalist Navy, intercepted and sank the *Komsomol* on December 14, 1936.[124] For their part, the Republican forces seized the German vessel *Palos*, which was bound for Nationalist Spain.

23.5.3 *Israel's Blockade of Gaza*

As a creature of the law of naval warfare, the contemporary law of blockade applies *a priori* to international armed conflicts (IACs). Common article 2 of the Geneva Conventions of 1949 states that IAC occurs when one or more states engage in armed conflict with another state, regardless of the intensity of the combat or even in the absence of hostilities. The Geneva Conventions are applicable to IACs involving "two or more High Contracting Parties, even if a state of war is not recognized by one of them." No formal declaration of war is required.

Common article 2 also applies in cases of military occupation. Some consider Gaza as occupied by Israel; but it is not. There are no Israeli troops in Gaza, which is a self-governing enclave cut from the Middle East. The Gaza Strip could be considered part of Egypt, which inherited governance of the area from the British Ottoman protectorate. But Egypt does not want it. An argument could be made that the territory is "constructively occupied" by virtue of the blockade, but this is

---

[122] Id., at 65–66.
[123] Hugh Thomas, The Spanish Civil War 715 (2001).
[124] Id., at 432 and 555.

rather circular, since the entire analysis is being conducted to determine whether Israel may conduct such a blockade.[125]

Article 1(4) of Additional Protocol I of 1977 extends the definition of IAC to include wars of national liberation—armed conflicts in which peoples are fighting against colonial domination, alien occupation or racist regimes in the exercise of their right to self-determination.

Whatever it is, the Gaza Strip is not a traditional *de jure* state, raising the question of whether the conflict between Israel and Gaza is not an IAC, but rather a "non-international armed conflict" (NIAC). Traditionally, a struggle between two states constitutes IAC, whereas a conflict between a state and non-state entity, such as an insurgency of a terrorist network, constitutes NIAC. The distinction is important because different rule sets apply to IACs and NIACs, and there is some debate as to whether blockade is available as a lawful measure in NIACs.

NIACs are fought between governmental forces and non-state armed groups, or among such groups only. Common article 3 applies to "armed conflicts not of an international character occurring in the territory of one of the High Contracting Parties." To further complicate matters, international humanitarian law recognizes a distinction between NIACs within the ambit of common Article 3 of the Geneva Conventions of 1949 and NIACs within the definition set forth in Article 1(4) of Additional Protocol II of 1977. The ICRC suggests that the requirement that the armed conflict occur in the territory of one of the High Contracting Parties has lost its importance in contemporary state practice since the Geneva law is universally accepted, and a conflict "has to but take place on the territory of one of the Parties to the Convention."[126]

Hamas is a non-state group formed in 1987 as the Palestinian branch of the Muslim Brotherhood. The group aims to establish an Islamic Palestinian state in the place of the State of Israel on the land of the former British mandate of Palestine. The U.S. Department of State has designated Hamas an international terrorist organization, but the group enjoys widespread support and sympathy throughout Gaza, strengthened by a network of social, religious and political patronage. Hamas opposes the 1993 Oslo peace process. The military forces of Hamas are called the *Izz-al-Din al-Qassam* Brigades, and they are responsible for thousands of missile strikes and hundreds of suicide bombings and terrorist attacks inside Israel and the West Bank.

The conflict between Israel and Hamas stretches back two decades, but it accelerated after the Hamas victory and the legislative elections of 2006 and the subsequent withholding of donor funds and closure of the Gaza strip in 2007. In

---

[125] We thank Eugene Kontorovich, Associate Professor of Law, Northwestern University Law School, for this observation.

[126] *How is the Term 'Armed Conflict' Defined in International Humanitarian Law?* INTERNATIONAL COMMITTEE OF THE RED CROSS OPINION PAPER 3 (ICRC, Mar. 2008).

June 2007, Hamas violently seized control of Gaza, and Israel promptly declared Gaza "hostile territory." Israel restricted and tightly controlled the movement of goods into and out of Gaza in order to turn back a wave of terrorists emanating from the territory.[127] On September 19, 2007, Israel issued a communiqué that stated:

> Hamas is a terrorist organization that has taken control of the Gaza Strip and turned it into hostile territory. This organization engages in hostile activity against the State of Israel and its citizens and bears responsibility for this activity....
>
> Additional sanctions will be placed on the Hamas regime in order to restrict the passage of various goods to the Gaza Strip and reduce the supply of fuel and electricity. Restrictions will also be placed on the movement of people to and from the Gaza Strip. The sanctions will be enacted following a legal examination, while taking into account both the humanitarian aspects relevant to the Gaza Strip and the intention to avoid a humanitarian crisis.[128]

In response to a large increase in the number and frequency of missile attacks into Israel from Gaza throughout 2008, on December 27 the Israeli Air Force launched *Operation Cast Lead*. The Israeli Security Cabinet's designation of Gaza as "hostile territory" is a factual (rather than a legal) determination, since Hamas is "an organization dedicated to the destruction of the State of Israel."[129] Israeli ground troops entered Gaza just days later—on January 3, 2009—the same day the naval blockade was established. The blockade boundaries were superimposed on the 20 nautical mile Gaza maritime zone.[130] The purpose of the naval blockade is to prevent Hamas from resupplying rockets and other weapons and to stop the infiltration of terrorists into Gaza. The IDF and Hamas were engaged in battle for nearly three weeks, and on January 21, 2009, Israeli forces withdrew from the Gaza territory. The naval blockade persisted and foreign vessels were barred from the Gaza offshore area. Vessels delivering humanitarian supplies to the civilian population were permitted to do so through the land crossings, subject to prior coordination with Israel and inspection of the cargoes.

The Oslo Accords recognize that the Palestinian Authority (PA) may exercise jurisdiction over the territorial waters off Gaza.[131] Israel, however, was granted the right to maintain external security of the Gaza Strip until such time as there

---

[127] Prime Minister Ehud Olmert, Communique of the State of Israel (Communicated by the Prime Minister's Media Adviser) Security Cabinet Declares Gaza Hostile Territory, Sept. 19, 2007.

[128] Id.

[129] Behind the Headlines: Israel Designates Gaza a "Hostile Territory," Israel Ministry of Foreign Affairs, Sept. 24, 2007.

[130] State of Israel Ministry of Transport and Road Safety, Notice to Mariners No. 1/2009 Blockade of the Gaza Strip, Jan. 6, 2009.

[131] Gaza-Jericho Agreement, Article 5, para. 1(a).

was a final status agreement.[132] Under the *Gaza-Jericho Agreement*, the PA was excluded from exercising functional authority for external security.[133] The Agreement also states, "Israel shall continue to carry the responsibility...for defense against external threats from the sea and from the air...and will have all the powers to take the steps necessary to meet this responsibility."[134]

In order to maintain coastal security, three maritime zones were established off Gaza. A central zone extends seaward from the beach to a distance of twenty nautical miles from the coastline. Along the north and south marine border of the central zone are strips of water adjacent to Egyptian and Israeli territorial seas and measuring one nautical mile in width. The two strips constitute military security areas and are under Israeli authority. The central zone is jointly managed by the government of Israel and the Palestinian Authority, and is open for fishing throughout the zone and for recreational boating out to a distance of three nautical miles from shore. Foreign shipping is not permitted to approach closer than 20 nautical miles from the coastline.

In May 2010, a flotilla of civilian ships registered in various flag States left Turkey filled with humanitarian supplies, apparently to challenge the blockade. The ships began to arrive at the specified maritime gathering point south of Cyprus on Friday, May 28. The largest vessel, the Comoros-flagged passenger ship *Mavi Marmara*, had 561 persons on board. Israeli naval forces boarded the large passenger liner on May 30, 2010, arousing one of the most interesting contemporary controversies regarding the law of irregular naval warfare.[135]

Israel's maritime interdiction of the "freedom flotilla" was designated *Operation Sea Breeze*. The *Mavi Marmara* was interdicted in the eastern Mediterranean Sea by Israeli commandoes, who rappelled vertically onto the top deck of the ship from a helicopter. The boarding incident and ensuing melee that unfolded on the deck of the ship left several Israeli military members seriously injured and resulted in the death of nine Turkish nationals. Seven Israeli soldiers were injured, two of them critically.

The boarding ignited a firestorm of debate in international humanitarian law and appears to have irreparably damaged Turkish-Israeli foreign relations. The nature of the tactical operation that unfolded on board the ship and the reaction of the vessel's passengers are bitterly disputed, inseparable from who used what force and when. The greatest legal wrinkle in the case of *Operation Sea Breeze* is whether the law of naval warfare applies in the struggle between Israel and Gaza.

---

[132] Id., at Article 5, para. 3.
[133] Id., at Article 5(1)(b).
[134] Id., at Article 8.
[135] Report of the international fact-finding mission to investigate violations of international law, including international humanitarian and human rights law, resulting from the Israeli attacks on the flotilla of ships carrying humanitarian assistance, UN Doc. A/HRC/15/21, Sept. 27, 2010, at 53.

Nearly everyone agrees that there exists some level of armed conflict between the state of Israel and Hamas, the armed group governing the Gaza Strip. What is less clear are the legal implications of the relationship between Israel and Hamas, mostly not because of a disagreement with the facts, which are rather minor, but rather disputes about the law that should apply. Is Israel in an armed struggle with only Hamas or at war with the Gaza Strip? Is the Gaza Strip a foreign area (or country) physically or constructively occupied by Israeli forces? Are standards for the use of force derived from international human rights law or international humanitarian law?

A report on the incident produced by the Human Rights Council, for example, concluded that the Israeli interception resulted in "...a series of violations of international law, including international humanitarian and human rights law...."[136] The Israeli Defence Force (IDF) concluded an inquiry on July 12, 2010, which found that the only way the IDF could have stopped the *Mavi Marmara* was to board the ship and that the commandoes acted properly.[137]

The Israeli-Gaza conflict does not fit squarely within the definition of IAC because Gaza is not a state, nor within the ambit of a NIAC because the conflict does not take place only in the territory of a High Contracting Party—namely, Israel. Gaza is not a High Contracting Party. Some scholars have tried to solve this dilemma by suggesting that the reference to common Article 3 to conflicts "occurring in the territory of one of the High Contracting Parties," and in Article I of Protocol II, to conflicts, "which take place in the territory of a High Contracting Party," are not geographic limitations, but simply recount that treaties apply only to their State parties. The argument is made that if the limitations excluded conflicts that spread over the territory of several states, there would be a gap in NIAC protection.

If the Gaza conflict constitutes IAC, then the law of blockade applies. If, however, the conflict is really only a NIAC, the application of the law of blockade is less clear. In some cases, it appears the rules governing conduct during armed conflict at sea apply in both IAC and NIAC, so the two bodies of law overlap. For example, the U.S. Civil War is a case study of blockade being used in a NIAC. One could question, however, whether there exists a right of blockade beyond the territorial sea during NIAC. It is not clear why parties to a NIAC should be entitled to interfere with foreign-flagged vessels and aircraft beyond the territorial sea. At the same time, it is just as murky why foreign-flagged, purportedly neutral merchant ships, should be immune from the belligerent right of visit and search in international waters while fomenting insurrection as part of a NIAC. Gaza is not a nation, but Gaza and Israel certainly are engaged in a war-like struggle.

---

[136] Id.
[137] Maj. Gen. (Res.) Eiland Submits Conclusions of Military Examination Team Regarding Mavi Marmara, July 12, 2010, Israeli Defense Force Blog, July 12, 2010.

Appendix 1: Agreement on the Gaza Strip and Jericho Area

Article XI, Annex I, Maritime Activity Zones (Map No. 6), Agreement on the Gaza Strip and the Jericho Area, Declaration of Principles on Interim Self-Government Arrangements [Declaration of Principles (DOP)], Sept. 13, 1993

1. Maritime Activity Zones
   a. Extent of Maritime Activity Zones
   The sea off the coast of the Gaza Strip will be divided into three Maritime Activity Zones, K, L, and M as shown on map No. 6 attached to this Agreement, and as detailed below:
   1. Zones K and M
      a. Zone K extends to 20 nautical miles in the sea from the coast in the northern part of the sea of Gaza and 1.5 nautical miles wide southwards.
      b. Zone M extends to 20 nautical miles in the sea from the coast, and one (1) nautical mile wide from the Egyptian waters.
      c. Subject to the provisions of this paragraph, Zones K and M will be closed areas, in which navigation will be restricted to activity of the Israel Navy.
   2. Zone L
      a. Zone L bounded to the south by Zone M and to the north by Zone K extends 20 nautical miles into the sea from the coast.
      b. Zone L will be open for fishing, recreation and economic activities, in accordance with the following provisions:
         i. Fishing boats will not exit Zone L into the open sea and may have engines of up to a limit of 25 HP for outboard motors and up to a maximum speed of 15 knots for inboard motors. The boats will neither carry weapons nor ammunition nor will they fish with the use of explosives.
         ii. Recreational boats will be permitted to sail up to a distance of 3 nautical miles from the coast unless, in special cases, otherwise agreed within the Maritime Coordination and Cooperation Center as referred to in paragraph 3 below. Recreational boats may have engines up to a limit of 10 horsepower. Marine motor bikes and water jets will neither be introduced into Zone L nor be operated therein.
         iii. Foreign vessels entering Zone L will not approach closer than 12 nautical miles from the coast except as regards activities covered in paragraph 4 below.
   b. General Rules of the Maritime Activity Zones
      1. The aforementioned fishing boats and recreational boats and their skippers sailing in Zone L shall carry licenses issued by the Palestinian Authority, the format and standards of which will be coordinated through the JSC.
      2. The boats shall have identification markings determined by the Palestinian Authority. The Israeli authorities will be notified through the JSC of these identification markings.
      3. Residents of Israeli settlements in the Gaza Strip fishing in Zone L will carry Israeli licenses and vessel permits.

4. As part of Israel's responsibilities for safety and security within the three Maritime Activity Zones, Israel Navy vessels may sail throughout these zones, as necessary and without limitations, and may take any measures necessary against vessels suspected of being used for terrorist activities or for smuggling arms, ammunition, drugs, goods, or for any other illegal activity. The Palestinian Police will be notified of such actions, and the ensuing procedures will be coordinated through the Maritime Coordination and Cooperation Center.

TWENTY-FOUR

SECURITY COUNCIL MARITIME ENFORCEMENT

Within the United Nations system, the International Court of Justice (ICJ) is not alone in its inability to successfully address the threat of low-intensity conflict at sea. The General Assembly has proven equally incapable of understanding the threat and devising effective international policy to deter and defeat it.[1] Dealing with asymmetric and state-sponsored attack was the major difficulty in the General Assembly reaching consensus on the Definition of Aggression in the UN General Assembly.

In contrast to the General Assembly, the UN Security Council has broad authority under Chapter VII of the UN Charter to maintain or restore international peace and security. Among the institutions of the World Court, the General Assembly, and the Security Council, the latter organization has been most effective in using legal authorities to maintain safety and security at sea. Recent Security Council efforts have focused on the threat of maritime piracy, and adoption of Resolution 1540 set forth a framework for maritime interdiction of weapons of mass destruction (WMD). On occasion, however, the Security Council has exercised its authority to impose a maritime blockade to enforce economic sanctions or arms embargoes against individual States. Article 39 of the UN Charter provides that:

> The Security Council shall determine the existence of any threat to the peace, breach of the peace, or act of aggression and shall make recommendations, or decide what measures shall be taken in accordance with Articles 41 and 42, to maintain or restore international peace and security.

Article 41 includes a list of measures not involving the use of force that may be applied to give effect to its decisions:

---

[1] UN Doc. A/Res/54/33, Results of the review by the Commission on Sustainable Development of the Sectoral theme of "Oceans and seas": International Coordination and Cooperation, Jan. 18, 2000.

> The Security Council may decide what measures not involving the use of armed force are to be employed to give effect to its decisions, and it may call upon the Members of the United Nations to apply such measures. These may include complete or partial interruption of economic relations and of rail, sea, air, postal, telegraphic, radio, and other means of communication, and the severance of diplomatic relations.

In cases in which measures adopted under Article 41 would be inadequate or have failed to achieve their desired outcome, the Security Council may utilize Article 42, which authorizes the Security Council to adopt measures that may be enforced through coercion or military action. This activity is also called "enforcement action."

> Should the Security Council consider that measures provided for in Article 41 would be inadequate or have proved to be inadequate, it may take such action by air, sea, or land forces as may be necessary to maintain or restore international peace and security. Such action may include demonstrations, blockade, and other operations by air, sea, or land forces of Members of the United Nations.

The Security Council has authorized maritime enforcement action under Article 42 in five situations: Rhodesia (1995), Iraq (1990), Federal Republic of Yugoslavia (1991–93), Haiti (1994), and Libya (2011). These five missions used ships and aircraft from the armed forces of member States to interdict shipping traffic, which was judged by the Security Council to be a threat to international peace and security.

24.1 Rhodesia Sanctions and the Beira Patrol (1965)

The first occasion for the use of maritime enforcement action to support Security Council sanctions arose from the situation in Rhodesia, as it progressed from a British colony to a majority-rule nation. On November 11, 1965, the white minority population of Southern Rhodesia unilaterally declared its independence from the United Kingdom. The Unilateral Declaration of Independence—or "UDI" as it was known—declared:

> That it is an indisputable and accepted historic fact that since 1923 the Government of Rhodesia have exercised the powers of self-government and have been responsible for the progress, development and welfare of their people;
>
> . . .
>
> That the people of Rhodesia have witnessed a process which is destructive of those very precepts upon which civilization in a primitive country has been built; they have seen the principles of Western democracy, responsible government and moral standards crumble elsewhere . . .;
>
> . . .
>
> Now Therefore, We The Government of Rhodesia, in humble submission to Almighty God who controls the destinies of nations . . . Do, By This Proclamation, adopt, enact

and give to the people of Rhodesia the Constitution annexed hereto God Save The Queen.[2]

The UN General Assembly immediately condemned the act by a vote of 107 to 2 (Portugal and South Africa).[3]

The boundaries of the newly created nation were coterminous with the colony of Southern Rhodesia, which was named after Cecil John Rhodes. The capital of the landlocked state was Salisbury. The colonies of Northern Rhodesia, which comprised the Federation of Rhodesia and Nyasaland, consisted of Zambia, Zimbabwe, and Malawi. In 1964, upon independence, Northern Rhodesia renamed itself Zambia and Nyasaland renamed itself Malawi. Thus, Southern Rhodesia changed its name simply to "Rhodesia." Ian Smith led the new white minority Rhodesian Front government.

The United Kingdom, as the administering power of Rhodesia, considered the declaration of independence to be an act of rebellion and condemned it as illegal. British policy insisted that there be no independence before institution of majority rule in the colony. The same day as the declaration of independence, on instructions from the Crown, the Governor of Rhodesia informed the Prime Minister and other Ministers of the Rhodesian Government that they had been dismissed from office, an order the Ministers promptly ignored.[4] The next day, the Security Council adopted Resolution 216, which supported the British position, and condemned the unilateral declaration.[5]

The following week, the Security Council adopted Resolution 217. The second resolution condemned the declaration of independence as lacking legal validity, and the Security Council called on the British Government to quell the rebellion. The Security Council also called on the United Kingdom to take all other appropriate measures to bring the unlawful regime to an immediate end. The resolution imposed an arms embargo and economic sanctions on the Rhodesian regime and authorized the United Kingdom to enforce an embargo and sanctions.

---

[2] Unilateral Declaration of Independence, Nov. 11, 1965, http://www.psywar.org/rhodesia.php.

[3] J. E. S. Fawcett, *Security Council Resolutions on Rhodesia*, 41 BRIT. Y.B. INT'L L. 103, 109 (1965–66).

[4] Prime Minister Harold Wilson: The Position of the British Government on the Unilateral Declaration of Independence by Rhodesia, Speech to Parliament, Nov. 11, 1965, http://www.fordham.edu/halsall/mod/1965Rhodesia-UDI.html.

[5] S/RES/216 (1965), Nov. 12, 1965. *See also*, Myres S. McDougal & W. Michael Reisman, *Rhodesia and the United Nations: The Lawfulness of International Concern*, 62 AM. J. INT' L. 1 (1968), J. E. S. Fawcett, *Security Council Resolutions on Rhodesia*, 41 BRIT. Y.B. INT'L L. 103 (1965–66), and VERA GOWLLAND-DEBBAS, COLLECTIVE RESPONSES TO ILLEGAL ACTS IN INTERNATIONAL LAW: UNITED NATIONS ACTION IN THE QUESTION OF SOUTHERN RHODESIA (1990).

Resolution 217 (1965)

...[T]he situation resulting from the proclamation of independence by the illegal authorities in Southern Rhodesia is extremely grave...the Government of the United Kingdom...should put an end to it and that its continuance in time constitutes a threat to international peace and security;

... *Calls upon* all States to refrain from any action which would assist and encourage the illegal regime and, in particular, to desist from providing it with arms, equipment and military material, and to do their utmost in order to break all economic relations with Southern Rhodesia, including an embargo on oil and petroleum products....[6]

On March 2, 1970, Rhodesia declared itself a Republic, but still the state received no grant of recognition from other nations. Security Council sanctions forbade states from trading or conducting financial exchange with Rhodesia. The maritime interdiction operation was code-named the Beira Patrol and included a naval blockade of the port of Beira in Mozambique to prevent oil shipments from reaching the renegade colony. The initial British commitment included an aircraft carrier, two frigates and a Royal Fleet Auxiliary support ship. Later, the British supported the blockade by maintaining two destroyers or frigates on station at all times and conducted daily air patrols of the Mozambique Channel with shore-based Royal Air Force Avro Shackleton long-range maritime patrol aircraft. The Royal Navy enforced the UN sanctions from March 1, 1966, to June 25, 1975, at which point Mozambique became an independent nation. Upon assurances from Mozambique to the United Kingdom that it would not allow the transshipment of oil to Rhodesia, the Beira Patrol ended.

By virtue of UN Security Council Resolution 217, the burden of enforcing the Beira Patrol fell on Britain. The Beira Patrol sought to stop oil tankers from entering port and it faced considerable difficulty in crafting coercive rules of engagement for visit and search on the high seas.[7] Politically, however, there never was a risk that Rhodesia's two supporters—South Africa and Portugal—would forcibly challenge the blockade.[8]

The Security Council adopted two more Resolutions—Resolution 221 of April 9, 1966, and Resolution 232 of December 16, 1966. Resolution 221 expressly authorized the use of force by the United Kingdom. The latter resolution stopped "the arrival at Beira of vessels reasonably believed to be carrying oil destined for Rhodesia, and empowers the United Kingdom to arrest and detain the tanker known a *Joanna V* upon her departure from Beira in the event her oil cargo is discharged there."[9] The *Joanna V* got underway from Beira without first discharging her oil, so the condition precedent was not triggered.

---

[6] S/RES 217 (1965), Nov. 20, 1965.
[7] D. P. O'CONNELL, THE INFLUENCE OF LAW ON SEAPOWER 174 (1975).
[8] JAMES CABLE, GUNBOAT DIPLOMACY 1919–1979 126 (1981).
[9] S/RES 221 (1965), Apr. 9, 1965.

Another ship, however, the tanker *Manuela*, was intercepted by *HMS Berwick* on the high seas and redirected from making port at Beira. The vessel was boarded, and the Master of the ship diverted to for Lourenço Marques, Mozambique.[10]

Portugal challenged the validity of the Security Council's finding in Resolution 221 that the situation in Rhodesia constituted a threat to international peace and security, arguing that there was no actual proof in the resolution that peace was threatened.[11] But the determination of the Security Council "has some of the characteristics of a judicial decision: it is definitive of a factual situation, it must be accepted by the United Nations members...and it has the consequence of providing a legal basis for action that might otherwise be unlawful."[12]

On December 6, 1966, the Security Council adopted Resolution 232, which stands out in contrast from earlier resolutions with its clarity and purpose.[13] The Resolution stated that the Security Council was acting in accordance with Articles 39 and 41 of the UN Charter. The Security Council decided that "all States shall prevent" commerce with Rhodesia including the sale of commodities, armaments, and oil and petroleum products. All Member States of the United Nations were called upon to comply with the decision of the Security Council in accordance with Article 25 of the Charter, and a declaration specified that refusal to implement the terms of the resolution shall constitute a violation of the *Charter of the United Nations*.

The nation of Rhodesia persisted as an unrecognized state from 1965 until 1979. Some states, including South Africa, Portugal, Israel, Iran, and several Arab states, continued to trade with Rhodesia during the period of the Beira Patrol. The United States enacted the Byrd Amendment in 1971 to permit limited trade with Rhodesia for certain industrial materials, such as nickel, chrome, and ferrochrome. Rhodesia (always referred to as "Southern Rhodesia" by the British government), achieved independence in April 1980, becoming the independent Republic of Zimbabwe.

24.2 The Maritime Blockade of Iraq (1990–91)

On August 2, 1990, Iraqi military forces invaded Kuwait, quickly subduing its smaller neighbor. The UN Security Council immediately adopted Resolution 660, which required withdrawal of all Iraqi military forces from Kuwait.[14]

---

[10] Report of the Sec'y General by Lord Caradon, United Kingdom Permanent Representative to the United Nations, S.C.O.R., S/7249, Apr. 11, 1966.
[11] Fawcett, *Security Council Resolution on Rhodesia*, at 116 (citing Stmt of the Portuguese Foreign Minister of Apr. 29, 1966).
[12] Id. at 116–17.
[13] Fawcett, *Security Council Resolution on Rhodesia*, at 121.
[14] S/RES/660 (1990), Aug. 2, 1990 and S/RES/661 (1990), Aug. 6, 1990.

Resolution 660 (1990)

...*Acting* under Articles 39 and 40 of the Charter of the United Nations,
1. *Condemns* the Iraqi invasion of Kuwait;
2. *Demands* that Iraq withdraw immediately and unconditionally [from Kuwait]....[15]

On August 6, having failed to secure the withdrawal of Iraqi forces from Kuwait, the Security Council adopted Resolution 661. The resolution imposed a general embargo on all trade with Iraq and Kuwait, and served as the principal means to induce Iraqi compliance with Resolution 660. The embargo specifically called on States to refrain from the use of their vessels to trade with Iraq.

Resolution 661 (1990)

...*Acting* under Chapter VII of the Charter of the United Nations... Decides that all States shall prevent:

(a) The import into their territories of all commodities and products originating in Iraq or Kuwait exported therefrom after the date of the present resolution;
(b) Any activities by their nationals or in their territories, which would promote or are calculated to promote the export or trans-shipment of any commodities or products from Iraq or Kuwait...;
(c) The sale or supply by their nationals or from their territories or using their flag vessels of any commodities or products, including weapons or any other military equipment... not including supplies intended strictly for medical purposes, and, in humanitarian circumstances, foodstuffs, to any person or body in Iraq or Kuwait....[16]

Iraq's noncompliance with UN Security Council Resolutions 660 and 661 led to adoption of UN Security Council Resolution 665 on August 25, 1990. Resolution 665 imposed a traditional maritime blockade, a belligerent act in the law of naval warfare, less than one month after the invasion—providing a means to enforce Resolution 661.[17] Specifically, Resolution 665 authorized states to "halt all inward and outward maritime shipping in order to inspect and verify their cargoes and destinations," under authority of Chapter VII of the Charter. The resolution removed any doubt that the sanctions and armaments embargo imposed by Resolution 661 constituted enforcement action under Article 42, and therefore could be enforced with military means.

---

[15] S/RES/660 (1990), Aug. 2, 1990.
[16] S/RES/661 (1990), Aug. 6, 1990.
[17] Interestingly, Security Council Resolution 665 requested states "cooperating with the Government of Kuwait" while executing the blockade of Iraq to also coordinate their actions using the mechanism of the Military Staff Committee in Articles 46 and 47 of the UN charter. The U.S.-led coalition refrained from doing so, however. *See*, YORAM DINSTEIN, WAR, AGGRESSION AND SELF-DEFENCE 306 (4th ed. 2005).

Resolution 665 (1990)

...Calls upon those Member States cooperating with the Government of Kuwait which are deploying maritime forces to the area to use such measures commensurate to the specific circumstances as may be necessary under the authority of the Security Council to halt all inward and outward maritime shipping in order to inspect and verify their cargoes and destinations and to ensure strict implementation of the provisions related to such shipping laid down in Resolution 661 (1990)....[18]

Under the coordination of the U.S.-led Commander, Middle East Force, coalition naval forces in the Persian Gulf, Gulf of Oman, and the Red Sea conducted the maritime interdiction mission. The primary focus of the operation was to halt the export of oil from Iraq and preclude the import of war materials into the country. Only humanitarian and medical supplies were allowed through the blockade. The area of maritime operations was defined by the U.S. Navy in Special Warning No. 80, which represented "a proximate and reasonable zone for ensuring that the prohibition of illicit trade with Iraq was given effect...."[19] Special Warning No. 80 reflects a classic application of the belligerent right of visit and search:

1. In response to requests from the legitimate Government of Kuwait and in exercising the inherent right of collective self-defense recognized under Article 51 of the UN Charter, United States forces will, in cooperation with regional and allied forces, conduct a maritime operation to intercept the import and export of commodities and products to and from Iraq and Kuwait that are prohibited by... Resolution 661.
2. Affected areas include the Strait of Hormuz, Strait of Tiran, and other choke points, key ports, and oil pipeline terminals....
3. All merchant ships perceived to be proceeding to or from Iraqi or Kuwaiti ports, or transshipment points, and carrying embargoed material to or from Iraq or Kuwait, will be intercepted and may be searched.
4. Ships which, after being intercepted, are determined to be proceeding to or from Iraq or Kuwait ports, or transshipment points, and carrying embargoed material to or from Iraq or Kuwait, will not be allowed to proceed with their planned transit.
5. The intercepting ship may use all available communications, primarily VHF channel 16, but including international code signals, flag hoists, other radio equipment, signal lamps, loudspeakers, and other appropriate means to communicate his directions to a ship. (Safe navigation may require vessels to be diverted to a port or anchorage prior to conducting a search.)
6. Failure of a ship to proceed as directed will result in the use of the minimum level of force necessary to ensure compliance.
7. Any ships, including waterborne craft and armed merchant ships, or aircraft, which threaten or interfere with U.S. forces engaged in enforcing this maritime interception will be considered hostile.[20]

---

[18] S/RES/665 (1990), Aug. 25, 1990.
[19] MARITIME OPERATIONAL ZONES Ch. 5 (Richard Jaques et al., ed. U.S. Naval War College, International Law Department, Center for Naval Warfare Studies 2006).
[20] United States Department of the Navy, Special Warning No. 80, *reprinted in* MARITIME OPERATIONAL ZONES, Appendix C.

Merchant ships throughout the Persian Gulf and its entrance into the Arabian Sea were tracked and identified. Vessels containing contraband trade bound for Iraq or Kuwait were challenged and warned, and then boarded and diverted to another port if they were found to be in violation of the UN sanctions. Ships determined not to be a threat, not to be en route to Iraq, Kuwait or one of its neighbors, and to be free of contraband goods, were allowed to proceed to their next port of call. By late December 1990, just months after implementation of the maritime operations, coalition forces had intercepted nearly 6,000 ships and boarded 713 vessels.

The Maritime Interdiction Force (MIF) received coordinated tasking and assigned patrol areas, and executed visit, board, search, and seizure missions. Naval forces from each participant state used their own national rules of engagement, which led to slight variation in the protocols for the use of force. There was no formal command and control structure, as the warships from contributing states worked together on an ad hoc basis. Overall, the maritime interception campaign was successful in stopping the flow of oil out of Iraq. Iraq was completely dependent upon oil exports, which produced 95 percent of the country's revenue. The MIF also prevented resupply of war materiel for the Iraqi Army, just as coalition airstrikes depleted ammunition, spare parts, and decimated internal lines of communication.

Over one million tons of prohibited cargo was diverted by the MIF, including surface-to-air missiles (SAMs), command and control equipment, early warning radar systems, weapons, ammunition, spare parts, and general supplies used to maintain Iraq's industrial base. Ultimately, more than 165 ships from 14 coalition nations participated in the operation. The warships challenged over 9,000 commercial vessels in the region. Of these 9,000 ships, over 1,100 were boarded and inspected, and more than 60 ships were diverted for a violation of UN sanctions.

The maritime sanctions regime continued throughout the 1990s and into the early-2000s, albeit with a tighter geographic focus. Operations in the Red Sea, Strait of Tiran, and Strait of Hormuz were halted, while maritime interceptions continued in the Persian Gulf and Gulf of Oman. On February 16, 2001, the following Special Warning reiterated what had become a familiar routine to international commercial carriers transiting the region:

1. In the Persian Gulf, Multi-national Naval Units continue to conduct a maritime operation to intercept the import and export of commodities and products to/from Iraq that are prohibited by UN Security Council resolutions 661 and 687.
2. Vessels transiting the Persian Gulf and the Gulf of Oman can expect to be queried and, if bound for or departing from Iraq or the Shatt-al-Arab Waterway, also intercepted and boarded. Safe navigation may require vessels to be diverted to a port or anchorage prior to conducting an inspection.
. . .
6. Ships which after being intercepted are determined to be in violation of UN Security Council Resolution 661 will not be allowed to proceed with their planned transit.

. . .

8. Failure of a ship to proceed as directed will result in the use of the minimum level of force necessary to ensure compliance.
9. Any ships, including waterborne craft and armed merchant ships, or aircraft, which threaten or interfere with the Multinational Forces engaged in enforcing a maritime interception, may be considered hostile.[21]

The economic sanctions imposed hardship on the Iraqi people, as well as the Iraq government. The regime of Saddam Hussein became adept at circumvention of the sanctions, exploiting the "oil for food" program intended to aid the civilian population. American and British military forces led a coalition of nations to invade the country in spring 2003, and the odious regime of Saddam Hussein was toppled. Economic sanctions against civilian and commercial trade were lifted by Security Council Resolution 1483, which was adopted on May 22, 2003, but the invasion also triggered a civil war that wrecked the nation's fragile economy and resulted in tragic human loss. Resolution 1483 specified that although the situation in Iraq had improved, it still constituted a threat to international peace and security. Acting under Chapter VII of the UN Charter, the Security Council decided that

> . . . with the exception of prohibitions related to the sale or supply to Iraq of arms and related materiel . . . all prohibitions related to trade with Iraq and the provision of financial or economic resources to Iraq established by Resolution 661 (1990) and subsequent relevant resolutions, including Resolution 778 (1992) of 2 October 1992, shall no longer apply. . .[22]

Thus, even after the removal of the Ba'athist regime in Iraq, the arms embargo, with limited exception, remained in place. While the United Nations still barred trade in arms and related material, commercial trade sanctions against Iraq were terminated by Resolution 1483, which helped to reintegrate the country into the global economy.

Coalition maritime forces continued to enforce the remaining sanction against armaments and weapons. As the country of Iraq was engulfed in civil war, international naval forces expanded their mission to include protection of the country's port facilities and internal waters and territorial seas. In particular, the Coalition forces patrolled the shipping lanes in the northern Gulf and provided security for Iraqi offshore oil terminals.

In 2004, the Maritime Liaison Office (MARLO) in Bahrain released on behalf of Coalition Maritime Security Forces new directions for commercial vessels bound for or departing from Iraqi ports. Commercial carriers were subject to two layers of security—the first maintained by Coalition naval forces and the second by the maritime forces of the government of Iraq.

---

[21] Special Warning No. 115, Persian Gulf, Feb. 16, 2001.
[22] S/RES/1483 (2003), May 22, 2003.

Vessels bound for or departing from Iraqi ports and offshore oil terminals must pass within a five nautical mile radius of [the Coalition checkpoint]. Approaching vessels must contact the on station coalition warship on marine VHF (bridge-to-bridge) radio-telephone, channel 16 within five nautical miles of this point and be prepared to be queried, boarded, and inspected for prohibited cargo by coalition Maritime Security Forces (MSF). Vessels will not be permitted to proceed from this point until cleared by the MSF. Clearance through the Iraqi maritime security checkpoint does not grant clearance to enter any specific Iraqi port or the internal waters of Iraq; such clearances must be obtained from appropriate authorities in Iraq.[23]

On June 8, 2004, about one year after Coalition military forces entered the country, the Security Council adopted Resolution 1546, which lifted the arms embargo on Iraq. The Security Council recognized the emergence of a new sovereign Interim Government of Iraq on June 1, 2004, and also its scheduled assumption of full and complete authority over the country on June 30, 2004. Under authority of Chapter VII, the Security Council decided that "... the prohibitions related to the sale or supply to Iraq of arms and related materiel under previous resolutions shall not apply to arms or related materiel required by the Government of Iraq or the multinational force to serve the purposes of this resolution...."[24]

24.3 Former Republic of Yugoslavia Armaments Embargo (1991–96)

After the fall of the Berlin Wall in 1989, the communist regime that governed the multiethnic Republic of Yugoslavia began to lose its grip on power. The country slowly fragmented into civil war, as historic Balkan grievances were unleashed. As ethnic warfare engulfed the former Yugoslavia, the warring factions signed and then violated cease-fire agreements. The European Union and the North Atlantic Treaty Organization failed to stop the spread of chaos, although the UN Security Council acted tentatively. Meeting on September 17 and 22, 1991, the Security Council imposed an arms embargo on Yugoslavia beginning on September 25, 1991.

Acting under authority of Chapter VII of the UN Charter, Resolution 713 decided:

> ... that all States shall, for the purposes of establishing peace and stability in Yugoslavia, immediately implement a general and complete embargo on all deliveries of weapons and military equipment to Yugoslavia until the Security Council decides otherwise following consultation between the Secretary-General and the Government of Yugoslavia; ...[25]

---

[23] Dep't of the Navy, MARLO Advisory Bull. 01–04, Jan. 12, 2004 (Maritime Liaison Office, Bahrain).
[24] S/RES/1546 (2004), June 8, 2004.
[25] S/RES/713 (1991), Sept. 25, 1991.

In July 1992, NATO and Western European Union (WEU) forces began operating in the Adriatic Sea to monitor compliance with the UN Security Council resolutions concerning the former Yugoslavia. While working closely together, both organizations conducted separate operations—named *Maritime Monitor* and *Sharp Vigilance*.[26] The maritime operations, however, did little to arrest the fighting. A Special Rapporteur who investigated the human rights situation in the former Yugoslavia found "massive and systematic violations of human rights and grave violations of international humanitarian law" in the Republic of Bosnia and Herzegovina.[27]

Violations of the armaments embargo imposed by Resolution 713 led the Security Council to adopt Resolution 787 on November 16, 1992. The Resolution authorized States individually or through regional arrangements to use naval forces to enforce the embargo:

> Acting under Chapters VII and VIII of the Charter of the United Nations, calls upon States, acting nationally or through regional agencies or arrangements, to use such measures commensurate with the specific circumstances as may be necessary under the authority of the Security Council to halt all inward and outward maritime shipping in order to inspect and verify their cargoes and destinations and to ensure strict implementation of the provisions of resolutions 713 (1991) and 757 (1992);...[28]

Resolution 787 is particularly interesting because it leveraged the authority of both chapters VII and VIII, and chapter VIII specifically opened the door for either the EU or NATO to take the lead in the Balkans—action neither was prepared to do, however. On November 22, 1992, *Maritime Monitor* and *Sharp Vigilance* were expanded to include the enforcement of UN Security Council resolutions 713, 757 and 787, which authorized military action to include boarding and search operations to ensure compliance. The operations were also renamed *Maritime Guard* and *Sharp Fence*.

In early-1993, the failure of the Bosnian Serbs to participate in the peace process resulted in implementation of an even tighter embargo. On April 17, 1993, the Security Council adopted Resolution 820, which prohibited unauthorized maritime traffic from entering the territorial sea of the Federal Republic of Yugoslavia (Serbia and Montenegro), except in cases of force majeure:

---

[26] NATO/WEU Operation Sharp Guard Fact Sheet, Oct. 2, 1996, http://www.nato.int/ifor/general/shrp-grd.htm. The joint NATO-WEU Operation SHARP GUARD began on June 15, 1993, to replace the separate NATO and WEU operations MARITIME GUARD and SHARP FENCE; the operation was suspended on June 19, 1996, and terminated following a United Nations Security Council resolution adopted on October 1, 1996.
[27] S/RES/787 (1992), Nov. 16, 1992.
[28] Id.

...*Acting* under Chapter VII of the Charter of the United Nations [the Security Council];

...*Decides* to prohibit all commercial maritime traffic from entering the territorial sea of the Federal Republic of Yugoslavia (Serbia and Montenegro) except when authorized on a case-by-case basis by the Committee established by resolution 724 (1991) or in case of force majeure;

...*Reaffirms* the authority of States... to enforce the present resolution and its other relevant resolutions, including in the territorial sea of the Federal Republic of Yugoslavia (Serbia and Montenegro)....[29]

Several months later, at a joint session of NATO and the Western European Union (WEU) on June 8, 1993, the respective Councils approved a combined operation for the implementation of UN Security Council Resolution 820. The combined operation, named *Sharp Guard*, launched Combined Task Force (CTF) 440 on June 15, 1993, as a unified command. Ships from NATO's Standing Naval Force Mediterranean (STANAVFORMED) and Standing Naval Force Atlantic (STANAVFORLANT), together with ships assigned to the WEU Contingency Maritime Force, were force providers for the CTF.

For the next three years, NATO and WEU forces operated under CTF 440 in the southern Adriatic to enforce sanctions against the Federal Republic of Yugoslavia (Serbia and Montenegro). The maritime interception operations were aimed at stopping weapons shipments into the Balkan war. NATO and WEU ships challenged 74,192 merchant vessels, inspected 5,951 ships at sea, and diverted 1,480 other vessels to Mediterranean ports for more exacting inspection. Ships that transited the area of operations were queried to determine the nature of their cargo, and port of origin and destination. Ships that were bound for the territorial sea of Yugoslavia were boarded and inspected (or diverted to an approved port or anchorage) to verify compliance with Security Council mandates. Ships in violation of the sanctions were escorted to Italian territorial waters and turned over to Italian authorities.

On November 22, 1995, Security Council Resolution 1021 suspended the general armaments embargo in favor of a more limited regime.[30] Thereafter, only heavy weapons (and their ammunition), mines, and military fixed wing and rotary aircraft were prohibited. Eleven months later, Resolution 1074 terminated the arms embargo entirely. On October 2, 1996, NATO and the WEU stood down Operation *Sharp Guard*.[31]

---

[29] S/RES/820 (1993), Apr. 17, 1993.
[30] S/RES/1021 (1995), Nov. 22, 1995.
[31] Res. 1074 (1996), S/RES/1074 (1996), Oct. 1, 1996.

24.4 Haiti Sanctions (1994)

In December 1990, Jean-Bertrand Aristide was elected president of Haiti by 67 percent of the popular vote. The election was considered to be free and fair by international observers. The new president took office two months later, on February 7, 1991. In September of that same year, however, Aristide was overthrown by a violent military coup led by Lieutenant General Raoul Cédras. For the next three years, the country was ruled by a *de facto* military regime that engaged in widespread human rights abuses. The government murdered several thousand Haitians.[32]

Following the coup, the Organization of American States (OAS) condemned the military action and imposed sanctions on the ruling junta aimed at restoration of the democratically elected government.[33] Likewise, the UN General Assembly condemned the use of military force to oust President Aristide and the widespread violation of human rights by the new regime. UN General Assembly Resolution 46/7, which was adopted on October 11, 1991, called on Member States of the United Nations to "take measures in support" of the OAS resolutions.[34] The General Assembly adopted a second resolution November 24, 1992, which "again demanded the restoration of the legitimate Government of President Aristide, together with the full application of the National Constitution and the full observance of human rights."[35]

These resolutions, however, failed to sway the military regime to return Aristide to power, so the UN Permanent Representative of Haiti sent a letter to the President of the Security Council on June 7, 1993, which stated that "despite the efforts of the international community, constitutional order had not yet been re-established in Haiti because the *de facto* authorities continued to obstruct all initiatives."[36] The displaced "[g]overnment of Haiti requested the Security Council to make universal and mandatory the sanctions against the *de facto* authorities adopted at the meeting of Ministers for Foreign Affairs of OAS and recommended

---

[32] Dep't of State Background Note: Haiti, Oct. 19, 2011, http://www.state.gov/r/pa/ei/bgn/1982.htm.

[33] MRE/RES.1/91, Oct. 3, 1991 OEA/Ser.F/V.1, MRE/RES.1/91 corr.1, Support to the democratic government of Haiti, Oct. 3, 1991 and MRE/RES.2/91, Oct. 8, 1991, OEA/Ser.F/V.1. *See also*, OEA/Ser.GCP/RES.567 (870/91), Support to the democratic government of Haiti, Sept. 30, 1991.

[34] UNGA Res. 46/7, A/RES/46/7 (1991), The Situation of Democracy and Human Rights in Haiti, Oct. 11, 1991.

[35] UNGA 47/20, The Situation of Democracy and Human Rights in Haiti, Nov. 24, 1992.

[36] S/25958, June 7, 1993, *excerpted in* Decision of June 16, 1993 (3238th meeting): Resolution 841 (1993), The question concerning Haiti, Chapter VIII. Consideration of questions under responsibility of the Security Council for the maintenance of international peace and security. Id., at 1.

in the General Assembly resolutions, giving priority to an embargo on petroleum products and the supply of arms and munitions."[37]

Accordingly, the Security Council adopted Resolution 841 on June 16, 1993. The resolution imposed an embargo on armaments and oil products, and it froze the assets controlled directly or indirectly by the *de facto* government in Haiti. The Security Council determined that "the continuation of [the] situation threatens international peace and security in the region." Acting under Chapter VII of the UN Charter, the Security Council imposed an embargo starting at 00.01 EST on June 23, 1993. The Security Council decided

> ... that all States shall prevent the sale or supply, by their nationals or from their territories or using their flag vessels or aircraft, of petroleum or petroleum products or arms and related materiel of all types, including weapons and ammunition, military vehicles and equipment, police equipment ... to any person or body in Haiti or to any person or body for the purpose of any business carried on in or operated from Haiti. ...;
>
> ... any and all traffic [is prohibited] from entering the territory or territorial sea of Haiti carrying petroleum or petroleum products, or arms and related materiel of all types, including weapons and ammunition, military vehicles and equipment, police equipment and spare parts. ...;[38]

The Security Council also established a committee to manage the embargo and licensed it to authorize exceptions for small "non-commercial quantities and only in barrels or bottles," of petroleum or petroleum products used [as fuel] in cooking and to meet "verified essential humanitarian needs."[39]

Several weeks later, UN mediator Dante Caputo drafted the *Governor's Island Accord*. The agreement was designed to pave the way for the restoration of democracy in Haiti and the return of President Aristide by October 30, 1993. President Aristide and General Cédras signed the accord on July 3, 1993. The agreement stipulated that Aristide would appoint a new commander-in-chief of the armed forces and would nominate a prime minister to be confirmed by the legally reconstituted parliament. Once the prime minister assumed office, the international sanctions imposed by the UN and OAS would be lifted. The text of the *Governor's Island Accord* would serve as the basis for a new regime in Haiti.[40]

In accordance with the terms of the agreement, on August 25, President Aristide nominated Robert Malval to be the new prime minister of Haiti. Subsequently, the Haiti Parliament ratified the appointment. Two days later, the Security Council adopted Resolution 861 (1993), which suspended the oil and arms embargo

---

[37] Id.
[38] S/RES/0841 (1993), June 16, 1993.
[39] Id.
[40] Governor's Island Accord, July 3, 1993, *reprinted in* OEA/Ser.L/II.85, Doc. 9 rev., Report on the Situation of Human Rights in Haiti, Annex ii, Feb. 11, 1994, at 63–66. *See also*, DEP'T OF STATE, BUREAU OF PUB. AFF., 4 DEP'T OF STATE DISPATCH, July 26, 1993.

against Haiti and unfroze government funds. The resolution warned that sanctions would be reinstated if the terms of the Governors Island Accord were not fully implemented.[41]

The military regime led by General Cédras, however, continued to resist implementation of the Accord. Therefore, on October 13, 1993, the UN Secretary-General recommended to the Security Council that it should immediately reinstitute the oil and gas embargo, as well as refreeze Haitian government funds.[42] Accordingly, the Security Council adopted UN Security Council Resolution 873. The new resolution stated that the military and police in Haiti "have not complied in good faith with the *Governor's Island Agreement*." Consequently, the suspension of the embargo was lifted on October 18, 1993.[43]

On October 14, 1993—the day after adoption of Resolution 873, but before the embargo was reinstated on October 18—François-Guy Malary, the Haitian Minister of Justice, was assassinated. Two days later the Security Council adopted Resolution 875, which cited authority of Chapters VII and VIII of the UN Charter. The resolution called on Member States to strictly implement the oil and arms embargo against Haiti, to include stopping and inspecting all ships travelling "towards Haiti in order to verify their cargoes and destinations."[44]

The military regime in Haiti was intransigent. As a result of a lack of progress by the ruling junta, the Security Council adopted Resolution 917 on May 6, 1994. Resolution 917 imposed a full embargo on all goods (except humanitarian supplies) from entry into Haiti. Member States also were authorized to use "all necessary means" to enforce the embargo and restore Aristide to power—the classic term of art for Security Council action under Article 42 of the Charter.[45]

Measures to enforce the embargo were immediately put in place by the international community, including a cooperative endeavor between the United States and other countries with the Dominican Republic "to monitor that country's enforcement of sanctions along its land border and in its coastal waters."[46] Eight U.S. warships worked in coordination with one Canadian vessel and an Argentine and a Dutch warship to enforce the sanctions at sea.

On July 13, 1994, the Haitian military expelled the international staff of the UN/OAS-sponsored International Civilian Mission in Haiti. The Security Council

---

[41] S/RES/861 (1993), Aug. 27, 1993.
[42] S/26573, Oct. 13, 1993.
[43] S/RES/873 (1993), Oct. 13, 1993.
[44] S/RES/875 (1993), Oct. 16, 1993.
[45] S/RES/917, May 6, 1994. Humanitarian supplies were specified as foodstuffs, propane for cooking, and medical supplies.
[46] Developments Concerning the National Emergency with Respect to Haiti, Message from the President of the United States, Transmitting a Report on Developments Since his Last Report of October 13, 1994, concerning the National Emergency with Respect to Haiti, pursuant to 50 U.S.C. § 1641(c) and 50 U.S.C. § 1703(c), 104th Congress, 1st Session, House Doc. 104–25.

responded to the continuing threat to peace and security in the region by adopting Resolution 940 on July 31, 1994. This resolution authorized "the formation of a multinational force to use all necessary means to facilitate the departure from Haiti of the military leadership and the return of legitimate authorities including President Aristide."[47]

> ... [The Security Council], Acting under Chapter VII of the United Nations Charter of the United Nations, authorizes Member States to form a multinational force under unified command and control and, in this framework, to use all necessary means to facilitate the departure from Haiti of the military leadership, consistent with the Governors Island Agreement, the prompt return of the legitimately elected President and the restoration of the legitimate authorities of the Government of Haiti, and to establish and maintain a secure and stable environment...;

By September 1994, 20 countries had agreed to contribute military forces to the multinational mission to restore democracy in Haiti. Faced with increasing international pressure and the threat of invasion, Cédras and his supporters relented and agreed to resign. On September 19, 1994, advance elements of a 28-nation multinational force landed in Haiti. Ten days later the Security Council lifted the sanctions on the impoverished Caribbean state.[48]

On October 15, 1994, President Aristide returned to Haiti and reassumed office. The Security Council lifted the remaining sanctions against Haiti on the same day.[49] The embargo against Haiti may be considered a success, but it is unlikely that sanctions alone would have achieved the same outcome. The threat of invasion by an overwhelming international military force targeted the regime elites, compelling them to step down from power. Although the Haiti experience demonstrates the efficacy of both Articles 41 and 42, it was really the latter authority, and the willingness of the international community to back it up with military force, that brought change on the ground.

24.5 Libya Embargo (2011)

The maritime interdiction operations targeting Libya grew out of the events of the Arab Spring. As with Haiti, the pressure of military intervention (and no small measure of military-related support to anti-regime forces) by the international community was decisive.

In February 2011, peaceful demonstrations in Benghazi by groups opposed to the continued rule of Colonel Muammar Qadhafi were violently repressed by government security forces. Dozens of protesters died over the next few days as

---

[47] Id.
[48] S/RES/944, Sept. 29, 1994.
[49] S/RES/948, Oct. 15 1994. The U.S. Government lifted sanctions and financial restrictions on the same day. *See*, E.O. 12932, October 14, 1994, 59 FR 52403, Oct. 18, 1994.

the demonstrations spread to other Libyan cities. The Arab League quickly condemned Qadhafi's brutal response to the demonstrations, as did the UN Security Council. The Security Council adopted Resolution 1970 on February 26, 2011, which acted under Article 41 to impose an arms embargo on the Qadhafi regime. Operative paragraph 9 of the Resolution states that:

> ...Member States shall immediately take the necessary measures to prevent the direct or indirect supply, sale or transfer to the Libyan Arab Jamahiriya, from or through their territories or by their nationals, or using their flag vessels or aircraft, of arms and related materiel of all types, including weapons and ammunition, military vehicles and equipment, paramilitary equipment, and spare parts for the aforementioned, and technical assistance, training, financial or other assistance, related to military activities or the provision, maintenance or use of any arms and related materiel, including the provision of armed mercenary personnel....[50]

Operative paragraph 11 called on States to inspect all cargo to and from Libya, including seaports and airports, if there was reasonable grounds to believe the items were unauthorized.[51] The resolution also established a travel ban on Libyan officials,[52] who were listed individually in Annex I of the text. By identifying regime members by name, and targeting them in the Resolution, the Security Council worked to separate the elites from the population of the country. Libyan financial assets also were ordered frozen, cutting off the regimes capital.[53]

With widespread violence by the government against the population of Libya, the situation in the country continued to deteriorate. On March 17, 2011, the Security Council adopted Resolution 1973, which authorized member States, *inter alia*, to use all necessary measures to enforce the arms embargo imposed by Resolution 1970. Resolution 1973 replaced operative paragraph 11 of Resolution 1970 with an even stronger remit to enforce an arms embargo and expand the scope of inspections of air and sea transportation into and out of Libya. The modified text called on flag States of ships and aircraft to cooperate with such inspections and it authorized Member States to use "all measures commensurate to the specific circumstances" to conduct maritime and aviation inspections.[54]

NATO responded to the Security Council's call for assistance by launching *Operation Unified Protector* on March 22, 2011. The first phase of the operation involved deployment of vessels into seaports to evacuate designated ("entitled") persons. The British Type 22 frigate *HMS Cumberland*, for example, evacuated 454 people from the port city of Benghazi to the safety of Malta during two voyages.[55]

---

[50] S/RES/1970 (2011), Feb. 26, 2011, para. 9.
[51] Id., at para. 11.
[52] Id., at paras. 15–16.
[53] Id., at paras. 17–21.
[54] S/RES/1973, Mar. 17, 2011, para. 13.
[55] Dave Sloggett, *A Unified Approach: How Naval Agility Help Win in Libya*, JANE'S NAVY INT'L, Mar. 2012, at 26, 27.

Naval forces from each participating state conducted non-combatant evacuation operations autonomously.

Operation Odyssey Dawn was the second phase. First, British and American submarines fired 124 cruise missiles into Libya, destroying the regime's air defense system.[56] Then, warships, submarines, and military aircraft stationed in the Mediterranean Sea destroyed high value regime targets. Fixed-wing strike packages from French, Italian, and U.S. aircraft carriers participated in the operation. Surface warships, such as the British destroyer *Liverpool* and the Type 23 frigates *Sutherland* and *HMS Iron Duke*, traded fire with Libyan government shore batteries.[57]

The longest and most varied multinational tasks were conducted by *Unified Protector*, the NATO maritime mission. *Unified Protector* enforced the arms embargo against Libya by screening commercial shipping cargo in bound to Libya. The operation also involved direct action against regime forces ashore. For example, a US Air Force A-10 Thunderbolt close air support aircraft and a P-3C maritime patrol aircraft engaged and destroyed a 12 meter Libyan Coast Guard ship that had been firing rounds into the besieged port of Misrata.[58] *Odyssey Dawn* was conducted over a large area of the central Mediterranean Sea, which encompassed nearly 2.5 million square kilometers of area.[59]

Under the command of Italian Vice Admiral Rinaldo Veri, Commander Maritime Command Naples, NATO forces had authority to stop, search and divert vessels suspected of carrying illegal arms or mercenaries to or from Libya. NATO developed and implemented special rules for visit, board, search and seizure. *Operation Odyssey Dawn* was under the tactical direction of Admiral Sam Locklear, commander of U.S. Naval Forces Africa, embarked aboard the *USS Mount Whitney* and operating within the maritime trade embargo zone.[60] Commercial ships transiting the area were expected to notify NATO of their cargo and destination via transmission of a detailed "navigation warning" message.[61] Warship commanding officers conducted patrols to enforce the embargo, and had authority to use necessary force to board and inspect vessels, to deny entry into Libya, or to divert the ships to alternate ports.

NATO used the Maritime Safety and Security Information System—also called MSSIS—to condense the maritime common operating picture in the Mediterranean Sea. Before using the shipboard VHF Automatic Identification System data source, the headquarters had to track 300 separate contacts each day. Combining

---

[56] Id.
[57] Id., at 32.
[58] Id., at 28.
[59] Id., at 26. Vice Admiral Harry B. Harris served on board the same ship as the Joint Forces Maritime Component Commander (JFMCC).
[60] Sloggett, *A Unified Approach*, JANE'S NAVY INT'L, at 26.
[61] Id., at 32.

AIS data from the MSSIS with covert intelligence, however, participating naval forces refined the list of possible suspect vessels.[62]

By March 24, 2011, naval and air forces from 12 NATO nations were engaged or en route to the area, including over 25 ships and submarines and more than 50 fighter aircraft and maritime patrol aircraft. The force laydown was strained by a geographic search zone that extended over a 61,000 square nautical mile area in the Central Mediterranean.[63]

Ships intending to transit through the embargo area were required to notify NATO of their cargo and destination. Any vessel suspected of violating the embargo was hailed by radio, and if satisfactory information about its cargo was not provided, NATO forces were authorized to stop and board the vessel to inspect the ship's log, and examine the crew list and cargo manifest. Lethal force was authorized to enforce the embargo, but only as a last resort. Any vessel could be denied the right to continue to its destination if it carried weapons, mercenaries or materials to support the regime, and there were reasonable grounds to believe that it posed a danger to Libyan civilians. Skeptics, which included China, began to suspect that NATO forces shoehorned authorization for a general war against Libya through the more narrow UN Security Council authority to protect Libyan civilians.

The maritime operation lasted for 228 days and included maritime interception operations as well as higher-profile attacks against targets inside Libya using Tomahawk land-attack cruise missiles from British and American warships and submarines.[64] As the regime weakened and collapsed, the Security Council ultimately adopted Resolution 2009 on September 16, 2011. The new Resolution lifted the arms embargo against Libya. Over the course of the operation, over 3,100 vessels were hailed. Of these ships encountered by coalition forces, approximately 300 were boarded, and 11 were "denied transit to or from Libya because the vessel or its cargo presented a risk to the civilian population."[65]

---

[62] Id., at 30–31.

[63] Military forces from the following nations participated in the operation: Belgium, Bulgaria, Canada, France, Greece, Italy, the Netherlands, Romania, Spain, Turkey, the United Kingdom, and the United States. JEREMIAH GERTLER, OPERATION ODYSSEY DAWN (LIBYA): BACKGROUND AND ISSUES FOR CONGRESS (Cong. Research Service Rpt. to Cong., Mar. 28, 2011).

[64] Sloggett, *A Unified Approach*, JANE'S NAVY INT'L at 26.

[65] OFFICE OF PUBLIC DIPLOMACY, NORTH ATLANTIC TREATY ORGANIZATION, OPERATION UNIFIED PROTECTOR FINAL MISSION STATISTICS, Nov. 2, 2011.

INDEX

1949 Geneva Conventions
  Common Article 2   895
  Common Article 3   896
1971 Seabed Treaty   8
1977 Additional Protocol I   896
1977 Additional Protocol II   896, 899
1988 Convention for the Suppression of Unlawful Acts against the Safety of Maritime Navigation. *See* 1988 SUA
1988 SUA   26, 803
1988 SUA Protocol   803
2005 SUA   494, 787, 789–790, 815, 820
  Armed conflict defined   824
  Boarding regime   833
  Flag state jurisdiction   836, 842
  IAEA   827
  Master consent   758
  NPT   828
  U.S. understanding   825
  UNSCR 1540   828
  UNSCR 1673   828
2005 SUA PROC   853

Achille Lauro   358, 380
Aeronautical Information Services
  Chicago Convention   103
  Federal Aviation Administration   105
  Notice to Airmen   104–106, 881
  Notice to Airmen, military   108–109
African Union Mission on Somalia. *See* AMISOM
AFS   421
Air-Sea Battle Concept   38, 45
Airspace
  FAA   300
  International, intercepts   294, 296, 298
  International, U.S. intercept procedures   300
Airspace Control Measures
  Air Defense Identification Zones   178–179
  Special Use Airspace   181
  Special Use Airspace, Alert Areas   183
  Special Use Airspace, Controlled Firing Areas   183
  Special Use Airspace, Military Operation Areas   182
  Special Use Airspace, National Security Areas   183
  Special Use Airspace, Prohibited Areas   181
  Special Use Airspace, Restricted Areas   181
  Special Use Airspace, Warning Areas   182
AIS   63, 404–407, 594, 716, 719, 920
Alberico Gentili   160
AMISOM   707–708, 710, 727, 729–730, 732
Amphibious Operations in the 21st Century   41
APEC   395, 442
APII
  Armed conflict defined   824
Arab League   919
Arab Spring   918
Automatic Identification System. *See* AIS

Baliam, Alexander Captain   684
Baltic and International Maritime Council   14
Battle of Leyte Gulf   8

Battle of Okinawa 8
Berlin Discothèque Bombing 251
Blockade 882
  1909 London Declaration 885
  1949 Geneva Convention IV 888
  Algeria blockade 884
  Breach of blockade 889
  Contraband 887, 889
  Contraband, 1909 London Declaration 887, 892
  Definition of Aggression 884
  Enemy merchant vessels 891
  Former Republic of Yugoslavia 885
  Gaza blockade 895
  Gaza blockade, Human Rights Council 899
  Gaza blockade, *Mavi Marmara* 898
  Gaza blockade, Operation Case Lead 897
  Gaza blockade, Operation Sea Breeze 898
  Graf Spee 891
  Hague Convention XII of 1907 885
  ILA Helsinki Principles 885, 890
  Iran-Iraq War 884
  Korean War 884
  Law of neutrality 891
  Lebanon 885
  Neutral ships 888–889
  Non-international armed conflict 892, 895
  Non-Intervention Patrol 895
  Orders-in-Council 884
  Paper blockade 883
  Paris Declaration Respecting Maritime Law 883
  Prize Cases 894
  Right of visit and search 888
  San Remo Manual 882
  Spanish Civil War 895
  Spanish-American War 883
  U.S. Civil War 892
  UN Charter, Article 42 882
  UN Security Council 885
  Vietnam War 884
  Visit and search 888, 899
  WWI 884
  WWII 884
Bush, George W. *See* PSI

Canals
  Panama 195
  Panama Canal 195, 404
  Suez Canal 195, 691, 865
  Suez Canal, Constantinople Convention 195
Captain of the Port 420, 429
CARICOM 566
CARSI 585
Central America Regional Security Initiate. *See* CARSI
CGPCS 699
Chicago Convention on Civil Aviation 202
Chicago Convention 289, 292, 559
  Annex 2 292, 296, 298
  ICAO 292
China National Offshore Oil Corp 322
China 42
  EP-3 Incident 44
CICAD 569
Coast Watch South 347
COLREGS 363, 367, 413
Confidence Building Measures
  U.S.-China Defense Policy Talks 309
  U.S.-China Military Maritime Consultative Agreement 309
Contact Group on Piracy off the Coast of Somalia. *See* CGPCS
Contact Group on Somali Piracy 10
Container Security Initiative. *See* CSI
Convention for the Suppression of Unlawful Acts against the Safety of Maritime Navigation. *See* Achille Lauro
Convention on International Civil Aviation. *See* Chicago Convention
Convention on the High Seas 659, 675, 698, 754
  Flag state jurisdiction 836
Convention on the International Regulations for Preventing Collisions at Sea. *See* COLREGS
Cooperative Strategy for 21st Century Seapower. *See* CS21
Corbett, Julian S. 13
Cordon Sanitaire 880
  Notice to Airmen 881
  Notice to Mariners 881
Counter-drug Operations
  Bilateral agreements 555
  Bilateral agreements, Mérida Initiative 582–583, 585
  CICAD 569
  Code of Conduct for Law Enforcement Officials 549

INDEX

Convention on Psychotropic Substances 521–523, 525, 529, 531, 540
Drug cartels 629, 636
Flag state jurisdiction 540, 561
IMO 541
IMO Guidelines for the Prevention and Suppression of the Smuggling of Drugs, Psychotropic Substances, and Precursor Chemicals on Ships Engaged in International Traffic 541
OAS 595
Philippines Coast Watch South 579, 582
Philippines National Coast Watch System 578, 581
Regional agreements 555
Regional agreements, Caribbean Basin Security Initiative 566–568, 634
Regional agreements, Caribbean Regional Maritime Agreement 555–562, 565–566, 569
Regional agreements, Caribbean Regional Maritime Agreement, U.S. declaration 563
Regional agreements, OAS Model SOP 569–572
Regional agreements, Paris Pact Initiative 573–578
Revised IMO Guidelines for the Prevention and Suppression of the Smuggling of Drugs, Psychotropic Substances and Precursor Chemicals on Ships Engaged in International Maritime Traffic 541, 543–548
Single Convention on Narcotic Drugs 523–525, 527–528
SPSS 591–593, 595, 596,
SPSS, model OAS legislation 595
Transnational criminal organizations 629–630, 650
U.S. legislation, Drug Trafficking Vessel Interdiction Act 592, 594, 596
U.S. legislation, immigration laws 607
U.S. legislation, Maritime Drug Law Enforcement Act 588, 589
U.S. maritime counterdrug agreements 639
U.S. maritime counterdrug agreements, U.S.-Colombia 641–643
U.S. maritime counterdrug agreements, U.S.-Colombia Air Bridge Denial Agreement 644–647, 649

U.S. operations 628
U.S. operations, CBP 587, 603
U.S. operations, DEA 635
U.S. operations, DOD policy guidance 612
U.S. operations, DOD policy guidance, CJCSI 3710.01 617, 619–620
U.S. operations, DOD policy guidance, DODD 5525.5 613, 615–616
U.S. operations, DOD policy guidance, JP 3-07.4 622–623
U.S. operations, DOD support 607
U.S. operations, DOD support, detection and monitoring 636
U.S. operations, DOD support, military support for civilian law enforcement 608, 610, 612
U.S. operations, DOD support, Posse Comitatus Act 607, 616
U.S. operations, DOD support, use of force 622
U.S. operations, Executive Order 12978 599
U.S. operations, JIATF 624–625
U.S. operations, JIATF-South 624–625, 637
U.S. operations, JIATF-West 624–625
U.S. operations, Kingpin Act 598–601
U.S. operations, National Drug Control Strategy 633–634
U.S. operations, NDIC 628
U.S. operations, Operation Martillo 625, 637
U.S. operations, SOUTHCOM Posture Statement 636–638
U.S. operations, Strategy to Combat Transnational Organized Crime 634–635
U.S. operations, USCG LEDET 622
UN Basic Principles on the Use of Force 549–550
UNCLOS 522, 540
UNODC 578, 627
UNODC World Drug Report 628
Vienna Convention 523–524, 532–538, 541, 555, 562, 639
Counter-piracy Operations
Armed robbery at sea 698
Barbary principalities 694
Best Management Practices 726, 737
Combined Maritime Forces 724
CTF Iraqi Maritime 725

926 INDEX

CTF-150 725
CTF-151 725, 728, 733
CTF-152 725
EU 728
EU Naval Force 727, 729–732
Exclusive economic zone 700
Faina 724
Flag state responsibilities 736
Gulf of Aden 721, 723
Gulf of Guinea 712
High Risk Areas 736–737
Horn of Africa 724–725, 733
IMB Piracy Reporting Centre 727
IMO 702, 713, 720
IMO, Djibouti Code of Conduct 718, 720–721
IMO, information sharing centers 721–722
IMO, MSC/Circ.443 713
IMO, MSC/Circ.622 715
IMO, MSC/Circ.623 717
Indian Ocean 724–725, 728, 721
Internationally Recognized Transit Corridor 709, 728, 733
Japan 733–734
Justinian Digest 692
Maritime Safety Center-Horn of Africa 731, 736
Maritime Security Centre—Horn of Africa 727
Maritime Security Patrol Area 728, 733
MARLO Bahrain 725
MOTR 722
National waters 700
NATO Shipping Center 727
NATO Shipping Centre 726
Operation Allied Protector 726
Operation Allied Provider 726
Operation Atalanta 727, 729, 731
Operation Ocean Shield 726–727
Piracy 692, 694–695
Piracy, U.S. Constitution 695
Piracy, UNCLOS 697–699
Privately contracted armed security personnel 736
Ransom 705, 724
ReCAAP Information Sharing Center 700
ReCAAP Information Sharing Centre 723
Seaborne Spirit 723

Self-Protection Measures 737
Ship Security Plan 736
Sirius Star 724
Somalia 699, 702, 707, 723, 860
Somalia, CGPCS 699
Somalia, Somali Transitional Federal Government 701, 707–708, 710, 732
SUA 699
U.S. Fifth Fleet 725
UK Maritime Component Commander 725
UN Security Council 699
UNCLOS 698, 702
UNCLOS, right of visist 700
UNSCR 1816 701
UNSCR 1838 702
UNSCR 1844 703
UNSCR 1918 704
CS21 36, 70
CSI 26
Cuban Missile Crisis 870
   OAS 874
   OAS Council 875
   OAS Resolution 875–876
   Proclamation of Interdiction 875
   Quarantine 873, 878–879
   Self-defense 879

DEA 584, 635
Defense Areas
   Administrative Areas 173
   Compact of Free Association 176
   Entry Control Commander 174
   Naval Airspace Reservations 173
   Naval Defensive Sea Areas 173–174
   Trust Territory of the Pacific Islands 173, 175
Drug Enforcement Agency. *See* DEA

East Asia Summit 347
EC 721
Environmental Control Measures 113
   Critical habitat, right whale 141
   Critical habitat, Undersea warfare training range 145
   Exclusive economic zone 115–116
   International agreements 116
   Marine National Monument, Marianas Trench 137
   Marine National Monument, Pacific Remote Islands 137

Marine National Monument,
  Papahānaumokuākea 131
Marine National Monument, Rose
  Atoll 136
Marine National Monuments, U.S. 16
Marine protected area 117
Particularly sensitive sea area 117–118,
  264
Particularly sensitive sea area,
  Associated protective measures 123
Particularly sensitive sea area, Criteria
  124
Particularly sensitive sea area, IMO
  guidelines 121
Particularly sensitive sea area, Malpelo
  Island 126–127, 129
Particularly sensitive sea area,
  Papahānaumokuākea 135
Special Area, MARPOL 117
Sovereign immunity exception
  280–281
Territorial sea 115
UNCLOS 116
Vessel source pollution 115
EU 29, 31, 33, 34, 35, 36, 58
  Chiefs of European Navies Maritime
    Operational Concept 66–67
  Counter-piracy operations 55
  EU Naval Force 730
  European Security Strategy 59
  Headline Goal 2010 64
  Integrated Maritime Policy 61
  Internal Security Strategy 59
  Maritime Security Centre—Horn of
    Africa 65
  Operation Atalanta 64
  Operation Concordia 729
  Regulation 725/2004 60
European Commission. *See* EC

FAA 105, 299
FAO 423
FARC 519, 633, 862
Federal Aviation Administration. *See* FAA
Flag State Jurisdiction 365, 412, 414, 495,
  664, 754, 757, 810, 836
  Consent 365
  Convention on the High Seas 754
  Counter-drug operations 540, 561
  Exceptions 366
  Exceptions, right of visit and search
    366

Flag state consent 757
High seas 365
Master consent 757–758, 782
MIO 366
Nottebohm Case 754
UNCLOS 754
UNCLOS, master consent 758
Visit, board, search and seizure 366
Freedom of Navigation
  Aäland Islands 865
  Aaland Strait 226
  Archipelagic sea lanes 416, 886
  Archipelagic sea lanes passage 120,
    138, 218, 227, 230, 261, 270, 866
  Archipelagic sea lanes passage, normal
    mode of operation 271
  Archipelagic sea lanes,
    designation 231
  Archipelagic sea lanes, partial
    designation 232, 275
  Archipelagic sea lanes,
    Philippines 273
  Archipelagic straits 227
  Archipelagic waters 227, 230, 416
  Archipelagic waters, IMO Guidance
    for Ships Transiting Archipelagic
    Waters 231–232
  Baselines, Conference for the
    Codification of International
    Law 216
  Baselines, straight 216
  Black Sea Bumping Incident 255–256
  Boundary Treaty between the Argentine
    Republic and Chile 226
  Condition of port entry 416, 754
  Contiguous zone 199, 431
  Contigous zone, coastal state authority
    254
  Continental shelf 241, 416
  Continental shelf, Outer Continental
    Shelf Lands Act 241
  Continental shelf, Truman
    Proclamation 241
  Convention for the Discontinuance of
    the Sound Dues 225
  Convention on the Non-Fortification
    and Neutralization of the Åaland
    Islands 226
  Corfu Channel case 220–221
  Corfu Channel, Operation Retail 220
  Creeping coastal state jurisdiction 196
  Danish Straits 225, 268

Danish Straits, Great Belt Fixed Link   268
Danish Straits, Øresund Bridge-Tunnel   268
Dead-end straits   223, 228
Distress entry   159, 217
EP-3 incident   44, 290, 314
Excessive claims, restrictions on archipelagic sea lanes passage   271, 275
Excessive claims, restrictions on transit passage   259
Excessive contiguous zone claims   254
Excessive maritime claims   193, 202, 243
Excessive straight baselines   246, 263
Excessive straight baselines, Strait of Hainan   261
Excessive territorial sea claims   252, 278
Exclusive economic zone   198, 388, 416
Exclusive economic zone, Chinese excessive claims   279–281, 288, 309, 311
Exclusive economic zone, coastal state authority   236
Exclusive economic zone, coatal state rights and duties   233
Exclusive economic zone, excessive claims   235, 284
Exclusive economic zone, high seas freedoms   235
Exclusive economic zone, intelligence collection   291–292, 304
Exclusive economic zone, marine data collection   285
Exclusive economic zone, marine scientific research   198
Exclusive economic zone, military activities   235–237, 284, 291–292, 304
Exclusive economic zone, peaceful purposes   284, 304–305, 308
Exclusive economic zone, restrictions in the exclusive economic zone   239
Exclusive economic zone, restrictions on military activities   239
Freedom of Navigation Program   201–202
Global commons   37, 40, 45, 57, 186, 188

Gulf of Aqaba   194
Gulf of Sidra   248, 250–251
Head Harbor Passage   262
High seas   242
High seas freedoms   75, 119, 198–199, 233, 235, 241–242, 891
Historic waters   247
Historic waters, Gulf of Sidra   247
Indonesian archipelago   271
Innocent passage   75, 115, 119, 136, 159, 198, 218–219, 226, 230, 237, 252–253, 257, 752, 777, 891
Innocent passage, prior notice or consent   253
INS Airavat incident   322
Internal waters   217, 226, 416
Internal waters, historic   217
Internal waters, Strait of Hainan   261
International straits   219, 224, 886
International straits, bordering state authority   260
International straits, bordering state rights and duties   223
International straits, high seas corridor   224
International straits, high seas freedoms   225
International straits, long-standing international convention   225
International straits, route of similar convenience   226
Jackson Hole Agreement   258
Korea Strait   227
Lausanne Convention   225
Line of Death   247–248, 250
Maritime mobility   189
Messina exception   223, 227
Montreux Convention   225
Non-suspendable innocent passage   223, 262, 866
Normal mode of operation   231
Northwest Passage   225, 262
Nuclear-powered ships   253
Osumi Strait   227
Palk Strait   356
Persian Gulf   867
Philippine Archipelago   273
Restrictions on innocent passage   253
Restrictions on military activities   282

South China Sea, high seas freedoms 336
Soya Strait 227
Stateless vessels 756
Stateless vessels, M/V *So San* 756
Strait of Hormuz 269
Strait of Magellan 195, 226, 865
Strait of Malacca, voluntary pilotage 269
Strait of Messina 227
Strait of Tiran 194
Strategic straits 219
Taiwan Strait 225, 264
Territorial sea 198, 218, 388, 495
Territorial sea, coastal state authority 252
Torres Strait 264
Torres Strait, compulsory pilotage 266
Transit passage 119, 138, 159, 218–219, 222, 227, 230, 237, 252, 259–260, 270, 866
Transit passage, approaches to strait 229
Treaty for the Redemption of the Sound Dues 225
Tsugaru Strait 226
Tsushima Strait 227
Turkish Straits 225
U.S. Freedom of Navigation Program 255
U.S. Ocean Policy Statement 197–198
U.S.-Peru C-130 incident 289
USNS Bowditch incident 287
USNS Impeccable Incident 310, 315
USNS Victorious Incident 311
VBSS 920
Visit and search 888
Warships 254
Freedom of the Seas 191
  Atlantic Charter 193
  Fourteen Points 192
From the Sea 36, 38
  Forward From the Sea 36, 38
Fuerzas Armadas Revolucionarias de Colombia. *See* FARC

General Provisions on Ships' Routeing 232, 274
Geneva Convention on the Territorial Sea and the Contiguous Zone 228, 413
Gentilli, Alberico. *See* Piracy

Global Maritime Distress and Safety System 408
  Daily Memorandum 88
  HYDROLANT 88
  HYDROPAC 88
  MARAD Advisories 88, 90, 98
  MARAD Advisory No. 05-01 98
  MARLO Advisory Bull 01-04 911
  National Geospatial-Intelligence Agency 90
  NAVAREA IV 87
  NAVAREA XII 88
  Notice to Mariners 881
  Special warnings 88, 90
  Special Warning No. 115 910
  Special Warning No. 80 909
  U.S. Notice to Mariners No. 1 90
Global Maritime Distress Safety System 388
Global Maritime Partnership 14, 19–20, 29, 32
Global Maritime Transportation System 355–356, 375
Globalization 16
Grotius, Hugo. *See* Freedom of the Seas, *See* Piracy
Gulf of Guinea 3, 357, 712–713, 763

Hezbollah 2
Homeland Security Presidential Directive. *See* HSPD
Homeland Security Strategy 35
HSPD
  13 27 n. 5
Hugo Grotius 190
Human Rights 659, 913
  International Covenant on Civil and Political Rights 549
  Universal Declaration of Human Rights 549
Human Rights Council 899

IAEA 795, 797, 827
ICAO 403
ICJ 755
ILA 885
ILO 376, 381, 385, 423
  Code of Practice 377
  International Labor Organization Merchant Shipping Convention No. 147 377
  Maritime Labor Convention 377

IMB
  International Chamber of Commerce 727
IMO 26, 223, 231–232, 355, 362–363, 366–368, 379–380, 397, 404–405, 407, 415, 418, 423, 435, 467, 471, 487–488, 495, 719–721, 723, 755, 802
  AIS 719
  Counter-drug Operations 541
  International Maritime Consultative Organization 368
  IMCO 755
  LRIT 719
  Member State Audit Scheme 375
IMO Measures
  Area to be avoided, right whale 144–145
  Guidelines 139
  Mandatory ship reporting 138, 140
  Mandatory ship reporting, right whale 141–143
  Ships' routeing systems 137
  Vessel traffic service 138
Information Sharing Center ReCAAP. See Piracy
Inmarsat-C SafetyNET 388
Inter-American Drug Abuse Control Commission. See CICAD
International Association of Classification Societies 397
International Civil Aviation Organization. See ICAO
International Convention for the Safety of Life at Sea. See SOLAS
International Convention on Load Lines. See Load Lines
International Convention on Maritime Search and Rescue. See SAR
International Convention on Standards of Training, Certification and Watchkeeping for Seafarers. See STCW
International Convention on the Control of Harmful Anti-Fouling Systems on Ships. See AFS
International Convention on Tonnage Measurement of Ships. See TONNAGE 69
International Court of Justice. See ICJ
International Labor Organization Merchant Shipping Convention No. 147 413
International Labor Organization. See ILO

International Law Association. See ILA
International Maritime Organization. See IMO
International Organization for Migration. See IOM
International Safety Management (ISM) Code and the International Ship and Port Facility Security (ISPS) Code. See ISPS Code
International Shipping and Port Facility Security Code. See ISPS Code
IOM 658
Iranian Revolutionary Guard Corps 3. See IRGC
IRCG 862
ISC 21, 721
ISM Code 422, 431, 467
ISPS 27
ISPS Code 368, 370–371, 377, 378–379, 384, 386, 394, 415, 417, 420–421, 431, 439, 440, 449, 467, 470, 515, 541
  Continuous Declaration of Security 391
  Declaration of Security 389
  Facility Security Survey 380
  International Ship Security Certificate 379, 392, 398, 420
  Maritime Transportation Security Act 382
  Port facility security 542
  Port Facility Security Plan 391–392, 415
  Security levels 387, 391–392
  Ship Security Plan 380, 391–393, 398

Jackson Hole Agreement 258
JMIE 400
Joint Maritime Information Element. See JMIE
Jurisdiction
  Nationality Principle 815
  Passive Personality Principle 810
  Protective Principle 811
  Territoriality Principle 815
  Universality Principle 812
just in time 5

Kananaskis Principles. See UNSCR 1540
Klinghoffer, Leon. See Achille Lauro
Koh, "Tommy" T. B. See Third UN Conference on the Law of the Sea

INDEX

Law Enforcement Detachment. *See* LEDET
Law of Naval Warfare 859
   1907 Hague Convention VII 867
   1936 London Protocol 869
   Blockade 867, 888–889
   Continental shelf 869
   Contraband 889
   Declaration of Paris 867
   Exclusive economic zone 867
   Fixed platforms 868
   Hague Conference of 1907 860
   Hybrid warfare 861–863
   IRGC 862, 868
   Jus ad bellum 859
   Jus in bello 859, 869
   Maritime zones 865
   Merchant ships 868
   Naval auxiliaries 867
   Neutral ships 888
   Neutralized waters 865
   Non-state actors 862
   Nuremberg Tribunal 882
   Operation Cast Lead 861
   Operation Enduring Freedom-Philippines 861
   Privateering 867
   Prizes 867, 889
   Right of visit and search 888
   Submarines 869
   Warships 867
LEDET 605, 622, 654–655
Littoral Combat Ship 25, 44, 351
Load Lines 363, 366, 372, 419, 421
Load Lines Protocol 421
Long Range Navigation. *See* LORAN
Long-Range Identification and Tracking of Ships. *See* LRIT
LORAN 399
LRIT 408

M/V *Limburg* 358
M/V *Saiga* 763
MAGNET 400
Mahan, Alfred Thayer 3, 12
Manila Declaration 347
Maritime Awareness Global Network. *See* MAGNET
Maritime Claims Reference Manual 203
Maritime Domain Awareness 399
   AIS 404–406, 408
   Baltic Sky 399
   Common operating picture 401

European Maritime Safety Agency 410
Global Maritime Intelligence Integration Plan 401
Intelligence Coordination Center 401
JMIE 400
LORAN 399
LRIT 403, 405, 408, 410
MAGNET 400
Maritime Safety & Security Information System 407
MDA Plan 401
NSPD-41 400–401
Office of Naval Intelligence 401
Sirius Star 407
Maritime Law Enforcement 2–3, 7, 91, 316, 323, 365, 557, 564–565, 587, 602–603, 623, 639, 651, 654, 686, 722, 802, 863
Maritime law enforcement definition 7
Maritime Organization of West and Central Africa. *See* Gulf of Guinea
Maritime Ports Convention 413
Maritime Rescue Coordination Centers 388
Maritime Rescue Coordination Centre 489
Maritime Safety and Security Information Systsem 920
Maritime Security Interagency Policy Committee. *See* MSIPC
Maritime Security Policy. *See* NSPD-41
Maritime Security 348
   Accidents 360
   Alternative Security Agreements 468
   Cargo Tampering, Sabotage, or Theft 359
   CTF-150 725
   CTF-151 725, 728, 733
   CTF-152 725
   Environmental Extremists 360
   Equivalent Security Arrangements 470
   Illegal Migrants, Stowaways, Refugees, and Asylum Seekers 359
   IMO/ILO Code of Practice on Port Security 382, 394, 415
   Maritime Security Measures 371, 383, 386–387, 392, 394–396, 398, 415, 435, 437, 467, 470, 487, 495, 500
   Maritime threats 358
   MARLO Bahrain 725
   Operation Active Endeavour 725

Organized Labor Activities and Labor Violence 361
Piracy and Armed Robbery at Sea 358
Recognized Security Organizations 395–397
Regional Organizations 395
Smuggling of Contraband 359
Weather and Natural Disasters 360
Maritime Terrorism 739
  Abu Sayyaf 744
  Achille Lauro 740
  Ahi Hanit 745
  Al Shabaab 745
  Al-Qaeda 743, 745
  Athena 742
  Hamas 741, 744
  Hezbollah 741, 745
  IRA 740–741
  Irish Mona 742
  Limassol 742
  Limburg 744
  Lord Mountbatten assassination 740
  LTTE 741–742
  M. Star 745
  M/V *Ahat* 741
  M/V *Cordiality* 742
  M/V *Progress Light* 742
  M/V *Sik Yang* 742
  Misen 742
  Morong Bon 742
  Operation Cactus 742
  Our Lady of Mediatrix 743
  PLF 740
  PLO 741
  Princess Kash 742
  Princess Wave 742
  Silk Pride 742
  Super Ferry 14 744
  USS *Ashland* 744
  USS *Cole* 743
  USS *Kearsarge* 744
  USS *The Sullivans* 743
Maritime Zones
  Archipelagic waters 227, 230, 416, 700, 752, 865, 891
  Contiguous zone 199, 233, 254, 431, 754, 891
  Contiguous zone, coastal state authority 254
  Continental shelf 241, 416, 866
  Exclusive economic zone 198, 233, 236, 416, 660, 698, 700, 866, 888, 891

Exclusive economic zone, marine scientific research 237, 285
High seas 242, 865
Historic waters 247
Internal waters 217, 416, 700, 752, 891
Internal waters, Strait of Hainan 261
Territorial sea 198, 218, 252, 388, 495, 558, 698, 700, 752, 865, 886, 891, 888, 898–899
Territorial seas, coastal state authority 252
MARPOL 366, 372–373, 413, 419, 421
Megaports 14
Megaports Initiative 26
Migrant Smuggling
  Balsero Crisis 687
  Bilateral agreements 666, 688
  Convention for the Unification of Certain Rules of Law Respecting Assistance and Salvage at Sea 675
  Convention on the High Seas 659, 675
  Cuba-U.S. Migration Accord 687
  Duty to Assist 675–676, 682
  Duty to Assist, COMDTINST M5000.3B 682
  Duty to Assist, U.S. law 682
  Duty to Assist, U.S. Navy Regulations 682
  Executive Order 12324 686
  Executive Order 12807 687
  Executive Order 13581 661–662
  IMO 689
  IMO initiatives, Interim Guidelines 668
  IMO initiatives, Interim Guidelines, MSC/Circ.896 669–670, 672
  IMO initiatives, Resolution A.773(18) 667
  IMO initiatives, Resolution A.867(20) 668
  IMO initiatives, SAR Convention, Guidelines on the Treatment of Persons Rescued at Sea 673–674
  IOM 658
  M/V *Golden Venture* 667
  M/V *Tampa* 678
  M/V *Yioham* 667
  Mariel Boatlift 686
  Migrant Smuggling Protocol 660, 662–665, 680
  Operation Able Manner 687
  Operation Able Response 688

INDEX 933

Operation Able Vigil   687
Presidential Proclamation 4865   686
Protocol Relating to the Status of
   Refugees   681
Refugee Convention   680–681
Salvage Convention   676
SAR Convention   673, 679
SOLAS   676
SOLAS, Regulation V/33   677–679
TOCC   660, 689
UNCLOS   659
UNHCR   669, 675, 678
UNODC   689
UNODC Model Law against the
   Smuggling of Migrants   689
USS Dubuque   684–685
USS Morton   683
Wet Foot, Dry Foot Policy   687
MIO
   2005 SUA   833
   Use of force, *I'm Alone Case*   760–761, 765
   Use of force, M/V *Saiga Case*   763–765
   Use of force, *The Red Crusader Case*   762–763, 765
   VBSS   920
Model Maritime Service Code U.S. Coast Guard. *See* Maritime Law Enforcement
MSIPC   28
   Maritime security policy coordinating committee   28

NACGF   20
National Defense Strategy   37
National Drug Intelligence Center.
   See NDIC
National Security Presidential Directive.
   See NSPD
National Security Strategy   30, 632
National Strategy for Global Supply Chain Security   34
National Strategy for Maritime Security.
   See NSMS
NATO   47, 725, 913–914, 919–920
   Alliance Maritime Strategy   48–49
   Collective defense   49
   Comprehensive Approach Action Plan   52
   Cooperative security   49
   Istanbul Cooperative Initiative   48
   Maritime Security and Safety Information System   63

Maritime security operations   52
Maritime Security Operations
   Concept   48
Military command structure   53
Operation Active Endeavour   64, 725
Operation Allied Provider   55
Operation Ocean Shield   47, 54
Response Force   54
Russia-Georgia Conflict   55
Standing NATO Maritime Groups
   52–53
Strategic Concept   48, 51, 54, 57
Standing Naval Force Atlantic   914
Standing Naval Force Mediterranean
   914
Naval Operation Concept. See NOC
Naval Operations Concept 2010   6
NAVTEX   388
NDIC   628
NOC   38
Non-SOLAS Vessels   515
   Declaration of Security   516
   S/V *Quest*   516
North Atlantic Coast Guard Forum. *See*
   NACGF
North Atlantic Treaty Organization. *See*
   NATO
North Pacific Coast Guard Forum. *See*
   NPCGF
NOTMAR   388
NPCGF   20
NPT   745, 828
   DPRK nuclear program   747, 750–751, 756, 768, 772, 774, 783, 795, 797
   DPRK nuclear test   746
   DPRK withdrawal   746, 768
   IAEA   746–747, 749, 774, 776, 778, 781, 795
   IAEA safeguard agreements   751, 776
   India nuclear program   751
   Iran nuclear program   747, 749, 751, 756, 768, 775–776, 778, 780, 782–784, 795, 797
   Israel nuclear program   751
   Non-nuclear weapons states   751
   Nuclear weapons states   751
   Pakistan nuclear program   751
   South Africa nuclear program   751
NSMS   29
NSPD
   41   27–28
Nuclear Non-Proliferation Treaty. *See* NPT

O'Connell, D.P. 11, 18
OAS 395, 874, 915–916
Officer in Charge of Marine Inspection 420
Organization of American States Model Operating Procedure for Combined Maritime Drug Operations. *See* OAS

Papal Bull 190
Paracel Islands
  Woody Island 319
PERSGA 428
Philippines Maritime Zones Act 273
Piracy 19, 358, 691, *See* Counter-piracy Operations
Pivot Toward Asia-Pacific 2, 42
Port Facility Security 434
  Cargo handling 445–446
  Declaration of Security 436–437
  Delivery of ships' stores 446–447
  Designated authority 436–439, 442, 449, 470
  Monitoring the port facility 448
  Port Facility Security Assessment 449
  Port Facility Security Organization 448
  Port Facility Security Plan 436–437, 439, 440–442
  Restricted areas with port facilities 444
  Restricted areas within port facilities 444–445
  Security levels 442–448
Port Facility Security Officer 487, 494
Port Security
  Maritime Transportation Security Act 412
Port State Control 412, 417, 420
  Code of Good Practices 428, 439
  Port and Tanker Safety Act 430
  Port Facility Security Officers 414, 437–438, 442, 448–449
  Port Security Committee 414
  Port Security Officer 414–415
  Port State Security Officer 436
  U.S. measures 429
  U.S. measures, customs waters 430
Port State Regional MOUs 423
  Abuja MOU 427
  Acuerdo de Viña del Mar 424
  Black Sea MOU 427
  Caribbean MOU 425
  Indian Ocean MOU 426
  Mediterranean MOU 425
  Paris MOU 424
  PERGSA 428
  Riyadh MOU 427
  Tokyo MOU 425
Ports and Waterways Safety Act
  Condition of port entry 158–159
  Regulated area 160
  Regulated navigation area 165
  Regulations 160
  Restricted waterfront area 165
  Safety zone 160–161
  Security zone 160, 162, 165
  Security zone, Cuba 163
  Traffic separation schemes 159
  Vessel traffic services 158
  Waterfront security 159
  Zones 156
Pound, Roscoe 4
Presidential Proclamation
  No. 5928 157
  No. 6867 163
  No. 7757 163
Proliferation Security Initiative. *See* PSI, *See* Weapons of Mass Destruction
Protocol against the Smuggling of Migrants by Land, Sea and Air. *See* Migrant Smuggling Protocol
Protocol II Additional to the Geneva Conventions of August 12, 1949. *See* APII
PSI 26, 771, 785, 788, 797, 821
  Bilateral boarding agreements 788, 794
  Boarding agreements 836
  Interdiction, legal basis 787
  National Security Strategy 785
  Opponents 785
  Statement of Interdiction Principles 786–787
  States of proliferation concern 786
  U.S.-Belize boarding agreement 771, 788

ReCAAP 21, 722
  Information Sharing Center. *See* ISC
Regional Agreement on Combating Piracy and Armed Robbery against Ships in Asia piracy. *See* ReCAAP

INDEX

Regional Organization for the Conservation of the Environment of the Red Sea and the Gulf of Aden. *See* PERSGA
Revolutionary Armed Forces of Columbia. *See* FARC
Richardson, Elliot. *See* Third UN Conference on the Law of the Sea
Rubin, Alfred. *See* Piracy

Safety of Life at Sea (SOLAS) Convention. *See* SOLAS
Safety Zones 417
    Continental shelf 76
    Exclusive economic zone 76
    IMO Guidelines 78, 80–81
    Outer Continental Shelf Lands Act 82–83
    Petroleum Act 1987 84
San Remo Manual on the Law of Armed Conflicts at Sea 307
Sansha City 318–319
SAR 363
Schengen Accord 520
Seafarers' Identity Documents Convention 423
Self-defense 758
    Collective self-defense 878
    Cordon sanitaire 880
    Rio Treaty 878
    The Caroline Case 758–760
    UN Charter, Article 51 838, 878
Senate Resolution 524 319
Shangri-La Dialogue 43
Shearer, Ivan 12
Ship Security
    Company Security Officer 486–487, 489–491, 494, 496
    Declaration of Security 483–484, 492, 494
    International Ship Security Certificate 499
    Recognized Security Organizations 494, 500
    Security levels 482, 484, 499
    Ship Security Alert System 489
    Ship security assessment 489
    Ship Security Officer 483–484, 486–487, 491, 493–494, 496
    Ship Security Plan 483, 490–493

SOLAS 27, 363, 366, 368–372, 375, 379, 381, 386, 392, 396, 404, 408, 413, 416–417, 419, 421, 422, 469, 541, 672
    Special Measures to Enhance Maritime Safety 384
    Special Measures to Enhance Maritime Security 384
SOLAS Protocol 420
Sonar Litigation 309
    Marine mammal mitigation measures 151–153
    Marine mammal research 151
    Winter v. Natural Resources Defense Council (NRDC) 147–149
South China Sea 313
    Amy Douglas Bank incident 330
    ARF 335
    ASEAN 333
    Australia-United States Ministerial Consultation 348–349
    Bali Declaration 332
    Balikatan exercise 328
    Binh Minh incident 323
    Brunei claims 315
    Challenges to Chinese claims 320
    China claims 315–316, 318
    Chinese economic coercion 321
    Core interest 318
    Declaration on the Conduct of Parties in the South China Sea 330, 335, 344–345
    Fishing incidents 323
    INS Airavat incident 321–322
    Invasion of Paracel Islands 313
    Iroquois Reef incident 330
    Jackson Atoll incident 340
    Johnson South Reef skirmish 314
    Kalayaan Island Group 325
    Occupation of Mischief Reef 326
    Pagasa Island improvements 327
    Philippine claims 325
    Reed Bank incident 327, 341
    U.S. interests 337, 345–347, 350
    U.S. position 334
    U.S. Senate Resolution 217, 336
    U.S. statement 319
    U.S.-Philippines Mutual Defense Treaty 329, 345
    U-shaped line 322
    Vietnam claims 321

INDEX

Viking 2 incident   323–324
Sovereign Immunity   414, 679, 697, 758
  SOLAS, Regulation I/3   679
  SOLAS, Regulation V/1   679
  Schooner Exchange Case   697
  Schooner Exchange v. M'Faddon   294
STCW   363, 366, 373–374, 393, 413, 419, 421, 488
  Knowledge, Understanding and Proficiency   488
Strategic Straits   260
  Lombok Strait   222, 271
  Strait of Bab el Mandeb   222, 728
  Strait of Gibraltar   55, 222, 252, 404
  Strait of Hormuz   222, 269, 744
  Strait of Malacca   259, 269
  Straits of Malacca and Singapore   222
  Sunda Strait   222, 259, 271
  Windward Passage   222
SUA
  Achille Lauro   801, 811
  IMO   802–804, 811

Tanker War   9
Terrorism   355, *See* Maritime Terrorism
  Abdullah Azzam Brigades   357
  Abu Sayyaf   359, 739
  Al Shabaab   708–710, 730
  Al-Qaeda in the Islamic Maghreb   712
  Al-Qaeda   357–358, 711–712, 739, 864
  Boko Haram   712
  Counter-terrorism conventions   829
  FARC   519, 633, 637, 712, 862
  Global Initiative to Combat Nuclear Terrorism   785
  Hague Conventions   802
  Hamas   712, 739, 862, 896, 899
  Hezbollah   712, 739, 782, 862, 885
  INS Hanit   863
  IRA   739
  Lashkar-e-taiba   356
  Liberation Tigers of Tamil Eelam   356
  Limburg   864
  LTTE   521, 739, 862
  Maritime terrorism   358
  Montreal Conventions   802
  Movement for the Emancipation of the Niger Delta   357, 712
  Operation Active Endeavour   725
  Operation Linda Nchi   711

Palestinian Islamic Jihad   739
Palestinian terrorists   358
PLF   739
Sendero Luminoso   637
UN General Assembly   766
UN Security Council   766
USS Cole   863
The Caroline Case   758–759
The Influence of Law on Sea Power. *See* O'Connell, D.P.
Third UN Conference on the Law of the Sea   17–18, 234–235, 271, 522, 698
Thirty Years War   16
Thousand Ship Navy. *See* Global Maritime Partnership
TOCC   660, 669, 689
TONNAGE   69, 363, 367, 374, 419, 421
Trans-Pacific Partnership   353
Treaty of Saragossa   190
Treaty of Tordesillas   190
Treaty of Westphalia   17

U.S. Army Corps of Engineers
  Danger areas   168
  Restricted areas   168
U.S. Coast Guard
  Maritime security and safety teams   156
  Naval vessel protection zones   166
U.S. Coast Guard Strategy for Maritime Safety, Security and Stewardship   36
U.S. Maritime Strategy for Homeland Security   36
U.S. Seventh Fleet   25, 43
U.S. Territorial Sea
  Presidential Proclamation 5928   157
UN Charter   304, 860
  Self-defense   308
UN Convention on Illicit Traffic of Narcotics and Psychotropic Drugs. *See* Vienna Convention
UN General Assembly   766, 915
  Definition of Aggression   884, 903
  Resolution 46/7   915
UN High Commissioner for Refugees. *See* UNHCR
UN Security Council   766, 795, 797, 915
  Article 39   766, 903
  Article 40   774
  Article 41   766–767, 770, 774, 776, 882, 903
  Article 42   767, 882, 904

INDEX

Chapter VII   702, 710, 767, 770, 838, 903, 919
Maritime enforcement actions   904
Maritime enforcement actions, Haiti   915
Maritime enforcement actions, Haiti, International Civil Mission in Haiti   917
Maritime enforcement actions, Haiti, UNGAR 46/7   915
Maritime enforcement actions, Haiti, UNSCR 841   916
Maritime enforcement actions, Haiti, UNSCR 873   917
Maritime enforcement actions, Haiti, UNSCR 875   917
Maritime enforcement actions, Haiti, UNSCR 917   917
Maritime enforcement actions, Haiti, UNSCR 940   918
Maritime enforcement actions, Haiti, UNSCR 944   918
Maritime enforcement actions, Haiti, UNSCR 948   918
Maritime enforcement actions, Iraq, Maritime Interdiction Force   910
Maritime enforcement actions, Iraq, MARLO Advisory Bull 01-04   911
Maritime enforcement actions, Iraq, Special Warning No. 115   910
Maritime enforcement actions, Iraq, Special Warning No. 80   909
Maritime enforcement actions, Iraq, UNSCR 1483   911
Maritime enforcement actions, Iraq, UNSCR 1546   912
Maritime enforcement actions, Iraq, UNSCR 660   907
Maritime enforcement actions, Iraq, UNSCR 661   908
Maritime enforcement actions, Iraq, UNSCR 665   908
Maritime enforcement actions, Libya   918
Maritime enforcement actions, Libya, Operation Odyssey Dawn   920
Maritime enforcement actions, Libya, Operation Unified Protector   919
Maritime enforcement actions, Libya, UNSCR 1970   919
Maritime enforcement actions, Libya, UNSCR 1973   919
Maritime enforcement actions, Rhodesia   904
Maritime enforcement actions, Rhodesia, Beira Patrol   906
Maritime enforcement actions, Rhodesia, UNSCR 216   905
Maritime enforcement actions, Rhodesia, UNSCR 217   905–906
Maritime enforcement actions, Yugoslavia   912
Maritime enforcement actions, Yugoslavia, CTF 440   914
Maritime enforcement actions, Yugoslavia, Operation Maritime Guard   913
Maritime enforcement actions, Yugoslavia, Operation Maritime Monitor   913
Maritime enforcement actions, Yugoslavia, Operation Sharp Fence   913
Maritime enforcement actions, Yugoslavia, Operation Sharp Guard   914
Maritime enforcement actions, Yugoslavia, Operation Sharp Vigilance   913
Maritime enforcement actions, Yugoslavia, UNSCR 1021   914
Maritime enforcement actions, Yugoslavia, UNSCR 1074   914
Maritime enforcement actions, Yugoslavia, UNSCR 713   912
Maritime enforcement actions, Yugoslavia, UNSCR 787   913
Maritime enforcement actions, Yugoslavia, UNSCR 820   913
UN Security Council Resolution 1540   27
UN Security Council Resolution 1838   55
UNCLOS   57, 196, 362–364, 368, 412, 414, 416, 659, 665, 698, 702, 752, 754, 758, 789, 810, 838, 860, 866–867
  Baselines, low-water line   216
  Baselines, straight   216
  Commission on the Limits of the Continental Shelf   241
  Constitution for the World's Oceans   197, 698
  Contiguous zone   233
  Continental shelf, defined   241
  Dead-end straits   262
  Exclusive economic zone   233

Flag state jurisdiction 561, 791, 836, 842
Freedoms of navigation and overflight 233
Internal waters 217
ITLOS 552, 763
ITLOS, M/V *Saiga Case* 552
Maritime zones 215
Negotiating history 234, 270
Negotiating history, exclusive economic zone 235, 291
Negotiating history, peaceful purposes 305
Part XI Implementing Agreement 196, 242
Piracy defined 697, 699
Right of visit 700, 758, 838
Straits regime 222
Suppression of illicit drug trafficking 522, 540
Territorial sea 218, 558
U.S. declarations, understandings, and conditions 196
U.S. interests 197, 200
U.S. support 200, 245
UNHCR 669, 675, 678
Uniform Interpretation of Rules of International Law Governing Innocent Passage. *See* Jackson Hole Agreement
Unilateral Declaration of Independence 904
United Kingdom 70
　Future Maritime Operational Concept 70
　Middle East presence 71
United Nations
　Division of Ocean Affairs and Law of the Sea (DOALOS) 14
United Nations Convention against Transnational Organized Crime. *See* TOCC
United Nations Convention on the Law of the Sea. *See* UNCLOS
United Nations Office of Drugs and Crime. *See* UNODC
UNODC 657, 722–723
UNSCR
　1021 914
　1074 914
　1441 797
　1483 911
　1540 767–768, 777, 783, 787, 828
　1546 912
　1673 783, 828
　1695 769, 774
　1696 747, 774, 776
　1701 782
　1718 747, 770, 772, 775
　1737 775–776
　1747 775–776, 782
　1803 776–777
　1816 701
　1835 778
　1838 702
　1844 703
　1872 731
　1874 747, 770–772, 788
　1918 704
　1929 779–780
　1970 919
　1973 919
　216 905
　217 905–906
　660 907
　661 908
　665 797, 908
　713 798, 912
　757 798
　787 798, 913
　820 798, 913
　825 768
　841 916
　873 917
　875 917
　917 917
　940 918
　944 918
　948 918
Use of Force
　Aggression 862
　Caribbean Regional Maritime Agreement 561
　M/V *Saiga* 763
　M/V *Saiga Case* 552
　OAS Model SOP 570
　SROE 621
　SRUF 622
　UN Basic Principles on the Use of Force 549–551
　USS Cole bombing 358

VBSS
  Use of force   762
Vienna Convention   524, 535, 541, 555, 562
Visit, Board, Search and Seizure   365, 394

Washington Declaration   352
Washington Treaty of 1922   7
WCO   381, 394, 423
  SAFE Framework of Standards   385
Weapons of Mass Destruction. *See* WMD
Webster, Daniel. *See The Caroline Case*
Western European Union. *See* WEU
WEU   913–914
  Contingency Maritime Force   914
WMD
  Deir ez-Zor reactor   798
  DPRK ballistic missile program   769, 772, 774
  DPRK nuclear test   769–770
  Executive Order 13599   796
  Interdictioin, M/V *So San*   756
  Interdiction   752
  Interdiction, archipelagic waters   752
  Interdiction, *BBC China*   756, 793
  Interdiction, condition of port entry   754
  Interdiction, contiguous zone   754
  Interdiction, flag state consent   757
  Interdiction, flag state jurisdiction   754, 757
  Interdiction, *Francop*   782
  Interdiction, *Hansa India*   782
  Interdiction, *Kam Nang 1*   771
  Interdiction, M/V *Light*   771, 788
  Interdiction, *Mahan 1*   782
  Interdiction, master consent   757–758
  Interdiction, *Monchegorsk*   782
  Interdiction, non-consensual boardings   758
  Interdiction, right of visit   758
  Interdiction, stateless vessels   756
  Interdiction, territorial sea   752
  Interdiction, UNCLOS   752
  Interdiction, use of force   758, 760, 762
  Natanz reactor   799
  National Strategy to Combat Weapons of Mass Destruction   785
  Operation Opera   798
  Operation Orchard,   798
  Osirak reactor   798
  Six-Party Talks   769
  Stuxnet malware virus   798
  UNSCR 1540   767–768, 777, 783
  UNSCR 1673   783
  UNSCR 1695   769, 774
  UNSCR 1696   747, 774, 776
  UNSCR 1718   747, 770, 772, 774–775
  UNSCR 1737   775–776
  UNSCR 1747   775–776, 782
  UNSCR 1803   776–777
  UNSCR 1835   778
  UNSCR 1874   747, 770–772, 788
  UNSCR 1929   779–780
  UNSCR 825   768
World Customs Organization. *See* WCO
World Food Program   727–729, 731
World-Wide Navigational Warning Service
  Coastal warnings   85–86
  Local warnings   85
  NAVAREA warnings   85
  NAVTEX   86
  SafetyNET   86
  Sub-Area warnings   85, 87

Yom Kippur War   8